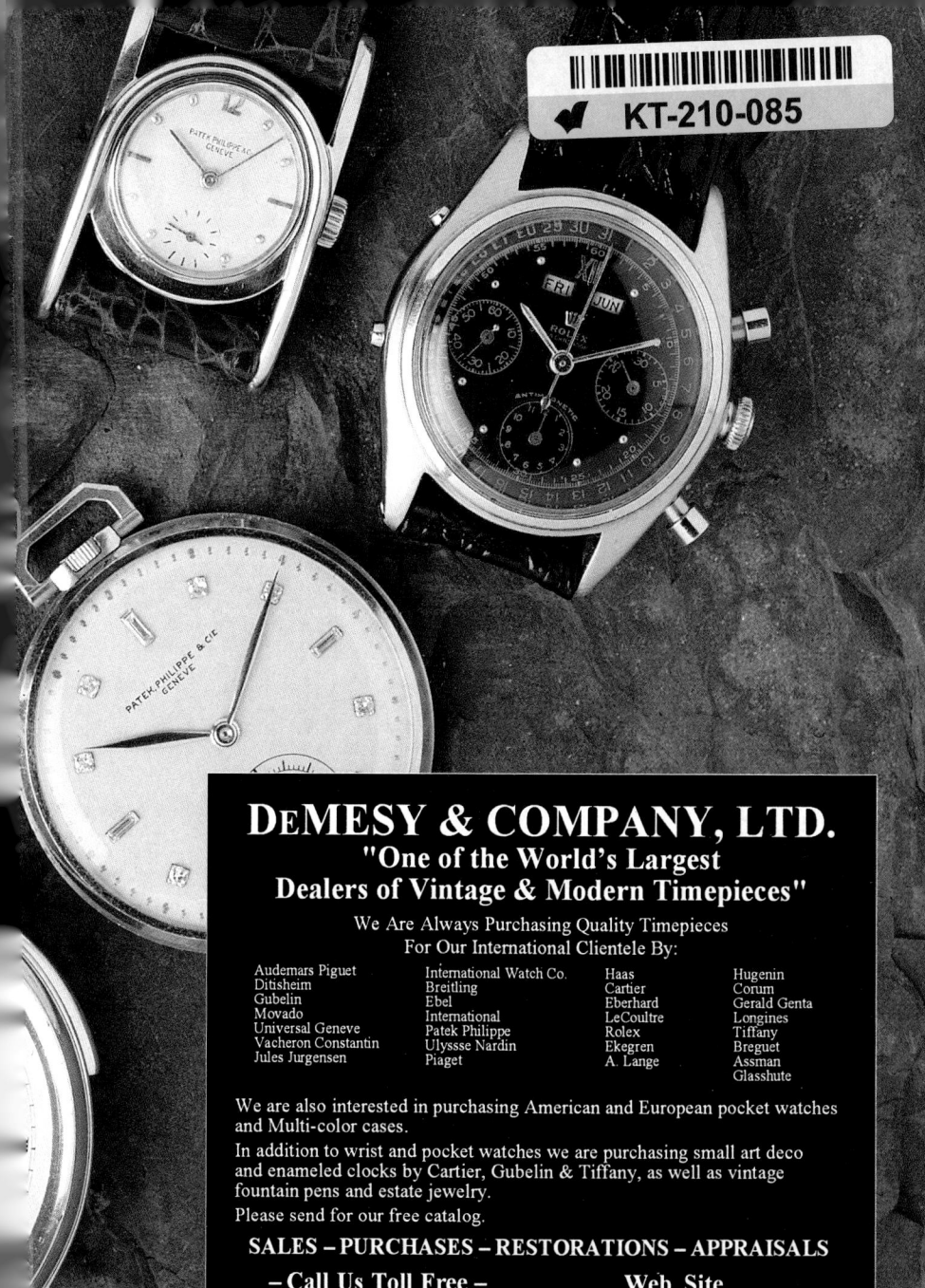

KT-210-085

DeMESY & COMPANY, LTD.
"One of the World's Largest Dealers of Vintage & Modern Timepieces"

We Are Always Purchasing Quality Timepieces
For Our International Clientele By:

Audemars Piguet	International Watch Co.	Haas	Hugenin
Ditisheim	Breitling	Cartier	Corum
Gubelin	Ebel	Eberhard	Gerald Genta
Movado	International	LeCoultre	Longines
Universal Geneve	Patek Philippe	Rolex	Tiffany
Vacheron Constantin	Ulyssse Nardin	Ekegren	Breguet
Jules Jurgensen	Piaget	A. Lange	Assman
			Glasshute

We are also interested in purchasing American and European pocket watches and Multi-color cases.

In addition to wrist and pocket watches we are purchasing small art deco and enameled clocks by Cartier, Gubelin & Tiffany, as well as vintage fountain pens and estate jewelry.

Please send for our free catalog.

SALES – PURCHASES – RESTORATIONS – APPRAISALS

– Call Us Toll Free –
1-800-635-9006

Web Site
www.demesy.com

Office: (214) 855-8777 ● Fax: (214) 871-6777
300 Crescent Court – Dallas, Texas 75201

ASHLAND

Over the past 35 years, the internationally recognized firm of ASHLAND has been building a clientele of astute collectors and investors. As a major buyer in the field of horology and vertu, ASHLAND possesses the expertise and purchasing power to acquire and offer to you the finest timepieces available. An in depth view of some of the extraordinary watches currently available may be obtained by sending for our most recent wrist or pocket watch catalog.

If you wish to receive these important publications free of charge, please send your name and address as soon as possible. Please specify if you are interested in pocket watches or wrist watches. Catalogs are already on reserve for our current customers. Keep ASHLAND in mind if the time comes to liquidate your investment. As a major force in the industry we are able to offer you top dollar for your valued collection.

ASHLAND INVESTMENTS
Sarasota Art & Antique Center, Suite 200
640 South Washington Blvd.
Sarasota, Florida 34236-7108

COMPLETE
PRICE GUIDE TO
WATCHES

COOKSEY SHUGART
TOM ENGLE • RICHARD E. GILBERT

EDITED BY MARTHA SHUGART

Important Notice. All of the information, including valuations, in this book has been compiled from the most reliable sources, and every effort has been made to eliminate errors and questionable data. Nevertheless, the possibility of error, in a work of such immense scope, always exists. The publisher or authors will not be held responsible for losses which may occur in the purchase, sale, statements of its advertisers or other transaction of items, because of information contained herein. Readers who feel they have discovered errors are invited to write and inform us, so they may be corrected in subsequent editions.

The Complete Price Guide To Watches is published independently and is not associated with any watch manufacturer.

This book endeavors to be a **Guide** or helpful manual and offers a wealth of material and information to be used as a tool not as a absolute document. The Complete Price Guide To Watches is like some *watches*, the worst may be better than none at all, but at best cannot be expected to be 100% accurate.

Copyright 1999 by Cooksey G. Shugart

All rights reserved under International and Pan-American Copyright Conventions. This **BOOK** and any part thereof must not be used or reproduced and / or made public in any form, by print, photoprint, microfilm, electronically or any other means without prior written consent of publisher, and author COOKSEY G. SHUGART.

Published by: **COOKSEY SHUGART PUBLICATIONS**
P. O. BOX 3147
CLEVELAND, TN. 37320-3147
TEL. OR FAX (423) 479 – 4813

Distributed by: **COLLECTOR BOOKS**
P. O. BOX 3009
5801 KENTUCKY DAM ROAD
PADUCAH, KY. 42001

ISBN 1 – 57432 – 130 – 7
NINETEENTH EDITION: JAN., 1999

European Distributor: **BUSHWOOD BOOKS**
6 Marksbury, Kew Gardens, Surrey TW9 4JF (U. K.)
Tel: 44 (0) 181 392 8585

Manufactured in the United States of America

COOKSEY SHUGART

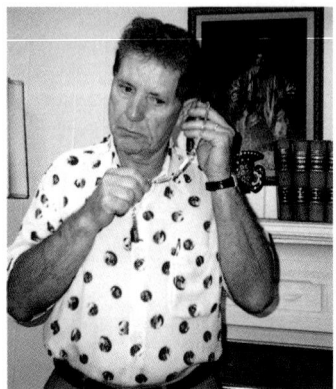

TOM ENGLE

RICHARD E. GILBERT

The *Complete Price Guide To Watches*, published by Shugart Publications, authored by Cooksey Shugart with co-authors Tom Engle and Richard E. Gilbert. All three have been active horologists since the early 1960's and members of the National Association of Watch and Clock Collectors since the early 1970's. They have searched for fine timepieces all over the world and are the foremost experts in the field of antique horology.

The co-authors travel extensively to auctions throughout the United States and Europe, to regional and national conventions, meets and shows, and keep an up-to-date pulse of the watch market. They continually expand their horological reference library and their extensive selection of watch photographs. Because of the unique knowledge of the market these co-authors possess, this volume should be considered one of the most authoritative watch references on the market today. Each edition contains updated and revised information and prices, and has become the accepted standard reference work of the watch market. "We see this book as an extension of the information we have been gathering for years and take great pride in sharing it with other collectors who have a deep and abiding interest in watches," the authors stated.

Mr. Shugart resides in Cleveland, Tenn., Mr. Engle resides in Louisville, KY. and Mr. Gilbert resides in Sarasota, FL.

TABLE OF CONTENTS

4

ACKNOWLEDGMENTS

I am especially appreciative of **Bob Overstreet**, author of The Overstreet Comic Book Price Guide, for his encouragement and without his assistance this book would have been impossible.

To my wife **Martha,** for her complete understanding and assistance in compiling this book.

To best friend **TOM ENGLE** whose help is invaluable a very special thanks.

A special thanks to Henry B. Fried, Dr. Adolphe Chapiro, Derek Pratt, Joe Cerullo, Philippe Dufour, and Dan Crawley.

To the NAWCC Museum, Hamilton Watch Co., and Bowman Technical School, for allowing us to photograph their watches.

To Christie's, Osvaldo Patrizzi, Dr. H. Crott, J. Wachsmann of Pieces of Time and Gisbert A. Joseph of Joseph Auctions for photographs of watches.

And to the following people whose help was invaluable and will be long remembered: Frank Irick, John Cubbins, Harold Harris, Paul Gibson, Robert L. Ravel, M.D., William C. Heilman Jr., M.D., Thomas McEntyre, Paul Morgan, Bill Selover, Oscar Laube, Ed Kieft, Charles Wallace, Bob Walters, Jack Warren, Howard Schroeder, Edward M. McGinnis, James Gardner, Paul Zuercher, Irving E. Roth, Don Bass, Stephen Polednak, Dick Stacy, Ernest J. Lewis, Herbert McDonald, David Steger, Fred Favour, Ralph Warner, Estus Harris, Norman Howard, Charles Cleves, Tom McIntyre, Ralph Ferone, Arnold C. Varey, Jeffrey Ollswang, Tom Rohr, Leon Beard, Glenn Smith, Kenneth Vergin, Thomas Rumpf, Frank Diggs, Tom Thacker, Bob Lavoie, Constantin Tanasecu, Rod Minter, Ernest Luffman, John Amneus, Lawrence D. Harnden, Mike Kirkpatrick, Clint B. Geller, Art W. Rontree, and a special thanks to Peter Kushnir, Dr. J. Mauss, Robert D. Gruen, Jeff Hess, Col. R. A. Mulholland, Dick Ziebell, Jack Warren, Dick Flaute, Ralph Vinge, Edward Fletcher, Richard Walker, Alex Wolanguk, Carl Goetz, Miles Sandler, Dave Mycko, Martin & Patrick Cullen, Benjy Rook, Phillip Welsh, Paul Craft, Fred Fox, Fred Andrus, Ellis Gifford, Steve Berger, Bruce Ellison, Lawrence D. Harnden, Geoff White, Bob & Pat Wingate, David Searles, Ray R. Tyulty Jr., Don Levison, Robert M. Toborowsky M.D., Dr. John R. Dimar, Jonathan Snellenburg, Tom Reindl, Paul A. Duggan, Gregory A. Hill, Don & Sandy Robbins, Bernie Kraus, Veron Willams, Fred Hansen, Drew Schmidt, Norman M. Tallan, Harry Blair, Jack Kurdzionak, Robert Schussel.

Special Consultant & Advisors

JIM WOLF

PAUL DUGGAN

MILES SANDLER

Send only corrections, additions, deletions and comments to
COOKSEY SHUGART, P. O. BOX 3147, CLEVELAND, TN. 37320-3147.
*When **corresponding**, please send a ✉ self-addressed, stamped envelope.*

INTRODUCTION

This book is dedicated to all watch collectors who we hope will find it an enjoyable and valuable reference to carry on buying trips or to trace the lost history of that priceless family heirloom.

The origin of this book began when I was given a pocket watch that had been in our family for many years. After receiving the prized heirloom I wanted to know its complete history, and thus the search began. Because of the lack of a comprehensive reference on American pocket watches the venture took me through volume after volume. Over the course of ten years many hours were accumulated in running down the history of this one watch. The research sparked my interest in the pocket watch field and pointed to the need for a book such as this one. We hope it will provide the information that you are looking for.

— The Authors

Watches are unique collectibles and since the beginning of civilization man has held a fascination for time. When man scooped up a handful of sand and created the hourglass, portable timepieces have been in demand for the wealthy and poor alike. Man has sought constantly to improve his time-measuring instruments and has made them with the finest metals and jewels. The pocket watch, in particular, became an ornamentation and a source of pride, and this accounts for its value among families for generation after generation.

The watch has become precious and sentimental to so many because it is one of the true personal companions of the individual night and day. Mahatma Gandhi, the father of India and one of the rare people in history who was able to renounce worldly possessions, was obsessed with the proper use of his time. Each minute, he held, was to be used in the service of his fellow man. His own days were ordered by one of his few personal possessions, a sixteen-year-old, eight-shilling Ingersoll pocket watch that was always tied to his waist with a piece of string.

Another factor that has made watches unique collectibles is the intricate artisanship with which they are put together. Many of the watches of yesteryear, which were assembled with extreme accuracy and fine workmanship, continue to be reliable timepieces today. They stand out as unique because that type of watch is no longer hand made. In today's world of mass production, the watch with individual craftsmanship containing precious jewels and metals can rarely be found—and, if found, it is rarely affordable.

The well-made watch is a tribute to man's skills, artisanship and craftsmanship at their finest level. That is why the watch holds a special place in the collectible field.

In America, there are about 80,000 avid watch collectors. About 5 million people own two or more watches, and an untold number possess at least one of these precious heirlooms.

The Complete Price Guide to Watches does not attempt to establish or fix values or selling prices in the watch trade market.

It does, however, reflect the trends of buying and selling in the collector market. Prices listed in this volume are based on data collected and analyzed from dealers and shops all over the country. These prices should serve the collector as a guide only. The price you pay for any watch will be determined by the value it has to you. The intrinsic value of any particular watch can be measured only by you, the collector, and a fair price can be derived only after mutual agreement between both the buyer and the seller.

Keep in mind the fair market values at **retail** level as outlined in this price guide and buying wisely, but don't hesitate, as the better and scarce pieces are quickly sold.

It is our hope that this volume can help make your watch collecting venture both pleasurable and profitable. Hopefully, everyone interested in horology will research the watch and add to his library on the subject.

Information contained herein may not necessarily apply to every situation. Data is still being found, which may alter statements made in this book. These changes, however, will be reflected in future editions.

COLLECTAMANIA
Hobby — Business — Pastime — Entertainment

Just name it. More than likely someone will want to buy or sell it: books, coins, stamps, bottles, beer cans, gold, glassware, baseball cards, guns, clocks, watches, comics, art, cars, and the list goes on and on.

Most Americans seem to be caught up in collectamania . More and more Americans are spending hour after hour searching through antique shops, auctions, flea markets and yard sales for those rare treasures of delight that have been lying tucked away for generations just waiting to be found.

This sudden boom in the field of collecting may have been influenced by fears of inflation or disenchantment with other types of investments. But more people are coming into the field because they gain some degree of nostalgic satisfaction from these new tangible ties with yesteryear. Collecting provides great fun and excitement. The tales of collecting and the resultant "fabulous finds" could fill volumes and inspire even the non-collector to embark upon a treasure hunt.

Collecting for the primary purpose of investment may prove to have many pitfalls for the amateur. The lack of sufficient knowledge is the main cause of disappointment. The inability to spot fakes or flawed merchandise can turn excitement into disappointment. And, in many fields, high-class forgers are at work, doing good and faithful reproductions in large quantities that can sometimes fool even the experts the first time they see them.

Collecting for fun and profit can be just that if you observe a fair amount of caution. Always remember, amidst your enthusiasm, that an object may not be what it would first appear. Next are a few guidelines that may be helpful.

FOCUS - LEARN - CONDITION - TRUST

" LOOK UNDER THE HOOD"

1. **Make up your mind** and **FOCUS** on what you want to collect and concentrate in this area. Your field of collecting should be one that you have a genuine liking for, and it helps if you can use the objects. It may also help to narrow your field even further, for instance, in collecting watches, to choose only one company or one type or style and have a method of collecting.

2. **Gain all the knowledge you can** and **LEARN** all about the objects you collect. The more knowledge you have the more successful you will be in finding valuable, quality pieces. The best way to predict the future is to study the past. Amassing the knowledge required to be a good collector is easier if you have narrowed your scope of interest. Otherwise, it may take years to become an "expert." Don't try to learn everything there is to know about a variety of fields. This will end in frustration and disappointment. Specialize and **learn** fair market **values**.

3. **Buy the best CONDITION you can afford**, assuming the prices are fair. The advanced collector may want only mint articles; but the novice collector may be willing to accept something far less than mint condition due to caution and economics. Collectible items in better condition continue to rise in value at a steady rate.

4. **Deal with reputable dealers** whom you can **TRUST**. Talk with the dealer; get to know the seller; get a business card; know where you can contact the dealer if you have problems, or if you want the dealer to help you find something else you may be looking for.

FAIR MARKET PRICE: Fair price may be defined as a fair **reasonable** range of prices usually paid for a watch or a watch of **good value** as used in this book (*at the RETAIL LEVEL*). This market level includes a particular time frame, desirability, condition and quality. A guide to fair purchase prices is subject to sales and transaction between a large number of buyers and sellers who are informed, up to date on all normal market influences (while keeping in mind the difference between compulsiveness and acceptable buying), and buy and sell on a large scale from coast to coast. A willing buyer and a willing seller acting carefully and judiciously in their own best interest while, doing business in a normal and fair manner and preferable with payment immediately.

The Complete Price Guide to Watches goal is to stimulate the orderly exchange of WATCHES between buyers and sellers.

Keep in mind the retail fair market **values** as outlined in this price guide and buying wisely, but don't *hesitate*, as the better and scarce watches are *quickly* sold. *The best way to predict the future is study the past.*

🕐 Pricing in this Guide are fair market price for **COMPLETE** watches which are reflected from the "**NAWCC**" National and regional shows.

HOW TO USE THIS BOOK

The Complete Price Guide to Watches is a simple reference, with clear and carefully selected information. The first part of the book is devoted to history, general information, and a how-to section. The second part of the guide consists mainly of a listing of watch manufacturers, identification guides, and prices. This is a unique book because it is designed to be taken along as a handy pocket reference for identifying and pricing watches. With the aid of this book, the collector should be able to make on-the-spot judgments as to identification, age, quality, and value. This complete guide and a pocket magnifying glass will be all you need to take on your buying trips.

Watch collecting is fast growing as a hobby and business. Many people collect for the enjoyment and profit. The popularity of watches continues to rise because watches are a part of history. The American railroad brought about the greatest watch of that time, the railroad pocket watch. Since that time America has produced some of the best quality pocket watches that money could buy. The gold-filled cases made in America have never been surpassed in quality or price in the foreign market. With the quality of movement and cases being made with guaranteed high standards as well as beauty, the American pocket watch became very desirable. Because they are no longer being made in the U. S. A., pocket watches continue to rise in value.

The watch is collected for its beauty, quality in movement and case, and the value of metal content. Solid gold and platinum are the top of the line; silver is also very desirable. (Consider that some watches in the early 1900's sold between $700 and $1,000. This is equal to or greater than the price of a good car of the same period.)

As with limited edition prints, a watch of supreme excellence is also limited and will increase in value. There is universal appeal and excitement in owning a piece of history, and your heirloom is just that. At one time pocket watches were a status symbol. Everyone competed for beauty and quality in the movement and case. Solid gold cases were adorned with elaborate engraving's, diamonds, and other precious jewels. The movements were beautiful and of high quality. Manufacturers went to great lengths to provide movements that were both accurate and lovely. Fancy damaskeening on the back plates of nickel with gold lettering, 26 jewels in gold settings, and a solid gold train (gears) were features of some of the more elaborate timepieces. The jewels were red rubies, or diamond-end stones, or sapphires for the pallet stones. There were gold timing screws, and more. The faces were made by the best artisans of the day. Hand-painted, jewel-studded, with fancy hands and double-sunk dials made of enamel and precious metals.

HOW TO DETERMINE MANUFACTURER

When identifying a watch, look on the face or dial for the name of the company and then refer to the alphabetical list of watch companies in this book. If the face or dial does not reveal the company name you will have to seek information from the movement's back plate. **First** determine from what country the watch originated. The company name or the town where it was manufactured will likely be inscribed there. The name engraved on the back plate is referred to as the "signature." After locating the place of manufacture, see what companies manufactured in that town. This may require reading the histories of several companies to find the exact one. Use the process of elimination to narrow the list. Note: Some of the hard-to-identify watches are extremely collectible and valuable. Therefore, it is important to learn to identify them.

In order to establish the true manufacturer of the movement, one must **study** the construction, taking note of the **SIZE**, number of jewels, shape, location of parts, plate layout (is it full or 3/4), shape of the balance cock and the regulator, location of jewels, location of screws, etc. Compare and match your watch movement with every photograph or drawing from each watch company in this volume until the manufacturer is located.

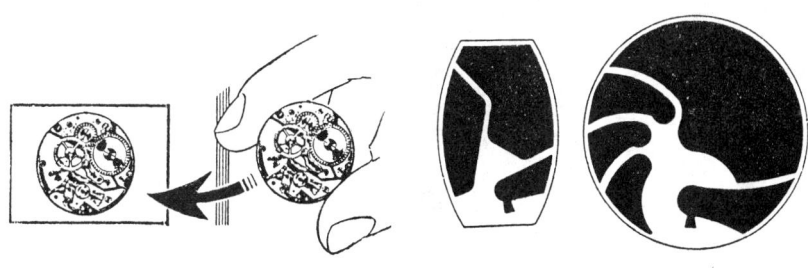

HOW TO DETERMINE AGE

After establishing the name of the manufacturer, you may be interested in the age of the watch (where production tables are listed). This information can be obtained by using the serial number inscribed on the back movement plate and referring to the production table. It is often difficult to establish the exact age, but this method will put you within a two or three-year period of the date of the manufacture.

To establish the age of a pre-1850 watch there are many points to be considered. The dial, hands, pillars, balance cock and pendant, for example, contain important clues in determining the age of your watch. However, no one part alone should be considered sufficient evidence to draw a definite conclusion as to age. The watch as a whole must be considered. First determine from what country the case originated and from what country did the movement originate for example, an English-made silver-cased watch will have a hallmark inside the case. It is quite simple to refer to the London Hallmark Table for hallmarks after 1697. The hallmark will reveal the age of the case only. This does not fix the age of the movement. Many movements are housed in cases made years before or after the movement was produced.

The case that houses the movement is not necessarily a good clue to the origin of the movement. It was a common practice for manufacturers to ship the movements to the jewelers and watchmakers uncased. The customer then married the movement and case. That explains why an expensive movement can be found in a cheaper case or vice versa.

If the "manufacturer's" name and location are no help, the inscription could possibly be that of a jeweler and his location. Then it becomes obvious there is no quick and easy way to identify some American made watches. However, the following steps may be helpful. Some watches can be identified by comparing the models of each company until the correct model is found. Start by sizing the watch and then comparing the varied plate shapes and styles. The cock or bridge for the balance may also be a clue. The general arrangement of the movement as to jeweling, whether it is an open face or hunting case, and style of regulators may help to find the correct identification of the manufacturer of the movement.

Numbers on a watch case should not be considered as clues to the age of the movement because cases were both American and foreign made, and many of the good watches were re-cased through the years.

APPRAISING WATCHES

Watch collecting is still young when compared to fields of the standard collectibles: coins and stamps. The watch collecting field is growing but information is still scarce, fragmented, and sometimes unreliable. To be knowledgeable in any field, one must spend the time required to study it.

The value of any collectible is determined first by demand. Without demand there is no market. In the watch trade, the law of supply and demand is also true. The supply of the American watches has stopped and the demand among collectors continues to rise. There are many factors that make a watch desired or in demand. Only time and study will tell a collector just which pieces are most collectible. After the collector or investor finds out what is desirable, then a value must be placed on it before it is sold. If it is priced too high, the watch will not sell; but, on the other hand, if it is priced too low, it will be hard to replace at the selling price. The dealer must arrive at a fair market price that will move the watch. As with limited edition prints, a watch of supreme excellence is also limited and will increase in value. There is universal appeal and excitement in owning a piece of history, and your heirloom is just that. At one time pocket watches were a status symbol. Everyone competed for beauty and quality in the movement and case. Solid gold cases were adorned with elaborate engraving's, diamonds, and other precious jewels.

The movements were beautiful and of high quality. Manufacturers went to great lengths to provide movements that were both accurate and lovely. Fancy damaskeening on the back plates of nickel with gold lettering, 26 jewels in gold settings, and a solid gold train (gears) were features of some of the more elaborate timepieces. The jewels were red rubies, or diamond-end stones, or sapphires for the pallet stones. There were gold timing screws, and more. The faces were made by the best artisans of the day. Hand-painted, jewel-studded, with fancy hands and double-sunk dials made of enamel and precious metals.

There are no two watches alike. This makes the appraising more difficult and often-times arbitrary. But there are certain guidelines one can follow to arrive at a fair market price. When watches were manufactured, most companies sold the movements to a jeweler, and the buyer had a choice of dials and cases. Some high-grade movements were placed in a low-grade case and vice versa. Some had hand-painted multi-colored dials; some were plain. The list of contrasts goes on. Conditions of watches will vary greatly, and this is a big factor in the value. The best movement in the best original case will bring the top price for any type of watch.

Prices are constantly changing in the watch field. Gold and silver markets affect the price of the cases. Scarcity and age also affect the value. These prices will fluctuate regularly.

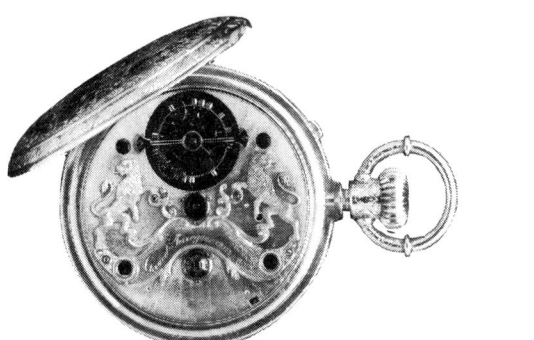

APPRAISING GUIDELINES

Demand, supply, condition, and value must be the prime factors in appraising an old watch. Demand is the most important element. Demand can be determined by the **number** of buyers for the particular item. The watch may be rare (only one or a few) but the *number* of collectors may be even more rare & the collector just as hard to find. A simple but true axiom is that value is determined by the price someone is willing to pay.

In order to obtain a better knowledge in appraising and judging watches, the following guidelines are most useful. Consider all these factors before placing a value on the watch. (There is no rank or priority to the considerations listed.)

1. Demand: Is it high or low? How many collectors **want** your watch.
2. Supply & Availability: How *rare* or *scarce* is the watch?
   How many of the total production remain?
3. Condition of both the case and movement (very important) .
4. Low serial numbers: The first one made would be more
   valuable than later models.
5. Historical value.   6. Age, how old is the Watch.
7. Value of metal content, style or type of case, beauty and eye appeal.

8. Is it in its **original** case? (very important).
9. Is it an early handmade watch?
10. Complications: Repeaters, for example.
11. Type of **escapement**.
12. Size, number of jewels, type of plates (3/4, full and bridge), type of balance, type of winding (key-wind, lever-set, etc.), number of adjustments, gold jeweled settings, damaskeening, gold train.
13. What grade of **condition** is it? Pristine, Mint, Extra Fine, Average, Fair, or Scrap?
14. Identification ability.
15. Future potential as an investment.
16. Quality (high or low grade), or low cost production watches (dollar watch).
17. How much will this watch scrap for?

GRADING WATCHES

Pricing in this book is based on the following grading system:

PRISTINE MINT (G-10): <u>*NEW OLD STOCK.*</u> Absolutely factory new; sealed in factory box with wax paper still intact & all tags & papers etc.

MINT PLUS (G-9): Still in factory box <u>*"BUT LOOKS UNUSED"*</u>.

MINT (G-8): Same as factory new but with very little use; **no** faint scratches & **no** trace of a screwdriver marks; is original in every way crystal, hands, dial, case, movement; used briefly & stored away, may still be in box. (Dealers **"RETAIL"** price after OVERHAUL)

NEAR MINT (G-7): Completely original in every way; faint marks may be seen with a loop only; expertly repaired; movement may have been cleaned and oiled.

EXTRA FINE (G-6): May or may not be in factory box; looks as though watch was used very little; crystal may have been replaced; original case, hands, dial, and movement. If watch has been repaired, all original replacement parts have been used. Faint case scratches are evident but hard to detect with the eye. No dents and no hairline on dial are detectable.

FINE (G-5): May have new hands and new crystal, but original case, dial and movement; **faint** hairline & no chips on dial; no large scratches & no brass seen on case; slight stain on movement; movement must be sharp with only **minor** scratches.

AVERAGE (G-4): Original case, dial and movement; movement may have had a part replaced, but part was near to original; no brass showing through on gold-filled case; no rust or chips in dial; may have hairlines in dial that are hard to see. All marks are hard to detect, but may be seen without a loop. (What some dealer "MAY" pay - **Wholesale** price)

FAIR (G-3): Hairlines in dial and small chips; slight amount of brass can be seen through worn spots on gold-filled case; rust marks in movement; a small dent in case; wear in case, dial, and movement; well used; may not have original dial or case.

POOR (G-2): Watch not working; needs new dial; case well worn, with many dents; hands may be gone; replacement crystal may be needed.

SCRAP (G-1): Movement not working; bad dial; rusty movement; brass showing badly; may not have case; some parts not original; no crystal or hands. Good for parts only.

🕐 Pricing in this Guide are fair market price for **COMPLETE** watches which are reflected from the "**NAWCC**" National and regional shows.

Hamilton 992B

G-10	$550
G-9	$500
G-8	**$475**
G-7	$350
G-6	**$275**
G-5	$250
G-4	**$225**
G-3	$175
G-2	$95
G-1	$65

MINT
G-8 = (Retail)

AVERAGE
G-4 = (Wholesale)

Above is an example of how the price is affected by the different grades of the same watch:

The value of a watch can only be assessed after the watch has been carefully inspected and graded. It may be difficult to evaluate a watch honestly and objectively, especially in the rare or scarce models.

If the watch has any defects, such as a small scratch on it, it can not be Pristine. It is important to realize that older watches in grades of Extra Fine or above are extremely rare and may never be found.

Watches listed in this book are priced at the collectable **retail level,** as **COMPLETE** watches having an original 14k gold-filled case and Key Wind with silver, an original white enamel single sunk dial, and with the entire original movement in good working order with no repairs needed.

Keep in mind the fair market values at **retail level,** as outlined in this price guide and buying wisely, but don't *hesitate*, as the better and scarce watches are *quickly* sold.

COLLECTING ON A LIMITED BUDGET

]ays looking for that sleeper, which is out there waiting to be found. One story goes that the collector went into a pawn shop and asked the owner if he had any gold pocket watches for sale. The pawn broker replied, "No, but I have a 23J silver cased pocket watch at a good price." Even though the pocket watch was in a cheaper case, the collector decided to further explore the movement. When he opened the back to look at the movement, there he saw engraved on the plates 24J Bunn Special and knew immediately he wanted to buy the pocket watch. The movement was running, and looked to be in first grade shape. The collector asked the price. The broker said he has been trying to get rid of the pocket watch, but had no luck and if he wanted it, he would sell it for $35. The collector took the pocket watch and replaced the bent-up silver case for a gold-filled J. Boss case, and sold it a month later for $400. He had a total of $100 invested when he sold it, netting a cool $300 profit.

Most collectors want a pocket watch that is in mint or near-mint condition and original in every way. But consider the railroad pocket watches such as the Bunn Special in a cheaper case. The railroad man was compelled to buy a watch with a quality movement, even though he may have only been able to afford a cheap case. The railroad man had to have a pocket watch that met certain standards set by the railroad company. A watch should always be judged on quality and performance and not just on its appearance. The American railroad pocket watch was unsurpassed in reliability. It was durable and accurate for its time, and that accounts for its continuing value today.

If you are a limited-budget collector, you would be well advised not to go beyond your means. But watch collecting can still be an interesting, adventurous, and profitable hobby. If you are to be successful in quadrupling your purchases that you believe to be sleepers, you must first be a hard worker, have perseverance and let shrewdness and skill of knowledge take the place of money. A good starting place is to get a working knowledge of how a pocket watch works. Learn the basic skills such as cleaning, mainspring and staff replacement. One does not have to be a watchmaker, but should learn the names of parts and what they do. If a watch that you are considering buying does not work, you should know how and what it takes to get it in good running order or pass it by. Stay away from pocket watches that do not wind and set. Also avoid "odd" movements that you hope to be able to find a case for.

Old watches with broken or missing parts are expensive and all but impossible to have repaired. Some parts must be made by hand. The odd and low-cost production watches are fun to get but hard to repair. Start out on the more common basic-jeweled lever pocket watches. The older the watch, the harder it is to get parts. Buy an inexpensive pocket watch movement that runs and play with it. Get the one that is newer and for which parts can be bought; and get a book on watch repairing.

You will need to know the ***pricing history*** and **demand** of a watch. Know what collectors are looking for in your area. If you cannot find a buyer, then, of course, someone else's stock has become yours.

JOIN THE NAWCC ®

The authors of this book Mr. Shugart, Mr. Richard Gilbert & Mr. Tom Engle recommend you join the NAWCC ® today and share a fascination for watches with other members.

The National Association of Watch and Clock Collectors (NAWCC ®) is a non-profit, scientific and educational corporation founded in 1943 and now serving the horological needs and interests of about 35,000 members (professional horologists and **amateurs**) in the United States and 40 others countries. Help to its members is only a telephone call away.

Participation in National & Regional *Conventions* also Local *Activities* and *Seminars.*

A **PUBLICATION** sent to you each month.

The **NAWCC ® Mart Sent to you every odd - month**

The **NAWCC ® Bulletin Sent to you every even - month**

The **Bulletin** sent to you every even - month is an absorbing, abundantly illustrated articles on historic, artistic and technical aspects of time keeping, answers by experts to your questions in the "Answer Box" , concise reviews of horological books, members' opinions and comments in "VOX TEMPORIS", research findings and request, slide programs available to Chapters, news and announcements of local Chapters, Regional and National activities.

The **Mart** sent to you every odd - month. An informal medium of exchange in which, for a nominal fee, you can list any horological item you may wish to **buy, sell or trade**... an absorbing and entertaining way to find items to fill out your collection or dispose of pieces you no-longer want. Announcements of Regional and National **Conventions & Seminars**.

TO JOIN THE NAWCC ® Call or Send for a FREE copy of their brochure with additional information on the NAWCC ®, membership and benefits.

NAWCC, INC.
514 Poplar Street
Columbia, PA   17512
(717) 684-8261

Recommended by member COOKSEY SHUGART membership number - **23,843.**
Also see AD in the ADVERTISING SECTION of this book.

THAT GREAT AMERICAN
RAILROAD POCKET WATCH

It was the late nineteenth century in America. The automobile had not yet been discovered. The personal Kodak camera was still not on the market. Women wore long dresses, and the rub board was still the most common way to wash clothes. Few homes had electricity, and certainly the radio had not yet invaded their lives. Benjamin Harrison was president. To be sure, those days of yesteryear were not quite as nostalgically simple as most reminiscing would have them be. They were slower, yes, because it took longer to get things done and longer to get from one place to another. The U.S. mail was the chief form of communication linking this country together, as America was inching toward the Twentieth Century.

The tremendous impact of the railroad on the country during this era should not be under estimated. Most of the progress since the 1830s had chugged along on the back of the black giant locomotives that belched steam and fire, up and down the countryside. In fact, the trains brought much life and hope to the people all across the country, delivering their goods and food, bringing people from one city to another, carrying the U.S. mail, and bringing the democratic process to the people by enabling candidates for the U.S. Presidency to meet and talk with people in every state.

Truly the train station held memories for most everyone and had a link with every family.

In 1891, the country had just eased into the period that historians would later term the "Gay Nineties." It was on April 19 of that year that events occurred near Cleveland, Ohio, that clearly pointed out that the nation's chief form of transportation was running on timepieces that were not reliable. The time had come for strict standards and guide lines for accurate pocket watches to be used by the railroad men and the railroad industry with precision in time keeping.

Above: **Allen A. Shugart** (my father) was photographed in the summer of 1981 at the Chattanooga Tenn. train station also called Chattanooga Choo-Choo Station.

That April morning the fast mail train, known as No. 4, was going East. On the same track an accommodation train was going West. It was near Elyria, about 25 miles from Cleveland, Ohio, that the engineer and conductor of the accommodation train were given written orders to let the fast mail train pass them at Kipton, a small station west of Oberlin.

As the accommodation train was leaving the station at Elyria, the telegraph operator ran to the platform and verbally cautioned the engineer and conductor, "Be careful, No. 4 is on time." The conductor replied, "Go to thunder. I know my business."

The train left Elyria on time according to the engineer's watch. What was not known was that the engineer's watch had stopped for four minutes and then started up again. Had the conductor looked at his own watch, the impending disaster could have been avoided.

The two trains met their destiny at Kipton; the accommodation train was under full brakes, but the fast mail was full speed ahead. Both engineers were killed as well as nine other people. The railroad companies (Lake Shore Railroad and Michigan Southern Railway) sustained great losses in property as did the U.S. Post Office.

Following this disaster, a commission was appointed to come up with standards for timepieces that would be accepted and adopted by all railroads. The commission learned that, up to the time of the Kipton crash, conductors on freight trains were depending on cheap alarm clocks. The railroading industry had grown, fast new trains were now in service, and the same lines were used by several different railways. Very often, in only a short space of time, two trains would cover the same track. The industry now had to demand precision in its time keeping.

From the ashes of this smoldering Ohio disaster rose the phoenix in the form of the great American railroad pocket watch, a watch unrivaled in quality and reliability.

By 1893 the General Railroad Timepiece Standards (below) were adopted, and **many** railroad lines used these standard in rail service by railroaders responsible for schedules were required to meet the following specifications:

Be open faced, size 18 or 16, have a minimum of 17 jewels, adjusted to at least five positions, keep time accurately to within a gain or loss of only 30 seconds a week, adjusted to temperatures of 34 to 100 degrees Fahrenheit, have a double roller, steel escape wheel, lever set, micrometric regulator, winding stem at 12 o'clock, grade on back plate, use plain Arabic numbers printed bold and black on a white dial, and have bold black hands.

Some also wanted a Breguet hairspring, adjusted to isochronism and 30 degrees Fahrenheit with a minimum of 19 jewels.

(These Standards changed from year to year.)

The railroad man was compelled to buy a timepiece more accurate than many scientific instruments of precision used in laboratories. The American pocket watch industry was compelled to produce just such an instrument which it did. The railroad watch was a phenomenal timekeeper and durable in long life and service. It had the most minute adjustments, no small feat because watchmaking was rendered far more difficult than clock making, due to the fact that a clock is always in one position and powered by a constant force-it's weights,while watches must be accurate in several positions with a variable power source.

The 1893 railroad pocket watch standards were adopted by almost every railroad line. While each company had its individual standards, most all of them included the basic recommendations of the commission.

The key figure in developing the railroad watch standards was Webb C. Ball of Cleveland, Ohio, the general time inspector for over 125,000 miles of railroad in the U.S., Mexico, and Canada. Ball was authorized by railroad officials to establish the timepiece inspection system. After Ball presented his guidelines, most American manufacturers set out to meet those standards and a list of the different manufacturers producing watches of the grade that would pass inspection, was soon available.

According to the regulations, if a watch fell behind or gained 30 seconds in 7 to 14 days, it must be sent in for adjustment or repair. Small cards were given to the engineers and conductors the railroad timekeepers and a complete record of the watch's performance was written in ink. All repairs and adjustments were conducted by experienced and approved watchmakers; inspections were conducted by authorized inspectors.

Because this system was adopted universally and adhered to, and because American watch manufacturers produced a superior railroad watch, the traveling public was assured of increased safety and indeed the number of railroad accidents occurring as a result of faulty timepieces was minimized.

Prior to the 1891 collision, some railroad companies had already initiated standards and were issuing lists of those watches approved for railroad use. Included were the Waltham 18s, 1883 model, Crescent Street Grade, and the B.W. Raymond, 18s, both in open & hunter cases with lever or pendant set.

By the mid 1890s hunter cases were being turned down as well as pendant set. Watches meeting approval then included Waltham, 18s, 1892 model; Elgin, 7th model; and Hamilton, 17j, open face, lever set.

Hamilton Grade **992**, 16 size, 21 jewels, nickel 3/4 plate movement, lever set only, gold jewel settings, gold center wheel, steel escape wheel, micrometric regulator, double roller, compensating balance. Adjusted to temperature, isochronism and 5 positions. Marked *Elinvar* under balance wheel. Serial number 2584307 & listed as **992E** under the "Hamilton serial numbers and grades" section.

By 1900 the double roller sapphire pallets and steel escape wheels with a minimum of five positions were required.

The early Ball Watch Co. movements, made by Howard, used initials of railroad labor organizations such as "B. of L.E. Standard" and ''B. of L.F. Standard." Ball also used the trademark "999" and "Official Railroad Standard." Some watches may turn up that are marked as "loaners." These were issued by the railroad inspectors when a watch had to be kept for repairs.

By 1920 the 18 size watch had lost popularity with the railroad men and by 1950 most railroad companies were turning them down all together.

In 1936 duty on Swiss watches were lowered by 50 percent, and by 1950 the Swiss imports had reached a level of five million a year.

In 1969 the last American railroad pocket watch was sold by Hamilton Watch Co.

NOTE: Railroad Standards, Railroad Approved & Railroad Grade **terminology,** as defined and used in this _**BOOK**_. **RAILROAD STANDARDS** = A commission or board appointed by the railroad companies outlined a set of **guidelines** to be accepted or approved by each railroad line. **RAILROAD APPROVED** = A _**LIST**_ of watches each railroad line would approve if purchased by their employee's. (this list changed through the years). **RAILROAD GRADE** = A watch made by manufactures to meet or exceed the railroad **standards**. Grades such as 992, Vanguard and B.W. Raymond, etc. Some GRADES **exceeded** the R.R. standards such as 23 jewels, diamond end stone, gold train, raised gold jewel settings, double sunk dial and the list goes on. Examples: such as Veritas, Sangamo, 950 & Riverside Maximus and many others.

RAILROAD GRADE WATCH ADJUSTMENTS

The railroad watch, as well as other fine timepieces, had to compensate for several factors in order to be reliable and accurate at all times. These compensations, called adjustments, were for heat and cold, isochronism, and five to six different positions. These adjustments were perfected only after experimentation and a great deal of careful hand labor on each individual movement.

All railroad grade watches were adjusted to a closer rate to compensate for heat and cold. The compensation balance has screws in the rim of the balance wheel which can be regulated by the watchmaker. The movement was tested in an ice box and in an oven, and if it did not keep the same time in both temperature extremes, as well as under average conditions, the screws in the balance wheel was shifted or adjusted until accuracy was achieved.

The isochronism adjustment maintained accuracy of the watch both when the mainspring was fully wound up and when it was nearly run down. This was achieved by selecting a hairspring of exact proportions to cause the balance wheel to give the same length of arc of rotation regardless of the amount of the mainspring that had been spent.

Railroad watches were adjusted to be accurate whether they were laying on their face or back, or being carried on their edges with pendants up or down, or with the three up or the nine up. These adjustments were accomplished by having the jewels, in which the balance pivots rest, of proper thickness in proportion to the diameter of the pivot and, at the same time, equal to the surface on the end of the pivot which rests on the cap jewel. To be fully adjusted for positions, the balance wheel and the pallet and escape wheel must be perfectly poised. Perfect poise is achieved when the pivots can be supported on two knife-edged surfaces, perfectly smooth and polished and when the wheel is placed in any edge, it will remain exactly as it is placed. If it is not perfectly poised, the heaviest part of the wheel will always turn to the point immediately under the lines of support.

Example: Of a Bunn 16 size, 17 jewels, nickel 3/4 plate movement, lever set, gold jewel settings, gold center wheel, double roller, steel escape wheel, micrometric regulator, compensating balance. Adjusted to temperature, isochronism and 5 positions, artistically damaskeened.

🕐 NOTE: Railroad grade watches had a compensation balance made of brass and steel. Brass was used on the outside rim and steel on the inside. Brass is twice as sensitive to temperature changes and twice as thick as the steel balance (one-piece is welded to the steel balance wheel) and after finishing, the rim is cut at one end near the arm of the balance and at the same spot 180 across. In higher temperature, the dominant brass would "grow" longer but welded to the steel rim, it would curve inward, thus, in effect, placing the mass of the balance closer to the center of the balance wheel. This would cause the balance to go faster. However, the steel hairspring in rising temperature would also grow longer but more important would also lose some of its resilience. This would cause the watch to lose time. The balance, remember under the same condition, in effect became smaller and this action by the balance compensated for the loss of the hairspring's elasticity and lengthening. In cold temperatures, the opposite effect took place. This is why the balance is called a "compensation" balance. (It compensates for the temperature errors in the hairspring.)

The micrometric regulator or the patent regulator is a device used on all railroad grade and higher grade watches for the purpose of assisting in the finer manipulation of the regulator. It is arranged so that the regulator can be moved the shortest possible distance without fear of moving it too far. There is always a fine graduated index attached which makes it possible to determine just how much the regulator has been moved.

E. Howard Watch Co. Railroad Chronometer, Series 11, 16 size, 21 jewels, expressly designed for the railroad trade.

The hairspring used on the so-called ordinary and medium-grade watches is known as the flat hairspring. The Breguet hairspring was an improvement over the flat hairspring and was used on railroad and high-grade watches. The inside coil of any hairspring is attached to a collet on the balance staff and the end of the outside coil of the hairspring is attached to a stud which is held firmly by a screw in the balance wheel bridge. Two small regulator pins are fastened to the regulator. These pins clasp the outer side of the hairspring a short distance from the hairspring stud. If the regulator index is moved toward the "S," the regulator pins will move, allowing the hairspring to lengthen and the balance wheel to make a longer arc of rotation. This causes the watch to run slower because it requires a longer time for the wheel to perform the longer arc.

Bunn Special

1924 AD
Jewellers listed cost for movement only =$24.00
&
Jewellers selling price for movement only = $45.00

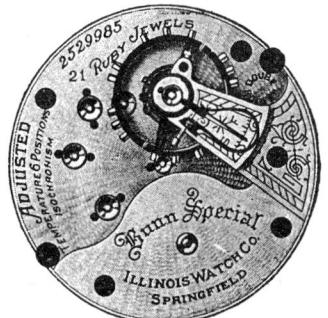

18 Size, 21 Jewels, Adjusted 6 Positions

21 ruby and sapphire jewels; gold settings; adjusted to temperature, SIX positions and isochronism; compensating balance; gold screws including timing screws; double roller; steel escape wheel; Breguet hairspring, patent micrometric screw regulator, safety screw center pinion, beautifully damaskeened with black enamel lettering, double sunk dial.

When the regulator is moved toward the "F" these regulator pins are moved from the stud which shortens the hairspring and makes shorter arcs of the balance wheel, thus causing the movement to run faster. Sometimes, after a heavy jolt, the coil next to the outside one will catch between these regulator pins and this will shorten the length of the hairspring just one round, causing a gaining rate of one hour per day. When this occurs, the hairspring can be easily released and will resume its former rate.

The Breguet <u>overcoil</u> hairspring, which is used on railroad grade movements, prevented the hairspring from catching on the regulator pins and protected against any lateral or side motion of the balance wheel ensuring equal expansion of the outside coil.

Railroad grade watches also used the patent or safety pinion which was developed to protect the train of gears from damage in the event of breakage of the mainspring. These pinions unscrewed in event of mainspring breakage, allowing the force to be harmlessly spent by the spinning barrel.

Some earlier railroad grade watches had non-magnetic movements. This was achieved by the use of non-magnetic metals for the balance wheel, hairspring, roller table and pallet. Two of the metals used were iridium and palladium, both very expensive.

Waltham, 18 size, unusual Railroad double sunk white porcelain dial is marked with uniquely placed minute numbers on the outer chapter and the hour chapter is in the center, the dial is also marked "Waltham Pat. Appl'd. For". This watch is a 1892 model & Appleton Tracy & Co. grade.

Ball Watch Co. Motto: "Carry a Ball and Time Them All." This case is base metal (20th Century Model) with Ball's patented Stirrup Bow. With the simple easy to read dial, this watch was a favorite among railroad men. 20th Century Model MODEL made of base metal, early 1900s.

RAILROAD WATCH DIALS

Railroad watch dials are distinguished by their simplicity. A true railroad watch dial contained no fancy lettering or beautiful backgrounds. The watches were designed to be functional and in order to achieve that, the dials contained bold black Arabic numbers against a white background. This facilitated ease of reading the time under even the most adverse conditions.

True railroad watches had the winding stem at the 12 o'clock position. The so-called "side winder," that winds at the 3 o'clock position, was not approved for railroad use. (The side winder is a watch movement designed for a hunter case but one that has been placed in an open-faced case.)

One railroad watch dial design was patented by a Mr. Ferguson. On this dial, the five minute numbers were much larger than the hour numbers which were on the inside. This dial never became very popular.

About 1910 the Montgomery dials began to appear. The distinguishing feature of the Montgomery dial is that each minute is numbered around the hour chapter. The five-minute divisions were in red, and the true Montgomery dial has the number "6" inside the minute register. These dials were favored by the railroad men.

The so-called Canadian dial had a 24-hour division inside the hour chapter.

The double-time hands are also found on some railroad grade watches. One hour hand was in blue or black and the other was in red or gold, one hour apart, to compensate for passing from one time zone to another.

Rockford Watch Co., Enamel Railroad double sunk dial, with two hour hands for a second time zone the hour hand at 2 O'clock is BLUE, the hour hand at 3 O'clock is RED or GOLD.

This style Illinois railroad watch cases were fitted with movements, re-rated and timed in their specially designed case at the factory as complete watches in a gold filled case with a hinged bezel . Note: This Illinois 60 hour single sunk dial, 17 size & referred to as a 16 size by the trade.

RAILROAD WATCH CASES

Open face cases were the only ones approved for railroad use. Railroad men sought a case that was tough and durable; one that would provide a dust-free environment for the movement.

The swing-out case offered the best protection against dust, but the screw-on back and bezel were the most popular open-face cases.

The lever-set was a must for railroad-approved watches and some of the case manufacturers patented their own styles of cases, most with a heavy bow. One example is the Stirrup Bow by the Ball Watch Co. Hamilton used a bar above the crown to prevent the stem from being pulled out. Glass was most commonly used for the crystal because it was not as likely to scratch.

RAILROAD GRADE OR
RAILROAD SERVICE

Note: Not all railroad GRADE watches were railroad **APPROVED**, to be approved each railroad line or company made a list of watch grades that they would approve for example, Southern Railway, Lake Shore Railroad & Santa Fe Railway System etc. Not all watches listed here are railroad approved, even though all are railroad grade.
(This list changed from year to year.)

BALL
All official R.R. standard with 19, 21, & 23J, hci5p, 18 &16S, open face.

COLUMBUS WATCH CO.
Columbus King, 21, 23, 25J; Railway King, 17-25J; Time King, 21-25J, 18S; Ruby Model, 16S.

ELGIN
1. "Pennsylvania Railroad Co." on dial, 18S, 15J & 17J, KW-KS, first model "B. W. Raymond."
2. "No. 349," 18S, seventh model, 17-21J.
3. Veritas, B. W. Raymond, or Father Time, 18S, 21-23J.
4: Grades 162, 270, 280, or 342 marked on back plate, 16S, 17-21J.
5. Veritas, Father Time, or Paillard Non-Magnetic, 16S, 19-23J.
6. 571, 21J or 572, 16S, 19J., also All wind indicator models.

HAMILTON
1. 18S= Grade 946= 23J, & 940, 942= 21J, & 944= 19J, & 924, 926, 934, 936, 938, 948 = 17J.
2. 16S = Grades 950, 950B, 950E= 23J, & 992, 992B, 992E, 954, 960, 970, 994, 990= 21J.
3. 16S = Grade 996= 19J & 972, 968, 964= 17J.

HAMPDEN
1. Special Railway, 17J, 21J, 23J; New Railway, 23J & 17J; North Am. Railroad, 21J;
   Wm. McKinley, 21J; John Hancock, 21J & 23J; John C. Duber, 21J, 18S.
2. 105, 21J; 104, 23J; John C. Duber, 21J; Wm. McKinley, 17, 21, & 23J;
   New Railway, 21J; Railway, 19J; Special Railway, 23J, 16S.

E. HOWARD & CO.
1. All Howard models marked "Adjusted" or deer symbol.
2. Split plate models, 18S or N size; 16S or L size.

Above: Double Hour Time Zone Hands, used on railroad watches & were reversible, available in RED & BLUE or GOLD & BLACK.

HOWARD WATCH CO.
All 16S with 19, 21, & 23J.

ILLINOIS
1. Bunn 15J marked "Adjusted," & Stuart, 15J marked "Adjusted," 18S.
2. Benjamin Franklin,17-26J; Bunn 17-21, 24J; Bunn Special,21-26J; Chesapeake & Ohio Sp.,24J;
   Interstate Chronometer, 23J;Lafayette, 24J; A. Lincoln, 21J; Paillard W. Co., 17-24J;
   Trainsmen, 23J; Pennsylvania Special 17-26J; The Railroader & Railroad King, 18S.
3. Benjamin Franklin,17-25J; Bunn,17-19J; Bunn Special,21-23J; Diamond Ruby Sapphire,21-23J;
   Interstate Chronometer,23J; Lafayette,23J; A.Lincoln,21J; Paillard Non-MagneticW.Co.,17-21J;
   Pennsylvania Special, 17, 21, & 23J; Santa Fe Special, 21J; Sangamo, 21-26J;
   Sangamo Special, 19-23J; grades 161, 161A=21J;163, 163A=23J & 187, and 189, 17J, 16S.

PEORIA WATCH CO.
15 & 17J with a patented regulator, 18S.

ROCKFORD
1. All 21 or more jewels, 16-18S, All and wind indicators.
2. Grades 900, 905, 910, 912, 918, 945, 200, 205, 18S.
3. Winnebago, 17-21J, 505, 515, 525, 535, 545, 555, 16S.

SETH THOMAS
Maiden Lane, 21-28J; Henry Molineux, 20J; 260 Model, 18S.

SOUTH BEND
1. Studebaker 329, Grade Nos. 323, and 327, 17-21J, 18S.
2. Studebaker 229, Grade Nos. 223, 227, 293, 295, 299, 17-21J, Polaris,21J; 16S.

UNITED STATES WATCH CO., MARION
United States, 19J, gold train.

U. S. WATCH CO., WALTHAM
The President, 17J, 18S.

WALTHAM
1. 1857 KW with Pennsylvania R.R. on dial, Appleton Tracy & Co. on movement.
2. Crescent Street, 17-23J; 1883 & 1892 Models; Appleton Tracy & Co., 1892 Model; Railroader,
   1892 Model; Pennsylvania Railroad; Special RR, Special RR King, Vanguard, 17 -23J, 1892
   Model; Grade 845, All wind indicators 18S.
3. American Watch Co., 17-21J, 1872 Models; American Watch Co., All wind indicators,
   ALL 17-23J Bridge Models; Crescent Street, 17-21J, 1899 & 1908 Models;
   Premier Maximus; Railroader; Riverside Maximus, 21-23J; Vanguard, 19-23J; 645 16S.

American Waltham Watch Co., Vanguard , 16 size, 19-23 jewels, winding indicator which alerts user to how far up or down the mainspring is wound. This watch was made to promote new sales in the railway industry.

Hamilton Watch Co., This was a favorite railroad style case by Hamilton model NO. 2 supplied in 10K or 14K gold filled. Note the Railroad style dial with red marginal figures as well as the bar-over-crown with "Hamilton Railroad" on crown.

CANADIAN PACIFIC SERVICE
RAILROAD APPROVED WATCHES 1899 to 1910

WALTHAM
Vanguard, 18-16S, 19-21-23 jewels
Crescent St., 18S, 19J; 18-16S, 21J
Appleton-Tracy 17J; also No. 845, 21J
Riverside 16S, 19J; Riverside Maximus, 16S, 23J;
No. 645, 16S, 21J, C. P. R. 18-16S, 17J; C.T. S. 18-16S, 17J
ELGIN
Veritas, 18-16S, 21-23J
B. W. R. 18-16S, 17-19-21J
Father Time 18-16S, 21J
Grade 349, 18S, 21J
HAMILTON
18S, 946, 23J; 940-942, 21J; 944, 19J; 936-938, 17J
16S, 950, 23J; 960-990-992, 21J; 952, 19J; 972, 17J
SOUTH BEND
18S, 327-329, 21J; 323, 17J
16S, 227-229, 21J; 223, 17J
BALL
All Balls 18S, 16S, 17-19-21-23J
ILLINOIS
Bunn Special, 18-16S, 21-23J; also Bunn 18-16S, 17-19J
A. Lincoln, 18-16S, 21J; Sangamo Special, 16S, 19-21-23J
SETH THOMAS
Maiden Lane, 18S, 25J; No. 260, 21J; No. 382, 17J
E. HOWARD WATCH CO.
16S Series, 0-23J, 5-19J, 2-17J, 10-21J; also No. 1, 21J
ROCKFORD
18S, Grade 918-905, 21J; Winnebago, 17J; also Grade 900, 24J
16S, Grades 545, 525, 515, 505, 21J; 655 W.I., 21J; and Grade 405, 17J
LONGINES
18S, Express Monarch, 17-19-21-23J
16S, Express Monarch, 17-19-21-23J
BRANDT-OMEGA
18S, D.D.R., 23J; C.C.C.R., 23J; C.D.R., 19J; C.C.R., 19J
(This list changed from year to year.)

AMERICAN RAILROAD APPROVED WATCHES 1930

The following requirements for railroad approved watches are outlined by Mr. R. D. Montgomery, General Watch Inspector of the Santa Fe Railway System:

"The regulation watch designated as of 1930 to be standard is described as follows:"

"16 size, American, lever-setting, 19 jewels or more, open face, winding at "12", double-roller escapement, steel escape wheel, adjusted to 5 positions,temperature and isochronism, which will rate within a variation not exceeding 6 seconds in 72 hour tests, pendant up, dial up and dial down, and be regulated to run within a variation not exceeding 30 seconds per week."

"The following listed makes and grades meet the requirements and comprise a complete list of watches acceptable. Watches bearing the name of jewelers or other names not standard trade marks or trade numbers will not be accepted:" (This list changed from year to year.)

AMERICAN WALTHAM W. CO.
(16 Size)
23J Premier Maximus
23J Riverside Maximus
23J Vanguard
  6 position
  winding indicator
23J Vanguard
  6 position
21J Crescent Street
21J No. 645
19J Vanguard
19J Riverside

BALL WATCH CO.
(16 Size)
23J Official R.R. Standard
21J Official R.R. Standard
19J Official R.R. Standard

ELGIN WATCH CO.
(16 Size)
23J Veritas
21J Veritas
21J B. W. Raymond
21J Father Time
21J No. 270

HAMILTON WATCH CO.
(16 Size)
23J No. 950
21J No. 990
21J No. 992
19J No. 952
19J No. 996

HAMPDEN WATCH CO.
(16 Size)
23J Special Railway
21J New Railway
19J Railway

HOWARD WATCH CO.
(16 Size)
All 23J
All 21J
All 19J

ILLINOIS WATCH CO.
(16 Size)
23J Sangamo Special
23J Sangamo
23J Bunn Special
21J Bunn Special
21J Sangamo
21J A. Lincoln
19J Bunn

SOUTH BEND WATCH CO.
(16 Size)
21J No. 227
21J No. 229
21J No. 295
19J No. 293

Union Pacific Railroad Time Inspectors , June, 1936

All new WATCHES must be <u>16 size with double roller</u> adjust to 5 positions & so stamped on plates, lever set, plain Arabic numbers , open-faced & wind at 12, maintain a rate of 30 seconds. The following will govern the NEW RAILROAD STANDARDS.
BALL=21&23 jeweled "Oficial Railroad Standard"; ELGIN=21&23 jeweled "B.W. Raymond"; HAMILTON="950 & 992"; ILLINOIS=21&23 jeweled "Bunn Special"; WALTHAM=23 jeweled "Vanguard".

CP RAIL SERVICE AS OF FEBRUARY 1, 1957

WALTHAM (16 SIZE)
23J Vanguard S. # 29, 634, 001 and up

ELGIN (16 Size)
21J B.W.R.
21J No. 571

HAMILTON (16 SIZE)
23J No. 950B
21J No. 992B

BALL W. Co.(16 Size)
21J (Hamilton) No. 992B
21J No. 435C

ZENITH (16 Size)
21J Extra RR 56

APPROVED WRIST WATCHES IN CP RAIL SERVICE

CYMA
17J RR 2852 M
25J RR 2872 A

GIRARD PERREGAUX
17J CP 307H.F.

LONGINES
17J RR 280

UNIVERSAL
19J RR 1205

ZENITH
18J RR 120 T

FERGUSON Patented Railroad Dial : Patent number on back. Valued at ; BALL = $350 to $550 and A.W.W.Co., Elgin, Hamilton, Illinois, etc., = $200 to $350 for MINT dials.

ELGIN WATCH CO., Montgomery Railroad Dial with red marginal numbers at 5, 10, 15, 20, 25, 30, 35, 40, 45, 50, 55, & 60. Valued at $75 to $135.

APPROVED WRIST WATCHES IN
CP RAIL SERVICE 1965
BATTERY POWERED

BULOVA ACCUTRON
17J 214
17J 218 Calendar

RODANIA
13J RR 2780 Calendar

WITTNAUER
13J RR 12 WT Calendar

APPROVED WRIST WATCHES SEMI-MECHANICAL
QUARTZ ANALOG BATTERY POWERED
IN CP RAIL SERVICE AS OF 1978

CYMA
7J Calendar RR 9361 Q
6J Calendar RR 960 Q

BULOVA
7J Calendar RR 9362 Q
6J Calendar RR 960.111Q

RODANIA
6J Calendar 9952.111RR
7J Calendar RR 9361 Q

ROTARY
7J Calendar RR 9366 Q

WYLER
7J Calendar RR 9361 Q

WITTNAUER
7J Calendar RR 2 Q 115 C

ADJUSTMENTS

There are **nine** basic adjustments for watch movements. They are:

heat 1
cold 1
isochronism 1
positions 6
TOTAL 9

THE SIX POSITION ADJUSTMENTS ARE:

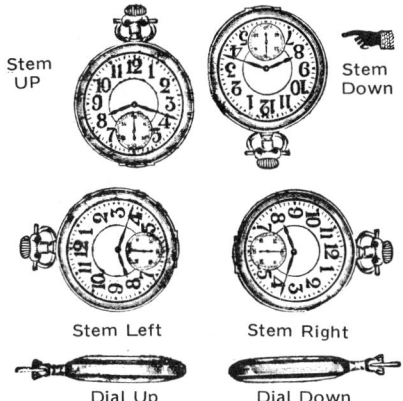

Stem UP

Stem Down

This position adjustment not required on railroad watches.

Stem Left

Stem Right

Dial Up

Dial Down

⏱ A watch marked as **5 positions** is equivalent to one marked *eight adjustments* (the most common found on RR watches) and will be listed in this book as: **"Adj.5P"** (adjusted to heat,cold, isochronism and 5 positions). A watch marked as **nine adjustments** is equivalent to one marked *6 positions* & listed as **"Adj.6P"** (adjusted to heat,cold, isochronism and 6 positions). A watch that is marked as *ADJUSTED* only is adjusted to isochronism & in poise in all temperatures & is listed as **"Adj."**.
* Later some manufactures used a variations of **8 adjustments, six to position, 1-isochronism, 1-temperature,** (*temperature* of heat & cold was combined to = one adjustment not two).

⏱ Not all railroad GRADE watches were railroad **APPROVED**, to be approved each railroad line or company made a list of watch grades that they would **approve** for example, Southern Railway, Lake Shore Railroad, CP Rail Service & Santa Fe Railway System etc.

WRIST WATCHES POSITION ADJUSTMENTS

CROWN UP - CROWN DOWN- CROWN LEFT - CROWN RIGHT - DIAL DOWN - DIAL UP
Main vertical position: Wrist Watches = CROWN DOWN & Pocket Watches = PENDANT UP.

The total number of pocket watches made for the railroad industry was small in comparison to the total pocket watches produced. Generally, watches defined as "Railroad Watches" fall into five categories:

1. **Railroad Approved-** A list of Grades and Models approved by the railway companies.
2. **Railroad Grade-**Those advertised as being able to pass or exceed railroad inspection.
3. **Pre-Commission Watches-**Those used by the railroads before 1893.
4. **Company Watches-**Those with a railroad logo or company name on the dial.
5. **Train Watches-**Those with a locomotive painted on the dial or inscribed on the case.

1.Not all railroad employees were required to purchase or use approved watches, just the employees that were responsible for schedules. But many employees did buy the approved watches because they were the standard in reliability.
2. These were used primarily by those railroaders who were not required to submit their watches for inspection.
3. There were many watches made for railroad use prior to 1893. Some of the key wind ones, especially, are good quality and highly collectible.
4 & 5. Some manufacturers inscribed logos & terms such as railroader, special railroad, dispatcher, etc. on the dials & back plates of the movements.

NOTE: Railroad Standards, Railroad Approved & Railroad Grade **terminology,** as defined and used in this **_BOOK_**. **RAILROAD STANDARDS** = A commission or board appointed by the railroad companies outlined a set of **guidelines** to be accepted or approved by each railroad line. **RAILROAD APPROVED** = A **_LIST_** of watches each railroad line would approve if purchased by their employee's. **(_this list changed through the years_). RAILROAD GRADE** = A watch made by manufactures to meet or exceed the railroad **standards.** Grades such as 992, Vanguard and B.W. Raymond, etc.
* Some GRADES **exceeded** the R.R. standards such as 23 jewels, diamond end stone, gold train, raised gold jewel settings, double sunk dial and the list goes on. Examples: such as Veritas, Sangamo, 950 & Riverside Maximus and many others.

COLONIAL WATCHMAKERS
(PRE—1850)

Early American watchmakers came from Europe; little is known about them, and few of their watches exist today. Their hand-fabricated watches were made largely from imported parts. It was common practice for a watchmaker to use rough castings made by several craftsmen. These were referred to as or "movements in the gray." The watchmaker finished the Ebauche movements and parts and assembled them to make a complete watch. He would then engrave his name on the finished timepiece.

Some of the early American watchmakers designed the cases or other parts, but most imported what they needed. The so called early **COLONIAL** watchmakers showed little originality as designers and we can only guess how many watches were really made in America.

These early hand-made watches are almost non-existent; therefore, only the name of the watchmaker will be listed. This compilation comes from old ads in newspapers and journals and other sources. It is not considered to be complete. Because of the rarity and condition of these early watches, prices may vary widely from **$800 to $12,000**.

As early as 1775 the first Swiss made watches came into the U.S.A. and made in the London style. In 1830, Vacheron & Constantin established a connection in New York through Jean Magnin. Later in mid 1830's extending their trade to Philadelphia and New Orleans and by 1838 Agassiz and later Jurgensen.

Early in the 1860's Swiss watches were sent to America. The Swiss Firms of Cortebert, E. Borel and Courvoisier made and **designed** watches to closely resemble the style of American watch case and movement. Examples the Ohio Watch Co. was distributed by Leon Lesquereaux and son (Junior) of Columbus, Ohio. E. Borel & Co. produced American style watches and shipped them to Lucien Morel & Ed. Droz at New York. These were followed later by the entire original designs of Omega, Tissot, Movado and Zenith.

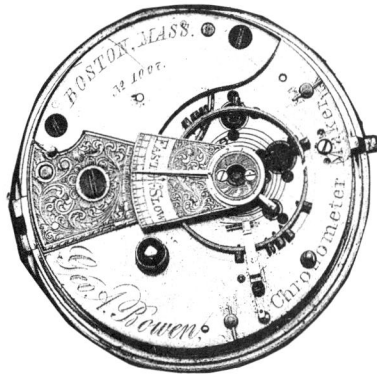

George Bowen, Boston Mass., engraved on movement "Chronometer Maker", KW KS, Spring Detent., Ca. 1850.

Davis Watson & Co. Boston, Fusee with right angle escapement lever, serial No. 8028 Ca. 1850.

Example of watch paper placed inside a pair-cased watch by a watch maker. This was a form of advertisement placed in the watch after repair was made.

Ephraim Clark, 18 size, non-jeweled, made between 1780-1790; a good example of a colonial watch. These early watches usually included chain driven fusees, verge type escapements, hand pierced balance cock, key wind & set; note the circular shaped regulator above the balance Cock.

Effingham Clark, New York, on dial & movement, the inner with Roman hour chapter and a sweep second outer dial, diamond stone, serial No. 720, Ca. 1815.

E. EMBREE, NEW YORK engraved on movement, serial # 790, chain driven fusee, silver pair cased watch, ca. early 1800's.

B. F. S. Patten, Bangor, Maine, LEFT & RIGHT; left a 48mm, 6 jewels, <u>Cylinder</u> escapement bar style Ebauche movement which may have been manufactured by Japy Freres with branches in France, Switzerland & England. Right; showing the movement cover that reads four holes jeweled but 6 jewels exits, Ca.1855 to 1865.("Continental Watch")

GREENLEUF & OAKES, Hartford, Ca. 1805, Greenleuf & Oakes formed a partnership in 1804, verge, pierced cock.

MARQUAND & CO., New York, Ca. 1850s, gold case, right angle lever escapement, fusee, gold dial.

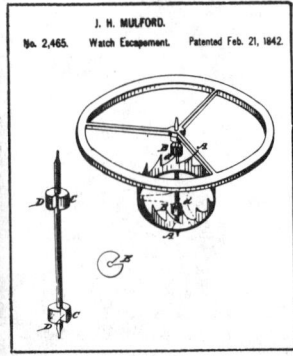

J. H. MULFORD, Albany, N. Y., produced watches from about 1835 to 1875, the two watch movements (A & B) are illustrated, A is about size 18, KWKS, gold jewel settings, compensated balance with gold screws. Movement B is 3 arm balance, diamond end stone. Note the J. H. Mulford patented verge style escapement patented # 2465,dated Feb. 21, 1842. illustrated to the far right.

EARLY AMERICAN WATCHMAKERS
(With Location and Approximate Date)

Adams, Nathan (Boston, MA, 1800)
Adams, William (Boston, MA, 1810)
Alden, & Eldridge (Bristol, Conn., 1820)
Aldrich, Jacob (Wilmington, DE, 1802)
Alrichs, Jonas (Wilmington, DE, 1880)
Allebach, Jacob (Phila., PA, 1825-1840)
Amant, Fester (Phila., PA, 1793)
Atherton, Nathan (Phila., PA, 1825)
Atkins & Allen (Bristol, Ct., 1820)
Atkinson, James (Boston, MA, 1745)
Austin, Isaac (Phila., PA, 1785)
Backhouse, John (Lancaster, PA, 1725)
Bagnall, Benjamin (Phila., PA, 1750)
Bailey, John (Boston, MA, 1810)
Bailey & Kitchen:(Phila,PA, 1832-46) name
changed to **Bailey, Banks & Biddle**
Bailey, William (Phila., PA, 1820)
Baker, Benjamin (Phila., PA, 1825)
Banks, Joseph (Phila., PA, 1790)
Banstein, John (Phila.,PA, 1790)
Barnes, Timothy (Litchfield, Conn. 1790)
Barnhill, Robert (Phila., PA, 1775)
Barrow, Samuel (Phila., PA, 1771)
Barry, Standish (Baltimore, MD, 1785)
Basset, John F. (Phila., PA, 1798)
Batterson, James (New York 1705-30)
Bayley, Simeon C., (Phila., PA 1795)
Beard, Duncan (Appoquinemonk, Del.1765)
Belk, William (Phila., PA 1796)
Belknap, William (Boston, MA, 1815)
Bell, William (Phila., PA, 1805)
Benedict, S. W. (New York, NY, 1835)
Bigger & Clarke (Baltimore, MD, 1783)
Billion, C. (Phila., PA, 1775-1800)
Billow, Charles & Co. (Phila., PA 1796
Bingham & Bricerly (Phila., PA, 1778-1799)
Birge, Mallory & Co. (Bristol, Conn. 1830)
Birge, Peck & Co. (Bristol, Conn. 1830)
Birnie, Laurence (Phila., PA, 1774)
Blundy, Charles (Charleston, SC, 1750)
Blunt & Nichols (New York, NY, 1850)
Boardman, Chauncey (Bristol, Conn.1815)
Boardman, & Dunbar (Bristol, Conn. 1811)
Boardman, & Wells (Bristol, Conn. 1815)
Bode, William (Phila., Pa 1796)
Bogardus, Evarardus (New York, 1698)
Bond, William (Boston,MA, 1800-1810)
Bonnaud (Phila., PA, 1799)
Bower, Michael (Phila., PA, 1790-1800)
Bowman, Joseph (Lancaster, PA, 1821-44)
Boyd & Richards (Phila., PA, 1808)
Boyter, Daniel (Lancaster, PA, 1805)
Brands & Matthey (Phila., PA, 1799)
Brandt, Aime (Phila., PA, 1820)
Brant, Brown & Lewis (Phila., PA, 1795)
Brazier, Amable (Phila., PA, 1795)
Brearley, James (Phila., PA, 1790-1800)
Brewer, William (Phila., PA, 1785-1791)
Brewster, Abel (Norwich, CT) 1802
Brewster &Ingraham(Bristol,CT,1827-39)
Brown, Davis (Boston, 1800)
Brown, Garven (Boston, MA, 1767)
Brown, John (Lancaster, PA, 1840)
Brown, Samuel (New York, 1820-1850)
Brownell, A. P. (New Bedford, MA.1840-60)
Burkelow, Samuel (Phila., PA, 1791-1799)

Burnop, Daniei (E. Windsor, Conn., 1793)
Bush, George (Easton, PA, 1790-1800)
Campbell, Charles (Phila., PA, 1796)
Campbell, William (Carlisle, PA, 1765)
Canby, Charles (Wilmington, Del., 1825)
Capper, Michael (Phila., PA, 1799)
Carey, James (Brunswick, ME, 1830)
Carrell, John (Phila., PA, 1791-1793)
Carter, Jacob (Phila., PA, 1805)
Carter, Thomas (Phila., PA, 1823)
Carver, Jacob (Phila., PA, 1790)
Carvill, James (New York, NY, 1803)
Chandlee, John(Wilmington,DE,1795-1810)
Chaudron, Co., (Phila., PA, 1799- 1815)
Chauncey & Joseph Ives (Bristol, CT, 1825)
Cheney, Martin (Windsor, VT, 1800)
Chick, M. M. (Concord, NH, 1845)
Clark,Benjamin(Wilmington,DE,1737-1750)
Clark, Charles (Phila., PA 1810)
Clark, Ephraim (Phila., PA, 1780-1800)
Clark, J.H. & Co. (Memphis Tenn, 1835)
Clark, John (New York, NY, 1770-1790)
Clark, John (Phila., PA, 1799)
Clark, Thomas (Boston, MA, 1764)
Claudon,John-George (Charleston SC,1773)
Cook, William (Boston, MA, 1810)
Crow, George (Wilmington, DE, 1740-1770)
Crow, John (Wilmington, DE, 1770-1798)
Crow, Thomas (Wilmington, DE, 1770-98)
Currier & Trott (Boston, MA, 1800)
Curtis, Solomon (Phila., PA, 1793-1795)
Dakin, James (Boston, MA, 1795)
Davis, Samuel (Boston, MA, 1820)
Davis,Watson & Co.(Boston, 1840-1850)
Delaplaine, James K.(New York, 1786-1800)
DeVacht, Joseph & Frances (Gallipolis, OH, 1792)
Dickinson, Thos. (Boston, 1810)
Dix, Joseph (Phila., PA, 1770)
Downes, Anson (Bristol, CT, 1830)
Downes, Arthur (Charleston, SC, 1765)
Downes, Ephriam (Bristol, CT, 1830)
Droz, Hannah (Phila., PA, 1840)
Droz, Humbert (Phila., PA, 1793-1799)
Duffield, Edward W. (Whiteland, PA, 1775)
Dunheim, Andrew (New York, NY, 1775)
Dupuy, John (Phila., PA, 1770)
Dupuy, Odran (Phila., PA, 1735)
Dutch, Stephen, Jr. (Boston, MA.1800-10)
Eberman, George (Lancaster, PA, 1800)
Eberman, John (Lancaster, PA, 1780-1820)
Ellicott, Joseph (Buckingham, PA, 1763)
Elsworth, David (Baltimore, MD.1780-1800)
Embree, Effingham (New York, NY, 1785)
Evans, David (Baltimore, MD, 1770-1773)
Fales, James (New Bedford, MA.1810-20)
Ferris, Tiba (Wilmington, DE, 1812-1850)
Fessler, John (Phila., PA, 1785-1820)
Feton, J. (Phila., PA, 1825-1840)
Filber, John (Lancaster, PA, 1810-1825)
Fister, Amon (Phila., PA, 1794)
Fix, Joseph (Reading, PA, 1820-1840)
Fowell, J & N (Boston, MA, 1800-1810)
Frances,Basil & Alexander Vuille(Baltimore,1766)
Galbraith, Patrick (Phila., PA, 1795)
Gibbons, Thomas (Phila., PA, 1750)
Goodfellow, William (Phila., PA,1793-1795)

Goodfellow & Son, William (Phila., PA,1796)
Gooding, Henry (Boston, MA, 1810-1820)
Green, John (Phila., PA, 1794)
Griffen, Henry (New York, 1790)
Groppengeiser, J. L. (Phila., PA, 1840)
Grotz, Issac (Easton, PA, 1810-1835)
Hall, Jonas (Boston, MA, 1848-1858)
Harland, Theodore (Norwich, CT,1750-90)
Harland, Thomas (New York, 1805)
Harland, Thomas (Norwich, CT, 1802)
Harrison, James (Shrewbury, MA, 1805)
Hawxhurst & Demilt (New York, 1800)
Hawxhurst, Nath. (New York, NY, 1784)
Heilig, Jacob (Phila., PA, 1770-1824)
Heilig, John (Germantown, PA, 1824-1830)
Hepton, Frederick (Phila., PA, 1785)
Heron, Isaac (New York, NY, 1770-1780)
Hill, D. (Reading, PA 1830)
Hodgson, William (Phila., PA, 1785)
Hoff, John (Lancaster, PA, 1800)
Hoffner, Henry (Phila., PA, 1791)
Howard, Thomas (Phila., PA, 1789-1791)
Howe, Jubal (Shrewbury, MA, 1800)
Huguenail, Charles (Phila., PA, 1799)
Hunt, Hiram (Robbinston, ME, 1800)
Hutchins, Abel (Concord, MA, 1785-1818)
Hutchins, Levi (Concord, MA, 1785-1815)
Hyde, John E. (New York, NY, 1805)
Hyde & Goodrich (New Orleans, LA, 1850)
Ingersoll, Daniel B. (Boston, MA, 1800-10)
Ingold, Pierre Frederick (NY, NY,1845-50)
Ives, Chauncy & Joseph (Bristol, CT, 1825)
Jacob, Charles & Claude (Annapolis, 1775)
Jackson, Joseph H. (Phila., PA, 1802-1810)
Jessop, Jonathan (Park Town, PA, 1790)
Jeunit, Joseph (Meadville, PA, 1763)
Johnson, Chauncy (AlbanyN.Y., (1825-1840)
Johnson, David (Boston, MA, 1690)
Johnson, John (Charleston, SC, 1763)
Jones, George (Wilmington, DE, 1815-35)
Jones, Low & Ball (Boston, MA, 1830)
Keith, William (Shrewbury, MA, 1810)
Kennedy, Patrick (Phila., PA, 1795-1799)
Kincaid, Thomas (Christiana Bridge, DE, Ca. 1775)
Kirkwood, John (Charleston, SC, 1761)
Kumble, Wm. (New York- 1776)
Launy, David F. (Boston & N. Y., 1800)
Leavenworth, Mark (Waterbury, CT, 1820)
Leavenworth, Wm. (Waterbury, CT, 1810)
Leslie & Co., Baltimore, MD, 1795)
Leslie & Price (Phila., PA, 1793-1799)
Leslie, Robert (Baltimore, MD, 1788-1791)
Levely, George (Phila., PA, 1774)
Levi, Michael & Issac (Baltimore,MD,1785)
Limeburner, John (Phila., PA, 1790)
Lind, John (Phila., PA, 1791-1799)
Lowens, David (Phila., PA, 1785)
Ludwig, John (Phila., PA, 1791)
Lufkins & Johnson (Boston, MA, 1800-10)
Lukins, Isaac (Phila., PA, 1825)
Macdowell, Robert (Phila., PA, 1798)
MacFarlane, John (Boston, MA, 1800-1810)
Mahve, Matthew (Phila., PA, 1761)
Manross, Elisha (Bristol, CT, 1827)
Martin, Patrick (Phila., PA, 1830)
Mathey, Louis (Phia., PA, 1800)
Maunroe & Whitney (Concord,MA,1800's)
Maus, Frederick (Phila., PA, 1785- 1793)

Maynard, George(New York,NY,1702-1730)
McCabe, John (Baltimore, MD, 1774)
McDowell, James (Phila., PA, 1795)
McGraw, Donald (Annapolis, MD, 1767)
Mends, James (Phila., PA, 1795)
Merriman, Titus (Bristol, CT, 1830)
Merry, Charles F. (Phila., PA, 1799)
Meters, John(Fredricktown, MD,1795-1825)
Miller, Abraham (Easton, PA, 1810-1830)
Mitchell & Atkins (Bristol, CT, 1830)
Mitchell, Henry (N. Y., NY, 1787-1800)
Mohler, Jacob (Baltimore, MD, 1773)
Moir, J & W (Waterbury, CT, 1790)
Montandon, Julien (Shrewbury, CT, 1812)
Moollinger, Henry (Phila., PA, 1794)
Morgan, Thomas (Phila. & Balti., 1774-93)
Moris, William (Grafton, MA, 1765-1775)
Mulford, J. H. (Albany, NY, 1845)
Mulliken, Nathaniel (Boston, MA, 1765)
Munroe & Whitney (Concord, MA, 1820)
Narney, Joseph (Charleston, SC, 1753)
Neiser, Augustine (Phila., PA, 1739-1780)
Nicholls, George (New York, NY, 1728-50)
Nicollette, Mary (Phila., PA, 1793-1799)
O'Hara, Charles (Phila., PA, 1799)
Oliver, Griffith (Phila., PA, 1785-1793)
Ormsby, James (Baltimore, MD, 1771)
Palmer, John (Phila., PA, 1795)
Palmer, John Peter (Phila., PA, 1795)
Park, Seth (Parktown, PA, 1790)
Parke, Solomon (Phila., PA, 1791-1795)
Parke, Solomon & Co. (Phila., PA, 1799)
Parker, James (Cambridge, OH, 1790)
Parker, Thomas (Phila., PA, 1783)
Parry, John J. (Phila., PA, 1795-1800)
Patton, Abraham (Phila., PA, 1799)
Patton, David (Phila., PA, 1800)
Payne, Lawrence (New York, NY,1732-55)
Pearman, W. (Richmond, VA, 1834)
Perkins, Thomas (Phila., PA. 1785-1800)
Perry, Marvin (New York, NY, 1770-1780)
Perry, Thomas (New York, NY, 1750-1775)
Phillips, Joseph (New York, NY, 1713-35)
Pierret, Mathew (Phila., PA, 1795)
Pope, Joseph (Boston, MA, 1790)
Price, Philip (Phila., PA, 1825)
Proctor, Cardan (New York, NY.1747-75)
Proctor, William (New York,NY.1737-1760)
Proud, R. (Newport, RI, 1775)
Potter, J.O.&J.R. (Providence,R.I.1849-59)
Purse, Thomas (Baltimore, MD, 1805)
Quimby, Phineas & William (Belfast, ME, 1825)
Reily, John (Phila., PA, 1785-1795)
Rich, John (Bristol, CT, 1800)
Richardson, Francis (Phila., PA, 1736)
Ritchie, George (Phila., PA, 1785-1790)
Roberts, John (Phila., PA, 1799)
Roberts, S & E (Trenton, NJ, 1830)
Rode, William (Phila., PA, 1785)
Rodger, James (New York, NY, 1822-1878)
Rodgers,Samuel (Plymouth,MA, 1800's)
Russell, George (Phila., PA, 1840)
Saxton & Lukens (Phila., PA, 1828)
Schriner, Martin (Lancaster, PA.1790-1830)
Schriner, M & P (Lancaster, PA, 1830-40)
Seddinger, Margaret (Phila., PA, 1846)
Severberg, Christian (NY, NY, 1755-1775)
Sherman, Robert(Wilmington, DE.1760-70)

Sibley, O. E. (New York, NY, 1820)
Simpson, Saml. (Clarksville,Tenn - 1855)
Smith, J. L. (Middletown, CT, 1830)
Smith & Goodrich (Bristol, CT, 1827-1840)
Soloman, Henry (Boston, MA, 1820)
Souza, Sammuel (Phila., PA, 1820)
Sprogell, John (Phila., PA, 1791)
Spurck, Peter (Phila., PA, 1795-1799)
Stanton, Job (New York, NY, 1810)
Stein, Abraham (Phila., PA, 1799)
Stever & Bryant (Wigville, CT, 1830)
Stillas, John (Phila., PA, 1785-1793)
Stinnett, John (Phila., PA, 1769)
Stokel, John (New York, NY, 1820-1840)
Store, Marmaduke (Phila., PA, 1742)
Strech, Thomas (Phila., PA, 1782)
Syderman, Philip (Phila., PA, 1785)
Taf, John James (Phila., PA, 1794)
Taylor, Samuel (Phila, PA, 1799)
Tonchure, Francis (Baltimore, MD, 1805)

Townsend, Charles (Phila., PA, 1799)
Townsend, David (Boston, MA, 1800)
Trott, Andrew (Boston, MA, 1800-1810)
Turrell, Samuel (Boston, MA, 1790)
Voight, Henry (Phila., PA, 1775-1793)
Voight, Sebastian (Phila., PA, 1775-1799)
Voight, Thomas (Henry's son) (Phila., PA, 1811-1835)
Vuille, Alexander (Baltimore, MD, 1766)
Warner, George T. (New York, NY, 1795)
Watson, Davis (Boston, 1840-50)
Weller, Francis (Phila., PA, 1780)
Wells, George & Co. (Boston, MA, 1825)
Wells, J.S. (Boston, MA, 1800)
Wetherell, Nathan (Phila., PA, 1830-1840)
Wheaton, Caleb (Providence, RI, 1800)
White, Sebastian (Phila., PA, 1795)
Whittaker, William (NY, NY, 1731-1755)
Wood, John (Phila., PA, 1770-1793)
Wright, John (New York, NY, 1712-1735)
Zahm, G.M. (Lancaster, PA, 1865)

Watch made by Andrew, Dunheim of New York in about 1775. Note the hand pierced case.

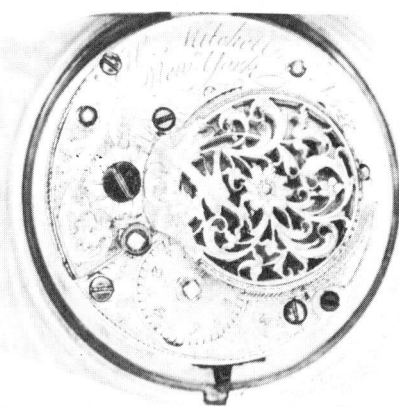

Louis Mathey, Philadelphia engraved on movement, about 18 size, very thin movement, **Virgule** escapement, key wind & set from back, Ca.1795-1805.

H. Mitchell, New York, 18 size, verge chain driven fusee; note the regulator below hand-pierced cock, Ca. 1790.

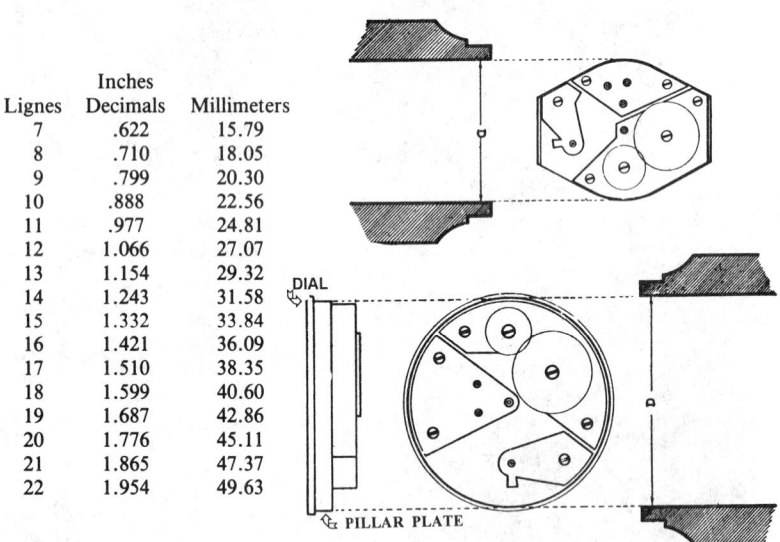

|10| 20| 30| 40| 50| 60| 70| 80| 90| 100| 110|

MILLIMETERS

HOW TO DETERMINE SIZE

AMERICAN MOVEMENT SIZES
LANCASHIRE GAUGE

Size	Inches	Inches	mm	Lignes	Size	Inches	Inches	mm	Lignes
18/0	18/30	.600	15.24	6 3/4	2	1 7/30	1.233	31.32	13 7/8
17/0	19/30	.633	16.08	7 1/8	3	1 8/30	1.266	32.16	14 1/4
16/0	20/30	.666	16.92	7 1/2	4	1 9/30	1.300	33.02	14 7/8
15/0	21/30	.700	17.78	7 7/8	5	1 10/30	1.333	33.86	15 1/8
14/0	22/30	.733	18.62	8 1/4	6	1 11/30	1.366	34.70	15 3/8
13/0	23/30	.766	19.46	8 5/8	7	1 12/30	1.400	35.56	15 3/4
12/0	24/30	.800	20.32	9 1/8	8	1 13/30	1.433	36.40	16 1/8
11/0	25/30	.833	21.16	9 3/8	9	1 14/30	1.466	37.24	16 1/2
10/0	26/30	.866	22.00	9 3/4	10	1 15/30	1.500	38.10	16 7/8
9/0	27/30	.900	22.86	10 1/8	11	1 16/30	1.533	38.94	17 1/4
8/0	28/30	.933	23.70	10 1/2	12	1 17/30	1.566	39.78	17 5/8
7/0	29/30	.966	24.54	10 7/8	13	1 18/30	1.600	40.64	18 1/8
6/0	1	1.000	25.40	11 1/4	14	1 19/30	1.633	41.48	18 3/8
5/0	1 1/30	1.033	26.24	11 5/8	15	1 20/30	1.666	42.32	18 3/4
4/0	1 2/30	1.066	27.08	12 1/8	16	1 21/30	1.700	43.18	19 1/8
3/0	1 3/30	1.100	27.94	12 3/8	17	1 22/30	1.733	44.02	19 1/2
2/0	1 4/30	1.133	28.78	12 3/4	18	1 23/30	1.766	44.86	19 7/8
0	1 5/30	1.166	29.62	13 1/8	19	1 24/30	1.800	45.72	20 1/4
1	1 6/30	1.200	30.48	13 1/2	20	1 25/30	1.833	46.56	20 3/4

SWISS MOVEMENT SIZES
Lignes With Their Equivalents in Millimeters and Decimal Parts of an Inch

Lignes	Inches Decimals	Millimeters
7	.622	15.79
8	.710	18.05
9	.799	20.30
10	.888	22.56
11	.977	24.81
12	1.066	27.07
13	1.154	29.32
14	1.243	31.58
15	1.332	33.84
16	1.421	36.09
17	1.510	38.35
18	1.599	40.60
19	1.687	42.86
20	1.776	45.11
21	1.865	47.37
22	1.954	49.63

DIAL

PILLAR PLATE

GAUGES FOR MEASURING YOUR WATCH SIZE

The size of a watch is determined by measuring the outside diameter of the dial side of the lower pillar plate. The gauges below may be placed across the face of your watch to calculate its approximate size.

AMER. MOVEMENT SIZES

SWISS MOVEMENT SIZES
LIGNES

SOLID GOLD MARKS

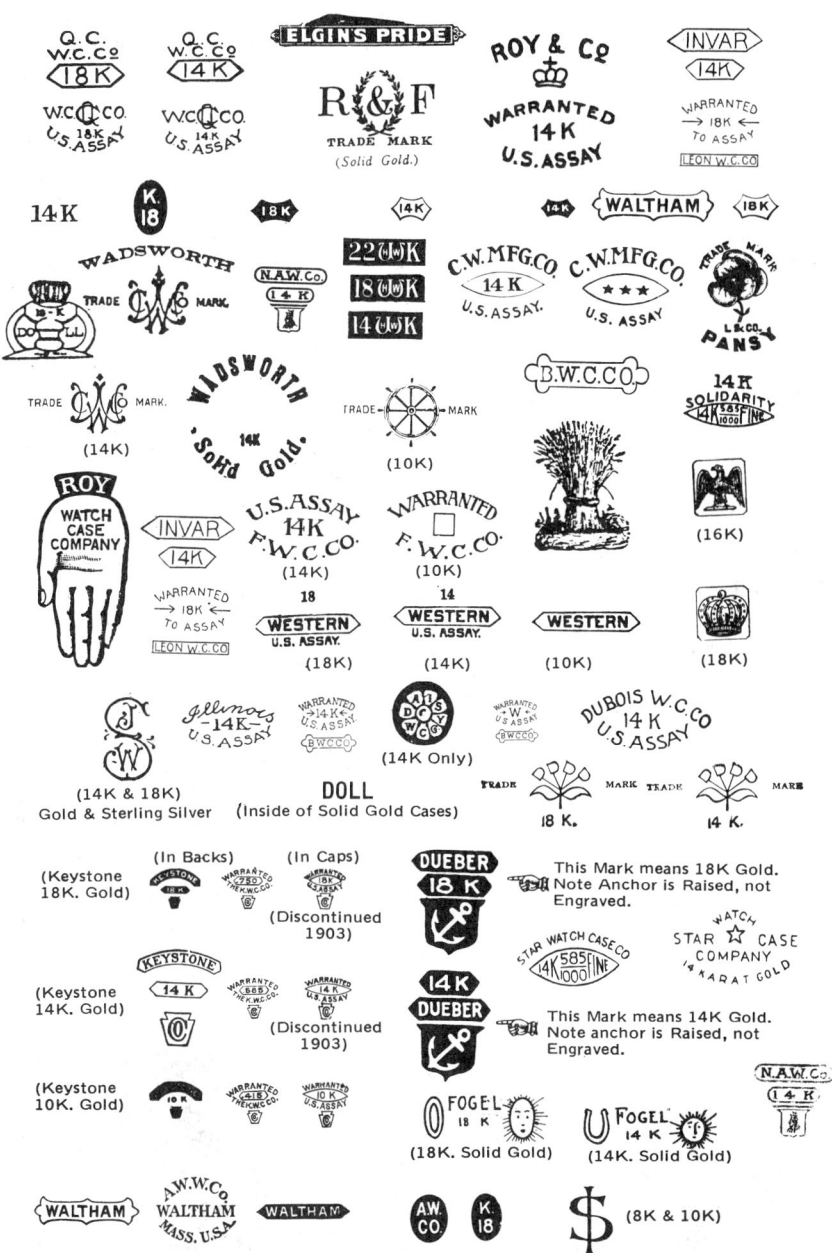

IMPORTANT NOTE: Have your watch case TESTED to make sure of gold quality or Karat.

The term **KARAT** is a word of definition in regards to the quality of gold, one 24th part (of pure gold). For example: Pure or fine gold is 24 karats; 18 Karat (abbreviated 18 K)consist of 18 parts of pure gold and mixed with 6 parts of other metal. The term **CARAT** is a unit of weight for gemstones, 200 milligrams equal 1 Carat. Karat = gold content & Carat = weight of GEMS.

GOLD-FILLED CASES

The first patent for gold-filled cases was given to J. Boss on **May 3, 1859.** Gold-filled cases are far more common than solid gold cases. Only about 5 percent of the cases were solid gold. In making the gold-filled case, the following process was used: two bars of gold, 12'' long, 2'' wide, and 1/2 '' thick were placed on either side of a bar of base metal. The bar of base metal was 3/4'' thick and the same length and width as the gold bars. These three bars were soldered together under pressure at high temperature. The bars were sent through rolling mills under tremendous pressure; this rolling was repeated until the desired thickness was reached. The new sandwich-type gold was now in a sheet. Discs were punched out of the sheet and pressed in a die to form a dish-shaped cover. Finally the lip, or ridge, was added. The bezel, snap, and dust caps were added in the finishing room. Gold-filled cases are usually 10k or 14k gold. The cases were marked ten-year, fifteen-year, twenty-year, twenty-five-year, or thirty-year. The number of years indicated the duration of guarantee that the gold on the case would not wear through to the base metal. The higher the number of years indicates that more gold used and that a higher original price was paid.

In 1924 the government prohibited any further use of the guarantee terms of 5, 10, 15, 20, 25, or 30 years. After that, manufacturers marked their cases 10k or 14k Gold-Filled and 10k Rolled Gold Plate. Anytime you see the terms ''5, 10, 15, 20, 25 and 30-year,'' this immediately identifies the case as being gold-filled. The word ''guaranteed'' on the case also denotes gold-filled.

Rolled Gold

Rolled gold involved rolling gold into a micro thinness and, under extreme pressure, bonding it to each sheet of base metal. Rolled gold carried a five-year guarantee. The thickness of the gold sheet varied and had a direct bearing on value, as did the richness of the engraving.

Gold Gilding

Brass plates, wheels and cases are often gilded with gold. To do this, the parts are hung by a copper wire in a vessel or porous cell of a galvanic battery filled with a solution of ferro-cyanide of potassium, carbonate of soda, chloride of gold, and distilled water. An electric current deposits the gold evenly over the surface in about a six-minute period. One ounce of gold is enough for heavy gilding of six hundred watches. After gilding, the plates are polished with a soft buff using powdered rouge mixed with water and alcohol. The older method is fire-gilt which uses a gold and mercury solution. The metal is subjected to a high temperature so the mercury will evaporate and leave the gold plating. This is a very dangerous method, however, due to the harmful mercury vapor.

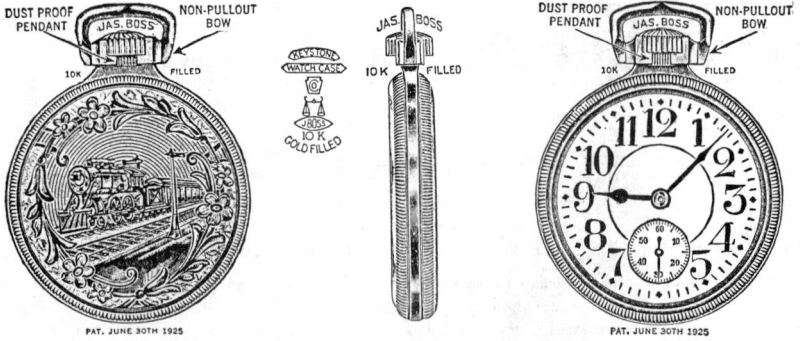

JAS. BOSS Railroad Model 10K Gold Filled cases sold for $14.00 in 1927

GOLD-FILLED MARKS

The following gold-filled and rolled gold plate marks are not complete, but if you have any doubt that the case is solid gold, **pay** only the _gold-filled_ price.

DUEBER WARRANTED 20 YEARS
(14K. 30 Years.)

WARRANTED DUEBER 25 YEARS

GUARANTEED ESSEX 14K SUPERIOR 25 YEARS

GUARANTEED 14K ESSEX 20 YEARS

GUARANTEED 14K ESSEX 10 YEARS

COLUMBIA TRADE MARK.

(Gold Filled, 10K.)

On Cap. GUARANTEED TO BE MADE OF TWO PLATES OF 14 KARAT GOLD OVER FINE HARD METAL AND TO WEARS FOR 20 YEARS.

On Cap. GUARANTEED TO BE MADE OF TWO PLATES OF 10 KARAT GOLD OVER FINE HARD METAL AND TO WEARS FOR 20 YEARS.

FAHYS (10K. Filled.)

On Back. TRADE MARK. CANTON.O. U.S.A.

DUEBER

NEWPORT

(Jas. Boss 14K. Filled. 25 Years.)

SOUTH BEND PILGRIM

SOUTH BEND PANAMA

SOUTH BEND PYRAMID

DERBY TRADE MARK.

(Jas. Boss 10K. Filled. 20 Years.)

DUEBER Engraved Anchor 10 K filled

WARRANTED Fahys

EMPRESS A.W.C.CO.

PHILADELPHIA WATCH CASE CO. VICTORY

10K RGP

☆ 10 K GOLDFILLED
☆ 14 K GOLDFILLED

DUEBER SPECIAL (Engraved) Anchor = 14 K filled

10 K GOLDFILLED
14 K GOLDFILLED

Illinois WATCH CASE CO. ELGIN U.S.A. GUARANTEED GIANT 20 YEARS

Illinois WATCH CASE CO. ELGIN U.S.A. GUARANTEED EMPIRE 25 YEARS

Illinois WATCH CASE CO. ELGIN U.S.A. GUARANTEED COMMANDER 25 YEARS

WATCH STAR CASE COMPANY 14 KT GOLD FILLED

ELGIN PRIDE GUARANTEED PERMANENT

GUARANTEED 10 YEARS

Elgin Suhrem

ONE-SIXTH GOLD PRIDE OF ELGIN

MONITOR

ILLINOIS WATCH CASE CO. ELGIN NAPOLEON GUARANTEED TEN YEARS

NAPOLEON I.W.C.CO.

WATCH STAR CASE COMPANY 10 KT GOLD FILLED

Elgin Giant WATCH CASE CO. ELGIN.U.S.A. 18K GOLD FILLED GUARANTEED 25 YEARS DoubleStock

Illinois WATCH CASE CO ELGIN U.S.A. ELGIN PRIDE GUARANTEED PERMANENT

Elgin Giant WATCH CASE CO. ELGIN.U.S.A. 14K GOLD FILLED GUARANTEED 25 YEARS DoubleStock

GUARANTEED GENERAL 10 YEARS

NE

WATCH STAR CASE COMPANY 10K GOLD FILLED P-6827

Important Notice. All of the information, including valuations, in this book has been compiled from the most reliable sources, and every effort has been made to eliminate errors and questionable data. Nevertheless, the possibility of error, in a work of such immense scope, always exists. The publisher or authors will not be held responsible for losses which may occur in the purchase, sale, or other transaction of items, because of information contained herein. Readers who feel they have discovered errors are invited to write and inform us, so they may be corrected in subsequent editions.

GOLD FILLED MARKS

☆ 10K ROLLED GOLD PLATE

BEE HIVE

(14K. Filled.)

*(Jas. Boss
10K. Filled.
20 Years.)*

*(Keystone Extra,
Substitute for
All-Gold Case.)*

CROWN 14K. FILLED
(25 Years.)

CROWN 10K. FILLED
(20 Years.)

(Rolled Gold.)

*(Jas. Boss
14K. Filled.
25 Years.)*

EMPRESS
(Gold Filled, 10 Years.)

FORTUNE
(Gold Filled, 20 Years.)

(10 Years.)

(14K. Filled.)

V.

XV.

(15 Years.)

**THE BELL
14K.**
(25 Years.)

XX.

(25 Years.)

PREMIER
(Gold Filled, 25 Years.)

CASHIER
(Gold Filled, 25 Years.)

THE COMET
(10 Years.)

(10K. Gold Filled.)

(5 Years.)

(20 Years.)

SILVER CASE MARKS

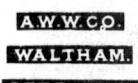

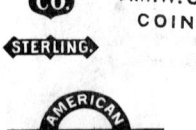

A.W.W. CO.
COIN.

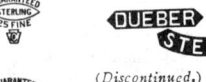

(Discontinued.)

(Discontinued.)

(Coin Silver with Albata Cap)
(Discontinued.)

(Coin Silver with Silver Cap)
(Discontinued.)

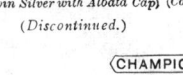

CHAMPION
COIN.

STAR W.C.CO

STERLING
925/1000
FINE

*(Coin Silver, with Silver Caps,
Gold Joints and Crowns.)*

N.A.W.Co
STERLING

(Sterling Silver.)

Sterling Silver

IMPORTANT NOTE: Have your watch case TESTED to make sure of gold quality or Karat.

NICKEL SILVER is 66% Copper, 24% Zinc, and 10% Nickel (also known as <u>Silveroid</u> etc.)

SILVER CASE MARKS

(Sterling Silver.)

STERLING
SILVER
UNITED STATES
ASSAY
925/1000
FINE.

ILLINOIS
W.C.CO,
ELGIN
STERLING

HUNTING CASES

A hunting case is identified by a cover over the face (concealed dial) of the watch. The case is opened by pressing the stem or the crown of the watch. The hunter style watch was used for protection of the watch and carried by men of status and used as a dress watch.

HOW TO HANDLE A HUNTING CASE WATCH

Hold the watch in your right hand with the bow or swing ring between the index finger and thumb. Press on the pendant-crown with the right thumb to release the cover exposing the face.

When closing, do not **SNAP** the cover. Press the crown to move the catch in, close the cover, then release the crown. This will prevent wear to the soft gold on the rim and catch.

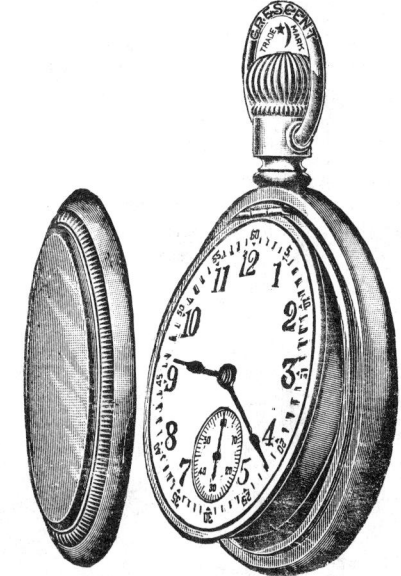

Above: Example of a hunting case

Right: Example of a swing-out case

SWING-OUT MOVEMENT

On some pocket watches the movement swings out from the front. On these type watches the movement can be swung out by unscrewing the crystal and pulling the stem out to **release** the movement. **SEE EXAMPLE ABOVE.**

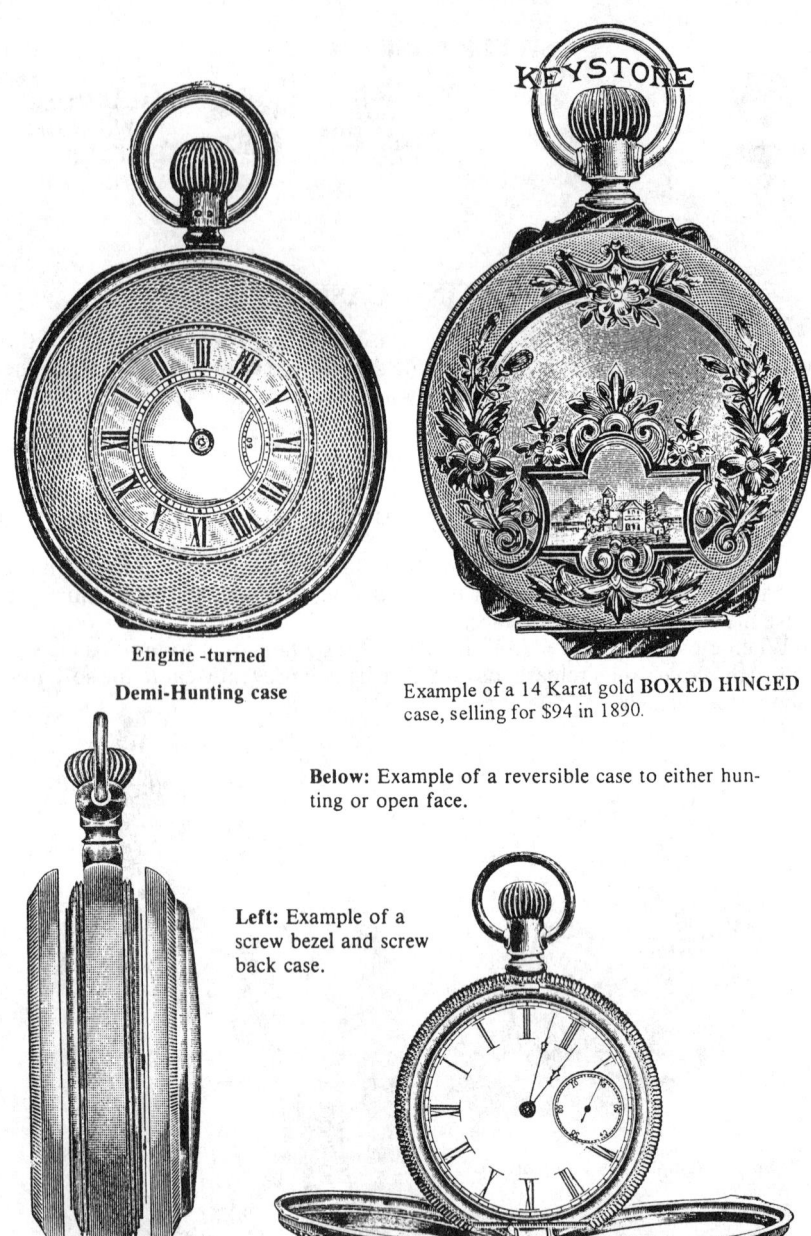

Engine -turned

Demi-Hunting case

Example of a 14 Karat gold **BOXED HINGED** case, selling for $94 in 1890.

Below: Example of a reversible case to either hunting or open face.

Left: Example of a screw bezel and screw back case.

Note: The screw on bezel was invented by E. C. Fitch in 1886.

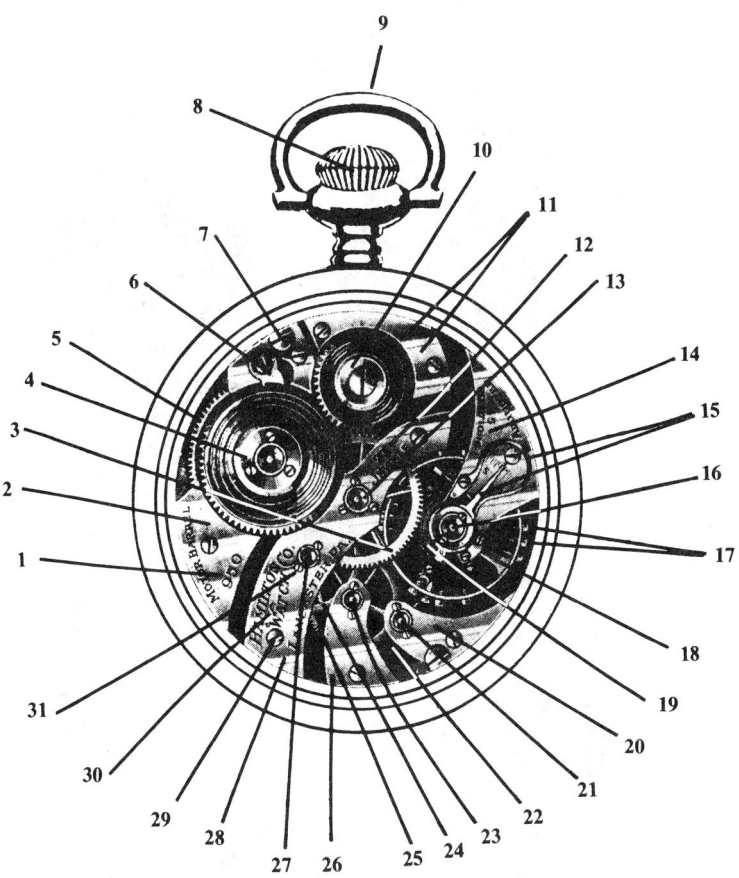

MOVEMENT IDENTIFICATION

1. Grade Number. **2.** Nickel Motor Barrel Bridge. **3.** Center Wheel (2nd Wheel). **4.** Winding Wheel with Jewel Setting. **5.** First Barrel Wheel. **6.** Winding Click. **7.** Case Screw. **8.** Pendant Crown. **9.** Pendant Bow or Swing Ring. **10.** Crown Wheel with Screw. **11** Damaskeening-horizontal pattern. **12.** Number of Jewels. **13.** Center Wheel Jewel with Setting. **14.** Adjusted to Heat, Cold, Isochronism & 5 Positions. **15.** Patented Regulator with Index & Spring. **16.** Balance End Stones (Diamonds, Rubys, & Sapphires were used). **17.** Balance Screws. **18.** Compensating Balance Wheel. **19.** Hairspring. **20.** Escapement Bridge. **21.** Escapement Wheel Jewel with Setting (Diamonds, Rubys, & Sapphires were used). **22.** Escapement Wheel. **23.** Fourth Wheel Jewel with Setting. **24.** Third Wheel. **25.** Fourth Wheel. **26.** Fourth Wheel Bridge. **27.** Third Wheel Jewel with Setting. **28.** Center & Third Wheel Bridge. **29.** Bridge Screw. **30.** Manufacturers Name & Location. **31.** Jewel Setting Screw.

NOMENCLATURE
OF
WATCH PARTS

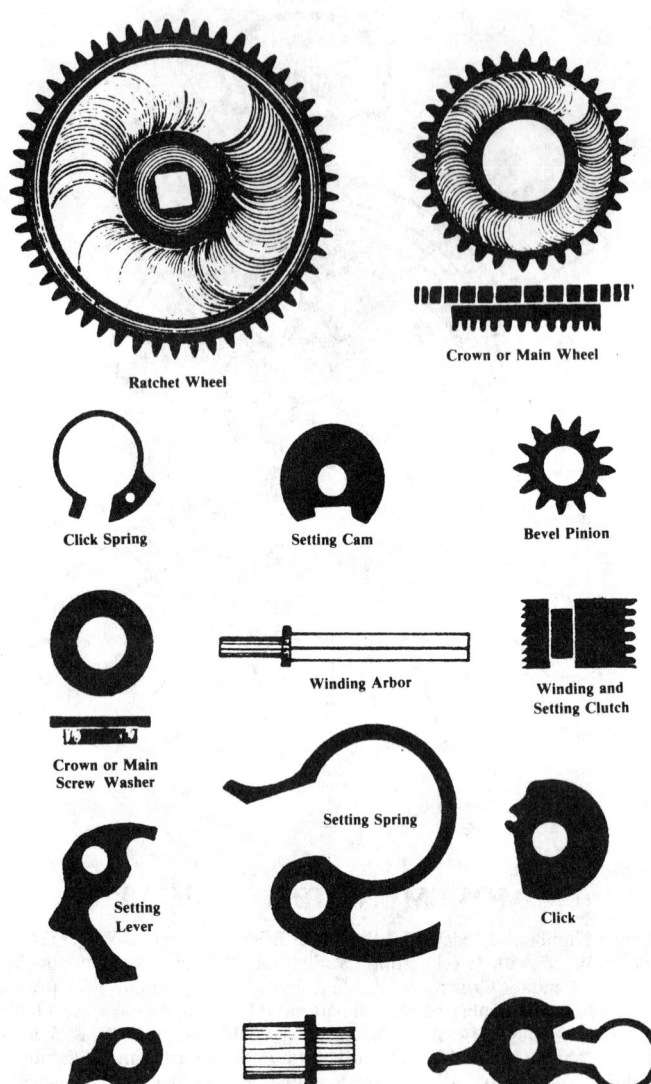

Ratchet Wheel

Crown or Main Wheel

Click Spring

Setting Cam

Bevel Pinion

Crown or Main
Screw Washer

Winding Arbor

Winding and
Setting Clutch

Setting
Lever

Setting Spring

Click

Setting
Spring Cam

Winding Sleeve

Clutch Lever

NOMENCLATURE
OF
WATCH PARTS

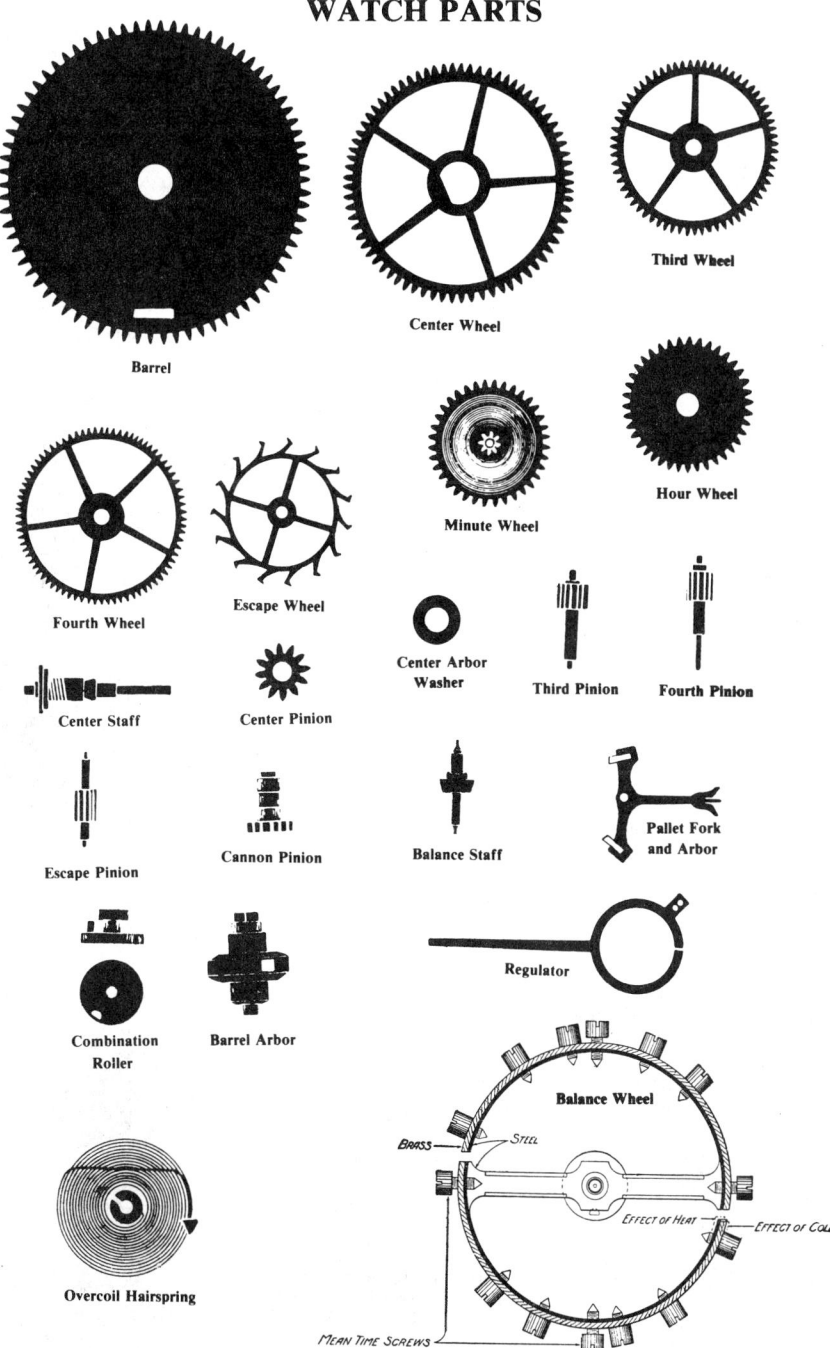

Barrel

Center Wheel

Third Wheel

Hour Wheel

Minute Wheel

Fourth Wheel

Escape Wheel

Center Arbor Washer

Third Pinion

Fourth Pinion

Center Staff

Center Pinion

Escape Pinion

Cannon Pinion

Balance Staff

Pallet Fork and Arbor

Combination Roller

Barrel Arbor

Regulator

Balance Wheel

BRASS — STEEL

EFFECT OF HEAT — EFFECT OF COLD

MEAN TIME SCREWS

Overcoil Hairspring

CASE PRICES

Case prices are for complete cases with bezel, crystal, stem, crown and bow. Hunting case style watches must have workable lift spring.

SILVEROID CASES

Size and Style	Avg	Ex-Fn	Mint
18S, OF, SW	$15	$20	$30
18S, OF, KW	35	40	50
18S, HC, SW	40	50	65
18S, HC, KW	50	60	80
16S, OF	20	25	30
16S, HC	40	45	50
12S, OF	10	15	20
12S, HC	40	45	50
6S-0S, OF	10	15	20
6S-0S, HC	35	40	50

COIN-SILVER CASES

Size and Style	Avg	Ex-Fn	Mint
18S, OF, SW	$50	$60	$85
18S, OF, KW	60	70	95
18S, HC, SW	70	80	100
18S, HC, KW	80	100	130
16S, OF	40	50	75
16S, HC	50	60	85
12S, OF	20	25	40
12S, HC	35	45	75
6S & 0S, OF	15	20	35
6S & 0S, HC	30	40	60

GOLD-FILLED CASES

Size and Style	Avg	Ex-Fn	Mint
18S, OF, Plain	$65	$85	$125
18S, OF, Fancy or **RR** or Ex-Heavy	90	125	200
18S, HC, Plain	85	100	175
18S, HC, BOX & Fancy or Ex-Heavy	150	185	300
18S, HC, MULTI-COLOR BOX & Fancy	350	400	500
16S, OF, Plain	60	75	100
16S, OF, Fancy or **RR** or Ex-Heavy	85	100	175
16S, HC, Plain	85	100	150
16S, HC, BOX & Fancy or Ex-Heavy	200	250	375
16S, HC, MULTI-COLOR BOX & Fancy	250	350	600
12S, OF, Plain	30	40	55
12S, OF, Fancy or Ex-Heavy	35	45	60
12S, HC, Plain	45	55	80
12S, HC, Fancy or Ex-Heavy	60	70	100
6S & 0S, OF, Plain	25	35	55
6S & 0S, OF, Fancy or Ex-Heavy	30	40	65
6S & 0S, HC, Plain	35	40	75
6S & 0S, HC, BOX or Ex-Heavy	75	90	175
6S & 0S, HC, MULTI-color BOX	135	165	250

🕐 **Note:** Plain enamel single sunk dial bring $20 to $40.

14K SOLID GOLD CASES

Size and Style	Avg	Ex-Fn	Mint
18S, OF, Plain	$300	$350	$450
18S, OF, Fancy or RR or Ex-Heavy	350	400	550
18S, HC, Plain	375	425	500
18S, HC, Fancy or Ex-Heavy	400	450	625
18S, HC, BOX & Fancy	600	800	1,200
16S, OF, Plain	250	285	375
16S, OF, Fancy or RR or Ex-Heavy	300	350	450
16S, HC, Plain	350	375	450
16S, HC, Fancy or Ex-Heavy	375	400	500
16S, HC, BOX & Fancy	425	550	800
12S, OF, Plain	150	160	200
12S, OF, Fancy or Ex-Heavy	200	235	300
12S, HC, Plain	225	255	325
12S, HC, Fancy or Ex-Heavy	265	295	350
6S & 0S, OF,	125	155	200
6S & 0S, HC, Plain	155	185	250
6S & 0S, HC, BOX or Heavy	200	225	350

18K SOLID GOLD CASES

Size and Style	Avg	Ex-Fn	Mint
18S, OF, Plain	$500	$550	$650
18S, OF, Fancy or RR or Ex-Heavy	550	625	775
18S, HC, Plain	650	725	850
18S, HC, Fancy or Ex-Heavy	750	850	1,400
18S, HC, BOX & Fancy	1,000	1,200	1,700
16S, OF, Plain	400	475	550
16S, OF, Fancy or RR or Ex-Heavy	450	525	675
16S, HC, Plain	500	600	775
16S, HC, Fancy or Ex-Heavy	550	650	875
16S, HC, BOX & Fancy	650	750	950
12S, OF, Plain	250	285	350
12S, OF, Fancy or Ex-Heavy	275	300	350
12S, HC, Plain	350	385	450
12S, HC, Fancy or Ex-Heavy	400	450	525
6S & 0S, OF,	155	185	250
6S & 0S, HC, Plain	200	250	350
6S & 0S, HC, BOX or Heavy	300	365	475

14K MULTI–COLOR SOLID GOLD CASES

Size and Style	Avg	Ex-Fn	Mint
18S, OF, Plain	$650	$700	$850
18S, OF, BOX or Ex-Heavy	1,000	1,200	1,600
18S, HC, Plain	850	900	1,000
18S, HC, BOX	1,500	2,000	2,600
18S, HC, BOX & Fancy or Ex-Heavy	1,800	2,500	4,000
16S, OF, Plain	500	650	750
16S, OF, BOX or Ex-Heavy	650	700	800
16S, HC, Plain	700	800	950
16S, HC, BOX	800	950	1,200
16S, HC, BOX & Fancy or Ex-Heavy	900	1,200	1,600
6S & 0S, OF,	300	350	425
6S & 0S, HC, Plain	400	450	525
6S & 0S, HC, BOX & Fancy or Ex-Heavy	450	500	600

🕐 Pricing in this Guide are fair market price for **COMPLETE** watches which are reflected from the "**NAWCC**" National and regional shows.

The Complete Price Guide to Watches goal is to stimulate the orderly exchange of **Watches** between "*buyers*" and "*sellers*".

INSPECTING OPEN-FACED WATCHES

For watches with a screw-on front and back, as in railroad models, hold the watch in the left hand and, with the right hand, turn the bezel counter clockwise. While removing the bezel, hold onto the stem and swing ring in order not to drop the watch. Lay the bezel down, check the dial for cracks and crazing, nicks, chips, etc. Look for lever and check to see that it will allow hands to be set. After close examination, **replace** the bezel and turn the watch over. Again, while holding the stem between the left thumb and index finger, remove the back cover. If it is a screw-on back cover, turn it counter clockwise. If it is a snap on cover, look for the lip on the back and use a watch opener to pry the back off.

Left: Example of **OPEN FACE** case.   Right: Example of **DAMASKEENING**.

DAMASKEENING

A special American factory terminology used in all their advertisements or a American **_IDIOM_** or expression. Damaskeening (pronounced dam-a-skeening) is the process of applying ornate designs on metal by inlaying gold or by etching. Damaskeening on watch plates became popular in the late 1870s. This kind of beauty and quality in the movement was a direct result of the competition in the watch industry. Illinois, Waltham, Rockford, and Seth Thomas competed fiercely for beauty. Some damaskeening was in two colors of metal such as copper and nickel. The process may derive its name from Damascus, a city in Syria, most famous for its metal work, called *"Damascening"* which is a type of steel that was made with designs of wavy or variegated lines etched or inlaid on their swords.

🕐 **Damaskeening** is a special American **Watch** factory terminology or a American idiom. In European this ornate designs on watches the terminology or expression is, *Fausse Cotes* or *Geneva Stripes*.

DISPLAY CASE WATCHES

Display case watches were used by salesmen and in jewelry stores to show the customer the movement. Both front and back had a glass crystal. These are not rare, but they are nice to have in a collection to show off a watch movement.

DISPLAY CASE with a bezel & glass crystal to view movement.

WATCH CASE PRODUCTION

Before the Civil War, watchmaking was being done on a very small scale, and most of the companies in business were making their own movements as well as their own cases. After the War, tradesmen set up shops specializing exclusively in cases, while other artisans were making the movements. The case factories, because of mass production, could supply watch manufacturers with cases more economically than the manufacturers could produce their own.

A patent granted to James Boss on May 3, 1859, were not the first gold-filled cases made from sandwich-type sheets of metal, but Boss did invent a new process that proved to be very successful, resulting in a more durable case that he sold with a 20-year money-back guarantee.

....Gold
···· Base Metal
··Gold

The illustrations at left is a sandwiched type gold-filled case.

GOLD CASE WEIGHTS BY SIZE

Size & Style of Case	Pennyweights (DWT)				
	Ex. Heavy	Heavy	Medium	Light	Ex. Light
18 size Hunting Case	60 to 65	50 to 55	45 to 50	40 to 45	35
16 size Hunting Case	55 to 60	45 to 50	40 to 45	35 to 40	32
18 size Open Face Case		40 to 45	38	35	
16 size Open Face Case		40	36	30	
12 size Open Face Case					
(Thin)					14
6 size Hunting Case	24	22	20	18	
0 size Hunting Case					14 to 16

An 18 size movement with a full plate weighs 50 DWT; a 16 size movement with a ¾ plate weighs 35 DWT. These weights do not include the case.

TROY WEIGHT = 24 grains=1dwt., 1 Grain= 0.0648 grams, 20dwt = 1 OZ., 12oz = 1 LB.
NOTE: Gold & Silver Standards Vary from Country to Country. U.S.A. Coin Gold =.900 or 21 3/5K, Silver Coin=.900.
Gold Standards: 24K=1,000%or 1.0, 23K=.958 1/3, 22K=.916 2/3, 21K=.875, 20K=.833 1/3, 19K=.791 2/3, 18K=.750, 17K=.708 1/3, 16K=.666 2/3, 15K=.625, 14K=.583 1/3, 13K=.541 2/3, 12K=.500, 11=.458 1/3, 10K=.416 2/3, 9K=. 375. 8K=.333 1/3, 7K=.291 2/3, 6K=.250, 5K=.208 1/3, 4K=.166 2/3, 3K=.125, 2K=.83 1/3, 1K=.41 2/3.

CARE OF WATCHES

To some people a watch is just a device that keeps time. They do not know the history of its development nor how it operates. They have no appreciation for improvements made over the years. That the watch is a true miracle of mechanical genius and skill, is seldom more than a fleeting thought. The average person will know it must be wound to run, that it has a mainspring and possibly a hairspring. Some even realize there are wheels and gears and, by some strange method, these work in harmony to keep time. If for some reason the watch should stop, the owner will merely take it to a watch repair shop and await the verdict on damage and cost.

To be a good collector one must have some knowledge of the components of a watch and how they work and the history of the development of the watch. To buy a watch on blind faith is indeed risky, but many collectors do it every day because they have limited knowledge.

How does a watch measure time and perform so well? Within the case one can find the fulcrum, lever, gear, bearing, axle, wheel, screw, and the spring which overcomes nature's law of gravity. All these parts harmonize to provide an accurate reading minute by minute. A good collector will be able to identify all of them.

After acquiring a watch, you will want to take good care of it. A watch should be cleaned inside and out. Dirt will wear it out much faster, and gummy oil will restrict it and keep it from running all together. After the watch has been cleaned it should be stored in a dry place. Rust is the No. 1 enemy. A watch is a delicate instrument but, if it is given proper care, it will provide many years of quality service. A pocket watch should be wound at regular intervals about once every 24 hours, early each morning so the mainspring has its full power to withstand the abuse of daily use. Do not carry a watch in the same pocket with articles that will scratch or tarnish the case. A fully wound watch can withstand a jar easier than a watch that has been allowed to run down. Always wind a watch and leave it running when you ship it. If you are one who enjoys carrying a watch be sure to have it cleaned at least once every two years.

EXAMINATION AND INSPECTION OF A WATCH BEFORE PURCHASING

The examination & inspection of a watch before purchasing is of paramount importance. This is by no means a simple task for there are many steps involved in a complete inspection.

The first thing you should do is to listen to a watch and see how it sounds. Many times the trained ear can pick up problems in the escapement and balance. The discriminating buyer will know that sounds cannot be relied on entirely because each watch sounds different, but the sound test is worthwhile and is comparable to the doctor putting the stethoscope to a patient's heart as his first source of data.

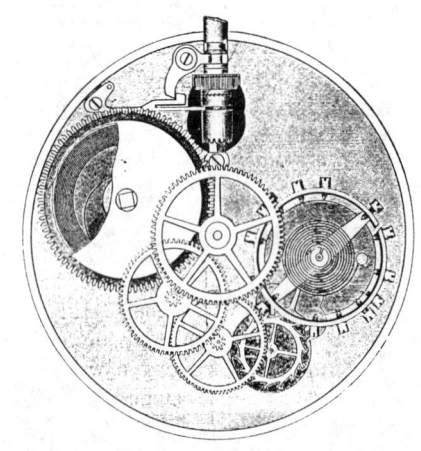

Check the bow to see if it is securely fastened to the case and look at the case to see if correction is necessary at the joints. The case should close firmly at both the back and front. (Should the case close too firmly, rub the rim with beeswax which will ease the condition and prolong the life of the rim.)

Take note of the dents, scratches, wear and other evidences of mis-use. Does the watch have a generally good appearance? Check the bezel for proper fit and the crystal to see if it is free of chips.

Remove the bezel and check the dial for chips and hairline cracks. Look for stains and discoloration; and check to see if the dial is loose. It is important to note that a simple dial with only a single sunk dial is by nature a stronger unit due to the fact that a double sunk dial is constructed of three separate pieces.

If it is a stem-winder, try winding and setting. Problems in this area can be hard to correct. Parts are hard to locate and may possibly have to be handmade. If it is a lever set, pull the lever out to see if it sets properly into gear. Also check to see that the hands have proper clearance.

Now that the external parts have been inspected, open the case to view the movement. Check to see that the screws hold the movement in place securely. Note any repair marks and any missing screws. Make a visual check for rust and discoloration, dust, dirt and general appearance. If the movement needs cleaning and oiling, this should be deducted from the price of the watch, as well as any repair that will have to be made.

Note the quality of the movement. Does it have raised gold jewel settings or a gold train (center wheel or all gears)? Are the jewels set in or pressed in? Does it have gold screws in the balance wheel? Sapphire pallets? Diamond end stones? Jeweled motor barrel? How many adjustments does it have? Does it have overall beauty and eye appeal?

Examine the balance for truth. First look directly down upon the balance to detect error truth in the roundness. Then look at it from the side to detect error in the flat swing or rotation. It should be smooth in appearance.

Examine the hairspring in the same manner to detect errors in truth. When a spring is true in the round, there will be no appearance of jumping when it is viewed from the upper side. The coils will appear to uniformly dilate and contract in perfect rhythm when the balance is in motion. Check the exposed portion of the train wheels for burred, bent, or broken teeth. Inspect pinions and pivots for wear. If a watch has complicated features such as a repeater, push the slides, plungers, and buttons to see that they are in good working order.

After the movement and case have been examined to your satisfaction and all the errors and faults are found, talk to the owner as to the history and his personal thoughts about the watch. Is the movement in the original case? Is the dial the original one? Just what has been replaced?

Has the watch been cleaned? Does it need any repairs? If so, can the seller recommend anyone to repair the watch?

Finally, see if the seller makes any type of guarantee, and get an address and phone number. It may be valuable if problems arise, or if you want to buy another watch in the future.

HOW A WATCH WORKS

There are five basic components of a watch:
1. The mainspring, and its winding mechanism, which provides power.
2. The train which consists of gears, wheels & pinions that turn the hands.
3. The escapement consisting of the escape wheel and balance that regulates or controls.
4. The dial and hands that tell the time & setting mechanism.
5. The housing consisting of the case and plates that protect.

A watch is a machine with a power source that drives the escapement through a train of gears, and it has a subsidiary train to drive a hand. The motion of the balance serves the watch the same as a pendulum serves a clock. The balance wheel and roller oscillate in each direction moving the fork and lever by means of a roller jewel or pin. As the lever moves back and forth it allows the escape wheel to unlock at even intervals (about 1/5 sec.) and causes the train of gears to move in one direction under the power of the mainspring. Thus, the mainspring is allowed to be let down or unwind one pulse at a time.

WATCH MOVEMENT PARTS

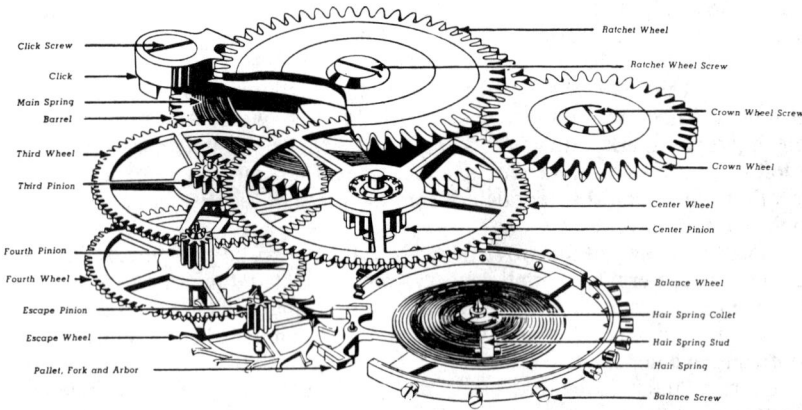

Mechanical watches are small engines powered by a main spring, which keeps the balance in motion. The **uniformity** of this motion relies on the balance and escapement; the **durability** rests on the quality of material and construction of the complete movement.

JOIN THE AWI

For those interested in Horology as a profession or a vocation the authors of this book recommend the **American Watchmakers-Clockmakers Institute**. This international non-profit corporation is dedicated to the advancement of the art and science of horology. The **AWI** publishes the *"Horological Times"* a monthly magazine. The AWI offers watch & clock repair programs of one-week and two-week classes in various phases of watch & clock repair techniques.

For a brochure & sample copy of *"Horological Times"* phone **(513) 367-9800** or write: **American Watchmakers-Clockmakers Institute**
701 Enterprise Drive
Harrison, OH 45030

TRAIN OF A ELGIN MOVEMENT
& EACH PART NAMED

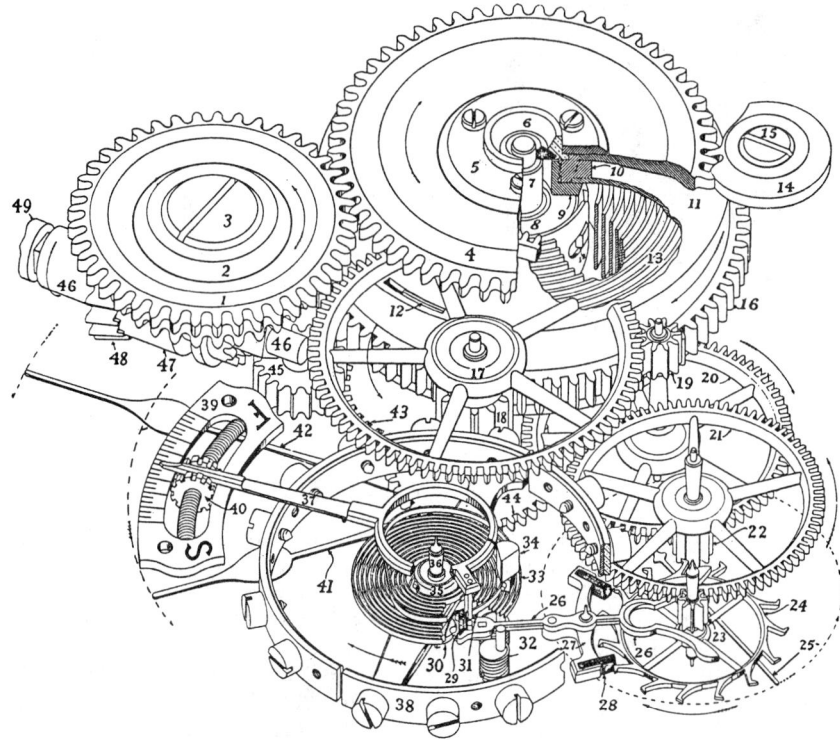

1 Main Wheel.	26 Fork.
2 Main Wheel Washer.	27 Pallet.
3 Main Screw.	28 Pallet Stones.
4 Ratchet Wheel.	29 Roller Jewel Pin.
5 Ratchet Wheel Washer.	30 Safety Roller.
6 Jewel Setting.	31 Table Roller.
7 Barrel Arbor.	32 Banking Screws.
8 Barrel Arbor Hub.	33 Breg. Hair Spring.
9 Barrel Hub Screw.	34 Hair Spring Stud.
10 Barrel Hub.	35 Hair Spring Collet.
11 Barrel.	36 Balance Staff.
12 Main Spring Hooked.	37 Regulator.
13 Main Spring.	38 Balance.
14 Recoiling Click.	39 Index.
15 Click Screw.	40 Reg. Adj. Nut.
16 First Wheel.	41 Hour Hand.
17 Center Wheel.	42 Minute Hand.
18 Center Pinion.	43 Minute Wheel.
19 Third Pinion.	44 Hour Wheel.
20 Third Wheel.	45 Setting Wheel.
21 Fourth Wheel.	46 Winding Arbor.
22 Fourth Pinion.	47 Wind. & Set. Clutch.
23 Escape Pinion	48 Bevel Pinion.
24 Escape Wheel.	49 Pendant Bar.
25 Second Hand.	

First Wheel 78 Teeth, 1 Rev. in 6 Hours, 30 Minutes.
Center Pinion 12 Teeth, 1 Rev. in 1 Hour.
Center Wheel 80 Teeth, 1 Rev. in 1 Hour.
3rd Pinion 10 Teeth, 1 Rev. in 7½ Minutes.
3rd Wheel 75 Teeth, 1 Rev. in 7½ Minutes.
4th Pinion 10 Teeth, 1 Rev. in 1 Minute.
4th Wheel 80 Teeth, 1 Rev. in 1 Minute.
Escape Pinion 8 Teeth, 1 Rev. in 6 Seconds.
Escape Wheel 15 Teeth, 1 Rev. in 6 Seconds.
Balance Vibrates 30 times in 6 Seconds.
300 times in 1 Minute.
18,000 times in 1 Hour.
432,000 times in 1 Day.
157,680,000 times in 1 Year.

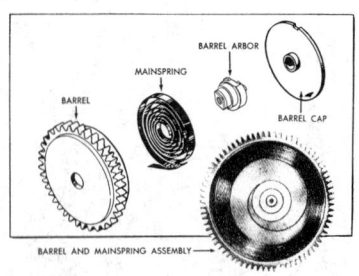

Power unit for modern watch showing the various parts.

Early style watch with a stackfreed (tear shaped cam). Note the balance is dumbbell shaped.

THE MAINSPRING

Watches were developed from the early portable clocks. The coiled spring or mainspring provided the drive power. The first coiled springs were applied to clocks about 1450. For the small portable watch, coiled springs were first used about 1470. The power from a mainspring is not consistent and this irregular power was disastrous to the first watches.

The Germans' answer to irregular power was a device called a stackfreed. Another apparatus employed was the fusee. The fusee proved to be the best choice. At first catgut was used between the spring barrel and fusee. By around 1660 the catgut was replaced by a chain. Today, the fusee is still used in naval chronometers. One drawback to the fusee is the amount of space it takes up in the watch. Generally, the simplest devices are best.

The mainspring is made of a piece of hardened and tempered steel about 20 inches long and coiled in a closed barrel between the upper and lower plates of the movement. It is matched in degree of strength, width, and thickness most suitable for the watch's need or design. It is subject to differing conditions of temperature and tensions (the wound-up position having the greatest tension). The lack of uniformity in the mainspring affects the time keeping qualities of a watch.

The power assembly in a watch consists of the mainspring, mainspring barrel, arbor, and cap. The mainspring furnishes the power to run the watch. It is coiled around the arbor and is contained in the mainspring barrel, which is cylindrical and has a gear on it which serves as the first wheel of the train. The arbor is a cylindrical shaft with a hook for the mainspring in the center of the body. The cap is a flat disk which snaps into a recess in the barrel. A hook on the inside of the mainspring barrel is for attaching the mainspring to the barrel.

The mainspring is made of a long thin strip of steel, hardened to give the desired resiliency. Mainsprings vary in size but are similar in design; they have a hook on the outer end to attach to the mainspring barrel, and a hole in the inner end to fasten to the mainspring barrel arbor.

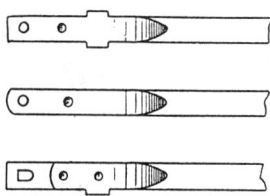

Mainspring Bridles showing a few different designs.

By turning the crown clockwise, the barrel arbor is rotated and the mainspring is wound around it. The mainspring barrel arbor is held stationary after winding by means of the ratchet wheel and click. As the mainspring uncoils, it causes the mainspring barrel to revolve. The barrel is meshed with the pinion on the center wheel, and as it revolves it sets the train wheels in motion. Pocket and wrist watches, in most cases, will run up to 40 hours on one winding.

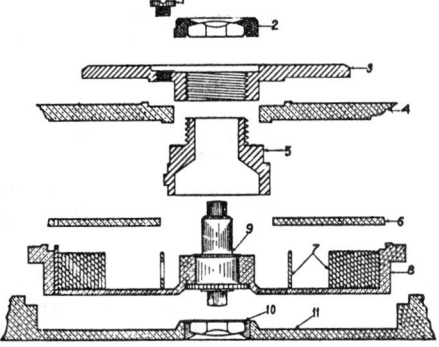

Jeweled Motor Barrel Unit: 1. Barrel top jewel screw. 2. Barrel top jewel and setting. 3. Ratchet wheel. 4. Barrel bridge. 5. Barrel hub. 6. Barrel head. 7. Mainspring (in barrel). 8. Barrel. 9. Barrel arbor (riveted to barrel). 10. Barrel lower jewel and setting. 11. Pillar plate.

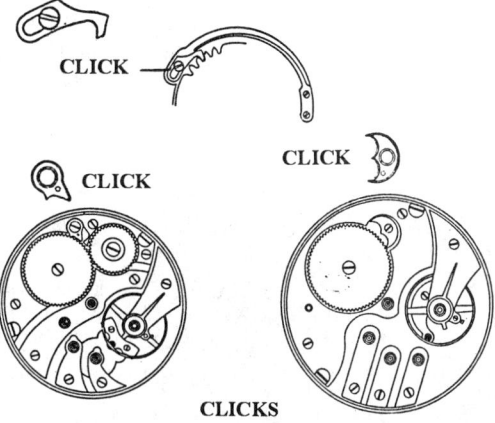

CLICKS

A **click** acts on the teeth of the ratchet wheel, so that the barrel-arbor can turn in one direction only, that of the winding. The click is made to mesh constantly with the ratchet teeth by the click spring. In older watches a device known as **stop-work** which restricted the two extremes of the mainspring was used. A modern watch uses the **click-work** which prevents the mainspring from being *over wound* by a certain amount of recoil.

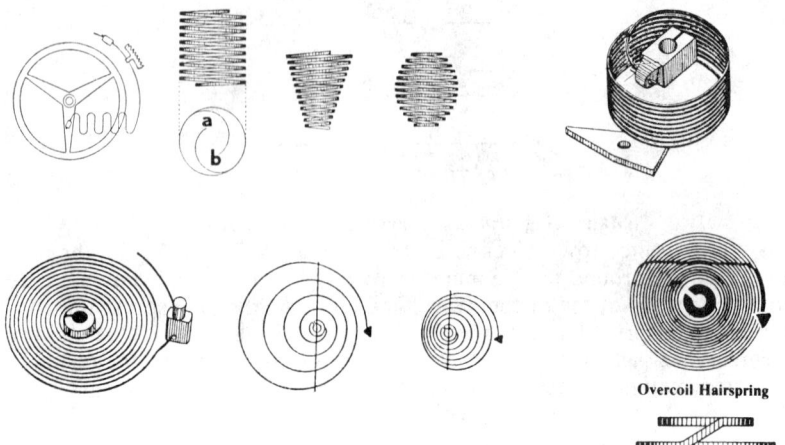

Overcoil Hairspring

BALANCE - SPRING

The balance-spring or hairspring is the brain of the watch and is kept in motion by the mainspring. The hairspring is the most delicate tension spring made. It is a piece of flat wire about 12 inches long, 1/100th of an inch wide, 0.05mm or 0.0019685 inches thick, and weighs only about 1/9,000th of a pound. Thousands of these hairsprings can be made from one pound of steel. The hairspring controls the action of the balance wheel. The hairspring steel is drawn through the diamond surfaces to a third the size of a human hair. There are two kinds of hairsprings in the watches of later times, the flat one and the Breguet. The Breguet (named for its French inventor) is an overcoil given to the spring.

There are two methods for overcoil, the oldest is the way the spring is bent by hand; and with the other method the overcoil is bent or completed in a form at one end and at the same time is hardened and tempered in the form. The hairspring contracts and expands 432,000 times a day.

A (Am. Waltham Co.) **PATENTED regulator**. Note the triangular shaped hairspring stud which is located on the balance bridge between the screw and curb pin.

REGULATORS
Identification

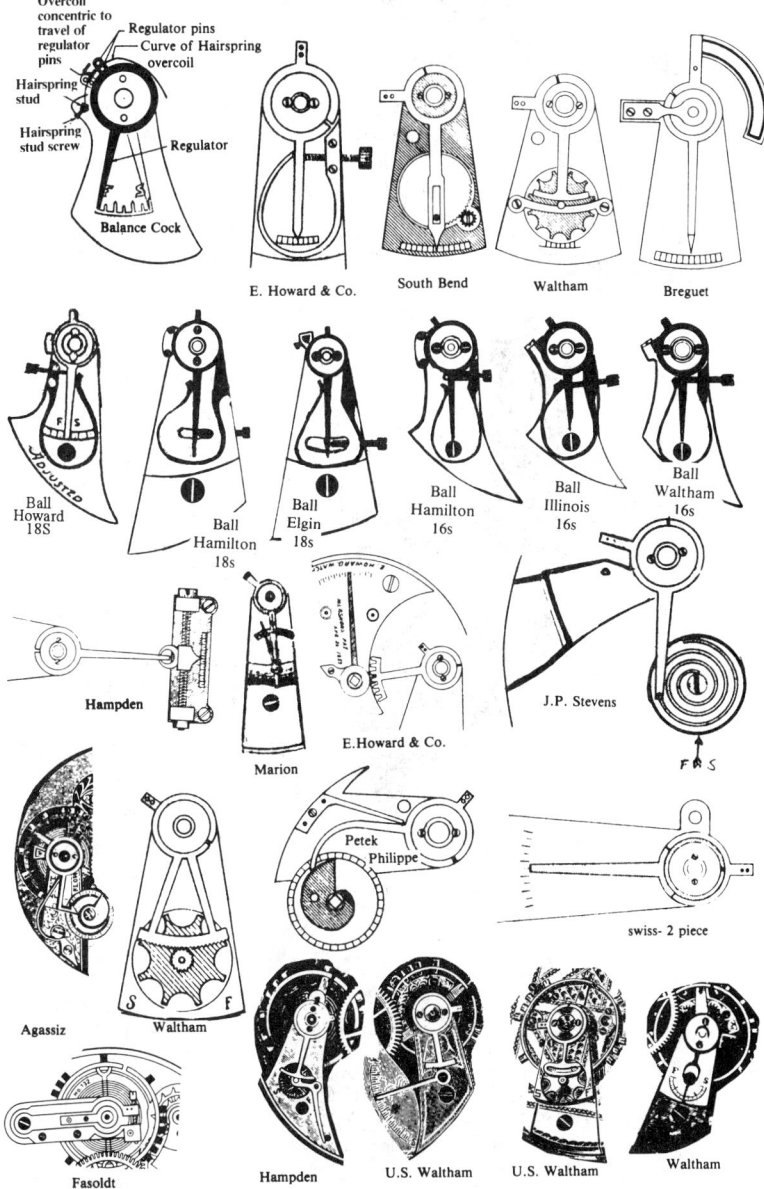

Overcoil concentric to travel of regulator pins

Regulator pins

Curve of Hairspring overcoil

Hairspring stud

Hairspring stud screw

Regulator

Balance Cock

E. Howard & Co.

South Bend

Waltham

Breguet

Ball Howard 18S

Ball Hamilton 18s

Ball Elgin 18s

Ball Hamilton 16s

Ball Illinois 16s

Ball Waltham 16s

Hampden

Marion

E. Howard & Co.

J.P. Stevens

Agassiz

Waltham

Petek Philippe

swiss- 2 piece

Fasoldt

Hampden

U.S. Waltham

U.S. Waltham

Waltham

REGULATORS
Identification

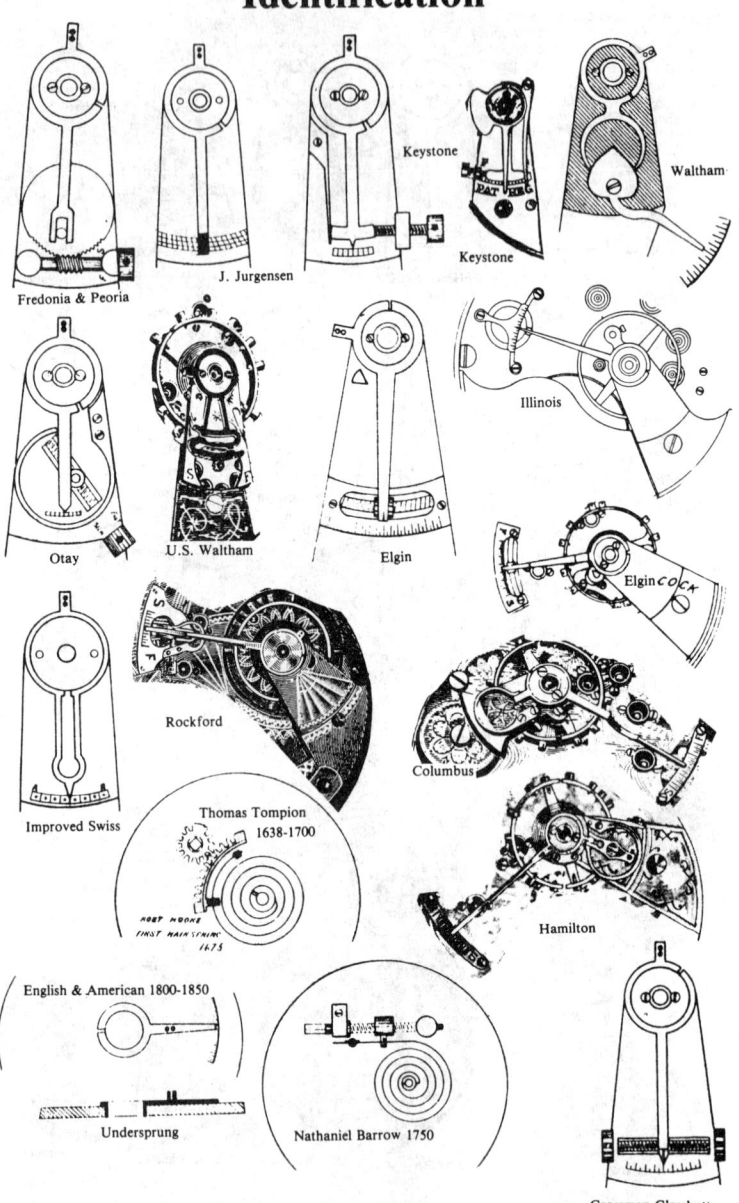

Fredonia & Peoria

J. Jurgensen

Keystone

Keystone

Waltham

Otay

U.S. Waltham

Elgin

Illinois

Elgin COCK

Improved Swiss

Rockford

Columbus

Thomas Tompion
1638-1700

Hamilton

English & American 1800-1850

Undersprung

Nathaniel Barrow 1750

Grossman Glasshutte

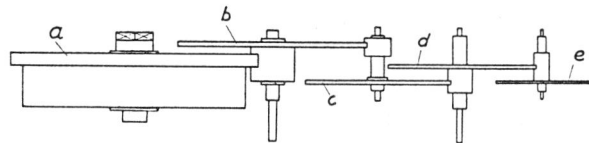

Elevation of a **GEAR-TRAIN**

(a.) mainspring barrel, (b.) center wheel (carries minute hand), (c.) third wheel, (d.) fourth wheel (carries seconds hand), (e.) escape wheel, 8 day watches use a intermediate (8 day wheel) placed between the barrel and the center wheel.

THE TRAIN

The gear-train which, transmits mainspring-barrel torque to the escape-wheel consists of a four-wheel multiplying train. The time train consists of the mainspring barrel, center wheel and pinion, third wheel and pinion, fourth wheel and pinion, and escape wheel which is part of the escapement. The function of the time train is to reduce the power of the mainspring and extend its time to 36 hours or more. The mainspring supplies energy in small units to the escapement, and the escapement delays the power from being spent too quickly. The Escapement is the turnstile of the watch, metering out a tiny unit of power for each tick and tock.

The long center wheel arbor projects through the pillar plate and above the dial to receive the cannon pinion and hour wheel. The cannon pinion receives the minute hand and the hour wheel the hour hand. As the mainspring drives the barrel, the center wheel is rotated once each hour.

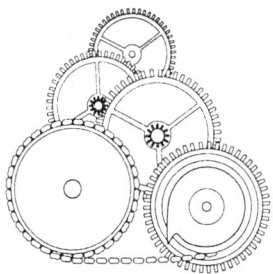
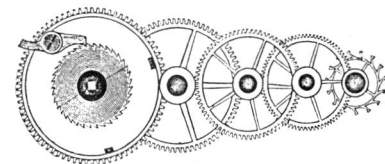

Alignment of chain driven fusee with train. **Fusee** at right and main-spring barrel at left. Note chain between fusee and main-spring barrel.

The gear-train which "transmits" mainspring-barrel torque to the escape wheel consists of a four-wheel multiplying train.

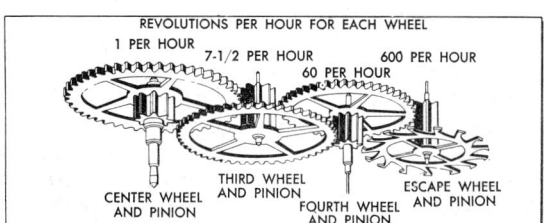

REVOLUTIONS PER HOUR FOR EACH WHEEL
1 PER HOUR
7-1/2 PER HOUR   600 PER HOUR
60 PER HOUR

THIRD WHEEL   ESCAPE WHEEL
AND PINION   AND PINION
CENTER WHEEL   FOURTH WHEEL
AND PINION   AND PINION

Actual alignment of **Train Unit**

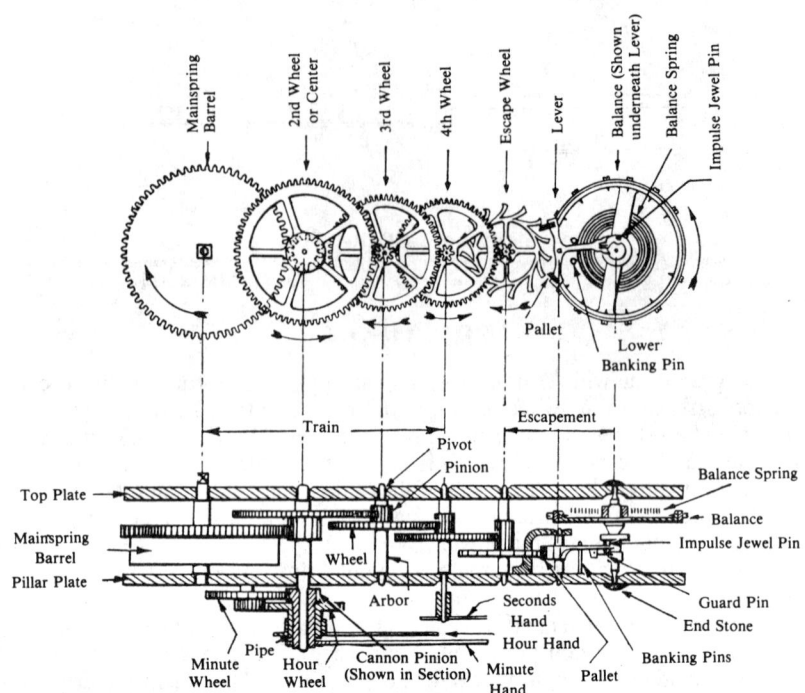

The second or center wheel of the watch turns once every hour. It is the second largest wheel in the watch, and the arbor or post of the center wheel carries the minute hand. The center wheel pinion is in mesh with the mainspring barrel (pinions follow and the wheel supplies the power). The center wheel is in mesh with the third wheel pinion (the third wheel makes eight turns to each turn of the center wheel). The third wheel is in mesh with the fourth wheel pinion, and the fourth wheel pinion is in mesh with the escape wheel pinion. The fourth wheel post carries the second hand and is in a 1:60 ratio to the center wheel (the center wheel turns once every hour and the fourth wheel turns 60 turns every hour). The escape wheel has 15 teeth (shaped like a flat foot) and works with two pallets on the lever. The two pallet jewels lock and unlock the escape wheel at intervals (1/5 sec.) allowing the train of gears to move in one direction under the influence of the mainspring. The lever (quick train) vibrates 18,000 times to one turn of the center wheel (every hour). The hour hand works from a motion train'. The mainspring barrel generally makes about five turns every 36 hours.

SOLID GOLD TRAIN

Some watches have a gold train instead of brass wheels. These watches are more desirable. To identify gold wheels within the train, look at a Hamilton 992; the center wheel is made of gold and the other wheels are made of brass. Why a gold train? Pure gold is soft, but it has a smooth surface and it molds easily. Therefore, the wheels have less friction and properly alloyed it is sturdy. These wheels do not move fast, and a smooth action is more important than a hard metal. Gold does not tarnish or rust and is non-magnetic. The arbors and pinions in these watches will be steel. Many watches have some gold in them, and the collector should learn to distinguish it.

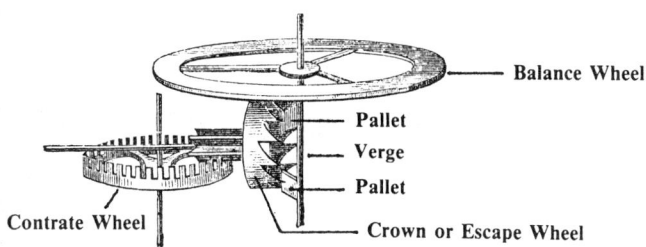

ABOVE: **Verge Escapement**

TYPES OF ESCAPEMENTS

The verge escapement is the earliest form of escapement. It was first used in clocks as far back as the early 1300s. The verge escapement consists of a crown escape wheel, a verge which has two flags called pallets, and a balance. Early German watches had a balance shaped like a dumbbell, called a "foliot." Later most other watches used a balance shaped like a wheel. The crude weights of the foliot could be adjusted closer to or farther from the center of the balance for better time keeping. Another design from that period was the circular balance. The circular balance was used by Christian Huygens in 1675 when he introduced the hairspring. This remarkable invention was used from that time onward.

The verge escapement was used by Luther Goddard in America as well as most of the Colonial watchmakers.

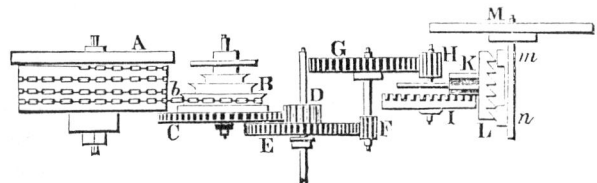

Movement of the common chain driven fusee & verge escapement.

A- is the **barrel** containing the mainspring. **B** - is the **fusee**, to which the key is applied in winding, and which is connected with the barrel by the chain **b**. **C**- is the **fusee-wheel**, called also the **first** or **great wheel**, which turns with the fusee, and works into the pinion **D**, called the **center-wheel pinion.** This pinion, with the **center-wheel**, or **second wheel**, **E**, turns once in an hour. The center-wheel E works into the **third-wheel** pinion **F**; and on the same arbor is **G**, the **third wheel**, which drives the **fourth** or **contrate-wheel pinion H**, and along with it the **contrate wheel I**. The teeth of this wheel are placed at right angles to its plane, and act in the pinion **K**, called the **balance-wheel pinion**, **L** being the **balance-wheel**, **escape-wheel**, or **crown-wheel**. The escape-wheel acts on the two **pallets**, **m** and **n**, attached to the **verge**, or arbor, of the balance **M**, which regulates the movement.

🕐 The isochronism test consists of reading your watch every two hours until the watch has run down. This will show how much the rate varies according to the time elapsed since winding.

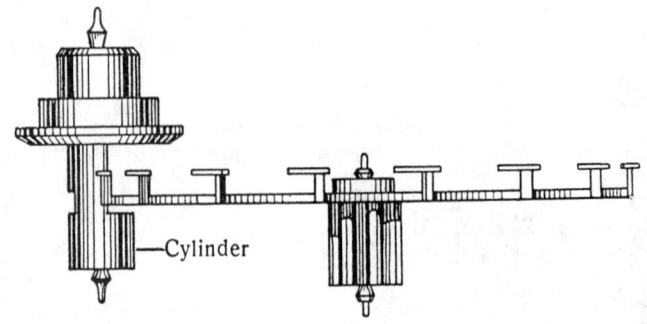

—Cylinder

ABOVE: **Cylinder Escapement**

About 1695 the cylinder escapement was invented by Tompion & improved by George Graham, an Englishman. The cylinder escapement was a great improvement over the verge. Even so, the cylinder escapement was not popular until Abraham Louis Breguet adopted the idea in the late 1790s.

Cylinder Escapement

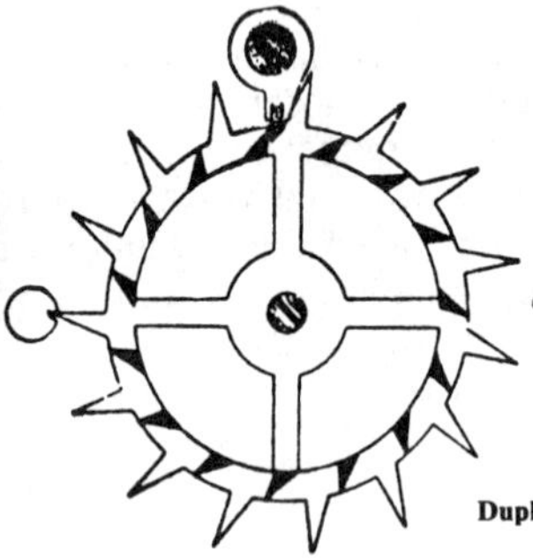

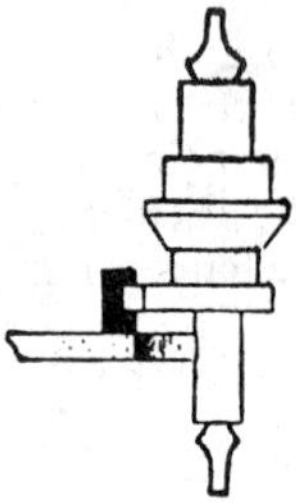

Duplex Escapement

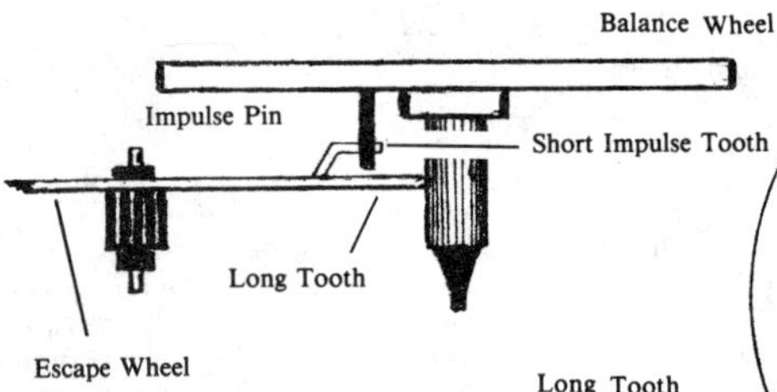

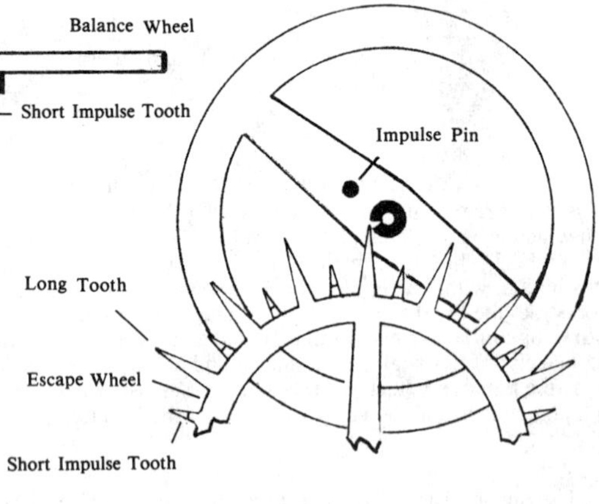

Balance Wheel

Impulse Pin

Short Impulse Tooth

Long Tooth

Escape Wheel

Illustrating and American form of the
Duplex Escapement as first employed
by the Waterbury Watch Co.

Impulse Pin

Long Tooth

Escape Wheel

Short Impulse Tooth

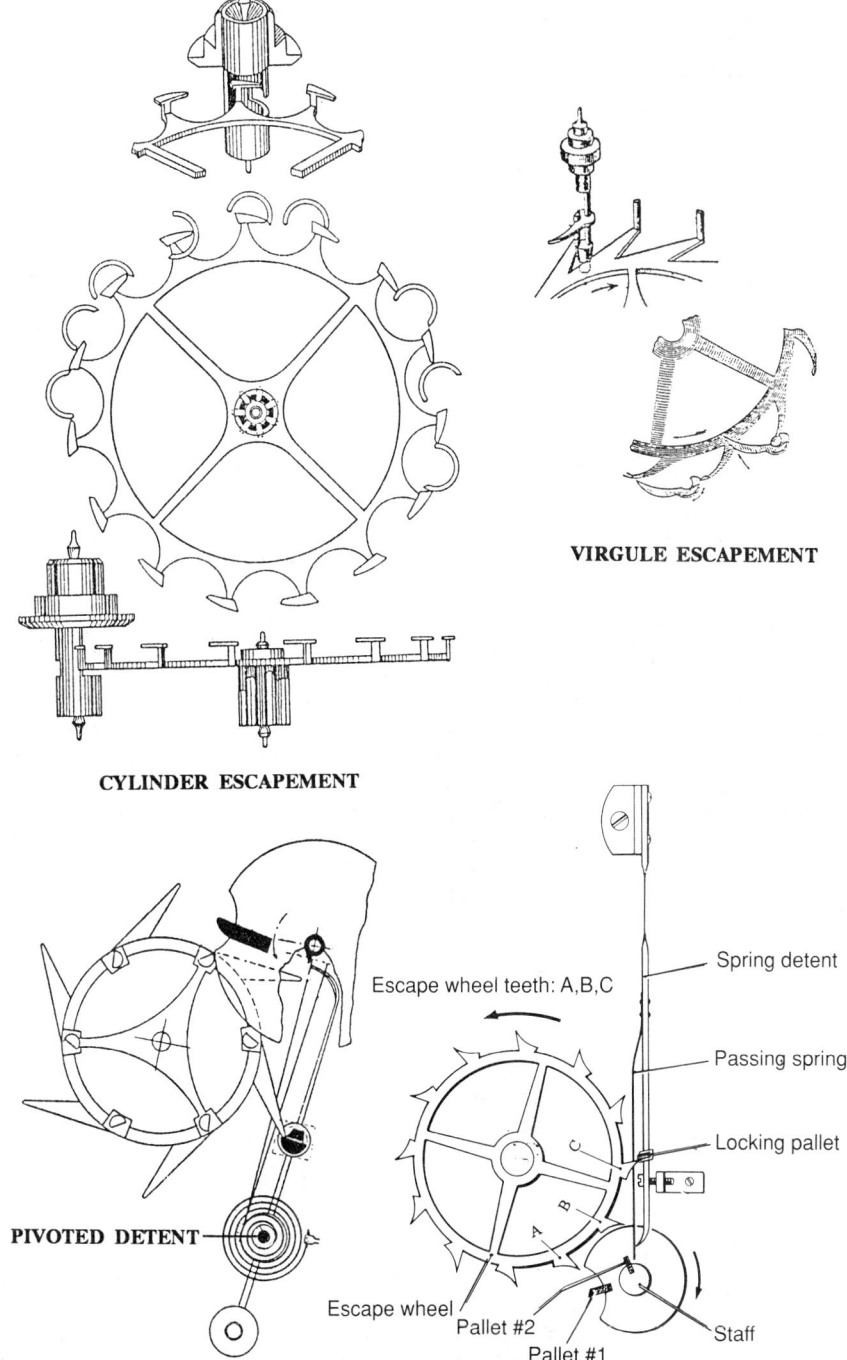

VIRGULE ESCAPEMENT

CYLINDER ESCAPEMENT

PIVOTED DETENT

Escape wheel teeth: A,B,C

Spring detent

Passing spring

Locking pallet

Escape wheel

Pallet #2

Pallet #1

Staff

SPRING DETENT (chronometer escapement)

The duplex escapement is accredited generally to Pierre LeRoy, a Frenchman, around 1750, but was never popular in France. This type of escapement was favored in England up to the mid 1850s. The New England Watch Co. of Waterbury, Conn., used the duplex from 1898 until 1910. The Waterbury Watch Company used it from 1880 to 1898. The roller and lever escapement was invented by Thomas Mudge in about 1750.

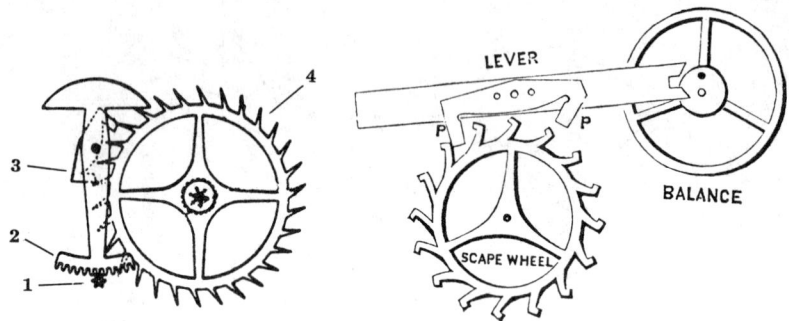

Rack and pinion lever escapement. **1.** Balance wheel pinion. **2.** Rack. **3.** Lever. **4.** Ratchet escape wheel.

Right Angle Lever used in earlier American made watches & **the Detached Escapement** which was used extensively in England. note: *P = pallet.*

The rack and pinion lever escapement was invented by Hautefeuille in 1722. The famous Breguet used the detached lever escapement early in the 1800s. By 1830 the English watchmakers had established the superiority of the lever escapement. In France and Switzerland the teeth of the lever escapement wheel were boot-shaped to provide a wider impulse plane. In England, pointed or ratchet teeth were preferred, and the right-angle lever was preferred over the straight line lever, also referred to as the Swiss lever. Pitkins and Custer both used the lever escapements. The right-angle lever was used in the early Am. Walthams, Elgin, Newark, Tremont, New York, Hampden, Illinois, Cornell, and other early American watches. The American factories settled on a Swiss style escapement (straight line lever & club tooth escape wheel) by the 1870s.

Purpose of Escape Wheel

If a movement consisted only of the mainspring and a train of wheels, and the mainspring were wound up, the train would run at full speed resulting in the power being spent in a few moments. For this reason, the escapement has been arranged to check it. The duty of the escapement is to allow each tooth of the escape wheel to pass at a regulated interval. The escapement is of no service alone and, therefore, must have some other arrangement to measure and regulate these intervals. This is accomplished by the balance assembly.

The escape wheel is in most cases made of steel and is staked on a pinion and arbor. It is the last wheel of the train and connects the train with the escapement. It is constructed so that the pallet jewels move in and out between its teeth, allowing but one tooth to escape at a time, turnstile fashion. The teeth are club-foot-shaped for addition of impulse face to the end of the teeth.

The pallet jewels are set at an angle to make their inside corners reach over three teeth and two spaces of the escape wheel. The outside corners of the jewels will reach over two teeth and three spaces of the escape wheel with a small amount of clearance. At the opposite end of the pallet, directly under the center of the fork slot, is a steel or brass pin called the guard pin. The fork is the connecting link to the balance assembly.

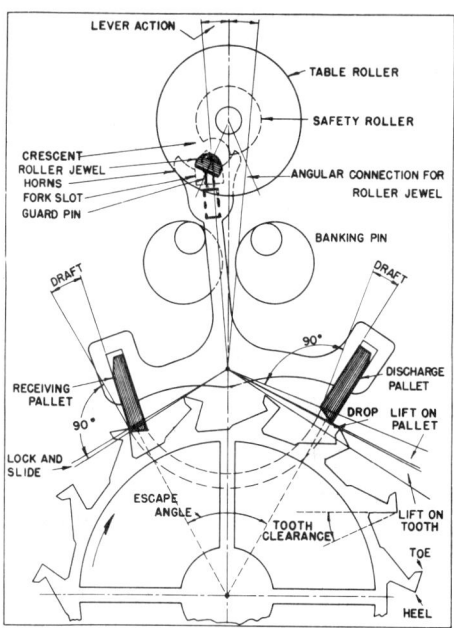

BALANCE AND HAIRSPRING

The rotation of the balance wheel is controlled by the hairspring. The inner end of the hairspring is pinned to the collet, and the collet is held friction-tight

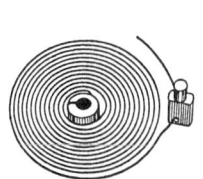

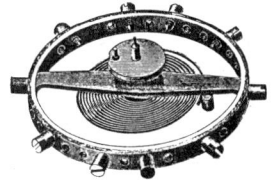

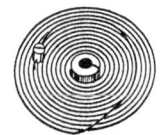

Left: example of **flat hairspring**.   Center: Balance & Hairspring.   Right: example of Breguet or **overcoil hairspring**.

66

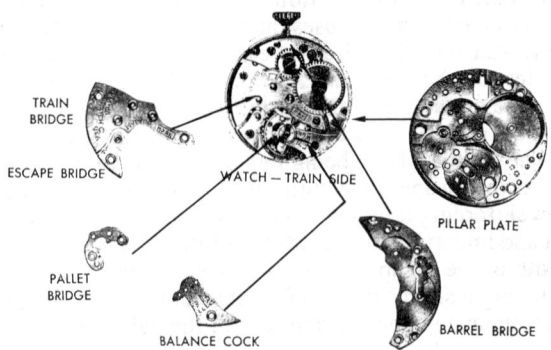

The plates and bridges which hold all the parts in proper relation to each other.

THE PLATES

The movement of a watch has two plates and the works are sandwiched in between. The plates are called the top plate and the pillar plate. The top plate fully covers the movement. The 3/4 plate watch and the balance cock are flush and about 1/4 of a full plate is cut out to allow for the balance, thus the 3/4 plate. The bridge style watch has two or three fingers to hold the wheels in place and together are called a bridge. The term bridge (horologically) is one that is anchored at both ends. A cock is a wheel support that is attached at one end only. English balance cock for verge watches and lever watches have but one screw. French and Dutch verge watches have their balance bridges secured at both ends. The metal is generally brass, but on better grade watches, nickel is used. The full plate is held apart by four pillars. In older watches the pillars were very fancy, and the plates were pinned, not screwed, together. The plates can be gilded or engraved when using brass. Some of the nickel plates have damaskeening. There are a few watches with plates made of gold. The plates are also used to hold the jewels, settings, etc. Over 30 holes are drilled in each plate for pillars, pivots, and screws.

The pinion is the smaller of the two wheels that exist on the shaft or arbor. They are small steel gears and usually have six teeth called leaves. Steel is used wherever there is great strain, but where there is much friction, steel and brass are used together; one gear of brass, and a pinion of steel. After the leaves have been cut, the pinions are hardened, tempered, and polished.

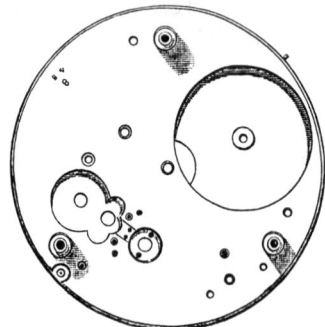

LEFT = PILLAR PLATE   RIGHT = TOP PLATE -(3/4 plate)

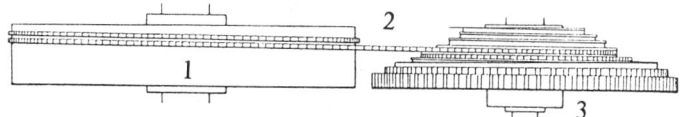

THE FUSEE FIRST UTILIZED IN 1525
1. MAINSPRING BARREL   2. FUSEE CHAIN   3. FUSEE WHEEL

THE FUSEE

A mainspring gives less and less power as it lets down. To equalize the power a fusee was first used. Fusee leverage increases as the main spring lets down. A fusee is smaller at the top for a full mainspring. When the chain is at the bottom, the mainspring is almost spent, and the fusee has more leverage. Leonardo da Vinci is said to have invented the fusee.

When the mainspring is fully wound, it also pulls the hardest. At that time the chain is at the small end of the fusee. As the spring grows weaker, the chain descends to the larger part of the fusee. In shifting the tension, it equalizes the power.

On the American watch, the fusee was abandoned for the most part in 1850 and an adjustment is used on the hairspring and balance wheel to equalize the power through the 24 hours. When a watch is first wound the mainspring has no more power than it does when it is nearly run down. With or without the fusee, the number of parts in a watch are about the same: close to 300.

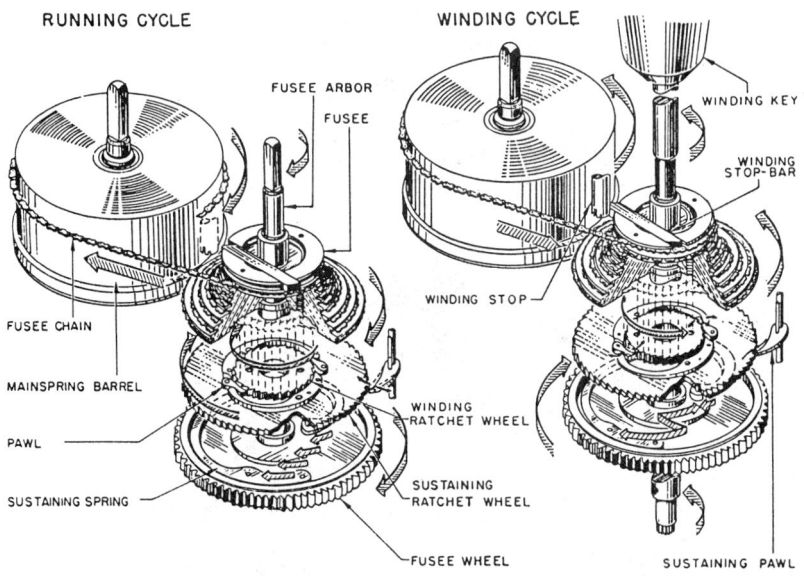

The above is a HAMILTON MODEL 21 **FUSEE** used in a Ships **Chronometer** .

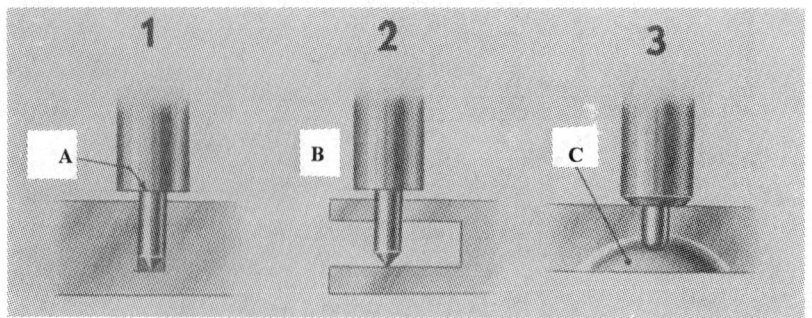

1. Illustration of pivot before 1700. 2. Pivot used in early 1700s. 3. Pivot used in late 1700s to present

JEWELS AND PIVOTS

Before 1700, holes were drilled only part way into the plates and the pivot rested directly on the bottom of the hole, as in Illustration No. 1. The shoulder of the pivot was above the plate, however, reducing part of the function, as in Illustration No. 1A.

In the early 1700s, a French watchmaker, Sully, improved the pivot friction as seen in Illustration No. 2B. Illustration No. 3 shows a later improvement. Perfected by Julien Le Roy.

N.F. de Duiller of Geneva, in conjunction with Peter and Jacob Debaufre, French immigrants living in London, developed a method of piercing jewels. This method was patented in 1704; however, it was not until around 1800 that holed jewels started to appear in watch movements and then only in high grade watches.

In the mid-1800s experiments were already being made for artificial rubies. In 1891 Fremy solved the problem and by the early 1900s the reconstructed ruby was popular.

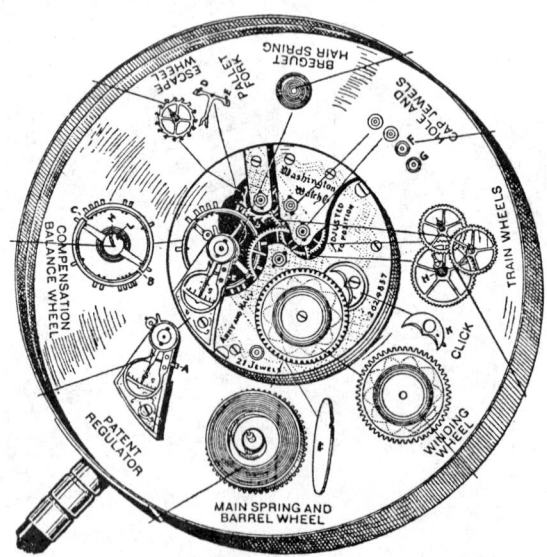

A WASHINGTON WATCH CO. WATCH UNDER A MAGNIFYING GLASS

SHOCK ABSORBERS

When a watch is dropped or subjected to a hard shock, the balance and pivots usually suffer the most.

A shock-resisting device was invented by Breguet in 1789; he called it a parachute. This device was a spring steel arm supporting the endstone. The parachute gives a cushioning effect to the balance staff.

The American pocket watch industry tried to find a device to protect pocket watch pivots, but it was the Swiss who perfected the devices for wristwatches around 1930.

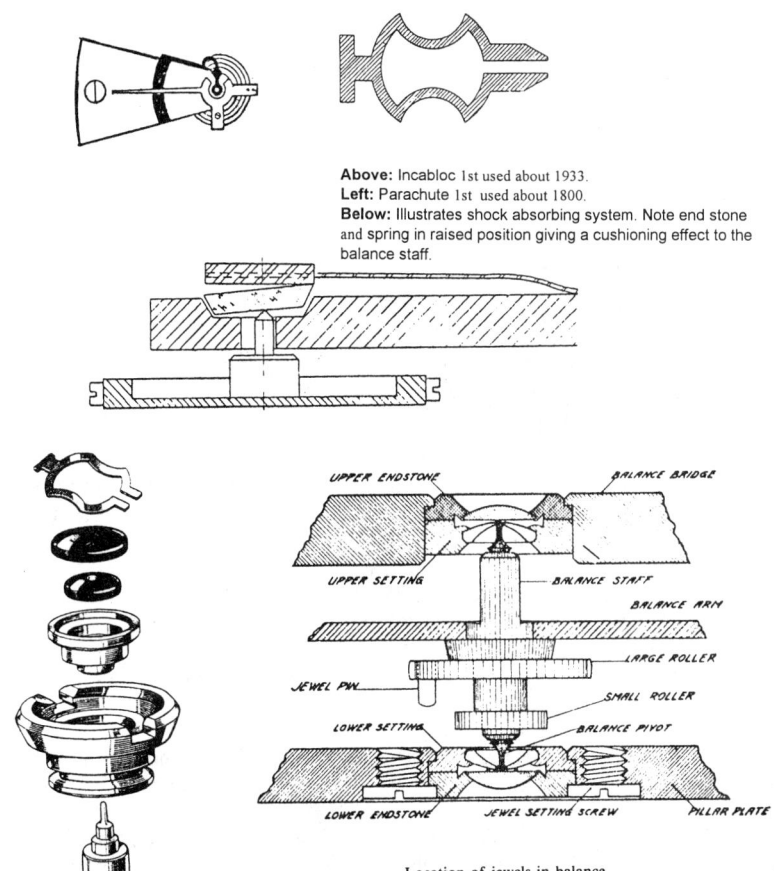

Above: Incabloc 1st used about 1933.
Left: Parachute 1st used about 1800.
Below: Illustrates shock absorbing system. Note end stone and spring in raised position giving a cushioning effect to the balance staff.

Location of jewels in balance

Above LEFT : Incabloc spring, cap-jewel, hole jewel, bearing block & balance-staff.

NOTE: Collectable watches with a higher jewel count usually demand a greater price, *when watches were produced the higher the jewel count the higher the cost,* however, lower production of some models this <u>collectable</u> **rule** does not apply. Example 7, 11 and 15 jewel Hamiltons will bring higher prices than a 17 jewel Hamilton, also a 19 jeweled "Sangamo Special" will bring a higher price than 21 jeweled "Sangamo Special". Most American made watches with 15 jewels and up are marked. **(Generally speaking it is accepted that good to medium quality watches have 15 to 17 jewels and are said to be "fully jeweled".)**
When counting **VISIBLE** jewels beware that some manufactures added <u>non-functional</u> jewels for eye appeal, disassembling the watch is the only way to get a true accurate count.

TYPES OF JEWELS.

Watch jewels are of four distinct types, each type having a particular function.

(1) **HOLE JEWELS.** Hole jewels are used to form the bearing surface for wheel arbors and balance staff pivots.

(2) **CAP JEWELS.** Cap jewels (also called end stones) are flat jewels. They are positioned at the ends of wheel staffs, outside the hole jewels, and limit the end thrust of the staff.

(3) **ROLLER JEWELS.** The roller jewel (pin) is positioned on the roller table to receive the impulse for the balance from the fork.

(4) **PALLET JEWELS.** The pallet jewels (stones) are the angular shaped jewels positioned in the pallet to engage the teeth of the escape wheel.

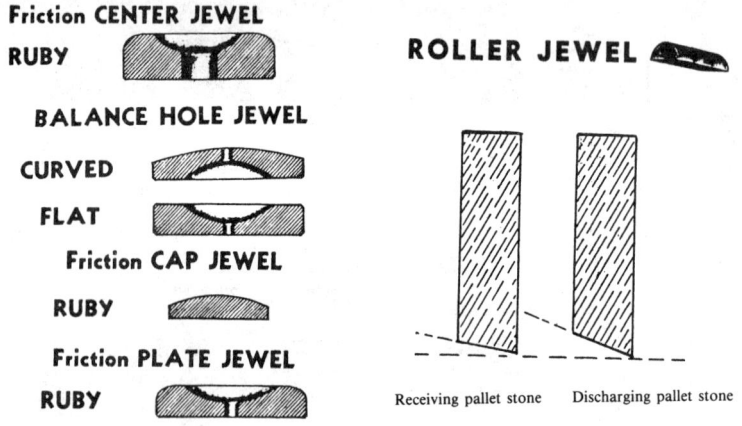

Friction **CENTER JEWEL**
RUBY

ROLLER JEWEL

BALANCE HOLE JEWEL
CURVED
FLAT

Friction **CAP JEWEL**
RUBY

Friction **PLATE JEWEL**
RUBY

Receiving pallet stone   Discharging pallet stone

JEWEL COUNT

Jewels are used as bearings to reduce metal-to-metal contacts which produce friction and wear. They improve the performance and accuracy of the watch, and materially prolong its usefulness. The materials used for making watch jewels are diamonds, sapphires, rubies, and garnets. The diamond is the hardest but is seldom used except for cap jewels. The sapphire is the next in hardness and is the most commonly used because of its fine texture. Garnets are softer than sapphires and rubies.

Number and Location of Jewels. Most watches have either 7, 9, 11, 15, 17, 19, 21, or 23 jewels. The location of the jewels varies somewhat in different makes and grades, but the general practice is as follows:

7-JEWEL WATCHES. Seven-jewel watches have: one hole jewel at each end of the balance staff; one cap jewel at each end of the balance staff; one roller jewel; and two pallet jewels.

9-JEWEL WATCHES. These have the seven jewels mentioned in 7-jewel watches, with the addition of a hole jewel at each end of the escape wheel.

11-JEWEL WATCHES. In these, seven are used in the escapement as in 7-jewel watches. In addition, the four top pivots (the third wheel, the fourth wheel, the escape wheel, and the pallet) are jeweled.

15-JEWEL WATCHES. These watches have the nine jewels found in 9-jewel watches, with the addition of the following: one hole jewel at each end of the pallet staff; one hole jewel at each end of the fourth wheel staff; and one hole jewel at each end of the third-wheel staff.

17-JEWEL WATCHES. The 15 jewels in 15-jewel watches are used with the addition of one hole jewel located at each end of the center wheel staff.

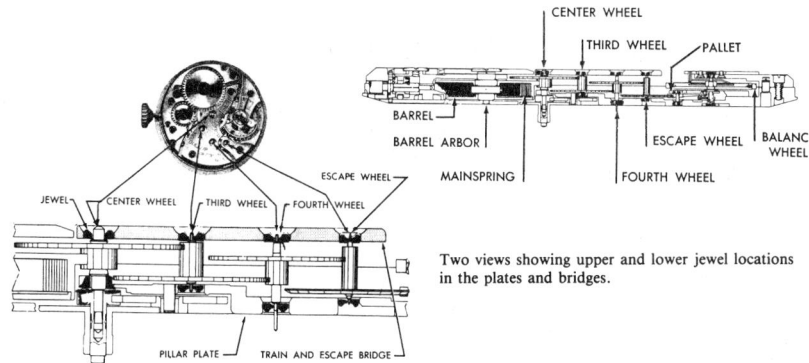

Two views showing upper and lower jewel locations in the plates and bridges.

19-JEWEL WATCHES. In these watches, the jewels are distributed as in the 17-jewel watch, with the addition of one for each pivot of the **barrel & mainspring.**

21-JEWEL WATCHES. The jewels in these are distributed as in the 17-jeweled grade, with the addition of two cap jewels (**USUALLY** placed on the pallet arbor and escape wheel) or 2 jewels for the barrel & mainspring.

Center Wheel — 2	Center Wheel— 2	Center Wheel— 2	Center Wheel— 2
Third Wheel — 2	Third Wheel — 2	Third Wheel — 2	Third Wheel — 2
Fourth Wheel — 2	Fourth Wheel— 2	Fourth Wheel— 2	Fourth Wheel— 2
Escape Wheel—2	Escape Wheel—2	Escape Wheel—2+2	Escape Wheel— 2+2
Pallet & Arbor— 4	**Barrel Arbor** — 2	Pallet & Arbor— 4+2	**Barrel Arbor** — 4+2
Balance Staff — 4	Pallet & Arbor— 4	Balance Staff — 4	Pallet & Arbor— 4+2
Roller jewel — 1	Balance Staff — 4	Roller jewel — 1	Balance Staff — 4
TOTAL — 17J	Roller jewel — 1	TOTAL—21J	Roller jewel — 1
	TOTAL — 19J		TOTAL— 23J

23-JEWEL WATCHES. The jewels are distributed as in the 21-jewel watch, with the addition of one for each pivot of the **barrel & mainspring.**

24J., 25J., and 26 JEWEL WATCHES. In all of these watches, the additional jewels were distributed as cap jewels. These were not very functional but were offered as **prestige** movements for the person who wanted more. **In many cases, these jewel arrangements varied according to manufacturer. All jeweled watches may NOT fit these descriptions.**

Collectable watches with a higher jewel count usually demand a greater price, *when watches were produced the higher the jewel count the higher the cost,* however, lower production of some models this collectable **rule** does not apply. Example 7, 11 and 15 jewel Hamiltons will bring higher prices than a 17 jewel Hamilton, also a 19 jeweled "Sangamo Special" will bring a higher price than 21 jeweled "Sangamo Special". Most American made watches with 15 jewels and up are marked. (**Generally speaking it is accepted that good to medium quality watches have 15 to 17 jewels and are said to be "fully jeweled".**)

When counting **VISIBLE** jewels beware that some manufactures added non-functional jewels for eye appeal, disassembling the watch is the only way to get a true accurate count. Note: When counting jewels from the movement back plate (with dial on) at the visible jewels a 11J. could appear to be a 15J. watch. A jewel which has a scribed circle around it plus two screws is a **mock** setting and usually have one jewel for top jewel only & no lower jewel.

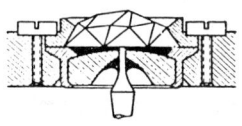

Right: Diamond faceted end stone.

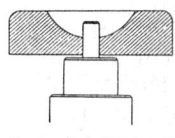

Center: Cylindrical pivot.

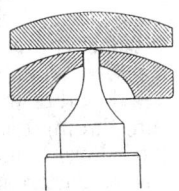

Right: Conical pivot & end stone.

WINDING AND SETTING

The simplest, but not the most practical method for winding up the mainspring of a pocket watch was to wind the barrel staff by means of a key, but then it is necessary to open up the watch case. The key method of winding proved unpopular, as oftentimes the key became lost.

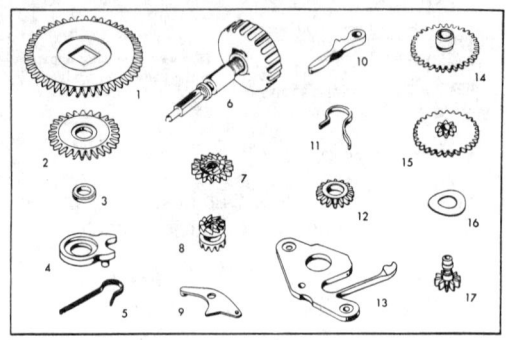

WINDING & SETTING PARTS

1. Ratchet Wheel	6. Stem and Crown	10. Clutch Lever	14. Hour Wheel
2. Crown Wheel	7. Winding Pinion	11. Clutch Lever Spring	15. Minute Wheel
3. Crown Wheel Center	8. Clutch Wheel	12. Setting Wheel	16. Dial Washer
4. Click	9. Setting Lever	13. Yoke	17. Cannon Pinion
5. Click Spring			

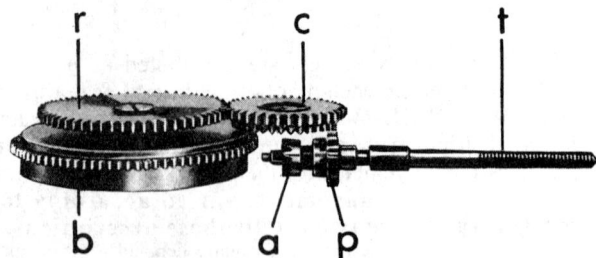

WINDING MECHANISM. a-Winding and setting clutch. p-Winding pinion. b-Barrel. r-Ratchet wheel. c-Crown or main wheel. t- Winding arbor.

The modern principle of the winding of the mainspring and hand setting by pulling on the crown, dates back to 1842. We owe this combination to Adrian Philippe, associate of Patek, of Geneva.

The winding and setting mechanism consists of the stem, crown, winding pinion, clutch wheel, setting wheel, setting lever, clutch lever, clutch spring, crown wheel, and ratchet wheel. When the stem is pushed in, the clutch lever throws the clutch wheel to winding position. Then, when the stem is turned clockwise, it causes the winding pinion to turn the crown and ratchet wheels. The ratchet wheel is fitted on the square of the mainspring arbor and is held in place with a screw. When the stem and crown are turned, the ratchet wheel turns and revolves the arbor which winds the mainspring, thereby giving motive power to the train. Pulling the stem and crown outward pushes the setting lever against the clutch lever, engaging the clutch wheel with the setting wheel. The setting wheel is in constant mesh with the minute wheel; therefore, turning the stem and crown permits setting the hands to any desired time.

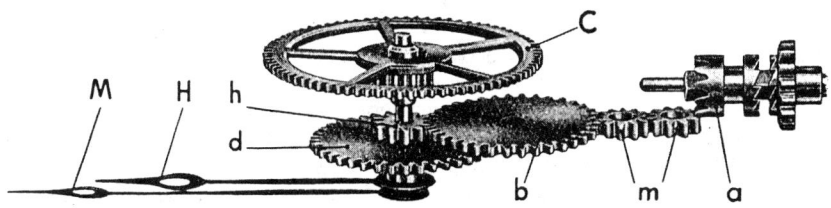

SETTING MECHANISM. Clutch a. meshes with m. and the minute works wheel b. The minute works wheel meshes with the cannon pinion h. The hour cannon d. bears the hour hand H. C. center wheel M. Minute hand.

The dial train consists of the cannon pinion, minute, and hour wheels. The cannon pinion is a hollow steel pinion which is mounted on the center wheel arbor. A stud which is secured in the pillar plate holds the minute wheel in mesh with the cannon pinion. A small pinion is attached to the minute wheel which is meshed with the hour wheel.

The center arbor revolves once per hour. A hand affixed to the cannon pinion on the center arbor would travel around the dial once per hour. This hand is used to denote minutes. The hour wheel has a pipe that allows the hour wheel to telescope over the cannon pinion. The hour wheel meshes with the minute wheel pinion. This completes the train of the cannon pinion, minute wheel, and hour wheel. The ratio between the cannon pinion and the hour wheel is 12 to 1; therefore, the hand affixed to the hour wheel is to denote the hours. With this arrangement, time is recorded and read.

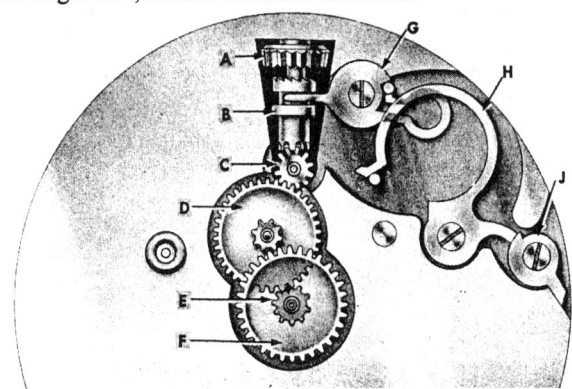

A—PINION
B—CLUTCH WHEEL
C—SETTING WHEEL
D—MINUTE WHEEL
E—CANNON PINION
F—HOUR WHEEL
G—CLUTCH LEVER
H—SETTING SPRING
J—SETTING SPRING CAM

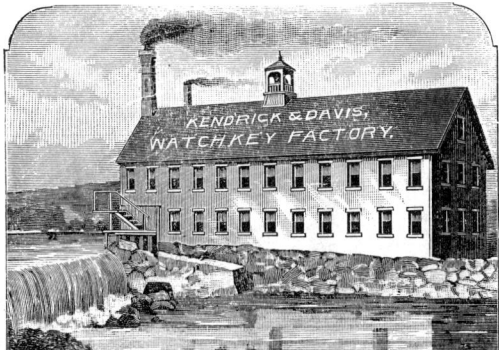

KENDRICK & DAVIS, WATCH KEY FACTORY was founded in 1876. They produced a dust-proof key which was looked upon as quite a wonderful patented watch key & sold world wide & also found with different foreign trade marks.

AUTOMATIC WINDING.

The self-winding watch uses the movements of the body in order to wind up the mainspring slowly and nearly continuously. The first pocket self-winding watches were executed by a watchmaker from Le Locle, Abraham-Louis Perrelet, around 1770. They were improved soon after by Abraham-Louis Breguet. In the case of the pocket watch, the movements causing the winding of the watch were essentially the result of walking. This system of winding was never widely adopted. The watch was a fancy model and not a really useful one. Herman von der Heydt was the only maker in America to work with the self-winding pocket watch. However, inventors always kept the idea of the self-winding watch in mind.

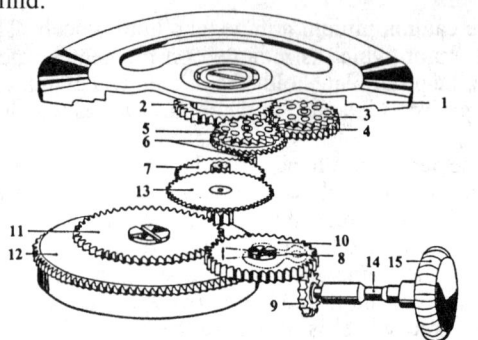 

Early self wind pocket watch by Breguet.

ETERNA-MATIC AUTOMATIC WINDING MECHANISM. 1–Oscillating weight. 2–Oscillating gear. 3–Upper wheel of auxiliary pawl-wheel. 4–Lower wheel of auxiliary pawl-wheel. 5–Pawl-wheel with pinion. 6–Lower wheel of pawl-wheel with pinion. 7–Transmission-wheel with pinion. 8–Crown-wheel yoke. 9–Winding pinion. 10–Crown-wheel. 11–Ratchet-wheel. 12–Barrel. 13–Driving runner for ratchet-wheel. 14–Winding stem. 15–Winding button.

In 1923, the British firm Harwood took up once again the solution of the problem of automatic winding, for wrist watches. This was the spark which rapidly resulted in research to improve and simplify this type of mechanism. A company was formed in London to manufacture Harwood's watch, and before long over 500 jewelers in the United Kingdom were selling his automatic watch. A second company was formed in France, and a third in the United States. The business flourished about two and one-half years. Then, in 1931, these companies were liquidated.

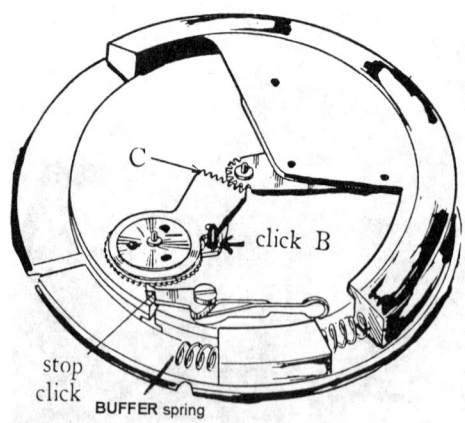 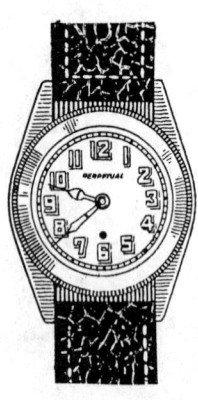

Illustration of Self Winding mechanism used by Harwood NOTE: The 2 **BUFFER** springs used on earlier movements.

This 1931 wrist watch made by Perpetual Self-Winding Watch Co. of America originally sold for $29.75.

THE BALANCE ARC OF VIBRATION

If the watch is to function with any degree of satisfaction, the proper arc of motion of a balance must be no less than 225 degrees in a single vibration direction. Wind up the watch, stop the balance; upon releasing the balance, carefully observe the extent of the swing or vibration. After 30 seconds it should have reached its maximum. If it takes longer, the full power of the mainspring is not being communicated strongly enough. With the watch fully wound, the balance should vibrate between 225 degrees and 315 degrees in a single vibration direction.

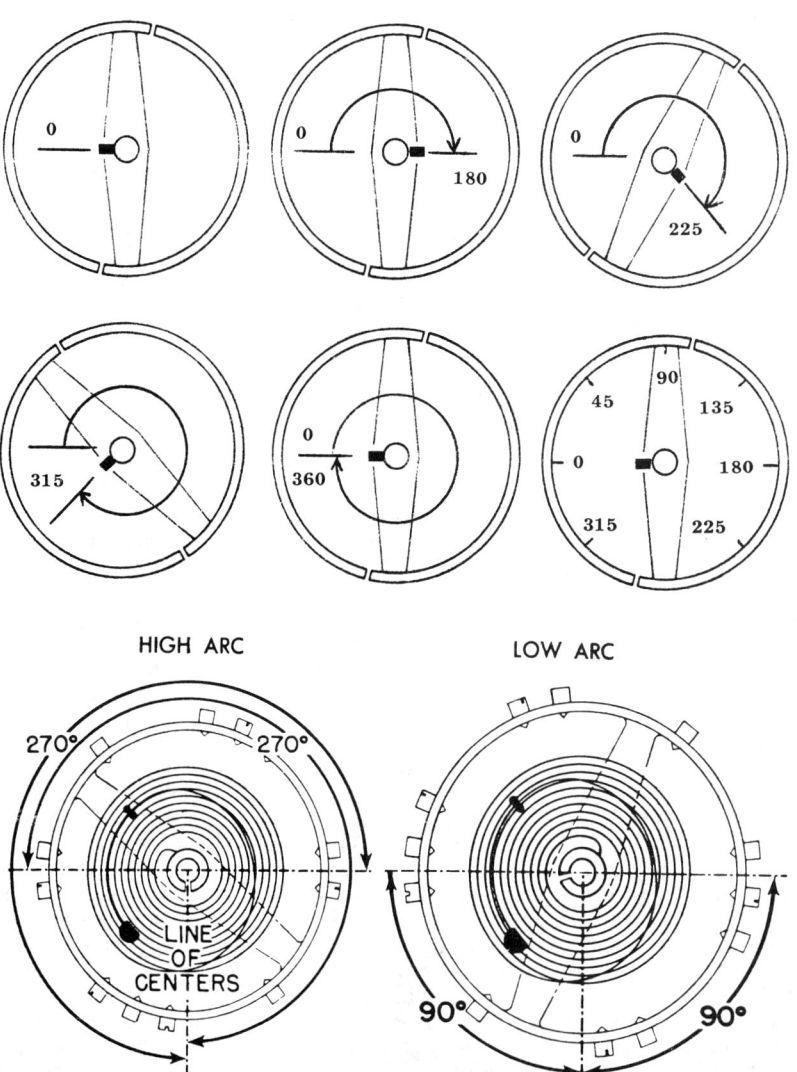

HIGH ARC   LOW ARC

JUDGING QUALITY

Judging the quality of a watch need not be difficult. While observing a watch movement there are two major determining factors to keep in mind. (1.) The quality or precious material. (2.) The amount of workmanship and time it takes to produce the parts for the movement. About **85% of the cost** of a _high-grade_ watch _movement_ is **labor**. The precious materials such as 18k or 14k gold, diamond or rubies, gold jewel settings or brass jewel settings. The amount of labor may be measured by the finished parts of the movement such as polishing, chamfered parts (removing sharp edges), and bluing of screws. The collector must learn to compare watches from the same time period because changes were made to improve the time keeping. To assist you the partial list below may be helpful in judging the quality of a watch.

LARGE CROWN for EASY WINDING — NON PULL-OUT BOW
EXTRA HEAVY PENDANT — DUST PROOF CASE
SAFETY RECOILING CLICK — RAISED SOLID GOLD JEWEL SETTINGS
CONCAVED AND POLISHED — 9 ADJUSTMENTS = 6 POSITIONS - 1 HEAT
WINDING WHEELS — 1 COLD AND 1 ISOCHRONISM
SAFETY CENTER PINION — POSITIVE MICROMETRIC REGULATOR
JEWELED MOTOR BARREL — SPRING TEMPERED COMPENSATING
19 TO 23 SELECTED RUBY AND — BALANCE WITH SOLID GOLD SCREWS
SAPPHIRE JEWELS — DOUBLE ROLLER & ENTIRE
GOLD TRAIN WHEELS — ESCAPEMENT IS CAP JEWELED
BREGUET OVER COILED HAIRSPRING — STEEL ESCAPE WHEEL

Escapement: detent, lever (with banking pins) or cylinder; **gold**, steel or brass escape wheel. _Balance wheel;_ number of platinum, gold or brass screws, mean-time screws are used in higher grade watches and two pair (4) of mean-time screws is higher than one pair (2), expansion full cut, 1/2 cut or uncut. In older movements gold or brass balance wheel. _Balance cock;_ diamond or ruby end stone, amount of engraving or hand pierced workmanship. _Regulator;_ free sprung, precision or simple. _Hair spring;_ helical, elinvar, overcoil or flat. _Adjustments;_ Isochronism, temperature, 6 to 3 positions, adjusted or unadjusted. _Note polished and finish to work under dial also under side of wheels and all parts._

The train of gears: Highly polished, **gold train** or brass gear; chamfered above & below, rounded, beveled or flat spokes. Wolf tooth gearing.

Finish to the plates: Engraved, carved, skeletonized, damaskeened with lavished or conservative finish, highly finished or polished, solid or plated, nickel, brass, gold inlaid, gilt or frosted plates. Hardening of various parts.

Screws: Highly finished or polished, chamfered or beveled, oval or flat heads, blued or plain, also chamfered screw holes.

Jewels and settings: Number of jewels; diamond, sapphire, ruby, other semi-precious jewels as garnet, aquamarine. Size of raised gold jewel settings held by 3 or 2 screws, flush gold jewel settings held by 3 or 2 screws, composition settings, fake engraved settings or jewels pressed directly into plates. Double roller with jeweled impulse pin. Entire escapement with capped jewels as lever, balance & escape wheel. Sapphire pallet jewels. **Jeweled mainspring barrel.**

Dials: _Enamel dial;_ enamel on gold or copper, harden or glass; triple, double single or unsunk. _Metal dial;_ gold or silver, hand carved or engraved, etched or plated; applied, raised, inlaid or hand painted numbers.

Cases: Platinum or white gold, 18k or 14k gold, boxed hinged or reversible, Hunting & Demi-hunter or open face case, **heavy** or light weight, multi-color gold, raised applied ornamentation, engraved or engine turned, diamonds or semi-precious jewels, porcelain, enamel or painted, gold or brass inter-dust cover, gold or brass bow, and silver or silveroid cases. Cases made of composition material that look like gold such as "Pinchbeck gold".

Metals used in watches: Bell metal or bronze, Beryllium white colored alloyed with iron, cobalt, copper, etc.; Bi-metallic (brass fused to steel), Brass, Carbon steel, Chromium, Chrome steel, Copper; Elinvar, German metal, gilding metal, Glucinum, Gold, Gold-filled, Gunmetal, Invar, Iron, Nickel, Palladium, Platinum, Pinchbeck, Silver, Silveroid, Silver plated, Stainless steel, Steel, Tin, White gold, and Zinc.

NOTE: Top **first** quality watches are fully chamfered, polished and finished, above and below on all the parts, as lever, escape wheel and train wheels, etc. The next down from Top First quality only the top or **visible** side are camfered, polished and finished. <u>Extra flat watches</u> the thinner the watch - the higher the production cost and Extra flat watches was considered the Highest or Top of the line.

OFFER VERSUS APPRAISALS

When you want to sell your watches you need a offer, not an appraisal. An offer is the actual price someone will pay for your item at a given point in time. The price will be determined by several factors: quality, size, age, metal content, style, grade, rarity and the collect ability at that time. Timing may be very critical in determining the price.

Jewelers and most appraisers use the insurance replacement cost, (an estimate of the retail replacement price). This type of appraisal is fine for contemporary watches and jewelry, but not for collectable watches and antique jewelry items. The "FAIR MARKET" value is a more realistic estimate of price. If done by an appraiser with "current market" knowledge, then a FAIR MARKET appraisal will be the correct evaluation of the dollar level at that *time* for your items.

Selling your watches may be a new experience. The task requires experience in the sale of watches. There is a market for watches, but as in any area of sales, knowledge of your BUYER is important. Collectors may not advertise that they are willing buyers; Collectors may not have enough ready cash at the time. Sending watches to a prospective buyer is a judgment call-- is the buyer trustworthy? Will it be worth the time involved? As a seller, you must guarantee the watch to work, offer return privileges, and refunds. The task of selling requires a knowledge of repair, shipping, the cost of advertising, time to market the watch, and someone standing by to talk to the collector. This is a short list and almost imperative that the seller be in the business of selling watches to be successful at selling. The collector may pay a higher price than a dealer, but the collectors are hard to find and may not have the ready cash at that time.

Selling to dealers may be more pleasant. Dealers will have a qualified staff, including buyers and seller, ready to respond to ads, as well as, a cash reserve for purchases. When dealing with an established business, that can provide you with good references and has a trustworthy record. Each customer is handled in a professional manner by a competent staff member. A dealer understands that selling maybe a new experience and will take you through the process one step at a time. Summation: Considering the cost, time and attempting to find a willing collector, you may be ahead to sell your watches to a qualified dealer.

When selling your watches to collectors or dealers it may involve sending the watch from one place to another. To receive the best price it will be vital to see the watches before a offer is made, this is a common practice in the watch market. Suggestions for mailing your package to the buyer. Make a detailed list of the items you are sending. Keep a copy and send a copy also list your name, address and daytime phone number. The jewelry industry sends millions of dollars worth of jewelry by REGISTERED MAIL. The Post Office Service has close control of the registered mail. Each person who handles the package must sign for it and be responsible for it's safety. Your package will be kept in a secure area much like a bank vault. Your package may be insured up to $25,000.00. Your package must also be able to withstand the shipping stress. Before sealing the box make sure to leave a inch of padded space between your watch and the sides, bottom and top of the box. Cushion these spaces with newspaper, tissue, cotton, bubble or foam padding. Seal the box securely then wrap the outside with gummed PAPER tape that can be written on.

When your package arrives at the dealer the mail staff will open and inspect your package, and log each item. One of the experts in charge will examine each item and call as soon as possible with the offer. If you accept the offer a check will be delivered to you. If the offer is turned down the items will be returned.

When buying watches for RESALE **know what the buyer will pay**. How many buyers are there for, prices above $1,000.00, $2,000.00, $5,000.00 $10,000.00 or as high as $50,000.00 to $100,000.00 and do they have ready cash. Can you find the collector that will pay more or pay your asking price. **The collector may be just as rare as your rare watch! (SUPPLY & DEMAND)**

"George Washington, New York", engraved on movement, patterned after the 1857 model by Waltham, **(SWISS)**

"The Nassau" on dial, "Hartford adjusted, jewels, heat & cold" on the movement. (SWISS FAKE)

COTTAGE INDUSTRY WATCHMAKING IN COLONIAL AMERICA

The cottage industry (pre-1700s to 1800s) consisted of organized, skilled craftsmen having separate divisions for the purpose of producing watches. The movements were handmade using manpowered tools. The parts generally were not given a final finish. The cottage industries were in most countries including France, England, Switzerland, Germany, and others, but not in America. Each skilled parts maker specialized in a specific part of the watch. There were fusee makers, wheel makers, plate and cock makers, spring makers, case makers and enamelers, to name a few. In the cottage industry each maker became an expert in his field. Expenses and overhead were less because fewer tools and less labor were required. Because all components were produced separately, a larger volume of watches resulted.

The enterprising colonial watchmaker in America would order all the parts and assemble them to complete a finished movement. This finisher, or watchmaker, would detail the parts, such as filing them to fit, polishing and gilding the parts, fitting the movement to a case, installing a dial, and adjusting the movement to perform. The finisher would then engrave his name and town of manufacture to the movement or dial. The finisher determined the time keeping quality of the completed watch, thus gaining a good reputation for some watchmakers.

Most watchmakers used this system during this period; even, to some extent, Abraham L. Breguet. A colonial watchmaker or finisher could produce about 50 watches a year. There were few colonial watchmakers because only the wealthy could afford such a prized possession as a watch. Most colonial watchmakers struggled financially, and supplemented their businesses with repair work on European-made watches. Since most of them understood the verge escapement, and imported this type of part from England to produce watches, many colonial watches have the verge escapement. Few colonial watches survive today.

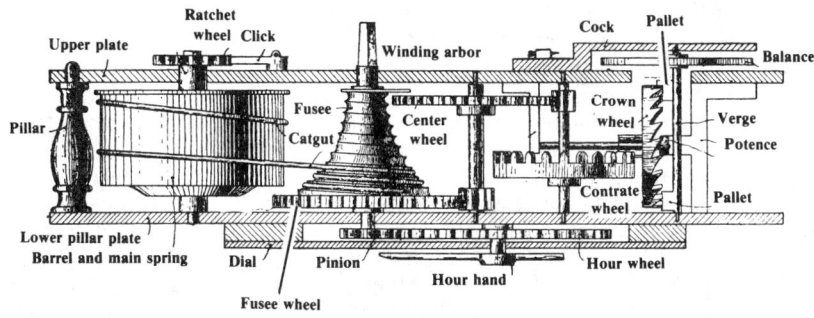

Side-view of 17th Century single-hand movement with fusee and catgut line to barrel. This three-wheel movement normally ran from 15 to 16 hours between windings. Also note the balance has no hairspring.

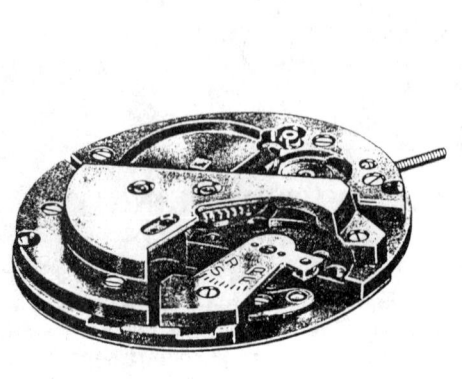 

EBAUCHES

The stamping out of plates and bridges began with Frederic Japy of Beaucourt, France, around 1770. At first, ebauches consisted of two plates with barrel and train bridges, the cock and fusee, pillars, and the clicks and assembly screws. The ebauches were stamped-out or rough movements. Japy invented machinery a common laborer could operate, including a circular saw to cut brass sheets into strips, a machine for cutting teeth in a wheel, a machine for making pillars, a press for the balance, and more. These machines were semi-automatic and hard to keep in alignment or register. But, with the aid of these new machines the principal parts of the movement could be produced in a short period of time with some precision. However, the parts of watches at this time were not interchangeable. These movements in the rough or "gray" were purchased by finishers. The finisher was responsible for fitting and polishing all parts and seeing to the freedom and depth of these wheels and working parts. He had to drill the holes to fit the dial and hands. The plates, cock and wheel, after being fitted and polished, were gilded. After the parts were gilded, the movement would be reassembled, regulated for good time keeping, and placed in a case. The finisher had to be a master watchmaker.

In England, during the 1800s, Lancashire became the center of the movement trade. One of the better known English ebauche makers was Joseph Preston & Sons of Prescot. The movements were stamped J. P. Some Swiss ebauches would imitate or stylize the movement for the country in which they were to be sold, making it even harder to identify the origin.

As the watch industry progressed, the transformation of the ebauche to a more completed movement occurred. Automation eventually made possible the watch with interchangeable parts, standard sizing, and precision movements that did not need retouching. This automation began about 1850 (in America) with such talented mechanics as Pierre Fredric Ingold, the Pitkins Brothers, A. L. Dennison, G. A. Leschot with Vacheron and Constantin, Patek, Philippe, and Frederic Japy of Beaucourt. The pioneers in the 1850s who set the standards for modern watchmaking included the American Pitkin Brothers, Dennison, Howard, and Jacob Custer. By 1880 most other countries had begun to follow the lead of America in the manufacture of the complete pocket watch with interchangeable parts.

In Switzerland there are **four** major categories of watch producers :
1. Complete, 2. Ebauche, 3. Parts or **Specialized 4. Finishers**. *Complete* watch producers manufacture 75% to 100% on their own premises as Le Coultre. *Ebauche* produce rough movements or movements in the gray called ebauche or blank movements such as ETA in Grenchen. These are made in the valley of Joux and Val-de-Ruz regions, in and around the towns of Granges, Grenchen, La Chaux-de-Fonds, Le Locle and Solothurn, in the Bernese Jura, the valley of St. Imier, Val-de-Travers, at Preseux, in the Ticino, and elsewhere. *Specialized or Parts* are made more or less all over the Swiss regions. Balances more so in Valley of Sagne and at Les Ponts. Lever assortments as the escape wheel, fork, & roller in Jour Valley, at Bienne, in Bernese Jura and especially, at Le Locle. Hairsprings as *"Nivarox"* are made near La Chaux-de-Fonds, Geneva, Bienne and St. Imier. Mainspring, dial, hands, cases, jewels, pendant, bow, crowns, crystals, screws, pins, generally speaking are made throughout Switzerland. *Finishers* buy blank movements, parts, cases, etc. and finish the watch as a complete watch with their own name engraved on the watch as *Tiffany & Co., Ball W. Co.* and many more.

By mid 1950s' the high quality watches made under **"one roof"** by Am.Waltham, Elgin, Hamilton and Illinois could not compete with the Swiss division of manufacturing. This Swiss system of manufacturing encourages improvement within its own field. Each **specialist** company has experience and can improved quality while speeding up large production at a competitive price. This specialized system is still used today with most Swiss Watch Companies.

Five typical Ebauches. Three with bar movements, one with a three -quarter plate, one with a half plate. Four with lever escapements, one with a cylinder escapement. The age ranges from 1860 to 1890.

Ebauches S.A.

Ebauches S.A. with its main office in Neuchatel, Switzerland, at one time the following 17 affiliated firms were part of Ebauche S.A. and in the year of 1968 they had produced ABOUT- 40,000, 000 WATCHES.

 A. Schild S.A., Grenchen

 Fabrique d'Horlogerie de Fontainemelon, fontainemelon

 Eta S.A., Fabrique d'Ebauches, Grenchen

 Fabrique d'Horlogerie de Fontainemelon, Succursale du Landeron, Le Landeron

 A. Michel S.A., Grenchen

 Felsa S.A., Grenchen

 Fabriques d'Ebauches Bernoises S.A., Etablissement Aurore, Villeret

 Fabrique d'Ebauches Venus S.A., Moutier

 Fabrique d'Ebauches Unitas S.A., Tramelan

 Fabrique d'Ebauches de Fleurier S.A., Fleurier

 Fabrique d' Ebauches de Peseux S.A., Peseux

 Fabriques d'Ebauches Reunies Arogno S.A., Arogno

 Fabriques d'Ebauches de bettlach, Bettlach

 Fabrique d'Ebauches de Chezard S.A., Chezard

 Derby S.A., La Chaux-de-Fonds

 Nouvelle Fabrique S.A., Tavannes

 Valjoux S.A., Les Bioux

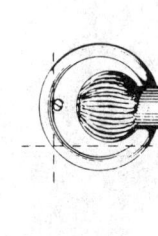 **FRENCH EBAUCHE**

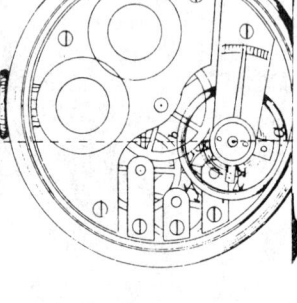

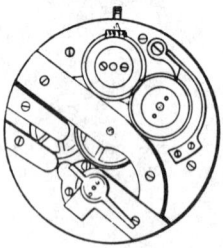

Examples of four ebauches: **Upper left:** Example of a Chinese duplex. **Lower left:** An ebauche circa 1900-1930. **Upper right:** A three-finger bridge movement, circa 1890-1910. **Lower right:** Bridge movement, circa 1885-1900.

WORM GEAR ESCAPEMENT

This oddity was advertised as, "The Watch With a Worm in It," Robert J. Clay of Jersey City was given a patent on October 16, 1886. Mr. Clay said, "The principal object of my invention is to provide a watch movement that is very simple and has but few parts." The worm gear or continuous screw was by no means simple. Mr. Clay and William Hanson of Brooklyn revamped the original worm gear and obtained another patent on January 18, 1887.

The first watch containing a worm gear escapement reached the market in 1887. However, the New York Standard Watch Co. soon converted to a more conventional lever escapement. About 12,000 watches with the worm gear were made, but few survived.

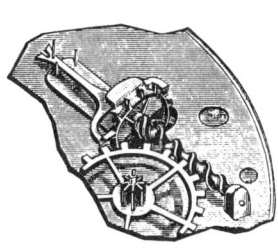

Enlarged **worm gear escapement.** Note endless screw was referred to by the New York Watch Co. as "A watch with a worm in it."

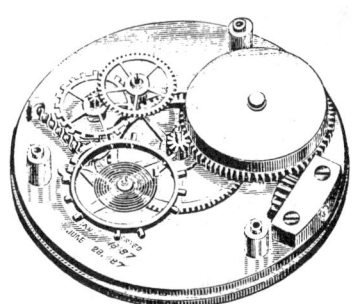

Movement with top plate removed.

DIAL MAKING

Watch dials were basically hand produced. The base is copper and the coating is generally enamel. In the process the copper plate is covered with a fine white enamel, spread with a knife to a thickness of 3/100ths of an inch. It is then allowed to dry at which time it is placed on a plate and inserted into a red hot furnace. The dial is turned frequently with a pair of long tongs. The copper would melt if it were not coated with the enamel. After the dial has been in the furnace for one minute it is removed and the resulting enamel is soft. The enamel is now baked onto the copper plate or "set." The surface is rough after cooling, and it is sanded smooth with sandstone and emery, then baked again. The dial is now ready for the painter, who draws six lines across the dial using a lead pencil. Then, with a pencil of black enamel, he traces the numbers, finishing the ends to make them symmetrical. Then the minute marks are made. Lastly, the name of the watch company is painted onto the dial. The dial is glazed and fired again, then polished. The dial artist used a magnifying glass and a fine camel hair brush to paint the dials and produced about one dozen per hour.

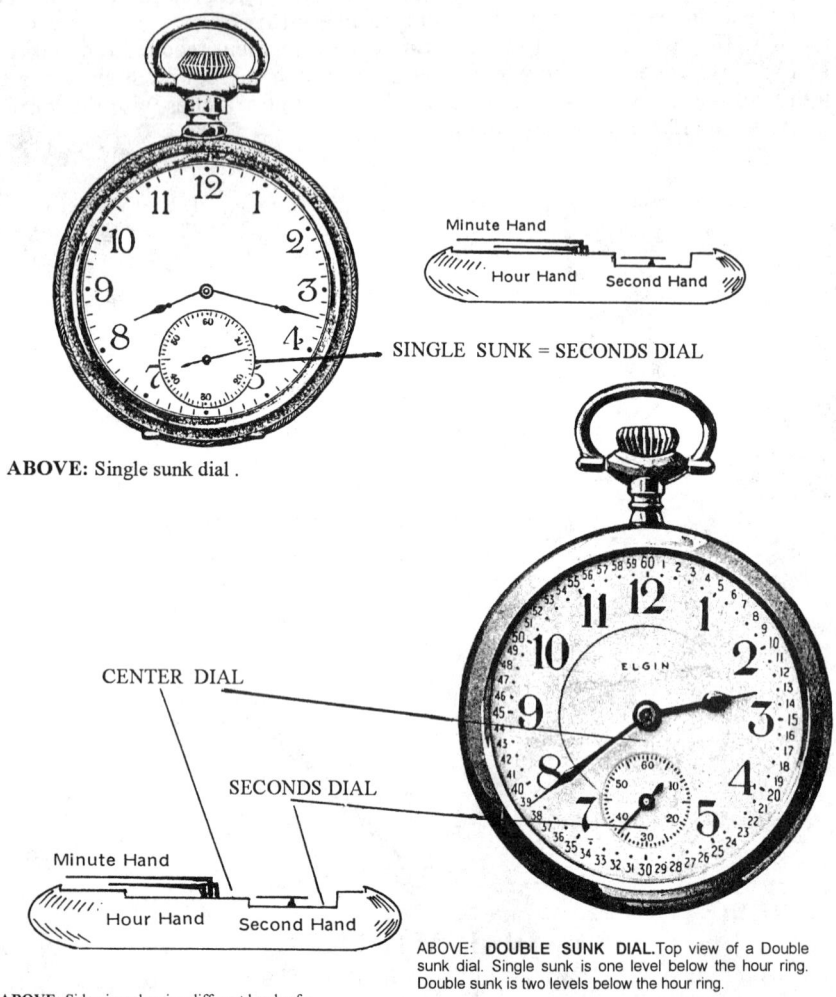

SINGLE SUNK = SECONDS DIAL

ABOVE: Single sunk dial .

CENTER DIAL

SECONDS DIAL

ABOVE: DOUBLE SUNK DIAL. Top view of a Double sunk dial. Single sunk is one level below the hour ring. Double sunk is two levels below the hour ring.

ABOVE: Side view showing different levels of a double sunk dial.

Note: Some single sunk dial have inner marked circle made to look like double sunk dial.

ENAMEL

Enamel, also called porcelain enamel, is a glass substance and may be transparent or colored. It acts as a protective surface on the metals and is resistant to acid, corrosion, and weather. Enamel is made of feldspar, quartz, silica, borax, lead, and mineral oxides for coloring. These materials are ground into a fine powder and then fired at a temperature of about 1500 degrees Fahrenheit. The heat melts the enamel powder and unites it with the surface of the metal.

CRAZING

The word "craze" means a minute crack in the glaze of the enamel. This is not a **crack** in the dial because the dial has a backing of copper. Crazing does little damage to the structure of the enamel, even though it may go all the way through to the copper.

FIRST DIALS

Thomas Gold was the first to make enamel dials in America in about 1838 in New York City. Thomas had a partner from 1846-51 named Thomas Reeves of Brooklyn. American Watch Co. (Waltham) made their own dial from the beginning by dial-makers John Todd & John T. Gold. Henry Foucy found employment in 1856 with the American Watch Co. he was from Geneva.

PIN LEVER ESCAPEMENT (DOLLAR WATCHES)

The pin lever escapement is sometimes erroneously referred to as "Roskopf escapement" and watches with pin lever escapements are sometimes referred to as "Roskopf watches."
The original Roskopf watch, which was publicly exhibited at the Paris Exposition in 1867, was a rugged "poor man's watch." The chief Roskopf patent, decreases the number of wheels by creating a large barrel whose diameter encroached upon the center of the watch. The loose cannon pinion and hour wheel were driven by a friction-clutch minute wheel mounted to the barrel cover and enmeshing with the loose cannon pinion and hour wheel. The cannon pinion rode loosely on a steel pin threaded to the center of the main plate. The true term, "Roskopf" applies to the barrel with its clutch fitted minute wheel driving the dial train. The Roskopf ebauches watch was made by **Cortebert** factory in La Chaux-de-Fonds, Switzerland. The first Roskopf watch was sold for 25 franks in January of 1870.
🕑NOTE: Some fakes use the name **"Rosskopf."**

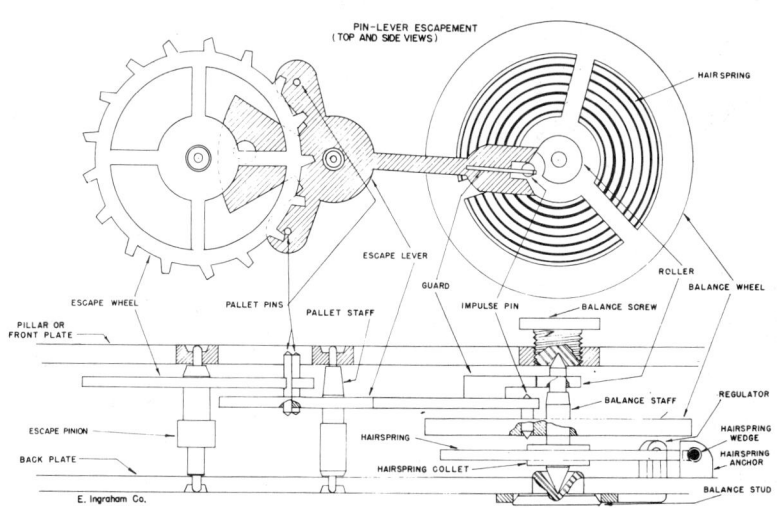

LOW COST PRODUCTION WATCHES
(DOLLAR WATCHES)

Jason R. Hopkins hoped to produce a watch that would sell for no more than 50 cents as early as the 1870s. He had a plan for which he received a patent (No. 161513) on July 20, 1875. It was a noble idea even though it was never fully realized. In 1876, Mr. Hopkins met a Mr. Fowle who bought an interest in the Hopkins watch. The movement was developed by the Auburndale Watch Co., and the Auburndale Rotary Watch was marketed in 1877. It cost $10, and 1,000 were made. The 20 size had two jewels and was open-face, pendant wind, lever set, and detent escapement. The 18 size had no jewels and was open-face.

In December, 1878, D. A. A. Buck introduced a new watch, at a record low price of $3.50, under the name of Benedict and Burnham Manufacturing Co. It was a rotary watch, open-face, with a skeleton dial which was covered with paper and celluloid. The movement turned around in the case, once every hour, and carried the minute hand with it. There were 58 parts and all of them were interchangeable. They had no jewels but did have a duplex style escapement. The teeth on the brass escape wheel were alternately long and short, and the short teeth were bent down to give the impulse. The main spring was about nine feet long and laid on a plate on the bed of the case. The click was also fastened to the case. The extremely long mainspring took 140 half turns of the stem to be fully wound. It came to be known as the "long wind" Waterbury and was the source of many jokes, "Here, wind my Waterbury for awhile; when you get tired, I'll finish winding it."

"Trail Blazer" by E. Ingraham Co. TOP view is the original Box, bottom. LEFT is Fob"Wings Over The Pole". RIGHT: Watch has original green crystal. Note: engraving on the back of watch is same scene as depicted on box.

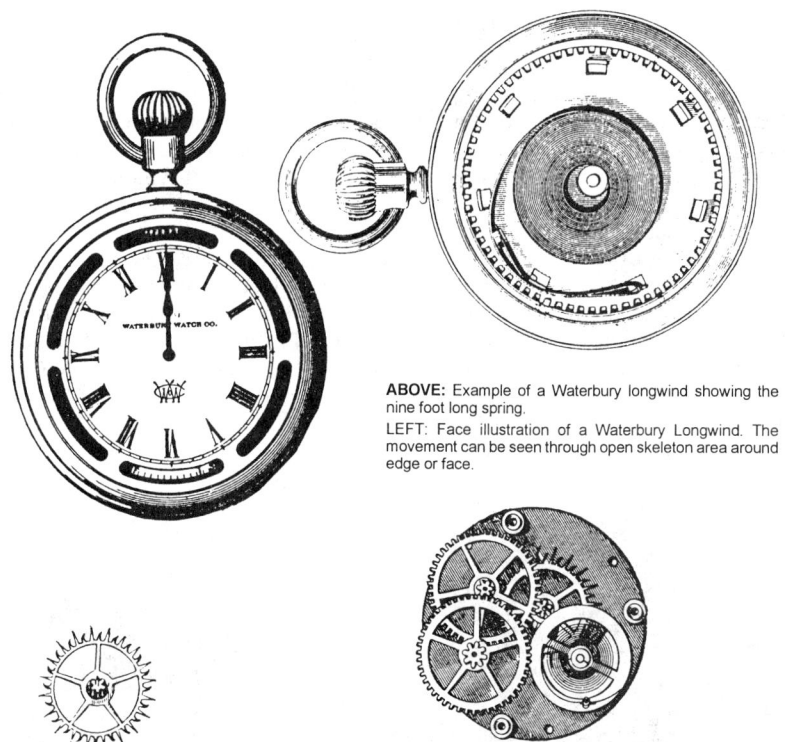

ABOVE: Example of a Waterbury longwind showing the nine foot long spring.
LEFT: Face illustration of a Waterbury Longwind. The movement can be seen through open skeleton area around edge or face.

LEFT: Escape wheel for the duplex escapement. **RIGHT:** Example of a two wheel train rather than the standard four wheel train.

In 1892 R. H. Ingersoll ordered 1,000 watches produced at a cost of 85 cents each. The watch for sale in his mail-order catalog for $1 ($12.00 / dozen) and in 1896 advertised it as, "The Watch that Made the Dollar Famous." These watches were thick, sturdy and noisy and were wound from the back like a clock. The wages in 1892 were about 8 cents per hour, so it took some 13 hours of work to buy a Dollar Watch. The Waterbury Jumbo & New Haven Sting appeared in about 1899.

The E. N. Welch Manufacturing Co. was the next low cost production watch manufacturer. Then came the New York City Watch Co., who in 1895, produced a watch with a unique pendant crank to wind the movement. In 1899 came the Western Clock Mfg. Co., which later became the Westclox Corporation.

Also, among the low cost production watches were the "comic character" watches. They have become prime collectibles in recent years.

About 70 percent of the watches sold in the U. S. were Dollar type. These watches were characterized by the pin lever, non-jeweled (for the most part), and with a face of paper or other inexpensive material. These watches were difficult to repair and the repairs cost more than the price of a new one. Thus they were thrown away, and today it is hard to find one in good condition.

DOLLAR WATCH CHARACTERISTICS:

1. Sold at a price that almost everyone could afford.
2. Used pin lever or duplex escapement.
3. Stamped or pressed out parts; also used fewer parts overall.
4. Were non-jeweled (except for a few) but rugged and practical.
5. Dial made of paper or other inexpensive material.
6. Case and movement were sold as one unit.

PRIVATE LABEL
PERSONALIZED & CUSTOM WATCHES

It was common practice for some watch manufacturers to personalize watches for **distributors**, jobbers, firms, jewelry companies and individuals. This was done either by engraving the movement or painting on the dial, such as Ball Watch Co., Sears, Montgomery Ward, and Burlington Watch Co..

Each manufacturer used its own serial number system even though there may have been a variety of names on the movements and/or dials. Knowledge of this will aid the collector in identifying watches as well as determining age.

In order to establish the true manufacturer of the movement, one must study the construction, taking note of the shape, location, plate layout (is it full or 3/4), shape of the balance cock and the regulator, location of jewels, location of screws, etc. Compare and match your watch movement with every photograph or drawing from each watch company in this volume until the manufacturer is located. The best place to start is at the Hamilton and Illinois sections because these two companies made most of the personalized & private label watches.

"Remington Watch Co."-marked on movement and case, made by N.Y. Standard Watch Co., NOTE: The CROWN wheel and RATCHET without a CLICK, these visible wheels are for show only, 16 size, 11 jewels.

"E.F. Randolph"-marked on movement, made by Illinois Watch Co., 23j, hunting, model No. 4. NOTE: The wavy ribbon damaskeening pattern

16 size, No. 390, made by New York Standard Watch Co. Same model as above.

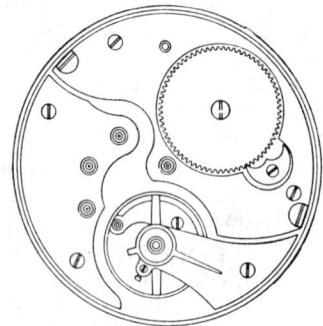

Model 4, 16 size, made by Illinois Watch Co. Same model as above.

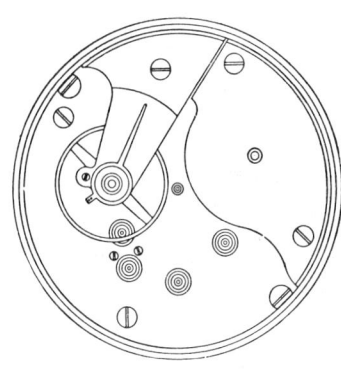

PRIVATE LABEL watch movement by ILLINOIS, engraved on movement & on dial B.A. BELL Chattanooga, Tenn., 18 size, adjusted, 15 jewels, OF.

MODEL 4, 18 size, open face, fine train, this matches the watch on the LEFT

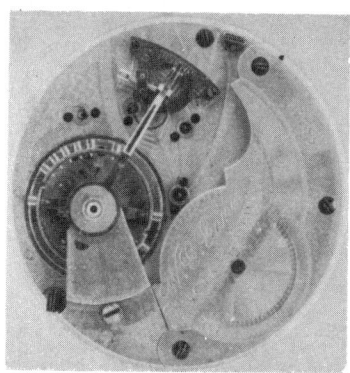

PRIVATE LABEL watch movement by ROCKFORD. Engraved on movement. "W.G. Gane, Special Railway, 17j, Adj, serial No. 344551." To identify, see the Identification of Movement section of all watch companies, noting plate design & screw locations to determine that it is a ROCKFORD Model No. 8.

PRIVATE LABEL watch movement by HAMILTON. Engraved on movement, "Mayer, Chattanooga, Tenn., Adjusted, 21 jewels, serial No. 254507." To identify, see the Identification of Movement section of all watch companies, noting plate design & screw locations to determine that it is an 18 size, open face HAMILTON model. Then by using the serial number, the grade can be determined.

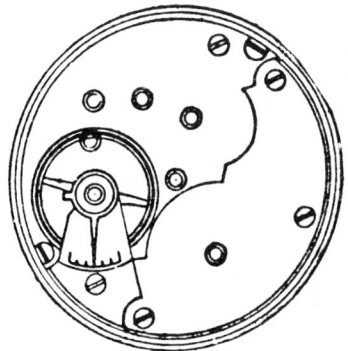

Model 8, 18 size, Rockford, full plate, hunting, lever set. This illustration from the identification section matches the model above.

Grade 936, 18 size, Hamilton, open face. This matches the model above.

The basic **model** will have the key mechanical features and construction. The *decoration,* damaskeening and jewel count determine the *grade.* Basic models will have such things as, size, hunting or open face, key or stem wind, lever or stem set, and basic layout design. The 18 size may be Transition models and note the location of the cock to the barrel bridge. The 16 size consider the winding parts may not be seen or they could be exposed (crown & ratchet wheel).

Example: Washington Watch Co. 16 size, 17 jewel, Senate grade. Illinois Watch Co. made a custom watch for (Montgomery Ward) using the name Washington Watch Co. and altered the appearance of the movement, however, the basic model was not significantly changed. The mechanical function remain the same to allow the parts to fit the altered model.

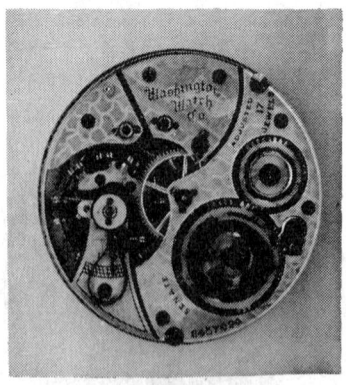 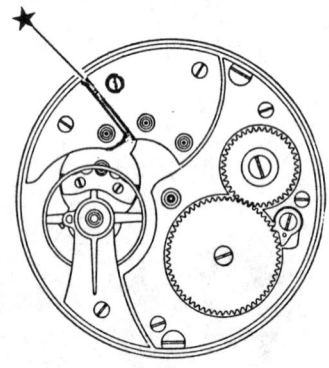

Washington Watch Co. , SENATE, 16 size, 17J, Adj. 3P, HC, polished jewel settings, damaskeen finish, double sunk enamel dial, pendant set, serial # 2457094.

ALTERED drawing of Illinois W. Co., this matches the watch to the left. NOTE: The extra screw & cut out . This also is the same model as below (MODEL # 6).

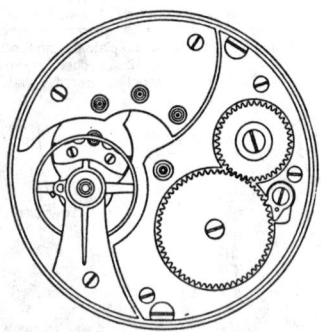

BASIC Illinois Watch Co. **MODEL** 6 as shown in the Illinois W. Co. section this drawing is NOT altered.

🕒 Generic, nameless, custom or private label watches or unmarked grades for watch movements are listed under the company name or initials of the company, etc. by size, jewel count and description.

After the correct manufacturer has been determined, the serial number can be used to determine the age. Taking the age, grade, size, and manufacturer into consideration, the approximate value can be determined by comparing similar watches from the parent company. If a jeweler's name and location are on the watch, this particular watch will command a higher price in that area.

The custom or **private label** watches are really just variations of a type or style of a grade and may show the serial number production dates. The production run may have called for 1,000 movements of a basic model and grade that may contain 700 with the Watch Co. name on movement and 300 of the custom or personalized watches with customers name on the watch. Therefore its difficult to determine how many of this type of custom made watches were produced. Usually the differences between the custom and basic grades can be seen with out a tear down of the movement. Unfortunately it may require a disassembling of the watch and you may want to have a watchmaker to help to make positive identification.

Compare and match the following list, it may aid you in the identification of your watches: first determine SIZE, then hunting or open face model, key or lever or pendant set, location of balance cock to winding barrel, location of jewels, location of screws, full, 3/4, 1/2, plate or bridge model. **Grade** differences may include: number of jewels (7-23J.), unadjusted - Adjusted to 3-5 positions, style of regulator & click, (some regulators and click were patented), style of decoration as damaskeening, *no name* or grade name. The grade without a name were the generic type or style of grade. Generic, nameless, private label, Jobber watches or unmarked grades for watch movements are listed under the company name or initials of the company, etc. by size, jewel count and description.

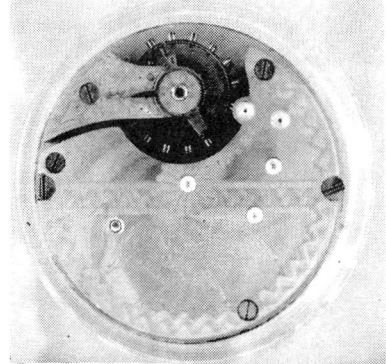

(A): ON MOVEMENT: J. P. STEVENS & BRO. 15 jewels, ON DIAL J.P. STEVENS & BRO. ATLANTA, GA. the size is 18 Size, hunting case model = a **Aurora new model.**

(B): ON DIAL *EAGLE* , On movement illustration of a *EAGLE* and serial number 512929, hunting case model, and is 18 size made by **Seth Thomas model #7**.

🕑 Generic, nameless, custom or private label watches or unmarked grades for watch movements are listed under the company name or initials of the company, etc. by size, jewel count and description.

FAKE 21 & 23 JEWEL WATCHES

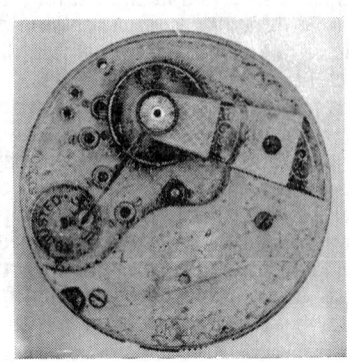

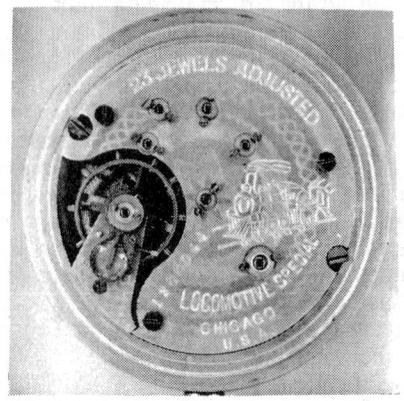

MARKED: 21 jewels, adjusted, R. R. SPECIAL on movement, the watch has 21 fake jewels and is not adjusted also the R. R. SPECIAL implies it is a railroad watch. Also a Locomotive is depicted on movement. (Swiss movement)

MARKED: 23 jewels adjusted, Locomotive Special Chicago U.S.A. on movement, the watch has 23 fake jewels and is not adjusted also Locomotive which implies it is a railroad watch. This is a Trenton M # 6, 18 size, OF.

SWISS IMPORTED FAKES

Before 1871 a flood of pocket watches were made with names strikingly similar to many well-known American watches. These were made in foreign countries as well as in America and looked and sounded like high quality watches. But they were fakes, inferior in quality.

These key-wind imitations of American pocket watches are a fascinating and inexpensive watch type that would make a good collection. The watches closely resembled the ones they were intended to emulate. Names such as "Hampton Watch Company" might fool the casual buyer into thinking he had purchased a watch from Hampden. "Rockville Watch Co." could easily be mistaken for the American Rockford Watch Co. Initials were also used such as H. W. Co., R. W. Co., and W. W. Co., making it even harder to determine the true identity.

In 1871 Congress passed a law requiring all watches to be marked with the country of origin. The Swiss tried to get around this by printing "Swiss" so small on the movement that it was almost impossible to see. Also the word "Swiss" was printed on the top of the scroll or on a highly engraved area of the movement, making it difficult to spot.

By 1885 these Swiss imitations were of better quality and resembled even more closely what was popular in America. But the Swiss fakes did not succeed, and by 1900 they were no longer being sold here.

Boston.

Example of a Swiss imported fake. Note misspelled signature "P.S. Barrett." The authentic American Waltham watch is spelled "P.S. Bartlett."

Example of a NEW HAVEN WATCH CO. imported Swiss fake. Marked on movement New Haven Watch Co. New Haven Conn. Serial # 778883.

HOW TO IDENTIFY A SWISS FAKE

1. At first they were keywind and keyset; then they became stem wind, full plate, about 18 size, large jewels on the plate side, and used Roman numerals.

2. Most had American-sounding names so close to the original that it looks merely like a misspelling.

3. The material was often crudely finished with very light gilding.

4. The dial used two feet; American watches used three.

5. The balance wheel was made to look like a compensated balance, but it did not have the cut in the balance wheel.

6. The large flat capped jewels were blue in color.

These characteristics are not present with all imported fakes. Some or none of these factors may be present. The later the date, the more closely the fake resembled the American watch.

Ohio Watch Co. imported Swiss fake distributed by Leon Lesquereaux of Columbus Ohio. This style watch may have been made by E. Borel & Co. (Swiss) about 1860.

Brooklyn Watch Co. New York serial # 6423, note the similarity to E. Howard & Co. Boston watch movement.

CONDENSED PRICE LIST

HIGH GRADE MOVEMENTS.

MANUFACTURED BY THE

HAMPDEN WATCH COMPANY.

1898 AD

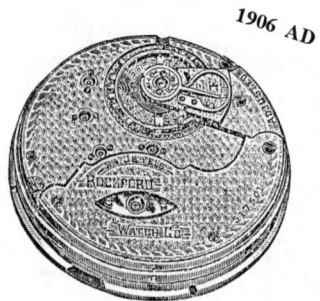

1906 AD

18 Size Movements.   O. F. and Htg.

Special Railway	23 Jewels, Nickel Adj.			$35.00
New Railway	23	"	"	28.00
John Hancock	21	"	"	23.00
Special Railway	17	"	"	30.00
New Railway	17	"	"	20.00
Anchor	17	"	"	16.00
No. 48 or 68	17	"	"	16 00
John C. Dueber Special	17	"	"	15.00
No. 47 or 67	17	"	"	15.00
John C. Dueber	17	"	"	12.00
No. 43 or 63	17	"	"	12.00
No. 80 or 81	17	"	"	10.00
No. 49 or 69	17	"	Gilt	9.50
Dueber	17	"	Nickel	8.00
The Dueber Watch Co.	15	"		6.50
No. 45 or 65	11	"	"	5.00
No. 46 or 66	11	"	Gilt	4.75
Champion	7	"	"	3.00

John C. Dueber, No. 48 and 63, damaskeened in two
colors when specially ordered.

18 Size

No. 800 Hunting }
No. 900 Open Face }   **$60.00**

24 extra fine ruby and sapphire jewels in gold
settings, sapphire jewel pin, double roller escapement, steel escape wheel, sapphire exposed
pallets, compensating balance in recess, adjusted
to temperature, isochronism and five positions,
mean time screws, Breguet hair spring, patent
micrometric regulator, safety pinion, poised
pallet and fork, handsomely damaskeened nickel
plates, gold lettering, champfered steel parts,
double sunk glass, enamel dial with red marginal
figures, Roman or Arabic, elegantly finished
throughout.   Certificate of rating furnished upon
application.

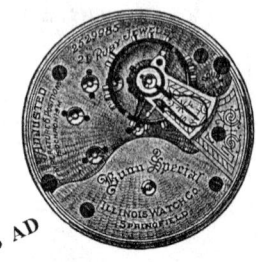

1926 AD

1926 AD

BUNN SPECIAL

9 Adjustments   21 Jewels

$45.00

SUGGESTED PRICES: Complete in any plain screw—
10K Filled Case, $55.00   14K Filled Case, $65.00
Fancy Cases and Fancy Dials Proportionately More.

21 ruby and sapphire jewels; gold settings; adjusted to SIX positions,
heat, cold and isochronism; compensating balance; gold screws including
timing screws; double roller; steel escape wheel; Breguet hairspring; patent
micrometric screw regulator; safety center pinion; beautifully damaskeened with black enamel lettering; double sunk dial.

—

No. 89

17 Jewels, Adjusted to Temperature

$22.50

SUGGESTED PRICES: Complete in any plain screw—
10K Filled Case, $32.50   14K Filled Case, $40.00
Fancy Cases and Fancy Dials Proportionately More.

17 jewels; polished settings; adjusted to temperature; compensating
balance with timing screws; Breguet hairspring; patent regulator; safety screw
center pinion; polished steel work; damaskeened in attractive pattern; double
sunk dial.

THE 60 HOUR 6 POSITION

BUNN SPECIAL

23 Jewels, $58.00 -:- 21 Jewels, $50.00

9 ADJUSTMENTS

SUGGESTED PRICES: Complete in any plain screw cases:
23J., 10K Filled Case, $65.00   14K Filled Case, $72.50
21J., 10K Filled Case, $57.50   14K Filled Case, $65.00
Special or Fancy Cases and Fancy Dials Proportionately More.

Ruby and sapphire jewels; raised gold settings; adjusted to SIX positions,
heat, cold and isochronism; spring tempered compensating balance with
gold screws including timing screws; double roller; steel escape wheel; gold
train wheels; safety screw center pinion; Illinois superior motor barrel; patent
micrometric screw regulator; recoiling safety click; concaved and polished
winding wheels; double sunk dial.

The 23 jewel grade contains the Illinois Superior Jeweled
Motor Barrel and two jewels in which barrel staff pivots operate.

THE 60 HOUR

BUNN

8 Adjustments   19 Jewels

$43.50

SUGGESTED PRICES: Complete in any plain screw—
10K Filled Case, $50.00   14K Filled Case, $57.50
Fancy Cases and Fancy Dials Proportionately More.

19 ruby and sapphire jewels; raised gold settings; adjusted to five
positions, heat, cold and isochronism; special quality hardened and tempered
compensating balance with gold screws, including mean time screws; gold
train wheels; double roller escapement; steel escape wheel; Breguet hairspring; safety screw center pinion; Illinois superior mainspring; patent micrometric screw regulator; recoiling click; Illinois superior jeweled motor barrel;
concaved and polished winding wheels; double sunk dial.

"Then vs. Now" MARKET REPORT
1984 - 1998

American Pocket Watches —MINT & with gold filled OF case	-1984-	-1998-
16 Size, 23J., Riverside Maximus, Wind-Ind, Adj.5P	$2,800	$5,500
16 Size, 23J., B.W. Raymond, Wind-Ind., Adj.5P	$475	$1,300
16 Size, 23J., 950 (Hamilton), gold train	$385	$1,200
16 Size, 21J., 992 (Hamilton), Gold Center Wheel	$135	$400
16 Size, 23J., Sangamo Sp., **marked** 60 Hour	$850	$2,000
16 Size, 21J., Rockford, Wind-Ind, Adj.5P	$850	$1,600
16 Size, 23J., Ball-Illinois, Off. RR Standard, Adj.5P	$950	$2,500
Total	**$6,445**	**$14,500**

Dollar & Comic Character Watches, MINT cases & dials	-1984-	-1998-
Ingersoll, Big Bad Wolf & Three Pigs, PW	$275	$800
Ingersoll, Dizzy Dean, PW	$175	$500
Ingraham, Buck Rogers, Ca. 1935, PW	$300	$800
New York City W. Co., "Lever Winder", (crank the pendant to wind)	$400	$1,200
New England W. Co., With Dogs, Horses, Cards, etc. on dial	$100	$300
Total	**$1,250**	**$3,600**

European Pocket Watches — Mint & Solid Gold OF cases	-1984-	-1998-
46-50mm, Audemars Piguet, Minute Repeater, 18K	$3,800	$7,000
46-50mm, A. Lange, Time Only, 18K	$1,900	$5,500
46-50mm, Longines, Chronog., Min. Rep., Moon Ph, 14K	$3,800	$20,000
46-50mm, P.P & Co., Perp. Cal., Min. Rep., Split Sec. Chron., 18K	$60,000	$110,000
46-50mm, V. & C., Min. Rep., Chronograph, 18K	$4,500	$10,000
Total	**$74,000**	**$152,500**

Wrist Watches –Mint & With 18K Gold cases	-1984-	-1998-
Rolex, Oyster, 35mm., Pink gold, Ca.1950s	$500	$2,400
Rolex, Bubble Back, 31mm, Pink gold, Ca.1940s	$1,500	$5,200
Rolex, Oyster, 35 mm, Moon Ph, & Cal., "Star Dial", Ca.1945	$6,200	$30,000
V & C, Round, Fancy lugs, 38mm, Manual wind, Ca.1948	$650	$2,500
V & C, Chronograph with 2 Registers, Ca.1950	$2,300	$9,000
P.P. & Co., Calatrava, 31mm. pink & screw back case, Ca.1950	$1,000	$5,000
P.P. & Co., RF# 2499, Perp.Cal. & Moon Ph., Chronograph with Round Pushers, Buckle, Papers, Box, etc., Ca.1955	$18,000	$80,000
Total	**$30,150**	**$134,100**
GRAND TOTAL	**$111,845**	**$304,700**

These are impressive numbers, and as with any commodity there are always *"peak and valleys."* The last few years have been active with DEALERS buying from the general PUBLIC and then selling to a COLLECTOR. As we have seen in the past, this *"Public-to-Dealer-to-Collector"*, leads to a stronger and orderly exchange of items. With the very new **Internet** boom and the U.S.A. & Global Market factored into the investment potential the future looks most promising.

The *"then vs. now"* price levels are very interesting so if you are a new or old collector the market is still relative new, the best way to predict the future is by looking at the past, now may be a good time to find and buy the minor names brand watches which are still very reasonable.

All of these areas will increase as SUPPLY DWINDLES and DEMAND in the Collectors Marketplace Expands just keep in mind the fair market values at **retail level,** as outlined in this price guide and buying wisely, but don't *hesitate*, as the better and scarce watches are *quickly* sold.

The **Complete Price Guide to Watches goal is to stimulate the orderly exchange of Watches between** *"buyers"* **and** *"sellers"*.

🕐 Pricing in this Guide are fair market price for **COMPLETE** watches which are reflected from the "**NAWCC**" National and regional shows.

AMERICAN LISTINGS

Pricing At Collectable Fair Market Value At Retail Level
(As Complete Watches With Case & Movement)

Watches listed in this book are priced at the collectable fair market **value** at the retail level (What a collector may expect to pay for a watch from a watch dealer) and as **complete** watches, having an original 14k gold-filled case with an original white enamel single sunk dial. The entire original movement is in good working order with no repairs needed, unless otherwise noted. Watches listed as 14k and 18k are solid gold cases. Coin or silveroid-type and stainless steel cases will be listed as such. Keywind and keyset watches are listed as having original coin silver cases. Dollar-type watches or low cost production watches are listed as having a base metal type case and a composition dial. Wrist watches are priced as having original gold-filled case with the movement being all original and in good working order, and the wrist watch band being made of leather except where bracelet is described.

Many of the watch manufacturers were commissioned to put jewelers' or jobbers' names on their movements in place of their own. Due to this practice, the true manufacturers of these movements are difficult to identify. These watch models are listed under the original manufacturer and can be identified by comparison with the model sections under each manufacturer. See ''Personalized & CustomWatches'' for more detailed information.

The watch manufacturers who personalized & custom made watches for jobbers or jewelry firms, with exclusive private signed or marked movements must first be found by using a illustration & matched to the manufacture shown in this book. After you identify the movement now the value can be determined. The valuable collectable watches are listed under the signed or marked movement. Other exclusive private signed or marked movements will have equivalent value are only slightly higher value & should be compared to Generic or Nameless movements. Railroad signed or marked (dials & movements) are usually more collectable & higher in value .

The prices shown were averaged from dealers' lists just prior to publication and are an indication of the collectable retail level or what collectors will pay. Prices are provided in three categories: average condition, extra fine, and mint condition, and are shown in whole dollar amounts only. The values listed are a guide for the collectable retail level and are provided for your information only. **Dealers** will not necessarily pay **full retail price**. Prices listed are for watches with original cases and dials.

Important Notice. All of the information, including valuations, in this book has been compiled from the most reliable sources, and every effort has been made to eliminate errors and questionable data. Nevertheless, the possibility of error, in a work of such immense scope, always exists. The publisher or authors will not be held responsible for losses which may occur in the purchase, sale, statements of its advertisers, or other transaction of items, because of information contained herein. Readers who feel they have discovered errors are invited to write and inform us, so they may be corrected in subsequent editions.

🕐 Descriptions and serial number ranges listed for early watches cannot be considered 100 percent accurate due to the manner in which records were kept by these companies.

🕐 Watch terminology or communication in this book has evolved over the years, in search of better and more precise language with a effort to improve, purify, adjust itself and make it easier to understand.

ABBREVIATIONS USED IN
THE COMPLETE PRICE GUIDE TO WATCHES

🕐—IMPORTANT NOTE.

★ ★ ★ ★ ★—only **ONE** to **FIVE** known
to exist (*proto type models etc.*)

★ ★ ★ ★—**Extremely Rare**; less than 25 to 50 known to exist.

★ ★ ★—**Rare**; about 250 known to exist.

★ ★ —**Scarce**; about 1,000 known to exist.

★ —**Uncommon**; about 2,500 known to exist.

⌂ — In Demand

ADJ —Adjusted (to temperature or heat & cold, also isochronism). Adj.5P = Adjusted to 5 positions, 3 positions or 4 positions etc

BASE—Base metal used in cases; e.g., silveroid

BB —Bubble Back (Rolex style case)

BRG—Bridge plate design movement

Ca. — Circa (about or approximate date)

Cal. —Calendar also Calibre (model)

C&B — Case and Band

Chrono.—Chronograph

Co.—Company

COIN—Coin silver

DES—Diamond end stones

DMK—Damaskeened

DSD—Double sunk dial

DR—Double roller

DWT—Penny weight: 1/20 Troy ounce

ETP—Estimated total production

ESC.—Escapement

EX—Extra nice; far above average

FULL—Full plate design movement

3/4—3/4 plate design movement

1F brg—One finger bridge design and a 3/4 plate (see Illinois 16s M#5)

2F brg—Two finger bridge design

3F brg—Three finger bridge design

GF—Gold filled

GJS—Gold jewel settings

G#—Grade number

GT—Gold train (gold gears)

GCW—Gold center wheel

GRO—Good running order

HC—Hunter case

id. — identification

(illo.) —Illustration of watches etc.

J—jewel (as 21J)

K—Karat (14k solid gold—not gold filled)

K(w) —WHITE GOLD as in 14K(w)

KS—Key set

KW—Key wind

KW/SW— transition (Key wind/stem wind)

LS—Lever set

MCC—Multi-color case

MCD—Multi-color dial

M#—Model number

mm —Millemeter (over all case size)

Mvt.— Only Dial and movement; no case

NI—Nickel plates or frames

OF—Open face

P—as Adj.5P = Adjusted to 5 positions, 3 positions or 4 positions etc.

PORC—Porcelain (porc. dial)

PS—Pendant set

PW — Pocket Watch

RF# —Reference Factory number

Reg.—Register on a chronograph

REP.—Repeater

RGJS—Raised gold jewel setting

RGP—Rolled gold plate

RR—Railroad

S—Size as 16S = 16 size

SBB—Screw back and bezel

SR—Single Roller

SRC—Swing ring case

SS—Stainless steel

SSD—Single Sunk Dial

SW—Stem wind

S#—Serial number

TEMP—Temperature

TP—Total production

2T—Two-tone

WGF—White gold filled

W.I. also W. Ind. —Wind indicator or (up and down indicator)

/ = WITH as KW/SW or SW/LS

WW—Wrist watch

YGF—Yellow gold filled

@ = AT or About

MODEL = Size, open face or hunter, full or 3/4 plate, key or stem wind, design & layout of parts.

GRADE= 1st., 2nd., & 3rd., Quality etc. some manufactures used names or numbers (**Bunn , 992**).

1. **Ebauche** = movement in the rough.
2. **Manufacture** = 75% to 100% completed on premises.
3. **Watchmaker** & Finisher = Finished movement in the rough & engraved their name.
4. **Jobber**, Distributor, Firms, Customized or Personalized = Retail only.

🕐 Pricing in this Guide are fair market price for **COMPLETE** watches which are reflected from the "**NAWCC**" National and regional shows.

INFORMATION NEEDED: We are interested in any facts and information you might have that should possibly be considered for future editions. Documented facts are needed, so please send photo or sources of information. Send to: Cooksey Shugart, P. O. BOX 3147, Cleveland, Tennessee 37320-3147.

(When *Corresponding, Please Include A* 🖃 *Self-addressed, Stamped Envelope.*)

Railroad Standards, Railroad Approved & Railroad Grade "TERMINOLOGY"

NOTE: Railroad Standards, Railroad Approved & Railroad Grade **terminology,** as defined and used in this **_BOOK_**.

1. **RAILROAD STANDARDS** = A commission or board appointed by the railroad companies outlined a set of **guidelines** to be accepted or approved by each railroad line.

2. **RAILROAD APPROVED** = A **_LIST_** of watches each railroad line would approve if purchased by their employee's. (this list changed through the years).

3. **RAILROAD GRADE** = A watch made by manufactures to meet or exceed the guidelines set by the railroad **standards**. Grades such as 992, Vanguard and B.W. Raymond, etc.

🕐 Some GRADES **exceeded** the R.R. standards such as 23 jewels, diamond end stone, gold train, raised gold jewel settings, double sunk dial and the list goes on. Examples: such as Veritas, Sangamo, 950 & Riverside Maximus and many others.

ABOVE: **GENERIC, NAMELESS OR UNMARKED MOVEMENTS**

Generic, Nameless or Unmarked grades for watch movements are listed under the Company name or initials of the Company, etc. by size, jewel count and description. Such as American Watch Co. or Amn Watch Co. or A.W.W.Co., Elgin W. Co. or Elgin National W. Co., Hampden W.Co. or Duber W.Co., Illinois W. Co.or I.W.Co., Rockford or R.W.Co., South Bend. **Example** name on movement Illinois Watch Co. and the watch is 18 size, 15 jewels, stem wind, adjusted, nickel, and damaskeened this watch can be found and will be listed under Illinois Watch Co. next look under the correct size (18 size) unmarked grade section as **Illinois Watch Co. or I.W.C., 15J, SW, ADJ, NI, DMK** these are Generic or unmarked grades. Movements with a grade **name** such as Bunn can be found and listed under **SIZE** then the name **Bunn** & jewels & etc..

MODEL = Size, open face or hunter, full or 3/4 plate, key or stem wind, design & layout of parts.
GRADE= 1st., 2nd., & 3rd., Quality etc. some manufactures used names or numbers (**Bunn , 992**).

🕐 Pricing in this Guide are fair market price for **COMPLETE** watches which are reflected from the "**NAWCC**" National and regional shows.

🕐 Watch terminology or communication in this book has evolved over the years, in search of better and more precise language with a effort to improve, purify, adjust itself and make it easier to understand.

ABBOTT'S STEM WIND

Henry Abbott first patented his stem wind attachment on June 30, 1876. The complete Abbott's stem wind mechanism is arranged in such a way as to convert key wind to stem wind. He also made a repeater-type slide mechanism for winding. On January 18, 1881, he received a patent for an improved stem wind attachment. On the new model the watch could be wound with the crown. Abbott sold over 50,000 of these stem-wind attachments, and many of them were placed on Waltham, Elgin, and Illinois watches.

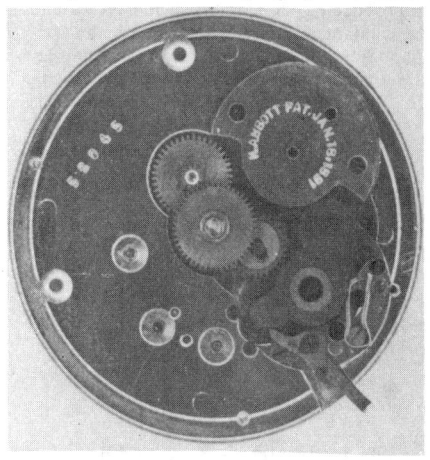

Abbott Stem Wind Attachment. LEFT: normal view of an Illinois watch movement with 'hidden' Abbott Stem Wind Attachment (pat. Jan., 18th, 1881). RIGHT: Same watch with dial removed exposing the Abbott Stem Wind Attachment. NOTE: Most Abbott's stem wind levers move up and down, while most standard levers move up & out.

ABBOTT WATCH CO.
(MADE BY HOWARD WATCH CO.) 1908 - 1912

Abbott Sure Time Watches were made by the E. Howard Watch Co.(Keystone), and are similar to Howard Watch Co. 1905 model. These watches sold for $8.75 and had 17 jewels. Some of the open face watches are actually hunting case models without the second bits register.

Description	Avg	Ex-Fn	Mint
Abbott Sure Time, 16S, 17J, OF, GF Case	$100	$135	$275
Abbott Sure Time, 16S, 17J, HC, GF Case	125	150	350
Abbott Sure Time, 16S, 17J, 14K **Abbott** HC ⬛	325	450	750

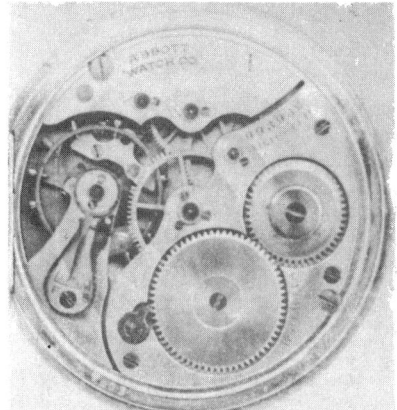

Abbott Watch Co., 16 size, 17 jewels, gold jeweled settings, hunting case. Note similarity to the Howard Watch Co. model 1905. Serial number 993932.

Abbott Watch Co., 16 size, 17 jewels, gold jeweled settings, open face. Note similarity to the Howard Watch Co. series 9.

ADAMS AND PERRY WATCH MANUFACTURING CO.

Lancaster, Pennsylvania
1874 - 1877

This company, like so many others, did not have sufficient capital to stay in business for long. The first year was spent in setting up and becoming incorporated. The building was completed in mid-1875, and watches were being produced by September. The first watches were limited to three grades, and the escapement and balance were bought from other sources. By December 1875, the company was short of money and,by the spring of 1876, they had standardized their movements to 18 size. The first movement went on sale (**very few watches were sold from this factory name**) April 7, 1876. The next year the company remained idle. In August 1877, the company was sold to the Lancaster Watch Company, after making only about 800 to 1,000 watches. In 1892 Hamilton acquired the assets.

Description		Avg	Ex-Fn	Mint
20S, 20J, GJS, PS, KW, 18K original	★ ★ ★	$2,000	$2,500	$4,000
18S, 20J, GJS, PS	★ ★	800	1,200	2,400
18S, 17J, GJS, PS	★	600	800	1,500
18S, 17J, GJS, PS, Coin, Original	★	800	1,200	2,200

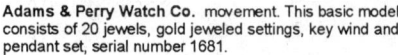

Adams & Perry Watch Co. movement. This basic model consists of 20 jewels, gold jeweled settings, key wind and pendant set, serial number 1681.

J. H. ALLISON movement 16 jewels,gold train and escape wheel with a pivoted detent, key wind and key set, serial number 19.

J. H. ALLISON

Detroit, Michigan
1853 - 1890

The first watch J. H. Allison made was in 1853; it was a chronometer with full plate and a fusee with chain drive. The balance had time screws and sliding weights. In 1864, he made a 3/4 plate chronometer with gold wheels. He also damaskeened the nickel movement. He produced only about 25 watches, of which 20 were chronometers. By 1883 he was making 3/4 plate movements with a stem wind of his own design.Allison made most of his own parts and designed his own tools. He also altered some key wind watches to stem wind. Allison died in 1890.

Description		Avg	Ex-Fn	Mint
Full Plate & 3\4 Plate, GT, NI, DMK	★ ★ ★ ★	$5,000	$6,500	$13,000
Detent Chronometer Escapement, 16J, KW/KS, GT	★ ★ ★ ★	9,000	10,000	18,000

AMERICAN REPEATING WATCH CO.

Elizabeth, New Jersey
1885 - 1892

Around 1675, a repeating mechanism was attached to a clock for the first time. The first repeating watch was made about 1687 by Thomas Tompion or Daniel Quare. Five-minute, quarter-hour and half-hour repeaters were popular by 1730. The minute repeater became common about 1830.

Fred Terstegen applied for a patent on August 21, 1882, for a repeating attachment that would work with any American key-wind or stem-wind watch. He was granted three patents: No. 311,270 on January 27, 1885; No. 421,844 on February 18, 1890; and No. 436,162 in September 1890. Waltham was the only watch company to fabricate repeating watches in America. It is not known how many repeaters were made, but it is estimated to be about **500** to **1,000**. This repeating attachment fits most American 18 size movements.

18 SIZE, with REPEATER ATTACHMENT

Name — Description		Avg	Ex-Fn	Mint
HOWARD, w/ 5 min. repeater attachment, COIN	★ ★	$2,500	$3,000	$4,500
GOLD CASE	★ ★	5,000	5,500	7,000
Keystone, or Lancaster, w/ 5 min. rep. attachment, COIN	★ ★	2,000	2,500	4,000
GOLD CASE	★ ★	3,000	4,000	5,500
SETH THOMAS, w/ 5 min. repeater attachment, COIN	★ ★	2,000	2,500	4,000
GOLD CASE	★ ★	3,000	4,000	5,500

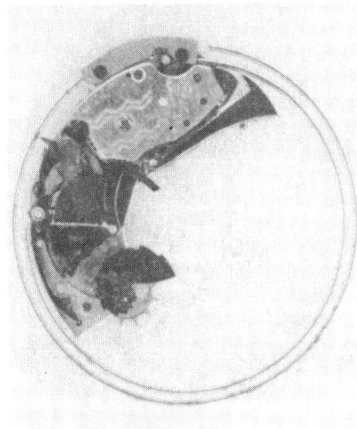 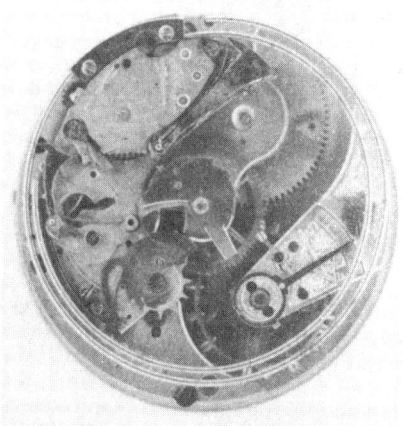

American Repeating Attachment. illustration at LEFT shows Terstegen's patented repeating attachment only. Illustration at RIGHT shows attachment as normally found on movement. The two outside circles on left illustration are wire gongs. The hammer can be seen at upper LEFT Illustration in the shape of a boot.

🕐 Watches listed in this book are priced at the **collectable fair market value** at the RETAIL level, as complete watches having an original 14k gold filled case, KEY WIND with silver, an original white enamel single sunk dial, and with the entire original movement in good working order with no repairs needed, unless otherwise noted.

🕐 Some grades are not included. Their values can be determined by comparing with **similar** age, size, metal content, style, models and grades listed.

16 SIZE, with REPEATER ATTACHMENT

Name — Description		Avg	Ex-Fn	Mint
COLUMBUS, w/ 5 min. rep. attachment, GF or COIN	★★	$2,000	$2,500	$4,000
GOLD CASE	★★	3,000	3,500	5,000
ELGIN, w/ 5 min. rep. attachment, GF or COIN	★★	2,000	2,500	4,000
GOLD CASE	★★	3,000	3,500	5,000
HAMPDEN, w/ 5 min. rep. attachment, GF or COIN	★★	2,000	2,500	4,000
GOLD CASE	★★	3,000	3,500	5,000
HOWARD, w/ 5 min. rep. attachment, GF or COIN	★★	3,000	3,500	5,000
GOLD CASE	★★	4,500	5,000	6,500
ILLINOIS, w/ 5 min. rep. attachment, GF or COIN	★★	2,000	2,500	4,000
GOLD CASE	★★	3,500	4,000	5,500
Non-magnetic (Paillard),w/ 5 min. rep. attachment, gold-filled	★★	2,000	2,500	4,000
GOLD CASE	★★	2,500	3,000	4,500

NOVEL STRIKING ATTACHMENTS

Five-Minute Repeaters.

(Manufactured under Terstegen's Patents.)

They are made to fit the following American Watch Movements :

16 SIZE	18 SIZE
ILLINOIS	ONLY TO
COLUMBUS	LANCASTER
HOWARD	or
HAMPDEN	KEYSTONE
NON-MAGNETIC PAILLARD	SETH THOMAS
WALTHAM and	and
ELGIN	HOWARD

HUNTING OR OPEN-FACE.

Handsome, Simple and Durable.

American
Repeating Watch Factory
of Elizabeth, N. J.

🕐 Watches listed in this book are priced at the **collectable fair market value** at the RETAIL level, as complete watches having an original 14k gold filled case, KEY WIND with silver, an original white enamel single sunk dial, and with the entire original movement in good working order with no repairs needed, unless otherwise noted.

🕐 Some grades are not included. Their values can be determined by comparing with **similar** age, size, metal content, style, models and grades listed.

🕐 Pricing in this Guide are fair market price for **COMPLETE** watches which are reflected from the "**NAWCC**" National and regional shows.

THE AMERICAN WALTHAM WATCH CO.
1851 - 1957

To trace the roots of the Waltham family one must start with the year 1850 in Roxbury, Massachusetts, No. 34 Water Street. That fall David Davis, a Mr. Dennison, and Mr. Howard together formed a watch company. Howard and Dennison had a dream of producing watches with interchangeable parts that were less expensive and did not result in less quality.

Aaron Dennison   E. Howard

Howard served an apprenticeship to Aaron Willard Jr. in about 1829. Several years later, in 1842, Howard formed a clock and balance scale manufacturing company with Davis. Howard and Dennison combined their ideas and, with financing provided by Samuel Curtis, the first of their watches was made in 1850. But they had problems. They were trying out ideas such as using jewels, making dials, and producing steel with mirror finishes. This required all new machinery and resulted in a great financial burden. They discovered, too, that although all watches were produced on the same machines and of the same style, each watch was individual with its own set of errors to be corrected. This they had not anticipated. It took months to adjust the watches to the point they were any better than any other timepieces on the market.

Example of a Warren model, about 18 size, 15 jewels, engraved on the movement *Warren N0 44 BOSTON,* plain dial, under sprung, steel balance, right angle lever, escape wheel has pointed teeth, key wind & key set from front, Ca.1853. Note: This movement was made to fit an English size case and will not fit a standard 18 size American case.

But Howard had perfected and patented many automatic watchmaking machines that produced precision watch parts. In 1851 the factory building was completed and the name American Horology Company was chosen. It was not until late 1852 that the first watches were completed bearing the signature "The Warren Mfg. Co.," after a famed Revolutionary War hero. The first 17 watches were not placed on the market but went to officials of the company. Watches numbered 18 through 110 were marked "Warren Boston;" the next 800 were marked "Samuel Curtis;" a few were marked "Fellows & Schell" and sold for $40.

The name was changed to the Boston Watch Company in September 1853, and a factory was built in Waltham, Massachusetts, in October 1854. The movements that were produced here carried serial numbers 1,001 to 5,000 and were marked "Dennison, Howard & Davis," "C. T. Parker," and "P. S. Bartlett." Boston Watch Company failed in 1857 and was sold at a sheriff's auction to Royal E. Robbins. In May 1857, it was reorganized as the Appleton, Tracy & Co., and the watches produced carried serial numbers 5,001 to 14,000, model 1857. The first movements were marked Appleton, Tracy & Co. The C. T. Parker was introduced as model 1857 and sold for $12.00, 399 of these models were made. In 1855 **brass clocks** were selling just over $1.00. Also 598 chronodrometers were produced and in January 1858 the P. S. Bartlett watch was made.

Engraved on movement *SAMUEL CURTIS ROXBURY. NO 112*, 18 size, 15 jewels, under sprung, steel balance, Ca. 1853. This movement was made to fit in the typical English size case.

Engraved on movement "*C.T. PARKER WALTHAM MASS. NO 1099*" , 7 jewels, under sprung, steel balance, Ca. November 1857. Note: Balance cock not engraved.

In January 1859, the Waltham Improvement Co. and the Appleton, Tracy & Co. merged to form the American Watch Company. In 1860, as Lincoln was elected president and the country was in Civil War, the American Watch Co. was faced with serious problems. The next year, business came to a standstill. There seemed to be little hope of finding a market for watches, and bankruptcy again seemed close at hand. At this point it was decided to cut expenditures to the lowest possible figure and keep the factory in operation.

American horology owes much to members of the Waltham Watch group such as Bacon, Church, Dennison, Fogg, Howard Marsh, Webster, and Woerd, who contributed much to its development and success. In early 1861, the name "J. Watson" appeared on model 1857 (first run: Nos. 23,601 to 24,300 total production 1,200).

The next model 1857 was the "R. E. Robbins" of which 2,800 were made. The William Ellery, marked "Wm. Ellery," (model 1857) was then introduced with the first serial number of 46,201. It was key wind and key set and had 7 to 15 jewels.

A size 10 woman's watch was made in July of 1861 with first serial numbers of 44,201. It was marked "Appleton, Tracy & Co." gold balance, key wind and key set, 3/4 plate, 13 to 15 jewels. Some were marked "P. S. Bartlett" and a 15 jewel was marked "Appleton, Tracy & Co." A special model, 10 size, serial numbers of 45,801 to 46,200, is extremely rare. The first stem wind, beginning with serial number 410,698, was produced in 1868. By 1880 all watches were quick train. The last key wind was serial No. 22,577,000, about 1919, 18 size, 1883 model, 7J, sterling, produced for export.

⊕ **Abraham Lincoln** owned & carried a "William Ellery" model, silver-cased, key wind, 11 jewels, serial no. 67613, so stated Carl Sandburg in his biography of Lincoln. The watch was produced by A.W.W.Co. in Jan.-Feb., of 1863 & was a 18 size, 1859 3/4 plate model with a steel balance.

WALTHAM ESTIMATED SERIAL NUMBERS AND PRODUCTION DATES

DATE — SERIAL NO.	DATE — SERIAL NO.	DATE — SERIAL NO.
1852 – 50	1888 – 3,800,000	1924 – 24,550,000
1853 – 400	1889 – 4,200,000	1925 – 24,800,000
1854 – 1,000	1890 – 4,700,000	1926 – 25,200,000
1855 – 2,500	1891 – 5,200,000	1927 – 26,100,000
1856 – 4,000	1892 – 5,800,000	1928 – 26,400,000
1857 – 6,000	1893 – 6,300,000	1929 – 26,900,000
1858 – 10,000	1894 – 6,700,000	1930 – 27,100,000
1859 – 15,000	1895 – 7,100,000	1931 – 27,300,000
1860 – 20,000	1896 – 7,450,000	1932 – 27,550,000
1861 – 30,000	1897 – 8,100,000	1933 – 27,750,000
1862 – 45,000	1898 – 8,400,000	1934 – 28,100,000
1863 – 65,000	1899 – 9,000,000	1935 – 28,600,000
1864 – 110,000	1900 – 9,500,000	1936 – 29,100,000
1865 – 180,000	1901 – 10,200,000	1937 – 29,400,000
1866 – 260,000	1902 – 11,100,000	1938 – 29,750,000
1867 – 330,000	1903 – 12,100,000	1939 – 30,050,000
1868 – 410,000	1904 – 13,500,000	1940 – 30,250,000
1869 – 460,000	1905 – 14,300,000	1941 – 30,750,000
1870 – 500,000	1906 – 14,700,000	1942 – 31,050,000
1871 – 540,000	1907 – 15,500,000	1943 – 31,400,000
1872 – 590,000	1908 – 16,400,000	1944 – 31,700,000
1873 – 680,000	1909 – 17,600,000	1945 – 32,100,000
1874 – 730,000	1910 – 17,900,000	1946 – 32,350,000
1875 – 810,000	1911 – 18,100,000	1947 – 32,750,000
1876 – 910,000	1912 – 18,200,000	1948 – 33,100,000
1877 – 1,000,000	1913 – 18,900,000	1949 – 33,500,000
1878 – 1,150,000	1914 – 19,500,000	1950 – 33,560,000
1879 – 1,350,000	1915 – 20,000,000	1951 – 33,600,000
1880 – 1,500,000	1916 – 20,500,000	1952 – 33,700,000
1881 – 1,670,000	1917 – 20,900,000	1953 – 33,800,000
1882 – 1,835,000	1918 – 21,800,000	1954 – 34,100,000
1883 – 2,000,000	1919 – 22,500,000	1955 – 34,450,000
1884 – 2,350,000	1920 – 23,400,000	1956 – 34,700,000
1885 – 2,650,000	1921 – 23,900,000	1957 – 35,000,000
1886 – 3,000,000	1922 – 24,100,000	
1887 – 3,400,000	1923 – 24,300,000	

⊕ The above list is provided for determining the __APPROXIMATE__ age of your watch. Match serial number with date. Watches were not necessarily *SOLD* and *DELIVERED* in the exact order of manufactured or production dates.

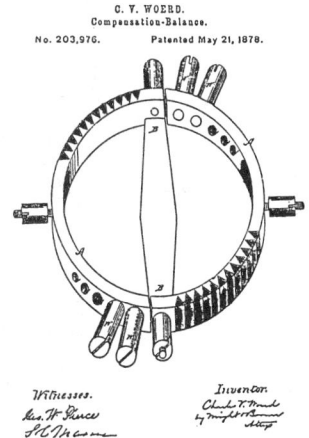

C. V. WOERD.
Compensation-Balance.

No. 203,976.   Patented May 21, 1878.

Witnesses.   Inventor.

HOWARD, DAVIS & DENNISON: 20 Size, 15 Jewels, 8 day, two mainsprings and gilt movement. The first 17 were made for the officials of the company, Ca. 1852.

Woerd's patented compensating balance the above illustration is a copy of the blue print of Mr. Woerd's patented SAW TOOTH BALANCE. The Saw Tooth Balance may be found on some 16 size 1872 models. (VERY RARE)

⊕   Generic, nameless or unmarked grades for watch movements are listed under the Company name or initials of the Company, etc. by size, jewel count and description.

20 SIZE
MODEL 1862 = 20 KW - (T. P. 3,500)

Grade or Name–Description	Avg	Ex -Fn	Mint
American Watch Co., 19J, KW, 18K, HC, all original .... ★★★	$4,000	$5,000	$8,000
American Watch Co., 15 to19J, KW, KS,3/4, vibrating hair-spring stud, silver case...................................... ★★	1,800	2,500	4,500
American Watch Co., 15 to 19J, KW, KS, 3/4, vibrating hair-spring stud, 18K HC, all original .... ★★	2,800	4,000	7,500
American Watch Co., 15 & 17J,3/4, KW, ADJ...........................★	400	650	1,200
American Watch Co., 19J,3/4, KW, ADJ .... ★★	2,000	2,600	4,000
American Watch Co., 19J,3/4, KW, ADJ, with Maltese cross stopwork, all original silver case...................................... ★★	2,200	2,500	4,500
Am'n W. Co., 7-11J,3/4, KW...★	300	400	700
American W. Co., Nashua S# under dial, (below 51,000).... ★★★	4,000	6,000	9,000
Am'n W. Co., 15J, KW,3/4, coin case..................................★	500	700	1,000
Appleton, Tracy & Co., 15J,3/4, KW, with Maltese cross stopwork, all original...★	600	800	1,200
Appleton, Tracy & Co., 15-17J,3/4, KW ....★	500	700	1,000
Appleton, Tracy & Co., 15 & 17J,3/4, KW, vibrating hair spring stud, silver case... ★★	1,400	1,800	2,800
Appleton, Tracy & Co., 15 & 17J,3/4, KW, vibrating hair spring stud, 18K HC .... ★★★	3,200	3,600	6,000
Appleton Tracy & Co., 15J, KW, vibrating hairspring stud Straton barrel, Foggs Pat. .... ★★	800	1,000	1,500
Appleton Tracy & Co., 15J, KW,3/4, **Mvt. only no case**	200	300	600
Appleton Tracy & Co., 19J, KW,3/4.. ★★	500	600	900
Howard, Davis & Dennison, S#1-17, 8 day, Ca.1852.... ★★★★★	30,000	40,000	80,000

NOTE: **RARE in original gold cases add ($1,200.00 in 14K) & ($1,600.00 in 18K).**

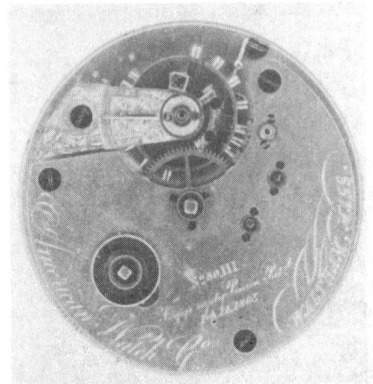 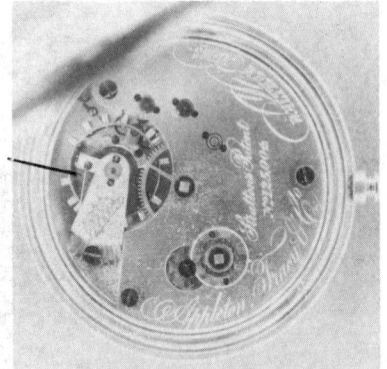

American Watch Co., Model 1862, 20 size, 17-19 jewels, gold balance and escape wheel, gold jeweled settings, key wind, key set from back, serial number 80111.

Appleton Tracy & Co., Model 20KW, 20 size, 15 jewels, serial number 125004. Note vibrating hairspring stud.

🕐 Generic, nameless or unmarked grades for watch movements are listed under the Company name or initials of the Company, etc. by size, jewel count and description.

🕐 Pricing in this Guide are fair market price for **COMPLETE** watches which are reflected from the "**NAWCC**" National and regional shows.

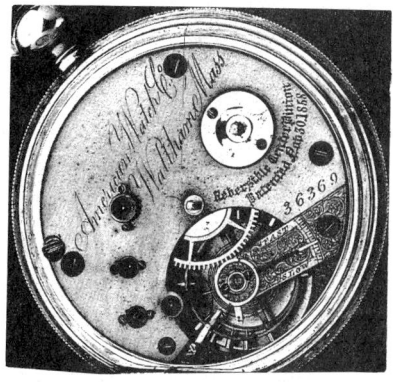

AMERICAN WATCH CO., Model 18KW, 18 size, 15 jewels, serial number 36369. Reversible center pinion, patented Nov. 30th, 1858.

Model 1857, 18 size, 15-16 jewels, "**Chronodrometer**" on dial, "Appleton Tracy & Co." or "P.S. Bartlett, key wind & set, 1/4 jump seconds, S.# 14,752. Listed under "**Appleton Tracy & Co.** Chronodrometer", Ist serial # 13,701.

18 SIZE
MODELS 1857, (18 KW =1859), 1870, 1877, 1879, 1883, 1892

Grade or Name – Description	Avg	Ex-Fn	Mint
American Watch Co., 17J,3/4, M#1859 or M#**18KW** .... ★★★	$2,400	$3,500	$5,000
American Watch Co., 19J, 3/4, M#1859............................★★★★	3,500	4,500	9,500
American Watch Co., 21J, M#1883, Special, ADJ, GJS ...... ★★★	650	850	1,500
American Watch Co., 15J, M#1859,3/4, Pat. Nov. 30, 1858,			
Reversible center pinion, original silver case .... ★★★	4,000	4,500	8,000
American Watch Co., 17J, M#1859,3/4, KW, Fitts Pat.			
Reversible center pinion, Originial 18K case .... ★★★★	5,500	6,500	9,000

🕐 Generic, nameless or unmarked grades for watch movements are listed under the Company name or initials of the Company, etc. by size, jewel count and description.

	Avg	Ex-Fn	Mint
AMn. Watch Co., 15J, M#1857, (*Waltham W. Co.*), KW, KS	$150	$200	$350
AMn. Watch Co., 15J, M#1857, (*Waltham W. Co.*), SW / KS@ dial★	200	325	500
AMn. Watch Co., 15J, M#1857, (*Waltham W. Co.*), SW / KW ..... ★	200	325	500
AMn. Watch Co., 15J, M#1857, (*Waltham W. Co.)*, SW / LS	200	325	500
AMn. Watch Co., 17J, M#1857, KW, KS ....★	175	225	375
AMn. Watch Co., 14K, HC, heavy box hinged, multi-color			
(4 colors)	2,000	2,500	4,000
AMn. Watch Co., 11J, thin model, KW, 3/4 plate ....★	150	200	500
AMn Watch Co., 15J, M#1870, KW..............	150	225	500
AMn. Watch Co., 17J, M#1870, KW, ADJ	175	275	550
AMn. Watch Co., 17J, M#1892	100	125	275
AMn. Watch Co., 21J, M#1892	150	200	400
AMn. Watch Co., 7J, M#1877, ...	70	100	250
AMn. Watch Co., 11J, M#1877	70	100	250
AMn. Watch Co., 7J, M#1883, SW/ KW	70	100	250
AMn. Watch Co., 11-13J, M#1883, SW/ KW	70	100	250
AMn Watch Co., 15-16-17J, M#1883..............	70	100	250
AMn. Watch Co., 15J, M#1883, SW/ KW	70	100	250
Appleton, Tracy & Co., 15J, M#1857, SW / LS...........................	150	200	300
Appleton, Tracy & Co., 7-11J, KW, M#1857	150	200	300
Appleton, Tracy & Co., 11J, thin model, KW,3/4 ....★	250	350	500
Appleton, Tracy & Co., 15J, M#1857, KW	150	200	300
Appleton, Tracy & Co., 15J, M#1857, KW,			
serial # below 10,000..★	600	700	1,500

🕐 Some watch manufacturers personalize watches for jobbers or jewelry firms, with exclusive private signed or marked movements. The valuable collectable watches are listed under the signed or marked movement. Other exclusive private signed or marked movements will have equivalent value are only slightly higher value and should be compared to Generic or Nameless movements. Railroad

Grade or Name–Description	Avg	Ex-Fn	Mint
Appleton, Tracy & Co., 15J, M#1859, 3/4, reverse pinion,			
Pat. Nov. 30, 1858, orig. silver case .... ★★★	$1,400	$1,600	$3,000
Appleton, Tracy & Co., 11-15-16-17J, KW, 3/4 .... ★	200	300	500
Appleton, Tracy & Co., 16J, M#1857, **1st run** (5,001-5,100)			
Am.W. Co. (Eagle) silver HC .... ★★	800	900	1,500
Appleton, Tracy & Co., 15J, M#1857, KW, 18K HC	700	800	1,200
Appleton, Tracy & Co., 16J, M#1857, KW	225	250	500
Appleton, Tracy & Co., 15J, 3/4, KW, with vibrating hairspring stud,			
Stratton's Pat., coin case .... ★★★	1,400	1,600	3,000
Appleton, Tracy & Co., 15J, 3/4, KW, with vibrating hairspring stud,			
orig. 18K case .... ★★★	2,000	2,400	3,800
Appleton,Tracy & Co., Sporting, (Chronodrometer),M#1857,			
16J, KW,KS, orig. case, with stop feature .... ★★	2,000	2,500	4,000
Appleton, Tracy & Co., 15J, 3/4, KW............................... ★	175	225	395
Appleton, Tracy & Co., 11-15J, M#s 1877, 1879, SW	70	95	200
Appleton, Tracy & Co., 15J, M#1877, KW	70	95	200
Appleton, Tracy & Co., 15J, M#s 1877-1879, SW, OF	70	95	200
Appleton, Tracy & Co., 15J, M#s 1877-1879, SW, HC	100	150	250
Appleton, Tracy & Co., 15J, M#1883, SW, OF	70	90	200
Appleton, Tracy & Co., 15J, M#1883, SW, **non- magnet**, OF	100	125	250
Appleton, Tracy & Co., 15J, M#1883, SW, HC	100	150	250
Appleton, Tracy & Co., 15J, M#1892, SW, OF	70	95	200
Appleton, Tracy & Co., 17J, M#1883, SW, HC........................	75	100	225
Appleton, Tracy & Co., 17J, M#1892, SW, Premiere	70	95	200
Appleton, Tracy & Co., 17J, M#1892, SW, OF	70	95	200
Appleton, Tracy & Co., 17J, M#1883, OF	70	95	200
Appleton, Tracy & Co., 17J, M#1892, SW, HC	125	150	250
Appleton, Tracy & Co., 19J, M#1892, SW, OF	200	300	400
Appleton, Tracy & Co., 19J, M#1892, SW, HC	225	300	450
Appleton, Tracy & Co., 21J, M#1892, SW, OF	225	300	450
Appleton, Tracy & Co., 21J, M#1892, SW, HC	300	350	550

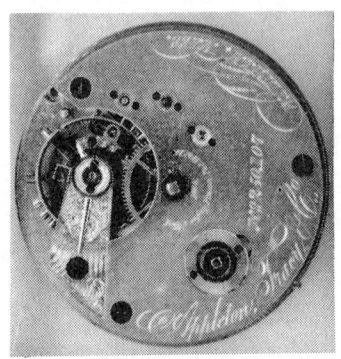

Appleton, Tracy & Co. (20 size), 15-17 jewels, Fogg's safety pinion pat. Feb 14 1865, key wind & set from back, serial number 250107.

P. S. Bartlett, Model 18KW or 1859, 18 size, 11 jewels, key wind & set from back, serial number 41597.

🕐 Pricing in this Guide are fair market price for **COMPLETE** watches which are reflected from the "**NAWCC**" National and regional shows.

🕐 Generic, nameless or unmarked grades for watch movements are listed under the Company name or initials of the Company, etc. by size, jewel count and description.

Grade or Name – Description	Avg	Ex-Fn	Mint
A. W. W. Co., 7-9J, M#1883, **KW,** OF	$150	$225	$400
A. W. W. Co., 7-9J, M#1883, SW, OF	70	90	150
A. W. W. Co., 11-13J, LS, HC	80	100	175
A. W. W. Co., 11-13J, M#1879, OF	70	90	150
A. W. W. Co., 11-13J, M#1883, SW, OF	70	90	150
A. W. W. Co., 15J, OF	70	90	150
A. W. W. Co., 15J, HC	80	100	175
A. W. W. Co., 15J, **14K multi-color boxcase HC**	2,000	2,500	4,000
A. W. W. Co., 15J, M#1879, OF	75	100	150
A. W. W. Co., 15J, M#1883	75	100	150
A. W. W. Co., 16 or 18J, OF or HC	100	125	200
A. W. W. Co., 17J, M#1857, gold bal. wheel, GJS, ★	275	350	500
A. W. W. Co., 17J, "for R.R. Service" on dial ★★	450	550	750
A. W. W. Co., 17J, M#1883, OF	70	95	150
A. W. W. Co., 17J, M#1883, HC	90	125	200
A. W. W. Co., 17J, M#1892, LS, OF	70	90	150
A. W. W. Co., 17J, M#1892, PS, OF	70	90	150
A. W. W. Co., 17J, M#1892, HC	100	125	175
A. W. W. Co., 19J, M#1892	150	185	350
A. W. W. Co., 21J, M#1892	250	300	450
A. W. W. Co., 23J, M#1892	275	325	500

P.S. Bartlett, 18 size, 15 jewels, Model 1857, Engraved on back "4 PR. Jewels." Serial number 13446.

Marked Canadian Railway Time Service, Model 1892, 18 size, 17 jewels, serial number 22,017,534.

Grade or Name – Description	Avg	Ex-Fn	Mint
P. S. Bartlett, 7J, M#1857, KW, 1st Run (1,401-1,500) ★★★			
Am.W. Co. (Eagle) silver HC	$1,500	$2,000	$4,500
P. S. Bartlett, 15J, M#1857, KW, 2nd Run (1,551-1,650)			
Am.W. Co. (Eagle) silver HC ★★	800	1,000	2,000
P. S. Bartlett, 11J, M#1857, KW, 2nd-3rd Run ★	600	700	1,100
P. S. Bartlett, 15J, M#1857, KW, 2nd-3rd Run ★	650	750	1,200
P. S. Bartlett, 11J, LS, **HC, 14K**	425	500	850
P. S. Bartlett, 15J, M#1857, KW, **below** S#8,000	600	700	1,200
P. S. Bartlett, 7-11J, M#1857, KW	125	150	225
P. S. Bartlett, 15J, M#1857, KW	150	175	300
P. S. Bartlett, 11J, M#1879, KW	70	90	175
P. S. Bartlett, 11J, M#1857, KW, Eagle inside case lid	270	350	500
P. S. Bartlett, 15J, M#1857, SW / LS, **(note let down screw)**	200	250	400

Grade or Name – Description	Avg	Ex-Fn	Mint
P. S. Bartlett, 15J, M#1879, KW	$85	$110	$175
P. S. Bartlett, 15J, M#1879, SW	75	100	150
P. S. Bartlett, 11-15J, M#1870, SW	75	100	150
P. S. Bartlett, 11-15J, M#1877, KW	80	120	200
P. S. Bartlett, 11J, M#1883, SW	75	100	150
P. S. Bartlett, 15J, M#1883, **KW**	100	150	250
P. S. Bartlett, 15J, M#1883, SW	75	100	150
P. S. Bartlett, 17J, M#1883, SW	75	100	150
P. S. Bartlett, 11J, M#1859, 3/4, thin model, KS from back	300	450	800
P. S. Bartlett, 11J, M#1859, 3/4, Pat. Nov. 30, 1858	400	500	950
P. S. Bartlett, 15J, **pinned plates**, M#1857, KW ★★	600	800	1,400
P. S. Bartlett, 15J, M#1892, SW ★	90	100	200
P. S. Bartlett, 17J, M#1892, SW, OF, LS	100	125	200
P. S. Bartlett, 17J, M#1892, SW, HC	125	175	275
P. S. Bartlett, 17J, M#1892, SW, OF, PS	100	125	200
P. S. Bartlett, 17J, M#1892, SW, 2-Tone	100	125	250
P. S. Bartlett, 19J, M#1892, SW	175	200	300
P. S. Bartlett, 21J, M#1892, SW	200	235	325
P. S. Bartlett, 21J, M#1892, SW, 2-Tone	250	300	500
Broadway, 7J, M#1857, KW, HC	100	125	200
Broadway, 11J, M#1857, KW, HC	125	150	200
Broadway, 7-11J, M#1877, KW, SW, NI, HC	125	150	200
Broadway, 7J, M#1883, KW, HC	125	150	200
Broadway, 11J, M#1883, KW, HC	125	150	200
Broadway, 11J, M#1883, SW, HC	125	150	200
Canadian Pacific R.R., 17J, M#1883 ★★	400	500	700
Canadian Pacific R.R., 17J, M#1892-1908 ★★	550	650	800
Canadian Pacific R.R., 21J, M#1892 ★★	600	700	1,000
Canadian Railway Time Service, 17J, M#1883-1892, Adj.5P	435	550	700
Central Park, 15J, M#1857, KW	160	185	300
Champion, 15J, M#1877, OF	80	100	150
Chronometro, 21J, M#1892, OF	225	300	450
Conklins Railroad Special, 21J, G#1892 ★★	500	550	800

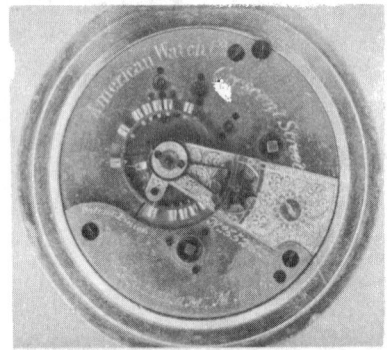

Appleton, Tracy & Co. 18 size, 15 jewels, Model # 1877, stem wind, quick train, hunting case, serial # 1,389,078.

Crescent Street, Model 1870, 18 size, 15 J., Key wind & set from back, serial number 552,526. This grade was the **first** American watch to be advertised as a railroad watch.

IMPORTANT NOTE: Railroad Standards, Railroad Approved & Railroad Grade **terminology,** as defined and used in this _BOOK_.
1. **RAILROAD STANDARDS** = A commission or board appointed by the railroad companies outlined a set of **guidelines** to be accepted or approved by each railroad line.
2. **RAILROAD APPROVED** = A _LIST_ of watches each railroad line would approve if purchased by their employee's. (this list changed through the years).
3. **RAILROAD GRADE** = A watch made by manufactures to meet or exceed the guidelines set by the railroad **standards**. Grades such as 992, Vanguard and B.W. Raymond, etc.
☉ Some GRADES **exceeded** the R.R. standards such as 23 jewels, diamond end stone, gold train, raised gold jewel settings, double sunk dial and the list goes on. Examples: such as Veritas, Sangamo, 950 & Riverside Maximus and many others.

Grade or Name–Description	Avg	Ex-Fn	Mint
Crescent Street, 15J, M#1870, KW	$150	$200	$400
Crescent Street, 15J, M#1870, **pin or nail set**	175	225	450
Crescent Street, 17J, M#1870, KW/SW ★	175	225	450
Crescent Street, 15J, M#1870, SW	100	135	265
Crescent Street, 15J, M#1883, SW, non-magnetic, OF	100	135	265
Crescent Street, 15J, M#1883, SW, non-magnetic, HC	150	175	300
Crescent Street, 15J, M#1883, SW, 2-Tone	100	125	225
Crescent Street, 17J, M#1883, SW, OF	70	90	175
Crescent Street, 17J, M#1883, SW, HC	100	120	200
Crescent Street, 19J, M#1883 ★	200	240	425
Crescent Street, 17J, M#1892, SW, **GJS**	100	150	250
Crescent Street, 17J, M#1892, SW, OF	95	125	200
Crescent Street, 17J, M#1892, SW, HC	110	135	200
Crescent Street, 19J, M#1892, SW, Adj.5P, GJS ,OF	125	150	300
Crescent Street, 19J, M#1892, SW, Adj.5P, GJS ,HC	225	265	350
Crescent Street, 21J, M#1892, SW, Adj.5P, GJS, OF	200	250	400
Crescent Street, 21J, M#1892, SW, Adj.5P, GJS, HC	250	275	425
Crescent Street, 21J, M#1892, Wind Indicator ★	1,000	1,200	1,800
Samuel Curtis, 11-15J, M#1857, KW, S# less than200, original 17S silver case ★★	3,000	3,500	5,000
Samuel Curtis, 11-15J, M#1857, KW, S# less than 400, original 17S silver case ★★	2,500	3,000	4,000
Samuel Curtis, 11-15J, M#1857, KW, S# less than 600, original 17S silver case ★★	2,200	2,400	3,500
Samuel Curtis, 11-15J, M#1857, KW, S# less than 1,000, original 17S silver case ★★	1,600	1,800	3,000
(Samuel Curtis **"not"** in original silver case, deduct $800 to $1,000 from value)			
Dennison, Howard, Davis, 7J, M#1857, KW, W/original case	900	1,000	1,500
Dennison, Howard, Davis, 11-13J, M#1857, KW, W/original case	950	1,100	1,600
Dennison, Howard, Davis, 15J, M#1857, KW, W/original case	1,000	1,200	1,800
Dennison, Howard, Davis, 15J, M#1857, KW, 1st. run (**1,002-1,100**) W/original case Am.W. Co. (Eagle)silver HC ★★★	1,500	2,000	3,000
Dennison, Howard, Davis, 15J, M#1857, KW, S# less than 2,000, W/original case Am.W. Co. (Eagle)silver HC ★	1,000	1,200	2,000

🕐 Pricing in this Guide are fair market price for **COMPLETE** watches which are reflected from the "**NAWCC**" National and regional shows.

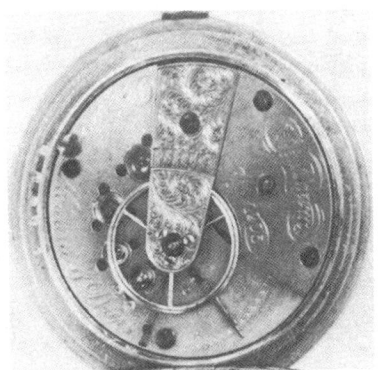

Dennison, Howard, Davis, Model 1857, 18 size, 15 jewels, under sprung, key wind, serial number 1205.

Howard & Rice, Model 1857, 18 size, 15 jewels, under sprung, serial number 6003.

🕐 Watches listed in this book are priced at the collectable retail level, as **complete** watches having an original 14k gold-filled case and Key Wind with silver, an original white enamel single sunk dial, and with the entire original movement in good working order with no repairs needed.

Grade or Name –Description		Avg	Ex-Fn	Mint
D.& R.G. Special (Denver & Rio Grande), 17J, M#1892, GJS, Adj.5P	★★★	$1,200	$1,500	$2,500
D.& R.G. Special (Denver & Rio Grande), 21J, M#1892, GJS, Adj.5P	★★★	1,200	1,500	2,500
Dominion Railways, 15-17J, M#1883, OF, SW, train on dial	★★★	1,000	1,300	2,300
Wm. Ellery, 7-11J, M#1857, Boston, Mass. all original silver HC case with Am. Watch Co.& eagle, serial # below **46,600**	★★	250	300	500
Wm. Ellery, 7-11J, M#1857, Boston, Mass.		100	150	275
Wm. Ellery, 7-11J, M#KW, 3/4		175	200	265
Wm. Ellery, 15J, KW, 3/4	★	225	300	495
Wm. Ellery, 7-11J, M#18KW, KW-KS from back, 18K, HC		1,000	1,200	2,000
Wm. Ellery, 7J, M#1857, KW, KS from back		200	300	500
Wm. Ellery, 15J, M#1857, SW / LS, (note let down screw)	★	200	300	500
Wm. Ellery, 7-15J, M#1877, M#1879, KW		70	100	200
Wm. Ellery, 11-15J, M#1877 & 1879, SW		70	100	200
Wm. Ellery, 7-13J, M#1883		70	100	200
Excelsior, M#1877, KW		70	100	200
Export, 7-11J, M#1877		70	100	200
Export, 7-11J, M#1883, KW		70	100	200
Express Train, 15-17J, M# 1883, LS, OF		325	400	550
Favorite, 15J, M#1877		90	125	225
Fellows & Schell, 15J, KW, KS, 1857 model	★★★	2,000	2,500	4,000
Franklin, 7J, M#1877, SW		150	175	300
Home Watch Co., 7-15J, M#1857-1883, KW		100	125	250
Home Watch Co., 7J, M#1877, KW		100	125	225
Home Watch Co., 7-11J, M#1879, SW		100	125	200
Howard & Rice, 15J, M#1857, KW, KS (serial numbers range from 6000 to 6500)	★★	2,000	2,500	3,500
E. Howard & Co., Boston (on dial & mvt.), English style escape wheel, upright pallets, 15J, M#1857, KW, KS, S#s about 6,400 to 6,500	★★★★	2,500	3,000	5,000
Lehigh Valley Railroad 17J, M#1883, SW, 2 tone mvt. Appleton, Tracy & Co. grade	★	750	900	1,500
Martyn Square, 7-15J, M#1857-1877-1879, KW, SW (exported)		125	150	300
Mermod, Jaccard & KingParagon Timekeeper, **23J,** M#1892, Vanguard, LS, GJS, HC		425	475	700

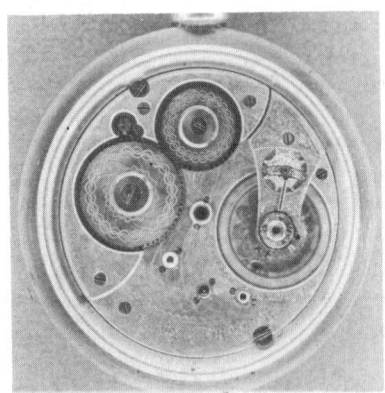

Pennsylvania Special, Model 1892, 18 size, 21 jewels, serial number 14,000,015.

American Waltham Watch Co., Model 1883, 18 size, 15 jewels, serial number 3,093,425.

🕑 Pricing in this Guide are fair market price for **COMPLETE** watches which are reflected from the "**NAWCC**" National and regional shows.

Grade or Name –Description	Avg	Ex-Fn	Mint
Non-Magnetic, 15J, SW, LS, NI	$100	$150	$250
Non-Magnetic, 17J, M#1892, SW, LS	125	175	300
Paragon, 15J, M#1883, HC	225	275	450
"Chas. T. Parker" marked, 11-15J, M#1857, KW, HC ★★	1,300	1,600	2,500
C. T. Parker, 7-11J, M#1857, KW, Am.W. Co. (Eagle) silver HC serial # below 1,200 ★★	1,400	2,000	2,800
C. T. Parker, 7-11J, M#1857, KW, Am.W. Co. 18K, HC serial # below 1,200 ★★	1,600	2,200	3,500
Pennsylvania R.R. on dial, Appleton, Tracy & Co. on Mvt., KW, KS, M# 1857 ★★★★	3,000	4,000	8,000
Pennsylvania Special, 21J, M#1892, HC ★★★	1,600	2,000	3,000
Pennsylvania Special, 21J, M#1892, OF ★★★	1,600	2,000	3,000
Pennsylvania Special, 21J, M#1892, HC GOLD DAMASKEENED, gold train ★★★★★	10,000	12,000	18,000
Pennsylvania Special, 23J, M#1892, OF ★★★★	2,500	3,000	5,000
Pioneer, 7J, M#1883	65	75	125
Premier, 17J, M#1892, LS, OF	90	100	150
Railroader, 17J, M#1892, LS ★★★	1,000	1,200	2,000
Railroader, 21J, M#1892, LS, ★★★	1,200	1,400	2,200
Railroad inspector, 21J, M#1892, LS, (loaner with # on case) ★★	500	600	900
Railroad King, 15J, M#1883, LS ★★	400	500	800
Railroad King, 15J, M#1883, 2-Tone ★★	400	500	800
Railroad King, 17J, Special, M#1883, LS ★★	400	500	800
Railroad Standard, 19J, G#1892, OF ★★★	1,000	1,400	2,000
Riverside, 17J, M#1892 ★	150	250	450
Roadmaster, 17J, M#1892, LS ★★	600	700	1,200
R. E. Robbins, 11-15J, M#1857, KW S# (25,101-25,200) ★★	1,400	1,600	2,500
R. E. Robbins, 13-15J, M#1877, KW	250	350	550
R. E. Robbins, 13J, M#1883	100	125	200
Royal, 17J, M#1892, OF	100	125	200
Royal, 17J, M#1892, HC	150	175	350

Sidereal, model #1892, 17j, 24 hour dial used by astronomers. (marked Sidereal on dial)

Vanguard, model 1892, 18S, 23J, diamond end stone, gold jewel settings, exposed winding gears, S# 10,533,465.

🕑 Pricing in this Guide are fair market price for **COMPLETE** watches which are reflected from the "<u>**NAWCC**</u>" National and regional shows.

Grade or Name – Description		Avg	Ex-Fn	Mint
Santa Fe Route, 17J, M#1883	★ ★	$400	$500	$700
Santa Fe Route, 17J, M#1892	★	525	650	800
Santa Fe Route, 21J, M#1892	★ ★	700	800	1,200
Sidereal, M#1892, 19J, (marked **Sidereal** on dial) OF	★ ★ ★	1,200	1,500	2,400
M#1892, 17J, Astronomical (marked **Sidereal** on dial) OF	★ ★ ★	1,000	1,300	2,000
Sol, 7-11J, M#1883, OF		75	100	150
Sol, 17J, OF, PS		75	100	150
Special Railroad, 17J, M#1883, LS, OF	★	325	400	650
Special R. R. King, 15-17J, M#1883	★ ★	350	400	700
Special R. R. King, 15-17J, M#1883, HC	★ ★	400	500	750
Sterling, 7J, M#1857, KW, Silver		100	125	200
Sterling, 7-11J, M#1877, M#1879		60	70	150
Sterling, 7-11J, M#1883, KW		60	70	150
Sterling, 11-15J, M#1883, SW		60	70	150
Tourist, 11J, M#1877		60	70	150
Tourist, 7J, M#1877		60	70	150
Tracy, Baker & Co., 15J, **18K original A.W.W. Co.** case	★ ★ ★ ★ ★	8,000	10,000	20,000
Vanguard, 17J, M#1892, GJS, HC	★ ★	400	500	700
Vanguard, 17J, M#1892, LS, Adj.5P, DR, GJS, OF	★ ★	300	400	600
Vanguard, 17J, M#1892, **Wind Indicator,** Adj.5P, DR, GJS		1,000	1,200	2,000
Vanguard, 19J, M#1892, LS, Adj.5P, Diamond end stones		200	225	400
Vanguard, 19J, M#1892, LS, Adj.5P, DR, GJS, OF		200	225	400
Vanguard, 19J, M#1892, **Wind Indicator,** LS, Adj.5P, DR, GJS		1,500	1,700	2,500
Vanguard, 19J, M#1892, Adj.5P, GJS, HC	★	325	375	600
Vanguard, 21J, M#1892, Adj.5P, PS		235	275	400
Vanguard, 21J, M#1892, GJS, Adj.5P, HC		325	350	500
Vanguard, 21J, M#1892, LS, Adj.5P, DR, GJS, OF		235	275	400
Vanguard, 21J, M#1892, LS, Adj.5P, Diamond end stone		235	275	400
Vanguard, 21J, M#1892, **Wind Indicator**, Adj.5P, GJS, OF	★	1,800	2,000	2,500
Vanguard, 23J, M#1892, LS, Adj.5P, DR, GJS, OF		300	350	550
Vanguard, 23J, M#1892, LS, Adj.5P, DR, GJS, HC	★	375	450	650
Vanguard, 23J, M#1892, LS, Adj.5P, DR, GJS, Diamond end stone		300	350	550
Vanguard, 23J, M#1892, PS, Adj.5P, DR, GJS, OF		300	350	550
Vanguard, 23J, M#1892, **Wind Indicator**, LS, Adj.5P, DR,GJS.	★	2,000	2,200	2,800
Waltham,17J, Adj., G#1892, **(non magnetic)**, OF		150	175	300
Waltham Standard,17J, Adj., G#1892, (locomotive)OF	★ ★	575	675	1,000
Waltham Standard,19J, Adj., G#1892, (locomotive), OF	★ ★ ★	1,000	1,400	2,000
Waltham Watch Co., 15J, **M#1857**, SW / LS, (let down screw)		200	250	325

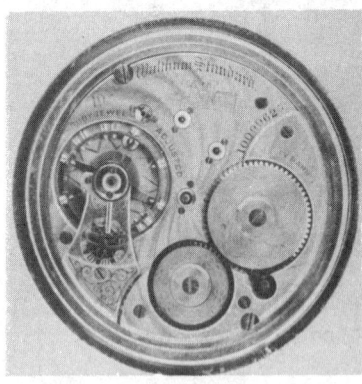

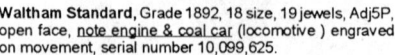

Waltham Standard, Grade 1892, 18 size, 19 jewels, Adj5P, open face, note engine & coal car (locomotive) engraved on movement, serial number 10,099,625.

Grade 845, Model 1892, 18 size, 21 jewels, railroad grade, Adj.5P, serial number 15,097,475

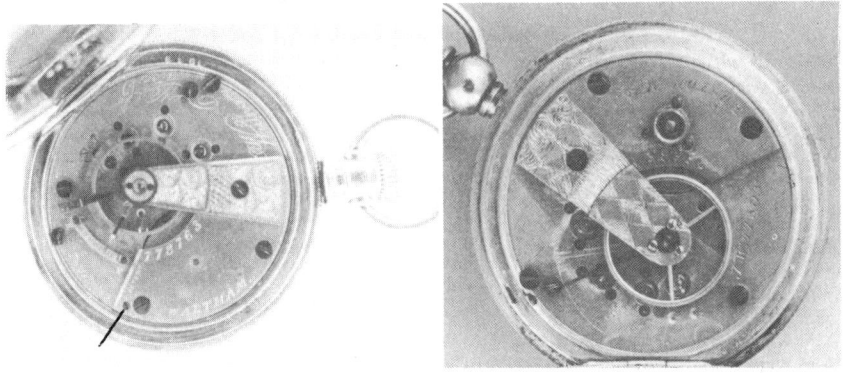

Waltham Watch Co., 1857 model with factory stem wind, 18S, 15J, S# 778763, Fogg's Patent, This is not a Abbott's stem wind conversion. NOTE **let down screw.** Most Abbott's stem wind with lever set the levers move up and down, while most stem winds the levers move up & out.

J. WATSON, Boston Mass engraved on movement, 18 size, 11 jewels, hunting case, key wind key set, serial number 28,635, Ca. April 1863.

Grade or Name – Description		Avg	Ex-Fn	Mint
Warren, 15J, M#1857, KW, KS, S#18-29, original 17S silver case	★★★★★	$20,000	$24,000	$40,000
Warren, 15J, M#1857, KW, KS, S#30-60, original 17S silver case	★★★★	18,000	20,000	30,000
Warren, 15J, M#1857, KW, KS, S#61-90, original 17S silver case	★★★★	15,000	18,000	25,000
Warren, 15J, M#1857, KW, KS, S#91-110, original 17S silver case	★★★★	14,000	16,000	22,000
(Warren not in original silver case, deduct $1,000 to $2,500)				
George Washington, M#1857, KW	★	400	550	900
J. Watson, 7J, M#1857, KW, marked"Boston" S# (28,201-28,270)	★★★	1,000	1,400	2,500
J. Watson, 7-11J, M#1857, KW, marked"London" S# (23,700-23,800)	★★★	1,000	1,400	2,500
454, 21J, GT, 3/4,		175	200	400
845, 21J, M#1892, OF		175	200	400
845, 21J, M#1892, HC		300	350	500
836, 17J, DR, Adj.4P, LS, OF		70	90	175

American Watch Co., Model 16KW or Model 1868, 16 size, key wind and set from back, Gold Train, serial number 501,561.

American Watch Co., Model 1888, 16 size, 19 jewels, gold jewel settings, gold train, high grade movement, serial number 5,000,297.

16 SIZE
MODELS 16KW =1860, 1868, 1872, 1888,
1899, 1908, BRIDGE MODEL

Grade or Name – Description	Avg	Ex-Fn	Mint
AMn. Watch Co., 7-15J, M#1872, KW KS, sweep sec. with a slide stop button ★ ★	$700	$800	$1,400
AMn. Watch Co., 7-11J, M#1888, 3/4, SW	70	80	200
AMn. Watch Co., 7-11J, M#1888-1899	70	80	200
AMn. Watch Co., 11J, M#16KW or 1868, KW & KS from back, original silver case ★ ★	800	1,000	1,800
AMn. Watch Co., 11J, M#1868, 3/4, KW	400	500	1,000
AMn. Watch Co., 13J, M#1888-1899	70	80	200
AMn. Watch Co., 15-17J, M#1868, 3/4, KW ★	600	800	1,400
AMn. Watch Co., 15J, M#1868-1872, 3/4, SW	250	400	800
AMn. Watch Co., 15J, M#16KW, KW & KS from back ★ ★	400	500	1,000
AMn. Watch Co., 15-16J, M#1888-1899, HC	100	125	275
AMn. Watch Co., 15J, M#1888-1899, SW, HC	100	125	275
AMn. Watch Co., 15J, M#1888-1899, SW,	70	100	200
AMn. Watch Co., 16-17J, M#1872, 3/4, SW	150	175	450
AMn. Watch Co., 17J, M#1888-1899	85	100	250
AMn. Watch Co., 19J, M#1872, 3/4, SW ★ ★ ★	1,000	1,300	1,600
AMn. Watch Co., 19J, M#1899	125	150	350

🕐 Generic, nameless or unmarked grades for watch movements are listed under the Company name or initials of the Company, etc. by size, jewel count and description.

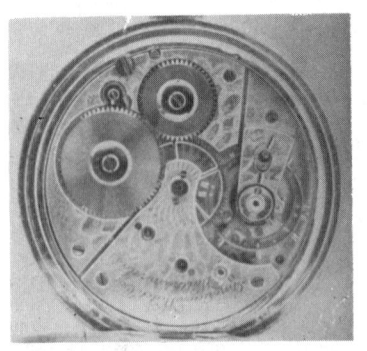

American Watch Co., Model 1888, 16 size, 21 jewels, gold train, note tadpole regulator.

American Watch Co., Bridge Model, 16 size, 23 jewels gold train, Adj.5P.

Grade or Name –Description	Avg	Ex-Fn	Mint
American Watch Co., 19J Maltese cross stopwork, gilt mvt. all original 1860 Model, **18Kcase** ★ ★	$1,600	$2,200	$3,500
American Watch Co., 17-19J, 3/4, KW & KS from back, vibrating hairspring stud, 1860 Model, **18Kcase** ★ ★ ★	1,800	2,500	4,000
American Watch Co., 19J, 3/4 , KW & KS from back, **nickel mvt.** 1860 Model, original case, **18K** case ★ ★ ★ ★	3,800	4,500	6,500
American Watch Co., 15J, M#1868, 3/4, KW, Silver ★ ★ ★	1,000	1,500	2,500
American Watch Co., 17J, M#1872,3/4,SW,**HC,14K** ★	1,400	1,600	2,500
American Watch Co., 17J, M#1868, 3/4, KW, ADJ, Silver ★ ★	1,000	1,400	2,000
American Watch Co., 17J, M#1899, Adj.5P, ★	400	500	700
American Watch Co., 18J, M#1868, SW, nickel mvt. ★	450	500	800
American Watch Co., 19J, M#1868, SW, nickel mvt. Silver case ★ ★ ★	2,000	2,500	4,000
American Watch Co., 19J, M#1888, SW, nickel mvt. ★ ★	450	500	800
American Watch Co., 19J, M#1899, SW, nickel mvt. ★ ★	600	700	1,000

🕐 Pricing in this Guide are fair market price for COMPLETE watches which are reflected from the **"NAWCC"** National and regional shows.

Grade or Name — Description	Avg	Ex-Fn	Mint
American Watch Co., 19-21J, M#1872, 3/4, SW .... ★★★	$1,200	$1,600	$2,400
American Watch Co., 19-21J, M# 1872, GJS, all original "Woerd's pat.- (see illo. below)			
compensating bal.", **With sawtooth bal.**,................. ★★★★	2,500	3,500	5,500
American Watch Co., 19-21J, M#1868-1872, 3/4, GJS,			
"Woerd's pat." on movt. **NO sawtooth bal.**.................... ★★	1,200	1,600	2,400
American Watch Co., 19-21J, M#1872, 3/4, SW, **18k**......... ★★★	1,600	2,000	3,000
American Watch Co., 19J, M#1888, **14K** .... ★★	1,000	1,200	2,000
American Watch Co., 19J, M#1888 .... ★★	500	700	1,200
American Watch Co., 21J, M#1888, NI, 3/4 .... ★★	500	700	1,200
American Watch Co., 23J, M# 1899, Adj.5P, GT, GJS .... ★★	550	750	1,400
American Watch Co., 23J, BRG, Adj.5P, GT, GJS, **14K**			
original case.. ★★	1,000	1,400	2,200
American Watch Co., 23J, BRG, Adj.5P, GT, GJS, **18K**			
original case.. ★★	1,100	1,600	2,500
American Watch Co., 23J, BRG, Adj.5P, GT, GJS .... ★★	600	800	1,200
American Watch Co., 21J, BRG, Adj.5P, GT, GJS .... ★	400	500	800
American Watch Co., 19J, BRG, Adj.5P, GT, GJS .... ★	350	400	600
American Watch Co., 17J, BRG, Adj.5P, GT, GJS	200	300	500
Appleton, Tracy & Co., 15J, M#1860, 3/4, KW & KS from			
back, all original silver case.....................................	600	700	1,000
Appleton, Tracy & Co., 15J, M#1868, 3/4, KW	400	500	1,100
Appleton, Tracy & Co., 15J, 3/4, KW, with vibrating			
hairspring stud, all original, silver case .... ★★	1,000	1,200	2,000
Appleton, Tracy & Co., 15J, 3/4, KW, with vibrating			
hairspring stud, **18K**, original case .... ★★★	1,600	1,900	2,800

🕐 Generic, nameless or unmarked grades for watch movements are listed under the Company name or initials of the Company, etc. by size, jewel count and description.

A. W. Co., 7J, M#1872, SW, HC......................................	$100	$125	$225
A. W. W. Co., 7J, SW, M#1888...	65	75	150
A. W. Co., 7J, SW, DMK...	65	75	150
A. W. Co., 9J, SW, ...	65	75	150
A. W. W. Co., 11-13J, SW	65	75	150
A. W. Co., 11J, M#1899, SW..	65	75	150
A. W. Co., 11-15J, M#1872, SW, HC....................................	100	125	225
A. W. W. Co., 13J, M#1888-99, OF	65	75	150

RIGHT: **Woerd's pat. compensating balance,**
this is a illustration copied from a blue print of
Mr. Woerd's patented **Saw Tooth Balance.**
This balance **must** be in watch for **top prices.**

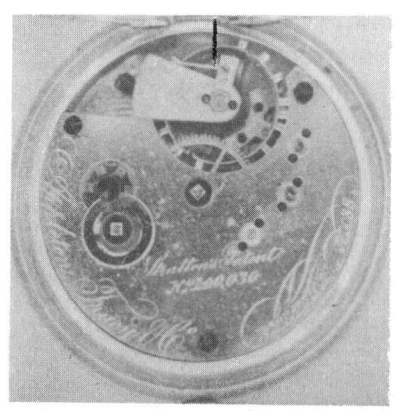

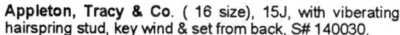

Appleton, Tracy & Co. (16 size), 15J, with viberating hairspring stud, key wind & set from back, S# 140030.

Crescent Street, Model 16–S (CENTER SECONDS), 16 size, movement, 22J, Adj6p, lever set, Wind indicator.

🕐 Generic, nameless or unmarked grades for watch movements are listed under the Company name or initials of the Company, etc. by size, jewel count and description.

Grade or Name—Descripion	Avg	Ex-Fn	Mint
A. W. W. Co., 15J, M#1899, OF	$75	$85	$175
A. W. W. Co., 15J, M#1888, SW, HC	85	100	175
A. W. W. Co., 16J, M#1888, SW, OF	75	80	175
A. W. W. Co., 16J, M#1899, SW, DMK, HC	85	100	175
A. W.W. Co., 17J, M#1872, SW, DMK, GJS, DES, HC ★	200	300	500
A. W. W. Co., 17J, SW, OF	85	95	150
A.W.W.Co., 19J, Adj.5P, LS, OF	100	125	175
A.W.W.Co., 19J, Adj.5P, LS, HC	125	150	200
A.W.W.Co., 21J, Adj.5P, PS, OF	200	225	350
A.W.W.Co., 21J, Adj.5P, PS, HC	225	250	400
A.W.W.Co., 23J, Adj.5P, PS, OF	225	250	400
A.W.W.Co., 23J, Adj.5P, PS, HC	250	275	450
P. S. Bartlett, 17J, M#1899, OF	60	80	150
P. S. Bartlett, 17J, M#1899, HC	100	125	175
P. S. Bartlett, 17J, M#1908, OF	60	80	150
Bond St., 7J, M#1888	40	50	100
Bond St., 11J, M#1888	40	50	100
Bond St., 15J, M#1888	40	50	100
Bond St., 7J, M#1899	40	50	100
Canadian Pacific RR, M#s 1888, 1899, 1908 ★ ★ ★	500	700	1,200
Canadian Railway Time Service, M#1908 ★ ★	400	500	800
CHRONOGRAPH are listed as 14 SIZE SEE Chronograph under 14 size			
Chronometro Superior, 21J, M#1899, LS, OF	200	250	500
Chronometro Victoria, 21J, M#1899, HC	200	250	550
Chronometro Victoria, 15J, M#1899, PS, OF	100	125	200
Crescent St., 19J, M#1899, Adj.5P, LS, OF	100	150	250
Crescent St., 19J, M#1899, Adj.5P, PS, OF	100	150	250
Crescent St., 19J, M#1899, Adj.5P,LS, HC	125	175	300
Crescent St., 21J, M#1899, Adj.5P, PS, OF	100	150	250
Crescent St., 21J, M#1899, Adj.5P, LS, OF	100	150	250
Crescent St., 21J, M#1899, Adj.5P, PS, HC	125	175	300
Crescent St., 19J, M#1908, Adj.5P, LS, OF	100	150	250
Crescent St., 19J, M#1908, Adj.5P, PS, OF	100	150	250
Crescent St., 21J, M#1908, Adj.5P, LS, OF	150	175	300
Crescent St., 21J, M#1908, Adj.5P, PS, OF	150	175	300
Crescent St., 21J, M#1908, Adj.6P, LS, OF	150	175	300
Crescent St., 21J, M#1908, Adj.5P, PS, HC	200	255	400
Crescent St., 21J, M#1908, Adj.5P, LS, **Wind Indicator**	600	725	1,000
Crescent St., 21J, M#1912, Adj.5P, LS, **Wind Indicator**	600	725	1,000
Crescent St., 22J, M#16–S, Adj.6P, **DECK WATCH**			
LS, center sec., **Wind Indicator.** ★ ★ ★	800	1,000	1,500
Diamond Express, 17J, M#1888, PS, OF,			
Diamond End Stones ★ ★	600	700	1,100
Electric Railway, 17J, OF, LS, Adj.3P	150	200	400
Equity, 7-11J, PS, OF, 16 1/2 Size	40	60	100
Equity, 7-11J, PS, HC, 16 1/2 Size	40	60	100
Equity, 15-17J, PS, OF, 16 1/2 Size	40	60	100
Equity, 15-17J, PS, HC, 16 1/2 Size	40	60	100
Giant, 7-11J, PS, OF, 16 1/2 Size	40	60	100
Giant, 7-11J, PS, HC, 16 1/2 Size	40	60	100
Hillside, 7J, M#1868, ADJ	100	125	200
Hillside, 7J, M#1868-1872, sweep sec. & STOP ★ ★ ★	900	1,000	2,000
Marquis, 15J, M#1899, LS	40	60	100
Marquis, 15J, M#1908, LS	40	60	100
Non-Magnetic, 15J, NI, HC	100	125	200
Park Road, 11-13-15J, M#1872, PS	100	125	200
Park Road, 16J, M#1872, PS	100	125	200

Premier Maximus, "Premier" on movement. "Maximus" on dial, 16 size, 23 jewels (two diamond end stones), open face, pendant set, serial number 17,000,014.

American Waltham Watch Co., 5 minute repeater, 16 size, 16 jewels, 3/4 plate, grade 1888, adj, 2 gongs, ca. 1900.

Grade or Name — Description	Avg	Ex-Fn	Mint
Premier, 9J, M#1908, PS, OF	$40	$50	$100
Premier, 11J, M#1908	40	50	100
Premier, 15J, M#1908, LS, OF	40	50	125
Premier, 17J, M#1908, PS, OF	50	70	150
Premier, 17J, M#1908, PS, OF, Silveroid	50	70	150
Premier, 21J, M#1908,	150	200	300
Premier, 22J, M#1908, LS, Adj.6P, **Stainless steel case**, OF	175	200	350
Premier, 23J, M#1908, LS, OF	225	275	450
Premier Maximus, 23J, M#1908, GT, gold case, LS,GJS, Adj.6P, WI, DR, **18K** Maximus case, **box & papers** ★ ★	8,000	9,000	12,000
Premier Maximus, 23J, M#1908, GT, gold case, LS, GJS,Adj.6P, WI, DR, **18K** Maximus case, **NO box** ★ ★	6,000	7,000	10,000
Premier Maximus, 23J, M#1908, GT, YGF **RECASED**	1,800	2,200	3,000
Railroader, 17J, M#1888, LS, NI ★ ★ ★	500	650	1,200
Railroad Time, 15-17J, ADJ, OF	200	250	450
REPEATER, 16J, M#1872, original **gold filled** case, 5 min. ... ★ ★	2,000	2,500	4,000
REPEATER, 16J, M#1872, original **coin** case, 5 min. ★ ★	2,200	2,700	4,400
REPEATER, 16J, M#1872, 5 Min., original **14K** case ★ ★	3,000	3,500	5,000
REPEATER, 16J, M#1872, 5 min., original **18K** case ★ ★ ★	4,000	4,200	5,500
REPEATER, 16J, M#1872, 5 min., chronograph with register, **18K** case, all original ★ ★ ★	6,000	7,000	9,000
REPEATER, **1 minute**, moon phase, M#1872, Perpetual Calendar, **18K** case, all original ★ ★ ★ ★	35,000	40,000	50,000

🕐 Watches listed in this book are priced at the collectable retail level, as **complete** watches having an original 14k gold-filled case and *Key Wind* with silver, an original white enamel single sunk dial, and with the entire original movement in good working order with no repairs needed.

🕐 Some watch manufacturers personalize watches for jobbers or jewelry firms, with exclusive private signed or marked movements. The valuable collectable watches are listed under the signed or marked movement. Other exclusive private signed or marked movements will have equivalent value are only slightly higher value and should be compared to Generic or Nameless movements. Railroad signed or marked (dials & movements) are usually more collectable & higher in value.

🕐 Pricing in this Guide are fair market price for COMPLETE watches which are reflected from the **"NAWCC"** National and regional shows.

Grade or Name — Description	Avg	Ex-Fn	Mint
Riverside, 15J, M#1872, PS, NI, OF	$85	$100	$175
Riverside, 15J, M#1872, PS, **gilted**, OF	75	100	175
Riverside, 16-17J, M#1888, NI, OF, **14K**	350	475	675
Riverside, 16-17J, M#1888, NI, OF	70	100	150
Riverside, 17J, M#1888, gilded, OF	70	100	150
Riverside, 15J, M#1888, gilded, OF	70	100	150
Riverside, 17J, M#1888, checker goldtone DMK, raised gold jewel settings, OF	100	125	200
Riverside, 17J, M#1899, LS, DR, OF	70	100	150
Riverside, 17J, M#1899, LS, DR, HC	90	125	200
Riverside, 19J, M#1899, LS, DR, OF	100	150	225
Riverside, 19J, M#1908, Adj.5P, LS, DR	90	125	200
Riverside, 19J, M#1908, Adj.5P, PS, DR, HC ★	100	150	250
Riverside, 21J, M#1888-1899-1908, LS, DR, OF	200	225	300
Riverside, 21J, M#1888-1899-1908, LS, DR, HC	250	275	450
Riverside Maximus, 21J, M#1888, LS, GT, Diamond end stones, OF ★★	650	775	1,100
Riverside Maximus, 21J, M#1888, LS, ADJ, GJS, GT, DR, HC, GF ★★	700	800	1,100
Riverside Maximus, 21J, M#1888, LS, ADJ, GJS, GT, DR, HC, **14K** ★★	1,000	1,100	1,500
Riverside Maximus, 21J, M#1899, PS, Adj.5P, GJS, GT, DR	375	450	700
Riverside Maximus, 21J, M#1899, LS, Adj.5P, GJS, GT, DR	375	450	700
Riverside Maximus, 21J, M#1899, LS, GT, Diamond end stone, OF	375	450	700
Riverside Maximus, 21J, M#1899, LS, GT, Diamond end stone, HC ★	500	600	900
Riverside Maximus, 23J, M#1899, LS, Adj.6P, GJS, GT, DR	400	500	750
Riverside Maximus, 23J, M#1908, PS, Adj.6P, GJS, GT, DR	400	500	750
Riverside Maximus, 23J, M#1908, LS, Adj.6P, GJS, GT, DR	400	500	750
Riverside Maximus, 23J, M#1908, Adj.6P, GJS, GT, **14K OF**	800	900	1,200
Riverside Maximus, 23J, M#1908, PS, Adj.6P, GJS, GT, DR, HC, GF ★	500	700	900
Riverside Maximus, 23J, M#1908, PS, Adj.6P, GJS, GT, DR, 14K, HC ★	900	1,000	1,500
Riverside Maximus, 23J, M#1899 or 1908, Adj.6P, Wind Indicator, OF ★★★	3,500	4,000	5,500

American Watch Co., model 1872, 16 size, 16-17-21 jewels, gold train, serial number 871199.

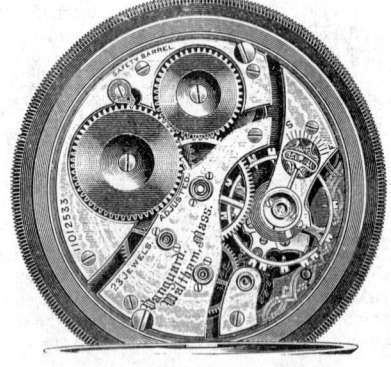

Vanguard, Model 1908, 16 size, 23 jewels, diamond end stone, gold jewel settings, exposed winding gears, serial number 11,012,533.

⊕ Some grades are not included. Their values can be determined by comparing with similar age, size, metal content, style, models and grades listed.

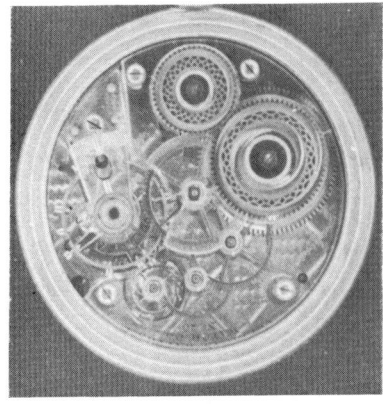

Stone Mountain, 16 size, 17 jewels, crystal plates, Model 1872, gold train, gold jeweled settings, Adj5p, serial # 20.

Vanguard, 16 size, 23 jewels, Adj6p, note pressed-in jewels rather than gold jewel settings. c. 1945.

Grade or Name — Description	Avg	Ex-Fn	Mint
Roadmaster, 17J, M#1899, LS, OF GJS .... ★★	$400	$500	$800
Royal, 15J, M#1872, PS, OF	50	70	150
Royal, 17J, M#1888, PS, OF	50	70	150
Royal, 17J, M#1888, PS, HC	100	120	200
Royal, 17J, M#1899, Adj.3P, OF	50	70	150
Royal, 17J, M#1899-1908, Adj.5P, OF	50	70	150
Royal, 17J, M#1899-1908, Adj.5P,HC	65	100	175
Royal Special, 17J, M#1888	100	125	200
Santa Fe Route, M#s 1888, 1899, 1908 .... ★★★	550	700	1,200
Sol, 7J, M#1888	45	55	95
Sol, 7J, M#1908	45	55	95
Stone Mountain, 17J, M#1872, GT, Crystal plates .... ★★★★	7,000	9,000	18,000
SWISS made, 17-25J, ...	40	50	75
Traveler, 7J, M#1888, 1899, 1908 & 16 1/2 size(Equity).............	40	50	70
Tennyson,15J, M#1888, OF	125	150	200
Vanguard, 19J, M#1899, PS, LS, Adj.5P, GJS, DR, OF	175	200	300
Vanguard, 19J, M#1899, PS, LS, Adj.5P, GJS, DR, HC	225	250	350
Vanguard, 21J, M#1899, Adj.5P, OF	225	250	350
Vanguard, 21J, M#1899, Adj.5P, **HC**	250	300	400
Vanguard, 23J, M#1899, LS, Adj.5P, GJS, DR, OF	250	300	350
Vanguard, 23J, M#1899, PS, Adj.5P, GJS, DR, OF	250	300	350
Vanguard, 23J, M#1899, Adj.6P, OF.................................	250	300	350
Vanguard, 23J, M#1899, Adj.5P, **HC**	275	325	475
Vanguard, 23J, M#1899, PS, **Wind Indicator**, Adj.5P, GJS, DR ★	600	700	900

🕐 Watches listed in this book are priced at the collectable retail level, as **complete** watches having an original 14k gold-filled case and *Key Wind* with silver, an original white enamel single sunk dial, and with the entire original movement in good working order with no repairs needed.

🕐 Some grades are not included. Their values can be determined by comparing with similar age, size, metal content, style, models and grades listed.

🕐 Watch terminology or communication in this book has evolved over the years, in search of better and more precise language with a effort to improve, purify, adjust itself and make it easier to understand.

🕐 Pricing in this Guide are fair market price for COMPLETE watches which are reflected from the **"NAWCC"** National and regional shows.

Grade or Name — Description	Avg	Ex-Fn	Mint
Vanguard, 19J, M#1908, LS & PS, Adj.5P, GJS, DR	$200	$225	$300
Vanguard, 21J, M#1908, Adj.5P, GJS, DR, Diamond end stone	225	275	400
Vanguard, 21J, M#1908, Adj.5P, GJS, DR, PS, LS, OF	225	250	375
Vanguard, 21J, M#1908, Adj.5P, GJS, DR, PS, LS, HC	300	350	475
Vanguard, 23J, M#1908, LS, Adj.5P, GJS, DR, OF	275	325	450
Vanguard, 23J, M#1908, LS, Adj.5P, GJS, DR, HC	325	400	500
Vanguard, 23J, M#1908, PS, Adj.5P, GJS, DR	275	325	450
Vanguard, 23J, M#1908, Adj.5P, Wind Indicator, GJS, DR	600	700	900
Vanguard, 23J, M#1908, Adj.5P, GJS , Diamond end stone	250	300	450
Vanguard, 23J, M#1908, Adj.5P, GJS, HC	325	350	500
Vanguard, 23J, OF, LS or PS, 14K	500	600	800
Vanguard, 23J, M#1908, Adj.6P, Wind Indicator, GJS, DR	600	700	900
Vanguard, 23J, M#1908, Adj.6P, Wind Ind., Lossier, GJS,DR	600	700	900
Vanguard, 23J, M#1912, Press Jewels	200	250	375
Vanguard, 23J, M#1912, PS, military (case), Wind Indicator	650	700	1,000
Vanguard, 24J, & marked 9J., center sec. .... ★ ★ ★	700	800	1,200
Weems, 21J, Navigation watch, Wind Indicator .... ★ ★ ★	900	1,000	1,500
Weems, 23J, Navigation watch, Wind Indicator .... ★ ★ ★	1,000	1,200	1,800
M#1888, G #s 650, 640	40	50	95
M#1899, G #s 615, 618, 620, 625, 628, ...	40	50	95
M#1908, G #s 611, 613, 614, 618, 621, 623, 628, 630, 641, 642	40	50	95
G#637-640=3 pos., G#636=4pos., G#1617=2 pos., ALL=17J.......	40	50	95
G#610=7-11J., un Adjusted & 620=15J	40	50	95
G#625-630-635=17J., Adj., OF...	40	50	95
G#645, 21J, GCW, OF, LS	150	200	350
G#645, 21J, GCW, OF, LS, wind indicator....................... ★ ★ ★	950	1,100	1,500
G#645, 19J, OF, LS	100	125	225
G#665, 19J, GJS, BRG, HC	600	700	900
G#16-A, 22J, Adj.3P, 24 hr. dial	200	250	300
G#16-A, & G#1024, 17J, Adj.5P	80	90	150
G#1617, 17J, adj.	80	90	150
G#1621, 21J, Adj.5P	150	175	250
G#1622, 22J, Adj.5P	175	200	300
G#1623, 23J, Adj.5P	250	300	450

Weems Navigation watch, 21j, Weems pat. seconds dial, pusher for seconds scale setting, ca. 1942.

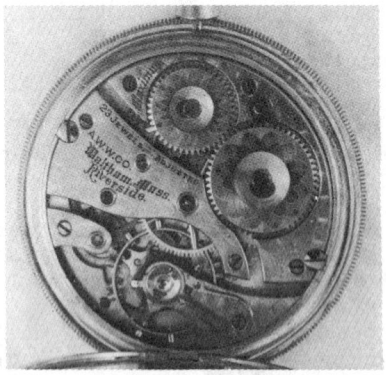

Riverside Maximus, Model 1899, 16 size, 23 jewels, gold train, raised gold jewel settings, a diamond end stone, adjusted to 5 positions, hunting case, serial # 12,509,200.

14 SIZE
MODELS 14KW FULL PLATE, 1874,
1884, 1895, 1897, COLONIAL-A

Grade or Name — Description	Avg	Ex-Fn	Mint
Adams Street, 7J, M#14KW, full plate, KW, Coin	$75	$90	$200
Adams Street, 11J, M#14KW, full plate, KW, Coin	80	100	225
Adams Street, 15J, M#14KW, full plate, KW	100	125	275

⊕ Generic, nameless or unmarked grades for watch movements are listed under the Company name or initials of the Company, etc. by size, jewel count and description.

A. W. Co., 7-11J, M#14KW, full plate, KW	40	60	125
A. W. W. Co., 7-11J, M#1874, SW, LS, HC	50	75	150
A. W. Co., 7-11J, M#s FP, 1884, & 1895	40	60	125
A. W. Co., 13J, M#1884	40	60	125
A. W. Co., 15-16J, M#1874, SW	40	60	125
A. W. Co., 17J, SW, OF	50	75	150
A.W.Co., 19J, GJS, GCW	75	90	175
Am. Watch Co., 7-11J, KW,	40	60	125
Am. Watch Co., 13J, M#1874-84, SW	40	60	125
Am. Watch Co., 15J, M#1874-84,	40	60	125
Am. Watch Co., 16J, M#1874, SW	50	70	150
Am. Watch Co., 7-11J, M#14KW, **Full Plate**, KW	75	95	175
Am. Watch Co., 16J, M#1884, SW	75	85	175
Am. Watch Co., 15J, M#1897, SW	40	60	125
Bond St., 7-11J, M#1895, SW	40	60	125
Bond St., 9-11J, M#1884, KW	40	60	125
Bond St., 7J, M#1884, SW, PS	40	60	125
Beacon, 15J, M#1897, SW	40	60	125
Chronograph, 13J, 1874, **14K**, OF, **Am. W. Co. case**	800	900	1,400
Chronograph, 13J, 1874, **14K**, OF, W/ register, Am. W. Co. case ★	1,000	1,300	1,800
Chronograph, 13J, 1874, **14K**, **HC**, W/ register, Am. W. Co. case ★	1,400	1,600	2,400
Chronograph, 13J, 1874, **18K**, HC, W/ register, **Am. W. Co. case** ★	1,500	1,800	2,800
Chronograph, 13J, 1874, **SILVER HC**, *Am. W. Co. case*	300	400	700
Chronograph, 16J, 1874, double dial, **"coin"**, Am. W. Co. case	2,000	2,500	4,000
Chronograph, 16J, 1874, double dial, **18K**, Am. W. Co. case	3,000	3,500	5,500

Chronograph, Model 1874, split-second, 14 size. Note two split second hands on dial and two pushers at 2 & 4.

Hillside, 14 size, 13 jewels, M#1874, stem wind, hunting case, Woerds Pat., serial number 1,696,188, 18K.

⊕ This book endeavours to be a GUIDE or helpful manual and offers a wealth of material to be used as a tool not as an absolute document. Price Guides are like watches the worst may be better than none at all, but at best cannot be expected to be 100% accurate.

Grade or Name — Description	Avg	Ex-Fn	Mint
Chronograph, 13J, M# 1884 , OF	$200	$250	$500
Chronograph, 13J, M# 1884, HC	300	400	600
Chronograph, 13J, 1884, 14K, HC, Am. W. Co. case	900	1,000	1,600
Chronograph, 13J, 1884, 18K, HC, Am. W. Co. case ★	1,000	1,300	1,800
Chronograph, 15J, M# 1874-1884 , OF	200	250	400
Chronograph, 15J, M#1874-1884, HC	250	300	500
Chronograph, 17J, M#1874-1884 , OF	200	250	400
Chronograph, 17J, M#1874-1884, HC	250	300	500
Chronograph, 17J, split second, Am. W. Co. case ★★★	700	800	1,200
Chronograph, 15J, split sec., 14K, HC ★★★	1,600	1,800	2,800
Chronograph, 15J, split second, min. register, 14K Am. W. Co. HC ★★★	1,800	2,200	3,500
Chronometro Victoria, 15J, M#1897, ★	100	135	200
Church St., 7J, M#1884,	80	90	150
Crescent Garden, 7-11J, M#14KW, KW	40	60	125
Crescent Garden, 7J, Full Plate, KW	40	60	125
Wm. Ellery, 7J, M#1874, SW	40	60	125
Gentleman, 7J, M#1884, SW	40	60	125
Hillside, 7-15J, M#1874, SW	40	60	125
Hillside, 7-11J, M#FP, SW	40	60	125
Hillside, 7-13J, M#1884, KW	40	60	125
Hillside, 9-11J, M#1884, KW	40	60	125
Hillside, 15J, M#1884, SW	40	60	125
Hillside, 16J, M#1874, (calendar date only on outside chapter) SW, GJS, OF,(calendar sets from back with lever)... ★★★★	500	600	750
Maximus, 21J, Colonial A	100	150	275
Maximus, 21J, Colonial A, 14K	275	300	500
Night Clock, 7J, M#1884, KW	80	100	175

Chronograph, M# 1884-double dial, 14 size, 15 jewels, hunting case.

Chronograph, Model 1884-Split Second, 14 size, 15 jewels, open face, gold escape wheel, gold train, serial number 303,094.

🕐 Watches listed in this book are priced at the collectable retail level, as **complete** watches having an original 14k gold-filled case and Key Wind with silver, an original white enamel single sunk dial, and with the entire original movement in good working order with no repairs needed.

🕐 Some watch manufacturers personalize watches for jobbers or jewelry firms, with exclusive private signed or marked movements. The valuable collectable watches are listed under the signed or marked movement. Other exclusive private signed or marked movements will have equivalent value are only slightly higher value and should be compared to Generic or Nameless movements. Railroad signed or marked (dials & movements) are usually more collectable & higher in value.

Five Minute Repeater, Model 1884, 14 size, 13-15 jewels, hunting case, slide activated, serial number 2,809,551.

Chronograph, 14 size, Model # 1874, Lugrin Pat., Sept. 28, 1880, serial # 3,162,800. Also Pat. date (Oct. 3,1876).

Grade or Name — Description		Avg	Ex-Fn	Mint
Repeater (5 min.), 16J, M#1884, SW, LS, **14K**	★	$3,500	$4,200	$5,500
Repeater (5 min.), 16J, M#1884, SW, LS, **18K**	★	3,800	4,400	6,000
Repeater (5 min.), 16J, M#1884, split second chronograph, 18K case	★★	5,000	6,500	9,000
Repeater (5 min.), 16J, M#1884, SW, LS, chronograph, with register, **14K** Am. W. Co. case		4,000	4,500	6,500
Repeater (5 min.), 16J, M#1884, SW, LS, chronograph, with register, **18K** Am. W. Co. case		4,500	5,000	7,500
Repeater (5 min.), 16J, M#1884, SW, LS, original **Coin** case		2,800	3,500	4,000
Repeater (5 min.), 16J, M#1884, SW, LS, original **gold filled** case		2,200	2,600	3,000
Repeater (5 Min.), **18K**, HC	★★	4,000	5,000	7,000
Repeater (**1 Min.**), perpetual calendar, moon ph., 18K	★★★★	30,000	40,000	60,000
Riverside, 11-15J, M#s 1874, HC		100	125	200
Riverside, 15J, M#1884, OF		40	60	125
Riverside, 19-21J, Colonial A, OF	★	100	165	250
Royal, 11-13-15J, M#s 1874, 1884		40	60	125
Seaside, 7-11J, M#1884, SW		40	60	125
Special, 7J, M#1895, HC		40	60	125
Sterling, 7J, M#1884		40	60	125
Waltham, Mass., 7J, Full Plate, KW		85	100	175

12 SIZE

MODELS KW, 1894, BRIDGE, COLONIAL SERIES

Grade or Name — Description		Avg	Ex-Fn	Mint
A. W. W. Co., 7J, M#1894, **14K**, OF		$150	$200	$300
A. W. W. Co., 11J, M#1894, also Colonial model		30	40	100
A. W. W. Co., 15J, M#1894, also Colonial model		30	40	100
A. W. W. Co., 15J, M#1894, Colonial, **14K**, HC		200	250	350
A. W. W. Co., 17J, M#1894, also Colonial model		30	45	100
A. W. W. Co., 17J, M#1894, also Colonial, **14K** OF		150	225	275
A. W. W. Co., 19J, OF		40	65	100
A. W. W. Co., 21J, OF		60	80	150
A. W. W. Co., 23J, OF		125	150	200
P. S. Bartlett, 19J, M#1894, **14K**, HC		200	250	400
P. S. Bartlett, 19J, M#1894		40	60	125
Bond St., 7-13J, M#1894		30	40	100
Bridge Model, 19J, GJS, Adj.5P, GT		75	100	200
Bridge Model, 19J, GJS, Adj.5P, GT, **18K**, HC	★	300	400	600
Bridge Model, 21J, GJS, Adj.5P, GT, OF		150	175	250
Bridge Model, 21J, GJS, Adj.5P, GT, **14K**, HC	★	350	400	500
Bridge Model, 23J, GJS, Adj.5P, GT		150	200	300

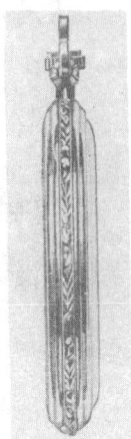

Actual size illustration of a cushion style shaped watch depicting thinness with emphasis on style and beauty. This watch was popular in the 1930s.

Grade or Name — Description	Avg	Ex-Fn	Mint
Duke, 7-15J, M#1894	$60	$50	$100
Digital Hour & Second Window, 17J	75	85	125
Elite, 17J, OF	40	60	100
Ensign, 7J, OF	40	60	100
Equity, 7J,adj.	40	60	100
Martyn Square, 7-11J, M#KW	100	125	175
Maximus, 21J, GJS, GT	150	200	300
Premier, 17-19J, M#1894	40	60	100
Premier, 21J, M#1894	100	150	250
Riverside, 17-19J, M#1894, Colonial	40	60	100
Riverside, 21J, M#1894, Colonial	100	150	250

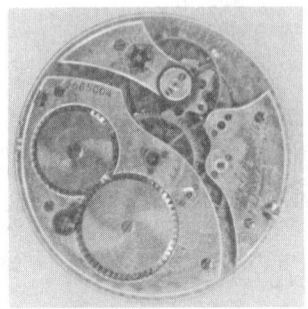

A.W.W.Co., Model 1894, 12 size, 7-11 jewels, open face, serial number 7,565,004.

Riverside, Colonial series, 12 size, 19 jewels, open face or hunting, Adj5p, double roller.

Grade or Name – Description	Avg	Ex-Fn	Mint
Riverside, 19-21J, M#1894, Colonial, **14K**, HC	$200	$300	$450
Riverside Maximus, 21J, M#1894, Colonial, GT, GJS, **14K**	350	400	500
Riverside Maximus, 21J, M#1894, Colonial, GT, GJS	200	250	325
Riverside Maximus, 23J, M#1894, Colonial, GT, GJS ★	250	300	400
Riverside Maximus, 23J, M#1894, Colonial, GT, GJS, **14K** ★	350	400	550
Royal, 17J, OF, PS, Adj, or Adj.3P	30	40	85
Royal, 19J, OF, PS, Adj.3P	30	40	85
Secometer, 17J, (revolving seconds dial only) OF	75	85	150

THE OPERA WATCH
10-12 size case & a 6/0 size Jewel Series movement

Grade or Name – Description	Avg	Ex-Fn	Mint
12-6/0 size, 17-19J, Adj, **18K gold case**	$300	$350	$450
12-6/0 size, 17-19J, Adj, **14K gold case**	200	250	350
12-6/0 size, 17-19J, Adj, **Platinum case**	400	450	550
12-6/0 size, 17-19J, Adj, **gold filled case**	85	100	200

A unique designed Gents dress watch about 10-12 size case with a fancy framed 6/0 movement (Jewel Series).

10 SIZE
MODEL KW, 1861, 1874

Grade or Name – Description	Avg	Ex-Fn	Mint
Am. W. Co., 7-15J, M#1874-1878, KW, **14K**	$150	$200	$350
A. W. Co., 7-11J, SW , OF	40	50	100
A. W. Co., 15-17J, SW , OF	40	50	100
A. W. Co., 19-21J, SW , OF	65	80	150
American Watch Co., 11-15J, M#1874, **14K, HC**	175	225	350
Appleton, Tracy & Co., 15J, M#1861 or 1874, **14K**, OF	200	250	400
Appleton, Tracy & Co., 15J, M#1861, **18K multi-color box case**	450	550	750
P. S. Bartlett, 7-11J, M#1861, KW, **14K**	200	250	400
P. S. Bartlett, 13J, M#KW, gold balance, 1st S# 45,801, last 46,200, **14K,** Pat. Nov. 3, 1858 ★ ★ ★	400	500	650
P. S. Bartlett, 13J, M#KW, gold balance, 1st S#45,801, last 46,200, **18K,** Pat. Nov. 3, 1858 ★ ★ ★	450	550	700
P. S. Bartlett, 13J, M#1861, KW, **14K**	200	250	400

Appleton Tracy & Co., Model 10KW, 10 size, 7-15 jewels, key wind and set from back, serial number 370,411.   **P. S. Bartlett**, 10 size, 7-15 jewels, serial # 181,602.

NOTE: These watches (excluding Colonial) are usually found with solid gold cases, and are therefore priced accordingly. Without cases, these watches have very little value due to the fact that the cases are difficult to find. Many of the cases came in octagon, decagon, hexagon, cushion and triad shapes.

Grade or Name – Description	Avg	Ex-Fn	Mint
Colonial A , 21J,OF	$50	$85	$125
Crescent Garden, 7J, M#1861, KW, **14K**	150	250	300
Wm. Ellery, 7,11,15J, M#1861, KW, **14K**	150	250	300
Home W. Co., 7J, M#1874, KW, **14K**	150	250	300
Martyn Square, 7-11J, M#1861, **14K**	150	250	350
Maximus "A", 21J, **14K** ★	200	275	400
Maximus "A", 23J, **14K** ★	200	275	400
Riverside, 19–21J, Adj.5P, GF	70	85	175
Riverside Maximus, 19-21J, Adj.5P, GJS, GF	90	100	275
Riverside Maximus, 19-21J, Adj.5P, GJS, **18K**	300	400	550
Riverside Maximus, 23J, Adj.5P, GJS, GF	150	200	300
Royal, 15J, Adj.5P, GF	35	50	95

8 SIZE
MODEL 1873

NOTE: Collectors usually want solid gold cases in small watches.

Grade or Name – Description	Avg	Ex-Fn	Mint
Am. W. Co., 15-17J, M#1873, **14K, Multi-Color Box Hinged case**	$400	$450	$850
Am. W. Co., 15-16J, M#1873	35	50	95
P. S. Bartlett, 15-16J, M#1873	35	50	95
Wm. Ellery, 7-11J, M#1873	35	50	95
Wm. Ellery, 7J, **14K, HC**	150	200	350
Riverside, 7-11J, M#1873, **18K, HC**	250	300	400
Riverside, 7-11J, M#1873	35	50	95
Royal, 7-16J, M#1873	35	50	95
Victoria, 11-15J, tu-tone movement, **18k HC** ★	200	250	500

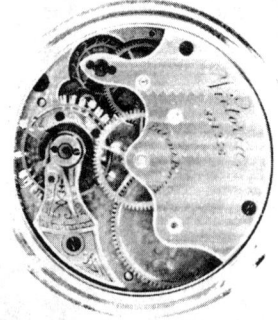

VICTORIA, 8 size 1873 model, 11-15 jewels, tu-tone high grade movement, HC, S# 871256

6 size Ladies movement this basic model came in the following grades: J=7 jewels, gilt; Y=7 jewels, nickel; N=15 jewels,gilded or nickel; X=15 jewels, nickel, gold jewel settings; K=16 jewels nickel, raised gold settings; RIVERSIDE=17 jewels, nickel, raised gold settings.

6 SIZE
MODEL 1873, 1889 , 1890

Grade or Name – Description	Avg	Ex-Fn	Mint
A,B,C,D,E,F,G,H,J,K	$35	$50	$95
A,B,C,D,E,F,G,H,J,K, **14K, HC**	150	200	325
A. W. W. Co., 19J, **18K, HC**	225	300	475
A. W. W. Co., 19J, **14K, Multi-Color gold case**	350	450	800
A. W. W. Co., 7J, M#1873	35	50	95

Grade or Name – Description	Avg	Ex-Fn	Mint
A. W. W. Co., 15J, multi-color GF, HC	$150	$225	$350
A. W. W. Co., 15J, 2 tone mvt., HC	60	80	200
A. W. W. Co., 11J, HC	30	40	95
Am. W. Co., 7-11J, M#1889 -1890	30	40	95
American W. Co., 7J, KW & KS from back, 10K, HC	125	175	300
Wm. Ellery, 7J, M#1873	30	40	95
Lady Waltham, 16J, M#1873, Demi, HC, 14K	150	200	400
Lady Waltham, 16J, M#1873, 18K	200	250	450
Riverside Maximus, 19J, GT, Adj., DR, HC ★	225	250	300
Riverside, 15-17J, PS	30	40	95
Seaside, 7-15J, M#1873	30	40	95
Royal, 16J, HC	55	65	135

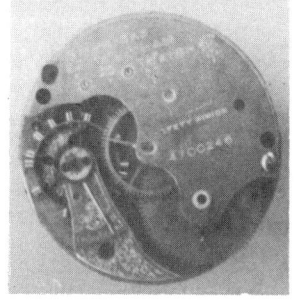 

American Watch Co., Model 1889, 6 size 7 jewels, serial number 4,700,246.

Stone Movement or Crystal clear see through Plates, size 4, 16 jewels, gold train, open face, serial number 28.

4 SIZE

Grade or Name – Description	Avg	Ex-Fn	Mint
Stone Movement or crystal movement, 4 size, crystal, 16 ruby jewels in gold settings, gold train, exposed pallets, compensation balance adjusted to temperature, isochronism, positions, Breguet hairspring, and crystal top plate, 14K case ★ ★ ★	$3,500	$4,500	$8,000

🕐 Watches listed in this book are priced at the collectable retail level, as **complete** watches having an original 14k gold-filled case and *Key Wind* with silver, an original white enamel single sunk dial, and with the entire original movement in good working order with no repairs needed.

1 SIZE & 0 SIZE
MODELS 1882, 1891, 1900, 1907

Grade or Name – Description	Avg	Ex-Fn	Mint
A.W.Co., 7-16J, OF	$30	$40	$95
A.W.Co., 7-16J, HC	50	60	175
A.W.Co., 7-15J, multi-color 14K HC	275	375	575
A. W. Co., 7J, 14K, HC	125	200	350
American Watch Co., 15J, SW, OF &HC	65	80	185

🕐 Generic, nameless or unmarked grades for watch movements are listed under the Company name or initials of the Company, etc. by size, jewel count and description.

🕐 Watch terminology or communication in this book has evolved over the years, in search of better and more precise language with a effort to improve, purify, adjust itself and make it easier to understand.

Lady Waltham, Model 1900, 0 size, 16 jewels, open face or hunting, adjusted, stem wind, pendant set.

A.W. Co., Model 1891, 0 size, 7 jewels, stem wind, originally sold for $13.00.

Grade or Name – Description	Avg	Ex-Fn	Mint
American Watch Co., 15J, S.W., **14K, HC**	$150	$225	$350
P. S. Bartlett, 11J, M#1891, OF, **14K**	150	175	200
P. S. Bartlett, 16J, **14K, HC**	200	275	350
Lady Waltham, 15J, SW, **14K, HC**	200	275	350
Lady Waltham, 15-16J, SW, HC	75	100	200
Maximus, 19J, SW, HC	150	175	225
Riverside, 15J,16J,17J, SW, HC	100	150	200
Riverside, 15J,16J,17J, SW, **14K, HC**	200	275	350
Riverside Maximus, 21J, GT, **multi-color gold HC, 14K** ...... ★ ★	500	600	850
Riverside Maximus, 21J, GT	200	225	300
Riverside Maximus, 19J, SW, HC	150	200	250
Riverside Maximus, 19J, **14K, HC** .... ★	275	350	475
Royal, 16J, SW, HC	50	70	150
Seaside, 15J, SW, **14K, HC**	125	175	350
Seaside, 11J, SW, OF, **multi-color dial, no chips**	150	200	250
Seaside, 11J, SW, HC	60	95	150
Seaside, 7J, HC	55	85	125
Seaside, 7J, **14K, HC**	150	200	350
Special, 11J, M#1891, **14K, OF**	150	200	275

Riverside, Jewel Series, 6/0 size, 17 ruby jewels, raised gold settings, gold center wheel.

Ruby, Jewel Series, 6/0 size, 15 jewels, adjusted to temperature, open face or hunting.

JEWEL SERIES or 6/0 SIZE

Grade or Name – Description	Avg	Ex -Fn	Mint
Diamond, 15J, Jewel Series, **14K, HC**	$150	$200	$300
Patrician, 15J, pin set, GJS, **18K, OF** .... ★	200	250	425
Riverside, 17J, Jewel Series, **14K, HC**	200	250	300
Ruby, 15J, Jewel Series, **14K, OF**	150	200	250
Sapphire, 15J, Jewel Series, **14K, OF**	150	200	250

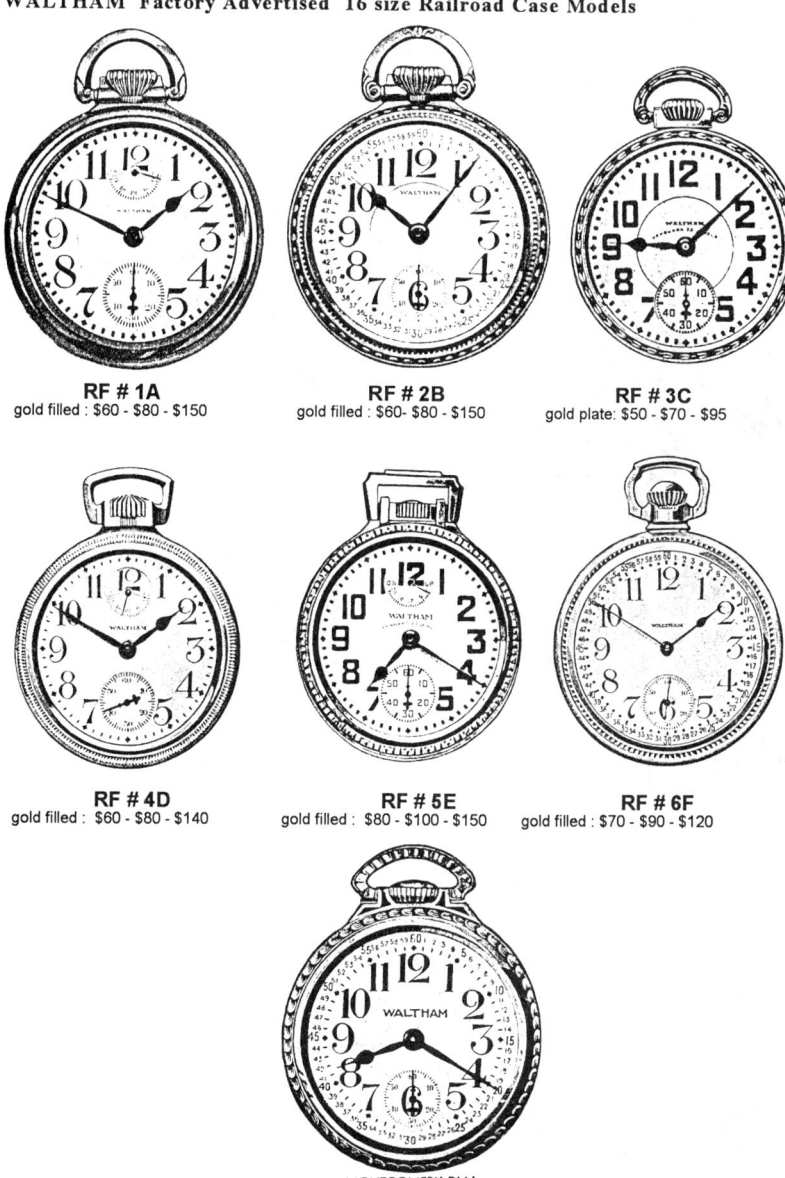

RF # 1A
gold filled : $60 - $80 - $150

RF # 2B
gold filled : $60- $80 - $150

RF # 3C
gold plate: $50 - $70 - $95

RF # 4D
gold filled : $60 - $80 - $140

RF # 5E
gold filled : $80 - $100 - $150

RF # 6F
gold filled : $70 - $90 - $120

MONTGOMERY DIAL

RF # 7G
LOCOMOTIVE model
gold filled : $70 - $90 - $135

1A, 2B, = Gold Filled White or Yellow & 3C = Yellow Gold Rolled Plate
4D, 5E, 6F, 7G = Yellow Gold Filled.

NOTE: Factory Advertised as a complete watch and were fitted with cases of exclusive and unusual design with special heavy bow & movement timed and rated at the factory. The factory also sold *uncased* movements to **JOBBERS** such as Jewelry stores & they cased the movement in a case styles the **CUSTOMER requested.** All the factory advertised complete watches came with the dial **SHOWN or CHOICE** of other **Railroad** dials.

AMERICAN WALTHAM WATCH CO.
IDENTIFICATION OF MOVEMENTS
BY MODEL NUMBER

How to Identify Your Watch: Compare the movement of your watch with the illustrations in this section. Upon matching the movement exactly, the model number and size can be determined. When comparing, note the location of the balance, jewels, screws, gears and type of back plate (Full, ¾, Bridge) which will be clues to identifying the movement you have. Having determined the size and model number, you can now find your watch in the main price listing by name or number (which is engraved on the movement).

20 size, 1862 or KW 20 model. Note vibrating hairspring stud. 1st serial number 50,001

18 size, 1859 or KW 18 model. 1st serial number 28,821

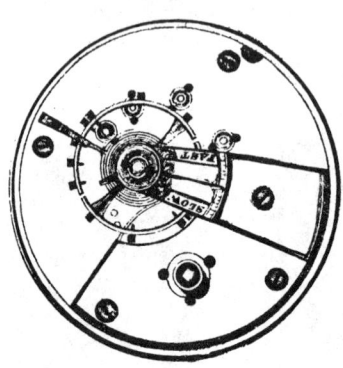

Model 1857, KW, KS. 1st serial number 1,001

Model 1870, KW, KS from back 1st serial number 500,001

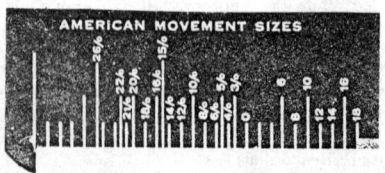

Model 1877, 18 size

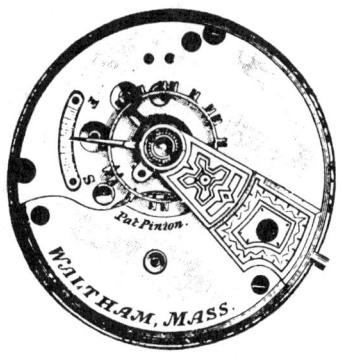

Model 1879, 18 size

Model 1883, hunting
1st serial number 2,354,001

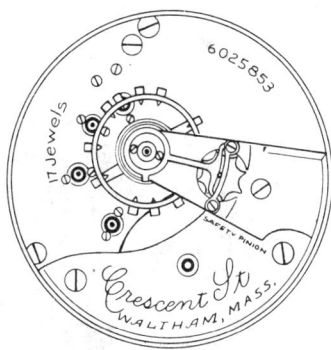

Model 1883, open face

Model 1892, open face

Model 1892, hunting.
1st serial number 6,026,001

16½ size, Equity open face

Model 1860=16KW or 1868

16 size

Model 1872, 16 size open face

Model 1872, 16 size hunting case

Model 1888, 16 size, hunting

Bridge Model, 16 size

**Model 1899 or Model 1908,
16 size, open face**

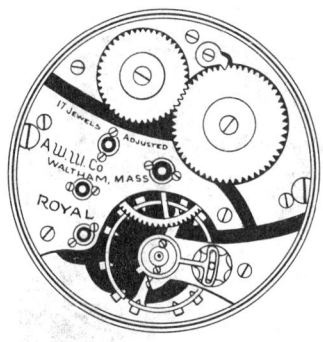

**Model 1899 or Model 1908,
16 size, hunting**

**Model 1899 or Model 1908,
16 size, open face**

Model 16-A, 16 size

**Model 1622, Deck Watch
16 size, sweep second**

Model 1874 & 1884, 14 size

Model 1874, 14 size, hunting

Model 1884, 14 size, open face

5 Minute Repeater, 14 size

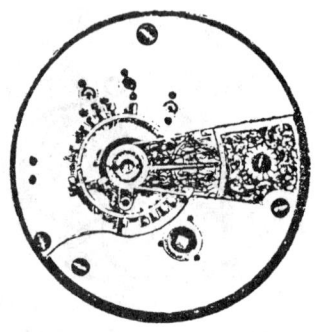

14 SIZE FULL PLATE KW KS
1 st. SERIAL # 909,001

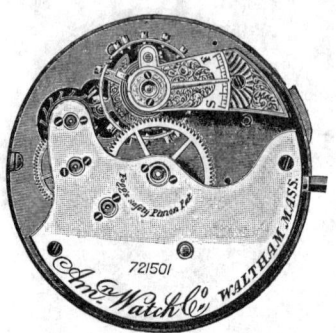

Model 1874, 14 size

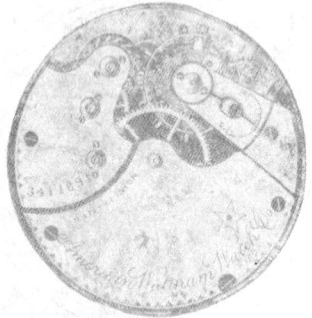

Model 1884, 14 size

Model 1895, 14 size,
open face

Model 1897, 14 size

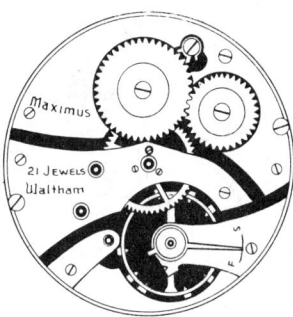

Colonial A Model, 14 size

Colonial Series, 14 size

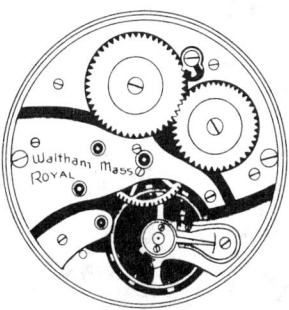

Model 1924, The Colonial

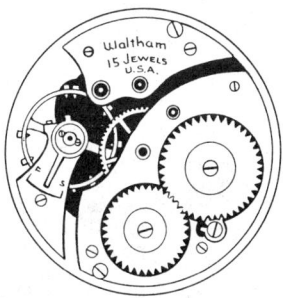

Model 1894, 12 size

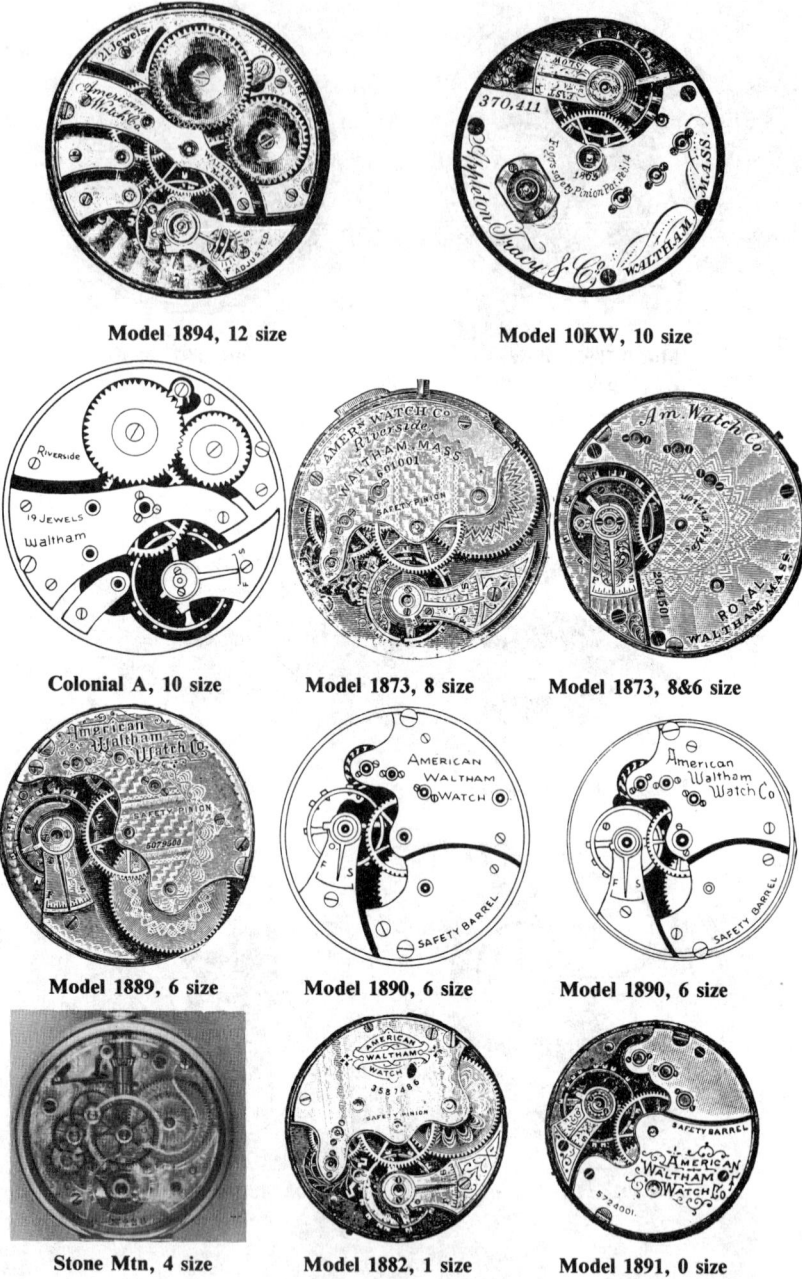

Model 1894, 12 size	**Model 10KW, 10 size**

Colonial A, 10 size	**Model 1873, 8 size**	**Model 1873, 8&6 size**

Model 1889, 6 size	**Model 1890, 6 size**	**Model 1890, 6 size**

Stone Mtn, 4 size	**Model 1882, 1 size**	**Model 1891, 0 size**

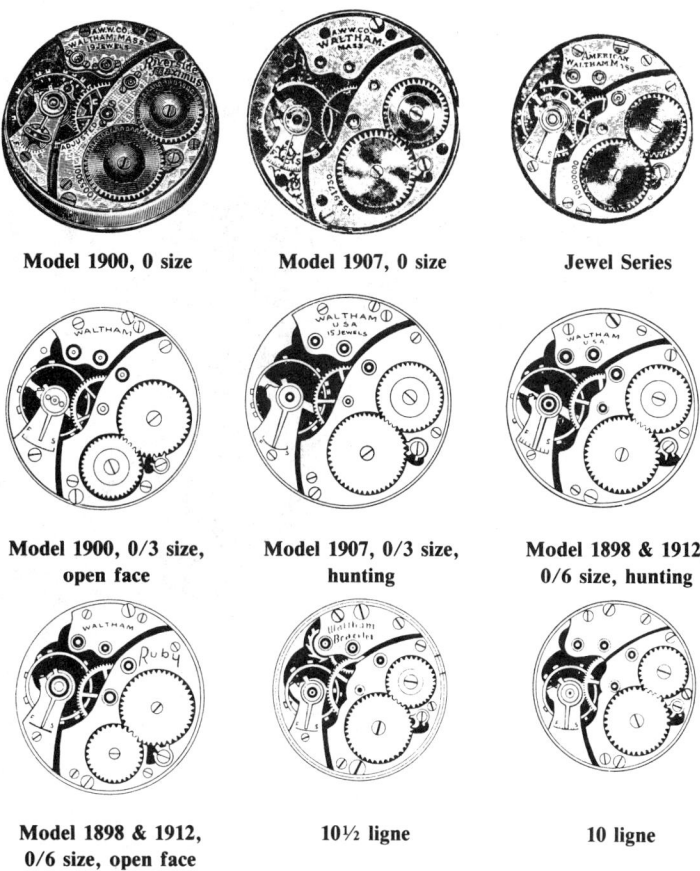

Model 1900, 0 size **Model 1907, 0 size** **Jewel Series**

Model 1900, 0/3 size, **Model 1907, 0/3 size,** **Model 1898 & 1912,**
open face **hunting** **0/6 size, hunting**

Model 1898 & 1912, **10½ ligne** **10 ligne**
0/6 size, open face

🕐 Generic, nameless or unmarked grades for watch movements are listed under the Company name or initials of the Company, etc. by size, jewel count and description.

🕐 Some grades are not included. Their values can be determined by comparing with similar age, size, metal content, style, models and grades listed.

🕐 Watches listed in this book are priced at the collectable retail level, as complete watches having an original 14k gold-filled case and Key Wind with silver, an original white enamel single sunk dial, and with the entire original movement in good working order with no repairs needed.

🕐 This book endeavours to be a GUIDE or helpful manual and offers a wealth of material to be used as a tool not as a absolute document. Price Guides are like watches the worst may be better than none at all, but at best cannot be.expected to be 100% accurate.

🕐 Characteristics of watches differ for the same age of both case and movement, because these features vary it may not be accurate to date a watch by one single influence. Example: the second hand was _not_ commonly found on watches before 1750, but common about 1800. The first second hand appeared in 1665 and another in 1690. Therefore statements are broad rather than accurate.

ANSONIA CLOCK CO.

Brooklyn, New York
1896 - 1929

The Ansonia Watch Co. was owned by the Ansonia Clock Company in Ansonia, Connecticut. Ansonia started making clocks in about 1850 and began manufacturing watches in 1896. They produced about 10,000,000 dollar- type watches. The company was sold to a Russian investor in 1930. "Patented April 17, 1888," is on the back plate of some Ansonia watches.

Ansonia Watch Company. Example of a basic movement, 16 size, stem wind.

Ansonia Watch Co., Sesqui-Centennial model.

Grade or Name–Description	Avg	Ex-Fn	Mint
Ansonia watch with a White Dial in Nickel case	$25	$35	$75
Ansonia watch with a Radium Dial in Nickel case	30	40	90
Ansonia watch with a Black Dial in Nickel case	40	50	100
Ascot	30	50	75
Bonnie Laddie Shoes	60	95	125
Dispatch	30	40	65
Faultless	40	50	75
Guide	40	50	75
Lenox	35	40	60
Mentor	35	45	65
Piccadilly	45	60	100
Rural	40	50	75
Sesqui-Centennial	250	275	400
Superior	45	60	80
Tutor	45	60	80

🕐 Some grades are not included. Their values can be determined by comparing with similar age, size, metal content, style, models and grades listed.

APPLETON WATCH CO.

(REMINGTON WATCH CO.)

Appleton, Wisconsin

1901 - 1903

In 1901, O. E. Bell bought the machinery of the defunct Cheshire Watch Company and moved it to Appleton, Wisconsin, where he had organized the Remington Watch Company. The first watches were shipped from the factory in February 1902; production ceased in mid-1903 and the contents were sold off before the end of that year. Most movements made by this firm were modified Cheshire movements and were marked "Appleton Watch Company." Advertisements for the firm in 1903 stated that they made 16 and 18 size movements with 11, 15, or 17 jewels. Serial numbers range from 90,000 to 104,950. During the two years they were in business, the company produced about 2,000 to 3,000 watches.

 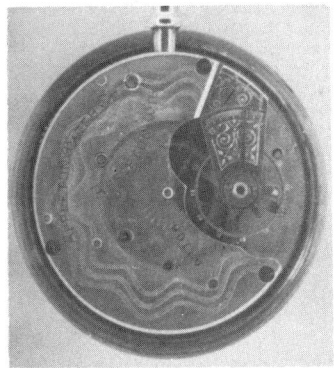

Appleton Watch Co., 18 size, 7 jewels, "The Appleton Watch Co." on dial. Engraved on movement "Appleton Watch Co., Appleton, Wis." Note that the stem is attached to movement. Serial number 93,106.

Description		Avg	Ex-Fn	Mint
18S, 7J, OF, NI, 3/4, DMK, SW, PS, stem attached	★★	$400	$500	$850
18S, 7J, OF, NI, 3/4, DMK, SW, PS, Coin, OF	★★	400	500	850
18S, 15J, NI, LS, SW, 3/4, M#2	★★	500	600	900
16S, 7-11J, 3/4, stem attached	★★	450	550	950

Note:With **ORIGINAL** APPLETON cases add **$200 to $300** more. This case is **difficult** to find.

AUBURNDALE WATCH CO.

Auburndale, Massachusetts

1876 - 1883

This company was the first to attempt an inexpensive watch. Jason Hopkins was issued two patents in 1875 covering the "rotary design." The rotary design eliminated the need of adjusting to various positions, resulting in a less expensive watch. The company was formed about 1876, and the first watches were known as the "Auburndale Rotary." In 1876, equipment was purchased from the Marion Watch Co., and the first rotary designed watches were placed on the market for $10 in 1877. Auburndale produced about 6,000 watches before closing in 1883.

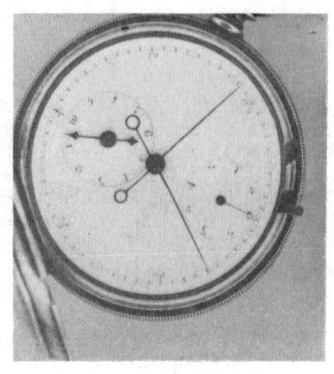 

Auburndale Timer, 18 size, 7 jewels, stem wind, 10 minute, second jump timer.

Auburndale 10 min. Timer, 1/4 beat jump seconds, sweep second hand, stop & fly back, back wind.

Grade or Name – Description	Avg	Ex-Fn	Mint
Auburndale Rotary, 20S, 2J, LS, SW, NI case, detent .... ★★★	$1,600	$2,000	$3,200
Auburndale Rotary, 18S, 2J, SW, LS, NI case, lever .... ★★★	1,000	1,500	2,500
Bentley, 18S, 7J, LS, NI case, SW, 3/4................................. ★★★	800	1,000	1,500
Lincoln, 18S, 7J, LS, NI case, KW, 3/4................................. ★★★	800	1,000	1,500
Auburndale Timer, 18S, 5-7J, SW, NI case, 10 min. timer, 1/4 sec. jump second..	350	400	500
Auburndale Timer, 18S, 5-7J, SW, NI case, 10 min. timer, 1/4 sec. jump seconds, with a 24 hour dial .... ★	400	450	600
Auburndale Timer, 18S, 5-7J, KW, NI case, 10 min. timer, 1/4 sec. jump seconds, **with split seconds** .... ★★	600	650	800
Auburndale Timer, 18S, marked "207", gold balance, OF..............	325	375	500

Bentley, 18 size, 7 jewels, 3/4 plate, stem wind, serial number 2.

Auburndale Rotary, 18 size, 2 jewels, stem wind, lever set, serial number 448.

🕐 Pricing in this Guide are fair market price for **COMPLETE** watches which are reflected from the "**NAWCC**" National and regional shows.

AURORA WATCH CO.

Aurora, Illinois
1883 - 1892

Aurora Watch Co. was organized in mid-1883 with the goal of getting one jeweler in every town to handle Aurora watches. The first movements were 18S, full plate, and were first sold in the fall of 1884. There were several watches marked No. 1. The total production was about 215,000; over 200,000 were 18 Size, and some were 6 size ladies' watches. For the most part Aurora produced medium to low grade; and at one time made about 150 movements per day. The Hamilton Watch Co. purchased the company on June 19, 1890.

AURORA WATCH CO.
Estimated Serial Nos. and Production Dates

1884 - 10,001	1888 - 200,000
1885 - 60,000	1889 - 215,000
1886 - 101,000	1891 - 230,901
1887 - 160,000	

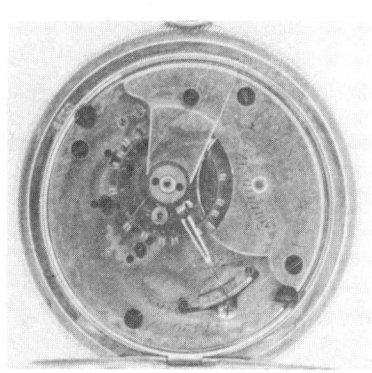

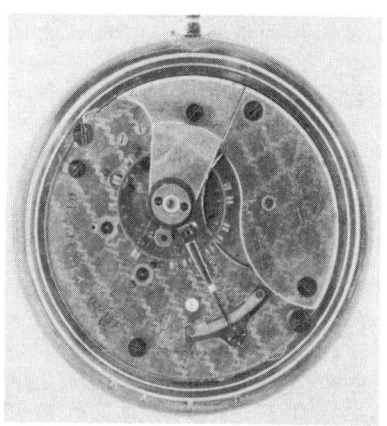

Aurora Watch Co., 18 size, 15 jewels, "NEW MODEL", serial number 142,060. Made for railroad service.

Aurora Watch Co., 18 size, 15 jewels, Adj, engraved on movement "Made expressly R.J.A.," 5th pinion serial number 73,529.

Description	Avg	Ex-Fn	Mint
18S, 7J, KW, KS, Gilded, OF	$135	$180	$300
18S, 7J, KW, KS, Gilded, HC	175	200	300
18S, 7J, 5th pinion, Gilded, LS, SW, OF	100	125	225
18S, 7J, LS, SW, Gilded, new model, HC	200	250	350
18S, 11J, KW, KS, Gilded, HC	175	200	300
18S, 11J, KW, KS, Gilded, OF	150	180	300
18S, 11J, 5th pinion, LS, SW, Gilded, new model, OF	110	175	275
18S, 11J, 5th pinion, LS, SW, NI, GJS, OF	120	200	300
18S, 11J, 5th pinion, LS, SW, NI, GJS, new model, OF	150	180	300
18S, 11J, LS, SW, Gilded, made expressly for the guild, HC.... ★	300	350	500
18S, 11J, 5th pinion, LS, SW, NI, OF made expressly for the guild ....★	300	350	500
18S, 15J, KW, KS, NI, GJS, DMK, OF or HC..........★	200	250	325
18S, 15J, 5th pinion, LS, SW, Gilded, OF	125	150	350
18S, 15J, 5th pinion, LS, SW, NI, GJS, DMK, ADT, OF	125	150	375
18S, 15J, 5th pinion, LS, SW, NI, GJS, DMK, ADJ, new model, OF	150	175	300
18S, 15J, LS, SW, NI, GJS, DMK, ADJ, new model, HC	150	175	300
18S, 15J, LS, SW, NI, GJS, ADJ, 2 Tone DMK, checkerboard or snowflake, Ruby Jewels, HC............ ★★	500	600	1,000
18S, 15J, LS, SW, NI, GJS, ADJ, 2 Tone DMK, checkerboard or snowflake, 5th pinion, Ruby Jewels, OF...... ★★★	600	800	1,500

MARKED "RUBY JEWELS", = Aurora's highest grade.

Size and Description	Avg	Ex-Fn	Mint
18S, 15J, LS, SW, NI, GJS, DMK, ADJ, Railroad Time Service or Caufield Watch, new model, HC .... ★★	$600	$700	$1,000
18S, marked **15 Ruby Jewels** but has 17J, 5th pinion, LS, SW, NI, GJS, 2 Tone, ADJ, OF .... ★★★	750	850	1,400
18S, marked **15 Ruby Jewels**, only 15J, LS, SW, NI, GJS, 2 Tone DMK, ADJ, HC............................. ★★	650	800	1,200
18S, marked **15 Ruby Jewels**, only 15J, LS, SW, NI, GJS, ADJ, 2 Tone DMK, OF .... ★★	600	750	1,000
18S, 15J, Chronometer, LS, SW, NI, DMK, ADJ, new model HC.................................... ★★	500	700	900
18S, 15J, Chronometer, LS, SW, NI, GJS, DMK, ADJ, HC .... ★	400	500	700
18S, 15J, LS, Gilded, "Eclipse, Chicago", new model, HC...........	250	300	400
18S, 15J, LS, SW, NI, DMK, made expressly for the guild, HC.. ★	300	375	500
18S, 15J, 5th pinion, LS, SW, Gilded, made expressly for the guild, OF .... ★	300	400	600
18S, 15J, LS, SW, Gilded, made expressly for the "RJA" (Retails Jeweler's Assoc.), HC........................... ★	400	450	650

6 SIZE

Size and Description	Avg	Ex-Fn	Mint
6S, 11-15J, LS, SW, Gilded, 3/4, HC	$70	$90	$200
6S, 11-15J, LS, SW, NI, GJS, DMK, 3/4, HC....................	80	100	225
6S, 11-15J, LS, SW, 3/4 plate, **14K, HC**........................	250	300	450

BALL WATCH CO.

Cleveland, Ohio

1879 - 1969

The Ball Watch Company did not manufacture watches but did help formulate the specifications of watches used for railroad service. Webb C. Ball of Cleveland, Ohio, was the general time inspector for over 125,000 miles of railroad in the U. S., Mexico, and Canada. In 1891 there was a collision between the Lake Shore and Michigan Southern Railways at Kipton, Ohio. The collision was reported to have occurred because an engineer's watch had stopped, for about four minutes, then started running again. The railroad officials commissioned Ball to establish the timepiece inspection system. Ball knew that the key to safe operations of the railroad was the manufacturing of sturdy, precision timepieces. He also knew they must be able to withstand hard use and still be accurate. Before this time, each railroad company had its own rules and standards. After Ball presented his guidelines, most American manufacturers set out to meet these standards and soon a list was made of the manufacturers that produced watches of the grade that would pass inspection. Each railroad employee had a card that he carried showing the record of how his watch performed on inspection. Ball was also instrumental in the formation of the Horological Institute of America. By 1908 Ball furnished over **100 different railroad** companies with watches.

🕐 NOTE: BALL WATCHES ARE PRICED AS HAVING A ORIGINAL BALL DIAL & CASE.

ESTIMATED SERIAL NUMBERS AND PRODUCTION DATES
FOR RAILROAD GRADE WATCHES

(Hamilton) Date – Serial #	(Waltham) Date – Serial #	(Elgin) 1904-1906
1895 - 13,000	1900 - 060,700	S # range:
1897 - 20,500	1905 - 202,000	11,853,000 - 12,282,000
1900 - 42,000	1910 - 216,000	
1902 - 170,000	1915 - 250,000	
1905 - 462,000	1920 - 260,000	(E. Howard & CO.)
1910 - 600,000	1925 - 270,000	1893-1895
1915 - 603,000		S # range:
1920 - 610,000		226,000 - 308,000
1925 - 620,000		
1930 - 637,000	(Illinois)	
1935 - 641,000	Date – Serial #	(Hampden)
1938 - 647,000	1929 - 800,000	1890-1892
1939 - 650,000	1930 - 801,000	S # range:
1940 - 651,000	1931 - 803,000	626,750 - 657,960 -
1941 - 652,000	1932 - 804,000	759,720
1942 - 654,000		

The above list is provided for determining the **APPROXIMATE** age of your watch. Match serial number with date. Watches were not necessarily sold in the exact order of manufactured date.

BALL — AURORA
18 SIZE

Description		Avg	Ex-Fn	Mint
15-17J, marked Webb C. Ball, OF .... ★ ★ ★		$2,000	$2,500	$3,500
15-17J, marked Ball, HC .... ★ ★ ★		2,500	3,000	4,500

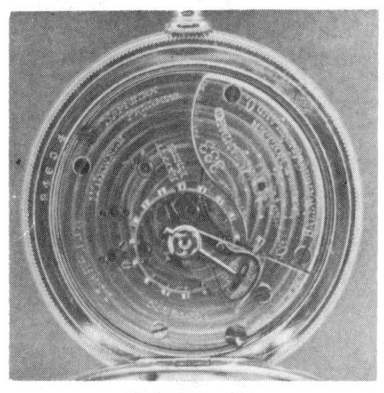
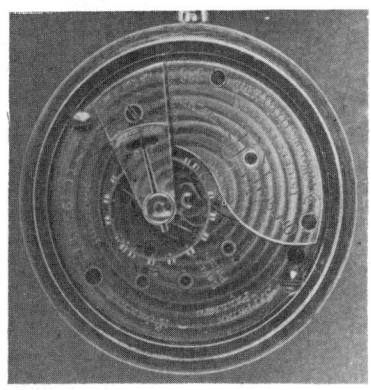

Ball-Elgin, Grade 333, 18 size, 17 jewels, rare hunting case model, serial number 11,958,002.

Ball-Elgin, Grade 333, 18 size, 17 jewels, open face model, serial number 11,856,801.

BALL — ELGIN
18 SIZE G. F. CASES

Description		Avg	Ex-Fn	Mint
16J, G#327, Commercial Standard, LS, OF .... ★		$200	$250	$450
17J, G#328, Commercial Standard, LS, HC .... ★		300	375	500

⏰ Pricing in this Guide are fair market price for **COMPLETE** watches which are reflected from the "**NAWCC**" National and regional shows.

Description		Avg	Ex-Fn	Mint
17J, G#328, Coin, LS, HC	★	$250	$325	$450
17J, G#329, NI, Adj.5P, LS, HC	★ ★	1,200	1,400	2,000
21J, G#330, LS, Official RR std., HC	★ ★ ★ ★	2,000	2,500	4,000
16J, G#331, NI, Adj.5P, PS, Commercial Std, OF.	★ ★	375	425	550
16J, G#331, NI, Adj.5P, PS, Commercial Std, HC	★ ★	400	450	600
17J, G#331, NI, Adj.5P, PS, OF		200	250	350
17J, G#332, Commercial Std, OF	★	300	350	450
17J, G#333, NI, Adj.5P, LS, OF		200	250	400
17J, G#333, NI, Adj.5P, LS, HC	★ ★ ★	1,300	1,600	2,000
21J, G#333, NI, Adj.5P, LS, OF		325	350	500
21J, G#334, NI, Adj.5P, LS, OF		375	450	600

🕐 Note: 18 Size Ball watches in **hunting cases** are scarce.

BALL — HAMILTON
18 SIZE G. F. CASES

Description		Avg	Ex-Fn	Mint
17J, M#936, **first trial run S# 601 to 625**	★ ★ ★	$2,500	$3,200	$5,000
17J, M#-937-939, Official RR std, LS, Adj., **HC**	★ ★	2,000	2,500	3,200
17J, M#938, NI, DR, OF	★ ★	575	625	850
17J, M#-939, Official RR std, LS, Adj., **HC**	★ ★	2,000	2,500	3,200
17J, M#999, Commercial Standard		300	400	600
17J, Off. Ball marked jewelers name on dial & mvt., OF	★	450	550	800
17J, M#999, NI, Official RR std, Adj.5P, LS, OF, Coin		300	400	600
17J, M#999, Official RR std, NI, Adj.5P, LS, OF		300	400	600
17J, M#999, "A" model adj. OF	★	350	400	700
17J, M#999, NI, Adj.5P, marked "Loaner" on case		350	450	750
19J, M#999, Official RR std, NI, Adj.5P, LS, OF		375	450	650
21J, M#999, Official RR std, NI, Adj.5P, LS, OF		400	450	700
23J, M#999, NI, Adj.5P, LS, Gold Filled OF Case	★ ★	4,000	4,500	6,000
23J, M#999, NI, Adj.5P, LS , OF, **14K case**	★ ★ ★	6,000	7,500	10,000
23J, M#999, NI, Adj.5P, LS, **HC,14K case**	★ ★ ★ ★	7,000	9,000	12,000
Early Ball & Co., 16-17J, (low serial # 13,001 to 13,400), OF marked dial & mvt. *Railroad Watch Co.* (second run)	★ ★	1,200	1,500	2,500
Early Ball & Co., 16-17J, (low serial # 14,001 to 15,000), OF marked dial & mvt. *Railroad Watch Co.* (third run)	★ ★	1,000	1,300	2,000
Ball & Co., 16-17J, marked dial & mvt. *Railroad Watch Co*	★ ★	1,000	1,200	1,800
Brotherhood of Locomotive Engineers, 17J, OF	★ ★	1,000	1,200	2,500
Brotherhood of Locomotive Engineers, 19J, OF	★ ★	1,200	1,400	2,600

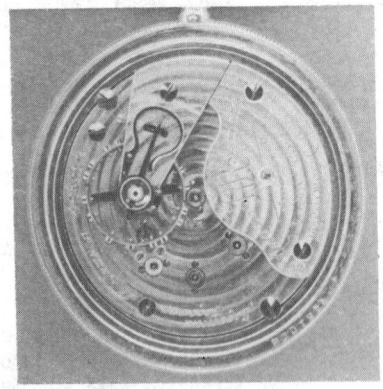 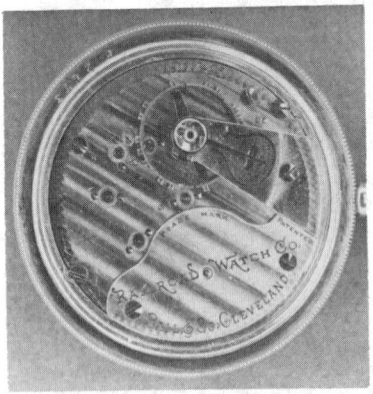

BALL-HAMILTON, Grade 999, 18 size, 17 jewels, serial number 458,623

BALL-HAMILTON, Grade 999, 18 size, 17 jewels, marked "*Railroad Watch Co.*" Ca. 1896, serial number 20,793.

Ball-Hamilton serial number **601** is known to exist.

Ball Watch Co., Brotherhood of RR trainmen, 18 size, 17J, movement made by Hamilton, serial number 13,020.

Ball Watch Co. (Hamilton). Grade 999, 18 size, 21-23 J., sun ray damaskeening, serial number 548,157, c.1906.

Description		Avg	Ex-Fn	Mint
Brotherhood of Locomotive Engineers, 21J, OF	★★	$1,400	$1,800	$2,600
Brotherhood of Locomotive Firemen, 17J, OF	★★	1,000	1,200	2,200
Brotherhood of Locomotive Firemen, 19J, OF	★★	1,200	1,400	2,400
Brotherhood of Locomotive Firemen, 21J, OF	★★	1,400	1,800	2,600
Brotherhood of Railroad Trainsmen, 17J, OF	★★	1,000	1,200	2,200
Brotherhood of Railroad Trainsmen, 19J, OF	★★	1,200	1,400	2,400
Brotherhood of Railroad Trainsmen, 21J, OF	★★	1,400	1,800	2,600
Order of Railroad Conductors, 17J, OF	★★	1,000	1,200	2,200
Order of Railroad Conductors, 19J, OF	★★	1,200	1,400	2,400
Order of Railroad Conductors, 21J, OF	★★★★	1,300	1,500	2,500
Order of Railroad Telegraphers, 17J, OF	★★★★	1,500	2,000	2,600
Order of Railroad Telegraphers, 19J, OF	★★★★	1,600	2,100	2,800
Order of Railroad Telegraphers, 21J, OF	★★★★	1,800	2,200	3,000
Private Label or Jewelers name, 17J, Adj., OF	★★	400	600	1,000

BALL WATCH Co. (OFFICIAL R.R. STANDARD) Dial, NOTE: 20th Century bow, W/ snap back.

BALL WATCH Co. DIAL (Order of Railroad Conductors), 18 size.

BALL– DeLONG ESCAPEMENT
16 SIZE

Description		Avg	Ex-Fn	Mint
21J, 14K OF Case	★ ★ ★ ★	$2,000	$2,500	$4,000

Ball-Hamilton, Model 998 Elinvar, 16 size, 23 jewels, with center bridge.   BALL W. CO. (HAMILTON),16 size, 21jewels, official RR standard, ADJ.5p, serial no.611429

BALL — HAMILTON
16 SIZE G. F. CASES

Description		Avg	Ex-Fn	Mint
16J, M#976, 977, NI, OF, LS	★	$350	$450	$750
17J, M#974, NI, OF, LS		200	250	400
17J, Official RR Standard, OF		250	300	450
19J, Official RR Standard, OF		250	300	475
19J, M#999, NI, Off. RR Stan., OF, LS		250	300	475
21J, M#999, NI, Off. RR Stan., OF, LS		350	375	500
21J, M#999B-marked, Off. RR Stan., OF, marked-Adj.6P		450	550	750
21J, M#999, Off. RR Stan., Coin case		350	400	550
21J, M#999 , Off. RR Stan., marked Loaner, coin case	★ ★	400	500	750
21J, M#992B, NI, marked 992B & Off RR Stan. Adj.6P	★ ★ ★	1,000	1,400	2,200
23J, M#999B, Off. RR Stan., NI, OF, LS, Adj.6P		600	800	1,200
23J, M#998 marked-Elinvar, Off. RR Stan., Adj.5P		775	850	1,400
23J, M#999, NI, Off. RR Stan., OF, LS	★ ★	700	800	1,200
Brotherhood of Locomotive Engineers, OF	★ ★	1,200	1,600	2,400
Brotherhood of Locomotive Firemen, OF	★ ★	1,200	1,600	2,400
Brotherhood of Railroad Trainmen, OF	★ ★	1,200	1,600	2,400
Order of Railroad Conductors, OF	★ ★	1,200	1,600	2,400
17-19J, Brotherhood or Order, HUNTING CASE	★ ★ ★	1,500	2,000	2,800
Private Label or Jewelers name, 21J, Adj., OF	★	400	500	800

BALL — HAMPDEN
18 SIZE

Description		Avg	Ex-Fn	Mint
15-17J, LS, SW, HC, marked Superior Grade	★ ★ ★	$1,250	$1,400	$2,500
15-17J, LS, SW, OF, marked Superior Grade	★ ★	1,000	1,200	1,800
15-17J, LS, SW, OF	★	400	450	800
15-17J, LS, SW, HC	★ ★ ★	600	800	1,300

BALL- NEW YORK WATCH CO.

Description		Avg	Ex-Fn	Mint
Whitcomb & Ball, E.W. Bond Style 3/4 plate, 17-19J, NI,	★ ★ ★	$2,500	$3,500	$5,500

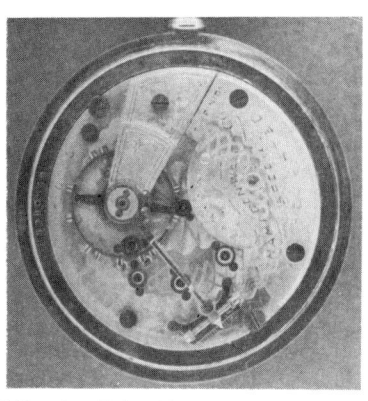

Ball-Hampden, 18 size, 17 jewels, serial number 759,728.

BALL & CO. (E. HOWARD & CO.), Series VIII, 18 size, 17 jewels. (Order of Railway Conductors), serial number 307,488. c.1900.

BALL — E. HOWARD & CO.
18 SIZE

Description		Avg	Ex-Fn	Mint
VII, Ball, 17J, nickel, SW, GF, HC	★ ★ ★	$2,200	$2,800	$5,000
VII, Ball, 17J, nickel, SW, **14K** orig. HC	★ ★ ★	3,500	4,000	8,000
VII, Ball ,17J, nickel, **18K** orig. HC	★ ★ ★	6,000	8,000	12,000
VIII, Ball, 17J, nickel, SW, GF, OF	★ ★ ★	1,000	1,500	3,000
VIII, Ball, 17J, nickel, SW, **14K** orig. OF	★ ★ ★	3,000	3,500	4,000
VIII, Ball, 17J, 3/4, PS, GJS, *Brotherhood of Locomotive Engineers, or Order of Railroad Conductors*, **14K** orig.OF,	★ ★ ★	5,000	6,000	9,000

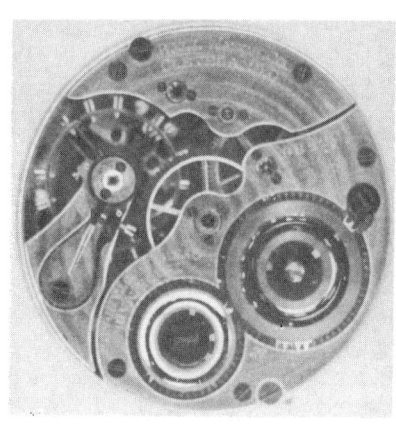

BALL W. Co. (E. HOWARD WATCH CO.), 16 size, 21J. (KEYSTONE). This watch believed to be one-of-a-kind prototype, serial number 982,201.

Ball Watch Co., Illinois Model, 16 size, 23 jewels. Note: The CORRECT HANDS FOR BALL ILLINOIS WATCH.

🕐 Some grades are not included. Their values can be determined by comparing with similar age, size, metal content, style, models and grades listed.

🕐 BALL Watches are priced as having a **ORIGINAL BALL DIAL & CASE.**

BALL — E. HOWARD WATCH CO. (Keystone)
16 SIZE

Description	Avg	Ex-Fn	Mint
17J, Keystone Howard, GJS, OF..	$2,000	$2,500	$3,500
21J, Keystone Howard, Adj, GJS, OF .... ★★★★	2,500	3,000	4,500

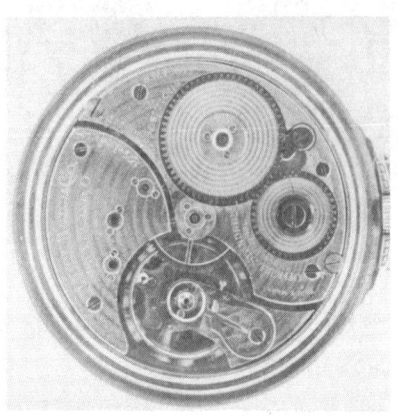

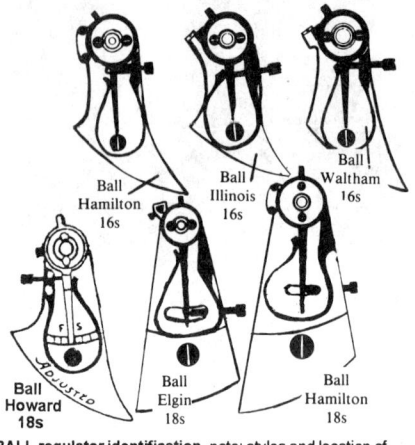

Ball Watch Co., Illinois Model, 16 size, 23 jewels. To identify, note back plates that circle around balance wheel, serial number B801,758.

BALL regulator identification, note: styles and location of hairspring stud.

BALL — ILLINOIS
18 & 16 SIZE

Description	Avg	Ex-Fn	Mint
18 size, 11-15J. or (Garland model), OF...	$200	$250	$400
16 size, 23J, 3/4, LS, Off. RR Stan., Adj. 5P, GJS, OF............ ★★	1,200	1,500	2,500

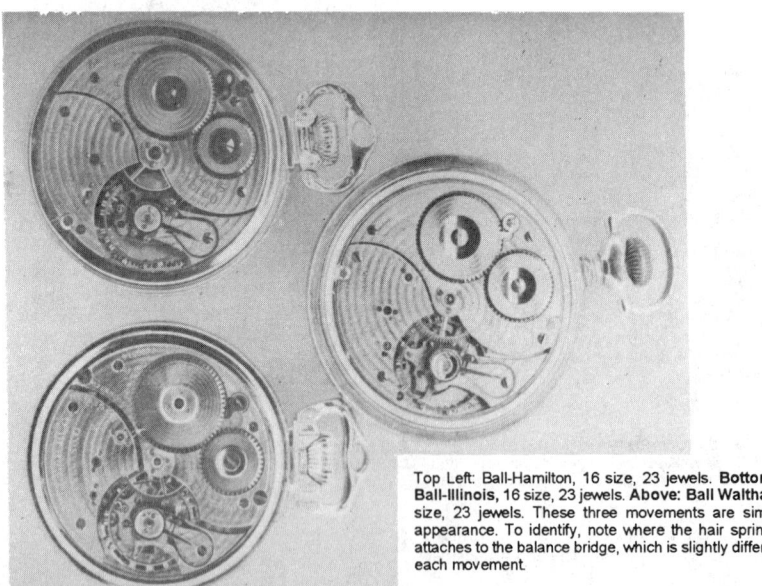

Top Left: Ball-Hamilton, 16 size, 23 jewels. Bottom left: Ball-Illinois, 16 size, 23 jewels. Above: Ball Waltham, 16 size, 23 jewels. These three movements are similar in appearance. To identify, note where the hair spring stud attaches to the balance bridge, which is slightly different on each movement.

BALL — SETH THOMAS
18 SIZE

Description		Avg	Ex-Fn	Mint
17J, M#3, LS, OF,3/4, GJS .... ★ ★ ★ ★		$5,000	$6,500	$8,500

BALL — WALTHAM
18 SIZE

Description		Avg	Ex-Fn	Mint
1892, 15-17J, OF, LS, SW,				
marked Webb C. Ball, Cleveland............................... ★ ★ ★		$2,500	$3,000	$4,500

BALL — WALTHAM
16 SIZE

Description		Avg	Ex-Fn	Mint
15J, Commercial Std.,3/4,HC, GCW .... ★ ★		$275	$400	$700
15-16J, Commercial std., OF..		125	150	300
16J, Commercial std., HC..		175	200	450
17-19J, Commercial std., OF		100	150	300
17-19J, Commercial std., HC		175	250	450
17J, LS, 3/4, Adj.5P, Multi-color case, GF, OF		250	400	700
17J, LS, 3/4, Adj.5P, Off. RR Stan., OF.................................		200	300	500
17J,Official RR std., HC... ★ ★		700	900	1,400

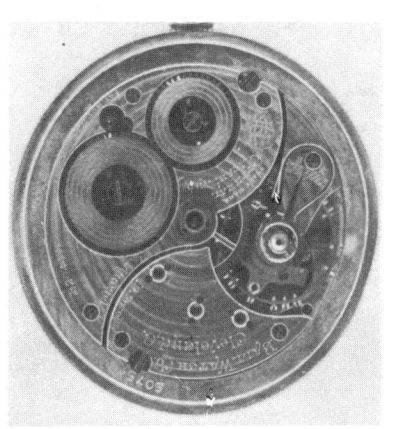 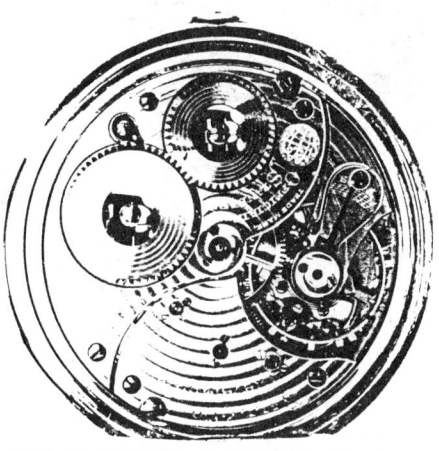

Ball-Waltham, 16 size, 19 jewels, ORC (Order of Railroad Conductors), serial number B204,475.

BALL–WALTHAM, 23 jewels, Official Railroad Standard, lever set, Adjusted to 5 positions, serial# B060,915.

Description		Avg	Ex-Fn	Mint
19J,Official RR std., LS, GCW,GJS, OF		$250	$300	$600
19J, LS, Off. RR Stan., stirrup style case, OF		275	325	600
19J, LS, Off. RR Stan., OF, Coin..		250	300	600
19J, LS, Off. RR Stan., **OF 14K** .... ★ ★		1,200	1,500	2,400
19J,Official RR std., LS, GCW,GJS, **HC** .... ★ ★		750	900	1,600
19J, LS, 3/4, Adj.5P, Off. RR Stan., OF, Wind Indicator .... ★ ★ ★		3,500	4,000	5,500
21J,Official RR std., LS, GCW,GJS, OF		325	400	550
21J, LS, 3/4, Adj.5P, Off. RR Stan., OF		325	400	550
21J, LS, OF, Adj.5P, Off. RR Stan., marked **Loaner**, OF........... ★		450	550	800
23J, LS, Adj.5P, NI, GJS, Off. RR Stand., OF,				
very rare .... ★ ★ ★ ★		3,000	4,000	6,500

Watches MARKED "BALL & Co." are more difficult to find than BALL WATCH Co.

Description		Avg	Ex-Fn	Mint
17J, Brotherhood, marked ORC, BOFLE & *other etc. dials*, OF	★ ★	$1,200	$1,400	$2,000
19J, Brotherhood, marked ORC, BOFLE & *other etc. dials*, OF	★ ★	1,200	1,400	2,000
17-19J, Brotherhood, marked ORC, BOFLE & *other etc. dials*, HC	★ ★	1,500	1,800	2,800
21J, Brotherhood, marked ORC, BOFLE & *other etc. dials*, OF	★ ★	1,300	1,500	2,200
21J, Brotherhood, marked ORC, BOFLE & *other etc. dials*, HC.	★ ★ ★	3,000	4,000	6,500

Ball Watch Co. by Illinois, Secometer, rotating digital sec, open face, 12 size, 19 jewels,

Record Watch Co. (BXC), 16 size, 21jewels, M#477-B, Adj.6P, Swiss made Ca.1961.

12 SIZE
(Not Railroad Grade)

Description	Avg	Ex-Fn	Mint
19J, Illinois, OF, PS	$100	$175	$300
19J, Illinois, HC, PS	200	300	400
19J, Illinois, Secometer, rotating digital sec, OF ★	250	300	500
17J, Waltham, Commercial Standard, OF, PS, ★	150	175	250

NO. 333
NO. 999

999
STANDARD

OFFICIAL RR STANDARD

OFFICIAL TIME SERVICE STANDARD

STANDARD B OF RT

B OF LE

Railway Queen

O OF RC

The B. of L. E. Standard Watch.
The B. of L. F. Standard Watch.
The B. of R. T. Standard Watch.
The O. of R. C. Standard Watch.
The Official R. R. Standard Watch.
The O. of R. T. Standard Watch.

B OF LF

SAFETY

FIRST

TRADE MARKS REGISTERED IN U. S. PATENT OFFICE

Ball-Audemars Piguet & Co., 14 size, 31 jewels, minute repeater, open face, serial number 4,220.

Ball-Vacheron & Constantin, 43mm, 18 jewels, hunting; note wolf-teeth winding.

BALL — SWISS
16 SIZE

Description	Avg	Ex-Fn	Mint
17J, "Garland"	$80	$125	$175
18-21J, Longines, OF	100	125	200
21J, Time Ball Special,OF	50	75	150
21J, M#435-B, LS, Adj.6P, Ball case, stirrup bow, OF	100	125	200
21J, M#435-C, LS, Adj.6P, Ball case, stirrup bow, OF	100	125	200
21J, M#477-B, Adj.6P (BXC-Record Watch Co.)	100	125	200
40mm Audemar Piguet, min. repeater, jeweled thru hammers, triple signed Webb C. Ball, **18K, OF** ★	4,000	5,000	7,000
43-44mm Vacheron & Constantin, 18J, **HC, 18K** ★	1,000	1,400	1,800

0 SIZE
(Not Railroad Grade)

Description	Avg	Ex-Fn	Mint
17-19J, Waltham, OF, PS	$225	$275	$400
19J, HC, PS, "Queen" in Ball case	300	350	500

PATENT SAFETY BOW

20 th CENTURY CASE

18 size: 14K=$450 - $500 - $600
18 size: gold filled= $120 - $130 - $150
16 size: 14K=$350 -$375 - $450
16 size: gold filled= $95 - $110 - $140

ANTIQUE STIRRUP BOW

18 size: 14K=$450 - $500 - $600
18 size: gold filled= $120 - $130 - $150
16 size: 14K= $350 -$375 - $450
16 size: gold filled= $95 - $110 - $140

CATALOG CASE # 106
gold filled case $100 - $175 - $200

CATALOG CASE # 110
gold filled case $150 - $175 - $275

"BOX CAR" Dial;
found on Hamilton & Illinois made Ball

"CONVENTIONAL" Dial;
found on Waltham made Ball

CATALOG CASE # 114
gold filled case $150 - $175- $250

CATALOG CASE # 118
gold filled case $175 - $200 - $300

🕐 NOTE: A 1902 advertisement for Ball Watch Company read, ''We do not sell movements or cases separately. BALL Advertised as a **COMPLETE** watch with a choice of BALL dials and was fitted with a certain matched, timed and rated movement and sold in the BALL designed case style as a **COMPLETE** watch. <u>**ALL THE ABOVE CASES ARE GOLD FILLED.**</u>

CATALOG CASE # 122
gold filled case $175 - $200 - $250

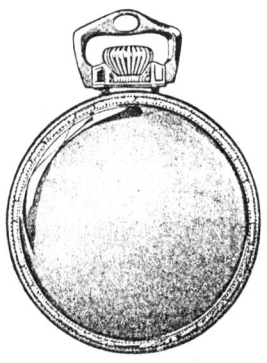

CATALOG CASE # 126
gold filled case $125 - $150 - $200

OFFICIAL **RR** STANDARD. BALL Dial

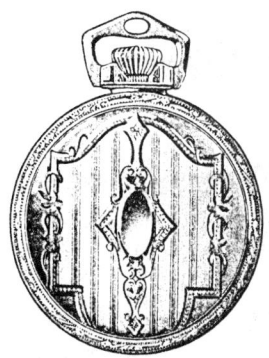

CATALOG CASE # 130
gold filled case $150 - $175 - $225

CATALOG CASE # 134
gold filled case $175 - $200 - $250

🕐 NOTE: A 1902 advertisement for Ball Watch Company read, ''We do not sell movements or cases separately. BALL Advertised as a **COMPLETE** watch with a choice of BALL dials and was fitted with a certain matched, timed and rated movement and sold in the BALL designed case style as a **COMPLETE** watch. <u>ALL THE ABOVE CASES ARE GOLD FILLED.</u>

BANNATYNE WATCH CO.
1905 - 1911

Mr. Bannatyne had previously worked for Waterbury Clock Co., in charge of watch production. Bannatyne made non-jeweled watches that sold for about $1.50. Ingraham bought this company in 1912.

ESTIMATED SERIAL NUMBERS AND PRODUCTION DATES

Date	Serial No.	Date	Serial No.	Date	Serial No.
1906	40,000	1908	140,000	1910	250,000

Description		Avg	Ex-Fn	Mint
16-18S, OF, SW, NI- case	★ ★	$300	$400	$700
12-14S, OF, SW, NI- case	★ ★	200	250	400

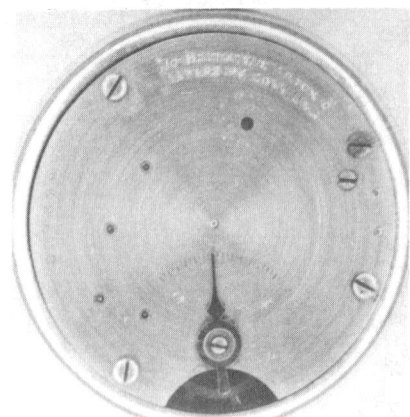 

Bannatyne Watch Co. (left), Ingraham Watch Co. (right). Note similarity of movements. Both patented Aug. 27th, 1907 & Sept. 3rd, 1907.

BENEDICT & BURNHAM MFG. CO.

Waterbury, Connecticut
1878 - 1880

This name will be found on the spring cover of the movement of the first 1,000 "long wind" Waterbury watches made in 1878. These watches had skeleton type movements with open dials that made the works visible. They contained 58 parts and were attractive. The company was reorganized in March 1880 as the Waterbury Clock Co. and in 1898 became the New England Watch Co.

🕐 Watches listed in this book are priced at the collectable retail level, as **complete** watches having an original 14k gold-filled case & *KEY WIND* with silver case, an original white enamel single sunk dial, and with the entire original movement in good working order with no repairs needed.

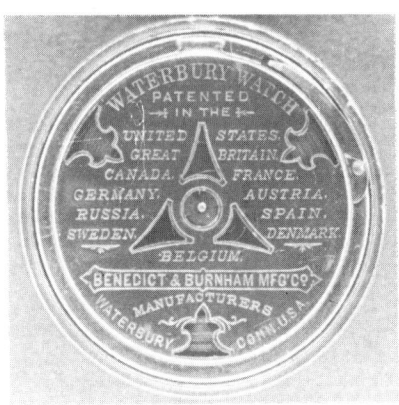

Benedict & Burnham Mfg. Co. dial & movement, 18 size, long wind, skeletonized dial.

Description		Avg	Ex-Fn	Mint
18S, duplex escapement, movement rotates as time advances long wind,Nickel OF case .... ★ ★ ★		$900	$1,000	$1,500

BOWMAN WATCH CO.

Lancaster, Pennsylvania
1879 - 1882

In March 1877, Ezra F. Bowman, a native of Lancaster, Pa., opened a retail jewelry and watch business. He employed William H. Todd to supervise his watch manufacturing. Todd had previously been employed by the Elgin and Lancaster Watch companies. Bowman made a 17 Size, 3/4 plate, fully-jeweled movement. The escape wheel was a star tooth design, fully capped, similar to those made by Charles Frodsham, an English watch maker. They were stem wind with dials made by another company. Enough parts were made and bought for 300 watches, but only about 50 watches were completed and sold by Bowman. These watches performed very well. The company was sold to J. P. Stevens of Atlanta, Ga.

Description	Avg	Ex-Fn	Mint
18S, 17J, Hamilton 928, OF, marked E. F. Bowman .... ★ ★	$400	$500	$800
17S, 19-21J, 3/4, GJS, NI, LS, SW .... ★ ★ ★ ★	9,000	11,000	20,000
16S, 21J, Hamilton 960, OF, marked E. F. Bowman .... ★ ★	500	600	800
16S, 21J, Hamilton 961, HC, marked E. F. Bowman............ ★ ★ ★	600	700	950

Bowman Watch Co., 16-18 size, 19-21 jewels, 3/4 plate, gold jewel settings, lever set, stem wind. Note free sprung balance. Serial number 17, c.1880.

Bowman Watch Co., 16-18 size, 19-21 jewels, 3/4 plate, gold jewel settings, lever set, stem wind. Note free sprung balance. Serial number 19, c.1880.

CALIFORNIA WATCH CO.

San Francisco - Berkeley, California
1876 - 1877

The Cornell Watch Co. was reorganized in early 1876 as the California Watch Co. The new company bought machinery to make watch cases of gold and silver. In a short time the company was in bad financial trouble and even paid its employees with watches. The business closed in the summer of 1876. Albert Troller bought the unfinished watches that were left. In about four months, he found a buyer in San Francisco. The factory was then closed and sold to the Independent Watch Co. Only about 5,000 watches were made by the California Watch Company. Serial numbers range from 25,115 to 30,174. Inscribed on the movements is "Berkeley."

Description		Avg	Ex-Fn	Mint
18S, 15J, FULL, KW, KS, "Berkeley"	★★★	$1,500	$2,000	$3,000
18S, 11-15J, FULL, KW, KS or SW	★	1,000	1,200	1,600
18S, 19J, FULL, KW, KS or SW	★★★	1,200	1,400	2,000

California Watch Co., 18 size, 15 jewels, full plate.

California Watch Co., 18 size, 7 jewels, full plate, serial number 29,029.

CHESHIRE WATCH CO.

Cheshire, Connecticut
1883 - 1890

In October 1883, the Cheshire Watch Company was formed by George J. Capewell with D. A. A. Buck (designer of the long-wind Waterbury) as superintendent. Their first movement was 18S, 3/4 gilt plate, stem wind, stem set, with the pendant attached to the movement. It fit into a nickel case which was also made at the Cheshire factory. The first watches were completed in April 1885. A new 18S nickel movement with a second hand was made to fit standard size American cases, and was introduced in 1887. By that date production was at about 200 watches per day.

NOTE: George J. Capewell inventor of the Capewell horse shoe nail.

⊕ Pricing in this Guide are fair market price for **COMPLETE** watches which are reflected from the "**NAWWC**" National and regional shows.

Serial numbers range from 201 to 89,650. All Cheshire watches were sold through L. W. Sweet, general selling agent, in New York City. The factory closed in 1890, going into receivership. The receiver had 3,000 movements finished in 1892. In 1901 O. E. Bell bought the machinery and had it shipped to Appleton, Wisconsin, where he had formed the Remington Watch Company. The watches produced by Remington are marked ''Appleton Watch Co.'' on the movements.

Cheshire Watch Co., 20 size, 4 jewels, model number 1. Note stem attached and will not fit standard size case, serial number 201. NOTE: Closed top plate near balance. The Cheshire Watch Co. may have started with S# 201.

Cheshire Watch Co., 20 size, 4 jewels, model number 1.

Description	Avg	Ex-Fn	Mint
20S, 4-7J, FULL, OF, SW, NI case, stem attached, low serial #			
1st model, closed top plate (S # 201 to 300)............ ★ ★ ★	$550	$650	$950
20S, 4-7J, FULL, OF, SW, NI case, stem attached,			
1st model, closed top plate .... ★ ★	450	550	700
18S, 4-7J, 3/4, SW, OF, NI case, stem attached, 2nd model .... ★	300	350	450
18S, 4-7J, HC/ OF fits standard case, 3rd model.......................... ★	250	300	400
18S, 11J, HC/ OF, standard case, 3rd model .... ★	275	325	425
18S, 15J, HC/ OF, NI, ADJ, standard case, 3rd model .... ★	300	350	450
18S, 21J, HC / OF, SW, Coin, standard case, 3rd model .... ★ ★	400	450	550
6S, 3/4, HC/ OF, SW, NI case.. ★	200	250	350

Cheshire Watch Co., 18 size, 4-7 jewels. This model number 2 was manufactured with the stem attached and requires a special case. NOTE: open top plate at Balance.

Cheshire Watch Co., 18 size, 4-7 jewels. This model fits standard 18 size cases. Model number 3.

🕀 1st & 2nd model Cheshire movements will not fit standard 18 size cases.
Model # 1, S# 201 to15,000 - Model # 2, S # 30,001 to 40,000 - Model # 3, S # 50,001 to 89,650.

CHICAGO WATCH CO.

Chicago, Illinois
1895 - 1903

The Chicago Watch Company's watches were 18 size, 7-15J & 12 size were made by other manufacturing companies and sold by Chicago Watch Co.

Description	Avg	Ex-Fn	Mint
18S, 7J, OF	$100	$145	$200
18S, 7-11J, HC or OF, Swiss	50	60	75
18S, 11J, KW	150	200	450
18S, 15J, OF, SW	125	200	300
Columbus, 18S, 15J, SW, NI, OF ★	200	250	400
Columbus, 18S, 15J, SW, NI, HC ★	225	300	425
Illinois, 18S, 11J, SW, NI ★	200	250	400
Waltham, 18S, 15J ★	200	250	400
12S, 15J, OF	60	100	200
12S, 15J, YGF, HC	100	150	325

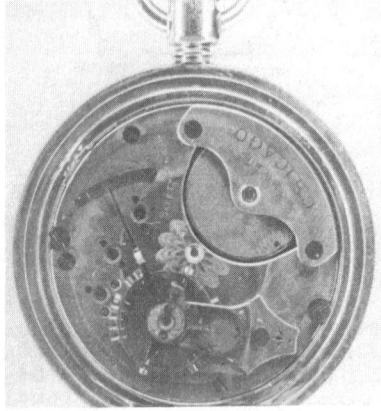

Chicago Watch Co., 18 size, 15 jewels, Hunting case, made by COLUMBUS Watch Co., nickel movement, lever set, serial # 209,145.

Columbia Watch Co., 0 size, 4 jewels, stem wind, open face and hunting, duplex escapement, the escape wheel teeth were milled to give better quality than the Waterbury movements.

COLUMBIA WATCH CO.

Waltham, Massachusetts
1896 - 1899

The Columbia Watch Company was organized in 1896 by Edward A. Locke, formerly General Manager of the Waterbury Watch Company. The firm began manufacturing an 0-size, 4-jewel gilt movement with duplex escapement in 1897. These movements were marked "Columbia Watch Co., Waltham, Mass." The firm also made movements marked "Hollers Watch Co., Brooklyn, NY," as well as nickeled movements marked "Cambridge Watch Co., New York."

Locke turned the business over to his son-in-law, Renton Whidden, in 1898, and the firm changed to an 0-size, 7- jewel nickel movement with lever escapement called the Suffolk. The firm name was not changed until early 1901.

Description	Avg	Ex-Fn	Mint
0S, 4J, SW, Duplex, gilded, HC	$55	$75	$135
0S, 4J, SW, Duplex, gilded, OF	50	60	125
0S, 7J, SW, lever escapement, OF	60	75	125

COLUMBUS WATCH CO.

Columbus, Ohio
1874 - 1903

Dietrich Gruen, born in Osthofen, Germany in 1847, started a business as the Columbus Watch Co. on Dec. 22 of 1874 in Columbus, Ohio. At the age of 27, he received a U.S. patent for an improved safety pinion. The new company finished movements made from Madretsch, Switzerland, a suburb of Beil. The imported movements were made in a variety of sizes and were in nickel or gilt. The early watches usually had the initials C.W.CO. intertwined in script on the dial. The serial numbers generally ran up to around 20,000's a few examples are in the 70,000's.

D. Gruen and W.J. Savage decided in late 1882 to manufacture watches locally. By August of 1883 the first movements were being produced with a train consisting of 72 teeth on the barrel, 72 on the center wheel, 11 on the center pinion, 60 on the third wheel with a pinion of 9, 70 on the fourth wheel with a pinion of 9 with a 7 leaf escape pinion. The new manufacture primarily made 18 size movements but also pioneered the 16 size watch while reducing the size and thickness. Several new innovations were used into the design including a completely covered main spring barrel, a new micrometric regulator and the ability to change the main spring without removing the balance cock. By 1884 they were making their own dials, but no cases were ever manufactured.

The company went into receivership in 1894 with new management. That same year Frederick Gruen started again as D. Gruen & Son. They had PAUL ASSMANN to produce 18 size & 16 size movements with 18 & 21 jewels with the escapement designed by Moritz Grossman of Glasshute. Soon after this time movements were obtained from Switzerland and the new Gruen veri-thin movement was developed. In 1898 this company moved to Cincinnati.

From 1894 through February 14, 1903 the Columbus Watch Co. produced watches both under the Columbus Watch Co. and the New Columbus Watch Co. name. The re-organized company produced the same models, but switched primarily to named grades such as Time King, Columbus King, etc. The higher grade watches were assigned a special block of serial numbers from 500,000 to 506,000 . In keeping with the industry several models with 25 jewels were produced in this block of serial numbers.

In 1903 the Columbus Watch Co. was sold to the Studebakers and the South Bend Watch Co. started. The machinery, unfinished movements, parts and approximately 3/4 of the 150 employees moved to South Bend, Indiana. Some marked Columbus Watch Co. movements were finished by the South Bend W. Co. Examples exist of dials made in the South Bend style and movements marked Columbus Watch Co.

COLUMBUS WATCH CO., 19 Lignes or about 14-16 size, 16 jewels, gold jewel settings, marked Gruen's Pat. pinion, OPEN FACE model, serial # 5,387. (Swiss contract)

COLUMBUS WATCH CO., 19 Lignes or about 14-16 size, 15 jewels, hunting case, engraved on movement "1874".

COLUMBUS
ESTIMATED SERIAL NUMBERS AND PRODUCTION DATES

DATE - SERIAL NO.		DATE— SERIAL NO.	
1874—	1	1888 – 97,000	
1875–	1,000	1889 – 119,000	
1876–	3,000	1890 – 141,000	
1877–	6,000	1891 – 163,000	SPECIAL BLOCK
1878–	9,000	1892 – 185,000	OF SERIAL NOS.
1879–	12,000	1893 – 207,000	DATE— SERIAL NO.
1880–	15,000	1894 – 229,000	1894 – 500,001
1881–	18,000	1895 – 251,000	1896 – 501,500
1882–	21,000	1896 – 273,000	1898 – 503,000
1883 – 25,000		1897 – 295,000	1900 – 504,500
1884 – 30,000		1898 – 317,000	1902 – 506,000
1885 – 40,000		1899 – 339,000	
1886 – 53,000		1900 – 361,000	
1887 – 75,000		1901 – 383,000	

The above list is provided for determining the **APPROXIMATE** age of your watch. Match serial number with date. Watches were not necessarily *SOLD* and *DELIVERED* in the exact order of manufactured or production dates.

SWISS, 3/4 PLATE, & MADE FROM 1874–1883
Most marked COL. WATCH CO. with single sunk dials and may be SW/KW Transitional, serial # up to 20,000.

Grade or Name — Description	Avg	Ex-Fn	Mint
18S, 7J, pressed J., nickel or gilded, OF/HC	$85	$100	$175
18S, 11J, pressed J., nickel or gilded, OF/HC	100	120	225
18S, 15J, GJS or pressed J., nickel, Adj., OF/HC	150	200	300
18S, 16J, raised GJS, 2 tone or nickel, Adj., OF/HC	200	300	400
Grade or Name — Description	**Avg**	**Ex-Fn**	**Mint**
16S, 11J, pressed J., nickel, OF/HC	$150	$200	$300
16S, 15J, pressed J. or GJS, Adj., nickel, OF/HC	150	200	300
16S, 16J, raised GJS, Adj., nickel, OF/HC	175	225	350
Grade or Name — Description	**Avg**	**Ex-Fn**	**Mint**
14S, 16J, GJS, nickel, Adj., OF/HC	$150	$200	$300
Grade or Name — Description	**Avg**	**Ex-Fn**	**Mint**
9S, 15J, GJS or pressed J., nickel, Adj., OF/HC	$100	$150	$225
Grade or Name — Description	**Avg**	**Ex-Fn**	**Mint**
8S, 11J, pressed J., nickel, OF/HC	$100	$150	$200
8S, 15J, pressed J., nickel, OF/HC	100	150	225

FOR ABOVE HUNTING CASED MODEL ADD $25.00 to $50.00
NOTE: These Odd size movements are difficult to case.

COLUMBUS WATCH CO., 19 Lignes or about 16 size, 15 jewels, exposed winding wheels, marked Gruen Patent, OPEN FACE model, serial # 1,661. (Swiss contract)

COLUMBUS WATCH CO., about 14 size, 16 jewels, gold jewel settings, nickel plates, marked Gruen's pat. pinion, HUNTING CASE model. (Swiss contract)

18 SIZE-KW, FULL PLATE, MODEL # 1 & TRANSITIONAL

Serial # up to 100,000, balance cock set flush to barrel bridge and may have pinned dial.

Marked Col. Watch Co., Ohio Columbus Watch Co.

Grade or Name — Description	Avg	Ex-Fn	Mint
11-13J, KW / KS, gilded, OF/HC	$250	$375	$525
13J, KW / KS, nickel,(marked 13 jewels), OF/HC................. ★ ★	400	500	700
15J, KW / KS, gilded, Adj., OF/HC....................................	325	400	500
16J, KW / KS, gilded, OF/HC..★	325	475	600
Grade or Name — Description	Avg	Ex-Fn	Mint
11-13J, SW/ KW, gilded or nickel, OF/HC	$150	$200	$300
15J, SW/ KW, gilded or nickel, GJS, OF/HC....................	175	250	350
16J, SW/ KW, gilded or nickel, GJS, OF/HC....................	200	275	375

FOR ABOVE HUNTING CASED MODEL ADD $25.00 to $50.00

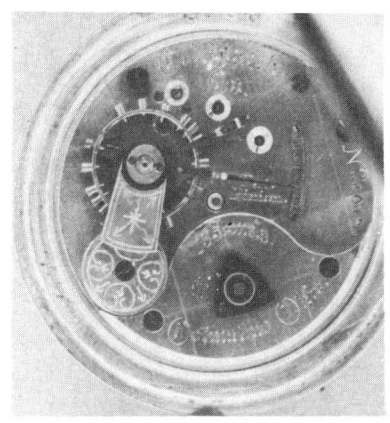 

COLUMBUS WATCH CO., 18 size, marked 13 jewels, pressed jewels, key wind key set, nickel plates, marked on movement Col. Watch Co. Columbus Ohio Pat. pinion, on dial "OHIO COLUMBUS WATCH CO.", serial #40,198.

COLUMBUS WATCH CO., 18 size, 15 jewels, key wind key set, hunting case, on movement "Columbus Watch Co. Columbus, Ohio Pat. Pinion", serial # 66,577.

18 SIZE, FULL PLATE, PRE-1894

Marked "Columbus Watch Co. Columbus, Ohio", all marked Safety Pinion

Grade or Name — Description	Avg	Ex-Fn	Mint
7J, G#90, pressed J., OF...	$50	$75	$150
7J, G#20, pressed J., HC...	60	85	200
11J, G#92, pressed J., nickel, OF	50	75	150
11J, G#22, pressed J., nickel, HC....................................	60	85	225
15J, G#64 / G#93, gilded, OF..	50	75	150
15J, G#24 / G#32, gilded, HC..	60	85	225
15J, G#63 / G#94, nickel, Adj., OF..................................	70	95	150
15J, G#23 / G#33, nickel, Adj., HC	80	125	250
15J, G#95, nickel, Adj., D.S. dial, OF	65	90	175
15J, G#34, nickel, Adj., D.S. dial, HC	85	125	275
16J, G#97, GJS, nickel, Adj., D.S. dial, OF	75	100	225
16J, G#27, GJS, nickel, Adj., D.S. dial, HC	95	150	300
16J, G#98, raised GJS, 2 tone nickel, Adj., D.S. dial, OF.............	85	125	250
16J, G#28, raised GJS, 2 tone nickel, Adj., D.S. dial, HC.............	100	150	325
16J, G#99, raised GJS, 2 tone nickel, Adj., D.S. dial, OF.............	100	150	350
16J, G#18, raised GJS, 2 tone nickel, Adj., D.S. dial, HC	125	175	400

18 SIZE-FULL PLATE, POST-1894

Some Marked "New Columbus Watch Co. Columbus Ohio"

Grade or Name — Description	Avg	Ex-Fn	Mint
7J, G#10, pressed J., gilded, OF	$50	$75	$165
7J, G#9, pressed J., gilded, HC	70	100	200
11J, G#8, nickel, OF	70	100	165
11J, G#7, nickel, HC	80	125	200
16J, G#6, nickel, OF	75	100	175
16J, G#5, nickel, HC	85	135	225
16J, G#4, GJS, 2 tone nickel, Adj., D.S. dial, OF	100	150	250
16J, G#3, GJS, 2 tone nickel, Adj., D.S. dial, HC	150	200	300
17J, G#204, GJS, 2 tone nickel, Adj., D.S. dial, OF	150	200	250
17J, G#203, GJS, 2 tone nickel, Adj., D.S. dial, HC	165	225	350
17J, G#2, raised GJS, 2 tone nickel, Adj., D.S. dial, OF	175	250	375
17J, G#1, raised GJS, 2 tone nickel, Adj., D.S. dial, HC	200	250	400

COLUMBUS WATCH CO., with a "Choo Choo" Railway King double sunk dial.

COLUMBUS WATCH CO., Railway King, 18 size, 17 jewels, 2 tone, serial # 313,005.

18 SIZE FULL PLATE, NAMED GRADES

Marked Names, Double Sunk Dials

Grade or Name — Description	Avg	Ex-Fn	Mint
Am. Watch Club, 15J, 2 tone, Adj., D.S. dial, OF/HC ★	$300	$400	$500
Burlington Route C.B. & QR.R., 15J, nickel, Adj., D.S. dial, OF ★★★	900	1,200	1,800
Champion, 15J, gilded, Adj., D.S. dial, OF	70	100	200
Champion, 15J, gilded, Adj., D.S.dial, HC	80	125	250
Champion, 15J, Nickel, Adj., D.S.dial, OF	70	100	200
Champion, 15J, Nickel, Adj., D.S.dial, HC	80	125	250
Champion, 16J, Nickel, Adj., D.S.dial, OF	80	125	250
Champion, 16J, Nickel, Adj., D.S.dial, HC	100	150	300

* Chicago W. Co. made by Columbus W. Co. (see listing under Chicago W. Co. HEADING)

🕐 Watches listed in this book are priced at the collectable retail level, as **complete** watches having an original 14k gold-filled case & *KEY W IND* with silver case, an original white enamel single sunk dial, and with the entire original movement in good working order with no repairs needed.

Grade or Name — Description	Avg	Ex-Fn	Mint
Columbus King, 17J, raised GJS, nickel, Adj., D.S. dial, OF	$200	$275	$425
Columbus King, 17J, raised GJS, nickel, Adj., D.S. dial, HC	275	350	500
Columbus King, 17J, raised GJS, nickel, Adj., choo choo D.S. dial, OF	450	550	850
Columbus King, 17J, raised GJS, nickel, Adj., Angled choo choo D.S. dial, OF	450	550	850
Columbus King, 21J, raised GJS, nickel, Adj., D.S. dial, OF	450	550	800
Columbus King, 21J, raised GJS, nickel, Adj., D.S. dial, HC	400	500	700
Columbus King, 23J, raised GJS, nickel, Adj., D.S. dial, OF ...... ★	950	1,100	1,800
Columbus King, 23J, raised GJS, nickel, Adj., D.S. dial, HC ..... ★	950	1,100	1,800
Columbus King, 25J, raised GJS, nickel, Adj., D.S. dial, OF .... ★ ★ ★	3,000	3,500	5,000
Columbus King, 25J, raised GJS, nickel, Adj., D.S. dial, HC .... ★ ★ ★	2,500	3,000	4,500
F.C. & P.R.R., 17J, GJS, nickel, Adj., D.S. dial, OF .... ★ ★ ★	700	800	1,000
Jackson Park, 15J, 2 tone, Adj., D.S. dial, OF .... ★	400	500	700
Jay Gould the Railroad King, 15J, nickel,Adj., D.S. dial, OF .. ★ ★	700	800	1,200
New York Susquehanna &Western R.R.,16J, GJS, SW/KW, gold flash, D.S. dial, OF .... ★ ★ ★	1,200	1,400	1,800
Non-magnetic, 16J, raised GJS, 2 tone, Adj., OF/HC	200	300	500
North Star, 11J, gilded, OF...	100	125	175
North Star, 11J, gilded, HC	125	150	200
North Star, 11J, nickel, OF...	100	125	175
North Star, 11J, nickel, HC	125	150	225
North Star, 15J, nickel, OF...	125	150	225
North Star, 15J, nickel, HC	150	175	300
The President, 17J, GJS, Adj, 2 tone, D.S. dial, OF	400	450	650
Railroad Regulator, 15J, GJS, nickel, Adj., D.S. dial, OF .... ★	450	550	750
Railroad Regulator, 16J, GJS, nickel, Adj., D.S. dial, OF .... ★	450	500	750
Railway, 17J, GJS, 2 tone, Adj., D.S. dial, OF .... ★	300	350	550

Columbus King, 18 size, 25 jewels, open face serial number 503,094. Note two screws between balance cock & barrel bridge.

Railway King, 18 size, 23 jewels, adjusted, stem wind, hunting case, serial number 503,315. Note one screw between balance cock & barrel bridge.

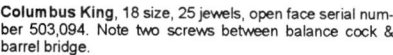

🕐 Watches listed in this book are priced at the collectable retail level, as **complete** watches having an original 14k gold-filled case & *KEY WIND* with silver case, an original white enamel single sunk dial, and with the entire original movement in good working order with no repairs needed.

🕐 Pricing in this Guide are fair market price for COMPLETE watches which are reflected from the **"NAWCC"** National and regional shows.

Grade or Name — Description	Avg	Ex-Fn	Mint
Railway King, 16J, GJS, 2 tone nickel, Adj., D.S. dial, OF............	$275	$300	$400
Railway King, 16J, GJS, 2 tone nickel, Adj., D.S. dial, HC	325	350	500
Railway King, 16J, GJS, 2 tone nickel, Adj., (black red blue) choo chooD.S. dial, OF................................	400	500	700
Railway King, 16J, GJS, 2 tone nickel, Adj., (black red blue) choo chooD.S. dial, HC................................	400	500	700
Railway King, 16J, GJS, 2 tone nickel, Adj., Angled choo choo dial, OF........................	475	575	750
Railway King, 16J, GJS, 2 tone nickel, Adj., Angled choo choo dial, HC........................	475	575	750
Railway King, 17J, raised GJS, nickel, Adj., D.S. dial, OF	250	300	425
Railway King, 17J, raised GJS, nickel, Adj., D.S. dial, HC............	300	375	500
Railway King, 21J, raised GJS, nickel, Adj., D.S. dial, OF	450	500	650
Railway King, 21J, raised GJS, nickel, Adj., D.S. dial, HC............	450	500	700
Railway King, 23J, raised GJS, nickel, Adj., Railway King D.S. dial, OF .... ★ ★ ★	900	1,200	1,800
Railway King, 25J, raised GJS, nickel, Adj., Railway King D.S. dial, OF .... ★ ★ ★ ★	2,500	3,000	4,000
Railway King, 25J, raised GJS, nickel, Adj., Railway King D.S. dial, HC .... ★ ★ ★ ★	3,000	4,000	5,000
Railway King Special, 17J, GJS, nickel, Adj., D.S. dial, OF...........	300	375	500
Railway Monarch, 17J, GJS, nickel, Adj., D.S. dial, OF .... ★	300	375	500
Railway Time Service, 17J, GJS, nickel, Adj., D.S. dial, OF ...... ★	375	450	550
The Regent, 15J, D.S. dial, OF..	150	200	300
R.W.K. Special, 15J, GJS, Adj., 2 tone, D.S. dial, OF...................	250	300	400
R.W.K. Special, 15J, GJS, Adj., 2 tone, D.S. dial, HC	250	300	400
R.W.K. Special, 16J, GJS, Adj., 2 tone, D.S. dial, OF...................	250	300	400
R.W.K. Special, 16J, GJS, Adj., 2 tone, D.S. dial, HC	300	350	500
Springfield Mo.W. Club, 16J, GJS, nickel, Adj., D.S. dial, HC ... ★	275	350	450
Special, 17J, GJS, nickel, D.S. dial, OF..	200	250	350
J.P. Stevens & Co. (see listing under J.P. Stevens & Co. HEADING)			
The New Menlo Park, 15J, HC .... ★	150	200	300
The Star, 11J, nickel, OF/HC	175	200	350
Time King, 21J, raised GJS, 2 tone nickel, Adj., D.S. dial, OF.......	300	400	500
Time King, 21J, raised GJS, 2 tone nickel, Adj., D.S. dial, HC	325	425	625
U.S. Army, 15J, nickel, HC.. ★	400	500	600

18 Size, 21 Jewels.

NEW COLUMBUS TIME KING.

Hunting and Open Face.

Nickel, 21 Genuine Ruby Jewels, set in red, Solid Gold Raised Settings, Escapement Cap Jeweled, Adjusted to temperature, Positions and Isochronism, Breguet Hair Spring, Patent Center Pinion, Patent Regulator, Polished Dust Band and Stem Wind, Beveled Steel Work, Pearled Plates; fine, white, cut and beveled edge, hard enameled, double sunk, Red marginal figured Roman or Arabic Dial; handsomely damaskeened in Gold on Nickel $25 00

1895 AD

🕐 Pricing in this Guide are fair market price for COMPLETE watches which are reflected from the **"NAWCC"** National and regional shows.

16 SIZE, 3/4 Plate

Marked "New Columbus Watch Co. Columbus Ohio"

Grade or Name — Description	Avg	Ex-Fn	Mint
7J, G#80 / G#20, gilded, OF	$60	$80	$150
7J, G#40 / G#19, gilded, HC	70	90	175
11J, G#81, gilded, OF	70	90	150
11J, G#41, gilded, HC	70	90	175
11J, G#83 / G#18, nickel, OF	70	90	150
11J, G#43 / G#17, nickel, HC	70	90	175
15J, G#84, Adj., gilded, OF	70	90	175
15J, G#44, Adj., gilded, HC	70	90	200
15J, G#86, GJS, Adj., nickel, D.S. dial, OF	70	90	175
15J, G#46, GJS, Adj., nickel, D.S. dial, HC	80	100	200
16J, G#87 / G#316, GJS, Adj., nickel, D.S. dial, OF	80	100	200
16J, G#47 / G#315, GJS, Adj., nickel, D.S. dial, HC	85	110	225
16J, G#14, GJS, Adj., 2 tone nickel, D.S. dial, OF	125	150	250
16J, G#13, GJS, Adj., 2 tone nickel, D.S. dial, HC	125	150	300
16J, G#88, raised GJS, Adj., 2 tone nickel, D.S. dial, OF	150	175	250
16J, G#48, raised GJS, Adj., 2 tone nickel, D.S. dial, HC	150	175	300
17J, G#12, raised GJS, Adj., 2 tone nickel, D.S. dial, OF	150	175	250
17J, G#11, raised GJS, Adj., 2 tone nickel, D.S. dial, HC	150	175	300
Ruby, 21J, raised GJS, Adj., 2 tone nickel, D.S. dial, OF ★ ★	400	600	900
Ruby, 21J, raised GJS, Adj., 2 tone nickel, D.S. dial, HC ★ ★	500	700	1,000

NEW Columbus Watch Co., 16 size, 16 jewels, gold train, 2-tone, serial number 341,339.

Columbus Watch Co., Ruby Model, 16 size, 21 jewels, three quarter plate, gold jewel settings, gold train, Adj.6p.

🕐 Some grades are not included. Their values can be determined by comparing with similar age, size, metal content, style, models and grades listed.

🕐 This book endeavours to be a GUIDE or helpful manual and offers a wealth of material to be used as a tool not as an absolute document. Price Guides are like watches the worst may be better than none at all, but at best cannot be expected to be 100% accurate.

🕐 Characteristics of watches differ for the same age of both case and movement, because these features vary it may not be accurate to date a watch by one single influence. Example: the second hand was not commonly found on watches before 1750, but common about 1800. The first second hand appeared in 1665 and another in 1690. Therefore statements are broad rather than accurate.

🕐 Pricing in this Guide are fair market price for COMPLETE watches which are reflected from the "NAWCC" National and regional shows.

6 SIZE

Grade or Name — Description	Avg	Ex-Fn	Mint
7J, G#102, gilded, OF..	$40	$65	$150
7J, G#102, gilded, HC..	50	70	185
11J, G#101 / G#51 / G#53, nickel or gilded, HC	50	70	185
13J, G#103, nickel, HC	50	70	185
15J, G#104 / G#55, GJS, nickel, D.S. dial, HC..............................	50	70	200
16J, G#57, raised GJS, nickel, D.S. dial, OF/HC............................	60	80	225
16J, G#100, raised GJS, 2 tone, D.S. dial, (marked 16J.), OF........	100	150	300
16J, G#100, raised GJS, 2 tone, D.S. dial, (marked 16J.), HC.........	100	150	275

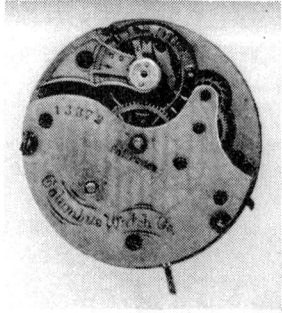

Columbus Watch Co., 8-10 size, 13 jewels, 3/4 plate, stem wind, serial number 13,372. For price see 2nd page of Columbus W. Co. under Swiss, 3/4 plate (1874-1883).

New Columbus Watch Co. Example of a basic model for 6 size, 3/4 plate, 7-16 jewels, gilded and nickel.

4 SIZE

Grade or Name — Description	Avg	Ex-Fn	Mint
11J, nickel or gilded, OF/HC.. ★	$75	$100	$275
15J, nickel or gilded, OF/HC.. ★	100	125	300

🕐 Watches listed in this book are priced at the collectable retail level, as **complete** watches having an original 14k gold-filled case & *KEY WIND* with silver case, an original white enamel single sunk dial, and with the entire original movement in good working order with no repairs needed.

🕐 Pricing in this Guide are fair market price for COMPLETE watches which are reflected from the **"NAWCC"** National and regional shows.

CORNELL WATCH CO.

Chicago, Illinois
1870 - 1874
San Francisco, California
1875 - 1876

The Cornell Watch Co. bought the Newark Watch Co. and greatly improved the movements being produced. In the fall of 1874, the company moved to San Francisco, Calif., with about 60 of its employees. The movements made in California were virtually the same as those made in Chicago. The company wanted to employ Chinese who would work cheaper, but the skilled employees refused to go along and went on strike. The company stayed alive until 1875 and was sold to the California Watch Co. in January 1876. But death came a few months later.

The Chronology of the Development of Cornell Watch Co.
Newark Watch Co. 1864-1870; S#s 6901-12,000.
Cornell Watch Co., Chicago, Ill. 1870-1874; S#s 12,001 to 25,000.
Cornell Watch Co., San Francisco, Calif. 1874-Jan. 1876; S# s 25,001 to 35,000.
California Watch Co., Jan. 1876-mid 1876.

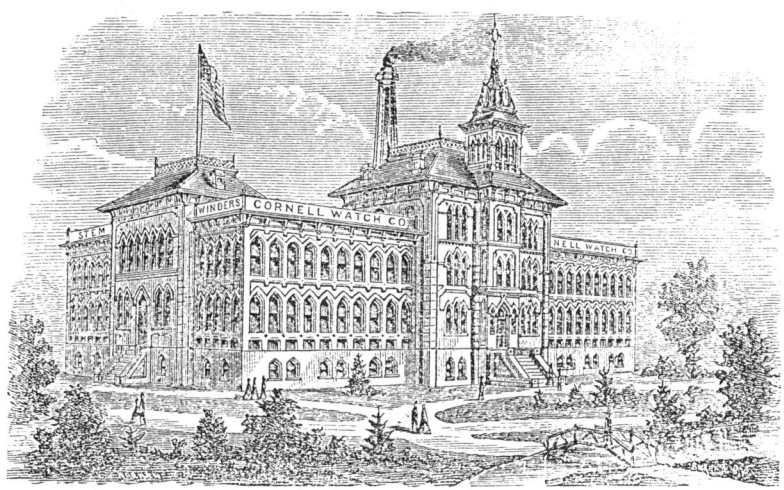

1871 AD for the Cornell Watch Co. Factory

18 SIZE

Grade or Name — Description		Avg	Ex-Fn	Mint
J. C. Adams, 11J, KW	★	$250	$350	$600
C. T. Bowen, FULL, KW	★	400	450	700
C. M. Cady, 15J, SW	★	400	500	700
Cornell W. Co., 7J, San Francisco on mvt., KW	★	800	1,400	2,200
Cornell W. Co., 11J, KW	★	250	300	600
Cornell W. Co., 11J, San Francisco on mvt., KW	★ ★	800	1,400	2,200
Cornell W. Co., 15J, KW	★	350	450	700
Cornell W. Co., 15J, San Francisco on mvt., KW	★	1,000	1,500	2,400
Cornell W. Co., 15J, San Francisco on mvt., SW	★ ★	1,200	1,400	2,000
Paul Cornell, 19J, GJS, HCI5P, SW	★ ★ ★	2,000	2,400	3,600
John Evans, 15J, KW		250	350	500
Excelsior, 15J, FULL, KW, KS	★	350	400	600

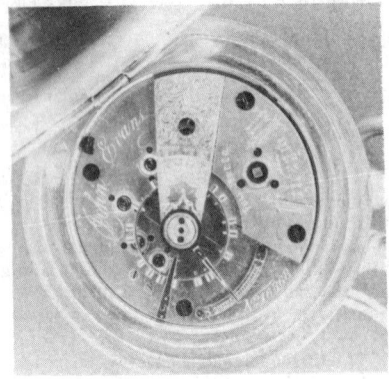

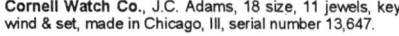

Cornell Watch Co., J.C. Adams, 18 size, 11 jewels, key wind & set, made in Chicago, Ill, serial number 13,647.

Cornell Watch Co., 18 size, 15 jewels, key wind & set, marked "John Evans," serial number 16,868.

Grade or Name — Description		Avg	Ex-Fn	Mint
H. N. Hibbard, 11J, KW, ADJ.	★	$350	$450	$700
C.L. Kidder, 7J, KWKS, OF	★	300	400	600
George F. Root, 15J, KW	★	400	500	800
George Waite, 7J, (Hyde Park), KW	★ ★	350	450	700
E. J. Williams, 7J, KW	★	250	350	500
Eugene Smith, 17J	★	350	450	650
Ladies Stemwind	★	150	200	375

JACOB D. CUSTER

Norristown, Pennsylvania

1840 - 1845

At the age of 19, Jacob Custer repaired his father's watch. He was then asked to repair all the watches within his community. Custer was basically self-taught and had very little formal education and little training in clocks and watches. He made all the parts except the hairspring and fusee chains. The watches were about 14 size, and only 12 to 15 watches were made. The 14S fusee watches had lever escapement, 3/4 plate and were sold in his own gold cases. He made a few chronometers, one with a helical spring.

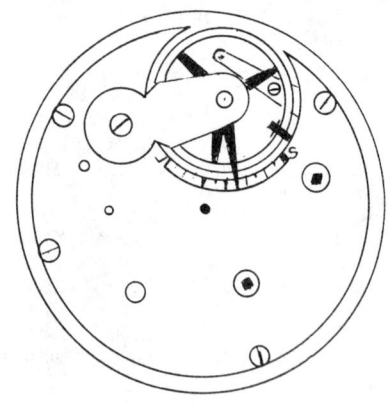

J.D. Custer, 14-16 size, engraved on movement is J.D. Custer, Norristown, Pa. Patented Feb. 4, 1843.

Description		Avg	Ex-Fn	Mint
14S, OF, engraved on mvt. (*J. D. Custer, Patented Feb. 4, 1843*)				
very RARE watch	★ ★ ★ ★ ★	$12,000	$18,000	$30,000

DUDLEY WATCH CO.

Lancaster, Pennsylvania
1920 - 1925

William Wallace Dudley became interested in watches and horology at the age of 13 and became an apprentice making ship chronometers in Canada. When he moved to America, he worked for the South Bend and Illinois Watch companies and the Trenton Watch Co. before going to Hamilton Watch Co. in Lancaster. He left Hamilton at age 69 to start his own watch company. In 1922 his first watches were produced; they were 14S, 19J, and used many Waltham Model 1894 – 1897, 14 size parts, including the train and escapement. The plates and winding mechanism were made at the Dudley plant. Dials and hands were made to Dudley's specifications in Switzerland. At first jewels were obtained from a manufacturer in Lancaster, but by 1925 they were Swiss supplied. The cases came from Wadsworth Keystone and the Star Watch Case Co. Dudley also made a 12S, 19J watch. By 1924, the company was heavily in debt, and on February 20, 1925, a petition for bankruptcy was filed. The Masonic Watch was his most unusual watch.

DUDLEY WATCHES			ESTAMATED TOTAL PRODUCTION	
Dudley Watch Co.	1920-1925	Model No.1	= S#	500—1,900 = 1,400
P. W. Baker Co.	1925-1935	Model No.2	= S#	2,001—4,800 = 2,800
XL Watch Co., N.Y.	1935-1976	Model No.3	= S#	4,801—6,500 = 1,700
				TOTAL = 5,900

🕐 NOTE: Not all movements were finished and sold as complete watches.

Model No. 1, 14S, 19J, OF, can be distinguished by the "Holy Bible" engraved on the winding arbor plate, and a gilded pallet bridge matching the plates.

Model No. 2, 12S, 19J, used the 910 and 912 Hamilton wheels and escapement, has a flat silver-colored Bible.

Model No. 3, 12S, can be distinguished by the silver Bible which was riveted in place and was more three-dimensional. The 3rd wheel bridge was rounded off at one end.

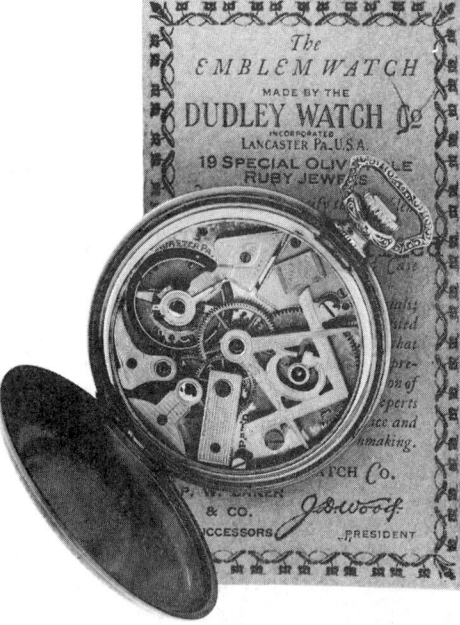

Dudley Watch Co., Model 1, 14 size, 19J., open face, Masonic form plates, flip back, serial # 1232, Ca. 1924.

Dudley Watch Co., Model 2, 14 size, 19J., open face, with original paper. The watch also came with a keystone shaped box, Ca 1927.

12 SIZE - 14 SIZE
"MASONS" MODEL

Grade or Name — Description	Avg	Ex-Fn	Mint
14S, Dudley, 19J, 14K, flip open back, Serial #1 (made 5 experimental models with Serial #1) .... ★	$5,000	$7,000	$10,000
14S, M#1, 19J, OF, 14K, flip open back .... ★	2,500	3,000	4,000
14S, M#1, 19J, OF, 14K, flip open back, w/box & papers .... ★	3,000	3,500	4,500
12S, M#2, 19J, OF, flip open back, GF .... ★	1,500	1,800	2,200
12S, M#2, 19J, OF, 14K, flip open back case .... ★	2,000	2,200	2,600
12S, M#2, 19J, OF, 14K display case .... ★	1,600	1,900	2,400
12S, M#3, 19J, OF, display case, GF .... ★	1,500	1,800	2,200
12S, M#3, 19J, OF, 14K flip open case .... ★	2,000	2,400	2,800

Dudley Watch Co., Model 2, 12 size, 19 jewels, open face, serial number 2,420.

Dudley Watch Co., Model 3, 12 size, 19 jewels, open face. NOTE: 3rd wheel bridge is rounded off at one end.

ELGIN WATCH CO.
(NATIONAL WATCH CO.)
Elgin, Illinois
1864 - 1964

This was the largest watch company in terms of production; in fact, Elgin produced half of the total number of pocket watches (dollar-type not included). Some of the organizers came from Waltham Watch Co., including P. S. Bartlett, D. G. Currier, Otis Hoyt, Charles H. Mason and others. The idea of beginning a large watch company for the mid-West was discussed by J. C. Adams, Bartlett and Blake. After a trip to Waltham, Adams went back to Chicago and approached Benjamin W. Raymond, a former mayor of Chicago, to put up the necessary capital to get the company started. Adams and Raymond succeeded in getting others to pledge their financial support also. The National Watch Co. (Elgin) was formed in August 1864. The factory site was in Elgin, Illinois, where the city had donated 35 acres of land. The factory was completed in 1866, & the 1st. movement was a B. W. Raymond, 18 size, full plate design.

Elgin 1st Movements

Movements	1st App.	1st S#	Movements	1st. App.	1st. S#
18S B. W. Raymond	April 1867	101	10S Lady Elgin	Jan. 1869	40,001
18S H. Z. Culver	July 1867	1,001	10S Frances Rubie	Aug. 1870	50,001
18S J. T. Ryerson	Oct. 1867	5,001	10S Gail Borden	Sept. 1871	185,001
18S H. H. Taylor	Nov. 1867	25,001	10S Dexter Street	Dec. 1871	201,001
18S G. M. Wheeler	Nov. 1867	6,001			
18S Matt Laflin	Jan. 1868	9,001	First Stem Wind	June 1873	
18S W.H. Ferry	No date	30,056	1st Nickel Movement	Aug.15, 1879	
18S J.V. Farwell	No date	30,296	Convertible	Fall 1878	
18S M.D. Ogden	No date	30,387	1st 16 Size watch	No date	600,001
18S Charles Fargo	No date	30,490	18 size with double roller	G# 214	8,400,001
18S Father Time	No date	2,300,001	16 size with double roller	G# 156	10,249,901
18S Overland	No date	6,653,401			
18S Veritas	No date	8,400,001			

The first watch a **B.W. Raymond** was sold April 1, 1867, selling for about $115.00, and was a 18 size, KW and quick train serial # 101. This **First** Pocket Watch, Serial No. 101, **was once again sold for $12,000.00** in 1988 at a SELL in NEW YORK. The first stem wind model was an H. Z. Culver with serial No. 155,001, lever set and quick train. In 1874, the name was changed to the Elgin National Watch Co., and they produced watches into the 1950s. The first **WRIST WATCH** made by Elgin was sold in 1910.

Some Serial Nos. have the first two numbers replace by a letter; i.e., 49,582,000 would be F 582,000.

X= 38 & 39	F= 49
C,E,T &Y= 42	S= 50
L= 43	R= 51
U= 44	P= 52
J= 45	K= 53
V= 46	I = 54
H= 47	
N= 48	

⊕ If the letters do not match the list above; the movement was produced after 1954.

ELGIN ESTIMATED SERIAL NUMBERS AND PRODUCTION DATES

DATE – SERIAL #	DATE–SERIAL #	DATE–SERIAL #
1867 — 10,000	1897 – 7,000,000 Oct.28th	1927 – 30,050,000
1868 — 25,001-Nov.20th	1898 – 7,494,001 May 14th	1928 – 31,599,001-Jan.11
1869 — 40,001-May 20th	1899 – 8,000,000 Jan.18th	1929 – 32,000,000
1870 — 50,001-Aug.24th	1900 – 9,000,000 Nov.14th	1930 – 32,599,001-July
1871 – 185,001-Sep. 8th	1901 – 9,300,000	1931 – 33,000,000
1872 – 201,001-Dec.20th	1902 – 9,600,000	1932 – 33,700,000
1873 – 325,001	1903 – 10,000,000 May 15th	1933 – 34,558,001-July 24th
1874 – 400,001-Aug.28th	1904 – 11,000,000 April 4th	1934 – 35,000,000
1875 – 430,000	1905 – 12,000,000 Oct.6th	1935 – 35,650,000
1876 – 480,000	1906 – 12,500,000	1936 – 36,200,000
1877 – 520,000	1907 – 13,000,000 April 4th	1937 – 36,978,001-July 24th
1878 – 570,000	1908 – 13,500,000	1938 – 37,900,000
1879 – 625,001-Feb.8th	1909 – 14,000,000 Feb.9th	1939 – 38,200,000
1880 – 750,000	1910 – 15,000,000 April 2nd	1940 – 39,100,000
1881 – 900,000	1911 – 16,000,000 July 11th	1941 – 40,200,000
1882 – 1,000,000- March,9th	1912 – 17,000,000 Nov.6th	1942 – 41,100,000
1883 – 1,250,000	1913 – 17,339,001- Apr.14th	1943 – 42,200,000
1884 – 1,500,000	1914 – 18,000,000	1944 – 42,600,000
1885 – 1,855,001-May 28th	1915 – 18,587,001-Feb.11th	1945 – 43,200,000
1886 – 2,000,000- Aug. 4th	1916 – 19,000,000	1946 – 44,000,000
1887 – 2,500,000	1917 – 20,031,001-June 27th	1947 – 45,000,000
1888 – 3,000,000 June 20th	1918 – 21,000,000	1948 – 46,000,000
1889 – 3,500,000	1919 – 22,000,000	1949 – 47,000,000
1890 – 4,000,000 Aug.16th	1920 – 23,000,000	1950 – 48,000,000
1891 – 4,449,001-Mar.26th	1921 – 24,321,001-July 6th	1951 – 50,000,000
1892 – 4,600,000	1922 – 25,100,000	1952 – 52,000,000
1893 – 5,000,000 July 1st	1923 – 26,050,000	1953 – 53,500,000
1894 – 5,500,000	1924 – 27,000,000	1954 -- 54,000,000
1895 – 6,000,000 Nov.26th	1925 – 28,421,001-July 14th	1955 – 54,500,000
1896 – 6,500,000	1926 – 29,100,000	1956 – 55,000,000

⊕The above list is provided for determining the **APPROXIMATE** age of your watch. Match serial number with date. Watches were not necessarily *SOLD* and *DELIVERED* in the exact order of manufactured or production dates.

It required several months for raw material to emerge as a finished movement. All the while the factory is producing all sizes, models and grades. The numbering system was basically *"consecutive"*, *due to demand a batch of movements could be side tracked, thus allowing a different size and model to move ahead to meet this demand. Therefore, the dates some movements were* **sold** *and delivered to the trade, may not be "consecutive".*

⊕   Generic, nameless or unmarked grades for watch movements are listed under the Company name or initials of the Company, etc. by size, jewel count and description.

The B. W. Raymond grade 571 was introduced in 1950 with the following three changes first, friction jewels; second, a solid balance wheel; third, a "DuraPower" mainspring. This was also the 47th model made by the Elgin Watch Co.. This model conformed with all railroad specifications as 16 size, 21 jewels and (8) eight adjustment; the movement is lever-set has a white enamel dial & black numbers.

Some collectors seek out low serial numbers and will usually pay a premium for them. The lower the number, the more desirable the watch. The table shown below lists the first serial number of each size watch made by Elgin.

Size	1st Serial Nos.	Size	1st Serial Nos.
18	101	10	40,001
17	356,001	6	570,001
16	600,001	0	2,889,001
14	351,001		

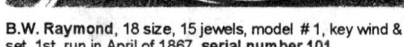

B.W. Raymond, 18 size, 15 jewels, model # 1, key wind & set, 1st. run in April of 1867, **serial number 101.**

Father Time, 18 size, 21 jewels, model #8 with wind indicator, free sprung model, serial number 22,888,020

18 SIZE

Grade or Name — Description	Avg	Ex-Fn	Mint
Advance, 11J, gilded, KW, HC, FULL	$65	$95	$200
Age, 7J, gilded, KW, FULL, OF/HC	65	95	200
Atlas Watch Co., 7J, HC, LS, FULL	65	95	200
California Watch, 15J, gilded, HC, KW, KS, FULL	175	200	350
Chief, 7J, gilded, KW, FULL, HC	65	95	200
Convertible, 7J= G#98, 11J=G399	100	150	225
Convertible, 15J=G#100, M#6	125	175	250
Culver, 15J, gilded, KW, KS, FULL, HC, ADJ, low S#	200	275	450
Culver, 15J, gilded, KW, KS, FULL, HC, ADJ	150	195	300
Culver, 15J, KW, KS, **14K, HC**	600	800	1,200
Culver, 15J, gilded, KW, KS, FULL, HC	100	175	250
Culver, 15J, gilded, SW, FULL, HC	65	125	175
Culver, 15J, gilded, KW, FULL, LS, HC	100	125	200

🕐 **Generic, nameless or unmarked** grades for watch movements are listed under the Company name or initials of the Company, etc. by size, jewel count and description.

Grade or Name — Description	Avg	Ex-Fn	Mint
Elgin W. Co., 7J, OF, SW	$50	$70	$125
Elgin W. Co., 7J, KW, gilded, HC	60	80	200
Elgin W. Co., 11J, SW/KW, LS	60	80	175
Elgin W. Co., 11J, LS, SW, HC, **9K-10K**	250	300	500
Elgin W. Co., 11J, LS, SW, HC, Silveroid	50	70	125
Elgin W. Co., 11J, LS,KW/ SW, OF	50	70	125
Elgin W. Co., 13J, KW/SW, PS/LS, OF	50	70	125
Elgin W. Co., 13J, KW/SW, PS/LS, HC	50	70	150
Elgin W. Co., 15J, SW, LS, OF	50	70	135
Elgin W. Co., 15J, KW, LS, HC	125	150	300
Elgin W. Co., 15J, KW/SW, LS, HC	50	70	165
Elgin W. Co., 15J, KW, **hidden key, COIN silver case**	200	275	450

🕐 Watches listed in this book are priced at the collectable retail level, **as complete** watches having an original 14k gold-filled case and *Key Wind* with silver, an original white enamel single sunk dial, and with the entire original movement in good working order with no repairs needed.

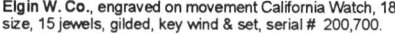

Elgin W. Co., engraved on movement California Watch, 18 size, 15 jewels, gilded, key wind & set, serial # 200,700.

Convertible, 18 size, 15 jewels, converts to either hunting or open face, Gilded, G#100, S#2,226,720.

Grade or Name — Description	Avg	Ex-Fn	Mint
Elgin W. Co., 15-17J, KW/SW, LS, **box–hinge YGF, HC**	$175	$250	$400
Elgin W. Co., 15-17J, KW/SW, LS, **box–hinge 14K, HC**	1,000	1,400	2,000
Elgin W. Co., 15-17, KW/SW, LS, **Multi-color box YGF, HC**	450	550	750
Elgin W. Co., 15-17J, KW/SW, **14K case, OF**	400	450	650
Elgin W. Co., 15-17J, KW/SW, **14K case, HC**	450	600	800
Elgin W. Co., 15-17J, KW/SW, **18K case, HC**	600	700	1,000
Elgin W. Co., 15-17J,KW/ SW, **Multi-color, 14K, HC**	2,000	2,500	3,500
Elgin W. Co., 15-17J, KW/SW, LS, **COIN Silver** 6 oz, OF	275	350	550
Elgin W. Co., 15-17J, KW/SW, LS, **COIN Silver**, OF	100	150	250
Elgin W. Co., 17J, KW/SW, LS, OF	60	90	150
Elgin W. Co., 17J, SW, LS or PS, HC	100	125	250
Elgin W. Co., 21J, SW, LS or PS, OF	225	250	400
Elgin W. Co., 21J, SW, LS, **box case, GF,OF**	325	350	500
Elgin W. Co., 21J, LS, **HC, 14K**	700	800	1,000
Elgin W. Co., 21J, SW, LS, Silveroid	225	250	350
Elgin W. Co., 21J, SW, LS, HC	325	350	500
Elgin W. Co., 21J, **Wind Indicator**	1,200	1,400	2,000
Elgin W. Co., 21J, **Wind Indicator, free sprung**	1,400	1,600	2,200
Elgin W. Co., 23J, SW, LS, OF	350	400	550
Elgin W. Co., 23J, SW, LS, HC ★	450	500	650

Above example of the *nameless* or unmarked *grades* for watch movements which are listed under the Company **name or initials** of the Company, (Elgin W. Co.) etc. by size, jewel count & description.

🕐 **Generic, nameless or unmarked** grades for watch movements are listed under the Company name or initials of the Company, etc. by size, jewel count and description.

Pennsylvania Railroad Co. on dial. B.W. Raymond on movement. One of the first railroad watches commissioned by Penn. RR Co., 18 size, 15 jewels, key wind and set, serial number 123,245, CA. 1874.

Grade or Name — Description	Avg	Ex-Fn	Mint
Charles Fargo, 7J, gilded, KW, HC	$175	$200	$400
J. V. Farwell, 11J, gilded, KW, HC ★	275	300	450
Father Time, 17J, NI, FULL, OF	125	150	300
Father Time, 17J, SW, OF, Silveroid	125	150	300
Father Time, 17J, SW, HC	200	250	400
Father Time, **20J**, NI, FULL, HC or OF ★	325	400	550
Father Time, 21J, NI, SW, FULL, GJS, OF	225	275	450
Father Time, 21J, NI, SW, 3/4, GJS, DMK, HC	300	375	500
Father Time, 21J, NI, SW, 3/4, GJS, OF	225	275	400
Father Time, 21J, GJT, ADJ.5P, Diamond end stone, OF	250	300	450
Father Time, 21J, NI, SW, 3/4, OF, GJS, **wind indicator**	1,300	1,600	2,000
Father Time, 21J, SW, 3/4, GJS, **wind indicator, HC** ★★★	3,000	3,500	5,500
Father Time, G#367, 21J, NI, SW, 3/4, OF, GJS, military style, **wind indicator,** free sprung, **602 sterling case**	1,600	1,800	2,600
Father Time, G#367, 21J, NI, SW, 3/4, OF, GJS, military style, **wind indicator,** free sprung, **35 size with gimbals & Box**	1,300	1,500	2,100
85 size, Model# 600, 14J, **free sprung,** helical hair spring, dent escapement, **wind indicator,** Gimbals & Box	1,400	1,600	2,200
W. H. Ferry, 15J, gilded, KW, HC	145	175	300
W. H. Ferry, 11J, gilded, KW, HC	145	175	300
Mat Laflin, 7J, gilded, KW, HC	145	175	300
National W. Co., 7J, KW, KS	95	125	200
National W. Co., 11J, KW, KS	95	125	200
National W. Co., 15J, KW, KS	100	135	200
M. D. Ogden, 15J, KW, HC	125	145	200
M. D. Ogden, 11J, gilded, KW, HC	125	145	200
Order of Railway Conductors, 17J, LS, OF ★★	700	800	1,200
Overland, 17J, NI, KW, HC	100	125	225
Overland, 17J, NI, SW, HC	75	100	200
Pennsylvania Railroad Co. on dial, B. W. Raymond on mvt., 15J, KW, KS (1st RR watches) ★★★	2,200	3,200	5,000
Railway Timer, 15J, FULL, HC ★	350	400	700

IMPORTANT NOTE: Railroad Standards, Railroad Approved & Railroad Grade **terminology,** as defined and used in this <u>*BOOK*</u>.
1. **RAILROAD STANDARDS** = A commission or board appointed by the railroad companies outlined a set of **guidelines** to be accepted or approved by each railroad line.
2. **RAILROAD APPROVED** = A <u>*LIST*</u> of watches each railroad line would approve if purchased by their employee's. (this list changed through the years).
3. **RAILROAD GRADE** = A watch made by manufactures to meet or exceed the guidelines set by the railroad **standards**. Grades such as 992, Vanguard and B.W. Raymond, etc.
🕐 **Some GRADES exceeded** the R.R. standards such as 23 jewels, diamond end stone, gold train, raised gold jewel settings, double sunk dial and the list goes on. Examples: such as Veritas, Sangamo, 950 & Riverside Maximus and many others.

B.W. **Raymond**, 18 size, 19 jewels, wind indicator. Note small winding indicator gear next to crown wheel.

H.H. **Taylor**, 18 size, 15 jewels, key wind & set, serial number 288,797.

Grade or Name — Description	Avg	Ex-Fn	Mint
B. W. Raymond, 15-17J, KW, low S# under 200	$700	$1,000	$1,500
B. W. Raymond, 15-17J, KW, low S# 201 to 500	500	600	1,000
B. W. Raymond, 15J, gilded, KW, FULL, HC	145	175	300
B. W. Raymond, 17J, gilded, KW, FULL, HC	145	175	300
B. W. Raymond, 15J, SW, HC	95	125	200
B. W. Raymond, 15J, **box case 14K**	900	1,200	2,000
B. W. Raymond, 17J, all G#s, NI, FULL, OF	75	100	200
B. W. Raymond, 17J, NI, FULL, HC	125	175	300
B. W. Raymond, 17J, gilded, NI, SW, FULL, ADJ	95	125	200
B. W. Raymond, 17J, **Wind Indicator**	750	850	1,000
B. W. Raymond, 19J, NI, 3/4, SW, OF, GJS, G#240, GT	200	225	300
B. W. Raymond, 19J, 3/4, GJS, **jeweled barrel, Wind Indicator**	850	1,000	1,400
B. W. Raymond, 19J, 3/4, GJS, GT, Diamond end stone	150	175	300
B. W. Raymond, 21J, 3/4, GJS, GT, Diamond end stone, OF	250	275	400
B. W. Raymond, 21J, SW, Silveroid	200	250	300
B. W. Raymond, 21J, SW, GJS, GT, G#274, HC ★★	350	400	600
B. W. Raymond, 21J, NI, 3/4, SW, GJS, G#389 & 390, GT, OF	225	275	425
B. W. Raymond, 21J, NI, 3/4, SW, GJS, **Wind Indicator**, DMK	1,200	1,400	2,000
J. T. Ryerson, 7J, gilded, FULL, KW, HC	125	145	300
Solar W. Co., 15J, Multi-color dial	135	165	300
Standard, 17J, OF, LS	125	150	300
Sundial, 7J, SW, PS	75	95	150
H. H. Taylor, 15J, gilded, FULL, KW, HC	100	125	200
H. H. Taylor, 15J, NI, FULL, KW, DMK, HC	100	125	200
H. H. Taylor, 15J, NI, FULL, **SW**, HC, DMK, quick train	125	150	250
H. H. Taylor, 15J, SW, Silveroid	95	125	150
H. H. Taylor, 15J, SW, slow train	95	125	150

⊕ Some watch manufacturers personalize watches for jobbers or jewelry firms, with exclusive private signed or marked movements. The valuable collectable watches are listed under the signed or marked movement. Other exclusive private signed or marked movements will have equivalent value are only slightly higher value and should be compared to **Generic or Nameless** movements. Railroad signed or marked (dials & movements) are usually more collectable & higher in value.

⊕ **Generic, nameless or unmarked grades** for watch movements are listed under the Company name or initials of the Company, etc. by size, jewel count and description.

⊕ Some grades are not included. Their values can be determined by comparing with **similar** age, size, metal content, style, models and grades listed.

Veritas, 18 size, 23 jewels, solid gold train, gold jewel settings, diamond end stone, serial number 9,542,678.

G.M. Wheeler, Grade 369, 18 size, 17 jewels, open face, gold jewel settings, serial number 14,788,315

The word **VERITAS** translated is *"TRUTH"*.

Grade or Name — Description	Avg	Ex-Fn	Mint
Veritas, 21J, 3/4, NI, GJS, DMK, GT, G#239, OF	$275	$300	$500
Veritas, 21J, 3/4, GJS, GT, Diamond end stones	285	325	525
Veritas, 21J, SW, PS, GJS, GT, HC	350	400	600
Veritas, 21J, SW, LS, GJS, GT, HC	350	400	600
Veritas, 21J, 3/4, GJS, GT, Diamond end stones, G#274, HC	350	425	600
Veritas, 21J, 3/4, NI, GJS, **Wind Indicator**, DMK, G#239, OF	1,600	1,800	2,600
Veritas, 21J, 3/4, NI, GJS, **Wind Indicator**, DMK, G#274, HC ★★	3,500	4,000	6,000
Veritas, 23J, 3/4, NI, GJS, OF, DMK, GT	400	450	500
Veritas, 23J, 3/4, NI, GJS, OF, DMK, GT, Diamond end stone	400	465	525
Veritas, 23J, G#214, 3/4, NI, GJS, **Wind Indicator,** OF	1,600	1,800	2,600
Veritas, 23J, G#94, **Wind Indicator**, *"Free Sprung"*, OF ★★★	2,000	2,200	3,000
Veritas, 23J, **G#214**, SW, OF	400	450	600
Veritas, 23J, 3/4, SW, NI, GJS, GT, LS, HC ★★★	450	550	800
Veritas, 23J, SW, **OF, 14K**	625	800	1,000
G. M. Wheeler, 11J, gilded, KW, HC	75	100	200
G. M. Wheeler, 13-15J, gilded, FULL, KW, SW	75	100	200
G. M. Wheeler, 15J, NI, FULL, KW, DMK, HC	100	125	225
G. M. Wheeler, 15J, SW, NI, FULL, DMK, OF	55	75	160
G. M. Wheeler, 17J, KW, NI, FULL, DMK, OF	100	125	225
G. M. Wheeler, 17J, SW, NI, DMK, OF	75	100	200

MOVEMENTS WITH NO NAME

Grade or Name — Description	Avg	Ex-Fn	Mint
No. 5 & No. 17, 7J, gilded, FULL, HC	$75	$95	$175
No. 23 & No. 18, 11J, gilded, FULL, HC	85	110	175
No. 69, 15J, M#1, KW, quick train, HC	95	125	200
No. 150, 21J, full plate, GJS, LS	200	225	400
No. 274, 21J., marked **274**, GT, Adj.5p, diamond end stone	225	250	450
No. 316, 15J, NI, FULL, HC, DMK	100	125	200
No. 317, 15J, NI, FULL, ADJ, OF, DMK	100	125	200

🕐 Generic, nameless or unmarked grades for watch movements are listed under the Company name or initials of the Company, etc. by size, jewel count and description.

🕐 Pricing in this Guide are fair market price for COMPLETE watches which are reflected from the **"NAWCC"** National and regional shows.

🕐 Watches listed in this book are priced at the collectable retail level, **as complete** watches having an original 14k gold-filled case and *Key Wind* with silver, an original white enamel single sunk dial, and with the entire original movement in good working order with no repairs needed.

🕐 Generic, nameless or unmarked grades for watch movements are listed under the Company name or initials of the Company, etc. by size, jewel count and description.

Grade or Name — Description	Avg	Ex-Fn	Mint
No. 326, 15J, OF	$85	$100	$200
No. 327, 15J, HC	100	125	200
No. 331, **16J,** M# 11, NI, OF ★	95	125	200
No. 335, 17J, HC	95	125	200
No. 336, 17J, NI, FULL, OF, DMK	95	125	200
No. 345, 19J, GJS, 2-Tone, HC ★	600	700	1,000
No. 348, 21J, NI, FULL, GJS, DMK, HC	225	250	500
No. 349, 21J, , LS, **MARKED LOANER,** OF ★	300	375	600
No. 378, 17-19J, NI, FULL, HC, DMK	125	150	300
No. 379, 17-19J, OF	125	150	300

Elgin Watch Co., Leader, 17 size, 11 jewels, key wind & set, made for English market, serial number 418,220.

Elgin Watch Co., 17 size, 7 jewels, key wind & set, serial number 199,076. Made for Kennedy & Co.

17 SIZE

Grade or Name — Description	Avg	Ex-Fn	Mint
Avery, 7J, gilded, KW, FULL, HC	$85	$100	$200
Inter-Ocean, 7J, KWKS, HC ★★	400	500	650
Leader, 7J, gilded, KW, FULL, HC	60	80	150
Leader, 11J, gilded, KW, FULL, HC,	60	80	150
Sunshine, 15J, KW, KS from back	100	125	175
M#11, 14, 15, 51, 59, 7J, gilded, KW, FULL, HC	100	125	175
17 Size, KW, Silveroid	60	80	125

16 SIZE

Grade or Name — Description	Avg	Ex-Fn	Mint
Braille or Blind Man's Watch, 9-17J, HC	$125	$150	$225
Convertible Model, 7J=G#47 & 11J=G#93, 13J=G#48, 3/4, gilded	100	125	200
Convertible Model, 13J=G#90, 3F BRG	125	150	225
Convertible Model, 15J=G#49, 3/4, gilded	100	125	200
Convertible Model, 15JG#50, 3/4, NI, ADJ,	125	150	225
Convertible Model, 15J=G#85 & G#86, 3F BRG	175	200	250
Convertible Model, 15J, 3/4, ADJ, DMK, GJS	125	150	300
Convertible Model, 15JG#50, 3/4, NI, ADJ, **14K,** HC	800	900	1,200

🕐 Pricing in this Guide are fair market price for COMPLETE watches which are reflected from the **"NAWCC"** National and regional shows.

Elgin Watch Co., 16 size, 21 jewels, 3/4, Convertible Model converts to open face or hunting case, S# 607,061.

Elgin W. Co., Convertible Model, 16 size, 21 jewels, three-fingered bridge model, adjusted, serial # 4,907,178.

Grade or Name — Description	Avg	Ex-Fn	Mint
Convertible Model, 21J=G#72 & G#91, 3/4, NI	$200	$250	$350
Convertible Model, 21J=G#91, 3F BRG ★★★	1,500	1,700	2,200
Convertible Model, 21J, G#72, 3/4, ADJ, GJS, **14K** ★★★	2,000	2,200	2,800
Convertible Model, 21J, G#91, 3F BRG, **14K** ★★★	2,200	2,400	3,000
Doctors Watch, 13J, 4th Model, NI, GT, sweep second hand, G#89 gilded, GF	250	350	550
Doctors Watch, 15J, 4th Model, NI, GT, sweep second hand, G# 83 gilded & G#84 nickel, GF case	250	350	550
Doctors Watch, 15J, 4th Model, gilded, sweep second hand, coin silver case	300	400	600
Doctors Watch, 15J, 4th Model, sweep second hand, **14K, OF**	700	800	1,200

Elgin Watch Co., 16 size, Multi- Color Gold hunting case, the locomotive has a **diamond** in the lantern, the case has white, yellow, rose flowers & green leaf designs, Ca.1880.

Doctors Watch, 16 size, 15 jewels, fourth model, gold jewel settings, gold train, sweep second hand, serial number 926,458.

🕐 **Generic, nameless or unmarked** grades for watch movements are listed under the Company name or initials of the Company, etc. by size, jewel count and description.

Grade or Name — Description	Avg	Ex-Fn	Mint
Elgin W. Co., 7-9J, OF	$45	$65	$125
Elgin W. Co., 7-9J, HC	60	80	150
Elgin W. Co., 11J, OF	45	80	125
Elgin W. Co., 11J, HC	60	80	165
Elgin W. Co., 13J, OF	45	65	125
Elgin W. Co., 13J, OF, Silveroid	45	65	125
Elgin W. Co., 13J, HC	50	70	150
Elgin W. Co., 15J, HC	50	70	175
Elgin W. Co., 15-16J, OF	50	70	150
Elgin W. Co., 15J, OF **14K case**	285	325	600
Elgin W. Co., 15J, HC, **14K**	450	550	750
Elgin W. Co., 15J, **multi-color gold +diamond, HC, 14K**	1,500	2,000	3,000
Elgin W. Co., 17J, OF	50	80	150
Elgin W. Co., 17J, LS, **multi-color HC, YGF**	250	300	600
Elgin W. Co., 17J, **multi-color HC, 14K**	1,000	1,200	2,500
Elgin W. Co., 17J, **14K, HC**	350	400	600
Elgin W. Co., 17J, G#280, 9th model, ADJ5P	90	150	200
Elgin W. Co., 17J, HC	90	165	250
Elgin W. Co., 19J, OF, LS	90	150	200
Elgin W. Co., 21J, HC	150	200	400
Elgin W. Co., 21J, OF, **Silveroid**	100	150	300
Elgin W. Co., 21J, OF	125	150	300
Elgin W. Co., 23J, OF	250	300	450
3F Bridge Model, 15J, NI, DMK	75	125	200
3F Bridge Model, 17J, Adj.3P, NI, DMK, GJS	100	125	200
3F Bridge Model, 17J, Adj.5P, NI, DMK, GJS, GT	125	150	275
3F Bridge Model, 21J, Adj.5P, NI, DMK, GJS, GT	400	500	650
Father Time, 17J, 3/4, NI, OF, GJS, DR, DMK	125	150	300
Father Time, 21J, 3/4, NI, HC, GJS, DR, DMK, ADJ.5P	225	250	400
Father Time, 21J, 3/4, NI, OF, GJS, DR, **Wind Indicator**	650	850	1,400
Father Time, 21J, 3/4, NI, GJS, DR, **pendant set**, ADJ.5P, OF ... ★	250	300	500
Father Time, 21J, NI, GJS, DR, ADJ.5P, GT, OF	200	250	400
Lord Elgin, 21J, GJS, DR, Adj.5P, 3F BRG, **14K, OF** .... ★ ★	1,450	1,750	2,400
Lord Elgin, 23J, GJS, DR, Adj.5P, 3/4, **14K, OF** .... ★ ★	1,500	1,800	2,500
Lord Elgin, 23J, GJS, DR, Adj.5P, 3/4, Gold filled OF .... ★ ★	1,000	1,200	1,800

ELGIN W. Co., Chronograph, 16 size, 16 jewels, model # 4, lever set.

Father Time, 16 size, 21 jewels, gold train; Note model 19 up and down wind indicator movement does not show the differential wheel as does the 18 size, S# 18,106,465.

🕐 Pricing in this Guide are fair market price for COMPLETE watches which are reflected from the **"NAWCC"** National and regional shows.

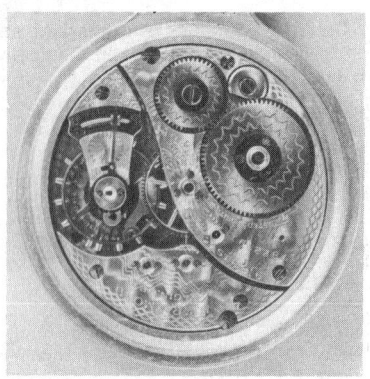

Lord Elgin, 16 size, 21 jewels, gold train, raised gold jewel settings, 3 finger bridge, serial number 10,249,819.

B.W. Raymond, 16 size, 19 jewels, gold jewel settings, Grade 350, serial number 17,822,991.

Grade or Name — Description	Avg	Ex-Fn	Mint
B. W. Raymond, 17J, 3/4, GJS, **14K, OF**	$400	$500	$700
B. W. Raymond, 17J, 3/4, GJS, SW, HC	300	400	500
B. W. Raymond, 17J, 3F BRG .... ★ ★	400	500	700
B. W. Raymond, 17J, LS, NI, **Wind Indicator** .... ★ ★	800	900	1,300
B. W. Raymond, 17J, GJS, SW, Adj., ALL G#s, OF	150	200	250
B. W. Raymond, 17J, 3/4, GJS, DR, Adj.5P, DMK	175	225	300
B. W. Raymond, 19J, 3/4, GJS, DR, Adj.5P, DMK, OF	195	225	300
B. W. Raymond, 19J, (Elgin **The Railroad**er on dial) Adj.5P, OF.	400	500	700
B. W. Raymond, 19J, OF, **14K, 30 DWT**	400	500	700
B. W. Raymond, 19J, 3/4, GJS, DR, Adj.5P, DMK, **Wind Indicator**	575	675	900
B. W. Raymond, 19J, M#8, G# 372, 455, Adj.5P, OF	175	200	300
B. W. Raymond, 19J, GJS, G#371, 401,Adj.5P, HC	200	250	400
B. W. Raymond, 21J, **14K, OF**	450	500	700
B. W. Raymond, 21J, G#472, 478, 506, 571, 581, 590, Adj.5P, OF	175	225	400
B. W. Raymond, 21J, 3/4, GJS, DR, Adj.5P, HC	300	350	500
B. W. Raymond, 21J, 3/4, GJS, DR, Adj.5P, DMK, OF	175	250	350
B. W. Raymond, 21J, **gold flashed movement**, OF	200	250	500
B. W. Raymond, 21J, 3/4, GJS, DR, Adj.5P, DMK,**Wind Indicator**	625	700	1,000
B. W. Raymond, 21J, 3/4, GJS, DR, **Adj.6P**, DMK,**Wind Indicator**	625	700	1,000
B. W. Raymond, 22J, WWII Model, sweep second hand	225	275	450
B. W. Raymond, 23J, 3/4, GJS, DR, Adj.5P, G#376, 494, 540	375	425	550
B. W. Raymond, 23J, 3/4, GJS, DR, Adj.5P, DMK, **Wind Indicator**	900	1,100	1,600
B. W. Raymond, 23J, 3/4, GJS, DR, **Adj.6P**, DMK, **Wind Indicator**	900	1,100	1,600
B. W. Raymond, 23J, 3/4, GJS, DR, Adj.5P, DMK,**Wind Indicator** military style	800	1,000	1,400

14K White or Green
Gold Filled
Specially Designed
Screw Case

Price $35.30

12K-Gold Filled
Specially Designed
Screw Case

Price $31.65

10K-Gold Filled
Specially Designed
Screw Case

Price $31.65

Winding Indicator $3.50 extra

AD
Oct. 15th, 1926

B. W. Raymond Movement
16 Size
21 Jewels
8 Adjustments, 5 of them position
Supplied with Montgomery Dial if desired

Veritas, 16 size, 23 jewels, (Veritas = "TRUTH"), solid gold train, gold jeweled settings, S# 16,678,681.

Elgin Watch Co., LORD ELGIN, Grade 351, 16 size, 23 J., gold train, gold jewel settings, serial number 12,718,340. NOTE: This watch came from the first run of Lord Elgins.

Grade or Name — Description		Avg	Ex-Fn	Mint
Veritas, 19J, G# 401, GJS, Adj. 5P., HC	★	$375	$450	$600
Veritas, 21J, GJS, DR, Adj.5P, DMK, 3/4, **Wind Indicator**		1,000	1,200	1,600
Veritas, 21J, 3F brg, GJS, G#360	★	375	400	600
Veritas, 21J, GJS, DR, Adj.5P, DMK, 3/4, G#401, HC		325	400	600
Veritas, 21J, GJS, SW, Grade 360	★	375	400	600
Veritas, 21J, GJS, SW, Adj.5P, OF, Grade 270 & 375		250	300	450
Veritas, 23J, GJS, Adj.5P, **14K, OF**		600	675	900
Veritas, 23J, GJS, Adj.5P, **HC**		500	550	750
Veritas, 23J, GJS, DR, Adj.5P, 3/4, G# 375- 376- 453, OF		350	400	600
Veritas, 23J, GJS, DR, Adj.5P, DMK, 3/4, Diamond end stone, Grade 350	★	350	400	700
Veritas, 23J, GJS, DR, Adj.5P, Grade 453 & 376 DMK, 3/4, **Wind Indicator**		1,200	1,400	2,200
G. M. Wheeler, 17J, DR, Adj.3P, DMK, 3/4		60	80	150
G. M. Wheeler, 17J, 3F BRG		60	80	200
G. M. Wheeler, 17J, **HC, 14K**		350	400	600
WWII Model, 17J, OF		100	150	200
WWII Model, 21J, OF		200	225	400
M#13, 9J, HC		85	100	150
M#48, 13J, HC		85	100	150

(Add $50 to $75 to hunting case models listed as open face)

MODELS WITH NO NAMES

Grade or Name — Description		Avg	Ex-Fn	Mint
Grade #72, 21J, M# 1, ADJ, HC	★ ★ ★	$1,500	$2,000	$3,000
Grade #91, 21J, 3F BRG	★ ★ ★	1,800	2,000	3,500
Grade #145, 19J, GJS, BRG, HC	★ ★	400	550	900
Grade #155, 17J, GT, GJS, HC		100	120	200
Grade #156, 21J, 3/4, NI, DR, DMK, GT, GJS, HC	★	375	425	700
Grade #156, 21J, 3/4, NI, DR, DMK, GT, GJS, HC, **14K**	★	600	700	900
Grade #162, 21J, SW, PS, NI, GJS, GT, OF	★	300	365	600
Grade #270, 21J, 3F BRG, GJS, marked mvt.		275	325	450
Grade #280, 17J, 3F BRG, marked on mvt.		125	150	300
Grade #290 HC& #291 OF, 7J, 3/4, NI, DMK		75	95	175

🕐 Generic, nameless or unmarked grades for watch movements are listed under the Company name or initials of the Company, etc. by size, jewel count and description.

🕐 Watches listed in this book are priced at the collectable retail level, as complete watches having an original 14k gold-filled case and Key Wind with silver, an original white enamel single sunk dial, and with the entire original movement in good working order with no repairs needed.

Grade or Name — Description	Avg	Ex-Fn	Mint
Grade #291, 7J, 3/4, HC, **14K**	$350	$450	$600
Grade #312 & #313, 15J, 3/4, NI, DR, DMK, OF	75	100	175
Grade # 340, 17J, 3 finger bridge, OF	95	100	150
Grade #372, 19J, M#15, LS, OF, Adj.5P	250	300	400
Grade #374, 21J, M#15, LS, OF, Adj.5P	275	325	500
Grade #381 & #382, 17J, 3/4, NI, DR, DMK, OF	85	125	250
Grade#401, 19J, M#17, LS, HC	250	300	400
Grade #540, 23J, Adj.5P, OF	250	350	450
Grade #572, 19J, Adj.5P, OF	100	150	250
Grade #573, 17J, Adj.5P, OF	90	110	175
Grade #575, 15J, Adj.3P, OF	60	70	150
Grade #581, 21J, Adj.5P, center sec, hacking, Army, OF	200	250	400
Grade # 845, 23J, Adj., (by **Buren** W. Co.) Swiss	60	70	150

14 SIZE

Grade or Name — Description	Avg	Ex-Fn	Mint
Lord Elgin, 17J, SS, OF	$80	$110	$200
7J, M#1, gilded, KW, **14K, HC**	250	300	400
7J, M#1, gilded, KW, YGF, HC	50	70	100
11J, M#1, gilded, KW, YGF, HC	50	70	100
11J, M#1, gilded, KW, YGF, OF	50	70	100
13J, M#1, gilded, KW, OF	50	70	100
15J, M#1, gilded, KW, OF	50	70	100
7J, M#2, SW, OF	50	70	100
15J, M#2, SW, OF	50	70	100
15J, M#2, SW, **14K, HC**	225	250	400
15J, M#1, grade # 46, KW, 3/4, HC	60	80	150

ELGIN, 14 size, model # 1, grade # 46, 3/4 plate design, key wind and key set, hunting case, serial # 474,414.

ELGIN EIGHT DAY, 12 size, 21 jewels, wind indicator, bridge movement, open face, serial number 12,345,678.

12 SIZE

Grade or Name — Description		Avg	Ex -Fn	Mint
Eight Day, 21J, 8-Day Wind Indicator, BRG	★ ★ ★ ★ ★	$2,500	$3,000	$3,500

🕐 Pricing in this Guide are fair market price for COMPLETE watches which are reflected from the **"NAWCC"** National and regional shows.

ELGIN W. Co., dial signed "U.S. Calendar Watch Co.",   ELGIN W. Co., 12 size with Masonic dial, Ca. 1930.
12 size, hand for date of month & day of week.

🕐 Generic, nameless or unmarked grades for watch movements are listed under the Company
name or initials of the Company, etc. by size, jewel count and description.

Grade or Name — Description	Avg	Ex-Fn	Mint
Elgin W. Co. #30, 7J, gilded, **KW, OF**	$70	$85	$200
Elgin W. Co. #189, 19J, HC	50	70	150
Elgin W. Co. #190-194, 23J, GJS, Adj.5P, NI, DMK, GT, OF	150	175	300
Elgin W. Co. #190-194, 23J, GJS, Adj.5P, NI, DMK, GT, HC	175	200	300
Elgin W. Co. #236 & #237, 21J, GJS, Adj.5P, NI, DMK, GT, OF	100	125	175
Elgin W. Co. #236 & #237, 21J, GJS, Adj.5P, NI, DMK, GT, HC.	125	150	200
Elgin W. Co. #301 & #302, 7J, HC	40	60	125
Elgin W. Co. #314 & #315, 15J, HC	50	80	175
Elgin W. Co. #383 & #384, 17J, HC	40	70	125
Elgin W. Co., 7-15J, **14K, Multi-color**	500	600	1,000
Elgin W. Co., 7-15J, OF, GF	65	75	125
Elgin W. Co., 7-15J, **HC, 14K**	225	275	500
Elgin W. Co., 17J, OF,GF	50	70	125
Elgin W. Co., 17J, **OF, 14K**	150	200	400
Elgin W. Co., 19J, OF, gold filled	50	80	165
Elgin W. Co., 19J, HC, gold filled	50	80	175
Elgin W. Co., 19J, **HC, 14K**	250	300	500
Elgin W. Co., 19J, **14K, OF**	125	200	400
Elgin W. Co., 21J, OF, gold filled case	75	100	200
12 size Model 2 & 3 spread to fit a 16 size			
Elgin W. Co., 15-17J, Model 2 **spread to 16 size**, OF	$40	$60	$120
Elgin W. Co., 15-17J, Model 3 **spread to 16 size**, HC	50	70	165
Elgin W. Co., 19-21J, Model 2 **spread to 16 size**, OF	70	100	175
Elgin W. Co., 19-21J, Model 3 **spread to 16 size, HC**	75	125	225
STANDARD 12 SIZE (continued)			
Elete, 17J, GJS, Adj,4P, OF	$35	$45	$95
C. H. Hulburd, 19J, thin BRG model (12/14 size) **18K case** ..... ★	800	1,000	1,500
C. H. Hulburd, 19J, thin BRG model (12/14 size) **Platinum** .... ★	1,000	1,200	1,800
Lord Elgin, 17J, OF	65	95	125
Lord Elgin, 17, HC	75	100	150
Lord Elgin ,19 , ADJ, OF	85	100	150
Lord Elgin, 19J, ADJ, HC	125	150	185
Lord Elgin, 21, GJS, DR, Adj.5P, DMK, NI, OF	125	150	185
Lord Elgin, 21J,GJS, DR, Adj.5P, DMK, NI, **14K, OF**	175	225	400
Lord Elgin, 21J, GJS, DR, Adj.5P, DMK, NI, HC	150	175	275
Lord Elgin ,23, GJS, DR, Adj.5P, DMK, NI, OF	150	175	275
Lord Elgin, 23J, GJS, DR, Adj.5P, DMK, NI, HC	225	250	400
Masonic dial, 15-17J, (with original Masonic dial), OF	175	200	400

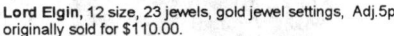

Lord Elgin, 12 size, 23 jewels, gold jewel settings, Adj.5p, originally sold for $110.00.

G.M. Wheeler, 12 size, 17 jewels, Adj3p, originally sold for $27.00.

Grade or Name — Description	Avg	Ex-Fn	Mint
Pierce Arrow, 17J, (with original dial), OF	$250	$300	$450
B. W. Raymond, 19J, GJS, Adj.5P, DR, DMK, NI, OF	60	80	175
B. W. Raymond, 19J, GJS, Adj.5P, DR, DMK, NI, HC	65	85	195
G. M. Wheeler, 17J, DR, Adj.5P, DMK, NI, OF	30	50	95
G. M. Wheeler, 17J, DR, Adj.5P, DMK, NI, HC	35	55	125
193, 19J, DR, GJS, Adj.5P, DMK, NI, OF	100	150	250

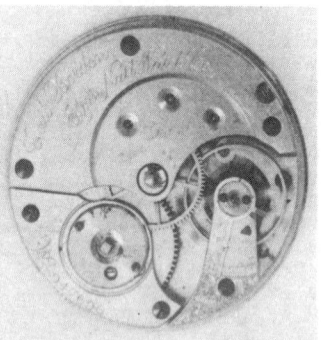

Frances Rubie, Grade 23, 10 size, 15 jewels, key wind & set.

Gail Borden, Grade 22, 10 size, 11 jewels, key wind & set, serial number 947,696.

10 SIZE
(HC)

Grade or Name — Description	Avg	Ex-Fn	Mint
Dexter St., 7J, KW, HC, **14K**	$200	$275	$500
Dexter St., 7J, KW, HC, **18K**	250	325	550
Dexter St., 7J, gilded, KW, HC, gold filled	75	100	150
Frances Rubie, 15J, gilded, KW, HC, **14K** ★	500	600	800
Frances Rubie, 15J, KW, HC, **18K** ★ ★	550	650	950

🕐 Watches listed in this book are priced at the collectable retail level, as **complete** watches having an original 14k gold-filled case and *Key Wind* with silver, an original white enamel single sunk dial, and with the entire original movement in good working order with no repairs needed.

🕐 Pricing in this Guide are fair market price for COMPLETE watches which are reflected from the **"NAWCC"** National and regional shows.

Grade or Name — Description	Avg	Ex-Fn	Mint
Gail Borden, 11J, gilded, KW, HC, **14K**	$225	$300	$500
Gail Borden, 11J, KW, HC, gold filled	75	100	125
Gail Borden, 11J, KW, HC, **18K**	270	325	500
Lady Elgin, 15J, gilded, KW, HC, **14K**	225	275	450
Lady Elgin, 15J, KW, HC, **18K**	275	325	500
Grade # 21 or 28, 7J, gilded, KW, HC, gold filled	75	100	125
Elgin, **multi-color case, gold filled**, HC	200	225	400
Elgin, 15J, Silveroid, HC	50	75	95
Elgin, 15J, YGF, HC	75	100	125

Elgin W. Co., Grade 121, 6 size, 15 jewels, hunting, serial number 4,500,445.

Elgin W. Co., 6 size, ENGRAVED movement, enamel & gold case, fancy dial, G# 94, S# 1,886,804.

6 SIZE
(HC Only)

Grade or Name — Description	Avg	Ex-Fn	Mint
Atlas, 7J, HC	$40	$60	$135
Elgin W. Co. #286, 7J, HC, DMK, NI	40	60	135
Elgin W. Co. #295, 15J, HC, DMK, NI	40	60	135
Elgin W. Co. #168, **16J,** nickel, HC	40	60	150
Elgin W. Co., 7J, HC, **14K**	150	225	350
Elgin W. Co., 11J, HC, **14K**	150	225	350
Elgin W. Co., ENGRAVED movement, enamel & gold case, fancy dial, G# 94, **14K** HC	800	1,000	1,400
Elgin W. Co., 15J, YGF, HC	60	80	135
Elgin W. Co., 15J, YGF demi-HC	60	80	150
Elgin W. Co., 15J, HC, **YGF** multi-color case	200	225	450
Elgin W. Co., 15J, HC, **10K**	175	200	300
Elgin W. Co., 15J, HC, **14K**	225	250	350
Elgin W. Co., 15J, **14K, Multi-color HC**	450	500	775
Elgin W. Co., 15J, HC, **18K**	300	350	450
Elgin W. Co., 15J, SW, HC, **Enamel case, 18K**	700	900	1,400
Elgin W. Co., **16J,** G# 230, gilded or nickel, HC	100	125	175

🕐 **Generic, nameless or unmarked** grades for watch movements are listed under the Company name or initials of the Company, etc. by size, jewel count and description.

Elgin W. Co., 6 size, 15 jewels

Elgin W. Co., Grade 201-HC, 205-OF, 0 size, 19 jewels, gold train.

Elgin W. Co., Grade 200-HC, 204-OF, 0 size, 17 jewels, gold jewel settings.

0 SIZE

Grade or Name — Description	Avg	Ex-Fn	Mint
Atlas W. Co., 7J, HC	$50	$70	$175
Elgin W. Co., 7J, NI, DR, DMK, OF	30	50	90
Elgin W. Co., 15J, NI, DR, DMK, OF	30	50	125
Elgin W. Co., 15J, NI, DR, DMK, HC	50	70	175
Elgin W. Co., 17J, NI, DR, DMK, ADJ, OF	50	70	140
Elgin W. Co., 19J, NI, DR, DMK, GJS, ADJ, OF	30	50	95
Elgin W. Co., 15J, OF, **14K**	125	150	300
Elgin W. Co., 15J, HC, **14K**	200	225	400
Elgin W. Co., 15J, HC, multi-color **GF**	150	200	350
Elgin W. Co., 15J, OF, multi-color **dial**	100	135	250
Elgin W. Co., 15J, HC, **10K**	150	175	225
Elgin W. Co., 15J, **14K**, Multi-color case	375	450	650
Elgin W. Co., 15J, **14K**, Multi-color case + diamond	400	500	700
Frances Rubie, 19J, HC ★★	250	300	500

Lady Elgin, 5/0 size, 17 jewels, gold jewel settings, originally sold for $42.50.

Lady Raymond, 5/0 size, 15 jewels, originally sold for $24.20.

3/0 and 5/0 SIZE
(HC ONLY)

Grade or Name — Description	Avg	Ex-Fn	Mint
Lady Elgin, 15J, PS, HC	$30	$70	$150
Lady Elgin, 15J, **14K**, HC	125	150	300
Lady Raymond, 15J, PS, HC	40	60	150
Elgin W. Co., 7J, HC	40	60	150

🕐 Generic, nameless or unmarked grades for watch movements are listed under the Company name or initials of the Company, etc. by size, jewel count and description.

🕐 Watch terminology or communication in this book has evolved over the years, in search of better and more precise language with a effort to improve, purify, adjust itself and make it easier to understand.

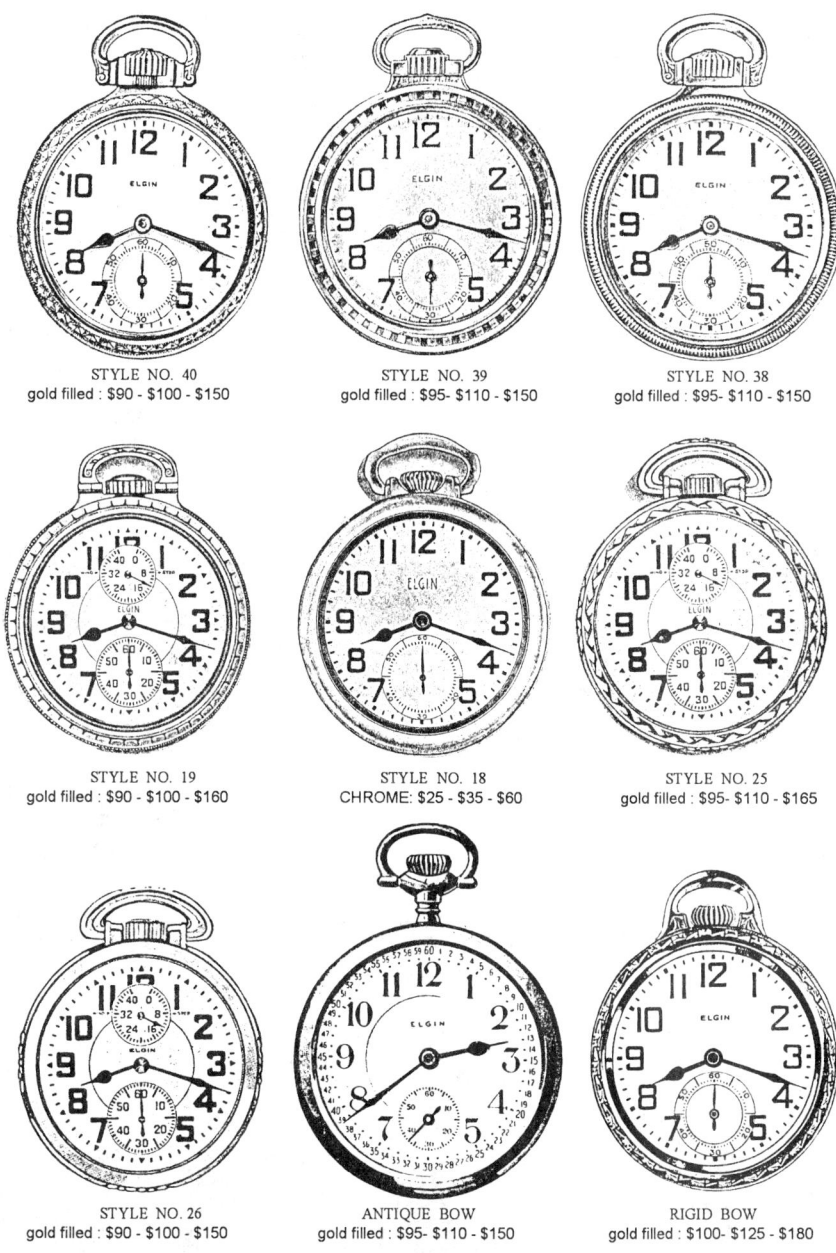

STYLE NO. 40
gold filled : $90 - $100 - $150

STYLE NO. 39
gold filled : $95- $110 - $150

STYLE NO. 38
gold filled : $95- $110 - $150

STYLE NO. 19
gold filled : $90 - $100 - $160

STYLE NO. 18
CHROME: $25 - $35 - $60

STYLE NO. 25
gold filled : $95- $110 - $165

STYLE NO. 26
gold filled : $90 - $100 - $150

ANTIQUE BOW
gold filled : $95- $110 - $150

RIGID BOW
gold filled : $100- $125 - $180

GOLD FILLED CASES = 40, 39, 38, 19, 25, 26, and some came with a **solid gold** bow.
CHROME CASES = 18 and ANTIQUE BOW & RIGID BOW= 20 year gold filled case

🕐 NOTE: Factory Advertised as a **complete** watch and was fitted with a certain matched, timed and rated movement and sold in the factory designed case style as a **complete** watch. The factory also sold _uncased_ movements to **JOBBERS** such as Jewelry stores & they cased the movement in a case styles the **CUSTOMER requested.** All the factory advertised **complete** watches came with a enamel dial **SHOWN or CHOICE** of other **Railroad** dials.

ELGIN NATIONAL WATCH CO.

GRADES OF MOVEMENTS
WITH
CLASSIFICATION AND DESCRIPTION
AS ORIGINALLY MADE

Grade.	Class.	Size.		Style.		Model.	Sett.	Train.	Jewels.
Advance	5	18	F. Pl.	Htg.	Gilded	1st to 4th	Key or Lever	Slow	11
Age	5	"	"	"	"	"	"	"	7
Avery	15	17	"	"	"	1st	Key	"	7
Chief	5	18	"	"	"	1st to 4th	Key or Lever	"	7
Culver	2	"	"	"	"	1st	"	Quick	15
Dexter St	48	10	¾ Pl.	"	"	1st	Key	"	7
Father Time	1	18	F. Pl.	"	Nickel	2d to 4th	Lever	"	20-21
Father Time	1	"	"	"	"	"	"	"	17
Father Time	7	"	"	O. F.	"	5th	Pend.	"	20-21
Father Time	7	"	"	"	"	"	"	"	17
Father Time	65	"	"	"	"	7th	Lever	"	17-21
Father Time	90	"	¾ Pl.	"	"	8th	"	"	21
Father Time	99	"	"	Htg.	"	9th	"	"	21
Father Time	134	"	"	O. F.	"	8th	"	"	21
Father Time	98	16	"	"	"	15th	"	"	21
Father Time	126	"	"	Htg.	"	14th	"	"	21
Father Time	126	"	"	"	"	17th	"	"	21
Fargo	5	18	F. Pl.	"	Gilded	1st	Key	Slow	7
Farwell	5	"	"	"	"	"	"	"	11
Ferry	4	"	"	"	"	"	"	"	15
Frances Rubie	46	10	¾ Pl.	"	"	"	"	Quick	15
Frances Rubie	76	0	"	"	Nickel	2d	Pend.	"	19
Frances Rubie	80	"	"	O. F.	"	3d	"	"	19
Gail Borden	48	10	"	Htg.	Gilded	1st	Key	"	11
Lady Elgin	47	"	"	"	"	"	"	"	15
Lady Elgin	133	5/0	"	"	Nickel	"	Pend.	"	15
Lady Elgin	96	10/0	"	O. F.	"	"	"	"	17
Lady Elgin	97	"	"	"	"	"	"	"	15
Lady Raymond	133	5/0	"	Htg.	"	"	"	"	15
Lady Raymond	136	"	"	O. F.	"	2d	"	"	15
Laflin	4	18	F. Pl.	Htg.	Gilded	1st to 4th	Key or Lever	Slow	7
Leader	15	17	"	"	"	1st to 2d	"	"	7
Lord Elgin	36	16	¾ Pl.	Htg. Br.	Nickel	6th	Pend.	Quick	21
Lord Elgin	41	"	"	O. F. Br.	"	7th	"	"	21
Lord Elgin	41	"	"	O. F.	"	"	"	"	23
Lord Elgin	67	12	"	Htg.	"	2d	"	"	23
Lord Elgin	71	"	"	O. F.	"	3d	"	"	23
Lord Elgin	135	"	"	"	"	4th	"	"	17
Lord Elgin	135	"	"	"	"	"	"	"	21
Ogden	5	18	F. Pl.	Htg.	Gilded	1st to 4th	Key or Lever	Slow	11
Overland	3	"	"	"	Nickel	2d to 4th	Lever	Quick	17
Overland	4	"	"	"	"	"	"	"	17
Overland	8	"	"	O. F.	"	5th	Pend.	"	17
Overland	9	"	"	"	"	"	"	"	17
Overland	66	"	"	"	"	7th	Lever	"	17
Overland	123	"	"	Htg.	"	2d to 4th	"	"	17
Overland	124	"	"	O. F.	"	7th	"	"	17
Raymond	1	"	"	Htg.	Gilded or Nickel	1st to 4th	Key or Lever	"	15-17
Raymond	7	"	"	O. F.	"	5th	Pend.	"	15-17
Raymond	65	"	"	"	Nickel	7th	Lever	"	17
Raymond	91	"	¾ Pl.	"	"	8th	"	"	19
Raymond	91	"	"	"	"	"	"	"	21
Raymond	99	"	"	Htg.	"	9th	"	"	21
Raymond	134	"	"	O. F.	"	8th	"	"	17
Raymond	98	16	"	"	"	15th	"	"	19
Raymond	98	"	"	"	"	"	"	"	21
Raymond	102	"	"	O. F. Br.	"	9th	"	"	17
Raymond	102	"	"	O. F.	"	13th	"	"	17
Raymond	102	"	"	"	"	15th	"	"	17
Raymond	125	"	"	Htg. Br.	"	8th	"	"	17
Raymond	126	"	"	Htg.	"	14th	"	"	19
Raymond	126	"	"	"	"	17th	"	"	19
Raymond	68	12	"	"	"	2d	Pend.	"	19
Raymond	72	"	"	O. F.	"	3d	"	"	19
Ryerson	4	18	F. Pl.	Htg.	Gilded	1st	Key	Slow	7
Taylor	3	"	"	"	"	2d to 4th	Lever	"	15
Taylor	3	"	"	"	Gilded or Nickel	1st to 4th	Key or Lever	Quick	15
Taylor	8	"	"	O. F.	Gilded	5th	Pend.	"	15
Veritas	89	"	¾ Pl.	"	Nickel	8th	Lever	"	23
Veritas	90	"	"	"	"	"	"	"	21
Veritas	99	"	"	Htg.	"	9th	"	"	21
Veritas	98	16	"	O. F. Br.	"	"	"	"	21
Veritas	98	"	"	O. F.	"	13th	"	"	21
Veritas	98	"	"	"	"	"	"	"	23
Veritas	98	"	"	"	"	15th	"	"	21
Veritas	132	"	"	"	"	"	"	"	23
Wheeler	4	18	F. Pl.	Htg.	Gilded	1st to 4th	Key or Lever	Slow	15
Wheeler	4	"	"	"	Gilded or Nickel	"	Lever	Quick	13-15
Wheeler	4	"	"	"	"	2d to 4th	"	"	15-17
Wheeler	9	"	"	O. F.	"	5th	Pend.	"	15-17

ELGIN NATIONAL WATCH CO.

Grades of Movements with Classification and Description as Originally Made

Grade.	Class.	Size.		Style.		Model.	Sett.	Train.	Jewels.
Wheeler	122	18	F. Pl.	O. F.	Nickel	7th	Lever	Quick	17
Wheeler	123	"	"	Htg.	"	2d to 4th	"	"	17
Wheeler	124	"	"	O. F.	"	7th	"	"	17
Wheeler	130	"	¾ Pl.	Htg.	"	9th	"	"	17
Wheeler	131	"	"	O. F.	"	8th	"	"	17
Wheeler	33	16	"	Htg. Br.	"	6th	Pend.	"	17
Wheeler	38	"	"	O. F. Br.	"	7th	"	"	17
Wheeler	127	"	"	"	"	9th	Lever	"	17
Wheeler	111	12	"	Htg.	"	2d	Pend.	"	17
Wheeler	112	"	"	O. F.	"	3d	"	"	17
No. 1	25	16	"	Htg.	Gilded	"	Lever	"	7
No. 2	25	"	"	"	"	"	"	"	13-15
No. 3	24	"	"	"	"	"	"	"	15
No. 4	24	"	"	"	Nickel	"	"	"	15
No. 5	5	18	F. Pl.	"	"	2d to 4th	"	Q. or S.	11
No. 6	6	"	"	"	Gilded	"	"	Slow	7
No. 7	6	"	"	"	"	1st	Key	"	7
No. 8	5	"	"	"	"	2d to 4th	Lever	"	7
No. 9	5	"	"	"	"	"	"	"	7
No. 10	5	"	"	"	"	"	"	Q. or S.	11
No. 11	15	17	"	"	"	"	2d	"	Slow	7
No. 12	5	18	"	"	"	"	1st	Key	"	7
No. 13	5	"	"	"	"	"	"	"	"	11
No. 14	15	17	"	"	"	"	"	"	"	7
No. 15	15	"	"	"	"	"	"	"	"	11
No. 16	4	18	"	"	"	"	"	"	"	7
No. 17	4	"	"	"	"	"	"	"	"	11
No. 18	5	"	"	"	"	"	"	"	"	11
No. 19	5	"	"	"	"	2d to 4th	Lever	"	11
No. 20	3	"	"	"	"	"	"	"	15
No. 21	48	10	¾ Pl.	"	"	1st	Key	Quick	7
No. 22	48	"	"	"	"	"	"	"	11
No. 23	47	"	"	"	"	"	"	"	15
No. 24	45	12	"	"	"	"	"	"	7
No. 25	45	"	"	"	"	"	"	"	11
No. 26	44	"	"	"	"	"	"	"	15
No. 27	1	18	F. Pl.	"	Nickel	2d to 4th	Lever	"	15-17
No. 28	48	10	¾ Pl.	"	Gilded	1st	Key	"	7
No. 29	47	"	"	"	"	"	"	"	11
No. 30	45	12	"	"	"	"	"	"	7
No. 31	45	"	"	"	"	1st	"	"	11
No. 32	44	"	"	"	"	"	"	"	11
No. 33	3	18	F. Pl.	"	Nickel	2d to 4th	Lever	"	15
No. 34	43	14	¾ Pl.	"	Gilded	1st	Key	"	7
No. 35	43	"	"	"	"	"	"	"	7
No. 36	43	"	"	"	"	"	"	"	11
No. 37	42	"	"	"	"	"	"	"	15
No. 38	3	18	F. Pl.	"	"	"	"	Slow	15
No. 39	43	14	¾ Pl.	"	"	"	"	Quick	13
No. 40	43	"	"	"	"	"	"	"	7
No. 41	42	"	"	"	"	"	"	"	13
No. 42	42	"	"	"	"	"	"	"	15
No. 43	10	18	F. Pl.	O. F.	Nickel	5th	Pend.	"	11
No. 44	9	"	"	"	"	"	"	"	15
No. 45	51	6	¾ Pl.	Htg.	"	1st	Lever	"	13
No. 46	42	14	"	"	"	"	Key	"	15
No. 47	19	16	"	Htg. and O.F.	Gilded	"	Lever	"	7
No. 48	18	"	"	"	"	"	"	"	13
No. 49	17	"	"	"	"	"	"	"	15
No. 50	17	"	"	"	Nickel	"	"	"	15
No. 51	15	17	F. Pl.	Htg.	Gilded	1st	Key	Slow	7
No. 52	15	"	"	"	"	"	"	"	11
No. 53	48	10	¾ Pl.	"	"	"	"	Quick	7
No. 54	48	"	"	"	"	"	"	"	13
No. 55	5	18	F. Pl.	"	"	"	"	Slow	7
No. 56	4	"	"	"	"	"	"	"	11
No. 57	4	"	"	"	"	"	"	"	13
No. 58	3	"	"	"	"	"	"	"	15
No. 59	15	17	"	"	"	"	"	"	7
No. 60	5	18	"	"	"	"	"	"	7
No. 61	2	"	"	"	"	2d to 4th	Lever	Quick	15
No. 62	2	"	"	"	"	1st	Key	"	15
No. 63	4	"	"	"	"	2d to 4th	Lever	Slow	13
No. 64	51	6	¾ Pl.	"	"	1st	"	Quick	7
No. 65	51	"	"	"	"	"	"	"	13
No. 66	50	"	"	"	"	"	"	"	15
No. 67	50	"	"	"	Nickel	"	"	"	15
No. 68	5	18	F. Pl.	"	Gilded	2d to 4th	"	Slow	7
No. 69	1	"	"	"	"	1st	Key	Quick	15
No. 70	1	"	"	"	"	2d to 4th	Lever	"	15-17
No. 71	49	6	¾ Pl.	"	Nickel	1st	"	"	17
No. 72	16	16	"	Htg. and O.F.	"	"	"	"	21
No. 73	11	18	F. Pl.	O. F.	Gilded	5th	Pend.	"	7
No. 74	10	"	"	"	"	"	"	"	11
No. 75	9	"	"	"	"	"	"	"	15
No. 76	8	"	"	"	"	"	"	"	15
No. 77	7	"	"	"	"	"	"	"	15-17
No. 78	5	"	"	Htg.	Nickel	1st	Key	Q. or S.	11
No. 79	3	"	"	"	Gilded	"	"	Quick	15

ELGIN NATIONAL WATCH CO.

Grades of Movement with Classification and Description as Originally Made.

Grade.	Class.	Size.		Style.		Model.	Sett.	Train.	Jewels.
No. 80	3	18	F. Pl.	Htg.	Gilded	2d to 4th	Lever	Quick	15
No. 81	4	"	"	"	"	1st	Key	"	13–15
No. 82	4	"	"	"	"	2d to 4th	Lever	"	13–15
No. 83	27	16	¾ Pl.	S. Sec.	"	4th	"	"	15
No. 84	27	"	"	"	Nickel	"	"	"	15
No. 85	22	"	"	Htg. and O.F.	Gilded	2d	"	"	15
No. 86	22	"	"	"	Nickel	"	"	"	15
No. 87	5	18	F. Pl.	Htg.	"	1st	Key	"	11
No. 88	5	"	"	"	"	2d to 4th	Lever	"	11
No. 89	28	16	¾ Pl.	S. Sec.	Gilded	4th	"	"	13
No. 90	23	"	"	Htg. and O.F.	"	2d	"	"	13
No. 91	21	"	"	"	Nickel	"	"	"	21
No. 92	26	"	"	Htg.	Gilded	3d	"	"	11
No. 93	20	"	"	Htg. and O.F.	"	1st	"	"	11
No. 94	52	6	"	Htg.	"	"	"	"	11
No. 95	52	"	"	"	"	"	"	"	7
No. 96	6	18	F. Pl.	"	"	2d to 4th	"	"	7
No. 97	6	"	"	"	"	1st	Key	"	7
No. 98	14	"	¾ Pl.	Htg. and O.F.	"	6th	Pend.	"	7
No. 99	13	"	"	"	"	"	"	"	11
No. 100	12	"	"	"	"	"	"	"	15
No. 101	52	6	"	Htg.	Nickel	1st	Lever	"	11
No. 102	5	18	F. Pl.	"	"	2d to 4th	"	"	11
No. 103	4	"	"	"	"	"	"	"	15
No. 104	31	16	¾ Pl.	O. F.	Gilded	5th	Pend.	"	7
No. 105	31	"	"	"	"	"	"	"	11
No. 106	30	"	"	"	"	"	"	"	13–15
No. 107	29	"	"	"	"	"	"	"	15
No. 108	29	"	"	"	Nickel	"	"	"	15
No. 109	60	0	"	Htg.	Gilded	1st	"	"	7
No. 110	60	"	"	"	Nickel	"	"	"	11
No. 111	58	"	"	"	"	"	"	"	15
No. 112	57	"	"	"	"	"	"	"	17
No. 113	60	"	"	"	Gilded	"	"	"	11
No. 114	26	16	"	"	"	3d	"	"	7
No. 115	59	0	"	"	Nickel	1st	"	"	13
No. 116	7	18	F. Pl.	O. F.	"	5th	"	"	15–17
No. 117	56	6	¾ Pl.	Htg.	Gilded	2d	"	"	7
No. 118	56	"	"	"	"	"	"	"	11
No. 119	56	"	"	"	Nickel	"	"	"	11
No. 120	55	"	"	"	"	"	"	"	13
No. 121	54	"	"	"	"	"	"	"	15
No. 122	53	"	"	"	"	"	"	"	17
No. 123	9	18	F. Pl.	O. F.	Gilded	5th	"	"	15
No. 124	9	"	"	"	Nickel	"	"	"	15
No. 125	4	"	"	Htg.	Gilded	2d to 4th	Lever	"	15
No. 126	4	"	"	"	Nickel	"	"	"	15
No. 127	26	16	¾ Pl.	"	"	3d	"	"	11
No. 128	31	"	"	O. F.	"	5th	Pend.	"	11
No. 129	60	0	"	Htg.	Gilded	1st	"	"	15
No. 130	60	"	"	"	Nickel	"	"	"	15
No. 131	58	"	"	"	"	"	"	"	15
No. 132	56	6	"	"	Gilded	2d	"	"	15
No. 133	56	"	"	"	Nickel	"	"	"	15
No. 134	54	"	"	"	"	"	"	"	15
No. 135	26	16	"	"	Gilded	3d	Lever	"	15
No. 136	26	"	"	"	Nickel	"	"	"	15
No. 137	25	"	"	"	Gilded	"	"	"	13–15
No. 138	31	"	"	O. F.	"	5th	Pend.	"	15
No. 139	31	"	"	"	Nickel	"	"	"	15
No. 140	30	"	"	"	Gilded	"	"	"	13–15
No. 141	5	18	F. Pl.	Htg.	"	2d to 4th	Lever	"	15
No. 142	5	"	"	"	Nickel	"	"	"	15
No. 143	4	"	"	"	Gilded	"	"	"	15–17
No. 144	4	"	"	"	Nickel	"	"	"	15–17
No. 145	10	"	"	O. F.	Gilded	5th	Pend.	"	15
No. 146	10	"	"	"	Nickel	"	"	"	15
No. 147	9	"	"	"	Gilded	"	"	"	15–17
No. 148	9	"	"	"	Nickel	"	"	"	15–17
No. 149	1	"	"	Htg.	"	2d to 4th	Lever	"	20–21
No. 150	7	"	"	O. F.	"	5th	Pend.	"	20–21
No. 151	35	16	¾ Pl.	Htg.	Gilded	6th	"	"	7
No. 152	35	"	"	"	Nickel	"	"	"	15
No. 153	34	"	"	"	"	"	"	"	17
No. 154	33	"	"	"	"	"	"	"	17
No. 155	32	"	"	"	"	"	"	"	17
No. 156	36	"	"	Htg. Br.	"	"	"	"	21
No. 157	40	"	"	O. F.	Gilded	7th	"	"	7
No. 158	40	"	"	"	Nickel	"	"	"	15
No. 159	39	"	"	"	"	"	"	"	17
No. 160	38	"	"	"	"	"	"	"	17
No. 161	37	"	"	"	"	"	"	"	17
No. 162	41	"	"	O. F. Br.	"	"	"	"	21
No. 163	3	18	F. Pl.	Htg.	"	2d to 4th	Lever	"	17
No. 164	1	"	"	"	"	"	"	"	17
No. 165	8	"	"	O. F.	"	5th	Pend.	"	17
No. 166	7	"	"	"	"	"	"	"	17
No. 167	58	0	¾ Pl.	Htg.	"	1st	"	"	16
No. 168	54	6	"	"	"	2d	"	"	16

ELGIN NATIONAL WATCH CO.

Grades of Movements with Classification and Description as Originally Made.

Grade.	Class.	Size.		Style.		Model.	Sett.	Train.	Jewels.
No. 169	5	18	F. Pl.	Htg.	Nickel	2d to 4th	Lever	Quick	15
No. 170	10	"	"	O. F.	"	5th	Pend.	"	15
No. 171	6	"	"	Htg.	"	2d to 4th	Lever	"	7
No. 172	11	"	"	O. F.	"	5th	Pend.	"	7
No. 173	60	0	¾ Pl.	Htg.	"	1st	"	"	7
No. 174	57	"	"	"	"	"	"	"	17
No. 175	56	6	"	"	"	2d	"	"	7
No. 176	53	"	"	"	"	"	"	"	17
No. 177	..	"	"	"	"	..	"	"	7
No. 178	..	18	F. Pl.	"	..	2d to 4th	Lever	"	7
No. 179	..	"	"	O. F.	..	5th	Pend.	"	7
No. 180	65	"	"	"	Nickel	7th	Lever	"	17
No. 181	65	"	"	"	"	"	"	"	21
No. 182	31	16	¾ Pl.	"	Gilded	5th	Pend.	"	7
No. 183	1	18	F. Pl.	Htg.	Nickel	2d to 4th	Lever	"	17
No. 184	7	"	"	O. F.	"	5th	Pend.	"	17
No. 185	35	16	¾ Pl.	Htg.	Gilded	6th	"	"	15
No. 186	40	"	"	O. F.	"	7th	"	"	15
No. 187	70	12	"	Htg.	Nickel	2d	"	"	15
No. 188	69	"	"	"	"	"	"	"	17
No. 189	68	"	"	"	"	"	"	"	19
No. 190	67	"	"	"	"	"	"	"	23
No. 191	74	"	"	O. F.	"	3d	"	"	15
No. 192	73	"	"	"	"	"	"	"	17
No. 193	72	"	"	"	"	"	"	"	19
No. 194	71	"	"	"	"	"	"	"	23
No. 195	31	16	"	"	Gilded	5th	"	"	15
No. 196	70	12	"	Htg.	Nickel	2d	"	"	7
No. 197	74	"	"	O. F.	"	3d	"	"	7
No. 198	79	0	"	Htg.	"	2d	"	"	7
No. 199	78	"	"	"	"	"	"	"	15
No. 200	77	"	"	"	"	"	"	"	17
No. 201	76	"	"	"	"	"	"	"	19
No. 202	83	"	"	O. F.	"	3d	"	"	7
No. 203	82	"	"	"	"	"	"	"	15
No. 204	81	"	"	"	"	"	"	"	17
No. 205	80	"	"	"	"	"	"	"	19
No. 206	75	6	"	Htg.	"	2d	"	"	7
No. 207	61	18	F. Pl.	"	"	2d to 4th	Lever	"	7
No. 208	63	"	"	O. F.	"	5th	Pend.	"	7
No. 209	75	6	¾ Pl.	Htg.	Gilded	2d	"	"	7
No. 210	92	16	"	"	Nickel	6th	"	"	7
No. 211	94	"	"	O. F.	"	7th	"	"	7
No. 212	92	"	"	Htg.	Gilded	6th	"	"	7
No. 213	94	"	"	O. F.	"	7th	"	"	7
No. 214	89	18	"	"	Nickel	8th	Lever	"	23
No. 215	63	"	F. Pl.	"	Gilded	5th	Pend.	"	7
No. 216	75	6	¾ Pl.	Htg.	Nickel	2d	"	"	15
No. 217	61	18	F. Pl.	"	"	2d to 4th	Lever	"	15
No. 218	63	"	"	O. F.	"	5th	Pend.	"	15
No. 219	84	0	¾ Pl.	Htg.	Gilded	1st	"	"	7
No. 220	92	16	"	"	Nickel	6th	"	"	15
No. 221	94	"	"	O. F.	"	7th	"	"	15
No. 222	84	0	"	Htg.	"	1st	"	"	7
No. 223	84	"	"	"	"	"	"	"	15
No. 224	85	"	"	"	"	2d	"	"	11
No. 225	86	"	"	O. F.	"	3d	"	"	11
No. 226	5	18	F. Pl.	Htg.	Gilded	2d to 4th	Lever	"	17
No. 227	10	"	"	O. F.	"	5th	Pend.	"	17
No. 228	5	"	"	Htg.	Nickel	2d to 4th	Lever	"	17
No. 229	10	"	"	O. F.	"	5th	Pend.	"	17
No. 230	56	6	¾ Pl.	Htg.	Gilded	2d	"	"	16
No. 231	56	"	"	"	Nickel	"	"	"	16
No. 232	87	12	"	"	"	"	"	"	7
No. 233	87	"	"	"	"	"	"	"	15
No. 234	88	"	"	O. F.	"	3d	"	"	7
No. 235	88	"	"	"	"	"	"	"	15
No. 236	68	"	"	Htg.	"	2d	"	"	21
No. 237	72	"	"	O. F.	"	3d	"	"	21
No. 238	61	18	F. Pl.	Htg.	Gilded	1st	Key	"	7
No. 239	90	"	¾ Pl.	O. F.	Nickel	8th	Lever	"	21
No. 240	91	"	"	"	"	"	"	"	19
No. 241	33	16	"	Htg. Br.	"	6th	Pend.	"	17
No. 242	33	"	"	"	"	"	"	"	17
No. 243	32	"	"	"	"	"	"	"	17
No. 244	38	"	"	O. F. Br.	"	7th	"	"	17
No. 245	38	"	"	"	"	"	"	"	17
No. 246	37	"	"	"	"	"	"	"	17
No. 247	93	"	"	Htg. Br.	"	6th	"	"	15
No. 248	95	"	"	O. F. Br.	"	7th	"	"	15
No. 249	62	18	F. Pl.	Htg.	Gilded	2d to 4th	Lever	"	17
No. 250	64	"	"	O. F.	"	5th	Pend.	"	17
No. 251	61	"	"	Htg.	"	2d to 4th	Lever	"	17
No. 252	65	"	"	O. F.	Nickel	7th	"	"	21
No. 253	87	12	¾ Pl.	Htg.	Gilded	2d	Pend.	"	7
No. 254	88	"	"	O. F.	"	3d	"	"	7
No. 255	97	10/0	"	"	Nickel	1st	"	"	15
No. 256	96	"	"	"	"	"	"	"	17
No. 257	92	16	"	Htg.	"	6th	"	"	15

ELGIN NATIONAL WATCH CO.

Grades of Movements with Classification and Description as Originally Made.

Grade.	Class.	Size.		Style.		Model.	Sett.	Train.	Jewels.
No. 258	94	16	¾ Pl.	O. F.	Nickel	7th	Pend.	Quick	15
No. 259	87	12	"	Htg.	"	2d	"	"	15
No. 260	88	"	"	O. F.	"	3d	"	"	15
No. 261	61	18	F. Pl.	"	"	2d to 4th	Lever	"	15
No. 262	63	"	"	O. F.	"	5th	Pend.	"	15
No. 263	77	0	¾ Pl.	Htg.	"	2d	"	"	17
No. 264	81	"	"	O. F.	"	3d	"	"	17
No. 265	66	18	F. Pl.	"	"	7th	Lever	"	17
No. 266	65	"	"	"	"	"	"	"	17-21
No. 267	85	0	¾ Pl.	"	"	2d	Pend.	"	15
No. 268	86	"	"	O. F.	"	3d	"	"	15
No. 269	85	"	"	Htg.	"	2d	"	"	7
No. 270	98	16	"	O. F. Br.	"	9th	Lever	"	21
No. 271	60	0	"	Htg.	"	1st	Pend.	"	16
No. 272	56	6	"	"	"	2d	"	"	16
No. 273	65	18	F. Pl.	O. F.	"	7th	Lever	"	17
No. 274	99	"	¾ Pl.	Htg.	"	9th	"	"	21
No. 275	100	12	"	"	"	2d	Pend.	"	17
No. 276	101	"	"	O. F.	"	3d	"	"	17
No. 277	65	18	F. Pl.	"	"	7th	Lever	"	21
No. 278	4	"	"	Htg.	"	2d to 4th	"	"	17
No. 279	9	"	"	O. F.	"	5th	Pend.	"	17
No. 280	102	16	¾ Pl.	O. F. Br.	"	9th	Lever	"	17
No. 281	85	0	"	Htg.	"	2d	Pend.	"	11
No. 282	86	"	"	O. F.	"	3d	"	"	7
No. 283	66	18	F. Pl.	"	"	7th	Lever	"	17
No. 284	75	6	¾ Pl.	Htg.	Gilded	2d	Pend.	"	15
No. 285	63	18	F. Pl.	O. F.	"	5th	"	"	15
No. 286	115	6	¾ Pl.	Htg.	Nickel	2d	"	"	7
No. 287	105	18	F. Pl.	"	"	2d to 4th	Lever	"	7
No. 288	106	"	"	O. F.	"	5th	Pend.	"	7
No. 289	115	6	¾ Pl.	Htg.	Gilded	2d	"	"	7
No. 290	109	16	"	"	Nickel	6th	"	"	7
No. 291	110	"	"	O. F.	"	7th	"	"	7
No. 292	109	"	"	Htg.	Gilded	6th	"	"	7
No. 293	110	"	"	O. F.	"	7th	"	"	7
No. 294	106	18	F. Pl.	"	"	5th	"	"	7
No. 295	115	6	¾ Pl.	Htg.	Nickel	2d	"	"	15
No. 296	105	18	F. Pl.	"	"	2d to 4th	Lever	"	15
No. 297	106	"	"	O. F.	"	5th	Pend.	"	15
No. 298	116	0	¾ Pl.	Htg.	Gilded	2d	"	"	7
No. 299	109	16	"	"	Nickel	6th	"	"	15
No. 300	110	"	"	O. F.	"	7th	"	"	15
No. 301	113	12	"	Htg.	"	2d	"	"	7
No. 302	113	"	"	"	"	"	"	"	15
No. 303	114	"	"	O. F.	"	3d	"	"	7
No. 304	114	"	"	"	"	"	"	"	15
No. 305	107	16	"	Htg. Br.	"	6th	"	"	15
No. 306	108	"	"	O. F. Br.	"	7th	"	"	15
No. 307	103	18	F. Pl.	Htg.	Gilded	2d to 4th	Lever	"	17
No. 308	104	"	"	O. F.	"	5th	Pend.	"	17
No. 309	105	"	"	Htg.	"	2d to 4th	Lever	"	7
No. 310	113	12	¾ Pl.	"	"	2d	Pend.	"	7
No. 311	114	"	"	O. F.	"	3d	"	"	7
No. 312	109	16	"	Htg.	Nickel	6th	"	"	15
No. 313	110	"	"	O. F.	"	7th	"	"	15
No. 314	113	12	"	Htg.	"	2d	"	"	15
No. 315	114	"	"	O. F.	"	3d	"	"	15
No. 316	105	18	F. Pl.	Htg.	"	2d to 4th	Lever	"	15
No. 317	106	"	"	O. F.	"	5th	Pend.	"	15
No. 318	116	0	¾ Pl.	Htg.	"	2d	"	"	15
No. 319	117	"	"	O. F.	"	3d	"	"	15
No. 320	116	"	"	Htg.	"	2d	"	"	7
No. 321	111	12	"	"	"	"	"	"	17
No. 322	112	"	"	O. F.	"	3d	"	"	17
No. 323	116	0	"	Htg.	"	2d	"	"	11
No. 324	117	"	"	O. F.	"	3d	"	"	7
No. 325	115	6	"	Htg.	Gilded	2d	"	"	15
No. 326	106	18	F. Pl.	O. F.	"	5th	"	"	15
No. 327	118	"	"	Htg.	Nickel	10th	Lever	"	16
No. 328	118	"	"	"	"	"	"	"	17
No. 329	119	"	"	"	"	"	"	"	17
No. 330	119	"	"	"	"	"	"	"	21
No. 331	120	"	"	O. F.	"	11th	Pend.	"	16
No. 332	120	"	"	"	"	"	"	"	17
No. 333	121	"	"	"	"	"	Lever	"	17
No. 334	121	"	"	"	"	"	"	"	21
No. 335	105	"	"	Htg.	"	4th	"	"	17
No. 336	106	"	"	"	"	5th	Pend.	"	17
No. 337	33	16	¾ Pl.	Htg. Br.	"	6th	"	"	17
No. 338	38	"	"	O. F. Br.	"	7th	"	"	17
No. 339	107	"	"	Htg. Br.	"	6th	"	"	17
No. 340	108	"	"	O. F. Br.	"	7th	"	"	17
No. 341	125	"	"	Htg. Br.	"	8th	Lever	"	17
No. 342	127	"	"	O. F. Br.	"	9th	"	"	17
No. 343	122	18	F. Pl.	O. F.	"	7th	"	"	17
No. 344	113	12	¾ Pl.	Htg.	"	2d	Pend.	"	17
No. 345	114	"	"	O. F.	"	3d	"	"	17
No. 346	111	"	"	Htg.	"	2d	"	"	17

ELGIN NATIONAL WATCH CO.

Grades of Movements with Classification and Description as Originally Made.

Grade.	Class.	Size.		Style.		Model.	Sett.	Train.	Jewels.
No. 347	112	12	¾ Pl.	O. F.	Nickel	3d	Pend.	Quick	17
No. 348	1	18	F. Pl.	Htg.	"	2d to 4th	Lever	"	21
No. 349	65	"	"	O. F.	"	7th	"	"	21
No. 350	98	16	¾ Pl.	"	"	13th	"	"	23
No. 351	41	"	"	"	"	7th	Pend.	"	23
No. 352	123	18	F. Pl.	Htg.	"	2d to 4th	Lever	"	17
No. 353	124	"	"	O. F.	"	7th	"	"	17
No. 354	116	0	¾ Pl.	Htg.	"	2d	Pend.	"	15
No. 355	117	"	"	O. F.	"	3d	"	"	15
No. 356	128	14	"	"	"	2d	"	"	7
No. 357	128	"	"	"	"	"	"	"	15
No. 358	128	"	"	"	"	"	"	"	17
No. 359	129	"	"	"	"	"	"	"	17
No. 360	98	16	"	"	"	13th	Lever	"	21
No. 361	102	"	"	"	"	"	"	"	17
No. 363	113	12	"	Htg.	Gilded	2d	Pend.	"	15
No. 364	114	"	"	O. F.	"	3d	"	"	15
No. 365	109	16	"	Htg.	"	6th	"	"	15
No. 366	110	"	"	O. F.	"	7th	"	"	15
No. 367	90	18	"	"	Nickel	8th	Lever	"	21
No. 368	130	"	"	Htg.	"	9th	"	"	17
No. 369	131	"	"	O. F.	"	8th	"	"	17
No. 370	102	16	"	"	"	15th	"	"	17
No. 371	126	"	"	Htg.	"	14th	"	"	19
No. 372	98	"	"	O. F.	"	15th	"	"	19
No. 373	126	"	"	Htg.	"	14th	"	"	21
No. 374	98	"	"	O₵ F.	"	15th	"	"	21
No. 375	98	"	"	"	"	"	"	"	21
No. 376	132	"	"	"	"	"	"	"	23
No. 377	116	0	"	Htg.	Gilded	2d	Pend.	"	15
No. 378	105	18	F. Pl.	O. F.	Nickel	2d to 4th	Lever	"	17
No. 379	106	"	"	O. F.	"	5th	Pend.	"	17
No. 380	133	5/0	¾ Pl.	Htg.	"	1st	"	"	15
No. 381	107	16	"	Htg. Br.	"	6th	"	"	17
No. 382	108	"	"	O. F. Br.	"	7th	"	"	17
No. 383	113	12	"	Htg.	"	2d	"	"	17
No. 384	114	"	"	O. F.	"	3d	"	"	17
No. 385	134	18	"	"	"	8th	Lever	"	17
No. 386	109	16	"	Htg.	"	6th	Pend.	"	17
No. 387	110	"	"	O. F.	"	7th	"	"	17
No. 388	98	"	"	"	"	15th	Lever	"	21
No. 389	134	18	"	"	"	8th	"	"	21
No. 390	91	"	"	"	"	"	"	"	21
No. 391	98	16	"	"	"	15th	"	"	21
No. 392	135	12	"	"	"	4th	Pend.	"	17
No. 393	113	"	"	Htg.	Gilded	2d	"	"	7
No. 394	114	"	"	O. F.	"	3d	"	"	7
No. 395	113	"	"	Htg.	"	2d	"	"	15
No. 396	114	"	"	O. F.	"	3d	"	"	15
No. 397	33	16	"	Htg. Br.	Nickel	6th	"	"	17
No. 398	38	"	"	O. F. Br.	"	7th	"	"	17
No. 399	136	5/0	"	O. F.	"	2d	"	"	15
No. 400	131	18	"	"	"	8th	Lever	"	17
No. 401	126	16	"	Htg.	"	17th	"	"	19
No. 402	126	"	"	"	"	"	"	"	21
No. 403	133	5/0	"	"	"	1st	Pend.	"	7
No. 404	97	10/0	"	O. F.	"	"	"	"	15
No. 405	96	"	"	"	"	"	"	"	17
No. 406	116	0	"	Htg.	Gilded	2d	"	"	13
No. 407	135	12	"	O. F.	Nickel	4th	"	"	21
No. 408	133	5/0	"	Htg.	"	1st	"	"	7
No. 409	117	0	"	O. F.	Gilded	3d	"	"	7
No. 410	117	"	"	"	"	"	"	"	15
No. 411	106	18	F. Pl.	"	Nickel	5th	"	"	21
No. 412	91	"	¾ Pl.	"	"	8th	Lever	"	21
No. 413	116	3/0	"	Htg.	"	2d	Pend.	"	7
No. 414	117	"	"	O. F.	"	3d	"	"	7
No. 415	116	"	"	Htg.	"	2d	"	"	15
No. 416	117	"	"	O. F.	"	3d	"	"	15

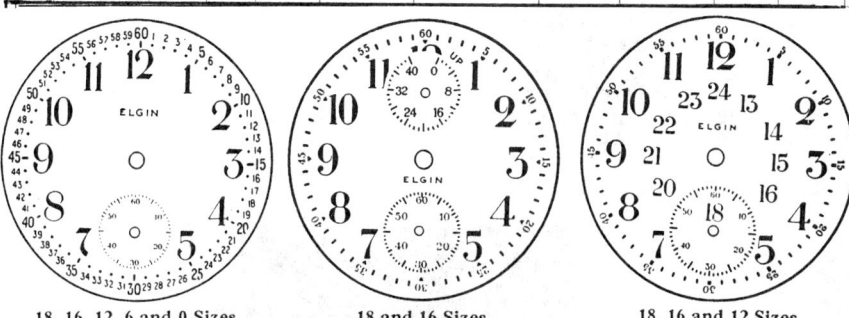

18, 16, 12, 6 and 0 Sizes   18 and 16 Sizes   18, 16 and 12 Sizes

ELGIN NATIONAL WATCH CO.
IDENTIFICATION OF MOVEMENTS
BY MODEL NUMBER

How to Identify Your Watch: Compare the movement of your watch with the illustrations in this section. Upon matching the movement exactly, the model number and size can be determined. While comparing, note the location of the balance, jewels, screws, gears and type of back plate (Full, ¾, Bridge) which will be clues in identifying the movement you have. Having determined the size and model number, you can now find your watch in the main price listing by name or number (which is engraved on the movement).

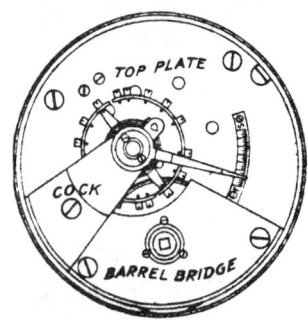

Model 1, 18 size, full plate, hunting, key wind & set, first serial number 101, Apr., 1867.

Model 2-4, 18 size, full plate, hunting, lever set, first serial number 155,001, June, 1873.

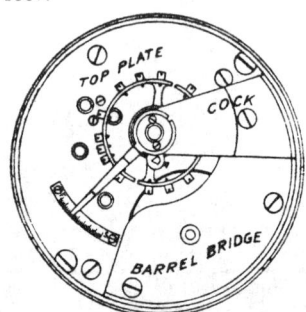

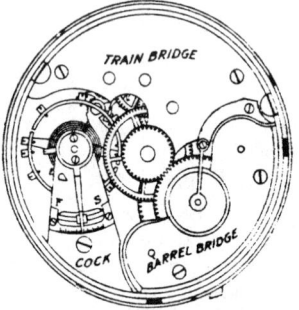

Model 5, 18 size, full plate, open face, pendant set, first serial number, 2,110,001, Grade 43, Dec., 1885.

Model 6, 18 size, three-quarter plate, hunting, open face, pendant set.

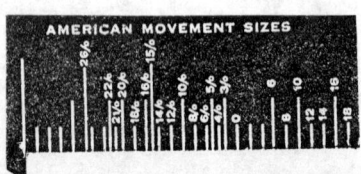

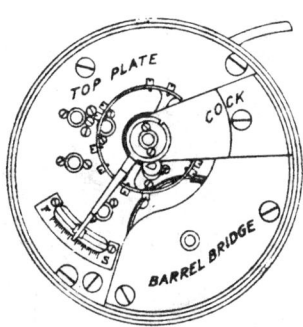

Model 7, 18 size, full plate, open face, lever set, first serial number 6,563,821, Grade 265, Apr., 1897.

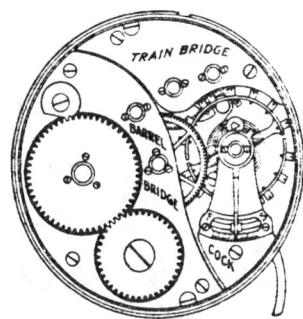

Model 8, 18 size, three-quarter plate, open face, lever set, first serial number 8,400,001, Grade 214, Dec., 1900.

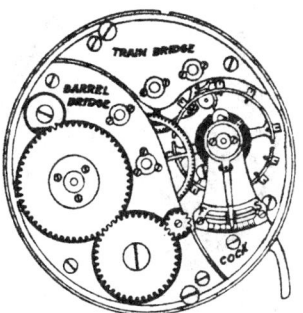

Model 8, 18 size, three-quarter plate, open face, lever set with winding indicator.

Model 9, 18 size, three-quarter plate, hunting, lever set, first serial number 9,625,001, Grade 274, May, 1904.

Model 9, 18 size, three-quarter plate, hunting, lever set with winding indicator.

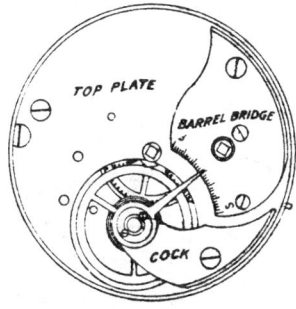

Model 1, 17 size, full plate, hunting, key wind and set.

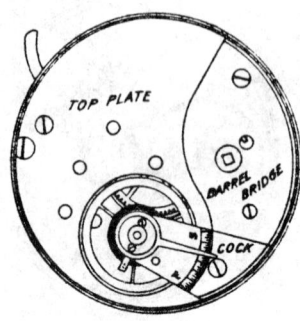

Model 2, 17 size, full plate, hunting, lever set.

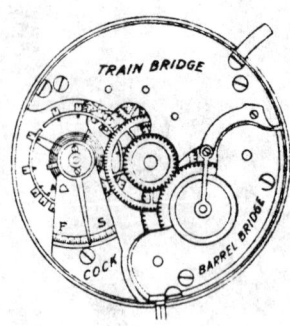

Model 1, 16 size, three-quarter plate, hunting & open face, lever set.

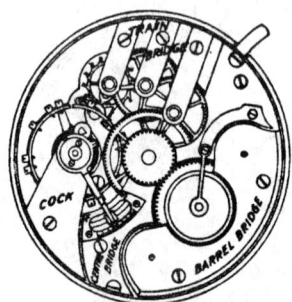

Model 2, 16 size, three-quarter plate, bridge, hunting & open face, lever set.

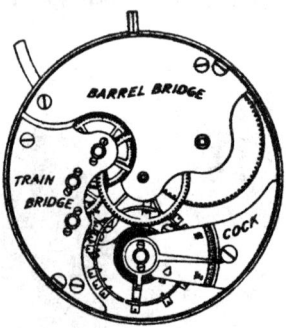

Model 3, 16 size, three-quarter plate, hunting, lever set, first serial number 625,001, Grade 1, Feb., 1879.

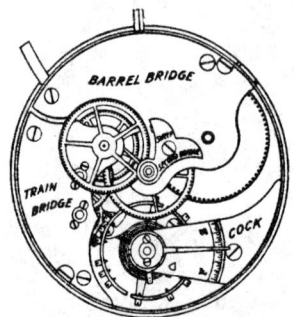

Model 4, 16 size, three-quarter plate, sweep second, hunting & open face, lever set.

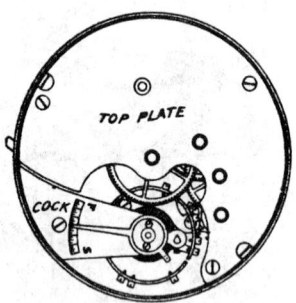

Model 5, 16 size, three-quarter plate, open face, pendant set.

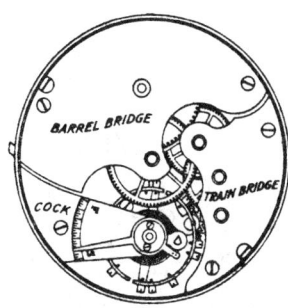

Model 5, 16 size, three-quarter plate, open face, pendant set, first serial number 2,811,001, Grade 105, Oct., 1887.

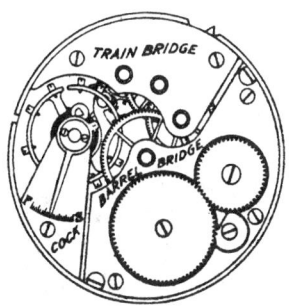

Model 6, 16 size, three-quarter plate, hunting, pendant set, first serial number 6,458,001, Grade 151, Aug., 1895.

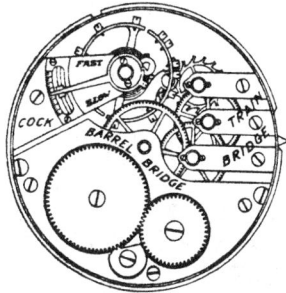

Model 6, 16 size, three-quarter plate, bridge, hunting, pendant set, first serial number 6,463,001, Grade 156, May, 1896.

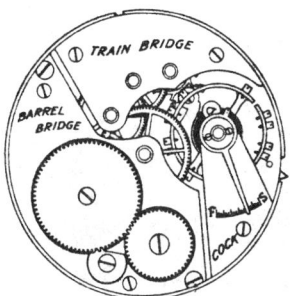

Model 7, 16 size, three-quarter plate, open face, pendant set, first serial number 6,464,001. Grade 157, Sept., 1895.

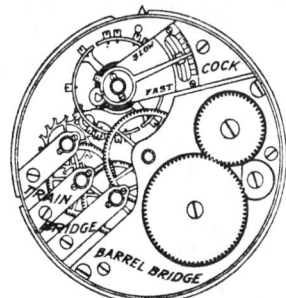

Model 7, 16 size, three-quarter plate, bridge, open face, pendant set, first serial number 6,469,001, Grade 162, Apr., 1896.

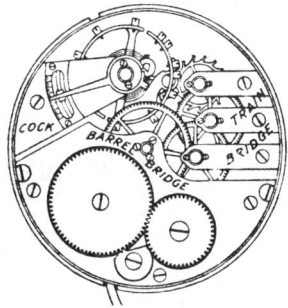

Model 8, 16 size, three-quarter plate, bridge, hunting, lever set, serial number 12,283,001, Grade 341, Jan., 1907.

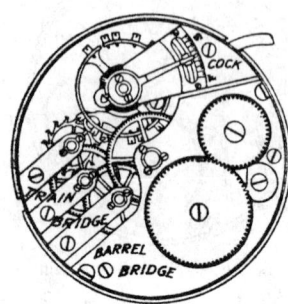

Model 9, 16 size, three-quarter plate, bridge, open face, lever set, first serial number 9,250,001, Grade 270, July, 1902.

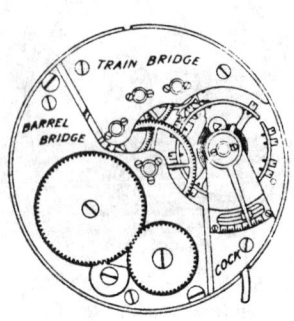

Model 13, 16 size, three-quarter plate, open face, lever set, first serial number 12,717,001, Grade 350, June, 1908.

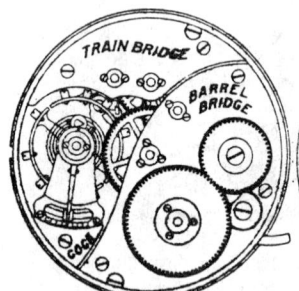

Model 14, 16 size, three-quarter plate, hunting, lever set.

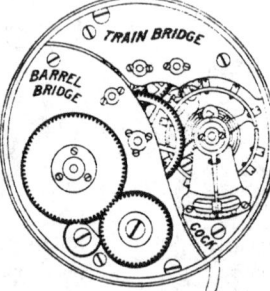

Model 15, 16 size, three-quarter plate, open face, lever set.

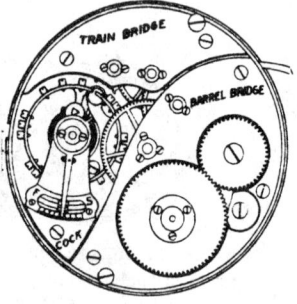

Model 17, 16 size, three-quarter plate, hunting, lever set.

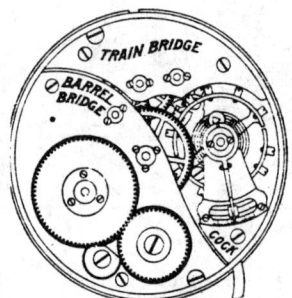

Model 19, 16 size, three-quarter plate, open face, lever set with winding indicator.

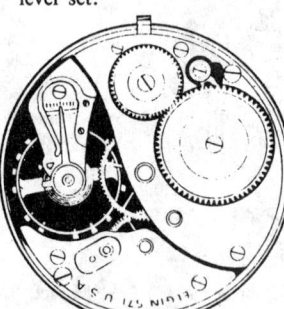

Model 20, 16 size, three-quarter plate, open face, Grades 571, 572, 573, 574, 575, 616.

Model 1, 14 size, three-quarter plate, hunting, key wind and set.

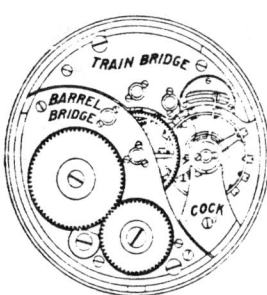

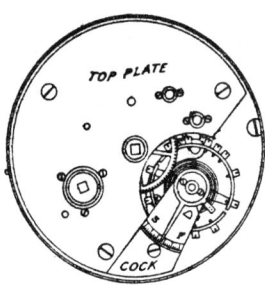

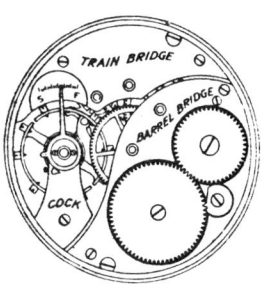

Model 2, 14 size, three-quarter plate, open face, pendant set.

Model 1, 12 size, three-quarter plate, hunting, key wind and set.

Model 2, 12 size, three-quarter plate, hunting, pendant set, first serial #7,410,001, Grade 188, Dec., 1897.

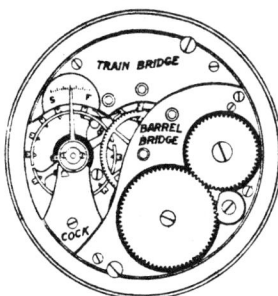

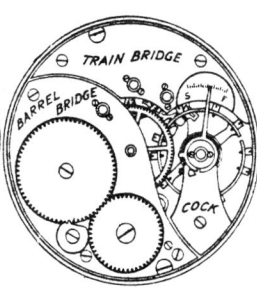

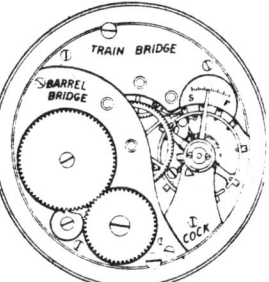

Model 2, 12 size, three-quarter plate, spread to 16 size, hunting, pendant set.

Model 3, 12 size, three-quarter plate, open face, pendant set, serial number 7,423,001, Grade 192, May 1898.

Model 3, 12 size, three-quarter plate, spread to 16 size, open face, pendant set.

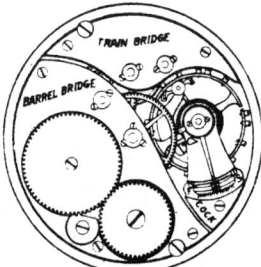

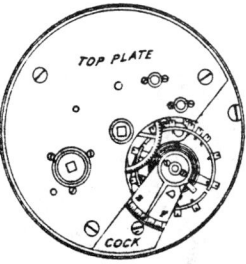

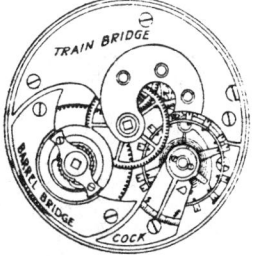

Model 4, 12 size, three-quarter plate, open face, pendant set, serial number 16,311,001, Grade 392, July, 1912.

Model 1, 10 size, three-quarter plate, style 1, hunting, key wind and set.

Model 2, 10 size, three-quarter plate, hunting, key wind and set.

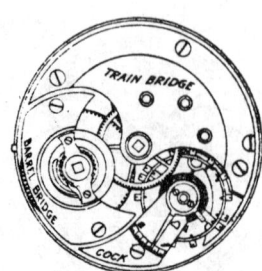

Model 3, 10 size, three-quarter plate, hunting.

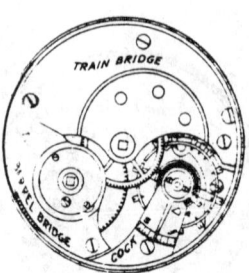

Model 4, 10 size, three-quarter plate, hunting.

Model 5 & 6, 10 size, three-quarter plate.

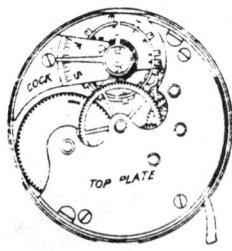

Model 1, 6 size, three-quarter plate, hunting.

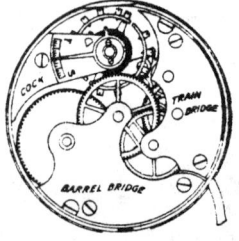

Model 1, 6 size, three-quarter plate, hunting.

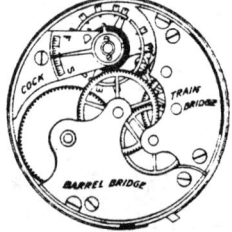

Model 2, 6 size, three-quarter plate, hunting.

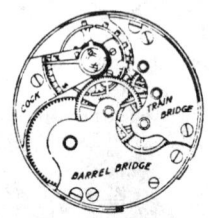

Model 1, 0 size, three-quarter plate, hunting.

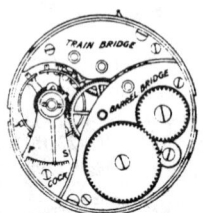

Model 2, 0 size, three-quarter plate, hunting.

Model 2, 0 size, three-quarter plate, hunting.

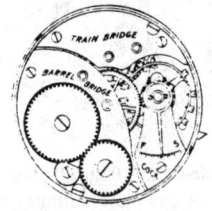

Model 3, 0 size, three-quarter plate, open face.

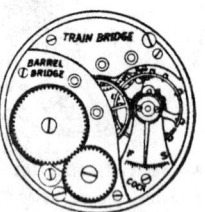

Model 3, 0 size, three-quarter plate, open face.

Model 2, 3-0 size, three-quarter plate, hunting.

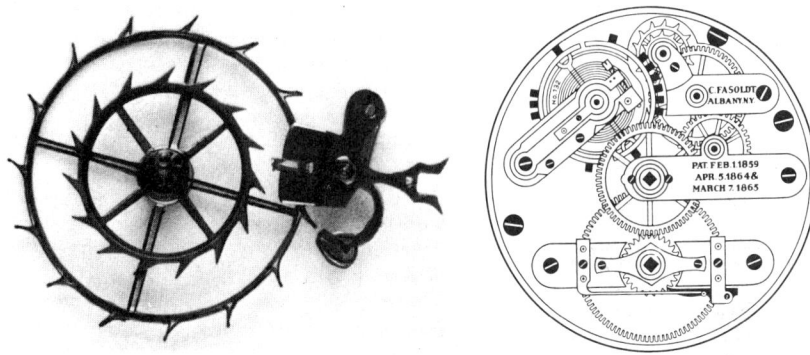

Charles Fasoldt's double escape wheel with odd shaped lever. The double escape wheel was designed to eliminate the use of oil at the escapement and prevent over-banking.

Charles Fasoldt, 18-20 size, 16 jewels, key wind & set, bar movement; S.# 132, note patented regulator, series II.

CHARLES FASOLDT WATCH CO.
Rome, New York   1849 - 1861
Albany, New York   1861 - 1878

Charles Fasoldt came from Dresden, Germany to Rome, New York in 1848. In 1861 he moved to Albany, New York where he set up a factory to make watches and clocks and other instruments. One of his first watches, Serial No. 27, was for General Armstrong and was an eight-day movement. At about that same time, he made several large regulators and a few pocket chronometers. He displayed some of his work at fairs in Utica and Syracuse and received four First-Class Premiums and two diplomas. In 1850, he patented a micrometric regulator (generally called the Howard Regulator because Howard bought the patent). He also patented a **chronometer** escapement with a double escape wheel in 1859 & 1865, a watch regulator in 1864, and a hairspring stud in 1877.

The reliability of his double escape wheel was demonstrated when Mr. Fasoldt **strapped** one of his watches (serial # 6), along with some other brand watches, to the **drive-rod** of the Empire Express locomotive. This round trip run from Albany to New York proved his point; all the other manufacturer's watches stopped about a minute after the train started. Mr. Fasoldt's watch, serial # 6, made the entire trip running, and was within a few minutes of the correct time.

Mr. Fasoldt's double escape wheel was designed to eliminate the use of oil at the escapement and prevent over-banking. Each watch he made has minor changes making no two watches alike and these masterpieces sold for about $300.00 dollars. Mr. Fasoldt was also known for his tower clocks, for which he received many awards and medals. He made about 400 watches in Albany and about 50 watches in Rome. Serial numbers 200 to 299 have not been seen.

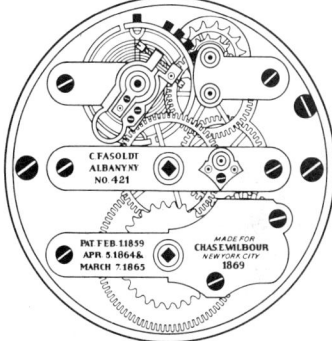

Charles Fasoldt, 18-20 size, 16 jewels, stem wind, key set, bar movement, note: the barrel ratchet wheel only having wolf tooth form, note: Single Winding Bridge, series III.

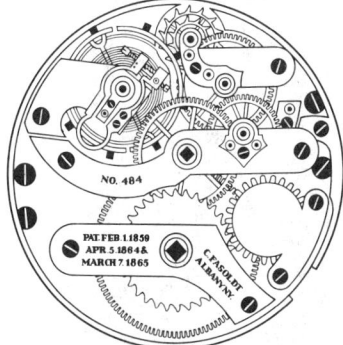

Charles Fasoldt, 18-20 size, 16 jewels, stem wind, key set, bar movement, note: the barrel ratchet wheel only having wolf tooth form, note: Double Winding Bridge, series III.

Estimated serial numbers & Production Dates
For Albany, New York MODELS (ONLY)

Year	Model	Style	Serial # Range
1861-1863	Series I	KW/KS, 1/2 plate	5-40
1864-1866	Series II	KW/KS, Bar	41-99
1867-1868	Series II	KW/KS, Bar	100-199
1868-1869	Series II	KW/KS, Bar	300-399
1869-1871	Series III	SW/KS, Bar	400-499
1872-1875	Series III	SW/KS, Bar	500-540

Serial numbers *200* to *299* have **not** been seen.

Serial # reported = 3, 5, 6, 27, 46, 59, 61, 64, 87, 90, 112, 113, 122, 124, 132, 161, 174, 335, 338, 349, 350, 384, 385, 390, 415, 421, 424, 437, 438, 439, 456, 484, 485, 496, 504, 508, 510, 512, 540.

Grade or Name — Description		Avg	Ex-Fn	Mint
18 - 20 SIZE, 22J, chronograph, Wind Ind., dual mainsprings & dual train, GJS, KW or SW, **18K case**	★★★★	$15,000	$20,000	$25,000
18 - 20 SIZE, 16J, GJS, **KW/ KS**, double escape wheel, **18K case**	★★★	8,500	12,000	18,000
18 - 20 SIZE, 16J, GJS, **SW/ KS**, double escape wheel, **18K case**	★★★	8,500	12,000	18,000
18 - 20 SIZE, 16J, GJS, double escape wheel, **movement only**		2,500	3,000	4,000
10 - 12 SIZE, 16J, by C. Fasoldt,GJS, KW & SW, KS, 14K		3,000	4,000	6,000
by **Otto H. Fasoldt**, **18S,** 15J, SW, Swiss made or American		375	450	600

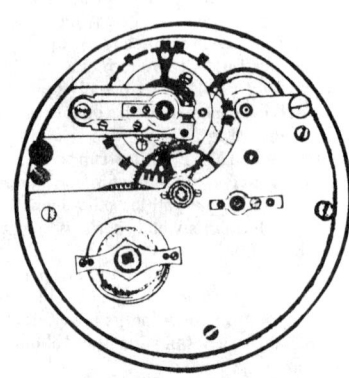

Charles Fasoldt, 18-20 size, 16 jewels, key wind, key set, half plate, double escape wheel, Serial **No. 6**, series I.

Charles Fasoldt, 18-20 size, 16 jewels, stem wind, key set, patented **chronometer** escapement with a double brass escape wheel, **gold regulator**, Serial No. 438, series III.

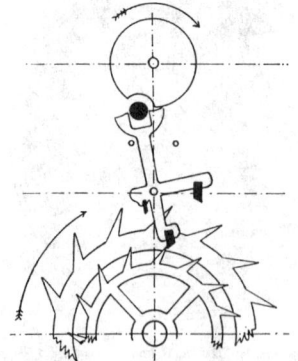

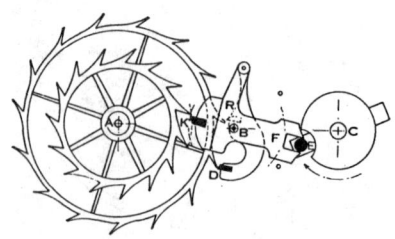

Charles Fasoldt patented **chronometer** escapement with a double brass escape wheel.

Fasoldt chronometer escapement, larger wheel for locking & smaller escape wheel for impulse to the escapement. The double escape wheel was designed to eliminate the use of oil at the escapement and prevent over-banking.

FITCHBURG WATCH CO.

Fitchburg, Massachusetts
1875 - 1878

In 1875, S. Sawyer decided to manufacture watches. He hired personnel from the U. S. Watch Company to build the machinery, but by 1878 the company had failed. It is not known how many, if any, watches were made. The equipment was sold to Cornell and other watch companies.

E. H. FLINT

Cincinnati, Ohio
1877 - 1879

The Flint watch was patented September 18, 1877, and about 100 watches were made. The serial number is found under the dial.

Grade or Name — Description		Avg	Ex-Fn	Mint
18 Size, 4–7J, KW, Full Plate, OF, Coin .... ★ ★ ★ ★		$3,500	$4,000	$6,000
18 Size, 4–7J, KW, Full Plate, 14K, HC .... ★ ★ ★ ★		5,000	6,000	9,000

 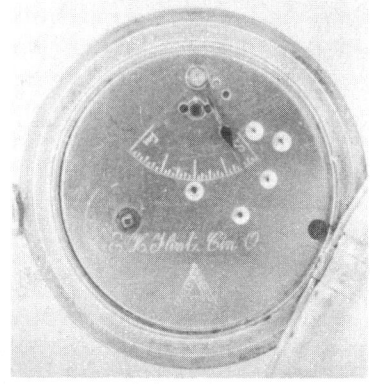

E.H. Flint dial and movement, 18 size, 4-7 jewels, open face, key wind & set, "Lancaster Pa." on dial, "Patented Sept. 18th,1877" on movement.

🕐 Watch terminology or communication in this book has evolved over the years, in search of better and more precise language with a effort to improve, purify, adjust itself and make it easier to understand.

🕐 Watches listed in this book are priced at the collectable retail level, as complete watches having an original 14k goldfilled case & KW with a Silver case, an original white enamel single sunk dial, and with the entire original movement in good working order with no repairs needed, unless otherwise noted.

🕐 Pricing in this Guide are fair market price for **COMPLETE** watches which are reflected from the "**NAWCC**" National and regional shows.

FREDONIA WATCH CO.

Fredonia, New York
1881 - 1885

This company sold the finished movements acquired from the Independent Watch Co. These movements had been made by other companies. The Fredonia Watch Company was sold to the Peoria Watch Co. in 1885, after having produced approximately 20,000 watches.

Chronology of the Development of Fredonia:

Independent Watch Co.	1875 –1881
Fredonia Watch Co.	1881 –1885
Peoria Watch Co.	1885 –1889

 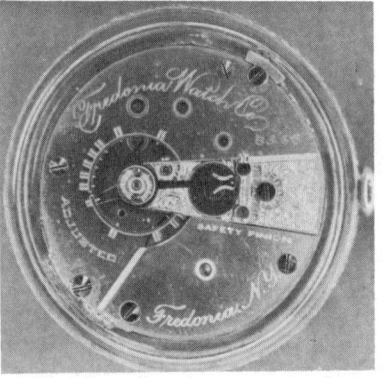

Fredonia Watch Co., 18 size, 15 jewels, signature on movement "Cyrus N. Gibbs, Mass.," key wind & set, serial number 4403.

Fredonia Watch Co., 18 size, 15 jewels, adjusted, serial number 8,368. NOTE: FREDONIA Regulator disc will have teeth all around the disc.

Fredonia Watch Co., with a reversible case; changes to either hunting or open face.

🕐 Pricing in this Guide are fair market price for **COMPLETE** watches which are reflected from the "**NAWCC**" National and regional shows.

Grade or Name — Description	Avg	Ex-Fn	Mint
18S, 7J, SW, OF	$200	$250	$400
18S, 7J, SW, HC	225	275	450
18S, 9J, SW, OF	250	300	450
18S, 9J, SW, HC	225	275	450
18S, 11J, SW, OF	250	300	450
18S, 11J, KW, KS, HC, Coin	225	275	450
18S, 15J, SW, Multi-color, **14K**, HC	1,400	1,800	2,800
18S, KW, Reversible case	500	600	900
18S, 15J, SW, LS, **Gilt**, OF	225	250	400
18S, 15J, straight line escapement, NI, marked **Adjusted**	300	400	500
18S, 15J, SW, LS, **Gold Plated**, OF	300	400	500
18S, 15J, HC, low serial number	300	400	500
18S, 15J, personalized mvt.	250	350	475
18S, 15J, KW, HC, marked Lakeshore W. Co.	250	350	450
18S, 15J, Anti-Magnetic, OF	300	400	500
18S, 15J, Anti-Magnetic, HC	325	425	525
18S, 15J, Special Superior Quality - Anti-Magnetic, OF ★★	450	600	850
18S, 15J, Special Superior Quality - Anti-Magnetic, HC ★★	475	650	900
18S, Mark Twain, 11J, KW, KS ★★★	800	900	1,500

FREEPORT WATCH CO.

Freeport, Illinois

1874 - 1875

Probably less than 20 nickel watches made by Freeport have survived. Their machinery was purchased from Mozart Co., and a Mr. Hoyt was engaged as superintendent. The building erected was destroyed by fire on Oct. 27, 1875. A safe taken from the ruins contained 300 completed brass movements which were said to be ruined.

Grade or Name — Description	Avg	Ex-Fn	Mint
18S, 19J, KW, SW, gold train, raised gold jewel settings 18K case ★★★★	$8,500	$12,000	$20,000
18S, 15J, KW, KS, gold train, friction jewels 18K case ★★★★	$8,000	$11,000	$18,000
Geo. P. Rose, Dubuque, Iowa, 18S, 15J, KW, KS, gold train, friction jewels, 18K case ★★★★	$6,000	$7,000	$9,000

Freeport Watch Co., Example of a basic movement, 18 size, 15 jewels, key wind & set, pressed jewels, gold train, high grade movement, serial number 11.

Freeport Watch Co., 15 jewels, gold train, damaskeened, large over coiled hairspring with a floating stud, steel lever & escape wheel with single roller.

208

SMITH D. FRENCH

Wabash, Indiana
1866 - 1878

On August 21, 1866, Mr. French was issued a patent for an improved escapement for watches. The escape wheel has triangular shaped pins and the lever has two hook-shaped pallets. The pin wheel escapement was probably first used by Robert Robin, about 1795, for pocket watches. Antoine Tavan also used this style escape wheel around 1800. Mr. French's improved pin wheel and hook shaped lever (about 70 total production) can be seen through a cutout in the plates of his watches.

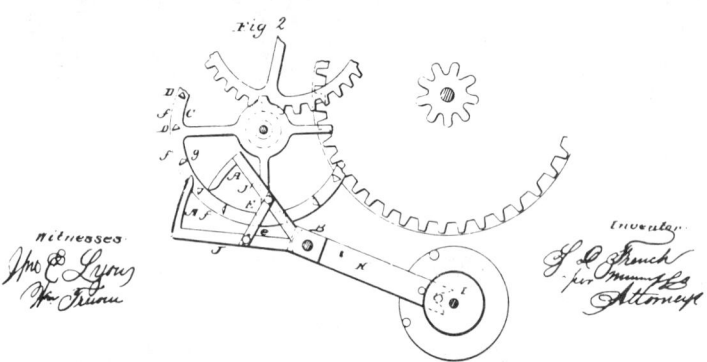

Illustration from the patent office, patent number 57,310, patented Aug. 21, 1866. Note pin wheel escapement with adjustable hook shaped lever.

Grade or Name — Description	Avg	Ex-Fn	Mint
18S, 15J, 3/4, KW, KS, gilt, pin wheel escapement, Silver case ★ ★ ★ ★	$8,000	$9,000	$13,000
18S, 15J, 3/4, KW, KS, gilt, pin wheel escapement, 18K case ★ ★ ★ ★	9,000	10,000	16,000

S.D. French, about 18 size, 15J., gilt 3/4 movement, key wind & set, with pin wheel escapement, engraved on movement "S.D. French, Wabash Ind., Aug. 21, 1866, No. 24."

L. Goddard, 55mm, 7 jewels, full plate movement with solid cock, chain driven fusee, flat steel balance, serial number 235, ca. 1809-1817.

LUTHER GODDARD

Shrewsbury, Massachusetts

1809 - 1825

The first significant attempt to produce watches in America was made by Luther Goddard. William H. Keith, who became president of Waltham Watch Co. (1861 -1866) and was once apprenticed to Goddard, said that the hands, dials, round and dovetail brass, steel wire, mainsprings and hairsprings, balance, verge, chains, and pinions were all imported. The plates, wheels, and brass parts were cast at the Goddard shop, however. He also made the cases for his movements which were of the usual style open faced, double case-and somewhat in advance of the prevalent style of thick bull's eye watches of the day. About 600 watches were made which were of good quality and more expensive than the imported type. The first watch was made about 1812 and was sold to the father of ex-governor Lincoln of Worcester, Massachusetts. In 1820 his watches sold for about $60.00.

Goddard built a shop one story high with a hip roof about 18' square; it had a lean-to at the back for casting. The building was for making clocks, but a need for watches developed and Goddard made watches there. He earned the distinction of establishing the first watch factory in America.

His movements were marked as follows: L. GODDARD, L.GODDARD & CO., LUTHER GODDARD & SON, P. GODDARD, L. & P. GODDARD, D.P. GODDARD & CO., D. & P. GODDARD.

Frank A. Knowlton purchased the company and operated it until 1933.

Chronology of the Development of Luther Goddard:

Luther Goddard, L. Goddard, L. Goddard & Son 1809-1825
L. Goddard & Son 1817-1825
P.& D. Goddard 1825-1842
D. Goddard & Son 1842-1850
Luther D. Goddard 1850-1857
Goddard & Co. 1857-1860
D. Goddard & Co., & Benj'n Goddard.. 1860-1872

D. Goddard, 18-20, 15 jewels," Worcester, Mass."on movement, key wind & set, solid balance, under sprung, serial number 8.

L. Goddard & Co.,16-18 size, pair case, open face-thick bulls-eye type, and of high quality for the time.

NOTE: Watches listed below are with original silver cases.

Grade or Name — Description		Avg	Ex-Fn	Mint
Benj'n Goddard..	★ ★	$1,500	$2,000	$3,500
Luther Goddard, S#1-35 with eagle on balance bridge......	★ ★ ★ ★	8,000	10,000	18,000
Luther Goddard without eagle on cock..................................	★ ★ ★	5,000	7,000	12,000
Luther Goddard,L.Goddard, Luther Goddard & Son	★ ★ ★	4,500	6,500	10,000
L. Goddard & Co., D. Goddard & Son	★ ★ ★	3,500	5,000	8,000
Luther D. Goddard, Goddard & Co., D. Goddard & Co.	★ ★ ★	2,500	3,500	6,000
P. Goddard, with eagle on cock..	★ ★ ★	4,000	6,000	9,000
P & D Goddard, 7J., (Worcester), fusee, KWKS, OF...............	★ ★	1,200	1,800	3,000

SEE ALSO OTHER **GODDARD** ILLUSTRATIONS ON PAGES- **208 & 210**

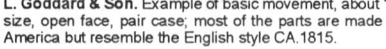

L. Goddard & Son. Example of basic movement, about 18 size, open face, pair case; most of the parts are made in America but resemble the English style CA.1815.

L. Goddard & Son, about 18 size, pair case, verge escapement, engraved on movement "L. Goddard & Son, Shrewsbury," serial number 460.

JONAS G. HALL
Montpelier, Vermont 1850 - 1870
Millwood Park, Roxbury, Vermont 1870 - 1890

Jonas G. Hall was born in 1822 in Calais, Vermont. He opened a shop in Montpelier where he sold watches, jewelry, silverware, and fancy goods. While at this location, he produced more than 60 full plate, lever style watches. Hall, later established a business in Roxbury, where he manufactured watch staking tools and other watchmaking tools. At Roxbury, he made at least one watch which was a three-quarter plate model. He also produced a few chronometers, about 20-size with a fusee and detent escapement and a wind indicator on the dial.

Hall was employed by the American Waltham Watch Co. for a short time and helped design the first lady's model. He also worked for Tremont Watch Co., E. Howard & Co., and the United States Watch Co. of Marion, New Jersey.

Style or Name–Description		Avg	Ex-Fn	Mint
18S, 15J, Full plate, KW KS	★ ★ ★	$3,000	$4,000	$7,000
18S, 15J, 3/4 plate, gilded, KW KS	★ ★ ★	4,500	6,000	8,000
20S, 15J, Detent Chronometer, KW KS	★ ★ ★ ★	5,000	7,000	12,000

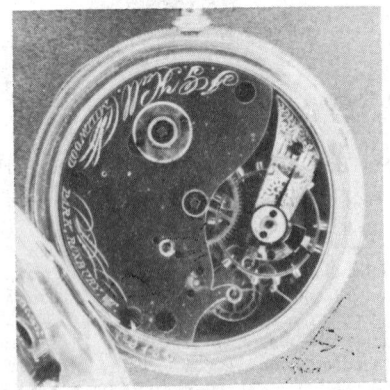

J.G. Hall, 18 size, 15 jewels, full plate, key wind & set, engraved on movement "J.G. Hall, Montpelier, VT.," serial number 25, ca. 1857.

J.G. Hall, 18 size, 15 jewels, 3/4 plate, key wind and set, engraved on movement "J.G. Hall, Millwood Park, Roxbury, VT," no serial number, ca. 1880.

HAMILTON WATCH CO.
Lancaster, Pennsylvania
December 14, 1892 - Present

Hamilton's roots go back to the Adams & Perry Watch Manufacturing Co. On Sept. 26, 1874, E. F. Bowman made a model watch, and the first movement was produced on April 7, 1876. It was larger than an 18S, or about a 19S. The movement had a snap on dial and the patented stem-setting arrangement. They decided to start making the watches a standard size of 18, and no more than 1,000 of the large-size watches were made. Work had commenced on Sept. 1, 1877, at the Lancaster Watch Co. The watches were designed to sell at a cheaper price than normal. It had a one-piece top 3/4 plate and a pillar plate that was fully ruby-jeweled (4 1/2 pairs). It had a gilt or nickel movement and a new stem-wind device designed by Mosely & Todd. By mid-1878, the Lancaster Watch Co. had made 150 movements. Four grades of watches were produced: Keystone, Fulton, Franklin, and Melrose. In September 1879 the company had manufactured 334 movements. In 1880 some 1,250 movements had been made. In mid-1882, about 17,000 movements had been assembled. All totaled, about 20,000 movements were made.

HAMILTON
No. 950 MOVEMENT

THE

THE RAIL ROAD TIMEKEEPER OF AMERICA.

LANCASTER, PA.

ABOVE: AD 1910

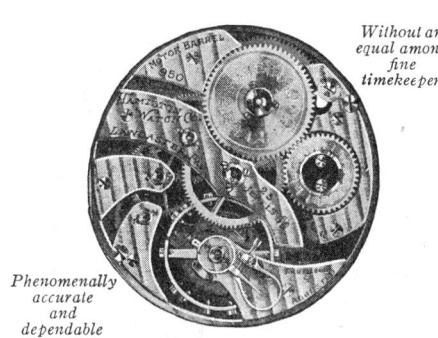

Without an equal among fine timekeepers

Phenomenally accurate and dependable

A most accurate and dependable movement designed by Hamilton to meet the most exacting standards of timekeeping.

No. 950 OPEN FACE—white gold finish, bridge movement, pendant or lever set, 23 extra fine ruby and sapphire jewels in gold settings, patent motor barrel, gold train, escapement cap jeweled, steel escape wheel, double roller escapement, sapphire pallets, Breguet hairspring, micrometric regulator, compensation balance, double sunk dial, adjusted to temperature, isochronism, and five positions.

GRADE 992 ELINVAR MOVEMENT
16 size, nickel, 3/4 plate, lever set, 21 extra fine ruby and sapphire jewels, double roller escapement, sapphire pallets, gold center wheel, steel escape wheel, micrometric regulator, ELINVAR hairspring, monometallic balance, friction set roller jewel, double sunk dial, two piece friction fit balance staff, beautifully damaskeened. Adjusted to five positions and automatically regulated to temperature. Sold cased only.

Note: Automatically regulated to temperature (1933 AD)

ABOVE: AD 1924
(TIME BOOK)

 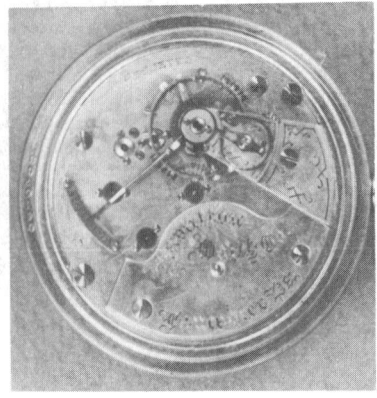

Grade 936, 18 size, 17 jewels, serial number 1. c. 1893.   Grade 936, 18 size, 17 jewels, serial number 2, c. 1893.

The first Hamilton movement to be sold was No. 15 to W. C. Davis on January 31, 1893. The No. 1 movement was finished on April 25, 1896, and was never sold. The No. 2 was finished on April 25, 1893, and was shipped to Smythe & Ashe of Rochester, N. Y. Nos. 1 & 2 are at the N.A.W.C.C. museum.

Chronology of the Development of Hamilton:

Adams & Perry Watch Co.	Sept. 1874-May 1876
Lancaster, Pa., Watch Co.	Aug. 1877-Oct. 1887
Lancaster, Pa., Watch Co.	Nov. 1877-May 1879
Lancaster Watch Co.	May 1883-1886
Keystone Standard Watch Co.	1886-1890
Hamilton Watch Co.	Dec. 14, 1892-Present

In 1893 the first watch was produced by Hamilton. The watches became very popular with railroad men and by 1923 some 53 percent of Hamilton's production were railroad watches. The 940 model watch was discontinued in 1910. Most Hamilton watches are fitted with a 42-hour mainspring.

Grade 937, 18 size, 17 jewels, hunting case. Note serial   Hamilton Watch Co., 18 size, 7 jewels, serial number 2934.
number 1047. **Hunting case models began with 1001.**   NOTE: Gilded plates.

The 950B was introduced in 1940 and by this time a total of about 25,000 grade (950) had been sold. The 992 watch sold for about $60.00 in 1929, the price remained the same $60.00 until 1940.

The Elinvar hairspring was patented in 1931 and used in all movements thereafter. On October 15, 1940, Hamilton introduced the 992B which were fitted with the Elinvar hairspring. Elinvar and Invar are trade names and are the same 36 percent nickel steel. Although the Hamilton Watch Co. is still in business today making modern type watches, they last produced American made watches in about 1969. Chronograph Grade 23 starts in 1943 ends in 1956 & total production = 23,146.

HAMILTON ESTIMATED SERIAL NUMBERS
AND PRODUCTION DATES

Date–Serial No.	Date–Serial No.	Date–Serial No.	Date–Serial No.
1893 -1 to 2,000	1906 — 590,000	1919—1,700,000	1932—2,500,000
1894 — 5,000	1907 — 756,000	1920—1,790,000	1933—2,600,000
1895 — 11,500	1908 — 921,000	1921—1,860,000	1934—2,700,000
1896 — 16,000	1909—1,087,000	1922—1,900,000	1935—2,800,000
1897 — 27,000	1910—1,150,500	1923—1,950,000	1936—2,900,000
1898 — 50,000	1911—1,290,500	1924—2,000,000	1937—3,000,000
1899 — 74,000	1912—1,331,000	1925—2,100,000	1938—3,200,000
1900—104,000	1913—1,370,000	1926—2,200,000	1939—3,400,000
1901—143,000	1914—1,410,500	1927—2,250,000	1940—3,600,000
1902—196,000	1915—1,450,500	1928—2,300,000	1941—3,800,000
1903—260,000	1916—1,517,000	1929—2,350,000	1942—4,025,000
1904—340,000	1917—1,580,000	1930—2,400,000	
1905—425,000	1918—1,650,000	1931—2,450,000	

The above list is provided for determining the <u>APPROXIMATE</u> age of your watch. Match serial number with date. Watches were not necessarily **SOLD** in the exact order of manufactured date.

Some serial numbers have the first numbers replaced by a (date) letter such as A, B, C, E, F, G, H, J, L, M, N, R, S, T, V, W, X, Y, CY, HW. These letters were used from late 30's to about late 50's. The date letter "2B + Ser.#" found on 950B = **1941 to 1943,** the date letter "C + Ser.#" found on 992B = **1940 to 1968,** the date letter "S + Ser.#" found on 950B = **1943 to 1968** and HA = SWISS.

992B with first letter of C + serial no.
```
1940=    C001
1941= C75000
1942=C160000
1943=C200000
1944=C240000
1945=C270000
1946=C300000
1947=C345000
1948=C365000
1950=C380000
1951=C400000
1952=C420000
1954=C430000
1956=C445000
1959=C462500
```

950B with first letter of 2B + serial no.
```
1941=2B001
1942=2B400
1943=2B800
```

950B with first letter of S + serial no.
```
1943=S001
1944=S1500
1945=S2900
1946=S4000
1947=S4500
1948=S6500
1949=S7500

1950=S8900
1951=S10000
1955=S18700
1962=S20000
1965=S25000
1968=S30000
```

NOTE: *It required several months for raw material to emerge as a finished movement. All the while the factory is producing all sizes, models and grades. The numbering system was basically "consecutive", due to demand a batch of movements could be side tracked, thus allowing a different size and model to move ahead to meet this demand. Therefore, the dates some movements were <u>sold</u> and delivered to the trade, the serial numbers may not be "consecutive".*

The Hamilton Masterpiece

The adjoining illustration shows the Hamilton Masterpiece. The dial is sterling silver with raised gold numbers and solid gold hands. This watch sold for $685.00 in 1930. All 922 **MP** Models included the following: 12 size, 23 jewels, were adjusted to heat, cold, isochronism, and five positions, with a motor barrel, solid gold train, steel escape wheel, double roller, sapphire pallets and a micrometric regulator.

HAMILTON SERIAL NUMBERS AND GRADES

To help determine the size and grade of your watch, the following serial number list is provided. Serial numbers 30,001 through 32,000, which are omitted from the list, were not listed by Hamilton. To identify your watch, simply look up its serial number which will identify the grade. After determining the grade, your watch can be easily located in the pricing section.

Serial Number	Grade
1-20	936
21-30	932
31-60	936
61-400	932
401-1000	936
1001-20	937
1021-30	933
1031-60	937
1061-1100	933
1101-300	937
1301-600	933
1601-2000	937
2001-3000	7J
3001-100	931
3101-500	935
3501-600	931
3601-900	935
3901-4000	931
4001-300	930
4301-5100	934
5101-400	926
5401-600	934
5601-6000	930
6001-600	936
6601-700	938
6701-800	936
6801-7000	932
7001-10	17J
7011-600	937
7601-700	939
7701-800	937
7801-8000	933
8001-700	936
8701-800	938
8801-9000	936
9001-300	937
9301-600	939
9601-800	937
9801-900	933
9901-10000	939
10001-200	938
10201-400	936
10401-50	932
10451-500	936
10501-700	938
10701-900	936
10901-11000	938
11001-12000	936
12001-200	939
12201-13000	937
13001-400	999
13401-14000	938
14001-15000	999
15001-300	939
15301-15401	21J
15302-700	937
15701-16000	939
16001-100	931
16101-200	930
16201-300	927
16301-400	931
16401-600	927
16601-17000	931
17001-500	929
17501-18000	931
18001-200	928
18201-300	926
18301-500	928
18501-19500	930
19501-700	926
19701-20000	930
20001-300	934
20301-500	926
20501-21000	999
21001-300	935
21301-500	927
21501-800	935
21801-22500	927
22501-800	931
22801-23000	935
23001-200	928
23201-500	7J
24001-500	926
24501-25000	934
25001-100	11J
25101-400	927
25401-800	931
25801-26000	935
26001-500	930
26501-27000	928
27001-28000	936
28001-29000	999
29001-800	927
29801-30000	935
32001-300	926
32301-700	930
32701-33000	934
33001-500	931
33501-800	927
33801-34000	935
34001-500	928
34501-700	930
34701-800	926
34801-35000	934
35001-800	931
35801-36000	935
36001-37000	928
37001-38000	929
38001-500	926
38501-600	930
38601-900	934
38901-39000	926
39001-200	931
39201-500	935
39501-700	927
39701-900	935
39901-40000	931
40001-200	930
40201-500	934
40501-41000	926
41001-500	929
41501-42000	927
42001-43000	999
43001-300	941
43301-500	943
43501-700	937
43701-900	941
43901-44000	943
44001-02	21J
44003-400	938
44401-500	942
44501-45000	936
45001-46000	929
46001-500	926
46501-800	934
46801-47000	930
47001-500	927
47501-700	935
47701-48000	931
48001-05	942
48006-300	940
48301-500	942
48501-900	940
48901-49000	942
49001-400	927
49401-900	925
49901-50	11J
50071-500	962
50501-750	960
50751-50850	964
50851-51000	960
51001-51300	16s
51301-400	963
51401-650	961
51651-750	965
51751-52000	961
52001-300	16s
52301-500	976
52501-700	974
52701-800	966
52801-53000	976
53001-53070	16s
53071-53500	977
53501-900	975
53901-54000	967
54001-200	972
54201-300	974
54301-500	976
54501-700	974
54701-800	968
54801-55000	976
55001-300	973
55301-600	977
55601-700	969
55701-800	977
55801-56000	975
56001-300	977
56301-500	974
56501-600	966
56601-800	972
56801-900	974
56901-57000	976
57001-300	977
57301-500	975
57501-600	973
57601-800	975
57801-58000	977
58001-100	972
58101-200	974
58201-300	972
58301-400	966
58401-500	976
58501-600	972
58601-800	974
58801-59000	976
59001-300	973
59301-500	967
59501-700	975
59701-60000	977
60001-500	976
60501-700	974
60701-61000	976
61001-200	975
61201-500	977
61501-600	973
61601-800	975
61801-62000	977
62001-100	972
62101-300	974
62301-500	976
62501-700	974
62701-900	972
62901-63000	974
63001-500	977
63501-600	975
63601-800	977
63801-900	975
63901-64000	973
64001-100	976
64101-200	972
64201-300	974
64301-600	972
64601-700	976
64701-900	974
64901-65000	976
65001-200	973
65201-300	977
65301-400	975
65401-500	973
65501-700	977
65701-900	975
65901-66000	977
66001-200	976
66201-300	974
66301-500	972
66501-600	976
66601-700	974
66701-800	972
66801-67000	974
67001-100	977
67101-300	975
67301-600	973
67601-800	975
67801-68000	977
68001-800	960
68801-69000	964
69001-100	977
69101-200	975
69201-400	973
69401-600	975
69601-70000	977
70001-200	976
70201-400	970
70401-600	968
70601-900	972
70901-71000	974
71001-200	975
71201-500	971
71501-700	975
71701-90	973
71791-800	969
71801-900	977
71901-72000	975
72001-100	974
72101-300	976
72301-600	974
72601-700	968
72701-900	976
72901-73000	972
73001-200	975
73201-300	973
73301-74000	977
74001-400	974
74401-600	972
74601-75000	976
75001-76799	HWW*
76002-76800	HWW*
77001-100	969
77101-300	973
77301-500	975
77501-600	971
77601-700	973
77701-900	975
77901-78000	977
78001-500	970
78501-700	972
78701-900	974
78901-79000	976
79001-100	973
79101-300	975
79301-700	977
79701-900	975
79901-80000	973
80001-200	972
80201-400	974
80401-600	970
80601-700	972
80701-900	974
80901-81000	976
81001-300	961
81301-500	965
81501-82000	961
82001-300	972
82301-500	974
82501-600	970
82601-700	972
82701-800	974
82801-900	968
82901-83000	976
83001-400	977
83401-500	971
83501-700	975
83701-800	973
83801-900	975
83901-84000	969
84001-400	974
84401-500	970
84501-700	972
84701-800	968
84801-85000	976
85001-200	937
85201-900	941
85901-86000	943
86001-87000	928
87001-88000	929
88001-500	926
88501-89000	930
89001-500	941
89501-90000	937
90001-100	926
90101-950	999
91001-92000	925
92001-200	940
92201-93000	936
93001-94000	927
94001-003	934
94004-95000	928
95001-96000	923
96001-100	942
96101-700	940
96701-97000	936
97001-900	929
97901-98000	927
98001-99000	924
99001-100000	925
100001-101000	924
101001-102000	925
102001-103000	922
103001-104000	927
104001-105000	940
105001-500	925
105501-106000	927
106001-107000	940
107001-400	941
107401-500	943
107501-800	941
107801-108000	943
108001-200	928

Serial	No.	Serial	No.	Serial	No.	Serial	No.
108201-109000	926	186001-187000	942	275202-460	HWW*	322001-323000	974
109001-500	927	187001-188000	927	275462-500	HWW*	323001-700	975
109501-110000	925	188001-189000	924	276001-277000	940	323701-324000	973
110001-900	940	189001-190000	925	277001-278000	941	324001-325000	960
110901-111000	942	190001-191000	926	278001-279000	940	325001-100	965
111001-500	937	191001-192000	927	279001-280000	925	325101-326000	961
111501-112000	941	192001-193000	924	280001-281000	936	326001-327000	974
112001-200	928	193001-194000	925	281001-282000	927	327001-300	971
112201-113000	926	194001-195000	926	282001-283000	926	327301-500	973
113001-114000	925	195001-500	935	283001-284000	925	327501-328000	975
114001-003	940	195501-196000	927	284001-500	934	328001-300	992
114004-115000	936	196001-197000	926	284501-900	924	328301-500	990
115001-116000	927	197001-198000	937	284901-285000	999	328501-329000	992
116001-117000	940	198001-199000	936	285001-286000	925	329001-330000	975
117001-118000	925	199001-200000	925	286001-287000	940	330001-100	992
118001-119000	999	200001-201000	926	287001-288000	927	330101-500	990
119001-120000	925	201001-202000	925	288001-289000	940	330501-331000	992
120001-121000	924	202001-500	926	289001-290000	927	331001-200	973
121001-500	941	202501-203000	934	290001-800	936	331201-400	975
121501-122000	943	203001-204000	927	290801-291000	938	331401-500	969
122001-300	940	204001-100	934	291001-292000	925	331501-700	971
122301-400	942	204101-500	926	292001-500	940	331701-800	973
122401-123000	940	204501-205000	934	292501-293000	942	331801-332000	975
123001-124000	941	205001-206000	941	293001-294000	925	332001-200	992
124001-100	942	206001-207000	940	294001-295000	926	332201-800	972
124101-800	940	207001-208000	927	295001-296000	927	332801-333000	974
124801-125000	942	208001-900	999	296001-297000	940	333001-500	975
125001-126000	927	208901-209000	940	297001-298000	927	333501-700	971
126001-127000	924	209001-210000	925	298001-299000	940	333701-900	973
127001-128000	941	210001-211000	940	299001-300000	925	333901-334000	975
128001-129000	936	211001-212000	927	300001-300	972	334001-200	972
129001-130000	925	212001-213000	940	300301-500	970	334201-800	992
130001-500	924	213001-500	941	300501-900	974	334801-335000	990
130501-131000	926	213501-600	937	300901-301000	968	335001-600	975
131001-132000	925	213601-214000	925	301001-400	975	335601-800	971
132001-100	926	214001-215000	924	301401-500	971	335801-900	973
132101-200	934	215001-216000	927	301501-302000	973	335901-336000	975
132201-500	926	216001-217000	940	302001-100	990	336001-200	972
132501-133000	924	217001-218000	927	302101-200	992	336201-337000	974
133001-134000	937	218001-219000	940	302201-300	990	337001-338000	975
134001-135000	924	219001-220000	925	302301-900	992	338001-200	974
135001-136000	925	220001-221000	924	302901-303000	990	338201-900	992
136001-137000	926	221001-222000	927	303001-100	973	338901-339000	990
137001-100	11J	222001-223000	926	303101-300	971	339001-300	971
137101-138000	927	223001-02	927	303301-800	975	339301-500	973
138001-139000	940	223003-04	941	303801-304000	973	339501-340000	975
139001-140000	937	223005	937	304001-100	970	340001-200	974
140001-300	938	223006-224000	927	304101-400	972	340201-300	972
140301-141000	942	224001-225000	924	304401-305000	974	340301-600	970
141001-142000	941	225001-226000	927	305001-100	973	340601-341000	974
142001-143000	940	226001-227000	940	305101-200	971	341001-200	973
143001-100	927	227001-228000	925	305201-300	969	341201-342000	975
143101-144000	925	228001-229000	924	305301-900	975	342001-300	990
144001-145000	924	229001-230000	925	305901-306000	973	342301-343000	992
145001-146000	925	230001-500	926	306001-400	972	343001-344000	975
146001-400	934	230501-231000	924	306401-307000	974	344001-200	970
146401-147000	924	231001-565	937	307001-100	975	344201-400	972
147001-148000	927	231566-232000	927	307101-300	971	344401-345000	974
148001-149000	940	232001-233000	940	307301-400	975	345001-346000	975
149001-150000	925	233001-234000	941	307401-500	973	346001-300	992
150001-151000	924	234001-235000	940	307501-600	975	346301-347000	974
151001-400	927	235001-236000	941	307601-700	971	347001-180	993
151401-500	935	236001-237000	936	307701-900	975	347181-200	991
151501-152000	927	237001-238000	941	307901-308000	969	347201-300	975
152001-153000	936	238001-239000	926	308001-700	990	347301-400	973
153001-154000	941	239001-500	943	308701-309000	992	347401-700	993
154001-155000	936	239501-240000	941	309001-100	971	347701-900	991
155001-156000	927	240001-241000	940	309101-400	973	347901-348000	973
156001-157000	940	241001-242000	941	309401-310000	975	348001-200	970
157001-158000	925	242001-243000	940	310001-400	970	348201-800	974
158001-159000	940	243001-244000	927	310401-311000	974	348801-349000	972
159001-160000	941	244001-245000	936	311001-700	975	349001-350000	975
160001-161000	940	245001-246000	925	311701-312000	973	350001-300	990
161001-162000	941	246001-247000	940	312001-200	970	350301-400	974
162001-163000	926	247001-248000	927	312201-500	972	350401-600	990
163001-164000	943	248001-249000	940	312501-600	968	350601-351000	992
164001-165000	940	249001-250000	927	312601-313000	974	351001-352000	975
165001-166000	925	250001-251000	926	313001-100	973	352001-100	968
166001-167000	924	251001-252000	927	313101-400	971	352101-353000	974
167001-168000	927	252001-253000	924	313401-600	969	353001-354000	975
168001-169000	940	253001-254000	925	313601-314000	975	354001-400	992
169001-400	935	254001-255000	940	314001-600	974	354401-355000	974
169401-170000	927	255001-256000	925	314601-900	972	355001-800	975
170001-171000	999	256001-257000	926	314901-315000	970	355801-900	973
171001-172000	925	257001-258000	941	315001-100	971	355901-356000	993
172001-100	934	258001-259000	924	315101-400	973	356001-500	990
172101-173000	926	259001-260000	941	315401-316000	975	356501-357000	974
173001-174000	925	260001-261000	940	316001-200	992	357001-358000	975
174001-175000	924	261001-262000	927	316201-300	972	358001-359000	974
175002-176000	HWW*	262001-263000	926	316301-500	992	359001-360000	975
175001-699	HWW*	263001-264000	925	316501-317000	972	360001-550	960
176001-177000	940	264001-265000	940	317001-600	975	360801-361000	960
177001-178000	927	265001-266000	927	317601-700	969	361001-100	993
178001-179000	942	266001-267000	940	317701-318000	973	361101-300	991
179001-500	935	267001-268000	925	318001-100	972	361301-400	993
179501-180000	927	268001-269000	940	318101-900	974	361401-700	975
180001-181000	940	269001-270000	927	318901-319000	970	361701-20	973
181001-182000	941	270001-271000	940	319001-100	971	361721-362000	975
182001-300	926	271001-272000	925	319101-320000	975	362001-900	974
182301-400	934	272001-273000	926	320001-300	972	362901-363000	990
182401-183000	926	273001-274000	941	320301-400	968	363001-364000	975
183001-184000	941	274001-275000	924	320401-321000	974	364001-365000	974
184001-185000	940	275002-100	HWW*	321001-200	973	365001-100	975
185001-186000	925	275102-200	HWW*	321201-322000	975	365101-300	973

Serial Range	No.
365301-366000	975
366001-367000	974
367001-500	975
367501-368000	993
368001-369000	974
369001-370000	992
370001-100	990
370101-400	992
370401-500	974
370501-800	990
370801-371400	992
371401-500	972
371501-373500	974
373501-700	990
373701-374000	992
374001-200	974
374201-700	990
374701-375000	974
375001-100	993
375101-500	991
375501-376000	975
376001-200	972
376201-500	974
376501-377000	992
377001-200	973
377201-378000	975
378001-379000	974
379001-380800	992
380801-381000	990
381001-382000	992
382001-100	990
382101-383000	974
383001-300	992
383301-700	990
383701-384000	972
384001-700	974
384701-900	972
384901-385000	974
385001-600	972
385601-800	974
385801-386000	990
386001-800	974
386801-900	992
386901-387000	972
387001-100	990
387101-900	992
387901-388000	972
388001-400	990
388401-389000	992
389001-391000	974
391001-300	972
391301-392000	974
392001-800	992
392801-393000	990
393001-400	975
393401-600	973
393601-394000	993
394001-200	972
394201-395000	974
395001-100	993
395101-900	991
395901-396000	993
396001-397000	992
397001-200	990
397201-398000	992
398001-200	972
398201-399000	993
399001-600	993
399601-400000	975
400001-401000	924
401001-402000	940
402001-404000	924
404001-405000	926
405001-406000	924
406001-407000	940
407001-408000	926
408001-416000	940
416001-417000	926
417001-418000	940
418001-419000	926
419001-420000	941
420001-421000	940
421001-422000	926
422001-423000	924
423001-425000	926
425001-426000	924
426001-500	936
426501-427000	944
427001-428000	924
428001-429000	926
429001-430000	925
430001-431000	924
431001-432000	925
432001-433000	940
433001-434000	924
434001-500	940
434501-500	942
434601-435000	946
435001-436000	924
436001-438500	940
438501-800	946
438801-900	942
438901-440000	946
440001-441000	924
441001-442000	940
442001-400	946
442401-500	942
442501-443000	946
443001-444000	926
444001-445000	924
445001-446000	927
446001-447000	924
447001-448000	925
448001-449000	926
449001-450000	924
450001-451000	926
451001-452000	925
452001-453000	940
453001-454000	924
454001-456000	940
456001-457000	999
457001-458000	940
458001-459000	999
459001-110	946
459111-118	942
459119-200	946
459201-700	942
459701-460000	946
460001-461900	940
461901-462000	940
462001-463000	999
463001-500	940
463501-464000	940
464001-466000	926
466001-467000	924
466701-468000	926
468001-469000	940
469001-470000	924
470001-471000	926
471001-472000	946
472001-473000	924
473001-474000	940
474001-475000	924
475001-476000	940
476001-477000	924
477001-478000	940
478001-479000	926
479001-480000	944
480001-481000	926
481001-482000	927
482001-483000	924
483001-484000	926
484001-485000	940
485001-486000	925
486001-487000	999
487001-488000	924
488001-489000	999
489001-492000	924
492001-493000	940
493001-494000	946
494001-495000	944
495001-496000	940
496001-497000	925
497001-498000	999
498001-499000	936
499001-501000	940
501001-900	926
501901-502000	934
502001-503000	926
503001-504000	999
504001-507000	940
507001-508000	999
508001-509900	940
509901-510000	942
510001-511500	940
511501-700	942
511701-517000	940
517001-519000	924
519001-521000	925
521001-523000	944
523001-524000	926
524001-531000	940
531001-532000	926
532001-10	934
532011-533000	926
533001-535550	999
535551-536000	940
536001-537000	936
537001-538000	924
538001-543000	940
543001-544000	927
544001-200	934
544201-545000	926
545001-546000	925
546001-547000	924
547001-548000	926
548001-549000	999
549001-551000	946
551001-553000	944
553001-555000	940
555001-556000	936
556001-558000	924
558001-560000	925
560001-561000	999
561001-562000	926
562001-564000	924
564001-565000	926
565001-568000	940
568001-569000	936
569001-571000	924
571001-576000	940
576001-200	942
576201-578000	940
578001-580000	924
580001-582000	926
582001-584000	925
584001-585000	927
585001-587000	999
587001-592000	940
592001-593000	926
593001-594000	924
594001-601000	940
B600001-601000	999 Ball
601001-601800	926
B601001-601800	999 Ball
601801-602000	934
B601801-602000	999 Ball
602001-603000	926
B602001-603000	999 Ball
603001-604000	926
B603001-604000	999 Ball
604001-605000	926
B604001-605000	999 Ball
605001-606000	925
B605001-606000	999 Ball
606001-607000	925
B606001-607000	999 Ball
607001-608000	·925
B607001-608000	999 Ball
608001-613000	924
B608001-613000	999 Ball
613001-614000	925
B613001-614000	999 Ball
614001-616500	924
B614001-616500	999 Ball
616501-617000	934
B616501-617000	999 Ball
617001-619000	926
B617001-619000	999 Ball
619001-620000	927
B619001-620000	999 Ball
620001-622700	940
B620001-622700	999 Ball
622701-623000	942
B622701-623000	999 Ball
623001-624000	941
B623001-624000	999 Ball
624001-625000	936
B624001-625000	999 Ball
625001-626000	925
B625001-626000	999 Ball
626001-627000	926
B626001-627000	999 Ball
627001-628000	924
B627001-628000	999 Ball
628001-630800	925
B628001-630800	999 Ball
631001-636000	940
B631001-636000	999 Ball
636001-637000	941
B636001-637000	999 Ball
637001-638000	936
B637001-638000	999 Ball
638001-639000	926
B638001-639000	999 Ball
639001-640000	925
B639001-640000	999 Ball
640001-642000	924
B640001-644400	999 Ball
644401-645000	940
645001-645500	927
B645001-645500	999 Ball
645501-646000	925
B645501-646000	999 Ball
646001-647000	926
B646001-647000	999 Ball
647001-648000	940
B647001-648000	999 Ball
648001-649000	940
B648001-649000	998 Ball
B649001-651000	999 Ball
650001-651000	999 Ball
651001-652000	940
B651001-652000	998 Ball
652001-652700	924
B652001-652700	999 Ball
652701-652800	924
652801-652900	927
652901-653000	937
653001-655000	940
B653001-655000	999 Ball
655001-655200	924
B655001-655200	999 Ball
655201-656000	924
656001-657000	926
657001-659000	927
659001-660000	925
660001-661000	927
661001-662000	924
662001-664000	940
664001-666000	924
666001-667000	940
667001-668000	941
668001-669000	926
669001-670000	999
670001-100	937
670501-673000	925
673001-675000	926
675001-677000	940
677001-678000	924
678001-679200	927
679201-680000	926
680001-685000	924
685001-687000	940
687001-688000	925
688001-689000	946
689001-694000	940
694001-696000	924
696001-697000	941
697001-700000	924
700001-702000	974
702001-703800	992
703801-704000	990
704001-400	992
704401-705000	990
705001-700	972
705701-706000	974
706001-707000	990
707001-800	972
707801-708000	990
708001-709500	975
709501-710000	973
710001-800	993
710801-711000	991
711001-300	973
711301-712000	975
712001-600	993
712601-713000	991
713001-714900	975
714901-715000	991
715001-716000	993
716001-100	972
716101-717000	974
717001-200	991
717201-718000	975L
718001-721500	974
721501-722000	992
722001-724000	974
724001-725000	972
725001-726000	974
726001-727000	992
727001-728000	974
728001-729000	992
729001-730000	975
730001-731000	992
731001-732000	975
732001-734000	990
734001-735000	975
735001-736000	974
736001-738000	975
738001-739000	974
739001-740000	975
740001-100	974
740101-200	972
740201-900	974
740901-741000	975
741001-742000	992
742001-743000	974
743001-300	975
743301-400	993
743401-744000	975
744001-500	974
744501-745000	992
745001-747000	975
747001-700	974
747701-748000	972
748001-749500	992
749501-750000	974
750001-100	961
750101-200	961
750201-700	950
750701-751000	952
751001-752000	960
752001-500	952
752501-753000	950
753001-500	952
753501-754000	950
754001-100	960
754101-500	952
754501-755000	960
755001-400	992
755401-500	974
755501-700	972
755701-900	974
755901-756000	972
756001-757000	974
757001-300	975
757301-500	993
757501-758000	975
758001-100	972
758101-759000	992
759001-760000	975
760001-400	992
760401-600	972
760601-800	974
760801-761000	992

Serial Range	Grade
761001-400	975
761401-600	993
761601-762000	975
762001-200	992
762201-300	972
762301-763000	974
763001-300	993
763301-600	973
763601-764000	975
764001-300	992
764301-400	972
764401-765000	974
765001-300	992
765301-767000	974
767001-600	992
767601-800	972
767801-768000	974
768001-769000	975
769001-700	992
769701-770000	972
770001-100	974
770101-771200	992
771201-400	972
771401-772000	974
772001-773000	975
773001-800	992
773801-774000	972
774001-775000	975
775001-500	952
775501-776000	950
776001-300	973
776301-700	993
776701-777000	975
777001-300	972
777301-778300	974
778301-800	992
778801-900	972
778901-779300	974
779301-780100	992
780101-300	972
780301-781300	992
781301-400	972
781401-500	974
781501-782000	992
782001-783000	975
783001-600	992
783601-784000	974
784001-785000	992
785001-500	952
785501-786000	950
786001-787000	992
787001-400	974
787401-788000	972
788001-791300	992
791301-792600	974
792601-900	972
792901-793700	992
793701-900	990
793901-794000	992
794001-200	972
794201-795000	974
795001-796400	992
796401-800	972
796801-797200	974
797201-500	954
797501-798000	974
798001-500	990
798501-800	972
798801-799000	974
799001-200	954
799201-600	992
799601-800000	954
800001-802000	974
802001-200	954
802201-2	972
802203-300	954
802301-500	972
802501-803700	974
803701-804200	954
804201-806000	974
806001-807000	975
807001-500	993
807501-808800	975
808801-809000	993
809001-500	974
809501-600	972
809601-810000	974
810001-300	990
810301-812000	974
812001-700	992
812701-813000	974
813001-814000	974P
814001-800	974L
814801-815900	992
815901-816000	974L
816001-817000	974P
817001-819000	974L
819001-820000	974P
820001-821500	974
821501-822000	990L
822001-700	992L
822701-823000	974L
823001-824000	974P
824001-826000	975P
826001-500	975L
826501-827000	993
827001-828000	975P
828001-829000	974L
829001-830000	974P
830001-500	990L
830501-831000	992L
831001-100	954P
831101-200	972P
831201-500	954P
831501-832000	974P
832001-400	974L
832401-833000	992L
833001-834000	990L
834001-600	974P
834601-800	974L
834801-835000	974P
835001-600	992L
835601-800	990L
835801-836000	974L
836001-500	974P
836501-900	954P
836901-837000	974P
837001-838000	975P
838001-839000	975L
839001-400	974L
839401-700	992L
839701-840000	990L
840001-400	952L
840401-900	950L
840901-841000	952L
841001-842000	975P
842001-843000	974L
843001-844000	974P
844001-200	993
844201-845000	975
845001-200	992
845201-400	972
845401-700	954
845701-846000	972
846001-500	952
846501-847000	950
847001-200	972
847201-849000	974
849001-850000	975
850001-300	992
850301-800	990
850801-851000	972
851001-400	993
851401-852000	975
852001-853000	992
853001-854000	974
854001-600	950
854601-900	952
854901-855100	960L
855101-856000	950L
856001-857840	975
857841-858000	975L
858001-500	974
858501-859000	972
859001-860000	974
860001-862300	992
862301-400	954
862401-500	972
862501-600	954
862601-800	972
862801-863000	974
863001-864000	992
864001-865000	975
865001-866000	992
866001-600	974
866601-700	954
866701-867000	972
867001-868000	975
868001-869000	992
869001-870000	975
870001-872000	992
872001-200	993
872201-874000	975
874001-800	974
874801-875000	975
875001-300	952
875301-876000	975
876001-600	993
876601-877000	975
877001-400	992
877401-700	975
877701-878000	993
878001-879400	992
879401-880000	975
880001-600	992
880601-882400	974
882401-883400	992
883401-884100	974
884101-885300	992
885301-886000	974
886001-887000	992
887001-300	974
887301-890300	992
890301-891000	974
891001-600	992
891601-892200	978
892201-896200	992
896201-897800	974
897801-898000	972
898001-899100	992
899101-500	978
899501-900000	974
900001-902000	940
902001-904000	926
904001-906000	924
906001-914000	940
914001-916000	926
916001-917000	927
917001-919000	925
919001-921000	940
921001-923000	924
923001-500	999
923501-924000	925
924001-926000	940
926001-100	927
927001-929000	926
929001-933000	924
933001-935000	925
935001-937000	926
937001-939000	940
939001-941000	924
941001-944000	940
944001-949000	926
949001-952000	925
952001-958000	924
958001-960000	926
960001-968000	940
968001-970000	926
970001-971700	924
971701-972000	948
972001-973000	924
973001-974000	936
974001-975400	924
975401-25 Spec.	926
975426-976000	924
976001-979000	940
979001-100	942
979101-981000	940
981001-982000	948
982001-984000	924
984001-986000	940
986001-987000	946
987001-988000	936
988001-992000	940
992001-996000	924
996001-999998	940
999999-1000000	947
1000001-1000300	972
1000301-1003000	992
1003001-1004000	974
1004001-900	992
1004901-1007100	974
1007101-1008300	992
1008301-1009500	974
1009501-1010700	992
1010701-1011200	972
1011201-1012700	974
1012701-1013000	992
1013001-1015000	978
1015001-300	974
1015301-1016000	992
1016001-300	975
1016301-600	973
1016601-1018000	993
1018001-1020000	992
1020001-1022600	950
1022601-1023000	952
1023001-700	992
1023701-1024500	974
1024501-600	992
1024601-1025000	972
1025001-1027000	975
1027001-400	993
1027401-1029600	975
1029601-1030000	973
1030001-1032000	992
1032001-1033000	974
1033001-200	972
1033201-800	954
1033801-1035300	974
1035301-600	972
1035601-1036000	974
1036001-300	972
1036301-800	974
1036801-1037000	992L
1037001-1038000	974
1038001-1039000	992
1039001-200	972
1039201-500	978
1039501-1040300	974
1040301-1041000	992
1041001-1042000	974
1042001-700	992
1042701-1043000	972
1043001-700	978
1043701-1044000	992
1044001-1045000	974
1045001-1046000	992
1046001-1047000	975
1047001-1048000	974L
1048001-1049000	992
1049001-500	990
1049501-1051000	992
1051001-200	975
1051201-1052000	993
1052001-500	972P
1052501-900	954
1052901-1053000	974
1053001-1054000	992
1054001-1056000	974
1056001-1057000	975
1057001-1061300	992
1061301-1062300	972
1062301-1066000	992
1066001-1068000	974
1068001-1069000	975
1069001-1070000	974
1070001-1071000	992L
1071001-1073000	975P
1073001-1075000	992
1075001-1076200	974L
1076201-700	972L
1076701-1077000	978L
1077001-1079000	974P
1079001-1080000	992L
1080001-100	952L
1080101-200	960L
1080201-400	994L
1080401-1081000	950L
1081001-1082000	978L
1082001-400	993L
1082401-1083000	973L
1083001-1084000	990L
1084001-1085000	992L
1085001-1086000	992L
1086001-1088000	974P
1088001-1091000	992L
1091001-200	978L
1091201-1092000	974L
1092001-1093000	992L
1093001-1095000	974P
1095001-1096000	992P
1096001-400	974L
1096401-1097000	974P
1097001-1098000	992L
1098001-400	975P
1098401-1099000	975L
1099001-600	993L
1099601-1100000	975P
1100001-1104000	992L
1104001-1105000	974P
1105001-1106000	992L
1106001-500	978L
1106501-1107000	972L
1107001-1109000	992L
1109001-1111000	972L
1111001-1112000	974L
1112001-1113000	974P
1113001-1116000	992L
1116001-900	974P
1116901-1117000	974L
1117001-1119000	992L
1119001-1120000	978L
1120001-1122000	992L
1122001-1123000	974P
1123001-500	972P
1123501-1125000	974P
1125001-1127000	992L
1127001-1128000	972L
1128001-1129000	974L
1129001-1130500	974P
1130501-1131000	956P
1131001-1132000	992L
1132001-1133000	990L
1133001-1134000	978L
1134001-1135000	972L
1135001-1137000	992L
1137001-1138000	956P
1138001-1139000	956P
1139001-1140000	978L
1140001-1141000	972L
1141001-1142000	956P
1142001-500	974P
1142501-1145000	974L
1145001-1146000	975P
1146001-500	956P
1146501-1149000	974P
1149001-1150000	974L
1150001-600	950L
1150601-1151800	952L
1151801-1152000	952P
1152001-900	950P
1152901-1153200	952P
1153201-300	994L
1153301-500	994L
1153501-800	994L
1153801-1154000	960L
1154001-500	950L
1154501-1155000	950P
1155001-200	994P
1155201-500	994L
1156001-1158000	996L
1158001-1160000	974P
1160001-1162000	992L
1162001-500	993L
1162501-1164000	993L
1164001-1166000	974P

Serial Range	Code	Serial Range	Code
1166001-1167000	974L	1291501-1292000	992P
1167001-1168000	956P	1292001-1297000	992L
1168001-1169000	975P	1297001-1298000	974P
1169001-1170000	974P	1298001-1299000	992L
1170001-1174000	956P	1299001-1300000	975P
1174001-1176000	974P	1300001-1301000	974P
1176001-1177000	992L	1301001-1302000	974L
1177001-1178000	956P	1302001-500	992L
1178001-1179000	974P	1302501-1303000	990L
1179001-1181000	996L	1303001-500	972L
1181001-1182000	992L	1303501-1304000	972P
1182001-1183000	996L	1304001-1305000	978L
1183001-1184400	974P	1305001-1306000	956P
1184401-1185400	956P	1306001-1307000	974P
1185401-1186000	974P	1307001-1308500	992L
1186001-1187000	992L	1308501-1309000	993L
1187001-1188000	996L	1309001-1310000	974L
1188001-1189000	992L	1310001-1311000	972L
1189001-1190000	974P	1311001-1312000	992L
1190001-1192000	996L	1312001-800	974P
1192001-1193000	975P	1312801-1313000	956P
1193001-1194000	974P	1313001-1317000	992L
1194001-1195000	956P	1317001-1318000	956P
1195001-1196000	974P	1318001-1321000	992L
1196001-1199000	992L	1321001-300	990L
1199001-1201000	974P	1321301-1322000	992L
1201001-1202000	975P	1322001-700	974L
1202001-1203000	992L	1322701-1323000	972L
1203001-1204000	974P	1323001-1324000	992L
1204001-500	956P	1324001-1325000	996L
1204501-1206000	974P	1325001-1326500	975P
1206001-1207000	992L	1326501-1327000	993L
1207001-1210000	974P	1327001-300	956P
1210001-1212000	992L	1327301-1329000	974P
1212001-1213000	974P	1329001-1330000	992L
1213001-500	996L	1330001-1331300	974L
1213501-1214000	992L	1331301-800	972L
1214001-1214600	993L	1331801-1332000	978L
1214601-1215000	975P	1332001-1334000	992L
1215001-1216000	974L	1334001-400	974P
1216001-1219000	992L	1334401-1335000	956P
1219001-1220000	974P	1335001-300	978L
1220001-1221000	992L	1335301-1336000	972L
1221001-1223500	974P	1336001-1337000	992L
1223501-1224000	956P	1337001-1338200	996L
1224001-1227000	992L	1338201-1339000	996L
1227001-1228000	972L	1339001-1340000	956P
1228001-700	992L	1340001-1341000	992L
1228701-1229000	990L	1341001-300	972L
1229001-500	956P	1341301-500	974L
1229501-1230000	974P	1341501-1342000	978L
1230001-1231000	974L	1342001-1343000	956P
1231001-1232000	992L	1343001-400	956P
1232001-1233000	974P	1343401-1344000	974P
1233001-1236000	992L	1344001-1345000	992L
1236001-500	974P	1345001-600	974L
1236501-1237000	956P	1345601-1346000	972L
1237001-500	996L	1346001-1348000	975P
1237501-1238000	992L	1348001-1349000	974P
1238001-1239000	956P	1349001-1350000	992L
1239001-1241000	992L	1350001-600	972L
1241001-1242000	975P	1350601-1351000	974L
1242001-400	974L	1351001-1352000	993L
1242401-1243000	972L	1352001-1352300	974L
1243001-500	996L	1352301-800	978L
1243501-1244000	992L	1352801-1353000	974L
1244001-1245000	974P	1353001-500	972P
1245001-1246000	992L	1353501-1354200	956P
1246001-300	974P	1354201-700	992P
1246301-800	956P	1354701-1355000	974P
1246801-1247000	974L	1355001-1356000	992L
1247001-1248000	992L	1356001-1357000	974P
1248001-1249700	974P	1357001-1359800	992L
1249701-1250000	956P	1359801-1361000	996L
1250001-1252000	983	1361001-1362000	992L
1252001-1253000	985	1362001-600	974P
1253001-1257000	983	1362601-1363000	956P
1257001-900	985	1363001-1364000	992L
1260001-970	Chro.*	1364001-1365000	975P
1260971-1265000		1365001-800	956P
1265001-1266000	956P	1365801-1367000	974P
1266001-1267000	974P	1367001-1369400	992L
1267001-1268200	978L	1369401-1370000	996L
1268201-1269000	978L	1370001-1371000	974L
1269001-600	992L	1371001-600	996L
1269601-1270000	992L	1371601-1373000	992L
1270001-1271700	956P	1373001-1374000	975P
1271701-1272000	974P	1374001-1375000	992L
1272001-1274000	996L	1375001-1376000	950L
1274001-500	993L	1376001-1377000	992L
1274501-700	992L	1377001-1378300	974P
1274701-1275000	992L	1378301-1379000	956P
1275001-1276000	972L	1379001-1380200	972L
1276001-1277000	974L	1380201-1381000	992L
1277001-1278000	992L	1381001-500	956P
1278001-1279000	975P	1381501-1383000	974P
1279001-1280000	992L	1383001-1384000	992L
1280001-1281000	992L	1384001-1386100	992L
1281001-800	974P	1386101-1387000	956P
1281801-1282000	956P	1387001-1388000	992L
1282001-1284000	996L	1388001-400	978L
1284001-1285000	992L	1388401-1389000	974P
1285001-1286000	956P	1389001-300	956P
1286001-1288000	978L	1389301-1390000	956P
1288001-500	993L	1390001-1391000	992L
1288501-1289100	992L	1391001-500	956P
1289101-700	990L	1391501-1392000	974P
1289701-1290000	992L	1392001-1393000	992L
1290001-1291500	974P	1393001-1394000	974P

Serial Range	Code	Serial Range	Code
1394001-1396000	992L	1569001-1571000	972L
1396001-500	972L	1571001-1572000	974P
1396501-1398000	974L	1572001-1573000	975P
1398001-400	974P	1573001-1575000	974P
1398401-1399000	956P	1575001-400	950L
1399001-1400000	992L	1575401-1576000	950P
1400001-1401000	936	1576001-1577000	950L
1401001-1403000	924	1577001-1578000	975P
1403001-1409000	940	1578001-1580000	992L
1409001-500	946	1580001-1581200	974L
1409501-1410000	940	1581201-1582000	956P
1410001-1414000	924	1582001-1583000	974P
1414001-300	941	1583001-1584000	992L
1414501-1415000	925	1584001-1585000	978L
1415001-1417000	924	1585001-1586000	972L
1417001-1419000	940	1586001-1587000	992L
1419001-1420000	924	1587001-500	992P
1420001-1421000	940	1587501-1589000	992L
1421001-1422000	924	1589001-500	956P
1422001-1424000	940	1589501-1590000	974P
1424001-1428000	924	1590001-1591000	974L
1428001-1430000	940	1591001-1592000	992L
1430001-200	924	1592001-1593000	974P
1430201-400	948	1593001-1595000	992L
1430401-1431000	924	1595001-200	974P
1431001-1433000	940	1595201-900	956P
1433001-1438000	924	1595901-1596000	974P
1438001-500	926	1596001-1611000	992L
1438501-1439500	924	1611001-1612100	974P
1439501-1440000	926	1612101-1613000	956P
1440001-1441000	940	1613001-600	996L
1441001-1442000	924	1614001-900	956P
1442001-500	926	1614901-1615000	974P
1442501-1444000	924	1615001-1625000	992L
1444001-1445000	940	1625001-200	950L
1445001-1447000	924	1625201-1626000	952L
1447001-1448200	940	1626001-1627000	974P
1449001-1450500	924	1627001-1633000	992L
1500001-600	974P	1633001-1635000	950L
1500601-1501200	956P	1635001-1636000	992L
1501201-1502000	974P	1636001-1637000	956P
1502001-1503000	993L	1637001-1638000	974P
1503001-1504000	996L	1638001-1642800	992L
1504001-500	974L	1642801-1643000	992P
1504501-1505200	972L	1643001-1644000	992L
1505201-700	978L	1644001-1646000	974L
1505701-1506000	974L	1646001-1648000	972L
1506001-1507000	975P	1648001-1649000	992L
1507001-1508000	992L	1649001-1652000	974P
1508001-400	974P	1652001-1653000	950L
1508401-1509000	956P	1653001-1654000	956P
1509001-1510000	992L	1654001-1657000	974P
1510001-1511000	974L	1657001-1660000	992L
1511001-1512000	975P	1660001-1661000	978L
1512001-1513200	992L	1661001-1663000	974P
1513201-600	992P	1663001-1664000	974L
1513601-1514000	992L	1664001-1665000	950L
1514001-200	956P	1665001-1666000	974P
1514201-1515000	974P	1666001-1667000	956P
1515001-1516000	992L	1667001-1669000	974P
1516001-1517000	974P	1669001-1670000	978L
1517001-1520000	992L	1670001-1671000	974P
1520001-1521200	974L	1671001-300	992L
1521201-1522000	978L	1671301-900	992P
1522001-600	974P	1671901-1672000	992L
1522601-1525000	956P	1672001-1676000	974P
1525001-1527000	996L	1676001-1678000	992L
1527001-1528000	992L	1678001-1679000	974P
1528001-1531000	974P	1679001-1681000	974L
1531001-1533000	992L	1681001-1682000	974P
1533001-600	974P	1682001-1683000	956P
1533601-1534000	956P	1683001-1685000	974P
1534001-100	992L	1685001-1686000	992L
1535101-200	975P	1686001-1688000	974P
1535201-600	975P	1688001-500	978L
1535601-1536000	993L	1689001-600	975P
1536001-1537000	972L	1690001-1691000	956
1537001-1538000	992L	1691001-1693000	992L
1538001-800	956P	1693001-1696000	956P
1538801-1539000	974P	1696001-1699000	992L
1539001-1540000	992L	1699001-1703000	974P
1540001-500	992P	1703001-1704000	992L
1540501-1541000	992L	1704001-1705000	956P
1541001-1542000	974P	1705001-1706000	974P
1542201-800	956P	1706001-1707100	992L
1542801-1543000	974P	1708001-1714000	992L
1543001-1544000	996L	1714001-1715000	974P
1544001-1545000	992L	1715001-1717000	992L
1545001-400	978L	1717001-800	956
1545401-1546000	974L	1718001-1750000	992L
1546001-1548000	992L	1750001-1761000	900
1548001-600	974L	1761001-1765000	914
1548601-1549000	972L	1765001-1767000	920
1549001-1550000	974P	1767001-1768000	914
1550001-500	972P	1768001-1769000	900
1550501-1552000	974P	1769001-1770000	920
1552001-1555000	992L	1770001-1778200	914
1555001-1557000	993P	1778201-1779000	910
1557001-800	972L	1779001-1780000	920
1557801-1558000	974L	1780001-1782000	910
1558001-500	956	1782001-500	920
1558501-1559700	956P	1782501-1783000	900
1559701-1560000	974P	1783001-1808000	910
1560001-1561000	975P	1808001-1810000	914
1561001-1563000	992L	1810001-1811000	910
1563001-1565000	978L	1811001-1813000	900
1565001-1567000	992L	1813001-1818000	910
1567001-1568000	974L	1818001-1819000	914
1568001-1569000	992L	1819001-1821000	910

Serial Range	Grade
1821001-1822000	914
1822001-1827000	910
1827001-600	914
1827601-1829100	910
1829101-500	914
1829501-1830000	910
1830001-1831000	900
1831001-1832000	920
1832001-700	910
1832701-1833300	914
1833301-1834500	910
1834501-1835400	914
1835401-1836900	910
1836901-1837400	914
1837401-1839000	910
1839001-500	914
1839501-1844700	910
1844701-1845700	914
1845701-1848300	910
1848301-1849500	914
1849501-1851900	910
1851901-1853100	914
1853101-1856800	910
1856801-1857900	914
1857901-1860300	910
1860301-1861000	914
1861001-1863000	900
1863001-700	920
1863701-1864300	900
1864301-1865000	920
1865001-500	914
1865501-1870300	910
1870301-1871500	914
1871501-1875100	910
1875101-600	914
1875601-1876500	910
1876501-1877500	914
1877501-1878700	910
1878701-1880000	914
1880001-300	920
1880301-1881500	900
1881501-700	920
1881701-900	900
1881901-1882900	920
1882901-1885000	900
1885001-1887400	910
1887401-1888600	914
1888601-1891000	910
1891001-1892200	914
1892201-1894600	910
1894601-1895800	910
1895801-1899000	910
1899001-300	900
1899301-1900000	920
1900001-400	910
1900401-1902100	914
1902101-1907000	910
1907001-1909000	914
1909001-1910000	910
1910001-500	920
1910501-1911000	900
1911001-1913000	920
1913001-1914000	900
1914001-1920000	910
1920001-1922000	920
1922001-1924000	910
1924001-1925000	900
1925001-1936000	910
1936001-1937000	920
1937001-900	900
1940001-1941000	914
1941001-1949000	910
1949001-1950000	914
1950001-1962000	910
1962001-1963000	914
1963001-1975000	910
1975001-1976000	914
1976001-1980000	910
1980001-1981000	914
1981001-1988500	910

Serial Range	Grade
1989001-400	914
2000001-2001700	988
2001701-2002400	986
2002401-800	988
2002801-2003100	986
2004001-2035000	986
2035001-2037200	981
2040001-2064900	986
2100001-2191300	986A
2200001-2248000	987
2248001-2300000	987F
2300001-2311000	992L
2311001-2312000	974L
2312001-2321700	992L
2321701-2323000	974L
2323001-2326000	992L
2326001-2327000	974P
2327001-2333000	992L
2333001-2336000	974P
2336001-2338000	992L
2338001-2339000	974P
2339001-2340000	974L
2340001-2341000	974P
2341001-2346000	992L
2346001-2347000	974P
2347001-2356000	992L
2356001-2358000	974P
2358001-2364000	992L
2364001-2365000	974P
2365001-2374000	992L
2374001-2375000	974P
2375001-2378000	992L
2378001-2380000	974L
2380001-2383000	992L
2383001-2384000	950L
2384001-2385000	992L
2385001-2396000	974P
2386001-2390000	992L
2390001-2391000	974P
2391001-2393000	992L
2393001-2395000	974P
2395001-2397000	992L
2397001-2398000	974L
2398001-2401000	992L
2401001-2402000	974P
2402001-2407000	992L
2407001-2409000	974P
2409001-2413000	992L
2413001-2414000	974P
2414001-2415000	974L
2415001-2418000	992L
2418001-2420000	974P
2420001-2422000	992L
2422001-2423000	974P
2423001-2432000	992L
2432001-2433000	974P
2433001-2434000	992L
2434001-2435000	974P
2435001-2437000	992L
2437001-2438000	974P
2438001-2442000	992L
2442001-2445000	974P
2445001-2451000	992L
2451001-2453000	974P
2453001-2455000	992L
2455001-2456000	974P
2456001-2457000	992L
2457001-2458000	950L
2458001-2459000	974L
2459001-2461000	992L
2461001-2462000	974L
2462001-2464000	992L
2464001-2466000	974P
2466001-2468000	992L
2468001-2469000	974P
2469001-2472000	992L
2472001-2473000	974P
2473001-2474000	992L
2474001-2475000	974P

Serial Range	Grade
2475001-2476000	992L
2476001-2477000	974P
2477001-2490000	992L
2490001-2492000	974L
2492001-2504000	992L
2504001-2505000	950L
2505001-300	950L
2506001-2526000	992L
2526001-2528000	974P
2528001-2533000	992L
2533001-2534000	974P
2534001-2535000	992L
2535001-2536000	974P
2536001-2537000	974L
2537001-2538000	974P
2538001-2539000	974L
2539001-2542000	974P
2542001-2543000	992L
2543001-2545000	974P
2545001-2547000	992L
2547001-2548400	974P
2548401-2548600	974L
2548601-2548700	974P
2548701-2550000	974L
2550001-2551000	992L
2551001-2552000	974L
2552001-2555000	992L
2555001-2555600	974L
2555701-2557000	974L
2558001-2560000	992L
2560001-2561000	974L
2561001-2563000	992L
2563001-2564000	974L
2564001-2566000	992L
2566001-2568600	974L
2567001-2581000	992L
2581001-2583900	992E
2583901-2584300	992L
2584301-2596000	992E
2596001-2597000	974L
2597001-2608000	992E
2608001-2608800	974L
2609001-2611000	992E
2611001-2611400	950L
2611401-2613000	950E
2613001-2618000	992E
2618001-2619000	950E
2619001-2631000	992E
2631001-2631600	950E
2631801-2632000	950E
2632001-2639000	992E
2639001-2641000	950E
2641001-2649000	992E
2649001-2650600	950E
2651001-2655300	992E
2900001-2911500	979
2911601-2931900	979F
3000001-3002300	922
3002301-3002500	922M.P.
3002501-3003800	922
3003801-3004000	922M.P.
3004001-3006100	922
3006101-3006300	922M.P.
3006301-3008000	922
3008001-3008600	922M.P.
3008601-3010000	922
3010001-3010500	922
3010501-3010700	922M.P.
3010701-3011900	922
3011901-3012500	922M.P.
3012501-3013100	922
3013101-3013700	922M.P.
3013701-3015700	922
3050001-3054800	902
3054801-3056000	922
3056001-3060800	902
3061001-3065100	904
3100001-3133800	916
3135001-3152700	918
3200001-3460900	912
4000001-4447201	987F
4447301-4523000	987E

Serial Range	Grade
A-001 to A-8900	980B
1B-001 to 1B-25300	999B
2B-001 to 2B-700	999B
2B-701 to 2B-800	950B
C-001 to C-396300	992B
E-001 to E-114000	989
E-114001 to E-140400	989E
F-101 to F-57600	995
F-57601 to F-59850	995A
F-59851 to F-62000	995
F-62001 to F-63000	995A
F-63001 to F-63800	995
F- 63801 to F-286200	995A
G-001 to G-13600	980
G-13601 to G-14600	980 & 980A
G-14601 to G-44500	980
G-44501 to G-45000	980A
G-45001 to G-47400	980
G-47401 to G-48400	980A
G-48401 to G-58200	980
G-58201 to G-58700	980A
G-58701 to G-61600	980
G-61601 to G-62500	980A
G-62501 to G-67500	980
G-67501 to G-68600	980A
G-68601- to G-651700	980
H-001 to H-1000	921
H-1001 to H-1800	400 & 921
H-1801 to H-2000	921
H-2001 to H-2800	400 & 921
H-2801 to H-3500	400
H-3501 to H-51700	921
H-50001 to H-57500	401
J-001 to J-670000	982
L-001 to L-165000	997
M-001 to M-201900	982M
N-001 to N-532200	721
O-1 to O-486300	987A
R-001 to R-3600	923
S-001 to S-18700	950B
SS-001 to SS-87400	987S
T-001 to T-783000	911
V-001 to V-127200	911M
X-001 to X-197600	917
Y-001 to Y-396200	747
CY-001 to CY-176700	748
O-01A to 622700-A	750
O-01C to 126000-C	751
001E to 47400E	752
001F to 63700F	753
001H to 26800H	754

*Hamilton 36 size chronometer watch

* Hayden W. Wheeler model

NOTE: The above serial number and grade listing is an actual Hamilton factory list and is accurate in most cases. However, it has been brought to our attention that in rare cases the serial number and grade number do not match the list. One example is the Hayden W. Wheeler model.

(See Hamilton Watch Co. **Serial Numbers and Grades** section located at the end of the Hamilton Watch price section to identify the movement, size and grade of your watch.)

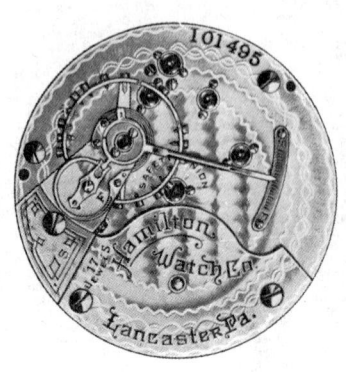

Grade 925, 18 size, 17 jewels, hunting case, serial number 101,495.

Grade 932, 18 size, 16 jewels, open face, serial number 6,888.

HAMILTON
18 SIZE

Grade or Name — Description		Avg	Ex-Fn	Mint
7J, LS, FULL, OF	★★	$800	$900	$1,500
11J, LS, FULL, HC	★★★	900	1,100	1,600
11J, LS, FULL, OF	★★★	1,000	1,200	1,650
922, 15J, OF	★★	400	500	700
923, 15J, HC	★★	550	650	900
924, 17J, NI, OF, DMK		100	125	200
925, 17J, NI, HC, DMK		125	150	200
926, 17J, NI, OF, DMK, ADJ		100	125	200
927, 17J, NI, HC, DMK, ADJ		125	150	200
928, 15J, NI, OF		150	175	250
929, 15J, NI, HC, **14K**		500	650	1,000
929, 15J, NI, HC		200	250	400
930, 16J, NI, OF		175	225	400
931, 16J, NI, HC		225	285	400
932 or 936, serial #s less than 50, OF	★★★	1,400	1,600	2,000
932, 16J, NI, OF	★★	375	485	650
932 (S#s less than 400 up to $1,200 to $2,000)				
933, 16J, NI, HC	★★	450	585	700
933 ((Serial #s started at 1021-30)				
934, 17J, NI, DMK, ADJ, OF		125	150	250
934, 17J, NI, ADJ, Coin OF		100	135	200
934 & 935 & 937, 17J, MARKED (**Main Line**)	★	300	400	600
935, 17J, NI, DMK, ADJ, HC.	★	275	325	400
936, 17J, NI, DMK, SR & DR, OF		100	135	200
936 (S#s less than 400 up to $1,200)				
937, 17J, NI, MARKED on Mvt.(**Official Standard**), HC	★	500	600	1,000
937, 17J, NI, DMK, SR & DR, HC		175	225	300
937, 17J, serial # 1001 to 1020 = 1st run HC	◻	500	600	1,000
937, 17J, serial # 1031 to 1060 = 2nd run HC	◻	400	500	900

FIRST Hunting Case serial was **1001.**
Grade 937 (Serial #s started at 1001)

🕐 Watches listed in this book are priced at the collectable retail level, as **Complete** watches having an original 14k gold-filled case for Stem Wind and *Key Wind* with silver case, an original white enamel single sunk dial, and with the entire original movement in good working order with no repairs needed.

Grade or Name — Description		Avg	Ex-Fn	Mint
938, 17J, NI, DMK, DR, OF	★ ★	$375	$450	$700
939, 17J, NI, DMK, DR, HC	★ ★	425	550	775
940, 21J, NI, Mermod Jaccards St. Louis Paragon , OF Time Keeper & a hour glass on mvt.	★	400	550	750
940, 21J, NI, DMK, SR & DR, Adj.5P, GJS, OF		185	250	400
940, 21J, NI, GF or Coin, OF		175	225	375
940, 21J, NI, SR & DR, 2-Tone, OF	★	325	350	600
940, 21J, NI, DR, Marked Extra, OF	★	450	500	800
940, 21J, NI, DR, Marked Special, OF	★	375	450	700
940, 21J, NI, DR, Marked Special for R R Service, OF	★ ★ ★	1,000	1,300	1,800
940, 21J, NI, DR, Marked Pennsylvania Special, OF	★	1,300	1,500	2,000
941, 21J, NI, DR, GJS, HC		275	335	450
941, 21J, NI, DR, GJS, Marked Special, HC	★	450	500	650
941, 21J, NI, DMK, SR & DR, Adj.5P, GJS, HC		285	375	425
942, 21J, NI, DMK, DR, Adj.5P, GJS, OF		275	350	400
942, 21J, NI, DMK, DR, Adj.5P, GJS Marked For Railroad Service. OF	★ ★	1,200	1,400	1,800
943, 21J, NI, DMK, DR, Adj.5P, GJS, HC	★	425	475	525
943, 21J, Marked Burlington Special	★	950	1,350	1,800
944, 19J, NI, DMK, DR, Adj.5P, GJS, OF		275	300	450
946, Anderson, (jobber name on movement), 14K		1,200	1,400	1,800
946, 23J, Marked Extra, GJS, OF	★	900	1,000	1,300
946, 23J, Marked "Loaner" on case	★	700	800	1,100
946, 23J, NI, DMK, DR, Adj.5P, GJS, OF		650	750	950
946, 23J, NI, DMK, Adj.5P, GJS, unmarked, OF		650	750	950
947, 23J, NI, DMK, DR, Adj.5P, GJS, 14K, HC, NOT MARKED "947"	★ ★ ★	3,000	4,000	5,500
947, 23J, NI, DMK, DR, Adj.5P, GJS, 14K, HC, MARKED "947"	★ ★ ★	4,000	4,500	7,000
947, 23J, NI, DMK, DR, Adj.5P, GJS, 14K, HC, MARKED "947" EXTRA	★ ★ ★ ★	4,500	5,500	7,500

MOVEMENTS WITH ODD GRADE NUMBERS ARE HUNTING CASE.
MOVEMENTS WITH EVEN GRADE NUMBERS ARE OPEN FACE.
Note: Some 18 size movements are **marked** with grade numbers, some are not. Collectors prefer marked movement.

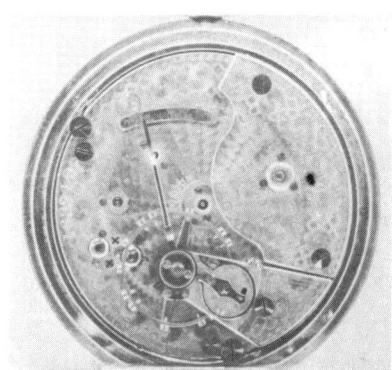

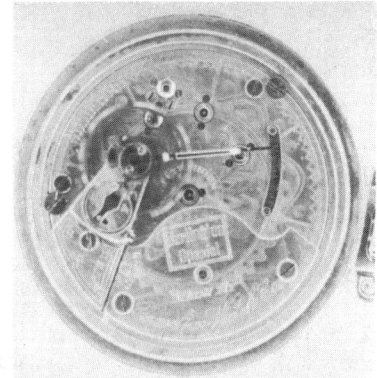

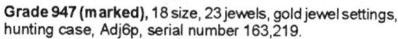

Grade 947 (marked), 18 size, 23 jewels, gold jewel settings, hunting case, Adj6p, serial number 163,219.   Burlington Special, 18 size, 21 jewels, Grade 943, open face, serial number 121,614.

🕐 Pricing in this Guide are fair market price for **COMPLETE** watches which are reflected from the "<u>NAWCC</u>" National and regional shows.

Grade or Name — Description		Avg	Ex-Fn	Mint
948, 17J, NI, DMK, DR, Adj.5P, GJS, OF	★	$350	$375	$600
948, 17J, NI, DMK, DR, Adj.5P, GJS, Coin, OF	★	350	375	600
The Banner, 928, 15J, NI, OF		150	175	300
The Banner, 940, 21J, NI, OF		275	325	400
The Banner, 940 **special**, 21J, NI, OF		375	425	575
The Banner, 941, 21J, NI, HC		325	375	500
The Banner, 17J, M#927, HC, ADJ		150	175	225
Burlington Special, 17J, Adj.5P, OF	★	900	1,000	1,400
Burlington Special, 17J, Adj.5P, HC	★	1,000	1,100	1,500
Burlington Special, 21J, Adj.5P, OF	★	1,100	1,200	1,600
Burlington Special, 21J, Adj.5P, HC	★	1,200	1,300	1,700
Chesapeake & Ohio, Special, (936)	★ ★ ★	1,200	1,400	1,800
Chesapeake & Ohio, Railway Special, (936)	★ ★ ★	1,200	1,400	1,800
Chesapeake & Ohio, Railway Special, (937)	★ ★ ★	1,300	1,500	2,000
Imperial Canada, GRADE 922, OF	★	550	700	900
Imperial Canada, GRADE 923, HC	★	600	700	1,000
Inspectors Standard, 21J, OF	★	500	600	900
The Union, 17J		150	185	300
The Union Special, 17J		150	185	300
The Union, 17J, G#925, HC		225	250	400

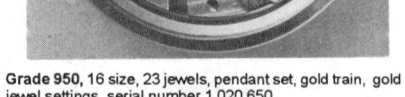

Grade 950, 16 size, 23 jewels, pendant set, gold train, gold jewel settings, serial number 1,020,650.

Grade 961, 16 size, 21 jewels, gold train, gold jewel settings, serial number 81,848.

16 SIZE

Grade or Name — Description		Avg	Ex-Fn	Mint
950, 23J, LS, BRG, DR, GT, **14K**, OF		$1,100	$1,200	$1,500
950, 23J, DR, BRG, GJS, Adj.5P, NI, GCW, OF		675	775	1,200
950, 23J, DR, GJS, BRG, Adj.5P, NI, Gold Tain, OF		675	775	1,250
950B, 23J, LS, Adj.6P, NI, DR, BRG, OF	◁	750	850	1,250
950B, 23J, LS, Adj.6P, NI, DR, BRG, **Gold Train**, OF	◁	775	875	1,300
950E, 23J, LS, Adj.6P, NI, DR, BRG, marked **Elinvar**, OF	◁	850	950	1,400
951, 23J, LS, BRG, Adj.5P, NI, GT, GJS, DR, HC	★ ★ ★	4,500	5,000	7,500
951, 23J, PS, BRG, Adj.5P, NI, GT, GJS, DR, HC	★ ★	4,000	4,500	7,000
951, 23J, PS, BRG, Adj.5P, NI, GT, GJS, DR, HC,**14K**	★ ★ ★	5,000	5,500	8,000
952, 19J, LS or PS, BRG, Adj.5P, NI, GJS, DR, OF		235	275	400
952, 19J, LS or PS, BRG, Adj.5P, OF, **14K**		450	550	750

🕐 Watches listed in this book are priced at the collectable retail level, as **Complete** watches having an original 14k gold-filled case for Stem Wind and Key Wind with silver case, an original white enamel single sunk dial, and with the entire original movement in good working order with no repairs needed.

🕐 Pricing in this Guide are fair market price for **COMPLETE** watches which are reflected from the "**NAWCC**" National and regional shows.

Grade or Name — Description	Avg	Ex-Fn	Mint
954, 17J, LS or PS, 3/4, DR, Adj.5P, OF	$100	$125	$275
956, 17J, PS, 3/4, DR, Adj.5P, OF	100	125	200
960, 21J, PS, BRG, GJS, GT, DR, Adj.5P, OF ★	350	400	650
960, 21J, LS, BRG, GJS, GT, DR, Adj.5P, OF ★	350	400	650
961, 21J, PS & LS, BRG, GJS, GT, DR, Adj.5P, HC ★	425	475	750
962, 17J, PS, BRG, OF ★★	475	500	800
963, 17J, PS, BRG, HC ★★	500	600	850
964, 17J, PS, BRG, OF ★★	500	600	875
965, 17J, PS, BRG, HC ★★	500	575	875
966, 17J, PS, 3/4, OF ★★	525	600	875
967, 17J, PS, 3/4 , HC ★★	500	600	875
968, 17J, PS, 3/4, OF ★	350	400	650
969, 17J, PS, 3/4, HC ★	450	475	650
970, 21J, PS, 3/4, OF	200	250	400
971, 23J, Adj.5P, SWISS MADE	55	70	150
971, 21J, PS, 3/4, HC	200	300	400
972, 17J, PS & LS, OF, 3/4, NI, GJS, DR, Adj.5P, DMK, OF	100	150	250
973, 17J, PS & LS, 3/4, NI, DR, Adj.5P, HC	100	150	300
974, 17J, LS, 3/4, NI, Adj.3P, OF	60	80	200
974, 17J, PS, Adj.3P, OF	60	80	200
974, 17J, 2-tone, OF	175	200	350
2974B, 17J, Adj.3P, **hacking**, U.S. GOV., OF. ★	250	285	450
975, 17J, PS & LS, 3/4, NI, Adj.3P, HC	125	150	200
976, 16J, PS, 3/4, OF	125	150	250
977, 16J, PS, 3/4, HC	125	150	250
978, 17J, LS, 3/4, NI, DMK, OF	125	150	200
990, 21J, LS, GJS, DR, Adj.5P, DMK, NI, 3/4, GT, OF	175	225	350
991, 21J, LS, 3/4, GJS, Adj.5P, DMK, NI, GT, HC	200	250	400

Grade 992B, 16 size, 21 jewels, Adj.6p.

Grade 4992B, 16 size, 22 jewels, Adj.6p.

Note: Prefix before serial no. was Hamilton's method of I.D.,(C & serial no.= 992B railroad watch), (2B & serial no. = 950B railroad watch also S), (3C & serial no. = 4992B G.T.C. Canada Gov't), (4C & serial no.= 4992B for U.S.A. Gov't), (2K & serial no.= 2974B used for comparing watch).

IMPORTANT NOTE: Railroad Standards, Railroad Approved & Railroad Grade **terminology,** as defined and used in this _**BOOK**_.
1. **RAILROAD STANDARDS** = A commission or board appointed by the railroad companies outlined a set of **guidelines** to be accepted or approved by each railroad line.
2. **RAILROAD APPROVED** = A LIST of watches each railroad line would approve if purchased by their employee's. (this list changed through the years).
3. **RAILROAD GRADE** = A watch made by manufactures to meet or exceed the guidelines set by the railroad **standards.** Grades such as 992, Vanguard and B.W. Raymond, etc.
☉ Some GRADES **exceeded** the R.R. standards such as 23 jewels, diamond end stone, gold train, raised gold jewel settings, double sunk dial and the list goes on. Examples: such as Veritas, Sangamo, 950 & Riverside Maximus and many others.

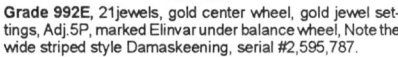

Grade 992E, 21jewels, gold center wheel, gold jewel settings, Adj.5P, marked Elinvar under balance wheel, Note the wide striped style Damaskeening, serial #2,595,787.

Grade 3992B, 22J, Adj.6P, "Navigation Master", note outside chapter on dial 1–10.

Grade or Name — Description	Avg	Ex-Fn	Mint
992, 21J, 3/4, Adj.5P, SR & DR, NI, OF	$175	$200	$350
992, 21J, 3/4, **gold center wheel**,GJS, Adj.5P, SR & DR, NI, OF..	200	250	400
992, 21J, 3/4, PS & LS, GJS, Adj.5P, DR, NI, DMK, **2 -Tone**, OF	250	325	500
992, 21J, **Extra**, 3/4, GJS, Adj.5P, DR, NI, DMK, OF ★	400	450	600
992, 21J, 3/4, DR, NI, **marked 8 Adj. for RR, Gold Flashed**, OF	425	475	675
992, 21J, marked **Special**, 3/4, PS & LS, GJS, Adj.5P, DR, NI, DMK, marked **Adj. for RR Service** on dial, OF ★★★	1,200	1,400	2,000
992E, 21J, marked **Elinvar, gold center wheel**, 3/4, GJS, Adj.5P .	250	300	450
992B, 21J, LS, Adj.6P, 3/4, OF	250	325	475
992B, 21J, Adj.6P, **2-Tone** ◲	375	475	600
992B, 21J, Adj.6P, 3/4, military silver case, OF	300	400	600
3992B, 22J, Adj.6P, 12 hr. dial, (Canadian), silver case ★	300	400	600
3992B, 22J, Adj.6P, "Navigation Master", Silver case ★	400	500	700
4992B, 22J, LS, 3/4, 24-hr. dial, Greenwich Civil Time, OF	200	300	450
993, 21J, PS, GJS, Adj.5P, DR, NI, DMK, HC	200	250	425
993, 21J, LS, GJS, Adj.5P, DMK, DR, NI, HC	200	250	425
993, 21J, marked **Special**, tu-tone, GJS, Adj.5P, DMK, DR, HC ★	375	400	600
993, 21J, LS, GJS, Adj.5P, DMK, DR, NI, **14K**, HC	550	600	875
993, 21J, LS, GJS, Adj.5P, DMK, DR, (GF multi color case), HC	400	475	650

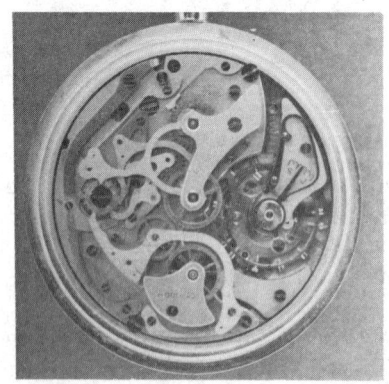

ADMIRAL,16 size, 16 jewels, Damaskeened on nickel 3/4 plate, serial no. 57821.

Chronograph, Grade 23, 16 size, 19 jewels, start-stop-reset to 0.

Grade or Name — Description	Avg	Ex-Fn	Mint
994, 21J, BRG, GJS, GT, DR, Adj.5P, DMK, PS, OF .... ★★	$800	$900	$1,300
994, 21J, BRG, GJS, GT, DR, Adj.5P, DMK, LS, OF .... ★★	900	1,000	1,400
996, 19J, LS, 3/4 GJS, DR, Adj.5P, DMK, OF	150	200	300
Admiral, 16J., Grade 977, 3/4 plate, OF, ...	100	150	250
Admiral,16J,NI, ADJ., DMK, HC..	135	165	275
DeLong Escapement, 21J, 992-B .... ★★★	1,500	1,700	2,200
Electric Interurban, 17J, G#974, OF	175	225	350
Official Standard, 17J, OF..	200	300	500
Union Special, 17J..	100	150	300
Hayden W. Wheeler, 17J, OF.....................................★	350	400	600
Hayden W. Wheeler, 17J, HC ....★	400	450	650
Hayden W. Wheeler, 21J...★	400	450	700
Hayden W. Wheeler, 21J, **14K** H.W.W. case...............★	750	900	1,100
Limited, 17J, G#974	150	175	250
Swiss Mfg., 17J, Adj.2P, G#669, GF case	40	60	135
Swiss Mfg., 23J, Adj.3P, (by Buren W. Co. G# 971), Ca. 1969-70s	75	100	200

CHRONOGRAPH
Grade 23

Grade or Name — Description	Avg	Ex-Fn	Mint
16S, 19J, chronograph with start-stop-reset to zero	$275	$300	$450

12 SIZE
(Some cases were octagon, decagon, cushion, etc.)

Grade or Name — Description	Avg	Ex-Fn	Mint
900, 19J, BRG, DR, Adj.5P, GJS, OF, **14K**	$225	$325	$500
900, 19J, BRG, DR, Adj.5P, GJS, OF	100	150	250
902, 19J, BRG, DR, Adj.5P, GJS...	100	150	250

 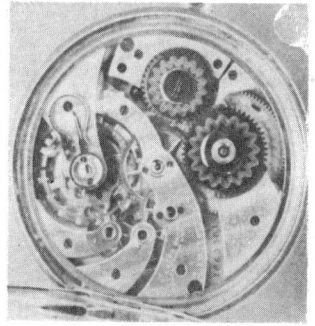

Grade 918, 12 size, 19 jewels, Adj3p, serial number 3,136,257.   Grade 920, 12 size, 23 jewels, gold train, gold jewel settings, serial number 1,863,381.

🕐 Watches listed in this book are priced at the collectable retail level, as **Complete** watches having an original 14k gold-filled case for Stem Wind and *Key Wind* with silver case, an original white enamel single sunk dial, and with the entire original movement in good working order with no repairs needed.

MOVEMENTS WITH ODD GRADE NUMBERS ARE HUNTING CASE.
MOVEMENTS WITH EVEN GRADE NUMBERS ARE OPEN FACE.

Grade or Name — Description	Avg	Ex-Fn	Mint
902, 19J, BRG, DR, Adj.5P, GJS, **14K**	$250	$300	$500
904, 21J, BRG, DR, Adj.5P, GJS, GT	125	150	300
910, 17J, 3/4, DR, ADJ	50	70	150
912, 17J, **Digital model, rotating seconds,** OF	150	200	350
912, 17J, 3/4, DR, ADJ	40	60	150
914, 17J, 3/4, DR, Adj.3P, GJS	40	60	150
914, 17J, 3/4, DR, Adj.3P, GJS, 14K	200	275	350
916, 17J, 3/4, DR, Adj.3P	40	60	125
916, 17J, Adj.3P, silver case	40	60	125
918, 19J, Adj.3P, WGF	100	125	250
918, 19J, 3/4, DR, Adj.3P, GJS, OF	100	125	250
920, 23J, BRG, DR, Adj.5P, GJS, GT, OF	225	275	400
920, 23J, BRG, DR, Adj.5P, GJS, GT, **14K**	425	475	600
922, 23J, BRG, DR, Adj.5P, GJS, GT, **14K**	425	475	600
922, 23J, BRG, DR, Adj.5P, GJS, GT, OF	225	275	400
922 MP, 23J, marked (MASTERPIECE), **18K case** ★	600	700	1,000
922 MP, 23J, marked (MASTERPIECE), **Iridium Platinum** ★	600	700	1,000
922 MP, GF, Hamilton case	325	425	600
400, 21J, (Illinois 13 size M#2, 5 tooth click), the Tycoon Series, **Hamilton on dial & case**, 18K, OF ★	325	425	600

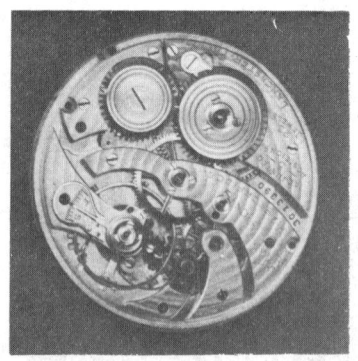

Grade 922MP, 12 size, 23 jewels, **marked** "masterpiece" serial number 3,013,390, c. 1930.

The MASTERPIECE
MODEL ''B''—18K GOLD

10 SIZE

Grade or Name — Description	Avg	Ex-Fn	Mint
917, 17J, 3/4, DR, Adj.3P	$40	$60	$125
917, 17J, 3/4, DR, Adj.3P, **14K**	200	250	325
921, 21J, BRG, DR, Adj.5P	125	150	200
923, 23J, BRG, DR, Adj.5P, **G.F.**	150	175	250
923, 23J, BRG, DR, Adj.5P, (**spread** to fit a 12 size CASE),14K	225	250	300
923, 23J, **18K, and box**	400	500	700
923, 23J, BRG, DR, Adj.5P, Iridium Platinum	300	350	450
945, 23J, Adj.5P, Masterpiece on DIAL	100	175	250

🕐 Watches listed in this book are priced at the collectable retail level, as complete watches having an original 14k goldfilled case & KW with a Silver case, an original white enamel single sunk dial, and with the entire original movement in good working order with no repairs needed, unless otherwise noted.

🕐   Watch terminology or communication in this book has evolved over the years, in search of better and more precise language with a effort to improve, purify, adjust itself and make it easier to understand.

0 SIZE

Grade or Name — Description	Avg	Ex-Fn	Mint
981, 17J, 3/4, Adj.3P, DR, **18K, HC**	$175	$225	$375
982, 17-19J, same as 981 & 983 HC but no seconds bit	70	90	150
983, 17J, Adj.3P, DR, GJS, **18K, HC**	175	225	375
985, 19J, BRG, Adj.3P, DR, GJS, GT, **18K, HC**	200	250	400
Lady Hamilton, 14K case, OF	200	250	400
Lady Hamilton, 23J, GJS, **gold filled OF**	150	175	275

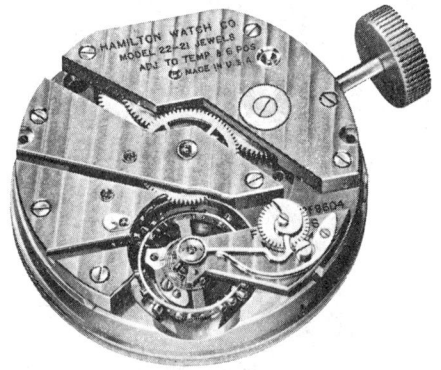

Model 22, 21 jewels, 35 Size or 70mm, wind indicator, adjusted to 6 positions, base metal case.

Chronometer Model 22, 21 jewels, 35 Size or 70mm, wind indicator, 54 hour mainspring, adjusted to 6 positions.

Above:Chronometer in padded box, stem wind.
Right: Chronometer in gimbals and box, wind indicator.

CHRONOMETER

Grade or Name — Description	Avg	Ex-Fn	Mint
35S, M#22, 21J, Wind Indicator, **Adj.6P**, in gimbals and box, lever	$700	$900	$1,400
35S, M#22, 21J, Wind Indicator, **Adj.6P**, in a large base metal OF case	500	600	800
36S, M#36, 21J, **Adj.5P**, Wind Indicator, in gimbals and box	1,300	1,500	2,000
36S, M#36, 21J, 56 hr.W. Ind.,"SID" (sidereal), chrome case ..... ★	1,500	1,700	2,200
36S, M#36, 21J, Wind Indicator, in Hamilton sterling pocket watch case with bow (s# 1,260,001 to 1,260,970) .... ★★★	1,600	1,800	2,500
37S, 21J, 940 movement S# range= 420,001 to 421,000, ONLY 220 made for U.S. Navy, true 24 hour black dial .... ★★★	1,500	1,700	2,400
85S, M#21, 14J, KW, KS, **Fusee, Detent Escapement** with helical hairspring, gimbals and box, (all original)	1,300	1,500	1,800

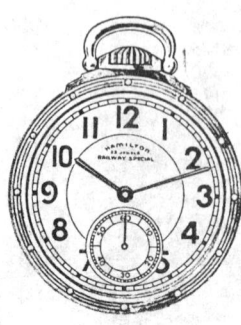

CASE MODEL # A
gold filled : $100 - $125 - $150

CASE MODEL #2
gold filled : $100- $125 - $250
14K Gold : $350 - $400 - $600
2 TONE caseGF:$125-$150-$300

CASE MODEL #3
gold filled : $95- $115 - $170

This Tag Identifies
The Improved
992

CASE MODEL # 4
gold filled : $90 - $115 - $180

CASE MODEL #5
gold filled : $100- $115 - $165

CASE MODEL #6
gold filled : $110- $130 - $200

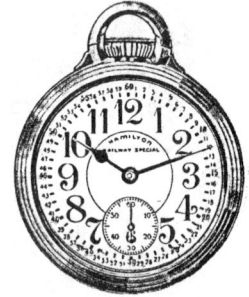

CASE MODEL # 7
White gold filled : $90 - $100 - $165

CASE MODEL #8
gold filled : $110- $130 - $200

CASE MODEL #10
gold filled : $100- $125 - $200

Model "A" was advertised in a Gold-filled Case & advertised with a grade 950 movement.
Models 2 & 17 came in 14K solid GOLD or gold-filled, model 2 advertised with 992 or 950.
Models 3, 4, 5, 6, (7 white G.F.), 8, 10, 11, Cross Bar, & Traffic Special II all gold-filled.
Model "16" gold plate and Model "15" & Traffic Special I was stainless steel case.

⊕ NOTE: Factory Advertised as a **complete** watch and was fitted with a certain matched, timed
and rated movement and sold in the factory designed case style as a complete watch. The factory
also sold _uncased_ movements to **JOBBERS** such as Jewelry stores & they cased the movement in
a case styles the **CUSTOMER requested.** All the factory advertised complete watches came with
the dial **SHOWN or CHOICE** of other **Railroad** dials.

CASE MODEL # 11
gold filled : $100 - $115 - $180

CASE MODEL #14
Nickel : $95- $110 - $165

CASE MODEL #15
S. steel : $30- $40 - $80

CASE MODEL # 16
gold plated : $80 - $90 - $140

CASE MODEL #17
gold filled : $100- $120 - $225
Gold : $400 - $450 - $500

CASE MODEL Cross Bar
gold filled : $100- $125 - $200

TRAFFIC SPECIAL I
S. Steel : $25 - $35 - $65

TRAFFIC SPECIAL II
gold plated : $45- $55 - $80

The MAINLINER
gold filled : $100 - $115 - $180

🕐 Railway Specials were packed & shipped in a plastic ivory cigarette style box and were sealed with a ribbon. To remove the watch break seal by cutting the ribbon which holds the watch in box.

Model "A" was advertised in a Gold-filled Case & advertised with a grade 950 movement.
Models 2 & 17 came in 14K solid GOLD or gold-filled, model 2 advertised with 992 or 950.
Models 3, 4, 5, 6, 8, 10, 11, & Cross Bar gold-filled.
Model "16" gold plate and Model "15" & Traffic Special I was stainless steel case.
Case Model 14 = Nickel-Chrome.

HAMILTON W. CO. IDENTIFICATION OF MOVEMENTS

How To Identify Your Watch: Compare the movement with the illustration in this section. While comparing, note the location of the balance, jewels, screws, gears, and back plate (Full, 3/4, Bridge) which will be clues in identifying the movement you have. Having determined the size, the **GRADE** can also be found by looking up the serial number of your watch in the Hamilton Serial Number & Grades List. Illustrations of selected grades of the different size movements are shown to assist you in identifying movements. Hamilton movements which do not have grade numbers engraved on them <u>do</u> carry serial numbers which can be checked against the serial number list to secure the *grade number.*

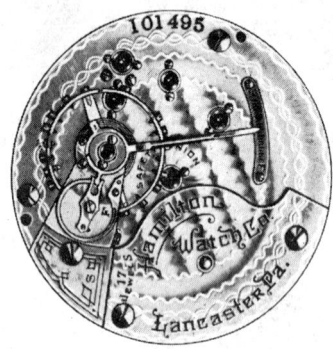

Grade 936, <u>18 SIZE</u>, **Full Plate, OPEN FACE** SHOWN. Also grades 922, 924, 926, 928, 930, 932, 934, 938, 940, 942, 944, 946, & 948 All look SIMILAR to the above.

Grade 925, <u>18 SIZE</u>, **Full Plate, Hunting Case** SHOWN. Also grades 923, 927, 929, 931, 933, 935, 937, 939, 941, 943, 945, and 947 All look SIMILAR to the above.

NOTE: 18 Size Grades 924, 925, 926, 927, 928, 929, 930, 931, 932, 933, 934, & 935 use 90% same parts but not plates. 18 Size Grades 936, 937, 938, 939, & 948 use 90% same parts but not plates. Grades 940, 941, 942, & 943 use 90% same parts but not plates. 18 Size Grades 944 & 946 use 90% same parts.

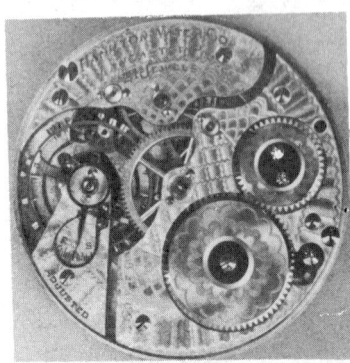

Grade 971, <u>16 SIZE</u>, **Hunting Case,** 3/4 Plate, 21 jewels, Shown. Note Crown Wheel with 2 Screws this movement uses a 4 Footed Dial. Also grades 969, 973, 975, 991, & 993 all look SIMILAR to the above. Note location of the larger ratchet wheel next to balance cock.

Grade 992, <u>16 SIZE</u>, **Open Face,** 3/4 Plate, 21 jewels, **1st.** model Shown. Note Crown Wheel with 2 Screws this movement uses a 4 Footed Dial. Also grades 954, 968, 970, 972, 974, & 990 all look SIMILAR to the above. Note location of the smaller Crown wheel next to balance cock. 1st. model.

NOTE: 16 Size Grades 950, 952, & 996 use 90% same parts. 16 Size Grades 954, 962, 963, 966, 967, 972, & 973 use 90% same parts but not plates. 16 Size Grades 956, 964, 965, 968, 969, 974, 975, 976, 977, & 978 use 90% same parts. 16 Size Grades 960, 961, 970, 971, 990, 991, 992, 993, & 994 use 90% same parts but not plates. Grades 950E & 950B differ from grade 950. Grades 992E & 992B differ from grade 992.

Grade 992 Note: with narrow stripes, 16 size, 3/4 plate, 21 jewels, 5 positions, **2nd model** Shown.   Note: Crown Wheel with 1 Screw. 2nd. model.

Grade 992 E = wide stripes Damaskeening with ELINVAR under balance wheel. 16 size, 3/4 plate, 21J., 5 positions, **3rd. model** Shown.

Grade 992 B, 16 size, 3/4 plate, 21J., **6 POSITIONS.** last model, model # 4.

Grade 950 16 size, BRIDGE, 23J., 5 positions. Note: with narrow stripes,

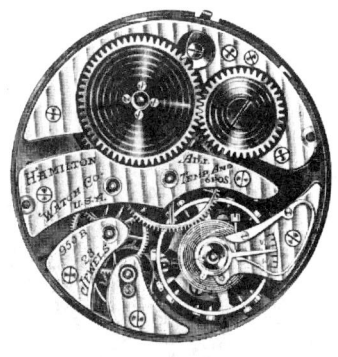

Grade 950 E = wide stripes Damaskeening with ELINVAR under balance wheel. 16 size, BRIDGE, 23J., 5 positions.

Grade 950 B, 16 size, BRIDGE, 23J., **6 POSITIONS.**

Grade 960, 16 SIZE, BRIDGE, OPEN FACE SHOWN. Also GRADES 950, 952, 962, 964, 994 all look SIMILAR to the above. Note location of the smaller Crown wheel next to balance cock.

Grade 961, 16 SIZE, BRIDGE, Hunting Case SHOWN. Also GRADES 951, 963, 965 all look SIMILAR to the above. Note location of the larger ratchet wheel next to balance cock.

SWISS MADE, 16 size, open face, 17 to 23 jewels, 3/4 plate.

Grade 902, 12 size
Open face, bridge movt., 19 jewels, double roller

Grade 912, 12 size
Open face, ¼ plate movt., 17 jewels, double roller

Grade 918, 12 size
Open face, ¼ plate movt., 19 jewels, double roller

Grade 922, 12 size
Open face, bridge movt., 23 jewels, double roller

Grade 917, 10 size
Open face, ¾ plate movt., 17 jewels, double roller

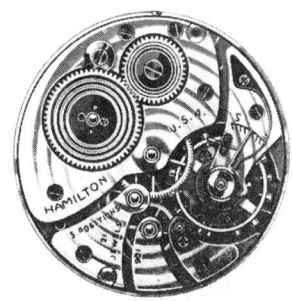

Grade 921, 10 size
Open face, bridge movt., 21 jewels, double roller

Grade 923, 10 size
Open face, bridge movt., 23 jewels, double roller

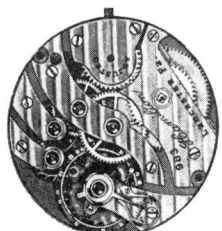

Grade 983, 0 size
Hunting, bridge movt., 17 jewels, double roller

Grade 979,6/0 size
Hunting, ¾ plate movt., 19 jewels, double roller

Grade 986, 6/0 size
Open face, ¾ plate movt., 17 jewels, double roller

🕐 Pricing in this Guide are fair market price for **COMPLETE** watches which are reflected from the "**NAWWC**" National and regional shows.

234

HAMPDEN WATCH CO.
(DUEBER WATCH CO.)
Springfield, Massachusetts
Canton, Ohio
1877 - 1930

The New York Watch Co. preceded Hampden, and before that Don J. Mozart (1864) produced his three-wheel watch. Mozart was assisted by George Samuel Rice of New York and, as a result of their joint efforts, the New York Watch Co. was formed in 1866 in Providence, Rhode Island. It was moved in 1867 to Springfield, Massachusetts. Two grades of watches were decided on, and the company started with a 18S, 3/4 plate engraved "Springfield." They were sold for $60 to $75. The 18S, 3/4 plate were standard production, and the highest grade was a "George Walker" that sold for about $200 and a 16S, 3/4 plate "State Street" which had steel parts and exposed balance and escape wheels that were gold plated.

John C. Dueber started manufacturing watch cases in 1864 and bought a controlling interest in a company in 1886. At about this time a disagreement arose between Elgin, Waltham, and the Illinois Watch companies. Also, at this time, an anti-trust law was passed, and the watch case manufacturers formed a boycott against Dueber. Dueber was faced with a major decision, whether to stay in business, surrender to the watch case companies or buy a watch company. He decided to buy the Hampden Watch Co. of Springfield, Mass. By 1889 the operation had moved to Canton, Ohio. By the end of the year the company was turning out 600 watches a day. The first 16 size watch was produced in 1890. About 1891 Hampden introduced the first 23J movement made in America. Hampden assigned serial numbers at random to the New York Watch Co. movements for years after they purchased the N.Y.W.Co.

HAMPDEN ESTIMATED SERIAL NUMBER AND PRODUCTION DATES

DATE-SERIAL NO.	DATE-SERIAL NO.	DATE-SERIAL NO.	DATE-SERIAL NO.
1877— 60,000	1889— 555,500	1901—1,512,000	1913—3,048,000
1878— 91,000	1890— 611,000	1902—1,642,000	1914—3,176,000
1879—122,000	1891— 666,500	1903—1,768,000	1915—3,304,000
1880—153,000	1892— 722,000	1904—1,896,000	1916—3,432,000
1881—184,000	1893— 775,000	1905—2,024,000	1917—3,560,000
1882—215,000	1894— 833,000	1906—2,152,000	1918—3,680,000
1883—250,000	1895— 888,500	1907—2,280,000	1919—3,816,000
1884—300,000	1896— 944,000	1908—2,408,000	1920—3,944,000
1885—350,000	1897—1,000,000	1909—2,536,000	1921—4,072,000
1886—400,000	1898—1,128,000	1910—2,664,000	1922—4,200,000
1887—450,000	1899—1,256,000	1911—2,792,000	1923—4,400,000
1888—500,000	1900—1,384,000	1912—2,920,000	1924—4,600,000

The above list is provided for determining the **APPROXIMATE** age of your watch. Match serial number with date. Watches were not necessarily sold in the exact order of manufactured date.

Chronology of the Development of Hampden Watch Co.:
The Mozart Watch Co., Providence, R. I. (1864-1866)
New York Watch Co., Providence, R. I. (1866-1867)
New York Watch Co., Springfield, Mass. (1867-1875)
New York Watch Mfg. Co., Springfield, Mass. (1875-1876)
Hampden Watch Co., Springfield, Mass. (1877-1886)
Hampden-Dueber Watch Co., Springfield, Mass. (1886-1888)
Hampden Watch Co., Canton, Ohio. (1888-1923)
Dueber Watch Co., Canton, Ohio. (1889-1923)
Dueber-Hampden Watch Co., Canton, Ohio. (1923-1931)
Amtorg, U.S.S.R (1930-Present)

Issued 1890

Issued 1892

Issued 1895

NR inside flag = New Railway and SR inside flag = Special Railway
D & ★ D & anchor inside flag = Duber and H inside flag = Hampden

Dueber Watch Co., 18 size, 15 jewels, nickel movement. Model 3, hunting case.

Dueber Grand, 18 size, 17 jewels, open face, originally sold for $20.00.

HAMPDEN
18 SIZE

Grade or Name — Description	Avg	Ex-Fn	Mint
Anchor (inside flag), 17J, ADJ, GJS, DMK, OF	$70	$90	$175
"3" Ball, 17J, ADJ, NI, DMK, OF	90	125	225
Boston W. Co. 11J, KW/SW	60	80	125
Canadian Pacific R.W., 17J, Adj., M# 4, OF ★ ★	1,000	1,200	1,800
Canadian Pacific RR, 17J, OF ★ ★	900	1,000	1,500
Canadian Pacific RR, 21J, OF ★ ★	1,000	1,100	1,600
Champion, 7-11J, ADJ, FULL, gilded, or, NI, OF	60	80	125
Champion, 7-11J, ADJ, FULL, gilded, or, NI, HC	80	100	175
Champion, 15-17J, ADJ, FULL, gilded, or, NI, OF	60	80	135
Champion, 15-17J, ADJ, FULL, gilded, or, NI, HC	75	90	200
Correct Time, 15J, HC	75	90	200
Dueber, 15J, gilded, DMK, HC	65	90	175
Dueber, 16J, gilded, DMK, OF	60	80	150
Dueber, 17J, gilded, DMK, OF	60	80	150
John C. Dueber, 15J, gilded, DMK, OF	60	80	150
John C. Dueber, 15J, gilded, DMK, HC	80	100	175
John C. Dueber, 17J, gilded, ADJ, DMK, OF	60	80	150
John C. Dueber, Special, 17J, ADJ, DMK, OF	75	90	175
John C. Dueber, Special, 17J, ADJ, DMK, HC	90	100	225
John C. Dueber, 17J, HC	70	90	200
John C. Dueber, 21J, HC	140	175	400
Dueber Grand, 17J, OF	60	80	150
Dueber Grand, 17J, ADJ, HC	60	90	200
Dueber Grand, 21J, ADJ, DMK, NI, HC	140	175	400

🕐 Generic, nameless or unmarked grades for watch movements are listed under the Company name or initials of the Company, etc. by size, jewel count and description.

	Avg	Ex-Fn	Mint
Dueber W. Co.,7-11J, OF	$50	$75	$150
Dueber W. Co., 15J, DMK, OF	50	75	150
Dueber W. Co., 15J, DMK, HC	65	85	200
Dueber W. Co., 16J, OF	50	75	150
Dueber W. Co., 16J, HC	65	85	200
Dueber W. Co., 17J, DMK, ADJ, OF	50	75	150
Dueber W. Co., 17J, Gilded	50	75	150
Dueber W. Co., 17J, DMK, ADJ, HC	60	85	200
Dueber W. Co., 19J, ADJ, GJS, HC ★	400	450	575
Dueber W. Co., 21J, Adj.5P, GJS, OF	150	200	295
Dueber W. Co., 21J, GJS, Adj.5P, HC	165	225	375

🕐 Pricing in this Guide are fair market price for **COMPLETE** watches which are reflected from the "**NAWCC**" National and regional shows.

John C. Dueber Special, 18 size, 17 jewels, serial number 949,097.

Oriental, 18 size, 15 jewels, open face, serial number 117,825.

Grade or Name — Description	Avg	Ex-Fn	Mint
Forest City, 15j, KW	$60	$75	$175
Gladiator, 7-9J, KW, OF	50	70	175
Gladiator, 9-11J, NI, DMK, OF	60	80	175
Gulf Stream Sp., 21J, R.R. grade, OF, LS ★★	500	600	1,000
Homer Foot, gilded, KW, OF (Early)	150	250	400

🕐 Generic, nameless or unmarked grades for watch movements are listed under the Company name or initials of the Company, etc. by size, jewel count and description.

	Avg	Ex-Fn	Mint
Hampden W. Co., 7J, KW, KS, coin silver OF	$80	$125	$175
Hampden W. Co., 7J, SW, OF	40	60	135
Hampden W. Co., 11J, OF, KW	40	60	135
Hampden W. Co., 11J, HC, KW	60	80	150
Hampden W. Co., 11J, OF, SW	40	60	135
Hampden W. Co., 11J, HC, SW	60	80	175
Hampden W. Co., 15J, OF, KW	65	85	150
Hampden W. Co., 15J, HC, KW	65	85	175
Hampden W. Co., 15J, HC, SW	65	85	175
Hampden W. Co., 15J, SW, Gilded, OF	40	60	135
Hampden W. Co., 15J, SW, NI, OF	40	60	150
Hampden W. Co., 15J, **Multi-color, 14K, HC**	1,600	2,000	3,000
Hampden W. Co., 16J, OF	50	70	175
Hampden W. Co., 17J, SW, Gilded	50	70	175
Hampden W. Co., 17J, SW, NI, OF	50	70	175
Hampden W. Co., 17J, SW, HC	50	70	175
Hampden W. Co., 17J, LS, HC, **14K**	425	575	750
Hampden W. Co., 17J, LS, HC, **10K**	225	350	500
Hampden W. Co., 21J, OF, SW	150	200	300
Hampden W. Co., 21J, HC, SW	200	250	335
John Hancock, 7J, Adj., OF	50	70	125
John Hancock, 15J, Adj.3P, OF	50	70	150
John Hancock, 17J, GJS, Adj.3P, OF	65	80	175
John Hancock, 17J, GJS, Adj.3P, HC	65	80	225
John Hancock, 21J, GJS, Adj.3P, OF	125	175	300
John Hancock, 23J, GJS, Adj.5P, OF	250	300	450
Hayward, 15J, KW	90	120	225
Hayward, 11J, SW	50	65	150

🕐 Watches listed in this book are priced at the collectable fair market value at the **RETAIL LEVEL**, as complete watches having an original 14k gold filled case, KEY WIND with silver, an original white enamel single sunk dial, and with the entire original movement in good working order with no repairs needed, unless otherwise noted.

Menlo Park, 18 size, 17 jewels, serial number 1,184,116.

New Railway, 18 size, 23 jewels, open face only, gold jewel settings, originally sold for $50.00, Model 2.

Grade or Name — Description	Avg	Ex-Fn	Mint
Lafayette, 11J, NI, HC	$60	$85	$150
Lafayette, 15J, NI, **KW**	200	250	400
Lafayette, 15J, NI, HC	70	85	200
Lakeside, 15J, NI, SW, HC	70	85	200
M. J. & Co. Railroad Watch Co., 15J, HC ★	300	400	600
Menlo Park, 15-17J, NI, ADJ, OF	125	150	300
Mermod, Jaccard & Co., 15J, KW, HC	150	175	300
Metropolis, 15J, NI, SW, OF	100	125	250
Wm. McKinley, 17J, Adj.3P, OF	60	80	150
Wm. McKinley, 17J, Adj.3P, HC	75	100	175
Wm. McKinley, 21J, GJS, Adj.5P	125	160	300
New Railway, 17J, GJS, Adj.5P, OF	100	125	275
New Railway, 19J, GJS, Adj.5P, OF	175	200	350
New Railway, 19J, GJS, Adj.5P, HC	200	250	400

Railway, 18 size, 17 jewels, key wind & set; early railroad watch.

Special Railway, 18 size, 23 jewels, Adj5p, serial number 3,357,284.

🕐 Watches listed in this book are priced at the collectable retail level, as **complete** watches having an original 14k gold-filled case and *Key Wind* with silver, an original white enamel single sunk dial, and with the entire original movement in good working order with no repairs needed.

NR inside flag = New Railway and SR inside flag = Special Railway
D & ★ D & anchor inside flag = Duber and H inside flag = Hampden

🕐 Pricing in this Guide are fair market price for **COMPLETE** watches which are reflected from the "<u>NAWCC</u>" National and regional shows.

Grade or Name — Description	Avg	Ex-Fn	Mint
New Railway, 21J, GJS, Adj.5P, OF	$160	$190	$295
New Railway, 21J, GJS, Adj.5P, HC	200	250	325
New Railway, 23J, GJS, Adj.5P	250	300	425
New Railway, 23J, GJS, Adj.5P, **14K**, OF	500	550	800
North Am. RR, 21J, GJS, Adj.5P, OF, LS	225	250	400
North Am. RR, 21J, GJS, Adj.3P, HC, PS	225	300	450
Order of Railroad Conductors, 17J, ADJ, OF ★★★	1,200	1,400	2,200
Pennsylvania Special, 17J, GJS, Adj.5P, DR, NI ★★★	1,200	1,400	2,000
J. C. Perry, 15J, KW, gilded, HC	90	120	225
J. C. Perry, 15J, NI, SW, OF	50	70	175
J. C. Perry, 15J, gilded, SW, OF	50	70	150
Railway, 11J, gilded, OF	100	125	200
Railway, 15-17J, NI, OF	125	150	225
Railway, 15-17J, **KW**, marked on mvt., HC ★★	600	700	1,000
Railroad with R.R. names on dial and movement:			
Private Label R.R. 17J, OF ★★	450	550	750
Special Railway, 17J, GJS, Adj.5P, NI, DR, OF	100	125	200
Special Railway, 21J, GJS, Adj.5P, NI, DR, 2-Tone, OF	185	225	400
Special Railway, 21J, GJS, Adj.5P, NI, DR, HC	250	275	400
Special Railway, 23J, GJS, Adj.5P, NI, DR, OF	300	335	400
Special Railway, 23J, GJS, Adj.5P, NI, DR, 2-Tone, OF	325	350	450
Special Railway, 23J, GJS, Adj.5P, NI, DR, HC	300	400	600
Special Railway, 23J, **14K, HC**	700	800	950
Springfield, 7-11J, KW, gilded, HC	85	120	200
Springfield, 7-11J, SW, NI, HC	85	120	200
Standard, 15J, gilded, HC	125	150	200
Train Service Standard, 17J, LS, M# 2, NI, HC ★	450	500	700
Theo. Studley, 15J, KW, KS, HC	85	150	200
Tramway Special, 17J, NI	175	200	250
Wisconsin Central R W, 17J, LS, OF ★	400	525	900
Woolworth, 11-15J, KW	90	110	200
Grade 30,31,45,46,49,54,57,65,66,69,70,71, **ALL =11J**	40	60	135
Grade 32,33,34,35,36,40,41,42,49,55,56,58,59,60,62, **All =15J**	45	65	150
Grade, 43,44,47,48,49,63,64,67,68,69,80,81, **ALL =16-17J**	50	70	165
Grade 85, **19J**, GJS, 2-Tone, HC ★★	500	600	750
Grade 95, **21J**, GJS, OF	170	200	300
Grade 125, **21J**, Adj.3P, OF	170	200	250

16 SIZE

Grade or Name — Description	Avg	Ex-Fn	Mint
Beacon, 7J, OF	$50	$60	$100
E.W. Bond & State Street models see New York W. Co. Springfield			
Champion, 7J, NI, 3/4, gilded, coin, OF	50	60	125
Champion, 7J, NI, 3/4, gilded, OF	50	60	125
Champion, 7J, NI, 3/4, gilded, HC	65	80	200
Chronometer,19- 21J, **detent escapement**, NI, Adj.3P, GJS ... ★★	650	750	1,000
John C. Dueber, 17J, GJS, NI, Adj.5P, 3/4	60	70	175
John C. Dueber, 21J, GJS, NI, Adj.5P, 3/4	125	175	250
John C. Dueber, 21J, GJS, NI, Adj.5P, DR, BRG	150	200	275
Dueber Watch Co., 17J, ADJ, 3/4	50	70	165

NOTE: Railroad Standards, Railroad Approved & Railroad Grade **terminology**, as defined and used in this *BOOK*.
1. **RAILROAD STANDARDS** = A commission or board appointed by the railroad companies outlined a set of **guidelines** to be accepted or approved by each railroad line.
2. **RAILROAD APPROVED** = A LIST of watches each railroad line would approve if purchased by their employee's. (this list changed through the years).
3. **RAILROAD GRADE** = A watch made by manufactures to meet or exceed the guidelines set by the railroad **standards**. Grades such as 992, Vanguard and B.W. Raymond, etc.
🕐 Some GRADES **exceeded** the R.R. standards such as 23 J,. diamond end stone, gold train, raised gold jewel settings, double sunk dial and the list goes on. Examples: such as Veritas, Sangamo, 950 & Riverside Maximus and many others.

🕐 Pricing in this Guide are fair market price for **COMPLETE** watches which are reflected from the "**NAWCC**" National and regional shows.

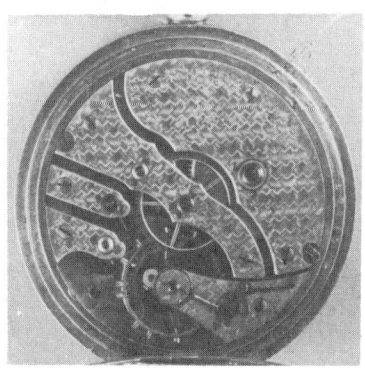 

Hampden W. Co., Bridge Model, 16 size, 23 jewels, 2-tone movement, serial number 1,899,430.

Hampden W. Co., 16 size, 17 jewels, gold jewel settings, serial number 3,075,235.

🕐 Generic, nameless or unmarked grades for watch movements are listed under the Company name or initials of the Company, etc. by size, jewel count and description.

Grade or Name — Description	Av	Ex-Fn	Mint
Hampden W. Co., 7J, SW, OF	$40	$60	$125
Hampden W. Co., 7J, SW, HC	40	60	150
Hampden W. Co., 11J, SW, OF	40	60	125
Hampden W. Co., 11J, SW, HC	40	60	150
Hampden W. Co., 15J, SW, OF	40	60	125
Hampden W. Co., 15J, SW, HC	40	60	150
Hampden W. Co., 17J, SW, OF	40	60	125
Hampden W. Co., 17J, **14K, Multi-color,** HC	1,300	1,500	2,000
Hampden W. Co., 17J, SW, HC	40	60	150
Hampden W. Co., 21J, SW, HC	150	200	400
Hampden W. Co., 21J, SW, OF	150	200	300
Hampden W. Co., 23J, Adj.5P, GJS, 3/4	300	400	500
Hampden W. Co., 23J, Series 2, **Freesprung,** GJS GT, HC ★ ★ ★	500	650	1,000
Masonic Dial, 23J, GJS, 2-Tone **porcelain dial**	500	600	900

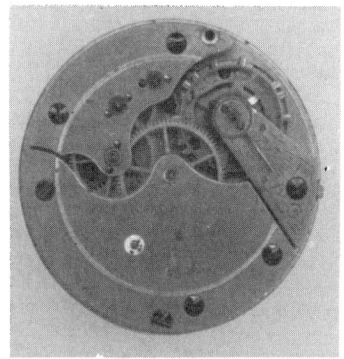 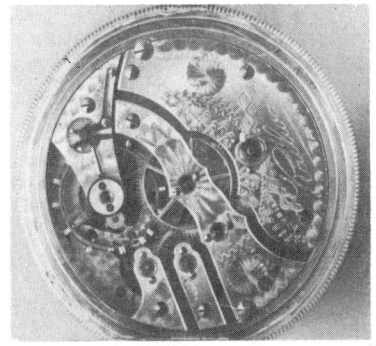

Hampden W. Co., Series 1, 16 size, 15 jewels, stem wind open face.

Railway, 16 size, 17 jewels, Adj.5P, gold jewel settings, serial number 2,271,866.

NR inside flag = New Railway and SR inside flag = Special Railway
D & ★ D & anchor inside flag = Duber and H inside flag = Hampden

🕐 Pricing in this Guide are fair market price for **COMPLETE** watches which are reflected from the "**NAWCC**" National and regional shows.

🕐 Generic, nameless or unmarked grades for watch movements are listed under the Company name or initials of the Company, etc. by size, jewel count and description.

Grade 104, 16 size, 23 jewels, gold jewel settings, gold train, Adj5p, open face, serial number 2,801,184.

Hampden style watch produced in Russia with the machinery purchased by the Russian factory. This watch is a 16 size 7 jewel movement Ca. 1935

Grade or Name — Description	Avg	Ex-Fn	Mint
Wm. McKinley, 17J, GJS, Adj.5P, NI, DR, 3/4	$50	$70	$175
Wm. McKinley, 21J, GJS, Adj.5P, NI, DR, 3/4	150	175	375
Wm. McKinley, 21J, GJS, Adj.5P, NI, DR, 3/4, **Coin**	150	200	300
Wm. McKinley, 21J, GJS, Adj.5P, NI, DR, BRG	150	200	275
New Railway, 21J, GJS, Adj.5P	200	250	350
New Railway, 23J, GJS, Adj.5P, LS, HC	300	350	475
Ohioan, 21J, Adj.5P, GJS, 3/4	200	300	400
Railway, 17-19J, GJS, Adj.5P, BRG, DR	140	170	300
Special Railway, 17J, Adj, NI, BRG, DR, OF	100	150	225
Special Railway, 17J, Adj, NI, BRG, DR, HC	100	150	225
Special Railway, 23J, Adj.5P, NI, BRG, DR	300	400	500
Russian made model, 7-17J, 16 size, 3/4 plate ★	75	100	200
Garfield, 21J., Adj.5P, OF	150	200	350
Gen'l Stark, 15J, DMK, BRG	50	70	150
Gen'l Stark, 17J, DMK, BRG	50	70	175
76, 21J, LS, Adj.3P	150	185	250
94-95, 21J, **marked "94 or 95"**, GJS, Adj.5P,	225	275	400
97 HC, 98 HC, 107 OF, 108 OF, **ALL = 17J**, Adj.3P, NI, 3/4	60	80	175
99, 15J, 3/4, HC	60	80	200
103, 21J, GJS, Adj.5P, NI, BRG, DR	200	275	400
104, 23J, GJS, Adj.5P, NI, 3\4 or BRG, DR, **marked**, OF	300	350	550
104, 23J, GJS, Adj.5P, NI, BRG, DR, **marked**, HC	350	400	600
105, 21J, GJS, Adj.5P, NI, 3/4, DR, **marked**,	225	250	300
106, 107 OF, & 108, **17J**, SW, NI, **marked**,	60	80	175
109, 15J, 3/4, **marked**, OF	60	80	175
110, 11J, 3/4	40	50	95
115, 21J, SW, NI, **marked**, OF	225	250	400
120, 21J, SW, NI, OF, **marked Chronometer on dial**	350	400	600
340, 17J, SW, NI	60	70	175
440, 15J, 2-tone	60	70	175
555, 21J, GT, GJS, **marked Chronometer on dial & mvt.**	600	700	900
555, 21J, GT, GJS, **marked Chronometer on dial ONLY**	375	400	500
600, 17J, SW, NI, **marked**,	50	60	175

🕐 Some watch manufacturers personalize watches for jobbers or jewelry firms, with ·exclusive private signed or marked movements. The valuable collectable watches are listed under the signed or marked movement. Other exclusive private signed or marked movements will have equivalent value are only slightly higher value and should be compared to Generic or Nameless movements. Railroad signed or marked (dials & movements) are usually more collectable & higher in value.

Dueber Grand, 12 size, 17 jewels, gold jewel settings, hunting case, serial number 1,737,354.

Dueber Grand, 12 size, 17 jewels, gold jewel settings, open face, pin set, serial number 1,732,255.

12 SIZE Standard Model

(SEE ALSO "12 SIZE " THIN MODEL)

Grade or Name — Description	Avg	Ex-Fn	Mint
Aviator, 17J, Adj.4P, OF .... ★	$90	$100	$150
Aviator, 19J, Adj.4P, OF	90	100	150
Beacon, 17J, OF	85	95	135
Biltmore, 17J, OF .... ★	85	95	135
Dueber Grand, 17J, BRG, OF	85	95	135
Dueber Grand, 17J, BRG, HC	100	125	165
Dueber Grand, 17J, 3/4 plate, OF	85	95	135
Duquesne, 19J, Adj., OF .... ★ ★	90	100	150
Gen'l Stark, 15J, (some models pin set)	60	75	100
Hampden W. Co., 7J, SW, OF	40	50	75
Hampden W. Co., 17J, **14K, Multi-color, HC**	600	800	1,000
John Hancock, 21J, Adj, OF	125	150	200
John Hancock, 21J, Adj, HC	150	175	250
Minute Man, 17J, (standard size), OF	85	95	135
Ohioan, 21J, Adj.3P, GJS, 3/4, OF ....★	125	150	200
Viking, 17J, Adj, OF ....★	85	95	135
No. 10, 7J, OF	40	50	75
300, 7J, HC	50	60	85
302, 7J, OF	40	50	75
304, 15J, HC	75	85	125
305, 17J, HC ....★	100	125	165
306, 15J, OF	60	75	100
307, 17J, Adj, OF	85	95	135
308, 17J, Adj, HC	100	125	165
310, 17J, Adj, OF	85	95	135
310, 17J, Adj, **marked**, 14K OF case	175	200	300
312, **marked**, 21J, 3/4, Adj.5P, DMK, HC	150	175	250
314, **marked**, 21J, DR, Adj. 5P, DMK, OF ....★	125	150	200
500, 17J, **marked**, OF	85	95	135
603, 17J, OF ....★	85	95	135
700, 15J, **marked**, OF	60	75	100

🕒 Pricing in this Guide are fair market price for **COMPLETE** watches which are reflected from the "**NAWCC**" National and regional shows.

Example of Hampden Watch Co.'s THIN MODEL showing dial and movement, 12 size, 17-19 jewels, Adj3-5p.

12 SIZE (THIN MODEL)

Grade or Name — Description	Avg	Ex-Fn	Mint
Nathan Hale, 15J	$70	$80	$100
Minute Man, 17J	85	95	135
Relgis, 15J, OF ★	85	85	135
Paul Revere, 17J, OF, **14K**	225	275	400
Paul Revere, 17J	85	95	135
Paul Revere, 19J	100	125	175

Hampden 12 size (thin model) case are **not** interchangeable with other American 12 style cases.
Note: Some 12 Sizes came in cases of octagon, decagon, hexagon, triad, and cushion shapes.

6 SIZE

Grade or Name — Description	Avg	Ex-Fn	Mint
200, 7J (add $25 for HC)	$25	$50	$100
206, 11J (add $25 for HC)	25	50	100
213, 15J (add $25 for HC)	25	50	100
215, 16J, (add $25 for HC)	25	50	100
220, 17J (add $25 for HC)	25	50	100
Hampden W. Co., 15J, **multi-color Gold Filled, HC**	225	275	425
Hampden W. Co., 15J, **multi-color, 14K, HC**	400	500	750

Molly Stark, 000 size, 7 jewels, hunting or open face, originally sold for $12.00.

000 SIZE

Grade or Name — Description	Avg	Ex-Fn	Mint
Diadem, 11-15J, **14K, OF Case**	$125	$150	$300
Diadem, 11-15J, **14K, HC Case**	225	275	400
Diadem, 11-15J, **Gold Filled, HC Case**	75	150	200
Molly Stark, 7J, **Gold Filled, HC Case**	75	150	200
Molly Stark, 7J, **14K, HC Case**	225	275	400
Molly Stark, 7J, Pin Set, OF	75	100	150
Four Hundred, 11, 15, 16, & 17J, HC	100	150	200
14K Multi-color, HC	400	500	700

HAMPDEN WATCH CO.
IDENTIFICATION OF MOVEMENTS

How to Identify Your Watch Size & Model: Compare the movement of your watch with the illustrations in this section. While comparing, note the location of the balance, jewels, screws, gears, and type of back plate (Full, 3/4, Bridge) which will be clues in identifying the movement you have.

Series I, 18 size
Hunting or open face, key wind & set

Series II, 18 size
Hunting, stem wind, pendant or lever set

Series III, 18 size
Hunting, stem wind, pendant or lever set

Series IV, 18 size
Open face, stem wind, lever set

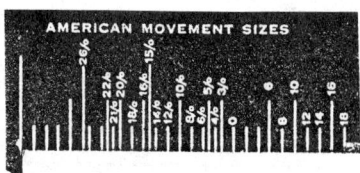

Series 1, 16 size
Open face, stem wind, pendant or lever set

Series II, 16 size
Hunting, stem wind, pendant or lever set

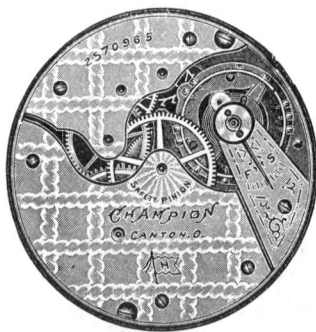

Series III, 16 size
Open face, stem wind, pendant set

Series IV, 16 size
Hunting, stem wind, pendant or lever set

Series V, 16 size
Open face, stem wind, pendant or lever set

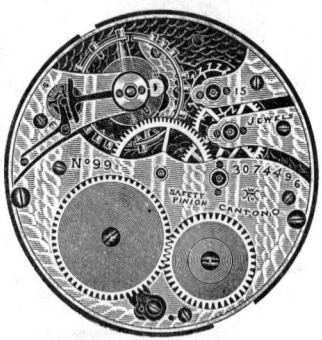

Series VI, 16 size
Hunting, stem wind, pendant set

Series VII, 16 size
Open face, stem wind, pendant set

Series III, 12 size
Open face, stem wind, pendant set

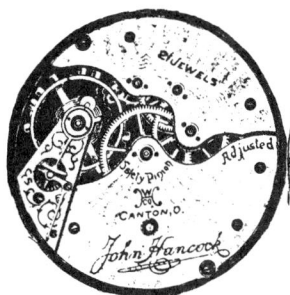

Series I, 12 size
Hunting, stem wind, lever set

Series II, 12 size
Open face, stem wind, lever set

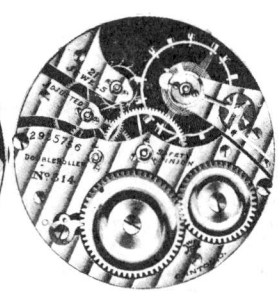

Series IV, 12 size
Open face, stem wind, pendant

Series V, 12 size
Open face, stem wind, pendant set

Series I, 6 size
Open face, stem wind

Series I, 3/0 size
Hunting, stem wind

🕐 Characteristics of watches differ for the same age of both case and movement, because these features vary it may not be accurate to date a watch by one single influence. Example: the second hand was not commonly found on watches before 1750, but common about 1800. The first second hand appeared in 1665 and another in 1690. Therefore statements are broad rather than accurate.

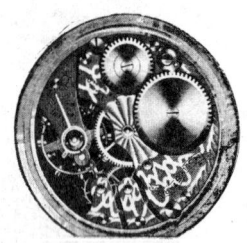

Series II, 3/0 size
Open face, stem wind, pendant

Series III, 3/0 size
Hunting, lever or pendant

Series IV, 3/0 size
Hunting, stem wind, pendant

HERMAN VON DER HEYDT

CHICAGO SELF-WINDING WATCH CO.

Chicago, Illinois
1883-1895

Herman von der Heydt patented a self-winding watch on Feb. 19, 1884. A total of 35 watches were hand-made by von der Heydt. The watches were 18S, full plate, lever escapement and fully-jeweled. The wind mechanism was a gravity type made of heavy steel and shaped like a crescent. The body motion let the heavy crescent move which was connected to a ratchet on the winding arbor, resulting in self-winding. Five movements were nickel and sold for about $90; the gilded model sold for about $75.

Grade or Name — Description		Avg	Ex-Fn	Mint
18S, 19J, FULL, NI	★★★★	$12,000	$13,000	$16,000
18S, 19J, FULL, gilded	★★★★	10,000	11,000	14,000

Herman Von Der Heydt, 18 size self winding watch, "Chicago S. W. Co." on dial. H. VON DER HEYDT, PATENTED, FEB.19, 84 on auxiliary dial.

Herman Von Der Heydt, 18 size, 19 jewels; America's only self winding pocket watch. Note crescent shaped winding weight serial number 19.

E. HOWARD & CO.
Boston (Roxbury), Massachusetts
December 11, 1858 - 1903

After the failure of the Boston Watch Company (1853-57), Edward Howard decided to personally attempt the successful production of watches using the interchangeable machine-made parts system. He and Charles Rice, his financial backer, were unable to buy out the defunct watch company in Waltham, however, they did remove (per a prior claim) the watches in progress, the tools and the machinery to Howard and Davis' Roxbury factory (first watch factory in America), in late 1857. During their first year, the machinery was retooled for the production of a revolutionary new watch of Howard's design. Also, the remaining Boston Watch Co. movements were completed (E. Howard & Co. dials, Howard & Rice on the movement). By the summer of 1858, Edward Howard had produced his first watch. On December 11, 1858 the firm of E. Howard & Co. was formed for the manufacture of high-grade watches. Howard's first model was entirely different from any watch previously made. It introduced the more accurate "quick beat" train to American watchmaking. The top plate was in two sections and had six pillars instead of the usual four pillars in a full plate. The balance was gold or steel at first, then later it was a compensation balance loaded with gold screws. Reed's patented barrel was used for the first time. The size, based on the Dennison system, was a little larger than the regular 18 size. In 1861, a 3/4 plate model was put on the market. Most movements were being stamped with "N" to designate Howard's 18 size. On February 4, 1868 Howard patented a new steel motor barrel which was to supersede the Reed's, but not before some 28,000 had been produced. Also, in 1868 Howard introduced the stemwinding movement and was probably the first company to market such a watch in the U. S. By 1869, Howard was producing their "L" or 16 size as well as their first nickel movements. In 1870, G. P. Reed's micrometer regulator was patented for use by E. Howard & Co. The Reed style "whiplash" regulator has been used in more pocket watches, worldwide, than any other type. In 1878, the manufacturing of keywind movements was discontinued. Mr. Howard retired in 1882, but the company continued to sell watch movements of the grade and style set by him until 1903 and beyond. This company was the first to adjust to all six positions. Their dials were always a hard enamel and always bore the name "E. Howard & Co., Boston." In 1902, the company transferred all rights to use the name "Edward Howard," in conjunction with the production of watches, to the Keystone Watch Case Co. Most of their models were stamped "Howard" on the dial and "E. Howard Watch Co., Boston. U.S.A." on the movement. Edward Howard's company never produced its own watch cases, the great majority of which were solid gold or silver. Keystone, however, produced complete watches, many of which were gold filled.

CHRONOLOGICAL DEVELOPMENT OF E. HOWARD & CO.:
Howard, Davis & Dennison, Roxbury, Mass., (1850)
American Horologue Company, Roxbury, Mass., (1851)
Warren Manufacturing Company, Roxbury, Mass., (1851-53)
Boston Watch Co., Roxbury, Mass., (1853-54) & Waltham, Mass., (1854-57)
Howard & Rice, Roxbury, Mass., (1857-58) with (E. Howard & Co. on dials)
E. Howard & Co., Roxbury, Mass., (1858-1903)
Keystone Watch Case Co. (Howard line), Jersey City, N. J., (1902-30)

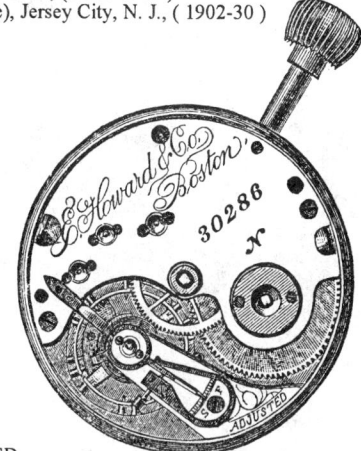

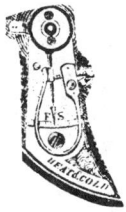

LEFT: Balance cock unmarked =UNADJUSTED
CENTER: Balance cock marked heat &cold =adjusted to TEMPERATURE
RIGHT: Balance cock on movement marked adjusted =FULLY ADJUSTED

A List of initials for **most** of the Solid Gold Watch **Case** companies used by E. Howard & Co.

A.W.C. Co.=American Watch Case Co.
B & T = Booz & Thomas
B.W.C. Co.=Brooklyn Watch Case Co.
C & M =Crosby & Mathewson
C.E.H. & Co. = C.E. Hale & Co.
C.W. Mfg. Co. = Courvoisier Wilcox Mfg. Co.
D T W & Co.= D.T. Warren & Co.
E.H. & Co. = E. Hale & Co.
F & Co. = Fellows & Co.
F & S = Fellows & Shell
J M H = J.M. Harper
J S (intertwined)= Jeannot & Shiebler

K (inside) U = Keller & Untermeyer
K E & F. Co.= Keller, Ettinger & Fink N.Y.
M B = Margot Bros.
M & B = Mathey Bros.
N.Y.G.W.C.Co =New York Gold Watch Case Co.
P & B = Peters & Boss
S & D = Serex & Desmaison
S & M B = Serex Maitre Bros.
S & R = Serex & Robert
W & S = Warren & Spadone
W P & Co = Wheeler Parsons & Co.
W W C Mfg. Co =Western Watch Case Co.

Crescent Watch Case Co.
Dueber Watch Case Co.
Keystone Watch Case Co.

Ladd Watch Case Co.
Marsh= Marsh Watch Case Co.
Muhr Watch Case Co.

Roy = Roy Watch Case Co.

NOTE: E. Howard & Co. movements will not fit standard cases properly.

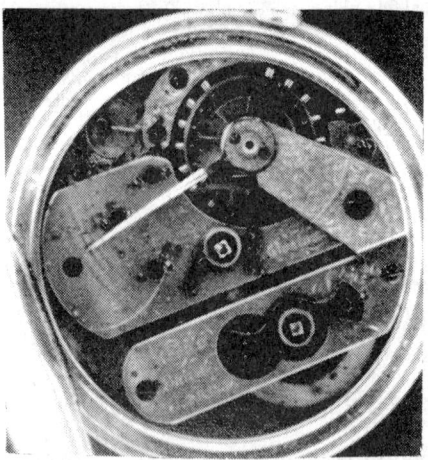

E. HOWARD & CO., Series I, helical hair-spring, detent escapement, KW KS, N (18)size, serial # 1120

E. HOWARD & CO., N (18) size, 15 jewels, chronometer escapement engraved on balance cock, Robin's escapement, serial # 3126.

E. HOWARD & CO., i (10) size, KW KS, note compensating balance above center wheel, serial # 3363.

E. HOWARD & CO., i (10) size, KW KS, **note** solid balance wheel below center wheel, serial # 3406.

E. HOWARD & CO.

APPROXIMATE DATES, SERIAL NOS., AND TOTAL PRODUCTION

Serial No.	Date	Series	Total Prod.
131-1,900—	1858-1860—	I (18S)—	1,800
1,901-3,000—	1860-1861—	II (18S)—	1,100
3,001-3,100—	1861—	K (14S)—	100
3,101-3,250—	1861—	III (18S)—	150
3,401-3,500—	1861—	i (10S)—	100
3,501-28,000—	1861-1871—	III (18S)—	4,500
30,001-50,000—	1868-1883—	IV (18S)—	20,000
50,001-71,000—	1869-1899—	V (16S)—	21,000
100,001-105,500—	1869-1899—	VI (6S)—	5,500
200,001-227,000—	1880-1899—	VII (18S)—	27,000
*228,001-231,000—	1895—	VII (18S)—	3,000
300,001-309,000—	1884-1899—	VIII (18S)—	9,000
*309,001-310,000—	1895—	VIII (18S)—	1,000
400,001-405,000—	1890-1895—	IX (18S)—	5,000
500,001-501,500—	1890-1899—	X (12S)—	1,500
*600,001-601,500—1896—1903—XI (16S)—			1,500
*700,001-701,500—1896—1903—XII (16S)—			1,500

(*) = 3/4 Split Plates with 17 Jewels. Total about 100,000

The above list is provided for determining the age & help identify the Series of your watch. Match serial number with date & Series.

E. HOWARD & CO. WATCH SIZES

Letter	Inches	Approx. Size
N	1 13/16	18
L	1 11/16	16
K	1 10/16	14
J	1 9/16	12
I	1 8/16	10
H	1 7/16	8
G	1 6/16	6
F	1 5/16	4
E	1 4/16	2
D	1 3/16	0

Below: Mershon's Patent center wheel rack regulator (April 26, 1859).

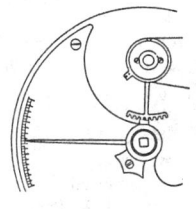

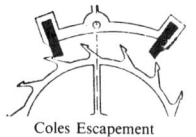

Coles Escapement

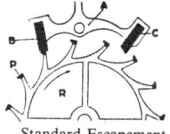

Standard Escapement

Deer
Adjusted to
Hcl6P

Horse
Adjusted to
HCI-No
positions

Hound
Unadjusted

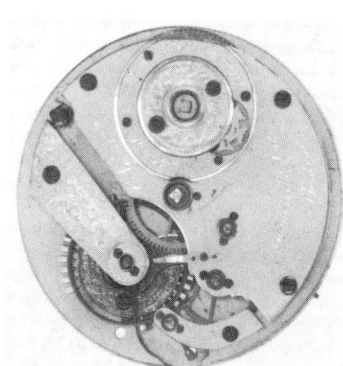
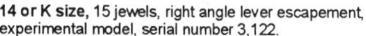

14 or K size, 15 jewels, right angle lever escapement, experimental model, serial number 3,122.

10 or I size, 15 jewels; note cut-out to view escape wheel, experimental model, serial number 3,472.

E. HOWARD & CO.

N SIZE (18) (In Original Cases)

Series or Name — Description		Avg	Ex-Fn	Mint
E. Howard & Co. on dial and movement, 15-16J, 1857 Model,				
(Howard & Rice style), KW & KS, silver case .... ★ ★ ★		$2,500	$2,800	$3,600
I, II or III, 15J, gilded, KW, helical hairspring .... ★ ★ ★ ★		10,000	15,000	25,000

The lowest known Series I serial # is **132**

Series 1, 18 size, 17 jewels, note the compensating balance on this early movement, serial number 133.

Series II, 18 size, 15 jewels, key wind & set, serial number 2,477.

Series or Name — Description	Avg	Ex-Fn	Mint
I, 15J, with serial # below 200.. ★ ★ ★	$5,000	$6,000	$10,000
I, 15J, with serial # below 300.. ★ ★ ★	2,500	3,000	6,000
I, 15J, gilded, KW, **18K,** HC, OF, upright or horizontal pallets ★ ★	2,500	3,500	6,000
I, 15J, gilded, KW, silver HC .... ★ ★	1,500	2,000	4,000
I, 15J, (movement only)... ★ ★	700	900	1,500
I, 17J, with unusual plate cut (movement only)................... ★ ★ ★	1,000	1,100	2,000
II, 15J, gilded, KW, **18K,** HC or OF.. ★ ★	2,000	2,500	4,000
II, 15J, gilded, KW, silver HC .... ★ ★	1,500	2,000	3,800
II, 15J, (movement only) .... ★ ★	700	900	1,500
II, 17J, with screw down jewel settings (movement only)...............	1,000	1,200	2,000
III, 15J, gilded, KW, **18K,** HC	1,200	1,500	2,200
III, 15J, gilded, KW, silver case...	700	800	1,400
III, 15J, **nickel,** KW, silver case...	1,000	1,200	2,000
III, 15J, gilded, KW, **18K,** Mershon's Patent.................................	1,500	1,800	2,500
III, 15J, gilded, KW, **18K,** Coles Escapement .... ★ ★	1,600	1,900	2,600
III, 15J, NI, Private label	800	1,000	1,400
III, 15J , (movement only)..	200	250	400
III, 15J, with RAY & nickel DMK (movement only)	500	700	1,000
IV, 15J, gilded, KW, **18K,** HC..	1,000	1,200	1,800
IV, 15J, **nickel,** KW, **18K,** HC..	1,200	1,400	2,000
IV, 15J, gilded or nickel, SW, **18K,** HC	900	1,100	1,600

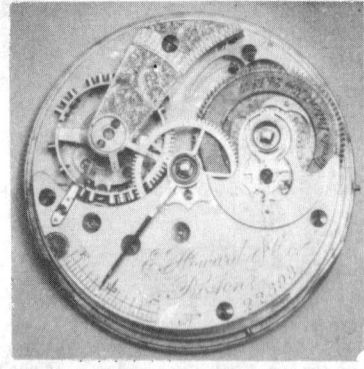

Series III, 18 size, 15 jewels, note **Mershon's Patent** center wheel rack regulator (April 26, 1859), serial # 22,693.

Series III, 18 size, 15 jewels, note high balance wheel over center wheel, serial number 7,000.

Series IV, 18 size, 15 jewels, key wind and set, serial number 37,893.

Series VII, 18 size, 15 jewels, nickel movement, note running deer on movement, "adjusted" on bridge, serial number 219,304.

Series or Name — Description		Avg	Ex-Fn	Mint
IV, personalized with jobber's name, silver	★ ★	$400	$600	$900
IV, 15J (movement only)		100	125	200
VII, 15J, gilded or nickel, SW, 14K, HC		750	1,000	1,500
VII, 17J, nickel, split plate, SW, 14K, HC	★ ★ ★	1,200	1,400	2,000
VII, 17J, nickel, split plate, SW, silver, HC	★ ★ ★	600	800	1,400
VII, 19J, nickel, SW, 14K, HC	★ ★ ★	2,500	3,000	4,000
VII, 15J (movement only)		100	125	250
VIII, 15J, gilded or nickel, SW, 14K, OF		675	800	1,400
VIII, 17J, nickel, split plate, SW, 14K, OF	★ ★ ★	1,200	1,400	2,000
VIII, 17J, nickel, split plate, SW, silver, OF	★ ★ ★	600	800	1,400
VIII, 17J, nickel, with **RR** on the side of balance cock, silver, OF		1,000	1,200	1,800
VIII, 15J (movement only)		100	150	300

BALL - HOWARDS SEE **BALL W. Co.**.

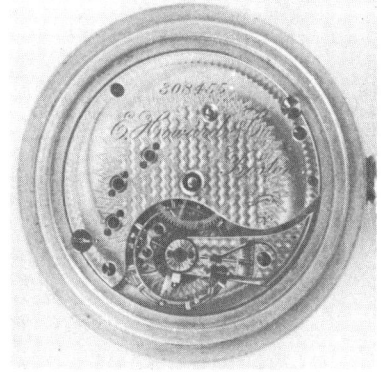

Series VII, 18 size, 17J, nickel, split plate, adjusted, Stem Wind, serial number 228,055.

Series VIII, 18 size, 15 jewels, serial number 308,455.

🕐 Pricing in this Guide are fair market price for **COMPLETE** watches which are reflected from the "<u>NAWCC</u>" National and regional shows.

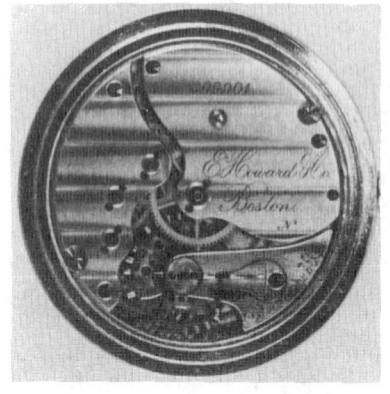

Series VIII, 18 size, 17 jewels, split plate model, gold jewel settings, serial number 309,904.

Series IX, 18 size, 15 jewels, hunting. This series is gilded only and hound grade exclusively, S # 402,873.

Series or Name — Description	Avg	Ex-Fn	Mint
IX, 15J, gilded, SW, 14K, HC	$900	$1,100	$1,800
IX, 15J, gilded, SW, silver, HC	450	550	900
IX, 15J (movement only)	100	125	250

L SIZE (16)

(In Original Cases)

Series or Name — Description	Avg	Ex-Fn	Mint
V, 15J, gilded, KW, 18K, HC	$900	$1,100	$1,600
V, 15J, gilded, KW, 18K, Coles Escapement ★★	1,000	1,300	1,800
V, 15J, gilded or nickel, SW, 14K, HC	800	1,000	1,400
V, 15J, gilded, SW, 14K, Coles Escapement ★★	1,000	1,200	1,600
Prescott, 15J., gilded, SW, Series V, original case, NOTE: case.....	2,500	3,000	4,500
may show evidence of filled key holes on dust cover . ★★★	1,000	1,300	2,800
Prescott, 15J., gilded, SW, (Series V movement only).......... ★★★	1,000	1,300	2,800

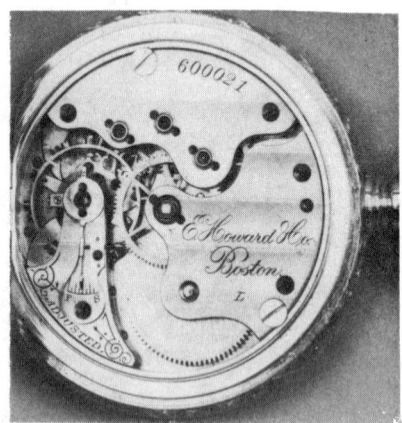

Series V, 16 or L size, Prescott Model, 15 jewels, hunting, serial number 50,434. NOTE: Original case may show evidence of filled key holes on dust cover. If the watch was returned to factory and converted from KW Coles movement to stem wind & lever set.

Series XI, 16 size, 17 jewels, split plate model, nickel movement, gold jewel settings, serial number 600,021.

🕐 Watches listed in this book are priced at the collectable retail level, as **complete** watches having an original 14k gold-filled case and *Key Wind* with silver, an original white enamel single sunk dial, and with the entire original movement in good working order with no repairs needed.

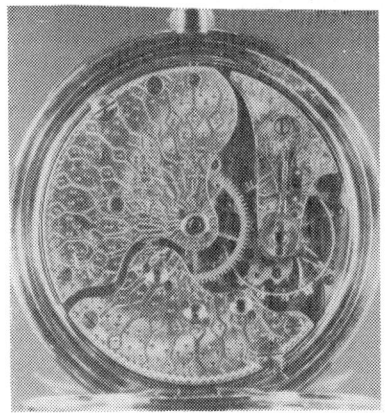

Series XII, L-16 size, 21 jewels, split plate model, nickel movement, gold lettering, gold jewel settings, serial number 700,899.

Series K, 14 or K size, 15 jewels, key wind & set, serial number 3,004.

Series or Name — Description		Avg	Ex-Fn	Mint
V, 15J (movement only)		$90	$100	$200
XI, 17J, nickel, split plate, SW, 14K, HC	★★★	1,100	1,300	1,800
XI, 17J, nickel, split plate, SW, silver, HC	★★★	600	800	1,400
XI, 17J (movement only)		300	400	700
XII, 17J, nickel, split plate, SW, 14K, OF	★★★	1,000	1,200	1,800
XII, 17J, nickel, split plate, SW, silver, OF	★★★	500	600	1,000
XII, 17J (movement only)		100	150	450
XII, 21J, nickel, split plate, SW, 14K OF	★★★★	2,500	3,000	6,000

K SIZE (14)
(In Original Cases)

Series or Name — Description		Avg	Ex-Fn	Mint
K, 15J, gilded, KW, 18K, HC	★★★★	$5,000	$6,000	$9,000

J SIZE (12)
(In Original Cases)

Series or Name – Description		Avg	Ex-Fn	Mint
X, 15J, nickel, hound, SW, 14K, OF	★	$700	$900	$1,300
X, 15J, nickel, horse, SW, 14K, OF	★	800	1,000	1,400
X, 15J, nickel, deer, SW, 14K, OF	★	900	1,100	1,500
X, 15J, hound (movement only)	★	150	200	400

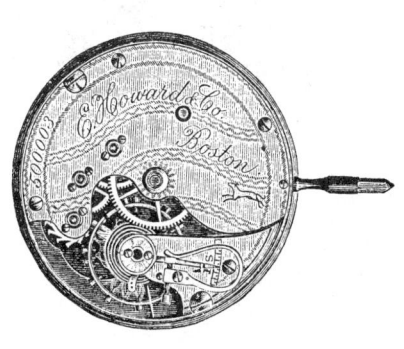

X, 15J, nickel, hound, SW, serial # 500,003

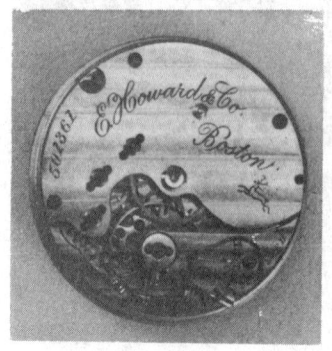

Series X, 12 or J size, 15 jewels, note deer on movement, serial number 501,361.

I size (10 size), 15 jewels, gilded, key wind, serial number 3,464.

I SIZE (10)
(In Original Cases)

Series or Name — Description		Avg	Ex-Fn	Mint
I, 15J, gilded, KW, 18K HC .... ★★★★		$4,000	$5,000	$8,000

G SIZE (6)
(In Original Cases)

Series or Name — Description		Avg	Ex-Fn	Mint
VI, 15J, gilded, **KW**, 18K, HC .... ★★★		$2,000	$2,500	$4,000
VI, 15J, gilded or nickel, SW, 18K, HC		1,000	1,200	1,500
VI, 15J, gilded or nickel, SW, 14K, HC		700	900	1,300
VI, 15J (movement only).................................		175	200	400

Series VI, 6 or G size, 15 jewels, stem wind.

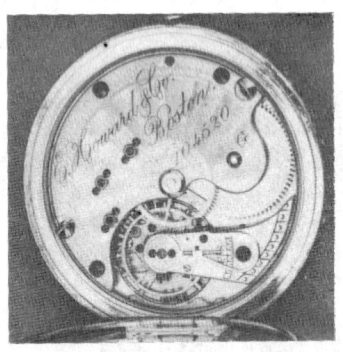

Series VI, 6 or G size, 15 jewels, stem wind, serial number 104,520.

🕐 Generic, nameless or unmarked grades for watch movements are listed under the Company name or initials of the Company, etc. by size, jewel count and description.

🕐 Pricing in this Guide are fair market price for **COMPLETE** watches which are reflected from the "<u>NAWCC</u>" National and regional shows.

E. HOWARD WATCH CO. (KEYSTONE)
Waltham, Massachusetts
1902 - 1930

The watches are <u>marked</u> "**E. Howard Watch Co. Boston, U. S. A.**" The Howard name was purchased by the Keystone Watch Case Co. in 1902. There were no patent rights transferred, just the Howard name. The "Edward Howard" chronometer was the highest grade, 16 size, and was introduced in 1912 for $350. All watches cased & timed at factory as a complete watch only.

Keystone Howard also gained control of U. S. Watch Co. of Waltham and New York Standard Watch Company. 16 size 21 jewel hunting case watches not made, 21 jewel were in open- face only.

ESTIMATED SERIAL NUMBERS
AND PRODUCTION DATES

The arrows denote number of jewels and adjustments in each grade.

Date	Serial No.
1902—	850,000
1903—	900,000
1909—	980,000
1912—1,100,000
1915—1,285,000
1917—1,340,000
1921—1,400,000
1930—1,500,000

Cross =23 jewel, 5 positions

Star =21 jewel, Adj.5P, & 19J with V under star

Triangle =19 jewel, 5 positions

Circle =17 jewel, 3 & 5 positions

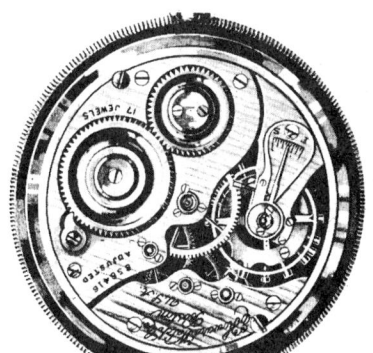

Model 1905, Series 7, 16 size, 17J., open face. This 3/4 model can be identified by the slant parallel damaskeening. This represents the 3/4 **top** grade, raised gold jewel settings, double roller, Adj.5P and sold for $115.00 in 1910.

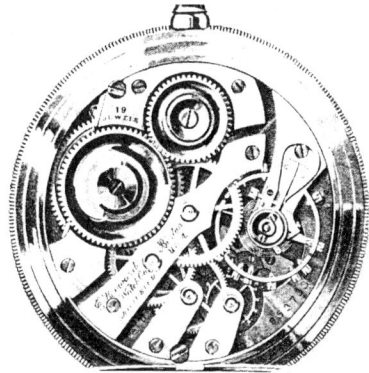

1907 Bridge Model, Series 5, 19 jewels, **open face**, Serial # 953,733. **NOTE:** The escape wheel bridge & the fourth wheel bridge is <u>not</u> notched out.

Model 1905, Series 9, 16 size, 17 jewels, open face. This 3/4 model can be identified by the checkerboard damaskeening. This represents the 3/4 **mid** grade, GJS, double roller, Adj.3 & 5P and sold for $105.00 in 1910.

Model 1905, Series 3, 16 size, 17 jewels open face. This 3/4 model can be identified by the circular damaskeening. This represents the 3/4 **lowest** grade of the three with single roller, Adj.3P and sold for $100.00 in 1910.

E. Howard Watch Co., Model 1907, marked Series 0, 16 size, 23 jewels, in original E. Howard Watch Co. swing-out movement Keystone Extra gold filled Open Face case.

E. HOWARD WATCH CO. Model 1907, Series 0 (not marked), 16S, 23J., Hunting Case,

🕐 Model 1907= **bridge** OF & HC and Series or No., 0, 1, 2, 5 & 10 , see above illustrations, 1907 = Series or No. 0=23J, Series or No.1&10=21J, Series2=17J, Series5 or No.5 =19J. Model 1905 = **3/4 plate** OF & HC

E. HOWARD WATCH CO. (KEYSTONE)
16 SIZE

Series or Name — Description	Avg	Ex-Fn	Mint
No. 0, & 1907, 23J, BRG, Adj.5P, DR, OF	$425	$500	$750
1907 model & No.0, 23J, BRG, Adj.5P, DR, HC	475	550	785
Unmarked, 23J, BRG, Adj.5P, DR, OF	400	450	600
Series 0, 23J, BRG, Adj.5P, DR, **Ruby banking pins**	425	500	750
Series 0, 23J, BRG, Adj.5P, DR, **jeweled barrel**	425	500	750
Series 0, 23J, BRG, Adj.5P, DR, OF, **14K**	750	850	1,200
Series 0, 23J, BRG, Adj.5P, DR, HC, **14K**	900	1,000	1,600
No. 1, 21J, BRG, Adj.5P, DR ....★	300	400	600
Series 1, 21J, BRG, Adj.5P, DR	300	400	600
Series 2, 17J, BRG, Adj.5P, DR, HC	150	200	400
Series 2, 17J, BRG, Adj.5P, DR, OF	85	110	175

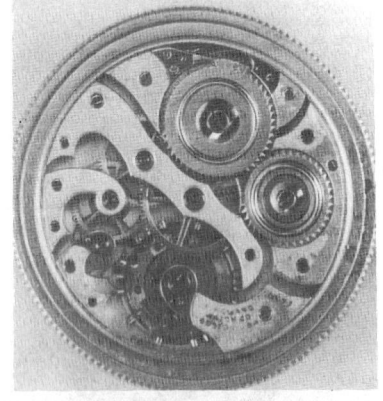

Series II, marked *Railroad Chronometer*, 16 size, 21 jewels, Adj5p, serial number 1,217,534.

Edward Howard Model, 16 size, 23 blue sapphire jewels, frosted gold bridge, wolfteeth wind, serial # 77.

🕐 Pricing in this Guide are fair market price for **COMPLETE** watches which are reflected from the "**NAWCC**" National and regional shows.

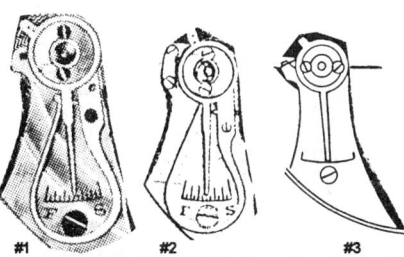

Above: Note illustrations #1 & #2 = Howard regulators with the 2 jewel screws vertical or upright and #1 has a **square** hairspring stud also note #2 has a **sliding** stud & a bean shaped cover. Howard-**Waltham** regulators (#3) the 2 jewel screws are horizontal and **triangular** hairspring stud.

E. Howard Watch Co., 16 size, 23 jewels, by Waltham, raised gold jewel settings, gold train, Adj5p, open face, bridge style movement. NOTE: Bow and S# on bridge 1,005,363 with the S# on top plate (not seen) 605,363.

E. Howard Watch Co., 16 size 19 jewels, by Waltham, gold jewel settings, Adj3p, hunting case, 3/4 plate movement.

Series or Name — Description	Avg	Ex-Fn	Mint
Series 3, 17J, 3/4, Adj.3P, circular DMK	$85	$110	$150
Series 3, 17J, Adj.3P, circular DMK, **14K** OF,	400	500	600
No. 5, 19J, BRG, GJS, HC ....★	250	300	475
Series 5, 19J, BRG, Adj.5P, DR, **14K**	450	550	650
Series 5, 19J, BRG, Adj.5P, DR, 1907 Model	175	200	300
Series 7, 17J, 3/4, Adj.5P, DR, RGJS, slant parallel DMK, OF	100	145	200
Series 7, 17J, 3/4, Adj.5P, DR, RGJS, slant parallel DMK, HC	125	150	250
Series 9, 17J, 3/4, Adj.3P, LS, checkerboard DMK, OF	100	125	200
Series 9, 17J, 3/4, Adj.5P, DR, checkerboard DMK, RR grade,14K	350	400	600
Series 10, 21J, BRG, Adj.5P, DR, Marked Non–Magnetic ....★	500	600	800
Series 10, 21J, BRG, Adj.5P, DR	275	325	450
No. 10, 21J, BRG, Adj.5P, DR	275	325	450
Series 11, 21J, **R.R. Chrono.**, Adj.5P, DR	300	400	600
Edward Howard, 23 blue sapphire pressed J, Free Sprung, Adj.5P, DR, Serial numbers below 300, without box .....★★	5,000	6,000	7,000
Edward Howard, 23 blue sapphire pressed J, Free Sprung, Adj.5P, DR, Serial numbers below 300, with original box and papers, **18K** Edward Howard case ....★★★	7,000	9,000	12,000
Climax,7J., (made for export), gilded, OF	40	50	125
23J, E. Howard W. Co. (mfg. by Waltham), **14K**, Brg model .★★	1,000	1,100	1,500
23J, E. Howard W. Co. (mfg. by Waltham), OF, gold filled	400	500	800
23J, E. Howard W. Co. (mfg. by Waltham), HC, gold filled	600	700	950
21J, E. Howard W. Co. (mfg. by Waltham), Bridge model, HC	300	350	600
21J, E. Howard W. Co. (mfg. by Waltham), 3/4, OF	200	250	400
19J, E. Howard W. Co. (mfg. by Waltham), Bridge model, HC	175	200	400
19J, E. Howard W. Co. (mfg. by Waltham), 3/4, OF	175	200	400
17J, E. Howard W. Co. (mfg. by Waltham), Bridge model, HC	175	200	400
17J, E. Howard W. Co. (mfg. by Waltham), 3/4, OF	175	200	350

12 SIZE - 1908 Model

Series or Name — Description	Avg	Ex-Fn	Mint
Series 6, 19J, BRG, DR, Adj.5P, 1908 Model, **14K**, HC	$250	$300	$500
Series 6, 19J, BRG, DR, Adj.5P, **14K**, OF	170	200	400
Series 6, 19J, BRG, DR, Adj.5P, OF	70	90	150
Series 7, 17J, BRG, DR, Adj.3P, **14K**, OF	170	200	375
Series 7, 17J, BRG, DR, Adj.3P, OF	65	85	125
Series 8, 21J, BRG, DR, Adj.5P, OF	100	150	250
Series 8, 23J, BRG, DR, Adj.5P, **14K**, OF	225	300	525
Series 8, 23J, BRG, DR, Adj.5P, OF	150	200	400
Series 8, 23J, BRG, DR, Adj.5P, **14K**, HC	400	450	700
23J, Waltham Model, BRG, HC	200	250	375
23J, Waltham Model, BRG, OF	150	200	325
21J, Waltham Model, BRG, HC	125	200	325
21J, Waltham Model, BRG, OF	125	200	275
17J, Waltham Model, BRG, HC	100	125	200
17J, Waltham Model, BRG, OF	100	125	175
17J, Waltham Model, 3/4, HC	100	150	175
17J, Waltham Model, 3/4, OF	70	90	150

NOTE: First Serial # for 12 size with 17J.=977,001; 19J.=977,451; 21J.=1,055,851.

Series 8, 12 size, 21 jewels, open face, stop works, extra thin. 1908 MODEL with 21 jewels engraved under balance, five positions and temperature.

E. Howard Watch Co., 10 size, 17J, Adj3p, serial # 61,230. (Serial # started at about 1,001 on this model.)

SERIES 8 GOING BARREL =21J.   SERIES 6 GOING BARREL =19J.   SERIES 7 GOING BARREL =17J.

10 SIZE

NOTE: 10 Size Serial numbers start at about **1,001** on this model.

Series or Name — Description	Avg	Ex-Fn	Mint
Thin Model, 21J, ADJ, 14K case, OF	$150	$225	$375
Thin Model, 19J, ADJ, 14K case, OF	150	200	300
Thin Model, 17J, ADJ, 14K case, OF	150	200	300

STYLE R.R. Chronometer
gold filled: $110 - $135 - $250

STYLE R.R. Antique Bow
note: Jointed- Inside Cap
gold filled: $100 - $125 - $200

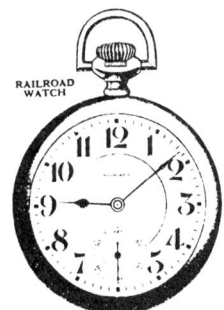

STYLE R.R. Plain swing out
gold filled: $100 - $125 - $200

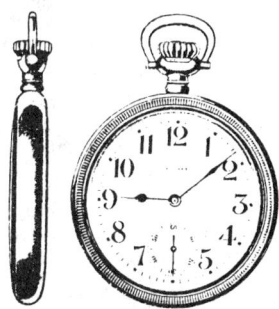

STYLE R.R. Engine Turned swing out
gold filled: $100 - $125 - $200

STYLE R.R. SWING OUT
gold filled: $100 - $125 - $200
14K GOLD: $300 - $325 - $400

Rail Road Chronometer = Gold Filled
Rail Road Antique Bow= solid 18K gold, 14K gold heavy, 14K gold, & 25 year **Gold Filled**
SWING OUT = Gold Filled and the swing out **Plain** also came 14K solid gold

🕐 NOTE: Factory Advertised as a **complete** watch and was fitted with a certain matched, timed and rated movement and sold in the factory designed case style as a **complete** watch. The factory advertised as *"Howard movements and cases are not sold separately"*. All the factory advertised **complete** watches came with a enamel dial **SHOWN or CHOICE** of other **Railroad** dials.

ILLINOIS WATCH CO.
Springfield, Illinois
1869 - 1927

The Illinois Watch Company was organized mainly through the efforts of J. C. Adams. The first directors were J. T. Stuart, W. B. Miller, John Williams, John W. Bunn, George Black and George Passfield. In 1879 the company changed all its watches to a quick train movement by changing the number of teeth in the fourth wheel. The first mainspring made by the company was used in 1882. The next year soft enamel dials were used.

The Illinois Watch Co. used more names on its movements than any other watch manufacturer. To identify all of them requires extensive knowledge by the collector plus a good working knowledge of watch mechanics. Engraved on some early movements, for example, are "S. W. Co." or "I. W. Co., Springfield, Ill." To the novice these abbreviations might be hard to understand, thus making Illinois watches difficult to identify. But one saving clue is that the location "Springfield, Illinois" appears on most of these watches. It is important to learn how to identify these type watches because some of them are extremely collectible. Examples of some of the more valuable of these are: the Benjamin Franklin (size 18 or 16, 25 or 26 jewels), Paillard's Non-Magnetic, Pennsylvania Special, C & O, and B & O railroad models.

The earliest movements made by the Illinois Watch Co. are listed below. They made the first watch in early 1872, but the company really didn't get off the ground until 1875. Going by the serial number, the first watch made was the Stuart. Next was the Mason, followed by the Bunn, the Miller, and finally the Currier. The first stem-wind was made in 1875.

STUART, FIRST Run was serial numbers .... 1 to 100.
MASON, FIRST Run was serial numbers .... 101 to 200.
BUNN, FIRST Run was serial numbers .... 201 to 300.
MILLER, FIRST Run was serial numbers .... 301 to 400.
CURRIER, FIRST Run was serial numbers............... 401 to 500.

The Illinois Watch Company was sold to Hamilton Watch Co. in 1927. The Illinois factory continued to produce Illinois watches under the new management until 1932. After 1933 Hamilton produced watches bearing the Illinois name in their own factory until 1939.

CHRONOLOGY OF THE DEVELOPMENT OF ILLINOIS WATCH CO.:
Illinois Springfield Watch Co...................................... 1869-1879
Springfield Illinois Watch Co...................................... 1879-1885
Illinois Watch Co. 1885-1927
Illinois Watch Co. sold to Hamilton Watch Co. 1927

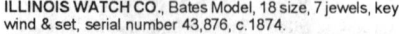

ILLINOIS WATCH CO., Bates Model, 18 size, 7 jewels, key wind & set, serial number 43,876, c.1874.

BUNN, 18 size, 16 jewels, hunting case, NOTE: Chalmer patented regulator, serial number 1,185,809.

🕐 NOTE: Numerous model 2 & 3 movements have key-wind style barrel arbors and stem wind *capabilities* they are referred to as **transition** Models. When model 2 & 3 were introduced the factory must have had a large supply of key-wind style barrel arbors so being frugal they were used.

ILLINOIS ESTIMATED SERIAL NUMBERS AND PRODUCTION DATES

DATE – SERIAL NO.	DATE – SERIAL NO.	DATE – SERIAL NO.
1872 – 5,000	1893 – 1,120,000	1914 – 2,600,000
1873 – 20,000	1894 – 1,160,000	1915 – 2,700,000
1874 – 50,000	1895 – 1,220,000	1916 – 2,800,000
1875 – 75,000	1896 – 1,250,000	1917 – 3,000,000
1876 – 100,000	1897 – 1,290,000	1918 – 3,200,000
1877 – 145,000	1898 – 1,330,000	1919 – 3,400,000
1878 – 210,000	1899 – 1,370,000	1920 – 3,600,000
1879 – 250,000	1900 – 1,410,000	1921 – 3,750,000
1880 – 300,000	1901 – 1,450,000	1922 – 3,900,000
1881 – 350,000	1902 – 1,500,000	1923 – 4,000,000
1882 – 400,000	1903 – 1,650,000	1924 – 4,500,000
1883 – 450,000	1904 – 1,700,000	1925 – 4,700,000
1884 – 500,000	1905 – 1,800,000	1926 – 4,800,000
1885 – 550,000	1906 – 1,840,000	1927 – 5,000,000
1886 – 600,000	1907 – 1,900,000	(Sold to Hamilton)
1887 – 700,000	1908 – 2,100,000	1928 – 5,100,000
1888 – 800,000	1909 – 2,150,000	1929 – 5,200,000
1889 – 900,000	1910 – 2,200,000	1931 – 5,400,000
1890 – 1,000,000	1911 – 2,300,000	1938 – 5,500,000
1891 – 1,040,000	1912 – 2,400,000	1948 – 5,600,000
1892 – 1,080,000	1913 – 2,500,000	

The above list is provided for determining the **APPROXIMATE** age of your watch. Match serial number with date. Watches were not necessarily sold in the exact order of manufactured date.

NOTE: It required several months for raw material to emerge as a finished movement. All the while the factory is producing all sizes, models and grades. The numbering system was basically "consecutive", due to demand a batch of movements could be side tracked, thus allowing a different size and model to move ahead to meet this demand. Therefore, the dates some movements were sold and delivered to the trade, may not be "consecutive".

(See Illinois Identification of Movements section located at the end of the Illinois price section to identify the movement, size and model number of your watch.)

ILLINOIS
18 SIZE (ALL FULL PLATE)

Grade or Name — Description	Avg	Ex-Fn	Mint
Alleghany, 11J, KW, gilded, OF	$60	$80	$175
Alleghany, 11J, M#1, NI, KW	60	90	200
Alleghany, 11J, M#2, NI, Transition	50	70	200
America, 7J, M#3, Silveroid	50	70	125
America, 7J, M#1-2, KW	80	125	225
America Special, 7J, M#1-2, KW	175	200	300
Army & Navy, 19J, GJS, Adj.5P, OF	200	225	350
Army & Navy, 19J, GJS, Adj.5P, HC	275	300	450
Army & Navy, 21J, GJS, Adj.5P, OF	250	300	400
Army & Navy, 21J, GJS, Adj.5P, HC	275	325	500
Baltimore & Ohio R.R. Special, 17J, GJS, ADJ ★★★	900	1,000	1,600
Baltimore & Ohio R.R. Special, 21J, GJS, NI, ADJ ★★★	1,200	1,400	2,000
Baltimore & Ohio R.R. Standard, 24J, GJS, ADJ ★★★	1,800	2,000	2,800
Bates, 7J, M#1-2, KW	80	100	200

🕐 Watches listed in this book are priced at the **collectable fair market value** at the **retail** level, as **complete** watches having an original 14k gold filled case, *KEY WIND* with silver, an original white enamel single sunk dial, and with the entire original movement in good working order with no repairs needed, unless otherwise noted.

🕐 GENERIC, NAMELESS OR **UNMARKED GRADES** FOR WATCH MOVEMENTS ARE LISTED UNDER THE COMPANY NAME OR INITIALS OF THE COMPANY, ETC. BY SIZE, JEWEL COUNT AND DESCRIPTION.

🕐 Some watch manufacturers personalize watches for jobbers or jewelry firms, with exclusive private signed or marked movements. The valuable collectable watches are listed under the signed or marked movement. Other exclusive private signed or marked movements will have equivalent value are only slightly higher value and should be compared to Generic or Nameless movements. Railroad signed or marked (dials & movements) are usually more collectable & higher in value.

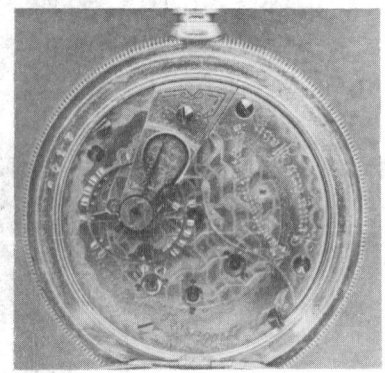

Illinois Watch Co., 18 size, railroad watch with a Ferguson dial with the numbers 1 through 12 in red.

Army and Navy, 18 size, 19 jewels, engraved on movement "Washington Watch Co.," serial number 1,606,612.

Grade or Name — Description	Avg	Ex-Fn	Mint
Benjamin Franklin U.S.A., 17J, ADJ, NI .... ★	$400	$500	$ 750
Benjamin Franklin U.S.A., 21J, GJS, **Adj.6P**, NI .... ★	900	1,000	1,450
Benjamin Franklin U.S.A., 21J, GJS, Adj.5P, NI .... ★	800	900	1,400
Benjamin Franklin U.S.A., 24J, GJS, Adj.6P, NI...................... ★	2,200	2,400	3,500
Benjamin Franklin U.S.A., 25J, GJS, Adj.6P, NI .... ★ ★ ★ ★	4,000	5,000	7,500
Benjamin Franklin U.S.A., 26J, GJS, Adj.6P, NI, ... ★ ★ ★ ★	5,000	6,000	8,000
Bunn, 15J, M#1, KW, KS, **1st. run S# 201 to 300**, OF ...... ★ ★ ★	2,000	2,400	3,400
Bunn, 15J, M#1, KW, KS, OF .... ★	450	550	800
Bunn, 15J, M#1, KW, KS, **"ADJUSTED"**, ...	400	500	850
Bunn, 15J, KW/SW transition	275	325	675
Bunn, 15J, M#1, KW, Coin	375	425	800
Bunn, 15J, KW, M#1, HC	400	450	800
Bunn, 15J, SW, M#2, HC	400	450	800
Bunn, 16J, KW, (not marked 16J.), OF	400	450	800
Bunn, 16J, KW, (not marked 16J.), HC	400	450	800
Bunn, 16J, SW, (not marked 16J.), HC................................	300	350	650
Bunn, 16J, SW, ADJ, (not marked 16J.), HC	300	350	650
Bunn, 17J, SW, NI, Coin	150	175	300
Bunn, 17J, SW, M#3, 5th pinion, gilded, OF	300	350	500
Bunn, 17J, M#4, SW, NI, OF...	150	175	300
Bunn, 17J, SW, M#5, NI, HC..	175	225	350
Bunn, 17J, SW, M#5, "Ruby Jewels", NI, Adj.5p, HC .... ★	500	600	900
Bunn, 17J, SW, M#6, SW, NI, OF	150	175	300
Bunn, 18J, SW, NI, ADJ., (not marked 18J.), OF .... ★ ★	500	600	850
Bunn, 19J, SW, NI, DR, LS, GJS, Adj.5P, **J. barrel** , OF.............	175	200	400
Bunn, 19J, SW, Adj.6P, DR, **J. barrel**, OF.................................	200	250	450
Bunn, 19J, SW, GJS, DR, Adj.5P, **J. barrel**, HC .... ★	300	400	600

IMPORTANT NOTE: Railroad Standards, Railroad Approved & Railroad Grade **terminology**, as defined and used in this ***BOOK***.
1. **RAILROAD STANDARDS** = A commission or board appointed by the railroad companies outlined a set of **guidelines** to be accepted or approved by each railroad line.
2. **RAILROAD APPROVED** = A **LIST** of watches each railroad line would approve if purchased by their employee.'s. (this list changed through the years).
3. **RAILROAD GRADE** = A watch made by manufactures to meet or exceed the guidelines set by the railroad **standards**. Grades such as 992, Vanguard and B.W. Raymond, etc.
☉ Some GRADES **exceeded** the R.R. standards such as 23 jewels, diamond end stone, gold train, raised gold jewel settings, double sunk dial and the list goes on. Examples: such as Veritas, Sangamo, 950 & Riverside Maximus and many others.

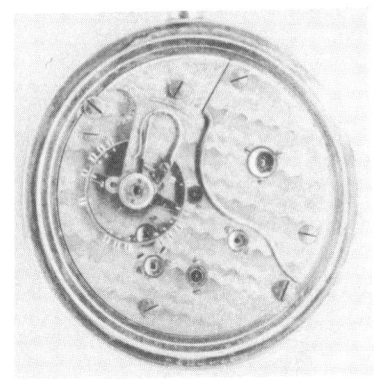

Bunn Special, 18 size, 24 jewels, adjusted, serial number 1,413,435

Bunn Special, 18 size, 26 Ruby jewels, "J. Home & Co." on dial, adjusted to six positions, gold jewel settings, serial number 2,019,415.

Grade or Name — Description	Avg	Ex-Fn	Mint
Bunn Special, 21J, SW, **Coin**	$200	$250	$350
Bunn Special, 21J, GJS, ADJ, HC	325	375	600
Bunn Special, 21J, GJS, ADJ, DR, OF	200	250	400
Bunn Special, 21J, GJS, DR, Adj.5P, OF	200	250	400
Bunn Special, 21J, GJS, DR, Adj.6P, OF	200	250	425
Bunn Special, 21J, GJS, Adj.5P, **HC, 14K**	600	700	1,000
Bunn Special, 21J, GJS, ADJ, 2-Tone	275	300	450
Bunn Special, 21J, GJS, Adj.5P, DR	250	275	400
Bunn Special, 21J," **EXTRA**", GJS ★★	800	900	1,500
Bunn Special, 23J, GJS, ADJ, DR, OF	550	600	800
Bunn Special, 23J, GJS, Adj.6P, DR, OF	550	600	800
Bunn Special, 23J, GJS, Adj.6P, DR, 2-Tone, OF ★★	600	700	900
Bunn Special, 23J, GJS, ADJ, DR, HC ★★★	1,800	2,200	3,000
Bunn Special, 24J, GJS, Adj.5P, DR, HC	650	750	1,100
Bunn Special, 24J, GJS, Adj.5P, DR, **14K, HC**	1,000	1,200	1,500
Bunn Special, 24J, GJS, Adj.5P, DR, OF	500	650	875
Bunn Special, 24J, GJS, Adj.6P, DR, OF	550	675	900
Bunn Special, 24J, GJS, Adj.6P, DR, HC	650	750	1,200
Bunn Special, 25J, GJS, Adj.6P, DR ★★★	5,000	6,000	8,000
Bunn Special, 26J, GJS, Adj.6P, DR ★★★	4,000	5,000	6,500
Central Truck Railroad, 15J, KW, KS ★★	600	700	1,300
Chesapeake & Ohio, 17J, ADJ, OF ★★	900	1,100	1,500
Chesapeake & Ohio Special, 21J, GJS, 2-Tone ★★	1,000	1,200	1,600
Chesapeake & Ohio Special, 24J, NI, ADJ, GJS ★★	1,800	2,200	2,800
Chronometer, 11-15J, KW, OF ★	250	300	500
Chronometer, 15J, M#2, HC ★	275	350	600
Columbia, 11J, M#3, 5th Pinion	60	100	200
Columbia, 11J, M#1 & 2, KW	60	100	200
Columbia, 11J, M#1 & 2, Silveroid	60	100	175
Columbia Special, 11J, M#1-2-3, KW	60	100	175
Columbia Special, 11J, M#1-2-3, KW/SW, transition	90	125	200
Comet, 11J, M#3, OF, LS, SW	100	125	200
Commodore Perry, 15-16J, HC	150	200	300
Criterion, 11-15J, HC	100	125	200

🕐 Some watch manufacturers personalize watches for jobbers or jewelry firms, with exclusive private signed or marked movements. The valuable collectable watches are listed under the signed or marked movement. Other exclusive private signed or marked movements will have equivalent value are only slightly higher value and should be compared to Generic or Nameless movements. Railroad signed or marked (dials & movements) are usually more collectable & higher in value.

Chesapeake & Ohio Special, 21 Ruby Jewels, Adjusted Temperature 6 Positions Isochronsim, OF, S# 1785680.

Diurnal, 18 size, 7 jewels, key wind & set, only one run, total production 2,000, serial number 86,757.

Grade or Name — Description	Avg	Ex-Fn	Mint
Currier, 11-12J, KW, OF	$70	$80	$200
Currier, 11-12J, KW, HC	80	90	225
Currier, 11-12J, **1st run S# 401 to 500** ★★★	400	500	800
Currier, 11-12J, KW/SW, transition, OF	70	80	150
Currier, 13–15J, M#3, OF	70	80	150
Currier, 13–15J, M#3, HC	70	80	200
Dauntless, 11J	70	80	150
Dean, 15J, M#1, KW, HC ★	175	225	475
Diurnal, 7J, KW, KS, HC, Coin ★	225	275	350
Dominion Railway, with train on dial ★★★	1,200	1,400	2,400
Eastlake, 11J, SW, KW, Transition	150	200	300
Emperor, 21J, M#6, LS, SW, ADJ	225	250	400
Enterprise, M#2, ADJ	125	150	200
Eureka, 11J	100	150	200
Favorite, 16J, LS, OF	100	150	200
Forest City, 7–11J, SW, LS, HC	100	175	200
Forest City, 17J, KW/SW, gilted,	100	175	225
General Grant or General Lee, 11J, M#1, KW	300	350	500
Hoyt, 7-9-11J, M#1-2, KW	70	85	165

🕐 **Generic, nameless,** Personalized Jobber Watches or unmarked grades for watch movements are listed under the Company name or initials of the Company, etc. by size, jewel count and description.

	Avg	Ex-Fn	Mint
Illinois Watch Co., 7-9J, M#1-2, KW	$50	$70	$150
Illinois Watch Co., 7-9J, M#2-6, SW	50	70	150
Illinois Watch Co., 11J, M#1-2, KW	50	70	150
Illinois Watch Co., 11J, M#3, SW	50	65	125
Illinois Watch Co., 13J, M#1-2, KW	50	85	200
Illinois Watch Co., 15J, M#1-2, KW	50	85	200
Illinois Watch Co., 15J, KW, ADJ, NI	100	125	225
Illinois Watch Co., 15J, SW, ADJ, DMK, NI	100	125	250
Illinois Watch Co., 15J, transition	50	65	135
Illinois Watch Co., 15J, SW, **Silveroid**	50	65	125
Illinois Watch Co., 15J, SW, **9K, HC**	225	300	500
Illinois Watch Co., 16J, SW, ADJ, DMK, NI	50	70	150
Illinois Watch Co., 16J, SW, ADJ, DMK, NI, marked **ADJ**	100	150	325
Illinois Watch Co., 17J, SW, **Silveroid**	40	60	125
Illinois Watch Co., 17J, M#3, **5th Pinion**	90	125	275
Illinois Watch Co., 17J, SW, 2 tone mvt,	70	80	150

🕐 Pricing in this Guide are fair market price for **COMPLETE** watches which are reflected from the "**NAWCC**" National and regional shows.

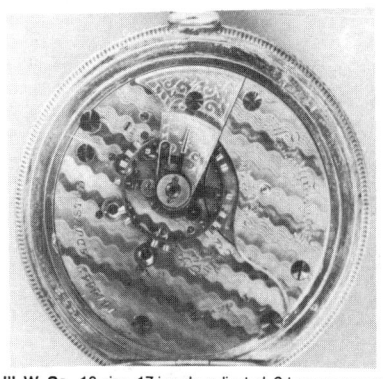

III. W. Co., 18 size, 17 jewels, adjusted, 2-tone movement, serial number 1,404,442.

Miller, 18 size, 17 jewels, 5th pinion model which changed hunting case to open face.

🕐 **Generic, nameless,** Personalized Jobber Watches or unmarked grades for watch movements are listed under the Company name or initials of the Company, etc. by size, jewel count and description.

Grade or Name — Description	Avg	Ex-Fn	Mint
Illinois Watch Co., 17J, SW, ADJ..	$70	$80	$150
Illinois Watch Co., 17J, SW, "EXTRA", Adj.4P.......................... ★	200	300	450
Illinois Watch Co., 17J, KW/SW, transition.................................	50	65	150
Illinois Watch Co., 19J, ADJ. **J. Barrel**, OF...............................	150	200	300
Illinois Watch Co., 21J, Adj.3P, OF...	200	250	350
Illinois Watch Co., 21J, ADJ5-6P, ...	300	350	450
Illinois Watch Co., 23J, ADJ6P, OF.............................. ★ ★ ★	1,500	1,700	2,500
Illinois Watch Co., 24J, ADJ, ...	500	575	650
Interior, 7J, KW & SW, OF..	60	80	200
Interstate Chronometer, 17J, HC, (sold by Sears)...........................	300	350	600
Interstate Chronometer, 17J, OF	250	300	500
Interstate Chronometer, 23J, Adj.5P, GJS, NI, OF...................... ★	900	1,000	1,200
Interstate Chronometer, 23J, Adj.5P, GJS, NI, HC .... ★ ★	1,000	1,200	1,600
Iowa W. Co., 7-11J, M#1-2, KW, ...	150	175	275
King of the Road, 16 &17J, NI, OF & HC, LS, ADJ .... ★	400	500	700
King Special, 17J, 2-tone, OF	125	150	300
King Philip Sp., 17J, (RR spur line)..................................... ★	300	400	600
Lafayette, 24J, GJS, Adj.6P, NI, SW, OF................................. ★	900	1,000	1,500
Lafayette, 24J, GJS, Adj.6P, NI, SW, HC .... ★ ★	1,300	1,500	2,200
Lakeshore, 17J, OF, LS, NI, SW..	100	150	200
Landis W. Co., 15-17J...	95	135	175
Liberty Bell, 17J, LS, NI, SW, OF...	90	125	150
Liberty Bell, 17J, LS, NI, SW, HC	90	150	200
Lightning Express, 11-13J, KWKS .... ★	200	250	400
A. Lincoln, 21J, Adj.5P, NI, DR, GJS, HC	400	450	600
A. Lincoln, 21J, Adj.5P, NI, DR, GJS,OF..................................	250	275	400
Lincoln Park, 15-17J, LS, OF..	70	80	175
Majestic Special, 17J, 2-tone, OF	125	150	200
Locomotive, 11J, M# 2 grade 4, Locomotive engraved on Mvt.	250	300	450
Maiden Lane, 16-17J, 5th Pinion	300	425	500
Manhattan, 11-13J, NI, KW, LS, HC or OF	100	175	250
Manhattan, 15–17J, NI, KW, LS,HC or OF	125	200	275
Mason, 7J, KW, KS, HC	90	110	225
Mason, 7J, KW, KS, HC, **1st run S# 101 to 200**.................... ★ ★	450	550	750
Miller, 15J,**1st run S# 301 to 400**................................... ★ ★	400	500	700
Miller, 15J, M#1, HC, KW...	100	125	250
Miller, 15J, M#1, HC, KW, ADJ	125	150	275
Miller, 15J, KW, OF...	100	125	225
Miller, 17J, 5th Pinion, ADJ..	150	175	300
Monarch W. Co., 17J, NI, ADJ, SW..	150	175	250

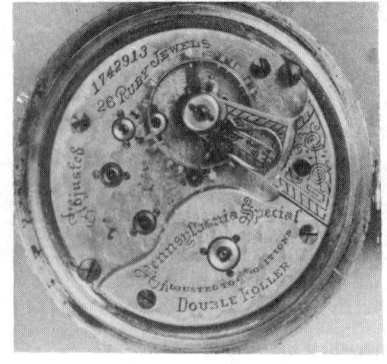

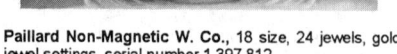

Paillard Non-Magnetic W. Co., 18 size, 24 jewels, gold jewel settings, serial number 1,397,812.

Pennsylvania Special, 18 size, 26 jewels, Adj6p, 2-tone movement, serial number 1,742,913.

Grade or Name — Description	Avg	Ex-Fn	Mint
Montgomery Ward, 15-17-19J, OF, GJS	$100	$135	$225
Montgomery Ward, 21J	150	225	300
Montgomery Ward Timer, 21J, ★	200	250	400
Montgomery Ward, 24J, OF	650	750	1,250
Montgomery Ward, 24J, HC ★	900	1,000	1,400
Montgomery Ward, 24J, marked double roller, HC ★	900	1,000	1,400
Muscatine W. Co., 15J, LS, NI, HC	135	160	300
The National, 11J, SW, LS, OF	70	90	150
(Paillard Non-Magnetic W. Co. SEE Non-Magnetic W. Co.)			
Pennsylvania Special, 17J, GJS, ADJ ★★	850	1,000	1,300
Pennsylvania Special, 21J, DR, Adj.5P ★★	1,200	1,400	2,000
Pennsylvania Special, 24J, DR, GJS, ADJ ★★	1,800	2,000	2,500
Pennsylvania Special, 25J, DR, GJS, ADJ, NI ★★★	4,500	5,000	7,000
Pennsylvania Special, 26J, DR, GJS, ADJ, NI ★★★	4,500	5,000	7,000
Pierce Arrow, 17J, "automaker logo" ★	375	450	600
Plymouth W. Co., 15-17J, SW, (sold by Sears)	70	90	200
Potomac, 17J, ADJ, NI, OF	150	175	275
Potomac, 17J, ADJ, NI, HC ★	225	275	400
The President, 15J, NI, OF	110	150	275
The President, 17J, DMK, **14K gold case**	500	600	900
Rail Road Construction, 17J, OF	225	275	400
Rail Road Dispatcher Extra or Special, 15-17J, OF	225	250	400
Rail Road Dispatcher Extra, 15-17J, HC	225	275	475
Rail Road Employee's Special, 17J, NI, LS, HC	275	325	450
Rail Road Timer Extra, 17-21J, (Montgomery Ward), OF ★	250	300	500
Rail Road King, 15J, NI, ADJ, OF ★	250	275	400
Rail Road King, 15J, NI, ADJ, HC ★	300	350	450
Rail Road King, 16J, NI, ADJ, OF ★	275	325	450
Rail Road King, 16J, NI, ADJ, HC ★	325	375	500
Rail Road King, 17J, NI, ADJ, OF ★	300	350	450
Rail Road King, 17J, NI, ADJ, HC ★	350	400	475
The Railroader, 15J, OF, ADJ, NI ★	250	300	450
Railway , 11J, KW, KS, gilt ★	100	125	300
Railway Engineer, 15J ★	275	325	500
Railway Regulator, 11-15J, LS, (R.W.Sears Watch Co.) ★★	425	525	800
Remington W.Co. 17J, OF	200	225	325
Remington W.Co. 17J, HC	225	275	400
Remington Special, 21J, Adj.6P, OF	300	350	500

The President, 18 size, 17 jewels, Chalmer patented regulator, serial number 1,240,909.

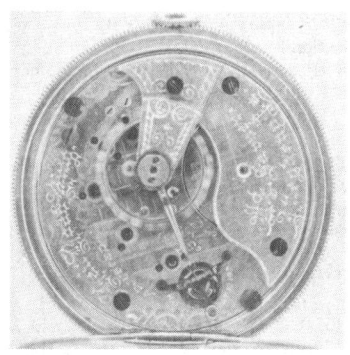

Railroad King, 18 size, 17 jewels, Fifth Pinion Model, adjusted. Note Chalmer patented regulator, S# 1,160,836.

Grade or Name — Description	Avg	Ex-Fn	Mint
Standard W. Co., 15J, several models	$110	$140	$225
S. W. Co., 15J, M#1, KW, HC	110	140	225
R.W. Sears Watch Co. Chicago,"Defiance" model, HC	600	700	900
Sears & Roebuck Special, 17J, GJS, NI, DMK, Adj	150	175	250
Senate, 17J, NI, DMK, Washington W. Co.	150	175	250
Southern R.R. Special, 21J, LS, ADJ, OF ★	1,200	1,400	2,000
Southern R.R. Special, 21J, M#5, LS, Adj., HC ★	1,600	1,800	2,400
Star Light, 17J, 5th pinion, Chalmers Reg. OF	150	200	325
Stewart Special, 11-15J, Adj.	80	125	150
Stewart Special, 17J, Adj.	110	175	200
Stewart Special, 21J, Adj.	170	225	300
Stuart, 15J, M#1, KW, KS	425	500	800
Stuart, 15J, M#1, KW/SW, transition	275	350	650
Stuart, 15J, M#1, KW, KS, marked Adj. ★	325	400	700
Stuart, 15J, ADJ, KW, Abbotts Conversion, 18K, HC ★	1,200	1,350	1,600
Stuart, 15J, M#1, KW, KS, Coin ★	500	600	800
Stuart, 15J, M#1, KW, KS, 1st run S# 1 to 10" ★★★★	4,000	6,000	8,500
Stuart, 15J, M#1, KW, KS, 1st run S# 11 to 100" ★★★	2,000	2,500	4,500
Stuart, 17J, M#3, 5th Pinion ★★	250	300	500
Stuart, 17J, M#3, 5th Pinion, ADJ ★★	275	325	600

Sears & Roebuck Special, 18 size, 17 jewels, serial number 1,481,879.

Washington W. Co., Lafayette model, 18 size, 24 Ruby jewels, gold jewel settings, adjusted, serial # 3,392,897.

Grade or Name — Description	Avg	Ex-Fn	Mint
Transition Models, 17J, KW/SW, OF	$80	$100	$175
Train Dispatcher Special, 17J, (Montgomery Ward), Adj, OF ..... ★	275	325	550
Time King, 17J, OF, LS, NI	125	150	275
Time King, 21J, OF, LS,	200	225	400
Union Pacific Sp., 17J, OF .... ★★	450	500	700
Vault Time Lock for Mosler, 15J, 72 hr.	70	125	175
Ward's Special, 15J, NI, FULL, LS,	70	125	150
George Washington,11J, HC	125	150	250
Washington,11-17J, also (U.S.A) sold by **Montgomery Ward,**	100	125	200
☉ **Washington W. Co.** (See Army & Navy, Liberty Bell, Lafayette, Senate)			
Wathiers Railway Watch, 15-17J, Adj., NI .... ★	400	475	700
N0. 5, 11J, KW KS, (**marked** No.5), HC	100	150	300
65, 15J, HC, LS, M#2	65	90	150
89, 17J, nickel, ADJ, OF	65	90	150
89, 21J, nickel, ADJ, HC	80	100	300
101, 11J, SW, KW, OF	60	80	165
101, 11J, SW, KW, Silveroid	60	80	135
101, 11J, SW, KW, HC	60	80	185
102, 13J, SW, KW, Silveroid	40	60	135
102, 13J, SW, KW, OF	60	80	160
102, 13J, SW, KW, HC	60	80	200
103, 15-16J, ADJ	60	80	150
104, 15J, M#2, HC .... ★★	300	400	600
104, 17J, M#3, early high grade for RR, Ca. 1885, OF........... ★★	350	425	700
105, 17J, M#3, early high grade for RR, Ca. 1885, OF....... ★★★	600	700	1,000
105, 15J, M#2, GJS, ADJ, KW, KS, HC .... ★★★	600	700	1,000
106, 15J, ADJ, KW, KS .... ★★	300	400	600
444, 17J, NI, ADJ, OF	70	90	150
445, 19J, GJS, 2-Tone, HC .... ★★	1,000	1,100	1,500
1908 Special, 21J, NI, Adj.5P,(**marked** 1908 special), OF	325	425	600

STUART, 17 jewels, Model #3, 5th Pinion, Transition Model.

First Model in 14K white or green gold filled Wadsworth case, showing Montgomery numerical dial.

☉ Pricing in this Guide are fair market price for **COMPLETE** watches which are reflected from the "**NAWCC**" National and regional shows.

ILLINOIS
16 SIZE

Grade or Name — Description	Avg	Ex-Fx	Mint
Adams Street, 17J, 3/4, SW, NI, DMK	$150	$200	$325
Adams Street, 21J, 3F brg, NI, DMK	250	300	450
Ak-Sar-Ben (Nebraska backward), 17J, OF, GCW	175	200	300
Ariston, 11J, OF & HC	75	100	150
Ariston, 15J, OF & HC	75	100	150
Ariston, 17J, Adj, HC	150	200	325
Ariston, 17J, Adj, OF	125	150	250
Ariston, 19J, Adj.5P, OF	175	200	300
Ariston, 21J, GJS, Adj.6P, OF	200	300	500
Ariston, 21J, GJS, Adj.6P, HC	250	350	600
Ariston, 23J, GJS, Adj.6P, OF	500	600	850
Ariston, 23J, GJS, Adj.6P, HC ★★	700	800	1,000
Arlington Special, 17J, OF	100	125	200
Arlington Special, 17J, OF, Silveroid	85	100	175
Army & Navy, 19J, GJS, Adj.3P, NI, 1F brg, OF	175	200	300
Army & Navy, 19J, GJS, Adj.3P, NI, 1F brg, HC	225	275	450
Army & Navy, 21J, GJS, Adj.3P, 1F brg, OF	200	250	350
Army & Navy, 21J, GJS, Adj.3P, 1F brg, HC	300	350	400
B & M Special, 17J, BRG, Adj.4P ★	400	500	800
B & O Standard, 21J ★★	900	1,100	1,600
Benjamin Franklin, 17J, ADJ, DMK, OF	300	325	550
Benjamin Franklin, 17J, ADJ, DMK, HC	375	450	700
Benjamin Franklin, 21J, GJS, Adj.5P, DR, GT, OF ★	550	625	800
Benjamin Franklin, 21J, GJS, Adj.5P, DR, GT, HC ★★	600	675	850
Benjamin Franklin, 25J, GJS, Adj.6P, DR, GT, OF ★★	3,000	3,500	4,500
Benjamin Franklin, 25J, GJS, Adj.6P, DR, GT, HC ★★★	3,500	4,000	5,000

Ben Franklin, 16 size, 25 jewels, gold jewel settings, gold train, **OF Getty Model**, serial number 2,242,138.

Bunn Special, Model 163, 16 size, 23J., gold jewel settings, gold train, 60 hour movement, serial # 5,421,504.

Note: Bunn Special original cases were marked Bunn Special except for Elinvars (Hamilton cased). also GRADES 161 & 163 were made by Hamilton W. Co.

🕑 Generic, nameless or **unmarked grades** for watch movements are listed under the Company name or initials of the Company, etc. by size, jewel count and description.

🕑 Watches listed in this book are priced at the **collectable fair market value** at the RETAIL level, as complete watches having an original 14k gold filled case, KEY WIND with silver, an original white enamel single sunk dial, and with the entire original movement in good working order with no repairs needed, unless otherwise noted.

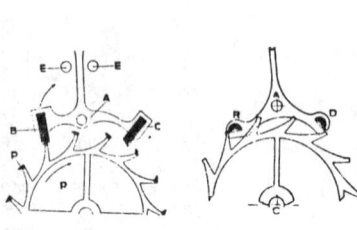

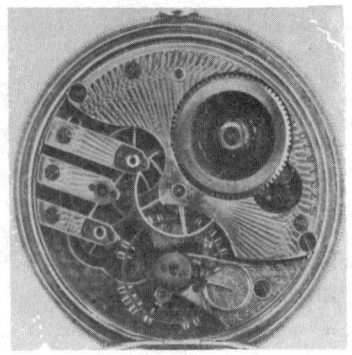

Left: Standard style escapement. Right: DeLong style escapement.

Illinois Watch Co., 16 size, 25J., 3 fingered bridge Getty Model, gold train, note click near balance cock = HC model, serial number S731,870.

Grade or Name — Description	Avg	Ex-Fn	Mint
Bunn, 17J, LS, OF, NI, 3/4, GJS, Adj.5P	$175	$200	$300
Bunn, 17J, LS, NI, 3/4, Adj.5P, HC ★★★	650	800	1,000
Bunn, 19J, LS, OF, NI, 3/4, GJS, Adj.5P	200	250	350
Bunn, 19J, LS, NI, 3/4, Adj.5P, HC ★★★	800	1,000	1,500
Bunn, 19J, LS, OF, NI, 3/4, GJS, Adj.5P, 60 hour	325	375	600
Bunn, 19J, **marked Jeweled Barrel**	225	250	350
Bunn Special, 19J, LS, OF, NI, 3/4, Adj.6P, GT	200	225	325
Bunn Special, 19J, LS, OF, NI, 3/4, Adj.5P, 60 hour	400	500	750
Bunn Special, 21J, NI, GJS, Adj.6P, GT, HC ★★	575	675	975
Bunn Special, 21J, LS, OF, NI, 3/4, GJS, Adj.6P, GT	250	300	450
Bunn Special, 21J, LS, GJS, Adj.6P, GT, **gold plated Mvt.** ★★	500	600	900
Bunn Special, 21J, LS,OF, NI, 3/4, GJS, Adj.6P, GT, 60 hour	275	325	550
Bunn Special, 21J, LS, OF, NI, 3/4, GJS, Adj.6P, GT, 60 hr. **marked Elinvar**	325	425	650
Bunn Special, 21J, 60 hr., 14K, OF, Bunn Special case ★	800	900	1,200
Bunn Special, 23J, LS, OF, NI, 3/4, GJS, Adj.6P, GT	450	500	800
Bunn Special, 23J, LS, OF, NI, 3/4, GJS, Adj.6P, GT, 60 hour	500	600	900
Bunn Special, 23J, LS, OF, NI, 3/4, GJS, Adj.6P, GT, with 23J, 60-hour on dial	600	700	1,200
Bunn Special, 23J, LS, NI, GJS, GT, Adj.6P, HC ★★★	1,500	1,800	2,500
161 Bunn Special, 21J, 3/4, Adj.6P, 60 hour	425	500	850
161A Bunn Special, 21J, 3/4, Adj.6P, 60 hour (**Elinvar** signed under balance or on top plate)	450	550	850
161 Elinvar Bunn Special, 21J, 3/4, Adj.6P, 60 hour (**Elinvar** signed at bottom of bridge)	450	550	850
161B, Bunn Special, 21J, 60 hour, pressed jewels ★★★★	4,000	5,000	8,000
163 Bunn Special, 23J, GJS, Adj.6P, 3/4, 60 hour	700	950	1,500
163 Elinvar Bunn Special, 23J, GJS, Adj.6P, 60 hour (**Elinvar** signed at bottom of cock, uncut balance) ★	1,100	1,250	1,600
163A Elinvar Bunn Special, 23J, GJS, Adj.6P, 3/4, 60 hour (**Elinvar** signed under balance) ◻	1,100	1,250	1,600
163A Elinvar Bunn Special, 23J, Adj.6P, 3/4, 60 hour (**Elinvar** signed on train bridge) ◻	1,200	1,300	1,700

🕐 Generic, nameless or unmarked grades for watch movements are listed under the Company name or initials of the Company, etc. by size, jewel count and description.

🕐 Some grades are not included. Their values can be determined by comparing with **similar** age, size, metal content, style, models and grades listed.

Grade or Name — Description	Avg	Ex-Fn	Mint
Burlington W. Co., 15J, OF	$75	$100	$200
BurlingtonW. Co., 15J, HC	100	150	250
BurlingtonW. Co., 17J, OF	85	125	200
Burlington W. Co., 17J, HC	100	175	275
Burlington W. Co., 19J, 3/4, NI, Adj.3P	90	150	225
Burlington W. Co., 19J, BRG, NI, Adj.3P	90	150	225
Burlington W. Co., 19J, 3/4, HC	100	150	250
Burlington W. Co., 19J, 3F brg, NI, Adj.3P	90	125	200
Burlington W. Co., 21J, 3/4, NI, Adj.3P	125	150	250
Burlington W. Co., 21J, Adj.6P, GJS	150	175	275
Burlington, Bull Dog- on dial, 21J, SW, LS, GJS, GT	275	300	450
C & O Special, 21J, 3/4, NI, ADJ ★★	900	1,100	1,600
Capitol, 19J, OF, 3/4, NI, Adj.3P	70	90	200
Central, 17J, SW, PS, OF	50	60	150
Commodore Perry Special, 21J, Adj.6P, GT, OF	250	300	450
Craftsman, 17J, OF	50	60	150
D. & R. G. Special, 21J, GJS, GT, Adj.5P, (Denver & Rio Grand RR), OF ★★★★	2,000	2,500	3,500
DeLong Escapement, 21J, GJS, (Bunn Sp. or A. Lincoln) Adj.6P, 14K OF ★★★★	1,500	1,800	2,500
Dependon, 17J, (J.V.Farwell)	150	175	300
Dependon, 21J, (J.V.Farwell)	200	245	400
Diamond, Ruby, Sapphire, 21J, GJS, GT, Adj.6P, BRG, OF ... ★★	1,000	1,200	2,000
Diamond, Ruby, Sapphire, 23J, GJS, GT, Adj.6P, BRG, OF ★★★	2,200	2,400	3,200
Diamond, Ruby, Sapphire, 23J, GJS, GT, Adj.6P, grade # 310, tall Arabic # on dial, BRG, DR, HC ★★★★	3,500	4,000	5,500
Diamond, Ruby, Sapphire, 23J, GJS, GT, Adj.6P, BRG, OF also marked Greenwich (Washington W.Co.) ★★★	2,500	3,000	4,000
Diamond, Ruby, Sapphire, 23J, GJS, GT, Adj.6P, 3/4 plate, OF ★★★	1,600	1,800	2,400
Dispatcher, 19J, Adj.3P	150	225	300
Fifth Ave:,19J, Adj.3P,GT,OF	110	130	200
Fifth Ave., 21J, Adj.3P,GT,OF	175	200	300
Franklin Street, 15J, 3/4, NI, ADJ	100	125	200
Grant, 17J, ADJ, LS, Getty Model, OF	150	200	300
Getty Model # 4 &5, 17J	100	125	175
Getty Model # 4 &5, 21J	200	250	375

Interstate Chronometer, 16 size, 23 jewels, one-fingered bridge, OF Getty Model, serial number 2,327,614.

A. Lincoln, 16 size, 21 jewels, gold jewel settings, gold train, Adj5p, OF Getty Model, serial number 2,237,406.

🕐 Pricing in this Guide are fair market price for COMPLETE watches which are reflected from the "NAWCC" National and regional shows.

Grade or Name — Description	Avg	Ex-Fn	Mint
Great Northern Special, 17J, BRG, ADJ	$225	$300	$400
Great Northern Special, 19J, BRG, ADJ	250	325	425
Great Northern Special, 21J, BRG, ADJ, Adj.3P	300	375	475
Illinois Central, 17-21J, 2-Tone, Adj.3P, GT	200	250	400

⊕ GENERIC, NAMELESS OR **UNMARKED GRADES** FOR WATCH MOVEMENTS ARE LISTED UNDER THE COMPANY NAME OR INITIALS OF THE COMPANY, ETC. BY SIZE, JEWEL COUNT AND DESCRIPTION.

Grade or Name — Description	Avg	Ex-Fn	Mint
Illinois Watch Co., 7-9J, M#1-2-3	$40	$60	$125
Illinois Watch Co., 11-17J, (**Rockland**)	60	70	150
Illinois Watch Co., 11-13J, 3/4, OF	40	60	135
Illinois Watch Co., 11-13J, M#7, 3/4, OF	40	60	135
Illinois Watch Co., 11-13, M#6, 3/4, HC	60	90	175
Illinois Watch Co., 15J, M#2, OF	60	90	135
Illinois Watch Co., 15J, M#1, HC	70	90	200
Illinois Watch Co., 15J, M#3, OF	40	70	135
Illinois Watch Co., 15J, 3/4, ADJ	40	70	135
Illinois Watch Co., 15J, 3F brg, GJS	40	70	135
Illinois Watch Co., 16-17J, **14K, HC**	375	400	650
Illinois Watch Co., 16-17J, Adj.3P, OF	60	70	150
Illinois Watch Co., 16-17J, M#2-3, SW, OF	60	70	150
Illinois Watch Co., 17J, M#6, SW, HC	60	70	200
Illinois Watch Co., 17J, M#7, OF	60	70	150
Illinois Watch Co., 17J, M#5, 3/4, ADJ, HC	70	80	175
Illinois Watch Co., 17J, M#4, 3F brg, GJS, Adj.5P, HC	150	175	300
Illinois Watch Co., 19J, 3/4, GJS, Adj.5P , **jeweled barrel**	150	175	300
Illinois Watch Co., 19J, 3/4, BRG, Adj.3-4P	100	125	175
Illinois Watch Co., 21J, Adj.3P, OF ★	200	225	325
Illinois Watch Co., 21J, ADJ, OF ★	200	225	325
Illinois Watch Co., 21J, GJS, HC ★	225	250	400
Illinois Watch Co., 21J, 3/4, GJS, Adj.5P ★	200	225	325
Illinois Watch Co., 21J, 3F brg, GJS, Adj.4P ★	175	195	300
Illinois Watch Co., 21J, 3F brg, GJS, Adj.5P ★	225	275	350
Illinois Watch Co., 23J, GJS, Adj.5P, OF ★★	400	500	650
Illinois Watch Co., 23J, GJS, Adj.5P, HC ★★	500	600	750
Illinois Watch Co., 25J, 4th model,3F brg, GJS, Adj.5P, HC ★★★	3,000	3,500	5,000
Imperial 8p., 17J, SW, LS, Adj.4P, OF	125	150	225
Interstate Chronometer, 17J, GCW, Adj.3P, HC, (sold by Sears)	300	325	450
Interstate Chronometer, 17J, GCW, Adj.3P, OF	275	300	450
Interstate Chronometer, 23J, 1F brg, ADJ, OF ★	700	800	1,250
Interstate Chronometer, 23J, 1F brg, ADJ, HC ★★	900	1,100	1,500
Lafayette, 23J, Washington W.Co., GJS, Adj.5P, GT, OF ★★★	1,000	1,200	1,600
Lafayette, 23J, Washington W.Co., GJS, Adj.5P, GT, HC ★★★	1,200	1,400	2,000
Lakeshore, 17J, OF	70	85	150
Lakeshore, 17J, HC	100	125	250
Landis W. Co., 15-17J	70	90	150
Liberty Bell, 15-17J, OF	70	90	175
Liberty Bell, 17J, HC ★	350	400	600
A. Lincoln, 21J,3/4, GJS, Adj.5P, OF	175	225	350
A. Lincoln, 21J,3/4, GJS, Adj.5P, HC	325	375	650
The Lincoln, 15J, 3F brg,	125	150	200
Logan, 15J, OF	40	70	125
Marvel, 19J, GT, GJS, Adj.3P, Of	60	80	150
Marine Special, 21J, 3/4, Adj.3P	150	185	325
Monarch W. Co., 17J, NI, ADJ, SW	70	90	200
Monroe, 17J, NI,3/4, OF (Washington W. Co.)	70	90	150
Monroe, 15J, 3/4, OF (Washington W. Co.)	70	90	150
Montgomery Ward, 17J, LS, Thin Model , OF	100	155	235
Montgomery Ward, 21J, "Extra RR Timer", 2 tone, G# 171 ★★	1,000	1,200	1.500
Our No. 1, 15J, HC, M#1	100	150	275
Overland Special, 19J, Adj., OF	100	150	225

⊕ Pricing in this Guide are fair market price for **COMPLETE** watches which are reflected from the "**NAWCC**" National and regional shows.

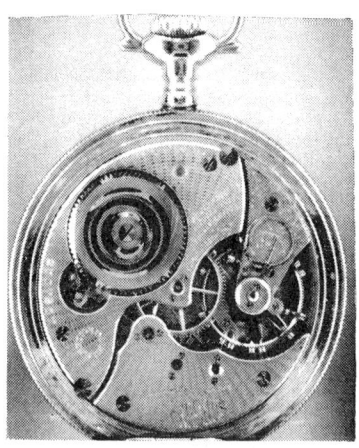

Sangamo, 16 size, 23 jewels, Adj.6p, gold jewel settings, gold train, OF Getty Model, serial number 2,307,867.

Sangamo Special, 17S, 23J., model 13, marked 60 hr. movement, Adj.6p, gold jewel settings, gold train, Serial # 4,758,199, Ca. 1926. NOTE: no red border on bal. cock.

Grade or Name Description	Avg	Ex-Fn	Mint
Pennsylvania Special, 17J, Adj.3P, HC .... ★	$400	$500	$800
Pennsylvania Special, 17J, Adj., 2 tone, G# 176, HC .... ★	800	900	1,100
Pennsylvania Special, 19J, OF .... ★	400	500	750
Pennsylvania Special, 21J, Getty model, 2-tone, Adj., OF .... ★	1,000	1,200	1,500
Pennsylvania Special, 21J, 2-tone, (Finely Adj.), HC .... ★ ★ ★	2,000	2,400	3,000
Pennsylvania Special, 23J, 3/4, GJS, Adj.5P .... ★	1,300	1,500	2,000
Plymouth W. Co., 15-17J, OF (Add $25 for HC), (sold by Sears) ..	60	70	150
Precise, 21J, OF, LS, Adj.3P	125	150	225
Quincy Street, 17J, 3/4, NI, DMK, ADJ	60	70	150
Railroad Dispatcher, 11-17J, DMK, 3/4	175	200	350
Railroad Dispatcher Extra or Special, 15-17J, DMK, 3/4	225	275	375
Railroad Employee's, 17J, ...	125	175	275
Railroad King, 16-17J, M#2 or 5-Getty model, NI, PS, OF	275	300	375
Railroad Official, 23J, 3 Finger bridge .... ★ ★ ★ ★ ★	2,000	2,200	2,700
Railway King, 17J, OF	175	200	300
Remington W.Co. 11-15J, OF	125	150	250
Remington W.Co. 17J, OF	200	225	325
Remington W.Co. 17J, HC	250	300	450
Rockland, 17-19J, GJS, GT, 7th model, grade 305, OF	65	85	125
Sangamo, 19J, model # 4, GJS, GT, ADJ., HC .... ★ ★ ★	4,000	5,000	7,000
Sangamo, 21J, GJS, Adj.6P, HC	250	300	450
Sangamo, 21J, GJS, Adj., OF	185	225	375
Sangamo, 21J, 3/4, GJS, DR, Adj.6P, OF	200	250	400
Sangamo, 21J, GJS, Adj.6P, EXTRA or SPECIAL, (Getty), HC ★	525	625	900
Sangamo, 21J, GJS, Adj.6P, EXTRA or SPECIAL, (Getty), OF . ★	475	575	800
Sangamo, 21J, GJS, Adj., marked SPECIAL 2-tone Mvt., Adj.6P, (straight ribbon - not wavy ribbon pattern), (Getty), OF ... ★	475	575	800
Sangamo, 23J, GJS, Adj., marked SPECIAL 2-tone Mvt., Adj.6P, (straight ribbon - not wavy ribbon pattern), (Getty), OF ... ★	625	725	1,000
Sangamo, 23J,3/4, GJS, DR, Adj.6P, OF	300	400	600
Sangamo, 23J, 3/4, GJS, DR, Adj.6P, HC	400	450	650
Sangamo, 25J, M#5, 3/4, GJS, DR, Adj.6P .... ★ ★ ★	4,000	5,000	7,000
Sangamo, 26J, M#5, 3/4, GJS, DR, Adj.6P .... ★ ★ ★	5,000	6,000	8,000
Sangamo Special, 19J, BRG, GJS, GT, Adj.6P, OF	350	375	650
Sangamo Special, 19J, BRG, GJS, GT, Adj.6P, HC .... ★ ★ ★	1,200	1,500	2,200
Sangamo, Extra, 21J, Adj.6P, gold train, Of .... ★ ★	425	475	800
Sangamo Special, 21J, M#7, OF	350	400	550
Sangamo Special, 21J, M#8, BRG, HC ....,.... ★ ★ ★	1,400	1,600	2,400
Sangamo Special, 21J, M#9, BRG, GJS, GT, Adj.6P, OF	350	400	650
Sangamo Special, 21J, BRG, GJS, GT, Diamond end cap	375	425	700

Grade or Name — Description	Avg	Ex-Fn	Mint
Sangamo Special, 23J, M#9-10, BRG, GJS, GT, Adj.6P, Sangamo Special **HINGED** case	$750	$850	$1,400
Sangamo Special, 23J, BRG, GJS, GT, Adj.6P, Diamond end stone, **screw back,** Sangamo Special case	650	700	1,100
Sangamo Special, 23J, M#8, GJS, GT, Adj.6P, **HC** ★★★	1,500	1,800	2,600
Sangamo Special, 23J, BRG, GJS, GT, Adj.6P, **not marked** 60 hour, rigid bow, Sangamo Special case	750	850	1,400
Sangamo Special, 23J, BRG, GJS, GT, Adj.6P, **marked 60 hour,** Sangamo Special case ★★★★	1,200	1,400	2,200
Sangamo Special, 23J, BRG, GJS, GT, Adj.6P, 60 hour, rigid bow, Sangamo Special case **14K gold case**	1,600	2,000	3,000
Santa Fe Special, 17J, BRG, Adj.3P	225	300	475
Santa Fe Special, 21J, 3/4, Adj.5P, OF	300	350	575
Santa Fe Special, 21J, 3/4, Adj.5P, HC	350	425	625
Sears, Roebuck & Co. Special, 15-17J, ADJ	60	80	135
Senate, 17J, (Washington W. Co.), NI, 3/4, ADJ	60	80	135
Standard, 15J	60	80	125
Sterling, 17J, SW, PS, Adj.3P, OF	60	80	125
Sterling, 19-21J, SW, PS, Adj.3P, OF	125	150	225
Stewart, 17J	75	100	125
Stewart Special, 21J, Adj.,	125	150	225
Stewart Special, 19J, Adj.3P	70	90	150
Stewart Special, 15-17J,	60	70	125
The General, 15J, OF	60	70	125
Time King, 17J, OF	60	70	135
Time King, 19J, Adj.3P, OF	100	125	150
Time King, 21J, Adj, OF	125	150	250
Trainmen's Special, 17J, HC ★	150	200	300
Union Pacific,17J, Adj.,DR, 2-tone, DMK, OF ★★	500	600	800
Victor, 21J, 3/4, Adj.3P	150	175	300

☉ **Washington W. Co.** (See Army & Navy, Liberty Bell, Lafayette, Senate)

Grade 163, 16 size, 23 jewels, adjusted to 6 positions, motor barrel, 60 hour model, serial number 5,421,504.

LAFAYETTE, 23J, 16 size, WASHINGTON W.CO., GJS, Adj.5P, GT, HC.

161 through 163A —See Bunn Special

Grade or Name — Description	Avg	Ex-Fn	Mint
167L, 17J, marked	$100	$125	$200
167, 17J	60	80	150
169, 19J, Adj.3P, OF	60	80	175
174, 23J, LS, GJS, Adj., OF, marked ★★	600	700	800
175, 17J, RR grade & a (RR inspectors name on dial &mvt.) ★★	450	550	800
177, 19J, SW, LS, 60 hour, Adj.5P, OF ★	300	400	600

⊕ Generic, nameless or unmarked grades for watch movements are listed under the Company name or initials of the Company, etc. by size, jewel count and description.

Grade or Name — Description	Avg	Ex-Fn	Mint
179, 21J, GJS, GT, Adj.6P, Getty model, **marked** Ruby Jewels HC or OF......★★	$300	$350	$600
181-189, 21J, 3F brg, Adj.6P, GJS, GT, **marked** Ruby Jewels, Getty model, HC or OF ......★	300	350	575
184, 19J, 3F brg, LS, OF......	90	120	200
187, 17J, 3F brg, Adj.5P, GJS, GT, **marked** 187, HC	250	300	400
333, 15J, HC	70	100	185
555, 17J, 3/4, ...	50	70	150
777, 17J, 3/4, ADJ	50	70	150
805, 17J, BRG, GJS, GT, DR, OF	50	70	150
809, 23J, Adj.6P, GT, **marked 809** ......★★★	400	500	700
900, 19J, LS, Adj.3P......	125	150	250

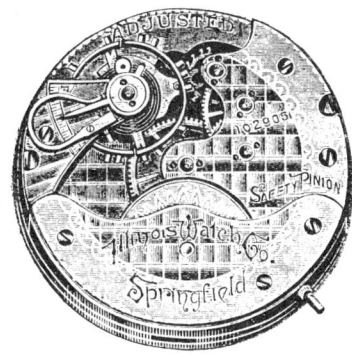

Illinois Watch Co., 14 size, 16 jewels, Adj5p.

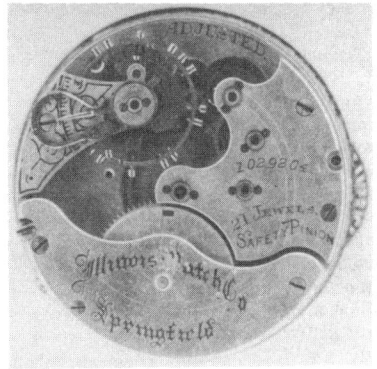

Illinois Watch Co., 14 size, 21J., adjusted, nickel movement, gold jewel settings, serial number 1,029,204.

ILLINOIS
14 SIZE

Grade or Name — Description	Avg	Ex-Fn	Mint
Illinois Watch Co., 7J, M#1, **GRADE 120, KW**, OF	$70	$80	$125
Illinois Watch Co., 7J, M#1-2-3, SW, OF	50	65	115
Illinois Watch Co., 11J, M#1-2-3, SW, OF	50	65	115
Illinois Watch Co., 15J, M#1-2-3, SW, OF	50	65	115
Illinois Watch Co., 16J, M#1-2-3, SW, OF	70	100	125
Illinois Watch Co., 21J, M#1-2-3, SW, OF ......★	125	150	225
Illinois Watch Co., 22J, ...★	125	150	375

NOTE: Add $35 for above watches in hunting case.

ILLINOIS
12 SIZE and 13 SIZE

Grade or Name — Description	Avg	Ex-Fn	Mint
Accurate, 21J, GJS, OF	$50	$70	$150
Aristocrat, 19J, OF......	50	70	125
Ariston, 11-17J, OF	60	70	150
Ariston, 19J, OF......	75	100	200
Ariston, 21J, Adj.5P, OF	100	125	300
Ariston, 23J, Adj.5P, OF ......★	225	275	400
Aluminum Watch, 17J, model #3, **movement plates made of aluminum** G#525, S# 3,869,251 to S# 3,869,300 ......★★★★	1,600	1,800	3,000

Characteristics of watches differ for the same age of both case and movement, because these features vary it may not be accurate to date a watch by one single influence. Example: the second hand was not commonly found on watches before 1750, but common about 1800. The first second hand appeared in 1665 and another in 1690. Therefore statements are broad rather than accurate.

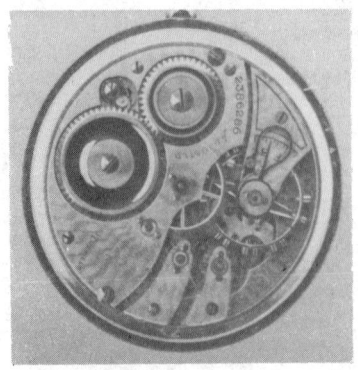

Ben Franklin, 12 size, 17 jewels, open face, gold train, serial number 2,366,286.

Illini, 13 size, 21 jewels, bridge model, serial number 3,650,129. Note five tooth click & jeweled barrel.

Grade or Name — Description	Avg	Ex-Fn	Mint
Autocrat, 17J, Adj.3P, 3/4	$40	$60	$95
Autocrat, 19J, Adj.3P, 3/4	40	60	135
Banker, 17J, Adj.3P, OF	40	60	135
Banker, 21J, Adj.3P, OF	70	90	175
Benjamin Franklin, 17J, OF	150	175	265
Benjamin Franklin, 21J, OF	200	250	400
Bunn Special, 21J, Adj 3P, (by Hamilton), OF ★★	400	450	600
Burlington Special, 19J, GT, OF	60	80	135
Burlington Special, 19J, GT, HC	80	100	175
Burlington W. Co., 21J, GT, OF	70	90	165
Burlington W. Co., 21J, GT, HC	100	125	195
Central, 17J, OF, 2-Tone	50	80	100
Commodore Perry Special, 17J., adj.3P	50	80	100
Criterion, 21J, OF	70	90	150
Dependon, 17, (J.V.Farwell), HC,	70	90	200
Diamond Ruby Sapphire, 21J, Adj.5P, GJS ★	400	450	600
Elite, 19J, OF	40	60	135
Garland, 17J, Adj.,GT, OF	40	60	95
Gold Metal, 17J, OF	40	60	90

Example of Illinois Thin Model, 12 size, 17 jewels, adjusted to 3 positions.

Maiden America, 12 size, 17 jewels, serial number 2,820,499.

Santa Fe Special, 12 size, 21 jewels, three-quarter plate, serial number 3,414,422.

Grade or Name — Description	Avg	Ex-Fn	Mint
Illini, 13 S., 21J, Adj.5P, BRG, jeweled barrel, 5 tooth click, OF ..	$65	$80	$150
Illini **Extra**, 13 S., 21J, Adj.5P, jeweled barrel, 5 tooth click, OF...	80	100	200
Illini, 12 Size, 23J, Adj.5P, BRG	100	120	225
Illini, 12 Size, 23J, Adj.6P, BRG, **14K**	240	300	450
Illinois Watch Co., 7-11J	35	50	85
Illinois Watch Co., 15J	35	50	85
Illinois Watch Co., 16-17J, OF, **14K**	200	240	400
Illinois Watch Co., 16-17J,OF, GF	35	50	125
Illinois Watch Co., 17J, GF, HC	60	90	175
Illinois Watch Co., 19J	60	90	150
Illinois Watch Co., 21J, OF	60	90	175
Illinois Watch Co., 21J, marked (21 SPECIAL), OF	90	120	200
Illinois Watch Co., 21J, HC	100	125	225
Illinois Watch Co., 23J, OF	150	175	265
Illinois Watch Co., 19J, OF, EXTRA THIN MODEL	50	65	125
Illinois Watch Co., 21J, OF, EXTRA THIN MODEL	60	85	175
Interstate Chronometer, 17J, OF, (sold by Sears)	95	125	190
Interstate Chronometer, 21J, GJS, OF	175	200	300
Interstate Chronometer, 21J, GJS, HC ★	225	250	400
Governor, 17J, OF	40	50	125
A. Lincoln, 19J, Adj.5P, GJS, DR, 3/4, marked on mvt.	90	110	175
A. Lincoln, 21J, Adj.5P, DR, GJS	90	110	175
Maiden America, 17J, ADJ	60	75	95
Marquis Autocrat, 17J, OF	60	75	95
Master, 21J, GT, GJS, OF	60	75	150
Masterpiece, 19J, Adj.3P, OF	85	100	150
A. Norton, 21J, OF	100	125	200
Plymouth Watch Co., 15-17J, HC, (sold by Sears)	75	100	125
Railroad Dispatch , 11-15J,	50	60	125
Railroad Dispatch , 17-19J, SW, GT	80	95	150
Rockland, 17J,	45	55	95
Roosevelt, 19J, Adj.3P, OF	60	95	150
Santa Fe Special, 21J	125	175	300
Sterling, 17J, OF	30	40	95
Sterling, 19-21J, OF	50	60	150
Stewart Special, 17J, SW, Adj.3P	40	50	95
Stewart Special, 19J, SW, OF, GT	40	50	100
Time King, 19J, SW, Adj.3P	45	60	125
Time King, 21J, SW, Adj.3P	60	80	150
Transit, 19J, OF, PS	45	60	125

🕐 Pricing in this Guide are fair market price for COMPLETE watches which are reflected from the **"NAWCC"** National and regional shows.

Grade or Name — Description	Avg	Ex-Fn	Mint
Vim, 17J, ADJ, BRG, GJS, DR, OF	$35	$50	$95
Washington W. Co., **Monroe,** 11J, sold by Montgomery Ward	50	65	175
Washington W. Co., **Army & Navy,** 19J	70	90	185
Washington W. Co., **Senate,** 17J, M#2, PS,	50	65	125
121, 21J, Adj.3P	60	75	150
127, 17J, ADJ	35	45	95
129, 19J, Adj.3P	45	60	125
219, 11J, M#1	30	40	75
403, 15J, BRG	30	40	85
405, 17J, BRG, ADJ, OF	30	40	95
409, 21J, BRG, Diamond, Ruby, Sapphire, Adj.5P, GJS ....★	275	325	500
410, 23J, BRG, GJS, Adj.6P, DR	175	225	400
410, 23J, BRG, GJS, Adj.6P, DR, **14K, OF**	275	350	500

ILLINOIS
8 SIZE

Grade or Name — Description	Avg	Ex-Fn	Mint
Arlington, 7J, ...★	$150	$175	$300
Rose LeLand, 13J, ...★★	225	250	400
Stanley, 7J, ...★★	200	250	400
Mary Stuart, 15J, ...★★	200	250	400
Sunnyside, 11J, ...★	50	70	100
151, 7J, 3/4	30	40	75
152, 11J, 3/4	30	40	85
155, 11J, 3/4	30	40	95
Illinois W. Co., 11-15J, (nameless unmarked grades)	30	40	100
Illinois W. Co., 16-17J, (nameless unmarked grades)	30	40	125

Note: Add $10 to $20 more for above watches in hunting case.

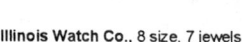

Illinois Watch Co., 8 size, 7 jewels

Grade 144, 6 size, 15 jewels, serial number 5,902,290.

ILLINOIS
6 SIZE

Grade or Name — Description	Avg	Ex-Fn	Mint
Illinois W. Co., 7J, LS, HC, **14K**	$175	$250	$325
Illinois W. Co., 7J, HC	30	40	150
Illinois W. Co., 7J, OF, Coin	30	40	100
Illinois W. Co., 11-12-13J, OF, HC	30	40	125
Illinois W. Co., 15J, OF, HC, **14K**	175	275	400
Illinois W. Co., 17J, OF, HC	35	50	125
Illinois W. Co., 19J, OF, HC	35	50	150
Plymouth Watch Co., 17J, OF, HC, (sold by Sears)	35	50	125
Sears & Roebuck Special, 15J, HC	35	50	85
Washington W. Co., 15J, Liberty Bell, HC	75	100	225
Washington W. Co., 11J, Martha Washington, HC	100	150	300

ILLINOIS
4 SIZE

Grade or Name — Description	Avg	Ex-Fn	Mint
Illinois W. Co., 7J, LS, HC	$40	$60	$125
Illinois W. Co., 11J, LS, HC	40	60	125
Illinois W. Co., 15-16J, LS, HC	40	60	125

ILLINOIS
0 SIZE

Grade or Name — Description	Avg	Ex-Fn	Mint
Accuratus, 17J, OF	$60	$70	$150
Ariste, 11-15-17J, OF & HC	100	135	200
Burlington Special, 15-17J, 3/4, OF	100	125	200
Illinois W. Co., 7 to 17J, LS, HC, 14K	200	250	400
201, 11J, BRG, NI	50	60	150
203, 15J, BRG, NI	50	60	150
204, 17J, BRG, NI	50	60	150
Interstate Chronometer, 15J, HC, SW	100	150	300
Interstate Chronometer, 17J, HC, SW	100	150	300
Lady Franklin, 15-17J, HC	50	60	165
Plymouth Watch Co., 15-17J, HC, (sold by Sears)	95	100	125
Santa Fe Special, 15-17J ★	150	200	300
Washington W. Co., Liberty Bell, 15J, ADJ	60	80	150
Washington W. Co., Mt. Vernon, 17J, ADJ	70	100	200

Washington W. Co., Mt. Vernon,
0 size, 17J, hunting case.

Grade **203**, 0 size, 15 jewels, originally sold for $10.40

Grade **204**, 0 size, 17 jewels, originally sold for $12.83.

ILLINOIS
CAPRICE

Grade or Name — Description	Avg	Ex-Fn	Mint
Caprice, 17J, handbag, pocket or desk watch, snake or ostrich	$100	$150	$250

Ca. 1929 AD

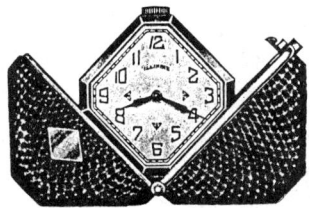

The CAPRICE

Just the watch for the handbag, pocket or desk; for sports wear or dress. It's an entirely practical timekeeper, too. In genuine coverings of snake or ostrich. 17 jewels, 14K gold filled inner case   **$50**

Rigid bow 60 HR. MODEL
gold filled: $175 - $225 - $300
14K gold: $300 - $400 - $550

Antique bow MODEL
gold filled: $100 - $120 - $160
14K gold: $275 - $380 - $450

FIRST MODEL
gold filled: $110 - $135 - $250

Stiff bow 60 HR. MODEL
gold filled: $200 - $250 - $300
14K gold: $360 - $400 - $700

Empire bow MODEL
gold filled: $100 - $120 - $180
14K gold: $300 - $400 - $575

MODEL 28
gold filled: $135 - $160 - $240
gold filled **2 tone**: $150 - $175 - $300

MODEL 29
gold filled: $110 - $135 - $200

MODEL 107
gold filled: $110 - $125 - $200

MODEL 28, 173 & 206=combination white & yellow gold-filled
models Solid Gold cases= rigid bow
Gold-filled cases (1st. model), (antique), (rigid bow), 28, 29, 107, 108, 128, 173, 181, 193, & 206

🕐 NOTE: Factory Advertised as a **complete** watch and was fitted with a certain matched, timed
and rated movement and sold in the factory designed case style as a **complete** watch. The factory
also sold _uncased_ movements to **JOBBERS** such as Jewelry stores & they cased the movement in
a case styles the **CUSTOMER requested.** All the factory advertised **complete** watches came with
the dial **SHOWN or CHOICE** of other **Railroad** dials.

MODEL 108
gold filled: $110 - $125 - $165

MODEL 128
gold **plated**: $60 - $75 - $110

MODEL 173
gold filled: $110 - $135 - $190
gold filled **2 tone**: $150 - $175 - $250

MODEL 193
gold filled: $110 - $135 - $190

MODEL 181
gold filled: $110 - $125 - $180

MODEL 206
gold filled: $100 - $120 - $175
gold filled **2 tone**: $110 - $140 - $200

BUNN SPECIALS were packed & shipped
in a ALUMINUM cigarette style box.
$50 — $75 — $150

MODEL 28, 173 & 206=combination white & yellow gold-filled
models Solid Gold cases= rigid bow
Gold-filled cases (1st. model), (antique), (rigid bow), 28, 29, 107, 108, 128, 173, 181, 193, & 206

🕐 NOTE: Factory Advertised as a **complete** watch and was fitted with a certain matched, timed and rated movement and sold in the factory designed case style as a **complete** watch. The factory also sold _uncased_ movements to **JOBBERS** such as Jewelry stores & they cased the movement in a case styles the **CUSTOMER** requested. All the factory advertised **complete** watches came with the dial **SHOWN** or **CHOICE** of other **Railroad** dials.

ILLINOIS SPRINGFIELD WATCH CO.
IDENTIFICATION OF MOVEMENTS
BY MODEL NUMBER

How to Identify Your Watch: Compare the movement of your watch with the illustrations in this section. Upon matching the movement exactly, the model number and size can be determined. While comparing, note the location of the balance, jewels, screws, gears, and type of back plate (Full, 3/4, Bridge) which will be clues in identifying the movement you have. Having determined the size and model number, you can now find your watch in the main price listing by name or number (which is engraved on the movement).

THE ILLINOIS WATCH CO. GRADE AND MODEL CHART

Size	Model	Plate Design	Setting	Hunting or Open Face	Type Barrel	Started w/ Serial No.	Remarks
18	1	Full	Key	Htg	Reg	1	Course train
	2	Full	Lever	Htg	Reg	38,901	Course train
	3	Full	Lever	OF	Reg	46,201	Course train, 5th pinion
	4	Full	Pendant	OF	Reg	1,050,001	Fast train
	5	Full	Lever	Htg	Reg	1,256,101	Fast train, RR Grade
	6	Full	Lever	OF	Reg	1,144,401	Fast train, RR Grade
16	1	Full	Lever	Htg	Reg	1,030,001	Thick model
	2	Full	Pendant	OF	Reg	1,037,001	Thick model
	3	Full	Lever	OF	Reg	1,038,001	Thick model
	4	¾ & brg	Lever	Htg	Reg	1,300,001	Getty model
	5	¾ & brg	Lever	OF	Reg	1,300,601	Getty model
	6	¾ & brg	Pendant	Htg	Reg	2,160,111	DR & Improved RR model
	7	¾ & brg	Pendant	OF	Reg	2,160,011	DR & Improved RR model
	8	¾ & brg	Lever	Htg	Reg	2,523,101	DR & Improved RR model
	9	¾ & brg	Lever	OF	Reg	2,522,001	DR & Improved model
	10	Cent brg	Lever	OF	Motor	3,178,901	Also 17S Ex Thin RR gr 48 hr
	11	¾	Lever & Pen	OF	Motor	4,001,001	RR grade 48 hr
	12	¾	Lever & Pen	Htg	Motor	4,002,001	RR grade 48 hr
	13	Cent brg	Lever	OF	Motor	4,166,801	Also 17S RR grade 60 hr
	14	¾	Lever	OF	Motor	4,492,501	RR grade 60 hr
	15	¾	Lever	OF	Motor	5,488,301	RR grade 60 hr Elinvar
14	1	Full	Lever	Htg	Reg	1,009,501	Thick model
	2	Full	Pendant	OF	Reg	1,000,001	Thick model
	3	Full	Lever	OF	Reg	1,001,001	Thick model
13	1	brg	Pendant	OF	Motor		Ex Thin gr 538 & 539
12	1	¾	Pendant	OF	Reg	1,685,001	
Thin	2	¾	Pendant	Htg	Reg	1,748,751	
	3	Cent brg	Pendant	OF	Reg	2,337,011	Center bridge
	4	Cent brg	Pendant	Htg	Reg	2,337,001	Center bridge
	5	Cent brg	Pendant	OF	Motor	3,742,201	Center bridge
	6	Cent brg	Pendant	Htg	Motor	4,395,301	Center bridge
12T	1	True Ctr brg	Pendant	OF	Motor	3,700,001	1 tooth click, Also 13S
	2	True Ctr brg	Pendant	OF	Motor	3,869,301	5 tooth click
	3	¾	Pendant	OF	Motor	3,869,201	2 tooth click
8	1	Full	Key or lever	Htg	Reg	100,001	Plate not recessed
	2	Full	Lever	Htg	Reg	100,101	Plate is recessed
6	1	¾	Lever	Htg	Reg	552,001	
4	1	¾	Lever	Htg	Reg	551,501	
0	1	¾	Pendant	OF	Reg	1,815,901	
	2	¾	Pendant	Htg	Reg	1,749,801	
	3	Cent brg	Pendant	OF	Reg	2,644,001	
	4	Cent brg	Pendant	Htg	Reg	2,637,001	

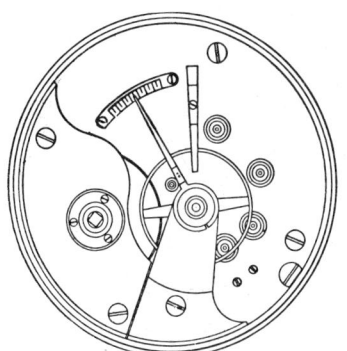

Model 1, 18 size, hunting, key wind & set.

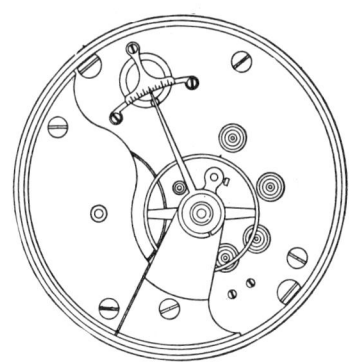

Model 2, 18 size, hunting, lever set, coarse train.

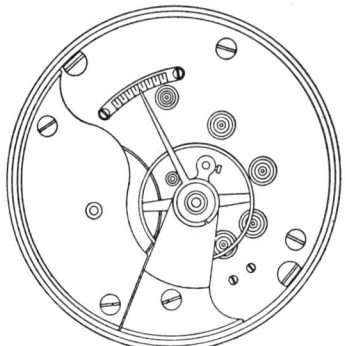

Model 3, 18 size, open face, lever set, coarse train, with fifth pinion.

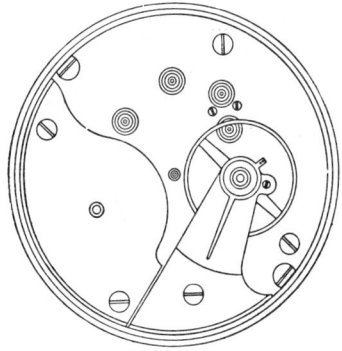

Model 4, 18 size, open face, pendant set, fine train.

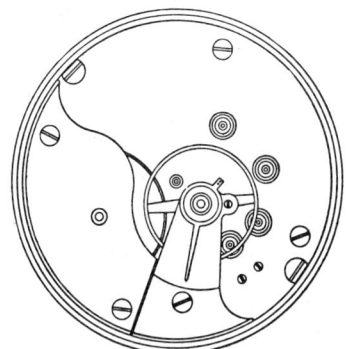

Model 5, 18 size, hunting, lever set, fine train.

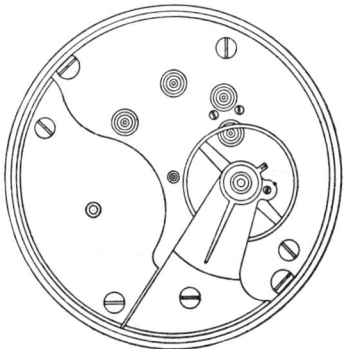

Model 6, 18 size, open face, lever set, fine train.

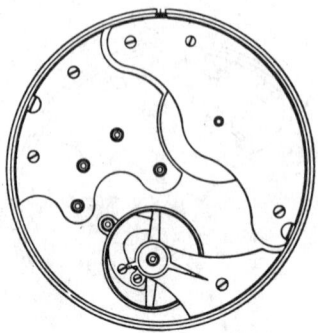

Model 1, 16 size, hunting, lever set.

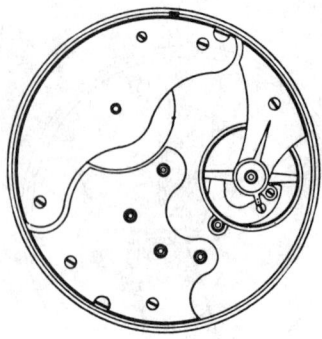

Model 2, 16 size, open face, pendant set.

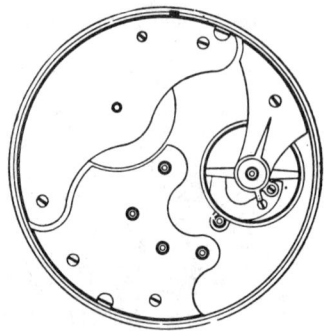

Model 3, 16 size, open face, lever set

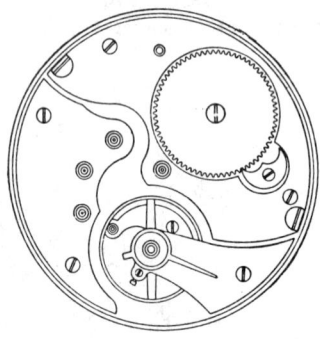

Model 4, 16 size, three-quarter plate, hunting, lever set.

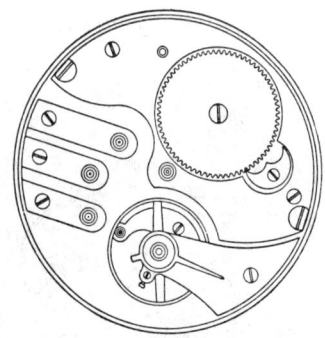

Model 4, 16 size, three-quarter plate, bridge, hunting, lever set.

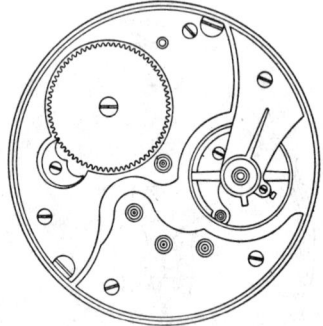

Model 5, 16 size, three-quarter plate, open face, lever set.

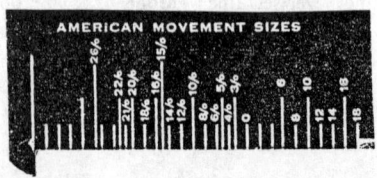

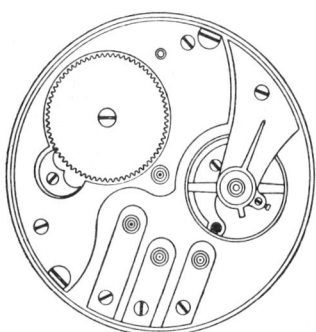

Model 5, 16 size, three-quarter plate, bridge, open face, lever set.

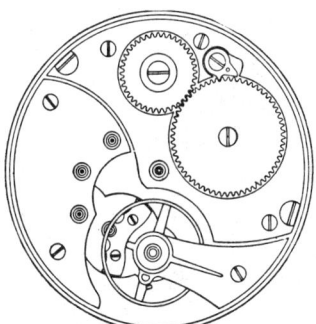

Model 6, 16 size - Pendant set
Model 8, 16 size - Lever set
hunting, three-quarter plate

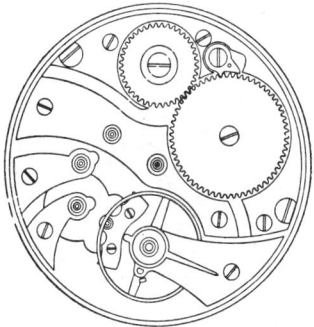

Model 6, 16 size - Pendant set
Model 8, 16 size - Lever set
hunting, bridge model

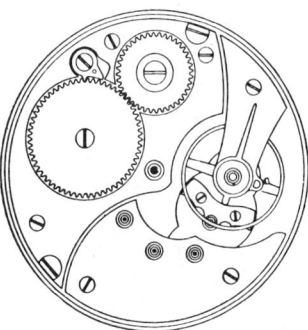

Model 7, 16 size - Pendant set
Model 9, 16 size - Lever set
open face, three-quarter plate

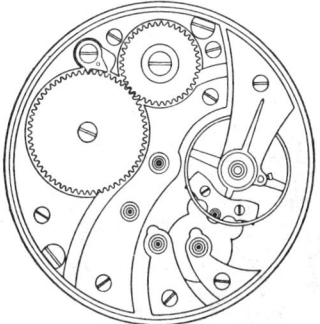

Model 7, 16 size - Pendant set
Model 9, 16 size - Lever set
open face, bridge model

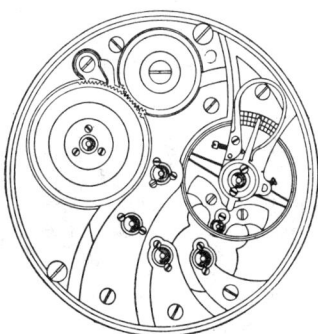

Model 10, 16 size, bridge, extra thin, open face, lever set, motor barrel.

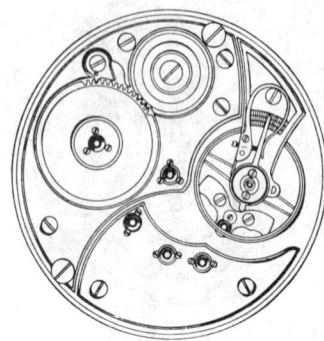

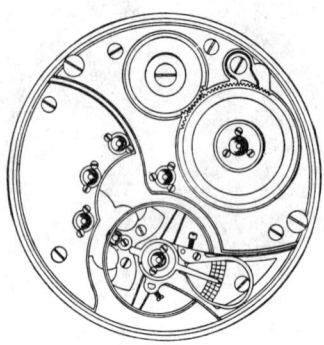

Model 11, 16 size, three-quarter plate, open face, pendant set, motor barrel.

Model 12, 16 size, three-quarter plate, hunting, pendant set, motor barrel.

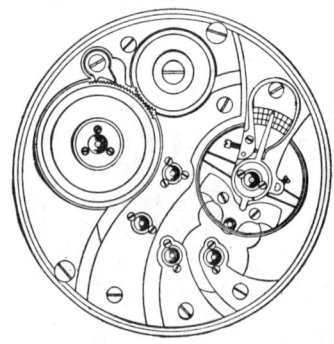

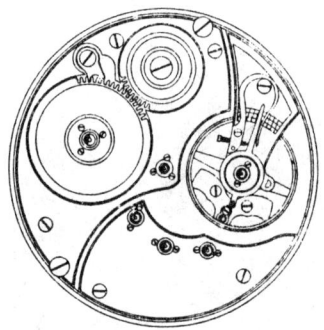

Model 13, 17 size, bridge, open face, lever set, motor barrel.(no red border on bal. cock)

Model 14, 16 size, three-quarter plate, open face, lever set, 60-hour motor barrel.

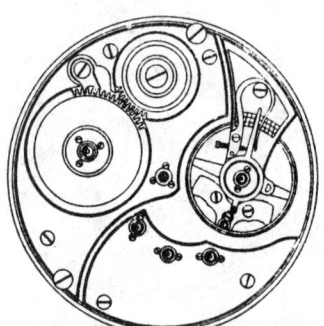

Model 15, 60 Hr. Elinvar.

Model B, 16 size, hunting case.

Model C, 16 size, open face

Model D, 16 size, open face

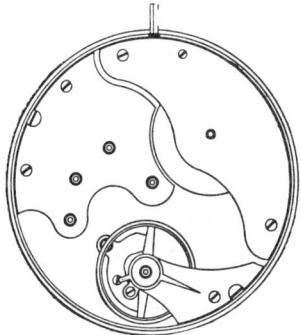

Model 1, 14 size, hunting, lever set.

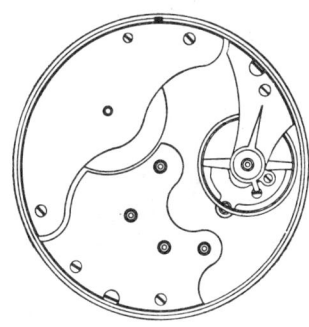

Model 2, 14 size, open face, pendant set.

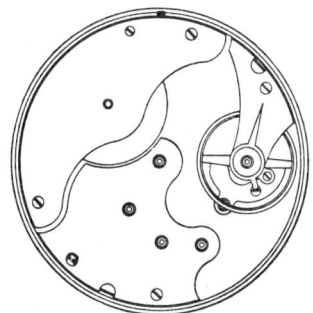

Model 3, 14 size, open face, lever set.

Model 1, 13 size, bridge, extra thin, open face, pendant set, motor barrel.

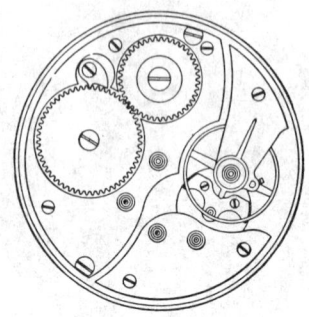 

Model 1, 12 size, three-quarter plate, open face, pendant set.

Model 1, 12 size, three-quarter plate, bridge, open face, pendant set.

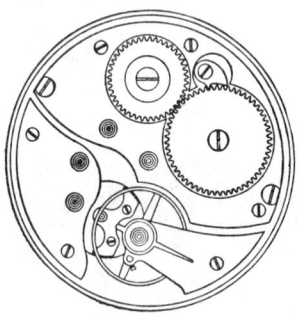 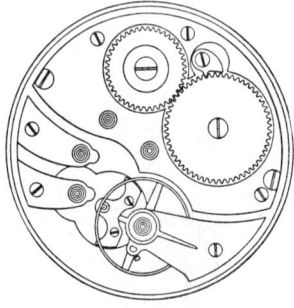

Model 2, 12 size, three-quarter plate, hunting, pendant set.

Model 2, 12 size, three-quarter plate, bridge, hunting, pendant set.

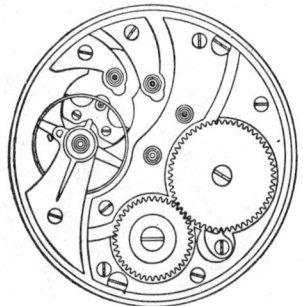 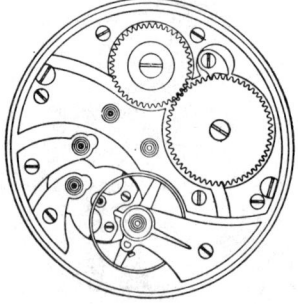

Model 3, 12 size, Model 4, 12 & 14 size, bridge, open face, pendant set.

Model 4, 12 size, bridge, hunting, pendant set.

Model 5, 12 size, bridge, open face, pendant set, motor barrel.

Model 1, 12 size, extra thin, bridge, open face, pendant set, motor barrel.

Model 2, 12 size, extra thin, bridge, open face, pendant set, motor barrel.

Model 3, 12 size, extra thin, three-quarter plate, open face, pendant set, motor barrel.

Model A, 12 size, bridge, open face.

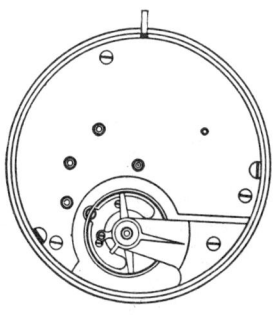

Model 1, 8 size, hunting, key or lever set.

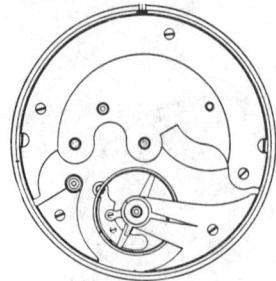  

Model 2, 8 size, hunting, lever set.

Model 1, 6 size, hunting, lever set.

Model 1, 4 size, hunting, lever set.

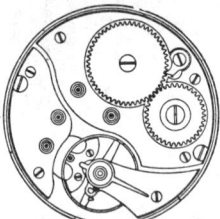 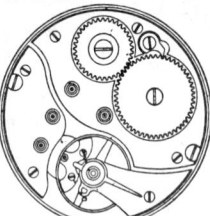 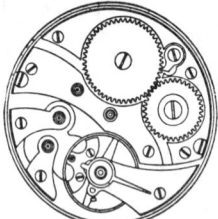

Model 1, 0 size, three-quarter plate, open face, pendant set.

Model 2, 0 size, three-quarter plate, hunting, pendant set.

Model 3, 0 size, bridge, open face, pendant set.

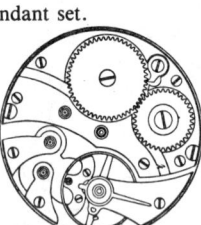 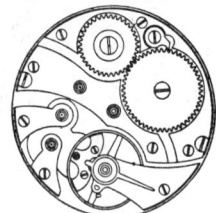

Model 4, 0 size, bridge, hunting, pendant set.

Model 3, 3/0 size, bridge, open face, pendant set.

Model 4, 3/0 size, bridge, hunting, pendant set.

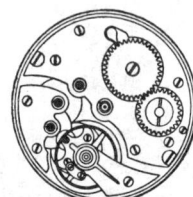

Model 1, 6/0 size, three-quarter plate, open face, pendant set.

Model 2, 6/0 size, bridge, open face, pendant set.

No. 5277–269-D

18, 16, 12 Sizes S. S. & D. S.

Spread 12, 8, 6, 4, 0 & 3/0 Sizes S. S. Only

INDEPENDENT WATCH CO.
Fredonia, New York
1875 - 1881

The California Watch Company was idle for two years before it was purchased by brothers E. W. Howard and C. M. Howard. They had been selling watches by mail for sometime and started engraving the Howard Bros. name on them and using American-made watches. Their chief supply came from Hampden Watch Co., Illinois W. Co., U. S. Watch Co. of Marion. The brothers formed the Independent Watch Co. in 1880, but it was not a watch factory in the true sense. They had other manufacturers engrave the Independent Watch Co. name on the top plates and on the dials of their watches. These watches were sold by mail order and sent to the buyer C. O. D. The names used on the movements were "Howard Bros.," "Independent Watch Co.," "Fredonia Watch Co.," and "Lakeshore Watch Co., Fredonia, N. Y."

The company later decided to manufacture watches and used the name Fredonia Watch Co., but they found that selling watches two different ways was not very good. The business survived until 1881 at which time the owners decided to move the plant to a new location at Peoria, Illinois. Approximately180,000 watches were made that sold for $16.00.

CHRONOLOGY OF THE DEVELOPMENT OF INDEPENDENT WATCH CO.

Independent Watch Co. 1875–1881
Fredonia Watch Co. ..,.............................. 1881–1885
Peoria Watch Co. 1885–1889

18 SIZE

Grade or Name — Description	Avg	Ex-Fn	Mint
18S, 7J, KW, KS, OF, made by U.S. W. Co. Marion, with expanded butterfly cutout ★	$350	$400	$600
18S, 11J, KW, KS, by Hampden	150	250	375
18S, 11J, KW, KS, Coin	175	225	350
18S, 11J, KW, KS	175	225	350
18S, 15J, KW, KS	200	300	350
18S, Howard Bros., 11J, KW, KS	300	400	550
18S, Independent W. Co., 11J, by Illinois W. Co.	175	250	400
18S, Independent W. Co., 15J, transition model by Illinois W. Co.	200	300	450
18S, Lakeshore W. Co., 15J, KW, HC, by N.Y. W. Co.	300	350	450

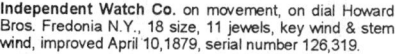

Independent Watch Co. on movement, on dial Howard Bros. Fredonia N.Y., 18 size, 11 jewels, key wind & stem wind, improved April 10,1879, serial number 126,319.

Independent Watch Co., 18 size, 15 jewels, key wind, made by U.S. Marion Watch Co., note expanded butterfly cutout, serial number 192,661.

🕐 Watches listed in this book are priced at the **collectable fair market value** at the RETAIL level, as complete watches having an original 14k gold filled case, KEY WIND with silver, an original white enamel single sunk dial, and with the entire original movement in good working order with no repairs needed, unless otherwise noted.

ROBERT H. INGERSOLL & BROS.
New York, New York
1892 - 1922

In 1892 this company published a catalog for the mail order trade. It listed men's watch chains and a "silverine" Swiss watch for $3.95. The first 1,000 said "The Universal Watch," and introduced that same year to the dealers. The watches with jewels; "Reliance" (seven) introduced about 1917. By 1899 the output was 8,000 per day and in 1901 Ingersoll advertised for sale by 10,000 dealers at $1.00 in U.S.A. and Canada. In 1916, Ingersoll's production was 16,000 a day. The slogan was "The Watch that Made the Dollar Famous." The first 1,000 watches were made by Waterbury Clock Co. Ingersoll bought the Trenton W. Co. in 1908 and the New England W. Co. in 1914. By 1922 the Ingersoll line was completely taken over by Waterbury. U. S. Time Corp. acquired Waterbury in 1944 and continued to use the Ingersoll name on certain watches.

ESTIMATED SERIAL NUMBERS
AND PRODUCTION DATES

DATE—SERIAL NO.	DATE—SERIAL NO.	DATE—SERIAL NO.	DATE—SERIAL NO.
1892 – 150,000	1902 – 7,200,000	1912 – 38,500,000	1922 – 60,500,000
1893 – 310,000	1903 – 7,900,000	1913 – 40,000,000	1923 – 62,000,000
1894 – 650,000	1904 – 8,100,000	1914 – 41,500,000	1924 – 65,000,000
1895 – 1,000,000	1905 –10,000,000	1915 – 42,500,000	1925 – 67,500,000
1896 – 2,000,000	1906 –12,500,000	1916 – 45,500,000	1926 – 69,000,000
1897 – 2,900,000	1907 –15,000,000	1917 – 47,000,000	1927 – 70,500,000
1898 – 3,500,000	1908 –17,500,000	1918 – 47,500,000	1928 – 71,500,000
1899 – 3,750,000	1909 –20,000,000	1919 – 50,000,000	1929 – 73,500,000
1900 – 6,000,000	1910 –25,000,000	1920 – 55,000,000	1930 – 75,000,000
1901 – 6,700,000	1911 –30,000,000	1921 – 58,000,000	1944 – 95,000,000

The above list is provided for determining the APPROXIMATE age of your watch. Match serial number with date. Watches were not necessarily sold in the exact order of manufactured date.

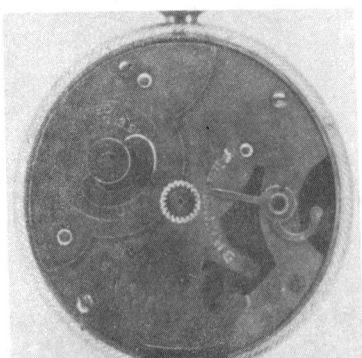

Ingersoll Back Wind & Set, patent date Dec. 23, 1890 and Jan. 13, 1891, c. late 1890s.

Ingersoll, engraved movement also pin set..

Ingersoll, Celluloid Case in Black or White.

Ingersoll, Blind Man's Watch.

INGERSOLL DOLLAR TYPE

NOTE: Prices are for complete watch in **good running order**. In some specialty markets, the comic character watches may bring higher prices in top condition.

Grade or Name — Description	Avg	Ex-Fn	Mint
Ingersoll Early **Back Wind** Models, (with cover plate)	$50	$60	$75
Ingersoll **Back Wind** Models	40	50	65
Ingersoll, Pin set or Rim set & Fancy **engraved** movement	75	100	135
Admiral Dewey, "Flagship Olympia" on back of case .... ★★★★	350	400	600
Advance, (revolving seconds)	40	45	65
American Pride	75	100	125
Are U My Neighbor	40	45	65
B. B. H. Special, Backwind	65	75	100
Blind Man Pocket Watch	50	75	120
Boer War, on dial **Souvenier of South African War 1900** .... ★★★★★	900	1,100	1,600
Buck	40	45	75
Calendar (on moveable calendar on back of case)	75	85	125
Celluloid Case in Black or White	100	135	185
Champion (many models)	50	75	125
Chancery	50	75	125
Chicago Expo. 1933 ★	300	400	600
Climax	40	45	95
Cloverine	60	70	85
Colby	40	45	65
Columbus (3 ships on back of case), 1893 ★★	300	400	600
Connecticut W. Co.	40	45	65
Cord	40	45	75
Crown	40	45	65
Dan Dee	40	45	65
Defiance	40	45	65
Delaware W. Co.	40	45	65
Devon Mfg. Co.	40	45	65
Eclipse (many models)	40	45	65
Eclipse Radiolite	45	65	75
Endura	40	45	65
Ensign	40	45	65
Escort	40	45	65

Scout watch (Be prepared)

Yankee watch with bicycle on dial.

NOTE : ADD $25 to $100 for original BOX and PAPERS

🕐 Pricing in this Guide are fair market price for **COMPLETE** watches which are reflected from the "**NAWCC**" National and regional shows.

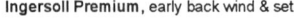

Ingersoll Premium, early back wind & set.   Ingersoll Triumph, note pin or rim setting.

Grade or Name — Description	Avg	Ex-Fn	Mint
Fancy Dials (unfaded to be mint)	$125	$150	$300
Freedom	40	45	65
Gotham	40	45	65
Graceline	45	50	65
Gregg	40	45	65
Junior (several models)	40	45	65
Junior Radiolite	40	45	65
Kelton	40	45	65
Lapel Watches	30	45	65
Leader	30	45	65
Leeds	30	45	65
Leonard Watch Co. ★★	60	75	95
Liberty U.S.A., backwind	75	100	200
Liberty Watch Co.	35	45	75
Limited, LEVER SET ON CASE RIM OF WATCH	50	60	120
Major	45	50	65
Maple Leaf	45	50	65
Master Craft	45	50	65
Midget (several models)	40	50	75
Midget , 6 size, "patd. Jan. 29 -01," Damaskeened, fancy case	75	100	150
Monarch	45	50	65
New West	45	50	65
New York World's Fair, 1939 ★	200	300	500
Overland	40	50	65
Pan American Expo., Buffalo, 1901 ★	275	350	500
Paris World Expo., 1900 ★	200	275	450
Patrol	45	50	65
Perfection	40	45	55
Pilgram	45	55	65
Premier, back wind, eagle on back, c. 1894 ★	95	125	300

NOTE : ADD $25 to $75 for original BOX and PAPERS

🕐 Pricing in this Guide are fair market price for **COMPLETE** watches which are reflected from the "**NAWCC**" National and regional shows.

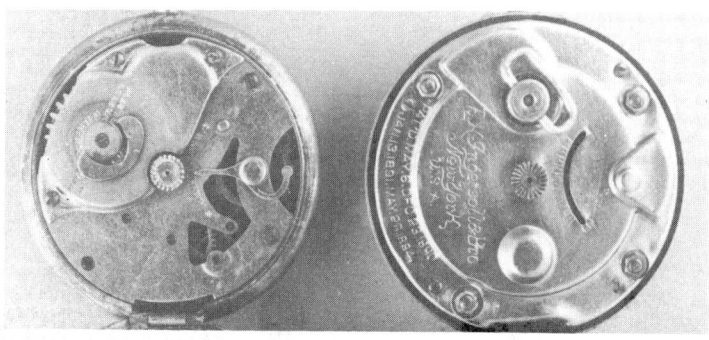

Left: Ingersoll Back Wind, c. 1895.   **Right:** Yankee Back Wind, c. 1893.

Grade or Name — Description	Avg	Ex-Fn	Mint
Premium Back Wind and Set	$60	$75	$125
Progress, 1933 World's Fair Chicago ★	250	275	500
Puritan	40	50	75
Quaker	40	45	65
Radiolite	45	65	75
Reliance, 7J	60	75	95
Remington W. Co. USA	60	75	100
Rotary International, c. 1920	50	65	80
Royal	45	50	65
St. Louis World's Fair (two models) ★ ★	250	300	500
The Saturday Post	70	100	225
Senator	40	50	65
Senior	45	50	65
Sir Leeds	35	40	50
Solar	35	40	50
Souvenir Special	50	75	100
Sterling	35	40	50
Ten Hune	60	70	85
Traveler with Bed Side Stand	35	45	65
Triumph	100	125	150
Triumph Pin set or rim set, large crown, engine turned case (early model) with engraved barrel or movement	125	150	275
True Test	35	45	55
Trump	35	45	55
USA (two models)	50	75	100
Universal, 1st model	200	250	300
Uncle Sam	45	55	65
George Washington	150	175	275
Waterbury (several models)	40	60	90

WATERBURY **CLOCK** CO. 35 size (Duke or Duchess models)
   pat. Jan.15,1878, May,6.90, Dec.23,90, Jan.13,91 on movement
   equivalent to Ingersoll BIG WATCH, (Waterbury on dial)...   100   150   250

NOTE : ADD $25 to $100 for original BOX and PAPERS

🕐 Pricing in this Guide are fair market price for **COMPLETE** watches which are reflected from the "**NAWCC**" National and regional shows.

Grade or Name — Description	Avg	Ex-Fn	Mint
Winner	$40	$45	$65
Winner, with Screw Back & Bezel.	65	75	100
Yankee Backwind	85	95	150
Yankee Bicycle Watch (sold for $1.00 in 1896)	175	200	300
Yankee Radiolite	55	65	85
Yankee Radiolite with Screw Back & Bezel.	75	100	135
Yankee Special (many models)	75	100	150
Yankee, Perpetual calendar on back of case	100	125	195

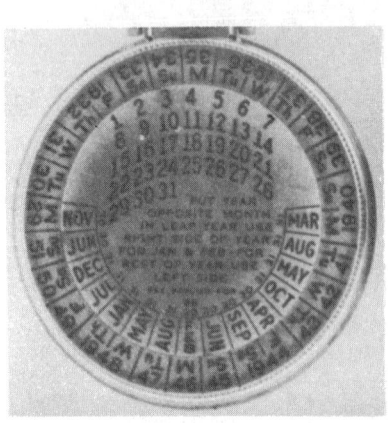

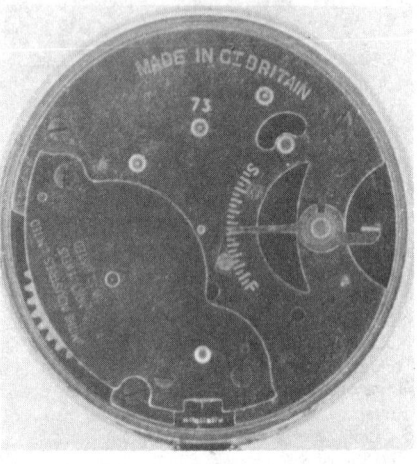

Ingersoll moveable calendar for years 1929-1951 located on back of case.

Ingersoll movement made in Great Britain.

INGERSOLL LTD.
(GREAT BRITAIN)

Grade or Name — Description	Avg	Ex-Fn	Mint
Ingersoll Ltd. (many models)	$65	$75	$100
Coronation, Elizabeth II on watch	175	200	300
Coronation, June 2, 1953 on dial	175	200	300
16S, 7J, 3F Brg	65	75	95
16S, 15J, 3F Brg	85	95	125
16S, 17J, 3F Brg, ADJ	125	145	175
16S, 19J, 3F Brg, Adj5P	150	175	325
12S, 4J	45	65	85

E. INGRAHAM CO.
Bristol, Connecticut 1912 - 1968

The E. Ingraham Co. purchased the Bannatyne Co. in 1912. They produced their first pocket watch in 1913. A total of about 65 million pocket watches and over 12 million wrist watches were produced before they started to import watches in 1968.

Grade or Name — Description	Avg	Ex-Fn	Mint
Ingraham W. Co. (many models)	$30	$40	$55
Allure	30	40	55
Aristocrat Railroad Special	50	65	75
Autocrat	30	45	65
Basketball & Football Timer	40	45	65
Beacon	30	40	55
Biltmore	30	40	55
Biltmore Radium dial	50	65	85
Bristol	30	40	55
Clipper	30	40	55
Co-Ed	30	40	55
Comet	50	60	90
Companion, sweep second hand	50	65	85
Cub	25	30	45
Dale	30	40	55
Demi–hunter style cover	65	75	100
Digital seconds dial, (no second hand but a digital seconds on dial)	60	70	90
Dixie	30	45	50
Dot	30	45	50
Endura	30	45	50
Everbrite (all models)	40	50	65
Graceline,	30	45	50
Ingraham USA	30	45	50
Jockey	30	45	50
Laddie	25	30	40
Laddie Athlete	40	45	55
Lady's Purse Watch, with fancy bezel	45	50	65
Lendix Extra	30	45	50
Master	25	30	40
Master Craft	30	45	50
Miss Ingraham	25	30	40
New York to Paris(with box for mint) ★	225	275	450
Overland	45	50	65
The Pal	30	45	50

INGRAHAM, Seven Seas, shows standard time, & Nautical time.

New York to Paris, with airplane model on dial, engraved bezel, commemorating Lindbergh's famous flight.

🕐 Prices are for complete watch in **good running order**. In some specialty markets, the comic character watches may bring higher prices in top condition.

NOTE : ADD $25 to $75 for original BOX and PAPERS

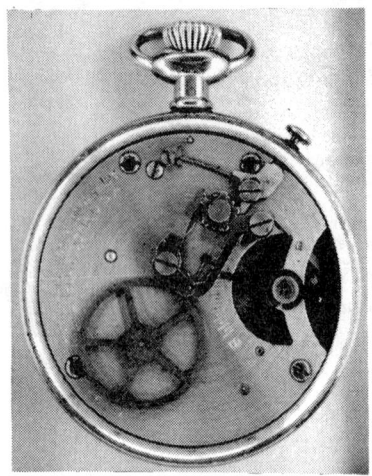

Pastor Stop Watch, Sterling W. Co. printed on dial, with start stop & fly back to zero function. The Sterling Watch Company, Inc. Waterbury, Conn. U.S.A. on movement

Grade or Name — Description	Avg	Ex-Fn	Mint
Pastor Stop Watch, (Sterling W. Co), fly back to zero...............★	$125	$175	$300
Pathfinder, compass on pendant..	95	125	200

Path Finder showing compass in crown.   Printed on dial, "Unbreakable crystal," ca. 1924.

Grade or Name — Description	Avg	Ex-Fn	Mint
Patriot	$125	$150	$250
Peerless..	30	35	55
Pilot	40	50	65
Pocket Pal..	30	45	50
Pony..	30	45	50
Pride	30	45	50
Princess	30	45	50
Prince..	30	45	50
Professional..	30	35	45
Pup...	30	45	50
Reliance...	45	50	65
Rex	30	45	50
Rite Time...	30	45	50
St. Regis	30	45	50
Secometer..	40	50	65
Sentinel..	30	45	50
Sentinel Click...	30	45	50
Sentinel Fold Up Travel	50	65	75
Sentry	30	45	50
Seven Seas, 24 hr. dial & nautical dial...............................	50	80	125
Silver Star..	30	45	50

Grade or Name — Description	Avg	Ex-Fn	Mint
Sturdy	$30	$45	$50
Target	30	45	50
The Best	30	45	50
The Pal	30	45	50
Time Ball	40	50	65
Time & Time	30	40	55
Top Flight	35	45	55
Top Notch	35	45	55
Tower	30	45	50

Trail Blazer, Commemorating Byrd's Antarctic Expedition.   Showing back side of Trail Blazer, also depicted on box.

FOB ☞   **ABOVE, BOX** - Same as depicted on BACK of watch.

Grade or Name — Description	Avg	Ex-Fn	Mint
Trail Blazer, Commemorating BYRD'S Antarctic Expedition	$200	$250	$500
Trail Blazer, Commemorating BYRD'S Antarctic Expedition, *all original* **watch**, with **fob** (wings over the pole), + **box** ★★★	500	600	1,000
Treasure	15	20	25
Unbreakable Crystal	45	50	65
Uncle Sam (all models)	50	75	95
Uncle Sam Backwind & Set	125	150	225
United	30	35	40
Viceroy	30	45	50
Victory	30	45	50
Wings	40	50	65

Example of a basic **International Watch Co.** movement with patent dates of Aug. 19, 1902, Jan. 27, 1903 & Aug. 11, 1903.

International Watch Co., "Highland" on dial.

INTERNATIONAL WATCH CO.

Newark City, New Jersey

1902 - 1907

This company produced only non-jeweled or low-cost production type watches that were inexpensive and nickel plated. Names on their watches include: Berkshire, Madison, and Mascot.

Grade or Name — Description		Avg	Ex-Fn	Mint
18 Size, skeletonized, pinlever escape., first model	★ ★	$200	$250	$300
Berkshire, OF	★	80	90	200
Highland	★	80	90	200
Madison, 18S, OF	★	80	90	200
Mascot, OF	★	80	90	200

KANKAKEE WATCH CO.

Kankakee, Illinois

1900

This company reportedly became the McIntyre Watch Co. Little or no information is available.

Grade or Name — Description		Avg	Ex-Fn	Mint
16S, BRG, NI	★ ★ ★ ★	$5,500	$6,500	$10,000

🕐 Watches listed in this book are priced at the **collectable fair market value** at the RETAIL level, as complete watches having an original 14k gold filled case, KEY WIND with silver, an original white enamel single sunk dial, and with the entire original movement in good working order with no repairs needed, unless otherwise noted.

KELLY WATCH CO.

Chicago, Illinois
c. 1900

Grade or Name — Description		Avg	Ex-Fn	Mint
16S, aluminum movement and OF case.............................. ★ ★ ★ ★		$250	$300	$450

Kelly Watch Co., 16 size, aluminum movement, straight line lever, quick train, porcelain dial, stem set, reversible ratchet stem wind, originally sold for $2.20, Ca. 1900.

KEYSTONE STANDARD WATCH CO.

Lancaster, Pennsylvania
1886 - 1890

Abram Bitner agreed to buy a large number of stockholders' shares of the Lancaster Watch Co. at 10 cents on the dollar; he ended up with 5,625 shares out of the 8,000 that were available. Some 8,900 movements had been completed but not sold at the time of the shares purchase. The company Bitner formed assumed the name of Keystone Standard Watch Co. as the trademark but in reality existed as the Lancaster Watch Co. The business was sold to **Hamilton Watch Co.** in 1891. Total production was 48,000.

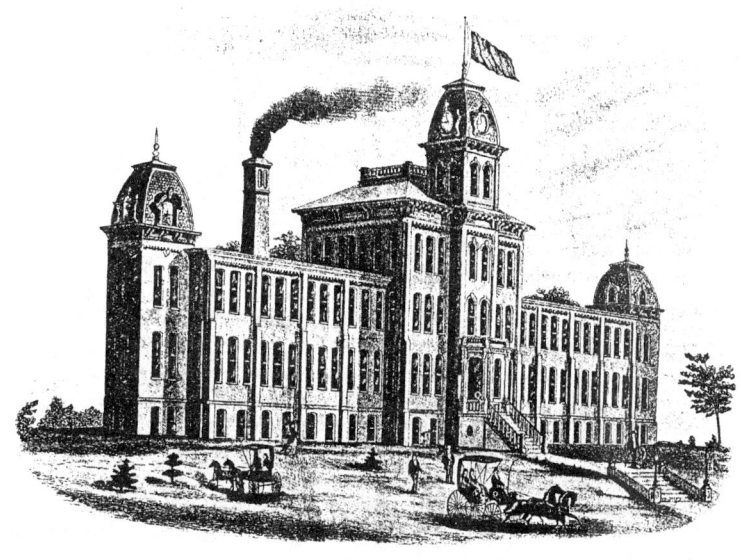

Grade or Name — Description	Avg	Ex-Fn	Mint
18S, 7-15J, OF, KW	$100	$120	$200
18S, 7-15J, OF, SW, 3/4, LS	70	100	150
18S, 15J, dust proof, ADJ...	100	120	225
18S, 11-15J, dust proof, OF...	100	125	175
18S, 11-15J, dust proof, HC..	120	150	225
18S, 17J, dust proof, HC...	150	175	250
18S, 20J, dust proof, HC......................................★ ★	300	450	600
18S, West End, 15J, HC	85	125	175
8S, 11J, dust proof	100	125	175
6S, 7-10J, HC...★	100	140	250

Keystone Watch Co., dust proof model, 18 size, 15 jewels, serial number 352,766.   Knickerbocker movement, 16-18 size, 7 jewels, duplex escapement.

KNICKERBOCKER WATCH CO.

New York, New York
1890 - 1930

This company imported and sold Swiss and low-cost production American watches.

Grade or Name — Description	Avg	Ex-Fn	Mint
18S, 7J, OF, PS, NI, duplex escapement...........................	$50	$65	$125
16S, 7J...	30	45	75
12S, 7J, OF..	30	45	85
10S, Barkley "8 Day" ....★ ★	100	125	200
6S, Duplex...	30	50	75

🕐 Some grades are not included. Their values can be determined by comparing with **similar** age, size, metal content, style, models and grades listed.

🕐 Watches listed in this book are priced at the **collectable fair market value** at the RETAIL level, as complete watches having an original 14k gold filled case, KEY WIND with silver, an original white enamel single sunk dial, and with the entire original movement in good working order with no repairs needed, unless otherwise noted.

🕐 Pricing in this Guide are fair market price for **COMPLETE** watches which are reflected from the "**NAWCC**" National and regional shows.

LANCASTER WATCH CO.

Lancaster, Pennsylvania

1877 - 1886

Work commenced on Sept. 1, 1877, at the Lancaster Watch Co. The watches produced there were designed to sell at a cheaper price than normal. They had a solid top, 3/4 plate, and a pillar plate that was fully ruby-jeweled (4 pairs). They had a gilt and nickel movement and a new stem-wind device, modeled by Mosly & Todd. By mid-1878 the Lancaster Watch Co. had produced 150 movements. Four grades of watches were made: Keystone, Fulton, Franklin, and Melrose. In September 1879 the company had made 334 movements. In 1880 the total was up to 1,250 movements, and by mid-1882 about 17,000 movements had been produced. All totaled, about 20,000 watch movements were made.

About 75, 8-size ladies' watches were also made.

CHRONOLOGY OF THE DEVELOPMENT OF THE LANCASTER WATCH CO.

Adams and Perry Watch Mfg. Co. 1874-1876
Lancaster Watch Co. 1877-1878
Lancaster Pa. Watch Co. 1878-1879
Lancaster Watch Co. 1879-1886
Keystone Standard Co. 1886-1890
Hamilton Watch Co. .... 1892 to present

LANCASTER
18 SIZE
(All 3/4 Plate)

Grade or Name — Description	Avg	Ex-Fn	Mint
Chester, 7-11J, KW, dust proof, gilded	$125	$150	$200
Comet, 7J, NI	125	150	200
Delaware, 20J, ADJ, SW, dust proof, gilded ★	300	350	500
Denver, 7J, dust proof, gilded	50	70	135
Denver, 7J, gilded, dust proof, Silveroid	50	70	100
Elberon, 7J, dust proof	125	150	200
Ben Franklin, 7J, KW, gilded	150	200	375
Ben Franklin, 11J, KW, gilded	175	250	425
Fulton, 7J, ADJ, KW, gilded	70	90	200
Fulton, 11J, ADJ, KW, gilded	70	90	200
Girard, 15J, ADJ, dust proof, gilded	70	90	200
Hoosac, 11J, OF	70	90	225
Keystone, 15J, ADJ, gilded, GJS, dust proof	70	90	175
Keystone, 15J, ADJ, gilded, GJS, Silveroid	70	90	125
Lancaster, 7J, SW	70	90	120
Lancaster, 15J, SW, Silveroid	40	75	100
Lancaster, 15J, OF	40	85	150
Lancaster Pa., 20J, ADJ, NI, ★★★	450	500	650

⊕ Some grades are not included. Their values can be determined by comparing with similar age, size, metal content, style, models and grades listed.

⊕ Watches listed in this book are priced at the **collectable fair market value** at the RETAIL level, as complete watches having an original 14k gold filled case, KEY WIND with silver, an original white enamel single sunk dial, and with the entire original movement in good working order with no repairs needed, unless otherwise noted.

⊕ Pricing in this Guide are fair market price for **COMPLETE** watches which are reflected from the "**NAWCC**" National and regional shows.

Lancaster Watch Co., 18 size, 20 jewels, gold jeweled settings, This is referred to as **Adams & Perry** S# 1747.

Stevens Model, 18 size, 15 jewels, adjusted, dust proof model, swing-out movement, c.1886.

Grade or Name — Description	Avg	Ex-Fn	Mint
Lancaster Watch Co., 20J, ADJ, GJS, about 19 or 20 size, low serial No.			
Referred to as **(Adams & Perry)** model .... ★★★	$1,000	$1,200	$2,000
Malvern, 7J, dust proof, gilded...	60	80	130
Melrose, 15J, NI, ADJ, GJS	75	90	175
Nation Standard American Watch Co., 7J, HC	200	225	300
New Era, 7J, gilded, KW, HC	60	100	150
New Era, 7J, gilded, KW, Silveroid.......................................	60	80	100
Paoli, 7J, NI, dust proof, ...	60	100	150
Wm. Penn, 20J, ADJ, NI, dust proof .... ★	400	500	700
Radnor, 7J, dust proof, gilded	60	80	175
Record, 7J, dust proof, Silveroid.......................................	60	80	125
Record, 15J, NI..	60	80	150

West End, 18 size, 15 jewels, key wind & set, serial number 158,080. c. 1878.

Lancaster movement, 8-10 size, 15 jewels, serial number 317,812.

🕐 Pricing in this Guide are fair market price for **COMPLETE** watches which are reflected from the "**NAWCC**" National and regional shows.

Grade or Name — Description	Avg	Ex-Fn	Mint
Ruby, 7-16J, NI	$140	$180	$300
Sidney, 15J, NI, dust proof,	100	125	200
Stevens, 15J, ADJ, NI, dust proof	150	175	250
West End, 19J, HC, KW, gilded	450	500	600
West End, 15J, HC, KW, KS	100	125	250
West End, 15J, SW	100	125	250
West End, 15J, SW, Silveroid	70	80	125

8 SIZE

Grade or Name — Description	Avg	Ex-Fn	Mint
Cricket, 11J	$40	$50	$100
Diamond, 15J	40	50	100
Echo, 11J	40	50	100
Flora, 7-11J, gilded	40	50	100
Iris, 13J	40	50	100
Lady Penn, 20J, GJS, ADJ, NI ★	300	350	450
Lancaster W. Co., 7J	40	60	100
Pearl, 7J	40	50	100
Red Rose, of Lancaster, 15J	40	50	100
Ruby, 15J	40	50	100

MANHATTAN WATCH CO.

New York, New York
1883 - 1891

The Manhattan Watch Co. made mainly low cost production watches. A complete and full line of watches was made, and most were cased and styled to be sold as a **complete** watch. The watches were generally 16S with full plate movements. The patented winding mechanism was different. These watches were both in hunter and open-face cases and later had a sweep second hand. Total production was 160,000 or more watches.

Manhattan Watch Co., stop watch, 16 size, note the escapement uses upright "D"—shaped pallets (steel), serial number 117,480.

Manhattan Watch Co., 16 size, stop watch. Note the two buttons on top; the right (at 2 o'clock) one sets the hands, the left (at 10 o'clock) starts and stops the watch.

16 SIZE

Grade or Name — Description		Avg	Ex-Fn	Mint
OF, with back wind, base metal case	★	$150	$200	$400
OF, 2 button stop watch, screw back & bezel, enamel dial, gold-filled case	★★	250	300	500
OF, 2 button stop watch, snap back & bezel, paper dial, base metal case	★	150	200	300
HC, 2 button stop watch, snap back & bezel, paper dial, base metal case	★	200	250	350
OF, 1 button, sweep sec., base metal case , paper dial	★	125	175	275
HC, 1 button, sweep sec., base metal case, paper dial	★	200	250	350
Ship's Bell Time Dial, OF or HC	★★★★	325	425	600
Twenty-Four Hour Dial, OF or HC	★★★★	325	425	600
Stallcup, 7J, OF	★	100	150	300

12 SIZE

Grade or Name — Description		Avg	Ex-Fn	Mint
12S	★	$80	$125	$275

Manhattan Watch Co., 16 size, time only watch & note no second hand, the button at Right sets the hands.

Manhattan Watch Co., 16 size, time only with Sweep-Second hand, the button at Right sets the hands.

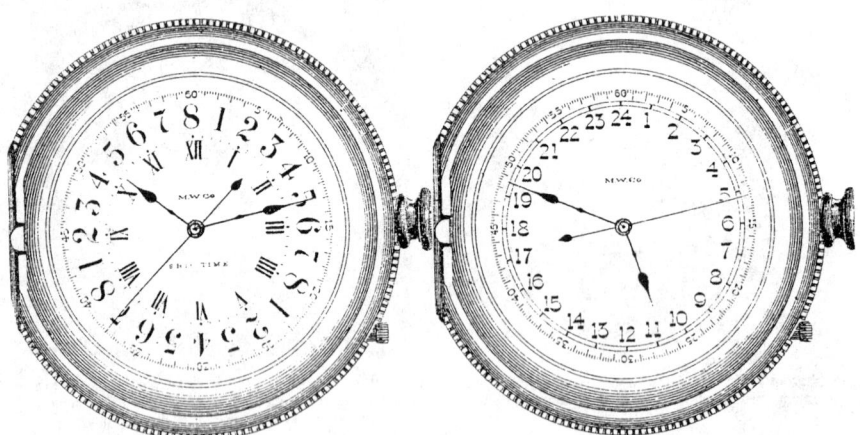

Manhattan Watch Co., 16 size, Ship's Bell Time DIAL for NAUTICAL USES & sweep second hand, Hunting Case.

Manhattan Watch Co., 16 size, with a 24-HOUR DIAL.& sweep second hand, Hunting Case.

MANISTEE WATCH CO.

Manistee, Michigan
1908 - 1912

The Manistee watches, first marketed in 1909, were designed to compete with the low-cost production watches. Dials, jewels, and hairsprings were not produced at the factory. The first movement was 18S, 7J, and sold for about $5. Manistee also made 5J, 15J, 17J, and 21J watches in cheap cases in sizes 16 and 12. Estimated total production was 60,000. Most were sold by Star Watch Case Co.

18 SIZE

Grade or Name —Description	Avg	Ex-Fn	Mint
18S, 7J, 3/4, LS, HC .... ★	$325	$375	$500
18S, 7J, 3/4, LS, OF... ★	275	325	400
18S, 7J, 3/4, LS, OF, gold train.. ★ ★	375	425	500

16 TO 12 SIZE

Grade or Name —Description	Avg	Ex-Fn	Mint
16S, 7J, OF.. ★	$200	$250	$400
16S, 15J, OF.. ★	225	250	400
16S, 15J, HC .... ★	250	275	425
16S, 17J, OF.. ★	225	250	400
16S, 19J, HC .... ★	300	350	500
16S, 21J, OF.. ★	325	375	525
12S, 15J... ★	150	175	300

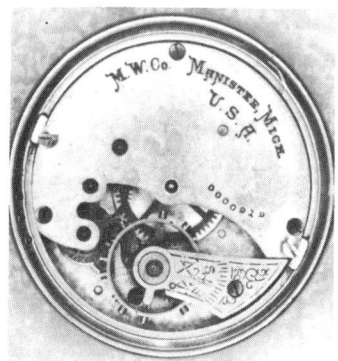
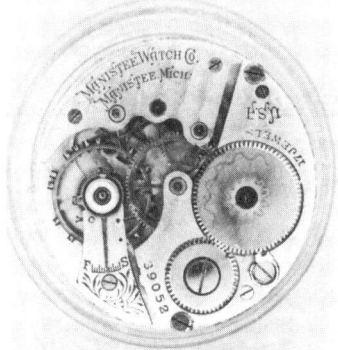

Manistee movement, 18 size, 7 jewels, 3/4 plate, open face, serial number 919.

Manistee movement, 16 size, 17 jewels, three-quarter plate, open face, serial number 39,052.

🕐 Watches listed in this book are priced at the collectable retail level, as **complete** watches having an original 14k gold-filled case and *Key Wind* with silver, an original white enamel single sunk dial, and with the entire original movement in good working order with no repairs needed.

🕐 Some grades are not included. Their values can be determined by comparing with **similar** age, size, metal content, style, models and grades listed.

🕐 Pricing in this Guide are fair market price for **COMPLETE** watches which are reflected from the "<u>**NAWCC**</u>" National and regional shows.

308

McINTYRE WATCH CO.

Kankakee, Illinois
1905 - 1911

This company probably bought the factory from Kankakee Watch Co. In 1908 Charles DeLong was made master watchmaker, and he designed and improved the railroad watches. Only a few watches were made, estimated total production being about **eight watches.**

Grade or Name — Description		Avg	Ex-Fn	Mint
16S, 21J, BRG, NI, WI	★★★★	$4,500	$5,000	$7,000
16S, 25J, BRG, NI, WI, Adj.5P, equidistant escapement	★★★★	5,500	6,000	8,000
12S, 19J, BRG	★★★★	2,000	2,500	3,500

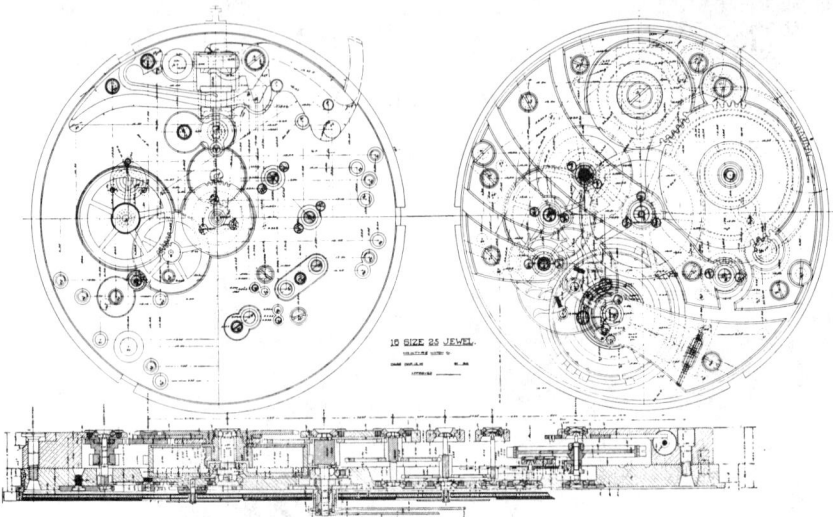

McIntyre Watch Co., 16 size, 25 jewels, adjusted to 5 positions with wind indicator, with equidistant escapement, manufactured about 1909. Above illustration taken from a blue print.

EXAMPLE OF A BREGUET STYLE DIAL   EXAMPLE OF A BOX CAR STYLE DIAL

MELROSE WATCH CO.

Melrose, Massachusetts
1866 - 1868

Melrose Watch Co. began as Tremont Watch Co., and imported the expansion balances and escapements. In 1866 the Tremont Watch Co. moved, changed its name to Melrose Watch Co., and started making complete watch movements, including a new style 18S movement engraved "Melrose Watch Co." About 3,000 were produced. Some watches are found with "Melrose" on the dial and "Tremont" on the movement. Serial numbers start at about 30,000.

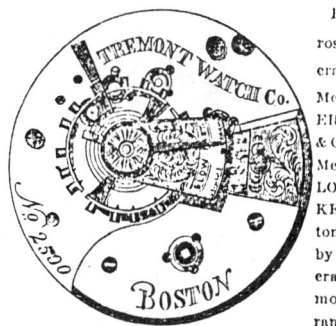

Factory at Melrose, Mass. General Agents, Messrs. WHEELER, PARSONS & CO.,New York, Messrs. BIGELOW BROS. & KENNARD, Boston, and for sale by the trade generally. Every movement warranted.

The TREMONT WATCH CO. manufacture the only DUST-PROOF Watch movement in this country. They have a branch establishment in Switzerland, under the personal superintendence of Mr. A. L. DENNISON, (the ORIGINATOR of the American system of watch-making), where they produce their Balances and Escapements of a superior quality. The cheap skilled labor of Europe, working thus on the AMERICAN SYSTEM, enables them to offer a superior article at a low rate.

Example of a basic **Melrose Watch Co.** movement, 18 size, 15 jewels, key wind & set.

1867 ADVERTISEMENT

Grade or Name — Description		Avg	Ex-Fn	Mint
18S, 7J, KW, KS	★★	$250	$300	$450
18S, 11J, KW, KS, OF	★★	250	300	450
18S, 15J, KW, KS	★★	350	400	550
18S, 15J, KW, KS, Silveroid	★★	250	300	400

Note: Add $25.00 - $70.00 to values of above watches in hunting case.

MOZART WATCH CO.
Providence, Rhode Island
Ann Arbor, Michigan
1864 - 1870

In 1864 Don J. Mozart started out to produce a less expensive three-wheel watch in Providence, R. I. Despite his best efforts, the venture was declared a failure by 1866. Mozart left Providence and moved to Ann Arbor, Mich. There, again, he started on a three-wheel watch and succeeded in producing thirty. The three-wheel watch was not a new idea except to American manufacturers. Three-wheel watches were made many decades before Mozart's first effort, but credit for the first American-made three-wheel watch must go to him. The size was about 18 and could be called a 3/4 or full plate movement. The balance bridge was screwed on the top plate, as was customary. The round bridge partially covered the opening in the top plate and was just large enough for the balance to oscillate. The balance was compensated and somewhat smaller in diameter than usual. Mozart called it a chronolever, and it was to function so perfectly it would be free from friction. That sounded good but was in no way true.

The watch was of the usual thickness for the American 18 size with a train that had a main wheel with the usual number of teeth and a ten-leaf center pinion, but it had a large center wheel of 108 teeth and a third wheel of 90 teeth, with a six-leaf third (escape)pinion. The escape wheel had 30 teeth and received its impulse directly from the roller on the staff, while the escape tooth locked on the intermediate lever pallet. The escape pinion had a long pivot that carried the second hand, which made a circuit of the dial, once in 12 seconds. The total number of Mozart watches produced was about 165, & 30 of these were the three-wheel type.

Grade or Name — Description	Avg	Ex-Fn	Mint
18S, 3/4, KW, KS, 3-wheel .... ★★★★★	$15,000	$20,000	$35,000
18S, 3/4, KW, KS .... ★★★★	10,000	15,000	25,000

Mozart Watch Co. movement, 18 size, three-quarter plate, key wind & set, three-wheel train, "Patent Dec. 24th, 1867" and Patent # was 72,528.

NASHUA WATCH CO. (marked), 20 size, 19 jewels, gold jewel settings, key wind & set from back, stop work, serial number 1,219.

NASHUA WATCH CO.

Nashua, New Hampshire

1859 - 1862

One of the most important contributions to the American Watch industry was made by the Nashua Watch Co. of Nashua, New Hampshire. Founded in 1859 by B. D. Bingham, the company hired some of the most innovative and creative watchmakers in America and produced an extremely high grade American pocket watch.

His company included N. P. Stratton, C. V. Woerd, Charles Moseley, James H. Gerry, and James Gooding, among others. Most of the people connected with the Nashua Watch Company became famous for various advances in watch manufacture, at one time or another. Many had extremely important American patents on various inventions that came to be regarded as a benchmark of the best watches America was capable of making at the time.

The Nashua Watch Co. is important for many reasons. It was the first American company to produce a truly superior high grade movement; the 3/4 plate design used by Nashua became the standard for over 40 years in the American marketplace. Perhaps most importantly, the watches designed by the Nashua Watch Co., and later by the Nashua division of the American Watch Co., became the leaders in the production of the highest quality watches made in America and forced the entire Swiss watch industry to change their technology to compete with the Nashua designs.

Nashua continually won awards for their various models of watches both here and in Europe. By virtue of their sheer technical superiority and classical elegance, Nashua became known universally as the most innovative producer of watches America ever knew.

The original Nashua company produced material for about 1,000 movements but, except for a handful, almost the entire production was finished by the American Watch Company at Waltham, Mass., after R. E. Robbins took over Nashua in 1862 when the company was in grave financial difficulty. Robbins was very happy about the arrangement since he got back almost all the watchmaking geniuses who had left him in 1859 to join Nashua. Robbins incorporated the Nashua Division into the American Watch Company as its high grade experimental division.

Over the years, many of the major advances were made by the Nashua division of Waltham, including the 1860 model 16-size keywind keyset, the 1862 model 20-size key wind keyset, the 1870 model 18-size keywind keyset, pin set, and lever set (which became the first American advertised Railroad watch), the 1868 model 16-size stem wind, and the 1872 model 17-size stemwind. The Nashua division also greatly influenced the 1888 model and the 1892 model by Waltham.

Since almost all the production material made by Nashua from 1859 until its incorporation into the American Watch Co. in 1862 was unfinished by Nashua, only about four examples of the 20-size keywind keyset from the back signed Nashua Watch Co. are known to exist.

20-size keywind keyset from the back signed Nashua Watch Co.

Grade or Name — Description	Avg	Ex-Fn	Mint
Nashua (marked), 19J, KW, KS, 3/4, 18K .... ★★★★★	$18,000	$22,000	$30,000
Nashua (marked), 15J, KW, KS, 3/4, silver case .... ★★★★	12,000	16,000	24,000

NEWARK WATCH CO.

Newark, New Jersey
1864 - 1870

Arthur Wadsworth, one of the designers for Newark Watch Co., patented an 18 Size full plate movement. The first movements reached the market in 1867. This company produced only about 8,000 watches before it was sold to the Cornell Watch Co.

CHRONOLOGY OF THE DEVELOPMENT OF NEWARK WATCH CO.

Newark Watch Co. 1864-1870; S#s 6,501 to 12,000;
Cornell Watch Co.,Chicago, Ill. 1870-1874; S#s 12,001 to 25,000;
Cornell Watch Co., San Francisco, Calif. 1874-Jan. 1876; S#s 25,001 to 35,000;
California Watch Co., Jan. 1876-mid 1876.

🕐 Watches listed in this book are priced at the **collectable fair market value** at the RETAIL level, as complete watches having an original 14k gold filled case, KEY WIND with silver, an original white enamel single sunk dial, and with the entire original movement in good working order with no repairs needed, unless otherwise noted.

Newark Watch Co. Robert Fellows movement, 18 size, 15 jewels, key wind & set, serial number 12, 044.

Grade or Name — Description		Avg	Ex-Fn	Mint
18S, 15J, KW, KS, HC .... ★★		$300	$325	$525
18S, 15J, KW, KS, OF .... ★★		325	375	450
18S, 7J, KW, KS .... ★★		250	300	400
J. C. Adams, 11J, KW, KS .... ★★		300	350	450
J. C. Adams, 11J, KW, KS, Coin .... ★★		300	350	450
Edward Biven, 11-15J, KW, KS .... ★★		375	425	550
Robert Fellows, KW, KS .... ★★		400	450	600
Keyless Watch Co., 15J, LS, SW .... ★★★		300	350	575
Newark Watch Co., 7-15J, KW, KS .... ★★		350	400	550
Arthur Wadsworth, SW .... ★★★		425	550	900
Arthur Wadsworth, 18S, 15J, 18K, HC ("Arthur Wadsworth, New York" on dial; "Keyless Watch, Patent #3655, June 19, 1866" engraved on movement) .... ★★★		1,200	1,600	2,400

NEW ENGLAND WATCH CO.
Waterbury, Connecticut
1898 - 1914

The New England Watch Co., formerly the Waterbury Watch Co., made a watch with a duplex escapement, gilt, 16S, open faced. Watches with the skeletonized movement are very desirable. The company later became Timex Watch Co.

Grade or Name — Description	Avg	Ex-Fn	Mint
16S, OF, duplex, **SKELETON**, good running order .... ★	$300	$350	$500
12S, 16S, 18S, OF, pictures on dial: ladies, dogs, horses, trains, flags, ships, cards, etc.	150	175	300
12S, 16S, 18S, OF, duplex escapement, good running order	65	75	120
12S, 16S, 18S, OF, pin lever escapement, good running order	45	55	100

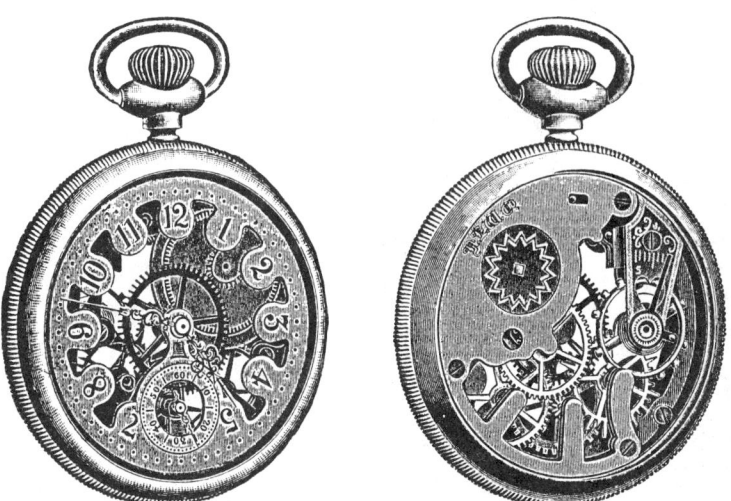

Front and back view of a **skeletonized** New England Watch Co. movement. This watch is fitted with a glass back and front, making the entire movement and wheels visible, 4 jewels, silver hands, black numbers, originally sold for $10-13.

Grade or Name — Description	Avg	Ex-Fn	Mint
6S, duplex	$40	$50	$65
0 S, 15-17 J, lever escapement	50	60	85
Addison, (all sizes)	50	60	85
Alden	40	50	65
Ambassador, 12S, duplex	40	50	65
Americus, duplex	40	50	75
Berkshire, duplex, 14K, **GF**	60	70	100

New England Watch Co., 16 size, 7 jewels, open face, double roller, Dan Patch stop watch.

New England Watch Co., Scout, about 16 size, 4 jewels, duplex escapement, New England base metal case.

🕐 Pricing in this Guide are fair market price for **COMPLETE** watches which are reflected from the "**NAWCC**" National and regional shows.

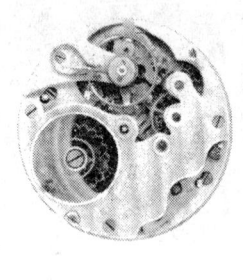

New England Watch Co., multi-colored paper dials, showing poker style playing cards. Watches complete with these type dials bring $300 - $600.00.

New England Watch Co., 0 size, 17 jewels, lever escapement, serial # 1,000,283.

Grade or Name — Description	Avg	Ex-Fn	Mint
Cadish, duplex escapement	$40	$50	$65
Cavour, duplex escapement	45	50	60
Columbian	45	55	65
Chronograph, 7J, Start, Stop & Reset	135	150	200
Cruiser, duplex	45	50	65
Dan Patch, 7J ★	275	350	500
Dominion, **0 size**	35	40	55
Excelsior, 7J	65	70	95
Enamel, full enamel cased watches back and bezel, blue red green, sizes from 6 size to 0 size	95	125	250
Embossed, base metal cases with duplex escapement	65	100	125
Fancy , "unfaded dial"	100	150	250
Gabour	65	70	85
General	45	50	65
Hale, 7J	45	50	65
Jockey, duplex	55	60	75
Oxford	45	50	65
Padishah, duplex	45	50	75
Putnam	65	70	85
Queen Mab, duplex escapement - **0 size**, 4J	40	50	65
Rugby, stop watch	65	70	85
Scout, 12 Size, duplex escapement, HC	40	45	60
Senator, duplex escapement	40	45	55
Trump, duplex	40	45	65
Tuxedo	45	50	65
Tuxedo, DUPLEX ESCAPEMENT	55	65	100

⊕ Some grades are not included. Their values can be determined by comparing with **similar** age, size, metal content, style, models and grades listed.

NEW HAVEN CLOCK AND WATCH CO.

New Haven, Connecticut
1853 - 1956

The company started making Marine clock movements with a balance wheel in about 1875, and used similar smaller movement to make watches in early 1880. The company soon reached a production of about 200 watches per day, making a total of some 40 million watches.

NEW HAVEN Clock & Watch Co., Angelus, with rotating dials, patented Jan 23, 1900.

NEW HAVEN, Ships Time, Ben Franklin dial. Note this watch uses only one hand.

Grade or Name – Description	Avg	Ex-Fn	Mint
Always Right	$45	$55	$75
Angelus, 2 rotating dials ★	135	200	300
Beardsley Radiant	65	75	95
Buddy	45	50	65
Bull Dog	40	45	60
Compensated	45	50	65
Captain Scout	85	100	150
Celluloid case (bold colors)	95	125	175
Chronometer	65	85	100
Earl	45	50	65
Elite	40	50	65
Elm City	45	50	65
Fancy dials, no fading	100	150	250
Football Timer	65	75	95
Ford Special	75	85	100
Hamilton	45	50	65
Handy Andy	50	60	85
Jerome USA	45	50	65

⏲ Note: Some styles, models and grades are not included. Their values can be determined by comparing with **similar** styles, size, age, models and grades listed.

NOTE : ADD $25 to $70 for original BOX and PAPERS

⏲ Pricing in this Guide are fair market price for **COMPLETE** watches which are reflected from the "**NAWCC**" National and regional shows.

Example of Kaiser Wilhelm.

Example of Traveler.

Grade or Name – Description		Avg	Ex-Fn	Mint
Kaiser Wilhelm	★ ★	$350	$450	$750
Kermit		40	45	55
Laddie		25	30	40
Lady Clare		25	30	40
Leonard Watch Co.		25	40	50
Leonard		45	50	65
Mastercraft Rayolite		75	85	95
Miracle		45	50	65
Motor		35	40	50
Nehi		50	70	85
New Haven, pin lever, SW		65	75	100
New Haven, back wind		100	135	200
Panama Official Souvenir, 1915	★	225	275	500
Paul Pry, 14 size with a Locomotive on back of case		35	45	65
Pedometer, 14 size, OF		45	50	65
Pentagon-shaped case		45	50	65
Playing cards on dial	★	350	450	650
Service		30	35	40
Ships Time & Franklin dial		75	95	125
Sports Timer		65	75	95
Surity		45	50	65
Tip Top		20	30	50
Tip Top Jr.		20	30	50
The American		45	50	60
Tommy Ticker		30	35	40
Tourist		45	50	65
Traveler, with travel case		40	45	60
True Time Teller Tip Top		40	45	60
United		30	35	40
USA		30	35	40
Victor		30	35	45

NOTE : ADD $25 to $70 for original BOX and PAPERS

🕐 Pricing in this Guide are fair market price for **COMPLETE** watches which are reflected from the "**NAWCC**" National and regional shows.

NEW HAVEN WATCH CO.

New Haven, Connecticut

1883 - 1887

This company was organized October 16, 1883 with the intention of producing W. E. Doolittle's patented watch; however, this plan was soon abandoned. They did produce a "Model A" watch, the first was marketed in the spring of 1884. Estimated total production is **200.** The original capital became absorbed by Trenton W. Co.

"**The New Haven Watch Co. Alpha, 149, Pat. Dec. 27-81,**" engraved on movement, lever escapement, open face, externally rare watch.

Grade or Name – Description		Avg	Ex-Fn	Mint
"A" Model, about 18S, pat. Dec. 27, '81 .... ★ ★ ★ ★		$625	$750	$1,000
Alpha Model, pat. Dec. 27, '81 .... ★ ★ ★ ★		625	750	1,000

NEW YORK CITY WATCH CO.

New York, New York

1890 - 1897

This company manufactured the Dollar-type watches, which had a pendant-type crank. The watch is wound by **cranking the pendant,** and has a pin lever escapement. The hands are set from the back of the watch movement. The" **patent number 526,871**", is engraved on movement, patent is dated October 1894, and was held by S. Schisgall. The New York City Watch Co., 20 size watch has the words "Lever Winder" printed on the paper dial.

⊕ Watches listed in this book are priced at the **collectable fair market value** at the RETAIL level, as complete watches having an original 14k gold filled case, KEY WIND with silver, an original white enamel single sunk dial, and with the entire original movement in good working order with no repairs needed, unless otherwise noted.

Grade or Name – Description	Avg	Ex-Fn	Mint
18-20S, no jewels, "Lever Winder on dial" .... ★★★★	$600	$800	$1,200
18-20S, no jewels, "SUN DIAL on dial" .... ★★★★	$700	$800	$1,200

New York City Watch Co., about 18-20 size, "Lever Winder" printed on paper dial. This watch is **WOUND by cranking the pendant back and forth**, pin lever escapement, also **back set,** & *"New York City Watch Co., patent No. 526,871"* engraved on movement.

NEW YORK CHRONOGRAPH WATCH CO.
NEW YORK, NEW YORK
1880 -1885

This company sold about 800 watches marked "New York Chronograph Watch Co." The 18 size stop watch was manufactured by Manhattan Watch Co.

Grade or Name –Description	Avg	Ex-Fn	Mint
18S, 7J, stop watch, HC .... ★	$125	$150	$250
18S, 7J, stop watch, OF .... ★	100	125	200
16S, 7J, SW, time only, OF .... ★	150	175	250
16S, 9-11J, SW, time only, OF....................................... ★	150	175	250
16S, 7-11J, SW, time only sweep sec., OF .... ★	125	150	275
16S, 7-11J, SW, **true CHRONOGRAPH,** OF .... ★★★	300	350	550

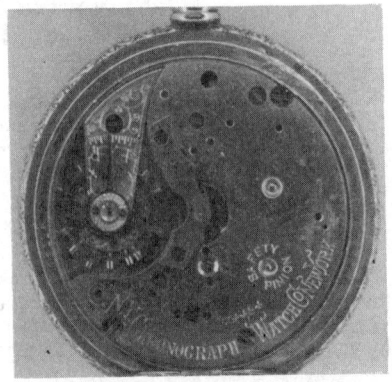

N.Y. Chronograph Watch Co., dial and movement, 16 size, 7 jewels, open face, time only, sweep second hand.

 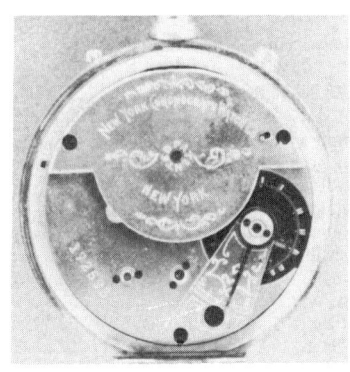

New York Chronograph Watch Co. dial and movement, 7 jewels, open face, buttons at the top of case set hands and stop watch.

NEW YORK STANDARD WATCH CO.

Jersey City, New Jersey
1885 - 1929

The first watch reached the market in early 1888 and was a 18S. The most interesting feature was a straight line lever with a ''worm gear escapement.'' This was patented by R. J. Clay. All watches were quick train and open-faced. The company also made its own cases and sold a complete watch. A prefix number was added to the serial number after the first 10,000 watches were made. Estimated total production was 7,000,000.

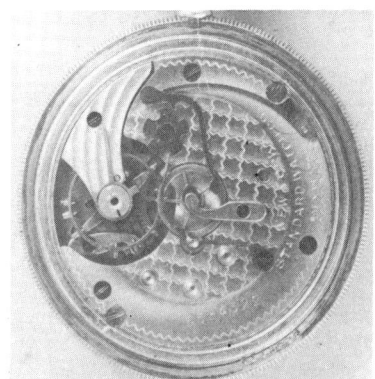 

New York Standard,Chronograph, 18 size, 7 jewels, stem wind, second hand start-stop and fly back, three-quarter plate, serial number 5,334,322.

New York Standard, converts to a hunting case movement or a open face movement, serial number 602,506.

N. Y. STANDARD
16 AND 18 SIZE

Grade or Name – Description	Avg	Ex-Fn	Mint
18S, 7J, N. Y. Standard, KW, KS	$250	$300	$375
18S, 7J, N. Y. Standard, SW	50	60	75
18S, 15J, N. Y. Standard, SW, LS, HC	100	125	175
Chronograph, 7-11J, 3/4, NI, DMK, SW, fly back hand	150	200	275
Chronograph, 10J, (marked 10J), fly back hand ★	195	235	350
Chronograph, 13J, sweep sec., stop & fly back hand	150	200	275
Chronograph, 15J, 3/4, NI, DMK, SW, fly back hand,	150	200	275
Columbus, 7J	50	60	75
Convertible,15J.,16 Size, HC or OF ★ ★ ★	300	400	650
Crown W. Co., 7J, OF or HC	50	60	65
Crown W. Co., 15J, HC	60	75	100
Dan Patch, 7J, stop watch(pat. DEC. 22 '08) ★	250	350	550
Dan Patch, 17J, stop watch(pat. DEC. 22 '08) ★ ★	375	450	600
Edgemere, 7J, OF & HC	50	60	75
Excelsior, 7J, OF or HC	50	60	75

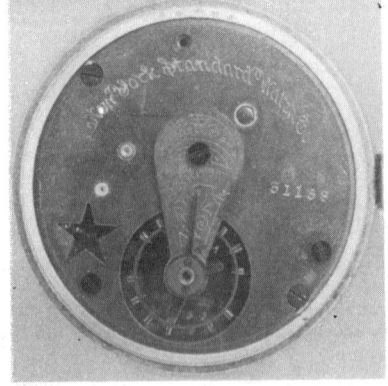

New York Standard, with WORM GEAR (located under cutout star), 18 size, 7 jewels, there was two runs of the worm-drive model 52,000 made, serial number 31,138.

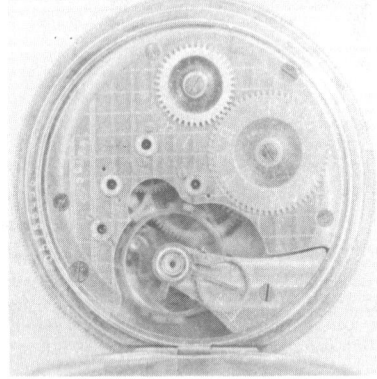

Remington W. Co. (marked on movement & case), 16 size, 11 jewels, 2-tone damaskeening, NOTE crown wheel & ratchet (no click), serial # CC021,331.

Grade or Name – Description	Avg	Ex-Fn	Mint
Harvard W. CO., 7-11J.,	$40	$50	$65
Hi Grade	50	60	75
Ideal	50	60	75
Jefferson, 7J.,	50	60	70
La Salle, 7J.,	35	45	55
New Era, 7J., OF or HC, skeletonized (Poor Man's Dudley)	250	275	425
New Era,7-11J.	40	50	65
New York Standard W. Co., 11J, 3/4	60	85	100
New York Standard, 7J, 3/4	60	85	100
New York Standard, 15J, BRG	75	100	125
N. Y. Standard, with (" WORM GEAR") ★	400	450	600

🕐 Note: Some styles, models and grades are not included. Their values can be determined by comparing with **similar** styles, size, age, models and grades listed.

🕐 Pricing in this Guide are fair market price for **COMPLETE** watches which are reflected from the "**NAWCC**" National and regional shows.

Grade or Name – Description	Avg	Ex-Fn	Mint
Pan American, 7J, OF	$60	$85	$100
Perfection, 7J, OF or HC	50	60	75
Perfection, 15J, OF or HC, NI	60	85	100
Remington W. Co., 11J, marked mvt. & case	75	100	150
Solar W. Co., 7J	50	60	75
Special USA, 7J	45	55	65
18S Tribune USA, 23J, HC or OF, Pat. Reg. Adj.	150	175	300
Washington, 7-11J	50	60	75
William Penn, 7-11J	50	60	75
Wilmington, 7-11J	50	60	75

For watches with **O'Hara Multi-Color Dials,** add $75 -$100 to value in **mint condition**; add $40-$60 for Hunting Cases.

12 SIZE

Grade or Name – Description	Avg	Ex-Fn	Mint
N. Y. Standard, 7J-11J, OF	$25	$30	$45
N. Y. Standard, 7J-11J, HC	40	55	60
N. Y. Standard, 7J, HC, Multi-Color dial	70	110	200
N. Y. Standard, 15J, OF	35	40	45
N. Y. Standard, 15J, HC	45	55	70
Crown W. Co., 7J, OF or HC	30	40	55

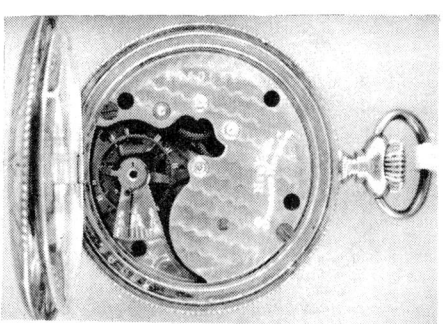

New York Standard Watch Co., 12 size, 7 jewels, open face, serial number 1,021,224.　　New York Standard W.Co., 6 size G# 144, Hunting Case.

6 SIZE AND 0 SIZE

Grade or Name – Description	Avg	Ex-Fn	Mint
Alton, 7-15J	$35	$40	$55
American,7J	35	40	55
Empire State W. Co., 7J	40	50	65
Excelsior, 7J, HC	40	50	65
Standard USA, 7J	40	50	65
6S, Columbia, 7J, HC	60	70	85
6S, N. Y. Standard, 7J, HC	60	70	85
6S, Orient, SW	30	40	55
6S, Progress, 7J, YGF	40	50	65
6S or 0S, Crown W. Co., 7J, OF or HC	20	30	45
0S, Ideal, 7J, HC	60	70	85
0S, N. Y. Standard, 7J, HC	60	70	85

🕐 Pricing in this Guide are fair market price for **COMPLETE** watches which are reflected from the "**NAWCC**" National and regional shows.

NEW YORK STANDARD WATCH CO.
IDENTIFICATION OF MOVEMENTS

How to Identify Your Watch: Compare the movement of your watch with the illustrations in this section. Upon matching the movement exactly, the model number and size can be determined. While comparing, note the location of the balance, jewels, screws, gears, and type of back plate (Full, 3/4, Bridge) which will be clues in identifying the movement you have. Having determined the size and model number, you can now find your watch in the main price listing by name or number (which is engraved on the movement).

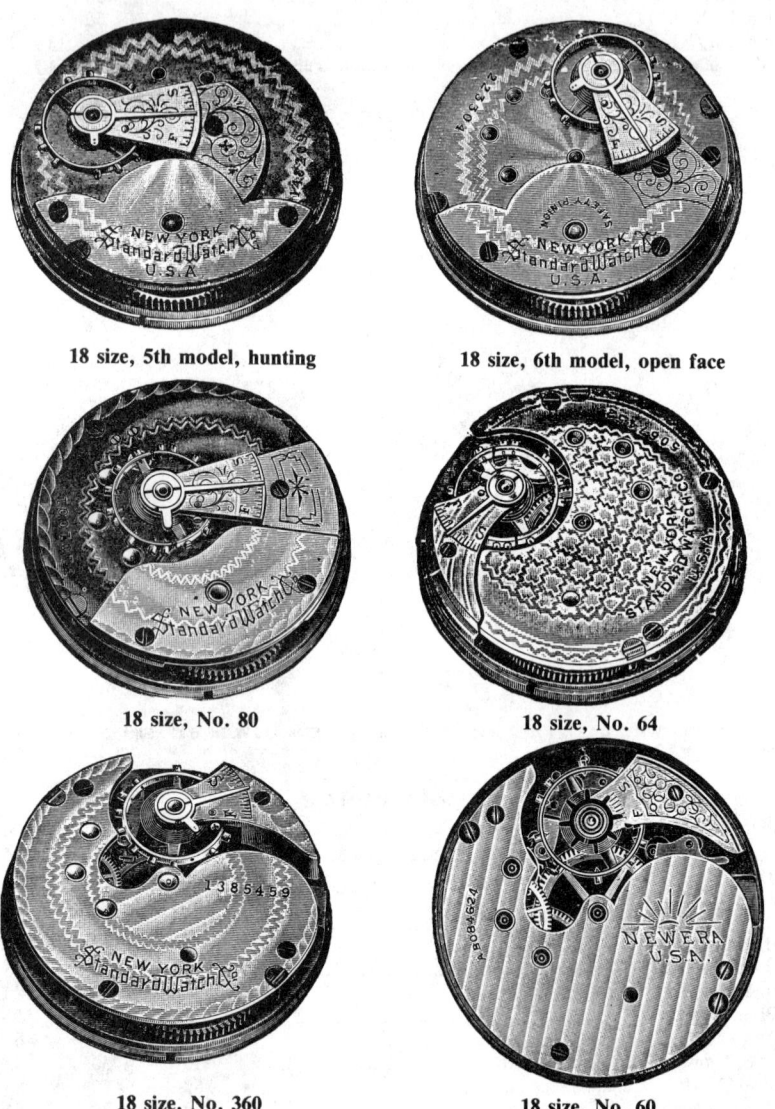

18 size, 5th model, hunting

18 size, 6th model, open face

18 size, No. 80

18 size, No. 64

18 size, No. 360

18 size, No. 60

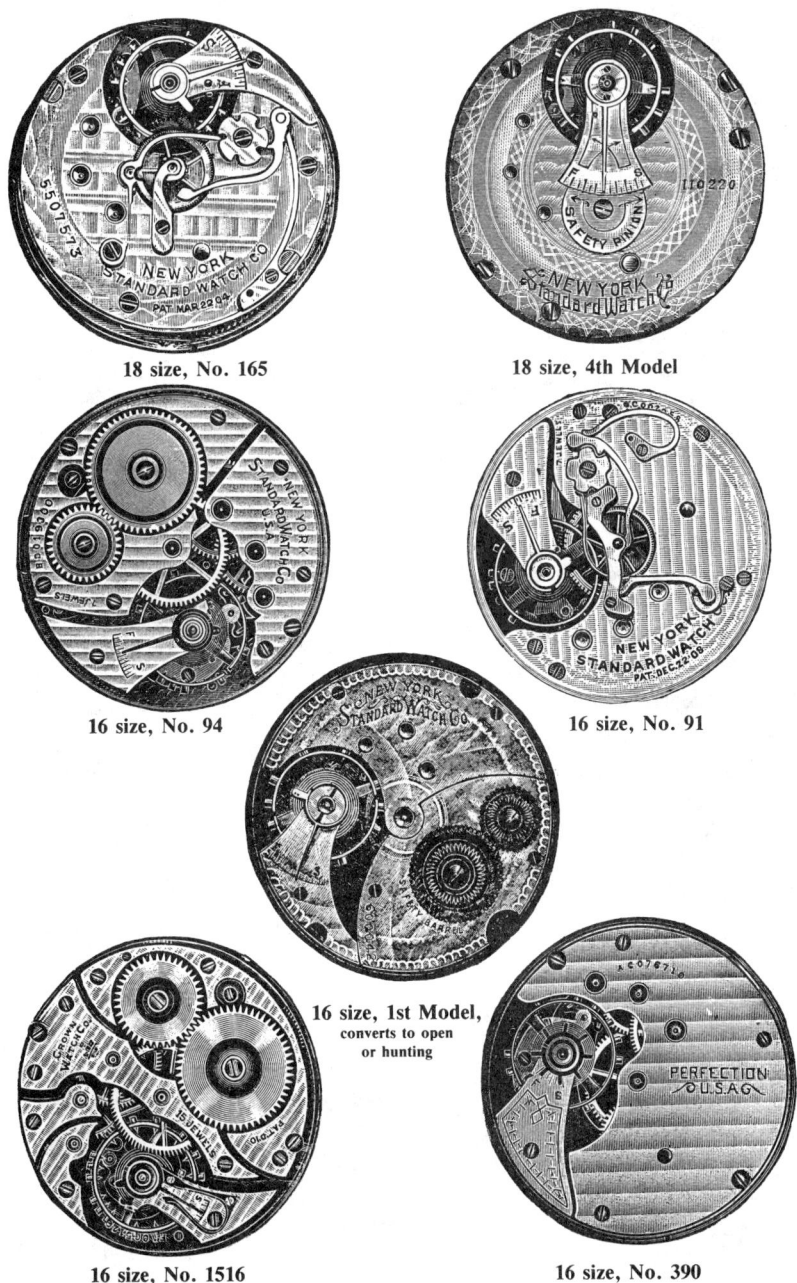

18 size, No. 165

18 size, 4th Model

16 size, No. 94

16 size, No. 91

16 size, 1st Model,
converts to open
or hunting

16 size, No. 1516

16 size, No. 390

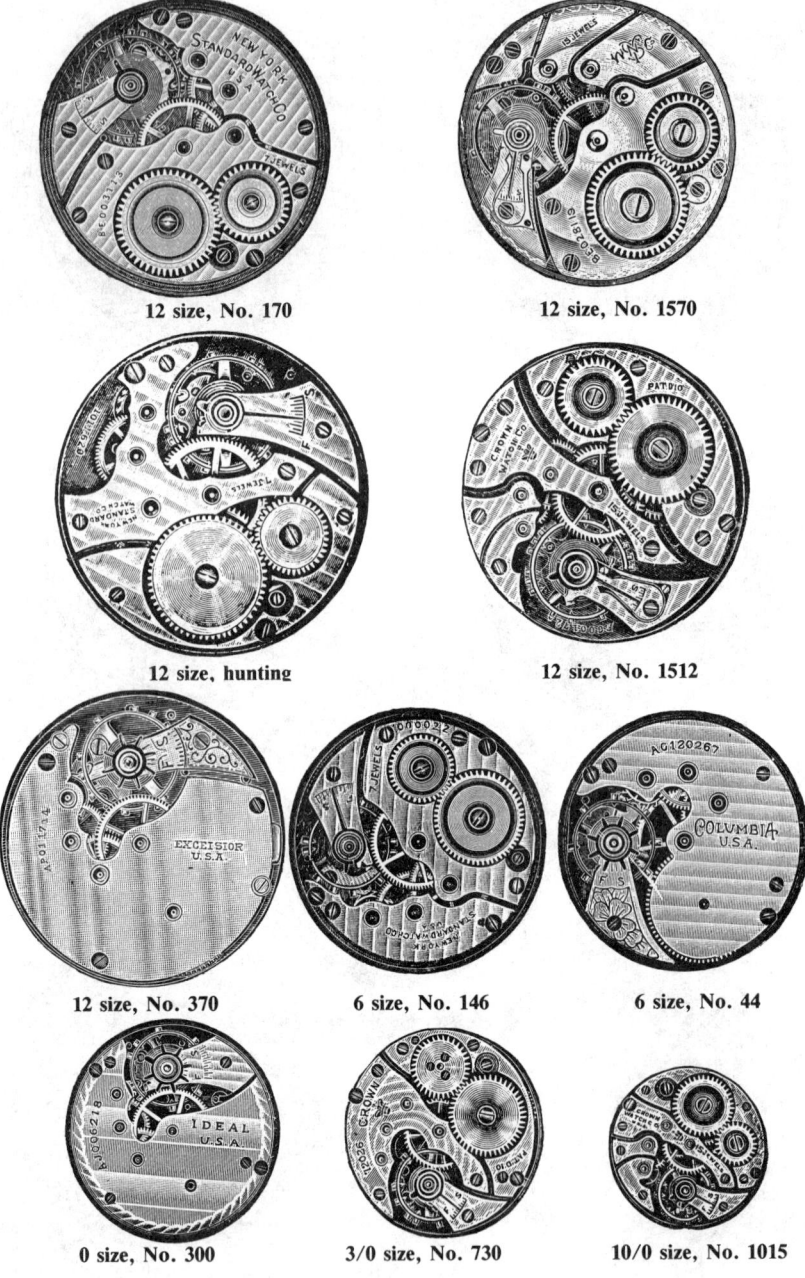

12 size, No. 170

12 size, No. 1570

12 size, hunting

12 size, No. 1512

12 size, No. 370

6 size, No. 146

6 size, No. 44

0 size, No. 300

3/0 size, No. 730

10/0 size, No. 1015

NEW YORK SPRINGFIELD WATCH CO.

Springfield, Massachusetts

1866 - 1876

The New York Watch Co. had a rather difficult time getting started. The name of the company was changed from the Mozart Watch Co. to the New York Watch Co., and it was located in Rhode Island. Before any watches had been produced, they moved to Springfield, Mass., in 1867. A factory was built there, but only about 100 watches were produced before a fire occurred on April 23, 1870. Shortly after the fire, in 1870, a newly-designed watch was introduced. The first movements reached the market in 1871, and the first grade was a fully-jeweled adjusted movement called "Frederick Billings." The standard 18S and the Swiss Ligne systems were both used in gauging the size of these watches. The New York Watch Co. used full signatures on its movements. The doors closed in the summer of 1876.

In January 1877, the Hampden Watch Co. was organized and commenced active operation in June 1877.

CHRONOLOGY OF THE DEVELOPMENT OF NEW YORK WATCH CO.

The Mozart Watch Co., Providence, R. I. 1864-1866
New York Watch Co., Providence, R. I. 1866-1867
New York Watch Co., Springfield, Mass. 1867-1875
New York Watch Mfg. Co., Springfield, Mass. 1875-1876
Hampden Watch Co., Springfield, Mass. 1877-1886
Hampden-Dueber Watch Co., Springfield, Mass. 1886-1888
Hampden Watch Co. Works, Canton, Ohio 1888-1923
Dueber-Hampden Watch Co., Canton, Ohio 1923-1930
Amtorg, U.S.S.R. 1930

NEW YORK WATCH CO. SPRINGFIELD
ESTIMATED SERIAL NUMBERS
AND PRODUCTION DATES

DATE – SERIAL NO.	DATE – SERIAL NO.
1866 – 1,000	1871 – 20,000
1867 – 3,000	1872 – 30,000
1868 – 5,000	1873 – 40,000
1869 – 7,000	1874 – 50,000
1870 – 10,000	1875 – 60,000

The above list is provided for determining the APPROXIMATE age of your watch. Match serial number with date. Watches were not necessarily sold in the exact order of manufactured date.

N. Y. W. SPRINGFIELD
18 TO 20 SIZE

Grade or Name – Description		Avg	Ex-Fn	Mint
Aaron Bagg, 7J, KW, KS .... ★		$225	$275	$400
Frederick Billings, 15J, KW, KS.................................... ★		225	275	400
E. W. Bond, 15J, 3/4.. ★ ★ ★		500	550	800
E. W. Bond, 18J, 3/4.. ★ ★ ★		600	700	900
J. A. Briggs, 11J, KW, KS, from back..................... ★ ★		325	350	550

🕐 Some grades are not included. Their values can be determined by comparing with **similar** age, size, metal content, style, models and grades listed.

🕐 Watches listed in this book are priced at the collectable retail level, as **complete** watches having an original 14k gold-filled case and *Key Wind* with silver, an original white enamel single sunk dial, and with the entire original movement in good working order with no repairs needed.

🕐 Pricing in this Guide are fair market price for **COMPLETE** watches which are reflected from the "**NAWCC**" National and regional shows.

E.W. Bond movement, 18 size, 15 jewels, three-quarter plate.

Chas. E. Hayward, 18 size, 15 jewels, key wind & set, note the hidden key, serial number 18,733.

Grade or Name – Description		Avg	Ex-Fn	Mint
Albert Clark, 15J, KW, KS, from back, 3/4	★★	$300	$350	$500
Homer Foot, 15J, KW, KS, from back, 3/4	★	300	350	500
Herman Gerz, 11J, KW, KS	★	200	250	400
John Hancock, 7J, KW, KS		125	150	275
John Hancock, 7J, KW, KS, Silveroid		70	100	200
John Hancock, 7J, KW, KS, Coin		125	150	275
Chas. E. Hayward, 15J, KW, KS, long balance cock		150	200	300
Chas. E. Hayward, 15J, KW, KS, Coin		150	200	300
J. L. King, 15J, KW, KS, from back, 3/4	★	400	450	600
New York Watch Co., 7J, KW, KS	★	150	200	300
New York Watch Co., 15-19J, KW, KS, Wolf's Teeth winding, (Serial #s below 75)	★★★★	900	1,200	2,000
New York Watch Co., 15-19J, KW, KS, Wolf's Teeth winding, all original	★★★	800	900	1,500
New York Watch Co., 11J, KW, KS	★★	250	300	400
H. G. Norton, 15J, KW, KS, from back, 3/4	★	250	300	400
H. G. Norton, 17J, KW, KS, from back, 3/4	★	300	350	450
H. G. Norton, 19J, KW, KS, from back, 3/4	★★★	450	550	750

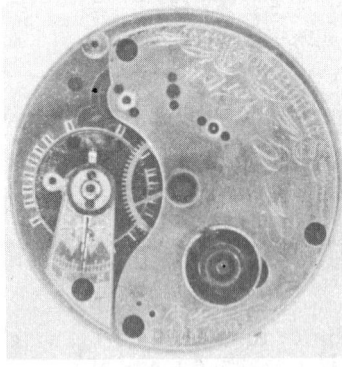
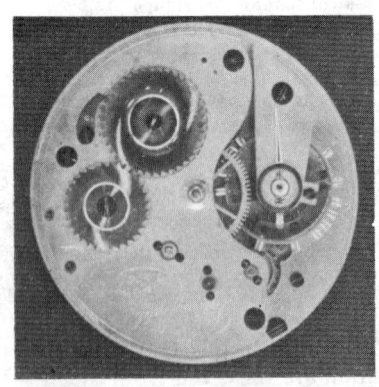

H.G. Norton, 18 size, 15 jewels, three-quarter plate, gold escape wheel, serial number 6592.

New York Watch Co., 18 size, 15-19 jewels, stem wind, hunting case, note wolf teeth winding, serial number 978.

State Street movement, 18 size, 15 jewels, three-quarter plate.

Theo E. Studley movement, 18 size, 15 jewels, key wind & set, full plate.

Grade or Name – Description	Avg	Ex-Fn	Mint
J. C. Perry, 15J..★	$80	$125	$300
J. C. Perry, 15J, Silveroid.....................................★	70	95	200
Railway, 15J, KW, FULL, Coin.........................★★★	600	650	1,000
Railway, 15J, KW, KS, FULL ....★★★	600	650	1,000
William Romp,15J,KW,KS from back,3/4 ....★★	425	600	700
Geo. Sam Rice, 7J, KW, KS..................................★	150	200	325
Springfield, 15J, KW, KS, from back, ADJ, Wolf teeth wind, serial Nos. below 1,000 ....★★★	800	900	1,500
Springfield, 19J, KW, KS, from back, ADJ, Wolf teeth wind, serial Nos. below 1,000 ....★★★	900	1,000	1,600
State Street, 11J, 3/4, SW ....★★	225	325	500
State Street, 15J, 3/4, SW ....★★	250	300	550
Theo E. Studley, 15J, KW, Coin	135	150	200
Theo E. Studley, 15J, KW, KS	125	150	200
George Walker, 17J, KW, 3/4, ADJ.....................★	300	350	500
Chester Woolworth, 15J, KW, KS	125	150	200
Chester Woolworth, 11J, KW, KS	125	150	200
Chester Woolworth, 11J, KW, KS, Silveroid	80	125	175
Chester Woolworth, 11J, KW, KS, ADJ..............	100	175	225
#4, 15J, ADJ, KW, KS	100	150	200
#5, 15J, KW, KS	75	125	175
#6, 11J, KW, KS	75	125	175
#6, 11J, KW, KS, Silveroid................................	75	95	150

🕐 Some KW, KS watches made by the New York Watch Co. have a hidden key. If you unscrew the crown, and the crown comes out as a key, add $100 to the listed value.

🕐 Watches listed in this book are priced at the collectable retail level, as **complete** watches having an original 14k gold-filled case and *Key Wind* with silver, an original white enamel single sunk dial, and with the entire original movement in good working order with no repairs needed.

🕐 This book endeavours to be a GUIDE or helpful manual and offers a wealth of material to be used as a tool not as an absolute document. Price Guides are like watches the worst may be better than none at all, but at best cannot be expected to be 100% accurate.

🕐 Characteristics of watches differ for the same age of both case and movement, because these features vary it may not be accurate to date a watch by one single influence. Example: the second hand was _not_ commonly found on watches before 1750, but common about 1800. The first second hand appeared in 1665 and another in 1690. Therefore statements are broad rather than accurate.

NON-MAGNETIC WATCH CO.

Geneva and America
1887 - 1905

The Non-Magnetic Watch Co. sold and imported watches from the Swiss as well as contracted watches made in America. Geneva Non-Magnetic marked watches appear to be the oldest type of movement. This company sold a full line of watches, high grade to low grade, as well as repeaters and ladies watches. An advertisement appeared in the monthly journal of "Locomotive Engineers" in 1887. The ad states that the "Paillard's patent non-magnetic watches are uninfluenced by magnetism of electricity." Each watch contains the Paillard's patent non-magnetic, inoxidizable compensation balance and hairspring. An ad in 1888 shows prices for 16 size Swiss style watches as low as $15 for 7 jewels and as high as $135 for 20 jewels.

18 SIZE
(must be marked Paillard's Patent)

Grade or Name – Description		Avg	Ex-Fn	Mint
Elgin, 17J, FULL, SW, LS, OF		$90	$150	$200
Elgin, 17J, FULL, SW, LS, HC		90	175	250
Elgin, 15J, FULL, SW, LS, OF		90	125	175
Elgin, 15-17J, FULL, SW, LS, HC		90	150	200
Illinois, 24J, GJS, NI, Adj.5P, OF		650	750	1,200
Illinois, 24J, GJS, NI, Adj.5P, HC	★★	800	900	1,500
Illinois, 23J, GJS, NI, Adj.5P, OF		700	750	950
Illinois, 23J, GJS, NI, Adj.5P, HC	★★★	1,600	1,800	2,200
Illinois, 21J, GJS, NI, Adj.5P, OF		225	275	400
Illinois, 21J, GJS, NI, Adj.5P, HC		300	400	600
Illinois, 17J, NI, ADJ, OF		125	150	200
Illinois, 17J, NI, ADJ, HC		175	225	300
Illinois, 15J, NI, OF		100	125	175
Illinois, 15J, NI, HC		125	150	200
Illinois, 11J, OF		60	90	175
Illinois, 11J, HC		70	100	200

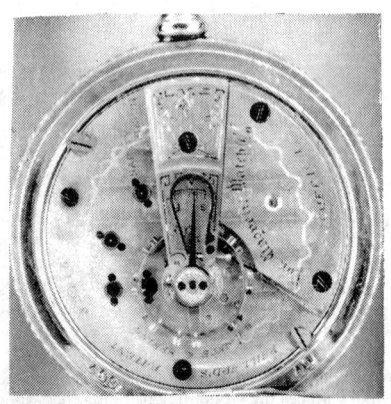
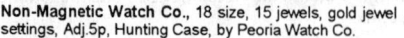

Non-Magnetic Watch Co., 18 size, 15 jewels, gold jewel settings, Adj.5p, Hunting Case, by Peoria Watch Co.

Non-Magnetic Watch Co., 18 size, 21 Ruby jewels, Adj.5p, note "Paillard" engraved on movement, made by Illinois Watch Co.

🕐 Watches listed in this book are priced at the collectable retail level, as **complete** watches having an original 14k gold-filled case and *Key Wind* with silver, an original white enamel single sunk dial, and with the entire original movement in good working order with no repairs needed.

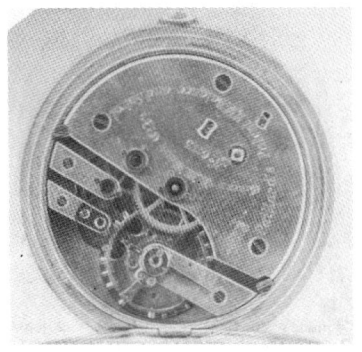

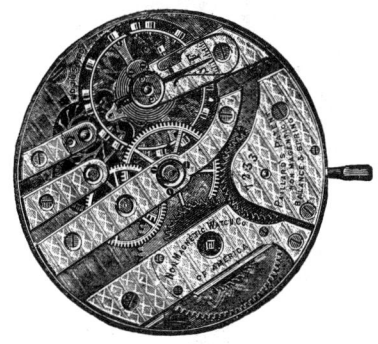

Non-Magnetic Watch Co., 18 size, 16J., 3/4 plate, hunting, note "Geneva" engraved on movement, serial # 6113.

Non-Magnetic Watch Co., 18 size, 16 jewels, Bar bridge model, example of a Swiss Ebauche.

Grade or Name – Description	Avg	Ex-Fn	Mint
Peoria, 17J, FULL, SW, LS, Adj., OF	$250	$300	$400
Peoria, 15J, FULL, SW, LS, Adj., OF	200	250	350
Peoria, 15J, FULL, SW, LS, Adj., HC	250	300	450
Peoria, 11J, FULL, SW, LS, OF	125	150	200
Peoria, 11J, FULL, SW, LS, HC	175	200	275
Swiss, 16J, 3/4 plate, SW, LS, Adj., OF	70	85	150
Swiss, 16J, 3/4 plate, SW, LS, Adj., HC	75	100	175
Swiss, 15-16J, bar bridge, SW, LS, Adj., OF	70	85	165
Swiss, 15-16J, bar bridge, SW, LS, Adj., HC	70	100	175
Swiss, 11J, 3/4 plate, SW, LS, OF, HC	70	80	150
Swiss, 11J, bar bridge, SW, LS, OF, HC	70	80	150

Non-Magnetic Watch Co., 18 size, 17 Ruby jewels, adjusted, made by Elgin Watch Co.

Non-Magnetic Watch Co., 16 size, 21 Ruby jewels, adjusted, made by Illinois Watch Co. Model 5, G# 179.

🕐 Watches listed in this book are priced at the **collectable fair market value** at the RETAIL level, as complete watches having an original 14k gold filled case, KEY WIND with silver, an original white enamel single sunk dial, and with the entire original movement in good working order with no repairs needed, unless otherwise noted.

🕐 Pricing in this Guide are fair market price for **COMPLETE** watches which are reflected from the "**NAWCC**" National and regional shows.

Non-Magnetic Watch Co., 16 size, 1/2 plate, 16 jewels, hunting case, adjusted. Swiss made.

Non-Magnetic Watch Co., 16 size, 1/2 plate, 15-20 jewels, note "Paillard's Patent, Balance And Spring" engraved on movement. Swiss made.

16 SIZE
(must be marked Paillard's Patent)

Grade or Name – Description	Avg	Ex-Fn	Mint
Elgin, 21J, ADJ 5P, OF	$135	$150	$300
Elgin, 21J, ADJ 5P, HC	225	250	400
Elgin, 17J, ADJ 5P, HC	90	125	200
Elgin, 17J, ADJ 5P, HC	100	150	250
Illinois, 21J, GJS, 3/4, DR, Adj.6P, OF	175	225	400
Illinois, 21J, GJS, 3/4, DR, Adj.6P, HC	250	300	600
Illinois, 17J, 3/4, DR, ADJ, OF	100	150	250
Illinois, 17J, 3/4, DR, ADJ, HC	125	175	275
Illinois, 15J, HC	100	150	175
Illinois, 15J, OF	70	125	150
Illinois, 11J, OF	70	90	125
Illinois, 11J, HC	70	125	150
Swiss, 20J, GJS, DR, Adj.6P, NI, 1/2 ,OF	70	125	150
Swiss, 20J, GJS, DR, Adj.6P, NI, 1/2, HC	70	125	175
Swiss, 18J, GJS, DR, Adj.6P, NI, 1/2, OF	150	175	250
Swiss, 18J, GJS, DR, Adj.6P, NI, 1/2, HC	150	175	250
Swiss, 16J, GJS, DR, Adj.6P, NI, 1/2, OF	70	90	150
Swiss, 16J, GJS, DR, Adj.6P, NI, 1/2, HC	70	90	175
Swiss, 15J, DR, NI, 3/4, OF	70	90	150
Swiss, 15J, DR, NI, 3/4, HC	70	90	175
Swiss, 7-11J, NI, 3/4, OF	50	60	100
Swiss, 7-11J, NI, 3/4, HC	70	90	175

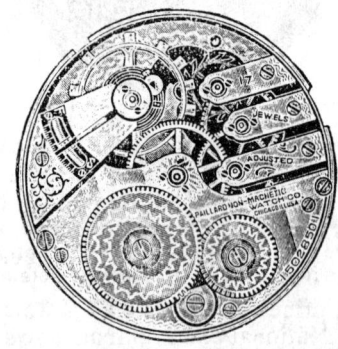

Non-Magnetic Watch Co., 16 size, 17J., by Elgin W. Co.

Non-Magnetic Watch Co., 16 size, 17J., by Elgin W. Co.

OTAY WATCH CO.

Otay, California
1889 - 1894

This company produced about 1,000 watches with a serial number range of 1,000 to 1,500 and 30,000 to 31,000. The company was purchased by a Japanese manufacturer in 1894. Names on Otay movements include: Golden Gate, F. A. Kimball, Native Sun, Overland Mail, R. D. Perry, and P. H. Wheeler. Machinery sold to Osaka of Japan. Only a few watches were made. Osaka watches look about the same as Otay watches.

Otay Watch Co. Dial; note hunting case style and lever for setting hands.

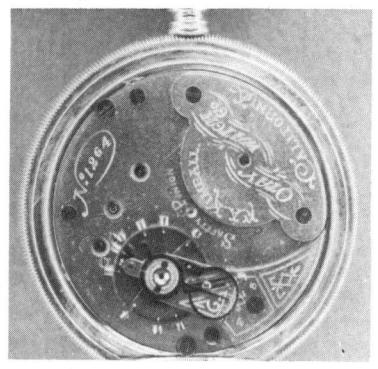

Otay Watch Co., F.A. Kimball, 18 size, 15 jewels, lever set, hunting, serial number 1,264.

18 SIZE

Grade or Name – Description		Avg	Ex-Fn	Mint
California, 15J., LS, HC, NI	★ ★ ★	$1,500	$1,800	$2,500
Golden Gate, 15J, LS, HC, OF, NI	★ ★ ★	2,400	2,600	3,300
F. A. Kimball, 15J, LS, HC, Gilt	★ ★	1,100	1,400	2,000
Native Son, 15J, LS, HC, NI	★ ★	1,800	2,000	2,800
Overland Mail, 15J, LS, HC, NI	★ ★ ★	2,400	2,700	3,500
R. D. Perry, 15J, LS, HC, Gilt	★ ★	1,200	1,400	1,900
P. H. Wheeler, 15J, LS, HC, Gilt	★ ★	1,200	1,400	1,900
Sunset, 7J, Gilt, HC	★ ★	1,400	1,600	2,200
Osaka W. Co., 15J, NI, or gilt, (made in Japan)	★ ★ ★ ★	2,200	2,400	3,000

D. D. PALMER WATCH CO.

Waltham, Massachusetts
1864 - 1875

In 1858, at age 20, Mr. Palmer opened a small jewelry store in Waltham, Mass. Here he became interested in pocket chronometers. At first he bought the balance and jewels from Swiss manufacturers. In 1864 he took a position with the American Watch Co. and made the chronometers in his spare time (only about 25 produced). They were, 18S, 3/4 plate, gilded, key wind, and some were nickel. At first they were fusee driven, but he mainly used going barrels. About 1870, Palmer started making lever watches and by 1875 he left the American Watch Co. and started making a 10S keywind, gilded movement, and a 16S, 3/4 plate, gilt and nickel, and a stem wind of his own invention (a vibrating crown wheel). In all he made about 1,500 watches. The signature appearing on the watches was "Palmer W. Co. Wal., Mass."

He basically had three grades of watches: Fine-Solid Nickel; Medium-Nickel Plated; and Medium-Gold Gilt. They were made in open-face and hunter cases.

D. D. Palmer Watch Co., 18 size, 15 jewels, Palmer's Pat. Stem Winder on movement, serial number 1,098.

Grade or name – Description		Avg	Ex-Fn	Mint
10-16S, 15-17J, 3/4 plate, spring detent chronometer .... ★ ★ ★ ★		$4,000	$5,000	$7,000
16-18S, 15-17J, NI, OF, **18K** .... ★ ★ ★		2,200	2,500	3,500

PEORIA WATCH CO.

Peoria, Illinois
1885 - 1895

The roots of this company began with the Independent Watch Co. (1880 - 1883). These watches marked Marion and Mark Twain were made by the Fredonia Watch Co. (1883 - 1885) Peoria Watch Co. opened Dec. 19, 1885, and made one model of railroad watches in about 1887.

Peoria watches were 18S, quick train, 15 jewel, and all stem wind. These watches are hard to find, as only about 3,000 were made. Peoria also made railroad watches for A. C. Smith's Non-Magnetic Watch Co. of America, from 1884-1888. The 18 size watches were full plate, adjusted, and had a whiplash regulator.

The Peoria Watch Co. closed in 1889, having produced about 47,000 watches.

Peoria Watch Co., 18 size, 15 jewels, nickel damaskeening plates, hunting, note patented regulator, serial number 11,532.

🕐 Watches listed in this book are priced at the **collectable fair market value** at the RETAIL level, as complete watches having an original 14k gold filled case, KEY WIND with silver, an original white enamel single sunk dial, and with the entire original movement in good working order with no repairs needed, unless otherwise noted.

Grade or Name – Description	Avg	Ex-Fn	Mint
18S, 9-11J, SW, OF	$200	$250	$375
18S, 15J, SW, personalized name	250	300	400
18S, Peoria W. Co., 15J, SW, OF	225	275	400
18S, Peoria W. Co., 15J, SW, HC	250	275	450
18S, Peoria W. Co., 15J, SW, low S# ★	400	500	700
18S, Anti-Magnetic, 15J, OF	300	325	400
18S, Anti-Magnetic, 15J, HC	350	375	500
18S, Anti-Magnetic, 15J, Made for Railway Service, OF ★	400	450	600
18S, Anti-Magnetic, 15J, Made for Railway Servic, HC ★	425	475	650
18S, Superior Quality Anti-Magnetic, 15J, NI, SW, GJS, Adj.5P, OF ★★	500	600	800
18S, Superior Quality Anti-Magnetic, 15J, NI, SW, GJS, Adj.5P, HC ★★★	550	650	900
18S, Made for Railway Service, 15J, NI, GJS, Adj.5P, OF ★	325	400	600
18S, Made for Railway Service, 15J, NI, GJS, Adj.5P, HC ★	350	450	700

PHILADELPHIA WATCH CO.

Philadelphia, Pennsylvania

1868 - 1886

Eugene Paulus organized the Philadelphia Watch Co. about 1868. Most all the parts were made in Switzerland, and finished and cased in this country. The International Watch Co. is believed to have manufactured the movements for Philadelphia Watch Co. Estimated total production of the company is 12,000 watches.

Issued by the U. S. Patent Office, August 25, and November 3, 1868.

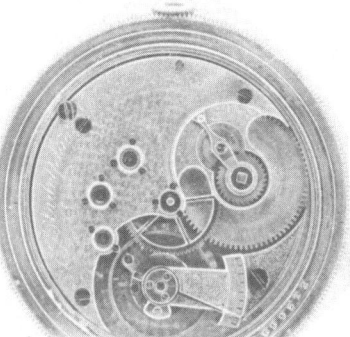

Philadelphia Watch Co., 16 size, 15 jewels, gold jewel settings, hunting case model. "Paulus' Patents 1868. Aug. 25th, Nov. 3rd" on movement, serial number 5,751.

NOV. 1871 advertising 15,16,19, & 21 size watches for sale at their New York City and Philadelphia offices.

Grade or Name – Description	Avg	Ex-Fn	Mint
18S, 15J, SW, HC ★	$225	$300	$500
18S, 15J, KW, KS ★	275	375	500
18S, 15J, SW, OF ★	200	250	450
18S, HC, KW, KS, **18K** original case marked Philadelphia Watch Co. ★★	1,000	1,200	1,600
18S, 11J, KW, KS ★	150	175	250
16S, 15J, KW, KS ★	150	175	250
16S, 19J, KW, KS, GJS ★	300	400	550
8S-6S, 11J, HC ★	125	175	250
8S-6S, 15J, HC ★	125	175	225
8S-6S, Paulus, 19J, KW, KS ★	150	200	350
000/S, 7J, HC, PS ★	125	200	300

JAMES & HENRY PITKIN

Hartford, Connecticut
New York, New York
1838 - 1852

Henry Pitkin was the first to attempt to manufacture watches by machinery. The machines were of Pitkin's own design and very crude, but he had some brilliant ideas. His first four workers were paid $30 a year plus their board. After much hardship, the first watches were produced in the fall of 1838. The watches had going barrels, not the fusee and chain, and the American flag was engraved on the plates to denote they were American made and to exemplify the true spirit of American independence in watchmaking.

The first 50 watches were stamped with the name "Henry Pitkin." Others bore the firm name "H. & J. F. Pitkin." The movements were about 16S and 3/4 plate. The plates were rolled brass and stamped out with dies. The pinions were lantern style with eight leaves. The movement had a slow train of 14,400 beats per hour. Pitkin's first plan was to make the ends of the pinions conical and let them run in the ends of hardened steel screws, similar to the Marine clock balances. A large brass setting was put in the plates and extended above the surface. Three screws, with small jewels set in their ends, were inserted so that they closed about the pivot with very small end shake. This proved to be too expensive and was used in only a few movements. Next, he tried to make standard type movements extend above the plates with the end shake controlled by means of a screw running down into the end of the pivots, reducing friction. This "capped jewel train" was used for a while before he adopted the standard ways of jeweling. The escape wheels were the star type, English style. The balance was made of gold and steel. These movements were fire gilded and not interchangeable. The dials, hands, mainsprings and hairsprings were imported. The rounded pallets were manufactured by Pitkin,and the cases for his watches were made on the premises. As many as 900 watches could have been made by Pitkin.

Grade or Name – Description		Avg	Ex-Fn	Mint
Henry Pitkin S#1-50 .... ★ ★ ★ ★ ★		$20,000	$25,000	$40,000
H. & J. F. Pitkin, S#50-377 .... ★ ★ ★ ★		15,000	20,000	30,000
Pitkin & Co., New York, S#378-900 .... ★ ★ ★		6,000	8,000	12,000
W. Pitkin, Hartford, Conn., S# approx. 40,000, fusee lever,				
KW, Coin .... ★ ★		800	900	1,600

H. & J. F. Pitkin, about 16 size,engraved on movement
"H. & J. F. PITKIN DETACHED LEVER", key wind & set.

Movements marked with New York are English made imports.

ALBERT H. POTTER WATCH CO.

New York, New York
1855 - 1875

Albert Potter started his apprenticeship in 1852. When this was completed he moved to New York to take up watchmaking on his own. He made about 35 watches in all that sold for $225 to $350. Some were chronometers, some were lever escapements, key wind, gilded movements, some were fusee driven, both bridge and 3/4 plate. Potter was a contemporary of Charles Fasoldt and John Mulford, both horological inventors from Albany, N. Y. Potter moved to Cuba in 1861 but returned to New York in 1868. In 1872 he worked in Chicago and formed the Potter Brothers Company with his brother William. He moved to Geneva about 1876. His company produced a total of about 600 watches, but only about 40 of those were made in the U. S.

below U.S. mfg.

Grade or Name – Description		Avg	Ex-Fn	Mint
18S, BRG lever, Chronometer, signed A. H. Potter, NewYork, 18K Potter case, U.S. mfg.	★ ★ ★ ★ ★	$12,000	$14,000	$20,000
18S, BRG lever with wind indicator, 18K Potter case	★ ★ ★	6,500	8,000	13,000
18S-20S, **Tourbillion,** signed A. H. Potter, **Boston,** gilded, **18K** Potter case, U.S. mfg.	★ ★ ★ ★ ★	20,000	25,000	35,000

below GENEVA Mfg.

Grade or Name – Description		Avg	Ex-Fn	Mint
16S, "Charmilles," 3/4 plate, Geneva, (Dollar Watch)	★	$250	$350	$550

(Note: For futher information on Potter Geneva timepieces, SEE European Section)

A.H. Potter Watch Co., BOSTON, 18 size, about 6 jewels, detent escapement, note similarity to E.H. Howard & Co. early watches, serial number 5.

"Charmilles Geneva" on dial, made in Charmilles Switzerland, 16S, low jewel count, 3/4 plate, Gun-Metal case, (dollar Watch), Ca. 1896.

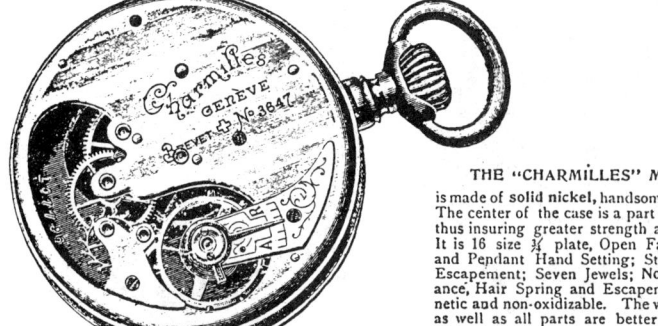

THE "CHARMILLES" MOVEMENT

is made of solid nickel, handsomely damaskeened. The center of the case is a part of the movement, thus insuring greater strength and reducing cost. It is 16 size ¾ plate, Open Face, Stemwinding and Pendant Hand Setting; Straight line Lever Escapement; Seven Jewels; Non-Magnetic Balance, Hair Spring and Escapement; is non-magnetic and non-oxidizable. The wheels and pinions as well as all parts are better finished than in higher priced movements, *and guaranteed perfect timekeepers.*

"Charmilles," AD Ca. 1896. in Marshall Field & Co. sales Catalog prices from $8.00 to $15.00.

GEORGE P. REED
Boston, Massachusetts 1865 - 1885

In 1854, George P. Reed entered the employment of Dennison, Howard and Davis, in Roxbury, Mass., and moved with the company to Waltham, Mass. Here he was placed in charge of the pinion finishing room. While there he invented and received a patent for the mainspring barrel and maintiming power combination. This patent was dated February 18, 1857. Reed returned to Roxbury with Howard who purchased his patented barrel. He stayed with the Howard factory as foreman and adjuster until 1865, when he left for Boston to start his own account.

He obtained a patent on April 7, 1868, for an improved chronometer escapement which featured simplified construction. He made about 100 chronometers with his improved escapement, to which he added a stem-wind device. His company turned out about 100 watches the first three years. Most, if not all, of his watches run for two days and have up and down indicators on the dial. They are both 18S and 16S, 3/4 plate, nickel, and are artistically designed. Reed experimented with various combinations of lever and chronometer escapements. One was a watch he made in 1862 and called the "Monitor." In all, Reed made a total of about **350** watches, and these are valuable to collectors.

Grade or Name – Description		Avg	Ex-Fn	Mint
18S, 15J, LS, OF or HC, Wind Indicator, chronometer escapement, 18K case	★★★★	$12,000	$15,000	$22,000
16S, 15J, LS, OF or HC, not chronometer, 18K case	★★★	7,500	8,000	15,000
16S, 15J, LS, OF, 31 day calendar, 18K case	★★★	7,500	8,000	14,000
16S, 15-17J, Wind Indicator, "Monitor", 14K, OF	★★★	6,500	7,000	13,000

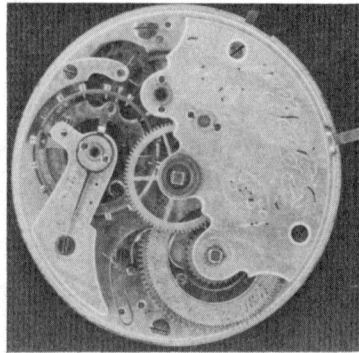

George P. Reed, 18 size, 15 jewels, key & stem wind, key & lever set, lever escapement, 48 hour up and down wind indicator, serial number 262.

George P. Reed, 18 size, 15 jewels, key & stem wind, key & lever set, lever escapement, 48 hour up and down wind indicator, serial number 5.

George P. Reed Boston, 18-16 size, 15 jewels, key wind, with key & lever set, lever escapement, serial # 282.

George P. Reed Boston, Monitor, 18-16 size, 15 jewels, wind indicator, serial # 322.

ROCKFORD WATCH CO.
Rockford, Illinois
1873 - 1915

The Rockford Watch Company's equipment was bought from the Cornell Watch Co., and two of Cornell's employees, C. W. Parker and P. H. Wheeler, went to work for Rockford. The factory was located 93 miles from Chicago on the Rock River. The first watch was placed on the market on May 1, 1876. They were key wind, 18S, full plate expansion balance & dials made by outside contract. By 1877 the company was making 3/4 plate nickel movements that fit standard size cases. Three railroads came through Rockford, and the company always advertised to the railroad and the demand was very popular with them. The company had some problems in 1896, and the name changed to Rockford Watch Co. Ltd. It closed in 1915.

ROCKFORD ESTIMATED SERIAL NUMBERS AND PRODUCTION DATES

DATE–SERIAL #	DATE–SERIAL #	DATE–SERIAL #	DATE–SERIAL #
1874 – 22,200	1884 – 226,000	1895 – 450,000	1906 – 670,000
1875 – 42,600	1885 – 247,000	1896 – 470,000	1907 – 690,000
1876 – 63,000	1886 – 267,000	1897 – 490,000	1908 – 734,000
1877 – 83,000	1887 – 287,500	1898 – 510,000	1909 – 790,000
1878 – 103,000	1888 – 308,000	1899 – 530,000	1910 – 824,000
1879 – 124,000	1889 – 328,500	1900 – 550,000	1911 – 880,000
1880 – 144,000	1890 – 349,000	1901 – 570,000	1912 – 936,000
1881 – 165,000	1891 – 369,500	1902 – 590,000	1913 – 958,000
1882 – 185,000	1892 – 390,000	1903 – 610,000	1914 – 980,000
1883 – 206,000	1893 – 410,000	1904 – 630,000	1915-1,000,000
	1894 – 430,000	1905 – 650,000	

The above list is provided for determining the APPROXIMATE age of your watch. Match serial number with date. Watches were not necessarily sold in the exact order of manufactured date.

ROCKFORD
18 SIZE

Grade or Name – Description	Avg	Ex-Fn	Mint
Belmont USA, 21J, LS, OF, NI, M#7	$225	$275	$400
Chronometer, 17J, ADJ, OF, G925 ....★	400	500	775
Dome Model, 9J, brass plates..★	100	150	275

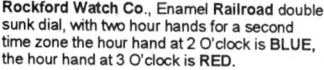

Rockford Watch Co., Enamel Railroad double sunk dial, with two hour hands for a second time zone the hour hand at 2 O'clock is BLUE, the hour hand at 3 O'clock is RED.

16-SIZE ROCKFORD

OUR SPECIAL No. 1000 21 JEWELS

Hunting or Open Face, nickel, 21 ruby and sapphire jewels in settings, adjusted to heat and cold. Compensating balance, Breguet hair spring, safety pinion, patent micrometric regulator, gold lettering, handsomely damaskeened, double sunk glass enameled dial, pendant set.

Above: 1913 AD
Note: S. # 825,020

🕐 Watches listed in this book are priced at the collectable retail level, as **complete** watches having an original 14k gold-filled case and *Key Wind* with silver, an original white enamel single sunk dial, and with the entire original movement in good working order with no repairs needed.

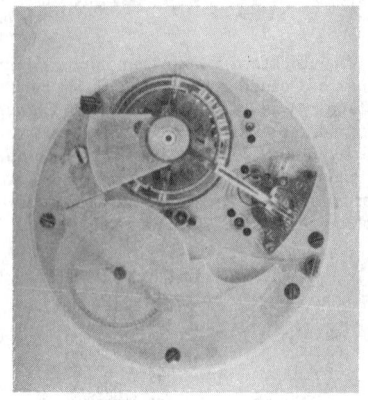

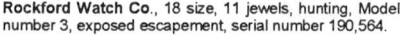

Rockford Watch Co., 18 size, 11 jewels, hunting, Model number 3, exposed escapement, serial number 190,564.   Special Railway, 18 size, 17 jewels, hunting, Model number 8, serial number 344,551.

Grade or Name – Description	Avg	Ex-Fn	Mint
King Edward, 21J, **Plymouth W. Co.**, 14K HC	$650	$700	$1,100
King Edward, 21J, **(Sears), Plymouth W. Co.** GJS, ADJ, NI, OF.	300	400	600
King Edward, 21J, **(Sears), Plymouth W. Co.** GJS, ADJ, NI, HC .	400	500	700
Nacirema is American backward, on dial Nacirema Watch Co.	80	100	200
Paxton's, 21J, **(Special on dial)**, OF	350	400	550
Pennsylvania Special, 25J, LS, Adj.6P, tu-tone, OF .... ★ ★ ★ ★	5,000	6,000	10,000
Railway King, 21J, OF .... ★	425	550	800
The Ramsey Watch, 11J, NI, KW or SW	150	175	250
The Ramsey Watch, 15J, NI, KW or SW	125	150	275
The Ramsey Watch, M#7, 21J, OF, NI, ADJ	350	425	600

🕐 Generic, nameless or **unmarked** grades for watch movements are listed under the Company name or initials of the Company, etc. by size, jewel count and description.

Rockford Early KW-KS, M#1-2, with low Serial #s less than 500 .... ★	$675	$775	$1,200
Rockford Early KW-KS, M#1-2, with low Serial #s from 500-1,000 .... ★	400	500	775
Rockford Early KW-KS, M#1-2, with **reversible case**	350	475	775
Rockford, 7-9J, SW, FULL, OF	75	95	200
Rockford, 7J, KW, FULL, OF	75	95	200
Rockford, 7J, KW, FULL, Silveroid	75	95	200
Rockford, 9J, SW, FULL, HC	85	100	225
Rockford, M#1, 9J, KW, FULL, HC	125	150	275
Rockford, 11J, SW, FULL, OF	70	90	200
Rockford, 11-13J, M#6, exposed escape wheel, FULL, HC .... ★	200	250	475
Rockford, M#1-2, 11J, KW, FULL	150	200	300
Rockford, M#1-2, 11J, transition case, FULL	100	150	225
Rockford, 11J, KW, Coin HC	150	200	250
Rockford, 9J, KW, M#5, 3/4 Plate, HC Coin	250	350	500
Rockford, 11J, KW, M#5, 3/4 Plate, HC Coin	275	400	550
Rockford, 15J, M#1 & 2, nickel, GJS, Adj, KW/KS, HC ..... ★ ★ ★	2,000	2,400	3,600
Rockford, 15J, KW/KS, M#5, 3/4 Plate, HC Coin	350	450	625
Rockford, 15J, KW/SW, M#5, 3/4 Plate, HC Coin	300	375	575
Rockford, 13J, HC	125	150	225
Rockford, 15J, SW, FULL	100	125	200
Rockford, 15J, KW, FULL, **multi-color dial**	375	450	875
Rockford, 15J, SW, 2-Tone movement	125	150	350

🕐 Watches listed in this book are priced at the collectable retail level, as **complete** watches having an original 14k gold-filled case and *Key Wind* with silver, an original white enamel single sunk dial, and with the entire original movement in good working order with no repairs needed.

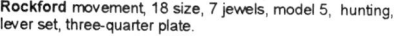

Rockford movement, 18 size, 7 jewels, model 5, hunting, lever set, three-quarter plate.

Grade 900, 18 size, 24J., Adj5p. Warning: 24J. fakes have been made from 21J. movements. The fakes are missing the eliptical jewel setting on the barrel bridge.

Grade or Name – Description	Avg	Ex-Fn	Mint
Rockford, 15J, KW, FULL, marked- ADJ	$185	$225	$375
Rockford, 15J, KW/SW	100	150	275
Rockford, 15J, KW/SW, Silveroid	100	150	240
Rockford, 15J, M#6, exposed escapement wheel, FULL, HC, LS, nickel mvt. ★	300	350	525
Rockford, 15J, M#6, exposed escapement wheel, FULL, HC, LS, gilded mvt.	200	275	425
Rockford, 15J, M#6, exposed wheel, nickel mvt., Coin	175	250	375
Rockford, M#1, 15J, KW, FULL	100	150	240
Rockford, 16J, GJS, NI, DMK, SW	100	150	225
Rockford, 16J, GJS, NI, DMK, SW, Silveroid	100	150	200
Rockford, 16J, GJS, NI, DMK, SW, Coin	100	150	200
Rockford, 17J, NI, DMK, SW, OF	100	150	200
Rockford, 17J, GJS, NI, DMK, SW, Adj.5P	100	165	250
Rockford, 17J, GJS, NI, SW, 2-Tone, OF	165	200	325
Rockford Early,19J, KW-KS, M#1-2, S# less than 100 ★★★	2,250	2,600	3,650
Rockford, M#1-2, 19J, KW, gilt, ADJ, HC ★★	1,850	2,000	2,450
Rockford, M#1-2, 19J, KW, nickel, GJS, ADJ, HC ★★★	2,500	3,000	3,850
Rockford, 21J, SW, Silveroid	250	275	425
Rockford, 21J, GJS, OF, Adj.5P, wind indicator ★★★	3,000	4,000	5,500
Rockford, 21J, SW, DMK, ADJ, HC	400	470	600
Rockford, 21J, NI, DMK, ADJ, OF	325	375	475
Rockford, 21J, GJS, NI, DMK, Adj.5P, marked "RG" OF	325	375	525
Rockford, ("22J", marked,) GJS, NI, Adj.5P, 2 tone, HC ★★	1,450	1,800	2,200
Rockford, ("22J", marked,) Adj, NI, SW,"RG," OF ★★	775	1,000	1,500
Rockford, 24J, GJS, SW, LS, Adj.5P, G# 900 or G# 918 marked "RG," OF	1,000	1,200	1,800
Rockford, 24J, GJS, SW, LS, Adj.5P, G# 800 marked "RG," HC ★	1,200	1,400	2,000
Rockford, 25J, GJS, SW, LS, Adj.5P, NI, DMK ★★★	3,800	5,500	7,500
Rockford, 26J, GJS, SW, LS, Adj.5P, NI, DMK ★★★	9,000	11,000	18,000

⊕ **Generic, nameless** or **unmarked** grades for watch movements are listed under the Company name or initials of the Company, etc. by size, jewel count and description.

	Avg	Ex-Fn	Mint
R.W. Co., 7-9-11J, NI or Gilded	$60	$85	$125
R.W. Co., 15J, NI or Gilded, OF	70	90	200
R.W. Co., 15J, NI or Gilded, HC	70	90	210
R.W. Co., 16-17J, Adj, NI, OF	70	90	210
R.W. Co., 16-17J, Adj, NI, HC	70	90	225
R.W. Co., 21J, Adj, NI, SW, OF	200	250	375
R.W. Co., 21J, Adj, NI, SW, HC	200	250	375

Rockford Watch Co., 18 size, 15 jewels, model # 5, 3/4 plate, key & stem wind.

Rockford Watch Co., 18 size, 15 jewels, model 4, open face, lever set, serial number 227,430.

Grade or Name – Description	Avg	Ex-Fn	Mint
Railway Special, 17J, ADJ, 2-tone, SW, HC ★	$425	$525	$775
The Syndicate Watch Co., M#7, 15J, LS, NI, HC	175	225	325
Winnebago, 17J, LS, GJS, Adj.5P, DR, NI, DMK, HC	200	250	450
Winnebago, 17J, LS, GJS, Adj.5P, DR, NI, DMK, OF	150	200	300
24 Hour Dial, 15J, SW or KW ★	200	300	550
40, 15J, M#3, HC ★★	275	375	575
43, 15J, M#3, HC, 2-Tone	125	150	250
66, 11J, M#7, OF	70	80	200
66, 11J, M#7, OF, Silveroid	70	80	175
66, 11J, M#7, HC	70	80	200
72, 15J, KW-SW, exposed escapement, HC ★	600	700	975
81, 9J, M#3, HC, Gilt	90	110	200
82, Special, 21J, SW ★★★	600	700	1,200
83, 15J, M#8, HC, 2-Tone	150	175	225
86, 15J, M#7, OF, NI ★	125	200	350
93, 9J, M#8, HC, Gilt	85	100	200
94, 9J, M#7, OF	70	100	185
200, 17J, M#9, NI, LS, HC	100	150	225
205, 17J, M#9, NI, LS, OF	100	150	175
800, 24J, GJS, DR, Adj.5P, DMK, HC ★	1,200	1,400	1,850
805, 21J, GJS, Adj.5P, NI, DMK, HC, marked "RG"	350	400	600
810, 21J, NI, DMK, ADJ, HC	335	385	500
820, 17J, HC, SW ★★	300	350	575
825, 17J, HC, FULL	150	175	225
830, 17J, HC, FULL	125	150	200
835, 17J, HC, FULL	125	150	200
835, 17J, HC, FULL, Silveroid	100	125	175
845, 21J, HC, GJS, FULL ★	425	500	575
870, 7J, HC, FULL	85	110	150

IMPORTANT NOTE: Railroad Standards, Railroad Approved & Railroad Grade **terminology,** as defined and used in this *BOOK*.
1. **RAILROAD STANDARDS** = A commission or board appointed by the railroad companies outlined a set of **guidelines** to be accepted or approved by each railroad line.
2. **RAILROAD APPROVED** = A **LIST** of watches each railroad line would approve if purchased by their employee's. (this list changed through the years).
3. **RAILROAD GRADE** = A watch made by manufactures to meet or exceed the guidelines set by the railroad **standards**. Grades such as 992, Vanguard and B.W. Raymond, etc.

🕐 Some GRADES **exceeded** the R.R. standards such as 23 jewels, diamond end stone, gold train, raised gold jewel settings, double sunk dial and the list goes on. Examples: such as Veritas, Sangamo, 950 & Riverside Maximus and many others.

Grade or Name – Description		Avg.	Ex-Fn	Mint
890, 24J, GJS, DR, Adj.5P, **HC**, NI, DMK	★ ★	$1,500	$1,700	$1,950
900, 24J, GJS, DR, Adj.5P, OF, NI, DMK	★ ★	1,000	1,200	1,700
900, 24J, GJS, DR, Adj.5P, 14K, OF case	★ ★	1,400	1,500	2,000
905, 21J, GJS, DR, Adj.5P, OF, NI, DMK		325	375	425
910, 21J, NI, DMK, ADJ, OF		175	200	325
912, 21J, Adj. 5P, LS, OF		475	600	750
915, 17J, M#9, OF, SW	★ ★ ★	700	800	1,000
918, **24J**, GJS, DR, Adj.5P, OF, NI, DMK	★ ★	1,200	1,400	1,850
918, 21J, OF, NI, GJS, Adj.5P, DR		300	350	400
918, 21J, OF, NI, GJS, Adj.5P, DR, Coin		275	325	375
920 & 930 , 17J, OF		175	225	275
925 & 935, 17J, OF		100	135	150
945, 21J, M#9, OF, SW		225	275	325
marked-950, 21J, OF, NI, GJS, Adj.5P, DR, **Wind Indicator** ★ ★		2,500	3,000	4,000
970, 7J, OF		70	90	125
970, 7J, OF, Silveroid		70	85	100

16 SIZE
(most HC grade numbers end with 0 & most OF grade numbers end with 5

Grade or Name – Description		Avg	Ex-Fn	Mint
Commodore Perry, 21J, OF, GJS, GT, marked "RG"	★	$300	$350	$500
Commodore Perry, 15-17J, ADJ		125	150	175
Cosmos, 17J, OF, GJS, LS, DMK, marked dial & mvt.		250	325	425
Cosmos, 17J, **HC**, GJS, LS, DMK, marked dial & mvt.		300	350	475
Doll Watch Co., 17J, marked dial & mvt., OF	★ ★ ★	750	1,000	1,600
Doll Watch Co., 21J, marked dial & mvt., OF	★ ★ ★	1,000	1,300	1,950
Doll Watch Co., 23J, marked dial & mvt., OF	★ ★ ★	1,500	1,700	2,500
Doll Watch Co., 23J, (G#504-M# 4), triple signed, HC	★ ★ ★ ★	1,700	1,900	2,800
Dome Model, 15J		75	100	125
Dome Model, 17J		75	100	125
Dome Model, 17J, 2-tone, HC		150	200	350
Herald Square, 7J, 3/4, OF		100	125	150
Iroquois, 17J, DR, **14K, HC**		550	585	775
Iroquois, 17J, DR, OF		150	200	350
Peerless, 17J, OF, NI, LS, DMK		100	125	250
Pocahontas, 17J, GJS, Adj.5P, DR, OF	★	200	250	475
Pocahontas, 17J, GJS, Adj.5P, DR, HC	★	275	350	550
Pocahontas, 21J, GJS, Adj.5P, DR, OF	★	300	450	650
Pocahontas, 21J, GJS, Adj.5P, DR, HC	★ ★	500	600	875
Prince of Wales (Sears), 21J, Plymouth W. Co.		275	300	500
Prince of Wales (Sears), 21J, Plymouth W. Co.**14K**		525	650	850

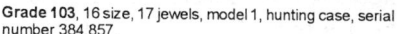

Grade 103, 16 size, 17 jewels, model 1, hunting case, serial number 384,857.

Cosmos movement, 16 size, 17 jewels, open face, gold jewel settings, grade 565, model 2.

Grade 500-HC, model 4, 16 size, 21 jewels, gold jewel settings, gold train, Adj6p, marked "RG," serial number 546,617, originally sold for about $100.00.

Grade 505-OF, model 5, 16 size, 21 jewels, gold jewel settings, gold train, Adj6p, marked "RG," serial number 593,929, originally sold for about $100.00.

🕐 **Generic, nameless or unmarked** grades for watch movements are listed under the Company name or initials of the Company, etc. by size, jewel count and description.

Grade or Name – Description	Avg	Ex-Fn	Mint
Rockford, 7J, 3/4, HC	$75	$100	$200
Rockford, 9J, 3/4, SW, OF	75	100	165
Rockford, 9J, SW, Silveroid	75	100	165
Rockford, 9J, SW, HC	75	100	225
Rockford, 11J, SW, Silveroid	75	100	150
Rockford, 11J, 3/4, HC	75	100	225
Rockford, 15J, 3/4, ADJ, OF	75	100	200
Rockford, 15J, 3/4, ADJ, Silveroid	75	100	150
Rockford, 15J, 3/4, ADJ, HC	75	100	225
Rockford, 16J, 3/4, SW, Silveroid	75	100	150
Rockford, 16J, 3/4, ADJ, NI, DMK	75	100	175
Rockford, 17J, 3/4	75	100	175
Rockford, 17J, 3/4, 2-Tone, marked "RG" ★	225	300	400
Rockford, 17J, BRG, Adj.3P, DR	125	150	250
Rockford, 17J, GJS, Adj.5P, DR, **Wind Indicator** (grade 665)	950	1,100	1,700
Rockford, 17J, BRG, Silveroid	70	100	175
Rockford, 17J, 3/4, Silveroid	70	90	170
Rockford, 21J, 3/4, SW, Silveroid	250	300	375
Rockford, 21J, BRG, SW, Silveroid	250	300	400
Rockford, 21J, 3/4, GJS, Adj.5P	300	375	425
Rockford, 21J, BRG, GJS, Adj.5P, GT, DR	325	350	500
Rockford, 21J, GJS, Adj.5P, DR, **Wind Indicator** ★	1,000	1,400	2,000
Winnebago, 17J, BRG, GJS, Adj.5P, NI, OF	200	250	350
Winnebago, 17J, BRG, GJS, Adj.5P, NI, HC ★	225	275	500
Winnebago, 21J, BRG, GJS, Adj.5P, NI ★	400	450	700
100, 16J, M#1, HC, 3/4, 2-Tone	225	275	350
100S, 21J, Special, HC, 3/4, LS ★	300	350	450
102, 15J, HC, M#1 ★	150	175	275
103, 15-17J, HC, M#1 ★ ★	275	325	425
104, 11J, HC, M#1	75	100	170
110, 17J, 2 tone dome style mvt.,HC	325	350	475
115-125, 17J, Special, HC ★ ★ ★	525	625	875
120-130, 17J, HC ★ ★ ★	425	525	775

🕐 Pricing in this Guide are fair market price for **COMPLETE** watches which are reflected from the "**NAWCC**" National and regional shows.

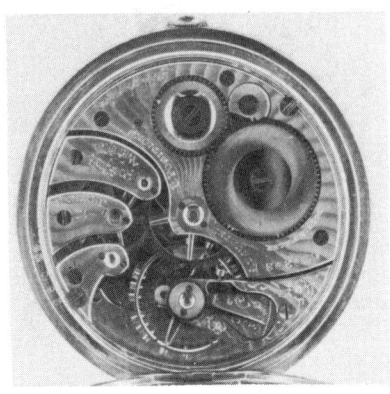

Rockford Watch Co., Pocahontas, 21 jewels., hunting case, bridge model, Adj.5P, serial # 670,203

Rockford Watch Co., 21j., Wind indicator, marked 655, adjusted to 5 positions, gold jewel settings, gold center wheel, double roller, Serial # 830,591.

Grade or Name – Description	Avg	Ex-Fn	Mint
400 & 405, 17J, NI, Adj.5P, GJS, DR, BRG	$125	$150	$250
440, 17J, GJS, HC	125	150	220
445, 19J, GJS, OF ★★	90	1,000	1,300
500, 21J, BRG, NI, GJS, Adj.5P, GT, HC ★★	500	550	775
501, 21J, GJS, HC ★★★	900	1,100	1,500
505, 21J, BRG, NI, GJS, Adj.5P, GT, OF ★★	500	575	875
510, 21J, BRG, NI, GJS, Adj.5P, GT, HC ★	425	475	675
515 - 525 -545, 21J, 3/4, OF	350	400	550
520, 21J, HC, 3/4	350	400	600
520 - 540, 21J, BRG, NI, GJS, Adj.5P, HC	450	500	650
525, 21J. M#5, GT, Adj.5P ★	350	400	500
530, 21J, HC, GJS, Adj.5P, marked "RG" ★	375	425	550
535, 21J, OF, 3/4 ★	300	325	425
537, 21J, OF, GJS, Adj.5P ★★★	1,000	1,100	1,400
540, 21J,GT, BRG, Adj.5P, OF	275	325	450
545, 21J,GT, BRG, Adj.5P, OF	275	325	450
561, 17J, BRG, HC	150	175	300
566, 17J, BRG, OF	150	175	250
572, 17J, BRG, NI, HC	150	175	275
573-575, 17J, 3/4 & BRG, NI, OF	150	175	250
578-579, 17J, PS, GJS ★★	300	350	550
584 15J, 3/4 NI, HC	65	75	150
585, 15J, 3/4, NI, OF	65	75	120
620-625, 21J, HC, 3/4 ★	325	400	600
655, 21J, **Wind Indicator**, Adj.5P, **marked 655**, OF ★★	1,100	1,500	2,100
665, 17J, **Wind Indicator**, Adj, 5P, OF ★	800	900	1,600

🕐 Watches listed in this book are priced at the collectable retail level, as **complete** watches having an original 14k gold-filled case and *Key Wind* with silver, an original white enamel single sunk dial, and with the entire original movement in good working order with no repairs needed.

🕐 This book endeavours to be a GUIDE or helpful manual and offers a wealth of material to be used as a tool not as a absolute document. Price Guides are like watches the worst may be better than none at all, but at best cannot be expected to be 100% accurate

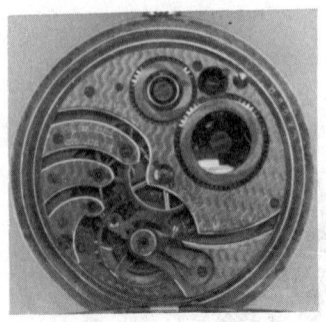

Rockford Watch Co., 12 size, 15 jewels, model 1, hunting, pendant set.

Rockford Watch Co., 12 size, 15 jewels, model 2, open face, pendant set.

12 SIZE
All 3/4 Bridge

Grade or Name – Description	Avg	Ex-Fn	Mint
Commodore Perry, 15-17J, ADJ.	$65	$80	$200
Doll Watch Co., 21J, marked on dial & movement, OF ★★	250	300	600
Iroquois, 17J, BRG, DR, ADJ	75	100	175
Pocahontas, 21J, GJS, Adj.5P, BRG, DR	175	200	325
Rockford, 15J, BRG	40	70	125
Rockford, 17J, BRG, NI, DR, ADJ	40	70	125
Rockford, 21J, BRG, NI, DR, ADJ	100	150	225
Rockford, 21J, BRG, NI, DR, ADJ, Silveroid	70	85	175
Winona, 15J, BRG	60	70	125
300, 23J, 3/4, GJS, Adj.5P, HC ★★	325	375	600
305, 23J, BRG, NI, GJS, Adj.5P, GT, OF ★★	325	375	600
310(HC)-315(OF), 21J, BRG, NI, GJS, Adj.5P ★	100	125	200
320(HC)-325(OF), 17J, BRG, NI, ADJ, DR	60	70	125
330, 17J, BRG, NI, DR, HC	60	70	150
335, 17J, BRG, NI, DR, OF	60	70	125
340(HC)-345(OF), 21J, M#1 ★	225	250	350
350, 17J, OF	60	70	125
355, 17J, HC	60	70	150

Note: Add $10 to $25 to above watches with hunting case.

0 - Size movement in 12 - Size Case ("Xtremethin")

Grade or Name – Description	Avg	Ex-Fn	Mint
0 - Size movement in 12 - Size Case, 15J., Plain GF case	60	85	150
0 - Size movement in 12 - Size Case, 15J., GF case & ENAMELED	125	150	225

8 SIZE

Grade or Name – Description	Avg	Ex-Fn	Mint
15J, 3/4, HC, LS, **14K, 40 DWT**	$400	$450	$675
9–15J, 3/4, KW or SW, LS, OF or HC,	65	85	175

🕐 Pricing in this Guide are fair market price for **COMPLETE** watches which are reflected from the "**NAWCC**" National and regional shows.

Rockford movement, 6 size, 17 jewels, quick train, straight line escapement, compensating balance, adjusted to temperature, micrometric regulator, 3/4 damaskeened plates.

6 SIZE

Grade or Name – Description	Avg	Ex-Fn	Mint
9J, NI, HC	$75	$100	$175
15J, 3/4, NI	75	100	150
16J, 3/4, NI	75	100	150
17J, 3/4, ADJ, NI	75	100	175

0 SIZE

Grade or Name – Description	Avg	Ex-Fn	Mint
Iroquois, 17J., HC	$125	$150	$325
Plymouth Watch Co., 15-17J, HC	225	250	350
7J, BRG, NI, DR, HC	50	70	200
11J, BRG, NI, DR, HC	50	70	200
15J, BRG, NI, DR, HC	60	80	225
17J, BRG, NI, DR, HC	75	90	225

🕐 Watches listed in this book are priced at the collectable retail level, as **complete** watches having an original 14k gold-filled case and *Key Wind* with silver, an original white enamel single sunk dial, and with the entire original movement in good working order with no repairs needed.

🕐 This book endeavours to be a GUIDE or helpful manual and offers a wealth of material to be used as a tool not as a absolute document. Price Guides are like watches the worst may be better than none at all, but at best cannot be expected to be 100% accurate.

🕐 Characteristics of watches differ for the same age of both case and movement, because these features vary it may not be accurate to date a watch by one single influence. Example: the second hand was not commonly found on watches before 1750, but common about 1800. The first second hand appeared in 1665 and another in 1690. Therefore statements are broad rather than accurate.

ROCKFORD WATCH CO.
IDENTIFICATION OF MOVEMENTS
BY MODEL NUMBER

How to Identify Your Watch: Compare the movement of your watch with the illustrations in this section. Upon matching the movement exactly, the model number and size can be determined. While comparing, note the location of the balance, jewels, screws, gears, and type of back plate (Full, 3/4, Bridge) which will be clues in identifying the movement you have. Having determined the size and model number, you can now find your watch in the main price listing by name or number (which is engraved on the movement).

The Rockford Watch Company, Ltd.

JANUARY 1907
NUMBER AND GRADE

WITH

DESCRIPTION OF MOVEMENTS MANUFACTURED TO DATE

Number and Grade of Movement	GRADE	Size	Style		Jewels	Wind	Sett	Model
1 to 114,000		18	Htg.	F. Pl.		Key Stem	Key Lever	1
114,001 " 115,000		"	"	¾ Pl.		"	"	5
115,001 " 126,000		"	"	F. Pl.		"	"	2
126,001 " 127,000		"	"	¾ Pl.		"	"	5
127,001 " 130,000		"	"	F. Pl.		"	"	2
130,001 " 131,000		"	"	¾ Pl.		"	"	5
131,001 " 133,000		"	"	F. Pl.		"	"	3
133,001 " 134,000		"	"	¾ Pl.		"	"	5
134,001 " 138,000		"	"	F. Pl.		"	"	3
138,001 " 139,000		"	"	¾ Pl.		"	"	5
139,001 " 143,000		"	"	F. Pl.		"	"	3
143,001 " 144,000		"	"	¾ Pl.		"	"	5
144,001 " 145,000		"	"	F. Pl.		"	"	3
145,001 " 146,000		"	"	¾ Pl.		"	"	5
146,001 " 149,000		"	"	F. Pl.		"	"	3
149,001 " 151,000		"	"	¾ Pl.		"	"	5
151,001 " 153,000		"	"	F. Pl.		"	"	3
153,001 " 154,000		"	"	¾ Pl.		"	"	5
154,001 " 158,000		"	"	F. Pl.		"	"	3
158,001 " 159,000		"	▪	¾ Pl.		"	"	5
159,001 " 169,000		"	"	F. Pl.		"	"	3
170,001 " 170,100		"	"	¾ Pl.		15	"	"	5
170,101 " 177,000		"	"	F. Pl.			"	"	3
177,001 " 177,800		"	"	"			"	"	6
177,901 " 189,500		"	"	"			"	"	3
189,601 " 190,900		"	"	"			"	"	6
191,001 " 191,100		"	"	"			"	"	3
191,101 " 196,400		"	O. F.	"			"	"	4
196,501 " 197,000		"	Htg.	"			"	"	6
197,101 " 197,500		"	"	"			"	"	3
197,601 " 198,000		"	O. F.	"			"	"	6
198,101 " 199,100		"	Htg.	"			"	"	4
199,201 " 199,500		"	"	"			"	"	6
199,600 " 200,000		"	"	¾ Pl.			"	"	5
200,001 " 213,100		8	"	"			"	"	1
213,101 " 218,900		6	"	"			"	"	"
219,001 " 219,500		18	"	"			"	"	5
219,501 " 224,500		"	"	F. Pl.			"	"	3
224,501 " 228,900		"	O. F.	"			"	"	4
229,001 " 232,000		"	Htg.	"			"	"	3
232,001 " 233,000		"	"	¾ Pl.			"	"	5
233,001 " 234,000	47	"	O. F.	F. Pl.	Nickel	15	"	"	4
234,001 " 235,000	45	"	"	"	"	"	"	"	"
235,001 " 236,000	43	"	Htg.	F. Pl.	"	"	"	"	3
236,001 " 237,000	44	"	"	"	Gilt	"	"	"	"
237,001 " 238,000	45	"	O. F.	F. Pl.	"	"	"	"	4
238,001 " 239,000		"	"	"	"	9	"	"	"
239,001 " 240,000	45	"	"	"	"	15	"	"	"
240,001 " 241,000	46	"	"	"	"	11	"	"	"
241,001 " 241,800	47	"	"	"	Nickel	15	"	"	"
241,801 " 242,000	40	"	Htg.	"	"	"	"	"	3
242,001 " 243,000	43	"	"	"	"	"	"	"	"
243,001 " 244,000	44	"	"	"	Gilt	"	"	"	"
244,001 " 244,300	49	"	"	"	Nickel	"	"	"	6
244,301 " 244,400	72	"	"	"	"	"	"	"	"
244,401 " 245,000	62	"	"	"	"	11	"	"	8
245,001 " 246,000	81	"	"	"	Gilt	9	"	"	3
246,001 " 247,000	44	"	"	"	"	15	"	"	"
247,001 " 248,000	64	"	O. F.	"	"	11	"	"	4
248,001 " 249,000	46	"	Htg.	"	"	15	"	"	6
249,001 " 250,000	49	"	"	"	Nickel	"	"	"	"
250,001 " 250,500	62	"	"	"	"	11	"	"	"
250,501 " 251,000	60	"	O. F.	"	"	"	"	"	7
251,001 " 252,000	66	"	"	"	"	"	"	"	"
252,001 " 253,000	67	"	"	"	Gilt	"	"	"	"
253,001 " 253,500	83	"	Htg.	"	Nickel	15	"	"	8
253,501 " 253,700	77	"	"	"	"	"	"	"	"
253,701 " 254,000	68	"	"	"	Gilt	11	"	"	"
254,001 " 254,600	86	"	O. F.	"	Nickel	15	"	"	7
254,601 " 254,800	76	"	"	"	"	"	"	"	"
254,801 " 255,000	78	"	"	"	Gilt	"	"	"	"
255,001 " 256,000	89	"	"	"	"	"	"	"	"
256,001 " 257,000	68	"	Htg.	"	"	11	"	"	8
257,001 " 258,000	93	"	"	"	"	9	"	"	"
258,001 " 259,000	69	"	"	"	Nickel	11	"	"	"

The Rockford Watch Company, Ltd.

Number and Grade of Movement	GRADE	Size		Style		Jewels	Wind	Sett	Model
259,001 to 260,000	66	18	O. F.	F. Pl.	Nickel	11	Stem	Lever	7
260,001 " 261,000	68	"	Htg.	"	Gilt	11	"	"	8
261,001 " 262,000	86	"	O. F.	"	Nickel	15	"	"	7
262,001 " 263,000	67	"	"	"	Gilt	11	"	"	7
263,001 " 264,000	83	"	Htg.	"	Nickel	15	"	"	8
264,001 " 265,000	69	"	"	"	"	"	"	"	8
265,001 " 266,000	68	"	"	"	Gilt	11	"	"	"
266,001 " 267,000	93	"	"	"	"	9	"	"	8
267,001 " 267,800	83	"	"	"	Nickel	15	"	"	"
267,801 " 268,000	77	"	"	"	"	"	"	"	"
268,001 ' 269,000	68	"	"	"	Gilt	11	"	"	7
269,001 " 270,000	67	"	O. F.	"	"	"	"	"	7
270,001 " 270,800	85	"	Htg.	"	"	15	"	"	8
270,801 " 271,000	79	"	"	"	"	"	"	"	8
271,001 " 272,000	66	"	O. F.	"	Nickel	11	"	"	7
272,001 " 272,100	77	"	Htg.	"	"	15	"	"	8
272,101 " 272,200	83	"	"	"	"	"	"	"	"
272,201 " 272,300	77	"	"	"	"	"	"	"	"
272,301 " 272,600	83	"	"	"	"	"	"	"	"
272,601 " 272,700	77	"	"	"	"	"	"	"	"
272,701 " 272,900	83	"	"	"	"	"	"	"	"
272,901 " 273,000	77	"	"	"	"	"	"	"	"
273,001 " 274,000	69	"	"	"	"	"	"	"	"
274,001 " 275,000	83	"	"	"	"	"	"	"	"
275,001 " 276,000	69	"	"	"	"	11	"	"	"
276,001 " 277,000	83	"	"	"	"	15	"	"	"
277,001 " 278,000	85	"	"	"	Gilt	"	"	"	"
278,001 " 279,000	66	"	O. F.	"	Nickel	11	"	"	7
279,001 " 279,200	76	"	"	"	"	15	"	"	"
279,201 " 280,000	86	"	"	"	"	"	"	"	"
280,001 " 281,000	66	"	"	"	"	11	"	"	"
281,001 " 282,000	85	"	Htg.	"	Gilt	15	"	"	8
282,001 " 283,000	83	"	"	"	Nickel	"	"	"	"
283,001 " 284,000	93	"	"	"	Gilt	9	"	"	"
284,001 " 285,000	89	"	O. F.	"	"	15	"	"	7
285,001 " 286,000	69	"	Htg.	"	Hickel	11	"	"	8
286,001 " 286,200	83	"	"	"	Nick.& Gilt	15	"	"	"
286,201 " 286,500	84	"	"	"	"	"	"	"	"
286,501 " 287,000	83	"	"	"	Nickel	"	"	"	"
287,001 " 288,000	66	"	O. F.	"	"	11	"	"	7
288,001 " 289,000	67	"	"	"	Gilt	"	"	"	"
289,001 " 289,500	84	"	Htg.	"	Spot Gilt	15	"	"	8
289,501 " 291,000	83	"	"	"	Nickel	"	"	"	"
291,001 " 292,000	69	"	"	"	"	11	"	"	"
292,001 " 293,000	67	"	O. F.	"	Gilt	"	"	"	7
293,001 " 294,000	85	"	Htg.	"	"	15	"	"	8
294,001 " 295,000	93	"	"	"	"	9	"	"	"
295,001 " 296,000	66	"	O. F.	"	Nickel	11	"	"	7
296,001 " 297,000	89	"	"	"	Gilt	15	"	"	"
297,001 " 298,000	69	"	Htg.	"	Nickel	11	"	"	8
298,001 " 299,000	67	"	O. F.	"	Gilt	"	"	"	7
299,001 " 300,000	93	"	Htg.	"	"	9	"	"	8
300,001 " 300,500	84	"	"	"	Nick.& Gilt	15	"	"	"
300,501 " 300,700	83	"	"	"	Nickel	"	"	"	"
300,701 " 301,000	70	"	"	"	Nick.& Gilt	16	"	"	"
301,001 " 302,000	66	"	O. F.	"	Nickel	11	"	"	7
302,001 " 303,000	93	"	Htg.	"	Gilt	9	"	"	8
303,001 " 304,000	69	"	"	"	Nickel	11	"	"	"
304,001 " 304,500	84	"	"	"	Nick.& Gilt	15	"	"	"
304,501 " 305,000	83	"	"	"	Nickel	"	"	"	"
305,001 " 305,500	84	"	"	"	Nick.&Gilt	"	"	"	"
305,501 " 306,000	83	"	"	"	Nickel	"	"	"	"
306,001 " 307,000	66	"	O. F.	"	"	11	"	"	7
307,001 " 308,000	83	"	Htg.	"	"	15	"	"	8
308,001 " 309,000	93	"	"	"	Gilt	9	"	"	"
309,001 " 310,000	83	"	"	"	Nickel	15	"	"	"
310,001 " 310,500	87	"	O. F.	"	Nick.& Gilt	"	"	"	7
310,501 " 310,700	88	"	"	"	Nickel	16	"	"	"
310,701 " 311,000	86	"	"	"	"	15	"	"	"
311,001 " 312,000	69	"	Htg.	"	"	11	"	"	8
312,001 " 313,000	93	"	"	"	Gilt	9	"	"	"
313,001 " 314,000	83	"	"	"	Nickel	15	"	"	"
314,001 " 317,000	93	"	"	"	Gilt	9	"	"	"
317,001 " 318,000	85	"	"	"	"	15	"	"	"
318,001 " 319,000	93	"	"	"	"	9	"	"	"
319,001 " 320,000	85	"	"	"	"	15	"	"	"
320,001 " 321,000	84	"	"	"	Nick.& Gilt	"	"	"	"
321,001 " 322,000	83	"	"	"	Nickel	"	"	"	"
322,001 " 323,000	84	"	"	"	Nick.& Gilt	"	"	"	"
323,001 " 325,000	83	"	"	"	Nickel	"	"	"	"
325,001 " 326,000	85	"	"	"	Gilt	"	"	"	"
326,001 " 327,000	93	"	"	"	"	9	"	"	"
327,001 " 328,000	83	"	"	"	Nickel	15	"	"	"
328,001 " 329,000	89	"	O. F.	"	Gilt	"	"	"	7
329,001 " 329,100	84	"	Htg.	"	Nick.& Gilt	"	"	"	8
329,101 " 329,200	83	"	"	"	Special	.....	"	"	"
329,201 " 329,700	84	"	"	"	Nick.& Gilt	15	"	"	"
329,701 " 330,000	70	"	"	"	"	16	"	"	"
330,001 " 330,800	87	"	O. F.	"	Nickel	15	"	"	7

The Rockford Watch Company, Ltd.

Number and Grade of Movement	GRADE	Description of Movement				Jewels	Wind	Sett	Model
		Size	Style						
330,801 to 331,000	88	18	O. F.	F. Pl.	Nick.& Gilt	16	Stem	Lever	7
331,001 " 332,000	68	"	Htg.	"	Gilt	11	"	"	8
332,001 " 333,000	86	"	O. F.	"	Nickel	15	"	"	7
333,001 " 334,000	69	"	Htg.	"	"	11	"	"	8
334,001 " 335,000	66	"	O. F,	"			"	"	7
335,001 " 336,000	94	"	"	"	Gilt	9	"	"	"
336,001 " 337,000	68	"	Htg.	"	"	11	"	"	8
337,001 " 338,000	94	"	O. F.	"	"	9	"	"	"
338,001 " 338,500	88	"	"	"	Nick.& Gilt	16	"	"	"
338,501 " 339,000	86	"	"	"	Nickel	"	"	"	"
339,001 " 339,500	70	"	Htg.	"	Nick.& Gilt		"	"	8
339,501 " 340,000	84	"	"	"	"	15	"	"	"
340,001 " 341,000	66	"	O. F.	"	Nickel	11	"	"	7
341,001 " 342,000	85	"	Htg.	"	Gilt	15	"	"	8
342,001 " 343,000	89	"	O. F.	"	"		"	"	7
343,001 " 344,000	94	"	"	"	"	9	"	"	"
344,001 " 345,000	84	"	Htg.	"	Nick.& Gilt	15	"	"	8
345,001 " 346,000	68	"	"	"	Gilt	11	"	"	"
346,001 " 347,000	87	"	O. F.	"	Nick.& Gilt	15	"	"	7
347,001 " 348,000	94	"	"	"	Gilt	9	"	"	"
348,001 " 348,300	88	"	"	"	Nick.& Gilt	16	"	"	"
348,301 " 348,500	87	"	"	"	"	15	"	"	"
348,501 " 349,000	86	"	"	"	Nickel	"	"	"	"
349,001 " 349,500	67	"	"	"	Gilt	11	"	"	"
349,501 " 350,000	89	"	"	"	"	15	"	"	"
350,001 " 350,500	70	"	Htg.	"	Nick.& Gilt	16	"	"	8
350,501 " 351,000	85	"	"	"	Gilt	15	"	"	"
351,001 " 352,000	87	"	O. F.	"	Nick & Gilt		"	"	7
352,001 " 352,500	88	"	"	"	"	16	"	"	"
352,501 " 353,000	67	"	"	"	Gilt	11	"	"	"
353,001 " 353,500	100	16	Htg.	¾ Pl.	Nick.& Gilt	16	"	"	1
353,501 " 353,800	101	"	"	"	Nickel	15	"	"	"
353,801 " 354,000	102	"	"	"	"		"	"	"
354,001 " 354,500	103	"	"	"	"	"	"	"	"
354,501 " 355,000	104	"	"	"	"	11	"	"	"
355,001 " 355,500	111	"	"	"	Gilt	15	"	"	"
355,501 " 356,000	112	"	"	"	"	11	"	"	"
356,001 " 356,500	113	"	"	"	"	9	"	"	"
356,501 " 357,000	114	"	"	"	"	11	"	"	"
357,001 " 358,500	68	18	"	F. Pl.	"	11	"	"	8
358,501 " 359,000	67	"	O. F.	"	"	9	"	"	7
359,001 " 359,500	87	"	"	"	Nick.& Gilt	15	"	"	"
359,501 " 360,000	86	"	"	"	Nickel	"	"	"	"
360,001 " 360,500	101	16	Htg.	¾ Pl.	Nick.& Gilt	"	"	"	1
360,501 " 361,000	102	"	"	"	Nickel	"	"	"	"
361,001 " 361,500	103	"	"	"	"	"	"	"	"
361,501 " 362,000	104	"	"	"	"	11	"	"	"
362,001 " 364,000	67	18	O. F.	F. Pl.	Gilt	"	"	"	7
364,001 " 365,000	112	16	Htg.	¾ Pl.	"	15	"	"	1
365,001 " 366,000	102	"	"	"	Nickel	"	"	"	"
366,001 " 367,000	103	"	"	"	"	"	"	"	"
367,001 " 368,000	67	18	O. F.	F. Pl.	Gilt	11	"	"	7
368,001 " 368,500	112	16	Htg.	¾ Pl.	"	15	"	"	1
368,501 " 369,000	101	"	"	"	Nick.& Gilt	"	"	"	"
369,001 " 370,000	104	"	"	"	Nickel	11	"	"	"
370,001 " 370,500	86	18	O. F.	F. Pl.	"	15	"	"	7
370,501 " 371,000	87	"	"	"	Nick.& Gilt	"	"	"	"
371,001 " 371,500	89	"	"	"	Gilt	"	"	"	"
371,501 " 372,000	94	"	"	"	"	9	"	"	"
372,001 " 372,500	113	16	Htg.	¾ Pl.	"	11	"	"	1
372,501 " 373,000	114	"	"	"	"	9	"	"	"
373,001 " 374,000	113	"	"	"	"	11	"	"	"
374,001 " 374,500	68	18	"	F. Pl.	"	"	"	"	8
374,501 " 375,000	94	"	O. F.	"	"	9	"	"	7
375,001 " 376,000	87	"	"	"	Nick.& Gilt	15	"	"	"
376,001 " 376,200	100	16	Htg.	¾ Pl.	"	16	"	"	1
376,201 " 376,700	101	"	"	"	"	15	"	"	"
376,701 " 377,000	102	"	"	"	Nickel	"	"	"	"
377,001 " 377,500	104	"	"	"	"	11	"	"	"
377,501 " 378,000	103	"	"	"	"	15	"	"	"
378,001 " 379,000	94	18	O. F.	F. Pl.	Gilt	9	"	"	7
379,001 " 379,500	86	"	"	"	Nickel	15	"	"	"
379,501 " 380,000	84	"	Htg.	"	Nick.& Gilt	"	"	"	8
380,001 " 380,500	101	16	"	¾ Pl.	"	"	"	"	1
380,501 " 381,000	104	"	"	"	Nickel	11	"	"	"
381,001 " 381,300	102	"	"	"	"	15	"	"	"
381,301 " 382,000	103	"	"	"	"	"	"	"	"
382,001 " 382,200	111	"	"	"	Gilt	"	"	"	"
382,201 " 383,000	112	"	"	"	"	11	"	"	"
383,001 " 383,500	113	"	"	"	"	9	"	"	"
383,501 " 384,000	114	"	"	"	"		"	"	"
384,001 " 384,500	100	"	"	"	Nick.& Gilt	16	"	"	"
384,501 " 385,000	103	"	"	"	Nickel	15	"	"	"
385,001 " 385,500	104	"	"	"	"	11	"	"	"
385,501 " 386,000	103	"	"	"	"	15	"	"	"
386,001 " 387,000	112	"	"	"	Gilt	"	"	"	"
387,001 " 387,500	93	18	"	F. Pl.	"	9	"	"	8
387,501 " 388,000	68	"	"	"	"	11	"	"	"

The Rockford Watch Company, Ltd.

Number and Grade of Movement	GRADE	Size	Style			Jewels	Wind	Sett	Model
388,001 to 388,500	94	18	O. F.	F. Pl.	Gilt	9	Stem	Lever	7
388,501 " 389,000	89	"	"	"	"	15	"	"	"
389,001 " 389,100	76	"	"	"	Nickel	"	"	"	"
389,101 " 390,000	86	"	"	"	"	"	"	"	"
390,001 " 391,000	69	"	Htg.	"	"	11	"	"	8
391,001 " 391,400	162	6	"	¾ Pl.	Gilt	9	"	"	2
391,401 " 391,700	161	"	"	"	"	11	"	"	"
391,701 " 392,000	160	"	"	"	"	15	"	"	"
392,001 " 392,300	154	"	"	"	Nickel	9	"	"	"
392,301 " 392,500	153	"	"	"	"	11	"	"	"
392,501 " 392,700	152	"	"	"	"	15	"	"	"
392,701 " 392,900	151	"	"	"	Nick.& Gilt	"	"	"	"
392,901 " 393,000	150	"	"	"	"	16	"	"	"
393,001 " 393,500	154	"	"	"	Nickel	9	"	"	"
393,501 " 394,000	153	"	"	"	"	11	"	"	"
394,001 " 394,500	152	"	"	"	"	15	"	"	"
394,501 " 394,800	151	"	"	"	Nick.& Gilt	"	"	"	"
394,801 " 395,000	150	"	"	"	"	16	"	"	"
395,001 " 396,000	162	"	"	"	Gilt	9	"	"	"
396,001 " 396,500	161	"	"	"	"	11	"	"	"
396,501 " 397,000	160	"	"	"	"	15	"	"	"
397,001 " 397,800	162	"	"	"	"	9	"	"	"
397,801 " 398,600	161	"	"	"	"	11	"	"	"
398,601 " 399,000	160	"	"	"	"	15	"	"	"
399,001 " 400,200	153	"	"	"	Nickel	11	"	"	"
400,201 " 400,700	152	"	"	"	"	15	"	"	"
400,701 " 401,000	152	"	"	"	Nick.& Gilt	"	"	"	"
401,001 " 401,500	93	18	"	F. Pl.	Gilt	9	"	"	8
401,501 " 402,000	68	"	"	"	"	11	"	"	"
402,001 " 402,500	69	"	"	"	Nickel	"	"	"	"
402,501 " 403,000	85	"	"	"	Gilt	15	"	"	"
403,001 " 403,500	94	"	O. F.	"	"	9	"	"	7
403,501 " 404,000	86	"	"	"	Nickel	15	"	"	"
404,001 " 404,300	60	"	"	"	Nick.& Gilt	11	"	"	"
404,301 " 405,000	66	"	"	"	Nickel	17	"	"	"
405,001 " 405,500	86	"	"	"	"	15	"	"	"
405,501 " 406,000	83	"	Htg.	"	"	"	"	"	8
406,001 " 407,000	69	"	"	"	"	11	"	"	"
407,001 " 407,500	68	"	"	"	Gilt	"	"	"	"
407,501 " 408,000	85	"	"	"	"	15	"	"	"
408,001 " 408,500	93	"	"	"	"	9	"	"	"
408,501 " 409,000	94	"	O. F.	"	"	"	"	"	7
409,001 " 410,000	69	"	Htg.	"	Nickel	11	"	"	8
410,001 " 410,500	93	"	"	"	Gilt	9	"	"	"
410,501 " 411,000	68	"	"	"	"	11	"	"	"
411,001 " 411,500	94	"	O. F.	"	"	9	"	"	7
411,501 " 412,000	67	"	"	"	"	11	"	"	"
412,001 " 412,500	86	"	"	"	Nickel	15	"	"	"
412,501 " 413,000	69	"	Htg.	"	"	11	"	"	"
413,001 " 414,000	93	"	"	"	Gilt	9	"	"	8
414,001 " 415,000	94	"	O. F.	"	"	"	"	"	7
415,001 " 415,200	81	"	Htg.	"	Plain	17	"	"	8
415,201 " 415,500	83	"	"	"	Nickel	15	"	"	"
415,501 " 415,600	80	"	"	"	Spot Gilt	17	"	"	"
415,601 " 416,000	82	"	"	"	Plain	"	"	"	"
416,001 " 416,100	61	"	O. F.	"	....	"	"	"	7
416,101 " 416,500	86	"	"	"	Nickel	15	"	"	"
416,501 " 417,000	62	"	"	"	Plain	17	"	"	"
417,001 " 417,500	66	"	"	"	Nickel	11	"	"	"
417,501 " 418,000	83	"	Htg.	"	"	17	"	"	8
418,001 " 419,000	93	"	"	"	Gilt	9	"	"	"
419,001 " 419,500	94	"	"	"	"	"	"	"	"
419,501 " 420,000	153	6	"	¾ Pl.	Nickel	11	"	"	2
420,501 " 421,500	161	"	"	"	Gilt	"	"	"	"
421,501 " 422,500	162	"	"	"	"	9	"	"	"
422,501 " 423,000	66	18	O. F.	F. Pl.	Nickel	11	"	"	7
423,001 " 424,000	93	"	Htg.	"	Gilt	9	"	"	8
424,001 " 425,000	69	"	"	"	Nickel	11	"	"	"
425,001 " 425,500	94	"	O. F.	"	Gilt	9	"	"	7
425,501 " 426,000	66	"	"	"	Nickel	11	"	"	"
426,001 " 427,000	83	"	Htg.	"	"	15	"	"	8
427,001 " 428,000	69	"	"	"	"	11	"	"	"
428,001 " 429,000	66	"	O. F.	"	"	"	"	"	7
429,001 " 430,000	83	"	Htg.	"	"	15	"	"	8
430,001 " 431,000	68	"	"	"	Gilt	11	"	"	"
431,001 " 431,500	66	"	O. F.	"	Nickel	"	"	"	7
431,501 " 432,000	82	"	Htg.	"	Plain	17	"	"	8
432,001 " 433,000	67	"	O. F.	"	Gilt	11	"	"	7
433,001 " 433,100	83	"	Htg.	"	Nickel	15	"	"	8
433,101 " 433,140	82a	"	"	"	"	"	"	"	"
433,141 " 433,400	82	"	"	"	"	"	"	"	"
433,401 " 433,500	82	"	"	"	"	17	"	"	"
433,501 " 433,600	83	"	"	"	"	15	"	"	"
433,601 " 433,700	82	"	"	"	Plain	17	"	"	"
433,701 " 433,750	80	"	"	"	Spot Gilt	"	"	"	"
433,751 " 433,800	81	"	"	"	Plain	"	"	"	"
433,801 " 434,000	83	"	"	"	Nickel	15	"	"	"
434,001 " 434,500	69	"	"	"	"	"	"	"	"

The Rockford Watch Company, Ltd.

Number and Grade of Movement	GRADE	Size			Style	Jewels	Wind	Sett	Model
434,501 to 434,600	86	18	O. F.	F. Pl.	Nickel	15	Stem	Lever	7
434,601 " 434,700	62	"	"	"	Plain	17	"	"	"
434,701 " 435,000	86	"	O. F.	"	Nickel	15	"	"	"
435,001 " 435,500	85	"	Htg.	"	Gilt	"	"	"	8
435,501 " 436,000	94	"	O. F.	"	"	9	"	"	7
436,001 " 436,100	67	"	"	"	"	11	"	"	"
436,101 " 436,200	89	"	"	"	"	15	"	"	"
436,201 " 436,300	67	"	"	"	"	11	"	"	"
436,301 " 437,000	89	"	"	"	"	"	"	"	"
437,001 " 437,800	82	"	Htg.	"	Nickel	17	"	"	8
437,801 " 438,000	81	"	"	"	Plain	"	"	"	"
438,001 " 438,500	83	"	"	"	"	15	"	"	"
438,501 " 438,900	62	"	O. F.	"	"	17	"	"	7
438,901 " 439,000	86	"	"	"	Nickel	15	"	"	"
439,001 " 439,500	82	"	Htg.	"	"	17	"	"	8
439,501 " 439,550	80	"	"	"	Nick.& Gilt	"	"	"	"
439,551 " 439,650	82a	"	"	"	"	"	"	"	"
439,651 " 439,700	81	"	"	"	Nickel	"	"	"	"
439,701 " 439,750	62a	"	O. F.	"	"	"	"	"	7
439,751 " 439,850	62	"	"	"	"	"	"	"	"
439,851 " 439,900	61	"	"	"	"	"	"	"	"
439,901 " 439,950	86	"	"	"	"	15	"	"	"
439,951 " 440,000	62a	"	"	"	"	17	"	"	"
440,001 " 441,000	93	"	Htg.	"	Gilt	9	"	"	8
441,001 " 441,500	62	"	O. F.	"	Nickel	17	"	"	7
441,501 " 442,000	83	"	Htg.	"	Plain	15	"	"	8
442,001 " 442,050	80	"	"	"	Nick.& Gilt	17	"	"	"
424,051 " 442,150	81	"	"	"	Plain	"	"	"	"
442,151 " 442,500	82	"	"	"	Nickel	"	"	"	"
500,001 " 500,054	930	"	O. F.	"	"	"	"	"	9
500,055	935	"	"	"	"	"	"	"	"
500,056 to 500,250	930	"	"	"	"	"	"	"	"
500,251 " 500,260	920	"	"	"	"	"	"	"	7
500,261 " 500,300	930	"	"	"	"	"	"	"	9
500,301 " 500,400	935	"	"	"	"	"	"	"	10
500,401 " 500,800	830	"	Htg.	"	"	"	"	"	"
500,801 " 500,900	835	"	"	"	"	"	"	"	"
500,901 " 501,100	830	"	"	"	"	"	"	"	"
501,101 " 501,900	835	"	"	"	"	"	"	"	"
501,901 " 502,400	830	"	"	"	"	"	"	"	"
502,401 " 502,481	930	"	O. F.	"	"	"	"	"	9
502,482 " 502,489	935	"	"	"	"	"	"	"	"
502,490 " 502 592	930	"	"	"	"	"	"	"	"
502,593	935	"	"	"	"	"	"	"	"
502,594 to 502,700	930	"	"	"	"	"	"	"	"
502,701 " 503,200	935	"	"	"	"	"	"	"	"
503,201 " 503,460	830	"	Htg.	"	"	"	"	"	10
503,461 " 503,470	820	"	"	"	"	"	"	"	8
503,471 " 503,483	830	"	"	"	"	"	"	"	10
503,484 " 503,489	820	"	"	"	"	"	"	"	8
503,490 " 503,520	830	"	"	"	"	"	"	"	10
503,521 " 503,531	820	"	"	"	"	"	"	"	8
503,532 " 503,536	830	"	"	"	"	"	"	"	10
503,537 " 503,540	820	"	"	"	"	"	"	"	8
503,541 " 503,550	825	"	"	"	"	"	"	"	10
503,551 " 503,610	830	"	"	"	"	"	"	"	"
503,611 " 503,620	820	"	"	"	"	"	"	"	8
503,621 " 503,700	830	"	"	"	"	"	"	"	10
503,701 " 504,000	835	"	"	"	"	"	"	"	"
504,001 " 504,100	830	"	"	"	"	"	"	"	"
504,101 " 505,150	835	"	"	"	"	"	"	"	"
505,151 " 505,200	830	"	"	"	"	"	"	"	"
505,201 " 505,300	835	"	"	"	"	"	"	"	"
505,301 " 505,350	830	"	"	"	"	"	"	"	"
505,351 " 505,360	835	"	"	"	"	"	"	"	"
505,361 " 505,370	830	"	"	"	"	"	"	"	"
505,371 " 505,398	835	"	"	"	"	"	"	"	"
505,399 " 505,400	830	"	"	"	"	"	"	"	"
505,401 " 505,700	835	"	"	"	"	"	"	"	"
505,701 " 506,000	830	"	"	"	"	"	"	"	"
506,001 " 506,800	935	"	O. F.	"	"	"	"	"	9
506,801 " 506,810	910	"	"	"	"	21	"	"	"
506,811 " 507,600	930	"	"	"	"	17	"	"	"
507,601 " 507,900	830	"	Htg.	"	"	"	"	"	10
507,901 " 508,500	835	"	"	"	"	"	"	"	"
508,501 " 509,000	830	"	"	"	"	"	"	"	"
509,001 " 509,100	820	"	"	"	"	"	"	"	8
509,101 " 509,700	925	"	O. F.	"	"	"	"	"	9
509,701 " 509,729	920	"	"	"	"	"	"	"	7
509,730	915	"	"	"	"	"	"	"	"
509,731 to 509,759	920	"	"	"	"	"	"	"	"
509,760	915	"	"	"	"	"	"	"	"
509,761 to 509,791	920	"	"	"	"	"	"	"	"
509,792	915	"	"	"	"	"	"	"	"
509,793 to 509,900	920	"	"	"	"	"	"	"	"
509,901 " 510,200	810	"	Htg.	"	"	21	"	"	10
510,201 " 510,700	825	"	"	"	"	17	"	"	"
510,701 " 511,300	830	"	"	"	"	"	"	"	"
511,301 " 511,600	835	"	"	"	"	"	"	"	"

The Rockford Watch Company, Ltd.

Number and Grade of Movement	GRADE	Size	Style			Jewels	Wind	Sett	Model
			Description of Movement						
511,601 to 512,500	935	18	O. F.	F. Pl.	Nickel	17	Stem	Lever	9
512,501 " 512,600	910	"	"	"	"	21	"	"	"
512,601 " 512,700	920	"	"	"	"	17	"	"	7
512,701 " 512,800	930	"	"	"	"	"	"	"	9
512,801 " 512,850	920	"	"	"	"	"	"	"	7
512,851 " 512,872	830	"	Htg.	"	"	"	"	"	10
512,873	915	"	O. F.	"	"	"	"	"	7
512,874 to 512,875	920	"	"	"	"	"	"	"	"
512,876	915	"	"	"	"	"	"	"	"
512,877 to 512,900	920	"	"	"	"	"	"	"	"
512,901 " 513,101	830	"	Htg.	"	"	"	"	"	10
513,102 " 513,181	820	"	"	"	"	"	"	"	8
513,182	815	"	"	"	"	"	"	"	"
513,183 to 513,251	820	"	"	"	"	"	"	"	"
513,252 " 513,259	810	"	"	"	"	21	"	"	10
513,260 " 513,300	820	"	"	"	"	17	"	"	8
513,301 " 513,400	830	"	"	"	"	"	"	"	10
513,401 " 513,500	835	"	"	"	"	"	"	"	"
513,501 " 513,600	830	"	"	"	"	"	"	"	"
513,601 " 513,900	835	"	"	"	"	"	"	"	"
513,901 " 514,000	930	"	O. F.	"	"	"	"	"	9
514,001 " 514,100	935	"	"	"	"	"	"	"	"
514,101 " 514,150	825	"	Htg.	"	"	"	"	"	10
514,151 " 514,500	835	"	"	"	"	"	"	"	"
514,501 " 514,600	930	"	O. F.	"	"	"	"	"	9
514,601 " 514,900	935	"	"	"	"	"	"	"	"
514,901 " 515,100	835	"	Htg.	"	"	"	"	"	10
515,101 " 515,400	935	"	O. F.	"	"	"	"	"	9
515,401 " 515,500	810	"	Htg.	"	"	21	"	"	10
515,501 " 515,600	910	"	O. F.	"	"	"	"	"	9
515,601 " 516,000	935	"	"	"	"	17	"	"	"
516,001 " 516,300	925	"	"	"	"	"	"	"	"
516,301 " 516,400	935	"	"	"	"	"	"	"	"
516,401 " 516,500	925	"	"	"	"	"	"	"	"
516,501 " 517,200	825	"	Htg.	"	"	"	"	"	10
517,201 " 519,300	910	"	O. F.	"	"	21	"	"	9
519,301 " 519,400	900	"	"	"	"	24	"	"	"
519,401 " 519,500	800	"	Htg.	"	"	"	"	"	10
519,501 " 519,600	805	"	"	"	"	21	"	"	"
519,601 " 519,700	905	"	O. F.	"	"	"	"	"	9
519,701 " 520,000	835	"	Htg.	"	"	17	"	"	10
520,001 " 521,000	935	"	O. F.	"	"	"	"	"	9
521,001 " 522,000	870	"	Htg.	"	"	7	"	"	10
522,001 " 522,400	970	"	O. F.	"	"	"	"	"	9
522,401 " 523,500	870	"	Htg.	"	"	"	"	"	10
523,501 " 524,800	970	"	O. F.	"	"	"	"	"	9
524,801 " 525,000	935	"	"	"	"	17	"	"	"
525,001 " 525,100	900	"	"	"	"	24	"	"	"
525,101 " 525,400	935	"	"	"	"	17	"	"	"
525,401 " 525,900	925	"	"	"	"	"	"	"	"
525,901 " 526,700	825	"	Htg.	"	"	"	"	"	10
526,701 " 526,900	930	"	O. F.	"	"	"	"	"	9
526,901 " 527,900	935	"	"	"	"	"	"	"	"
527,901 " 528,800	930	"	"	"	"	"	"	"	"
528,801 " 529,800	935	"	"	"	"	"	"	"	"
529,801 " 530,800	925	"	"	"	"	"	"	"	"
530,801 " 531,800	835	"	Htg.	"	"	"	"	"	10
531,801 " 532,450	825	"	"	"	"	"	"	"	"
532,451 " 532,500	835	"	"	"	"	"	"	"	"
532,501 " 533,400	925	"	O. F.	"	"	"	"	"	9
533,401 " 534,000	935	"	"	"	"	"	"	"	"
534,001 " 534,012	920	"	"	"	"	"	"	"	7
534,013	915	"	"	"	"	"	"	"	"
534,014 to 534,035	920	"	"	"	"	"	"	"	"
534,036	915	"	"	"	"	"	"	"	"
534,037 to 534,039	920	"	"	"	"	"	"	"	"
534,040	915	"	"	"	"	"	"	"	"
534,041 to 534,064	920	"	"	"	"	"	"	"	"
534,065	915	"	"	"	"	"	"	"	"
534,066 to 534,112	920	"	"	"	"	"	"	"	"
534,113 " 534,115	915	"	"	"	"	"	"	"	"
534,116 " 534,119	920	"	"	"	"	"	"	"	"
534,120	915	"	"	"	"	"	"	"	"
534,121	920	"	"	"	"	"	"	"	"
534,122 to 534,123	915	"	"	"	"	"	"	"	"
534,124 " 534,127	920	"	"	"	"	"	"	"	"
534,128	915	"	"	"	"	"	"	"	"
534,129 to 534,130	920	"	"	"	"	"	"	"	"
534,131	915	"	"	"	"	"	"	"	"
534,132	920	"	"	"	"	"	"	"	"
534,133	915	"	"	"	"	"	"	"	"
534,134	920	"	"	"	"	"	"	"	"
534,135	915	"	"	"	"	"	"	"	"
534,136 to 534,138	920	"	"	"	"	"	"	"	"
534,139	915	"	"	"	"	"	"	"	"
534,140 to 534,144	920	"	"	"	"	"	"	"	"
534,145	915	"	"	"	"	"	"	"	"
534,146 to 534,147	920	"	"	"	"	"	"	"	"
534,148	915	"	"	"	"	"	"	"	"

The Rockford Watch Company, Ltd.

Number and Grade of Movement	GRADE	Size	Style			Jewels	Wind	Sett	Model
534,149..........................	920	18	O. F.	F. Pl.	Nickel	17	Stem	Lever	7
534,150..........................	915	"	"	"	"	"	"	"	"
534,151 to 534,155...............	920	"	"	"	"	"	"	"	"
534,156 " 534,157...............	915	"	"	"	"	"	"	"	"
534,158 " 534,163...............	920	"	"	"	"	"	"	"	"
534,164..........................	915	"	"	"	"	"	"	"	"
534,165 to 534,171...............	920	"	"	"	"	"	"	"	"
534,172..........................	915	"	"	"	"	"	"	"	"
534,173..........................	920	"	"	"	"	"	"	"	"
534,174..........................	915	"	"	"	"	"	"	"	"
534,175..........................	920	*	"	"	"	"	"	"	"
534,176 to 534,179...............	915	"	"	"	"	"	"	"	"
534,180 " 534,182...............	920	"	"	"	"	"	"	"	"
534,183..........................	915	"	"	"	"	"	"	"	"
534,184..........................	920	"	"	"	"	"	"	"	"
534,185..........................	915	"	"	"	"	"	"	"	"
534,186 to 534,188...............	920	"	"	"	"	"	"	"	"
534,189..........................	915	"	"	"	"	"	"	"	"
534,190 to 534,196...............	920	"	"	"	"	"	"	"	"
534,197..........................	915	"	"	"	"	"	"	"	"
534,198..........................	920	"	"	"	"	"	"	"	"
534,199..........................	915	"	"	"	"	"	"	"	"
534,200..........................	920	"	"	"	"	"	"	"	9
534,401 to 534,600...............	930	"	"	"	"		"	"	9
534,601 " 535,200...............	910	"	"	"	"	21	"	"	"
535,201 " 535,400...............	900	"	"	"	"	24	"	"	"
535,401 " 535,600...............	910	"	"	"	"	21	"	"	"
535,601 " 535,700...............	800	"	Htg.	"	"	24	"	"	10
535,701 " 535,800...............	805	"	"	"	"	21	"	"	"
535,801 " 536,300...............	910	"	O. F.	"	"	17	"	"	9
536,301 " 536,600...............	930	"	"	"	"	17	"	"	"
536,601 " 536,700...............	945	"	"	"	"	21	"	"	Special
536,701 " 537,400...............	910	"	"	"	"	"	"	"	9
537,401 " 539,400...............	935	"	"	"	"	17	"	"	"
539,401 " 540,400...............	910	"	"	"	"	21	"	"	"
540,401 " 541,400...............	935	"	"	"	"	17	"	"	"
541,401 " 541,500...............	905	"	"	"	"	21	"	"	"
541,501 " 542,000...............	835	"	Htg.	"	"	17	"	"	10
542,001 " 542,300...............	800	"	"	"	"	24	"	"	"
542,301 " 542,500...............	810	"	"	"	"	21	"	"	"
542,501 " 542,700...............	900	"	O. F.	"	"	24	"	"	9
542,701 " 542,800...............	905	"	"	"	"	21	"	"	"
542,801 " 543,300...............	805	"	Htg.	"	"	"	"	"	10
543,301 " 543,500...............	905	"	O. F.	"	"	"	"	"	9
543,501 " 544,000...............	835	"	Htg.	"	"	17	"	"	10
544,001 " 544,100...............	560	16	"	¾ Pl.	"	"	"	"	3
544,101 " 544,200...............	570	"	"	"	"	"	"	"	"
544,201 " 544,400...............	560	"	"	"	"	"	"	"	"
544,401 " 544,500...............	530	"	"	"	"	21	"	"	"
544,501 " 544,800...............	550	"	"	"	"	17	"	"	4
544,801 " 545,000...............	540	"	"	"	"	21	"	"	"
545,001 " 545,500...............	535	"	O. F.	"	"	"	"	"	2
545,501 " 546,500...............	570	"	Htg.	"	"	17	"	"	3
546,501 " 546,600...............	540	"	"	"	"	21	"	"	4
546,601 " 546,700...............	500	"	"	"	"	"	"	"	"
546,701 " 546,800...............	510	"	"	"	"	"	"	"	"
546,801 " 546,900...............	520	"	"	"	"	"	"	"	"
546,901 " 547,000...............	530	"	"	"	"	17	"	"	3
547,001 " 548,000...............	560	"	"	"	"	"	"	"	"
548,001 " 549,000...............	565	"	O. F.	"	"	"	"	"	2
549,001 " 550,000...............	575	"	"	"	"	"	"	"	"
550,001 " 550,500...............	560	"	Htg.	"	"	"	"	"	3
550,501 " 550,600...............	515	"	O. F.	"	"	21	"	"	5
550,601 " 550,700...............	525	"	"	"	"	"	"	"	"
550,701 " 550,900...............	545	"	"	"	"	"	"	"	"
550,901 " 551,200...............	555	"	"	"	"	17	"	"	"
551,201 " 551,700...............	530	"	Htg.	"	"	21	"	"	3
551,701 " 552,700...............	575	"	O. F.	"	"	17	"	"	2
552,701 " 553,200...............	565	"	"	"	"	"	"	"	3
553,201 " 554,200...............	570	"	Htg.	"	"	"	"	"	2
554,201 " 554,700...............	565	"	O. F.	"	"	"	"	"	5
554,701 " 554,900...............	555	"	"	"	"	21	"	"	2
554,901 " 554,920...............	535	"	"	"	"	"	"	"	3
554,921 " 554,927...............	570	"	Htg.	"	"	17	"	"	2
554,928 " 554,930...............	575	"	O. F.	"	"	"	"	"	3
554,931 " 554,940...............	560	"	Htg.	"	"	11	"	Pend.	Special
554,941 " 554,960...............	605	"	O. F.	"	"				
554,961..........................	......	"	"	"	Gilt	"	"	"	"
554,962..........................	......	"	"	"	"	"	"	"	"
554,963..........................	......	"	"	"	"	"	"	"	"
554,964..........................	......	"	Htg.	"	Nickel	17	"	"	"
554,965..........................	......	"	"	"	Gilt	"	"	"	"
554,966..........................	......	"	"	"	Nickel	"	"	"	"
554,967..........................	......	"	"	"	Gilt	"	"	"	"
554,968..........................	......	"	O. F.	"	"	15	"	"	"
554,699..........................	......	"	"	"	....	"	"	"	"
554,970..........................	......	"	"	"	....	"	"	"	"
554,971..........................	......	"	Htg.	"	....	"	"	"	"
554,972..........................	......	"	"	"	....	"	"	"	"

The Rockford Watch Company, Ltd.

Number and Grade of Movement	GRADE	Size	Style			Jewels	Wind	Sett	Model
554,973...		16	Htg.	¾ Pl.	Gilt	11	Stem	Pend.	Special
554,974...	935	18	O. F.	F. Pl.	Nickel	17	"	Lever	9
554,975...		16	Htg.	¾ Pl.	Nickel	11	"	Pend.	Special
554,976...		"	"	"	.....	"	"	"	"
554,977...		"	"	"		"	"	"	"
554,978...		"	O. F.	"	Nickel	17	"	"	"
554,979...		"	"	"	"	"	"	"	"
554,981 to 554,992	25	18	"	F. Pl.	"	25	"	Lever	"
555,001 " 556 000	560	16	Htg.	¾ Pl.	"	17	"	"	3
556,001 " 558,000	575	"	O. F.	"	"	"	"	"	2
558,001 " 558,500	550	"	Htg.	"	"	"	"	"	4
558,501 " 559,000	540	"	"	"	"	21	"	"	"
559,001 " 560,000	560	"	"	"	"	17	"	"	3
560,001 " 560,500	545	"	O. F.	"	"	21	"	"	5
560,501 " 561,000	555	"	"	"	"	17	"	"	"
561,001 " 562,000	835	18	Htg.	F. Pl.	"	"	"	"	10
562,001 " 563,000	935	"	O. F.	"	"	"	"	"	9
563,001 " 565,000	570	16	Htg.	¾ Pl.	"	"	"	"	3
565,001 " 566,000	575	"	O. F.	"	"	"	"	"	2
566,001 " 566,500	918	18	"	F. Pl.	"	24	"	"	9
566,501 " 566,600	930	"	"	"	"	17	"	"	"
566,601 " 566,800	935	"	"	"	"	"	"	"	"
566,801 " 566,900	830	"	Htg.	"	"	"	"	"	10
566,901 " 566,940	500	16	"	¾ Pl.	"	21	"	"	4
566,941 " 567,000	501	"	"	"	"	"	"	"	"
567,001 " 568,000	575	"	O. F.	"	"	17	"	"	2
568,001 " 570,000	570	"	Htg.	"	"	"	"	"	3
570,001 " 571,000	575	"	O. F.	"	"	"	"	"	2
571,001 " 571,300	545	"	"	"	"	21	"	"	5
571,301 " 571,500	575	"	"	"	"	17	"	"	2
571,501 " 571,530	505	"	"	"	"	21	"	"	5
571,531 " 571,600	515	"	"	"	"	"	"	"	"
571,601 " 571,700	570	"	Htg.	"	"	17	"	"	3
571,701 " 571,900	575	"	O. F.	"	"	"	"	"	2
571,901 " 572,000	585	"	"	"	"	15	"	"	"
572,001 " 572,700	565	"	"	"	"	17	"	"	"
572,701 " 573,000	560	"	Htg.	"	"	"	"	"	3
573,001 " 573,500	810	18	"	F. Pl.	"	21	"	"	10
573,501 " 573,510	590	16	"	¾ Pl.	"	11	"	"	3
573,511 " 574,000	584	"	"	"	"	15	"	"	"
574,001 " 574,500	905	18	O. F.	F. Pl.	"	21	"	"	9
574,501 " 575,000	835	"	Htg.	"	"	17	"	"	10
575,001 " 577,000	570	16	"	¾ Pl.	"	"	"	"	3
577,001 " 577,500	584	"	"	"	"	15	"	"	"
577,501 " 577,800	565	"	O. F.	"	"	17	"	"	2
577,801 " 577,900	520	"	Htg.	"	"	21	"	"	4
577,901 " 578,000	525	"	O. F.	"	"	"	"	"	5
578,001 " 579,150	835	18	Htg.	F. Pl.	"	17	"	"	10
579,201 " 579,370	935	"	O. F.	"	"	"	"	"	9
579,401 " 579,500	570	16	Htg.	¾ Pl.	"	"	"	"	3
579,501 " 579,600	575	"	O. F.	"	"	"	"	"	2
579,601 " 579,700	560	"	Htg.	"	"	"	"	"	3
579,701 " 579,735	565	"	O. F.	"	"	"	∴	"	2
579,801 " 579,900	830	18	Htg.	F. Pl.	"	"	"	"	10
579,901 " 580,000	930	"	O. F.	"	"	"	"	"	9
580,001 " 580,200	560	16	Htg.	¾ Pl.	"	"	"	"	3
580,201 " 580,300	565	"	O. F.	"	"	"	"	"	2
580,301 " 580,500	570	"	Htg.	"	"	"	"	"	3
580,501 " 580,600	575	"	O. F.	"	"	"	"	"	2
580,601 " 581,000	930	18	"	F. Pl.	"	"	"	"	9
581,001 " 582,000	585	16	"	¾ Pl.	"	15	"	"	2
582,001 " 583,000	584	"	Htg.	"	"	"	"	"	3
583,001 " 584,000	560	"	"	"	"	17	"	"	"
584,001 " 585,000	584	"	"	"	"	15	"	"	"
585,001 " 585,500	935	18	O. F.	F. Pl.	"	17	"	"	9
585,501 " 585,600	515	16	"	¾ Pl.	"	21	"	"	5
585,601 " 585,700	525	"	"	"	"	"	"	"	"
585,701 " 585,800	830	18	Htg.	F. Pl.	"	17	"	"	10
585,801 " 585,900	930	"	O. F.	"	"	"	"	"	9
585,901 " 586,000	835	"	Htg.	"	"	"	"	"	10
586,001 " 588,000	584	16	"	¾ Pl.	"	15	"	"	3
588,001 " 590,000	835	18	"	F. Pl.	"	17	"	"	10
590,001 " 591,000	570	16	"	¾ Pl.	"	"	"	"	3
591,001 " 592,000	584	"	"	"	"	15	"	"	"
592,001 " 593,000	835	18	"	F. Pl.	"	17	"	"	10
593,001 " 593,100	560	16	"	¾ Pl.	"	"	"	"	3
593,101 " 593,200	570	"	"	"	"	"	"	"	"
593,201 " 593,300	100	"	"	"	"	21	"	Pend.	Special
593,301 " 593,400	101	"	O. F.	"	"	"	"	"	"
593,401 " 593,600	925	18	"	F. Pl.	"	17	"	Lever	9
593,601 " 593,700	835	"	Htg.	"	"	"	"	"	10
593,701 " 593,800	825	"	"	"	"	"	"	"	"
593,801 " 593,900	520	16	"	¾ Pl.	"	21	"	"	4
593,901 " 594,000	505	"	O. F.	"	"	"	"	"	5
594,001 " 596,000	590	"	Htg.	"	"	11	"	Pend.	3
596,001 " 597,000	595	"	O. F.	"	"	"	"	"	2
597,001 " 598,000	590	"	Htg.	"	"	"	"	"	3
598,001 " 599,000	586	"	"	"	"	15	"	"	5
599,001 " 599,500	587	"	O. F.	"	"	"	"	"	2

The Rockford Watch Company, Ltd.

Number and Grade of Movement	GRADE	Description of Movement							
		Size		Style		Jewels	Wind	Sett	Model
599,501 to 599,502	575	16	O. F.	¾ Pl.	Nickel	17	Stem	Lever	2
599,503 " 599,504	565	"	"	"	"	"	"	"	"
599,505	575	"	"	"	"	"	"	"	"
599,506 to 600,000	587	"	"	"	"	15	"	Pend.	"
600,001 " 601,000	935	18	"	F. Pl.	"	17	"	Lever	9
601,001 " 602,000	590	16	Htg.	¾ Pl.	"	11	"	Pend.	3
602,001 " 603,000	595	"	O. F.	"	"	"	"	"	2
603,001 " 605,000	561	"	Htg.	"	"	17	"	"	4
605,001 " 605,700	573	"	O. F.	"	"	"	"	"	5
605,701 " 605,850	845	18	Htg.	F. Pl.	"	21	"	Lever	Special
605,851 " 605,900	945	"	O. F.	"	"	"	"	"	"
605,901 " 605,950	540	16	Htg.	¾ Pl.	"	"	"	"	4
606,001 " 608,000	935	18	O. F.	F. Pl.	"	17	"	"	9
608,001 " 609,000	572	16	Htg.	¾ Pl.	"	"	"	Pend.	4
609,001 " 610,000	566	"	O. F.	"	"	"	"	"	5
610,001 " 613,000	605	"	"	"	"	11	"	"	2
613,001 " 614,000	587	"	"	"	"	15	"	"	"
614,001 " 615,000	600	"	Htg.	"	"	11	"	"	3
615,001 " 617,000	605	"	O. F.	"	"	"	"	"	2
617,001 " 617,500	586	"	Htg.	"	"	15	"	"	3
617,501 " 617,800	845	18	"	F. Pl.	"	21	"	Lever	Special
617,801 " 618,000	810	"	"	"	"	"	"	"	10
618,001 " 618,500	587	16	O. F.	¾ Pl.	"	15	"	Pend.	2
618,501 " 618,600	578	"	Htg.	"	"	17	"	"	3
618,601 " 618,700	579	"	O. F.	"	"	"	"	"	2
618,701 " 618,800	600	"	Htg.	"	"	11	"	"	3
618,801 " 618,900	586	"	"	"	"	15	"	"	"
618,901 " 618,950	120	"	"	"	"	17	"	"	Special
618,951 " 619,000	125	"	O. F.	"	"	"	"	"	"
619,001 " 619,300	525	"	"	"	"	21	"	Lever	5
619,301 " 619,700	600	"	Htg.	"	"	11	"	Pend.	3
619,701 " 619,900	565	"	O. F.	"	"	17	"	Lever	"
619,901 " 620,000	101	"	"	"	"	21	"	Pend.	Special
620,001 " 621,000	545	"	"	"	"	"	"	Lever	5
621,001 " 622,000	935	18	"	F. Pl.	"	17	"	"	9
622,001 " 622,300	160	0	Htg.	¾ Pl.	"	15	"	Pend.	1
622,301 " 622,350	140	"	"	"	"	17	"	"	"
622,351 " 622,500	150	"	"	"	"	"	"	"	"
622,501 " 623,000	160	"	"	"	"	15	"	"	"
623,001 " 623,100	200	18	O. F.	F. Pl.	"	17	"	Lever	10
623,101 " 623,500	605	16	"	¾ Pl.	"	11	"	Pend.	2
623,501 " 624,000	160	0	Htg.	"	"	15	"	"	1
624,001 " 624,200	205	18	O. F.	F. Pl.	"	17	"	Lever	10
624,201 " 624,300	945	"	"	"	"	21	"	"	Special
624,301 " 624,400	930	"	"	"	"	17	"	"	9
624,401 " 624,450	110	16	Htg.	¾ Pl.	"	"	"	Pend.	Special
624,451 " 624,500	115	"	O. F.	"	"	"	"	"	"
624,501 " 624,525	130	"	Htg.	"	Gilt	"	"	"	"
624,526 " 624,550	135	"	O. F.	"	"	"	"	"	"
624,601 " 624,800	540	"	Htg.	"	Nickel	21	"	Lever	4
625,001 " 625,400	400	"	"	"	"	17	"	Pend.	"
625,401 " 626,000	405	"	"	"	"	21	"	"	5
626,001 " 626,200	510	"	"	"	"	"	"	Lever	4
626,201 " 626,400	515	"	O. F.	"	"	"	"	"	5
626,401 " 626,600	520	"	Htg.	"	"	"	"	"	4
626,601 " 626,700	525	"	O. F.	"	"	"	"	"	5
626,701 " 626,900	845	18	Htg.	F. Pl.	"	"	"	"	Special
626,901 " 627,000	572	16	"	¾ Pl.	"	17	"	Pend.	4
627,001 " 627,300	500	"	"	"	"	21	"	Lever	"
628,001 " 628,100	520	"	"	"	"	"	"	"	"
628,101 " 628,300	515	"	O. F.	"	"	"	"	"	5
628,301 " 628,500	505	"	"	"	"	"	"	"	5
628,501 " 628,600	510	"	Htg.	"	"	"	"	"	4
628,601 " 628,800	100	"	"	"	"	"	"	Pend.	Special
628,801 " 628,950	101	"	O. F.	"	"	"	"	"	"
628,951 " 629,000	935	18	"	F. Pl.	"	17	"	Lever	9
629,001 " 630,000	835	"	Htg.	"	"	"	"	"	10
630,001 " 630,600	162	0	"	¾ Pl.	"	"	"	Pend.	1
630,601 " 630,700	150	"	"	"	"	"	"	"	"
630,701 " 630,800	160	"	"	"	"	15	"	"	"
630,801 " 631,000	586	16	"	"	"	"	"	"	3
631,001 " 632,000	825	18	"	F. Pl.	"	17	"	Lever	10
632,001 " 632,500	925	"	O. F.	"	"	"	"	"	9
632,501 " 633,000	587	16	"	¾ Pl.	"	15	"	Pend.	2
633,001 " 633,500	935	18	"	F. Pl.	"	17	"	Lever	9
634,001 " 635,000	160	0	Htg.	¾ Pl.	"	15	"	Pend.	1
635,001 " 636,000	150	"	"	"	"	17	"	"	"
636,001 " 636,500	160	"	"	"	"	15	"	"	"
636,501 " 636,600	600	16	"	"	"	11	"	"	3
636,601 " 638,000	160	0	"	"	"	15	"	Pend.	1
638,001 " 639,000	162	"	"	"	"	"	"	"	"
639,001 " 640,000	610	16	"	"	"	7	"	"	Special
640,001 " 641,000	615	"	O. F.	"	"	"	"	"	3
641,001 " 642,000	587	"	"	"	"	15	"	"	2
642,001 " 643,000	142	0	Htg.	"	"	17	"	"	"
643,001 " 644,000	162	"	"	"	"	15	"	"	1
644,001 " 644,500	610	16	"	"	"	7	"	"	Special
645,001 " 646,600	615	"	O. F.	"	"	"	"	"	3
646,001 " 647,000	160	0	Htg.	"	"	15	"	Pend.	1
647,001 " 648,000	605	16	O. F.	"	"	11	"	"	2
648,001 " 649,000	160	0	Htg.	"	"	15	"	Pend.	1
649,001 " 650,000	605	16	O. F.	"	"	11	"	"	2

The Rockford Watch Company, Ltd.

Number and Grade of Movement	GRADE	Description of Movement						
		Size	Style		Jewels	Wind	Sett	Model
650,001 " 651,000	573	16	O. F.	¾ Pl.	Nickel	17	Stem	Pend.	5
651,001 to 656,000	160	0	Htg.	"	"	15	"	"	1
656,001 " 656,100	152	"	"	"	"	17	"	"	
657,001 " 657,200	182	"	"	"	"	7	"	"	Special
658,001 " 659,000	600	16	"	"	"	11	"	"	3
659,001 " 659,200	930	18	O. F.	F. Pl.	"	17	"	Lever	9
660,001 " 660,100	910	"	"	"	"	21	"	"	
661,101 " 661,200	810	"	Htg.	"	"	"	"	"	10
662,001 " 662,600	100	16	"	¾ Pl.	"	"	"	Pend.	Special
663,001 " 663,100	101	"	O. F.	"	"	"	"	"	
664,001 " 664,100	845	18	Htg.	F. Pl.	"	"	"	Lever	"
665,001 " 665,100	830	"	"	"	"	17	"	"	10
666,001 " 666,100	900	"	O. F.	"	"	24	"	"	9
667,001 " 667,100	905	"	"	"	"	21	"	"	
668,001 " 669,000	605	16	"	¾ Pl.	"	11	"	Pend.	2
669,001 " 669,100	912	18	"	F. Pl.	Spot Gilt	21	"	Lever	9
670,001 " 670,100	537	16	"	¾ Pl.	"	"	"	"	2
671,001 " 671,300	200	18	"	F. Pl.	Nickel	17	"	"	10
672,001 " 673,000	205	"	"	"	"	"	"	"	2
674,001 " 675,000	405	16	"	¾ Pl.	"	"	"	Pend.	5
675,001 " 675,500	525	"	"	"	"	21	"	Lever	
676,001 " 677,000	566	"	"	"	"	17	"	Pend.	"
677,001 " 678,000	573	"	"	"	"	"	"	"	
678,001 " 678,500	586	"	"	"	"	15	"	"	3
679,001 " 680,500	587	"	"	"	"	"	"	"	2
681,001 " 682,000	600	"	Htg.	"	"	11	"	"	3
682,001 " 686,000	605	"	O. F.	"	"	"	"	"	2
686,001 " 693,000	615	"	"	"	"	7	"	"	"
693,001 " 694,000	610	"	Htg.	"	"	7	"	"	3
694,001 " 694,500	935	18	O. F.	F. Pl.	"	17	"	Lever	9
695,001 " 695,500	945	"	"	"	"	21	"	"	Special

STYLE & NAMES OF U.S.A. HANDS

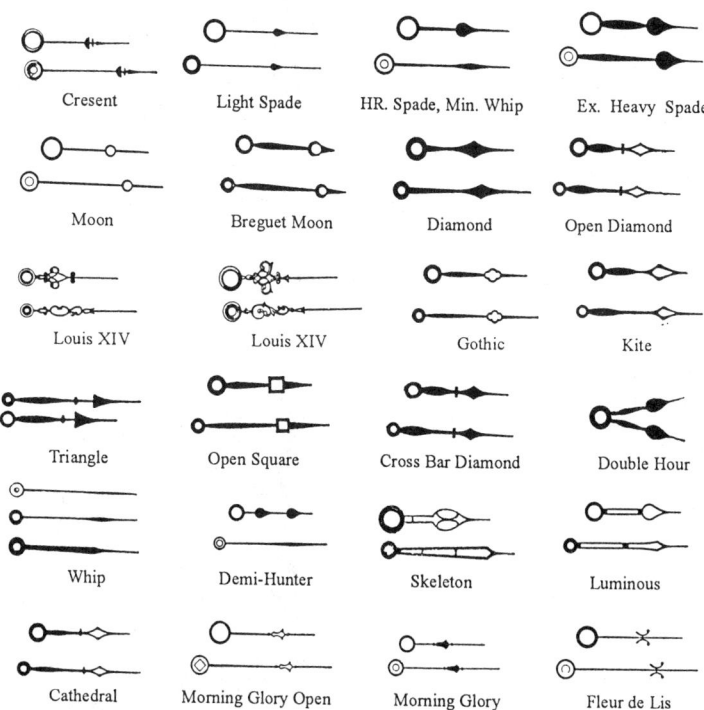

Cresent　Light Spade　HR. Spade, Min. Whip　Ex. Heavy Spade

Moon　Breguet Moon　Diamond　Open Diamond

Louis XIV　Louis XIV　Gothic　Kite

Triangle　Open Square　Cross Bar Diamond　Double Hour

Whip　Demi-Hunter　Skeleton　Luminous

Cathedral　Morning Glory Open　Morning Glory　Fleur de Lis

SERIAL NUMBER — GRADE,SIZE-STYLE, JEWELS,MODEL

695501-696000=945,18S.O.F.21J,M#SP.
696001-697000=838,18S.H.C.17J,M#10
697001-698000=938,18S.O.F.17J.M# 9
698001-699000=150, 0S. H.C.17J.M# 1
699001-700000=140, 0S. H.C.17J.M# 1
700001-702100=180, 0S. H.C. 7J.M# 1
702101-703000=160, 0S. H.C.15J.M# 1
703001-703500=170, 0S. H.C.11J.M# 1
703501-704000=160, 0S. H.C.15J.M# 1
704001-704300=935,18S.O.F.17J.M# 9
704301-704400=930,18S.O.F.17J.M# 9
704401-704500=935,18S.O.F.17J.M# 9
704501-704600=930,18S.O.F.17J.M# 9
704601-705000=935,18S.O.F.17J.M# 9
705001-706000=572,16S.H.C.17J.M# 4
706001-707000=600,16S.H.C.11J.M# 3
707001-708000=918,18S.O.F.21J.M# 9
708001-709000=586,16S.H.C.15J.M# 4
709001-710000=587,16S.O.F.15J.M# 3
710001-710100=930,18S.O.F.17J.M# 9
710101-710600=935,18S.O.F.17J.M# 9
710601-710700=930,18S.O.F.17J.M# 9
710701-711000=935,18S.O.F.17J.M# 9
711001-711100=830,18S.H.C.17J.M# 9
711101-711500=835,18S.O.F.17J.M#10
711501-711600=830,18S.H.C.17J.M#10
711601-712000=835,18S.H.C.17J.M#10
712001-712700=573,16S.O.F.17J.M# 5
712701-713000=635,16S.O.F.17J.M# 5
713001-714000=610,16S.O.F. 7J.M#SP.
714001-715000=572,16S.H.C.17J.M# 4
715001-716000=586,16S.O.F.15J.M# 3
716001-717000=587,16S.O.F.15J.M# 2
717001-718000=600,16S.O.F.11J.M# 3
718001-719000=605,16S.O.F.11J.M# 2
719001-720000=615,16S.O.F. 7J.M# 3
720001-721000=610,16S.O.F. 7J.M#SP.
721001-721500=600,16S.H.C.11J.M# 3
721501-722000=586,16S.H.C.15J.M# 3
722501-722700=573,16S.O.F.17J.M# 5
722701-722800=635,16S.O.F.17J.M# 5
722801-722900=573,16S.O.F.17J.M# 5
722901-723000=635,16S.O.F.17J.M# 5
723001-724000=935,18S.O.F.17J.M#10
724001-725000=205,18S.O.F.17J.M# 9
725001-725100=930,18S.O.F.17J.M# 9
725101-726000=935,18S.O.F.17J.M# 9
726001-727000=405,16S.O.F.17J.M# 5
727001-728000=587,16S.O.F.15J.M# 2
728001-728500=573,16S.O.F.17J.M# 5
728501-728600=635,16S.O.F.17J.M# 5
728601-728800=573,16S.O.F.17J.M# 5
728801-729000=635,16S.O.F.17J.M# 5
729001-729800=600,16S.H.C.11J.M# 3
729801-730000=586,16S.O.F.15J.M# 3
730001-730700=610,16S.O.F. 7J.M#SP.
730701-731000=586,16S.O.F.17J.M# 3
731001-732000=615,16S.O.F. 7J.M# 3
732001-732500=162, 0S.H.C.17J.M# 1
732501-733000=150, 0S.H.C.17J.M# 1
733001-734000=572, 6S.H.C.17J.M# 4
734001-735000=586,16S.O.F.15J.M# 2
735001-735200=610,16S.H.C. 7J.M#SP.
735201-736000=586,16S.O.F.15J.M# 2
736001-738000=935,18S.O.F.17J.M# 9
738001-739000=938,18S.O.F.17J.M#10
739001-740000=925,18S.O.F.17J.M# 9
740001-740200=830,18S.H.C.17J.M#10
740201-741000=835,18S.H.C.17J.M#10
741001-741100=600,16S.H.C.11J.M# 3
741101-742000=586,16S.H.C.15J.M# 3
742001-742500=605,16S.O.F.11J.M# 2
742501-743000=587,16S.O,F.15J.M# 2
743001-745000=935,18S.O.F.17J.M# 9
745001-746000=930,18S.O.F.17J.M# 9
746001-747000=586,16S.O.F.15J.M# 2
747001-748000=935,18S.O.F.17J.M# 9
748001-749000=938,18S.O.F.17J.M#10
749001-749600=572,16S.H.C.17J.M# 4
749601-750000=630,16S.H.C.17J.M# 4
750001-750200=573,16S.O.F.17J.M# 5
750201-750600=635,16S.O.F.17J.M# 5
750601-751000=573,16S.O.F.17J.M# 5
751001-751200=605,16S.O.F.15J.M# 2
752001-752100=572,16S.H.C.17J.M# 4
752101-752200=630,16S.H.C.17J.M# 4
752201-753000=572,16S.H.C.17J.M# 4
753001-754000=573,16S.O.F.17J.M# 5
754001-755000=586,16S.H.C.15J.M# 3
755001-756000=587,16S.O.F.15J.M# 2
756001-757000=935,18S.O.F.17J.M# 9
757001-758000=925,18S.O.F.17J.M# 9
758001-759000=150, 0S.H.C.17J.M# 1
759001-759500=572,16S.H.C.17J.M# 4

FROM ROCKFORD PARTS CATALOG 1909 - 1910

SERIAL NUMBER — GRADE,SIZE-STYLE, JEWELS,MODEL

759501-756000=620,16S.H.C.21J.M# 5
760001-760500=573,16S.O.F.17J.M# 5
760501-761000=625,16S.O.F.21J.M# 5
761001-762000=160, 0S.H.C.15J.M# 1
762001-762500=400,16S.H.C.17J.M# 4
762501-764000=405,16S.O.F.17J.M# 5
764001-765000=205,18S.O.F.17J.M#10
765001-765500=515,16S.O.F.21J.M# 5
765501-766000=545,16S.O.F.21J.M# 5
766001-767000=930,18S.O.F.17J.M# 9
767001-768000=572,16S.H.C.17J.M# 4
768001-769000=935,18S.O.F.17J.M# 9
769001-770000=918,18S.O.F.21J.M#10
770001-770500=938,18S.O.F.17J.M#10
770501-771000=835,18S.H.C.17J.M#10
771001-772000=586,16S.O.F.15J.M# 3
772001-772100=320,12S.H.C.17J.M# 1
772001-772200=330,12S.H.C.17J.M# 1
772201-772300=310,12S.H.C.17J.M# 1
772301-772400=300,12S.H.C.23J.M# 1
772401-772600=325,12S.O.F.17J.M# 2
772601-772800=335,12S.O.F.17J.M# 2
772801-772900=315,12S.O.F.21J.M# 2
772901-773000=305,12S.O.F.23J.M# 2
773001-773100=300,12S.H.C.23J.M# 1
773101-773200=310,12S.H.C.21J.M# 1
773201-773400=320,12S.H.C.17J.M# 1
773401-773500=305,12S.O.F.23J.M# 2
773501-773600=315,12S.O.F.21J.M# 2
773601-773800=325,12S.O.F.17J.M# 2
773801-774000=330,12S.H.C.17J.M# 1
774001-774500=335,12S.O.F.17J.M# 2
774501-774700=325,12S.O.F.17J.M# 2
774701-774000=320,12S.H.C.17J.M# 1
774901-775000=320,12S.H.C.17J.M# 1
775001-776000=587,16S.O.F.15J.M# 2
776001-777000=630,16S.H.C.17J.M# 5
777001-778000=635,16S.O.F.17J.M# 5
778001-779000=838,18S.H.C.17J.M#10
779001-779500=938,18S.H.C.17J.M#10
779501-780000=935,18S.O.F.17J.M# 9
780001-781000=835,18S.H.C.17J.M#10
781001-782000=545,16S.O.F.21J.M# 5
782001-783000=404,16S.O.F.17J.M# 5
783001-784000=561,16S.H.C.17J.M# 4
784001-784500=930,18S.O.F.17J.M# 9
784501-786000=205,18S,O.F.17J.M# 9
786001-787000=935,18S.O.F.17J.M# 9
787001-787200=310,12S.H.C.21J.M# 1
787201-788000=335,12S.O.F.17J.M# 2
788001-788100=315,12S.O.F.21J.M# 2
788101-789000=335,12S.O.F.17J.M# 2
789001-789100=330,12S.H.C.17J.M# 1
789001-789500=320,12S.H.C.21J.M# 1
789501-790000=330,12S.H.C.17J.M3 1
790001-791000=325,12S.O.F.17J.M# 2
791001-792000=330,12S.H.C.17J.M# 1
792001-792900=335,12S.O.F.17J.M# 2
72901-793000=355,12S.O.F.17J.M# 2
793001-796000=935,18S.O.F.17J.M# 9
796001-797000=930,18S.O.F.17J.M# 9
797001-798000=938,18S.O.F.17J.M# 9
798001-799000=830,18S.H.C.17J.M# 8
799001-800000=587,16S.O.F.15J.M# 2
800001-801000=572,16S.H.C.17J.M#.4
801001-802000=573,16S.O.F.17J.M# 5
802001-802500=573,16S.O.F.17J.M# 5
802501-803000=566,16S.O.F.17J.M# 5
803001-804000=573,16S.O.F.17J.M# 5
804001-805000=150, 0S.H.C.17J.M# 1
805001-806000=335,12S.O.F.17J.M# 2
806001-806100=300,12S.H.C.23J.M# 1
806101-807000=335,12S.O.F.17J.M# 2
807001-807100=305,12S.O.F.23J.M# 2
807101-808000=335,12S.O.F.17J.M# 2
808001-810000=573,16S.O.F.17J.M# 5
810001-811000=572,16S.H.C.17J.M# 4
811001-812000=160, 0S.H.C.15J.M# 1
812001-813000=330,12S.H.C.17J.M# 1
813001-814000=355,12S.O.F.17J.M# 2
814001-814500=350,12S.O.F.17J.M# 2
814501-814600=345,12S.O.F.21J.M# 2
814601-814700=340,12S.O.F.21J.M# 2
814701-815000=350,12S.H.C.17J.M# 1
815001-816000=335,12S.O.F.17J.M# 2
816001-817000=190, 0S.H.C.15J.M# 1
817001-818000=185 0S.H.C.17J.M# 1
818001-819000=335,12S.O.F.17J.M# 2
819001-820000=355,12S.O.F.17J.M# 2
820001-821000=190, 0S.H.C.15J.M# 1
821001-822000=335,12S.H.C.17J.M# 1
822001-823000=350,12S.O.F.17J.M# 1
823001-824000=330,12S.H.C.17J.M# 1

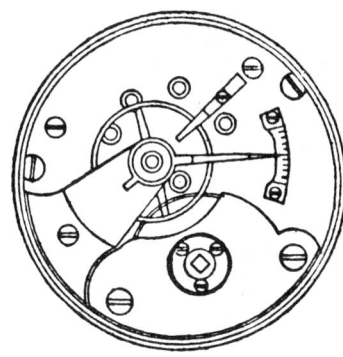

Model 1, 18 size, full plate, hunting, key wind & set.

Model 2, 18 size, full plate, hunting, lever set.

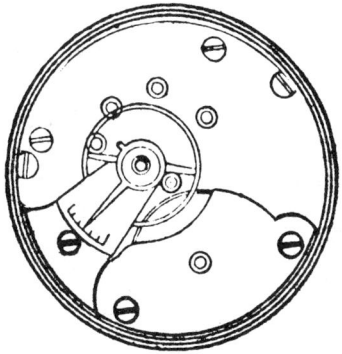

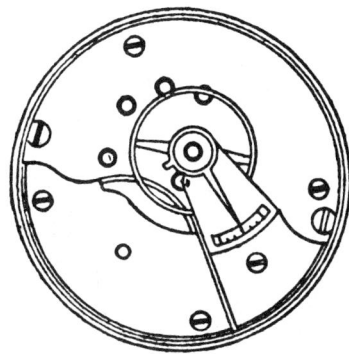

Model 3, 18 size, full plate, hunting, lever set.

Model 4, 18 size, full plate, open face, lever set.

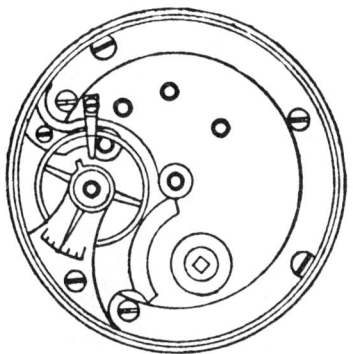

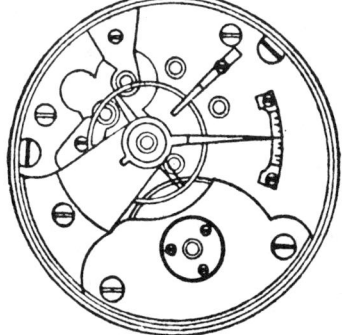

Model 5, 18 size, three-quarter plate, hunting, lever set.

Model 6, 18 size, full plate, hunting, lever set, exposed escapement.

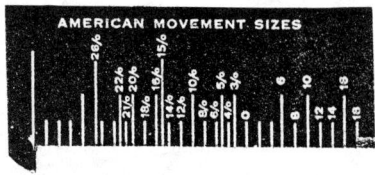

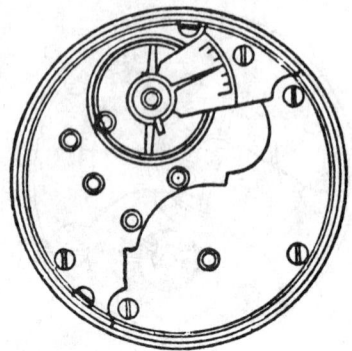

Model 7, 18 size, full plate, open face, lever set.

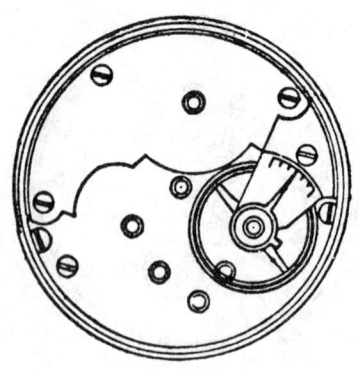

Model 8, 18 size, full plate, hunting, lever set.

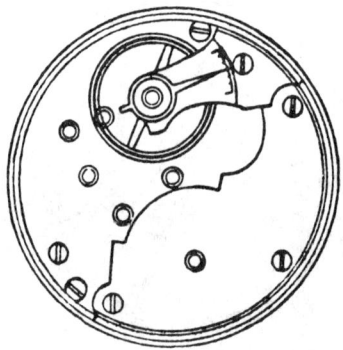

Model 9, 18 size, full plate, open face, lever set.

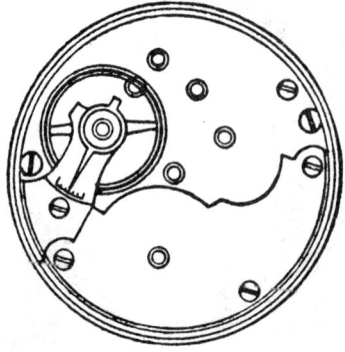

Model 10, 18 size, full plate, hunting, lever set.

Model 1, 16 size, three-quarter plate, hunting, lever set.

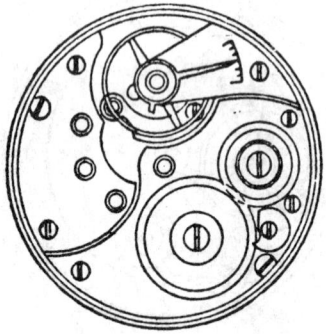

Model 2, 16 size, three-quarter plate, open face, pendant & lever set.

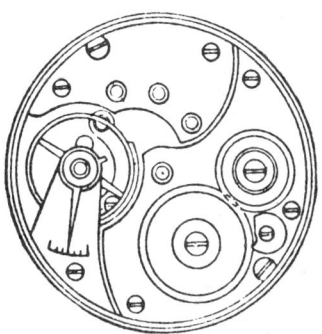

Model 3, 16 size, three-quarter plate, hunting, pendant & lever set.

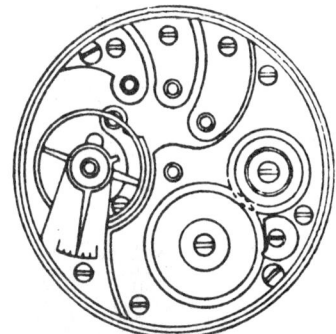

Model 4, 16 size, three-quarter plate, bridge, hunting, pendant & lever set.

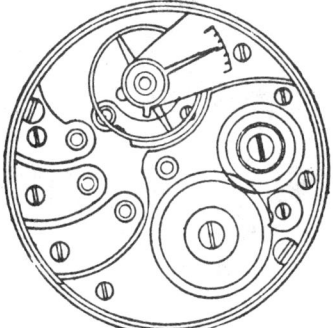

Model 5, 16 size, three-quarter plate, bridge, open face, pendant & lever set.

Model 1, 12 size, three-quarter plate bridge, hunting, pendant set.

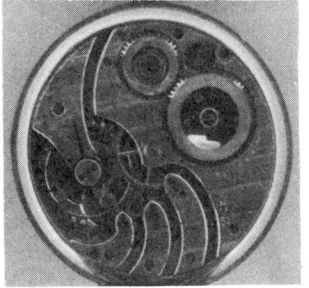

Model 2, 12 size, three-quarter plate bridge, open face, pendant set.

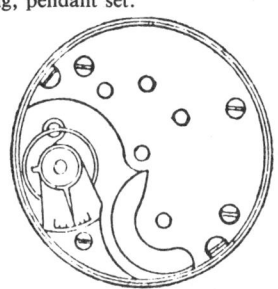

Model 1, 6 & 8 size, three-quarter plate, hunting, lever set.

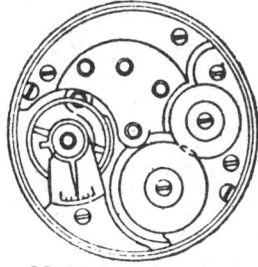

Model 2, 6 size, three-quarter plate, hunting, lever set.

Model 1, 0 size, three-quarter plate, bridge, hunting, pendant set.

Model 2, 0 size, three-quarter plate, bridge, open face, pendant set.

SAN JOSE WATCH CO.
California 1891

Very few watches were made by the San Jose Watch Co., and very little is known about them. The company purchased the Otay Watch Company and machinery and remaining watch movements. The San Jose Watch Co. produced about a few dozen watches. Engraved on a San Jose Watch Co. movement S# 30,656 (First watch manufactured by San Jose Watch Co. November 1891). The San Jose W. Co was sold to Osaka, in Japan.

Grade or Name – Description		Avg	Ex-Fn	Mint
18S, 15J, LS, SW .... ★★★		$2,200	$2,600	$3,600

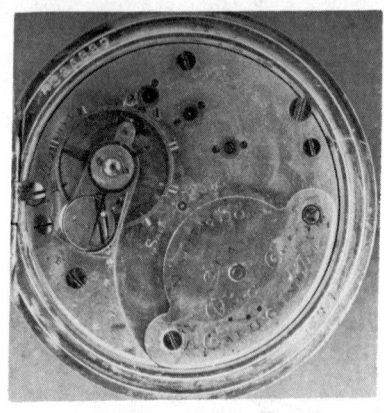

SAN JOSE WATCH CO. movement 18 size 15 jewels, Otay W. Co. material & machinery used to produce movement.

M.S. Smith & Co. movement, 18 size, 19 jewels, three-quarter plate, key wind & set.

M. S. SMITH & CO.
Detroit, Michigan 1870 - 1874

Eber B. Ward purchased the M. S. Smith & Co. which was a large jewelry firm. These watches carried the Smith name on them. A Mr. Hoyt was engaged to produce these watches and about 100 were produced before the Freeport Watch Co. purchased the firm. These watches are very similar to the "J.H.Allison" movements.

Grade or Name – Description		Avg	Ex-Fn	Mint
18S, 19J, 3/4, KW, KS, Freeport Model, 18K case........... ★★★★		$3,000	$3,500	$5,500
18S, 19J, 3/4, KW, KS, Freeport Model .... ★★★★		1,800	2,200	3,500
18S, 15J, 3/4, wolf's tooth -wind, Swiss, 14K HC .... ★		800	900	1,200
6S, 15J, KW, KS, HC 18K case .... ★		500	600	900
6S, 15J, SW .... ★		200	300	500

M. S. Smith & Co., 18S, 15J, 3/4, wolf's tooth -wind, Swiss, Ca. 1874.

M. S. Smith, 6-8 size, 15 jewels, KW KS, Swiss, 18K HC, Ca. 1870.

SOUTH BEND WATCH CO.
South Bend, Indiana
March 1903 - December 1929

Three brothers, George, Clement and J. M. Studebaker, purchased the successful Columbus Watch Co. The first South Bend watches were full plate and similar to the Columbus watches. The serial numbers started at 380,501 where as the Columbus serial numbers stopped at about 500,000. The highest grade watch was a "Polaris," a 16S, 3/4 plate, 21 jewels, and with an open face. This watch sold for about $100. The 227 and 229 were also high grade. The company identified its movements by model numbers 1, 2, and 3, and had grades from 100 to 431. The even numbers were hunting cases, and the odd numbers were open-faced cases. The lowest grade was a 203, 7J, that sold for about $6.75. The company closed on Dec. 31, 1929.

SOUTH BEND ESTIMATED SERIAL NUMBERS
AND PRODUCTION DATES

DATE – SERIAL NO.	DATE – SERIAL NO.	DATE – SERIAL NO.	DATE – SERIAL NO.
1903 – 380,501	1910 – 620,000	1917 – 865,000	1924 – 1,110,000
1904 – 410,000	1911 – 655,000	1918 – 900,000	1925 – 1,145,000
1905 – 445,000	1912 – 690,000	1919 – 935,000	1926 – 1,180,000
1906 – 480,000	1913 – 725,000	1920 – 970,000	1927 – 1,215,000
1907 – 515,000	1914 – 760,000	1921 – 1,005,000	1928 – 1,250,000
1908 – 550,000	1915 – 795,000	1922 – 1,040,000	1929 – 1,275,000
1909 – 585,000	1916 – 825,000	1923 – 1,075,000	

The above list is provided for determining the APPROXIMATE age of your watch. Match serial number with date. Watches were not necessarily sold in the exact order of manufactured date.

SOUTH BEND
18 SIZE (Lever set)

Grade or Name – Description	Avg	Ex-Fn	Mint
South Bend, 15J, OF	$80	$125	$175
South Bend, 15J, HC	100	150	200
South Bend, 17J, OF	100	125	175
South Bend, 17J, HC	125	150	200
South Bend, 21J, OF	250	275	325
South Bend, 21J, HC, 14K	600	700	1,000
South Bend, 21J, OF, HC, Silveroid	250	275	350
South Bend, 21J, SW, HC	400	450	550
The Studebaker, G#323, 17J, GJS, NI, Adj.5P, OF	300	400	500
The Studebaker, G#328, 21J, GJS, NI, FULL, Adj.5P, HC ★	650	800	1,100
The Studebaker, G#329, 21J, GJS, NI, FULL, Adj.5P, OF	450	525	775

IMPORTANT NOTE: Railroad Standards, Railroad Approved & Railroad Grade **terminology**, as defined and used in this *BOOK*.
1. **RAILROAD STANDARDS** = A commission or board appointed by the railroad companies outlined a set of **guidelines** to be accepted or approved by each railroad line.
2. **RAILROAD APPROVED** = A LIST of watches each railroad line would approve if purchased by their employee's. (this list changed through the years).
3. **RAILROAD GRADE** = A watch made by manufactures to meet or exceed the guidelines set by the railroad **standards**. Grades such as 992, Vanguard and B.W. Raymond, etc.
☉ Some GRADES **exceeded** the R.R. standards such as 23 jewels, diamond end stone, gold train, raised gold jewel settings, double sunk dial and the list goes on. Examples: such as Veritas, Sangamo, 950 & Riverside Maximus and many others.

🕑 Generic, nameless or **unmarked** grades for watch movements are listed under the Company name or initials of the Company, etc. by size, jewel count and description.

🕑 Watches listed in this book are priced at the collectable retail level, as **complete** watches having an original 14k gold-filled case and *Key Wind* with silver, an original white enamel single sunk dial, and with the entire original movement in good working order with no repairs needed.

🕑 Pricing in this Guide are fair market price for **COMPLETE** watches which are reflected from the "**NAWCC**" National and regional shows.

South Bend movement, 18 size, 17 jewels, stem wind, hunting, serial number 426,726.

The Studebaker in (SCRIPT), 18 size, 21 jewels, gold jewel settings, marked 329, stem wind.

Grade or Name – Description	Avg	Ex-Fn	Mint
304, 15J, HC	$90	$125	$200
305, 15J, OF	90	125	175
305, 15J, OF, Silveroid	75	100	150
309, 17J, OF	100	125	200
312, 17J, HC, NI, ADJ	100	125	200
313, 17J, OF, NI, ADJ, **marked 313** ★	225	275	350
315, 17J, OF, NI, Adj.3P	100	125	200
G#s 323, 328 & 329 see "The Studebaker"			
327, 21J, OF, Adj.5P, marked 327 ★	300	350	450
327, 21J, OF, Adj.5P, marked 327, Silveroid ★	225	250	350
330, 15J, M#1, LS, HC	90	125	250
331, 15J, M#1, LS, OF	90	125	200
332, 15J, HC	100	150	325
333, 15J, OF	90	125	200
337, 17J, OF	100	125	200
340, 17J, M#1, Adj.3P, NI, HC	125	150	225
341, 17J, M#1, ADJ, NI, Adj.3P, OF	100	125	200
342, 17J, M#1, LS	100	125	200
343, 17J, M#1, LS, OF	100	125	200
344, 17J, HC, NI, Adj.3P ★★	325	375	450
345, 17J, OF, NI, Adj.3P ★★	300	350	425
346, 17J, HC, NI	325	375	450
347, 17J, OF, NI	100	125	200
355, 19J, GJS, 2-Tone, HC ★★	1,000	1,200	1,500

🕐 Generic, nameless or **unmarked** grades for watch movements are listed under the Company name or initials of the Company, etc. by size, jewel count and description.

🕐 Watches listed in this book are priced at the collectable retail level, as **complete** watches having an original 14k gold-filled case and *Key Wind* with silver, an original white enamel single sunk dial, and with the entire original movement in good working order with no repairs needed.

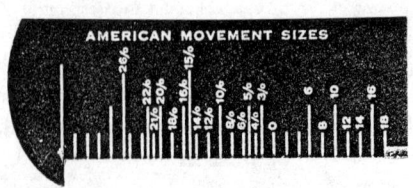

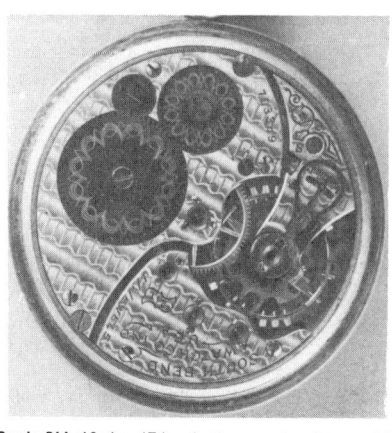 

Grade 211, 16 size, 17 jewels, three-quarter plate, serial number 703,389.

Grade 295, 16 size, 21 jewels, first model, gold jewel settings, gold train, open face, serial number 518,022.

16 SIZE
M#1 Lever set

Grade or Name – Description		Avg	Ex-Fn	Mint
Polaris, 21J, M#1, Adj.5P, 3/4, NI, DR, GJS, GT,				
14K South Bend case with Polaris dial ★ ★		$1,800	$2,200	$3,000
South Bend, 7J, OF		75	100	150
South Bend, 7J, HC		100	125	175
South Bend, 9J, OF		75	100	150
South Bend, 9J, HC		100	125	175
South Bend, 15J, OF		75	100	150
South Bend, 15J, HC		100	125	175
South Bend, 15J, OF, Silveroid		75	100	150
South Bend, 17J, OF		75	100	150
South Bend, 17J, HC, ADJ		125	150	200
South Bend, 17J, 14K HC		450	500	600
South Bend, 21J, OF, Adj, 5P		250	275	375
South Bend, 21J, HC, ADJ		325	375	450
The Studebaker 223, 17J, M#2, Adj.5P, GJS, DR, GT ★ ★		325	400	650
The Studebaker 229, 21J, M#2, Adj.5P, GJS, DR, GT ★ ★		375	425	700
Studebaker, 21J, OF, PS, Adj.5P		225	250	425
203, 7J, 3/4, NI, OF		75	100	150
204, 15J, 3/4, NI, HC		75	100	150
207, 15J, OF, PS		75	100	150
209, 9J, M#2, OF, PS		75	100	150
211, 17J, M#2, 3/4, NI, OF		75	100	150
212, 17J, M#2, HC, LS, heat & cold		125	150	250
215, 17J, M#2, OF, LS, heat & cold		75	100	150
215, 17J, M#2, OF, SILVEROID		75	100	150
217, 17J, M#2, OF, NI, BRG, DR, GT, ADJ.3P.		100	125	200
219, 19J, OF, NI, PS, BRG, DR, ADJ.4P		150	175	250

🕐 Generic, nameless or unmarked grades for watch movements are listed under the Company name or initials of the Company, etc. by size, jewel count and description.

🕐 Pricing in this Guide are fair market price for **COMPLETE** watches which are reflected from the "**NAWCC**" National and regional shows.

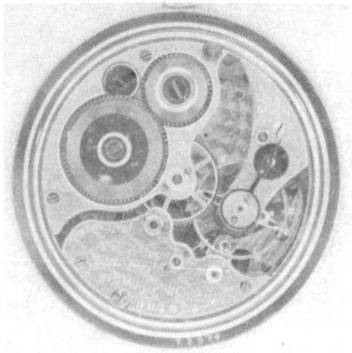

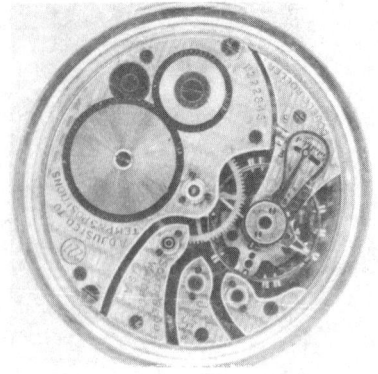

South Bend Watch Co. **Polaris**, 16 size, 21 jewels, model number 1, Adj5p, gold jewel setting, gold train, open face, serial number 518,236.

Grade 227, 16 size, 21 jewels, RR approved, gold jewel settings, Adj5p, serial number 1,222,843.

Grade or Name – Description		Avg	Ex-Fn	Mint
223, 17J, M#2, OF, LS, ADJ.5P		$75	$100	$150
227, 21J, M#2, 3/4, NI, LS, DR, ADJ.5P, OF		225	250	375
260, 7J, M#1, HC		75	100	150
261, 7J, M#1, OF		75	100	150
280, 15J, M#1, HC		85	100	150
281, 15J, M#1, OF		85	100	150
290, 17J, M#1, LS, ADJ.3P, HC	★★	225	275	350
291, 17J, M#1, OF, ADJ.3P	★★	200	225	300
292, 19J, M#1, HC, 3/4, GJS, NI, DR, Adj,5P	★	275	325	400
293, 19J, M#1, OF, 3/4, GJS, NI, DR, Adj,5P	★	200	250	300
294, 21J, M#1, ADJ.5P, GJS, GT, HC, marked 294	★★★	400	500	700
295, 21J, M#1 OF, LS, ADJ.5P, GJS, GT, marked 295	★★	400	450	650
298, 17J, M#1, HC, ADJ.3P	★★	225	275	400
299, 17J, M#1, OF, ADJ.3P	★★	200	250	350

12 SIZE
Chesterfield Series style cases (OF Only)

Grade or Name – Description	Avg	Ex-Fn	Mint
407, 15J, Gold Filled case	$60	$70	$90
411, 17J, DR, GJS, Gold Filled case	70	80	100
415, 17J, ADJ to temp, Gold Filled case.	80	90	125
419, 17J, Adj.3P, Gold Filled case	90	110	150
429, 19J, Adj.4P, DR, GJS, Gold Filled	100	125	200
14K case	150	200	300
431, 21J, Adj.5P, DR, GJS, Gold Filled Case	125	150	250
14K Case	150	200	300
18K Case	200	250	350

⏱ Chesterfield Series (OF Only) comprises of a variety of case and dial combinations. Case styles such as Delmar, Carlton, Fairfax, Girard, Savoy, Senior, Tremont, Warwick, & Wellington. Chesterfield Series were cased and timed at the factory only as complete watches. Chesterfield Series case are **not** interchangeable with other American 12 standard style cases.

South Bend **Digital**, 19J, BRG, NI, DR, GJS, ADJ.4P
(marked 429), 12 size .... ★★ $225 $295 $400

⏱ Pricing in this Guide are fair market price for **COMPLETE** watches which are reflected from the "**NAWCC**" National and regional shows.

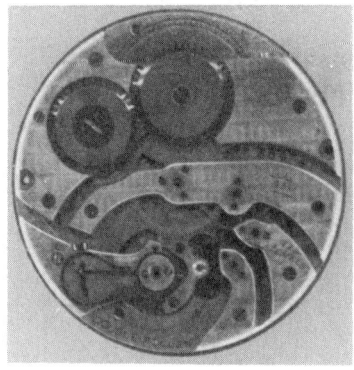

Grade 411, 12 size, 17 jewels, open face, double roller.

Chesterfield, 12 size, 21 jewels, grade # 431, bridge, gold jewel settings, pendant set, double roller, Adj5p.

6 SIZE

Grade or Name – Description	Avg	Ex-Fn	Mint
South Bend, 11J, G#160, HC	$50	$60	$150
South Bend, 15J, G#170, HC	60	75	150
South Bend, 17J, G#180, HC ★	60	75	200
South Bend, 17J, G#180, **14K,HC** ★	225	275	350

South Bend, 6 size, grade # 170, 15 jewels.

Grade 120-HC, 121-OF, 0 size, 17 jewels, bridge, nickel, double roller, pendant set.

0 SIZE

Grade or Name – Description	Avg	Ex-Fn	Mint
South Bend, 15J, M# 1 & 2, OF, PS	$40	$60	$150
Grade 100 HC & 101 OF, 7J, PS	40	60	175
Grade 110 HC & 111 OF, 15J, 3F Brg, DR	60	75	175
Grade 120 HC & 121 OF, 17J, BRG, NI, DR, PS ★	70	80	225
Grade 150 HC & 151 OF, 17J, M# 3, BRG, NI, PS ★	80	90	225

IDENTIFICATION OF MOVEMENTS BY MODEL NUMBER

How to Identify Your Watch: Compare the movement of your watch with the illustrations in this section. Upon matching the movement exactly, the model number and size can be determined. While comparing, note the location of the balance, jewels, screws, gears, and type of back plate (Full, 3/4, Bridge) which will be clues in identifying the movement you have. Having determined the size and model number, you can now find your watch in the main price listing by name or number (which is engraved on the movement).

Record of Serial and Grade Numbers of South Bend Watch Movements

Serial Number	Grade	Size	Model	Jewels	Serial Number	Grade	Size	Model	Jewels
1000 to 4000...	Htg.	18	1	7	400001 to 401200...	331	18	1	15
4001 to 7000...	"	18	1	7	401201 to 403200...	330	18	1	15
7001 to 10000...	"	16	1	15	403201 to 407200...	341	18	1	17
10001 to 21000...	"	18	1	15	407201 to 408500...	340	18	1	17
21001 to 29500...	"	16	1	7	408501 to 408700...	342	18	1	17
29501 to 37000...	"	18	1	7	408901 to 409200...	342	18	1	17
37001 to 41000...	"	16	1	15	409201 to 412200...	330	18	1	15
41001 to 52000...	"	18	1	15	412201 to 413800...	290	16	1	17
52001 to 61000...	"	18	1	7	413801 to 414800...	342	18	1	17
61001 to 76000...	"	18	1	15	414801 to 415800...	291	16	1	17
76001 to 83000...	"	16	1	15	415801 to 417700...	331	18	1	15
83001 to 92000...	"	16	1	7	417701 to 418700...	342	18	1	17
92001 to 97000...	"	18	1	7	418701 to 419700...	343	18	1	17
97001 to 105000...	"	18	1	15	419701 to 420600...	290	16	1	17
105001 to 114000...	"	16	1	17	420601 to 421900...	291	16	1	17
114001 to 127000...	"	18	1	15	421901 to 422400...	281	16	1	15
127501 to 138000...	"	18	1	17	422401 to 423200...	280	16	1	15
138001 to 156000...	"	16	1	7	423201 to 423800...	343	18	1	17
156001 to 165000...	"	18	1	15	423801 to 425800...	261	16	1	7
165001 to 171000...	"	16	1	7	425801 to 426100...	281	16	1	15
171001 to 196000...	"	16	1	17	426101 to 428100...	342	18	1	17
196001 to 201000...	"	18	1	7	428101 to 431100...	260	16	1	7
201001 to 214000...	"	16	1	15	431101 to 431600...	280	16	1	15
214001 to 218000...	"	16	1	7	431601 to 432100...	281	16	1	15
218001 to 220000...	"	18	1	15	432101 to 433100...	342	18	1	17
220001 to 232000...	"	16	1	15	433101 to 435100...	340	18	1	17
232001 to 250000...	"	18	1	7	435101 to 436600...	280	16	1	15
250001 to 261000...	"	16	1	7	436601 to 437900...	281	16	1	15
261001 to 267000...	"	16	1	15	437901 to 438200...	280	16	1	15
267001 to 271000...	"	18	1	15	438201 to 438500...	290	16	1	17
271001 to 274000...	"	18	1	15	438501 to 439500...	293	16	1	19
274001 to 281000...	"	16	1	7	439501 to 440500...	280	16	1	16
281001 to 292000...	"	16	1	7	440501 to 441500...	290	16	1	17
292001 to 294000...	"	16	1	17	441501 to 441600...	260	16	1	7
294001 to 295500...	"	18	1	17	441601 to 441700...	261	16	1	7
295501 to 299100...	"	16	1	7	441701 to 441800...	290	16	1	17
299101 to 302000...	"	18	1	7	441801 to 445900...	293	16	1	19
302001 to 311000...	"	16	1	7	441901 to 445900...	280	16	1	16
311001 to 314000...	"	16	1	15	445901 to 446000...	Htg.	16	1	21
314001 to 321000...	"	18	1	15	446001 to 447000...	261	16	1	7
321001 to 329000...	"	16	1	7	447001 to 450000...	260	16	1	7
329001 to 334000...	"	18	1	7	450001 to 451000...	261	16	1	7
334001 to 341000...	"	16	1	15	451001 to 453000...	260	16	1	7
341001 to 347000...	"	16	1	7	453001 to 455000...	261	16	1	7
347001 to 349500...	"	16	1	17	455001 to 457000...	343	18	1	17
349501 to 354000...	"	16	1	15	457001 to 461000...	260	16	1	7
354001 to 361000...	"	18	1	7	461001 to 462500...	331	18	1	15
361001 to 366000...	"	16	1	7	462501 to 464000...	281	16	1	16
366001 to 368000...	"	18	1	17	464001 to 465300...	331	18	1	16
368001 to 371000...	"	16	1	15	465301 to 467300...	261	16	1	7
371001 to 374000...	"	18	1	15	467301 to 468800...	331	18	1	15
374001 to 376000...	"	16	1	17	468801 to 469300...	290	16	1	17
376001 to 377000...	"	16	1	15	469301 to 469800...	294	16	1	21
377001 to 378000...	"	18	1	17	469801 to 470100...	295	16	1	21
378001 to 379500...	"	18	1	15	*470101 to 470200...	295	16	1	21
379501 to 380500...	"	16	1	15	470201 to 470300...	295	16	1	21
380501 to 381000...	160	6	1	11	470301 to 471300...	281	16	1	15
381001 to 381500...	170	6	1	15	471301 to 472300...	280	16	1	15
381501 to 382500...	330	18	1	15	472301 to 473300...	281	16	1	15
382501 to 383000...	160	6	1	11	473301 to 474800...	330	18	1	15
383001 to 383500...	170	6	1	15	474801 to 475800...	331	18	1	15
383501 to 384000...	302	18	1	15	475801 to 476800...	290	16	1	17
384001 to 384500...	160	6	1	11	477001 to 478000...	261	16	1	7
384501 to 384900...	291	16	1	17	478001 to 479000...	330	18	1	15
384901 to 385200...	281	16	1	15	479001 to 480000...	261	16	1	7
385201 to 385500...	291	16	1	17	480001 to 480200...	295	16	1	21
385501 to 386400...	290	16	1	17	*480201 to 480500...	295	16	1	21
386401 to 386900...	280	16	1	15	480501 to 481500...	290	16	1	17
386901 to 387400...	170	6	1	15	481501 to 483500...	291	16	1	17
387401 to 387900...	330	18	1	15	483501 to 485000...	280	16	1	15
387901 to 388400...	331	18	1	15	485001 to 486000...	331	18	1	15
388401 to 389400...	180	6	1	17	486001 to 487000...	330	18	1	15
389401 to 389900...	170	6	1	15	487001 to 489000...	331	18	1	15
389901 to 390400...	341	18	1	17	489001 to 490000...	341	18	1	17
390401 to 390900...	331	18	1	15	*490001 to 490500...	294	16	1	21
390901 to 391200...	330	18	1	15	490501 to 490800...	293	16	1	19
391201 to 391700...	341	18	1	17	*490801 to 490900...	293	16	1	19
391701 to 392600...	330	18	1	15	490901 to 491000...	293	16	1	19
392601 to 394100...	331	18	1	15	491001 to 492000...	281	16	1	15
394101 to 396000...	330	18	1	15	492001 to 493000...	330	18	1	15
396001 to 400000...	340	18	1	17	493001 to 494000...	340	18	1	17

Although grade numbers appear in this list some of the earlier watches did not have grade numbers stamped upon them. In all instances odd grade numbers indicate open face movement, even grade numbers indicate hunting movement.

*Watches with these serial numbers have double roller.

Serial Number	Grade	Size	Model	Jewels	Serial Number	Grade	Size	Model	Jewels
494001 to 495000...	290	16	1	17	570001 to 571000...	261	16	1	7
495001 to 497000...	331	18	1	15	*571001 to 572000...	313	18	2	17
497001 to 498000...	261	16	1	7	572001 to 573000...	280	16	1	15
498001 to 499000...	291	16	1	17	573001 to 574000...	347	18	2	17
499001 to 500000...	261	16	1	7	*574001 to 575000...	323	18	2	17
500000 to 501000...	281	16	1	15	*575001 to 576000...	217	16	2	17
501001 to 502000...	290	16	1	17	576001 to 577000...	333	18	2	15
502001 to 503000...	331	18	1	15	577001 to 578000...	281	16	1	15
503001 to 503500...	341	18	1	17	*578001 to 579000...	223	16	2	17
503501 to 504000...	343	18	1	17	*579001 to 580000...	329	18	2	21
504001 to 505000...	290	16	1	17	*580001 to 581000...	212	16	2	17
505001 to 505100...	293	16	1	19	*581001 to 582000...	333	18	2	15
*505101 to 505500...	293	16	1	19	582001 to 583000...	261	16	1	7
506501 to 506500...	261	16	1	7	*583001 to 584000...	227	16	2	21
506501 to 507500...	280	16	1	15	*584001 to 585000...	229	16	2	21
507501 to 508500...	261	16	1	7	585001 to 586000...	207	16	2	15
508501 to 509000...	280	16	1	15	586001 to 587000...	211	16	2	17
509501 to 510500...	281	16	1	15	*587001 to 588000...	215	16	2	17
510501 to 511400...	291	16	1	17	588001 to 589000...	260	16	1	7
511401 to 511500...	299	16	1	17	*589001 to 590000...	217	16	2	17
511501 to 511900...	292	16	1	19	590001 to 591000...	204	16	2	15
*511901 to 512000...	292	16	1	19	591001 to 592000...	203	16	2	7
512001 to 513000...	333	18	2	15	592001 to 593000...	207	16	2	15
513001 to 514000...	280	16	1	15	*593001 to 594000...	212	16	2	17
514001 to 515000...	261	16	1	7	594001 to 595000...	203	16	2	7
515001 to 516000...	260	16	1	7	595001 to 596000...	332	18	2	16
516001 to 516500...	298	16	1	17	*596001 to 597000...	215	16	2	17
*516501 to 516600...	298	16	1	17	*597001 to 598000...	223	16	2	17
516601 to 516800...	298	16	1	17	*598001 to 599000...	229	16	2	21
*516801 to 516900...	298	16	1	17	599001 to 600000...	260	16	1	7
516901 to 517000...	298	16	1	17	600001 to 601000...	211	16	2	17
517001 to 517700...	345	18	2	17	*601001 to 602000...	313	18	2	17
*517701 to 518000...	345	18	2	17	602001 to 603000...	203	16	2	7
*518001 to 518500...	295	16	1	21	603001 to 604000...	204	16	2	15
*518501 to 519000...	294	16	1	21	604001 to 605000...	207	16	2	15
519001 to 520000...	347	18	2	17	605001 to 606000...	333	18	2	15
520001 to 521000...	332	18	2	15	606001 to 607000...	347	18	2	17
*521001 to 522000...	329	18	2	21	*607001 to 608000...	215	16	2	17
*522001 to 523000...	293	16	1	19	608001 to 609000...	211	16	2	17
523001 to 523400...	299	16	1	17	609001 to 610000...	203	16	2	7
*523401 to 524000...	299	16	1	17	*610001 to 611000...	215	16	2	17
524001 to 524300...	344	18	2	17	611001 to 612000...	207	16	2	15
*524301 to 524800...	344	18	2	17	612001 to 613000...	203	16	2	7
524801 to 525000...	344	18	2	17	*613001 to 614000...	212	16	2	17
525001 to 526000...	346	18	2	17	614001 to 615000...	305	18	2	16
526001 to 527000...	333	18	2	15	615001 to 616000...	204	16	2	15
527001 to 528000...	347	18	2	17	616001 to 617000...	207	16	2	15
*528001 to 529000...	345	18	2	17	617001 to 618000...	203	16	2	7
*529001 to 530000...	292	16	1	19	*618001 to 619000...	415	12	1	17
530001 to 531000...	260	16	1	7	*619001 to 620000...	431	12	1	21
531001 to 532000...	281	16	1	15	620001 to 621000...	211	16	2	17
532001 to 533000...	333	18	2	15	*621001 to 622000...	223	16	2	17
*533001 to 534000...	323	18	2	17	*622001 to 623000...	229	16	2	21
*534001 to 535000...	345	18	2	17	*623001 to 624000...	411	12	1	17
535001 to 536000...	347	18	2	17	*624001 to 625000...	215	16	2	17
536001 to 537000...	333	18	2	15	625001 to 626000...	203	16	2	7
537001 to 538000...	312	18	2	17	626001 to 627000...	305	18	2	15
538001 to 539000...	332	18	2	15	627001 to 628000...	207	16	2	15
*539001 to 539500...	298	16	1	17	*628001 to 629000...	419	12	1	17
539501 to 539700...	298	16	1	17	629001 to 630000...	260	16	1	7
*539701 to 540000...	298	16	1	17	*630001 to 631000...	407	12	1	15
*540001 to 540400...	299	16	1	17	*631001 to 632000...	217	16	2	17
540401 to 541000...	299	16	1	17	632001 to 633000...	204	16	2	15
*541001 to 542000...	328	18	2	21	633001 to 634000...	347	18	2	17
*542001 to 543000...	313	18	2	17	*634001 to 635000...	329	18	2	21
543001 to 544000...	261	16	1	7	635001 to 636000...	203	16	2	7
544001 to 545000...	260	16	1	7	*636001 to 637000...	217	16	2	17
545001 to 546000...	333	18	2	15	*637001 to 638000...	411	12	1	17
546001 to 547000...	332	18	2	15	638001 to 639000...	211	16	2	17
547001 to 548000...	333	18	2	15	*639001 to 640000...	212	16	2	17
548001 to 549000...	346	18	2	17	*640001 to 641000...	217	16	2	17
549001 to 550000...	261	16	1	7	*641001 to 642000...	415	12	1	17
550001 to 551000...	280	16	1	15	642001 to 643000...	203	16	2	7
551001 to 552000...	281	16	1	15	*643001 to 644000...	229	16	2	21
552001 to 553000...	347	18	2	17	644001 to 645000...	260	16	1	7
*553001 to 554000...	313	18	2	17	*645001 to 646000...	215	16	2	17
*554001 to 555000...	323	18	2	17	646001 to 647000...	207	16	2	15
*555001 to 556000...	327	18	2	21	*647001 to 648000...	407	12	1	15
*556001 to 557000...	298	16	1	17	*648001 to 649000...	419	12	1	17
*557001 to 558000...	299	16	1	17	649001 to 650000...	207	16	2	15
558001 to 559000...	347	18	2	17	650181 to 655200...	Htg.	0	1	7
559001 to 560000...	346	18	2	17	655201 to 656200...	"	0	1	15
*560001 to 561000...	313	18	2	17	656201 to 659700...	"	0	1	7
561001 to 562000...	333	18	2	15	659701 to 662400...	"	0	1	7
562001 to 563000...	332	18	2	15	662401 to 662500...	O.F.	0	2	7
563001 to 564000...	261	16	1	7	662501 to 665400...	Htg.	0	2	7
564001 to 565000...	347	18	2	17	665401 to 665500...	O.F.	0	2	7
565001 to 566000...	260	16	1	7	665501 to 666000...	Htg.	0	2	7
566001 to 567000...	211	16	1	17	666001 to 666500...	"	0	2	17
567001 to 569000...	333	18	2	15	666501 to 666600...	"	0	2	15
*569001 to 570000...	215	16	2	17	666601 to 666650...	O. F.	0	2	15

Although grade numbers appear in this list some of the earlier watches did not have grade numbers stamped upon them. In all instances odd grade numbers indicate open face movement, even grade numbers indicate hunting movement.

*Watches with these serial numbers have double roller.

Serial Number	Grade	Size	Model	Jewels		Serial Number	Grade	Size	Model	Jewels
666651 to 667500...	Htg.	0	2	15		*739001 to 740000...	217	16	2	17
667501 to 671500...	"	0	2	7		*740001 to 740200...	101	0	2	7
671501 to 671600...	O. F.	0	2	7		*740201 to 741000...	100	0	2	7
671601 to 672800...	Htg.	0	2	7		*741001 to 741200...	111	0	2	15
672801 to 672900...	O. F.	0	2	7		*741201 to 742000...	110	0	2	15
672901 to 673000...	Htg.	0	2	7		742001 to 743000...	207	16	2	15
673001 to 674000...	"	0	2	15		743001 to 744000...	203	16	2	7
674001 to 675000...	"	0	2	17		*744001 to 745000...	212	16	2	17
675001 to 676000...	"	0	2	7		*745001 to 746000...	227	16	2	21
676001 to 679400...	"	0	2	15		*746001 to 746100...	111	0	2	15
679401 to 679500...	O. F.	0	2	16		*746101 to 747000...	110	0	2	15
679501 to 680400...	Htg.	0	2	15		747001 to 748000...	305	18	2	15
680401 to 680500...	O. F.	0	2	15		748001 to 749600...	309	18	2	17
680501 to 681000...	Htg.	0	2	15		*749601 to 750000...	223	16	2	17
681001 to 682000...	"	0	2	17		750001 to 751000...	207	16	2	16
682001 to 682800...	"	0	2	15		*751001 to 751100...	101	0	2	7
682801 to 682900...	O. F.	0	2	15		*751101 to 752000...	100	0	2	7
682901 to 683000...	Htg.	0	2	15		752001 to 753000...	211	16	2	17
683001 to 684000...	"	0	2	17		*753001 to 754000...	229	16	2	21
684001 to 684600...	"	0	2	7		754001 to 755000...	203	16	2	7
684601 to 684700...	O. F.	0	2	7		*755001 to 756000...	215	16	2	17
684701 to 685000...	Htg.	0	2	7		*756001 to 757000...	313	18	2	17
685001 to 686000..	'	0	2	15		*757001 to 758000...	323	18	2	17
686001 to 686100...	101	0	2	7		758001 to 759000...	204	16	2	15
686101 to 687000...	100	0	2	7		*759001 to 759500...	Htg.	0	2	17
687001 to 687100...	111	0	2	15		759501 to 759510...	150	0	3	17
687101 to 688000...	110	0	2	15		759511 to 759520...	103	0	3	7
688001 to 688100...	101	0	2	7		759521 to 759530...	102	0	3	7
688101 to 689000...	100	0	2	7		759531 to 759540...	151	0	3	17
689001 to 689100...	111	0	2	15		759541 to 760000...	Htg.	0	2	17
689101 to 690000...	110	0	2	15		760001 to 761000...	305	18	2	15
690001 to 690100...	101	0	2	7		761001 to 762000...	207	16	2	16
690101 to 691000...	100	0	2	7		*762001 to 762100...	111	0	2	15
691001 to 691100...	101	0	2	7		762101 to 763000...	110	0	2	17
691101 to 692000...	100	0	2	7		763001 to 764000...	203	16	2	7
692001 to 692100...	111	0	2	15		*764001 to 765000...	215	16	2	17
692101 to 693000...	110	0	2	15		*765001 to 766000...	217	16	2	17
693001 to 693100...	101	0	2	7		766001 to 767000...	211	16	2	17
693101 to 694000...	100	0	2	7		*767001 to 768000...	217	16	2	17
*694001 to 695000...	217	16	2	17		*768001 to 769000...	212	16	2	17
695001 to 696000...	305	18	2	15		*769001 to 770000...	217	16	2	17
696001 to 696100...	111	0	2	15		*770001 to 771000...	151	0	3	17
696101 to 697000...	110	0	2	15		*771001 to 772000...	217	16	2	17
697001 to 697100...	101	0	2	7		*772001 to 773000...	150	0	3	17
697101 to 698000...	100	0	2	7		*773001 to 774000...	215	16	2	17
*698001 to 699000...	215	16	2	17		*774001 to 775000...	107	0	3	15
*699001 to 700000...	415	12	1	17		*775001 to 776000...	106	0	3	15
*700001 to 701000...	431	12	1	21		776001 to 777000...	207	16	2	15
*701001 to 702000...	313	18	2	17		*777001 to 778000...	102	0	3	7
702001 to 702100...	111	0	2	15		*778001 to 779000...	103	0	3	7
702101 to 703000...	110	0	2	15		779001 to 780000...	211	16	2	17
703001 to 704000...	211	16	2	17		780001 to 781000...	203	16	2	7
*704001 to 705000...	212	16	2	17		781001 to 782000...	305	18	2	15
705001 to 706000...	305	18	2	15		*782001 to 783000...	217	16	2	17
*706001 to 707000...	215	16	2	17		*783001 to 784000...	215	16	2	17
707001 to 708000...	203	16	2	7		784001 to 785000...	207	16	2	16
*708001 to 709000...	407	12	1	15		*785001 to 786000...	215	16	2	17
709001 to 710000...	204	16	2	15		*786001 to 787000...	227	16	2	21
710001 to 711000...	305	18	2	15		*787001 to 788000...	407	12	1	15
711001 to 712000...	260	16	1	7		*788001 to 789000...	217	16	2	17
712001 to 713000...	207	16	2	16		789001 to 790000...	211	16	2	17
*713001 to 713000...	111	0	2	15		*790001 to 791000...	215	16	2	17
*713101 to 714000...	110	0	2	15		*791001 to 792000...	217	16	2	17
*714001 to 715000...	227	16	2	21		*792001 to 793000...	407	12	1	15
715001 to 716000...	211	16	2	17		*793001 to 794000...	215	16	2	17
*716001 to 717000...	411	12	1	17		*794001 to 795000...	212	16	2	17
*717001 to 717100...	101	0	2	7		*795001 to 796000...	411	12	1	17
*717101 to 718000...	100	0	2	7		796001 to 797000...	203	16	2	7
*718001 to 719000...	215	16	2	17		*797001 to 798000...	407	12	1	15
719001 to 720000...	309	18	2	17		*798001 to 799000...	429	12	1	19
720001 to 721000...	203	16	2	7		*799001 to 800000...	411	12	1	17
*721001 to 722000...	227	16	2	21		*800001 to 801000...	219	16	2	19
722001 to 723000...	204	16	2	15		*801001 to 802000...	429	12	1	19
723001 to 724000...	207	16	2	15		*802001 to 804000...	219	16	2	19
724001 to 725000...	211	16	2	17		*804001 to 805000...	411	12	1	17
725001 to 726000...	217	16	2	17		*805001 to 806000...	407	12	1	15
*726001 to 727000...	227	16	2	21		*806001 to 808000...	429	12	1	19
*727001 to 728000...	223	16	2	17		*808001 to 809000...	219	16	2	19
*728001 to 729000...	212	16	2	17		*809001 to 810000...	411	12	1	17
729001 to 730000...	305	18	2	15		*810001 to 811000...	429	12	1	19
730001 to 731000...	304	18	2	15		*811001 to 812000...	211	16	2	17
*731001 to 732000...	313	18	2	17		*812001 to 814000...	219	16	2	19
732001 to 733000...	309	18	2	17		*814001 to 815000...	429	12	1	19
733001 to 734000...	211	16	2	17		*815001 to 816000...	407	12	1	15
*734001 to 735000...	215	16	2	17		*816001 to 817000...	219	16	2	19
735001 to 736000...	217	16	2	17		*817001 to 818000...	429	12	1	19
*736001 to 737000...		0	2	17		*818001 to 819000...	219	16	2	19
*737001 to 738000...	227	16	2	21		*819001 to 820000...	429	12	1	19
*738001 to 739000...	215	16	2	17						

Although grade numbers appear in this list some of the earlier watches did not have grade numbers stamped upon them. In all instances odd grade numbers indicate open face movement, even grade numbers indicate hunting movement.

*Watches with these serial numbers have double roller.

A-112

18 SIZE—MODEL 1
Open Face and Hunting Lever Set

No. 341—Open Face, 17 Jewels, Lever Set, Adjusted to Temperature & 3 Positions.
No. 340—Hunting, 17 Jewels, Lever Set, Adjusted to Temperature & 3 Positions.
No. 343—Open Face, 17 Jewels, Lever Set.
No. 342—Hunting, 17 Jewels, Lever Set.
No. 331—Open Face, 15 Jewels, Lever Set.
No. 330—Hunting, 15 Jewels, Lever Set.

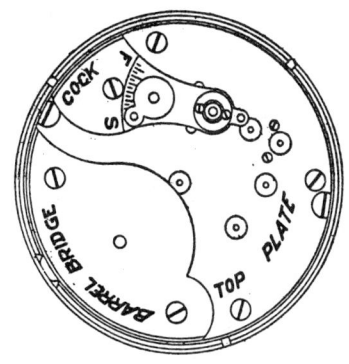 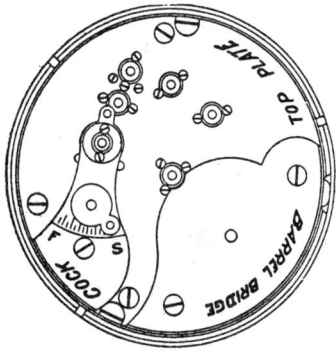

Model 1, Full Plate, Open face.　　　　Model 1 , Full Plate, Hunting

18 SIZE—MODEL 2
Open Face and Hunting, Lever Set

No. 329—21J, Open Face, "Studebaker," Adjusted to Temperature and 5 Positions.
No. 328—21J, Hunting, "Studebaker," Adjusted to Temperature and 5 Positions.
No. 327—21J, Open Face, Adjusted to Temperature and 5 Positions.
No. 323—17J, Open Face, "Studebaker," Adjusted to Temperature and 5 Positions.
No. 345—17J, Open Face, Adjusted to Temperature and 3 Positions.
No. 344—17J, Hunting, Adjusted to Temperature and 3 Positions.
No. 313—17J, Open Face, Adjusted to Temperature.
No. 312—17J, Hunting, Adjusted to Temperature.
Nos. 309, 337, 347—17J, Open Face.
No. 346—17J, Hunting.
Nos. 333, 305—15J, Open Face.
Nos. 332, 304—15J, Hunting.

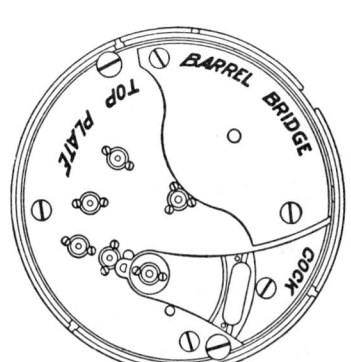 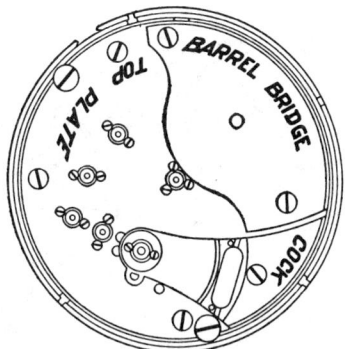

Model 2, Full Plate, Open face.　　　　Model 2, Full Plate, Hunting.

16 SIZE—MODEL 1
Open Face and Hunting, Lever Set

No. 295—Open Face, 21 Jewels, Adjusted to Temperature and 5 Positions.
No. 294—Hunting, 21 Jewels, Adjusted to Temperature and 5 Positions.
No. 293—Open Face, 19 Jewels, Adjusted to Temperature and 5 Positions.
No. 292—Hunting, 19 Jewels, Adjusted to Temperature and 5 Positions.
No. 299—Open Face, 17 Jewels, Adjusted to Temperature and 3 Positions.
No. 298—Hunting, 17 Jewels, Adjusted to Temperature and 3 Positions.
No. 291—Open Face, 17 Jewels, Adjusted to Temperature and 3 Positions.
No. 290—Hunting, 17 Jewels, Adjusted to Temperature and 3 Positions.
No. 281—Open Face, 15 Jewels, & No. 280—Hunting, 15 Jewels.
No. 261—Open Face, 7 Jewels, & No. 260—Hunting, 7 Jewels.

Model 1, 3/4 Plate, Open Face.   Model 1, 3/4 Plate, Hunting.

16 SIZE—MODEL 2
Open Face and Hunting, Pendant and Lever Set.

No. 229—21J, Open Face, Lever Set, "Studebaker," Adjust. to Temp. and 5 Positions.
No. 227—21J, Open Face, Lever Set, Adjusted to Temperature and 5 Positions.
No. 219—19J, Open Face, Pendant Set, Adjusted to Temperature and 4 Positions.
No. 223—17J, Open Face, Lever Set, "Studebaker," Adjust. to Temp. and 5 Positions.
No. 217—17J, Open Face, Lever Set, Adjusted to Temperature and 3 Positions.
No. 215—17J, Open Face, Pendant Set, Adjusted to Temperature.
No. 212—17J, Hunting, Lever Set, Adjusted to Temperature.
No. 211—17J, Open Face, Pendant Set
No. 207—15J, Open Face, Pendant Set, & No. 204—15J, Hunting, Lever Set.
No. 209—9J, Open Face, Pendant Set, & No. 203—7J, Open Face, Pendant Set.

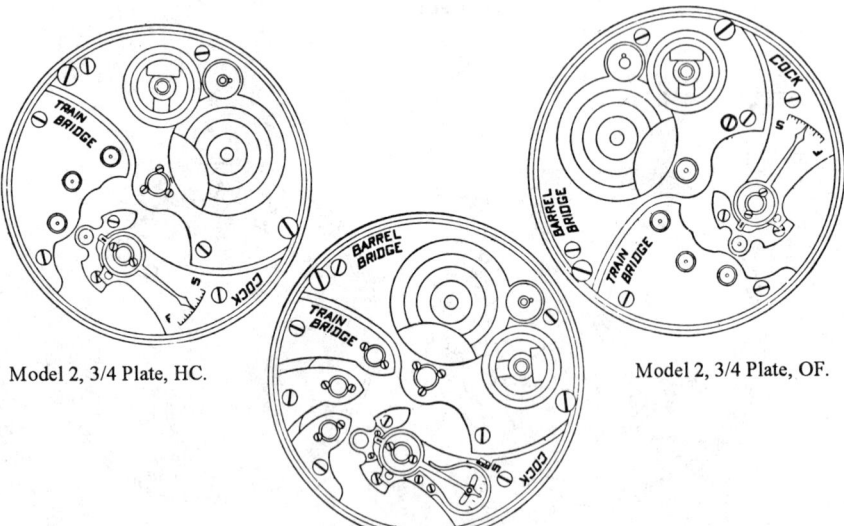

Model 2, 3/4 Plate, HC.   Model 2, 3/4 Plate, OF.

Model 2, Bridges, Open Face.

12 SIZE—MODEL 1
Chesterfield Series and Grade 429 Special
Made in Pendant Set, Open Face Only

No. 431—21J, Adjusted to Temperature and 5 Positions.
No. 429—19J, Adjusted to Temperature and 4 Positions.
No. 419—17J, Adjusted to Temperature and 3 Positions.
No. 415—17J, Adjusted to Temperature.
No. 411—17J.
No. 407—15J.

Model 1, Bridges, Open Face.

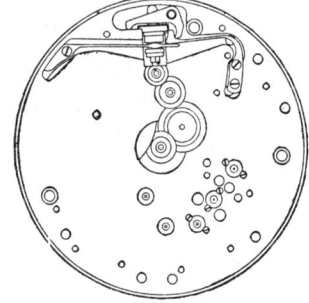

Model 1, Lower Plate, Dial Side.

6 SIZE— MODEL 1
Hunting
Grade No. 180, 17 Jewels
Grade No. 170, 15 Jewels
Grade No. 160, 11 Jewels

Serial Number Range
380,501 to 389,900

Model 1, 3/4 Plate, 6 size

0 SIZE—MODEL 1
Open Face, No second hand, Hunting has second hand

Model numbers 1 & 2 serial numbers under 659,700. All open face and hunting parts for this model except dial and fourth pinion are interchangeable.

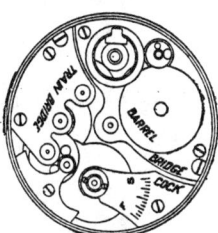

Model 1, Open Face, 3/4 Plate, 7 jewels.

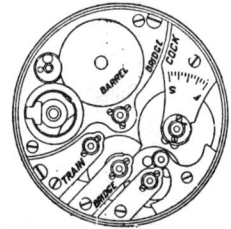

Model 1, Hunting, Bridges, 15-17 jewels.

0 SIZE—MODEL 2
Open Face, No second hand, Hunting has second hand

No. 100— 7 Jewels, Hunting, 3/4 Bridge.
No. 101— 7 Jewels, Open Face, 3/4 Plate.
No. 110— 15 Jewels, Hunting, 3/4 Bridge.
No. 111— 15 Jewels, Open Face, 3/4 Plate.
No. 120— 17 Jewels, Hunting, 3/4 Bridge.
No. 121— 17 Jewels, Open Face, 3/4 Plate.

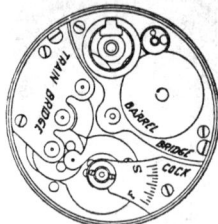

Model 2, Open Face, 3/4 Plate.

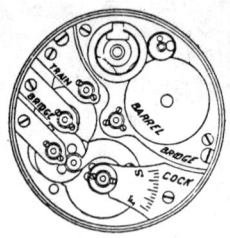

Model 2, Hunting, 3/4 Bridge.

Model numbers 1 & 2 serial numbers under 659,700. All open face and hunting parts for this model except dial and fourth pinion are interchangeable.

0 SIZE—MODEL 3
Both Open Face and Hunting have second hand

No. 151— 21J, Open Face, Bridge Model.
No. 150— 21J, Hunting, Bridge Model.
No. 121— 17J, Open Face, Bridge Model.
No. 120— 17J, Hunting, Bridge Model.

Model 3, Open Face, Bridges.

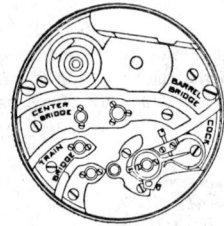

Model 3, Hunting, Bridges.

J. P. STEVENS & CO.

J. P. STEVENS & BRO.
J. P. STEVENS WATCH CO.

Atlanta, Georgia
1882 - 1887

In mid-1881 J. P. Stevens bought part of the Springfield Watch Co. of Massachusetts; and some unfinished watch components from E. F. Bowman. He set up his watchmaking firm above his jewelry store in Atlanta, Ga., and started to produce the Bowman unfinished watches which were 16 size and 18 size, to which was added the "Stevens Patent Regulator." This regulator is best described as a simple disc attached to the plate which has an eccentric groove cut for the arm of the regulator to move in. This regulator is a prominent feature of the J. P. Stevens, and only the top is jeweled. These watches were 16S, 3/4 plate, stem wind and had a nickel plate with damaskeening. The pallets were equidistant locking and needed greater accuracy in manufacturing. About 50 of these watches were made. A line of gilt movements was added. The pallet and fork are made of one piece aluminum. The aluminum was combined with 1/10 copper and formed an exceedingly tough metal which will not rust or become magnetized. The lever of this watch is only one-third the weight of a steel lever. The aluminum lever affords the least possible resistance for overcoming inertia in transmitting power from the escape wheel to the balance. In 1884, the company was turning out about ten watches a day at a price of $20 to $100 each. In the spring of 1887 the company failed. Only 174 true Stevens watches were made, but other watches carried the J. P. Stevens name.

Original J. P. **Stevens** movement, 16-18 size, 15 jewels, note patented eccentric style regulator, serial number 65.

J.P. **Stevens Watch Co.** movement by Columbus Watch Co., 18 size, 11-15 jewels.

16 TO 18 SIZE

Grade or Name – Description		Avg	Ex-Fn	Mint
Original Model, Serial Nos. 1 to 174,(recased)	★ ★ ★	$1,500	$2,000	$2,800
Original Model, Serial Nos. 1 to 174 with original J. P. Stevens dial & **18K** case	★ ★ ★ ★	6,000	7,000	10,000
Aurora, 15-17J	★	350	400	675
Chronograph, 17J, Swiss made, fly back hand	★	500	550	850
Columbus W. Co., 15-17J	★	400	450	700

🕐 Watches listed in this book are priced at the collectable retail level, as **complete** watches having an original 14k gold-filled case and *Key Wind* with silver, an original white enamel single sunk dial, and with the entire original movement in good working order with no repairs needed.

J. P. Stevens & Bro., on movement & dial, made by **Aurora,** 18 size, 15 jewels, Hunting Case, S # 39806.

J. P. Stevens & Bro., Swiss chronograph movement, about 18 size, with fly back hand.

Grade or Name – Description		Avg	Ex-Fn	Mint
Elgin, 15-17J	★	$300	$350	$450
Hamilton, 17J	★	400	450	650
Hampden, 15-17J		300	350	450
Illinois, 15-17J	★	600	650	750
N. Y. W. Co., 17J, Full Plate, S#s range in 500s	★	700	750	1,000
N. Y. W. Co. "Bond" Model, S#s range in 500s	★ ★	900	1,000	1,400
A. Potter, 14K case, Swiss made	★ ★ ★	3,000	3,500	5,000
Rockford, 15J, Full Plate, HC	★	400	450	700
18S Swiss, 15-17J, bar style movement, wolf teeth winding		400	450	600
16S Swiss, 15-17J, Longines		175	200	250
16S Swiss, 15-17J, 3/4 plate		175	200	250
Waltham, 11-15-17J	★	400	450	675

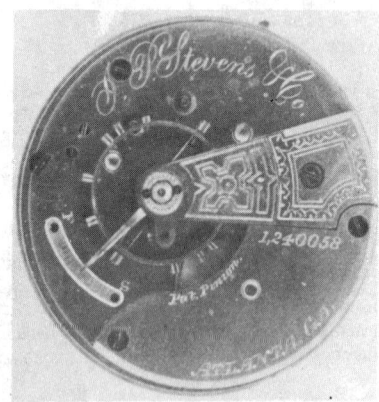

J.P. Stevens & Bro., about 18 size, 17 jewels, wolf teeth winding, Ca. about 1889.

J.P. Stevens Watch Co. movement by **Waltham,** 18 size, 11 jewels, serial number 1,240,058.

J.P. Stevens movement made by Hampden, 18 size, 17 jewels, note eccentric style regulator, serial # 515.

J.P. Stevens & Bro., movement made by Hampden, model 4, 18 size, 17jewels, model 4, S#732,085.

6 SIZE

Grade or Name – Description	Avg	Ex-Fn	Mint
Ladies Model, 15J, LS, HC, 14K	$500	$575	$650
Ladies Model, 15J, LS, GF case, HC	225	275	350
Ladies Model, 15J, LS, GF cases, OF	200	250	325
Ladies Model, 15J, LS, GF cases, Swiss made	150	175	250

J.P. Stevens Watch Co., 16 size, 15 jewels, Adjusted to temperature & positions, serial number 21,814.

J.P. Stevens Watch Co., 6 size, 11 jewels, exposed winding gears.

🕐 Generic, nameless or **unmarked** grades for watch movements are listed under the Company name or initials of the Company, etc. by size, jewel count and description.

🕐 Watches listed in this book are priced at the collectable retail level, as **complete** watches having an original 14k gold-filled case and *Key Wind* with silver, an original white enamel single sunk dial, and with the entire original movement in good working order with no repairs needed.

🕐 Pricing in this Guide are fair market price for **COMPLETE** watches which are reflected from the "**NAWCC**" National and regional shows.

SUFFOLK WATCH CO.

Waltham, Massachusetts 1899 - 1901

The Suffolk Watch Company officially succeeded the Columbia Watch Company in March 1901. However, the Suffolk 0-size, 7-jewel nickel movement with lever escapement was being manufactured in the Columbia factory before the end of 1899. More than 25,000 movements were made . The factory was closed after it was purchased by the Keystone Watch Case Company on May 17, 1901. The machinery was moved to the nearby factory of the United States Watch Company (purchased by Keystone in April 1901), where it was used to make the United States Watch Company's 0-size movement, introduced in April 1902. Both the Columbia Watch Company and the Suffolk Watch Company made 0-size movements only.

Grade or Name – Description		Avg	Ex-Fn	Mint
0S, 7J, NI, HC...★		$70	$90	$175

Suffolk Watch Co., 0 Size, 7 jewels, serial number 216,841.   Seth Thomas, *Colonial U.S.A.* on movement, 18 size, 7 jewels, model # 11.

SETH THOMAS WATCH CO.

Thomaston, Connecticut

1883 - 1915

Seth Thomas is a very prominent clock manufacturer, but in early 1883, the company made a decision to manufacture watches. The watches were first placed on the market in 1885. They were 18S, open face, stem wind, 3/4 plate, and the escapement was between the plates. The compensating balance was set well below the normal. They were 11J, 16,000 beats per minute train, but soon went to 18,000 or quick train. In 1886, the company started to make higher grade watches and produced four grades: 7J, 11J, 15J, and 17J. That year the output was 100 watches a day.

SETH THOMAS ESTIMATED SERIAL NUMBERS AND PRODUCTION DATES

DATE – SERIAL NO.	DATE – SERIAL NO	DATE–SERIAL NO.	DATE – SERIAL NO.
1885 – 5,000	1893 – 510,000	1901 – 1,230,000	1909 – 2,500,000
1886 – 20,000	1894 – 600,000	1902 – 1,320,000	1910 – 2,725,000
1887 – 40,000	1895 – 690,000	1903 – 1,410,000	1911 – 2,950,000
1888 – 80,000	1896 – 780,000	1904 – 1,500,000	1912 – 3,175,000
1889 – 150,000	1897 – 870,000	1905 – 1,700,000	1913 – 3,490,000
1890 – 235,000	1898 – 960,000	1906 – 1,900,000	1914 – 3,600,000
1891 – 330,000	1899 – 1,050,000	1907 – 2,100,000	
1892 – 420,000	1900 – 1,140,000	1908 – 2,300,000	

The above list is provided for determining the APPROXIMATE age of your watch. Match serial number with date. Watches were not necessarily sold in the exact order of manufactured date.

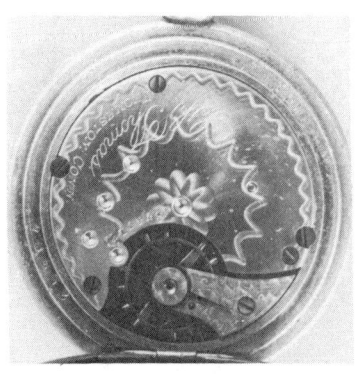

Seth Thomas movement, 18 size,17 jewels, Molineux model, 2 tone yellow gold, heavy damaskeening, H. C.

Seth Thomas 18 size,"Molineux" 17 J., 2 tone yellow gold gilt & nickel heavy damaskeening model #2 ,HC

18 SIZE

Grade or Name – Description	Avg	Ex-Fn	Mint
Century, 7J, OF	$55	$70	$150
Century, 7J, HC	70	90	175
Century, 15J, OF	50	70	150
Century, 15J, HC	60	80	175
Chautauqua, 15J, GJS, M#5 ★	150	175	325
Colonial U.S.A., 7J, model # 11	55	65	125
Early model # 1, low serial # under **1,000**	275	350	500
Eagle Series, No. 36, 7J, OF	100	125	150
Eagle Series, No. 37, 7J, HC	125	150	175
Eagle Series, No. 106, 11J, OF	100	125	150
Eagle Series, No. 107, 11J, HC	125	150	175
Eagle Series, No. 206, 15J, OF	100	125	150

Liberty, Eagle Series,18 size, 7 jewels, hunting or open face, eagle on movement.

Maiden Lane, 18 size, 28 jewels, gold jewel settings, Adj5p, engraved dated as =8,1,99. No serial number.

🕐 Pricing in this Guide are fair market price for **COMPLETE** watches which are reflected from the "**NAWCC**" National and regional shows.

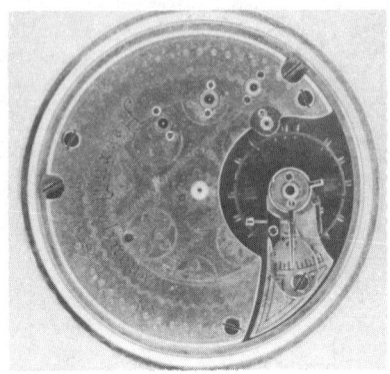

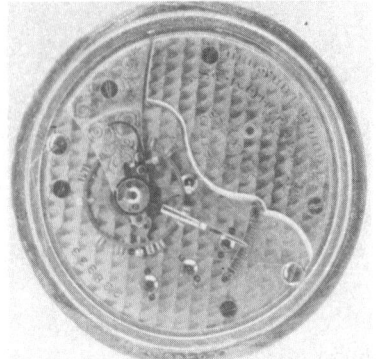

Henry Molineux, 18 size, 17 jewels, "Corona W. Co. USA" on dial, open face, serial number 54,951.

Seth Thomas, 18 size, 23 jewels, gold jewel settings, adjusted, serial number 298,333.

Grade or Name – Description	Avg	Ex-Fn	Mint
Eagle Series, No. 207, 15J, HC	$150	$175	$200
Eagle Series, 15J, M# 2, HC	125	150	200
Eagle Series, No. 210, 17J, OF	125	150	175
Eagle Series, No. 211, 17J, HC	175	200	250
Eagle Series, 17J, NI, 3/4, OF	125	150	175
Edgemere, 11J	50	65	150
Edgemere, 17J	50	65	175
Keywind M#2, 7J, 11J, & 15J, 3/4	175	225	325
Keywind M#4, 7J, 11J, & 15J, 3/4	175	225	325
Lakeshore, 17J, GJS, ADJ, NI	150	200	325
Liberty, 7J, 3/4, eagle on back plate	100	125	200
Maiden Lane, 17J, GJS, DR, Adj.6P, NI, marked ★★	1,200	1,400	1,700
Maiden Lane, 19J, GJS, DR, Adj.6P, NI, marked ★★	1,300	1,500	1,800
Maiden Lane, 21J, GJS, DR, Adj.6P, NI, marked ★★	1,400	1,600	1,900
Maiden Lane, 24J, GJS, DR, Adj.6P, marked ★★★	1,600	1,800	2,200
Maiden Lane, 25J, GJS, DR, Adj.6P, NI, marked ★★	2,000	2,400	3,000
Maiden Lane, 28J, GJS, DR, Adj.5P, NI, marked ★★★★★	15,000	18,000	25,000
Henry Molineux, M#3, 17J, 3/4, GJS, ADJ ★★	575	625	775
Henry Molineux, M#2, 17J, GJS, ADJ ★★	575	625	775
Henry Molineux, M#2, 20-21J, GJS, ADJ ★★★	800	950	1,500
Monarch Watch Co., 7-15J, 2-tone	60	75	175
R. R. Special USA, 7J, with a locomotive on dial	125	150	200
Republic USA, 7J, OF	50	65	125

🕐 Generic, nameless or **unmarked** grades for watch movements are listed under the Company name or initials of the Company, etc. by size, jewel count and description.

	Avg	Ex-Fn	Mint
S. Thomas, 7J, 3/4, **multi-color dial**	$175	$225	$400
S. Thomas, 7J, 3/4	50	75	150
S. Thomas, 11J, 3/4, HC	50	75	175
S. Thomas, 11J, 3/4, OF	50	75	150
S. Thomas, 15J, 3/4, HC	50	75	200
S. Thomas, 15J, 3/4, gilded, OF	50	75	150
S. Thomas, 15J, 3/4 , OF	50	75	150
S. Thomas, 16J, 3/4	50	75	175
S. Thomas, 17J, 3/4, OF, nickel	50	75	200

🕐 Pricing in this Guide are fair market price for **COMPLETE** watches which are reflected from the "**NAWCC**" National and regional shows.

Grade or Name – Description	Avg	Ex-Fn	Mint
S. Thomas, 17J, 3/4, 2-Tone	$90	$125	$225
S. Thomas, 17J, 3/4, OF, gilded	50	70	175
S. Thomas, 17J, 3/4, HC	70	90	200
S. Thomas, 19J, GJS, DR, Adj.5P, OF ★★	600	700	950
S. Thomas, 21J, GJS, DR, Adj.5P	350	425	500
S. Thomas, 23J, GJS, DR, Adj.5P ★★	900	1,200	1,500
Special Motor Service,17J, 2 tone, LS, OF ★	350	400	650
20th Century (Wards), 11J	75	95	175
20th Century (Wards), 11J, 2-Tone	75	95	200
Wyoming Watch Co., 7J, OF	90	120	225
S. Thomas, G# 33, 7J, 3/4, gilded, OF	60	80	150
S. Thomas, G# 37, 7J, 3/4, NI, HC	60	80	175
S. Thomas, G# 44, 11J, 3/4, gilded, OF	60	80	150
S. Thomas, G# 47, 7J, gilded, FULL, OF	60	80	150
S. Thomas, G# 58, 11J, FULL, gilt, OF	60	80	150
S. Thomas, G# 70, 15J, 3/4, gilded, OF	60	80	150
S. Thomas, G# 80, 17J, 3/4, gilded, ADJ, HC	90	120	200
S. Thomas, G# 101, 15J, 3/4, gilded, ADJ, OF	60	80	150
S. Thomas, G# 149, 15J, gilded, FULL, OF	60	80	150
S. Thomas, G# 159, 15J, NI, FULL, OF	60	80	150
S. Thomas, G# 169, 17J, NI, FULL, OF	60	80	150
S. Thomas, G# 170, 15J, 3/4, NI, OF	60	80	150
S. Thomas, G# 179, 17J, 3/4, NI, ADJ, OF	90	120	175
S. Thomas, G# 180, 17J, 3/4, NI, HC	135	175	225
S. Thomas, G# 182, 17J, DR, NI, FULL, OF	100	125	175
S. Thomas, G# 201, 15J, 3/4, NI, ADJ, OF	100	130	175
S. Thomas, G# 245, 19J, GJS, 2-Tone, HC ★★	1,000	1,200	1,500
S. Thomas, G# 260, 21J, DR, Adj.6P, NI, FULL, OF	250	350	500
S. Thomas, G# 281-282, 17J, FULL, DR, Adj.3P, OF, 2-tone	200	250	350
S. Thomas, G# 382, 17J, FULL, DR, Adj.5P, OF, 2-tone	200	250	350
Trainsman Special, fake "23"J Adj, seen in model 10 or 12	75	125	175

Trainsman Special, fake 23 jewels, Adjusted, Chicago U.S.A., jewels made of glass, seen in model 10 or 12.

Grade 36, 16 size, 7 jewels, open face, three-quarter nickel plate.

🕐 Generic, nameless or **unmarked** grades for watch movements are listed under the Company name or initials of the Company, etc. by size, jewel count and description.

🕐 Watches listed in this book are priced at the collectable retail level, as **complete** watches having an original 14k gold-filled case and *Key Wind* with silver, an original white enamel single sunk dial, and with the entire original movement in good working order with no repairs needed.

16 SIZE
(OF Only)

Grade or Name – Description	Avg	Ex-Fn	Mint
Centennial, 7J, 3/4, NI, OF	$50	$70	$125
Locust, 7J, NI, 3/4, OF	50	70	125
Locust, 17J, NI, ADJ, 3/4, OF	60	80	150
Republic USA, 7J, OF	50	70	125

🕐 Generic, nameless or **unmarked** grades for watch movements are listed under the Company name or initials of the Company, etc. by size, jewel count and description.

	Avg	Ex-Fn	Mint
S. Thomas, G# 25, 7J, BRG, OF	$40	$60	$125
S. Thomas, G# 26, 15J, BRG, GJS, OF	40	60	125
S. Thomas, G# 27, 17J, BRG, GJS, OF	40	60	125
S. Thomas, G# 28, 17J, BRG, Adj.3P, GJS, OF	80	100	175
S. Thomas, G# 326, 7J, 3/4, NI, OF	40	60	125
S. Thomas, G# 328, 15J, 3/4, NI, OF	40	60	125
S. Thomas, G# 332, 7J, 3/4, NI, OF	40	60	125
S. Thomas, G# 334, 15J, NI, ADJ,3/4, DMK, OF	40	60	125
S. Thomas, G# 336, 17J, ADJ, 3/4, DMK, OF	70	85	150

Seth Thomas, 12 size, 7 jewels, open face, pendant set.

Seth Thomas, 12 size, 17 jewels, gold jewel settings, gold center wheel, open face, Adj3p.

12 SIZE
(OF Only)

Grade or Name – Description	Avg	Ex-Fn	Mint
Centennial, 7J	$35	$45	$95
Republic USA, 7J, OF	35	45	95
S. Thomas, G# 25, 7J, BRG, OF	35	45	95
S. Thomas, G# 26, 15J, BRG, GJS, OF	35	45	95
S. Thomas, G# 27, 17J, BRG, GJS, OF	35	45	95
S. Thomas, G# 28, 17J, OF, BRG, Adj.3P, GJS	40	60	125
S. Thomas, G# 326, 7J, OF, 3/4, NI	35	45	95
S. Thomas, G# 328, 15J, OF, 3/4, NI	35	45	95

🕐 Watches listed in this book are priced at the collectable retail level, as complete watches having an original 14k gold-filled case and Key Wind with silver, an original white enamel single sunk dial, and with the entire original movement in good working order with no repairs needed.

🕐 Generic, nameless or unmarked grades for watch movements are listed under the Company name or initials of the Company, etc. by size, jewel count and description.

Seth Thomas movement, 6 size, 7 jewels, serial number 441,839. Sometimes appears in a 12 size case.

SETH THOMAS, 0 size, 15 jewels, pendant set, hunting case, serial number 200,449.

6 SIZE
(Some 6 Size were used to fit 12 Size cases)

Grade or Name – Description	Avg	Ex-Fn	Mint
Century, 7J, NI, 3/4	$35	$55	$100
Countess Janet, 17J, Adj., HC	75	125	150
Eagle Series, 7J, No. 45, 3/4, NI, DMK, OF	65	85	100
Eagle Series, 7J, No. 205, 3/4, HC	60	125	150
Eagle Series, 15J, No. 35, 3/4, NI, DMK, OF	65	85	125
Eagle Series, 15J, No. 245, 3/4, HC	70	125	150
Edgemere, 7-11J,	35	50	125
Republic USA, 7J	35	50	100
Seth Thomas, 7J, 3/4, HC, **14K, 26 DWT**	250	275	325
Seth Thomas, 11J, 3/4, HC	70	80	125
Seth Thomas, 11J, 3/4, OF	35	45	100
S. Thomas, G# 35, 7J, HC, NI, DMK,3/4	35	45	100
S. Thomas, G# 119, 16J, HC, GJS, NI, DMK, 3/4	70	125	150
S. Thomas, G# 205, 15J, HC	70	125	150
S. Thomas, G# 320, 7J, OF, NI, DMK, 3/4	35	50	100
S. Thomas, G# 322, 15J, OF	35	50	100

NOTE: Add $25 to $50 for HC.

0 SIZE

Grade or Name – Description	Avg	Ex-Fn	Mint
Seth Thomas, 7J, OF, No. 1	$40	$60	$125
Seth Thomas, 7J, HC, No. 1	50	70	150
Seth Thomas, 15J, OF, GJS, No. 3	50	70	150
Seth Thomas, 15J, HC, No. 3	50	70	150
Seth Thomas, 17J, GJS, PS, No. 9, OF	50	70	150
Seth Thomas, 17J, GJS, PS, No. 9, HC	55	65	150

NOTE: Add $25 to $50 for HC.

🕐 Pricing in this Guide are fair market price for **COMPLETE** watches which are reflected from the "**<u>NAWCC</u>**" National and regional shows.

SETH THOMAS WATCH CO.
IDENTIFICATION OF MOVEMENTS
BY MODEL NUMBER

How to Identify Your Watch: Compare the movement of your watch with the illustrations in this section. Upon matching the movement exactly, the model number and size can be determined. While comparing, note the location of the balance, jewels, screws, gears, and type of back plate (Full, 3/4, Bridge) which will be clues in identifying the movement you have. Having determined the size and model number, you can now find your watch in the main price listing by name or number (which is engraved on the movement).

Model 1, 18 size, Open Face

Model 2, 18 size, Hunting

Model 3, 18 size, Open Face

Model 4, 18 size, Key Wind

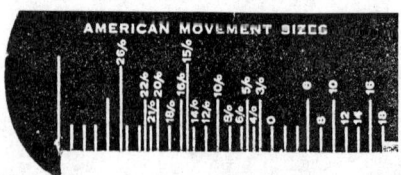

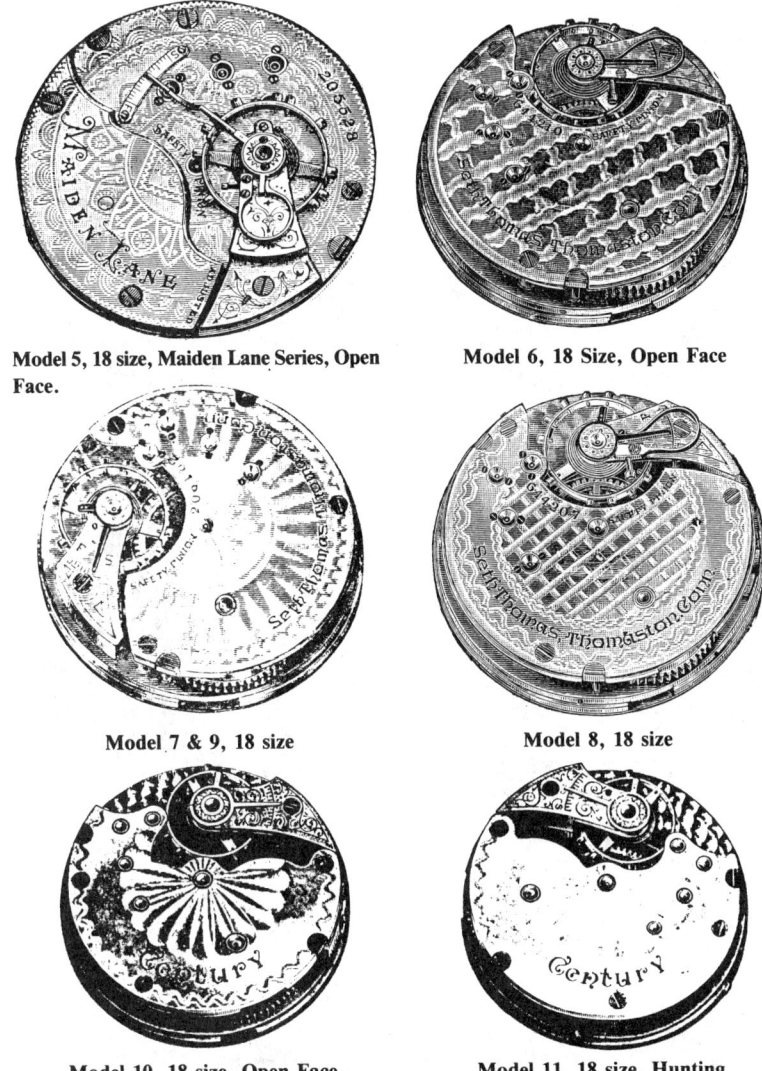

Model 5, 18 size, Maiden Lane Series, Open Face.

Model 6, 18 Size, Open Face

Model 7 & 9, 18 size

Model 8, 18 size

Model 10, 18 size, Open Face

Model 11, 18 size, Hunting

🕐 This book endeavours to be a GUIDE or helpful manual and offers a wealth of material to be used as a tool not as a absolute document. Price Guides are like watches the worst may be better than none at all, but at best cannot be expected to be 100% accurate.

🕐 Characteristics of watches differ for the same age of both case and movement, because these features vary it may not be accurate to date a watch by one single influence. Example: the second hand was not commonly found on watches before 1750, but common about 1800. The first second hand appeared in 1665 and another in 1690. Therefore statements are broad rather than accurate.

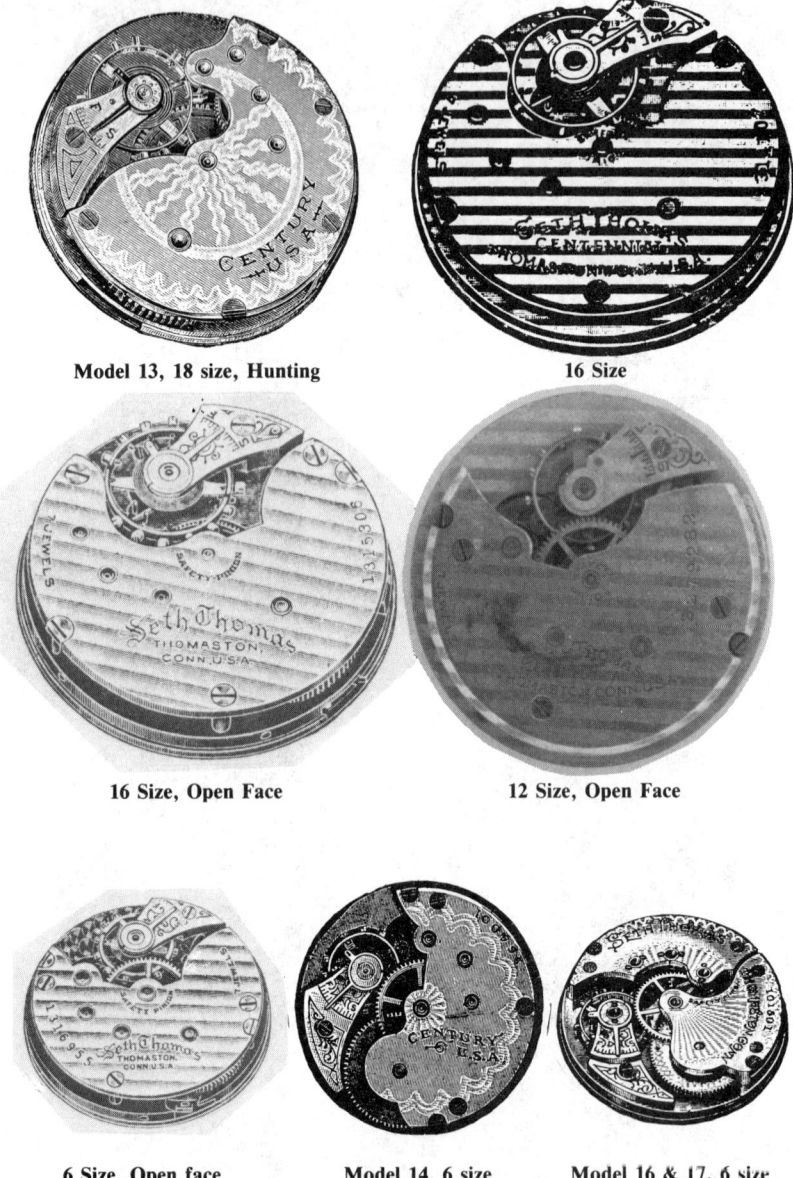

Model 13, 18 size, Hunting　　　　**16 Size**

16 Size, Open Face　　　　**12 Size, Open Face**

6 Size, Open face　　**Model 14, 6 size**　　**Model 16 & 17, 6 size**

TREMONT WATCH CO.

Boston, Massachusetts
1864 - 1866

In 1864 A. L. Dennison thought that if he could produce a good movement at a reasonable price, there would be a ready market for it. Dennison went to Switzerland to find a supplier of cheap parts, as arbors were too high in America. He found a source for parts, mainly the train and escapement and the balance. About 600 sets were to be furnished. Dials were first made by Mr. Gold and Mr. Spurr, then later by Mr. Hull and Mr. Carpenter. Tremont had hoped to produce 600 sets of trains per month. In 1865, the first movements were ready for the market. They were 18S, key wind, fully jeweled, and were engraved "Tremont Watch Co." In 1886, the company moved from Boston to Melrose. The Tremont Watch Co. produced about 5,000 watches before being sold to the English Watch Co.

Tremont Watch Co., with "Washington Street Boston" engraved on movement, 18 size, 15 jewels, key wind and set, serial number 5,264.

Tremont movement, 18 size, 15 jewels, key wind & set, serial number 8,875.

Grade or Name – Description	Avg	Ex-Fn	Mint
18S, 7J, KW, KS	$250	$275	$350
18S, 11J, KW, KS	250	275	350
18S, 7-11-15J, KW, KS, gilded Silveroid	200	225	300
18S, 7-11-15J, KW, KS, gilded, marked LONDON	250	300	400
18S, 15J, KW, KS, gilded	250	275	400
18S, 15J, KW, KS, HC, 14K	775	850	1,000
18S, 15J, KW, KS, gilded, Washington Street ★★	500	600	800
18S, 17J, KW, KS, gilded	300	325	400
18S, 15J, KW, Key Set from back, 3/4 plate ★★★	1,800	2,200	3,200

🕐 Watches listed in this book are priced at the collectable retail level, as **complete** watches having an original 14k gold-filled case and *Key Wind* with silver, an original white enamel single sunk dial, and with the entire original movement in good working order with no repairs needed.

🕐 Pricing in this Guide are fair market price for **COMPLETE** watches which are reflected from the "**NAWCC**" National and regional shows.

TRENTON WATCH CO.
Trenton, New Jersey
1885 - 1908

Trenton watches were marketed under the following labels: Trenton, Ingersoll, Fortuna, Illinois Watch Case Company, Calumet U.S.A., Locomotives Special, Marvel Watch Co., and Reliance Watch Co.

Serial numbers started at 2,001 and ended at 4,100,000. Total production was about 1,934,000.

CHRONOLOGY OF THE DEVELOPMENT OF TRENTON WATCH CO.:

New Haven Watch Co., New Haven, Conn. 1883-1887
Trenton Watch Co., Trenton, N. J. 1887-1908
Sold to Ingersoll 1908-1922

TRENTON MODELS AND GRADES
With Years of Manufacture and Serial Numbers

Date	Numbers	Size	Model	Date	Numbers	Size	Model
1887-1889	2,001-61,000	18	1	1900-1903	2,000,001-2,075,000	6	2
1889-1891	64,001-135,000	18	2	1902-1905	2,075,001-2,160,000	6	3 LS
1891-1898 *1	135,001-201,000	18	3	"	"	12	2 LS
1899-1890	201,001-300,000	18	6	1905-1907	2,160,001-2,250,000	6	3 PS
1891-1900	300,001-500,800	18	4	"	"	12	2 PS
1892-1897	500,001-600,000	6	1	1899-1902	2,500,001-2,600,000	3/0	1
1894-1899	650,001-700,000	16	1	ca. 1906	2,800,001-2,850,000	6	3 PS
1898-1900	700,001-750,000	6	2	"	"	12	2 PS
1900-1904 * 2	750,001-800,000	18	4	1900-1904	3,000,001-3,139,000	16	2
1896-1900	850,001-900,000	12	1	1903-1907	3,139,001-3,238,000	16	3 OF
1898-1903	900,001-1,100,000	18	5	1903-1907	3,500,001-3,600,000	16	3 HC
1902-1907	1,300,001-1,400,000	18	6	1905-1907	4,000,001-4,100,000	0	1

1—7 jewel grades made only during 1891; 9 jewel chronograph Pat. Mar. 17, 1891, made 1891-1898.
2—A few examples are KWKS for export to England.

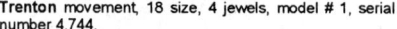

Trenton movement, 18 size, 4 jewels, model # 1, serial number 4,744.

Trenton movement, 18 size, 7 jewels, 4th model, serial number 788,313.

🕐 Pricing in this Guide are fair market price for **COMPLETE** watches which are reflected from the "**NAWCC**" National and regional shows.

18 SIZE

Grade or Name – Description	Avg	Ex-Fn	Mint
Trenton W. Co., M#1-2, gilded, OF..★	$150	$175	$300
Trenton W. Co., M#3, 7J, 3/4..	60	75	125
Trenton W. Co., M#3, 9J, 3/4..	60	75	125
Trenton W. Co., M#4, 7J, FULL...	60	75	125
Trenton W. Co., M#4, 11J, FULL...	60	75	125
Trenton W. Co., M#4, 15J, FULL...	60	75	125
Trenton W. Co., M#4-5, FULL, OF, NI	60	75	125
Marvel W. Co. Fake 23 jewels..	60	75	125
New Haven Watch Co. style, M#1, 4J ....★ ★ ★	250	325	450
Railroad Special, fake 23J, tu-tone, locomotive on dial & mvt.	100	150	250
Trenton, 7J, KW, KS ....★	175	225	500

Note: Add $25 to value of above watches in hunting case.

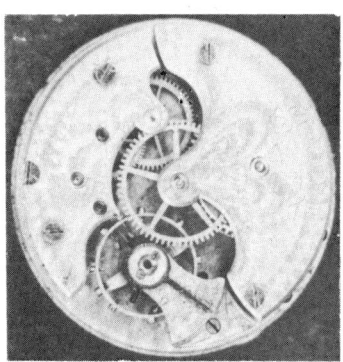

Trenton movement, 18 size, 7 jewels, model #3, serial number 148,945.

Chronograph, 16 size, 9 jewels, third model; start, stop & fly back, sweep second hand.

16 SIZE

Grade or Name – Description	Avg	Ex-Fn	Mint
Trenton W. Co., M#1-2, 7J, 3/4, NI, OF....................................	$30	$50	$125
Trenton W. Co., M#3, 7J, 3F BRG	30	50	125
Trenton W. Co., M#3, 11J, 3F BRG	30	50	125
Trenton W. Co., M#3, 15J, 3F BRG	30	50	135
Trenton W. Co., 7,11,15J, 3F BRG, NI	30	50	135
Chronograph, 9J, start, stop, & fly back, DMK ....★ ★ ★ ★	275	350	550
Chronograph, 9J, start, stop, & fly back, GILDED ....★ ★ ★ ★	275	350	550
Convertible Model, 7J, OF...★	100	125	175
Trenton W. Co., Grade #30 & 31, 7J..	50	75	125
Trenton W. Co., Grade #35, 36 & 38, 11J................................	50	75	125
Trenton W. Co., Grade #45, 16J...	60	70	150
Trenton W. Co., Grade #125, 12J..	50	75	125
Ingersoll Trenton, 7J, 3F BRG	40	50	125

🕐 Generic, nameless or **unmarked** grades for watch movements are listed under the Company name or initials of the Company, etc. by size, jewel count and description.

🕐 Watches listed in this book are priced at the collectable retail level, as **complete** watches having an original 14k gold-filled case and *Key Wind* with silver, an original white enamel single sunk dial, and with the entire original movement in good working order with no repairs needed.

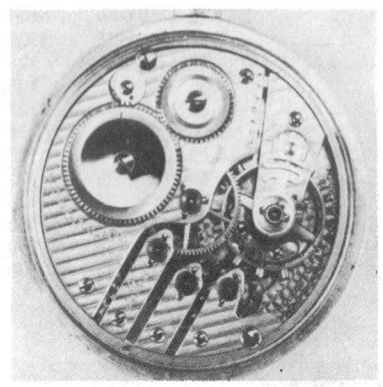

Ingersoll **Trenton** movement, 16 size, 19 jewels, three fingered bridge, adjusted, serial number 3,419,771.

Ingersoll **Trenton** movement, 16 size, 12 jewels; "Edgemere" engraved on movement.

Grade or Name – Description	Avg	Ex-Fn	Mint
Ingersoll Trenton, 15J, 3F BRG, NI, ADJ	$75	$100	$150
Ingersoll Trenton, 17J, 3F BRG, NI, ADJ	85	110	160
Ingersoll Trenton, 19J, 3F BRG, NI, Adj.5P ★ ★	150	250	300
Peerless, 7J, SW, LS	50	65	80
Railroad Reliance, 17J, OF ★	100	125	150
Reliance, 7J	40	65	80

Note: Add $25 to value of above watches in hunting case.

Railroad Special, 18 size, 23 jewels, tu-tone, locomotive on dial & movement, model # 6, S# 1,3660,044.

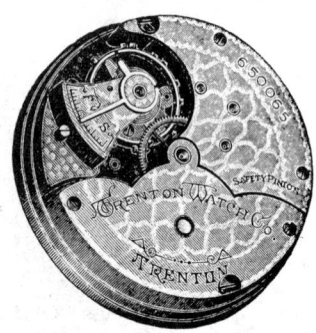

Trenton movement, convertible model converts to open face or hunting case, 16 size, 7 J.

🕐 Pricing in this Guide are fair market price for **COMPLETE** watches which are reflected from the "**NAWCC**" National and regional shows.

10 - 12 SIZE

Grade or Name – Description	Avg	Ex-Fn	Mint
"Fortuna," 7J, 3 finger BRG	$30	$50	$65
Trenton W. Co., M#1, 7J, 3/4	30	50	65
Monogram, 7J, SW	30	40	55

Trenton Watch Co. movement, 12 size, *Fortuna*, 7 jewels, 3 finger BRG., quick train, cut expansion balance.

Trenton Watch Co. movement, 6 size, 7 jewels, open face & hunting, nickel damaskeened.

6 SIZE

Grade or Name – Description	Avg	Ex-Fn	Mint
Trenton W. Co., 7J, 3/4, NI	$20	$40	$55
Trenton W. Co., 7J, 3Finger BRG	20	40	55
Trenton W. Co., 15J, 3Finger BRG	30	50	65
"Fortuna," 7J, 3 Finger Bridge	20	40	55

Note: Add $25 to value of above watches in hunting case.

0 SIZE

Grade or Name – Description	Avg	Ex-Fn	Mint
Trenton W. Co., 7J, 3F BRG	$25	$50	$65
Trenton W. Co., 15J, 3F BRG	30	60	75

Note: Add $25 to value of above watches in hunting case.

Trenton Chronograph, 9J, start, stop, & fly back, Model # 3.

UNITED STATES WATCH CO.

Marion, New Jersey
1865 - 1877

The United States Watch Company was chartered in 1865, and the factory building was started in August 1865 and was completed in 1866. The first watch, called the "Frederic Atherton," was not put on the market until July 1867. It was America's first mass produced stem winding watch. This first grade was 18S, 19J, full plate and a gilt finish movement. A distinctive feature of the company's full plate movements was the butterfly shaped patented opening in the plate which allowed escapement inspection. That same year a second grade called the "Fayette Stratton" was introduced. It was also a gilt finish, full plate movement.

Most of these were 15J, but some of the very early examples have been noted in 17J. In 1868 the "George Channing," "Edwin Rollo," and "Marion Watch Co." grades were introduced. All were 18S, 15J, full plate movements in a gilt finish. In February 1869 the gilt version of the "United States Watch Co." grade was introduced. It was 18S, 19J, full plate and was the company's first entry into the prestige market. Later that year the company introduced their first nickel grade, a 19J, 18S, full plate movement called the "A. H. Wallis." About this same time, in December 1869, they introduced America's most expensive watch; the first nickel, 19J, 18S, full plate "United States Watch Co." grade. Depending on case weight, these prestige watches retailed between $500 and $600, more than the average man earned in a year at that time. The company also introduced damaskeening to the American market; first on gilt movements and later on the nickel grades. The damaskeening process was later improved by using **IVORY** disc in place of wooden disc. The United States and Wallis 19J prestige grades were beautifully finished with richly enameled engraving including a variety of unique designs on the balance cock. It is significant to note that no solid gold trains have been seen with these prestige items in the extant examples presently known.

FREDERIC ATHERTON & CO., 18 size, 19 J., gold jewel settings, key wind the pin set will bring a HIGHER price. Note butterfly cut-out.

United States Watch Co. Marion, N.J., 1871 advertisement.

In 1870 the company introduced their first watch for ladies, a 10S, 15J, plate, cock & bridge movement which was made to their specifications in Switzerland. This model was first introduced in two grades, the "R. F. Pratt" and "Chas. G. Knapp," both in a 15J, gilt finish movement. Later it was offered in a high grade, 19J "I. H. Wright" nickel finish movement. During 1870 and 1871 several other full plate grades in both gilt and nickel finish were introduced. In 1871 development on a new line of full plate, 3/4, plate, and plate & bridge was started but not introduced to the market until late in 1872 and early in 1873. The 10S and 16S new grades in 3/4 plate and bridge were probably delayed well into 1873 and were not available long before the "Panic of 1873" started in September; this explains their relative scarcity.

By July 1874 the "Panic" had taken its toll and it was necessary for the company to reorganize as the Marion Watch Company, a name formerly used for one of their grades. At this time jewel count, finish standards, and prices were lowered on the full plate older grades, but this proved to be a mistake. That same year they introduced a cased watch called the "North Star", their cheapest watch at $15 retail.

The year of 1875 hit the watch industry the hardest; price cutting was predatory and the higher priced watches of the United States Watch Co. were particularly vulnerable. Further lowering of finish standards and prices did not help and in 1876 the company was once again reorganized into the Empire City Watch Co. and their products were displayed at the Centennial that year. The Centennial Exhibition was not enough to save the faltering company and they finally closed their doors in 1877. The Howard brothers of Fredonia, New York (Independent and Fredonia Watch Co.) purchased most of the remaining movement stock and machinery. In the ten year period of movement production, current statistical studies indicate an estimated production of only some 60,000 watches, much smaller than the number deduced from the serial numbers assigned up to as high as 289,000.

NOTE: The above historical data and estimated production figures are based on data included in the new NAWCC book **MARION, A History of the United States Watch Company,** by William Muir and Bernard Kraus. This definitive work is available from NAWCC, Inc., 514 Poplar St., Columbia, PA. (Courtesy, Gene Fuller, MARION book editor.) This book is recommended for your library.

EMPIRE CITY W. CO. & EQUIVALENT U.S.W. CO. GRADES

Empire City W. Co.	United States W. Co.
W. S. Wyse	A. H. Wallis
L. W. Frost	Henry Randel
Cyrus H. Loutrel	Wm. Alexander
J. L. Ogden	S. M. Beard
E. F. C. Young	John W. Lewis
D. C. Wilcox	George Channing
Henry Harper	Asa Fuller
Jesse A. Dodd	Edwin Rollo
E. C. Hine	J. W. Deacon
New York Belle	A. J. Wood
The Champion	G. A. Read
Black Diamond	Young America

NOTE: Courtesy Gene Fuller, NAWCC "MARION" book editor.

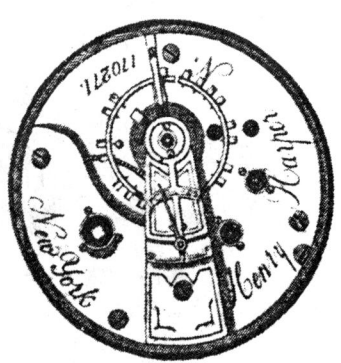

Empire City W. Co., Henry Harper, note: movement does not have **Butterfly Cut-out.**

United States Watch Co. movement, 18 size, 19 jewels, gold jewel settings, key wind. Their highest grade watch.

United States Watch Co., Henry Randel, 15jewels, KWKS, FROSTED plates, S.# 24,944

MARION
18 SIZE
(All with Butterfly Cut-out Except for 3/4 Plate)

Grade or Name – Description	Avg	Ex-Fn	Mint
Wm. Alexander, 15J, NI, KW, HC	$225	$300	$550
Wm. Alexander, 15J, NI, KW, OF	225	300	500
Wm. Alexander, 15J, NI, SW, OF	225	300	500
Frederic Atherton & Co., 15J, SW, gilded	275	325	450
Frederic Atherton & Co., 17J, KW, gilded, HC	350	375	575
Frederic Atherton & Co., 17J, KW, gilded, OF	300	350	475
Frederic Atherton & Co., 17J, SW, gilded, HC	300	350	475
Frederic Atherton & Co., 17J, SW, gilded, OF	275	325	425

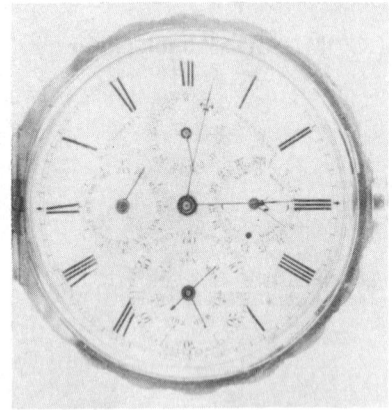

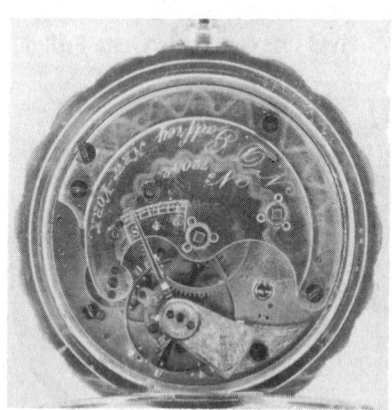

U.S. Watch Co., dial and movement, 18 size, 20 jewels, hunting case, 3/4 plate, engraved on movement "N.D. Godfrey," serial number 72,042. Painted on the dial "New York 1873." The dial consists of day-date-month and moon phases.

NOTE: The **PIN** or **NAIL** set feature is considered more desirable & will bring a **HIGHER** price.

Grade or Name – Description	Avg	Ex-Fn	Mint
Frederic Atherton & Co., 19J, SW, gilded, ... ★ ★	$750	$850	$1,300
Frederic Atherton & Co., 19J, KW, gilded .... ★ ★	650	700	1,000
BC&M R.R., 11J, KW... ★ ★ ★ ★	1,600	1,800	2,500
BC&M R.R., 15J, gilded, KW .... ★ ★ ★ ★	1,600	1,800	2,500
S. M. Beard, 15J, KW, NI, OF...	200	250	400
S. M. Beard, 15J, SW, NI, OF...	200	250	400
S. M. Beard, 15J, SW or KW, HC	250	300	450
Centennial Phil., 11-15J, SW or KW, NI .... ★ ★ ★ ★	1,800	2,200	3,600
George Channing, 15J, KW, NI...	250	300	400
George Channing, 15J, KW, gilded	250	295	350
George Channing, 15J, KW, NI, 3/4 Plate	300	350	500
George Channing, 17J, KW, NI...	300	350	425
J. W. Deacon, 11-13J, KW, gilded......................................	150	225	300
J. W. Deacon, 15J, KW, gilded	200	250	400
J. W. Deacon, 11-15J, KW, 3/4 Plate............................... ★	300	350	600
Empire City Watch Co., 11J, SW, no butterfly cut-out ...... ★ ★ ★	650	775	1,200
Empire City Watch Co., 15-19J, no butterfly cut-out .... ★ ★ ★	800	900	1,400
Empire Combination Timer, 11J, FULL, time & distance on dial.. ★ ★ ★	1,000	1,200	2,000
Empire Combination Timer, 15J, 3/4, time & distance on dial... ★ ★ ★	900	1,300	2,200
Fellows, 15J, NI, KW	400	450	600
Benjamin Franklin, 15J, KW..	400	450	600
Asa Fuller, 7-11J, gilded, KW..	150	225	300
Asa Fuller, 15J, gilded, KW	150	225	300
Asa Fuller, 15J, gilded, KW, 3/4 Plate............................. ★ ★	300	325	500
N. D. Godfrey, 20J, NI, 3/4 plate, day date month, moon phases, c. 1873, HC, 18K .... ★ ★ ★ ★	5,000	6,000	10,000
John W. Lewis, 15J, NI, KW	150	200	375
John W. Lewis, 15J, NI, SW	250	300	400

 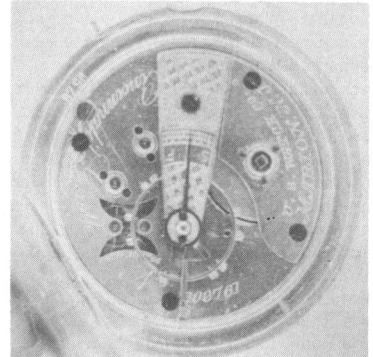

Edwin Rollo, 18 size, 15 jewels, gilded, key wind & set, note butterfly cut-out, serial number 110,214.

Marion Watch Co. personalized Watch, 18 size, about 15J., pin set, note butterfly cut-out, serial # 106,761.

🕑 Watches listed in this book are priced at the collectable retail level, as **complete** watches having an original 14k gold-filled case and *Key Wind* with silver, an original white enamel single sunk dial, and with the entire original movement in good working order with no repairs needed.

🕑 Pricing in this Guide are fair market price for **COMPLETE** watches which are reflected from the "**NAWCC**" National and regional shows.

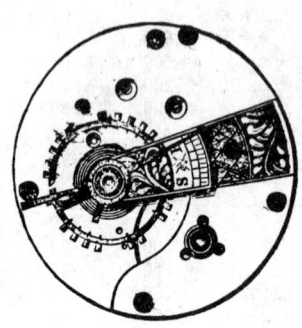

Empire City Watch Co. on movement, U.S. Marion Watch Co. on dial, 18 size, 15 jewels, note **no butterfly cut-out** on this model. **Second Quality**

United States Watch Co., 18 size, 19 jewels, gold jewel settings, key wind & pin set, serial number 24,054.

Grade or Name – Description	Avg	Ex-Fn	Mint
John W. Lewis, 15J, NI, 3/4 Plate ....★	$300	$350	$500
Marion Watch Co., 11J, KW, gilded...............................	150	250	375
Marion Watch Co., 15J, KW, gilded...............................	150	250	375
Marion Watch Co., 15J, SW, gilded, 3/4 Plate ....★★	300	350	475
Marion Watch Co., 17-19J, KW, gilded ....★	400	425	600
N.J. R.R.&T. Co., 15J, gilded, KW..............................★★	1,200	1,400	2,000
Newspaper Special Order, 11-15J, gilded, SW or KW ....★	400	500	700
North Star, 7J, KW, NI case...................................★	350	400	550
North Star, 7J, SW, KS..★	350	400	550
North Star, 7J, 3/4 Plate.....................................★	450	500	600
Pennsylvania R.R., 15J, NI, KW, HC ....★★★★	2,000	2,800	4,000
Personalized Watches, 7-11J, KW, 3/4 Plate....................★	250	300	450
Personalized Watches, 11J, KW, gilded.........................★	250	300	450
Personalized Watches, 15J, KW, gilded ....★	250	300	450
Personalized Watches, 15J, KW, NI ....★	275	325	500
Personalized Watches, 15J, KW, 3/4 Plate ....★	300	350	500
Personalized Watches, 19J, KW, Full Plate.....................★	400	450	600
Henry Randel, 15J, KW, NI	250	300	425
Henry Randel, 15J, KW, frosted plates.........................	275	350	450
Henry Randel, 15J, SW, NI......................................	250	300	450
Henry Randel, 15J, 3/4 Plate ....★	300	350	550
Henry Randel, 17J, KW, NI ....★	275	325	500
G. A. Read, 7J, gilded, KW.....................................	150	250	325
G. A. Read, 7J, 3/4 Plate......................................	200	300	425
Edwin Rollo, 11J, KW, gilded...................................	150	250	325
Edwin Rollo, 15J, KW, gilded...................................	150	250	325
Edwin Rollo, 15J, SW, gilded	150	250	325
Edwin Rollo, 15J, 3/4 Plate ....★	225	350	425
Royal Gold, 11J, KW...★	400	500	750
Royal Gold, 15J, KW...★	450	550	775
Royal Gold, 15J, 3/4 Plate.................................★★	500	600	850

🕐 Watches listed in this book are priced at the collectable retail level, as **complete** watches having an original 14k gold-filled case and *Key Wind* with silver, an original white enamel single sunk dial, and with the entire original movement in good working order with no repairs needed.

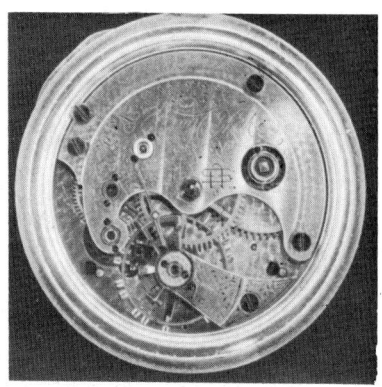 

A.H. Wallis on movement, Empire City Watch Co. on dial, 18 size, 19 jewels, three-quarter plate, hunting. This combination timer has listed on the dial, 16 cities showing the time of day and distance in comparison with New York City, serial number 54,409.

Grade or Name – Description	Avg	Ex-Fn	Mint
Rural New York, 15J, gilded........★	$400	$475	$700
Fayette Stratton, 11J, gilded	225	275	425
Fayette Stratton, 15J, KW, gilded	250	325	425
Fayette Stratton, 15J, SW, gilded	250	325	375
Fayette Stratton, 17J, KW, gilded	275	350	450
Fayette Stratton, 17J, SW, gilded	300	350	475
Union Pacific R.R., 15J, KW, gilded ★★★	1,800	2,000	3,000
United States Watch Co., 15J, NI, KW ★	700	750	1,000
United States Watch Co., 15J, NI, SW ★	800	850	1,100
United States Watch Co., 15J, 3/4 Plate, NI ★	800	850	1,200
United States Watch Co., 15J, 3/4 Plate, gilded ★	800	850	1,200
United States Watch Co., 19J, GJS, Adj.5P, 18K HC, dial mvt. & case all marked, Pin Set, SW ★★★	3,500	4,000	5,000
United States Watch Co., 19J, NI, KW ★★	1,200	1,500	2,200
United States Watch Co., 19J, NI, SW ★★	1,350	1,650	2,200
A. H. Wallis, 15J, KW, NI	250	300	400
A. H. Wallis, 15J, SW, NI	250	300	400
A. H. Wallis, 17J, KW, NI	275	325	425
A. H. Wallis, 17J, SW, NI	300	350	450
A. H. Wallis, 19J, KW, NI ★★★	450	500	700
A. H. Wallis, 19J, SW, NI ★★★	450	500	700
D. C. Wilcox, 15J, SW, no butterfly cut-out	250	300	450
I. H. Wright, 11J, KW, gilded	225	275	350
I. H. Wright, 15J, KW, gilded	225	275	350

⊕ Watches listed in this book are priced at the collectable retail level, as **complete** watches having an original 14k gold-filled case and *Key Wind* with silver, an original white enamel single sunk dial, and with the entire original movement in good working order with no repairs needed.

⊕ Some grades are not included. Their values can be determined by comparing with **similar** age, size, metal content, style, models and grades listed.

⊕ Pricing in this Guide are fair market price for **COMPLETE** watches which are reflected from the "**NAWCC**" National and regional shows.

16 SIZE
1/4 Plate

Grade or Name – Description		Avg	Ex-Fn	Mint
S. M. Beard, 15J, NI, KW,	★★★	$400	$450	$550
John W. Lewis, 15J, NI, KW	★★★	400	450	550
Personalized Watches, 15J, NI, SW	★★★	400	450	550
Edwin Rollo, 15J, KW	★★★	400	450	550
United States Watch Co., 15J, NI, SW	★★★	600	700	1,200
A. H. Wallis, 19J, NI, SW,	★★★	700	800	1,200

Note: 16S, 1/4 plate are the scarcest of the U.S.W.Co.–Marion watches.

Asa Fuller, 16 size, 15 jewels, stem wind, one-quarter plate, serial number 280,018. Note: 3 screws on barrel bridge.

United States Watch Co., 14 size, 15 jewels, three-quarter plate, engraved on movement "Royal Gold American Watch, New York, Extra Jeweled."

14 SIZE
3/4 Plate

Grade or Name – Description		Avg	Ex-Fn	Mint
Centennial Phil., 11J, KW, gilded	★★★	$650	$775	$1,300
J. W. Deacon, 11J,	★★	275	325	400
Asa Fuller, 15J,	★★	375	425	500
John W. Lewis, 15J, NI	★★	325	375	425
North Star, 15J,	★★	300	325	450
Personalized Watches, 7-11J,	★★	375	425	500
Edwin Rollo, 15J,	★	325	375	450
Royal Gold, 15J,	★	375	425	500
Young America, 7J, gilded		250	300	450

🕑 Watches listed in this book are priced at the collectable retail level, as **complete** watches having an original 14k gold-filled case and *Key Wind* with silver, an original white enamel single sunk dial, and with the entire original movement in good working order with no repairs needed.

🕑 Some grades are not included. Their values can be determined by comparing with **similar** age, size, metal content, style, models and grades listed.

10 SIZE
1/4 Plate

Grade or Name – Description	Avg	Ex-Fn	Mint
Wm. Alexander, 15J, KW, NI	$125	$150	$350
S. M. Beard, 15J, KW, NI, 1/4 Plate	125	150	350
Empire City Watch Co., 15J, KW ★★	400	500	700
Chas. G. Knapp, 15J, **Swiss**, 1/4 Plate, KW	100	150	250
Personalized Watches, 11-15J, 1/4 Plate	200	250	350
R. F. Pratt, 15J, **Swiss,** 1/4 Plate, KW	100	150	200
Edwin Rollo, 11-15J, 1/4 Plate	150	175	400
A. H. Wallis, 17-19J, KW, 1/4 Plate	170	200	350
A. J. Wood, 15J, 1/4 Plate, KW ★★	300	350	450
I. H. Wright, 19J, **Swiss**, NI, Plate, KW ★★	250	300	400

S. M. Beard, 10 size, 15 jewels, key wind, quarter plate, serial number 248,407. Note: 2 screws on barrel bridge. **Chas. G. Knapp,** 10 size, 15 jewels, Swiss, quarter plate, key wind.

U. S. WATCH CO.
OF WALTHAM
Waltham, Massachusetts
1884 - 1905

The business was started as the Waltham Watch Tool Co. in 1879. It was organized as the United States Watch Co. in 1884. The first watches were 16S, 3/4 plate pillar movement in three grades. They had a very wide mainspring barrel (the top was thinner than most) which was wedged up in the center to make room for the balance wheel. These watches are called dome watches and are hard to find. The fork was made of an aluminum alloy with a circular slot and a square ruby pin. The balance was gold at first, as was the movement which was a slow train, but the expansion balance was changed when they went to a quick train. The movement required a special case which proved unpopular. By 1887, some 3,000 watches had been made. A new model was then produced, a 16S movement that would fit a standard case. These movements were quick train expansion balance with standard type lever and 3/4 plate pillar movement. This company reached a top production of 10 watches a day for a **very short period.** The company was sold to the E. Howard Watch Co. (Keystone) in 1903. The United States Watch Co. produced some 890,000 watches total. Its top grade watch movement was the **"President."**

🕐 Pricing in this Guide are fair market price for **COMPLETE** watches which are reflected from the "**NAWCC**" National and regional shows.

U. S. WATCH CO. OF WALTHAM
ESTIMATED SERIAL NUMBERS AND PRODUCTION DATES

Date	Serial No.	Date	Serial No.
1887	3,000	1896	300,000
1888	6,500	1897	350,000
1889	10,000	1898	400,000
1890	30,000	1899	500,000
1891	60,000	1900	600,000
1892	90,000	1901	700,000
1893	150,000	1902	750,000
1894	200,000	1903	800,000
1895	250,000		

U.S. Watch Co. of Waltham, The President , 18 size, 17 jewels, hunting, serial number 150,000.

U.S. Watch Co. of Waltham, The President, 18 size, 17 jewels, open face, 2-tone, adj., note regulator, serial number 150,350.

18 SIZE

Grade or Name – Description	Avg	Ex-Fn	Mint
Express Train, 15J, ADJ, OF	$150	$200	$425
Express Train, 15J, ADJ, HC	175	225	500
The President, 17J, HC ★ ★	350	400	650
The President, 17J, GJS, Adj.6P, DR, NI, DMK, OF ★	350	400	650
The President, 21J, GJS, Adj.6P, DR	400	450	700
The President, 21J, GJS, Adj.6P, DR, **14K** ★ ★	800	900	1,200
U. S. Watch Co., 15J, OF, **2-tone, stem attached** ★	275	325	400
Washington Square, 15J, HC ★	175	225	300
U. S. Watch Co., 39 (HC) & 79 (OF), 17J, GJS, ADJ, NI, DMK, Adj.5P, BRG	90	150	200
U. S. Watch Co., 40 (HC) & 80 (OF), 17J, GJS	90	150	200
U. S. Watch Co., 48 (HC) & 88 (OF), 7J, gilded, FULL	90	150	200
U. S. Watch Co., 48 (HC) & 88 (OF), 7J, gilded, FULL, Silveroid	55	85	100
U. S. Watch Co., 52 (HC)	90	125	200
U. S. Watch Co., 92 (OF), 17J, Silveroid	60	95	110

🕐 Generic, nameless or unmarked grades for watch movements are listed under the Company name or initials of the Company, etc. by size, jewel count and description.

🕐 Some grades are not included. Their values can be determined by comparing with **similar** age, size, metal content, style, models and grades listed.

Grade or Name – Description	Avg	Ex-Fn	Mint
U. S. Watch Co., 52 (HC) & 92 (OF), 17J	$80	$90	$175
U. S. Watch Co., 53 (HC) & 93 (OF), 15J, NI, FULL, DMK	80	90	175
U. S. Watch Co., 54 (HC) & 94 (OF), 15J	80	90	175
U. S. Watch Co., 56 (HC) & 96 (OF), 11J	80	90	175
U. S. Watch Co., 57 (HC) & 97 (OF), 15J	80	90	175
U. S. Watch Co., 58 (HC) & 98 (OF), 11J, NI, FULL, DMK	80	90	175

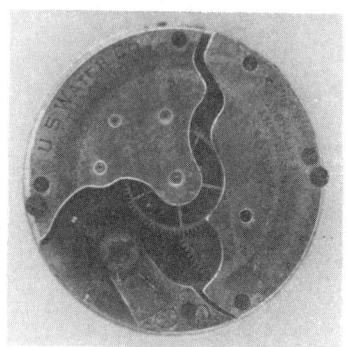

U.S. Watch Co. of Waltham, 16 size, 7 jewels, gilded, note raised dome on center of movement, engraved on movement "Chas. V. Woerd's Patents," serial number 3,564.

U.S. Watch Co. of Waltham, 16 size, 7 jewels, "A New Watch Company At Waltham, Est'd 1885" on movement, serial number 770,771.

16 SIZE

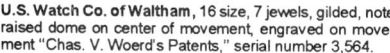

Grade or Name – Description	Avg	Ex-Fn	Mint
Dome Plate Model, 7J, gilded	$100	$125	$225
U. S. Watch Co., 103, 17J, NI, 3/4, ADJ	50	70	135
U. S. Watch Co., 104, 17J, NI, 3/4	50	70	135
U. S. Watch Co., 104, 17J, NI, 3/4, Silveroid	50	70	120
U. S. Watch Co., 105, 15J, NI, 3/4, HC	70	90	175
U. S. Watch Co., 105, 15J, NI, 3/4, OF	50	70	135
U. S. Watch Co., 105, 15J, NI, 3/4, Silveroid	50	70	125
U. S. Watch Co., 106, 15J, gilded,3/4, Silveroid	50	70	125
U. S. Watch Co., 106, 15J, gilded,3/4	50	70	135
U. S. Watch Co., 108, 11J, gilded, 3/4	50	70	135
U. S. Watch Co., 109, 7J, NI, 3/4	50	70	125
U. S. Watch Co., 110, 7J, 3/4, HC	50	70	150
U. S. Watch Co., 110, 7J, 3/4, OF	50	70	125

Note: Add $20 - $40 to value of above watches in hunting case.

🕐 Generic, nameless or **unmarked** grades for watch movements are listed under the Company name or initials of the Company, etc. by size, jewel count and description.

🕐 Watches listed in this book are priced at the collectable retail level, as complete watches having an original 14k gold-filled case and Key Wind with silver, an original white enamel single sunk dial, and with the entire original movement in good working order with no repairs needed.

🕐 Pricing in this Guide are fair market price for **COMPLETE** watches which are reflected from the "<u>NAWCC</u>" National and regional shows.

U.S. Watch Co., 16 size, 15 jewels, three-quarter plate.

6 SIZE

Grade or Name – Description	Avg	Ex-Fn	Mint
U. S. Watch Co., 60, 17J, GJS, NI, 3/4, Adj.3P	$30	$40	$95
U. S. Watch Co., 60, 17J, GJS, NI, 3/4, Adj.3P, **HC, 14K**	200	275	350
U. S. Watch Co., 62, 15J, NI, 3/4	30	40	95
U. S. Watch Co., 63, 15J, gilded	30	40	95
U. S. Watch Co., 64, 11J, NI	20	35	95
U. S. Watch Co., 65, 11J, gilded	20	35	65
U. S. Watch Co., 66, 7J, gilded	30	40	65
U. S. Watch Co., 66, 7-11J, NI, 3/4	30	40	95
U. S. Watch Co., 68, 16J, GJS, NI, 3/4	45	60	125
U. S. Watch Co., 69, 7J, NI, HC	45	60	150
U. S. Watch Co., 69, 7J, NI, OF	20	30	65

Grade 64, 6 size, 11 jewels

U.S. Watch Co. of Waltham, 0 size, 7 jewels, serial number 808,231.

0 SIZE

Grade or Name – Description	Avg	Ex-Fn	Mint
Betsy Ross, HC, GF case	$100	$125	$250
U. S. Watch Co., 15J, HC, GF case	70	90	200
U. S. Watch Co., 7-11J, HC, GF case	70	90	200

THE WASHINGTON WATCH CO.

Washington, D. C.

1872 - 1874

J. P. Hopkins, though better known as the inventor of the Auburndale Rotary Watch, was also connected with the Washington Watch Co. they may have produced about 50 watches. They were 18S, key wind, 3/4 plate and had duplex escapements. Before Hopkins came to Washington Watch Co. he had handmade about six fine watches. The company had a total production of 45 movements with duplex escapements.

Grade or Name – Description		Avg	Ex-Fn	Mint
18S, 15J, 3/4, KW, KS .... ★ ★ ★ ★		$5,000	$6,000	$10,000

WATERBURY WATCH CO.

Waterbury, Connecticut

1880 - 1898

The Waterbury Watch Co. was formed in 1880, and D. A. A. Buck made its first watch. The watches were simple and had only 58 parts. The mainspring was about nine feet long and coiled around the movement. It had a two-wheel train rather than the standard four-wheel train. The Waterbury long wind movement revolved once every hour and had a duplex escapement. The dial was made of paper, and the watch was priced at $3.50 to $4.00. Some of these watches were used as give aways. The Waterbury Watch Co. was reorganized and renamed the New England Watch Company in 1898. Ingersoll bought the New England Watch Co. in 1914. The Waterbury Watch Co. took over Ingersoll in 1922, and became part of the US Time Corp. in 1944 which is now the TIMEX Corp..

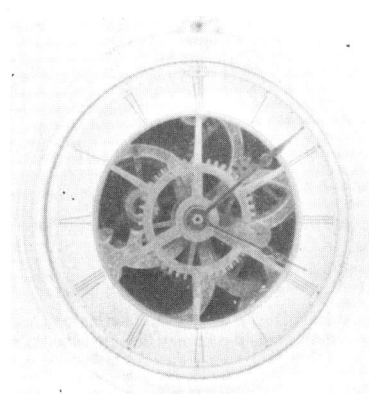

Waterbury Watch Co., skeletonized movement; so called a poor man's tourbillon due to the fact it rotated as a tourbillon does.

Waterbury Watch Co., long wind movement. Note six spokes on dial.

CHRONOLOGY OF THE DEVELOPMENT OF THE WATERBURY WATCH CO.:

Waterbury Watch Co., Waterbury, Conn. 1880-1898
re-named New England Watch Co.......... 1898-1912
Purchased Ingersoll.. 1922
Became U. S. Time Corp. (maker of Timex) 1944

Waterbury Watch Co. movement, Series C.   Series L, Waterbury W. Co. Duplex Escapement, about 16 size.

18 TO 0 SIZES

Grade or Name – Description	Avg	Ex-Fn	Mint
Long wind, skeletonized, 3 spokes.. ★ ★	$250	$300	$550
Long wind, skeletonized, 4 spokes...................................... ★ ★ ★	400	450	800
Long wind, skeletonized, 6 spokes.. ★	300	350	700
Long wind, skeletonized, 6 spokes, **celluloid case**............... ★ ★ ★	400	450	800
Series A, long wind, skeletonized .... ★	250	300	550
Series B, long wind...	150	225	300
Series C or E, long wind...	150	225	300
Series C or E, long wind (with advertising embossed on backs)	200	225	400
Series D, long wind... ★ ★ ★	300	400	550
Series F, Duplex escapement...	60	75	125

Waterbury CLOCK Co. see Ingersoll

🕐 Some grades are not included. Their values can be determined by comparing with **similar** age, size, metal content, style, models and grades listed.

🕐 Watches listed in this book are priced at the collectable retail level, as **complete** watches having an original 14k gold-filled case and *Key Wind* with silver, an original white enamel single sunk dial, and with the entire original movement in good working order with no repairs needed.

🕐 This book endeavours to be a GUIDE or helpful manual and offers a wealth of material to be used as a tool not as a absolute document. Price Guides are like watches the worst may be better than none at all, but at best cannot be expected to be 100% accurate.

🕐 Characteristics of watches differ for the same age of both case and movement, because these features vary it may not be accurate to date a watch by one single influence. Example: the second hand was not commonly found on watches before 1750, but common about 1800. The first second hand appeared in 1665 and another in 1690. Therefore statements are broad rather than accurate.

Series I, The Trump, about 18 size, no jewels, pin lever escapement.

Series T, Oxford Duplex Escapement, about 18 size, no jewels.

Grade or Name – Description	Avg	Ex-Fn	Mint
Series G, 3/4 lever escapement.. ★	$150	$225	$300
Series H, Columbian Duplex.................................... ★ ★	300	350	475
Series I, Trump, duplex, ...	50	75	125
Series I, Trump, 3/4	50	75	125
Series J, Americus Duplex	50	75	125
Series K, Charles Benedict Duplex...............................	125	150	300
Series L, Waterbury W. Co. Duplex	85	100	125
Series N, Addison Duplex..	65	70	110
Series P, Rugby Duplex...	60	70	150
Series R, Tuxedo Duplex...	60	70	125
Series S, Elfin	60	70	85
Series T, Oxford Duplex..	60	70	100
Series W, Addison	60	70	135
Series Z	60	70	100
Free Press Watch, Series E.. ★	200	250	450
Old Honesty, Series C, longwind, ...	250	300	500
Oxford, ...	40	60	95
The Trump..	40	60	90
Waterbury W. Co., 7J, 3/4, low Serial No.	300	375	500
18size, Waterbury W. Co., KW, LS............................. ★	350	425	550

NOTE: Dollar -watches must be in **Running** condition to bring these prices.

🕐 Some grades are not included. Their values can be determined by comparing with **similar** age, size, metal content, style, models and grades listed.

🕐 Watches listed in this book are priced at the collectable retail level, as **complete** watches having an original 14k gold-filled case and *Key Wind* with silver, an original white enamel single sunk dial, and with the entire original movement in good working order with no repairs needed.

🕐 This book endeavours to be a GUIDE or helpful manual and offers a wealth of material to be used as a tool not as a absolute document. Price Guides are like watches the worst may be better than none at all, but at best cannot be expected to be 100% accurate.

🕐 Pricing in this Guide are fair market price for **COMPLETE** watches which are reflected from the "**NAWCC**" National and regional shows.

E. N. WELCH MFG. CO.

Bristol, Connecticut
1834 - 1897

Elisha Welch founded this company about 1834. His company failed in 1897, and the Sessions Clock Co. took over the business in 1903. E. N. Welch Mfg. Co. produced the large watch which was displayed at the Chicago Exposition in 1893. This watch depicted the landing of Columbus on the back of the case.

E.N. Welch Mfg. Co., 36 size, back wind & set, made for the Chicago Exposition in 1893. Die debossed back depicting the landing of Columbus in America, Oct, 12th, 1492.

Grade or Name – Description		Avg	Ex-Fn	Mint
36S, Columbus Exhibition watch................................ ★		$400	$450	$650

WESTCLOX

United Clock Co. – Western Clock Mfg. Co.– General Time Corp.
Athens, Georgia
1899 - Present

The first Westclox pocket watch was made about 1899; however, the Westclox name did not appear on their watches until 1906. In 1903 they were making 100 watches a day, and in 1920 production was at 15,000 per day. This company is still in business in Athens, Georgia.

Grade or Name – Description	Avg	Ex-Fn	Mint
M#1, SW, push to set, GRO...............................	$50	$65	$125
M#2, SW, back set, GRO...............................	50	60	75
18S, Westclox M#4, OF, GRO...............................	50	60	75
1910 Models to 1920, GRO...............................	35	45	60
Anniversary...............................	35	45	60
Antique...............................	20	30	45
Boy Proof...............................	60	70	80
Bingo...............................	30	40	55
Bulls Eye (several models)...............................	15	20	25
Campus...............................	15	20	25
Celluloid case, 70mm...............................	30	35	45
Coronado...............................	15	20	25
Country Gentleman...............................	40	50	60

Boy Proof Model, about 16 size, designed to be tamper proof.

Westclox movement, stem wind, back set.

Grade or Name – Description	Avg	Ex-Fn	Mint
Dax (many models)	$10	$15	$20
Dewey	10	15	20
Elite	25	35	40
Everbrite (several models)	30	45	65
Explorer	150	200	325
Farm Bureau	65	85	100
Glo Ben	65	85	100
Glory Be	20	25	30
Johnny Zero (several models)	100	150	200
Ideal	30	35	40
Lighted Dial	25	30	40
Magnetic	20	25	30
Major	25	30	35
Man Time	15	20	25
Mark IV	35	45	55
Mascot	20	25	30
Maxim	30	40	50

Zep, about 16 size with radiant numbers and hands, c. 1929.

Explorer, back of case and dial, "Wings Over The Pole, The Explorer" on back of case.

World's Fair watch & fob, (1982 -Knoxville Tn.){Wagner Time Inc.}, total production for watch 4,200 and 200 for the FOB, Ca. 1982 .

Grade or Name – Description	Avg	Ex-Fn	Mint
Military Style, 24 hour	$65	$85	$100
Monitor	15	20	25
Mustang	40	45	60
NAWCC, TOTAL PRODUCTION = 1,000	65	85	110
Panther	45	50	60
Pocket Ben (many models)	10	20	30
Ruby	25	30	45
Scepter	20	25	30
Scotty (several models)	15	20	25
Silogram	15	20	25
Smile	25	30	40
Solo	15	20	25
St. Regis	20	25	35
Sun Mark	30	35	40
Team Mate (various major league teams)	25	35	40
Tele Time	25	35	45
Texan	35	45	65
The Airplane	45	55	65
The American, **back SET**	50	60	150
The Conductor	45	55	85
Tiny Tim	150	200	300
Trail Blazer	40	65	150
Uncle Sam	40	50	60
Victor	80	100	130
Vote	25	35	45
Westclox	15	20	25
World's Fair (1982 -Knoxville Tn.){Wagner Time Inc.}	60	75	95
above wth box & fobTOTAL PRODUCTION=200 ★ ★	100	135	200
Zep, (Zepplin)	200	225	400
Zodiak Time	35	40	45

🕐 Pricing in this Guide are fair market price for **COMPLETE** watches which are reflected from the "**NAWCC**" National and regional shows.

WESTERN WATCH CO.

Chicago, Illinois
1880

Albert Trotter purchased the unfinished watches from the California Watch Co. Mr. Trotter finished and sold those watches. Later he moved to Chicago and, with Paul Cornell and others, formed the Western Watch Company. Very few watches were completed by the Western Watch Co.

Grade or Name – Description		Avg	Ex-Fn	Mint
Western Watch Co., 18S, FULL .... ★ ★ ★ ★		$2,000	$2,500	$4,000

Western Watch Co. movement, 18 size, 15 jewels, key wind & set.

WICHITA WATCH CO.

Wichita, Kansas
July, 1887 - 1888

This company completed construction of their factory in Wichita, Kansas in June 1888, and only a half dozen watches were produced during the brief period the company was in operation. The president was J. R. Snively. These watches are 18S, 1/2 to 3/4 plate, adjusted, 15 jewels.

Grade or Name – Description		Avg	Ex-Fn	Mint
18S, 15J, 3/4 plate, ADJ .... ★ ★ ★ ★		$3,500	$4,500	$6,500

🕐 Watches listed in this book are priced at the collectable retail level, as **complete** watches having an original 14k gold-filled case and *Key Wind* with silver, an original white enamel single sunk dial, and with the entire original movement in good working order with no repairs needed.

🕐 Pricing in this Guide are fair market price for **COMPLETE** watches which are reflected from the "**NAWCC**" National and regional shows.

COMIC AND CHARACTER WATCHES

When discussing the topic of watches and someone mentions Comic Character Watches, we immediately picture a watch with Mickey Mouse. Isn't Mickey Mouse the most famous of all watches in the world? Before Mickey appeared in the 1930's there were a handful of lesser known comic watches with characters like Skeezix, Smitty and Buster Brown, but it was the Mickey Mouse Watch that paved the way for all other comic character watches. As a collaboration between Walt Disney (the creator of Mickey Mouse) and Robert Ingersoll and his brother the founders of the Ingersoll-Waterbury Watch Company. The Mickey Mouse Watch was one of this century's greatest marketing concepts. In a two year period Ingersoll had sold nearly 2.5 million Mickey Mouse wrist and pocket watches. Throughout the 1930's they also introduced other watches with Disney characters such as Big Bad Wolf in 1934, as well as, the Donald Duck wrist watch. The Donald Duck pocket watch was produced several years later in 1939. The Mickey Lapel and Mickey Deluxe Wrist were produced in the late 1930's.

Ingersoll dominated the character watch market in the early 1930's due to the incredible popularity of the Disney characters, however by the mid 1930's other companies mainly Ingraham and New Haven secured the rights to other popular characters. Throughout the 1930's kids fell in love with these watches featuring their favorite comic character or hero, such as, Popeye, Superman, Buck Rogers, Orphan Annie, Dick Tracy and The Lone Ranger. There was also a couple of other well known characters, Betty Boop and Cowboy Tom Mix produced but for some reason these watches did not become popular like all the others, so very small quantities were produced.

During World War II production of comic watches ceased, but after the war comic watches came back stronger than ever. Once again Disney was the overall leader. The Ingersoll name only appeared on some of the watches to keep the trade name still familiar, as Ingersoll was sold to U.S. Time Watch Company.

The late 1940's was very good to the character watch market and proof being the many character watches produced as the Twentieth Birthday Series for Mickey in 1948 that included with Mickey, Donald Duck, Pinocchio, Pluto, Bambi, Joe Carioca, Jiminy Cricket, Bongo Bear and Daisy Duck. Other watches from this time include Porky Pig, Puss-N-Boots, Joe Palooka, Gene Autry, Captain and Mary Marvel and others featuring characters of the comic and cartoons, space and western heroes.

The early to mid 1950's was also a vibrant time for character watch production with more Disney characters, western heroes and comic characters than ever before, but by 1958 manufacturing of character watches had almost completely stopped as manufacturing costs went up, popularity of some characters faded and many other circumstances led to a complete stop of any of these watches until the late 1960's. The watches were never the same again.

In the 1970's Comic Character Watch once again made it's come back with the Bradley Watch Company (Elgin W. Co.) leading the way just as Ingersoll did in the first years of comic watches.

Today there are hundreds of character watches to choose from, Disney Super Hero movie characters like E.T., and Roger Rabbit and a wealth of others, but today's fascination is not just with the new but with the old as we see in the re-issue of the original Mickey watches. There is a growing awareness and appreciation for all the originals. It is a very unusual attraction that draws people to love and collect the character watches of the past. Collectors appreciate the original boxes (that are fascinating works of art) and the face of the watch that features the character that we love. The manufacturing method of these simple pin lever movements were not the best of timekeepers, but were solidly constructed. All in all, when you put together the watches and boxes they are pieces of functional art and history that brings back memories of our youth. Something that no other kind of watch can do.

LEFT: SNOOPY & WOODSTOCK - CENTER: SNOOPY 1 to 12 DIAL - RIGHT: SNOOPY 12-3-6-9 DIAL (all 3 Ca. 1968)

Babe Ruth, by Exact Time, ca. 1948.

Betty Boop, by Ingraham, ca. 1934.

Style or Grade – Description	Avg	Ex-Fn	Mint	Mint +Box
Alice in Wonderland, WW, c. 1951, by U.S. Time	$40	$50	$100	$275
Alice, Red Riding Hood, & Marjory Daw, WW, c. 1953, by Bradley	40	50	100	250
Alice in Wonderland, WW, c. 1958, by Timex	40	50	100	300
Alice in Wonderland & Mad Hatter, WW, c. 1948, by New Haven	65	100	200	300
All * Stars, c.1965, autographed by Mickey Mantel, Rodger Maris, Willie Mays, Sandy Koufax, Swiss, GREEN DIAL	125	200	300	550
All * Stars, c.1965, autographed by Mickey Mantel, Rodger Maris, Willie Mays, Sandy Koufax, Swiss, BLACK DIAL	100	150	250	450
Annie Oakley, WW, (Action Gun) c. 1951, by New Haven	150	200	300	450
Archie, WW, c.1970s, Swiss,	50	60	100	150
Babe Ruth, WW, c. 1948, by Exact Time, box baseball pledge card	★ 175	325	575	1,500
Ballerina, WW, c.1955, Ingraham, Action legs,	40	50	60	100
Bambi, WW, c. 1949, by U.S. Time, Birthday series	100	200	300	500
Barbie, WW, c.1964, by Bradley, facing "3",	75	100	175	300
Barbie, WW, c.1970, by Bradley, action arms	75	100	175	275
Batman, WW, c. 1970 by Gilbert (band in shape of bat)	100	175	225	500
Batman, WW, c. 1978, by Timex	100	125	175	250
Betty Boop, PW, c. 1934, by Ingraham, (all original) (with diedebossed back)	★★★450	750	1,000	2,000
Betty Boop, WW, c.1980s, with hearts on dial & band	40	50	60	100
Bert & Ernie, WW, c.1970s, swiss	40	50	60	100
Big Bad Wolf & 3 Pigs, PW, c. 1936, by Ingersoll	★ 400	600	900	2,000
Big Bad Wolf & 3 Pigs, WW, c. 1936, by Ingersoll	★ 400	650	1,000	2,200
Big Bird, WW, c.1970s, Swiss, action arms, (pop up box)	40	50	60	75
Blondie & Dagwood, WW, c.1950s, Swiss	150	200	250	475
Bongo Bear, WW, c.1946, Ingersoll, Birthday series	100	150	200	300
Boy Scout, PW, c.1937, by Ingersoll, be prepared hands	250	275	350	600
Boy Scout, WW, c.1938, by New Haven	75	85	100	150
Buck Rogers, PW, c.1935, Ingraham (lightning bolt hands)	350	500	900	1,500
Bud Man, WW, Swiss, c.1970s	40	50	60	75
Bugs Bunny, WW, c. 1951, Swiss, (carrot shaped hands)	100	200	300	600
Bugs Bunny, WW, c. 1951, Swiss, (without carrot hands)	70	100	175	300
Bugs Bunny, WW, c. 1970, Swiss, (standing bugs)	45	50	60	100

🕐 NOTE: Beware (**COLOR COPY DIALS**) are being faked as Buck Rodgers, Babe Ruth, Hopalong Cassidy and others. *BUYER BEWARE*

The Complete Price Guide to Watches goal is to stimulate the orderly exchange of Watches between "*buyers*" and "*sellers*".

BIG BAD WOLF & 3 PIGS, + FOB INGERSOLL

BUSTER BROWN, INGERSOLL, Ca. 1925

BUGS BUNNY, EXACT TIME, Ca. 1949

BUCK ROGERS, INGRAHAM, Ca. 1935

BIG BAD WOLF & 3 PIGS

– DICK TRACY, NEW HAVEN, Ca.1948

– DICK TRACY, (six shooter action arm) Ca.1952

DIZZY DEAN, By Everbright W. Co.

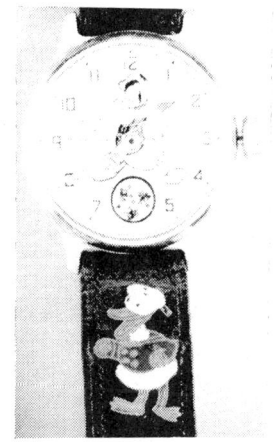

DONALD, with mickey seconds hand, 3 grades.

DONALD DUCK, by INGERSOLL, C. 1942.

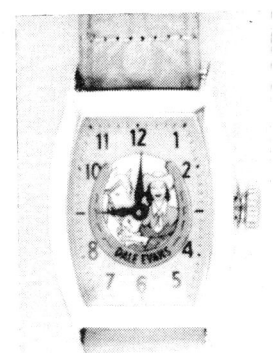

DALE EVANS, INGRAHAM

DAN DARE, INGERSOLL made in England

FROM OUTER SPACE, INGERSOLL made in England

Style or Grade – Description	Avg	Ex-Fn	Mint	Mint +Box
Buster Brown, PW, c. 1928, by Ingersoll	$125	$175	$250	$500
Buster Brown, PW, c. 1928, by Ingersoll (Buster in circle)	125	175	300	500
Buster Brown, WW, c.1930, engraved case	125	150	200	275
Buzz Corey, WW, c. 1952, by U.S. Time	75	125	200	450
Buzzy the Crow, in red hat	40	50	60	100
Captain Liberty, WW, c. 1950, by U.S.Time, multi-color band	50	80	150	450
Captain Marvel, PW, c. 1945, by New Haven	200	250	550	800
Captain Marvel,WW, c.1948, New Haven (small w.w.)	85	100	300	550
Captain Marvel, WW, c. 1948, by New Haven (larger size)	100	150	350	700
Captain Marvel, WW, c. 1948, Swiss made	100	200	400	750
Captain Marvel Jr., c. 1948, Swiss	100	130	200	350
Captain Midnight, PW, c. 1948, by Ingraham	250	300	450	900
Casper, WW, c.1970s, Swiss, action arms	40	50	60	100
Cat In The Hat, WW, c.1970s, Swiss, Action arms	40	50	60	100
Cinderella, WW, c. 1950, by U.S. Time (slipper box)	40	45	65	275
Cinderella, WW, c. 1955, by Timex (box with imitation cel)	40	50	60	275
Cinderella, WW, c. 1958, by Timex (box with plastic statue)	25	30	60	275
Cinderella, WW, c. 1958, by Timex (box & porcelain statue)	40	50	75	275
Coca Cola, PW, c. 1948, by Ingersoll	125	150	200	300
Cowboy, WW, c.1955, by Muros, Swiss, action gun	40	50	60	100
Cowgirl, WW, c.1951, by New Haven, Action Gun	40	45	65	120
Cub Scout, WW, by Timex	40	50	60	100
Daisy Duck, WW, c. 1947, by Ingersoll (tonneau style)	100	175	250	500
Daisy Duck, WW, c. 1948, by U.S. Time (fluted bezel, birthday series)	100	175	250	500
Daisy Duck, WW, c. 1949, by U.S. Time, (grooved bezel)	95	135	175	350
Dale Evans, WW, c.1949,by Ingraham,Dale standing,(tonneau)	80	100	175	300
Dale Evans, WW, c. 1950, by Bradley (western style leather band & necklace &lucky horseshoe), tonneau style case	75	100	150	400
Dale Evans, WW, c. 1960, by Bradley (round)	40	50	65	150
Dan Dare, PW, c. 1950, by *Ingersoll Ltd. England*, action arm	200	300	400	900
Davy Crockett, WW, c. 1951, by Bradley (round dial)	80	100	175	400
Davy Crockett, WW, c. 1954, Action gun, (round dial)	75	90	150	350
Davy Crockett, WW, c. 1954, Liberty , (round dial)	50	70	120	300
Davy Crockett, WW, c. 1955, by U.S. Time (& powder horn)	125	175	250	575
Davy Crockett, WW, c. 1956, by Bradley (barrel shaped dial)	40	55	100	275
Dennis the Menace, WW, c. 1970, by Bradley	45	55	75	100
Dick Tracy, PW, c. 1948, by Ingersoll	250	350	500	1,100
Dick Tracy, WW, c. 1948, by New Haven (round dial)	95	110	200	500
Dick Tracy, WW, c. 1948, by New Haven (small tonneau)	75	100	200	450
Dick Tracy, WW, c. 1935, by New Haven (large)	150	225	300	500
Dick Tracy, WW, c. 1951, by New Haven (6 shooter action)	195	275	350	600
Dizzy Dean, PW, c. 1935, by Ingersoll ★★	200	350	500	1,000
Dizzy Dean, WW, c. 1938, by Everbright.W.Co. ★★	200	300	500	1,000

🕐Note: To be mint condition, character watches must have **unfaded dials**, and boxes must have ALL inserts. (PW=Pocket Watch; WW=Wrist Watch)

COCA COLA, PW, Ca. 1948, by Ingersoll.

ADOLF HITLER, character wrist watch, Swiss movement "Roskopf" caliber, Ca. 1935.

Dizzy Dean, Ingersoll, ca. 1935   Donald Duck, Ingersoll, ca. 1940. Mickey on back of case.

Style or Grade – Description	Avg	Ex-Fn	Mint	Mint +Box
Donald Duck, PW, c. 1939, by Ingersoll (Mickey on back)..★★	$350	$500	$1,000	$2,000
Donald Duck, WW, c. 1935, by Ingersoll (Mickey on second hand) ....★★	500	800	1,200	2,500
Donald Duck, WW, c. 1942, by U.S. Time (tonneau style, silver tone)...	100	150	350	750
Donald Duck, WW, c. 1948, by U.S. Time (tonneau style, gold tone)...	150	200	400	800
Donald Duck, PW, , c. 1954, Swiss made	75	150	250	500
Donald Duck, WW, c. 1948, by Ingersoll (fluted bezel, birthday series)...	150	175	300	700
Donald Duck, WW, c. 1955, by U.S. Time, (plain bezel, pop-up in box)	65	85	200	550
Dopey, WW, c. 1948, by Ingersoll (fluted bezel, birthday series)...	100	150	300	650
Dudley Do-Right, WW, 17J (Bullwinkle & Rocky)..............★	175	250	400	600
Elmer Fudd, WW, c.1970s, Swiss...	55	75	150	300
Elvis, WW, c.1970s, Bradley	55	60	75	175
Flash Gordon, PW, c. 1939, by Ingersoll...............................★	350	475	900	1,600
Flash Gordon, WW, c.1970, Precision......................................	100	225	400	750
From Outer Space, PW, Ingersoll G.Britian, ...	100	150	225	450
Fred Flintstone, WW, (Fred on dial).......................................	100	125	175	300
Garfield, WW, (The Cat Jumped Over The Moon)......................	40	45	85	150
Gene Autry, WW, c. 1939, by Ingersoll (Gene and Champion on dial)	100	150	300	550

Donald Duck, Ingersoll, ca.1947. -- Gene Autry, (action gun), by Ingersoll, ca.1950. -- Gene Autry (Swiss made), ca.1956.

MICKEY MOUSE, by Ingersoll, original band, Ca.1938

MICKEY MOUSE, by Ingersoll,

MICKEY MOUSE by Ingersoll, center LUGS.

MICKEY MOUSE, by Bradley, 1972 -1985

MICKEY MOUSE, made in England by Ingersoll, Ca.1934

Who's afraid of the Big Bad Wolf

Hopalong Cassidy, U.S. Time, ca. 1950s.

Hopalong Cassidy, Ingersoll, ca. 1955.

Style or Grade – Description	Avg	Ex-Fn	Mint	Mint +Box
Gene Autry, WW, c. 1939, by Ingersoll	$95	$125	$200	$600
Gene Autry, WW, c. 1950, by New Haven, (action gun)	200	275	350	650
Gene Autry, WW, c. 1956, Swiss made	65	75	95	300
Girl Scouts, WW, c.1955, by Timex	40	50	60	100
Goofy, WW, c. 1972, by Helbros, 17J (watch runs backward)	385	500	750	1,200
Hoky Poky, WW, c.1950, **action arm**	35	50	75	150
Hopalong Cassidy, WW, by U.S. Time (metal watch, box with saddle)	40	50	100	400
Hopalong Cassidy, WW, by U.S. Time (plastic watch, box with saddle)	45	55	75	300
Hopalong Cassidy, WW, by U.S. Time (small watch, leather Western band, flat rectangular box)	45	55	100	400
Hopalong Cassidy, WW, by U.S. Time (regular size watch, black leather cowboy strap)	45	55	125	425
Hopalong Cassidy, PW, c. 1955, by U.S. Time (rawhide strap and fob)	125	225	300	600
Hot Wheels, WW, c.1971, Bradley -Swiss, checkered hands	45	55	75	100
Hot Wheels, WW, c.1971, Bradley -Swiss, rotating bezel	35	45	65	100
Hot Wheels, WW, c.1983, Swiss, LCD QUARTZ	25	35	45	65
Howdy Doody, WW, c. 1954, by Ingraham (with moving eyes)	100	150	300	650
Howdy Doody, WW, c. 1954, by Ingraham (with friends)	75	125	250	650
Jamboree, PW, c. 1951, by Ingersoll, Ltd.	75	100	250	400

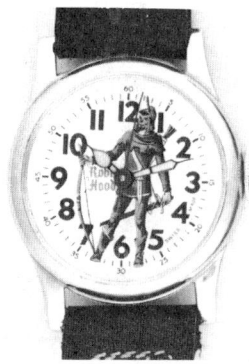

Howdy Doody (& friends) — BUD MAN Ca.1970s — Li'l Abner (waving flag)

LONE RANGER, New Haven, ca.1939

LONE RANGER, New Haven, ca.1939

MICKEY MOUSE Ingersoll, ca.1933

MICKEY MOUSE Ingersoll, ca.1933

LEFT: Mickey Mouse, Ingersoll, w/ Mickey seconds, ca.1939. **CENTER:** Mickey Mouse, Ingersoll, no seconds, ca.1939.. **RIGHT:** Mickey Mouse, Ingersoll, grooved bezel NOT birthday series, ca.1948

Note: To be **mint** condition, character watches must have unfaded dials, and boxes must have all inserts. (PW=Pocket Watch; WW=Wrist Watch)

Style or Grade – Description	Avg	Ex-Fn	Mint	Mint +Box
James Bond 007, WW, c. 1972, by Gilbert	$70	$125	$200	$600
Jeff Arnold, PW, c. 1952, by Ingersoll (English watch with moving gun)	150	200	325	550
Jiminy Cricket, WW, c.1948, Ingersoll, Birthday series (fluted)	75	100	200	500
Jiminy Cricket, WW, c.1949, Ingersoll, Not Birthday (grooved)	75	100	200	500
Joe Carioca, WW, c. 1948, by U.S. Time (fluted bezel, birthday series)	75	100	200	400
Joe Palooka, WW, c. 1948, by New Haven	150	200	300	550
Li'l Abner, WW, c. 1948, by New Haven (waving flag)	150	175	250	500
Li'l Abner, WW, c. 1948, by New Haven (moving mule)	150	175	200	400
Li'l Abner, WW, c. 1955, all black dial	100	135	175	200
Little King, WW, c. 1968, by Timex	55	125	225	425
Little Pig Fiddler, WW, c.1947, by Ingersoll	125	200	300	450
Lone Ranger, PW, c. 1939, by New Haven (with fob)	★ 150	250	400	900
Lone Ranger, WW, c. 1938, by New Haven (large)	95	185	295	500
Lone Ranger, WW, c. 1948, New Haven, (Fluted lugs)	75	125	200	400
Lone Ranger, WW, c. 1950's, round case	65	100	175	300
Louie, WW, c.1940s, by Ingersoll, (Donalds nephew)	100	150	200	400
Mary Marvel, WW, c. 1948, by U.S. Time (paper box)	65	85	125	350
Mary Marvel, WW, c. 1948, by U.S. Time (plastic box)	65	85	125	350
Mickey Mouse, PW, c.1933, by Ingersoll, #1&2 (tall stem)	285	400	500	800
Mickey Mouse, PW, c. 1936, by Ingersoll, #3&4 (short stems)	200	300	425	750
Mickey Mouse, PW, c. 1938, by Ingersoll (Mickey decal on back)	275	400	700	1,000
Mickey Mouse, PW, c. 1933, by Ingersoll Ltd. (English)	300	450	750	1,400
Mickey Mouse, PW, c. 1934, by Ingersoll (Foreign)	275	325	450	650
Mickey Mouse, PW, c.1976, by Bradley (bicentennial model)	40	50	75	200
Mickey Mouse, PW, c. 1974, by Bradley (no second hand)	40	50	60	85
Mickey Mouse, PW, c. 1974, by Bradley ("Bradley" printed at 6)	40	50	60	75

MICKEY MOUSE, Ingersoll, model no.3 on the left.   Right: Model no.4 is shown with lapel button

NOTE: Beware (COLOR COPY DIALS) are being FAKED as Buck Rodgers, Babe Ruth, Hopalong Cassidy and others. *BUYER BEWARE*

The Complete Price Guide to Watches goal is to stimulate the orderly exchange of <u>Watches</u> between "*buyers*" and "*sellers*".

Style or Grade – Description	Avg	Ex-Fn	Mint	Mint +Box
Mickey Mouse, WW, c. 1933, by Ingersoll (metal band with 3 Mickeys' on seconds disc)	$200	$300	$375	$800
Mickey Mouse, WW, c. 1933, by Ingersoll (English Mickey with 3 Mickeys' on seconds disc, 24 hr. outer dial)	200	300	375	800
Mickey Mouse, WW, c. 1938-9, by Ingersoll (one Mickey for second hand)	125	200	300	900
Mickey Mouse, WW, c. 1938-9, by Ingersoll, plain seconds	85	125	200	400
Mickey Mouse, WW, c. 1938-9, by Ingersoll (girl's watch, 1 Mickey for second hand)	175	200	300	900
Mickey Mouse, WW, c. 1948, by Ingersoll (fluted Bezel, birthday series, 2 styles Mickey in a circle & no circle)	150	175	200	500
Mickey Mouse, WW, c. 1949, by Ingersoll, **grooved** bezel	125	150	200	350
Mickey Mouse, WW, c. 1946, by U.S. Time (10k gold plated)	100	125	200	400
Mickey Mouse, WW, c. 1946, **Kelton**, 2 Styles	100	125	200	300
Mickey Mouse, WW, c. 1947, by U.S. Time (tonneau, plain, several styles)	75	95	150	350
Mickey Mouse, WW, c. 1947, by U.S. Time (same as above, gold tone)	85	100	175	350
Mickey Mouse, WW, c. 1950s, by U.S. Time (round style)	40	50	100	300
Mickey Mouse, WW, c. 1958, by U.S. Time (statue of Mickey in box)	50	60	100	300
Mickey Mouse, WW, c. 1965 to 1970, by Timex (Mickey Mouse electric)	85	100	175	275
Mickey Mouse, WW, c. 1965-70s, Timex (manual wind)	55	65	100	140
Mickey Mouse, WW, c. 1975, Elgin (**ELECTRIC MODEL**), 14K GOLD CASE & leather band, 13 jewels	400	500	600	850
Mickey Mouse, WW, c. 1970s, by Bradley	40	50	60	90
Mickey Mouse, WW, c. 1980, by Bradley (colored min. chapter)	60	70	85	150
Mickey Mouse, WW, c. 1983, by Bradley (limited commemorative model)	60	75	100	150

Mickey Mouse, Bradley, ca. 1969.

Mickey Mouse, with wide bezel, Ingersoll, it is believed dealers have used a Wrist Watch dial in a Hopalong case, ca. 1955.

Note: To be **mint** condition, character watches must have unfaded dials, and boxes must have all inserts. (PW=Pocket Watch; WW=Wrist Watch)

Left: Captain Marvel, Ca. 1948. **Center:** Minnie Mouse, U.S.Time, Ca.1961. **Right:** Orphan Annie, New Haven, Ca.1939

ORPHAN ANNIE, New Haven, Ca. 1940   2 styles of POPEYE & friends, New Haven, Ca. 1936

 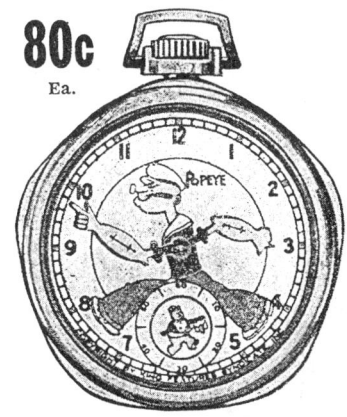

POPEYE, New Haven, (with friends), Ca. 1935   POPEYE, New Haven, Ca. 1936, (Wimpy only), originally sold for .80 in 1936.

🕐Note: To be **mint** condition, character watches must have unfaded dials, and boxes must have all inserts. (PW=Pocket Watch; WW=Wrist Watch)

LEFT: GOOFY watch runs backward.   CENTER: Little Pig & fiddle.   RIGHT: Porky Pig

Left: Pluto, Birthday Series, by Ingersoll.   **Center:** Rocky Jones, Ca.1955.   **Right:** Speedy Gonzales, Swiss

DONALD DUCK on face, with MICKEY on back side of watch.

Style or Grade – Description	Avg	Ex-Fn	Mint	Mint +Box
Mickey Mouse, WW, c. 1985, by ETA (clear plastic bezel and band)	$40	$50	$65	$85
Mickey Mouse, WW, c.1980s, Bradley, (Tachometer dial)	45	50	60	75
Mighty Mouse, WW, c.1980s, Swiss, (Plastic case)	25	30	35	40
Minnie Mouse, WW, c. 1958, by U.S. Time (statue of Minnie in box)	40	50	100	300
Moon Mullins, PW, c. 1930, by Ingersoll	★ 200	300	500	900
Orphan Annie, WW, c. 1939, by New Haven (fluted bezel)	75	100	150	400
Orphan Annie, WW, c. 1935, by New Haven (large style)	100	120	150	400
Orphan Annie, WW, c. 1948, by New Haven smaller model)	50	65	100	300
Orphan Annie, WW, c. 1968, by Timex	45	55	75	110
Pee Wee Herman, WW, (Swiss), FLIP TOP	25	30	35	40
Peter Pan, PW, c. 1948, by Ingraham	150	200	300	650
Pinocchio, WW, c. 1948, by Ingersoll (fluted bezel, birthday series)	125	150	250	400
Pinocchio, WW, c. 1948, by U.S. Time (Happy Birthday cake box)	125	150	250	450
Pluto, WW, c. 1948, by U.S. Time(birthday series)	100	150	250	450
Popeye, PW, c. 1935, by New Haven (with friends on dial)	★ 275	450	650	1,100
Popeye, PW, c. 1936, by New Haven (plain dial)	225	375	500	1,000
Popeye, WW, c. 1936, by New Haven (tonneau style, with friends on dial)	★ 250	375	650	1,200
Popeye, WW, c. 1966, by Bradley (round style)	75	100	125	200
Popeye, WW, c. 1948, Swiss, Olive Oyl at 3	75	150	250	400
Porky Pig, WW, c. 1948, by Ingraham (tonneau)	100	175	250	450
Porky Pig, WW, c. 1949, by U.S. Time (round)	100	175	250	450
Punkin Head, WW, c.1946, Ingraham,	55	65	85	135
Puss-N-Boots, WW, c. 1959, by Bradley	100	175	250	400
Quarterback, WW, c.1965, Swiss, (Football action arm)	65	75	85	125
Red Ryder, WW, c.1949, Swiss, (with Little Beaver)	100	135	175	250
Robin, WW, c. 1978, by Timex	40	45	65	90
Robin Hood, WW, c. 1955, by Bradley (tonneau style)	85	125	200	400
Robin Hood, WW, c. 1958, by Viking (round)	75	125	200	400
Rocky Jones Space Ranger, WW, c. 1955, by Ingraham	125	235	350	700
Roy Rogers, PW, c. 1960, by Ingraham, rim set	70	100	150	300
Roy Rogers, WW, c. 1954, by Ingraham (Roy and rearing Trigger)	75	100	200	450

Joe Palooka, Ca.1948.

— Snow White U.S.Time. —

Roy Rogers, Ingraham, ca. 1954.

ROY ROGERS, Ingraham, note rim set, Ca. 1960.

ROY ROGERS, Ingraham (large), Ca. 1951.

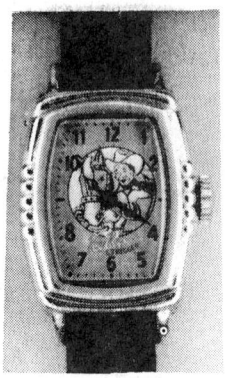

ROY ROGERS, Ingraham, Ca. 1951

SKEEZIX, Ingraham, Ca. 1936.

Left: Smitty, New Haven, Ca.1936. **Center**: Superman, New Haven, Ca.1939. **Right**: Superman, New Haven, Ca.1939.

Style or Grade – Description	Avg	Ex-Fn	Mint	Mint +Box
Roy Rogers, WW, c. 1954, by Ingraham (Roy and Trigger)	$60	$75	$100	$350
Roy Rogers, WW, c. 1954, by Ingraham (expansion band).........	60	75	100	350
Roy Rogers, WW, c. 1956, by Ingraham (round dial).................	60	75	100	250
Rudolf the Red Nose Reindeer, c.1946, Ingersoll	85	125	200	400
Rudy Nebb, PW c. 1930, by Ingraham	150	200	275	500
Shirley Temple, PW, c.1958, by Westclox .... ★ ★	275	375	450	550
Skeezix, PW, c. 1928, by Ingraham	225	275	350	650
Sky King, WW, (action gun)...	75	100	150	275
Smitty, PW, c. 1928, by New Haven	225	275	350	650
Smitty, WW, c. 1936, by New Haven	150	200	300	550
Smokey Stover, WW, c. 1968, by Timex	75	100	150	225
Snoopy, WW, c. 1958 (tennis racket)	40	50	60	100
Snoopy, WW, c. 1958 (Woodstock).......................................	40	50	60	100
Snow White, WW, c. 1938, by Ingersoll (tonneau)..................	100	125	200	400
Snow White, WW, c. 1952, by U.S. Time (round)....................	45	50	65	300
Snow White, WW, c. 1956, by U.S. Time (statue in box)	40	45	70	300
Snow White, WW, c. 1962, by U.S. Time (plastic watch)..........	40	45	65	275
Space Explorer, c.1953, COMPASS watch	75	95	135	200
Speedy Gonzales, WW, Swiss	75	95	150	225
Spiro Agnew, WW,c.1970s, Swiss	40	50	75	150
Superman, PW, c. 1956, by Bradley	150	200	350	600
Superman, WW, c. 1938, by New Haven	200	250	400	650
Superman, WW, c.1946, by Ingraham(lightning bolt hands)....	150	200	250	500
Superman, WW, c. 1978, by Timex (large size)........................	50	65	95	150
Superman, WW, c. 1978, by Timex (small size)........................	45	50	75	125
Superman, WW, c.1975, Dabs & Co.; yellow min. chapter.........	45	50	75	150
Superman, WW, c.1965, Swiss, rotating superman....................	55	75	125	225
Superman, WW, c.1976, Timex, sweep sec. hand......................	60	65	95	150
Texas Ranger, WW, c.1950, by New Haven, action gun	100	125	150	200
Three Little Pigs, PW, c. 1939, by Ingersoll..................... ★ ★	400	600	900	1,800
Tom Corbett, WW, c. 1954, by New Haven	75	100	150	450
Tom Mix, PW, c. 1936, by Ingersoll (with fob) .... ★ ★ ★	450	750	1,000	2,500
Tom Mix, WW, c. 1936, by Ingersoll .... ★ ★ ★	400	600	900	3,000
Winnie the Pooh Bear, c.1970s, Swiss....................................	40	50	60	75
Wizard of Oz, c.1972, swiss...	40	55	70	120
Wonder Woman,WW, c.1975, stars at 1,2,4,5,7,8,10,11	65	70	95	160
Wonder Woman,WW, c.1975, Dabs & Co.	50	65	95	150
Woody Woodpecker, WW, c. 1948, by Ingersoll (tonneau)	100	125	250	600
Woody Woodpecker, WW, c. 1952, by Ingraham (round dial)...	100	125	175	500
Yogi Bear, WW, c. 1964, by Bradley	50	55	75	100
Zorro, WW, c. 1956, by U.S. Time..	55	60	100	300

Left: Tom Corbett, Space Cadet, New Haven, ca. 1935. **Center:** Tom Mix, Ingersoll, ca. 1936. **Right:** Woody Woodpecker, U.S. Time, ca. 1948.

Moon Mullins, by Ingersoll, ca. 1928

Rudy Nebb, by Ingersoll, ca. 1928

Shirley Temple, by Westclox, ca. 1958

1952 AD, by Ingersoll, Dan Dare Watch and Box.

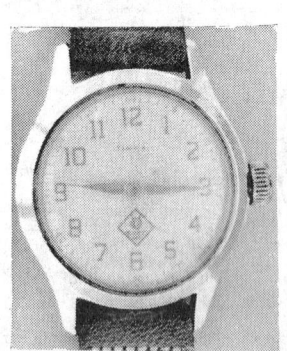

CUB SCOUT by Timex   BOY SCOUT by New Haven   DAVY CROCKETT, by Ingraham

MICKEY MOUSE WRIST WATCH with metal or leather strap bearing Mickey's picture. The watch itself is smartly styled ... round and therefore entirely practical for a very little girl's wrist. Packed in Mickey Mouse display carton. Retails $2.75. List $3.90

MICKEY MOUSE WATCH AND FOB— a wonderful buy at $1.50 complete. Mickey on the dial of the watch pointing out the time—Mickey on the fob—three little Mickies on the second-circle chasing each other around. List $2.20

New Mickey Mouse Lapel Watch. A handsome lapel model with Mickey's hands telling time on small dial. Mickey on dial and back of a black glossy finished case with nickel trim. Black lapel cord and button. Each in a display box.

No. 1W61.   Each......................$2.10

LONE RANGER FOB WATCH

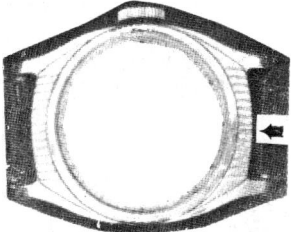

ABOVE: 20th Birthday series style case note **fluted** bezel. The Birthday series used ten different characters & sold for $6.95. The TEN CHARACTERS are: Mickey Mouse, Daisy Duck, Pluto, Bambi, Joe Carioca, Bongo, Donald Duck, Pinnochio, Dopey, and Jiminy Cricket.

New De Luxe Mickey Mouse Wrist Watch. A smarter thinner chromium plated rectangular case. Mickey appears in bright colors on the dial. Fitted with a perspiration proof leather band. Each in display box.

No. 11W440.   Each..................$5.54

EARLY ANTIQUE WATCHES

The early antique watches looked quite similar to small table clocks. The **mainspring** was introduced to clocks in about **1450**. These drum-shaped watches were about two inches in diameter and usually over one-half inch thick. The drum-shaped watch lost popularity in the late 1500s. The earliest portable timepieces did not carry the maker's name, but initials were common. The cases generally had a hinged lid which covered the dial. This lid was pierced with small holes to enable ready identification of the position of the hour hand. They also usually contained a bell. The dial often had the numbers "I" to "XII" engraved in Roman numerals and the numbers "13" to "24" in Arabic numbers with the "2" engraved in the form of a "Z." Even the earliest of timepieces incorporated striking. The oldest known watch with a date engraved on the case was made in 1548. A drum-shaped watch with the initials "C. W.," it was most likely produced by Casper Werner, a protege of Henlein.

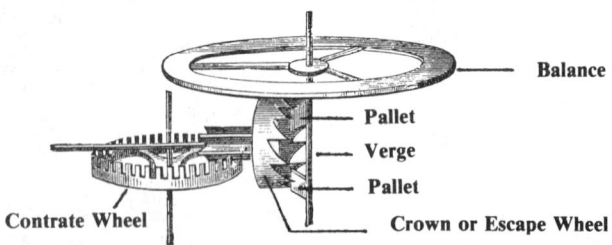

- Balance
- Pallet
- Verge
- Pallet
- Contrate Wheel
- Crown or Escape Wheel

Early pocket watches were designed to run from 12 to 16 hours. The pinions usually bore five leaves, the great wheel 55 teeth, the second wheel 45 teeth, the third wheel 40 teeth, and the escape wheel 15 teeth. With one less pinion and wheel the escape wheel ran reverse to a standard four-wheel watch. During the 1500s, 1600s, and much of the 1700s, it was stylish to decorate not only the case and balance cock but all parts including the clicks, barrel, studs, springs, pillars, hands, and stackfreed. The plates themselves were decorated with pierced and engraved metal scrolls, and in some instances the maker's name was engraved in a style to correspond with the general decoration of the movement. During these periods the most celebrated artists, designers, and engravers were employed. The early watches were decorated by famous artists such as Jean Vauquier 1670, Daniel Marot 1700, Gillis l'Egare 1650, Michel Labon 1630, Pierre Bourdon 1750, and D. Cochin 1750. Most of the artists were employed to design and execute pierced and repousse cases.

Alarm watch made by Bockel of London Ca. 1648.

THE MID-1700s

In the mid-1700s relatively minor changes are noticed. Decoration became less distinctive and less artistic. The newer escapements resulted in better time keeping, and a smaller balance cock was used. The table and foot became smaller. The foot grew more narrow, and as the century and the development of the watch advanced, the decoration on the balance cock became smaller and less elaborate. About 1720 the foot was becoming solid and flat. No longer was it hand pierced; however, some of the pierced ones were produced until about 1770. Thousands of these beautiful hand pierced watch cocks have been made into necklaces and brooches or framed. Sadly, many of the old movements were destroyed in a mad haste to cater to the buyers' fancy.

THE 1800s

As the 1800s approached the balance cocks became less artistic as the decoration on movements gradually diminished. Breguet and Berthoud spent very little time on the beauty or artistic design on their balance cocks or pillars. But the cases were often magnificent in design and beauty, made with enamels in many colors and laden with precious stones. During this period the movements were plain and possessed very little artistic character.

As early as 1820 three-quarter and one-half plate designs were being used with the balance cock lowered to the same level as the other wheels. The result was a slimmer watch. **Flat enamel** dials are being used in about 1810.

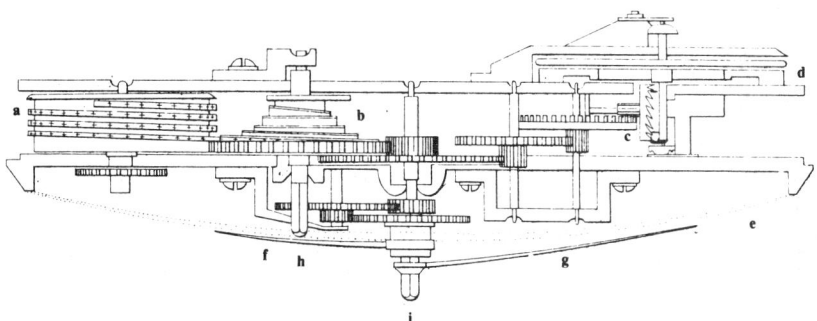

Exposed illustration of an early watch movement, c. 1800-1850. Note that movement is key wind and set from the dial side. The illustrated example is a chain driven fusee with a verge escapement: a- Main spring barrel and chain. b- Fusee. c - Verge escapement. d- Balance wheel. e- Dial. f - Hour hand. g- Minute hand. h- Winding arbor. i- Setting arbor.

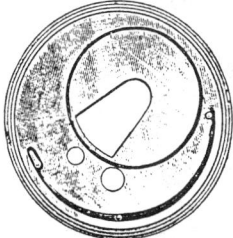

The DUST CAP Ca. 1734 to 1875
Popular in England.

Characteristics of watches differ for the same age of both case and movement, because these features vary it may not be accurate to date a watch by one single influence. Example: the second hand was not commonly found on watches before 1750, but common about 1800. The first second hand appeared in 1665 and another in 1690. Therefore statements are **broad** rather than absolute.

WATCH-MAKER

The term watch-maker might originally denote the *maker* of *watches* from base material or one who manufactures watches. But as we shall see a watch-maker may better be described as the expert in charge of producing watches. One other note before we move on, a watch may be considered as a miniature spring driven clock, so early on many **clock-makers** were also *watch-makers.*

There are surviving artifacts that make it possible to make certain assumptions. Thomas Tompion (also a English clock-maker) born 1639, death 1713, used a production system for making watches. About 1670 Tompion divided and sub-divided laborers into various branches of manufacturing of watches. This meant each craftsman specialized in making single watch parts, thus the division of labor led to a faster rate of production, with higher quality and a lower cost to the ebauche movement. About 1775 John Elliott and John Arnold had much of their work done by other sub-divided workers. The quality of the employees work depends upon the watch-maker. Thus, the **PRICE depends** on the **reputation** of the master (watch-maker). The same holds true for todays prices, the reputation of the maker helps to determine the price they can fetch for the timepieces. The parts and materials are of little value in their original state, but the various pieces require such delicacy of manipulation and the management of production of watches, thus the responsibility for the action of the watch depends on the committee in the house of the maker. Prior to 1870 rough movements were mainly produced in the **Prescot** area then finished in London, Liverpool, & etc.

In about 1760 to 1765 Lepine introduced the French or Lepine style calibre of ebauche movements. The Lepine style used separate bridges instead of the single top plate design. Frederic Japy (Japy Freres & Cie.) of Beaucourt, France, later manufactured ebauche Swiss bar style movements in the early 1770's. About 1776, Japy aids in setting up a factory in the LeLocle area and latter in England. Japy Freres & Co. were producing 30,000 movements each year by 1795, and over 60,000 ebauche style movements each year by 1860. Other "BAR" style Ebauche Companies: 1804-Sandoz & Trot of Geneva, 1840-G.A. Leschot with Vacheron & Constantin and about 1850- LeCoultre. These bar style ebauche movements were imported into the U.S.A. about 1850 and were used in the jewelry trade with the jewelers name on the case and dial until about 1875.

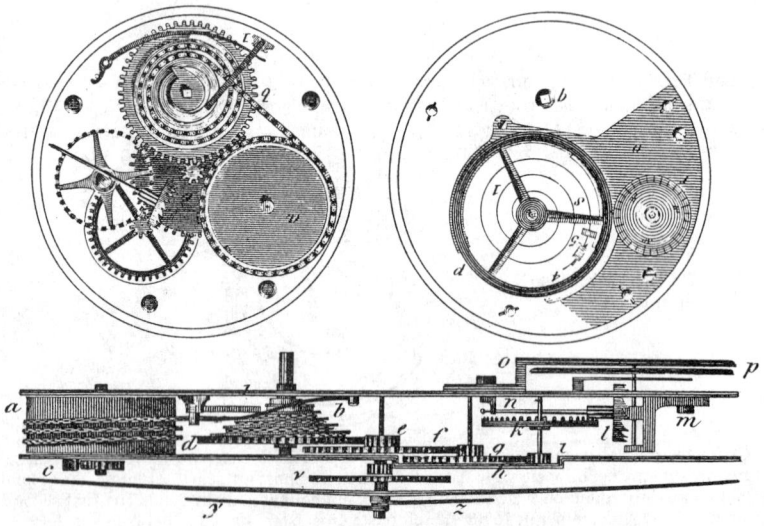

MOVEMENTS " IN THE GRAY "
Movements in an early stage of manufacture.

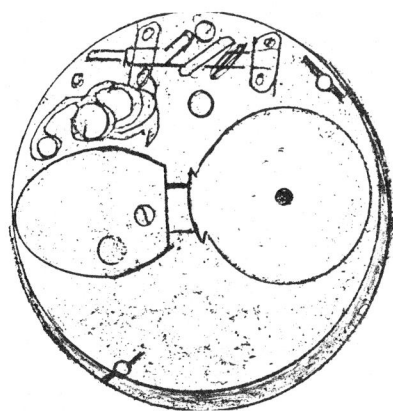

ABOUT MID 1600'S

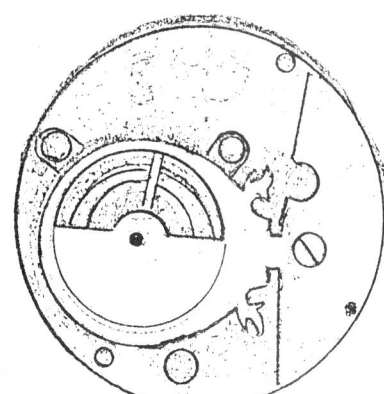

ABOUT 1700'S

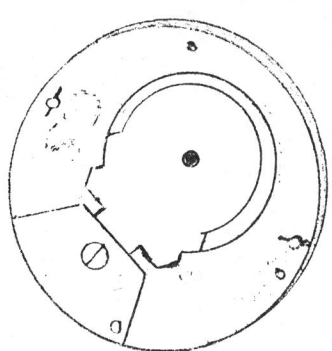

**ABOUT 1790—1830
ENGLISH STYLE**

EBAUCHE style movement with verge,
chain driven fusee, under sprung, KW,
ABOUT 1810 — 1860.

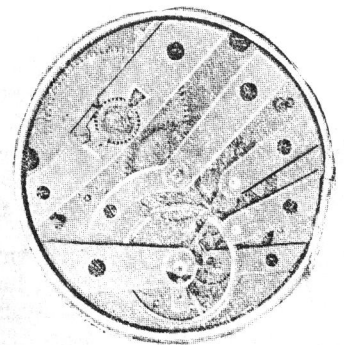

BAR STYLE movement, cylinder, **ABOUT 1840-80.**

Le Locle style EBAUCHE **ABOUT 1870 to 1890.**

🕐 **Multi-color** cases became popular by 1800, 1st. used in 1760 & **Engine Turning** rarely found before early 1760s. **Tortoise Shell** 1st. used in 1620, but did not become popular till about 1780.

The ebauche makers and the cottage industry made different models designed to conform or answer the needs of each country to which they were trying to do business with such as French style, English style, Chinese style, etc. This makes it hard to determine the origin of the ebauche watch. The case may be made in England, the movement Swiss, and the dial French.

Below are some of the principle workmen employed in the sub-divided production of plain parts or ebauche simple watch movements (in the rough)from about 1800s. Some of these were small family specialist that formed a **cottage industry**, (some being females) they usually produced only one product.

1. Cock-maker (made brass blanks)
2. Pillar-maker (turn the pillars, etc.)
3. Frame-maker (two full plates, bars, bridges, etc.)
4. Wheel-maker (small and large)
5. Wheel-cutter (cuts the teeth on the wheels)
6. Balance-makers (made of steel or brass)
7. Spring-maker(hair & main springs)
8. Fusee-maker
9. Verge-makers
10. Chain-makers
11. Pinion- maker
12. Escapement-maker
13. Hand-maker
14. Dial-maker

Below a list of craftsman making cases.
1. Case-maker (makes cupped lids for cases)
2. Side-maker (makes the side of the case)
3. Cap-maker (makes the lids of the case)
4. The joint-finisher (joints for cases)
5. Glass-maker (made crystals for bezels)
6. Bezel-makers & Pendant-maker

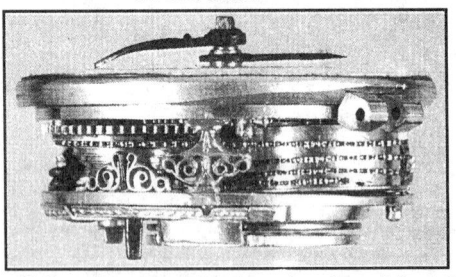

RIGHT: A English made movement,
  Ca. Early 1800s.

These blank movements, parts, dials and cases were bought, then shipped on to the final destination. The *watch-maker* or *finisher,* such as, the house of (CARTIER). The Finisher would often house or contract decorators to finish the cases. The Finisher completed, polished, engraved, timed, regulated and made all the adjustments to the movements. They added and fitted the case to the movement. They added and fitted the complications such as repeaters to the movements. The *finished* watch is now ready for sale.

This type of system of producing watches left time for the Master watch-makers or famous watch-makers to invent, design new and better ways to make watches, such as, Abraham Louis Breguet. In early 1800's Breguet firm received parts and Swiss ebauches from 18 different suppliers. Thus the more famous the maker the higher the price of the watch even though the watch-maker may not have **made** the smallest piece for the *finished* watch.

The cottage industry with its one man, one task system, make it difficult to establish who, when and where some watches were actually made. It is some what simpler to determine the origin or area, as Swiss, English, French or American, however it is rewarding with further research to unmask the disguise of watch-making. Close study, inspection and comparing movements over the years will prove helpful and may reveal the origin and age of your watch.

Most Swiss manufactures do not make the complete watch on their own premises. Some parts are supplied by specialized firms, such as; balance wheels, escape wheels, jewels, hairsprings, mainsprings, pendant bows and crowns, crystals, hands, cases, screws, pins and other small parts. There were a few factories in Le Locle Switzerland that manufactured the Cylinder and escape wheel but most were made in the *Maiche district of France*. Brass plates were plated with RHODIUM for the most part in Swiss Industry. Ebauche or rough movement were made in the Valley of Joux and the Val-de-Ruz regions, in and around towns such as Granges, Bienne, Solothurn, La Chaux- de-Fonds also near by Le Locle, in the Bernese Jura, the Valley of St.Imier, and elsewhere.

CLUES TO DATING YOUR WATCH

To establish the age of a watch there are many points to be considered. The dial, hands, pillars, balance cock and pendant, for example, contain important clues in determining the age of your watch. However, no one part alone should be considered sufficient evidence to draw a definite conclusion as to age. The watch as a whole must be considered. For example, an English-made silver-cased watch will have a hallmark inside the case. It is quite simple to refer to the London Hallmark Table for hallmarks after 1697. The hallmark will reveal the age of the case only. This does not fix the age of the movement. Many movements are housed in cases made years before or after the movement was produced.

An informed collector will note that a watch with an **enamel dial**, for instance, could not have been made before 1635. **A pair of cases** indicates it could not have been made prior to 1640. The **minute hand** was introduced in 1687. The presence of a **cylinder escapement** would indicate it was made after 1710. **1750 the duplex escapement** was first used. A **dust cap** first appeared in 1774. *1776 Lepine* introduced the **thin** watch. **Flat enamel dial** being used in about 1810. **Keyless winding** came into being after 1820, but did not gain widespread popularity until *after* about 1860. All of these clues and more must be considered before accurately assessing the age of a watch. *Some watches were also updated such as minute hand added or new style escapement added.*

Example of an early pocket watch (**Ca. 1548**) with a stackfreed design to equalize power much as a fusee does. Note dumbbell shaped foliot which served as a balance for verge escapement, and the tear shaped cam which is part of the stackfreed.

⊕ **Characteristics of watches differ for the same age of both case and movement, because these features vary it may not be accurate to date a watch by one single influence. Example: the second hand was not commonly found on watches before 1750, but common about 1800. The first second hand appeared in 1665 and another in 1690. Therefore statements are broad rather than absolute.**

⊕ **Multi-color** cases became popular by 1800, 1st. used in 1760 & **Engine Turning** rarely found before early 1760s. **Tortoise Shell** 1st. used in 1620, but did not become popular till about 1780. **Flat enamel** dials are being used in about 1810.

PILLARS

Pillars are of interest and should be considered as one of the elements in determining age. Through the years small watches used round pillars, and the larger watches generally used a square type engraved pillar.

(*Illus.* 1) This pillar is one of the earliest types and used in the 1800s as well. This particular pillar came from a watch which dates about 1550. It is known that this type pillar was used in 1675 by Gaspard Girod of France and also in 1835 by James Taylor of England.

(*Illus.* 2) This style pillar is called the tulip pattern. Some watchmakers preferred to omit the vertical divisions. This style was popular between 1660 and 1750 but may be found on later watches. It was common practice to use ornamentation on the tulip pillar.

(*Illus.* 3) The ornament shown was used by Daniel Quare of London from 1665 to 1725 and by the celebrated Tompion, as well as many others.

(*Illus.* 4) This type pillar is referred to as the Egyptian and dates from 1630 to the 1800s. The squared Egyptian pattern was introduced about 1630 and some may be found with a wider division with a head or bust inserted. This style was used by D. Bouquet of London about 1640 and by many other watchmakers.

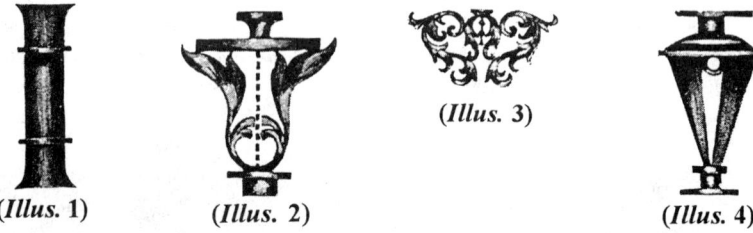

(*Illus.* 3)

(*Illus.* 1)   (*Illus.* 2)   (*Illus.* 4)

(*Illus.* 5) This pillar was used by Thomas Earnshaw of London about 1780. The plain style was prominent for close to two hundred years 1650 to 1825.

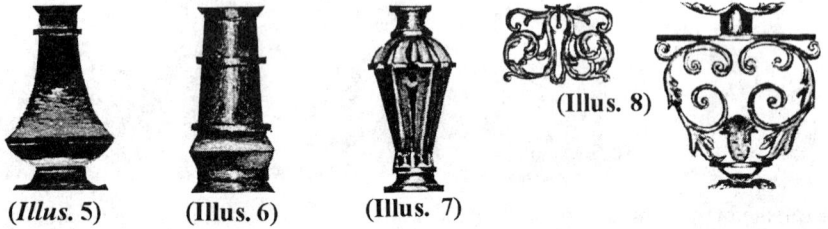

(Illus. 8)

(*Illus.* 5)   (Illus. 6)   (Illus. 7)

(Illus. 6) This style was popular and was used by many craftsmen. Nathaniel Barrow of London put this in his watches about 1680.

(Illus. 7) This pillar may be seen in watches made by Pierre Combet of Lyons, France, about 1720. It was also used by many others.

(Illus. 8) This style pillar and the ornament were used by John Ellicott of England and other watchmakers from 1730 to 1770.

These illustrations represent just a few of the basic pillars that were used. Each watchmaker would design and change details to create his own individual identity. This sometimes makes it more difficult to readily determine the age of watches.

🕐 **Multi-color** cases became popular by 1800, 1st. used in 1760 & **Engine Turning** rarely found before early 1760s. **Tortoise Shell** 1st. used in 1620, but did not become popular till about 1780. **Flat enamel** dials are being used in about 1810.

Example of 2 Egyptian pillars left & right also a hand pierced ornament that is not a pillar. (Ca.1700)

BALANCE COCKS OR BRIDGES

The first balance cocks or bridges used to support the balance staff were a plain "S" shape. The cocks used on the old three-wheel watches were very elaborate; hand-pierced and engraved. At first no screws were used to hold the cock in place. It is noteworthy that on the three wheel watch the regulator was a ratchet and click and was used on these earlier movements to adjust the mainspring. About 1635 the balance cock was screwed to the plate and pinned on its underside, which helped steady the balance. The first cock illustrated is a beautifully decorated example made by Josias Jeubi of Paris about 1580. Note that it is pinned to a stud which passes through a square cut in the foot of the cock. Next is a balance cock made by Bouquet of London about 1640. The third balance cock is one made by Jean Rousseau and dates around 1650. The fourth one dates around 1655.

The next two bridges are supported on both sides of the balance bridge by means of screws or pins. They are strikingly different and usually cover much of the plate of the movement. This French & Swiss style of balance bridge was used around 1665 and was still seen as late as 1765.

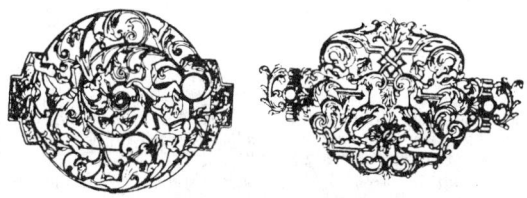

434

The beautiful balance cock below at left, with the ornate foot, dates about 1660. The next illustrated balance cock with the heavy ornamentation was used from about 1700 to 1720 or longer. By 1720 a face was added to the design. The face shows up where the table terminates on most balance cocks.

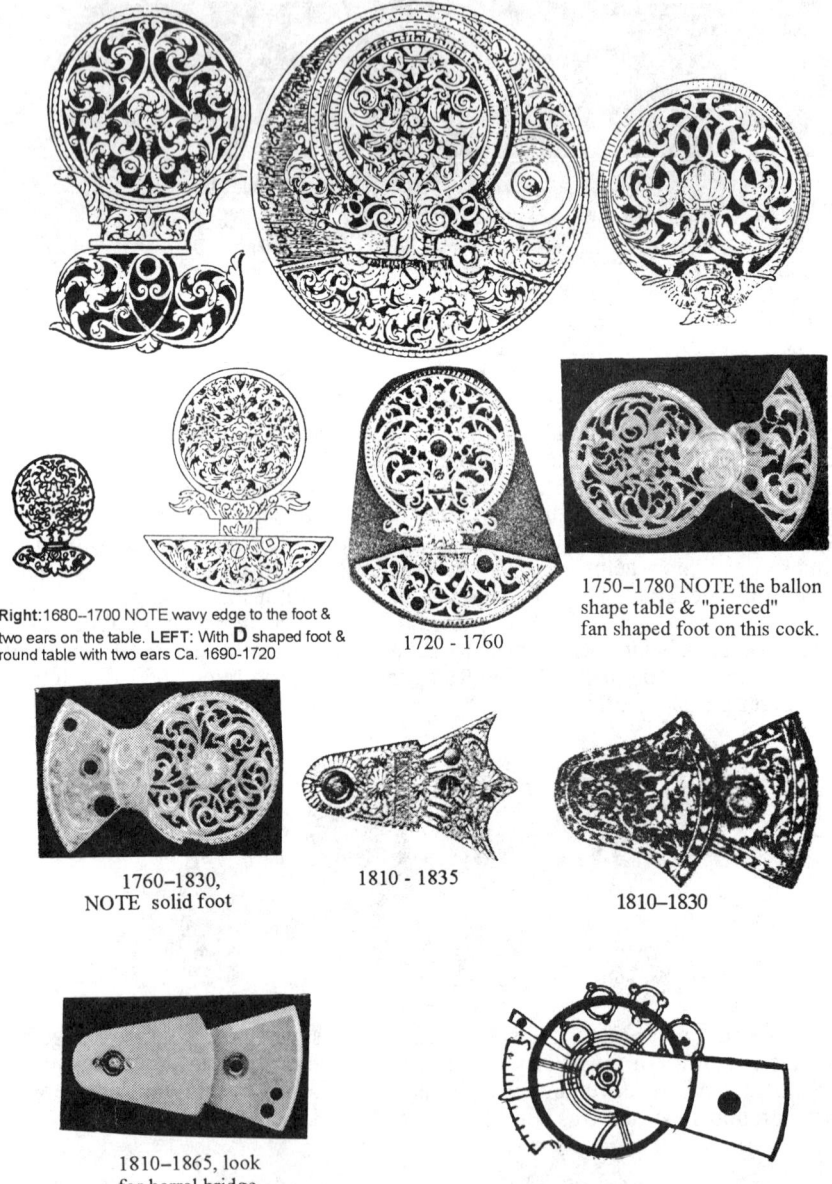

Right: 1680–1700 NOTE wavy edge to the foot & two ears on the table. **LEFT:** With **D** shaped foot & round table with two ears Ca. 1690-1720

1720 - 1760

1750–1780 NOTE the ballon shape table & "pierced" fan shaped foot on this cock.

1760–1830, NOTE solid foot

1810 - 1835

1810–1830

1810–1865, look for barrel bridge

1850 NOTE under-sprung

Characteristics of watches differ for the same age of both case and movement, because these features vary it may not be accurate to date a watch by one single influence. Example: the second hand was <u>not</u> commonly found on watches before 1750, but common about 1800. The first second hand appeared in 1665 and another in 1690. Therefore statements are **broad** rather than absolute.

Lepine style movement Ca. 1790-1820, with free standing barrel, also note the horse shoe shaped bridge, this denotes center seconds.

Lepine, or FRENCH style ebauche caliber, NOTE the step shaped and tapered bridges, also note the free standing barrel, Ca. 1800--1825.

Lepine, or FRENCH style ebauche caliber, NOTE the step shaped and tapered bridges, also note the COVERED barrel bridge, this style movement was popular from Ca.1820–1840.

Lepine, or FRENCH style ebauche caliber, NOTE the step shaped and tapered bridges, also note the CURVED barrel bridge, this style movement was popular from Ca.1830–1845.

🕐 Characteristics of watches differ for the same age of both case and movement, because these features vary it may not be accurate to date a watch by one single influence. Example: the second hand was not commonly found on watches before 1750, but common about 1800. The first second hand appeared in 1665 and another in 1690. Therefore statements are **broad** rather than absolute.

Muti-colored cases became popular by 1800, 1st. used in 1760 & **Engine Turning** rarely found before early 1760s. **Tortoise Shell** 1st. used in 1620, but did not become popular till about 1780. An informed collector will note that a watch with an enamel dial, for instance, could not have been made before 1635. A pair of cases indicates it could not have been made prior to 1640. The minute hand was introduced in 1650. The presence of a cylinder escapement would indicate it was made after 1710. 1750 the duplex escapement was first used. A dust cap first appeared in 1774. 1776 Lepine introduced the thin watch. **Flat enamel** dials are being used in about 1810. Keyless winding came into being after 1820 but did not gain widespread popularity until after about 1860. All of these clues and more must be considered before accurately assessing the age of a watch. Some watches were also **updated** such as minute hand added or new style escapement added.

Bar (Le Coultre) SWISS style ebauche caliber, NOTE the flat straight bridges and parallel design, also the CURVED barrel bridge this movement was popular Ca.1830–1850.

Bar (Le Coultre) SWISS style ebauche caliber, NOTE the flat straight bridges and parallel design, also the STRAIGHT barrel bridge this movement was popular Ca.1840–1885.

JULES JURGENSEN Style Bar SWISS La Chaux de Fonds ebauche caliber, Ca.1870–1895.

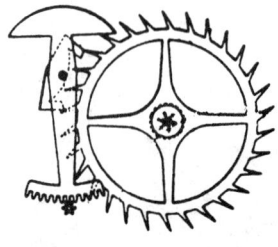

Rack and lever escapement

Invented in 1722

ESCAPEMENTS

Virgule Escapement

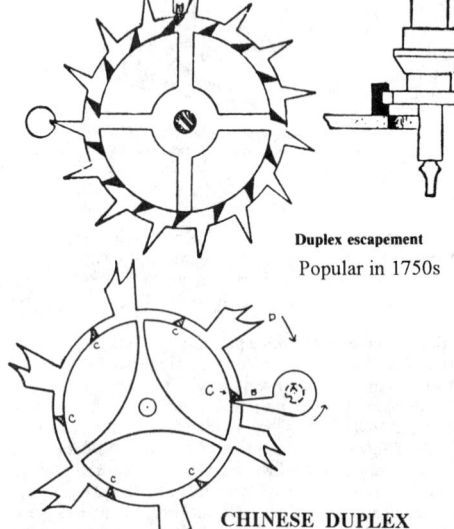

Duplex escapement

Popular in 1750s

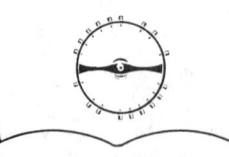

The "Glucydur" Balance can be recognized by the **shape** of its spokes.

CHINESE DUPLEX
or CRAB LEG DUPLEX

CHRONOLOGICAL LIST TO HELP ESTABLISH THE AGE OF YOUR WATCHES
DATES BELOW ARE WHEN COMPONENTS WERE FIRST INTRODUCED OR BECAME POPULAR.

1510 - Mainspring also large watches made entirely of **IRON** & were round in shape.

1525 - Fusee by Jacob of Prague.

1535-1545 - Brass plates.

1550 - Screws & Oval shaped watches.

1564 - Swiss Watchmaking begins.

1570 - Hexagonal and octagonal shaped watches.

1590 - Rock Crystal & Form style watches.

1590 - Fusee CHAIN being used.

1600 - English Watchmaking.

1615 - Watch glasses to protect dials.

1620 - Tortoise shell covered cases & used till 1800.

1625 - Colored enamel cases.

1635 - Enamel dial invented by Paul Viet, of Blois, France.

1640 - Pair cased watches.

1650 - Repousse Cases & Form watches.

1657 - Balance spring by Hooke.

1660 - Virgule escapement.

1670 - Large Bulb shaped or Oignon watches, shagreen cases being seen.

1670 - Minute hand **popular** on watches.

1675 - Wathcmaking in Scotland.

1680 - Watches now run for about 24 hours; before 1680 for about 15 hours only.

1687 - Repeating watches.

1690 - Enamel watch dials now being used in ENGLAND.

1695 - Cylinder escapement by Tompion.

1700 - Pinchbeck "Gold" (Zink & Copper)

1704 - Watch JEWELS invented.

1715 - Dust band also seconds hand with tails.

1720 - Improved cylinder escapement by Graham, but not popular.

1722 - Rack lever escapement.

1724 - Duplex escapement invented.

1734 - Dust caps seen on Movements.

1750 - Duplex escapement **popular**.

1760 - Engine Turning & multi- color gold found on cases.

1761 - John Harrison's chronometer # 4 went to sea for first trial.

1765 - Center seconds.

1765 - Lever escapement by Mudge.

1766 - Compensation balance by Le Roy.

1767 - Virgule escapement.

1770 - Ebauche style watches by Japy.

1775 - Helical balance spring by Arnold.

1776 - Thin modern watches by Lepine.

1782 - Spring detent by Arnold & Earnshaw.

1790 - Musical works & Automaton style watches, 4 color gold dials.

1800 - Watches decorated with pearls.

1800-10 - Flat Enamel dials being used.

1820 - Reproduction of **1600 Form** watches.

1830 - Club tooth escape wheel. Min repeater

1835 - Chinese Duplex.

1844 - Heart shaped cam for chronograph.

1848 - Rocking bar keyless winding.

1867 - Roskopf (Dollar) watches.

1896 - Invar "Guillaume" balance.

1900 - Wrist Watches being used.

1924 - Auto-wind Wrist Watch.

1957 - 1st electric W. W. sold by Hamilton.

1960 - First Electronic Wrist Watch by Max Hetzel & sold by Bulova "Accutron".

1967 - Quartz crystal watch developed.

⊕ Characteristics of watches differ for the same age of both case and movement, because these features vary it may not be accurate to date a watch by one single influence.

EARLY EUROPEAN WATCHMAKERS

NOTE ABBREVIATIONS USED
art = maker used this enamel case painter
enamel = enamel case painter or artist
pat. = patent or inventor
ca. = circa or about
since = founded to present

Achard, J. Francois (Geneva, ca. 1750)
Addison, J. (London, 1760-1780)
Adamson, Gustave (Paris, 1775-1790)
Alfred, W. Humphreys (London, ca. 1905)
Alibut (Paris, ca. 1750s)
Alliez, Buchelard & Teron Co. (French, ca. 1830)
Amabric, Abraham (Geneva, ca. 1750-1800)
Amabric, Freres (Geneva, ca. 1760-1795)
Amon (Paris, 1913)
Andre, Jean (enamel) (Geneva, 1660-1705)
Anthony, Willams (London, 1785-1840)
Antram, J. (London, ca. 1700-1730)
Appleby, Edward (London, ca. 1675)
Appleby, Joshua (London, ca. 1720-1745)
Ardin, Coppet (ca. 1710)
Arlaud, Benjamin (London, c. 1680)
Arlaud, Louis (Geneva, ca. 1750)
Anord & Dent (London) ca. 1839
Arnold & Frodsham, Charles (London, 1845)
Arnold, Henery (London, ca. 1770-1780)
Arnold, John (London, ca. 1760-1790)
Arnold, John Roger, son of (London, ca. 1800-1830)
Arnold, Nicolas (ca. 1850)
Arnold & Lewis, Lote Simmons (Manchester, ca. 1860)
Arnold & Son (London, ca. 1787-1799)
Assman, Julius (Glasshutte, 1850-1885)
Auber, Daniel (London, ca. 1750)
Aubert, D. F. (Geneva, ca. 1825)
Aubert, Ferdinand (1810-1835)
Aubert & Co. (Geneva, ca. 1850)
Aubry, Irenee (Geneva, 1885-1910)
Audebert (Paris, 1810-1820)
Audemars, Freres (Swiss, 1810 until Co. splits in 1885)
Audemars, Louis-Benjamin (Swiss, 1811-1867)
Aureole (Swiss, 1921)
Auricoste, Jules (Paris, ca. 1910)
Bachhofen, Felix (Swiss, 1675-1690)
Badollet, Jean-Jacques (Geneva, 1779-1891)
Baillon, Jean-Hilaire (Paris, ca. 1727)
Baird, Wm. (London, 1815-1825)
Balsiger & Fils (ca. 1825)
Barberet, J. (Paris, ca. 1600)
Barbezat, Bole (Swiss, 1870)
Baronneau, Jean-Louis (France, 1675-1700)
Barnett, John (England) 1690
Barraud & Lunds (England) 1872
Barraud & Lunds (1812-1840)
Barraud, Paul-Philip (London, 1752-1820)
Barrow, Edward (London, ca. 1650-1710)
Barrow, Nathaniel (London, 1653-1689)
Barry, M. (French, ca. 1620)
Bartholony, Abraham (Paris, 1750-1752)
Barton, J. (London, 1760-1780)
Barwise J.(London, 1800)
Bassereau, Jean-Hilaire (Paris, ca. 1800-1810)
Bautte, Jean-Francois (Geneva, 1800-1835)
Bautte & Moynier (Geneva, ca. 1825)
Beaumarchais, Caron (Paris, 1750-1795)
Beauvais, Simon (London, ca. 1690)
Beckman, Daniel (London, 1670-1685)
Beckner, Abraham (London, ca. 1640)
Beliard, Dominique (Paris, ca. 1750)
Bell, Benj. (London, 1650-1668)
Bennett, John (London, 1850-1895)
Benson, J. W. (London, 1825-1890)
Benson, J. W. (London, 1850-1900)
Bergstein, L. (London, ca. 1840)
Bernard, Nicholas (Paris, 1650-1690)

Bernoulli, Daniel (Paris, 1720-1780)
Berrollas, J. A. (Denmark, 1800-1830)
Berthoud, Augusta-Louis (Paris, ca. 1875)
Berthoud, Ferdinand (Paris, 1750-1805)
Beihler & Hartmann (Geneva, ca. 1875)
Blanc, Henri (Geneva, ends 1964)
Blanc, Jules (Geneva, 1929-1940)
Blanc & Fils (Geneva, 1770-1790)
Bock, Johann (German, 1700-1750)
Bockel (London, ca. 1650)
Bolslandon, Metz (ca. 1780)
Bolviller, Moise (Paris, 1840-1870)
Bommelt, Leonhart (Nuremburg, Ger., ca. 1690)
Bonney (London, ca. 1790)
Bonniksen, Bahne (England, 1890-1930) invented karrusel
Booth, Edward (name change to Barlow)
Bordier, Denis (France, ca. 1575)
Bordier, Freres (Geneva, 1787-1810)
Bordier, Jacques (enamel) (ca. 1670)
Bornand, A. (Geneva, 1895-1915)
Boubon (Paris, 1810-1820)
Bouquet, David (London, ca. 1630-1650)
Bovet (England) 1815 (used J.L.Richer Art)
Bovet, Edouard (Swiss, 1820-1918)
Bovier, G. (enamel painter) (Paris, c. 1750)
Brandt, Iacob (Swiss, ca. 1700)
Brandt, Robert & Co. (Geneva, ca. 1820)
Breitling, "Leon" (Swiss, since 1884)
Brookbank (London, 1776)
Brocke (London, ca. 1640)
Brodon, Nicolas (Paris, 1674-1682)
Bronikoff, a Wjatka (Russia, 1850 "watches of wood")
Bruguier, Charles A. (Geneva, 1800-1860)
Bull, Rainulph (one of the first British) (1590-1617)
Burgis, Eduardus (London, 1680-1710)
Burgis, G. (London, 1720-1740)
Burnet, Thomas (London, ca. 1800)
Busch, Abraham (Hamburg, Ger., ca. 1680)
Buz, Johannes (Augsburg, Bavaria, ca. 1625)
Cabrier, Charles (London, ca. 1690-1720)
Capt, Henry Daniel (Geneva, 1802-1880)
Caron, Augustus (Paris, ca. 1750-1760)
Caron, Francois-Modeste (Paris, 1770-1788)
Caron, Pierre (Paris, ca. 1700)
Caron, Pierre Augustin (pat. virgule escap.) (Paris,1750-1795)
Carpenter, William (London, 1750-1800)
Carte, John (London, 1680-1700)
Champod, P. Amedee (enamel) (Geneva, 1850-1910)
Chapeau, Peter (England) 1746
Chapponier, Jean (Geneva, 1780-1800)
Charlton, John (England) 1635
Charman (London, 1780-1800)
Charrot (Paris, 1775-1810)
Chartiere (enamel) (France, ca. 1635)
Chaunes (Paris, ca. 1580-1600)
Chauvel, J. (England) 1720-25
Chavanne & Pompejo (Vienna, 1785-1800)
Cheneviere, Louis (Geneva, 1710-1740)
Cheneviere, Urbain (Geneva, 1730-1760)
Cheriot or Cherioz, Daniel (ca. 1750-1790)
Cheuillard (Blois, France, ca. 1600)
Chevalier & Co. (Geneva, 1795-1810)
Cisin, Charles (Swiss, 1580-1610)
Clark, Geo. (London, 1750-1785)
Clay, Charles (England) 1750
Clerc (Swiss, ca. 1875)
Clouzier, Jacques (Paris, 1690-1750)
Cochin, D. (Paris, ca. 1800)

Cocque, Geo. (ca. 1610)
Cogniat (Paris, ca. 1675)
Coladon, Louis (Geneva, 1780-1850)
Cole, James Ferguson (London, 1820-1875)
Cole, Thomas (London, 1820-1864)
Collins, Clement (London, ca. 1705)
Collins, John (London, ca. 1720)
Collins, R. (London, ca. 1815)
Colondre & Schnee (ca. 1875)
Combret, Pierre (Lyons, France, ca. 1610-1625)
Cooper, T.F. (England) 1842-80 later "T.M."
Cotton, John (London, ca. 1695-1715)
Coulin, Jaques & Bry, Amy (Paris & Geneva, 1780-1790)
Court, Jean-Pierre (ca. 1790-1810)
Courvosier, Freres (Swiss, 1810-1852)
Courvoisier & Houriet (Geneva, ca. 1790)
Cox, James (London, 1760-1785)
Crofswell J.N. (London), ca. 1825
Csacher, C. (Prague, Aus., ca. 1725)
Cumming, Alexander (London, 1750-1800)
Cummins, Charles (London, 1820)
Cuper, Barthelemy (French, 1615-1635)
Curtis, John (London, ca. 1720)
Cusin, Charles (Geneva, ca. 1587)
Darling, William (British, ca. 1825)
Daniel, de St. Leu (England) 1815
De Baghyn, Adriaan (Amsterdam, ca. 1750)
Debaufre, Peter (French, 1690-1720) (Debaufre escap.)
Debaufre, Pierre (Paris, London, Geneva, 1675-1722)
De Bry, Theodore (German, 1585-1620)
De Charmes, Simon (London, France, 1690-1730)
De Choudens (Swiss & French, 1760-1790)
Decombaz, Gedeon (Geneva, 1780-1820)
Degeilh & Co. (ca. 1880-1900)
De Heca, Michel (Paris, ca. 1685)
De L Garde, Abraham (Paris, "Blois," ca. 1590)
Delynne, F. L. (Paris, ca. 1775)
"Dent", (Edward John)(London, 1815-1850)
Denham, Go. (London, 1750)
Derham, William (English, ca. 1677-1730)
Deroch, F. (Swiss, 1730-1770)
Des Arts & Co. (Geneva, 1790-1810)
Desquivillons & DeChoudens (Paris, ca. 1785)
Destouches, Jean-Francois-Albert (Holland, ca. 1760)
Devis, John (London, 1770-1785)
Dimier & Co. (Geneva, 1820-1925)
Dinglinger (enamel) (Dresden, Ger., ca. 1675)
Ditisheim & Co. "Maurice" (Swiss, 1894)
Ditisheim, Paul (Swiss, 1892)
Dobson, A. (London, 1660-1680)
Droz, Daniel (Chaux-de-Fonds, Sw., ca. 1760)
Droz, Henri (Chaux-de-Fonds, Sw., ca. 1775)
Droz, Pierre Jacquet (Chaux-de-Fonds, Sw., 1750-1775)
Droz, Pierre (Swiss, 1740-1770)
Droz & Co. (Swiss, ca. 1825)
Dubie (enamel) (Paris, ca. 1635)
Dubois & Fils (Paris, ca. 1810)
Duchene & Co. "Louis" (Geneva, 1790-1820)
Ducommun, Charles (Geneva, ca. 1750)
Duduict, Jacques (Blois, France, ca. 1600)
Dufalga, Philippe (Geneva, 1730-1790)
Dufalga, P. F. (Geneva, ca. 1750)
Dufour, Foll & C. (Geneva, 1800-1830)
Dufour, J. E. & Co. (ca. 1890)
Dufour & Ceret (Ferney, Fr., ca. 1770-1785)
Dufour & Zentler (ca. 1870)
Duhamel, Pierre (Paris, ca. 1680)
Dunlop, Andrew (England) 1710
Dupin, Paul (Paris, 1730-1765)
Dupont (Geneva, ca. 1810-1830)
Dupont, Jean (enamel) (Geneva, 1800-1860)
Duru (Paris, ca. 1650)
Dutertre, Baptiste (ca. 1730) (pat. duplex escapement)
Dutton, William (London, 1760-1840)

Dyson, John & Sons (England) 1816
Earnshaw, Thomas (London, 1780-1825)
East, Edward (London, 1630-1670)
Edmonds, James (London to U.S.A., 1720-1766)
Edward, George & Son (London, ca. 1875)
Ekegren, Henri-Robert (Geneva, 1860)
Ellicott, John (London, 1728-1810)
Emanuel, E.& E (England) 1861
Emery, Josiah (Geneva, 1750-1800)
Etherington, George (England) 1700
Esquivillon & De Choudens (Paris, 1710-1780)
Ester, Jean Henry (Geneva, 1610-1665)
Etherington, George (London, 1680-1730)
Etienne Guyot & Co. (Geneva, ca. 1880)
Facio De Duillier, Nicholas (British, 1665-1710)
Fallery, Jacques (Geneva, ca. 1760)
Farmer, G. W. (wooden watches) (Germany, 1650-1675)
Fatio, Alfred (Geneva, 1920-1940)
Fatton, Frederick Louis (London, ca. 1822)
Favre Marius & Fils (Geneva, 1893)
Fenie, M. (ca. 1635)
Ferrero, J. (ca. 1854-1900)
Fiarce, Clement (Paris, ca. 1700)
Fitter, Joseph (London, ca. 1660)
Fontac (London, ca. 1775)
Forfaict, Nicolas (Paris, 1573-1619)
Fowles, Allen (Kilmarnock, Scot., ca. 1770)
French (London, 1810-1840)
Fureur (Swiss, 1910)
Gallopin "Henri Capt" (Geneva, 1875)
Gamod, G. (Paris, ca. 1640)
Garnier, Paul (Paris, 1825) (pat. Garnier escapement)
Garon, Peter (England) 1700
Garrault, Jacobus (Geneva, ca. 1650)
Garty & Constable (London, ca. 1750)
Gaudron, Antoine (Paris, 1675-1707)
Gaudron, Pierre (Paris, 1695-1740)
Geissheim, Smod (Augsburg, Ger., ca. 1625)
Gent, James & Son (London, 1875-1910)
Gerbeau, V. (Paris, 1900-1930)
Gerrard (British, 1790-1820)
Gibs, William (Rotterdam, ca. 1720)
Gibbons Joshua (London), ca. 1825
Gibson & Co., Ltd. (Ireland, ca. 1875-1920)
Gidon (Paris, ca. 1700)
Gillespey, Charles (Ireland, 1774-1171)
Girard, Perregaux (Swiss, 1856)
Girard, Theodore (Paris, 1623-1670)
Girardier, Charles (Geneva, 1780-1815)
Girod, B. (Paris, ca. 1810)
Girod, Gaspard (Paris, ca. 1670-1690)
Godod, E. (Paris, ca. 1790)
Godon, F. L. (Paris, ca. 1787)
Golay, A. Leresche & Fils (Geneva, 1844-1857)
Golay, H. (Swiss, 1969-1911)
Golay, Stahl & Fils (1878-1914)
Gollons (Paris, ca. 1663)
Gould, Christopher (England) 1650
Gounouilhou, P. S. (Geneva, 1815-1840)
Gout, Ralph (London, 1790-1830)
Graham, George (London, 1715-1750)
Grandjean, Henri (Swiss, 1825-1880)
Grandjean, L. C. (Swiss, 1890-1920)
Grant, John & Son (English, 1780-1867)
Grantham, William (London, ca. 1850-60)
Grasset, Isaac (Geneva, ca. 1896)
Gray & Constable (London, ca. 1750-90)
Grazioza (Swiss, ca. 1901)
Grebauval, Hierosme (ca. 1575)
Gregory, Jermie (London, ca. 1652-1680)
Gregson, Jean P. (Paris, 1770-1790)
Grendon, Henry (England) 1645
Griblin, Nicolas (French, 1650-1716)
Griessenback, Johann G. (Bavaria, ca. 1660)

Grignion "family" (London, 1690-1825)
Grignion, Daniel & Thomas (London, 1780-1790)
Grinkin, Robert (England) 1625
Grosclaude, Ch. & Co. (Swiss, ca. 1865)
Grosjean, Henry (French, ca. 1865)
Gruber, Hans (Nurnberg, Ger., ca. 1520-1560)
Gruber, Michel (Nurnberg, Ger., ca. 1605)
Gruet (Geneva, Sw., ca. 1664)
Gubelin, E. (Lucern, Switzerland, ca. 1832)
Guillaume, Ch. (pat. Invar, Elinvar)
Haas Nevevx & Co. (founder B. J. Haas) (Swiss, 1828-1925)
Hagen, Johan (German, ca. 1750)
Haley, Charles (London, 1781-1825)
Hallewey (London, 1695-1720)
Hamilton & Co. (London, 1865-1920)
Hamilton G.(London), Ca.1800s
Harper, Henry (London, ca. 1665-1700)
Harrison, John (England, b.1693-1776) **Marine No.1-2-3-4**
Hasluck Brothers (London, ca. 1695)
Hautefeuille, Jean (Paris, 1670-1722)
Hautefeuille, John (Paris, 1660-1700)
Hawley, John (London, ca. 1850)
Hebert, Juliette (enamel) (Geneva, ca. 1890)
Helbros (Geneva, since 1918)
Hele or Henlein, Peter (Nurnberg, 1510-1540)
Heliger, J. (Zug, Sw., ca. 1575)
Henner, Johann (Wurtzburg, Ger., ca. 1730)
Henry, F. S. (Swiss, ca. 1850)
Hentschel, J. J. (French, ca. 1750)
Hess, L. (Zurich, Sw., ca. 1780)
Hessichti, Dionistus (ca. 1630)
Higgs & Evans (London, 1775-1825)
Hill, Ben. (London, 1640-1670)
Hindley, Henry (England) 1758
Hoddell, James, & Co. (England) 1869
Hoguet, Francois (Paris, ca. 1750)
Hooke, Robert (England, 1650-1700)
Hoseman, Stephen (London, ca. 1710-1740)
Houghton, James (England, ca. 1800-1820)
Houghton, Thomas (Chorley, England, ca. 1820-1840)
Houriet, Jacques Frederic (Paris 1810-1825)
Howells & Pennington (England) 1795
Huaud, Freres (enamel) (Geneva, ca. 1685)
Huber, Peter (German, ca. 1875)
Hubert, David (London, 1714-1747)
Hubert, James (England) 1760
Hubert, Oliver (London, ca. 1740)
Hubert, Etienne (French, 1650-1690)
Hues, Peter (Augsburg, Ger., ca. 1600)
Huguenin, David L. (Swiss, 1780-1835)
Humbert-Droz, David (Swiss, ca. 1790)
Hunt & Roskell (England) 1846
Huygens, Christian (Paris, 1657-1680)
Iaquier or Jacquier, Francois (Geneva, 1690-1720)
Ilbery, *William* (London, 1800-35) (used J.L. Richer art)
Ingold, Pierre-Frederic (Swiss, Paris, London, 1810-1870)
Invicta ("R. Picard") (Swiss, 1896)
Jaccard, E. H. & Co. (Swiss, ca. 1850)
Jacot, Charles-Edouard (Swiss, 1830-1860) (pat. Chinese duplex)
Jaeger, Edmond (Paris, 1875-1920)
Jaeger Le Coultre & Co. (Swiss, since 1833)
Jamison, Geo. (London, 1786-1810)
Janvier, Antide (Paris, 1771-1834)
Japy, Frederic & Sons "family" (French, Swiss, ca. 1776)
Jaquet, Pierre (Swiss, 1750-1790)
Jean Richard, Daniel (Swiss, 1685-1740)
Jean Richard, Edouard (Swiss, 1900-1930)
Jeannot, Paul (ca. 1890)
Jefferys & Gildert (London, 1790)
Jessop, Josias (London, 1780-1794)
Jeubi, Josias (Paris, ca. 1575)
Joly, Jacques (Paris, ca. 1625)
Jovat (London, ca. 1690)

Johnson Joseph. Liverpool (English), ca.1805-1855
Jones, Henry (London, ca. 1665-1690)
Jump, Joseph (English, ca. 1827-1850)
Junod, Freres (Geneva, ca. 1850)
Jurgensen, Urban & Jules (Copenhagen, Swiss,1745-1912)
Just & Son (London, 1790-1825)
Juvet, Edouard (Swiss, 1844-1880)
Juvet, Leo (Swiss, 1860-1890)
Keates, William (London, ca. 1780)
Keely, W. (London, ca. 1790)
Kendall, Larcum (London, ca. 1786)
Kendall, James (London, 1740-1780)
Kessels, H. J. (Holland, 1800-1845)
Kirkton, R. (London, ca. 1790)
Klein, Johann Heinr (Copenhagen, Den., ca. 1710)
Klentschi, C. F. (Swiss, 1790-1840)
Koehn, Edward (Geneva, 1860-1908)
Kreizer, Conard (German, 1595-1658)
Kuhn, Jan Hendrik (Amsterdam, 1775-1800)
Kullberg, Victor (Copenhagen to London, 1850-1890)
Lamy, Michel (Paris, 1767-1800)
Lang & Padoux (ca. 1860)
Larcay (Paris, ca. 1725)
Lardy, Francois (Geneva, ca. 1825)
Larpent, Isacc & Jurgensen (Copenhagen, 1748-1811)
Laurier, Francois (Paris, 1654-1675)
Le Baufre (Paris, ca. 1650)
Lebet (Geneva, ca. 1850)
Lebet & Fils (Swiss, 1830-1892)
Le Coultre, Ami (Geneva, ca. 1887)
Le Coultre, Eugene (Geneva, ca. 1850)
Leekey, C. (London, ca. 1750)
Leeky, Gabriel (London, ca. 1775-1820)
Lepaute, Jean-Andre (Paris, 1750-1774)
Lepine or L'Epine, Jean-Antoine (Paris, 1744-1814)
Le Prevost (Swiss), ca.1810
Leroux, John (England, 1758-1805)
Le Roy & Co. (Paris, ca. 1853)
Le Roy, Charles (Paris, 1733-1770)
Le Roy, Julien (Paris, 1705-1750)
Le Roy, Pierre (French, 1710-80) (improved duplex escap.)
Levy, Hermanos (Hong Kong, "Swiss," 1880-1890)
L'Hardy, Francois (Geneva, 1790-1825)
Lichtenauer, G. (London, ca. 1740-1770)
Lindesay, G. (London, ca. 1740-1770)
Lindgren, Erik (England, 1735-1775) (pat. rack lever)
Litherland, Peter (English, 1780-1876)
Loehr, (Von) (Swiss, ca. 1880)
Long & Drew (enamel) (London, ca. 1790-1810)
Losada, Jose R. (London, 1835-1890)
Lowndes, Jonathan (London, ca. 1680-1700)
MacCabe, James (London, 1778-1830)
Maillardet & Co. (Swiss, ca. 1800)
Mairet, Sylvain (Swiss, 1825-1885) (London, 1830-1840)
Malignon, A. (Geneva, ca. 1835)
Marchand, Abraham (Geneva, 1690-1725)
Margetts, George (London, 1780-1800)
Markwick Markham, "Perigal" "Recordon"
(London, 1780-1825)
Marshall, John (London, ca. 1690)
Martin (Paris, ca. 1780)
Martin, Thomas (London, ca. 1870)
Martineau, Joseph (London, 1765-1790)
Martinot, "family" (Paris, 1570-1770)
Martinot, James (London, ca. 1780)
Mascarone, Gio Batt (London, ca. 1635)
Massey, Edward (England, 1800-1850)
Massey, Henry (London, 1692-1745)
E. Mathey-Tissot & Co. (Swiss, 1886-1896)
Matile, Henry (Swiss, ca. 1825)
Maurer, Johann (Fiessna, Ger., ca. 1640-1650)
May, George (English, 1750-1770)
Mayr, Johann Peter (Augsburg, Ger., ca. 1770)

McCabe, James (London, 1780-1710)
McDowall, Charles (London, ca. 1820-1860)
Meak, John (London, ca. 1825)
Mecke, Daniel (ca. 1760)
Melly, Freres (Geneva, Paris, 1791-1844)
Mercier, A. D. (Swiss, 1790-1820)
Mercier, Francois David (Paris, ca. 1700)
Meuron & Co. (Swiss, ca. 1784)
Meylan, C. H. "Meylan W. Co." (Swiss, ca. 1880)
Michel, Jean-Robert (Paris, ca. 1750)
Miller, Joseph (London, ca. 1728)
Milleret & Tissot (ca. 1835)
Miroir (London, ca. 1700-1725)
Mistral (Swiss, ca. 1902)
Mobilis (Swiss, ca. 1910)
Modernista (Swiss, ca. 1903)
Moillet, Jean-Jacques (Paris, 1776-1789)
Molina, Antonio (Madrid, Spain, ca. 1800)
Molinie (Swiss, ca. 1840)
Molyneux, Robert (London, ca. 1825-1850)
Montandon, Chs. Ad. (Swiss, 1800-1830)
Morand, Pierre (Paris, ca. 1790)
Moricand & Co. (Swiss, ca. 1780)
Moricand & Desgranges (Geneva, 1828-1835)
Moricand, Christ (Geneva, 1745-1790)
Morin, Pierre (English, French & Dutch style, ca. 1700)
Morliere (enamel) (Blois, Fr., ca. 1636-1650)
Moser, George Michael (London, ca. 1716-1730)
Motel, Jean Francois (French, 1800-1850)
Moulineux, Robert (London, 1800-1840)
Moulinier, Aine & Co. (Swiss, 1828-1851)
Moulinier, Freres & Co. (Swiss, ca. 1822)
Mudge, Thomas (London, 1740-1790)
Mulsund (enamel) (Paris, ca. 1700)
Munoz, Blas (Madrid, Spain, ca. 1806-1823)
Mussard, Jean (Geneva, 1699-1727)
Musy Padre & Figlo (Paris, 1710-1760)
Myrmecide (Paris, ca. 1525)
Nardin, Ulysse (Swiss, ca. 1846)
Nelson, W. (London, 1777-1818)
Nocturne (ca. 1920)
Noir, Jean-Baptiste (Paris, 1680-1710)
Norris, J. (Dutch, 1680-1700)
Norton (London), ca.1805
Nouwen, Michael (1st English, 1580-1600)
Noyean (ca. 1850)
Oldnburg, Johan (German, ca. 1648)
Oudin, Charles (Paris, 1807-1900)
Owen, John (English, ca. 1790)
Palmer, Samuel (London, ca. 1790-1810)
Panier, Iosue "Josue" (Paris, ca. 1790)
Papillon (ca. 1690)
Papillon, Francesco (Florence, ca. 1705)
Parr, Thomas (London, ca. 1735-1775)
Payne, H. & John (London, ca. 1735-1775)
Pellaton, Albert (Swiss, ca. 1873)
Pellaton, James (Swiss, 1903) (Tourbillon)
Pendleton, Richard (London, 1780-1805)
Pennington, Robert (English, 1780-1816)
Perigal, Francis (English, 1770-1790)
Pernetti, F. (Swiss, ca. 1850)
Perrelet, Abram (Swiss, 1780) (self wind)
Perret, Edouard (Swiss, 1850)
Perrin, Freres (Swiss, 1810)
Phillips, Edouard (Paris, ca. 1860)
Phleisot (Dijon, Fr., ca. 1540)
Piaget, George (Swiss, ca. 1881)
Picard, James (Geneva, ca. 1850)
Piguet & Capt (Geneva, 1802-1811)
Piguet & Meylan (Geneva, 1811-1828)
Piguet, Victorin-Emile (Geneva, 1870-1935)
Plairas, Solomon (Blois, Fr., ca. 1640)
Plumbe, David (ca. 1730)
Poitevin, B. (Paris, 1850-1935)

Poncet, J. F. (Dresden, 1750)
Poncet, Jean-Francois (Swiss, 1740-1800)
Potter, Harry (London, 1760-1800)
Pouzait, Jean-Moise (Geneva, 1780-1800)
Poy, Gottfrey (London, ca. 1725-1730)
Prest, Thomas (English, 1820-1855)
Prevost, Freres (ca. 1820)
Prior, Edward (London, 1825-1865)
Prior, George (London, 1800-1830) (used J.L. Richer art)
Pyke, John (English, 1750-1780)
Quare, Daniel (London, 1700-1724)
Quarella, Antonio (ca. 1790)
Racine, Cesar (Swiss, ca. 1902)
Racine, C. Frederic (la Chaux-de-Fonds, Swiss, ca.1810-32)
Raillard, Claude (Paris, 1662-1675)
Raiss (1890-1910) (enamel)
Rait, D. C. (German, ca. 1866)
Ramsay, David (Scotland, France, London, 1590-1654)
Ramuz, Humbert U. & Co. (Swiss, ca. 1882)
Ratel, Henri (Paris, 1850-1900)
Recordon, Louis (London, 1778-1824)
Redier, Antoine (Paris, 1835-1883)
Renierhes (London, ca. 1850)
Rey, Jn. Ante, & Fils (Paris, 1790-1810)
Reynaud, P. & Co. (1860)
Rich, John (Geneva, London, 1795-1825)
Richard, Daniel Jean (1685-1740)
Richer, J. L. (outstanding enamel artist) (Geneva, 1786-1840)
Rigaud, Pierre (Geneva, 1750-1800)
Rigot, Francois (Geneva, ca. 1825)
Robert & Courvoisier & Co. (Paris, 1781-1832)
Robin, Robert (Paris, 1765-1805)
Robinet, Charles (Paris, ca. 1640)
Robinson, Olivier & Fredmahn (Naples, 1727-1790)
Robinson William (Liverpool), ca.1850
Rogers, Isaac (London, 1770-1810)
Romilly, Sieur (Geneva, ca. 1750-1775)
Rooker, Richard (London, 1790-1810)
Rose, Joseph (London, 1752-1795)
Rosier, John (Geneva, ca. 1750)
Roskell, Robert (London, 1798-1830) (rack-lever)
Roskopf, G. (German to Swiss, 1835-1885)
Rosselet, Louis (Geneva, 1855-1900) (enamel)
Rousseau, Jean (Paris, 1580-1642)
Roux, Bordier & Co. (Geneva, ca. 1795)
Ruegger, Jacques (ca. 1800-1840)
Ruel, Samuel (Rotterdam, ca. 1750)
Rugendas, Nicholas (Augsburg, Ger., ca. 1700-1750)
Rundell & Bridge (London, ca. 1772-1825)
Russel, Thomas & Son (England) 1898
Sailler, Johann (Vienna, Aus., ca. 1575)
Sanchez, Cayetano (Madrid, Spain, c. 1790-1800)
Sandoz, Henri F. (Tavannes W. Co.) (ca. 1840)
Savage, George (London, 1808-1855) (Inv. pin lever)
Savage, William (London 1800-1850)
Savile, John (London, ca. 1656-1679)
Schatck, Johann Engel (Prague, ca. 1650)
Schultz, Michael (ca. 1600-1650)
Schuster, Caspar (Nunburg, ca. 1570)
Sermand, J. (Geneva, ca. 1640)
Sellar - Reading (England) 1854
Shepherd, Thomas (England) 1632
Sherman De Neilly (Belfort, ca. 1910)
Sherwood, J. (London, ca. 1750-1775)
Sidey, B. (England) 1770
Solson (London, 1750)
Soret (Geneva, ca. 1810)
Soret, Frederic II (1735-1806)
Soret, Isaac & Co. (1690-1760)
Sleightholm & Co. (England) 1800
Smith, C. (England) 1829
Smith, George (England) 1630
Smith, S, & Son (England) 1910
Snelling,J.50

Speakman, Edward (England) 1690
Spencer & Perkins (London, 1770-1808)
Stadlin, Francois (Swiss, 1680-1735)
Staples, James (1755-1795)
Stuffer, M. T. (Swiss, 1830-1855)
Stauffer "Stauffer Son & Co." (London, 1880)
Strasser & Rohde (Glashutte, 1875)
Sudek, J. (ca. 1850)
Sully, Henry (French, London, 1700-1725)
Swift, Thomas (London, ca. 1825-1865)
Tavan, Antoine (Geneva, 1775-1830)
Tavernier, Jean (Paris, 1744-1795)
Tempor Watch Co. (1930) (Masonic watch)
Terond, Allier & Bachelard (ca. 1805-1830)
Terrot & Fazy (ca. 1767-1775)
Terrot, Philippe (Geneva, ca. 1732)
Terroux (ca. 1776)
Theed & Pikett (ca. 1750)
Thierry, J. (London, ca. 1760)
Thierry, Niel (ca. 1810)
Thiout, Antoine (Paris, 1724-1760)
Tobias & Co. M.I. (England) 1805-68 (Michael Isac)
Tobias large family very active in exporting watches
Thomlinson, George (England) 1675
Thorne, Robert (London, 1850)
Thoroton, James (London, 1860)
Thuret, Jacques (Paris, ca. 1695)
Thomason J.N. (Edinburgh), ca.1830
Timing & Repeating W. Co. (Geneva, 1900)
Tompion, Thomas (English, 1671-1715)
Tonkin, Tho. (London, ca. 1760)
Torin, Daniel (England) 1750
Toutaia, Henri (French, 1650) (enamel)
Toutin, Jean (enamel) (Blois, Fr., ca. 1630)
Treffler, Sebastain (ca. 1750)
Tregent, J. (English, 1765-1800)
Truitte, Louis & Mourier (Geneva, ca. 1780)
Tupman (England) 1828
Tyrer, Thomas (London, ca. 1782)
Uhren Fabrik Union (Glashutte, 1893-1970)
Ullman, J. & Co. (Swiss, 1893)
Ulrich, Johann (London, 1820-1870)
Upjohn, W. J. (London, 1815-1824)
Vacheron, Abraham Girod (German, 1760-1843)
Valere (Paris, 1860)

Vallier, Jean (Lyons, Fr., ca. 1630)
Valove, James (London, ca. 1740)
Vanbroff, James (Germany, ca. 1600)
Van Ceule, J. (ca. 1799-1725)
Vandersteen (ca. 1725)
Vaucher, C. H. (Geneva, ca. 1835)
Vaucher, Daniel (Paris, 1767-1790)
Vaucher, Freres (Swiss, 1850)
Vauquer, Robert (French, ca. 1650) (enamel)
Veigneur, F. I. (ca. 1780)
Verdiere A. (Paris), ca.1810
Vernod, Henriette (Paris, ca. 1790)
Vigne, James (London, ca. 1770)
Viner (England) 1834
Vrard, L., & Co. (Pekin, 1860-1872)
Vulliamy, *Justin* (London, ca. 1830-1854)
Vully, Jaques (London, ca. 1890-1900)
Vuolf (Swiss, ca. 1600)
Waldron, John (London, 1760)
Wales, Giles & Co. (Swiss, ca. 1870)
Walker, Allen (England) 1784
Waltrin (Paris, ca. 1820)
Webb, Benjamin (England) 1799
Weston, D. & Willis (enamel) (London, ca. 1800-1810)
Welldon, I. (England) 1731
Wichcote, Samuel (England) 1733
Widenham (England) 1824
Windmills,J. (England) 1710
Whitney, A. (Enniscorthy- S.of Dublin) Ca. 1810-1830
Whitthorne, James (Dublin, since 1725)
Willats, John (London, ca. 1860)
Williamson, Timothy (London, 1770-1790)
Wilter, John (London, ca. 1760)
Winckles, John (London, 1770-1790)
Winnerl, Joseph Thaddeus (Paris, 1829-1886)
Wiss, Freres & Menu (Swiss, ca. 1787-1810)
Wiss, G. (Geneva, ca. 1750)
Wood, William (England) 1860
Wright, Charles (London, 1760-1790)
Wright, Thomas (English, ca. 1770-1790)
Yates, Thomas (England) 1855
Young, Richard (London, 1765-1785)
Zech, Jacob (Prague, Aus. 1525-1540)
Zolling, Ferdinand (Frankfurt, Ger. ca. 1750)

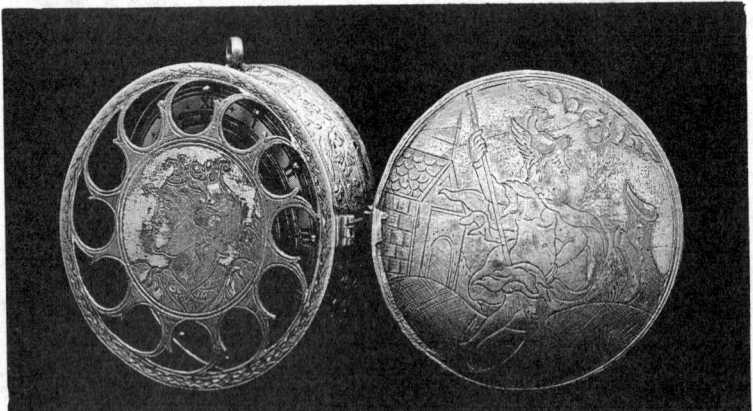

Tambour style case, probably Nuremburg, ca. 1575, hinged cover, pierced to reveal engraved Roman chapter I-XII and Arabic 13-24 Central chapter, 60mm.

HALLMARKS OF ENGLAND

Hallmarks were used on gold and silver **cases** made in England. These **case** marks, when interpreted, will help determine **age** of the **case** and location of the assay office. Hallmarks were used to denote information for the **case only**. The Maker's Mark (*W.C.Co.*) when interpreted is who made the **case only**.

The **London** date-marks (a single letter) used 20 letters, A-U, never using the letters W, X, Y, or Z. The letters J & I or U & V, because of their similarity in shape, were never used together within the same 20-year period.

A total of four marks maybe found on English **cases**, which are:

The **CASE MAKER'S MARK** with two or more letters was used to denote the manufacturer of the case **ONLY**.
The **STANDARD MARK** was used to denote a guarantee of the quality of the metal.
The **ASSAY OFFICE MARK** (also known as the town mark) was used to denote the location of the assay office.
The **DATE LETTER MARK** was a letter of the alphabet used to denote the year in which the article was stamped. The stamp was used on gold and silver cases by the assay office.

Case Maker's Mark   The Standard Mark

The Assay Office Mark   The Date Letter Mark   DUTY MARK

1822 - UP
NO CROWN   1478 to 1821

With George looking to the right 1786 to 1798 are uncommon.

Chester   Birmingham   Edinburgh   Dublin   Glasgow

SWISS HALLMARKS

18k .750   14k .585   Platinum .950

Sterling Silver .925   Sterling Silver   Silver .800

Lucerne   Neuchatel, Poincons d'essai de décembre 1852.    German silver mark    German gold mark

.800

FRENCH .800   FRENCH .950

TROY WEIGHT = 24 grains=1dwt., 1 Grain= 0.0648 grams, 20dwt = 1 OZ., 12oz = 1 LB.
NOTE: Gold & Silver Standards Vary from Country to Country. U.S.A. Coin Gold =.900 or 21 3/5K, Silver Coin=.900.
Gold Standards: 24K=1,000%or 1.0, 23K=.958 1/3, 22K=.916 2/3, 21K=.875, 20K=.833 1/3, 19K=.791 2/3, 18K=.750, 17K=.708 1/3, 16K=.666 2/3, 15K=.625, 14K=.583 1/3, 13K=.541 2/3, 12K=.500, 11=.458 1/3, 10K=.416 2/3, 9K=. 375.
8K=.333 1/3, 7K=.291 2/3, 6K=.250, 5K=.208 1/3, 4K=.166 2/3, 3K=.125, 2K=.83 1/3, 1K=.41 2/3.

LONDON DATE LETTER MARKS

Mark	Year	Mark	Year	Mark	Year	Mark	Year	Mark	Year	Mark	Year	Mark	Year	Mark	Year
❁	1551	M	1589	k	1627	J	1666	⬥	1709	r	1752	B	1797	J	1841	I	1884
P	1552	N	1590	l	1628	K	1667	S	1710	ſ	1753	C	1798	G	1842	K	1885
Q	1553	O	1591	m	1629	L	1668	q	1711	t	1754	D	1799	h	1843	L	1886
R	1554	P	1592	n	1630	M	1669	R	1712	u	1755	E	1800	j	1844	M	1887
S	1555	Q	1593	o	1631	N	1670	S	1713	a	1756	F	1801	k	1845	N	1888
T	1556	R	1594	p	1632	O	1671	t	1714	w	1757	G	1802	l	1846	O	1889
V	1557	S	1595	q	1633	P	1672	u	1715	c	1758	H	1803	M	1847	P	1890
a	1558	T	1596	r	1634	Q	1673	A	1716	D	1759	I	1804	n	1848	Q	1891
b	1559	V	1597	s	1635	R	1674	B	1717	e	1760	K	1805	o	1849	R	1892
C	1560	A	1598	t	1636	S	1675	C	1718	f	1761	L	1806	p	1850	S	1893
d	1561	B	1599	u	1637	T	1676	D	1719	G	1762	M	1807	Q	1851	T	1894
e	1562	C	1600	a	1638	V	1677	E	1720	h	1763	N	1808	R	1852	U	1895
f	1563	D	1601	b	1639	a	1678	F	1721	j	1764	O	1809	S	1853	a	1896
g	1564	E	1602	c	1640	b	1679	G	1722	k	1765	P	1810	T	1854	b	1897
h	1565	F	1603	d	1641	c	1680	H	1723	l	1766	Q	1811	U	1855	c	1898
i	1566	G	1604	e	1642	d	1681	I	1724	m	1767	R	1812	a	1856	d	1899
k	1567	h	1605	f	1643	e	1682	K	1725	n	1768	S	1813	b	1857	e	1900
l	1568	I	1606	g	1644	f	1683	L	1726	O	1769	T	1814	c	1858	f	1901
m	1569	K	1607	h	1645	g	1684	M	1727	p	1770	U	1815	d	1859	g	1902
n	1570	L	1608	i	1646	h	1685	N	1728	C	1771	a	1816	e	1860	h	1903
o	1571	M	1609	B	1647	u	1686	O	1729	R	1772	b	1817	f	1861	i	1904
p	1572	N	1610	c	1648	k	1687	P	1730	S	1773	c	1818	g	1862	k	1905
q	1573	O	1611	d	1649	i	1688	Q	1731	T	1774	d	1819	h	1863	l	1906
r	1574	P	1612	R	1650	m	1689	R	1732	U	1775	e	1820	i	1864	m	1907
S	1575	Q	1613	S	1651	n	1690	S	1733	a	1776	f	1821	k	1865	n	1908
t	1576	R	1614	P	1652	o	1691	T	1734	b	1777	g	1822	l	1866	o	1909
u	1577	S	1615	q	1653	p	1692	V	1735	c	1778	h	1823	m	1867	p	1910
A	1578	T	1616	t	1654	q	1693	a	1736	d	1779	i	1824	n	1868	q	1911
B	1579	V	1617	s	1655	r	1694	b	1737	e	1780	k	1825	o	1869	r	1912
C	1580	a	1618	d	1656	s	1695	c	1738	f	1781	l	1826	p	1870	s	1913
D	1581	b	1619	B	1657	t	1696	d	1739	g	1782	m	1827	q	1871	t	1914
E	1582	C	1620	a	1658	u	1697	d	1739	h	1783	n	1828	r	1872	u	1915
F	1583	d	1621	B	1659	c	1698	e	1740	i	1784	o	1829	s	1873	a	1916
G	1584	e	1622	C	1660	s	1699	f	1741	k	1785	p	1830	t	1874	b	1917
H	1585	f	1623	D	1661	t	1700	g	1742	l	1786	q	1831	u	1875	c	1918
I	1586	g	1624	E	1662	ff	1701	h	1743	m	1787	r	1832	A	1876	d	1919
K	1587	h	1625	F	1663	g	1702	j	1744	n	1788	s	1833	B	1877	e	1920
L	1588	i	1626	G	1664	b	1703	k	1745	o	1789	t	1834	C	1878	f	1921
				H	1665	j	1704	l	1746	P	1790	u	1835	D	1879	g	1922
						k	1705	m	1747	q	1791	a	1836	E	1880	h	1923
						l	1706	n	1748	r	1792	B	1837	F	1881	i	1924
						n	1707	o	1749	s	1793	c	1838	G	1882	k	1925
								p	1750	t	1794	D	1839	H	1883	l	1926
								q	1751	u	1795	e	1840				
										A	1796						

DATE LETTER MARKS FOR
BIRMINGHAM & CHESTER

BIRMINGHAM ASSAY OFFICE DATE LETTERS

A 1773	a 1798	A 1824	A 1849	a 1875
B 1774	b 1799	B 1825	B 1850	b 1876
C 1775	c 1800	C 1826	C 1851	c 1877
D 1776	d 1801	D 1827	D 1852	d 1878
E 1777	e 1802	E 1828	E 1853	e 1879
F 1778	f 1803	F 1829	F 1854	f 1880
G 1779	g 1804	G 1830	G 1855	g 1881
H 1780	h 1805	H 1831	H 1856	h 1882
I 1781	i 1806	I 1832	I 1857	i 1883
K 1782	j 1807	K 1833	J 1858	k 1884
L 1783	k 1808	L 1834	K 1859	l 1885
M 1784	l 1809	M 1835	L 1860	m 1886
N 1785	m 1810	N 1836	M 1861	n 1887
O 1786	n 1811	O 1837	N 1862	o 1888
P 1787	o 1812	P 1838	O 1863	p 1889
Q 1788	p 1813	Q 1839	P 1864	q 1890
R 1789	q 1814	R 1840	Q 1865	r 1891
S 1790	r 1815	S 1841	R 1866	s 1892
T 1791	s 1816	T 1842	S 1867	t 1893
U 1792	t 1817	U 1843	T 1868	u 1894
V 1793	u 1818	V 1844	U 1869	v 1895
W 1794	v 1819	W 1845	V 1870	w 1896
X 1795	w 1820	X 1846	W 1871	x 1897
Y 1796	x 1821	Y 1847	X 1872	y 1898
Z 1797	y 1822	Z 1848	Y 1873	z 1899
	z 1823		Z 1874	

CHESTER ASSAY OFFICE DATE LETTERS

A 1701	A 1726	a 1751	a 1776	A 1797	A 1818	A 1839	a 1864
B 1702	B 1727	b 1752	b 1777	B 1798	B 1819	B 1840	b 1865
C 1703	C 1728	c 1753	c 1778	C 1799	C 1820	C 1841	c 1866
D 1704	D 1729	d 1754	d 1779	D 1800	D 1821	D 1842	d 1867
E 1705	E 1730	e 1755	e 1780	E 1801	D 1822	E 1843	e 1868
F 1706	F 1731	f 1756	f 1781	F 1802	E 1823	F 1844	f 1869
G 1707	G 1732	g 1757	g 1782	G 1803	F 1824	G 1845	g 1870
H 1708	H 1733	h 1758	h 1783	H 1804	G 1825	H 1846	h 1871
I 1709	I 1734	i 1759	i 1784	I 1805	H 1826	I 1847	i 1872
K 1710	K 1735	k 1760	k 1785	K 1806	I 1827	K 1848	k 1873
L 1711	L 1736	l 1761	l 1786	L 1807	K 1828	L 1849	l 1874
M 1712	M 1737	m 1762	m 1787	M 1808	L 1829	M 1850	m 1875
N 1713	N 1738	n 1763	n 1788	N 1809	M 1830	N 1851	n 1876
O 1714	O 1739	o 1764	o 1789	O 1810	N 1831	O 1852	o 1877
P 1715	P 1740	p 1765	p 1790	P 1811	O 1832	P 1853	p 1878
Q 1716	Q 1741	q 1766	q 1791	Q 1812	P 1833	Q 1854	q 1879
R 1717	R 1742	r 1767	r 1792	R 1813	Q 1834	R 1855	r 1880
S 1718	S 1743	s 1768	s 1793	S 1814	R 1835	S 1856	s 1881
T 1719	T 1744	t 1769	t 1794	T 1815	S 1836	T 1857	t 1882
U 1720	U 1745	tt 1770	u 1795	U 1816	T 1837	U 1858	u 1883
V 1721	V 1746	u 1771	y 1796	V 1817	U 1838	V 1859	A 1884
W 1722	W 1747	v 1772				W 1860	B 1885
X 1723	X 1748	w 1773				X 1861	C 1886
Y 1724	Y 1749	x 1774				Y 1862	D 1887
Z 1725	Z 1750	y 1775				Z 1863	E 1888
							F 1889

REPEATING WATCHES

Repeaters are those watches with an attachment added that will sound the time at the wish of the user. The repeating mechanism is operated by either a slide, plunger, or button in the case of the watch. There are basically five types of repeating mechanisms, some more common than others:

(1). **QUARTER REPEATERS**– The quarter repeater strikes the previous hour and quarter hour. In the older watches usually verge the striking is on a single bell attached to the inside of the case and the hour and quarter striking uses the same tone. There is first a series of hammer blows on the bell to indicate the hours, followed, after a short pause, by up to three twin strikes to denote the number of quarters elapsed. In later watches the striking is on wire gongs attached to the movement itself. The hours are struck on a single deep gong and the quarters on a higher-pitched gong followed by the deeper gong, producing a "ting-tang" sound.

(2). **HALF-QUARTER REPEATERS** -These strike the hours, the last quarter (ting-tang) and the previous half-quarter; i.e., seven and a half minutes. Half-quarter repeaters are mostly all verge escapement watches and are rarely seen by the average collector.

(3). **FIVE-MINUTE REPEATERS**– These fall into two types. One system is similar to the half-quarter repeater but follows the 1/4 "ting-tang" by a single higher-pitched strike for each 5 minute interval elapsed since the last quarter. The other system strikes the hours on a deep gong and follows this with a single higher note for each 5 minute period after the hour, omitting a 1/4 striking.

(4).**MINUTE REPEATERS**– The most complicated of the repeater is similar to the 1/4 repeater with the addition of the minutes. The minute repeater strikes the last recorded hour, quarter and minutes. At 10:52; a minute repeater will strike 10 deep chimes for the hour, 3 double chimes (deep & high) producing a "ting-tang for 3/4 hours & 7 high pitched chimes for 7 minutes (45+7=52).

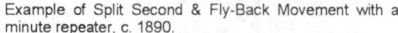
Example of Split Second & Fly-Back Movement with a minute repeater, c. 1890.

Example of English Clock Watch, 20 size, jeweled through hammers, minute repeater.

(5). **CLOCK WATCHES**– The clock watch is essentially a repeater with the features of a striking clock. Where as the above-mentioned repeaters are all operated by a plunger or slide which winds the repeating function and which runs down after the last strike, the clock watch is wound in the same way as the going train usually with a key and is operated by the touch of a button in the case. The repeat function can be operated many times before the watch needs to be rewound. The CLOCK part of the name comes from the watch also striking the hours and sometimes the quarters or half hour in passing. The clock watch is easily recognizable by the two winding holes in either the case or the dial.

In addition to the five types described above, the features of striking are sometimes found with not only two but three and even four gongs, this producing a peal of notes. These repeaters are known as **"CARILLONS."**

At the other end of the scale from the carillon is the "dumb" repeater. This strikes on a block of metal in the case or on the movement and is felt rather than heard. It is said that the idea was to produce a watch that would not embarrass its owner when he wished to know when to slip away from boring company. Although the dumb repeater is less desirable for the average collector, it certainly should not be avoided– Breguet himself made dumb repeaters.

Grande Sonnerie and **Petite Sonnerie** have been used since early 1700's. The clock watch striking system at first was called *Dutch Striking* because it was used in clock making in about 1665. The older system used striking on bells and struck the hours of the day. Then came the Dutch Striking which also struck the half-hour. This system later developed into a chiming function called **Grande Sonnerie** (grand strike or tone) which struck <u>both</u> the hour and quarter hours are struck ever 15 minutes (thus the hour is repeated ever 15 minutes). The **Petite Sonnerie** is a simpler variation of *Grande Sonnerie* in which the 1/4 hour are struck, but the hour is struck only at the o'clock (not repeated).

L.Audemars 2 train Grande or Petite Sonnerie minute repeating clock watch. Note: Marked on bezel sonne & silence at 12 o'clock also Petite Sonnerie & Grande Sonnerie at 6 o'clock, Ca. 1870's.

L. Audemars 2 train Grande or Petite Sonnerie 1/4 repeating clock watch. Note: The push button in the pendant that activate the repeating gongs, Ca. 1850.

A BIT OF HISTORY

Now that we have seen what repeaters are supposed to do, it might be in order to look briefly at their origins. Before the days of electric light, it was a major project to tell the time at night, since striking a tinderbox was said to have taken up to fifteen minutes to accomplish. Clocks, of course, had striking mechanisms, but they tended to keep the occupants of the house awake listening for the next strike. The repeating addition to the clock meant that the master of the house could silence the passing strike at night and, at his whim, simply pull a cord over his bed to activate the striking in another part of the house and thus waking everyone. To silence those members of the household who did not appreciate a clock booming out in the early hours of the morning, the horologists of the day turned their thoughts to the idea of a repeating watch.

The first mention of repeating watches is in the contest between Daniel Quare (1649-1724) and the Rev. Edward Barlow (1639-1719) to miniaturize the repeating action of a clock. Barlow, who for some reason had changed his name from Booth, was a theoretical horologist of outstanding ability. Barlow's design made for him by Thomas Tompion and Quare's watch were both submitted to King James II and the Privy Council for a decision as to whom should be granted a patent. The King chose Quare's design because the repeating mechanism was operated by a single push-button, whereas Barlow's required two. Quare was granted a patent in 1687. Barlow had had his share of fame earlier, however, with the invention of rack-striking for clocks in 1676.

Quare went into production with his new repeater watches, but changed the design to replace the push-button in the case with a pendant that could be pushed in. The first of these watches showed a fault that is still found on the cheaper repeaters of this century – that is, if the pendant was not pushed fully in, then the incorrect hours were struck. To overcome this problem, he invented the so-called "all-or-nothing" piece. This is a mechanism whereby if the pendant was not pushed fully home, then the watch would not strike at all.

The half-quarter appeared shortly after the all-or-nothing piece, and then by about 1710 the five-minute repeater was on the market. Some five years after this, a "deaf-piece" was often fitted to the watch. This was a slide or pin fitted to the case which, when activated, caused the hammers to be lifted away from the bell and had the same effect as a dumb repeater.

Sometime around 1730, Joseph Graham decided to dispense with the idea of a bell and arranged for the hammers to strike a dust-cover, thus making the watch slimmer and preventing dust from entering the pierced case.

About the middle of the century, the French master Le Roy carried the idea a stage further and dispensed with both bells and dust covers, and used a metal block which revolutionized the thickness of the repeating watch and introduced the dumb repeater. Breguet used wire gongs around 1789 and the pattern for the modern repeater was set. The minute repeater came into more common use after 1800, and earlier examples are definitely very rare, although it is known that Thomas Mudge made a complicated watch incorporating minute repeating for Ferdinand VI of Spain about 1750.

By the last quarter of the 1700s, Switzerland had gone for the repeater in a big way and the center of fine craftsmanship for complicated watches was in the Vallee de Joux. Here the principle of division of labor was highly refined and whole families were hard at work producing parts for repeating and musical watches. Since one person concentrated only on one part of the watch, it is hardly surprising that parts of excellent quality were turned out. The basic movements were then sold to watchmakers/finishers all over the Continent and even to England, where the principle of one man, one watch, among the stubborn majority eventually led to the downfall of what had once been the greatest watchmaking nation in history. Minute repeaters first appeared about 1830.

The greatest popularity of the repeater came, however, in the last quarter of the 1800s, when Switzerland turned them out in the tens of thousands. Although there were many different names on the dials of the watches, most seem to have been produced by the company "Le Phare" and only finished by the name on the dial. The production of repeaters in quantity seems to have ground to a finish in about 1921 due to (a) the invention of luminous dials and universal electric or gas lighting, and (b) a lack of watchmakers willing to learn the highly demanding skills. The interest in horology over the past decade has, however, revived the idea of the repeater and several companies in Switzerland are now producing limited editions of expensive models.

BUYING A REPEATER

Since so many repeaters seem to have been repaired at some time in the past by incompetent watchmakers, it is often too expensive a purchase if the buyer does not know what he is doing.

Rule One should be: if it does not work perfectly, avoid it like the plague unless a competent repairer first gives you an estimate which suits your pocket. All too often in the past the repairer was under the impression that metal grows with age and he has filed the teeth of a rack in order to get the full striking to work again. When it dawned on him that the problem was a worn bearing, the tooth was stretched with a punch and refiled, making it weak. It was then goodbye to a fine piece of craftsmanship.

A better quality repeater is usually one which is "jeweled to the hammers." This simply means that the hammers have jeweled bearing which can be seen by searching the movement for the hammers, locating the pivots around which they swing, and looking for the jeweled bearing in which they sit.

All repeaters have some system for regulating the speed of the repeating train. On the older fusee types, there was usually a rather primitive arrangement of a pinion in an eccentric bushing which could be turned to increase or decrease the depth of engagement of the pinion with the next wheel. Another system, a little better, uses an anchor and a toothed wheel as in an alarm clock. This system is usually located under the dial but can be detected by the buzzing sound it makes when the train is operated. The far superior system is the centrifugal governor which can be seen whizzing around in the top plate of the watch when the repeating action is operated. On the whole, the watch with the centrifugal governor is more desirable, although it must be mentioned that the Swiss turned out some inferior watches with this system.

Minute repeating movement by Dent of London. Minute repeating on two gongs and slide activated. Also note the watch has a split second chronograph, Ca. early 1900s.
IMPORTANT NOTE: If possible & it should be possible if you are investing a lot of money have a watchmaker check it.

Test the watch by operating the repeating train over a full hour, seeing that the quarters and minutes function correctly, then test each individual hour. Finally, set the hands to just before 1 o'clock (about 12:45) and test the striking. Any defect due to dirt or worn bearings will show up by the final blow(s), being either sluggish or not striking at all. If there is incorrect striking, have an expert look at it before you buy.

Try a partial operation of the slide or push-piece. If the watch has an all-or-nothing piece (as a reasonable grade movement should have), then the watch will not strike. Partial striking indicates either a low grade watch or a non-functioning all-or-nothing piece.

Note: Additional features such as chronograph functions, calendar, moon phase, etc., and will obviously affect the price of the watch.

Important note: Remember Rule One, if any function does not work, **BUYER BEWARE!**

TOURBILLON

Breguet invented the tourbillon in 1795. A tourbillon is a device designed to reduce the position errors of a watch. This device has the escape wheel, lever and balance wheel all mounted in a **carriage** of light frameworks. The carriage turns 360 degrees at regular intervals (usually once per minute). The fourth wheel is fixed, and is concentric with the carriage pinion and arbor. The escape wheel pinion meshes with the fourth wheel and will roll around the fixed fourth wheel. The escape wheel and lever are mounted on the carriage, and the third wheel drives the carriage pinion, turning the carriage once every minute. This rotation of the escapement will help reduce the position errors of a watch. One of the major objections is that the carriage and escapement weight mass must be stopped and started at each release of the escapement. The tourbillon design requires extreme skill to produce and is usually found on watches of high quality. Somewhat similar to the tourbillon is the karrusel, except it rotates about once per hour and the fourth wheel is not fixed. It also takes less skill to produce.

Charles Frodsham, TOURBILLON escapement, minute repeating, split second chronograph, about 600 to 700 tourbillons are known to exist. About 85 % of the English tourbillon movements were made by Albert Pellaton, Favre and Nicole Nielson & Co. as in this watch. The TOURBILLON escapement, is located near the top of this movement.

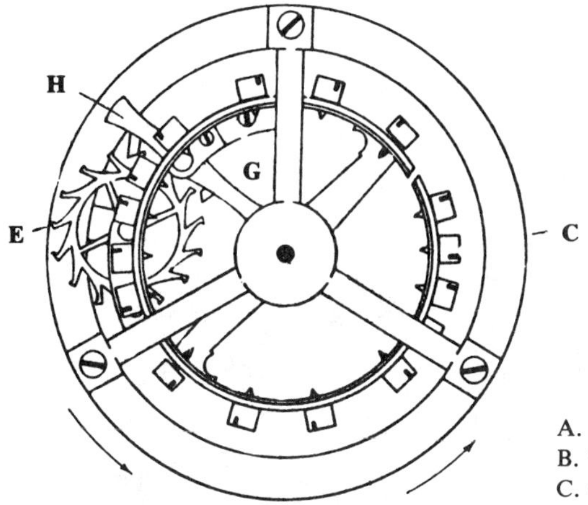

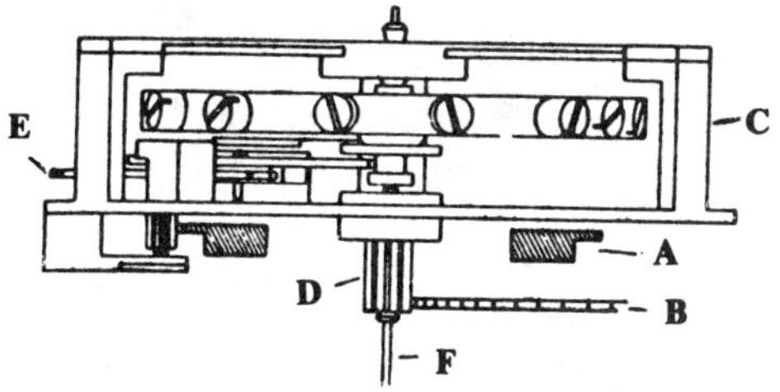

Tourbillon

A. Fixed fourth wheel
B. Third wheel
C. Carriage (one revolution per minute)
D. Carriage pinion
E. Escape Wheel & pinion
F. Arbor for seconds hand
G. Escape cock
H. Lever & pallets

MUSICAL WATCHES
(Three basic types)

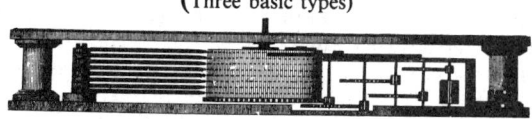

Stacked Tooth

Disc Type with individual teeth

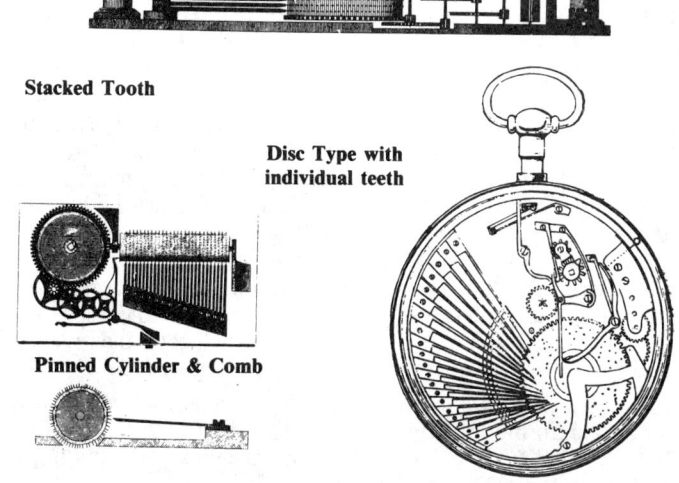

Pinned Cylinder & Comb

Where Watches Are Born

A trip to *"Where Watches Are Born,"* is recommended. In this area persists a strong cottage industry where in every small village and almost every street corner, a famous watch-maker or watch factory was born, and after this modern age of electronic and quartz watches still some survive. This area is the Jura Mountain chain which borders the French & Swiss countries.

A micro-techniques route may start at Montbeliard, France and go south to Geneva Switzerland. This micro-techniques route adjacent to the French & Swiss borders should include Factories, Museums, Workshops, and *Antique watch shops galore.* In Besancon, France its Fine Arts Museum with a collection that includes the LeRoy watch that has 25 indicators in addition to the time, also the Museum of Time to be finished in the year 2000, this is also home of the Lip watch factory. Next to Beaucourt, France to see the Frederic Japy Museum. Japy, a very productive maker which at one time produced 3,500 Ebauches a month. On to Valdahon and Morteau (Villers-le-Lac) and visit the Museum of Clock and Watch Making (Musee de Horlogerie du Haut-Doubs). Next LeLocle, Switzerland, home of Cyma, Ulysse Nardin, Tissot and Zenith also see the Watch Museum of the Chateau des Monts. Then La Chaux-de-Fonds home of Corum, Ebel, Girard-Perregaux and many more watch factories. Also visit the International Museum of Horology with a wealth of items also near by Antique Watch & Clock shops. In Neuchatel the Art Museum with the Jaquet Droz collection of mechanical dolls. Now go North to the area of Solothurn, Grenchen & Biel (Bienne) where the Rolex, Omega movement factory and many more as Mido, Urban Jurgensen, Swatch, Breitling, Movado and ETA factory. Further south the Vallee de Joux to see watch factories as Jaeger-LeCoultre, also smaller watch-makers as Daniel Roth & Philippe Dufour in LeSentier. Near by Le Brassus to see Audemars Piguet, Blancpain, and Breguet. On south to Geneva home of Patek Philippe, Rolex, Vacheron Constantin and many more also the see the Clock and Watch Museum Geneva. You may wish to start in Geneva and reverse the above trip. (*Basel 99 Watch Fair is from April 29 to May 6, 1999.*)

NOTE: **Nick Lerescu of Advantage Tours** has a Horological tour & seminar each year in late Spring or early Summer. *ADVANTAGE TOURS - P.O. BOX 936 - HIGHLAND LAKES, NJ 07422* or call Nick at 1-800-262-4284. Ask about the trip for the TIME TRIPPERS.

EUROPEAN POCKET WATCH LISTINGS
Pricing at Collectable Fair Market Retail Level
(Complete Watches Only)

Unless otherwise noted, watches listed in this section are priced at the collectable **fair market** retail level and as **complete** watches having an original 14k gold-filled case with an original white enamel single sunk dial, and the entire original movement in good working order with no repairs needed. Watches listed as 14k and 18k are solid gold cases. Coin or silveroid type and stainless steel cases will be listed as such. Keywind and keyset pocket watches are listed as having original coin silver cases. Dollar type watches, or low cost production watches, are listed as having a base metal type case and a composition dial.

The prices shown were averaged from dealers' lists just prior to publication and are an indication of the retail level or what collectors will pay. Prices are provided in three categories: average condition, extra fine, and mint condition, and are shown in whole dollar amounts only. The values listed are a guide for the *collectable* retail level and are provided for your information only. Dealers will not necessarily pay FULL RETAIL PRICE. Prices listed are for watches with *original cases* and *dials*.

🕐 Descriptions and serial number ranges listed for early watches cannot be considered 100 percent accurate due to the manner in which records were kept by these companies. Watches were not necessarily sold in the exact order of manufactured date.

Important Notice. All of the information, including valuations, in this book has been compiled from the most reliable sources, and every effort has been made to eliminate errors and questionable data. Nevertheless, the possibility of error, in a work of such immense scope, always exists. The publisher or authors will not be held responsible for losses which may occur in the purchase, sale, statements of its advertisers, or other transaction of items, because of information contained herein. Readers who feel they have discovered errors are invited to write and inform us, so they may be corrected in subsequent editions.

The Complete Price Guide to Watches goal is to stimulate the orderly exchange of Watches between "*buyers*" and "*sellers*".

🕐 WATCH terminology or communication in this book has evolved over the years, in search of better and more precise language with a effort to improve, purify, adjust itself and make it easier to understand.

INFORMATION NEEDED

This price guide is interested in any facts and information you might have that should possibly be considered for future editions. Documented facts are needed. Please send photo or **sources** of information to:

COOKSEY SHUGART
P.O. BOX 3147
CLEVELAND, TENNESSEE
37320-3147

(WHEN CORRESPONDING, PLEASE INCLUDE A ✉
SELF-ADDRESSED, STAMPED ENVELOPE.)

AGASSIZ
Swiss

Auguste Agassiz of Saint Imier & Geneva started manufacturing quality watches in 1832. They later became interested in making a flat style watch which proved to be very popular. Some of these movements can be fitted inside a $20 gold piece.

The company was inherited by Ernest Francillion who built a factory called **Longines**. The Longines factory continued the Agassiz line until the Great Depression.

Agassiz, 43mm, 17 jewels, World Time, 42 Cities, ca. 1940.   Agassiz, 40mm, 21 jewels, 8 day with wind indicator.

TYPE – DESCRIPTION	Avg	Ex-Fn	Mint
Early, KW KS, Swiss bar Mvt., time only, Ca.1870, Silver case ...	$65	$85	$135
Time only, gold, 40–44mm, 10-12 size, OF	175	225	325
HC	225	275	400
Time only, gold, 45- 50mm, OF	195	250	350
Time only, gold & **enamel**, 45- 50mm, OF	450	650	950
HC	500	700	1,100
Cole's Resilient Escapement, 20J, gold, 45mm, Of	800	900	1,200

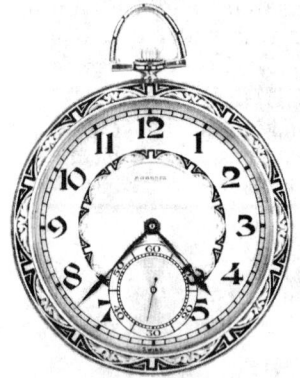 

Agåssiz, Time only, gold & enamel, 45- 50mm, OF   Agassiz, $20 gold 22 / 18K coin watch, Ca. 1950s.

Watches listed in this book are priced at the collectable fair market value at the retail level, as complete watches having an original case, an original white enamel dial, and with the entire original movement in good working order with no repairs needed, unless otherwise noted.

TYPE – DESCRIPTION	Avg	Ex-Fn	Mint
8 day, 21J, wind indicator, **18K gold,** 44mm, OF	$600	$800	$1,400
14K gold, OF	500	700	1,000
S. S. case, OF	275	325	425
$20 gold 22 to 18K coin watch, 34mm, Ca. 1950s.	1,600	1,800	2,300
World Time, 42 Cities, gold, 43mm, OF	4,000	4,800	6,000
Chronograph, gold, 45-50mm, register, OF	475	550	650
HC	675	750	850
Split second chronograph, register, gold, OF	700	825	1,000
HC	800	925	1,200
1/4 hr. repeater, gold, 46-52mm, OF	650	750	1,000
HC	1,000	1,250	1,600
Minute repeater, gold, 46-52mm, OF	1,500	1,800	2,500
OF w/chrono.	1,800	2,100	2,800
Minute repeater, gold, 46-52mm, HC	2,000	2,400	3,100
HC w/chrono.	2,200	2,600	3,300

ASSMANN
Glasshute

Julius Assmann began producing watches with the help of Adolf Lange in 1852. His watches are stylistically similar to those produced by Lange. Later on he adopted his own lever style. Assmann made highly decorative watches for the South American market that are highly regarded by some collectors.

Assmann, 50mm, 19 jewels, diamond cap jewels, gold jewel settings, gold lever escapement, serial number 3,086, BRIDGE MODEL, ca. 1875.

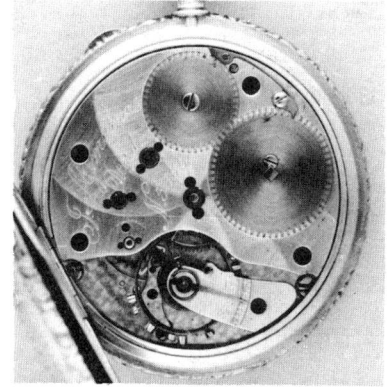

Assmann, 50mm, 19 jewels, diamond cap jewels, gold jewel settings, gold lever escapement, serial number 3,739, ca. 1877.

TYPE – DESCRIPTION	Avg	Ex-Fn	Mint
Time only, 45- 50mm, **2nd Quality,** 14K OF	$1,200	$1,600	$2,200
14K HC	1,400	1,800	2,400
Chronograph, **1st Quality,** 55mm, 18K OF	4,000	5,500	8,500
18K HC	5,000	7,000	8,900
Split second chronograph, **1st Quality,** 57mm, 18K OF	6,000	9,000	15,000
18K HC	8,000	12,000	20,000
1/4 hr. repeater, gold, 50-55mm, OF	7,500	9,000	12,000
HC	8,500	10,000	14,000
Minute repeater, gold, 50-55mm, OF	14,000	17,000	22,000
HC	15,000	18,000	24,000
Perp. moonph. cal. w/min. repeater, gold, HC	50,000	65,000	90,000

Some models and grades are not included. Their values can be determined by comparing with similar age, size, metal content, style, models and grades listed.

AUDEMARS, PIGUET & CIE
Swiss

Audemars, Piguet & Cie was founded in 1875 by Jules Audemars and Edward Piguet, both successors to fine horological families. This company produced many fine high grade and complicated watches, predominantly in nickel and, with a few exceptions, fully jeweled. Their complicated watches are sought after more than the time only pocket and wrist watches.

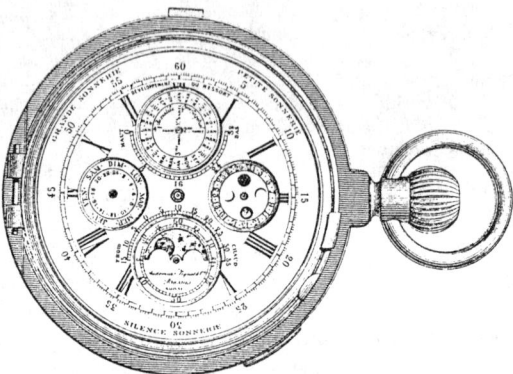

Audemars Piguet, 40mm, about 10 size, 19 jewels, cabochon on winding stem, Platinum, OF.

Audemars Piguet, 50mm, hunting case, Grand & Petite Sonnerie, minute repeater on demand, split-second Chronograph, Perpetual Calendar, wind indicator & thermometer, taken from a French ad, ca. 1900.

TYPE – DESCRIPTION	Avg	Ex-Fn	Mint
Early, KW KS, Swiss bar Mvt., time only, Ca.1870, **Gold case**	$350	$450	$600
Time only, gold, 40-44mm, OF	650	775	1,000
HC	750	875	1,100
Platinum, OF	800	900	1,200
Time only, gold, 45- 50mm, OF	800	900	1,200
HC	900	1,000	1,300
Jumping hour w/ day-date-month, gold, 43mm., ca. 1925.	4,000	6,500	8,500
Rising Arms (Bras en L'Air), 44mm, one arm points to the hours & the other to the minute, 18K, OF	6,000	8,000	12,000
Chronograph, gold, 45-50mm, OF	2,000	3,000	4,000
HC	2,500	3,000	4,500
OF w/register	2,500	3,000	4,500
HC w/register	3,500	4,000	5,000

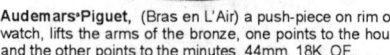

Audemars Piguet, (Bras en L'Air) a push-piece on rim of watch, lifts the arms of the bronze, one points to the hour and the other points to the minutes, 44mm, 18K, OF.

Audemars Piguet, Perpetual moon phase calendar, Astronomic watch showing the moon phases, and perpetual calendar showing day, date, & month, Ca.1920s.

AUDEMARS PIGUET, 46mm, 36 jewels, minute repeater, split-second chronograph, serial # 3853, Ca.1888.

AUDEMARS PIGUET, 46mm, Min. repeater, moon-phase, Chronograph, 18K, HC, Ca.1928.

TYPE – DESCRIPTION	Avg	Ex-Fn	Mint
Split second chronograph, gold, 45-52mm, OF	$3,000	$4,500	$5,000
HC	3,500	4,500	6,000
OF w/register	4,000	5,000	7,000
HC w/register	5,000	6,000	8,000
5 minute repeater, gold, 46-52mm, OF	3,500	4,000	5,000
HC	4,000	4,500	5,750
Minute repeater, gold, 46-52mm, OF	4,500	5,500	7,000
HC	5,000	6,000	8,000
OF w/chrono.	4,750	5,750	7,500
HC w/chrono.	5,000	6,000	8,000
OF w/chrono. & register	5,250	6,250	8,500
HC w/chrono. & register	5,250	6,750	9,000
OF w/split chrono. & register	7,000	10,000	15,000
HC w/split chrono. & register	8,000	12,000	18,000
Perpetual moonphase calendar, gold, OF	7,000	9,000	12,000
HC	8,000	10,000	13,000
Perp. moonphase cal. w/min.repeater, chronograph, gold, OF	30,000	36,000	45,000
HC	32,000	38,000	48,000

PRODUCTION TOTALS

Date- Serial #	Date- Serial #	Date- Serial #	Date- Serial #	Date- Serial #
1882 - 2,000	1905 - 9,500	1925 - 33,000	1945 - 48,000	1965 - 90,000
1890 - 4,000	1910-13,000	1930 - 40,000	1950 - 55,000	1970-115,000
1895 - 5,350	1915-17,000	1935 - 42,000	1955 - 65,000	1975-160,000
1900 - 6,500	1920-25,000	1940 - 44,000	1960 - 75,000	1980-225,000

REPEATER IDENTIFICATION

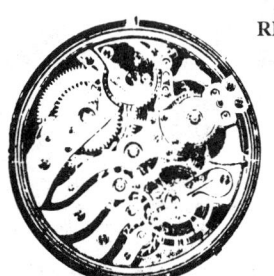

Calibre SMV

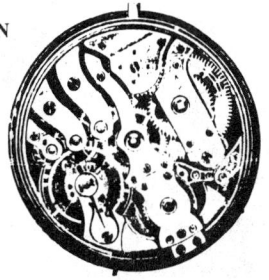

Calibre SMS

BARRAUD & LUNDS
LONDON (1750-1929)

The Barraud family (of which) there were several makers, one of them being Paul Philip Barraud. Paul was in the trade at 86 Cornhill from about 1796 to 1813. His sons John and James, traded at 41 Cornhill as Barraud & Sons from 1813 till 1838. After 1838 the firm became known as Barraud & Lunds. About 1885 their address was 49 Cornhill and 14 Bishopsgate about 1895. Advertised "machine-made" watches in about 1880 until 1929.

TYPE – DESCRIPTION	Avg	Ex-Fn	Mint
Time only, gold, 45- 50mm, OF	$450	$550	$700
HC	550	650	850
Time only, gold, 45- 50mm, OF, (wind indicator)	550	650	800
Chronograph, gold, 45-50mm, OF	850	1,000	1,400
HC	900	1,100	1,500
Split second chronograph, gold, 45-52mm, OF	1,500	1,800	2,250
HC	1,600	1,900	2,400
1/4 hr. repeater, gold, 46-52mm, OF	1,000	1,250	1,550
HC	1,250	1,450	1,750
Minute repeater, gold, 46-52mm, OF	1,800	2,200	2,750
HC	2,000	2,400	3,200
OF w/chrono.	2,200	2,600	3,500
HC w/chrono.	2,400	2,800	4,000

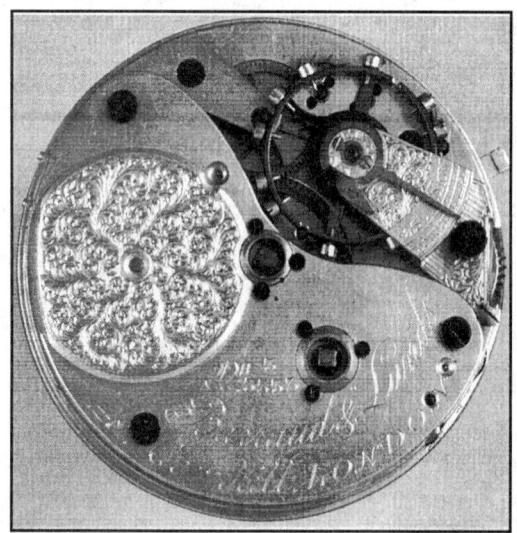

Barraud & Lunds, English lever and movement signed *"Barraud & Lunds 49 Cornhill London 3/3333"*, 3/4 plate with a fusee and chain, stem wind, Note: Engraved and raised barrel. With a white enamel signed *"Barraud & Lunds-Cornhill London 3/3333"*, with wind-indicator, Ca. 1886.

⊕*Some models and grades are not included. Their values can be determined by comparing with similar age, size, metal content, style, models and grades listed.

⊕ Watches listed in this book are priced at the collectable fair market value at the retail level, as complete watches having an original case, an original white enamel dial, and with the entire original movement in good working order with no repairs needed, unless otherwise noted.

BARWISE
LONDON

John Barwise a leading watchmaker born 1790 died 1843. Dealer at 29 St.Martin's Lane, and with Weston Barwise from 1820 to 1842. John Barwise was also the chairman of British Watch Co., 1842 to 1843. The firm moved back to 29 St.Martin's Lane, 1845 to 1851, and 69 Piccadilly from 1856 to 1875.

TYPE – DESCRIPTION	Avg	Ex-Fn	Mint
Time only, gold, 45- 50mm, OF	$950	$1,150	$1,400
HC	1,200	1,400	1,800
Chronograph, gold, 45-50mm, OF	1,200	1,400	1,800
HC	1,500	1,700	2,000
Split second chronograph, gold, 45-52mm, OF	2,000	2,300	2,700
HC	3,000	3,200	3,500
7-1/2 Min. Repeater, gold, 46-52mm, 18K-OF	4,800	5,200	6,000
1/4 hr. repeater, gold, 46-52mm, OF	1,800	2,000	2,300
HC	2,500	2,800	3,200
Minute repeater, gold, 46-52mm, OF	3,000	3,500	4,500
HC	3,500	4,000	5,000
OF w/chrono.	3,500	4,000	5,000
HC w/chrono.	4,000	5,250	6,000
Dent Chronometer, gold, 48-52mm, OF	6,000	6,600	7,500
HC	7,000	8,000	9,000

BARWISE, Rare 7-1/2 MINUTE REPEATER with ruby cylinder escapement, open face, key wind & key set, Signed BARWISE LONDON No. 5369, Ca. 1800.

COMPARISON OF WATCH SIZES

U. S. A.	EUROPEAN
10-12 SIZE	40—44 MM
16 SIZE	45—48 MM
18 SIZE	50—52 MM

J. W. BENSON
London (1749)

The Benson signature is found on many medium to high grade gilt movements. Factory English machine-made market circa 1870-1930. "Makers to the Admiralty" & "By Warrant to H.M. the Queen" can be found signed on the movements. Named models ("Bank", "Field", "Ludgate")about 16 or 14 size.

TYPE – DESCRIPTION	Avg	Ex-Fn	Mint
KWKS, side lever, Silver hallmarked, 48-52mm, OF, C. 1875	$125	$150	$185
SW, 15-17J, side lever, ("Bank", "Field", "Ludgate") Silver, 49mm, Demi-hunter, C. 1870-1930	150	175	225
Fusee, lever escape., high grade, SW, 18K, 54mm, OF, C.1875	600	700	900
Fusee w/indicator, KWKS, side lever, Silver, 54mm, OF, C.1870	450	550	750
Fusee, w/indicator, free spring, lever escape.,18K, 50mm, OF	750	950	1,200
Time only, gold, 45-48mm, OF..................................	450	550	700
HC..	550	650	800
Split second chronograph, gold, 45-52mm, OF..........................	3,000	3,500	4,750
HC	3,200	4,000	5,000
Minute repeater, gold, 46-52mm, OF.............................	2,800	3,400	4,400
HC	3,000	3,600	4,600

J. W. Benson, 13-15 jewels, 3/4 plate, "The Field, Best London Make, By Warrant to H.M. the Queen" engraved on Movement. Serial Number C8764.

J. W. Benson, 45mm, Split Second Chronograph, 20 jewels, 3/4 plate, free sprung, hunting case, Ca. 1890.

COMPARISON OF WATCH SIZES

U. S. A.	EUROPEAN
10-12 SIZE	40—44 MM
16 SIZE	45—48 MM
18 SIZE	50—54 MM

MILLIMETERS 10   20   30   40   50

BOVET
FRENCH & SWISS

Edouard Bovet starts a company in the village of Fleuier Switzerland about 1818 and another firm in Besancon in 1832. The Bovet firm specialized in watches for the chinese market. The Bovet Companies was purchased by Leuba Freres (Cesar & Charles). Bovet also signed watches "TEVOB" making his signature easily read by the Chinese. The new Bovet firm discontinued making watches for the Chinese market. The company was purchased by the Ullmann & Co. in 1918.

Above: *Superior quality* finely painted turquoise enamel watch set in pearls, 18K, 58mm, time only, Duplex Escapement, signed BOVET, Ca. 1845.

TYPE – DESCRIPTION	Avg	Ex-Fn	Mint
Time only, LEVER escapement, KW, Silver, 58mm, OF	$200	$275	$375
HC	225	325	450
Time only, DUPLEX escapement, KW, Silver, 58mm, OF	225	300	400
HC	250	350	475
Time only, DUPLEX escapement, KW, GOLD, 58mm, OF	700	900	1,200
HC	800	1,000	1,300
Enamel, Time only, DUPLEX escap., KW, Silver, 58mm, OF	900	1,100	1,500
HC	1,000	1,200	1,600
(below *SUPERIOR QUALITY* Gold & Enamel, on OF & HC watches)			
Gold &Enamel, Time only, Duplex escap., KW, 55- 58mm, OF	6,500	9,500	14,000
HC	9,500	12,500	17,500

⊕ Some models and grades are not included. Their values can be determined by comparing with similar age, size, metal content, style, models and grades listed.

⊕ Watches listed in this book are priced at the collectable retail level, as complete watches having an original case, an original dial, and with the entire original movement in good working order with no repairs needed.

ABRAHAM-LOUIS BREGUET
also BREGUET ET FILS
Paris

Abraham-Louis Breguet, one of the worlds
most celebrated watchmakers.

ABRAHAM-LOUIS BREGUET was born at Neuchatel in 1747 and died in
1823. He was perhaps the greatest horologist of all time in terms of design,
elegance, and innovation. He is responsible for the development of the tourbil-
lion, the perpetual calendar, the shock-proof parachute suspension, the isochronal overcoil, and many other improvements. It is difficult to include him in this
section because of the complexity surrounding identification of his work which
was frequently forged, and the fact that so many pieces produced by his shop
were unique. Suffice it to say that the vast majority of watches one encounters
bearing his name were either marketed only by his firm or are outright fakes
made by others for the export market. Much study is required for proper
identification.

Abraham-Louis Breguet, PRODUCTION TOTALS

Date —	Serial #	Date —	Serial #
1795 —	150	1815 —	2700
1800 —	500	1820 —	3500
1805 —	1500	1825 —	4000
1810 —	2000	1830 —	4500

Abraham-Louis Breguet died on 17th day of September, 1823. The Breguet
firm continues today with the tradition started by Abraham-Louis. At first in the
hands of his immediate successors and later under the guidance of the "Browns",
when the interest of the Breguet family diversified. Today the firm of Breguet
continues to produce high quality and exclusive range of watches based on the
classic style that has made the Breguet name so famous. The Company makes
jewelry, wrist watches, clocks, as well as, fine pocket watches. They produce
choice examples, with complicated movements and should be signed on dial,
case and movement.

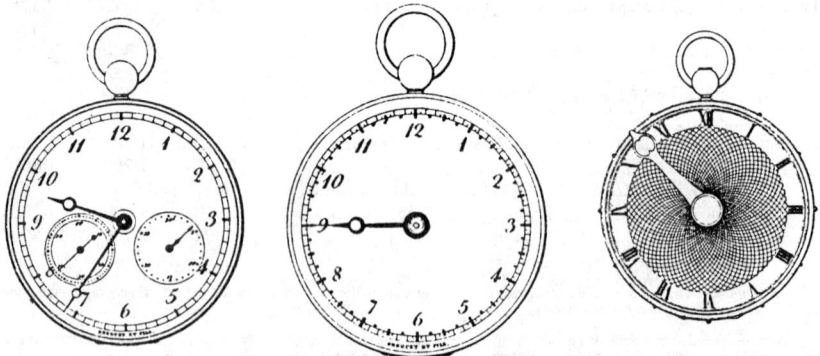

Above: Reprints (Reduced) issued by the firm Breguet Ca. 1820s.

60 to 62mm. Example of Breguet **SOUSCRIPTION** style face and movement. Gilt movement with central winding arbor, balance with parachute suspension, HANGING ruby cylinder escapement. White enamel dial with secret signature at 12 o'clock. NOTE: Winds from center either front or back, also most had a silver case and gold bezel. Total production of SOUSCRIPTION style watches about 1,600. "**The above Example is actual size**".

TYPE – DESCRIPTION	Avg	Ex-Fn	Mint
1/4 repeater, Breguet & Fils, silver, OF, fusee, 54mm C.1820	$500	$700	$1,000
1/4 repeater, Breguet & Fils, fusee, 18K, 54mm, OF, C.1820	800	1,000	1,300
1/4 repeater, Breguet & Fils, verge, automated, 18K, 55mm, OF	3,500	4,000	5,500
Ruby cylinder, parachute, KW, 18K, 49mm, OF, C. 1800	3,000	4,000	5,500
Repeater Horologer De La Marine , silver dial, ruby cylinder escapement	8,000	10,000	14,000
Min. repeater, split sec. chrono., min. register 18K, 2 tone case, 53mm, OF, C. 1945	15,000	17,000	24,000
Jump hr.w/ aperture, revolving min.disc, 18K, 46mm, OF, C.1930	4,500	5,500	6,750
Hanging ruby cylinder, enamel "souscription" dial, center wind, all original,18K, 60 to 62mm, OF, C. 1800	8,000	10,000	14,000
Montre'a tact, 6J ruby cylinder, pearl & enamel case, 18K, 36mm, C. 1810	15,000	18,000	24,000

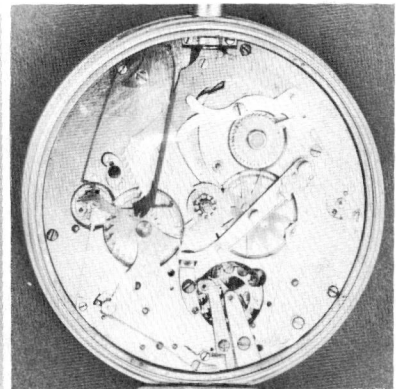

Abraham Louis Breguet, repeating, ruby cylinder watch. Left: gilt movement with standing barrel. Note jeweled parachute suspension. Right: Dial side of movement, repeating train with exposed springs.

Important repeater Horologer De La Marine by Breguet. Left: Guilloche silver dial with roman numerals and typical Breguet hands. Right: Gilt brass movement with ruby cylinder escapement and triple arm balance.

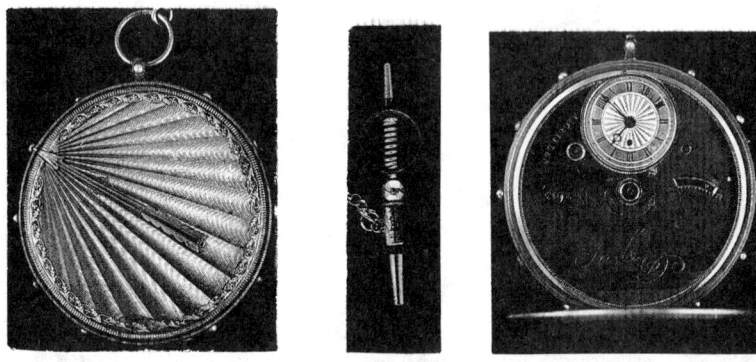

Breguet "montre a tact" or touch time watch, 36mm. Case embellished with 12 pearls for tactile hours (Braille style watch). The arrow on case revolves. Souscription movement with 6 jewels, central barrel, ruby cylinder escapement.

BREGUET, 51mm, chronograph with perpetual calendar and minute repeater. Note sector style wind indicator.

BREGUET, 53mm, minute repeating, split-second chronograph. Chronograph activated by crown and button on band. Repeater activated by slide.

Generic Breguet, 45-48mm, ruby cylinder, KW KS, Swiss bar Mvt., time only, Ca.1830, 18K case

TYPE – DESCRIPTION	Avg	Ex-Fn	Mint
Min. repeater, perpetual calendar chronograph, wind indicator, 18K, 51mm, OF, C. 1932	$43,000	$50,000	$64,000
Min. repeater, split sec. chronograph, two tone gold case, 53mm, C.1948	12,000	15,000	18,500
Perpetual calendar, thin digital watch, 18K case, 45mm	7,500	8,500	12,000
Tactile braille watch, 18K enamel case w/ pearls, 36mm	15,000	18,000	24,000
Small keyless watch, platinum balance, gold case, 18mm	14,000	16,000	22,000
Early, KW / KS, **generic Swiss bar Mvt.**, time only, Ca.1830, 18K case, (NOT TRUE BREGUET)	350	400	550

BULOVA
U. S. A. & Swiss

Bulova was a leader in the mass production of quality wristwatches; however, their pocket watch output was small and limited to mostly basic time only varieties. The ultra thin "Phantom" was one of their limited production models.

Joseph Bulova started with a wholesale jewelry business in 1875. The first watches were marketed in the early 1920s. Bulova manufactured millions of movements in their own Swiss plant. The company cased these movements in the U.S.A. and imports all production today. The ACCUTRON was introduced in 1960 and sold about 5 million watches.

Some models and grades are not included. Their values can be determined by comparing with similar age, size, metal content, style, models and grades listed.

Watches listed in this book are priced at the collectable retail level, as complete watches having an original case, an original dial, and with the entire original movement in good working order with no repairs needed.

TYPE – DESCRIPTION	Avg	Ex-Fn	Mint
GF, 17J, 42mm, OF, C. 1940	$50	$60	$85
Rose GF, art deco, 17J, 42mm, OF, C. 1930	70	90	125
14K, 17J, 42mm, OF, C. 1950	200	225	275
Platinum, ultra-thin, "Phantom", 18J, 43mm, OF, C. 1920	500	600	750
Accutron, date, GF, 43mm, HC	135	150	175

BULOVA Accutron, with date, gold filled hunting case, about 43mm, ca. 1970s.

HENRY CAPT, 52mm, 32 jewels, minute repeater, serial number 34,711, ca. 1900.

HENRY CAPT
Geneva

Henry Daniel Capt of Geneva was an associate of Isaac Daniel Piguet for about 10 years from 1802 to 1812. Their firm produced quality watches and specialized in musicals, repeaters and chronometers. By 1844, his son was director of the firm and around 1880 the firm was sold to Gallopin.

TYPE – DESCRIPTION	Avg	Ex-Fn	Mint
Early, KW KS, Swiss bar Mvt., time only, Ca.1870, Silver case	$125	$150	$200
Early, KW KS, Swiss bar Mvt., time only, Ca.1870, Gold	400	500	800
Time only, gold, 45- 50mm, OF	500	600	750
HC	600	700	850
Chronograph, gold, 45-50mm, register, OF	750	850	1,000
HC	800	900	1,100
Split second chronograph, gold, 45-52mm, register, OF	1,000	1,200	1,500
HC	1,100	1,300	1,600
1/4 hr. repeater, gold, 46-52mm, OF	1,400	1,600	1,900
HC	1,500	1,800	2,200
Minute repeater, gold, 46-52mm, OF	2,000	2,800	3,500
HC	2,200	3,100	4,000
OF, w/split chrono.	5,000	6,500	8,000
HC, w/split chrono.	6,000	7,500	9,000
Perpetual moonphase calendar, gold, OF	7,500	8,500	10,000
HC	8,000	9,000	11,000
Perp. moonphase cal., w/min.repeater, gold, OF	18,000	25,000	30,000
Perp. moonphase cal. ,w/min.repeater and chrono., gold, HC	20,000	35,000	40,000

🕐 Characteristics of watches differ for the same age of both case and movement, because these features vary it may not be accurate to date a watch by one single influence. Example: the second hand was _not_ commonly found on watches before 1750, but common about 1800. The first second hand appeared in 1665 and another in 1690. Therefore statements are broad rather than absolute.

CARTIER

Paris

CARTIER was a famous artisan from Paris who first made powder flasks. By the mid-1840s the family became known as the finest goldsmiths of Paris. Around the turn of the century the Cartier firm was designing watches and in 1904 the first wrist watches were being made. In 1917 Cartier created a watch design that was to become known as the tank-style case. The tank-style case was made to look like tank caterpillars of the U. S. A and is still popular today.

Cartier, 52mm, 40 jewels, triple complicated-perpetual calendar, minute repeater, split-second chronograph.

Cartier, 45mm, 18 jewels, flat, astronomic with moon phases triple calendar, platinum watch, Ca. 1930s.

TYPE – DESCRIPTION	Avg	Ex-Fn	Mint
Time only, gold, 40- 44mm, signed E.W.C., OF	$1,400	$1,650	$2,000
HC	1,500	1,750	2,200
Time only, gold, 45- 50mm, signed E.W.C., OF	1,600	1,800	2,200
HC	1,750	2,000	2,400
Flat, astronomic w/ moon ph. triple calendar, signed E.W.C., platinum,OF	10,000	12,000	15,000
Chronograph, gold, 45-50mm, signed E.W.C., OF	3,500	4,200	5,000
5 minute repeater, gold, 46-52mm, signed E.W.C., OF	4,000	5,000	6,500
HC	4,500	5,500	7,000
Minute repeater, gold, 46-52mm, signed E.W.C., OF	7,500	9,500	12,000
HC	8,000	10,000	12,500
Triple complicated, astronomical moon ph. perpetual triple cal., signed E.W.C. min. repeater, split sec. chron. w/min. recorder, 18 K	70,000	90,000	120,000

Above: **Cartier**, 43mm, 18 jewels, dial has raised gold Arabic numbers, 18k, OF, Ca.1930s.

T. F. COOPER
Liverpool

The Cooper name is usually marked on inner dust covers which protect Swiss ebauche keywind bar movements. Numerous watches produced from 1850-1890 are found with this Liverpool name. The T.F. Cooper & later the T.W. Cooper firms supplied the U.S. market with low cost silver-cased keywinds.

TYPE – DESCRIPTION	Avg	Ex-Fn	Mint
KWKS, "full-jeweled", Silver, 44-48mm, OF, Ca.1850-1875	$75	$90	$125
KWKS, 15J, Silver, 46-50mm, HC, Ca.1850-1870	85	110	150
KW, Fusee, lever, silver, 48mm, OF, C. 1870	130	150	185
KW, 15J, metal dust cover, gilt dial, 18K, OF, C. 1875	275	300	375
KW, 15J, Lady's, 18K, 44mm, fancy HC, C. 1875	300	325	400
KW, gold dial, bar movement w/side lever escap., parachute shock on balance, 18K, 50mm, OF, C. 1870	285	325	400
Captains double time, 15J, KWKS, silver, 48mm, OF, C.1865	400	465	550

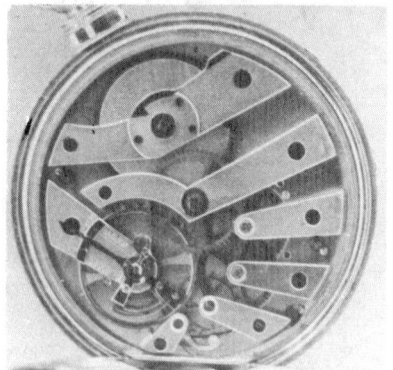  

T.F. Cooper, KW, bar movement with right angle lever escapement, parachute shock on balance, 18K, 50mm, OF, Ca. 1852.

Courvoisier, Freres, 37mm, cylinder escap. with wolf-tooth winding, front & back view, 18K & enamel HC, Ca.1880.

COURVOISIER, Freres
SWISS (La Chaux de Fonds)

Started as Courvoisier & Cie in 1810-11, by 1845 Henri-Louis and Philippe-Auguste became owners. In 1852 name changes to Courvoisier, Freres. The watches circa 1810 are signed with the older signature. They exported very ornate pieces for the Chinese market (Lepine bar caliber).They also obtained a Chinese *TRADEMARK* for their signature.

TYPE – DESCRIPTION	Avg	Ex-Fn	Mint
Time only, KW, SILVER, 45- 50mm, OF	$125	$150	$200
HC	135	175	225
Time only, KW, Gold, 45- 50mm, OF	350	450	575
HC	400	500	625
Captains Watch, SILVER, 2 hour dials, 2 trains, Key Wind, center seconds, 50mm, OF	500	575	675
HC, (SAME AS ABOVE)	550	625	725
Captains Watch, GOLD, 2 hour dials, 2 trains, Key Wind, center seconds, 50mm, OF	900	1,000	1,200
HC, (SAME AS ABOVE)	1,000	1,150	1,350
1/4 hr. repeater, SILVER, 46-52mm, OF	600	750	900
1/4 hr. repeater, GOLD, 46-52mm, OF	850	1,000	1,250
Detent* Chronometer, gold, 48-52mm, OF	2,000	2,200	2,500
HC	2,200	2,400	2,700

DENT (M. F. & Co.)
LONDON

Edward John Dent, born in 1790 died in 1853. Edward worked for J.R. Arnold, at 84 Strand, from 1830-1840 and worked alone at 82 Strand from 1841 to 1849. Then moved to 61 Strand 1850 till 1853. The year before his death the Westminster Place gave Dent the contract for making BIG BEN with a big bell weighing over 13 tons. The clock was built by Frederick Rippon Dent. The Dent firm was in business until 1920.

DENT, PIVOTED Detent chronometer, about 15 jewels, fusee, gold, 48-52mm, Ca. 1870, open face.

DENT, 1/4 hr. repeater, marked " Dent Watch Maker to the Queen 61 Strand London", S# 30077, gold, 46-52mm, OF

TYPE – DESCRIPTION	Avg	Ex-Fn	Mint
Time only, gold, 45- 50mm, OF	$550	$650	$800
HC	650	800	1,000
Chronograph, gold, 45-50mm, OF	750	900	1,100
HC	800	1,000	1,200
Split second chronograph, gold, 45-52mm, OF	1,000	1,200	1,500
HC	1,100	1,300	1,600
1/4 hr. repeater, gold, 46-52mm, OF	1,800	2,250	2,750
HC	2,000	2,400	3,000
HC w/chrono., cal. & moonphase	5,700	6,700	8,000
Minute repeater, gold, OF	3,000	3,800	4,800
HC	3,200	4,000	5,000
OF w/chrono.	3,200	4,000	5,000
HC w/split chrono.	5,500	6,300	7,500
HC w/cal. & moonphase	8,000	10,000	12,500
Detent chronometer, gold, 48-52mm, OF	3,400	4,000	4,800
Perpetual moonphase calendar, gold, OF	8,000	10,000	14,000
HC	9,000	11,000	15,500
Perp. moonphase cal. w/min. repeater, OF	22,000	26,000	32,000
HC	24,000	28,000	34,000

⊕ Some models and grades are not included. Their values can be determined by comparing with similar age, size, metal content, style, models and grades listed.

⊕ Watches listed in this book are priced at the collectable fair market value at the retail level, as complete watches having an original case, an original white enamel dial, and with the entire original movement in good working order with no repairs needed, unless otherwise noted.

DUBOIS et FILS
Le Locle (SWISS)

Dealer and Watchmaker, one of the most active in the Le LOCLE region. Founded in 1785 by Philippe (1738-1808). They exported all over the world and specialized in automaton watches, skeleton watches and watches with false pendulums. The company is still in business today.

TYPE – DESCRIPTION	Avg	Ex-Fn	Mint
Verge, KW, pair case, silver, 48-52mm	$275	$325	$400
Verge, enamel w/scene & automata windmill, silver or gilt, 48-52mm	1,100	1,400	1,800
Verge w/mock pendulum, silver, OF, 48-52mm	650	850	1,150
Verge, KW, GOLD, OF, 50-54mm	600	750	950
Verge, KW, GOLD w/enamel, OF,52mm	900	1,400	2,200
1/4 hr. repeater, SILVER, OF, 50-54mm	650	850	1,150
1/4 hr. repeater, GOLD, OF, 50-54mm	850	1,050	1,350
1/4 hr. repeater w/automaton, 18K, OF, 50-52mm	3,000	3,800	4,500

Dubois et Fils, Verge with mock pendulum, silver, OF, enamel dial, 48-52mm, Ca. 1830.

Dubois et Fils, Verge, enamel w/scene, silver or gilt, OF, painted enamel scene with windmill automata, 48-52mm. Ca. 1810.

COMPARISON OF WATCH SIZES

U. S. A.	EUROPEAN
10-12 SIZE	40—44 MM
16 SIZE	45—48 MM
18 SIZE	50—54 MM

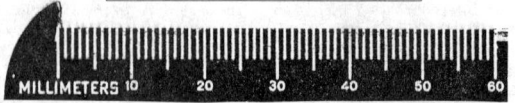

DUCHENE L., & Fils
GENEVA

Watchmaker, well known for their large and small pieces, including coach clocks, calendar watches and minute repeater watches. The firm was known also for decorative work with polychrome champleve enamel and painted enamel, and fantasy watches. The movements are classically-designed, with fusee & verge escapements. Cases are in "Empire-style", engraved or guilloche.

TYPE – DESCRIPTION	Avg	Ex-Fn	Mint
KW, cylinder, silver, 46mm, OF	$85	$125	$175
HC	100	140	200
KW, verge fusee, silver, 46-52mm, OF	275	300	400
KW, verge fusee, enamel case ,gilt, 52mm, OF	600	800	1,100
1/4 hr. repeater, silver, 54mm, OF	500	700	900
1/4 hr. repeater, gold, 52mm, OF	875	1,000	1,250
Ball form, KWKS, cylinder, 29mm, 18K OF	500	650	900

Duchene L. & Fils, 1/4 Hour Repeater, fusee and cylinder escapement, repeats on gongs, 52mm, Ca. 1820.

Dunand, 1/4 hour repeater, about 15 jewels, repeater is slide activated, 49MM, OF, Ca. 1905

DUNAND
Swiss

The Dunand factory produced repeaters, timers & chronographs during the 1890-1930 time period.

TYPE – DESCRIPTION	Avg	Ex-Fn	Mint
Time only, gold, 45-50mm, OF	$350	$400	$500
HC	450	500	600
Chronograph, gold, 45-50mm,OF	500	600	725
HC	550	700	925
Split second chronograph, gold, 45-52mm, OF	800	950	1,100
HC	900	1,050	1,250
1/4 hr. repeater, gold, 46-52mm, OF	750	900	1,050
HC	850	1,000	1,200
OF w/chrono.	950	1,050	1,250
HC w/chrono.	1,100	1,250	1,500
Minute repeater, gold, 46-52mm, OF	1,500	1,800	2,200
HC	1,800	2,000	2,400

🕐 Pricing in this Guide are fair market price for **COMPLETE** watches which are reflected from the "**NAWCC**" National and regional shows.

EARNSHAW, THOMAS
LONDON

Thomas Earnshaw born in 1749 died in 1829. In about 1781 he improves the spring detent. Earnshaw also contributed to the development of the chronometer. He pioneered the method of fusing brass and steel together to form a laminate of the compensation rims as in the modern method of today. Known for his chronometers he also made 1/4 and 1/2 hour repeaters with cylinder and duplex escapements.

THOMAS EARNSHAW, chronometer, KWKS, spring detent, Z or S balance with trapezoidal weights, helical hairspring, serial # 589, silver case, Ca.1810.

Signed: "T. EARNSHAW Invt et Fecit 665 London 9117" KW KS, spring detent chronometer, NOTE: compensation curb so called "sugar-tongs", silver case, Ca.1803.

TYPE – DESCRIPTION	Avg	Ex-Fn	Mint
Time only, KW, SILVER, 45- 48mm, OF	$1,200	$1,500	$2,000
Time only, KW, GOLD, 45- 48mm, OF	2,200	2,800	3,500
1/4 hr. repeater, GOLD, 46-52mm, OF	4,500	5,700	7,250
Spring detent escapement, chronometer, gold, 48-54mm, OF	7,000	9,000	12,000
Spring detent escapement, chronometer, (Sugar-Tongs), OF	10,000	12,000	15,000

H. R. EKEGREN
Copenhagen & Geneva

Henry Robert Ekegren, a Swiss maker of quality watches, started in business around 1870. The firm specialized in flat watches, chronometers and repeaters. Ekegren became associated with F. Koehn in 1891.

TYPE – DESCRIPTION	Avg	Ex-Fn	Mint
Time only, gold, 45- 50mm, register, OF	$550	$700	$900
HC	650	850	1,100
Chronograph, gold, 45-50mm, register, OF	800	1,000	1,250
HC	900	1,100	1,350
Split second chronograph, gold, 45-52mm, OF	1,200	1,400	1,650
HC	1,300	1,500	1,900
FIVE-Minute repeater, gold, 46-52mm, OF	1,800	2,000	2,400
HC	2,000	2,200	2,600

Some models and grades are not included. Their values can be determined by comparing with similar age, size, metal content, style, models and grades listed.

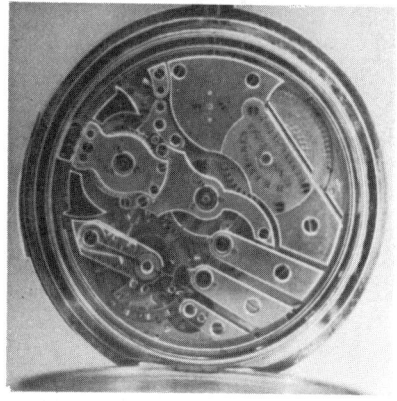

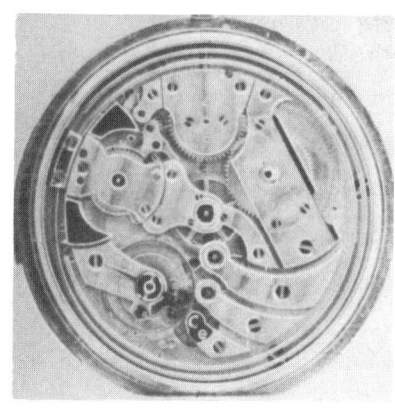

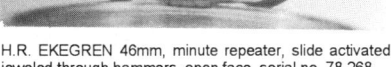

H.R. EKEGREN 46mm, minute repeater, slide activated, jeweled through hammers, open face, serial no. 78,268.

H.R. EKEGREN, 47mm, minute repeater, jeweled through hammers, hunting case.

TYPE – DESCRIPTION	Avg	Ex-Fn	Mint
Minute repeater, gold, 46-52mm, OF	$2,400	$2,900	$3,400
HC	2,750	3,200	4,000
OF w/chrono.	2,500	3,000	3,700
HC w/chrono.	3,000	3,500	4,300
OF w/split chrono.	3,700	4,500	5,500
HC w/split chrono.	4,500	5,250	6,500
Perpetual moonphase calendar, gold, OF	8,000	9,500	12,500
Perpetual moonphase cal. w/ min. repeater, OF	18,000	21,000	26,000
HC	20,000	23,000	28,000
Perp. moonphase cal. w/min. rep. and chrono., OF	22,000	24,000	30,000
HC	25,000	32,000	40,000
Karrusel, gold, 48-55mm, OF	8,000	9,500	12,000
Tourbillion, gold, 48-55mm, OF	40,000	50,000	65,000
Detent chronometer, gold, 48-52mm, OF	4,500	5,750	7,000
World time watch, gold, 48-52mm, OF	5,000	7,000	9,500

FAVRE–LEUBE
Le Locle & Geneva

Faver-Leube firm is still active and production has covered more than eight generations of watchmakers. The company has made watches since 1815.

FAVER-LEUBE, 53mm, Minute repeater, 15 jewels, slide on rim activates the repeater mechanism, Ca.1895.

TYPE – DESCRIPTION	Avg	Ex-Fn	Mint
Early, KW KS, Swiss bar Mvt., time only, Ca.1870, Silver case ...	$100	$125	$175
KW, Gold w/enamel, 35-40mm, HC	800	1,000	1,300
KW, silver w/enamel, 45mm, HC	225	300	400
KW, Gold w/enamel, 45-48mm, OF	600	800	1,100
Chronograph, gold, 45-50mm, OF	500	650	850
HC	600	750	1,000
Split second chronograph, gold, 45-52mm, OF	700	850	1,100
HC	800	950	1,200
1/4 hr. repeater, gold, 46-52mm, OF	800	950	1,200
HC	1,100	1,300	1,600
Minute repeater, gold, 46-52mm, OF	1,200	1,400	1,800
HC	1,500	1,800	2,200

CHARLES FRODSHAM
London

Charles Frodsham followed in the footsteps of his father, William, whose father was close with Earnshaw. Charles became the most eminent of the family, producing very fine chronometers and some rare tourbillon and complicated watches. He died in 1871. His quality movements endorse the letters A.D. FMSZ. Originally Arnold & **Frodsham** was located at 84 Strand, London until 1858. He later moved to New Bond Street, London.

Frodsham, 84 Strand, London engraved on movement, 16-18 jewels, platinum balance screws, Ca. 1850s

Chas. Frodsham, 84 Strand London, 25 jewels, Fusee, Freesprung, Diamond end stone, serial number 3520.

TYPE – DESCRIPTION	Avg	Ex-Fn	Mint
Time only, early mvt. **84 Strand**, silver, 45- 48mm, OF, C.1850 ...	$250	$350	$475
Time only, early mvt. **84 Strand,** gold, 45- 48mm, OF, C.1850	700	900	1,200
Time only, gold, 45- 50mm, OF	700	900	1,200
HC	900	1,100	1,500
Chronograph, gold, 45-50mm, OF	1,600	1,800	2,400
HC	1,800	2,100	2,700
Split second chronograph, gold, 45-52m, OF	2,600	3,200	4,200
HC	2,800	3,500	4,500

⊕ Pricing in this Guide are fair market price for **COMPLETE** watches which are reflected from the "**NAWCC**" National and regional shows.

Frodsham, 46-50mm, jeweled through the center wheel, stem wind, 18K case, Ca. 1895.

Frodsham, 59mm, 60 minute Karrusel, 15 jewels, stem wind, open face, 18K gold case, Ca. 1895.

TYPE – DESCRIPTION	Avg	Ex-Fn	Mint
Minute repeater, gold, 46-52mm,OF	$4,500	$5,400	$6,500
HC	5,000	6,000	7,500
OF w/split chrono.	12,000	16,000	22,000
HC w/split chrono.	15,000	18,000	25,000
Perpetual moonphase calendar, gold, OF	18,000	22,000	28,000
Perp. moonphase cal. w/min. repeater, OF	35,000	45,000	60,000
HC	40,000	52,000	65,000
Karrusel, 16J, (59 to 60 Min. Karrusel), 18K, C.1895	4,500	5,500	7,000
Tourbillion, gold, 48-55mm, OF	45,000	55,000	68,000
Marine chronometer, Parkinson-Frodsham, helical hairspring, w/ detent escape., 48 hr. WI, C. 1840, 97mm deck box	2,400	2,800	3,500
Detent chronometer, w/wind ind., silver, OF, KWKS, C. 1850	2,000	2,500	3,300

GIRARD-PERREGAUX
La Chaux-de-Fonds Switzerland

In 1856, The Constant Girard and Henry Perregaux families founded the Swiss firm of Girard-Perregaux. About 1860, the firm made a tourbillon with three golden bridges. A replica of this watch was made in 1982. Both were a supreme expression of horological craftsmanship. Towards 1880 the first wrist watch is made for the German Navy officers. In 1906, the company purchased the Hecht factory in Geneva. Girard-Perregaux has been recognized many times and still makes prestigious quartz and mechanical watches.

TYPE – DESCRIPTION	Avg	Ex-Fn	Mint
Skeletonized "Shell" (Shell Oil Co. advertising watch), 7J, Base metal display case, total production = 30,000 Ca.1940	$100	$135	$185

Skeletonized **"Shell Watch"** (Golden Shell Oil) advertising a watch filled with Shell car motor oil they wanted to prove even a watch would run on this top quality car motor oil. Most stopped with heavy car oil, so the oil was removed from some watches. Girard-Perregaux used a ebauche by A. Scheld calibre 1052, Base metal display case, only 7J, total production = 30,000, & sold for $5.00, Ca. June 5, 1940.

GIRARD-PERREGAUX, three golden bridges movement patented March 25th, 1884.

GIRARD-PERREGAUX, Chronometer, with pivoted dentent, gold train, 20 jewels, nickel movement, Ca. 1878.

TYPE – DESCRIPTION	Avg	Ex-Fn	Mint
Time only, gold 40-44mm, OF	$275	$300	$375
HC	350	450	575
Time only, gold 45- 50mm, OF	325	375	450
HC	475	525	700
3 gold bridges, with **silver** case, C. 1884,	4,000	5,000	6,500
with **gold** case	6,000	7,500	10,500
Chronometer, pivoted detent, 20J., gold train, 18K, C.1878	4,500	5,500	7,000
Chronograph, gold, 45-50mm, OF	800	1,000	1,300
HC	1,000	1,200	1,500
1/4 hr. repeater, gold, 45-52mm, OF	1,400	1,650	2,000
HC	1,600	1,900	2,400
HC w/chrono., cal. & moonphase	2,400	2,700	3,300
Minute repeater, gold, 46-52mm, OF	2,500	2,800	3,200
HC	2,700	3,000	3,500
OF w/chrono.	2,700	3,000	3,400
OF w/split chrono.	4,000	4,500	5,500
HC w/cal. & moonphase	4,500	5,500	6,800
Detent chronometer, gold, 48-54mm, OF	4,500	5,500	6,800
HC	5,000	6,000	7,000

🕐 Note: Some models and grades are not included. Their values can be determined by comparing with similar age, size, metal content, style, models and grades listed.

🕐 Watches listed in this book are priced at the collectable fair market **value** at the **retail** level, as complete watches having an original case, an original white enamel dial, and with the entire original movement in good working order with no repairs needed, unless otherwise noted.

🕐 This book endeavors to be a GUIDE or helpful manual and offers a wealth of material to be used as a tool not as a absolute document. Price Guides are like watches the worst may be better than none at all, but at best cannot be expected to be 100% accurate.

COMPARISON OF WATCH SIZES

U. S. A.	EUROPEAN
10-12 SIZE	40—44 MM
16 SIZE	45—48 MM
18 SIZE	50—54 MM

GOLAY A., LERESCHE & Fils
SWISS

Manufactured under the name Golay-Leresche from 1844-1857, then his son changed the name to Golay A., Leresche & Fils, he worked until the beginning of the 20th Century. Watches were primarily exported to U.S.A., he was well known for watches of all kinds and "grande complications".

TYPE – DESCRIPTION	Avg	Ex-Fn	Mint
Time only, gold, 45- 50mm, OF	$500	$650	$800
HC	650	750	950
Chronograph, gold, 45-50mm, OF	600	750	950
HC	700	875	1,050
Split second chronograph, gold, 45-52mm, OF	750	925	1,200
HC	850	1,050	1,400
1/4 hr. repeater, gold, 46-52mm, OF	1,400	1,800	2,200
HC	1,600	2,000	2,450
HC w/chrono., cal. & moonphase	4,500	5,500	6,500
Minute repeater, gold, OF	2,000	2,500	3,200
HC	2,200	2,800	3,400
OF w/chrono.	2,200	2,800	3,400
HC w/split chrono.	3,500	5,000	7,500
HC w/cal. & moonphase	6,000	7,500	9,500
Detent chronometer, gold, 48-52mm, OF	2,200	2,600	3,400
Perpetual moonphase calendar, gold, OF	8,000	10,000	12,500
HC	8,500	10,500	13,500
Perp. moonphase cal. w/min. repeater, OF	24,000	29,000	35,000
HC	26,000	32,000	40,000

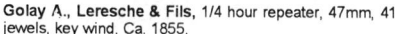

Golay A., Leresche & Fils, 1/4 hour repeater, 47mm, 41 jewels, key wind, Ca. 1855.

Golay A., Leresche & Fils, minute repeater, split seconds chonograph, moon phases, day date month, open face, Ca. 1896.

COMPARISON OF WATCH SIZES

U. S. A.	EUROPEAN
10-12 SIZE	40—44 MM
16 SIZE	45—48 MM
18 SIZE	50—54 MM

H. GRANDJEAN

The son of David-Henri (1774-1845), this respected maker produced high quality complicated watches, chronometers and ornately decorated watches for the South American market. A Grandjean specialty was magnificent enamel and gem set ladies watches.

TYPE – DESCRIPTION	Avg	Ex-Fn	Mint
Time only, gold, 45- 50mm, OF	$550	$650	$800
HC	700	900	1,200
Chronograph, gold, 45-50mm, OF	650	750	950
HC	750	900	1,100
Split second chronograph, gold, 45-52mm, OF	1,100	1,400	1,800
HC	1,200	1,600	2,200
1/4 hr. repeater, gold, 46-52mm, OF	1,400	1,600	2,000
HC	1,600	1,800	2,200
HC w/chrono., cal. & moonphase	2,400	2,800	3,500
Minute repeater, gold, OF	2,200	2,500	3,000
HC	2,400	2,800	3,500
OF w/chrono.	2,400	2,800	3,500
HC w/split chrono.	3,800	4,500	5,500
HC w/cal. & moonphase	4,500	5,500	6,750
Detent chronometer, gold, 48-52mm, OF	3,000	3,600	4,500
Perpetual moonphase calendar, gold, OF	8,000	10,000	12,500
HC	8,500	10,500	14,000
Perp. moonphase cal. w/min. repeater, OF	20,000	24,000	30,000
HC	24,000	28,000	32,500
Grande & Petite Sonnnerie repeating clock watch, 38J, fancy dial, 18k gold, 53mm, HC	11,000	13,500	17,000

H. GRANDJEAN, Grande & Petite Sonnnerie repeating clock watch, 38J, with tandem wind mechanism, fancy dial, 18k gold, 53mm, HC

🕐 Pricing in this Guide are fair market price for **COMPLETE** watches which are reflected from the "**NAWCC**" National and regional shows.

GRUEN WATCH CO.
Swiss & U. S. A. (1894 - 1953)

The early roots of the Gruen Company are found in Columbus, Ohio where Dietrich Gruen and W.J. Savage formed a partnership in 1876. The D. Gruen & Son legacy began in 1894 and flourished with the introduction of fine quality "Precision" movements. Curvex movements, ultra-thins and the prestigious 50th anniversary model are highlights of this prolific company.

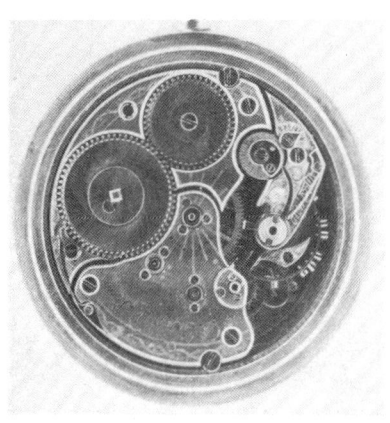

D. Gruen & Son, 44mm, jeweled through center wheel, made for railroad service, serial number 62,428.

Gruen 50th Anniversary Watch, 40mm or 10 size, 21 jewels, (two diamonds) placed in a five-sided pentagon case, solid gold bridges.

TYPE – DESCRIPTION	Avg	Ex-Fn	Mint
17J, veri-thin or precision, GF, 40-43mm, OF, C. 1920's	$75	$95	$125
17J, veri-thin-precision, **14K**, 40-43mm, C.1930	175	200	275
Pentagon case ,17J, GF, 40-43mm, OF, C.1920's..........................	125	150	195
Pentagon case, 17-19J, precision, **14K**, 40-43mm, C. 1930	275	325	400
21-23J, D. Gruen, Swiss, Gold, 45-54mm, OF, C. 1900-20	225	300	450
21J, D. Gruen, (by Assmann),14K, OF, C. 1905............................	425	500	600
21J, D. Gruen, (by Assmann),14K, HC, C. 1910	750	900	1,100
50th anniversary , 12K gold movement, 21J & 2 diamonds, pentagon case, 18K, 40mm, OF, C. 1924	1,800	2,200	2,800

Gruen W. Co., Swiss made, 23 jewels in screwed settings, 47mm, wind indicator, micrometer regulator, Ca.1900's.

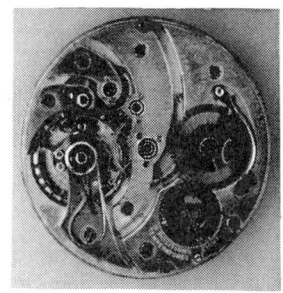

Gruen W. Co., 40mm, Precision V1 1/2 verithin, 21 jewels, 8 positions, serial number 535,203.

E. GUBELIN

Swiss

Jacques Edouard Gubelin joined the firm of Mourice Brithschmid in Lucerne around 1854. By 1919, Edouard Gubelin headed the firm. In 1921 they opened an office in New York & produced fine jewelry and watches for 5 generations.

E. GUBELIN, 50mm, 29J., minute repeater, chronograph, day-date-month-moon phase.

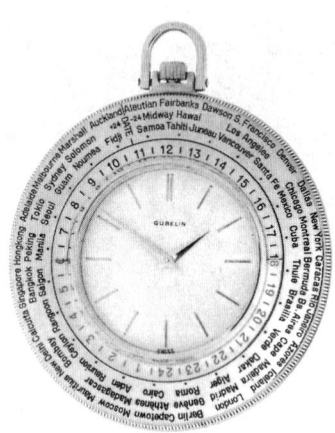

E. GUBELIN, 48mm, world time with 68 cities on outside bezel 24 hour on inter bezel, Gold Filled open face.

TYPE – DESCRIPTION	Avg	Ex-Fn	Mint
Time only, gold, 40- 44mm, OF	$375	$425	$550
HC	475	550	700
Time only, gold, 45- 50mm, OF	425	475	600
HC	575	675	850
Chronograph, gold, 45-50mm, OF	550	650	800
HC	650	775	900
Split second chronograph, gold, 45-52mm, OF	750	800	1,100
HC	850	1,100	1,450
1/4 hr. repeater, gold, 46-52mm, OF	1,200	1,600	2,200
HC	1,400	1,900	2,600
OF w/chrono.	1,300	1,700	2,300
HC w/chrono.	1,500	2,000	2,750
HC w/chrono., calendar & moonphase	3,200	3,800	4,500
5 minute repeater, gold, 46-52mm, OF	1,800	2,200	2,800
HC	2,000	2,400	3,000
Minute repeater, gold, 46-52mm, OF	2,200	2,700	3,500
OF w/chrono.	2,500	3,200	4,000
OF w/split chrono.	3,200	4,000	5,000
OF w/chrono., calendar & moonphase	4,500	5,500	6,800
World time watch, **Gold Filled**, 48-52mm, OF	350	450	575
Perpetual moonphase calendar, gold, OF	8,500	10,000	12,500
Perp. moonphase cal. w/min. repeater, OF	24,000	28,000	35,000
Perp. moonphase cal. w/min.rep. and chrono., OF	26,000	32,000	40,000

The following will explain the French days of the week abbreviations, Sunday =**DIM** (Dimanche), Monday = **LUN** (Lundi), Tuesday = **MAR** (Mardi), Wednesday = **MER** (Mercedi), Thursday = **JEU** (Jeudi), Friday = **VEN** (Vendredi), Saturday = **SAM** (Samedi).

C. L. GUINAND & CO.

Swiss

Founded Ca. 1865 and became know for their Timers and Chronographs.

TYPE – DESCRIPTION	Avg	Ex-Fn	Mint
Timer, with register, base metal, OF, 46mm	$50	$60	$75
Timer, split second, register, base metal, OF, 46mm	65	75	85
Chronograph, 30 min. register,14K, 50mm, OF, C. 1910	500	600	800
HC	650	750	950
Split sec. chrono., 30 min. register, 14K, OF, 50mm, C. 1915	1,000	1,200	1,600
Minute repeater, **18K**, OF, 50mm, C. 1915	2,500	2,800	3,500
HC	3,000	3,400	4,000
Minute repeater, split sec. chrono., 18K, OF, 50mm, C. 1915	4,000	4,500	5,500

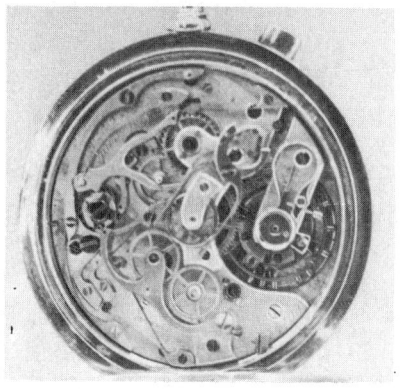 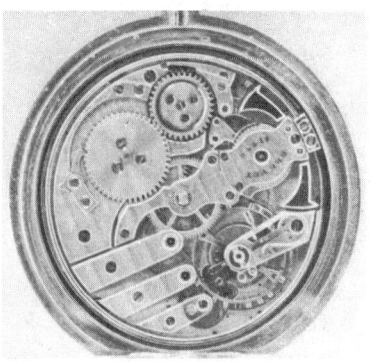

C.L. Guinand, 50mm, split-second chronograph, serial number 44,109.

Haas, Neveux & Co., 40mm, 31 jewels, minute repeater, 18k open face case, serial number 11,339.

HAAS, NEVEUX

Swiss

The Haas Neveux firm is one of the oldest in Switzerland, founded by Leopold & Benjamin Haas in 1848. High grade precision timepieces and chronometers were characteristic of this reputable firm's output.

TYPE – DESCRIPTION	Avg	Ex-Fn	Mint
Time only, gold, 40- 44mm, OF	$325	$400	$500
HC	425	500	600
Time only, gold, 45- 50mm, OF	425	500	600
HC	650	750	900
Chronograph, gold, 45-50mm, OF	800	825	900
HC	850	950	1,100
Split second chronograph, gold, 45-52mm, OF	1,200	1,700	2,000
HC	1,500	1,800	2,400
1/4 hr. repeater, gold, 46-52mm, OF	1,000	1,200	1,500
HC	1,200	1,400	1,700
Minute repeater, gold, 46-52mm, OF	1,500	1,800	2,500
OF w/split chrono.	3,500	4,200	5,000
OF w/cal. & moonphase	4,000	4,500	5,500
Perpetual moonphase calendar, gold, OF	7,000	8,000	10,000
Perp. moonphase cal. w/min. repeater, OF	25,000	28,000	35,000
HC	26,000	30,000	37,000
Perp. moonphase cal. w/min. rep. and chrono., OF	28,000	32,000	38,000

HEBDOMAS
Swiss

The Hebdomas name is commonly found on imported Swiss novelty "8" day watches. Produced from the early 1900's to the 1960's, these popular timepieces featured fancy colored dials with an opening at the bottom of dial to expose the balance wheel and pallet-fork. This style watch is now being made by Arnex Time Corp. under the name of (Lucien Piccard) & other Co. names.

Hebdomas, 8 day (JOURS) 6 jewels, balance seen from the face of the watch, Ca.1920s. This style watch is now being made by Arnex Time Corp. (Lucien Piccard).

Hebdomas, 8 day (JOURS), 6 jewels, 1 adjustment, exposed balance, day date, center seconds, Ca.1920s

TYPE – DESCRIPTION	Avg	Ex-Fn	Mint
8 day, exposed balance, 7J, gun metal, 50mm, OF, C. 1920............	$150	$175	$225
8 day, exposed balance, 7J, base metal, fancy dial, 50mm, OF, C.1920	200	235	300
8 day, exposed balance, 7J, silver, 50mm, OF, C. 1920..................	200	235	300
8 day, exposed balance, 7J, silver, 50mm, HC, C. 1920's .... ★	250	300	400
8 day, exposed balance, 7J, **day date calendar**, center sec., with fancy dial, silver, 55mm, OF, C. 1920's........................	350	400	485

⊕ Note: Some models and grades are not included. Their values can be determined by comparing with similar age, size, metal content, style, models and grades listed.

⊕ Watches listed in this book are priced at the collectable fair market **value** at the **retail** level, as complete watches having an original case, an original white enamel dial, and with the entire original movement in good working order with no repairs needed, unless otherwise noted.

COMPARISON OF WATCH SIZES

U. S. A.	EUROPEAN
10-12 SIZE	40—44 MM
16 SIZE	45—48 MM
18 SIZE	50—54 MM

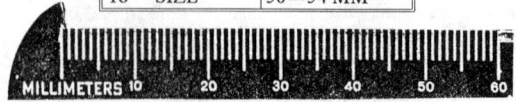

HUGUENIN & CO.

Swiss

Founded by Adolphe Huguenin and the firm name registered in 1880.
Purchased by Hamilton W. Co. in March of 1959.

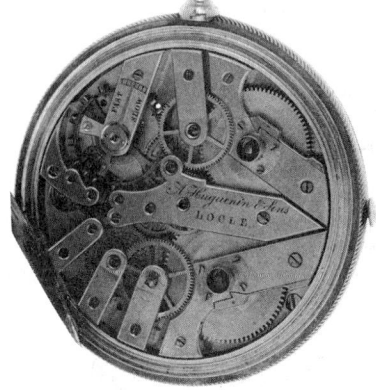

Huguenin & Co., 2-Train 1/4 second jump watch, center
sweep hand, enamel dial, 54mm, KW KS, 18K, Ca. 1880.

Huguenin & Co., 2-Train 1/4 second jump watch, 2 main
barrels & 2 gear trains, 54mm, KW KS, Ca. 1880.

TYPE – DESCRIPTION	Avg	Ex-Fn	Mint
KW, cylinder, silver, 46- 48mm, OF, C. 1870s	$85	$95	$125
KW, silver, 46- 48mm, HC, C. 1870s	125	150	185
KW, cylinder escapement, **18K,** 48mm, OF, C.1870s	250	325	425
KW, fancy engraved, **18K,** 47mm, HC, C. 1870s	700	800	900
1/4 Sec. Jump, 2-train, **silver**, 50-54mm	2,000	2,300	2,800
1/4 Sec. Jump, 2-train, **gold**, 50-54mm	2,500	2,800	3,500
Chronograph, gold, 45-52mm, OF	1,000	1,200	1,500
HC	1,200	1,400	1,800
1/4 hr. repeater, gold, 46-52mm, OF	1,500	1,700	2,000
HC	1,700	2,000	2,400
Minute repeater, gold, 46-52mm, OF	1,800	2,200	2,800
HC	2,500	2,800	4,000
OF, w/ chrono.	2,200	2,400	2,800
OF, w/ split chrono.	5,000	5,600	6,500
HC, w/ split chrono.	6,000	6,600	7,500
HC, w/ chrono., cal. & moonphase	5,000	5,500	6,800

Huguenin & Co., Chronograph, enamel dial, 51mm,
18K, Hunting Case, Ca. 1890.

Huguenin & Co.,Chronograph, 3/4 plate movement,
51mm, 18K, Hunting Case, Ca. 1890.

International Watch Co.
Swiss

The founder of the prestigious Swiss International Watch Co. was an American engineer F.A. Jones from Boston and previously worked for E. Howard Watch & Clock Company. F.A. Jones and C. L. Kidder for 3 years worked together from about 1869 to 1872 building up a new firm which was the only North-eastern watch factory founded in Switzerland by **Americans**. Mr. C. L. Kidder returned to U.S.A. in 1872 and took on a position with Cornell Watch Co. as first Superintendent in the new Newark factory. Mr. Jones stayed to continue building up the factory which was completed in spring of 1875. F.A. Jones in December of 1875 filed for bankruptcy and soon returned to U.S.A. in 1876. The short lived I.W.Co. produced about 5,000 watches. In 1877 the production of the factory (now called "Internationale Uhrenfabrik") was delegated to F.F. Seeland of New York. In 1879 Mr. Seeland was removed from his position by managing director Johann Rauschenbach. The company today is still making precision, hand crafted watches. IWC is well known for its super-light watch constructed of titanium.

International W. Co., apertures for jump hour and minute disc, 11-15 jewels, enamel dial, **Pallweber** movement.

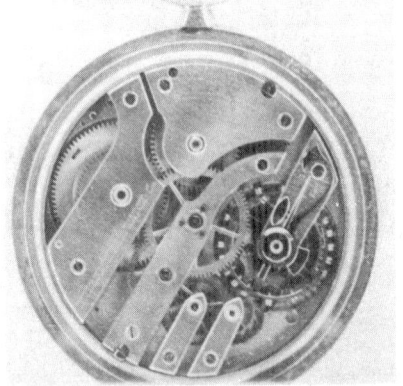

International Watch Co., 54mm, 17 jewels, adj.6P, serial number 741,073.

TYPE – DESCRIPTION	Avg	Ex-Fn	Mint
Early, KW, Time only, Swiss bar, silver case	$150	$175	$225
Time only, gold, 40-44mm, OF	425	485	550
HC	675	750	850
Time only, gold, 45-50mm, OF	625	700	800
HC	900	1,100	1,500
Jump hour and minute disc, 11-15 jewels, **silver, HC**	1,800	2,000	2,500
Jump hour and minute disc, 11-15 jewels, **14K**, HC	2,400	3,000	3,500
Chronograph, gold, 45-50mm, OF	1,800	2,000	2,500
HC	2,000	2,500	3,000
Split second chronograph, gold, 45-52mm, OF	3,000	3,400	4,000
HC	4,000	4,400	5,000
Minute repeater, gold, 46-52mm, OF	2,800	3,200	4,000
HC	3,200	4,200	5,500
OF, w/split chrono.	6,500	7,200	8,500
HC, w/split chrono.	8,000	8,500	10,000
OF, w/cal. & moonphase	7,000	8,000	10,000
HC, w/chrono., cal. & moonphase	9,000	9,500	11,000
Detent chronometer, gold, 48-52mm, OF	7,000	7,500	9,000
World Time watch, gold, 48-52mm, OF	12,000	14,000	18,000
Perpetual moonphase calendar, gold, OF	7,000	7,500	9,000
Perpetual moonphase calendar, w/minute repeater, HC	30,000	35,000	45,000

A new numbering system was started with serial # 01 in **1884**. The old register can not be found and the new uninterrupted serial numbers list started on the 9th of January 1885 with serial number 6,501. The highest known serial number for the "JONES" Caliber is 42,327, & the lowest "SEELAND" Caliber serial number is 26,211, the highest number for "SEELAND" Caliber is 60,014.

PRODUCTION TOTALS

OLD DATE – SERIAL #	DATE – SERIAL #	DATE – SERIAL #	DATE – SERIAL #
1875 ---- 7,000	1901 - 253,500	1926 - 845,000	1951 - 1,253,000
1877 ---- 25,000	**1902 - 276,500**	**1927 - 866,000**	**1952 - 1,291,000**
1879 ---- 50,000	1903 - 298,500	1928 - 890,500	1953 - 1,316,000
1881 ---- 80,000	1904 - 321,000	1929 - 919,500	1954 - 1,335,000
1883 ---- 100,000	1905 - 349,500	1930 - 929,000	**1955 - 1,361,000**
NEW	1906 - 377,500	1931 - 937,500	1956 - 1,399,000
DATE – SERIAL #	1907 - 406,000	1932 - 938,000	1957 - 1,436,000
1884 ---- 6,500	1908 - 435,000	1933 - 939,000	1958 - 1,480,000
1885 ---- 15,500	1909 - 463,500	1934 - 940,000	1959 - 1,513,000
1886 ---- 23,500	1910 - 492,000	1935 - 945,500	1960 - 1,553,000
1887 ---- 29,500	1911 - 521,000	1936 - 955,500	1961 - 1,612,000
1888 ---- 37,500	1912 - 557,000	1937 - 979,000	1962 - 1,666,000
1889 --- 49,000	1913 - 594,000	1938 - 1,000,000	1963 - 1,733,000
1890 ---- 63,000	1914 - 620,500	1939 - 1,013,000	1964 - 1,778,000
1891 ---- 75,500	1915 - 635,000	1940 - 1,019,000	1965 - 1,796,000
1892 ---- 87,500	1916 - 657,000	1941 - 1,039,000	1966 - 1,820,000
1893 ---- 103,000	1917 - 684,000	1942 - 1,062,000	1967 - 1,889,000
1894 ---- 117,000	1918 - 714,000	1943 - 1,078,000	1968 - 1,905,000
1895 ---- 133,000	1919 - 742,000	1944 - 1,092,000	1969 - 1,970,000
1896 ---- 151,500	1920 - 765,000	1945 - 1,106,000	1970 - 2,026,000
1897 ---- 170,500	1921 - 780,000	1946 - 1,131,000	1971 - 2,113,000
1898 ---- 194,000	1922 - 783,500	1947 - 1,153,000	1972 - 2,218,000
1899 ---- 212,000	1923 - 793,500	1948 - 1,177,000	1973 - 2,230,000
1900 ---- 231,000	1924 - 807,000	1949 - 1,205,000	1974 - 2,265,000
	1925 - 827,500	1950 - 1,222,000	1975 - 2,275,000

The above list is provided for determining the APPROXIMATE age of your watch. Match serial number with date. Watches were not necessarily sold in the exact order of manufactured date.

OLD STYLE MOVEMENTS

NOTE: **"Jones"** Caliber, had 6 different grades, the highest grade was E = 20J, SW, 3/4 plate in nickel, 3 sets of screwed gold settings; next was grade H = 16J, SW, 3/4 plate in nickel; grade D =16J, SW, 3/4 plate in nickel; grade S = 15J, SW, 3/4 plate in nickel; grade R = 15J, 3/4 plate; grade B = 13J, 3/4 plate. The **"Jones"**model used a stem- wind & set, a long index regulator & exposed winding gears. The *key- wind* models did not have exposed winding gears but used long index regulator. **"SEELAND"** Caliber, usually were full or 3/4 plate, with short index regulator, and lever or pin set.

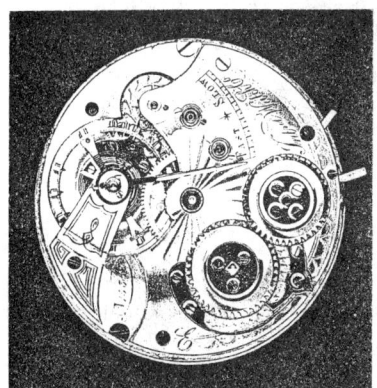 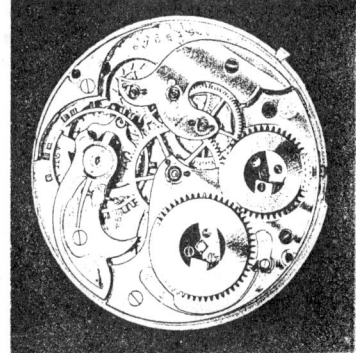

"Jones" Caliber, grade "E", 20J., long index regulator, exposed wind gears, 3 sets of screw style gold jewel settings, SW, 3/4 plate, overcoil hair-spring, Ca. 1876.

"71" Caliber, 16J., OF, 4 sets of screw style gold jewel settings, 300 made in 1904 & 300 in 1917, also HC Caliber "72", 300 made in 1904 & 300 in 1917, 71 & 72 total=1,200.

⊕ Some models and grades are not included. Their values can be determined by comparing with similar age, size, metal content, style, models and grades listed.

INVICTA
Swiss

Founded by R. Picard in 1837. Invicta trade-mark was registered on May 18, 1896 by Files de R. Picard, of La Chaux-de-Fonds. Other names used Seeland Watch Co. and Eno Watch Co.

TYPE – DESCRIPTION	Avg	Ex-Fn	Mint
1/4 hr. repeater, gun metal ,48mm, OF, C. 1900s	$425	$475	$550
1/4 hr. repeater, silver, 48mm, OF, C. 1900s	525	625	750
1/4 hr. repeater, silver, 50mm, HC, C. 1900s	750	800	950
1/4 hr. repeater, **gold,** 58mm, HC, C. 1900s	1,000	1,100	1,300
with chronograph	1,200	1,300	1,500
Min. repeater, gun metal, 52mm, HC, C. 1900s	800	1,000	1,300
silver	900	1,100	1,400
gold	1,000	1,200	1,500

INVICTA, 1/4 hour repeater with chronograph, 18 jewels, Hunting Case about 58MM, Ca. 1895.

JACOT, HENRI
PARIS

Henri Jacot settled in Paris in 1820 and developed the carriage clock industry. He also invented and improved watchmaking and clock making tools. Henri Jacot died July 31, 1867.

TYPE – DESCRIPTION	Avg	Ex-Fn	Mint
KW, cylinder, silver, 46mm, OF	$85	$100	$125
HC	125	150	185
KW, LADIES, **18K**, 40-44mm, OF	225	275	350
HC	300	350	425
KW, GENTS, **18K**, 48mm, OF	400	450	550
HC	500	550	650
1/4 hr. repeater, SILVER, 50mm, OF	900	1,000	1,200
1/4 hr. repeater, GOLD, 50mm, OF	1,700	1,800	2,000

CHARLES E. JACOT
New York & Swiss

In 1837 Charles worked with his uncle, Louis Matthey in New York City. During the 20 year period of working in the U.S.A. he was sold a interest in the firm and the name was changed to Jacot, Courvoisier & Co. Charles E. Jacot had a patent for a star duplex escapement on July 20, 1852. He had about 12 or more watch patents.

In 1857 he returned to Switzerland he forms a company of Jacot & Saltzman. 1876 the name of the firm was Charles E. Jacot. He remained in close contact with his New York connections and in 1897 he died. In 1925 the firm Chas.E. Jacot was listed in Le Locle.

TYPE – DESCRIPTION	Avg	Ex-Fn	Mint
Early, KW, Time only, silver case	$200	$250	$450
Time only, gold, 40-44mm, OF	450	500	750
HC	700	800	1,000
Time only, gold, 45-50mm, OF	625	725	875
HC	850	1,000	1,500
Time only, 30J., independent 1/4 seconds, 2 train, gold, OF	1,000	1,200	2,000
HC	1,400	2,000	3,000

Cha's E. Jacot, Patents, Sept. 64, Nov. 67, Apr, 70; 50mm, lever escapement, SW, HC, Ca. 1871, S# 8133.

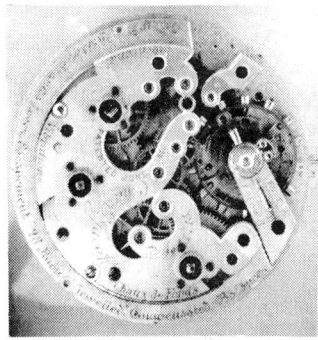

Cha's E. Jacot, on movement "Chaux de Fonds, Indep't Quarter Seconds Lever Escapement 28 Ruby Jewels Compensated Balance. Isochronal Vibrations. Patented June, 1858, S# 7715", 2 train, KW & KS from back.

Cha's E. Jacot, on movement "Chaux de Fonds, Improved Straight Line Lever, full jeweled in Ruby & Sapphire, Pat. Sept. 1859, S# 1637", KW & KS.

Ch's E. Jacot, on movement, " Pat, Oct. 1867, N=25338", KW & KS from back, 15 jewels, 40mm.

RIGHT: Cha's E. Jacot's STAR DUPLEX escapement with 3 pointed star, also seen 4 pointed star PATENTED JULY 20, 1852.

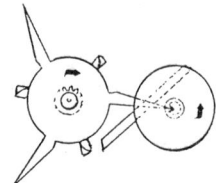

JOSEPH JOHNSON
LIVERPOOL, (1810-1850)

Josh. Johnson of Liverpool started his firm in the early 1800's and lasted till mid 1800's. The Johnson firm supplied the U.S. market with low to medium cost key-wind watches.

TYPE – DESCRIPTION	Avg	Ex-Fn	Mint
KW, 7-15J, silver, 47mm, OF	$85	$100	$125
KW,7- 15J, silver, 47mm, HC	100	125	175
KW,7-15J, swiss, gilt dial, fancy case, 18K, 48mm,OF	265	300	375
KW, lever, fusee, gold dial, Heavy 18K, 52mm, HC	900	1,200	1,500
KW, rack lever escapement, Silver, 56mm, OF	400	450	600
HC	500	550	700
KW, rack lever escapement, Gold, 56mm, OF	900	1,000	1,200
HC	1,100	1,200	1,500
KW, verge fusee, multi-color gold dial & THIN case, 52mm, OF	500	550	700
HC	700	800	950
KW, 15 sec. dial, detached lever, fusee,			
multi-color gold dial & case, 50mm, OF	900	1,000	1,200

Signed on movement *Josh. Johnson Liverpool Detached Patent*, Key wind Key Set, diamond end stone, Massey style side lever, the escape wheel coverts the second hand to rotate once every 15-seconds rather than the normal 60-seconds. Multi-color gold case and dial with carved decorations on the back of case and outer rim of the case, S # 5563, 50mm open face case, Ca. 1850.

🕑 Note: Some models and grades are not included. Their values can be determined by comparing with similar age, size, metal content, style, models and grades listed.

🕑 Watches listed in this book are priced at the collectable fair market **value** at the retail level, as complete watches having an original case, an original white enamel dial, and with the entire original movement in good working order with no repairs needed, unless otherwise noted.

COMPARISON OF WATCH SIZES

U. S. A.	EUROPEAN
10-12 SIZE	40—44 MM
16 SIZE	45—48 MM
18 SIZE	50—54 MM

JULES JURGENSEN
Swiss

The firm of Jules Jurgensen was an extension of the earlier firm of Urban Jurgensen & Sons, which was located, at various times, in Copenhagen and Le Locle. Jules ultimately established his firm in Le Locle after his father's death in the early 1830's. From that time forward the company produced, generally speaking, very fine watches that were high grade and complicated. It appears that by 1850 the company had already established a strong market in America, offering beautiful heavy 18K gold watches of exemplary quality. Until around 1885, most stem-winding watches exhibited the **bow-setting feature.**

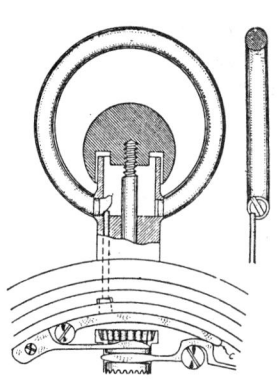
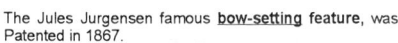

The Jules Jurgensen famous **bow-setting** feature, was Patented in 1867.

Jules Jurgensen, 27 jewels, 1/5 second jump watch, 2 main barrels & 2 gear trains, 54mm, Ca. 1890.

Jules Jurgensen, LEFT: fully signed dial *"Jules Jurgensen Copenhagen"*; RIGHT: movement signed on barrel bridge *"Jules Jurgensen Copenhagen No.6319"*, 18K Hunting Case, 17 jewels, with gold escape wheel & chronometer pivoted detent escapement, KWKS, Ca. 1875.

Almost any collectible Jurgensen watch will be fully signed on the dial and movement, with an impressively embossed "JJ" stamping on all covers of the case. Watches not so marked should be examined carefully; and untypical or inelegant stamping should be viewed suspiciously, as there have been some forgeries of these fine watches. Frequently one finds the original box and papers accompanying the watch, which enhances the value. After 1885, as the firm started to buy movements from other companies, we begin to see variations in Jurgensen watches. By 1930, Jurgensen watches barely resembled the quality and aesthetics of the early period, and they are not as desirable to the collector.

JULES JURGENSEN, 46mm, 21J., hands set by inclination of pendant ring, serial # 14,492, ca.1890.

JULES JURGENSEN, 46-52mm, Minute repeater, 32 jewels, Ca.1887.

TYPE – DESCRIPTION	Avg	Ex-Fn	Mint
Time only, gold, 40- 42mm, Ca. 1930, OF	$350	$400	$500
HC	650	700	850
Time only, gold, 45- 50mm, OF	2,000	2,400	3,000
HC	3,000	3,400	4,000
Flat digital watch, 18J., gold, 40-44mm, OF, Ca. 1930	4,500	5,000	6,000
1/5 second jump watch, 2 main barrels & 2 gear trains, 18K OF	3,500	4,500	6,000
Chronograph, gold, 45-50mm, OF	2,500	2,800	3,500
HC	4,000	4,400	5,000
HC w/register	4,500	4,800	5,500
Split second chronograph, gold, 45-52mm, OF	5,500	5,800	6,500
HC	6,500	6,800	7,500
5 minute repeater, gold, 46-52mm, OF	5,000	5,400	7,000
HC	7,000	7,500	9,000
Minute repeater, gold, 46-52mm, OF	6,000	8,000	12,000
HC	10,000	14,000	20,000
OF, w/ chrono.	8,000	10,000	14,000
HC, w/ chrono.	12,000	15,000	22,000
OF, w/split chrono.	12,000	15,000	22,000
HC, w/split chrono.	15,000	20,000	28,000
Detent chronometer, gold, 48-52mm, OF	10,000	12,000	15,000
HC	15,000	16,000	18,000
Perpetual moonphase calendar, gold, OF	20,000	24,000	30,000
HC	25,000	28,000	35,000
Perp. moonphase cal. w/min. repeater, OF	45,000	48,000	65,000
HC	50,000	55,000	70,000

EDWARD KOEHN

Swiss

Koehn was an innovative watchmaker and a specialist in the design of thin calibre watches. Formerly associated with Patek Phillipe and H. R. Ekegren, he produced watches under his own name from 1891-1930.

TYPE – DESCRIPTION	Avg	Ex-Fn	Mint
Time only, gold, 40- 44mm, OF	$400	$450	$550
HC	550	650	800
Time only, gold, 45- 50mm, OF	800	850	1,000
HC	1,000	1,200	1,500
Chronograph, gold, 45-50mm, OF	1,200	1,400	1,800
HC	1,500	1,700	2,000
Split second chronograph,gold, 45-52mm, OF	1,800	1,900	2,200
HC	2,500	2,800	3,200
5 minute repeater, gold, 45-52mm, OF	3,000	3,400	4,000
HC	3,500	3,800	4,500
Minute repeater, gold, 46-52mm, OF	2,200	2,700	3,500
HC	2,800	3,200	4,000
OF, w/split chrono.	4,500	4,800	5,500
HC, w/split chrono.	6,500	6,800	7,500

E. Koehn, of Geneve, 46mm, 18 jewels, note: **free standing barrel,** lever escapement, Ca. 1900.

🕐 Note: Some models and grades are not included. Their values can be determined by comparing with similar age, size, metal content, style, models and grades listed.

🕐 Watches listed in this book are priced at the collectable fair market **value** at the retail level, as complete watches having an original case, an original white enamel dial, and with the entire original movement in good working order with no repairs needed, unless otherwise noted.

COMPARISON OF WATCH SIZES

U. S. A.	EUROPEAN
10-12 SIZE	40—44 MM
16 SIZE	45—48 MM
18 SIZE	50—54 MM

A. LANGE & SOHNE
Germany

A. Lange & Sohne was established with the aid of the German government at Glashutte, Germany in 1845. Lange typically produced 3/4 plate lever watches in gilt finish for the domestic market, and in nickel for the export market. High grade and very practical, these watches had a banking system for the pallet that was later used briefly by E. Howard in America. Lange complicated watches are scarce and very desirable. On May 8, 1945 Russian bombers destroy workshops.

PRODUCTION TOTALS

DATE– SERIAL #	DATE– SERIAL #	DATE– SERIAL #
1870— 5,000	1895— 35,000	1920— 75,000
1875— 10,000	1900— 40,000	1925— 80,000
1880— 20,000	1905— 50,000	1930— 85,000
1885— 25,000	1910— 60,000	1935— 90,000
1890— 30,000	1915— 70,000	1940—100,000

TYPE – DESCRIPTION	Avg	Ex-Fn	Mint
Time only, A.L.S. first. quality , GJS, **18k gold**, 45- 52mm, OF	$4,000	$4,500	$5,500
HC	4,500	5,000	6,000
Time only, D.U.F. grade, pressed jewels, **14k gold**, 45- 52mm, OF	1,200	1,500	2,000
HC	1,400	1,700	2,200
Time only, O.L.I.W. grade, pressed jewels, not adjusted	500	600	800
World War II model, wind indicator, 52mm, OF (before 1945)	1,500	1,800	2,200
Chronograph, gold, 45-50mm, OF	6,000	7,500	9,500
HC	6,500	8,000	10,500
Split second chronograph, gold, 45-52mm, OF	16,000	21,000	27,000
HC	17,000	22,500	30,000
1/4 hr. repeater, gold, 45-52mm, OF	8,000	10,000	12,500
HC	9,000	11,000	13,500
Minute repeater, gold, 45-52mm, OF	12,000	16,000	24,000
HC	14,000	18,000	25,000
OF, w/split chrono.	22,000	25,000	30,000
HC, w/split chrono.	23,000	27,000	32,000
Detent chronometer, gold, 48-52mm, OF	20,000	25,000	32,000
Perpetual moonphase calendar, gold, OF	30,000	38,000	50,000

A. LANGE & SOHNE, 52mm, serial number 87250, hunting case, Ca. 1926. The A.L.S. top grade watches had gold jewel settings which are screwed to the plates, diamond end stone, gold lever, Adj. to 5 positions, a second A.L.S. grade the gold settings are not screwed into plates, and most had no diamond end stone, both A.L.S. grades are in 18K cases.

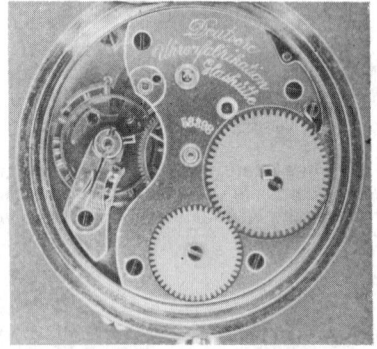

D. U. F. grade by Lange, 50mm, 3/4 plate, engraved on movement "Deutsche Uhren Fabrikation Glashutte,"serial number 58,398. The D. U. F. grade had pressed jewels, brass & nickel balance, adjusted to 3 positions, the D.U.F. grades came in 14K cases and introduced in about 1885 with lower production cost to compete other Companies,

TYPE – DESCRIPTION

TYPE – DESCRIPTION	Avg	Ex-Fn	Mint
Perp. moonphase cal. w/min. repeater, OF	$45,000	$80,000	$125,000
Perp. moonphase cal. w/min. rep. and chronograph, HC .... ★	100,000	125,000	165,000
Perp. moonphase cal. w/min. rep. and **split sec.**			
2 button chronograph, HC .... ★★★★	185,000	200,000	275,000

A. Lange & Sohne, 60mm Hunter Cased Minute Repeating instantaneous Perpetual calendar with day, date, month and leap year indicator, full split second chronograph operated by two buttons with minute recorder and the phases of the moon. The white enamel dial has Arabic numbers, pierced gold hands, four subsidiary dials indicating day, date and the month is combined with leap year indicator and 30 minutes recorder, and the moon phases is combined constant seconds.

A. Lange & Sohne, the movement made in the typical Glashutte 3/4 plate style with a nickel finish, gold lever escapement with convex entry pallet & concave exit pallet, compensation balance, diamond endstone, gold escape wheel, gold lever, repeating on two gongs. This type watches have 40 to 60 jewels, 75 wheels, over 300 screws and 24 bridges. The movement was supplied by Audemars Piguet in 1908-1909 and may be one of fourteen with a two button chronograph finished and cased by A. Lange & Sohne. Audemars Piguet supplied about 35 watches of this type to Glashutte market.

LE COULTRE & CO.
Swiss

Antoine Le Coultre in 1833 formed a company to make ebauches. He created a machine to cut pinions from solid steel as well as other machines for manufacturing clocks and watches. By 1900 they were making flat or thin watches. 1936 Jaeger & Le Coultre officially merge. The signed watches with Jaeger - Le Coultre logo may fetch more money, but have the same quality grade movement as the signed Le Coultre dial and movement. They made parts for Vacheron & Constantin, P. P. & Co., Omega, Longines and many others.

TYPE – DESCRIPTION	Avg	Ex-Fn	Mint
Early, KW, Time only, Swiss bar, Pre. 1870, silver case	$75	$100	$175
Time only, gold, 40- 44mm, OF	200	250	400
HC	250	350	500
Time only, gold, 45- 50mm, OF	225	300	400
HC	375	450	575
8 day, 15J, wind indicator, 45mm, **18K**, OF	700	800	1,100
8 day, 14K, OF	550	650	900
8 day, S.S., OF	300	400	600
Roulette wheel style bezel, gold, 40mm, OF	600	800	1,100
World time watch, gold, 48-52mm, OF	4,500	5,500	7,500
Chronograph, gold, 45-50mm, OF	700	850	1,100
HC	800	1,000	1,300
OF, w/register	700	900	1,200
Split second chronograph,gold, 45-52mm, OF	1,200	1,400	2,000
HC	1,400	1,600	2,200

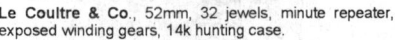

Le Coultre & Co., 52mm, 32 jewels, minute repeater, exposed winding gears, 14k hunting case.

Le Coultre & Co., runs on one winding for **8 DAYS**, wind-indicator at 6 O'clock, 45mm, OF, Ca. 1930.

TYPE – DESCRIPTION	Avg	Ex-Fn	Mint
1/4 hr. repeater, gold, 46-52mm, OF	$1,100	$1,400	$1,800
HC w/chrono., cal. & moonphase	2,400	3,200	3,800
Minute repeater, gold, 46-52mm, OF	2,200	2,500	3,200
HC	2,500	2,800	3,400
OF, w/chrono. & register	2,500	2,800	3,400
HC, w/chrono. & register	2,700	3,100	3,800
HC, w/split chrono.	4,000	5,000	6,500
HC w/chrono., cal. & moonphase	5,500	6,500	7,750
Perpetual moonphase calendar, gold, OF	7,000	8,000	9,500
HC	7,500	8,500	10,000
Perp. moonphase cal. w/min. repeater, OF	15,000	18,000	22,000
HC	17,000	20,000	24,000
Perpetual moonphase cal. w/ min. rep. & chrono., OF	18,000	22,000	27,000
HC	20,000	24,000	29,000

Note: Ebauche movements look under hammers for initials *L.C. & Co.*

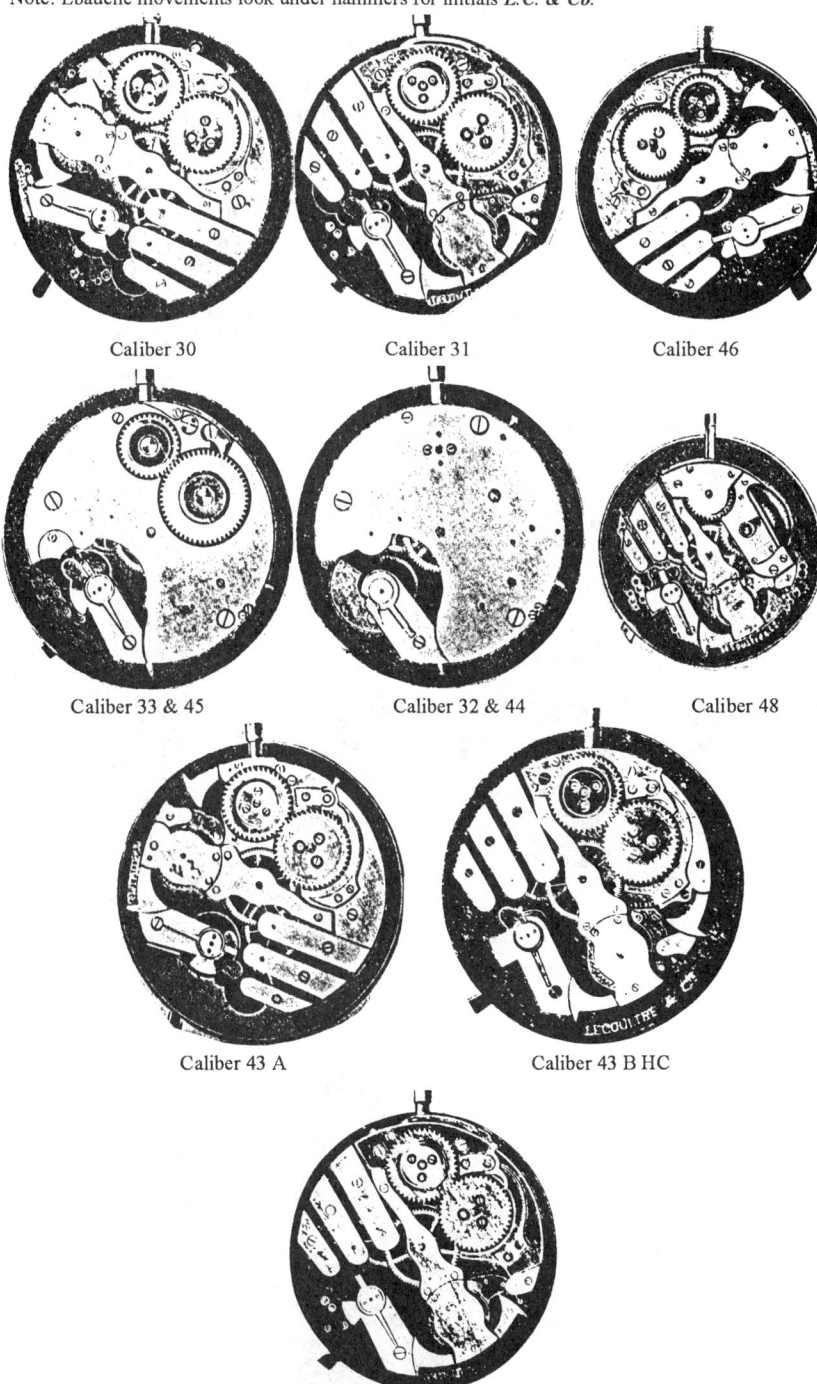

Caliber 30   Caliber 31   Caliber 46

Caliber 33 & 45   Caliber 32 & 44   Caliber 48

Caliber 43 A   Caliber 43 B HC

Caliber 49

LE PHARE
Swiss

Le Phare specialized in the production of repeater ebauches from 1890-1940. They were the first to mass produce or manufacture inexpensive repeaters with interchangeable parts. Le Phare *patented* a **centrifugal force governor**.

TYPE – DESCRIPTION	Avg	Ex-Fn	Mint
Chronograph, gold, 45-50mm, OF	$650	$800	$1,000
HC	750	900	1,100
Split second chronograph, gold, 45-52mm, OF	1,200	1,300	1,600
HC	1,400	1,500	1,800
1/4 hr. repeater, gold, 46-52mm, OF	1,200	1,400	1,500
HC	1,400	1,500	1,800
HC w/chrono., cal. & moonphase	2,500	2,800	3,500
Minute repeater, gold, 46-56mm, OF	1,500	1,800	2,200
HC	1,800	2,000	2,400
OF w/chrono. & register	1,800	2,000	2,400
HC w/chrono.	1,900	2,200	2,600
HC w/chrono., cal. & moonphase	3,000	3,500	4,500

Le Phare, 56mm, minute repeater, chronograph and calendar with moon phases, Note the governor at 6 0'clock..   Le Phare, 57mm, 1/4 repeater, chronograph , Ca. 1905.

Below: Centrifugal style governor.

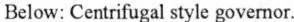

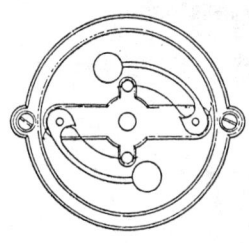 

Le Phare, Min. repeater, 54mm, HC, 17J., 3/4 plate, push button, Ca. 1895, Note centrifugal force governor at 6 o'clock.

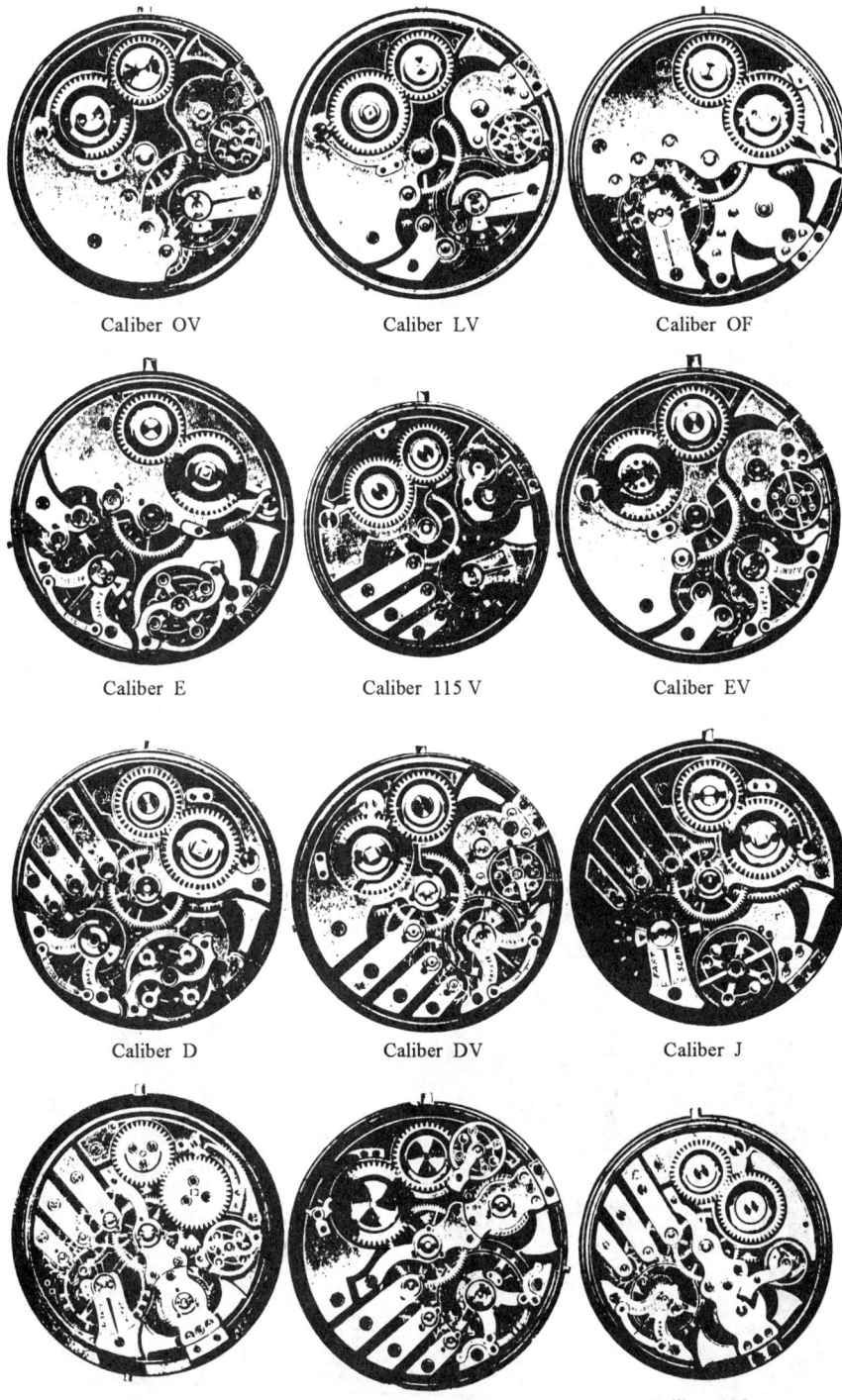

Caliber OV   Caliber LV   Caliber OF

Caliber E   Caliber 115 V   Caliber EV

Caliber D   Caliber DV   Caliber J

Caliber 110 M   Caliber ZM   Caliber 105

L'Epine or Lepine
Paris France (1720 - 1814)

Jean-Antoine L'Epine more than any other one man, revolutionized the **form** of the watch. He developed and first used the following list of improvements in 1770 to 1790, bar bridges, suspended use of the fusee, free-standing barrel, new style virgule, cylinder and lever escapements, stylized arabic numbers, center seconds, moon style hands, wolf's teeth gearing, gongs for repeaters, much thinner watches about 12-13mm, concealed case hinge, cuvette dust cover, engine turned cases, back wind & back set of the hands, pump wind, and open faced style case which is called L'Epine calibre by the Swiss watch makers. The House of Lepine was sold in 1914.

George Washington was the owner of a L'Epine *Gold Watch*. Governor Morris was commissioned to acquire for his friend, the President, a reliable watch while on a business trip to Paris, France. On April 23, 1789, Governor Morris selected a Lepine large gold watch with Virgule escapement as the best. Thomas Jefferson was asked to deliver the watch due to the fact the Governor had a delay in Paris. The watch is on exhibit in the Museum of the Historical Society of Pennsylvania, Pittsburgh, Pa.

TYPE – DESCRIPTION	Avg	Ex-Fn	Mint
Time only, **Silver,** KW, verge or cylinder escap., 46-52mm OF	$200	$300	$600
Time only, **Silver,** KW, virgule escap., 46-52mm OF	600	700	1,000
Time only, **Gold,** KW, verge or cylinder escap, , plain, 50mm, OF	500	650	900
Time only, **Gold,** KW, virgule escap., enamel & scene, 50mm, OF	2,000	2,500	3,800
Time only, **Gold,** KW, *lever with 40 tooth gold escape wheel,*			
Ca. 1778-1790, 50mm, OF .... ★ ★ ★	2,500	3,500	5,000
1/4 repeater, **SILVER**, 52mm, OF..	800	1,100	1,500
1/4 repeater, **GOLD**, 54mm, OF..	1,100	1,500	2,000

Signed *L'Epine a Paris*, virgule escapement, open face, standing barrel, note hinged cuvette, key wind key set from back, 50mm, Ca. 1790-95.

Lepine, virgule escapement, note horse-shoe shaped centerbridge for center seconds, Ca. 1790-95.

LE ROY ET CIE

Paris

Le Roy et Cie was the final product of a dynasty of great watchmakers, starting with Julien Le Roy and his son Pierre, whose credits are numerous in the development of horology in the 18th century. There is, however, much confusion and hoopla over "Le Roy" watches. Frequently, you will see watches signed "Le Roy" that have nothing to do with the original family. These watches are unimportant. You have to distinguish between the works of Julien, of Pierre, of Charles, and of their contemporary namesakes. The modern firm, Le Roy et Cie., established in the late 19th century, contracted and finished some very fine and, in some cases, extremely important complicated watches, using imported Swiss ebauches.

TYPE – DESCRIPTION	Avg	Ex-Fn	Mint
Verge, KW, paircase, silver, 49-50mm, C. 1775	$325	$400	$500
Verge, fusee, Enamel w/scene, 18K, 38- 40mm, C. 1760	2,400	3,000	3,800
Miniature, 22mm, diamonds & pearls on enamel, OF	800	1,000	1,300
Time only, gold, 45- 50mm, OF	600	750	1,000
1/4 hr. repeater, gold, 46-52mm, OF	1,200	1,500	2,400
Min. repeater, two train, tandem winding wheels, fully jeweled jump center seconds, gold, 50mm	6,500	7,500	10,000

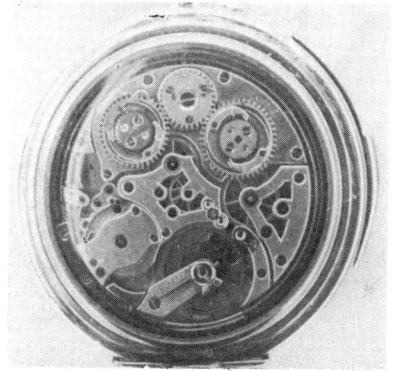 

Le Roy, 50mm, minute repeater, two train, tandem winding wheels, jump center seconds.

Le Roy, 22mm, miniature watch with enamel, pearls, with a Diamond on the pin, 18K, OF, Ca. 1910.

⊕ This book endeavours to be a GUIDE or helpful manual and offers a wealth of material to be used as a tool not as a absolute document. Price Guides are like watches the worst may be better than none at all, but at best cannot be expected to be 100% accurate.

⊕ Characteristics of watches differ for the same age of both case and movement, because these features vary it may not be accurate to date a watch by one single influence. Example: the second hand was not commonly found on watches before 1750, but common about 1800. The first second hand appeared in 1665 and another in 1690. Therefore statements are broad rather than accurate.

LONGINES
Swiss

The beautiful Fabrique des Longines is situated in St. Imier, Switzerland. The company was founded by Ernest Francillon in 1866. They manufacture all grades of watches.

PRODUCTION TOTALS
LONGINES DATE OF MOVEMENT MANUFACTURE

DATE– SERIAL #	DATE– SERIAL #	DATE– SERIAL #
1867 ––– 1	1911 - 2,500,000	1937 - 5,500,000
1870 ––– 20,000	1912 - 2,750,000	1938 - 5,750,000
1875 ––– 100,000	1913 - 3,000,000 - Aug.	1940 - 6,000,000 - June
1882 ––– 250,000	1915 - 3,250,000	1945 - 7,000,000 - July
1888 ––– 500,000	1917 - 3,500,000	1950 - 8,000,000 - May
1893 ––– 750,000	1919 - 3,750,000	1953 - 9,000,000 - July
1899 - 1,000,000 - Feb.	1922 - 4,000,000 - Oct.	1956-10,000,000 - May
1901 - 1,250,000	1925 - 4,250,000	1959-11,000,000 - April
1904 - 1,500,000	1926 - 4,500,000	1962-12,000,000 - May
1905 - 1,750,000	1928 - 4,750,000	1966-13,000,000 - June
1907 - 2,000,000 - July	1929 - 5,000,000 - Oct.	1967-14,000,000 - Feb.
1909 - 2,250,000	1934 - 5,250,000	1969-15,000,000 - Feb.

The above list is provided for determining the APPROXIMATE age of your watch. Match serial number with date. Watches were not necessarily sold in the exact order of manufactured date.

LONGINES, 44mm, 21 jewels, U.S. Army AC, adjusted to temp. & 5 positions, World War II model, cal. 2129.

LONGINES, 59mm, 21 jewels, Railroad Model , gold filled open face case, Ca. 1910-1925.

TYPE – DESCRIPTION	Avg	Ex-Fn	Mint
15 -17J, GF, 40- 50mm, OF, C. 1930	$55	$65	$85
21J, GF, 40- 50mm, OF, C. 1930	135	155	195
15 -17J, silver, 48- 50mm, HC, C. 1890	100	125	165
15-17J, for Tiffany, Sterling, 45- 50mm OF, C. 1905	135	155	195
KW, for Turkish market, .800 silver, HC, C. 1900	100	125	175
17J, "Express Leader", Adj., LS, GF, 48- 50mm, OF, C.1900-20...	125	150	200
21J, "Express Leader", Adj., LS, GF, 48- 50mm, OF, C.1900-20...	200	225	275
23J, "Express Leader", Adj., LS, GF, 48- 50mm, OF, C.1900-20...	225	250	300
21J, "Express Monarch", LS, GF, 48- 50mm, OF, C.1900-20........	200	225	275
24J, "Express Monarch", LS, GF, 48- 50mm, OF, C.1900-20........	250	275	375
21J, Trans-Continental Express, LS, GF, 48- 50mm, OF, C.1910-20	200	225	275
23J, Trans-Continental Express, LS, GF, 48- 50mm, OF, C.1910-20	225	250	300
U.S. Army AC, World War II, 21J., silver, 44mm, **WI.**, OF..........	600	700	850
U.S. Army, World War II, 17-21J., silver, 44mm, OF....................	350	425	525
Time only, gold, 40- 44mm, OF..	250	325	425
HC	350	400	475
Time only, gold, 45- 48mm, OF..	300	375	500
HC	450	550	750

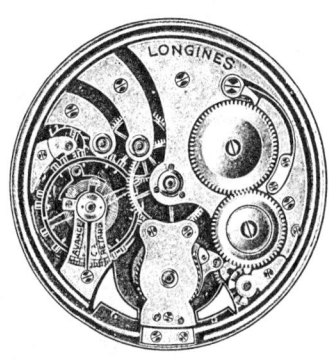

Longines, open face minute repeater movement

Longines, 46mm, Min. repeater, 24 jewels, 3/4 plate design, open face, Ca. 1915.

TYPE – DESCRIPTION	Avg	Ex-Fn	Mint
World time watch, gold, 48-52mm, OF	$4,500	$5,500	$7,000
8 day watch with wind-indicator, **14K OF**	1,500	1,700	2,200
Chronograph w/register, silver, OF, 48- 50mm, C. 1905	250	300	400
Chronograph, gold, 45-50mm, OF	450	500	700
HC	700	800	1,000
Split second chronograph, gold, 45-52mm, OF	1,000	1,200	1,600
HC	1,200	1,400	1,800
Chronograph, Lugrin's Pat., fly back, silver OF case	375	400	500
1/4 hr. repeater, gold, 46-52mm, OF	1,200	1,400	1,800
HC	1,500	1,700	2,000
HC w/chrono., cal. & moonphase	4,000	5,000	6,500
Minute repeater, gold, 46-52mm, OF	2,000	2,500	3,500
HC	2,500	3,000	4,000
OF w/chrono.	2,500	3,000	4,000
HC w/chrono.	3,000	3,500	4,500
OF w/split chrono.	3,500	4,000	5,000
HC w/split chrono.	4,500	5,000	7,000
HC w/cal. & moon- phase	5,000	6,000	7,500
Perpetual moonphase calendar, gold, OF	6,000	8,000	10,000
Perp. moonphase cal. w/min.repeater & chrono., OF	15,000	17,000	20,000
HC	18,000	20,000	25,000

Longines, Chronograph, H.A. Lugrin's Pat. June 13, Oct. 3, 1876, Start, Stop, Fly Back.

Longines, 8 day with wind-indicator, Ca. 1930.

MARKWICK, MARKHAM
LONDON (1725-1825)

He enjoyed selling clocks and watches to the Turkish Market. Watches can be found with his name & that of another maker added, Example: Markwick, Markham "Perigal", or "Recordon". Also watches with the names "Story" Ca.1780, "Borrel" Ca.1813 and "Perigal" Ca.1825 are known.

TYPE – DESCRIPTION	Avg	Ex-Fn	Mint
Pair case, verge, silver plain, 50mm, OF	$300	$375	$500
GOLD	800	1,000	1,300
Pair case, verge, silver w/ **repousee**, 50mm, OF	450	650	1,000
GOLD	1,100	1,400	1,850
Triple cased, verge, silver & **Tortoise shell** outer case,	750	1,000	1,500
Triple cased, verge, Painted enamel on first & second case, for Turkish Market, 18K gold cases, Ca. 1800	7,500	9,500	12,500
1/4 hr. repeater, SILVER, 54mm, OF	700	900	1,200
GOLD	1,100	1,300	1,600

Markwick, Markham, Triple cased , 18K gold cases, Painted enamel on first & second case, made for Turkish Market, Ca. 1800.

COMPARISON OF WATCH SIZES

U. S. A.	EUROPEAN
10-12 SIZE	40—44 MM
16 SIZE	45—48 MM
18 SIZE	50—52 MM

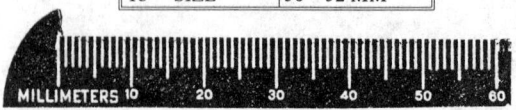

MATHEY – TISSOT
Swiss

Firm founded in June 1886 by Edmond Mathey-Tissot. Makers of complicated and simple watches of good quality.

TYPE – DESCRIPTION	Avg	Ex-Fn	Mint
Early, KW, Time only, Swiss bar, Pre 1870, silver	$95	$125	$200
Time only, gold, 40- 44mm, OF	285	350	425
HC	425	500	585
Time only, gold, 45- 50mm, OF	435	500	650
HC	600	700	850
1/4 hr. repeater, gold, 46-52mm, OF	1,200	1,300	1,600
HC	1,500	1,600	2,000
OF w/chrono., cal. & moonphase	2,200	2,400	3,000
HC w/chrono., cal. & moonphase	2,500	2,800	3,500

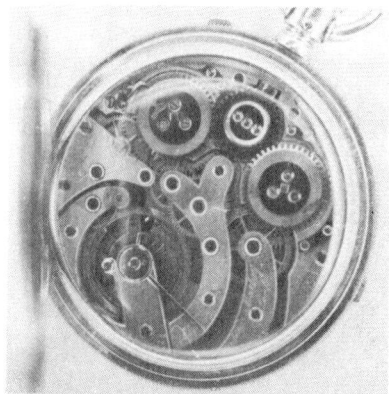

Mathey-Tissot, 52mm, 27 jewels, quarter jump sweep second chronograph, two train, 18k HC.

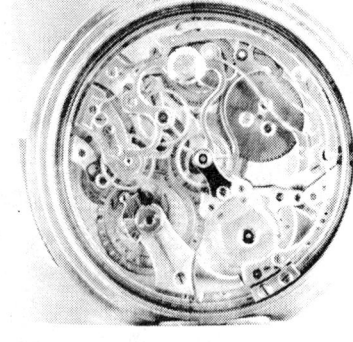

Mathey-Tissot, min. repeater with chronograph, day date month & moon phases, HC.

TYPE – DESCRIPTION	Avg	Ex-Fn	Mint
Minute repeater, gold, 46-52mm, OF	$1,800	$2,200	$2,800
HC	2,000	2,400	3,000
OF w/chrono. & register	2,000	2,400	3,000
HC w/chrono. & register	2,200	2,700	3,400
HC w/chrono. & moon ph,. day date month,	4,500	5,500	6,700
OF w/split chrono.	4,200	4,700	5,500
HC w/split chrono.	4,700	5,300	6,250
OF w/cal. & moonphase	3,800	4,600	5,500
HC w/cal. & moonphase	4,000	4,800	6,000
World time watch, gold, 48-52mm, OF	4,500	5,500	6,500
Perpetual moonphase calendar, gold, OF	6,000	7,000	9,000
Perp. moonphase cal. w/min. repeater, OF	18,000	20,000	26,000
HC	20,000	22,000	28,000
Perp. moonphase cal. w/min. rep. and chrono., OF	20,000	22,000	28,000
HC	22,000	24,000	30,000

☉ Note: Some models and grades are not included. Their values can be determined by comparing with **similar** age, size, metal content, style, models and grades listed.

🕐 Pricing in this Guide are fair market price for **COMPLETE** watches which are reflected from the "**NAWCC**" National and regional shows.

McCabe
London

William McCabe of Ireland was a clock & watch-maker who moved to London. This long lived firm has a good reputation for making watches. The son of William, James McCabe became the owner in about 1822. The business was carried on by nephew, Robert Jeremy till about 1883.

TYPE – DESCRIPTION	Avg	Ex-Fn	Mint
Time only, Verge escapement, KW, Silver, 58mm, OF	$200	$275	$375
HC	225	325	450
Time only, DUPLEX escapement, KW, Silver, 58mm, OF	225	300	400
HC	250	350	475
Time only, DUPLEX escapement, KW, GOLD, 58mm, OF	700	900	1,200
HC	800	1,000	1,400
Enamel, Time only, DUPLEX escap., KW, Silver, 58mm, OF	900	1,200	1,500
HC	1,000	1,300	1,700
Gold &Enamel, Time only, Duplex escap., KW, 55- 58mm, OF	6,500	9,000	14,000
HC	9,500	12,000	17,000
Time only, Lever escapment, gold, 45- 50mm, OF	950	1,250	1,400
HC	1,200	1,400	1,800
1/4 hr. repeater, gold, 46-52mm, OF	1,800	2,000	2,300
HC	2,500	2,800	3,200
Dent Chronometer, gold, 48-52mm, OF	6,000	6,600	7,500
HC	7,000	7,500	9,000

Ja. McCabe, "Royal Exchange London", key-wind with fusee, diamond stone, three arm gold balance, right angle lever, Ca. 1835.

🕐 Pricing in this Guide are fair market price for **COMPLETE** watches which are reflected from the "**NAWCC**" National and regional shows.

MEYLAN WATCH CO.

Swiss

Meylan Watch Co., founded by C.H. Meylan in 1880, manufactured fine watches, with complications, in Le Brassus, Switzerland.

TYPE – DESCRIPTION	Avg	Ex-Fn	Mint
Time only, gold, 40- 44mm, OF	$350	$425	$500
HC	450	525	650
Time only, gold, 40- 44mm, 18K case & **enamel on bezel**, OF	1,500	1,800	2,200
Time only, gold, 45- 50mm, OF	500	550	700
HC	850	950	1,100
Chronograph, gold, 45-50mm, OF	700	750	900
HC	900	1,000	1,200
Split second chronograph, gold, 45-52mm, OF	1,200	1,300	1,600
HC	1,800	1,900	2,200
1/4 hr. repeater, gold, 46-52mm, OF	1,500	1,600	2,000
HC	2,000	2,100	2,400
HC w/chrono., cal. & moonphase	3,000	3,500	4,500

C. H. Meylan, 42mm, 21 jewels, straight line lever escapement, 18K case with enamel on bezel.

C. H. Meylan, Minute Repeater, split second Chronograph, minute register, 18K gold OF case, Ca. 1895

TYPE – DESCRIPTION	Avg	Ex-Fn	Mint
5 minute repeater, gold, 46-52mm, OF	$1,700	$2,000	$2,400
HC	1,900	2,200	2,600
Minute repeater, gold, OF	2,400	2,700	3,100
HC	2,600	2,900	3,400
OF w/chrono.	2,600	2,900	3,300
HC w/chrono.	2,700	3,000	3,500
OF w/split chrono.	3,800	4,500	5,500
HC w/split chrono.	4,000	4,800	6,000
OF w/cal. & moonphase	4,000	4,800	6,000
HC w/cal. & moonphase	5,000	5,500	7,000
HC w/chrono., cal. & moonphase	5,500	6,000	7,500
Tourbillion, gold, 48-55mm, OF	25,000	30,000	40,000
Detent chronometer, gold, 48-52mm, OF	3,000	4,000	5,200
World time watch, gold, 48-52mm, OF	4,500	5,000	6,000
Perpetual moonphase calendar, gold, OF	8,000	9,000	12,000
HC	9,000	10,000	14,000
Perp. moonphase cal. w/min. rep. and chrono., OF	18,000	20,000	24,000
HC	20,000	22,000	27,000

MORICAND, CH.
GENEVA

Firm specialized in making verge watches with cases highly decorated with stones and enameled portraits. Associates with brother Benjamin and Francois Colladon from 1752 to 1755, with a firm name of Colladon & Moricand. Later, with Jean Delisle then later in 1780 as Moricand.

Delisle & Moricand, 36MM, 1/4 hour repeater pendant activated, two-footed balance bridge, Ca.1775.

Ch. Moricand, 46mm, gilt and enamel with two ladies in a floral garden, KW KS, Ca.1800.

TYPE – DESCRIPTION	Avg	Ex-Fn	Mint
Verge, KW, paircase, **silver**, 50mm, OF	$250	$375	$500
Verge, enamel w/ portrait, **silver/ gilt,** 49-52mm, OF	700	900	1,300
Verge, KW, **gold**, 50-54mm, OF	800	950	1,200
Verge, KW, **gold** w/ enamel, 52mm, OF	1,600	2,200	3,000
1/4 hr. repeater, **silver,** 54mm, OF	600	700	1,000
1/4 hr. repeater, **gold**, 50-54mm, OF	900	1,100	1,400
1/4 hr. repeater, **gold** w/ enamel, 54mm, OF	2,400	2,800	3,500

C. MONTANDON
Swiss

This 19th century maker was associated with Perret & Company as well as other Le Locle and Chaux-de-Fonds factories. Montandon specialized in low cost keywind watches for the American market.

TYPE – DESCRIPTION	Avg	Ex-Fn	Mint
KW, cylinder escap., silver, 46mm, OF, C. 1870	$85	$95	$125
KW, silver, 46-48mm, HC, C. 1875	100	125	150
KW, 15J, lady's , **18K**, 40-44mm, OF, C. 1870	175	200	250
HC, C. 1870	250	300	385
KW, 15J, gent's, **18K**, 48mm, OF, C. 1875	275	325	395
Chronograph, gold, 45-50mm, OF	600	700	1,000
HC	700	800	1,100
1/4 hr. repeater, gold, 46-52mm, OF	800	900	1,200
HC	1,000	1,100	1,500
Minute repeater, gold, 46-52mm, OF	2,200	2,400	2,800
HC	2,600	2,800	3,500
Minute repeater, w/cal. & moonphase, OF	3,500	3,800	4,500
HC	4,500	4,800	6,500
Minute repeater, **w/chrono.**, cal. & moonphase, HC	5,000	5,800	7,000

MOVADO
Swiss

L. A. I. Ditesheim & Freres (L.A.I. the initials of the 3 Ditesheim brothers) formed their company in 1881. The name Movado ("always in motion") was adopted in 1905. The Swiss company invented a system of watch making which they called "Polyplan." This was an arrangement of three different angles to the watch movement which produced a curve effect to the case so as to fit the curvature of the arm. Another unusual watch produced by this company in 1926 was the "Ermeto." This watch was designed to be protected while inside a purse or pocket and each time the cover was opened to view the time, the watch was partially wound.

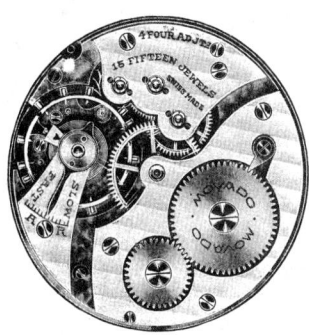 

Movado, 44mm, 15J., with jewel settings, Adjusted to 4 Positions, calibre # 800M.

Top: Movado, Purse watch, Sting Ray leather, 17 jewels.
Bottom: Movado, Purse watch, silver case, 17 jewels.

TYPE – DESCRIPTION	Avg	Ex-Fn	Mint
SW, 17J, LS, Silver, 43mm, OF, C. 1920	$125	$150	$185
SW, 15J, LS, Silver, 47mm, HC, C. 1920	150	175	200
Time only, gold, 40-44mm, OF	225	250	325
HC	350	400	500
Time only, gold, 45-50mm, OF	425	500	600
HC	625	700	850
Purse watch, black leather, 50 x 33mm, C. 1930's	200	250	350
silver	250	300	450
Sting Ray leather	275	325	475
leather, moonph. & calendar	800	900	1,200
Coin form, 17J, St. Christopher coin, 18K, closed case, 29mm	600	700	900
Chronograph, gold, 45-50mm, OF	800	900	1,200
Minute repeater, gold, 46-52mm, OF	2,400	2,600	3,200
HC	2,600	3,000	3,600
HC w/split chrono. & register	5,500	6,000	7,000

Movado, Purse watch with moonph. & calendar, auto-wind by opening & closing case, leather.

ULYSSE NARDIN
Swiss

Ulysse Nardin was born in 1823. The company he started in 1846 produced many fine timepieces and chronometers, as well as repeaters and more complicated watches. This firm, as did Assmann, found a strong market in South America as well as other countries. Ulysse's son, Paul David Nardin, succeeded him, as did Paul David's sons after him.

Ulysse Nardin, Key wind, 18 jewels, pivoted detent, bridge movement, 48mm, Ca. 1860.

Ulysse Nardin, pocket chronometer with date, 19J. pivoted detent, gold jewel settings, Ca.1890.

TYPE – DESCRIPTION	Avg	Ex-Fn	Mint
Early KW, 18J., pivoted detent, bar style mvt., gold, HC, C.1860 ..	$1,400	$1,600	$2,000
Time only, gold, 40-44mm, OF	300	350	500
HC	450	500	650
Time only, gold, 45- 50mm, OF	600	650	700
HC	750	800	850
Chronograph, gold, 45-50mm, OF	800	1,000	1,250
HC	1,000	1,200	1,500
Deck chronometer **w/box**, detent chronometer, C. 1905	1,400	1,600	2,000
Pocket chronometer, lever escape., 21J., GJS, **18K**, HC, C.1910....	1,200	1,400	1,800
Pocket chronometer, **pivoted detent, with date**, gold, 57mm	4,000	4,500	5,500
World time watch, gold, 48-52mm, OF	4,500	5,000	6,000
Karrusel, 52 Min. karrusel, free sprung balance, silver case	6,000	7,000	10,000

Ulysse Nardin, 53mm, 52 minute karrusel, free sprung balance, ca. 1905.

Ulysse Nardin, pocket chronometer, lever escapement, 21 jewels, gold jewel settings, Ca. 1910

TYPE – DESCRIPTION	Avg	Ex-Fn	Mint
1/4 hr. repeater, gold, 46-52mm, OF	$1,400	$1,600	$2,250
OF w/chrono., cal. moonphase	2,400	2,800	3,400
HC	1,600	2,000	2,700
HC w/chrono., cal. & moonphase	2,600	3,000	3,800
Minute repeater, gold, 46-52mm, OF	2,800	3,200	4,000
HC	3,200	3,600	4,500
OF w/split chrono.	3,800	4,400	5,500
HC w/split chrono.	4,200	4,800	6,000
OF w/cal. & moonphase	7,000	9,000	12,000
HC w/cal. & moonphase	8,000	10,000	13,000
HC w/chrono., cal. & moonphase	8,500	10,500	14,000
Perpetual moonphase calendar, gold, OF	10,000	12,000	15,000
HC	11,000	13,000	16,000
Perp. moonphase cal. w/min . repeater, OF	22,000	26,000	34,000
HC	24,000	28,000	36,000
Perp. moonphase cal. w/min. rep. and chrono. , OF	23,000	27,000	35,000
HC	25,000	30,000	38,000

NICOLE, NIELSEN & CO.
London

Adolphe Nicole in 1840 came to London from Switzerland and joined Henry Capt. In 1876 Emil Nielsen became a partner in the firm. The company was purchased by S. Smith & Sons in 1904. Tourbillons were made by V. Kullberg and Nicole, Nielsen for the England market. Last watches made Ca. 1933.
(Made ebauche for Dent, Frodsham, and Smith)

Nicole, Nielsen, 50mm, chronograph, 15 jewels, 3/4 plate, gilded movement, Ca. 1890.

Nicole, Nielsen, 64mm, min. repeater, split-second chronograph, tourbillon, free sprung escapement, most were made for Frodsham.

TYPE – DESCRIPTION	Avg	Ex-Fn	Mint
Time only, gold, 45- 50mm, OF	$600	$800	$1,200
HC	700	900	1,300
Chronograph, gold, 45-50mm, HC	1,200	1,400	1,800
Minute repeater, gold, 46-52mm, OF	2,700	3,000	3,500
HC	3,000	3,300	3,800
OF w/chrono. & register	3,000	3,300	3,800
HC w/chrono. & register	3,400	3,800	4,300

TYPE – DESCRIPTION	Avg	Ex-Fn	Mint
Minute repeater, tourbillon, split-second chronograph, free sprung escapement, gold, 64mm,	$100,000	$125,000	$160,000
Karrusel, gold, 48-55mm, OF	6,000	7,000	10,000
Tourbillion, gold, 48-55mm, OF	28,000	32,000	44,000
Perpetual moon phase calendar, gold, OF	12,000	14,000	18,000
HC	14,000	16,000	22,000
Perp. moonphase cal. w/min.rep. and chrono., OF	24,000	26,000	32,000
HC	26,000	28,000	35,000

NON–MAGNETIC WATCH CO.
Swiss.
(NOT MARKED *PAILLARD'S PATENT*)

TYPE – DESCRIPTION	Avg	Ex-Fn	Mint
Time only, gold, 45- 50mm, OF	$350	$400	$500
HC	375	475	650
Chronograph, gold, 45-50mm, OF	550	650	800
HC	650	750	1,000
Split second chronograph, gold, 45-52mm, OF	750	850	1,100
HC	850	950	1,200
1/4 hr. repeater, gold, 46-52mm, OF	1,200	1,400	1,800
HC	1,300	1,500	2,000
Minute repeater, gold, 46-52mm, OF	2,200	2,400	2,800
HC	2,400	2,600	3,250
OF w/split chrono.	4,000	4,500	5,500
HC w/split chrono.	4,500	5,000	6,000
HC w/chrono., cal. & moonphase	5,000	5,500	6,500

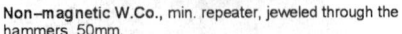

Non–magnetic W.Co., min. repeater, jeweled through the hammers, 50mm.

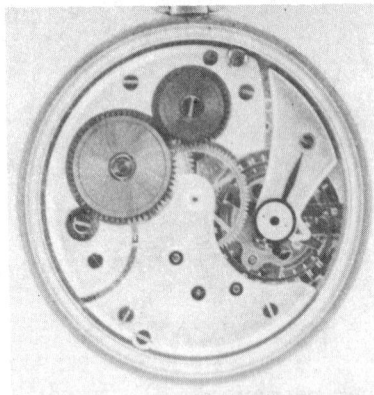

Omega pocket watch movement, 45-48mm, 15 jewels, serial number 9,888,934.

🕐 Watches listed in this book are priced at the collectable fair market **value** at the retail level, as complete watches having an original case, an original white enamel dial, and with the entire original movement in good working order with no repairs needed, unless otherwise noted.

OMEGA WATCH CO.
Swiss

Omega Watch Co. was founded by Louis Brandt in 1848. They produced watches of different grades. In 1930, they began to produce different lines with Tissot under the name Societe Sussie pour l'Industrie Horlogere. Omeg is now part of the SMH (Societe Suisse de Microelectronique et d' Horlogerie).

PRODUCTION TOTALS

DATE- SERIAL #	DATE- SERIAL #	DATE- SERIAL #
1895 –1,000,000	1944-10,000,000	1962-19,000,000
1902 - 2,000,000	1947-11,000,000	1963-20,000,000
1908 - 3,000,000	1950-12,000,000	1964-21,000,000
1912 - 4,000,000	1952-13,500,000	1965-22,000,000
1916 - 5,000,000	1954-14,000,000	1966-23,000,000
1923 - 6,000,000	1956-15,000,000	1967-25,000,000
1929 - 7,000,000	1958-16,000,000	1968-26,000,000
1935 - 8,000,000	1960-17,000,000	1969-28,000,000
1939- 9,000,000	1961-18,000,000	1970-29,000,000

Note: By 1980 ETA Calibers were being used by Omega.

The above list is provided for determining the APPROXIMATE age of your watch. Match serial number with date. Watches were not necessarily sold in the exact order of manufactured date.

TYPE – DESCRIPTION	Avg	Ex-Fn	Mint
15J, gilt, silver, 48mm, OF, C. 1905	$75	$95	$125
15J, SW, silver, 47mm, HC, C. 1910	100	125	150
21J, **R.R. model,**" Gold Filled", 52mm, OF, C. 1915	185	225	275
Time only, gold, 45- 48mm, OF	400	475	600
HC	500	575	700
Chronograph, gold, 45-50mm, OF	700	900	1,100
HC	800	1,000	1,200
Chronograph, gold, 45-50mm, **Double-Dial,** OF	2,600	3,000	4,000
Minute repeater, gold, 46-52mm, OF	2,000	2,500	3,200
HC	2,200	2,700	3,500
OF w/split chrono.	4,000	4,500	5,500
HC w/split chrono.	4,200	4,750	5,800
HC w/chrono., cal. & moonphase	5,500	6,000	7,500

Omega, **Chronograph**, gold, 45-50mm, **Double-Dial**, open face, Multi-color enamel dials.

CHARLES OUDIN
PARIS

Oudin was a pupil of Breguet and became a talented maker from 1807-1830. He produced quality timepieces and invented an early "keyless" watch.

Charles Oudin, Dial & Movement, 51mm, 32J., Minute repeater with Chronograph, Ca.1910.

TYPE – DESCRIPTION	Avg	Ex-Fn	Mint
Verge, KW, silver single case, 45mm, OF, C. 1865......................	$300	$350	$500
Early, KW, Time only, Swiss bar, silver , OF	75	95	125
GOLD, OF	400	500	700
Split sec. chrono., 29J, w/ register,18K, 51mm, HC, C. 1900	800	900	1,200
Minute repeater, gold, 46-52mm, OF...	2,200	2,400	3,000
HC	2,400	2,600	3,100
OF w/chrono. & register...	2,700	3,000	3,500
HC w/chrono. & register	2,900	3,300	3,850

"CHs. OUDIN, Paris," engraved on movement, Key Wind, cylinder escapement, Swiss bar, Ca. 1865.

PATEK, PHILIPPE & CIE.
Swiss

Patek, Philippe & Cie. has produced some of the world's most desirable factory-made watches. Antoine Norbert de Patek began contracting and selling watches in the 1830's, later became partners with Francois Czapek and generally produced lovely decorative watches for a high class of clientele. In 1845 Adrien Philippe, inventor of the modern stem-winding system, joined the firm of Patek & Cie., and in 1851, the firm established its present name. Between Philippe's talent as a watchmaker and Patek's talent as a businessman with a taste for the impeccable, the firm rapidly established an international reputation which lasts to this day. Early Patek, Philippe & Cie. watches are generally signed only on the dust cover, but some are signed on the dial and cuvette. It was not until the 1880's that the practice began of fully signing the dial, movement and case-perhaps in response to some contemporary forgery but more likely a necessity to conform to customs' regulations for their growing international market. Many early and totally original Patek watches have suffered from the misconception that all products of the company are fully signed. Never the less, collectors find such pieces more desirable. It requires more experience, however, to determine the originality of the earlier pieces. As with Vacheron & Constantin, some watches were originally cased in U.S.A., but this lowers their value in general.

PRODUCTION TOTALS

DATE—SERIAL #	DATE—SERIAL #	DATE—SERIAL #
1840— 100	1950—700,000	1940— 900,000
1845— 1,200	1955—725,000	1945— 915,000
1850— 3,000	1960—750,000	1950— 930,000
1855— 8,000	1965—775,000	1955— 940,000
1860— 15,000	1970—795,000	1960— 960,000
1865— 22,000		1965— 975,000
1870— 35,000	DATE—SERIAL #	1970— 995,000
1875— 45,000	1920— 800,000	
1880— 55,000	1925— 805,000	DATE—SERIAL #
1885— 70,000	1930— 820,000	1960—1,100,000
1890— 85,000	1935— 824,000	1965—1,130,000
1895—100,000	1940— 835,000	1970—1,250,000
1900—110,000	1945— 850,000	1975—1,350,000
1905—125,000	1950— 860,000	1980—1,450,000
1910—150,000	1955— 870,000	1985—1,600,000
1915—175,000	1960— 880,000	1990—1,850,000
1920—190,000	1965— 890,000	
1925—200,000	1970— 895,000	

The above list is provided for determining the APPROXIMATE age of your watch. Match serial number with date. Watches were not necessarily sold in the exact order of manufactured date.

EARLIER KEY WIND
NOTE: Watches signed *PATEK & CIE.* usually have serial numbers from about 1,129 to 3,729, Ca. 1845 to 1850. Usually signed on cuvette with serial number & Patek & Cie., and not on the movement. *"Patek et Czapek"* found signed on cuvette for earlier <u>KEY WIND</u> watches.

Important note: From about 1880 forward all watches were signed on dial, case & movement.

1854 Tiffany & Co. became a official customer of the Patek firm.

Patek, Philippe & Cie. 43mm, time only, 18K, open face.

Patek, Philippe & Cie., 18 jewels, engraved gold dial with enamel center, 18K, 43mm, Ca. 1920's.

Patek, Philippe & Cie. , KWKS, lever escapement, gilt movement, signed on 18K case, 47mm, Ca. 1865.

Patek, Philippe & Co., Perpetual calendar, moonphase, min. repeater & split second chronograph, 18K, OF.

Patek, Philippe & Co., "Chronometro Gondolo", 19 jewels, signed, lever escapement, 51mm, Ca. 1908.

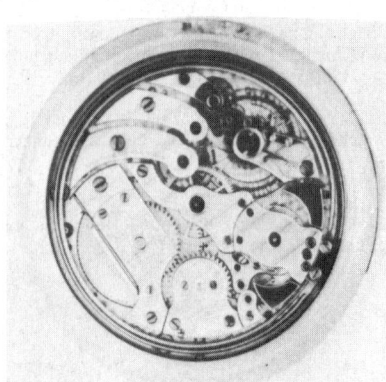

Patek, Philippe & Co., dial & movement, min. repeater, 29J, perpetual calendar, day, date, month, moon-phases, 18K.

TYPE – DESCRIPTION

TYPE – DESCRIPTION	Avg	Ex-Fn	Mint
Time only, gold, 25- 30mm, ladies, OF	$800	$900	$1,100
HC	1,000	1,300	1,800
Time only, gold, 32- 44mm, OF	1,800	2,000	2,500
HC	2,500	2,800	3,500
Time only, **enameled bezel**, gold, 32- 44mm, OF	2,500	2,800	3,500
Time only, gold, 45- 50mm, OF	2,000	2,200	2,500
HC	3,000	3,200	3,500
Time only, with **Wind Indicator**, gold, 45- 50mm, OF	4,000	5,000	7,000
EARLY Time only, KWKS, gilt mvt., lever or cylinder escapement pre 1865, signed on gold case, 40-45mm,	1,500	1,700	2,000
Time only, Chronometre Gondolo, gold, 38mm, OF	2,000	2,400	3,000
Time only, Chronometre Gondolo, gold, 50mm, OF	2,500	2,900	3,500

Patek, Philippe & Co., enameled bezel, 18K OF, 42mm

Patek, Philippe & Co., perpetual calendar with moon phases, signed, 18 jewels, 49mm, Ca. 1949

TYPE – DESCRIPTION

TYPE – DESCRIPTION	Avg	Ex-Fn	Mint
Chronograph, gold, 45-50mm, OF	$3,200	$3,400	$4,000
HC	4,000	4,400	5,000
OF w/register	3,600	4,000	4,500
HC w/register	4,200	4,700	5,500
Split second chronograph, gold, 45-52mm, OF	5,200	6,000	7,500
HC	5,800	6,500	8,500
OF w/register	5,500	6,300	8,000
HC w/register	6,500	7,300	9,000
1/4 hr. repeater, gold, 46-52mm, OF	2,500	3,000	3,800
HC	2,900	3,400	4,200
5 minute repeater, gold, 46-52mm, OF	4,000	4,600	5,500
HC	5,000	5,600	6,500
OF w/split chrono.	8,000	9,000	12,000
HC w/split chrono.	9,000	10,000	15,000
Minute repeater, gold, 46-52mm, OF	7,000	8,000	10,500
HC	10,000	12,000	14,500
OF w/chrono.	10,000	11,000	12,500
HC w/chrono.	12,000	14,000	16,500
OF w/chrono. & register	11,000	12,000	13,500
HC w/chrono. & register	14,000	16,000	18,500

TYPE – DESCRIPTION	Avg	Ex-Fn	Mint
Minute repeater, w/split chrono., gold, 46-52mm, OF	$15,000	$18,000	$22,000
HC w/split chrono.	18,000	22,000	26,000
OF w/split chrono. & register	16,000	20,000	24,000
HC w/split chrono. & register	22,000	25,000	30,000
Perpetual moonphase calendar, gold, OF	25,000	30,000	35,000
HC	27,000	32,000	38,000
Perp. moonphase cal. w/min. repeater, OF	50,000	60,000	70,000
HC	55,000	65,000	75,000
Perpetual moonphase cal. w/ min. rep. & chrono. , OF	60,000	70,000	80,000
HC	65,000	75,000	85,000
Perpetual moonphase cal. w/ min. rep. & split sec. chrono. , OF	80,000	90,000	120,000
HC	85,000	95,000	150,000

Patek, Philippe & Co., Digital Jump Hour, with minute hand & second hand, 18 jewels, 45mm, 18K.

Patek, Philippe & Co., gold coin watch, 100 pesetas, secret push-piece opens lid to disclose dial, 35mm, Ca.1928.

TYPE – DESCRIPTION	Avg	Ex-Fn	Mint
Lady's pendant watch w/ brooch,18K & small diamonds, 27mm	$2,400	$2,800	$3,300
Gold Coin, 100 pesetas 18K, 18J., coin opens to disclose dial	4,000	4,300	5,000
Digital Jump Hour, W/minute hand & sec. hand, 45mm, 18K	30,000	38,000	50,000
Karrusel, gold, 48-55mm, OF	85,000	95,000	100,000
Tourbillion, gold, 48-55mm, OF	100,000	120,000	150,000
HC	110,000	130,000	175,000
Detent chronometer, gold, 48-52mm, OF	25,000	30,000	40,000
HC	30,000	35,000	50,000
World time watch, gold, 48-52mm, OF	35,000	40,000	50,000

🕐 Pricing in this Guide are fair market price for **COMPLETE** watches which are reflected from the "**NAWCC**" National and regional shows.

COMPARISON OF WATCH SIZES

U. S. A.	EUROPEAN
10-12 SIZE	40—44 MM
16 SIZE	45—48 MM
18 SIZE	50—54 MM

PICARD, JAMES

GENEVA

Watch dealer and finisher in the latter part of the 19th Century. Known for his complicated watches and pocket chronometers of high quality.

TYPE – DESCRIPTION	Avg	Ex-Fn	Mint
Time only, gold, 45- 50mm, OF	$450	$550	$700
HC	600	700	850
Chronograph, gold, 45-50mm, OF	750	850	1,000
Split second chronograph, gold, 45-52mm, OF	1,700	1,900	2,200
HC w/register	2,700	3,000	3,500
5 minute repeater, gold, 45-52mm, OF	3,200	3,400	3,700
HC	3,500	3,700	4,000
Minute repeater, gold, 45-52mm, OF	3,500	3,700	4,000
HC	3,700	4,000	4,500
OF w/split chrono.	4,800	5,200	6,000
HC w/split chrono.	7,000	7,500	8,200
OF w/cal. & moonphase	9,000	9,500	11,000
HC w/chrono., cal. & moonphase	10,000	11,000	13,000
Tourbillion, gold, 48-55mm, OF	30,000	35,000	45,000
Detent chronometer, gold, 48-52mm , OF	4,000	4,500	6,000
HC	5,000	5,500	7,000
Perp. moonphase cal. w/min.rep. and chrono, OF	20,000	25,000	35,000
HC	25,000	30,000	45,000

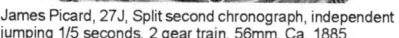

James Picard, 27J, Split second chronograph, independent jumping 1/5 seconds, 2 gear train, 56mm, Ca. 1885.

Albert Potter, 22 jewels, hunting case, helical hair spring, detent escapement

ALBERT H. POTTER & CO.

(Note: For further information on Potter timepieces, see U.S. Watch Section.)

TYPE – DESCRIPTION	Avg	Ex-Fn	Mint
Time only, gold, 45- 48mm, OF	$4,000	$5,000	$7,000
HC	4,500	5,500	7,500
Pocket chronometer, pivoted detent ,free-spring balance, porcelain dial, bridge mvt., **re-cased** (silver), 58mm, C.1879	4,000	4,500	5,000
Calendar, nickel, offset seconds and days of week dials, SW, 18K, 50mm, OF, C.1800	8,000	9,000	12,000
Rare lever, SW, 19J, nickel mvt., 1/2 moon-shaped plate for barrel & train, white enamel dial, triple signed, lever with counterpoise on pallet,18k, 52mm, HC, C.1882	100,000	115,000	140,000

TYPE – DESCRIPTION	Avg	Ex-Fn	Mint
Regulator dial (center minute hand, offset hours, offset seconds),			
half moon- shaped nickel mvt., 18K, 50mm, OF, C.1880.......	$18,000	$23,000	$30,000
Minute repeater, gold, 46-52mm, OF...	15,000	18,000	22,000
HC	20,000	22,000	26,000
Detent chronometer, gold, 48-52mm, OF	15,000	17,000	20,000
HC	18,000	20,000	23,000
Perp. moonphase cal. w/min. repeater, HC.....................................	30,000	35,000	45,000
Perp. moonphase cal. w/min. rep. & chrono.,HC	32,000	37,000	47,000
4 SIZE, 21J., hour repeater, 18K HC .... ★★	4,000	5,000	7,000

PRIOR, GEORGE
PRIOR, EDWARD
LONDON

George Prior born in 1793 and died in 1830. He was a recipient of two prestigious awards and well known for his pieces for the turkish market. He also produced tortoise shell and triple-case watches with the outer case featuring wood with silver inlay. He made gold watches with Oriental chased cases, watches with pierced outer cases and triple-cased enamel engraved and repeaters.

Edward Prior born in 1800 and died in 1868. Well known for his pieces for the turkish market.

TYPE – DESCRIPTION	Avg	Ex-Fn	Mint
Verge, pair case, plain silver, 50mm, OF...	$450	$500	$600
Verge, pair case w/ repousee, silver, 50mm, OF	1,000	1,200	1,500
Verge, triple case w/ tortoise shell, silver, 56mm, OF	1,500	1,700	2,000
Verge, pair case, GOLD, 48-52mm, OF	2,000	2,300	2,800
Verge, pair case, GOLD & enamel, 48-54mm, OF	2,800	3,000	3,500
1/4 hr. repeater, pair case, GOLD & enamel, 50mm, OF.................	6,000	6,500	7,500

George Prior, 52mm, white porcelain signed dial, and engine turned silver hunter's case, verge with fusee, KW KS, Ca. 1830.

Edward Prior, outer case made of tortoise shell, leather travel case, verge escapement, note the stag beetle hour hand and poker minute hand, Ca. 1830.

ROLEX WATCH CO.
Swiss

Rolex was founded by Hans Wilsdorf in 1905 & in <u>1908</u> the trade-mark **"Rolex"** was officially registered. In 1926, they made the first real waterproof wrist watch and called it the **"Oyster."** In 1931, Rolex introduced a self-wind movement which they called **"Perpetual"**. In 1945, they introduced the **"Date-Just"** which showed the day of the month. The **"Submariner"** was introduced in 1953 and in 1954 the **"GMT Master"** model. In 1956, a "Day-Date" model was released which indicates the day of the month (in numbers) and the day of the week (in letters.)

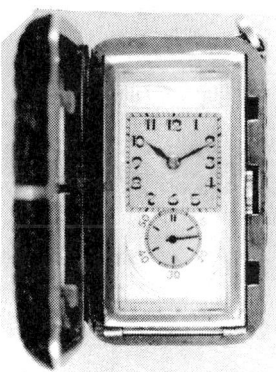

Rolex, **SPORTING PRINCE**, 17 jewels, Adjusted to six positions, silver & leather case,

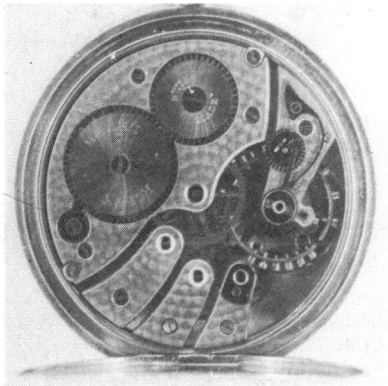

Rolex, 42-43mm, 17 jewels, three adjustments, cam regulator, exposed winding gears.

ROLEX ESTIMATED PRODUCTION DATES

DATE–SERIAL #	DATE–SERIAL #	DATE–SERIAL #
1925 — 25,000	1949 — 608,000	1973— 3,741,000
1926 — 27,500	1950 — 673,500	1974— 4,000,000
1927 — 30,500	1951 — 735,500	1975— 4,260,000
1928 — 33,000	1952 — 804,000	1976— 4,530,000
1929 — 35,500	1953 — 869,000	1977— 5,000,000
1930 — 38,000	1954 — 935,000	1978— 5,480,000
1931 — 40,000	1955—1,010,000	1979— 5,960,000
1932 — 43,000	1956—1,095,000	1980— 6,430,000
1933 — 49,000	1957—1,167,000	1981— 6,910,000
1934 — 55,000	1958—1,245,000	1982— 7,380,000
1935 — 62,000	1959—1,323,000	1983— 7,860,000
1936 — 82,000	1960—1,401,000	1984— 8,340,000
1937 — 98,000	1961—1,485,000	1985— 8,810,000
1938—118,000	1962—1,557,000	1986— 9,300,000
1939—136,000	1963—1,635,000	1987— 9,760,000
1940—165,000	1964—1,713,000	1987 1/2-9,999,999
1941—194,000	1965—1,791,000	1987 3/4-R000,001
1942—224,000	1966—1,870,000	1988 —- R999,999
1943—253,000	1967—2,164,000	1989 — L000,001
1944—284,000	1968—2,426,000	1990 — L999,999
1945—348,000	1969—2,689,000	1990 1/2-E000,001
1946—413,000	1970—2,952,000	1991 1/4-E999,999
1947—478,000	1971—3,215,000	1991 1/2-X000,001
1948—543,000	1972—3,478,000	1991 3/4-N000,001
		1992 1/4-C000,001

The above list is provided for determining the APPROXIMATE age of your watch. Match serial number with date. Watches were not necessarily sold in the exact order of manufactured date.The above list was furnished with the help of TOM ENGLE.

Hans Wilsdorf started in 1905 with his brother-in-law using the name of Wilsdorf & Davis. They used movement supplier Aegler in Bienne and bought cases in London. In 1919 Wilsdorf started the "Manufacture des Montres Rolex", the movements were manufactured in Bienne but finished in Geneva. 1950 the **Turn-o-graph** was used, the forerunner of the **SUBMARINER.**

ROLEX, split seconds Chronograph, register, S.S. case.

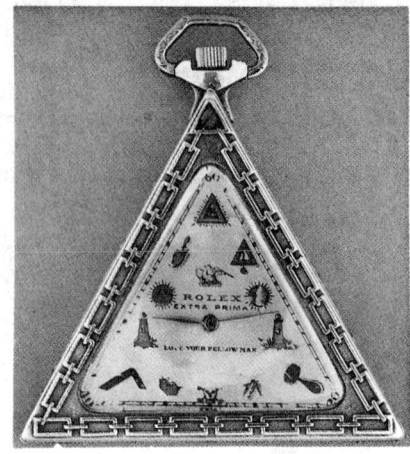

ROLEX, Masonic watch, mother of pearl dial, 15J.

TYPE – DESCRIPTION	Avg	Ex-Fn	Mint
17J, silver, 45mm, OF, C. 1920's....................................	$225	$250	$325
17J, 3 adj., CAM regulator, **14K**, 43mm, OF, C. 1920	450	550	750
1/4 Century Club, 17J, **14K**, 41mm, OF, C. 1940..........................	650	750	900
Thin line, 17J, **18K**, 42mm, OF, C. 1940..	650	750	900
Time only, gold, 40-44mm, **18K**, OF	500	600	750
HC	700	800	1,000
Time only, gold, 45-50mm, **18K**, OF	800	900	1,100
HC	1,200	1,300	1,500
Rolex, **SPORTING PRINCE**, 17J, Adj. 6P .... ★★	3,000	3,500	4,500
Duo dial, fancy-shaped, 17J, **18K/WG**, OF, 41mm, C. 1930	2,000	2,500	3,500
$20 dollar coin watch in closed case, triple signed, C.1950.............	2,500	3,000	4,000
World time watch, gold, 45-52mm	9,000	10,000	12,000
Chronograph, split seconds, register, S.S. case, 50mm...................	3,000	4,000	6,000
Masonic, mother of pearl dial, silver case, Ca.1930s .... ★★★	4,000	4,200	5,000

Romilly, Gold , verge, pair case with polychrome enamel & scene, 52mm, OF, Ca.1730.

ROMILLY, JEAN
PARIS

Became a master Watchmaker in 1752 after studying in Geneva and Paris. In 1755, he completed a repeater with beating seconds and a large balance (at one oscillation per second). He also made watches with a 8 day power reserve. Also known for his very ornate paintings on enamel.

TYPE – DESCRIPTION	Avg	Ex-Fn	Mint
Time only, KW, verge, silver, 46-52mm OF	$700	$900	$1,200
Time & Calendar, verge, silver, 50mm, OF	1,500	1,600	1,800
Gold , verge, pair case, plain, 48mm, OF	2,000	2,100	2,300
Gold , verge, pair case w/ enamel & scene, Ca.1730, 52mm, OF...	4,000	4,200	4,800
1/4 repeater, SILVER, 52mm, OF	2,500	2,800	3,500
1/4 repeater, GOLD, 54mm, OF	3,500	3,800	4,500

ROBERT ROSKELL
Liverpool

Roskell was active from 1798-1830 and worked in both Liverpool and London. He made fine rack lever fusees and gold dial watches. Other family members also produced watches for many years in Liverpool.

R. Roskell, 47mm, bar style movement, cylinder escapement, Ca. 1850.

Roskell, Monochrome Scene, Hour & Min. Hand removed to show scene, KW KS, Ca. 1810-20.

TYPE – DESCRIPTION	Avg	Ex-Fn	Mint
KW, (Swiss ebauche) 15J, silver, 48mm, OF, C. 1830-70	$75	$95	$125
KW, (Swiss) 15J, silver, 46-48mm, HC, C. 1830-70	100	125	150
KW, 13J, dust cover, fancy gold dial, 18K, 47mm, OF, C.1830-70	275	300	375

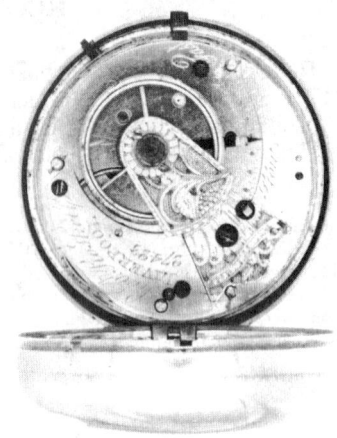

Roskell, 48mm, lever escapement, KW KS, Ca.1830.   Roskell, 55mm, KW KS, Ca. 1825

TYPE – DESCRIPTION	Avg	Ex-Fn	Mint
Rack lever fusee, porcelain dial, silver, hallmarked, OF, C.1870....	$350	$400	$500
2 day marine chronometer fusee, spring detent escapement, helical hairspring, 54 hr. wind ind., gimbal & box	1,800	2,000	2,500
Debaufre escapement, KW KS, silver, 55mm, OF..................... ★ ★	3,000	3,200	3,600

Debaufre escapement,
D-shaped & inclined pallet.

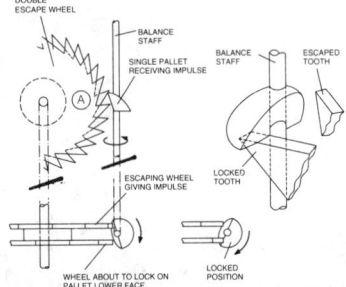

Roskell, 55mm, movement with Debaufre escapement, D-shaped and inclined pallet, KW KS, Ca. 1840.   Robert Roskell, 52mm, London, fusee, spring detent escapement, helical hairspring, 54 hr. wind ind., KW KS.

ROSKOPF
Swiss

Maker of pin lever, early low cost stem wind watches, often found with fancy dials. A **true** Roskopf watch has only *3 wheels* in its train of gears.

Roskopf, multi-colored blue enamel dial, nail set.
Roskopf, 45mm, pin lever escapement, 3 wheel train.

TYPE – DESCRIPTION	Avg	Ex-Fn	Mint
4J, pin lever, 3 wheel train, nail set, base metal, OF, Ca. 1885	$65	$75	$95
Fancy dial, oversize plain case, 55mm, OF, Ca. 1880	75	95	125
Fancy enamel dial, **fancy enamel case**, 55mm, OF, Ca. 1880	125	150	195

Roskopf, multi-colored enamel with blue & purple Butterflies & silver case, nail set.

THOMAS RUSSELL & SONS
London

Thomas Russell & Sons produced quality early keyless watches including Karrusels and chronometers. (Circa 1870-1910)

TYPE – DESCRIPTION	Avg	Ex-Fn	Mint
Time only, gold, 45-48mm, OF	$600	$700	$900
Chronograph, gold, 45-50mm, OF	1,200	1,300	1,600
Split second chronograph, gold, 45-52mm, OF	1,800	2,000	2,500
Minute repeater, gold, 46-52mm, OF	2,500	3,000	4,000
HC	3,000	3,800	4,500
Karrusel, 18K, 51mm, OF, C. 1890	4,000	4,500	5,000

Signed *Thomas Russell & Sons Liverpool*, KW KS, lever with a club foot escape wheel, Ca. 1905.   **Sandoz**, 52mm, KW, nickel bridge, gold train, Ca.1880.

SANDOZ & FILS
SWISS

Large family of watchmakers in the La Chaux-de-Fonds area. Known for repeating watches and pocket chronometers of fine quality.

TYPE – DESCRIPTION	Avg	Ex-Fn	Mint
Time only, gold, 40- 44mm, OF	$325	$375	$450
HC	450	500	600
Time only, gold, 45- 50mm, OF	525	600	700
HC	650	725	850
Chronograph, gold, 45-50mm, OF	700	750	800
Split second chronograph, gold, 45-52mm, OF	1,600	1,800	2,000
HC w/register	2,250	2,500	2,750
5 minute repeater, gold, 45-52mm, OF	2,000	2,200	2,800
HC	2,200	2,500	3,700
Minute repeater, gold, 45-52mm, OF	2,000	2,400	3,000
HC	2,500	3,000	4,000
OF w/split chrono.	4,000	4,800	6,000
HC w/split chrono.	6,000	7,000	8,500
OF w/cal. & moonphase	8,000	8,500	10,000
HC w/chrono., cal. & moonphase	9,000	10,000	14,000
Tourbillion, gold, 48-55mm, OF	20,000	25,000	35,000
Detent chronometer, gold, 48-52mm , OF	5,000	6,000	7,000
HC	5,500	6,500	7,500
World time watch, gold, 48-52mm, OF	6,000	8,000	12,000
Perp. moonphase cal. w/min.rep. and chrono, OF	25,000	28,000	35,000
HC	30,000	33,000	40,000

TAVANNES
Swiss
Creates watches in 1895, other names used Dvina, La Tavanes, Obi, Lena Azow, and Kawa.

TYPE – DESCRIPTION	Avg	Ex-Fn	Mint
15J, GF, 35mm, HC, C. 1910	$80	$95	$125
15J, **14K,** 35mm, HC, C. 1910	200	225	275
17J, **14K,** 45mm, OF, C. 1915	225	250	300
21J, **14K,** 45mm, OF, C. 1920	250	275	325
Enamel Bezel & gold, 14K, 40mm, OF	400	500	650
Enamel Scene & gold, 18K, 45mm, OF, C. 1925	5,000	5,500	7,000

TAVANNES, Enamel Scene, 45mm, 18K, OF, C. 1925.   Tiffany & Co., P.P.Co., 43mm, enamel on bezel, 18K.

TIFFANY & CO.

In 1837 Charles Lewis Tiffany opened a store with John P. Young. They enlarged this operation in 1841, with the help of J.L. Eliss, and imported fine jewelry, watches and clocks from Europe. They incorporated as Tiffany & Co. in 1853. Tiffany made clocks, on special order, in New York around the mid-1800's. About 1874 Tiffany & Co. started a watch factory in Geneva but with little success. Four years later Patek, Philippe & Co. assumed the management of their Geneva watch business. The watch machinery was returned to America. Tiffany, Young & Ellis had been a client of Patek, Philippe & Co. since 1849. Tiffany & Co. introduced Patek, Philippe to the American market in 1885. Audemars, Piguet and International Watch Co. also made watches for this esteemed company. Tiffany & Co. sells watches of simple elegance as well as watches with complications such as chronographs, moon phases, repeaters, etc.

TYPE – DESCRIPTION	Avg	Ex-Fn	Mint
Time only, gold, 40- 44mm, OF	$375	$425	$500
HC	525	600	700
Time only, gold, 40-44mm, (P.P.Co.), 18K, **enamel on bezel,** OF.	1,500	1,700	2,200
Time only, gold, 45- 50mm, OF	700	800	950
HC	900	1,000	1,200
Chronograph, gold, 45-50mm, OF	1,400	1,500	1,800
HC	1,800	1,900	2,100
OF w/register	1,600	1,700	1,900
Split second chronograph, gold, 45-52mm, OF	2,800	3,000	3,400
HC	3,200	3,400	4,000

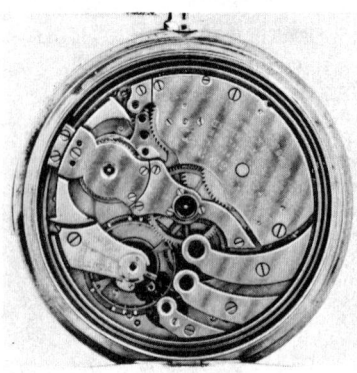

Tiffany & Co., 50mm, 25J., split-second chronograph.

Tiffany & Co., flat minute repeater, 45mm, 29 jewels, made by Patek, Philippe & Co., ca. 1911.

TYPE – DESCRIPTION	Avg	Ex-Fn	Mint
5 minute repeater, gold, 46-52mm, OF	$3,000	$3,800	$4,500
HC	3,500	4,000	5,000
OF w/split chrono.	5,000	6,000	7,000
HC w/split chrono.	6,000	7,000	7,500
Minute repeater, gold, 46-52mm, OF	3,000	3,200	4,000
HC	4,000	4,500	5,500
by P. P. & Co., flat, 29J., gold, 45mm, OF, C.1912	9,000	11,000	15,000
OF w/split chrono. & register	7,000	8,000	10,000
HC w/split chrono. & register	8,000	9,000	12,000
HC w/chrono., cal. & moonphase	10,000	12,000	16,000
World time watch, gold, 48-52mm, OF	10,000	14,000	16,000
Perpetual moonphase calendar, gold, OF	8,000	9,000	12,000
Perp. moonphase cal. w/min. rep. and chrono, OF	30,000	35,000	42,000
HC	35,000	40,000	52,000

TIMING & REPEATING WATCH CO.
Geneva

Timing & Repeating W. Co., chronograph movement Patented Sept. 23, 1880 - England Pat. # 3224.

Timing & Repeating W. CO., chronograph movement Patented Sept. 23, 1880 - England Pat. # 3224.

TYPE – DESCRIPTION	Avg	Ex-Fn	Mint
Chronograph, 17J, GF, 48mm, OF, C. 1900	$150	$160	$175
Chronograph w/register, 17J, GF, 48mm, OF, C. 1900	185	200	250
Chronograph, 17J, gilt mvt., silver, 49mm, HC, C. 1900	200	225	275

TISSOT
Swiss

The firm of Chs. Tissot & Fils was founded in 1853 in Le Locle by Charles Tissot. This skilled watchmaker worked from his home and in 1907 a factory was started. In 1971 the worlds first plastic wrist watch was made.

TYPE – DESCRIPTION	Avg	Ex-Fn	Mint
Time only, gold, 40- 44mm, OF	$350	$400	$500
HC	450	500	600
Time only, gold, 45- 50mm, OF	500	550	700
HC	600	700	850
2-Train 1/4 second jump watch, silver, 50mm,	700	800	950
2-Train 1/4 second jump watch, gold, 50mm,	1,700	2,000	2,500
Chronograph, gold, 45-50mm, OF	800	850	900
Split second chronograph, gold, 45-52mm, OF	1,800	2,000	2,200
HC w/register	2,800	3,000	3,400
5 minute repeater, gold, 45-52mm, OF	2,700	2,900	3,300
HC	3,000	3,200	3,500
Minute repeater, gold, 45-52mm, OF	3,000	3,200	3,500
HC	3,200	3,500	4,000
OF w/split chrono.	4,000	4,500	6,000
HC w/split chrono.	6,500	7,000	8,500
OF w/cal. & moonphase	8,000	8,500	10,000
HC w/chrono., cal. & moonphase	9,000	10,000	12,000
Tourbillion, gold, 48-55mm, OF	38,000	40,000	55,000
Detent chronometer, gold, 48-52mm , OF	4,000	5,000	7,000
HC	5,000	6,000	7,500
World time watch, gold, 48-52mm, OF	10,000	12,000	15,000
Perp. moonphase cal. w/min.rep. and chrono, OF	20,000	25,000	35,000
HC	25,000	30,000	40,000

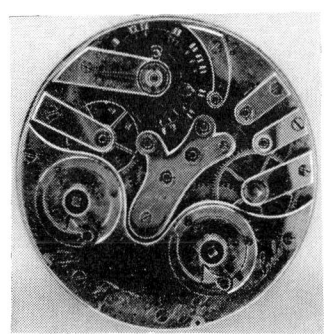

Tissot, 2-Train 1/4 second jump watch, center sweep hand, enamel dial, 28 J., gold train, 54mm, KWKS, 18K, Ca. 1880.

Tissot, Minute repeater, with chronograph, day date month, moonphase, 27 jewels, 18K, HC, Ca. 1910.

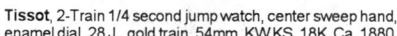

Watches listed in this book are priced at the collectable fair market **value** at the retail level, as complete watches having an original case, an original white enamel dial, and with the entire original movement in good working order with no repairs needed, unless otherwise noted.

TOBIAS & CO.

M. I. Tobias started a watchmaking career in Liverpool, about 1805. He specialized in exporting watches to U.S.A. About 1820 the company started using movements made in Switzerland the watches were engraved, *Liverpool*. The script M.I.Tobias can be misleading the script letter (I) may look like a **(J)**. The watches with a (J style) are made in the Swiss manner with a club-tooth escape-wheel made of steel and straight line lever, the Liverpool or English style watches used a (I) & a "ratchet" (sharp-pointed) escape wheel made of brass and right angle lever. The Tobias family activity extends from about 1805 to 1868.

 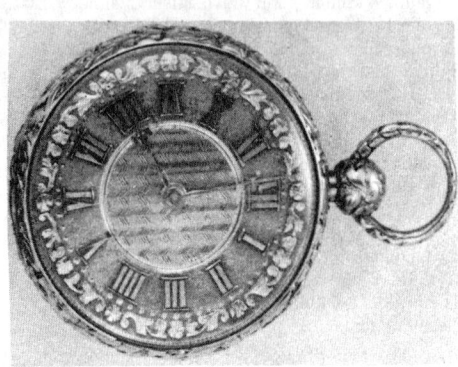

M. I. **Tobias & Co.**, Lord Street, Liverpool, 2 train independent sec., Pat.21 Feb, 1848, 52mm, right angle lever.   M. I. **Tobias**, multi-color gold dial & thin gold case, 52mm.

TYPE – DESCRIPTION	Avg	Ex-Fn	Mint
KW, 7-15J, silver, 47mm, OF	$75	$95	$135
KW,7- 15J, silver, 47mm, HC	100	125	175
KW,7-15J, swiss, **gilt dial,** fancy case, **18K,** 48mm,OF	265	300	375
KW, lever, fusee, **gold dial, Heavy 18K,** 52mm, HC	700	900	1,200
KW, rack lever escapement, **Silver,** 56mm, OF	350	400	500
HC	400	450	600
KW, verge fusee, **multi-color gold dial & THIN case,** 52mm, OF	450	500	700
HC	600	700	950
KW, rack lever escapement, **Gold,** 56mm, OF	700	800	1,000
HC	900	1,000	1,200
Captain's watch, center sec., sub-sec., gold dial, **18K,** 51mm, OF..	1,100	1,400	1,800
18K, 51mm, HC	1,200	1,500	2,000

 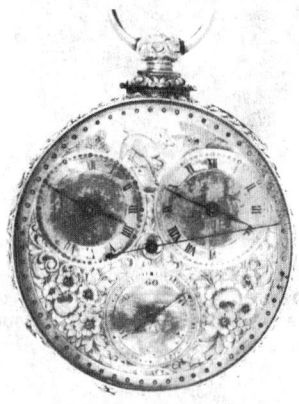

Tobias, (Liverpool), 51mm, OF, 18K, Captain's watch, center sec., subseconds, gold dial.

TOUCHON & CO.

Swiss

Touchon & Co. started using this name as a trade mark in 1907. They manufactured complex and simple watches. In 1921 they associated with the firm of Wittnauer & Co.

Touchon & Co., 47mm, 29 jewels, minute repeater, open face, jeweled through hammers.

Touchon & Co., 47mm, 29 jewels, split-second chronograph and minute repeater, ca. 1910.

TYPE – DESCRIPTION	Avg	Ex-Fn	Mint
Time only, gold, 45- 50mm, OF	$450	$500	$600
HC	550	600	750
1/4 hr. repeater, gold, 46-52mm, OF	800	1,000	1,100
HC	1,000	1,200	1,500
OF w/chrono.	900	1,100	1,400
HC w/chrono.	1,100	1,300	1,700
OF w/chrono., cal. & moonphase	2,200	2,600	3,500
HC w/chrono., cal. & moonphase	2,400	2,800	3,700
5 minute repeater, gold, 46-52mm, OF	1,800	2,200	3,000
HC	2,000	2,400	3,200
Minute repeater, gold, 46-52mm, OF	2,500	3,000	4,000
HC	2,700	3,200	4,200
OF w/chrono. & register	2,700	3,200	4,200
HC w/chrono. & register	2,900	3,400	4,400
OF w/split chrono.	4,500	5,000	6,000
HC w/split chrono. & register	4,800	5,500	6,400
HC w/chrono., cal. & moonphase	5,500	6,000	7,500
HC, **Perp.** moonphase cal.	22,000	24,000	28,000
HC, **Perp.** moonphase cal. and chrono.	25,000	28,000	32,000
World time watch, gold, 48-52mm, OF	4,500	5,000	6,500
Perpetual moonphase calendar, gold, OF	7,000	8,000	10,000

COMPARISON OF WATCH SIZES

U. S. A.	EUROPEAN
10-12 SIZE	40—44 MM
16 SIZE	45—48 MM
18 SIZE	50—52 MM

VACHERON & CONSTANTIN
Swiss

The firm of Vacheron & Constantin was officially founded by Abraham Vacheron in 1785, but the association bearing the name today did not come into being until 1819. In these early periods, different grades of watches produced by Vacheron & Constantin bore different names.

ESTIMATED PRODUCTION DATES

DATE–SERIAL #	DATE–SERIAL #	DATE–SERIAL #
1830 - 30,000	1880-170,000	1930-410,000
1835 - 40,000	1885-180,000	1935-420,000
1840 - 50,000	1890-190,000	1940-440,000
1845 - 60,000	1895-223,000	1945-464,000
1850 - 75,000	1900-256,000	1950-488,000
1855 - 95,000	1905-289,000	1955-512,000
1860-110,000	1910-322,000	1960-536,000
1865-125,000	1915-355,000	1965-560,000
1870-140,000	1920-385,000	1970-585,000
1875-155,000	1925-400,000	

The above list is provided for determining the APPROXIMATE age of your watch. Match serial number with date. Watches were not necessarily sold in the exact order of manufactured date.

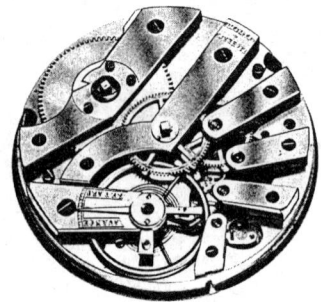

Early movements manufactured with the machines invented by George-Auguste Leschot. The machines were built in the Vacheron Constantin factory Ca. 1839 to 1840. In about 1863 to 1865 V. & C. manufactured a inexpensive watch using the names Abraham Vacheron or Abm. Vacheron also the name of Chossat & Cie.

The association with Leschot, around 1840, catapulted the firm into its position as a top quality manufacturer. Before that time, their watches were typical of Genevese production. Vacheron & Constantin exported many movements to the United States to firms such as Bigelow, Kennard & Co., which were cased domestically, typically in the period 1900-1935. In its early period the firm produced some lovely ladies' enameled watches, later it produced high grade timepieces and complicated watches, and to this day produces fine watches.

Vacheron & Constantin, 44mm, 18 jewels, enamel bezel, 18K, Ca. 1930.

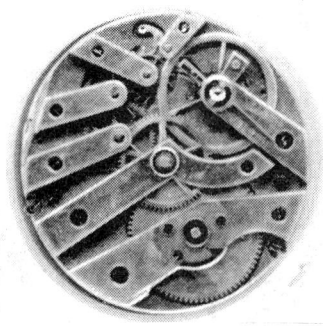

Early bar movement, lever escap., **signed "VACHERON & CONSTANTIN"** time only, KW KS, silver case, Ca.1840-1875.

TYPE – DESCRIPTION	Avg	Ex-Fn	Mint
Early bar movement, lever escap., **signed Vacheron & Constantin**			
time only, KW KS, silver case, 30-39mm, OF	$135	$165	$250
(same as above) 40-44mm, OF	185	235	325
(same as above) 45-48mm, OF	200	250	350
(same as above) 45-48mm, **HC**	250	300	400
Early Le-Pine bar movement, duplex escap., GOLD & ENAMEL			
KW KS, **signed Vacheron & Constantin**, 49mm, OF	4,500	5,500	6,500
Time only, 18K gold & **enamel bezel**, 40-44mm, OF	1,200	1,300	1,500

Vacheron & Constantin, 49mm, Early Lepine bar style movement, duplex escapement, GOLD & ENAMEL, KW KS, **signed Vacheron & Constantin**, 49mm, OF, Ca. 1840.

Vacheron & Constantin, Gold coin 50 pesos 900 fine, coin hollowed out to receive watch, LEFT view shows dial & movement.

TYPE – DESCRIPTION	Avg	Ex-Fn	Mint
Time only, 18K gold, 40-44mm, OF	$600	$800	$1,000
HC	1,000	1,200	1,500
Time only, gold, 45-50mm, OF	1,200	1,400	1,800
HC	1,800	2,000	2,400
X-thin, 17J., **Aluminum,** weight =20 grains, OF, C. 1940	1,600	1,800	2,200
Desk chronometer, wooden box, 21J., silver, 60mm, OF, C.1943	2,000	2,500	3,200
Gold coin 50 pesos 900 fine, coin hollowed out to receive watch	3,000	3,500	4,000

V. & C., Chronograph, for the corps of engineers USA, 20 jewels, enamel dial, nail set, 50mm, 3,000 made, Ca.1917.

V. & C., Astronomic with moon phases, perpetual calendar, minute repeater, split-second chronograph, 1905.

TYPE – DESCRIPTION	Avg	Ex-Fn	Mint
Chronograph, corps of engineers USA, **SILVER**, 45-50mm, OF	$1,200	$1,500	$1,800
Chronograph, gold, 45-50mm, **V& C case**, OF	2,500	2,700	3,000
HC	3,000	3,200	4,000
OF w/register	2,700	3,000	3,500
HC w/register	3,500	3,800	4,000

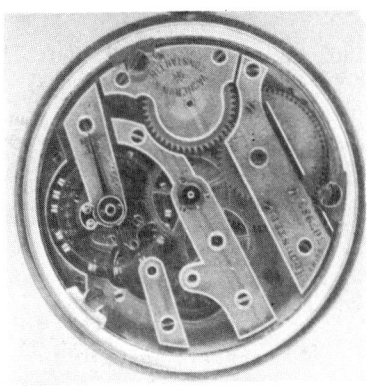

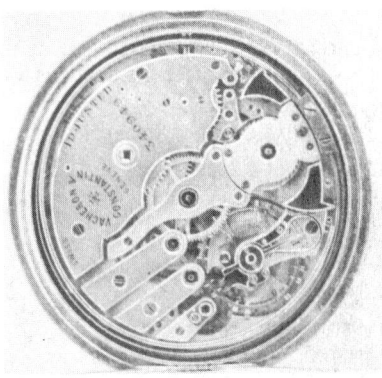

V. & C., 40mm, wolf tooth winding, open face.   V. & C., 40mm, 31J., Min. repeater, slide activated, OF.

TYPE – DESCRIPTION	Avg	Ex-Fn	Mint
Split second chronograph, gold, 45-52mm, OF	$5,500	$5,800	$6,500
HC	6,500	6,800	7,500
OF w/register	6,000	6,300	7,000
HC w/register	7,500	7,800	8,500
Minute repeater, gold, 46-52mm, OF	6,000	6,500	8,000
HC	7,000	8,000	11,000
OF w/chrono.	7,000	9,000	10,000
HC w/chrono.	12,000	14,000	17,000
OF w/chrono. & register	8,000	9,000	11,000
HC w/chrono. & register	12,000	14,000	18,000
OF w/split chrono.	10,000	11,000	13,000
HC w/split chrono.	14,000	16,000	20,000
OF w/split chrono. & register	10,000	12,000	15,000
HC w/split chrono. & register	15,000	18,000	22,000
OF w/chrono., cal. & moonphase	15,000	18,000	22,000
Tourbillion, gold, 48-55mm, OF	50,000	65,000	90,000
World time watch, gold, 48-52mm, OF	25,000	28,000	35,000
Perp. moonphase cal. w/min. repeater, OF	45,000	50,000	65,000
HC	50,000	55,000	70,000
Perp. moonphase cal. w/min. rep. and split sec. chrono., OF	55,000	60,000	75,000
Perp. moonphase cal. w/min. rep. and split sec. chrono., HC	65,000	75,000	85,000

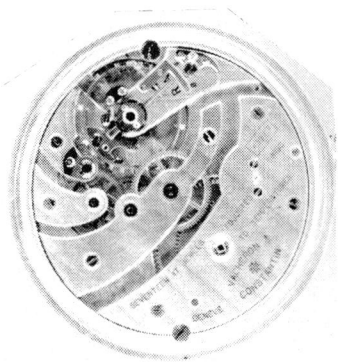

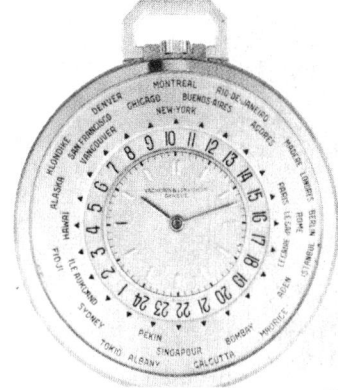

V. & C., extra thin and light weight **Aluminum,** (20 grains), about 12 size, 44mm, OF, 17 jewels, Ca. 1940.   V. & C., World time, revolving 24 hour dial, 31 citys of the world, 18 jewels, 45mm, Ca. 1945

VINER
LONDON

Charles Viner apprenticed in about 1802 and in records till 1840. The company continued after his death as Viner & Co. Viner also made clocks.

TYPE – DESCRIPTION	Avg	Ex-Fn	Mint
VINER, Verge Fusee / Alarm, 50MM, Silver, OF, Ca.1835..........	$1,200	$1,400	$1,800

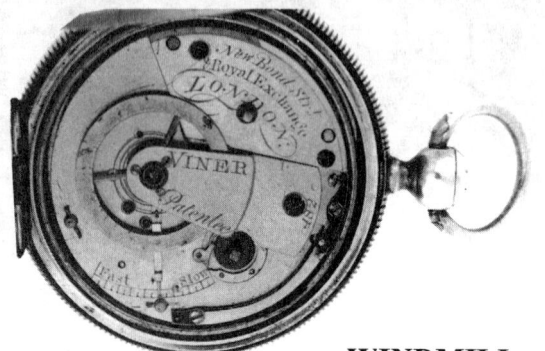

VINER, Verge Fusee with Alarm, marked on cuvette for the two arbors "*wind up*" & the other marked "*warning*", under sprung hairspring, 50MM, Silver Open Face Case, Ca. 1835.

WINDMILL
LONDON

Joseph and his son Thomas made clocks and watches and at one time employed 10 workers. Started in business in 1671 and lasted till about 1732.

TYPE – DESCRIPTION	Avg	Ex-Fn	Mint
Tho. WINDMILL, 1/4 hr. repeater, 55MM, silver OF, Ca.1690	$6,500	$7,000	$8,000

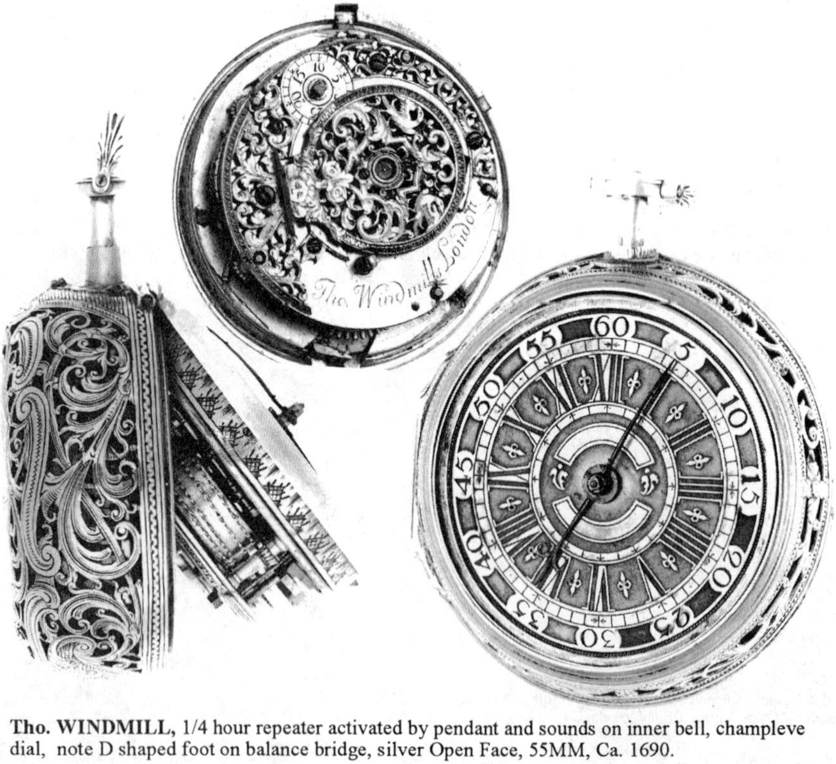

Tho. WINDMILL, 1/4 hour repeater activated by pendant and sounds on inner bell, champleve dial, note D shaped foot on balance bridge, silver Open Face, 55MM, Ca. 1690.

ZENITH
Swiss

Zenith watch and clock factory was founded in 1865 by George Farvre Jacot. By 1920 they had manufactured 2,000,000 watches.

ZENITH, alarm watch, enamel dial, 17J., 50mm, Ca. 1930   ZENITH, Military Deck Watch, 51mm, nickel case, Ca.1940.

TYPE – DESCRIPTION	Avg	Ex-Fn	Mint
Time only, gold, 40-44mm, OF	$250	$300	$400
HC	400	450	500
Time only, gold, 40-44mm, with **enamel** on bezel, **18K**, OF	600	650	800
Time only, gold, 45-50mm, OF	450	500	600
HC	550	600	700
RR Extra, 21J., Grade 56, (16 size), **Gold Filled** OF	150	200	275
Military Deck Watch, 51mm, nickel case, Ca.1940	250	300	375
Alarm watch, 17J., nail set, **two barrels**, gold, 50mm, C.1930	1,500	1,600	1,800
Chronograph, gold, 45-50mm, OF	800	900	1,100
HC	900	1,000	1,200
Minute repeater, gold, 46-52mm, OF	2,800	3,000	3,500
HC	3,500	3,700	4,000
OF w/split chrono.	4,500	4,700	5,200
HC w/split chrono.	5,000	5,500	6,500
OF w/chrono., cal. & moonphase	6,500	7,000	8,000
HC w/chrono., cal. & moonphase	9,000	9,500	10,000
Perp. moonphase cal. w/min. rep. and chrono., OF	22,000	25,000	30,000
HC	25,000	28,000	32,000

ZENITH, 42mm, 18K, enamel on case, open face, 17J., signed ZENITH, Ca. 1930's.

PRE–1850 REPEATERS

Swiss 1/4 hr. repeater, verge or cylinder, silver, 55mm, Ca. 1820, OF. Note: Parachute (illo.1)

Swiss 1/4 hr. rep., pump, verge or cylinder, 18K, 52mm, OF, Ca.1800s. (illo.2)

TYPE – DESCRIPTION	Avg	Ex-Fn	Mint
Swiss 1/4 hr. rep., verge or cylinder, silver, 55mm, OF (illo.1).......	$1,200	$1,400	$2,000
Swiss 1/4 hr. rep., pump, verge or cylinder, 18K, 52mm, OF, C.1800s (illo.2)	1,800	2,100	3,000
Swiss 1/4 hr., automaton on dial (2 figures), gilt, verge, KW, 55mm, OF, early 1800s	2,500	3,000	3,700
Swiss 1/4 hr. musical repeater disc-driven, KW KS, cylinder,18K, 57mm, OF, C. 1825 (illo.3)	4,000	5,000	6,000
Swiss 1/4 hr. repeater, 32-35mm, KW KS, gold, Ca. 1850 (illo.4).	1,800	2,200	2,800

Swiss 1/4 hr. musical repeater disc-driven, cylinder, Kw KS, 18k, 57mm, OF, C. 1825, (illo.3)

Swiss 1/4 hr. repeater, 32-35mm, cylinder escapement, Swiss bar movement, KW KS, gold, Ca. 1850, (illo.4)

French, 1/4 hr. repeater, gold and enamel superior quality, enameled scene, outer case with pearls, verge, 20K, 52mm, OF, C.1785. **(illo.5)**

1/4 hr. repeater, Virgule escap., KW, 18K, 46mm, OF, Ca. 1840. **(illo.6)**

TYPE – DESCRIPTION	Avg	Ex-Fn	Mint
Skeletonized 1/4 hr., cylinder, Swiss, 18K, 58mm, OF, C.1810......	$3,500	$4,000	$5,000
French 1/4 hr. repeater, **20K** gold and enamel, verge, enameled scene, superior quality, outer pearls, 52mm, OF, C.1785 (illo.5)......	6,000	6,500	7,500
1/4 hr. repeater, Virgule escap., KW, 18K, 46mm, OF (illo.6)........	3,000	3,200	3,600
1/4 hr. rep., erotic scene (concealed in cuvette), automated, multi-color gold figures, verge, pump 1/4 hr., 18K, 54mm, OF, C.1800...	3,500	3,700	4,500
French or Swiss pump 1/4 hr. repeater, free standing barrel, **Thin gold** case, cylinder escape., tapered bridges , Ca.1790-1835 (illo.7)......	2,000	2,400	3,200
Early 1/4 hr. rep., Paris (Clouzier) gilt dial w/ enamel hour cartouches, verge, gilt & shagreen case, 58mm, OF, C.1700....................	6,500	7,000	8,000
1/4 hr. repeater, London, gilt & shagreen paircase, verge, extremely fine, 56mm, OF, C.1700s	5,000	5,500	6,500

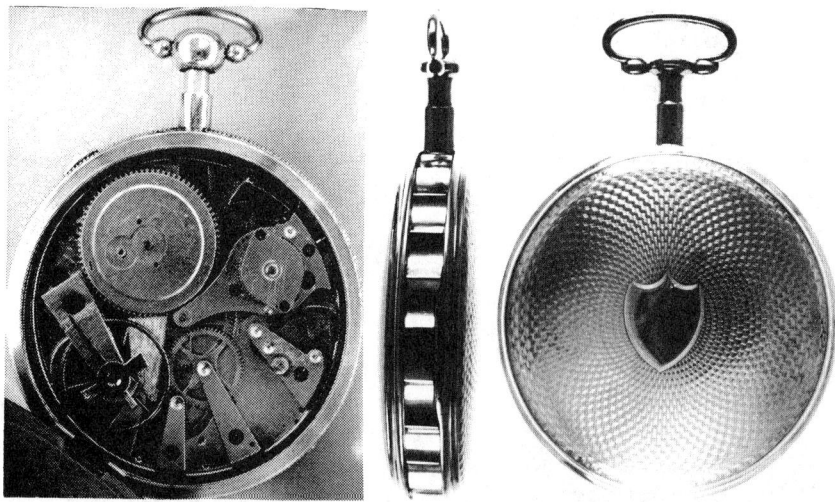

French or Swiss pump 1/4 hr. repeater, free standing barrel, cylinder escapement, tapered bridges, **Thin** gold engine turned case, Ca. 1790-1835. **(illo.7)**

1/4 hour verge repeater, 49mm, 22K gold repousse pair case, repeating on an inner bell, repeat mechanism is activated from the pendant, ca. 1750-1780, **(illo.8)**

1/4 hour repeater, musical, 25 musical tines, cylinder, center seconds, KW, 18K, 58mm, OF, Ca.1820, **(illo.9)**

1/4 hour repeater, verge (London, Dutch), pierced inner case, repousee outer case, gold, 49mm, C.1750, **(illo.10)**

1/4 Hr. repeating coach watch, with alarm,120mm diameter, verge fusee, silver repousse case, ca.1730-40. **(illo. 11)**

TYPE – DESCRIPTION	Avg	Ex-Fn	Mint
1/4 hr. repeater, repousse pair case, verge, **22K**, 49mm (illo.8)	$5,500	$6,000	$7,000
1/4 hr. repeater, musical, 25 musical tines, cylinder, center seconds, KW, 18K, 58mm,OF, C. 1820 (illo.9)	6,000	6,500	7,500
1/4 hr. rep., verge (London, Dutch), pierced inner case, repousee outer case, gold, 49mm, C.1750 (illo.10)	5,500	6,000	7,000
1/4 hr. repeating coach watch w/alarm, verge, fusee, silver repousee case, 120mm, C. 1730 (illo. 11)	8,000	9,000	11,000
1/4 hr. repeater with automaton dial, verge, Swiss, KW, 3 automated figures on dial and carillon chimes, silver, 52mm, OF, C. 1790.	2,500	2,800	3,500
Gold & enamel, 1/4 hr. repeater, London, cylinder, Fusee, paircase, enamel on outer case, 18K, 48mm, C. 1790	4,000	4,500	5,500
Swiss, 1/4 hr. pump repeater, w/ automaton, verge, 18K, 54mm, OF, C. 1800	4,500	5,000	6,000
Virgule escapement, 1/4 hr. repeater, fancy gold & multi-dial, London, KW, 18K, OF, C. 1840	2,800	3,000	3,500

REPEATERS

1/4 hour repeater, 17 jewels, nail set, gun metal case, 49mm, C. 1910. (illo.12)

1/4 hour repeater with chronograph, gun metal base-metal or gold filled, 49-50mm, (illo.13)

TYPE – DESCRIPTION	Avg	Ex-Fn	Mint
1/4 hr. repeater, 17J, gun metal, 49-50mm, C. 1910 (illo.12)	$450	$500	$600
1/4 hr. repeater, 17J, silver, 49-50mm, OF, C. 1910	550	600	700
1/4 hr. repeater, 17J, silver, 49-50mm, HC, C. 1910	600	650	800
1/4 hr. rep. **w/chrono.**,17J, base metal, gun metal or GF, OF 49-50mm, C.1910 (illo.13)	650	700	800
1/4 hr. rep. **w/chrono.**,17J, base metal, gun metal or GF, HC 49-50mm, C.1910	750	800	1,000

🕐 Pricing in this Guide are fair market price for **COMPLETE** watches which are reflected from the "**NAWCC**" National and regional shows.

1/4 hr. repeater with Calendar, 17J, gold filled, 3/4 plate, open face, 50mm, C. 1910 (illo.14)

1/4 hour repeater, 55mm, 2 Jacquemarts, gilt case, Ca. 1820. (illo.15)

TYPE – DESCRIPTION	Avg	Ex-Fn	Mint
1/4 hr. repeater with Calendar, 17J, gun metal or gold filled, 3/4 plate, OF, 49-50mm, C. 1910 (illo.14)	$600	$650	$750
Swiss 1/4 hr. repeater w/moonphase & calendar, 17J, 18K, 53mm, HC, C. 1900..	3,000	3,200	4,000
55mm, 1/4 repeater, 2 Jacquemarts, gilt case, Ca. 1820 (illo.15) ...	2,000	2,300	2,900
Swiss 1/4 hr. repeater, **Erotic Scene,** 14K, HC, 50-54mm, ALL ORIGINAL, (note: beware of fakes) (illo.16)............	8,000	9,000	12,000

Swiss 1/4 hour repeater, **Erotic Scene** with automaton action dial, 14K, HC, 50-54mm, (illo.16)
This has CONVERSION not original (note: beware of fakes)

COMPARISON OF WATCH SIZES

U. S. A.	EUROPEAN
10-12 SIZE	40—44 MM
16 SIZE	45—48 MM
18 SIZE	50—54 MM

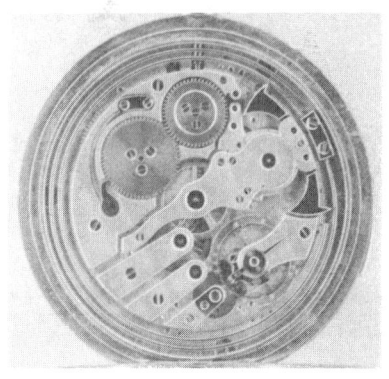

Minute Repeater, 48 jewels, 2 train Independent seconds **TANDEM** wind, 55mm, Ca. 1890, 18K HC. (illo.17)

Swiss minute repeater, 54mm, jeweled through hammers, 14k case. (illo.18)

TYPE – DESCRIPTION	Avg	Ex-Fn	Mint
Min. rep., 20J, Swiss, gilt mvt., gun metal, 52mm, **OF**, 1910	$700	$900	$1,200
Min. rep., 48 jewels, 2 train Independent seconds **TANDEM** wind, 55mm, Ca. 1890, 18K HC. (illo.17)......................................	7,000	8,000	10,000
Min. rep., 17J, Swiss, gilt, 18K, 52mm, HC, C. 1910	1,600	2,000	2,800
Min. rep., 32 J, Swiss, gilt, 18K, 54mm, HC, C. 1910	2,000	2,400	3,000
Min. rep., 32 J, Swiss, NI, porc. dial, 14K, OF, C. 1905 (illo.18) ...	2,200	2,600	3,200
Min. rep., 32 J, Swiss, NI, porc. dial, 18K, OF, C. 1905 (illo.19) ...	2,500	2,800	3,400
Min. repeater, Self contained, (activated from button on crown) 25J, 14K, OF, C. 1915...	3,500	4,000	5,000
Min. repeater, Swiss, ultra thin, 32J, 18K, OF, C. 1930..................	4,000	4,500	6,000
Min. repeater, automated Father & Baby Time, 18K, 54mm (illo.20) ....,..............	5,000	5,500	6,500

Minute Repeater, 32 J, Swiss, porcelain dial, wolf tooth winding, 18K, OF, C. 1905. (illo.19)

Father & Baby Time, automated min. repeater, 54mm, note father and baby striking bell, 18K. (illo.20)

Minute repeating **Clock Watch**, 3/4 plate, a on or off strike activated mechanism, three gongs, tandem-winding barrels, 18K, 48-50mm, HC, Ca.1900 (illo.21)

Minute repeater, split second chronograph, Swiss, 18K, 47-50mm, OF, Ca.1900 . (illo.22)

TYPE – DESCRIPTION	Avg	Ex-Fn	Mint
Min. repeating Clock Watch, 18K, 48-50mm, HC, Ca.1900 (illo.21)	$7,500	$8,500	$10,500
Min.rep. w/ chrono, Swiss ,SW, 18K, large 58mm, OF, C.1900.....	2,000	2,200	3,000
Min. repeater w/chrono. register, 32J, nickel, very high quality, 18K, 50mm, OF, C. 1900	3,500	4,000	5,000
Min. rep.w/chrono, 30 min. register, Swiss, 36J, 18K ,HC, C.1895	3,500	4,000	5,000
Min. rep., split sec. chrono, Swiss, 18K, 47-50mm, OF, C.1900 (illo.22)	5,000	5,500	7,000
Min. rep., split sec. chrono, Swiss, 18K, 47-50mm, HC,C.1900	6,000	6,500	8,000
Swiss min. repeater, chrono, moonphase and calendar, 30J or more, 18K, 60mm, HC, C. 1895 (illo.23)...	5,500	6,000	7,000
Swiss min. repeater, moonphase and **perpetual calendar,** 30J or more, 18K, 60mm, HC, C. 1895 (illo.24)................. ★	12,000	14,000	18,000
Swiss min. rep., Grand Sonnerie, clockwatch w/ carillon chimes, 2 train, nickel, tandem wind, 30J, 3 hammers, ornate case, 18K, 55mm, HC, C. 1900...	10,000	12,000	15,000

Swiss minute repeater, chronograph, start - stop - return to zero, moonphase and calendar, 30J or more, 18K, 60mm, HC, C. 1895. (illo.23)

Swiss minute repeater, moonphase and **perpetual calendar,** 30J or more, 18K, 60mm, HC, C. 1895. (illo.24)

PRE–1850 ALARMS

TYPE – DESCRIPTION	Avg	Ex-Fn	Mint
Alarm, (**Blois, France**), double silver case pierced and engraved, gilt mvt., cut gut cord fusee, 2 wheel train + verge escape. w/foliot, silver balance cock, 44mm, Ca. 1640 (illo.25)	$15,000	$17,000	$22,000
Alarm, 2 cases pierced, 3 wheel train, Egyptian pierced pillers, verge & foliot, 51mm, Ca. 1675 (illo.26)	7,000	9,000	14,000

ALARM, **from BLOIS,** FRANCE, double silver case pierced and engraved, silver crown dial with roman numbers, alarm center dial with arabic numbers, gilt movement, cut gut cord fusee, 2 wheel train plus verge escapement with foliot, silver balance cock, 44mm, Ca. 1640. It is believed French watch-making started in the town of **Blois, France.** (illo.25)

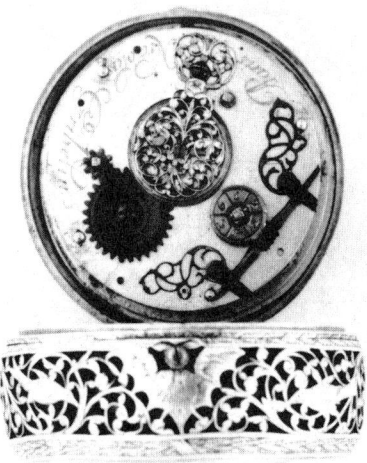

ALARM, 2 cases pierced & engraved, roman outer dial, alarm center dial, blued hands , 3 wheel train, Egyptian pierced pillars, verge & foliot, endless screw adjustment, Paris, 51mm, Ca. 1675. (illo.26)

ALARM, strikes on bell, pair cased, verge, C. 1650. (illo.27)

Alarm, pair cased, first case pique nailed skin, second case pierced, 4 wheel train, verge, amphora pillers, 56mm, Ca. 1680. (illo.28)

TYPE – DESCRIPTION	Avg	Ex-Fn	Mint
Alarm, strikes on bell, pair cased, verge, C. 1650 (illo.27)	$5,000	$6,000	$8,000
Alarm, pair cased, first case pique nailed skin, 4 wheel train, verge, 56mm, Ca. 1680 (illo.28)	9,000	11,000	15,000
Alarm, Rotterdam, silver pierced case, gilt, tulip pillars, verge, fusee, 48mm, Ca. 1685 (illo.29)	5,000	6,000	8,000
Alarm, "oignon", verge, fusee, large pierced bal. bridge (illo.30)	6,000	7,000	10,000

ALARM, Rotterdam, silver pierced case, gilt, tulip pillars, verge, fusee, 48mm, Ca. 1685. (illo.29)

ALARM, "oignon", verge, fusee, large pierced balance bridge. (illo.30)

ALARM, nailed pique shagreen skin, second case pierced silver, balance cock has short feet, 4 wheel train verge, 60mm, London, Ca. 1685. (illo.31)

ALARM, nailed pique shagreen (**Sting-Ray**) skin, triple cases, entirely pierced throughout, richly decorated, 4 wheel train, verge, fusee, English-Swiss, Ca. 1700. (illo.32)

TYPE – DESCRIPTION	Avg	Ex-Fn	Mint
Alarm, nailed pique shagreen skin, second case pierced silver,			
4 wheel train verge, 60mm, London, Ca. 1685 (illo.31)	$6,500	$7,500	$9,000
Alarm, nailed pique shagreen (**Sting-Ray**) skin, English-Swiss, verge,			
fusee, Ca.1700s, (illo.32)	6,000	6,500	8,000
Oignon alarm, verge, French, silver and animal skin cover,			
movement wound from center arbor on dial,			
silver champleve dial, 60mm, OF, C. 1710	5,000	5,500	7,000

ALARMS

The most common Swiss and German alarms are usually in base metal or gun metal cases. Early makes with porcelain dials are more desirable than later (post 1920's) metal dial alarms.

TYPE – DESCRIPTION	Avg	Ex-Fn	Mint
Swiss alarm sounding on bell,7J, base metal, 49mm,OF, C.1915 ...	$95	$110	$135
Swiss alarm sounding on gongs, 15J, tandem wind,			
gun metal, 50mm, OF, C. 1900	175	200	275
Cricket alarm, w/cricket design, Swiss , SW,			
silver case, 48mm, OF, C.1890	500	600	750

COMPARISON OF WATCH SIZES

U. S. A.	EUROPEAN
10-12 SIZE	40—44 MM
16 SIZE	45—48 MM
18 SIZE	50—54 MM

TIMERS & CHRONOGRAPHS
Gallet, Racine & other names are commonly found on timers & chronographs.

Timer, 1/5 sec., 7J, register, base metal, 48mm, OF.   Timer, **split second**, register, base metal, 46mm, OF.

TYPE – DESCRIPTION	Avg	Ex-Fn	Mint
Timer, 1/5 sec., register,7J, base metal, 48mm, OF, C. 1940	$40	$50	$75
Timer, 1/5 sec. register, **17J,** base metal, 48mm, OF, C. 1940	60	70	95
Timer, **split sec.,** register, base metal, 46mm, OF, C. 1940	75	90	125
Timer or Stop Watch, **silver,** 48mm, **HC,** 1925	135	155	195
Chronograph, **7J, GF or silver,** 48mm, OF, C. 1905	130	150	190
HC	155	175	200
Chronograph, **15-17J, porcelain** dial, GF or silver, 50mm, OF,	200	225	300
HC,	250	275	350
Chronograph, **20J, 18K,** 52mm, OF, C. 1895	500	575	700
HC	600	700	850

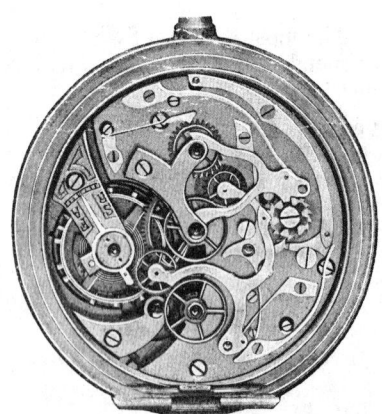

Timer or Stop Watch, **silver,** 48mm, HC.   Chronograph, 7-17J, GF, 48mm, OF, C. 1905.

Chronograph, w/register, porc. dial, **20J, 14K**, 52mm, HC, Ca. 1890. (illo.A)

Chronograph, Split Seconds, w/register, porc. dial, **20J, 18K**, 52mm, OF, Ca. 1910. (illo.B)

TYPE – DESCRIPTION	Avg	Ex-Fn	Mint
Chronog. w/register, porc. dial, **15J, silver,** 52mm, OF, C. 1890....	$250	$300	$400
HC (illo.A)	300	350	450
Chronog. w/register, porc. dial, **20J, 14K,** 52mm, OF, C. 1890......	400	450	550
HC	500	550	650
Chronog. w/register, porc. dial, **20J, 18K,** 52mm, OF, C. 1890......	600	650	750
HC	800	850	1,100
Split sec. chronograph, 15-17J, **.800 silver,** 52mm, OF, C. 1900..	300	325	400
Split sec. chronograph, 19-32J, **18K,** 52mm, OF, C. 1900	800	900	1,200
HC (illo.B)	1,000	1,100	1,400
Double dial (time on front, chrono. on back), Swiss , 17J, **14K** display case , 51mm, OF, Ca. 1885 (illo.C)	900	1,100	1,500
1/4 second jump watch, 26J, two gear train, SW , **18K,** HC, C.1880 (illo.D)..	2,200	2,500	3,500

Double dial (time on front, Chronograph on back), Swiss, 17J, 14K display case, 51mm, OF, Ca. 1885. (illo.C)

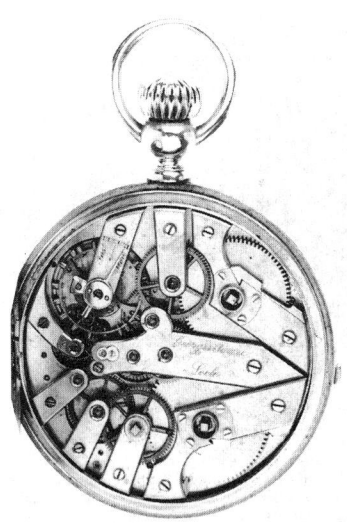

1/4 second jump watch, 26J, two gear train, two main spring barrels, KW , 18K, 53mm, HC, C.1880. (illo.D)

POCKET CHRONOMETER

JOHN ARNOLD, chronometer, KWKS, spring detent, Z balance with adjustable weights, helical hair spring, 18K case, serial # 14, upright escape wheel, "INV ET FECT" engraved on movement (made by), his chronometer factory was located in Chigwell (London), #36 pocket chronometers sold for about $500.00 in 1776. (illo.33)

TYPE – DESCRIPTION	Avg	Ex-Fn	Mint
Chronometer, KWKS, spring detent, Z bal., helical hair-spring, "JOHN ARNOLD", 18K case, C. 1776 (illo.33)	$10,000	$13,000	$18,000
Chronometer, KWKS, spring detent, Z bal., helical hair-spring, silver case, C. 1795 (illo.34)	2,200	2,600	3,200
Chronometer, KWKS, spring detent, Z bal., helical hair-spring, "J. R. ARNOLD", 18K case, C. 1805 (illo.35)	8,000	10,000	14,000

Chronometer,13 jewels, KWKS, spring detent, Z balance with screw counterpoise on terminal curves, helical hair-spring, silver case, Ca. 1795. (illo.34)

J. R. ARNOLD, chronometer, KWKS, spring detent, Z balance with screw counterpoise on terminal curves, helical hair-spring, 18K case, 58mm, C. 1805. (illo.35)

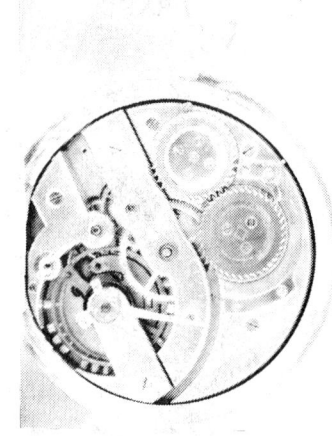

JOHANNES KESSELS "ALTON", deck chronometer, KWKS, spring detent, fusee, silver case, C. 1830 . (illo.36)

Detent chronometer, Helical hairspring, Swiss, SW, 18K, 56mm, HC, C. 1900. (illo.37)

TYPE – DESCRIPTION	Avg	Ex-Fn	Mint
Chronometer, KWKS, spring detent, Z bal., helical hair-spring,			
"KESSELS", **silver case,** C. 1830 (illo.36)	$2,200	$2,800	$3,800
Chronometer, KW, spring detent, **coin,** OF, C. 1875......................	600	700	900
Detent chronometer, Swiss, SW, **18K**, 56mm, HC, Ca.1900 (ill0.37)	1,500	1,700	2,000
Detent chronometer, English, w/ wind indicator, **18K**, 48mm, OF .	3,500	4,000	5,000
Chronometer, pivoted detent, helical hairspring, (French),			
SW, **silver,** 56mm, OF (illo.38)	300	400	550
Pocket chronometer, Swiss, 20 jewel, fancy case, silver and gilt dial,			
detent, w/ helical spring, **18K**, 49mm, HC, C. 1890 (illo.38A)	2,600	3,000	4,000

Engraved on movement "*Chronome'tre*" (French), 16 jewels, pivoted detent, helical hairspring, stem wind, manufactured by **LIP** in **Besancon France,** silver, 56mm, OF, Ca. 1910-30. (illo.38)

Detent chronometer, English, w/ fusee, helical hairspring, note: Trapezoidal weights on balance. (illo.38A)

⊕ Note: Some models and grades are not included. Their values can be determined by comparing with **similar** age, size, metal content, style, models and grades listed.

⊕ Note: Watches listed in this book are priced at the **collectable retail** level, as **complete** watches having an original case, an original dial, and with the entire original movement in good working order with no repairs needed.

TOURBILLON, KARRUSEL, RARE & UNUSUAL MOVEMENTS

One minute so called "Poor Man's Tourbillon", center seconds silver watch with centered dial & visible system. Swiss, 54mm. (illo.39)

Visible Tourbillon, 53mm, 13 jewels, tourbillon system is visible from dial side, ca. 1913. (illo.40)

TYPE – DESCRIPTION	Avg	Ex-Fn	Mint
Tourbillon, Swiss, base metal, 54mm, OF (illo.39)	$1,700	$1,900	$2,300
Tourbillon, 53mm, 13J, visible from dial, Ca. 1913 (illo.40)	1,800	2,000	2,500
Tourbillon, **4 min.**, 15J, enamel dial, silver, C.1930 (illo.41)	2,800	3,000	3,800
Karrusel, **52 min.**, English, 3/4, gilt, 16J, SW, silver case, 56mm, OF, C.1885 (illo.42)	3,000	3,400	4,000
Helicoil mainspring, Swiss, 15J , cylinder esc., base metal, 51mm, OF, C. 1910 (illo.43)	1,200	1,400	1,800

TOURBILLON, in 4 minutes, 15 jewels, enamel dial, silver case, Ca.1930. (illo.41)

52 minute KARRUSEL, 57mm, 14J., English, silver case, Ca.1885. (illo.42)

COMPARISON OF WATCH SIZES

U. S. A.	EUROPEAN
10-12 SIZE	40—44 MM
16 SIZE	45—48 MM
18 SIZE	50—54 MM

Helicoil Mainspring, 51mm, 15J., rare winding system, cylindrical spring replaces standard mainspring. (illo.43)

Lever with Fusee, KW KS, (Liverpool), hallmarked, silver, **undersprung**, 46mm, OF, Ca. 1850-70.(illo.44)

EARLY PRE–1850 NON—GOLD

TYPE – DESCRIPTION	Avg	Ex-Fn	Mint
Lever, Fusee, (Liverpool), silver, 46mm, OF, Ca. 1850-70 (illo.44)	$135	$175	$250
Lever or cylinder, BAR, KW KS, silver, 46-52mm, OF (illo.45)...	125	150	175
Lever or cylinder, **engraved** BAR, KW KS, silver, 46-52mm, OF, Ca. 1840-85 (illo.46)......	135	155	200
Lever or cylinder, **Le-PINE**, KW KS, silver, 46-52mm (illo.47)...	135	155	200
Rack & pinion escap., KW KS, silver, 46-52mm, OF (illo.48).....	300	400	575

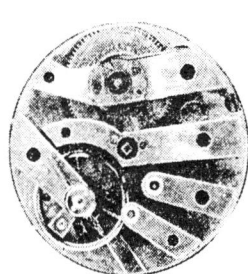
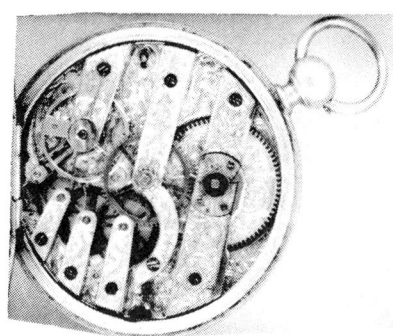

Lever, KW KS, bar style movement, note **curved barrel bridge**, silver, 46-52mm, OF, C. 1830-50. (illo.45)

Lever, **Lepine style bar, engraved**, KW KS, silver, 46-52mm, OF, Ca. 1840-85. (illo.46)

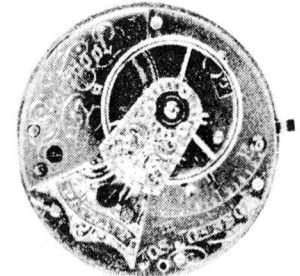

Lever, **Lepine style tapered bar movement**, KW KS, silver, 46-52mm, OF, Ca. 1820-35. (illo.47)

Rack & pinion escapement, KW KS, silver, 46-52mm, Ca. 1830. (illo.48)

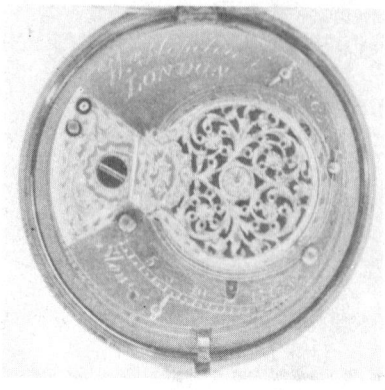
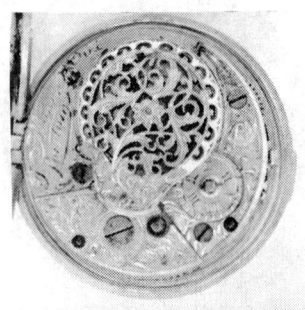

Verge, chain driven fusee, (English) paircase, 52mm, OF, C.1800- 40. (illo.49)

Verge, fusee, (English) paircase, hallmarked, KW, 52mm, OF, Ca. 1780-90. (illo.50)

TYPE – DESCRIPTION	Avg	Ex-Fn	Mint
Verge, Fusee (Swiss), KW, (unmarked) single case, silver, 49mm, OF, C. 1810-40	$250	$300	$400
Verge (English) paircase, 52mm, OF, C.1800- 40 (illo.49)	250	300	400
Painted "farmer's dial," verge, Swiss / London, silver, 52-55m, OF	500	600	750
Cylinder, Fusee, silver, 48-52mm, OF, C. 1830s	250	300	400
Verge, Fusee (Swiss), KW, silver single case, 49mm OF, C. 1810-1840	250	300	400
Verge (English) paircase, hallmarked, KW, 52mm, OF, C. 1780-90 (illo.50)	275	325	450
Miniature, verge, lady's, plain, porcelain dial, hallmarked silver, 24mm, OF, C. 1810	700	800	1,100
Gilt & enamel, verge, Swiss or French, 46mm, OF, C. 1800	800	900	1,200
Skeletonized, verge, Swiss, double case, hand-carved movement, case silver & horn, 53mm,OF, C. 1800	500	600	800
Repousee paircase, fancy dial, verge, London, hallmarked silver, 49mm, OF, C. 1800 (illo.51)	800	1,100	1,600
Erotic Repousee paircase, Swan & Lady, verge, London (illo.52)	1,000	1,400	2,000

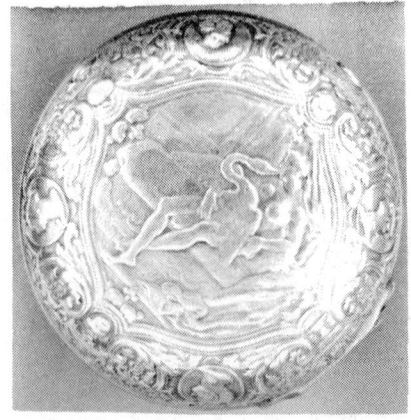

Repousee paircase, fancy dial, verge, English hallmarked silver case, 49mm, OF, C. 1800. (illo.51)

Erotic Repousee silver paircase, Swan & Lady, verge, Fusee, London. (illo.52)

OIGNON watch with mock pendulum, 58mm, Ca. 1700-1720. (illo.53)

Lady & mock pendulum, mock pendulum can be seen at top of Ladies head , 58mm, Ca. 1690 (illo.54)

TYPE – DESCRIPTION	Avg	Ex-Fn	Mint
Oignon watch with mock pendulum, 58mm, ca. 1700-20 (illo.53) .	$2,800	$3,500	$4,800
Lady & mock pendulum, enamel Lady, 58mm, Ca. 1690 (illo.54) .	3,200	4,200	5,500
Verge w/ calendar, repousee paircase, London hallmarked, 51mm, OF, C. 1690	2,200	2,600	3,200
Dublin, early verge, silver paircase, champleve silver dial (signed), 54mm, OF, C. 1720	1,600	2,000	2,600
Early verge, large winged cock, signed silver dial, London, Egyptian pillars, silver, 55mm, OF, C. 1700 (illo.55)	1,800	2,200	2,800
Viennese enamel on gilt, verge, fusee, multi-scenes on case, KW, 55mm, HC, C. 1780	2,000	2,600	3,500
English, verge w/ calendar, signed champleve dial, silver & horn, 54mm OF, C. 1680	2,400	3,000	4,000

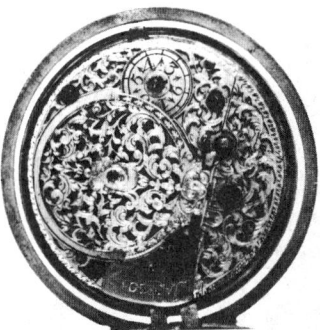

Early verge, large D shaped foot on the cock, London, signed silver dial, Egyptian pillars, silver, 55mm, OF, C. 1700 . (illo.55)

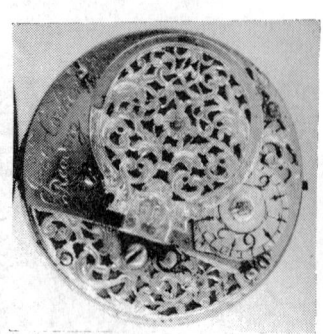

Tortoise shell case, verge with chain driven fusee, calendar, D shaped foot balance cock, C. 1700, (illo.56)

English, verge, hand pierced cock, fusee, silver, note face on balance cock, C. 1720, (illo.57)

TYPE – DESCRIPTION	Avg	Ex-Fn	Mint
Tortoise shell, verge, calendar, Ca. 1700 (illo.56)...........................	$1,400	$1,800	$2,500
English, verge, hand pierced cock, fusee, silver, Ca. 1720, (illo.57)	1,200	1,400	2,200
Pumpkin Form Case, verge, silver, 40mm, Ca. 1775 (illo.58)........	1,800	2,200	2,900
Garooned Case, verge, fusee, 44mm, silver, Ca. 1650 (illp.59)......	6,500	8,500	11,000
Painted scene on horn, verge, gilt, 57mm, OF, Ca. 1780 (illo.60)..	1,000	1,600	2,500

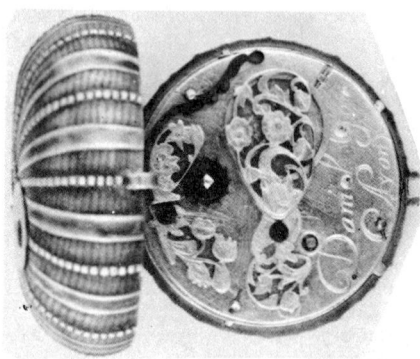

Pumpkin Form Case, verge, silver, Ca. 1775. (illo.58)

Garooned Case, verge, fusee, 44mm, Ca. 1650. (illp.59)

Painted horn (full scene in color) London, verge, gilt, 57mm, OF, C. 1780. (illo.60)

EARLY NON—GOLD

Early Astronomic watch with day date month calendar, lunar calendar, 57mm, Ca. 1680. (illo.61)

TYPE – DESCRIPTION	Avg	Ex-Fn	Mint
Early Astronomic watch with day date month calendar, lunar calendar, 57mm, Ca. 1680 (illo.61)	$7,000	$9,000	$15,000
Early Astronomic watch with moon phases and triple date, fusee with cut-gut cord, 3 gear train, foliot, Ca.1660 (illo.62)	12,000	15,000	20,000

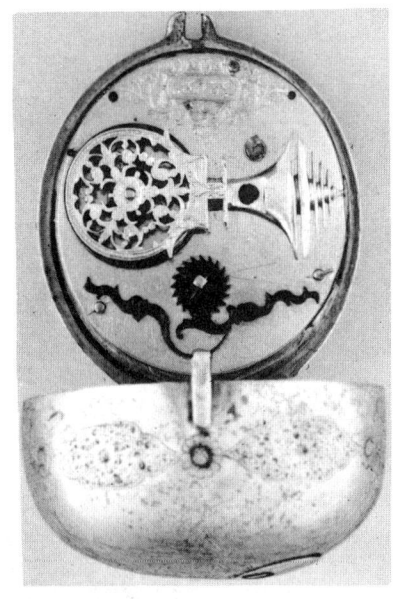

Early Astronomic watch with moon phases and triple date, fusee with cut-gut cord, 3 gear train, 6 armed foliot, Ca.1660. (illo.62)

Early German made silver watch, verge and foliot, silver pierced dial, "Hamburg", Ca. 1660. (illo.63)

TYPE – DESCRIPTION	Avg	Ex-Fn	Mint
Early German made silver watch, verge and foliot, silver pierced dial, "Hamburg", Ca. 1660 (illo.63)	$4,500	$6,000	$8,000
Early silver watch, blued steel hand, cut-gut fusee, foliot, rosette for adj., 53mm, Ca.1660 (illo.64)	12,000	15,000	20,000

Early silver watch, silver dial with blued steel hand, cut gut fusee, 3 wheel train, foliot, rosette for adjustment of the motor-spring tension, 53mm, Ca.1660. (illo.64)

Pair cased, first case silver covered with nailed skin, verge, cut-gut cord fusee, 3 wheel train, foliot, pierced cock, endless screw adjustment for main spring tension, 45mm, Ca. 1660. (illo.65)

Early French watch movement with hour and minute hand, striking bell each hour, hand pierced case & gilt brass movement, cut-gut fusee, c. 1600s. (illo.66)

TYPE – DESCRIPTION	Avg	Ex-Fn	Mint
Pair cased, first case silver & nailed skin, verge, fusee, 3 wheel train, foliot, pierced cock, 45mm, Ca. 1660 (illo.65)	$5,500	$7,000	$9,000
Early French watch hour and minute hand, striking on bell, cut-gut fusee, c. 1600s (illo.66)	12,000	15,000	20,000
Early Drum Clock, iron plates, 4 wheel train, brass fusee on a steel great wheel, steel contrate wheel with brass teeth, steel verge and foliot balance w/ T-shaped ends, 34mm high (illo.67)	28,000	35,000	45,000

43mm, Early Drum Clock, iron plates, 4 wheel train, brass fusee on a steel great wheel, steel contrate wheel with brass teeth, steel verge and foliot balance with T-shaped ends . The cylindrical gilt brass case is finely engraved and is 34mm high, Ca. 1550 - 1560. (illo.67)

🕐 Pricing in this Guide are fair market price for **COMPLETE** watches which are reflected from the "**<u>NAWCC</u>**" National and regional shows.

PRE–1850 *GOLD*

 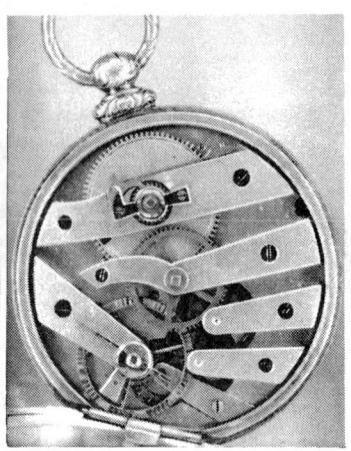

Lever or verge, (Liverpool), 18K, multi-colored gold dial, 52mm, OF, C.1820-75. (illo.68).

Lever or cylinder, BAR style movement, GOLD, 45-52mm, OF, 1840-1865. (illo.69)

TYPE – DESCRIPTION	Avg	Ex-Fn	Mint
Lever or verge, (Liverpool), **18K**, 52mm, OF, C.1820-75 (illo.68).	$500	$600	$900
Lever or verge, (Liverpool), 15J, **18K**, 52mm, HC, C. 1820-75	600	700	1,000
Lever or cylinder, BAR, GOLD, 45-52mm, OF(illo.69)	250	325	425
(same as above) w / skeletonized movement,**18K** (illo.70)	350	425	575
Lever or cylinder, Le-Pine style, GOLD, 45-52mm, OF (illo.71)	250	300	425
Cylinder Fusee, paircase, London, plain case, porcelain dial,**18K**, 48mm, OF, C. 1880	1,100	1,400	1,900
Verge, multi-color case, Swiss/ French, porcelain dial, **18K**, 42mm,OF, Ca. 1770-1800	1,000	1,300	1,800
Verge, French, gold & enamel patterns on case, KWKS, OF, C. 1805	1,200	1,500	2,000
Verge, (Swiss), **18K**, 52-54mm, plain case, OF, C. 1790-1820	550	700	1,000
Verge ,Swiss, gold scene, high quality ,**18K**, 50mm, OF, C.1790	1,200	1,600	2,200

Lever or cylinder, skeletonized & engraved bar movement, Swiss, 45-52mm, OF,18K. (illo.70)

Lever or cylinder escapement, Lepine style movement, Ca. 1820-1835, GOLD, 45-52mm, OF. (illo.71)

Verge, repousee paircase, 20K gold case, 43mm, Open Face, Ca.1780, (illo.72)

Early verge, D shaped balance cock, signed dial, London, Egyptian pillars, gold, 55mm, OF, Ca. 1760. (illo.73)

TYPE – DESCRIPTION	Avg	Ex-Fn	Mint
Verge, repousee paircase, 20K, 43mm, OF, C.1780 (illo.72)	$1,800	$2,300	$3,200
Early verge, large winged cock, signed dial, London,Egyptian pillars, gold, 55mm, OF, C. 1760 (illo.73).............................	2,000	2,400	3,000
Virgule, Fusee, Swiss or French, **18K**, 50-55mm, OF, C. 1790	1,200	1,400	1,800
Fusee, made in HOLLAND, Ca. 1800, GOLD case (illo.74)	450	550	700
Skeletonized French, diamonds on bezel, 39mm, C.1780 (illo.75) .	1,200	1,500	2,000
Rack & Pinion lever escapement, **18K**, OF, Ca. 1830 (illo.75A)....	600	700	900

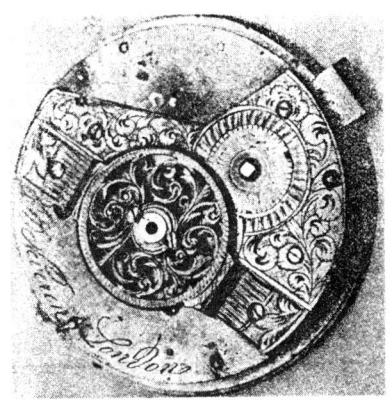

Fusee, movement made in HOLLAND, GOLD case, note the bridge style, 60mm, OF, Ca. 1800 (illo.74)

Skeletonized French watch, diamonds on bezel, 39mm, C.1780 (illo.75)

Rack and Lever Escapement, 18K, OF, Ca. 1830 (illo.75A)

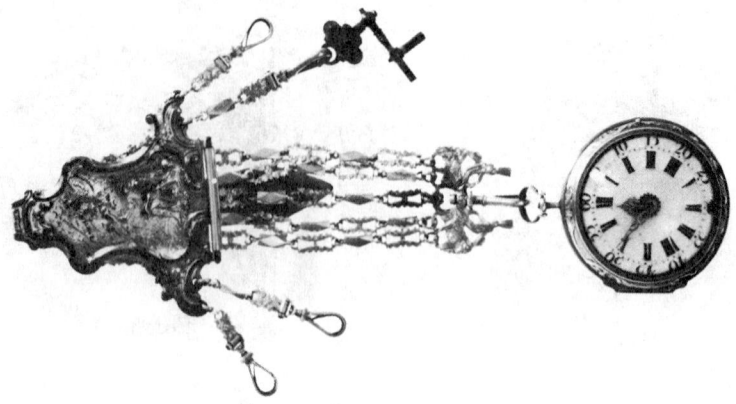

CHATELAINE, verge, fusee, 22k pair case, 45mm, (illo.76)

TYPE – DESCRIPTION	Avg	Ex-Fn	Mint
Chatelaine, verge, fusee, 22k pair case (illo.76)	$3,500	$3,800	$4,500
Early gold & nailed double case watch, foliot, C.1670 (illo.77)	22,000	24,000	29,000

Early gold & nailed double case watch, Champleve gold dial, 3 wheel train, verge, foliot, rosette adjustment and endless screw, 50mm, C.1670 (illo.77)

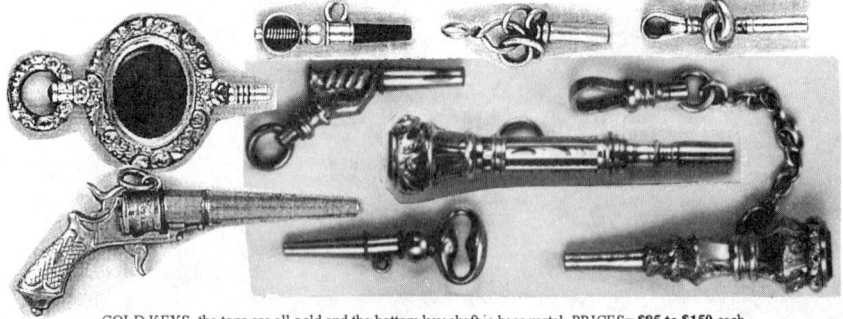

GOLD KEYS, the tops are all gold and the bottom key shaft is base metal, PRICES= **$85 to $150** each.

MISC. MEN'S GF / SILVER / BASE METAL

Dollar watch **German**, base metal ,OF, C.1895. (illo.78)

Dollar watch **German**, with camera, back wind, **waterproof style model,** base metal, OF, C.1885. (illo.79)

TYPE – DESCRIPTION	Avg	Ex-Fn	Mint
Dollar watch **German**, base metal ,OF, C.1895 (illo.78)	$40	$50	$75
Dollar watch **German,** back wind, **waterproof,** OF, C.1885 (illo.79)	325	350	400
Base metal, 7-17J, SW, 43-48mm, OF, C. 1900-1930	40	50	75
GF or silver, 7-17J, SW, 43-48mm, OF, C. 1895-1940	60	70	95
GF or silver, 7-17J, SW, 43-52mm, **HC,** C. 1895-1940	85	100	150
Swiss Fakes , 7J, KW, base metal, OF, 52mm, C. 1870-90	65	85	100
Non-magnetic, pat.# 7546/780, **Moeris,** base metal (illo.80)	100	125	165
Cylinder, (Liverpool), 1/2 plate design (illo.81)	85	100	125

Non-magnetic, pat.#7546-780, **Moeris**, base metal, thumb-nail set, SW, OF. (illo.80)

Cylinder escapement, (Liverpool), 1/2 plate design, marked 4 hole jeweled=8 jewels. (illo.81)

COMPARISON OF WATCH SIZES

U. S. A.	EUROPEAN
10-12 SIZE	40—44 MM
16 SIZE	45—48 MM
18 SIZE	50—54 MM

KW KS, **Chinese Duplex** escapement, 3/4 plate design, note **BAT** style balance, OF. (illo.82)

KW KS, with a **Compass** on movement, lever escapement. (illo.83)

TYPE – DESCRIPTION	Avg	Ex-Fn	Mint
KWKS, **Chinese Duplex,** 3/4 plate design, OF (illo.82)	$250	$300	$400
KWKS, **Compass** on movement, lever escap., (illo.83)	100	125	175
KWKS, 6-15J, silver, 45-52mm, OF, C. 1860-85	65	80	100
KWKS, 8-17J, silver, 45-52mm, HC, C. 1860-85	75	90	130
Engraved movement, KWKS, 15J, silver, 46mm, HC, C.1870	90	100	150
KWKS, marked railway, pin lever, Swiss (illo.84)	45	55	75
21J, RR type, GF, 48mm, OF, C. 1910-30	80	100	150
25J, Waltham (Swiss made), GF, 48mm, OF, C. 1950	100	125	175
Niello enamel, 17J, SW, silver, 45mm, HC, C. 1940	125	165	225
Niello enamel & **embossed** hunting scene on case, enamel dial, 3/4 plate, made in **Beaucourt France,** OF (illo.85)	100	125	200

KWKS, marked railway, pin lever, Swiss. (illo.84)

Niello enamel & embossed hunting scene on case, enamel dial, 3/4 plate, made in Beaucourt France, OF, Ca. 1890. (illo.85)

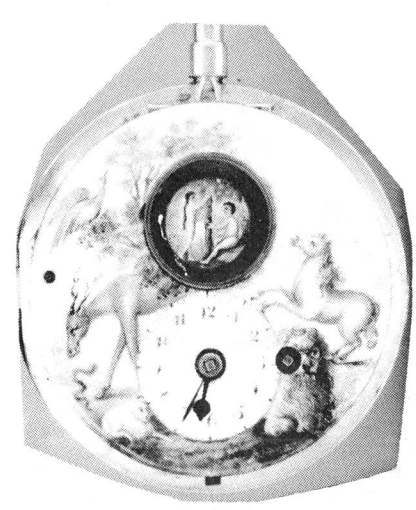

1/4 repeater early rim activated, Swiss or French, silver, OF, Ca.1820. (illo.86)

Automaton, **Adam & Eve**, note snake circles Adam & Eve, hand painted enamel dial, KW KS, OF. (illo. 87)

TYPE – DESCRIPTION	Avg	Ex-Fn	Mint
1/4 repeater early rim activated, silver, OF, Ca.1820 (illo.86).........	$700	$900	$1,200
Automaton, **Adam & Eve**, w/ snake, KW KS, OF (illo. 87)...........	3,800	4,500	5,500
Spring detent chronometer w/**Tandem** wind, fusee,			
56mm, Ca.1875 (illo.88)..	700	850	1,200
Gamblers playing cards on dial porcelain, Swiss, silver, OF (illo.89)	275	375	500

Spring Detent chronometer with **Tandem** wind, chain driven fusee, Helical hair spring, 56mm, Ca.1875. (illo.88)

Gamblers playing cards on porcelain dial, Swiss, silver, OF. (illo.89)

Exposed Skeletonized Balance from dial, enamel painted dial, verge, fusee, KW KS, large advance-retard index, Ca.1790. (illo.90)

TYPE – DESCRIPTION	Avg	Ex-Fn	Mint
Exposed Balance from dial, enamel painted dial, Ca.1790 (illo.90)	$1,600	$1,800	$2,400
Wandering Digital Jump Hour Hand, 45mm, Ca. 1880 (illo.91)....	3,500	4,000	5,500
Jump Digital Hour, W/ Date, at 6, sec. hand at 3, Ca. 1820 (illo.92)	1,200	1,400	1,800

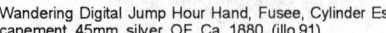

Wandering Digital Jump Hour Hand, Fusee, Cylinder Escapement, 45mm, silver, OF, Ca. 1880, (illo.91)

Jump Digital Hour, W/ Date, at 6, sec. hand at 3, silver, engine turned dial, OF, Ca. 1820 (illo.92)

COMPARISON OF WATCH SIZES

U. S. A.	EUROPEAN
10-12 SIZE	40—44 MM
16 SIZE	45—48 MM
18 SIZE	50—54 MM

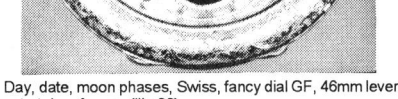

Day, date, moon phases, Swiss, fancy dial GF, 46mm lever set at rim of case. (illo.93)

Day, date, Swiss, fancy dial, **base metal**, 46mm. (illo.94)

TYPE – DESCRIPTION	Avg	Ex-Fn	Mint
Day, date, moon phases, Swiss, fancy dial, **GF**, 46mm (illo.93).....	$200	$250	$350
Day, date, moon phases, Swiss, fancy dial, **gun metal**, 46mm	150	200	300
Day, date, Swiss, fancy dial, **base metal**, 46mm (illo.94)	85	125	175
Self winding, (Loehr patent), KW, set from back (illo.95)	400	500	600
Mock pendulum (dial side), **all original**, duplex escap. (illo.96) ..	350	400	500

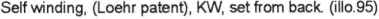

Self winding, (Loehr patent), KW, set from back. (illo.95)

Mock pendulum (seen from face side), duplex escap. Multicolor dial. FAKES SEEN (illo.96)

MISC. MEN'S *GOLD* / PLATINUM

TYPE – DESCRIPTION	Avg	Ex-Fn	Mint
SW, 17J, **14K**, 43-46mm, OF, C. 1910-1940	$200	$225	$275
SW, 17J-19J, **18K**, 43-46mm, OF, C. 1910-1940	250	275	350
SW, 17J, **14K**, 48mm, HC, C. 1910-1940	375	400	500
SW, 17J, **Platinum**, 42mm, OF, C. 1940's	500	550	650
KWKS, 15J, lever, fancy ,gilt dial, **18K**, 45mm, C. 1870...............	275	300	400
KWKS, 15-20J, lever **18K**, 49-53mm, C. 1870-1885	400	500	650
Lever, Fusee, (Liverpool), 15J, porcelain dial, **18K**, 52mm, C.1860	450	550	700

UNUSUAL NON—GOLD

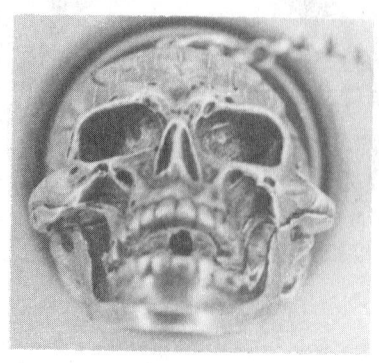

Skull (miniature) form watch, fusee, cylinder escapement, 25mm. Reproduction Ca. 1950 w/ early movement. (illo.97)

Blinking Eyes, pin set animated eyes, 46mm. (illo.98)

TYPE – DESCRIPTION	Avg	Ex-Fn	Mint
Skull (miniature) form, fusee, cylinder escape., 25mm, (illo.97)	$350	$475	$700
Blinking Eyes, pin set animated eyes, 46mm, (illo.98)	250	275	375
8 day, exposed balance, 7J, gun metal, 50mm, C. 1920s (illo.99)...	85	125	175
8 day, exposed balance, 7J, Swiss, **DAY & DATE,** gun metal, 50mm, C. 1920s	125	175	250
Roulette wheel dial, 7J, SW, base metal, 46mm, OF, C.1915	130	150	225
Game spin wheel novelty watch, 6 horses, gun metal, (illo.100).....	200	250	350

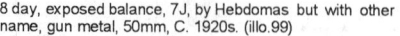

8 day, exposed balance, 7J, by Hebdomas but with other name, gun metal, 50mm, C. 1920s. (illo.99)

Game spin wheel novelty watch, 6 horses, gun metal. (illo.100)

🕐 Note: Some models and grades are not included. Their values can be determined by comparing with **similar** age, size, metal content, style, models and grades listed.

🕐 Note: Watches listed in this book are priced at the collectable retail level, as **complete** watches having an original case, an original dial, and with the entire original movement in good working order with no repairs needed.

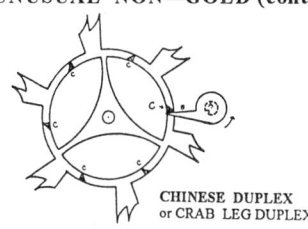

CHINESE DUPLEX
or CRAB LEG DUPLEX

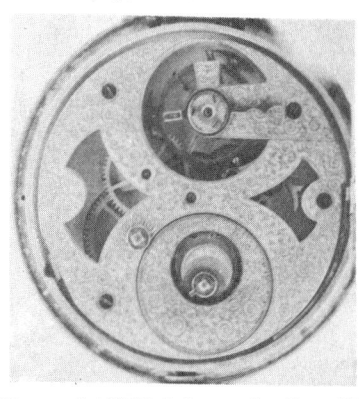

Chinese market, KWKS, duplex esc. silver, 58mm, OF, note BAT style balance, C.1870. (illo.101)

Chinese market, KW, duplex esc. silver, 58mm, OF, C.1870. (illo.102)

TYPE – DESCRIPTION	Avg	Ex-Fn	Mint
For Chinese market, lever esc., 12J, KWKS, silver, BAT style balance, 55mm, OF, C. 1880	$175	$225	$325
Chinese market, KW, duplex esc. silver, 58mm, OF, C.1870 (illo.101)	200	250	350
Chinese market, KW, duplex esc. silver, 58mm, OF, C.1870 (illo.102)	200	250	350
same as above with a GOLD CASE	450	550	700
Chinese market, KW, duplex esc. silver, carved movement, 58mm, OF, C.1870 (illo.103)	250	300	450
Carved movement, lever escap., KWKS, silver, 58mm, OF(illo.104)	95	125	200
KW, for Turkish market, 15J, .800 silver, 47mm, HC, C. 1880	75	100	175

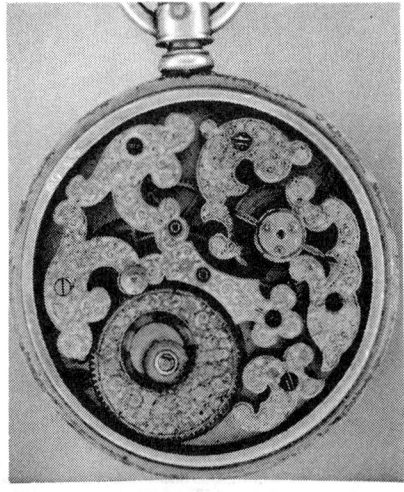

Chinese market, KW, duplex esc. silver, carved movement,58mm, OF, C.1870. (illo.103)

Carved movement, lever escap., KWKS, silver, 58mm, OF. (illo.104)

Oversize, moon phase & calendar, silver, 65-70mm,
Ca.1900. (illo.105)

Moonphase triple cal., Swiss, gun metal, 50mm, OF,
Ca. 1905. (illo.106)

TYPE – DESCRIPTION	Avg	Ex-Fn	Mint
Oversize PW, 15J, base metal, 65-70mm, C. 1900-1915	$125	$175	$250
Oversize, moon ph. & calendar, silver,65-70mm, Ca.1900 (illo.105)	750	950	1,250
Moonphase triple cal., Swiss, gun metal , 50mm, OF, C.1905(illo.106)	300	350	425
Moonphase triple cal., Swiss, silver or GF, 50mm, OF, C.1905	350	450	575
Moonphase triple cal., Swiss, silver, 52-54mm, HC, C. 1905	550	700	900
Moonphase calendar, sterling, , oversize 65mm, OF, C. 1895	650	800	1,000
Verge (Swiss) skeletonized KW movement, silver & horn pair-case, 61mm, C. 1800	650	750	1,000
Captain's watch, 2 hour dials, 1 train, KW KS, center second, silver, 50mm, HC, C. 1870 (illo.107)	325	400	525
Digital dial (porcelain), 15J, SW, Swiss, jump hr. & min. discs, silver,HC, C. 1900 (illo.108)	250	325	450

Captain's watch, 2 hour dials, 1 train, KW KS, center second, silver, 50mm, HC, C. 1870. (illo.107)

Digital dial (porcelain), 15J, SW, Swiss, jump hr. & min.
discs, silver,HC, C. 1900. (illo.108)

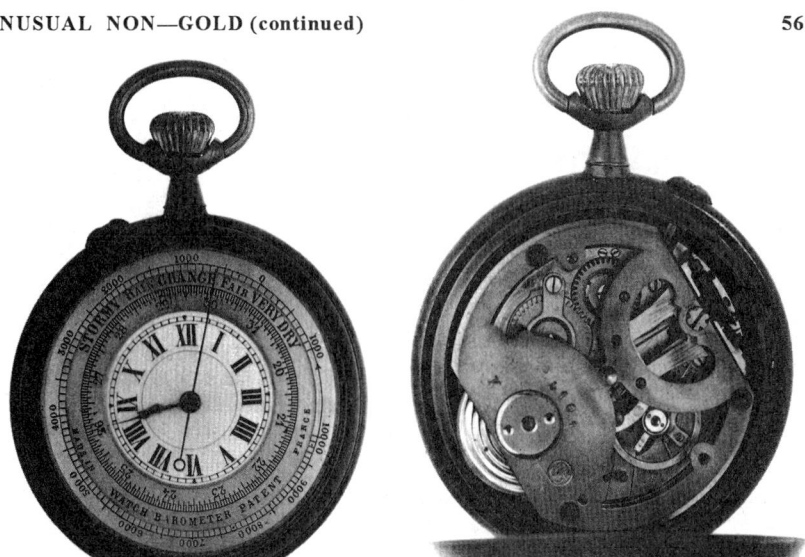

Swiss Pocket Watch with **BAROMETER**, Left: White enamel dial and outer barometer chapter is signed "Made in France, Watch barometer Patent", Right: Barometer is attached to movement, 7 jeweled, Cylinder escapement, 54MM, Gun Metal, Ca. 1890. (illo.108A)

TYPE – DESCRIPTION	Avg	Ex-Fn	Mint
Swiss Pocket Watch with **BAROMETER**, Made in France,			
54MM, Gun Metal, Ca. 1890. (illo.108A)..............................	$900	$1,200	$2,000
Oversized 1/4 Hour Repeater, 3-1/4" diameter Gun Metal Watch Case,			
leather box, Ca. 1890. (illo.108B)..	500	700	1,000

Oversized 1/4 Hour Repeater, 3-1/4" diameter Gun Metal Case, 29 jewels, 3/4 plate gilt movement, large white enamel dial, velvet-lined leather box , Ca. 1890. (illo.108B)

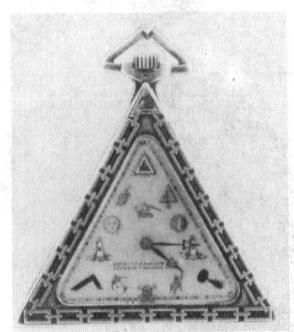

Automated with moving windmill on dial, Swiss, colored scene, exposed balance, 8 day , base metal, OF, C.1910. (illo.109)

Masonic triangular watch, Swiss ,17J, **mother of pearl** masonic dial, sterling, C. 1920's. (illo.110)

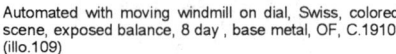

TYPE – DESCRIPTION	Avg	Ex-Fn	Mint
Automated w/moving windmill on dial, Swiss, colored scene, exposed balance, 8 day , base metal, OF, C.1910 (illo.109)...	$400	$500	$625
Masonic triangular watch, Swiss ,17J, **mother of pearl** masonic dial, sterling, C. 1920's (illo.110)..............................	1,100	1,500	2,000
Masonic, as above, with blue stone in crown, 1905	1,500	1,800	2,500
World-time w/ 6 zones, Swiss, **Gun Metal**, OF, C. 1900 (illo.111)	500	650	800
World time w/ 6 zones, Swiss, **silver**, 52mm, OF, C. 1900	700	800	1,000
World time, 24 Cities, w/ coded color rotating dial, **18K GOLD**, 61mm (illo.112)...	2,200	3,000	4,000

World time, with 6 zones, Swiss, GUN METAL, 52mm, OF, Ca.1900. (illo.111)

World time, 24 Cities, with coded color rotating dial, Ca. 1895, 61mm. (illo.112)

Note: Some models and grades are not included. Their values can be determined by comparing with **similar** age, size, metal content, style, models and grades listed.

Note: Watches listed in this book are priced at the collectable retail level, as **complete** watches having an original case, an original dial, and with the entire original movement in good working order with no repairs needed.

TYPE – DESCRIPTION	Avg	Ex-Fn	Mint
Mysterieuse watch, Swiss, see-through dial, hidden movement silver, 52mm, OF, Ca. 1895 (illo.113-114).............................	$800	$1,000	$1,300
GOLD, 52mm, OF, Ca. 1895 (illo.113-114).................... ★ ★	2,000	2,300	2,800
Wooden works, wooden wheels, wooden case, 50mm (illo.115)...	1,400	1,800	2,400
Sector watch, fan-shaped, fly back hour & min. hands, 17J, "Record Watch Co.," silver, 49x34mm, Ca. 1900 (illo.116)..	1,100	1,500	2,200
Musical, play's 2 tunes, silver, HC, 50mm, Ca. 1900 (illo.117)......	2,400	3,000	3,900

Mysterieuse watch, Swiss, see-through dial, showing dial side of watch, 52mm, OF, Ca. 1895. (illo.113)

Mysterieuse watch, Swiss, see-through dial, showing the hidden movement, 52mm, OF, Ca. 1895. (illo.114)

Wooden works, wooden wheels, wooden case, all wooden watch, 50mm, made in Russia in, Ca. 1860. (illo.115)

Sector watch, fan-shaped, fly back hour & min. hands, 17J, "Record Watch Co.," silver, 49x34mm, Ca. 1900. (illo.116)

Musical, play's 2 tunes, silver, 30 Tynes, HC, 50mm, 1900. (illo.117)

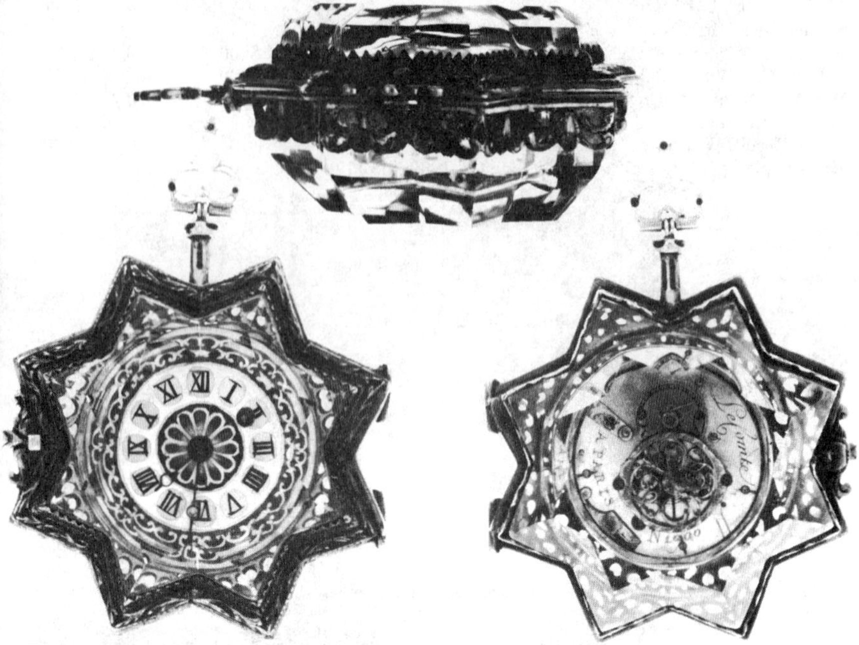

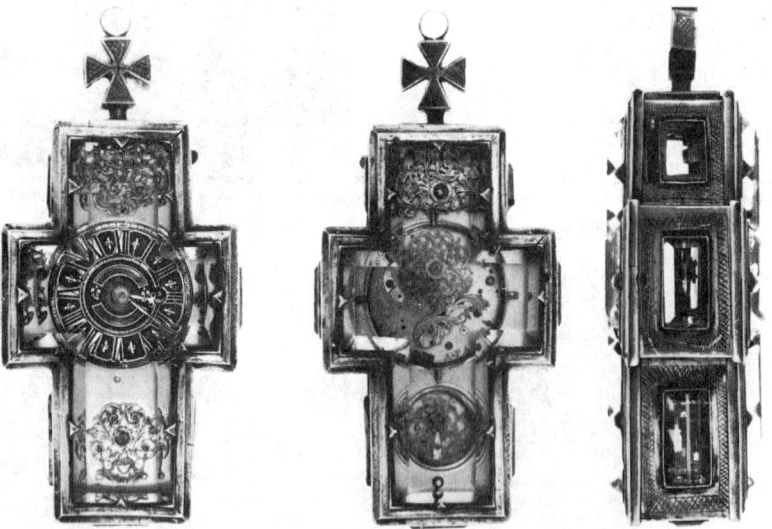

Rock crystal & enamel, star shape case, champleve enameled dial, verge, gilt & crystal case, 57x27mm, original French form Ca. 1600-1660, **Shown** Viennese form Ca. 1780-1800. (illo.118)

TYPE – DESCRIPTION	Avg	Ex-Fn	Mint
Rock crystal & enamel, star shape case, champleve dial, **Shown** Viennese verge, gilt & crystal case, 57x27mm, C.1800 (illo.118)	$4,000	$4,500	$5,500
Crucifix form 1/4 hr. repeater & musical, crystal & silver form case, **Shown** Viennese (illo.119)...	6,500	8,000	10,000

Crucifix form 1/4 hr. repeater & musical, crystal & silver form case, original French form Ca. 1600-1660, **Shown** Viennese form Ca. 1780-1800. (illo.119)

MEN'S UNUSUAL *"GOLD"*

Above note thin watch.
Extra flat watch, **1.5mm thick,** Swiss, 18K, HC, <u>ACTUAL SIZE</u>,50mm. (illo.120)

TYPE – DESCRIPTION	Avg	Ex-Fn	Mint
Extra flat watch, 1.5mm thick, Swiss, **18K**, HC, 50mm (illo.120)..	$2,500	$3,000	$4,500
Jump 1/4 seconds, 2 train, 30J, KW, nickel, (Swiss), **18K**, 56mm, HC, C. 1870-90	1,200	1,500	1,900
Captain's watch, enameled portraits on case, Maharaja & Queen Victoria, KW, lever movement, **18K**, 44mm, HC, C.1870	2,500	2,800	3,500
Captain's watch, KW, 15J, engraved case & enamel dial, **2 train, 18K**, 52-58mm, OF, C. 1870 (illo.121)	800	1,100	1,500
1776-1876 centennial watch, H.O. Stauffer, bridges in 1776 form, 17J, **18K**, 53mm, HC, C. 1876 (illo.122)...............................	1,400	1,800	2,400

Captain's watch, KW, 15J, engraved case & enamel dial, **2 train,**18K, 52-58mm, OF, Ca. 1870. (illo.121)

1776-1876 centennial watch, H.O. Stauffer, bridges in 1776 form, 17J, 18K, 53mm, HC, Ca. 1876. (illo.122)

Moonphase, double dial, calendar, Swiss, 17J, back lid opens to reveal cal. dial, 14K, HC, C.1890. (illo.123)

TYPE – DESCRIPTION	Avg	Ex-Fn	Mint
Captain's watch, KW KS, 15J, ornate case, Swiss, single train, **18K**, 52mm, HC, C. 1870	$600	$700	$1,000
Digital dial, hrs. & min. on digital jump discs, Swiss, 15J, SW, **18K**, 51mm, HC, C. 1905	600	800	1,200
Moonphase, double dial, calendar, Swiss, 17J, back lid opens to reveal cal. dial, **14K**, HC, C.1890 (illo.123)	800	1,000	1,700
Two train, center independent sec.,2 going barrels, lever escap., KW KS, GOLD, 42mm, Ca. 1880, HC (illo. 124)	700	900	1,200
Art Deco dial, Swiss, **18K**, 45mm,OF (illo.125)	600	700	1,000

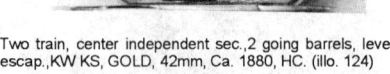

Two train, center independent sec.,2 going barrels, lever escap.,KW KS, GOLD, 42mm, Ca. 1880, HC. (illo. 124)

Art Deco style with **exaggerated** numbers on dial, Swiss, 18K, 45mm,OF. (illo.125)

TYPE – DESCRIPTION	Avg	Ex-Fn	Mint
Double dials, world time & moon ph. triple date,**18K** (illo.126)	$4,500	$5,300	$6,500
Perpetual calendar with moonphase and chrono., Swiss , 20J, porcelain dial, 3/4 plate, 18K, 51mm, OF, C.1890-1900	5,500	7,200	8,500
Rare verge, w/ automaton "Serpent, Adam & Eve" on dial with moving serpent, verge, French , 18K, OF, C. 1800	4,500	5,300	6,500
Musical, two train of gears, pin cylinder & 24 blades, one tune, 18K (illo.127)	2,200	2,800	3,700
Waterproof watch w/wind ind. 17J., C.1885 (illo.128)	1,000	1,200	1,500
Cigarette lighter & Swiss watch, Dunhill, Silver, C.1926 (illo.129)	300	350	500
9K case	900	1,100	1,400
14K case	1,200	1,400	1,700
$20.00 U.S. gold coin, 17J, mvt. in coin, 35mm, Ca.1920's (illo.130)	1,200	1,400	1,700

Double dials, world time & moon ph. triple date,18K. (illo.126)

Musical, two train of gears, pin cylinder & 24 blades, one tune, 18K. (illo.127)

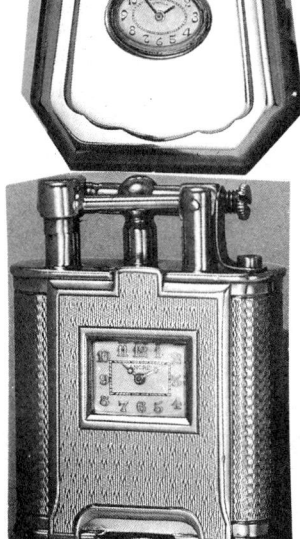

Waterproof watch w/wind ind. 17J., C.1885. (illo.128)

Cigarette lighter & Swiss watch, Dunhill, Silver, Ca.1926. (illo.129)

$20.00 U.S. gold coin, 17J, Swiss mvt. in coin, 35mm, Ca.1920's. (illo.130)

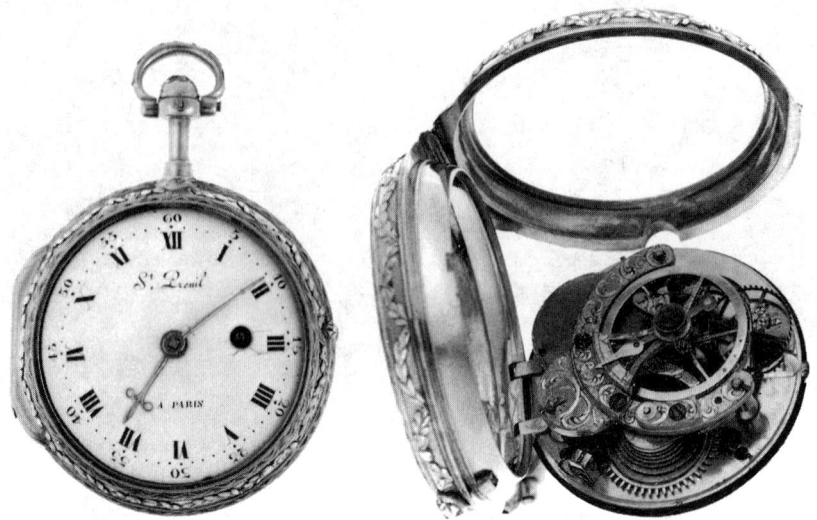

Skeletonized Verge & Fusee (*French*), Multi-color 18K Case & rose cut diamonds, horseshoe shaped plate, balance end stone is a large Cabochon Ruby,45MM, KW KS, Ca. 1785.(illo.130A)

TYPE – DESCRIPTION	Avg	Ex-Fn	Mint
Skeletonized Verge & Fusee movement, 45MM, KWKS with Multi-color 18K Case, Ca. 1785 (illo.130A)...................	$2,800	$3,000	$4,000
Lorgnette Form Watch, 3/8" x 7/8 x 3-1/4", *18K Closed Case*, KWKS, Ca. 1850. (illo.130B)...	3,700	4,000	5,000

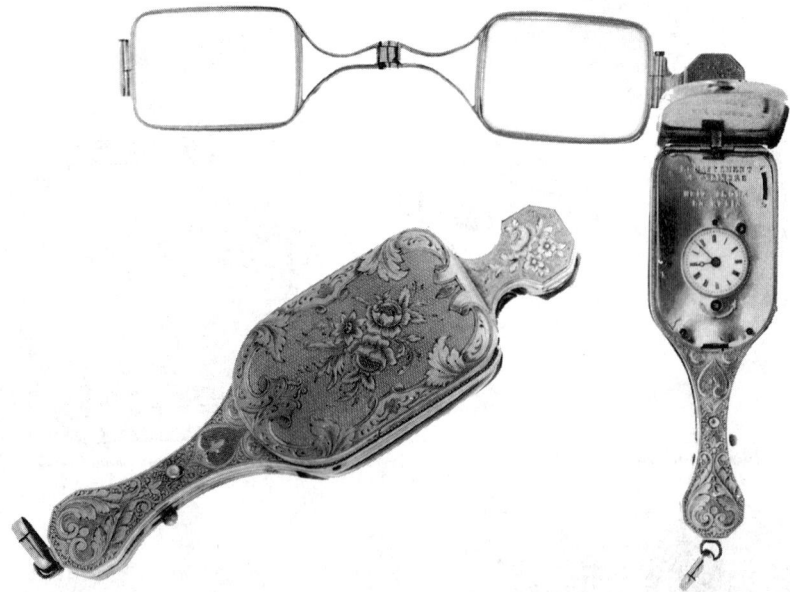

Lorgnette Form Watch, 3/8" x 7/8 x 3-1/4", *18K Closed Case*, the case is chased with leaf patterns and arabesque, signed "Echappement a Cylindre Huit Trous en Rubis", the looking frames are rose gold and flip out with a push button, KWKS, Ca. 1850. (illo.130B)

MISC. SWISS LADY'S Ca. 1850–1950 SILVER or GOLD FILLED

TYPE – DESCRIPTION	Avg	Ex-Fn	Mint
GF or silver, 7-17J, SW, 35mm, OF, C. 1900-1930	$45	$55	$75
GF or silver, 10-15J, SW, 35mm, fancy dial, OF, C. 1910	65	75	100
GF or silver, 7-17J, SW, 35- 40mm, HC, C. 1890-1930	75	95	125
Enamel or silver, cylinder, pinset, 35mm, OF, C. 1910	85	90	125
KWKS, silver, 40- 45mm, OF, C. 1865-1885	75	90	125
KWKS, silver, 37- 45mm, HC, C. 1865-1885	100	125	150
Ball shaped, 17J, 35mm, SW, GF or silver with chain	100	135	195

MISC. LADYS Ca. 1850–1950 *GOLD* (NO ENAMEL)

TYPE – DESCRIPTION	Avg	Ex-Fn	Mint
SW, 7-15J, 14K, 35- 40mm, OF, C. 1910-1930	$100	$135	$195
SW, 7-15J, 14K, 35- 40mm, HC, C. 1910-1930	235	300	325
KWKS, 10J, cylinder, 18K, 34- 40mm, OF, C.1865-90	165	225	275
KWKS, 10J, cylinder, 18K, 38- 43mm, HC, C. 1865-85	300	350	400
Fusee, lever, fancy dial, 18K, 38- 43mm, OF, C. 1845-75	350	450	550
Fusee, lever, fancy dial, 18K, 38- 43mm, HC, C. 1850s	400	500	600
Ball shaped w/pin, 10J, 14K, 25mm, OF, C. 1890	500	600	650

MISC. LADYS Ca. 1850–1950 ENAMEL ON *GOLD*

TYPE – DESCRIPTION	Avg	Ex-Fn	Mint
KW, enamel (black outlines) 18K, 40- 42mm HC, C. 1860	$250	$375	$475
KW, enamel & dia., Swiss, 10J, 18K, OF, C. 1860	350	450	650
Pattern enamel & demi-hunter, 15J, 18K , 35mm, HC, C.1885	400	550	800
Portrait enamel, KWKS, Swiss, 14K, 34- 42mm, HC, C. 1870	400	600	900
Enamel , with pearls and/ or dia., 10-17J, w/ matching pin, 18K, 23-26mm, OF	700	900	1,400
Enamel, w/dia. or pearls, w/ pin, 18K, 26-30mm, HC, C. 1895	900	1,250	1,700
Miniature verge, gold & enamel w/ pearls, superior enamel, Swiss, KW, gold case, 27mm, OF, C. 1770,	2,750	3,500	5,000
Miniature HC enamel & dia., 17J, Swiss, with orig. pin, 18K, 23mm, HC, C. 1890	1,200	1,600	2,300
Ball-shaped (Duchene) Geneva, verge, KW, enamel and gold, 25mm, C. 1800	1,200	1,700	2,500

Ⓛ Note: Some models and grades are not included. Their values can be determined by comparing with similar age, size, metal content, style, models and grades listed.

Ⓛ Note: Watches listed in this book are priced at the collectable retail level, as complete watches having an original case, an original dial, and with the entire original movement in good working order with no repairs needed.

COMPARISON OF WATCH SIZES

U. S. A.	EUROPEAN
10-12 SIZE	40—44 MM
16 SIZE	45—48 MM
18 SIZE	50—54 MM

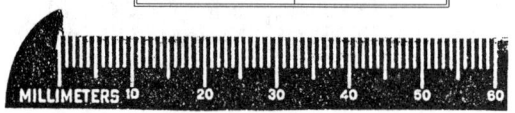

LADY'S UNUSUAL *GOLD* & ENAMEL

LEFT; Ball-shaped, bezel wind, 18K, enamel & diamonds, Swiss, 16mm, OF, C. 1920. (illo.131) CENTER: Ring watch w/enamel & dia., Swiss, 18K, 18mm, C.1910. (illo.132) RIGHT: Padlock form enamel and gold, Swiss, KW. (illo.133)

TYPE – DESCRIPTION	Avg	Ex-Fn	Mint
Ball-shaped, bezel wind, Swiss, enamel & diamonds on 18K case, 16mm, OF, C. 1920 (illo.131)	$900	$1,200	$1,600
Ring watch w/enamel & dia., Swiss, 18K, 18mm, C.1910 (illo.132)	750	1,000	1,400
Cherry form enamel & 18K, 17J, closed case, bezel wind, Swiss, 22mm,	1,500	2,300	3,500
Flower basket form, enamel and 18K, Swiss, KWKS, with heart form movement, 10J, 18K, 30x24mm, HC, C. 1860	2,500	3,200	4,200
Padlock form enamel and gold, Swiss, KW (illo.133)	900	1,200	1,600
Padlock form enamel and gold (cover over dial,) Swiss, KW, diamonds on case, heart shaped mvt.,18K, 28x51mm, HC, C.1870	1,200	1,500	2,200
Form watch in shape of **leaf**, gold & enamel, Bar mvt. (illo.134)	1,200	1,500	2,200

 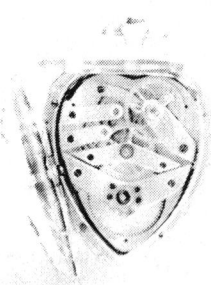

Form watch in shape of **leaf**, gold & enamel, cylinder escapement, Bar movement., KW KS, Ca.1865. (illo.134)

🕐 Pricing in this Guide are fair market price for **COMPLETE** watches which are reflected from the "**NAWCC**" National and regional shows.

Scarab form gold & enamel, 10J, cylinder, diamonds, closed case w/wings that open, 18K, 54x23mm, C.1885. (illo.135)

Rare enamel & gold harps, matched pair w/ music, verge, diamonds, lapis and enameled scenes, 3 3/4" high, C.1830. (illo.136)

TYPE – DESCRIPTION	Avg	Ex-Fn	Mint
Scarab form gold & enamel, 10J, cylinder, diamonds, closed case w/wings that open, 18K, 54x23mm, C.1885 (illo.135)	$4,000	$5,200	$7,000
Lorgnette with enamel & gold, KW, 10J, Swiss, 3 1/4" x 1" cover ornamented w/dia., 18K	3,500	4,500	6,000
Rare enamel &gold harps, matched pair w/ music, verge, diamonds, lapis and enameled scenes, 3 3/4" high, C.1830 (illo.136)	18,000	24,000	32,000
Rock crystal case, silver dial, **Viennese** made, C. 1830 (illo.137) ..	3,500	4,500	5,800

Rock crystal case, silver dial, Viennese made, C. 1830. Reproduction, (illo.137)

ENAMEL WATCHES

Floral enamel watch. Bouquet of flowers within a champleve border of scrolls enclosing panels of flowers. (illo.E-2)

Floral enamel watch. Finely painted floral enamel panel within border of seed pearls. (illo.E-1)

SIZE AND DESCRIPTION	Avg	Ex-Fn	Mint
55mm, finely painted floral, seed pearls, (Bovet also Ilbery),18K (illo.E.1)	$7,500	$9,500	$15,000
47mm, gold enamel repeater, with chatelaine of pierced gold links & enamel plaques with enamel key & fob seals (illo.E.2)	4,000	4,500	6,500
Enamel & pearls, hunting scene of lion, for China market, silver gilt duplex escapement, 62mm, Ca. 1845 (illo.E-3)	4,500	5,000	6,500
Enamel and 18K case, automated horseman and windmill also fountain, horse drinks water (illo.E-4)	25,000	29,000	35,000
Enamel floral scene, enamel and pearls on gold case, finely painted floral bouquet, 55mm (illo.E-5)	24,000	32,000	40,000
Enamel and 18K case, MINUTE- REPEATER, HC, surrounded with pearls, 55mm, (illo.E-5A)	12,000	14,500	19,000
VIENNESE enamel watch, the front cover shows a lady and gentleman in a scene, the back cover pictures three boys in a scene, 55mm (illo.E-6 & E-6A)	1,500	1,800	2,200
54mm, 29J., 1/4 repeater, pearls & enamel, silver case (illo.E-8)	1,800	2,200	3,000
VIENNESE Lapis Lazuli enamel watch, verge fusee, top and bottom covers are finely cut solid lapis stone, champleve enamel dial, Ca. 1830 reproduction (illo.E-9)	2,500	3,000	4,000

🕑 French watch-making believed to have started in town of Blois, France. French Enamel Watches also believed to have started in Blois, in early 1600's.

Enamel & pearls, hunting scene of lion, for China market, duplex escapement, 62mm, Ca. 1845. (illo.E-3)

Enamel and 18K case, automated horseman and windmill also fountain, horse drinks water. (illo.E-4)

Enamel floral scene, enamel and pearls on gold case, finely painted floral bouquet, 55mm (illo.E-5)

Enamel and 18K case, MINUTE- REPEATER, Hunting Case, surrounded with pearls, 55mm, Ca.1890. (illo.E-5A)

VIENNESE enamel watch, the front cover shows a lady and gentleman in a scene, the back cover pictures three boys in a scene, 55mm. see movement below. (illo.E-6)

VIENNESE enamel watch, same watch as above, two-footed balance bridge, the inner lids are decorated with polychrome enamelled scenes. (illo.E-6A)

54mm, 29J, 1/4 hour repeater, Pearls and enamel on a silver case, ca. 1885. (illo.E-8)

VIENNESE Lapis Lazuli enamel watch, verge fusee, top and bottom covers are finely cut solid lapis stone, champleve enamel dial, Ca. 1830 Reproduction (illo.E-9)

Floral enamel watch, 57mm, bouquet of flowers within a gold case set with split pearls. (illo.E-10)

Enamel scene watch, 58mm, finely painted scene of ships in harbor. (illo.E-11)

SIZE AND DESCRIPTION	Avg	Ex-Fn	Mint
57mm, floral enamel, duplex, (Bovet), pearls, 18K, (illo.E-10)	$6,500	$8,000	$10,000
58mm, harbor scene enamel, duplex, 18k, Ca. 1790 (illo.E-11)	20,000	24,000	32,000
43mm, basket form champleve enamel, 18k, Ca.1800 (illo.E.12)...	2,600	3,200	4,000
42mm, champleve border, finely painted flowers, (Le Roy), gold case & chain..	2,500	2,800	3,500
37mm, rose gold guilloche enamel demi-hunter.............................	350	450	600
36mm, gold enamel & champleve enamel, verge, Ca. 1800	1,600	2,000	2,800
35mm, gold champleve enamel, (L'Epine), cylinder	650	900	1,200
35mm, gold enamel & seed pearls, rose cut diamonds	275	400	600
34mm, gold egg-shaped form enamel, verge, (Austrian)	1,200	1,800	2,500
30mm, gold miniature enamel, verge, seed pearls, Ca. 1800	750	900	1,200
27mm, gold enamel lapel brooch with seed pearls & rose cut diamonds, Ca. 1890	550	700	900
27mm, gold fine enamel lapel brooch with cut diamonds by C. H. Meylan (illo.E.13)	1,500	1,800	2,500

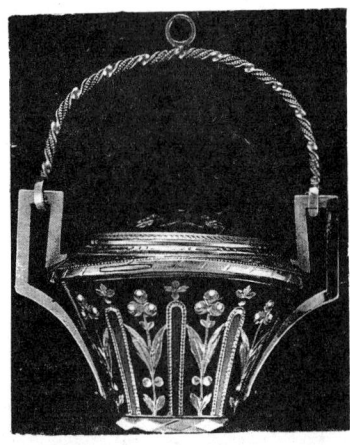

Enamel form tapered oval basket with rising rope handle, enhanced with panels of flowers, 18K case. (illo.E-12)

A chased enamel gold lady's pendant watch. Enamel portrait of a lady. (illo.E-13)

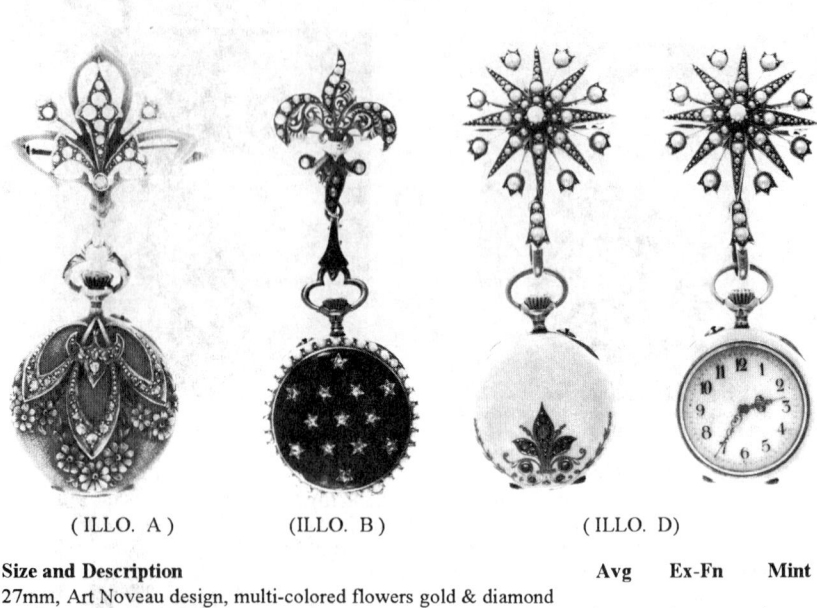

(ILLO. A)   (ILLO. B)   (ILLO. D)

Size and Description	Avg	Ex-Fn	Mint
27mm, Art Noveau design, multi-colored flowers gold & diamond pendant watch & pin, 18K, OF, Ca.1890 (illo. A)	$800	$1,000	$1,400
25mm, Enamel & pearls & diamonds, star shaped gold settings , pendant and pen, 18K, OF, Ca. 1890 (illo. B)	650	750	1,000
25mm, enamel pendant with pin, golden frame of vines around a scene of a lady , 14K, OF, Ca. 1900	900	1,100	1,400
24mm, pearl pendant watch with pin, seed pearls also on classic fleur-de-lis designed pin, 14K OF, Ca.1885 (illo. C)	800	1,000	1,300
24mm, enamel and gold pendant watch with a starburst gold and pearl pin, 10 J, cylinder movement, 18K, OF, Ca.1900 (illo. D)	700	900	1,200
22mm, ball-shaped enamel & pearl pendant watch, exposed balance, lever escapement can be seen back crystal (illo. E)	1,400	1,700	2,200
20mm, 17J, three-finger bridge miniature movement, Adj.5P, by Didsheim platinum OF case, Ca.1930s (illo. F)	1,100	1,400	1,800

(ILLO. E)

(ILLO. C)   (ILLO. F)

Am. Waltham W. Co

Date	Serial #
1852	50
1853	400
1854	1,000
1855	2,500
1856	4,000
1857	6,000
1858	10,000
1859	15,000
1860	20,000
1861	30,000
1862	45,000
1863	65,000
1864	110,000
1865	180,000
1866	260,000
1867	330,000
1868	410,000
1869	460,000
1870	500,000
1871	540,000
1872	590,000
1873	680,000
1874	730,000
1875	810,000
1876	910,000
1877	1,000,000
1878	1,150,000
1879	1,350,000
1880	1,500,000
1881	1,670,000
1882	1,835,000
1883	2,000,000
1884	2,350,000
1885	2,650,000
1886	3,000,000
1887	3,400,000
1888	3,800,000
1889	4,200,000
1890	4,700,000
1891	5,200,000
1892	5,800,000
1893	6,300,000
1894	6,700,000
1895	7,100,000
1896	7,450,000
1897	8,100,000
1898	8,400,000
1899	9,000,000
1900	9,500,000
1901	10,200,000
1902	11,100,000
1903	12,100,000
1904	13,500,000
1905	14,300,000
1906	14,700,000
1907	15,500,000
1908	16,400,000
1909	17,600,000
1910	17,900,000
1911	18,100,000
1912	18,200,000
1913	18,900,000
1914	19,500,000
1915	20,000,000
1916	20,500,000
1917	20,900,000
1918	21,800,000
1919	22,500,000
1920	23,400,000
1921	23,900,000
1922	24,100,000
1923	24,300,000
1924	24,550,000
1925	24,800,000
1926	25,200,000
1927	26,100,000
1928	26,400,000
1929	26,900,000
1930	27,100,000
1931	27,300,000
1932	27,550,000
1933	27,750,000
1934	28,100,000
1935	28,600,000
1936	29,100,000
1937	29,400,000
1938	29,750,000
1939	30,050,000
1940	30,250,000
1941	30,750,000
1942	31,050,000
1943	31,400,000
1944	31,700,000
1945	32,100,000
1946	32,350,000
1947	32,750,000
1948	33,100,000
1949	33,500,000
1950	33,560,000
1951	33,600,000
1952	33,700,000
1953	33,800,000
1954	34,100,000
1955	34,450,000
1956	34,700,000
1957	35,000,000

AURORA W. CO.

Date	Serial #
1884	10,001
1885	60,000
1886	101,000
1887	160,000
1888	200,000
1889	215,000
1891	230,901

COLUMBUS W. CO.

Date	Serial #
1875	1,000
1876	3,000
1877	6,000
1878	9,000
1879	12,000
1880	15,000
1881	18,000
1882	21,000
1883	25,000
1884	30,000
1885	40,000
1886	53,000
1887	75,000
1888	97,000
1889	119,000
1890	141,000
1891	163,000
1892	185,000
1893	207,000
1894	229,000
1895	251,000
1896	273,000
1897	295,000
1898	317,000
1899	339,000
1900	361,000
1901	383,000

SPECIAL BLOCK OF SERIAL NOS.

Date	Serial #
1894	500,001
1896	501,500
1898	503,000
1900	504,500
1902	506,000

ELGIN WATCH CO.

Date	Serial #	
1867	10,000	
1868	25,001	Nov,20th
1869	40,001	May, 20th
1870	50,001	Aug. 24th
1871	185,001	Sep. 8th
1872	201,001	Dec. 20th
1873	325,001	
1874	400,001	Aug 28th
1875	430,000	
1876	480,000	
1877	520,000	
1878	550,000	
1879	625,001	Feb 8th
1880	750,000	
1881	900,000	
1882	1,000,000	March, 9th
1883	1,250,000	
1884	1,500,000	
1885	1,855,001	May,28th
1886	2,000,000	Aug 4th
1887	2,500,000	
1888	3,000,000	June 20th
1889	3,500,000	
1890	4,000,000	Aug 16th
1891	4,449,001	Mar 26th
1892	4,600,000	
1893	5,000,000	July 1st
1894	5,500,000	
1895	6,000,000	Nov. 26th
1896	6,500,000	
1897	7,000,000	Oct. 28th.
1898	7,494,001	May,14th
1899	8,000,000	Jan. 18th
1900	9,000,000	Nov. 14th
1901	9,300,000	
1902	9,600,000	
1903	10,000,000	May 15th
1904	11,000,000	April 4th
1905	12,000,000	Oct. 6th
1906	12,500,000	
1907	13,000,000	April 4th
1908	13,500,000	
1909	14,000,000	Feb. 9th
1910	15,000,000	April 2nd
1911	16,000,000	July 11th
1912	17,000,000	Nov. 6th
1913	17,339,001	Apr. 14th
1914	18,000,000	
1915	18,587,001	Feb. 11th
1916	19,000,000	
1917	20,031,001	June,27th
1918	21,000,000	
1919	22,000,000	
1920	23,000,000	
1921	24,321,001	July,6th
1922	25,100,000	
1923	26,050,000	
1924	27,000,000	
1925	28,421,001	July,14th
1926	29,100,000	
1927	30,050,000	
1928	31,500,000	
1929	32,000,000	
1930	32,599,001	July
1931	33,000,000	
1932	33,700,000	
1933	34,558,001	July,24th
1934	35,000,000	
1935	35,650,000	
1936	36,200,000	
1937	36,978,001	July,24th
1938	37,900,000	
1939	38,200,000	
1940	39,100,000	
1941	40,200,000	
1942	41,100,000	
1943	42,200,000	
1944	42,600,000	
1945	43,200,000	
1946	44,000,000	
1947	45,000,000	
1948	46,000,000	
1949	47,000,000	
1950	48,000,000	
1951	50,000,000	
1952	52,000,000	
1953	53,500,000	
1954	54,000,000	
1955	54,500,000	
1956	55,000,000	

HAMILTON WATCH CO.

Date	Serial No.
1893	1-2,000
1894	5,000
1895	11,500
1896	16,000
1897	27,000
1898	50,000
1899	74,000
1900	104,000
1901	143,000
1902	196,000
1903	260,000
1904	340,000
1905	425,000
1906	590,000
1907	756,000
1908	921,000
1909	1,087,000
1910	1,150,500
1911	1,290,500
1912	1,331,000
1913	1,370,000
1914	1,410,500
1915	1,450,500
1916	1,517,000
1917	1,580,000
1918	1,650,000
1919	1,700,000
1920	1,790,000
1921	1,860,000
1922	1,900,000
1923	1,950,000
1924	2,000,000
1925	2,100,000
1926	2,200,000
1927	2,250,000
1928	2,300,000
1929	2,350,000
1930	2,400,000
1931	2,450,000
1932	2,500,000
1933	2,600,000
1934	2,700,000
1935	2,800,000
1936	2,900,000
1937	3,000,000
1938	3,200,000
1939	3,400,000
1940	3,600,000
1941	3,800,000
1942	4,025,000

DATE LETTERS
2B on 950B=1941-43
C on 992B=1940-59
S on 950B=1943-68
OTHER DATE LETTERS = 1930s to 1950s

HAMPDEN W. CO.

Date	Serial #
1877	60,000
1878	91,000
1879	122,000
1880	153,000
1881	184,000
1882	215,000
1883	250,000
1884	300,000
1885	350,000
1886	400,000
1887	450,000
1888	500,000
1889	555,500
1890	611,000
1891	666,500
1892	722,000
1893	775,000
1894	833,000
1895	888,500
1896	944,000
1897	1,000,000
1898	1,128,000
1899	1,256,000
1900	1,384,000
1901	1,512,000
1902	1,642,000
1903	1,768,000
1904	1,896,000
1905	2,024,000
1906	2,152,000
1907	2,280,000
1908	2,408,000
1909	2,536,000
1910	2,664,000
1911	2,792,000
1912	2,920,000
1913	3,048,000
1914	3,176,000
1915	3,304,000
1916	3,432,000
1917	3,560,000
1918	3,680,000
1919	3,816,000
1920	3,944,000
1921	4,072,000
1922	4,200,000
1923	4,400,000
1924	4,600,000

E. HOWARD & CO.

Date	Serial #
1858-60)	131-1,900
1860-61)	1,901-3,000
1861)	3,001-3,100
1861)	3,101-3,250
1861)	3,401- 3,500
1861-71)	3,501-28,000
1868-83)	30,001-50,000
1869-99)	50,001-71,000
1869-90)	100,001-105,000
1880-99)	200,001-227,000
1895)	228,001-231,000
1884-99)	300,001-309,000
1895)	309,001-310,000
1890-95)	400,001-405,000
1890-99)	500,001-501,500
1896-1903)	600,001-601,500
1896-1903)	700,001-701,500

HOWARD WATCH CO.
(KEYSTONE)

Date	Serial #
1902	850,000
1903	900,000
1909	980,000
1912	1,100,000
1915	1,285,000
1917	1,340,000
1921	1,400,000
1930	1,500,000

ILLINOIS WATCH CO.

Date	Serial #
1872	5,000
1873	20,000
1874	50,000
1875	75,000
1876	100,000
1877	145,000
1878	210,000
1879	250,000
1880	300,000
1881	350,000
1882	400,000
1883	450,000
1884	500,000
1885	550,000
1886	600,000
1887	700,000
1888	800,000
1889	900,000
1890	1,000,000
1891	1,040,000
1892	1,080,000
1893	1,120,000
1894	1,160,000
1895	1,220,000
1896	1,250,000
1897	1,290,000
1898	1,330,000
1899	1,370,000
1900	1,410,000
1901	1,450,000
1902	1,500,000
1903	1,650,000
1904	1,700,000
1905	1,800,000
1906	1,840,000
1907	1,900,000
1908	2,100,000
1909	2,150,000
1910	2,200,000
1911	2,300,000
1912	2,400,000
1913	2,500,000
1914	2,600,000
1915	2,700,000
1916	2,800,000
1917	3,000,000
1918	3,200,000
1919	3,400,000
1920	3,600,000
1921	3,750,000
1922	3,900,000
1923	4,000,000
1924	4,500,000
1925	4,700,000
1926	4,800,000
1927	5,000,000
(Sold to Hamilton)	
1928	5,100,000
1929	5,200,000
1931	5,400,000
1938	5,500,000
1948	5,600,000

ROCKFORD W.Co.

Date	Serial #
1874	22,200
1875	42,600
1876	63,000
1877	83,000
1878	103,000
1879	124,000
1880	144,000
1881	165,000
1882	185,000
1883	206,000
1884	226,000
1885	247,000
1886	267,000
1887	287,500
1888	308,000
1889	328,500
1890	349,000
1891	369,500
1892	390,000
1893	410,000
1894	430,000
1895	450,000
1896	470,000
1897	490,000
1898	510,000
1899	530,000
1900	550,000
1901	570,000
1902	590,000
1903	610,000
1904	630,000
1905	650,000
1906	670,000
1907	690,000
1908	734,000
1909	790,000
1910	824,000
1911	880,000
1912	936,000
1913	958,000
1914	980,000
1915	1,000,000

SOUTH BEND W. CO.

Date	Serial #
1903	380,501
1904	410,000
1905	445,000
1906	480,000
1907	515,000
1908	550,000
1909	585,000
1910	620,000
1911	655,000
1912	690,000
1913	725,000
1914	760,000
1915	795,000
1916	825,000
1917	865,000
1918	900,000
1919	935,000
1920	970,000
1921	1,005,000
1922	1,040,000
1923	1,075,000
1924	1,110,000
1925	1,145,000
1926	1,180,000
1927	1,215,000
1928	1,250,000
1929	1,275,000

SETH THOMAS W. Co.

Date	Serial #
1885	5,000
1886	20,000
1887	40,000
1888	80,000
1889	150,000
1890	235,000
1891	330,000
1892	420,000
1893	510,000
1894	600,000
1895	690,000
1896	780,000
1897	870,000
1898	960,000
1899	1,050,000
1900	1,140,000
1901	1,230,000
1902	1,320,000
1903	1,410,000
1904	1,500,000
1905	1,700,000
1906	1,900,000
1907	2,100,000
1908	2,300,000
1909	2,500,000
1910	2,725,000
1911	2,950,000
1912	3,175,000
1913	3,490,000
1914	3,600,000

BALL WATCH CO.
(Hamilton)

Date	Serial #
1895	13,000
1897	20,500
1900	42,000
1902	170,000
1905	462,000
1910	600,000
1915	603,000
1920	610,000
1925	620,000
1930	637,000
1935	641,000
1938	647,000
1939	650,000
1940	651,000
1941	652,000
1942	654,000
(Waltham)	
1900	060,700
1905	202,000
1910	216,000
1915	250,000
1920	260,000
1925	270,000
(Illinois)	
1929	800,000
1930	801,000
1931	803,000
1932	804,000

(Elgin)
1904-1906
S # range
11,853,000-12,282,000
(E. Howard & CO.)
1893-1895
S # range
226,000-308,000
(Hampden)
1890-1892
S # range
626,750-657,960-759,720

Audemars Piguet

DATE	SERIAL #
1882	2,000
1890	4,000
1895	5,350
1900	6,500
1905	9,500
1910	13,000
1915	17,000
1920	25,000
1925	33,000
1930	40,000
1935	42,000
1940	44,000
1945	48,000
1950	55,000
1955	65,000
1960	75,000
1965	90,000
1970	115,000
1975	160,000
1980	225,000

International W.Co.
(Schaffhausen)

DATE	SERIAL #
1884	6,500
1886	23,500
1888	37,500
1890	63,000
1892	87,500
1894	117,000
1896	151,500
1898	194,000
1900	231,000
1902	276,500
1904	321,000
1906	377,500
1908	435,000
1910	492,000
1912	557,000
1914	620,500
1916	657,000
1918	714,000
1920	765,000
1922	783,500
1924	807,000
1926	845,000
1928	890,500
1930	929,000
1932	938,000
1934	940,000
1936	955,500
1938	1,000,000
1940	1,019,000
1942	1,062,000
1944	1,092,000
1946	1,131,000
1948	1,177,000
1950	1,222,000
1952	1,291,000
1954	1,335,000
1956	1,399,000
1958	1,480,000
1960	1,553,000
1962	1,666,000
1964	1,778,000
1966	1,820,000
1968	1,905,000
1970	2,026,000
1972	2,218,000
1974	2,265,000
1975	2,275,000

A. Lange & Sohne

DATE	SERIAL #
1870	5,000
1875	10,000
1880	20,000
1885	25,000
1890	30,000
1895	35,000
1900	40,000
1905	50,000
1910	60,000
1915	70,000
1920	75,000
1925	80,000
1930	85,000
1935	90,000
1940	100,000

LONGINES

DATE	SERIAL #
1867	1
1870	20,000
1875	100,000
1882	250,000
1888	500,000
1893	750,000
1899	1,000,000
1901	1,250,000
1904	1,500,000
1905	1,750,000
1907	2,000,000
1909	2,250,000
1911	2,500,000
1912	2,750,000
1913	3,000,000
1915	3,250,000
1917	3,500,000
1919	3,750,000
1922	4,000,000
1925	4,250,000
1926	4,500,000
1928	4,750,000
1929	5,000,000
1934	5,250,000
1937	5,500,000
1938	5,750,000
1940	6,000,000
1945	7,000,000
1950	8,000,000
1953	9,000,000
1956	10,000,000
1959	11,000,000
1962	12,000,000
1966	13,000,000
1967	14,000,000
1969	15,000,000

OMEGA

DATE	SERIAL #
1895	1,000,000
1902	2,000,000
1908	3,000,000
1912	4,000,000
1916	5,000,000
1923	6,000,000
1929	7,000,000
1935	8,000,000
1939	9,000,000
1944	10,000,000
1947	11,000,000
1950	12,000,000
1952	13,000,000
1956	15,000,000
1958	16,000,000
1961	18,000,000
1963	20,000,000
1965	22,000,000
1967	25,000,000
1968	26,000,000
1970	29,000,000

PATEK PHILIPPE & CO.

DATE	SERIAL #
1840	100
1845	1,200
1850	3,000
1855	8,000
1860	15,000
1865	22,000
1870	35,000
1875	45,000
1880	55,000
1885	70,000
1890	85,000
1895	100,000
1900	110,000
1905	125,000
1910	150,000
1915	175,000
1920	190,000
1925	200,000
1950	700,000
1955	725,000
1960	750,000
1965	775,000
1970	795,000
1920	800,000
1925	805,000
1930	820,000
1935	824,000
1940	835,000
1945	850,000
1950	860,000
1955	870,000
1960	880,000
1965	890,000
1970	895,000
1940	900,000
1945	915,000
1950	930,000
1955	940,000
1960	960,000
1965	975,000
1970	995,000
1960	1,100,000
1965	1,130,000
1970	1,250,000
1975	1,350,000
1980	1,450,000
1985	1,600,000
1990	1,850,000

ROLEX (Case S #)

DATE	SERIAL #
1925	25,000
1926	27,500
1927	30,500
1928	33,000
1929	35,500
1930	38,000
1931	40,000
1932	43,000
1933	49,000
1934	55,000
1935	62,000
1936	82,000
1937	98,000
1938	118,000
1939	136,000
1940	165,000
1941	194,000
1942	224,000
1943	253,000
1944	284,000
1945	348,000
1946	413,000
1947	478,000
1948	543,000
1949	608,000
1950	673,500
1951	735,500
1952	804,000
1953	869,000
1954	935,000
1955	1,010,000
1956	1,095,000
1957	1,167,000
1958	1,245,000
1959	1,323,000
1960	1,401,000
1961	1,485,000
1962	1,557,000
1963	1,635,000
1964	1,713,000
1965	1,791,000
1966	1,870,000
1967	2,164,000
1968	2,426,000
1969	2,689,000
1970	2,952,000
1971	3,215,000
1972	3,478,000
1973	3,741,000
1974	4,000,000
1975	4,260,000
1976	4,530,000
1977	5,000,000
1978	5,480,000
1979	5,960,000
1980	6,430,000
1981	6,910,000
1982	7,380,000
1983	7,860,000
1984	8,340,000
1985	8,810,000
1986	9,300,000
1987	9,760,000
1987 1/2	9,999,999
1987 3/4	R000,001
1988	R999,999
1989	L000,001
1990	L999,999
1990 1/2	E000,001
1991 1/4	E999,999
1991 1/2	X000,001

VACHERON

DATE	SERIAL #
1830	30,000
1835	40,000
1840	50,000
1845	60,000
1850	75,000
1855	95,000
1860	110,000
1865	125,000
1870	140,000
1875	155,000
1880	170,000
1885	180,000
1890	190,000
1895	223,000
1900	256,000
1905	289,000
1910	322,000
1915	355,000
1920	385,000
1925	400,000
1930	410,000
1935	420,000
1940	440,000
1945	464,000
1950	488,000
1955	512,000
1960	536,000
1965	560,000
1970	585,000

The above list is provided for determining the **approximate** age of your watch. Match serial number with date. Watches were not necessarily sold in the exact order of manufactured date.

ROMANCING THE WRIST WATCH

The wrist watch is considered by many watch collectors to be "today's collectable." This phenomenon is due, in part, to the development of the quartz movement which began in the 1970's and virtually revolutionized the watch market. Although these quartz watches are quiet, accurate timekeepers, and are inexpensive to manufacture, the watches of the past hold a special fascination in the heart of the collector. They enjoy collecting the timepieces with jeweled and moving parts that produce a rhythmic heartbeat inside their gold cases.

The watch collector has seen the prices of wrist watches soar in the past years, as wrist watches have become more and more in demand as an object of fashion, function and jewelry. A Patek Philippe man's platinum minute repeater wrist watch sold for the record price of 345,000 Swiss francs, about $250,000 U.S. Not far behind this record setting sale was a Patek Philippe "Calatrava" that brought $198,000. A Patek Philippe enameled white gold "World Time" man's wrist watch sold for about $130,000. Some collectors have seen the values of their wrist watches double and, in many cases, triple in recent years. For example, in the early 1980s, a Patek Philippe perpetual calendar chronograph watch would have sold for $10,000. In 1987, the same watch would have sold for $50,000, and in 1988 for $80,000. In 1989, the price was up to $100,000. Such dramatic increases in values have brought about a feverish demand for wrist watches. The Swiss wrist watch has the attention of the wealthiest collectors, with Patek, Philippe & Co. at the top of their list and Audemars Piguet, Cartier, Rolex, and Vacheron & Constantin close behind. Other wrist watches showing appreciable value are Ebel, A. Lange, Gubelin, International Watch Co., Le Coultre, Ulysse Nardin, and Piaget. Next are Jules Jurgensen, Baume & Mercier, Gerard Perregaux, Movado, and Omega; then Benrus, Bulova, Agassiz, Elgin, Gruen, Hamilton, Illinois, Longines, and Waltham, the character watches, chronographs, and complicated watches.

Many wrist watch collectors have focused on fashion and take pride in wearing their unique watches. Women have been buying high fashion men's watches to wear, making women candidates for collecting. Young men appear to enjoy collecting wrist watches rather than pocket watches. The intense competition within their increasing numbers has influenced the rising prices.

$$*\qquad*\qquad*$$

Important Notice. All of the information, including valuations, in this book has been compiled from the most reliable sources, and every effort has been made to eliminate errors and questionable data. Nevertheless, the possibility of error, in a work of such immense scope, always exists. The publisher or authors will not be held responsible for losses which may occur in the purchase, sale, or other transaction of items, because of information contained herein. Readers who feel they have discovered errors are invited to write and inform us, so they may be corrected in subsequent editions.

European and Japanese collectors are making the biggest impact on the wrist watch market with their volume of buying, as well as the higher prices being paid. The American collector has been inspired by the heated market which has been, in part, fueled by the weakened U.S. dollar. The general appearance of a wrist watch seems to be the main factor in the price of the watch, but high mechanical standards, along with the various functions of the watch, also determine the price. Some of these features include repeaters, chronographs, duo-dials, bubble backs, curvex, flip-up tops, reverso, day-date-month moon phase, jump hour, diamond dial, world time, sector, skeletonized, character, first versions as early auto winds, very early electronics, unusual shapes, and enamel bezels.

EBEL WATCH CO., chronograph with triple day & moon phases, outside chapter shows tachymetre, 18k gold.

Today's watches are a "mixed bag," ranging from gold luxury watches priced at $10,000, and mid-priced watches at $1,000, to the low-end plastic quartz watches at $30, and all keep time equally well. The gold watch is still a status symbol today; a mark of affluence and of appreciation for the finer things in life. The Swiss control about 85 percent of the luxury watch market, while the Japanese have about the same percentage of the market for more moderately-priced watches. The predominant companies producing the "top of the line" watches are Patek, Philippe & Co., Cartier, Gubelin, Audemars Piguet, Piaget, Vacheron Constantin. Just below in price, but higher in volume, are names like Rolex, International Watch Co., Girard Perregaux, and Le Coultre. Collectors are also wearing high grade new watches by Ebel, Blancpain, Gerald Genta, Hublot, Raymond Weil, and watches produced for and bearing the names of Chanel, Christian Dior, and Dunhill. Prices of Ebel watches start at about $1,000 and go upward to $24,000. This company also manufactures watches for Cartier. Patek, Philippe watches range in price from $3,000 to $100,000.

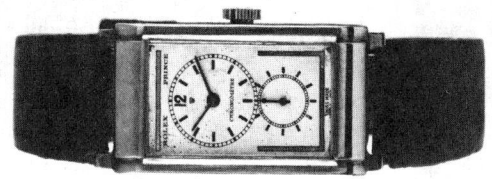

NOTE: **Sapphire** glass has a hardness of 9 (Mohs.), **Mineral** glass has a hardness of 5 (Mohs.).

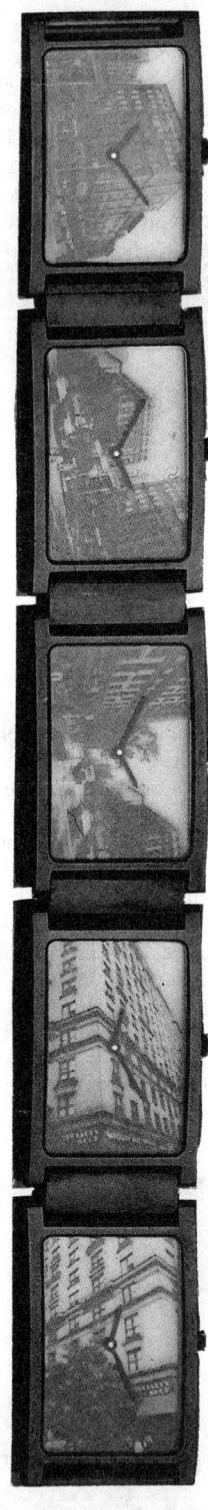

Audemars Piguet produces a tourbillon wrist watch that retails for about $28,000. Blancpain, owned by Omega, produces only about 100 ultrathin handmade watches per year. Rolex is the most recognizable name in today's luxury wrist watch market. The Rolex 18k gold President with fluted bezel, champagne cabochon dial, and 18k gold bracelet, sells for $9,400, while the same watch with diamond bezel and dial sells for $14,400. Rolex makes the Oyster Quartz day-date, 18k gold, pave diamond dial with sapphire, bezel case, and bracelet set with 107 diamonds totaling 8.06 carats, which bears a price tag of $100,000.

The Warhol collection, which included about 200 watches, was sold on April 27, 1988 at Sotheby's for a reported price of $461,000. The artist collected watches of various styles and types. A set of three vinyl quartz character watches brought the price of $2,400. A stainless steel Gene Autry watch listed and pre-determined to bring about $100 sold for $1,700. The so-called "heavy weight" wrist watches such as Patek Philippe, Cartier, Rolex, and Vacheron Constantin sold for two to three times the estimated prices.

The trend or vogue for older watches has motivated some watch companies to reproduce favorite watches from their past models. Companies have searched their archives to find older models that sold well, and are now marketing replicas of those watches. Hamilton Classics Authentic Reproductions From America's Past include the Ventura (1957), Wilshire City (1939), Cabot (1935), and Ardmore (1934). Jaeger LeCoultre's Reverso has been reintroduced, as well as Longines' hour angle watch developed and worn by Charles Lindbergh. Also, the Lorus Company has marketed a close look-a-like to the Mickey Mouse wrist watch first sold by Ingersoll in the early 1930s.

The romancing of the wrist watch is moving at a steady upward pace. Price adjustments may be needed, but should hold for a few more years. The quality American movements may still be undervalued, and the novelty or comic character wrist watches may still be a good value for the investor.

Left: Movado designed by Andy Warhol the "Times Five" were made in Quartz and limited to 250 pieces. The dials have New York scenes are in black and white with red hands. The five time zones cases are black with black links Ca. 1988.

A SHORT HISTORY OF WRIST WATCHES

While no one is sure who invented the first wrist watch or when the first wrist watch was ever worn. Watch-bracelets were created by great makers for ladies of great wealth and a few ladies wrist watches began to appear around 1790. Small miniature watches had been made earlier than this, however. David Rosseau made a watch which was about 18mm in diameter (the size of a dime) in the late 1600s.

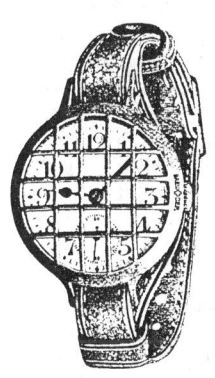

Early BRACELET that holds a small pendant-watch, a lid opens on this 18K & enamel case to view the watch, Ca.1840.

About 1880 Girard-Perregaux created the first wristwatch which was to be used by officers of the German Navy. The order was for 1,000 watches with a protective GRID.

Miniaturization was a great challenge to many of the famous watch makers including Louis Jaquet, Paul Ditisheim, John Arnold and Henri Capt. The smallest watch in semi-mass production was 12mm by 5mm. In early 1930, the American Waltham Watch Co. made a 9mm by 20mm Model 400 watch.

Wrist watches were at first thought to be too small and delicate to be practical for men to wear. However, during World War I a German officer was said to have strapped a small pocket watch to his wrist with a leather webbed cup. This arrangement freed both hands and proved to be most useful. After the war, the wrist watch gained in popularity. Mass production of wrist watches was started around 1880 by the **Girard - Perregaux** factory which were designed to be used by officers of the German Navy. The Swiss introduced wrist watches to the United States around 1895, but they did not prove to be very popular at first. Around 1907 the Elgin and Illinois watch companies were manufacturing wrist watches and by 1912 Hampden and Waltham had started.

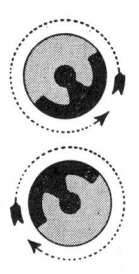

Miniaturized wrist watch by Waltham model # 400. Note size comparison to dime.

ROTOR for self winding Wrist Watch.

HARWOOD self-winding wrist watch, RIM SET, Ca.1928.

590

By 1920 the round styles were being replaced with square, rectangular and tonneau shapes and decorated with gems. By 1928 wrist watches were outselling pocket watches, and, by 1935, over 85 percent of the watches being produced were wrist watches.

Self-wind pocket watches were first developed by Abraham Louis Perrelet in 1770 and by Abraham Louis Breguet about 1777. Louis Recordon made improvements in 1780, but is was not until 1923 that the principle of self-winding was adapted to the wrist watch by John Harwood, an Englishman who set up factories to make his patented self-wind wrist watches in Switzerland, London, France, and the United States. His watches first reached the market about 1929. The firm A. Schild manufactured about 15,000 watches in Switzerland. Mr. Harwood's watch company removed the traditional stem or crown to wind the mainspring, but in order to set the hands it was necessary to turn the bezel. The Harwood Watch Co. failed around 1931 and the patent expired.

Snap on protector used on some early Wrist Watches.

Rolex Oyster Perpetual, BUBBLE BACK, Ca. 1940.

Early in 1930 the Rolex Watch Co. introduced the Rolex Oyster Perpetual, the first waterproof and self-winding wrist watch. In 1933 the first "Incabloc" shock protection device was used. By 1940 wrist watches came in all shapes and types including complicated chronographs, calendars, and repeaters. Novelties, digital jump hour and multi-dial were very popular, as well.

A dramatic change occurred in 1957 when the Hamilton Watch Co. eliminated the mainspring and replaced it with a small battery that lasted well over one year. In 1960 the balance wheel was removed in the Accutron by Bulova and replaced by a tuning fork with miniature pawls.

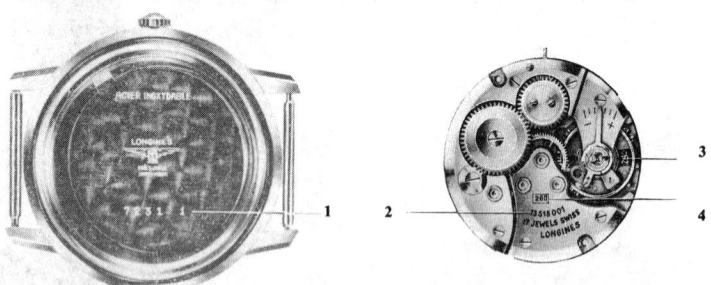
1. Case number.   2. Movement serial number.   3. Caliber number.   4. Caliber number.

NOTE: Some wrist watches have a grade or caliber number engraved on the movement. For example, Patek, Phillipe & Co. has a caliber number 27-460Q. The '27' stands for 27mm; the '460Q' is the grade; the 'Q' designates Quantieme (Perpetual calendar and moon phases).

AUTOMATIC WINDING

The self-winding watch uses the movements of the body in order to wind up the mainspring slowly and nearly continuously. The first pocket self-winding watches were executed by a watchmaker from Le Locle, Abraham-Louis Perrelet, around 1770.

Early self wind pocket watch by Breguet Ca. 1785.

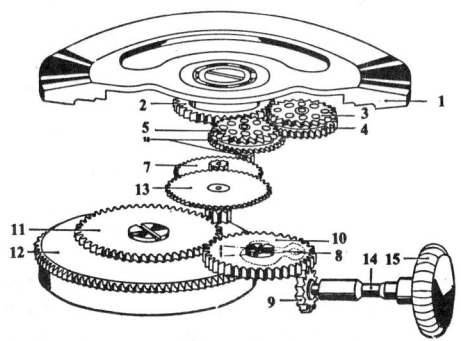

ETERNA-MATIC automatic winding mechanism with rotor oscillating on *5 ball bearings 1st introduced in 1949*. 1.–Oscillating weight. 2. –Oscillating gear. 3. –Upper wheel of auxiliary pawl-wheel. 4. –Lower wheel of auxiliary pawl-wheel. 5. –Pawl-wheel with pinion. 6. –Lower wheel of pawl wheel with pinion. 7. –Transmission-wheel with pinion. 8. –Crown-wheel yoke. 9. –Winding pinion. 10. –Crown-wheel. 11. –Ratchet-wheel. 12. –Barrel. 13. –Driving runner for ratchet-wheel. 14. –Winding stem. 15. –Winding button.

They were improved soon after by Abraham-Louis Breguet. In the case of the pocket watch, the movements causing the winding of the watch were essentially the result of walking. This system of winding was never widely adopted. The watch was a fancy model and not a really useful one. Herman von der Heydt was the only maker in America to work with the self-winding pocket watch. However, inventors always kept the idea of the self-winding watch in mind.

In 1923, the British firm Harwood took up once again the solution of the problem of automatic winding, for wrist watches. This was the spark which rapidly resulted in research to improve and simplify this type of mechanism. A company was formed in London to manufacture Harwood's watch, and before long over 500 jewelers in the United Kingdom were selling his automatic watch. A second company was formed in France, and a third in the United States. The business flourished about two and one-half years. Then, in 1931, these companies were liquidated.

Early self-winding wrist watch by FREY W. Co., Ca. 1930's. NOTE: The pendulum style weight for self-winding.

Early self-winding wrist watch by AUTORIST W. Co. Ca.1930's. Winding by moving flexible lugs.

  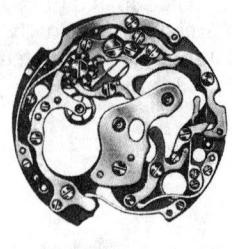

LEFT: CHRONOGRAPH with 1 push piece & **CENTER** 2 push pieces. **RIGHT**: CHRONOGRAPH module or attachment

Chronograph with two push pieces:

Action and movement of hands : The pusher No .1 sets the hands in action and second action stops the same hands.

Pusher No. 2 brings the hands back to zero. During their movement this pusher is a fixture, thus preventing the accidental return of the hands to zero. The double pusher chronograph permits an interruption in the reading, the hands are set going again from the position they stopped, thus indispensable for any time lost during a control of any description.

HOW TO READ THE TACHOMETER-TELEMETER DIAL

The **TACHOMETER** may have a spiral scale around center of dial indicates miles per hour, based on a trial over one mile. It indicates speeds from 400 to 20 miles per hour on three turns. Each turn of spiral corresponds to one minute (scale for first 8 seconds being omitted), the outer turn from 400 to 60 (0 to 1 minute) and the center turn from 30 to 20 miles per hour (2 to 3 minutes).

When passing the first marker of mile zone, start chronograph hand by pressing push piece. When passing following mile marker, press push piece again. The chronograph hand now indicates the speed in miles per hour on the spiral. If a mile has been made in less than one minute the speed will be indicated on outside turn of spiral; from 1 to 2 minutes on middle turn and 2 to 3 minutes on center turn.

EXAMPLE: If a mile has been made in 1 minute and 15 seconds the chronograph hand indicates 48 miles per hour on middle turn of spiral.

The **TELEMETER** scale around margin of dial is based on the speed of sound compared with the speed of light. Each small division is 100 meters. The scale is read in kilometers & hundreds of meters. Approximately 16 divisions equal 1 mile.

To determine the distance of a storm: When you see the flash of lightning press push piece of chronograph. When hearing thunder press again, the chronograph hand will indicate on the Telemeter scale the distance in kilometers and hundreds of meters. One kilometer equals 5/8 of a mile.

NOTE: The chronograph is a fitted attachment to a time only watch movement, with a additional function that can be used independently of the time indication. The chronograph ebauche factories who make 80% of the raw chronograph attachments (about 10 ebauche manufactures), are rarely known by the public. The chronograph module or attachment are made to be fitted or added to a time only movement. The same is true of repeaters. Companies as Patek Philippe, Rolex, Audemars Piguet and many more are fitted with ebauche chronograph attachments to their own time only movement. Watch Companies as Breitling, Heuer, Eberhard and many more are finished with ebauche chronograph attachments fitted to raw movements made by other wrist-watch ebauche factories.

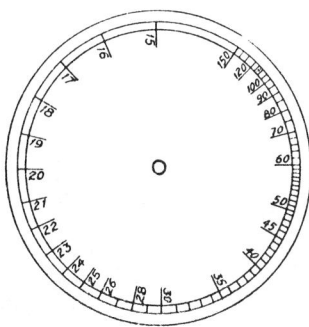

Dial No. 1 is a simple stop watch and chronograph dial. Graduated into fifths of seconds.

Dial No. 2 is used to time a car over a quarter-mile track and read the numbers of miles per hour directly from dial.

Dial No. 3 is used to measure speed in kilometers per hour over a course of one fifth of a kilometer.

Dial No. 4 used by physicians to count the pulse beats of a patient.

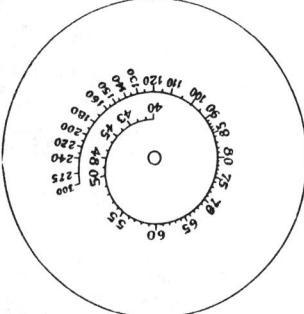

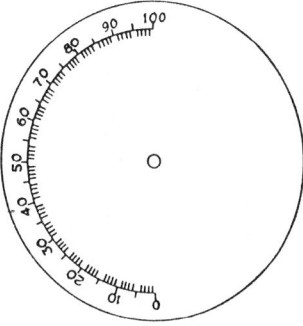

Dial No. 5 is used by artillery officers for determining distance by means of sound in kilometers.

Dial No. 6 shows a tachometer: many watches are made with several scales on the same dial in order to cover a greater range of functions. The figures are sometimes grouped in a spiral form or in several circles, thus the hand may make more than one complete revolution.

CHRONOGRAPH MECHANISM
NUMBERS & NAMES USED IN THE EBAUCHE BOOK
" TECHNOLOGICAL DICTIONARY OF WATCH PARTS " Ca. 1953

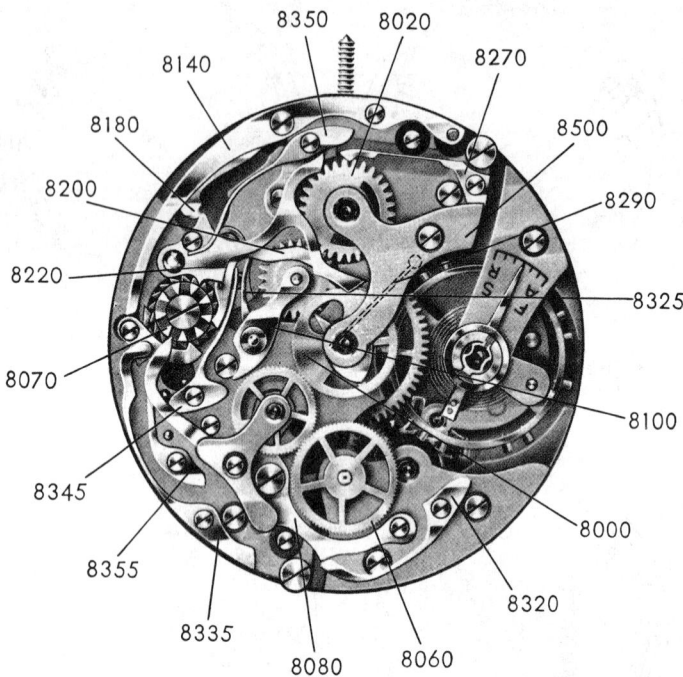

8000 Chronograph central wheel, w/ finger.
8020 = Minute-recording wheel, register.
8060 = Driving wheel.
8070 = Pillar or Crown wheel, 3 functions.
8080 = Coupling clutch w/ transmission wheel, 2 functions.
8100 = Sliding or star gear, 2 functions.
8140 = Operating or starting lever, 2 functions.
8180 = Fly-back lever, reset to zero.
8200 = Blocking lever, 2 functions.
8220 = Hammer or heart piece striker, 2 functions.
8270 = Minute-recording jumper spring.
8290 = Friction spring , for chronograph central wheel.
8320 = Coupling clutch spring.
8325 = Sliding gear spring, 2 functions.
8335 = Operating or starting lever spring.
8345 = Blocking lever spring.
8350 = Hammer or heartpiece lever spring, 2 functions.
8355 = Pillar or crown wheel jumper or block.
8500 = Chronograph bridge, for center & min. recording wheels.

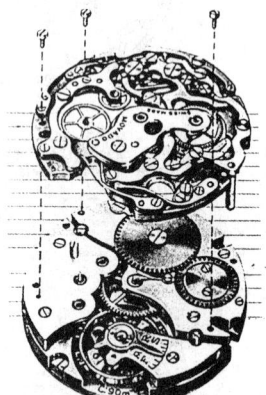

ABOVE: Illustration of a
Modular construction or
Attachment to a chronograph.

   The chronograph is a fitted attachment to a time only watch movement, with a additional function that can be used independently of the time indication. The chronograph ebauche factories who make 80% of the raw chronograph attachments (about 10 ebauche manufactures), are rarely known by the public. The chronograph modular or attachment are made to be fitted or added to a time only movement. The same is true of repeaters. Companies as Patek Philippe, Audemars Piguet, Rolex and many more are fitted with ebauche chronograph attachments to their <u>own</u> time only movement. Watch Companies as Breitling, Heuer, Eberhard and many more are finished with ebauche chronograph attachments fitted to raw movements made by other wrist-watch ebauche factories.

CHRONOGRAPH

The term chronograph is derived from the Greek words chronos which means "time" and grapho which means "to write." The first recording of intervals of time was around 1822 by the inventor Rieussec. His chronograph made dots of ink on a dial as a measure of time. Around 1862 Adolph Nicole introduced the first chronograph with a hand that returned to zero. The split second chronograph made its appearance around 1879. Today a chronograph can be described as a timepiece that starts at will, stops at will, and can return to zero at will. A mechanical chronograph had a sweep or center second hand that will start, stop, and fly back to zero. The term chronometer should not be confused with chronograph. A chronometer is a timepiece that has superior time keeping qualities at the time it is made. The CHRONOGRAPH **1 button** wrist watch was 1st. advertised in 1910 & a 2 **button** CHRONOGRAPH in 1939 by Breitling.

A. Day window. B. Split second hand. C. Calendar pusher. D. Register for seconds. E. Calendar pusher. F. Date hand. G. Register for total hours. H. Sweep center second hand. I. Month window. J. Start/stop pusher. K. Register for total minutes. L. Return pusher. M. Date of month.

TRADE MARK	MANUFACTURER	TRADE MARK	MANUFACTURER

 VALJOUX
Now part of the ETA group

 LANDERON

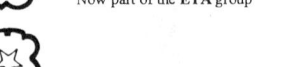 VENUS

FONTAINEMELON

WRIST WATCH CASE AND DIAL STYLES

Barrel

Maxine

Square

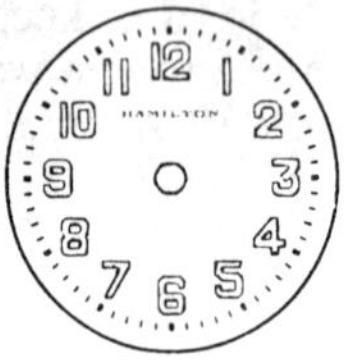

Round

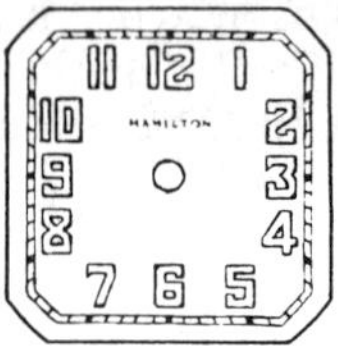

Square Cut Corner

Cushion

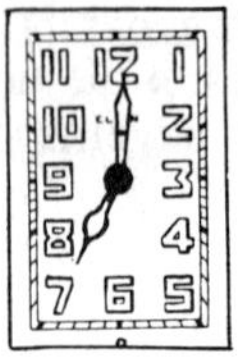

Rectangle

Flared

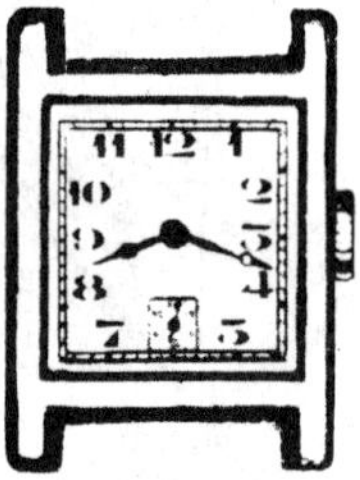

Tank

Round
(Ladies style; converts to lapel or wrist)

Curved or Curvex

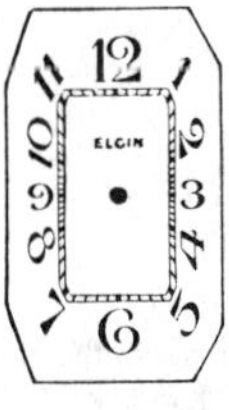

Rectangle Cut Corner

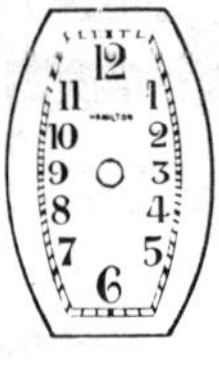

Tonneau

Baguette

Oval

EXAGGERATED

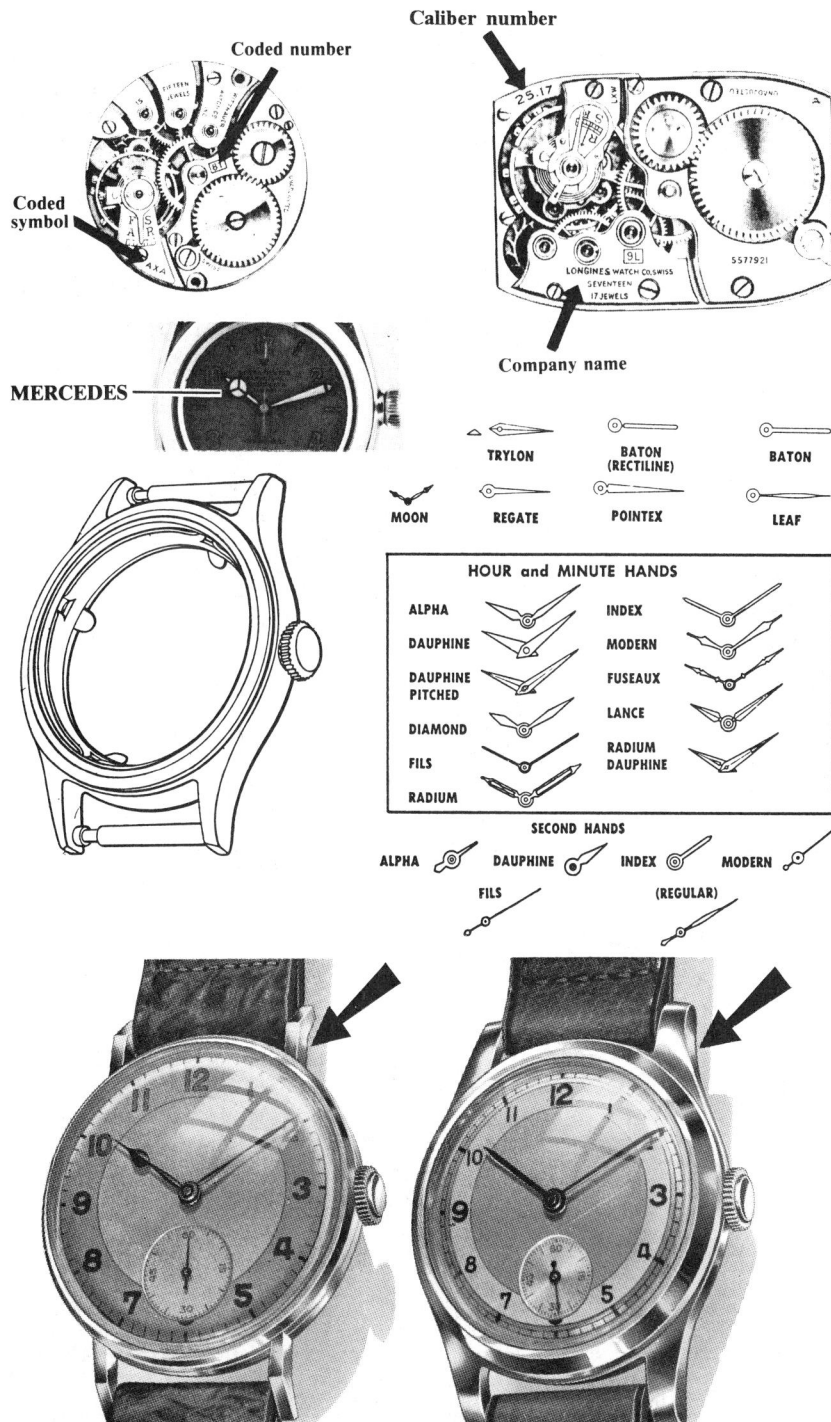

Coded number

Caliber number

Coded symbol

Company name

MERCEDES

TRYLON   BATON (RECTILINE)   BATON

MOON   REGATE   POINTEX   LEAF

HOUR and MINUTE HANDS

ALPHA   INDEX

DAUPHINE   MODERN

DAUPHINE PITCHED   FUSEAUX

DIAMOND   LANCE

FILS   RADIUM DAUPHINE

RADIUM

SECOND HANDS

ALPHA   DAUPHINE   INDEX   MODERN

FILS   (REGULAR)

LEFT: Watch has SOLDERED lugs. **RIGHT**: Watch has SOLID lugs or ONE PIECE lug.

SWISS CODE INITIALS

Between the years of 1880 & 1927 over 8,000 trademarks and brand names were registered in Switzerland. Some Swiss watches have three initials on the balance bridge. These initials are not model identification but are for house identification. Following is a list of import initials with the name of the firm.

AOC--Roamer
AOL--Adolph Schwarcz & Son
AOX--Alstate W. Co.
AXA--Wittnauer
AZZ--Benrus
AYP-Audemars Piguet
BOL--Lemania
BXC--Avia
BXJ--Midland
BXN--Benrus
BXP--Imperial, Bayer, Pretzfelder & Mills
BXW--Bulova
COC--Crawford
COW--Croton
CXC--Concord
CXD--Cypres
CXH--Clinton
CXV--Cort
CXW--Central; Benrus
DOB--Dreffa W. Co.
DOW--Deauville
EOE--Elrex
EON--Avalon
EOP--Harvel
EOT--Lavina
EXA--ETERNA
EXC--Everbrite
FXE--Provis
FXU--Louis Aisenstein & Bros.
FXW--Louis
GXC--Gruen
GXI--Gotham (Ollendorff)
GXM--Girard-Perregaux
GXR--Grant
GXW--Gothic
HOM--Homis
HON--Tissot; A. Hirsch
HOR--Lanco; Langendorf

HOU--Oris
HXF--Harman
HXM--R. H. Macy & Co.
HXN--Harvel
HXO--Harold K. Oleet
HXW--Helbros
HYL-- Hamilton
HYO--Hilton W Co.
JXE--Normandie
JXJ--Jules Jurgensen
JXR--Gallet
KOT--Landau
KXJ--Wm. J. Kappel
KXV--Louis
KXZ--Kelton; Benrus, Central
LOA--Emil Langer
LOD--Latham
LOE--Packard
LXA--Laco, Winton, Elbon
LXE--Evkob
LXJ--Jaegar-LeCoultre
LXW--Longines
MOG--Mead & Co.; Boulevard
MOU--Tower; Delbana
MXE--Monarch
MXH--Seeland
MXI--Movado
MXT--Mathey-Tissot
NOA--U.Nardin
NOS--Heritage
NOU--Louvic
NXJ--National Jewelers Co.
NXO--Oris
OXG--Omega
OXL--Wyler
OYT--Shriro (Sandoz)
POY--Camy; Copley
PXA--Pierce
PXP--Patek, Philippe

PXT--Paul Breguette
PXW--Parker
PYS--Langel
QXO--Kelbert
ROC--Raleigh
ROL--Ribaux
ROP--Rodania
ROR-Audemars Piguet
ROW--Rolex
RXG--R. Gsell & Co.
RXM--Galmor
RXW--Rima
RXY--Liengme
RYW--Ritex
SOA--Felca
SOE--Semca
SOW--Seeland
SOX--Cortebert, Orvin
SXE--Savoy; Banner
SXK--S. Kocher & Co.
SXS--Franco
UOA--Actua
UOB--Aero
UOW--Universal
UXM--Medana
UXN--Marsh
UYW--Stanley W. Co.
VOS--Sheffield
VXN--V & C & LeCoultre
VXT--Kingston
WOA--Tower
WOB--Wyler
WOG--Breitling
WOR--Creston
WXC--Buren
WXE--Welsbro
WXW--Westfield
ZFX--Zenith W.Co.
ZOV--Titus
ZYV--Hampden (new company)

Between the years 1880 & 1927 over 8,000 trade-mark titles were registered in Switzerland. Such as ALPHA, BULOVA, CAMY, JAEGER, REVERSO, SUBMARINER, VALJOUX, ZODIAC & ETC.

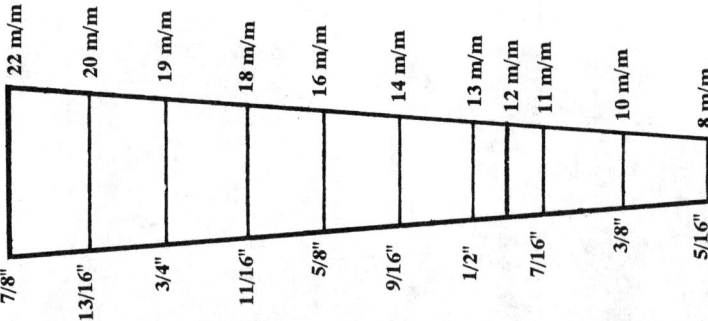

To determine your wrist watch band size use the **ABOVE GAUGE** and measure between the lugs. The band sizes are listed on each side of the gauge.

When performing any underwater activity, the dynamic pressure generated through movement is greater than the static pressure. Below a ranking of water resistance for most watches.
1 **meter** = 3.28 ft., 330 ft. =about 100 **meters**. 33.89 ft. =1 **atmosphere,** 100 ft. = about 3 **atmospheres.**

50M = shower only, rain, sweat-resistant (1 AT.)
100M = swimming (**no diving**) -330 ft.
200M = snorkeling, skin diving -600 ft.
1000M =scuba diving -3,300 ft.

WRIST WATCH LISTINGS
Pricing At Collectable Fair Market Value At Retail Level
(Complete Watches Only)

Unless otherwise noted, wrist watches listed in this section are priced at the *collectable* fair market RETAIL level (What a collector may expect to pay for a watch from a watch dealer) and as **complete** watches having an original gold-filled case and stainless steel back, also with original dial, and the entire original movement in good working order with no repairs needed. They are also priced as having a watch band made of **leather** except where a bracelet is described. Watches listed as 14k and 18k are solid gold cases. Coin or base-metal and stainless steel cases will be listed as such. Low cost production watches, are listed as having a base metal type case and a composition dial.

Many of the watch manufacturers were commissioned to put jewelers' or jobbers' **names** on their movements in place of their own. Because of this practice, the true manufacturers of these movements are difficult to identify. Between the years 1880 & 1927 over 8,000 trade-mark titles were registered in Switzerland, such as Alpha, Bulova, Camy, Jaeger, Reverso, Submariner, Valjoux, Zodiac & Etc.

The prices shown were averaged from dealers' lists just prior to publication and are an indication of the retail level or what collectors will pay. **Prices** are provided in three categories: **average condition, extra fine, and mint condition,** and are shown in whole dollar amounts only. The values listed are a guide for the *collectable* retail level and are provided for your information only. **Dealers** will not necessarily pay full retail price. Prices listed are for watches with **original** cases, movement and dials and in good running order.

Warning: There are currently fake wrist watches being sold on the world-wide market. These watches have the appearance of authenticity but are merely cheap imitations of prestigious companies such as Rolex (all types), Gucci, Cartier, & Piaget.

Important Notice. All of the information, including valuations, in this book has been compiled from the most reliable sources, and every effort has been made to eliminate errors and questionable data. Nevertheless, the possibility of error, in a work of such immense scope, always exists. The publisher or authors will not be held responsible for losses which may occur in the purchase, sale, statements of its advertisers, or other transaction of items, because of information contained herein. Readers who feel they have discovered errors are invited to write and inform us, so they may be corrected in subsequent editions.

🕐 Wist Watch terminology or communication in this book has evolved over the years, in search of better & more precise language with a effort to improve, purify, adjust itself & make it easier to understand.

INFORMATION NEEDED — The authors are interested in any facts and information you might have that should possibly be considered for future editions. Documented facts are needed, so please send photo or sources of information. Send to:

COOKSEY SHUGART
P.O. BOX 3147
CLEVELAND, TN. 37320-3147

When **CORRESPONDING**, Please send a 🖃 self addressed, stamped **ENVELOPE**.

ABERCROMBIE & FITCH, 17J., chronog.by Valj.,3 reg.
14K...$900 $1,000 $1,200
s.steel $350 $400 $500

Abercrombie & Fitch, 17J., **Seafarer,** chronog., waterproof
18k $1,100 $1,300 $1,600
s. steel $350 $400 $500

Abercrombie & Fitch, 17J., chronog.by Valj.,3 reg., Ca.1950
s.steel $350 $400 $500

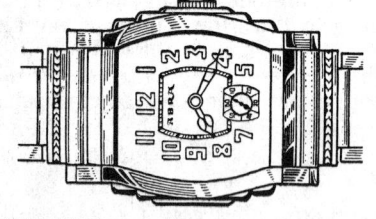

ABRA, 17J., step case, c.1930s
base metal $30 $35 $55

🕐 Pricing in this Guide are fair market price for **COMPLETE**
watches which are reflected from the "**NAWCC**" National and
regional shows.

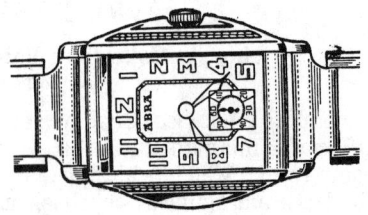

ABRA,17J., carved case, c.1930s
base metal $30 $35 $55

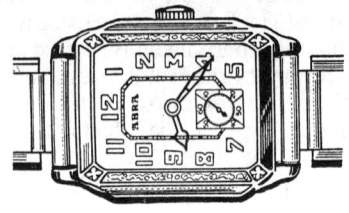

ABRA, 17J., engraved case
base metal $30 $35 $55

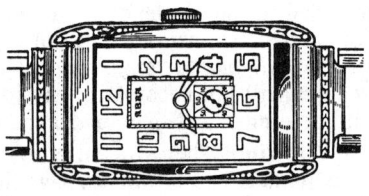

ABRA,15J., curved case, c.1930s
base metal $30 $35 $55

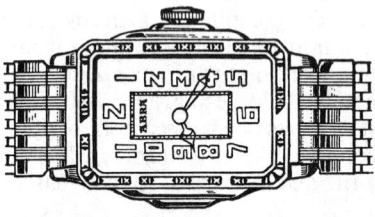

ABRA,15J., engraved case, c.1930s
gold plate $30 $35 $55

ABRA, 17J., **jump hour**
s. steel $250 $300 $395

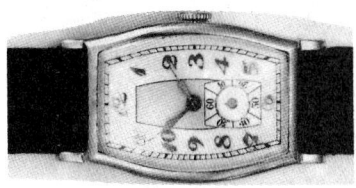

ACRO W. CO., 17 jewels, **hinged back**
18k $225 $250 $350

ADMES, 17 jewels, self wind, waterproof, center sec.,
14K...$95 $125 $150
  gold filled................................ $40 $50 $85

AGASSIZ, 17 jewels, **World Time**
18k $5,000 $5,500 $7,000

AGASSIZ, 17 jewels, fancy bezel,
18k $600 $650 $800

AGASSIZ, 18 jewels, for Tiffany & Co., 48mm, oversize
18k $800 $850 $1,000

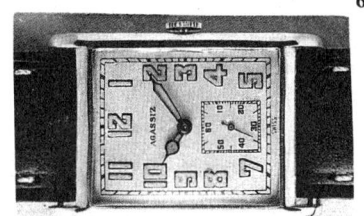

AGASSIZ,17J., C. 1940s
18K(W)................................. $600 $650 $800

AGASSIZ, 18 jewels, barrel shaped dial, 40mm,
18k $400 $450 $600

AGASSIZ, 17 jewels, for Tiffany & Co., 45mm
18k $700 $800 $950

ALPHA, 17J., chrono. 2 reg., cal.48, c.1950s
14K $400 $450 $550
  s.steel $150 $175 $225

ALPHA, 17J., **Fancy lugs,** sweep sec., c. 1948
18k $250 $275 $350

ALPHA, 17J, autowind, c.1950s
18K...$175 $200 $250

ALPINA, 15 jewels, automatic, water proof, center sec.
gold filled..................................$45 $55 $85

ALPINA, 17 jewels, automatic, water proof, aux. sec.
18k $175 $200 $250

ALSTA, 17J., **chronograph**, 3 reg.
14K..$425 $475 $525
base metal $200 $250 $325

ALSTA, 17 jewels, **wrist alarm**
gold filled $85 $110 $150

ALTON, 17J., fancy lugs, c.1950s
14K $150 $175 $225

ALTUS, 17 jewels, ref. 827
18k $150 $175 $225

AM. WALTHAM, 15J.,"Harley-Davidson", c.1935
gold filled $125 $150 $200

AM. WALTHAM, 17J., aux, sec. c.1930s
14k $150 $175 $250

AM. WALTHAM, 17J., Driver style, Ca. 1935
gold filled..............................$125 $150 $225

AM. WALTHAM, 21J., cal.750B, GJS, c.1950s
14k $125 $150 $250

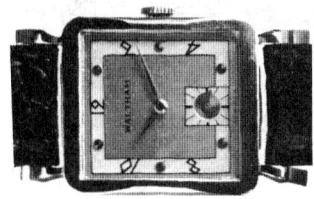

AM. WALTHAM, 17J., cal.750B, c.1951
gold filled..................................$75 $85 $125

AM. WALTHAM, 15J., "Masonic" model, c.1925
14k (original dial).................$250 $275 $350

AM. WALTHAM, 15-17J, **solid lugs,** c.1920s
sterling silver $200 $250 $325

AM. WALTHAM, 15-17J, "Ruby"model, c.1920s
gold filled $125 $150 $200

AM. WALTHAM, 17 J, barrel shaped dial, c. 1920
14k $150 $175 $250

AM. WALTHAM, 17 jewels, "Cromwell"
gold filled $55 $65 $100

AM. WALTHAM, 17 jewels, "Oberlin"
gold filled $55 $65 $100

AM. WALTHAM, 15 jewels, engraved bezel
gold filled $100 $125 $175

AM. WALTHAM, 17J., for Tiffany & Co.
14k $250 $300 $400

AM.WALTHAM, 19J., **enamel dial**, C. 1905
silver $135 $165 $225

AM. WALTHAM, 17 jewels, wire lugs
14k $300 $350 $500

AM. WALTHAM, 17 jewels, "Duxbury"
gold filled.................................$65 $75 $100

AM. WALTHAM, 21J, stepped case, curved back
14k $225 $275 $350

AM. WALTHAM, 7-15 jewels, wandering sec., c. 1930
gold filled $150 $200 $300

AM. WALTHAM, 17 jewels, **wandering sec.**, c. 1930
gold filled $175 $225 $325

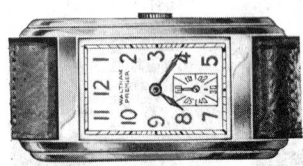

AM. WALTHAM, 17 jewels, "Fairmont"
gold filled $75 $100 $135

AM. WALTHAM, 17 jewels, "Stan Hope"
gold filled $65 $75 $100

AM. WALTHAM, 17 jewels, "Winfield"
gold filled $65 $75 $100

AM. WALTHAM, wandering min., **jumping hour.**, c. 1933
gold filled $500 $600 $750

AM. WALTHAM, 15J., aux. sec.
gold filled..................................$50 $60 $85

AM. WALTHAM, 21 jewels, "Albright"
14k $125 $150 $200

AM. WALTHAM, 21 jewels, "Sheraton"
14k $125 $150 $200

AM. WALTHAM, 17 jewels, center sec.
gold filled.................................$45 $55 $85

AM. WALTHAM, 15 jewels, **winds at 12,** wire lugs, c. 1916
silver $250 $300 $400

AM. WALTHAM, 15 J., case by **Rolland Fischer**
silver $300 $350 $450

AM. WALTHAM, 15J., **enamel dial, center lugs,** c.1915
silver $200 $250 $350

AM. WALTHAM, 17J., aux.sec., multi color dial, c.1910s
gold filled $150 $200 $250

AM. WALTHAM, 15J, **multi-color enamel dial,** Ca. 1920
base metal $200 $250 $300

AM. WALTHAM, 7-15J., **pulsations**, solid lugs, c.1925
silver $300 $350 $450

AM. WALTHAM, 17J.,"**Riverside**", **GJS**, c.1918
silver $450 $500 $600

AM. WALTHAM, 15 jewels, c. 1930
gold filled.................................. $60 $70 $95

AM. WALTHAM, 7J., **oxidized case**, c.1930s
gold filled.................................. $75 $100 $135

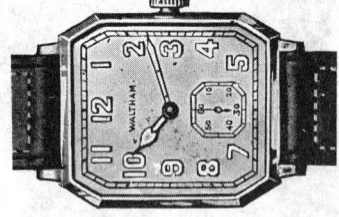

AM. WALTHAM, 7-15J., **cut corner dial**, c.1930s
gold filled.................................. $65 $85 $125

AM. WALTHAM, 15 jewels,
gold filled $60 $70 $100

AM. WALTHAM, 15J., **engraved oxidized case**, c.1930s
gold filled $75 $85 $125

AM. WALTHAM, 15J.,engraved case
gold filled $75 $85 $125

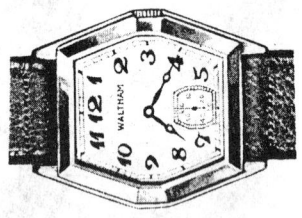

AM. WALTHAM, 17 jewels, 18K applied #s
silver $175 $200 $250

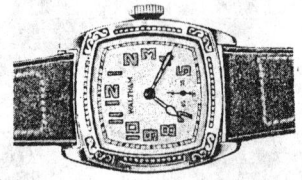

AM. WALTHAM, 7-15 jewels, engraved case
gold filled $75 $85 $125

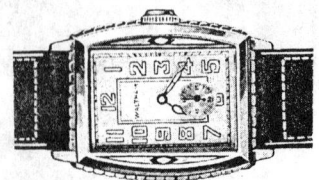

AM. WALTHAM, 7-15 jewels, **carved** case
gold filled $75 $85 $125

AM. WALTHAM, 15 jewels, **curved back**
14k $200 $225 $300

AM. WALTHAM, 7-15 jewels, engraved case
gold filled..................................$75 $85 $125

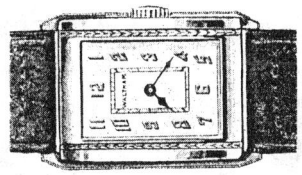

AM. WALTHAM, 17 jewels, tank style, **18K applied #s**
14kw $200 $225 $275

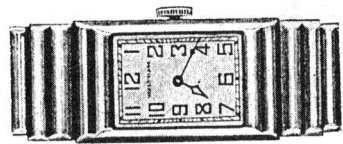

AM. WALTHAM, 15-17 jewels,
gold filled..................................$60 $70 $95

AM. WALTHAM, 7-15 jewels,
gold filled..................................$75 $85 $125

AM. WALTHAM, 15-17J, Premier, note **screwed on case**
water-resistant, Ca. 1920
14K..$300 $350 $450

AM. WALTHAM, 15J., case by Rolland Fischer,
silver $400 $500 $650

AM. WALTHAM, 15 jewels, "Depollier," **early water
proof, (Canteen style)**, c. 1917
silver $400 $500 $700

AM. WALTHAM, 15 jewels, protective grill, c. 1907
gold filled $250 $300 $385
14k $750 $850 $1,000

AM. WALTHAM, 17 jewels, military with **hack setting**
s. steel $85 $100 $150

AM. WALTHAM, 17 jewels, **cut-corner dial**
14k $175 $200 $300

🕐 Some grades are not included. Their values can be
determined by comparing with **similar** age, size, metal
content, style, grades, or models such as **time only**,
chronograph, repeater etc. listed.

AM. WALTHAM, 17 jewels, luminous dial
14k $150 $175 $250

AM. WALTHAM, 17 jewels, **WINDS at 12**, wire lugs
gold filled..............................$150 $175 $250

AM. WALTHAM, 17 jewels, **center lugs**
14k $175 $200 $275

AM. WALTHAM, 17 jewels, "**Allen**"
gold filled..................................$60 $75 $100

AM. WALTHAM, 17 jewels, "**Penton**"
gold filled $50 $65 $100

AM. WALTHAM, 9-17 jewels, "**Side-wrist**"
gold filled $125 $150 $225

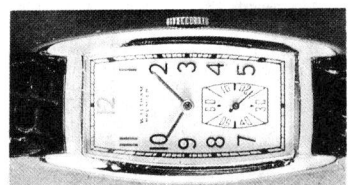

AM. WALTHAM, 17 jewels, **curvex, 42mm**
14k $300 $350 $450

AM. WALTHAM, 17 jewels, **curvex, 52mm**
14k $450 $550 $700

AM. WALTHAM, 17 jewels, **curvex, 42mm**
gold filled $100 $125 $175

🕐 Pricing in this Guide are fair market price for **COMPLETE**
watches which are reflected from the "<u>NAWCC</u>" National and
regional shows.

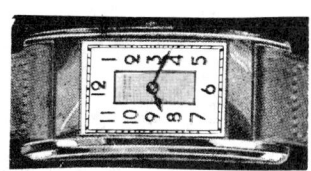

AM. WALTHAM, 17-21 jewels, curved
14k $150 $200 $275
gold filled..................................$65 $75 $100

AM. WALTHAM, 17 jewels, curved, aux. sec.
gold filled..................................$65 $75 $100

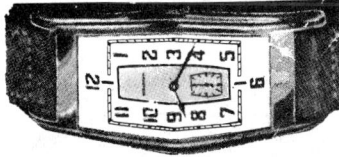

AM. WALTHAM, 17 jewels, curved
gold filled..................................$75 $85 $120

AM. WALTHAM, 21 jewels, C.1938
14K..$150 $200 $250

AM. WALTHAM, 17 jewels, curved
gold filled..................................$75 $85 $125

AM. WALTHAM, 17 jewels, curved
gold filled..................................$60 $75 $100

AM. WALTHAM, 15J., **note bow swings, screw back case, solid lugs, enamel dial, early water proof** , c. 1920s
14K .... ★★$450 $550 $750

AM. WALTHAM, 17 jewels, enamel bezel
14k $650 $750 $950
14k (w) $500 $600 $800
gold filled $150 $200 $300

AM. WALTHAM,21J., enamel bezel,**"ruby"** model,c.1928
14k(w)................................... $550 $650 $800

AM. WALTHAM,17J., **stepped case**
gold filled $65 $85 $125

AM. WALTHAM, 17 jewels, **"Jeffrey"**
gold filled $65 $85 $125

AM. WALTHAM, 21 jewels, "**Tulane**"
gold filled...................................$45 $55 $85

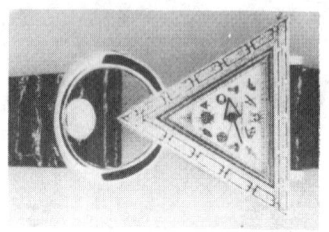

AM. WALTHAM, 17J., triangular, masonic symbols
fancy hands, **mother of pearl dial**, Ca. 1950
gold filled................................$700 $800 $1,000

AM. WALTHAM, 7-15J., luminous dial, c.1928
base metal $40 $50 $75

AM. WALTHAM, 7-15J., cushion case, c.1928
gold filled................................$50 $65 $100

AM. WALTHAM, 7-15J., tonneau case, c. 1928
gold filled................................$50 $65 $100

AM. WALTHAM, 7J., luminous dial, c.1928
base metal $65 $75 $100

AM. WALTHAM, 7J., luminous dial, c. 1928
gold filled $70 $90 $125

AM. WALTHAM, 17J., luminous dial, c.1929
gold filled $60 $70 $85
14k(w)....................................$175 $200 $275

AM. WALTHAM, 17J., aux. sec., c. 1928
14k(w)....................................$175 $200 $275

AM. WALTHAM,7-15J., **lugless case**, c.1928
gold filled $60 $75 $125

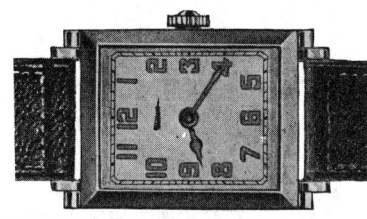

AM. WALTHAM,15J., luminous dial, c.1928
14k $150 $175 $275

AM. WALTHAM,15J., Tank style brush finish, c.1928
14k $175 $225 $325

AM. WALTHAM,7J., luminous dial, c.1928
gold plate $65 $75 $100

AM. WALTHAM,17J.,GJS, ca.1940
14K..$125 $150 $200

AM. WALTHAM,7-15J., cut corner case, c.1929
gold filled................................$70 $80 $100

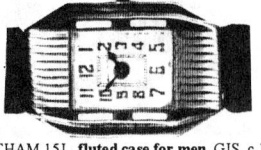

AM. WALTHAM,15J., **fluted case for men,** GJS, c.1925
14k(w)+enamel......................$150 $175 $300

AM. WALTHAM,7-15J., **Butler finish** = (smooth), c.1928
gold filled $60 $75 $100

AM. WALTHAM, 7-15J., GJS, Ca.1927
14K(w)....................................$150 $200 $300

AM. WALTHAM,7-15J., engraved case, etched dial, c.1929
14k(w)....................................$60 $70 $100
gold filled $30 $40 $70

AM. WALTHAM,15J., engraved case, etched dial, c.1928
14K(W)....................................$95 $125 $175
gold filled $30 $45 $65

AM. WALTHAM,7-15J., enamel case, c. 1928
14k(w)....................................$100 $150 $250

AM. WALTHAM,15J., enamel case, c.1929
gold filled (w)..........................$65 $75 $125

AMERICAN WALTHAM WATCH CO. IDENTIFICATION BY MOVEMENT

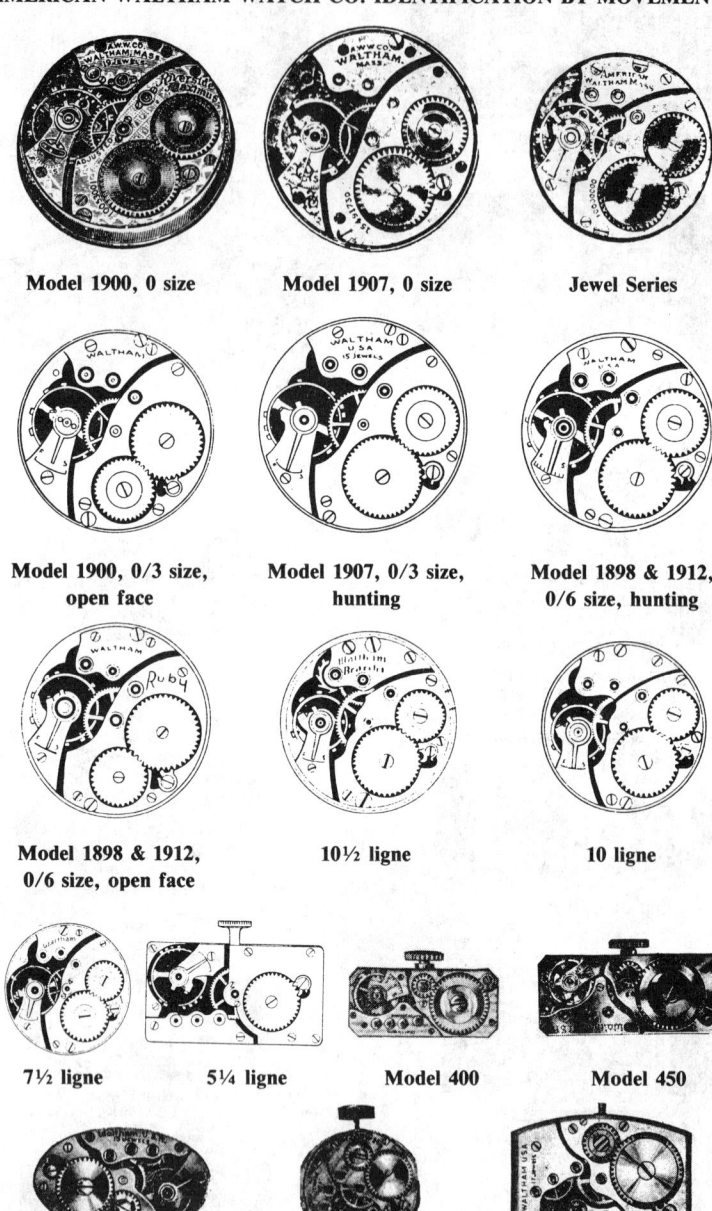

Model 1900, 0 size   Model 1907, 0 size   Jewel Series

Model 1900, 0/3 size,   Model 1907, 0/3 size,   Model 1898 & 1912,
open face   hunting   0/6 size, hunting

Model 1898 & 1912,   10½ ligne   10 ligne
0/6 size, open face

7½ ligne   5¼ ligne   Model 400   Model 450

Model 650   Model 675   Model 750

AMERICUS, 17 jewels, **8 day** movement, c. 1933
18k .... ★★$1,000 $1,200 $1,500
gold filled .... ★$400 $500 $700
s. steel .... ★$300 $400 $600

ANGELUS, 17J., day, date, moon ph.,C. 1949
s. steel $300 $350 $450

AMERICUS, 7 jewels, curved, c.1935
gold filled $75 $100 $150

ANGELUS, 17 jewels, chronograph, 2 reg., water proof
14k $500 $550 $700
18k $700 $750 $900
s. steel $200 $250 $350

ANGELUS, 17 jewels, chronograph, 2 reg., c. 1943
18k $600 $700 $900
14k $400 $500 $700
gold filled $150 $175 $250

ANGELUS, 17J., **date and alarm**, c.1955
s. steel $125 $150 $200

ANGELUS, 17J., chronograph, **triple date**, C. 1949
s. steel $350 $400 $500
14k $700 $800 $1,000
18k $1,300 $1,400 $1,600

ANGELUS, 27 jewels, **1/4 hour repeater**
s. steel $3,000 $3,300 $3,800

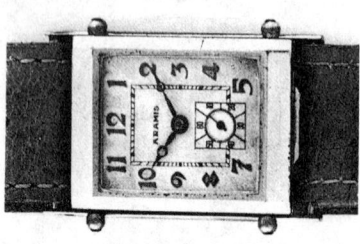

ARAMIS, 15 jewels, **early self wind, lug action winding by back & forth motion of watch case**, c. 1933
s. steel ....★★$600 $700 $900

ARCTOS, 17J., "PARAT", world map on dial, c.1955
base metal...............................$100 $125 $200

ARBU, 17 jewels, triple date, **moon phase**
18k $800 $900 $1,200
s. steel $300 $350 $450

ARDATH, 17J., chronograph, triple date, c.1947
s. steel...................................$200 $250 $350

ARBU, 17 jewels, chronograph, 3 reg., day-date-month
18k $600 $700 $900
s. steel $250 $300 $400

ARISTO, 17 jewels, chronog., water proof
14k...$500 $600 $750
s. steel...................................$150 $175 $225

ARBU, 17 jewels, **split second chronograph**
18k $3,000 $3,300 $4,000

ARISTO, 17J., chronog., 3 reg., **triple date**
14k...$1,500 $1,700 $2,000
s. steel...................................$400 $500 $650

ARISTO, 17 jewels, day-date-month, moon phase
s. steel ....$300　　$350　　$450

ARSA, 17 jewels, chronog., day-date-month, Ca. 1950
18k ....$1,000　　$1,100　　$1,400

ARSA, 17 jewels, day-date-month, moon phase
18k ....$800　　$900　　$1,100
s. steel ....$300　　$350　　$450

ARSA, 15 jewels, day-date-month, moon phase
18k ....:.$700　　$800　　$1,000
s. steel ....$275　　$325　　$400

ASPREY, 16 jewels, **curved hinged back**
9k...$125　　$150　　$225

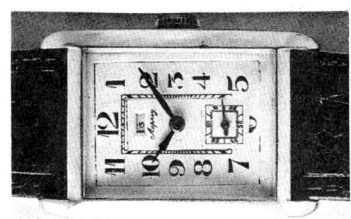

ASPREY, 17J., **date**, ca. 1930s
14k.......................................$350　　$400　　$475
gold filled...............................$150　　$200　　$275

ASPREY, 15 jewels, **duo dial**
18k.....................................$1,500　　$1,700　　$2,000

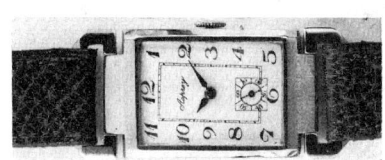

ASPREY, 17 jewels, **enamel dial, center lugs**
9k...$200　　$250　　$350

AUDAX, 15J., Ca.1938
9k...$100　　$125　　$200

🕐 Some grades are not included. Their values can be determined by comparing with similar age, size, metal content, style, grades, or models such as time only, chronograph, repeater etc. listed.

AUDEMARS PIGUET, 33J., **minute** repeater, gold train, platinum & 18K with **40** diamond bezel, diamond dial & diamonds on band
18K & platinum.................$70,000 $80,000 $100,000

AUDEMARS PIGUET, 29 J., **minute repeater**, c. 1917
18k $60,000 $70,000 $90,000

AUDEMARS PIGUET, 29 J., **minute repeater**, c. 1925
platinum $60,000 $70,000 $90,000

AUDEMARS PIGUET, 19 J., **tourbillon,** self-winding tourbillon can be seen from dial side
18k $7,000 $8,000 $10,000

AUDEMARS PIGUET, 36 J., octagonal shaped case, triple date, moon phase, perpetual
18k C&B $9,000 $10,000 $12,000

AUDEMARS PIGUET, 33J., day date, moon ph., c.1989
18k...$2,500 $2,800 $3,500

AUDEMARS PIGUET, day date, moon ph., C. 1980s
18k...$2,500 $2,800 $3,500

AUDEMARS PIGUET, chronograph, triple date, moon ph., tear drop lugs, Ca. 1940s
18k..................................... $20,000 $22,000 $26,000

🕐 Pricing in this Guide are fair market price for **COMPLETE** watches which are reflected from the "**NAWCC**" National and regional shows.

AUDEMARS PIGUET, 36 jewels, gold rotor, day-date
month, moon phase, perpetual
18 k C&B $9,000 $10,000 $12,000

AUDEMARS PIGUET, skeletonized, triple date,
moon phase, perpetual , C. 1980s
platinum...........................$18,000 $20,000 $24,000

AUDEMARS PIGUET, 17 J., chronog., 3 reg., c. 1945
s.steel $8,000 $9,000 $11,000
18k $12,000 $13,000 $15,000

AUDEMARS PIGUET, 18 J., "Le Brassus," **chronog.**
skeletonized
18k C&B..........................$12,000 $14,000 $18,000

AUDEMARS PIGUET, 22 jewels, chronog., 2 reg.,
s.steel $7,000 $8,000 $10,000
18k $14,000 $15,000 $16,000

AUDEMARS PIGUET, 18 jewels, skeletonized
18k $4,000 $5,000 $6,500

AUDEMARS PIGUET, 17 jewels, thin skeletonized
18k $3,500 $4,500 $6,000

🕐 Pricing in this Guide are fair market price for **COMPLETE**
watches which are reflected from the "**NAWCC**" National and
regional shows.

AUDEMARS PIGUET, 18 J., triple date, moonphase
18k $4,000 $5,000 $6,500

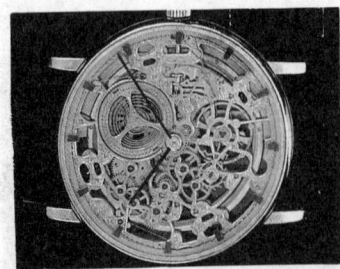

AUDEMARS PIGUET, 36 jewels, skeletonized
18k $5,000 $6,000 $8,000

AUDEMARS PIGUET, 17 J., center lugs, skeletonized
18k $5,000 $6,000 $8,000

AUDEMARS PIGUET, 17J., Dodecagonal, black dial
18k $1,200 $1,300 $1,600

AUDEMARS PIGUET, 17J., diamond dial, c. 1970
18k $1,500 $1,600 $1,900

AUDEMARS PIGUET, 12 diamond dial c.1960
platinum $2,000 $2,200 $2,500

AUDEMARS PIGUET, 11 diamond dial
18k $1,400 $1,600 $2,000

AUDEMARS PIGUET, 12 sapphire dial, c.1950
18k $1,800 $2,000 $2,500

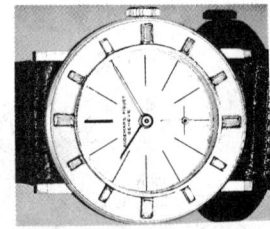

AUDEMARS PIGUET, 17 jewels, 12 diamond dial
18k (w) $1,600 $1,800 $2,000

AUDEMARS PIGUET, 36 jewels, self-winding
18k $1,200 $1,400 $1,700

AUDEMARS PIGUET, 17 jewels, adj. to 5 positions
18k C&B.............................$1,400 $1,600 $2,000

AUDEMARS PIGUET, 17 jewels, rope style bezel
18k C&B $1,500 $1,700 $2,000

AUDEMARS PIGUET, 36 jewels, self-winding
18k $1,500 $1,700 $2,000

AUDEMARS PIGUET, 17J., diamond bezel, center lugs
18k $2,000 $2,200 $2,500

AUDEMARS PIGUET, 36 jewels, lazuli dial
18k C&B.............................$2,000 $2,200 $2,600

AUDEMARS PIGUET, 20J., rope style bezel, c. 1980s
18k case, 14k band $1,000 $1,100 $1,300

AUDEMARS PIGUET, 17 jewels, thin style
18k C&B.............................$2,000 $2,200 $2,600

AUDEMARS PIGUET, 20J., "Le Brassus," c. 1970
18k C&B.............................$2,000 $2,200 $2,600

AUDEMARS PIGUET, 17 jewels, fancy bezel, c. 1950
18k $2,000 $2,400 $2,800

AUDEMARS PIGUET, fancy shaped, c.1960s
18k $3,000 $3,700 $5,000

AUDEMARS PIGUET, 17J., **"Philosopher"**, hour hand only
18k $3,000 $3,300 $3,800

AUDEMARS PIGUET, 20 jewels, thin model
18k $800 $1,000 $1,300

AUDEMARS PIGUET, 17J., engraved bezel, c. 1963
18k $1,200 $1,400 $1,800

AUDEMARS PIGUET, 17J., wide bezel, thin model
14k C&B $1,200 $1,400 $1,800

AUDEMARS PIGUET, 21J., auto wind, center sec.
18k $1,600 $1,800 $2,200

🕐 Pricing in this Guide are fair market price for **COMPLETE**
watches which are reflected from the "**NAWCC**" National and
regional shows.

AUDEMARS PIGUET, **painted world time**, fancy lugs
s. steel $8,000 $9,000 $11,000

AUDEMARS PIGUET, **painted world time** , c. 1940s
14k $9,000 $10,000 $12,000

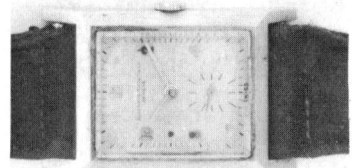

AUDEMARS PIGUET, 18 jewels, gold train
18k $2,500 $2,800 $3,500

AUDEMARS PIGUET, 18J., **hidden lugs**, Ca. 1950
18k $1,000 $1,200 $1,600

AUDEMARS PIGUET, 18 jewels, aux. sec. c. 1940
18k $1,200 $1,400 $1,800

AUDEMARS PIGUET, 17 jewels, for Tiffany & Co.
18k C&B $2,000 $2,200 $2,600

AUDEMARS PIGUET, 18J., no second hand, Ca. 1965
18k $800 $900 $1,100

AUDEMARS PIGUET, 18 jewels, aux. sec.
18k $1,600 $1,700 $2,000

AUDEMARS PIGUET, 18 jewels, center sec., c. 1950
18k $1,400 $1,500 $1,800

AUDEMARS PIGUET, 18 jewels, tank style, c. 1960
18k (w)..............................$1,400 $1,500 $1,800

AUDEMARS PIGUET,18J., straight line lever escape.
18k $900 $1,000 $1,300

AUDEMARS PIGUET, 18 jewels, hooded lugs
18k $1,400 $1,500 $1,800

AUDEMARS PIGUET, 17 jewels, mid-size
18k $500 $600 $800

AUDEMARS PIGUET, 17J., engraved bezel, c.1966
18k $1,300 $1,400 $1,600

AUDEMARS PIGUET, 18J., mid size, **flat bezel**, Ca. 1969
18k $900 $1,000 $1,300

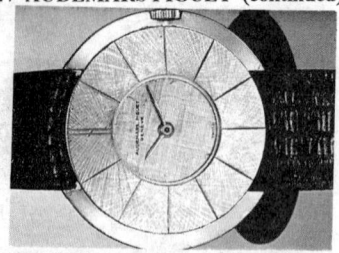

AUDEMARS PIGUET, gold textured dial, c.1960s
18k $900 $1,000 $1,200

AUDEMARS PIGUET,18J., aux. sec., c. 1950s
18k $1,000 $1,200 $1,500

AUDEMARS PIGUET, 18J., auto wind, waterproof
18k $1,600 $1,800 $2,200

AUDEMARS PIGUET, 18 jewels, **painted dial**, c. 1970
18k $800 $900 $1,100

AUDEMARS PIGUET, 21J, sweep sec., automatic -18k rotor
18k $1,700 $1,900 $2,300

AUDEMARS PIGUET, 19J., center sec.
18k $1,400 $1,600 $2,000

AUDEMARS PIGUET, 18J., Manual wind, waterproof
18k $1,500 $1,700 $2,000

AUDEMARS PIGUET, 17 jewels, gold train
18k $1,000 $1,200 $1,500

AUDEMARS PIGUET, **triple date, moon ph.,** c.1930s
18k $25,000 $30,000 $38,000

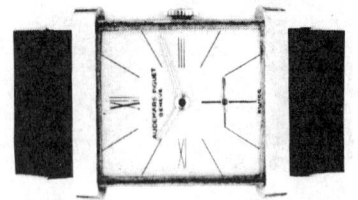

AUDEMARS PIGUET, 18 J.," **top hat**", aux. sec., c. 1950
platinum..............................$3,000 $3,500 $4,500

Wrist Watches listed in this section are priced at the collectable
fair market **retail** level as **complete** watches having an original
gold-filled case and stainless steel back, also with original dial,
leather watch band, and the entire original movement in good
working order with no repairs needed.

AUDEMARS PIGUET, 17J., gold train, 2 tone case in platinum & gold
18k (w) C&B $2,500 $2,700 $3,000

AUDEMARS PIGUET, Breguet style no., c.1927s
18k $1,500 $1,800 $2,500

AUDEMARS PIGUET, 17 jewels, gold train
14k C&B $1,200 $1,400 $2,000

AUDEMARS PIGUET, 18 J., textured bezel, c. 1950
18k $1,200 $1,400 $1,800

AUDEMARS PIGUET, 2 tone dial, c.1930s
18k $2,500 $3,000 $4,000

🕐 Some grades are not included. Their values can be determined by comparing with **similar** age, size, metal content, style, grades, or models such as **time only**, chronograph, repeater etc. listed.

AUDEMARS PIGUET, 17 jewels, gold train, c. 1940
18k (w) $2,200 $2,500 $3,000

AUDEMARS PIGUET, 18J, curvex, large bezel, c. 1950
18k $1,500 $1,700 $2,000

AUDEMARS PIGUET, 18 jewels, tank style, c. 1950's
18k $1,500 $1,700 $2,000

AUDEMARS PIGUET, Royal Oak, **date,** auto wind, c.1973
18K $2,500 $2,800 $3,500
18k C&B $5,000 $5,500 $7,000

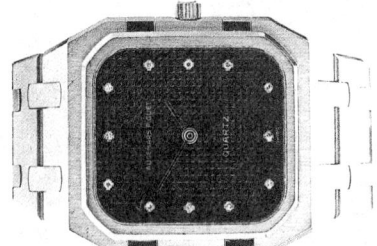

AUDEMARS PIGUET, quartz, 12 diamonds, c. 1981
s. steel $1,200 $1,300 $1,600

AUDEMARS PIGUET, ladys, 72 small diamonds, c.1930s
plat.case & band $1,500 $1,700 $2,000

AUDEMARS PIGUET, ladys, 36 diamonds, c.1930s
plat.case $1,500 $1,700 $2,000

AUTOMATIQUE, 17J., cal.F699, c. 1955
s. steel $55 $60 $75

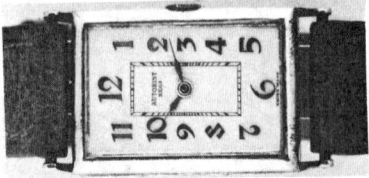

AUTORIST, 15 jewels, **lug action wind**, enamel dial
s. steel $400 $450 $600

AUTORIST, 15 jewels, **lug action wind**, c. 1930
s. steel $400 $450 $600

Wrist Watches listed in this section are priced at the collectable
fair market **retail** level as **complete** watches having an original
gold-filled case and stainless steel back, also with original dial,
leather watch band, and the entire original movement in good
working order with no repairs needed.

🕐 Pricing in this Guide are fair market price for **COMPLETE**
watches which are reflected from the "**NAWCC**" National and
regional shows.

AUTORIST, 15 jewels, **lug action wind**, c. 1930
gold filled $500 $550 $700

AUTORIST, 15 jewels, **lug action wind**, (lady's)
s. steel $200 $250 $400

AVALON,17J., aux.sec.
gold filled $30 $40 $75

AVALON,17J., aux.sec.
gold filled $50 $60 $80

BALL W. CO., 25 jewels, auto wind, adj. to 5 pos., E.T.A.
10k $200 $275 $350

BALL W. CO., 25 jewels, auto wind, adj. to 5 pos., E.T.A.
gold filled...............................$150 $200 $250

BALL W. CO., 25 jewels, auto wind, adj. to 5 pos., E.T.A.
s. steel $150 $200 $250

BAUME & MERCIER, 18J., triple date, moon phase
s. steel $400 $450 $600

BAUME & MERCIER, 17J., chronog., 2 reg., c.1949
gold filled...............................$250 $300 $400

BAUME & MERCIER, 17J., chronog., 2 reg.,c.1950s
18k $500 $600 $750

BAUME & MERCIER, 18J., chronog., 3 reg. & dates
s. steel $350 $400 $550

BAUME & MERCIER, 18 J., chronog., 3 reg. & dates
18k $1,000 $1,200 $1,400

BAUME & MERCIER, 18 jewels, tachymeter, c. 1940
s. steel, original black dial $350 $400 $500

BAUME & MERCIER, 17J., triple date, chronog.
moon ph., c.1950s
18k $1,300 $1,500 $1,900

BAUME & MERCIER, 17J., 2 dials, 2 time zones &
2 movements
18k $700 $800 $1,000

BAUME & MERCIER, 18 J., chronog., fancy lugs
18k $1,800 $2,100 $2,600

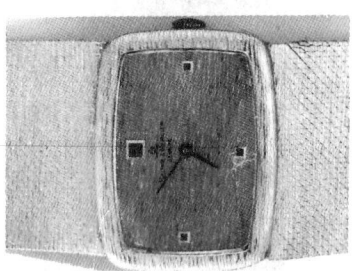

BAUME & MERCIER, 18 jewels, gold dial, date
14k C&B................................$500 $600 $800

BAUME & MERCIER, 17J., chronog., triple date
18k $1,000 $1,200 $1,500

BAUME & MERCIER, 18 jewels, thin model
14k C&B................................$400 $450 $550

BAUME & MERCIER, 18J., triple date, moon phase
18k $800 $1,000 $1,300

BAUME & MERCIER, 17 jewels, center sec., c. 1956
14k $200 $250 $350

BAUME & MERCIER, 17J, fancy lugs, aux. sec., c. 1955
14k $250 $300 $400

BAUME & MERCIER, 17J., RF#49300, c. 1965
14k $150 $175 $225

BAUME & MERCIER, 18 J., "Riviera", date, c. 1980s
18k & s. steel $400 $450 $525

BAUME & MERCIER, **quartz**, enamel dial, tank, c.1990s
14k $200 $250 $350

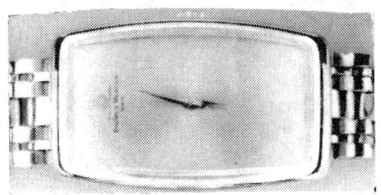

BAUME & MERCIER, 17J., curved, c. 1990s
14k C&B $500 $600 $800

BAUME & MERCIER,17J., sec. window, auto-w., c.1950s
base metal $100 $125 $175

BAUME & MERCIER, 17J.,diam. mystery dial, c.1950s
14k(W)....................................$500 $600 $800

BAYLOR, 17J., hidden lugs
gold filled $40 $55 $75
14k $125 $150 $195

BAYLOR, 17J., diamond on bezel & dial, c.1948
14k $175 $200 $275

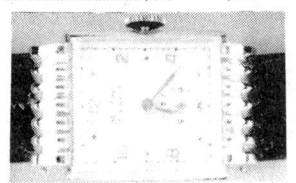

BELTONE, 17J., fancy hidden lugs
14k $125 $150 $200

BEMONTOIR, 15J., enamel dial, c.1920
14k $125 $150 $200

BENRUS,17J., day date
base metal $30 $35 $50

BENRUS, 18J., mystery-diamond dial
18k $400 $500 $650
gold filled................................$100 $125 $200

BENRUS, 15 jewels, day, date, c. 1948
s. steel $55 $65 $100

⊕ Pricing in this Guide are fair market price for **COMPLETE**
watches which are reflected from the "**NAWCC**" National and
regional shows.

BENRUS, 15 jewels, quick change date
gold filled $75 $85 $125

BENRUS,17J.,"Sky Chief", chronog., c.1945
s. steel $225 $250 $325

BENRUS,17J., "Sky Chief", chronog., center lugs, c.1945
gold filled $225 $250 $325

BENRUS,17J.,"Sky Chief",triple date,chronog.,c.1940s
s. steel $325 $350 $425

BENRUS, 15 jewels, calendar, auto wind, fancy lugs, c.1950
14k $150 $200 $250
gold filled..................................$65 $75 $100

BENRUS, 15J., auto wind, fancy bezel, by ETA, c. 1950
gold filled..................................$50 $60 $85
14k $125 $150 $200

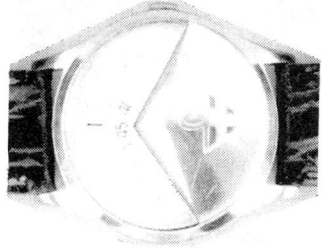

BENRUS,17J., jumping hour, wandering min.
gold filled..................................$150 $175 $250

BENRUS,17J., dial-0-rama, direct read, c. 1958
gold filled..................................$150 $175 $250

Wrist Watches listed in this section are priced at the collectable
fair market **retail** level as **complete** watches having an original
gold-filled case and stainless steel back, also with original dial,
leather watch band, and the entire original movement in good
working order with no repairs needed.

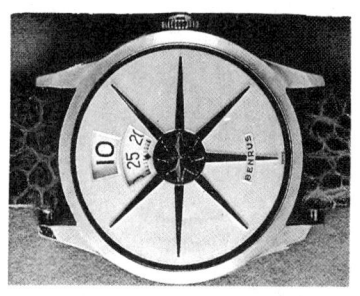

BENRUS, 15 jewels, jumping hour, wandering min.
gold filled $125 $150 $175
s. steel $100 $125 $150

BENRUS,17J., fancy lugs
gold filled $65 $75 $125

BENRUS,17J., fancy lugs
gold filled $50 $60 $85

BENRUS,17J., center sec., heavy lugs,
gold filled $40 $50 $85

🕐 Some grades are not included. Their values can be
determined by comparing with **similar** age, size, metal
content, style, grades, or models such as **time only**,
chronograph, repeater etc. listed.

BENRUS, 15 jewels, fancy lugs, c. 1948
14k $150 $175 $250
gold filled..................................$75 $85 $125

BENRUS, 15J., auto-wind, **water-proof**
gold filled...................................$35 $40 $60

BENRUS, 15 jewels, fancy bezel, cal. BB14
14k $150 $175 $250
gold filled...................................$80 $90 $125

BENRUS, 21J., aux. sec., c. 1950s
14k $100 $125 $175

🕐 Pricing in this Guide are fair market price for **COMPLETE** watches which are reflected from the "**NAWCC**" National and regional shows.

🕐 Some grades are not included. Their values can be determined by comparing with similar age, size, metal content, style, grades, or models such as time only, chronograph, repeater etc. listed.

BENRUS, 17J., **wind indicator,** c.1955
gold filled $65 $75 $125

BENRUS, 21J., aux. sec., fancy lugs, c.1950
gold filled $65 $75 $125

BENRUS, 17J., hidden lugs
14K $125 $150 $200

BENRUS, 17J., cadillac logo, c.1950s
gold plate $45 $55 $85

BENRUS, 17J., by ETA, c.1955
gold filled $50 $60 $95

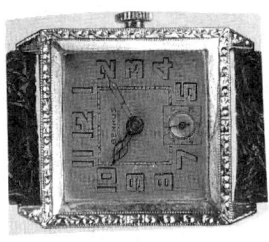

BENRUS, 15J., engraved bezel, c.1935
14k $125 $150 $200

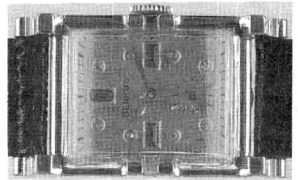

BENRUS, 17J., Rhinestone dial, c. 1945
gold filled..................................$60 $70 $100

BENRUS, 17J., date, fancy lugs, c.1950
gold filled..................................$75 $100 $150

BENRUS, 17J., aux. sec., c.1940
14k $100 $125 $175

BENRUS, 15J.,aux sec.
gold filled..................................$55 $60 $90

🕐 Pricing in this Guide are fair market price for **COMPLETE**
watches which are reflected from the "**NAWCC**" National and
regional shows.

BENRUS,17J., **flared case**, cal.180, c. 1951
gold filled $55 $65 $90

BENRUS, 7J., rhinestone dial, fancy lugs, c. 1948
base metal $30 $40 $60

BENRUS,17J., rhinestone dial, cal. bb1, c. 1945
gold plate $30 $40 $60

BENRUS, 15J.,stepped case
gold filled $30 $40 $60

BENRUS, 15J.,fancy lugs
14kC&B................................$300 $350 $450

BENRUS, 17J., hidden lugs, cal.11ax, Ca.1951
14k $150 $175 $250

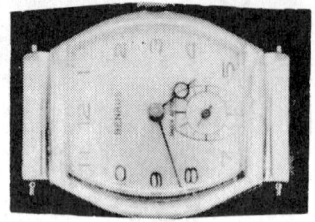

BENRUS, 15J., hooded lugs, cal#bb3
gold filled.................................$30 $40 $60

BENRUS, 15J., **enamel bezel**, c. 1930
14k (w)....................................$200 $250 $325

BENRUS, 15 jewels, 26 diamond bezel
14k (w)....................................$250 $300 $400

BENRUS,17J., aux sec., Ca.1935
gold filled.................................$40 $50 $75

BENRUS, 15 jewels, **flip-top case**, c. 1940
gold filled $250 $300 $400

BENRUS,17J., hooded lugs, c.1948
14k $125 $150 $200

BENRUS,17J., hooded lugs, cal.AX11, c. 1950
14k $175 $200 $250

BENRUS, 15 jewels, hooded lugs
gold filled $60 $70 $100

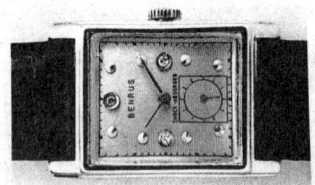

BENRUS, 15 jewels, cal. AX, 3 small diam. dial, c. 1950
14k $125 $150 $225

Wrist Watches listed in this section are priced at the collectable
fair market **retail** level as **complete** watches having an original
gold-filled case and stainless steel back, also with original dial,
leather watch band, and the entire original movement in good
working order with no repairs needed.

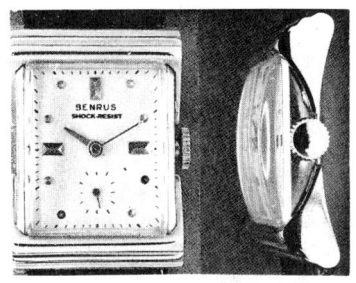

BENRUS, 17 jewels, curved, rhinestones , hooded lugs
14k $150 $175 $250

BENRUS, 15 jewels, curved back, c. 1942
gold filled...................................$60 $70 $90

BENSON, 15 jewels, of London, aux sec. c.1930s
9k $100 $125 $175

BENSON, 15J., of London, Ca.1938
9k $100 $125 $175

BENSON, 15 jewels, enamel dial, tank style case
9k $200 $235 $300

🕐 Some grades are not included. Their values can be
determined by comparing with **similar** age, size, metal
content, style, grades, or models such as **time only**,
chronograph, repeater etc. listed.

BENSON, 15 jewels, enamel dial, flared case
9k $200 $250 $350

BENSON, 15 jewels, enamel dial, 2-tone flared case
9k $275 $325 $425

BERG, 25J., auto-wind, c.1959
14k $125 $140 $175

BLANCPAIN, 23J, day-date-month, perpetual, auto-wind
s. steel- perpetual.................$3,000 $3,500 $4,500
18K - perpetual...................$7,000 $8,000 $10,000

BLANCPAIN, 17J.,hooded lugs, c.1945
14k $200 $225 $300

BLANCPAIN, 16J., c.1925
silver $125 $150 $200

BOILLAT FRERES, 17 jewels, "Blita," waterproof
s. steel $35 $45 $60

E. BOREL, 17 jewels, chronometer, aux. sec.
18k $200 $250 $325
gold filled................................$30 $40 $65

E. BOREL, 17J., cocktail style, c.1960s
gold filled................................$60 $70 $100
s. steel $55 $60 $80

⏱ Some grades are not included. Their values can be determined by comparing with **similar** age, size, metal content, style, grades, or models such as **time only**, chronograph, repeater etc. listed.

E. BOREL, 17J., cocktail dial, date, c. 1969
base metal $30 $40 $65

E. BOREL, 15J., hour dial, min. dial, center sec., c.1940
s. steel $150 $175 $250

E. BOREL, 17 jewels, auto wind, date
gold filled $55 $75 $125

BOUCHERON, 17J., c.1930s
18k $200 $250 $350

Wrist Watches listed in this section are priced at the collectable fair market **retail** level as **complete** watches having an original gold-filled case and stainless steel back, also with original dial, leather watch band, and the entire original movement in good working order with no repairs needed.

⏱ Pricing in this Guide are fair market price for **COMPLETE** watches which are reflected from the "**NAWCC**" National and regional shows.

BOULEVARD, 17J., "STOP", c.1950s
s. steel $65 $75 $125

BOVET, 17 jewels, chronog., 2 reg., c. 1940
s. steel $150 $175 $250

BOVET, 17 jewels, chronog., triple date & 3 reg.
14k $700 $800 $1,000
gold filled...............................$375 $425 $500

BREGUET, 21 jewels, skeletonized
18k C&B..............................$8,000 $9,000 $11,000

BREGUET, 17J., chronog., triple date, Ca.1950
s. steel $6,000 $7,000 $9,000

BREGUET, auto-w., triple date, moon ph., perpetual
18k $14,000 $16,000 $19,000

BREGUET, jump hour, c.1980s, **total made =50**
18k $9,000 $10,000 $12,000

BREGUET, 37J., auto-w., date, moon ph., 45 hr. wind ind.
18k $12,000 $13,000 $15,000

BREGUET, 17 jewels, silver dial, thin model
18k $1,200 $1,300 $1,600

BREGUET, 17 jewels, curvex
platinum...............................$3,000 $3,500 $5,000

P. BREGUETTE, 17J., gold jewel settings, Ca.1948
14k $125 $150 $225

P. BREGUETTE, 17J., gold jewel settings, flared case
14k $200 $225 $275

P. BREGUETTE, 17J., gold jewel settings, Ca.1948
gold filled.................................$60 $70 $100

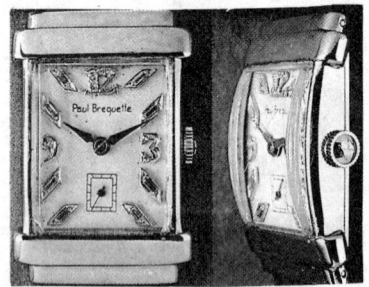

P. BREGUETTE, 17 jewels, top hat, diamond dial, c. 1940
14k $500 $600 $750

P. BREGUETTE, 17J., triple date, c.1960s
gold filled $125 $150 $200
s. steel $100 $125 $175

Breitling, 17 J., "Chronomat," slide rule bezel
18k $2,000 $2,200 $2,500
gold filled $900 $1,000 $1,200
s. steel $800 $900 $1,100

Breitling, 17 J., **Navitimer,** date, slide rule bezel, RF 7806
s. steel $1,100 $1,200 $1,400

BREITLING, 17J., **Chronomat.**, RF 808, c.1950
gold filled...............................$900 $1,000 $1,200

BREITLING, 17J., chronog., RF#1199, sq. button, c.1958
s. steel $400 $450 $525

BREITLING, 17J., chronog., "Navitimer," **24 hour,** 3 reg.
18k $4,500 $5,000 $5,700
s. steel $1,000 $1,100 $1,400

BREITLING, 17 jewels, split sec. chronog., 2 reg.
s. steel $4,000 $5,000 $6,500

BREITLING, 18J., date, moon ph., split chronog. 3 reg.
18k $8,000 $9,000 $11,000

BREITLING, 17 J, chronog., "Navitimer," RF 806
18K C&B............................$5,000 $5,500 $6,000
18K case only $4,500 $5,000 $5,700
gold filled $1,100 $1,200 $1,500
s. steel $1,000 $1,100 $1,400

BREITLING, 17 J., chronog., "Cosmonaute," 24 HR.
s. steel $1,000 $1,100 $1,400

AOPA logo ☞

A.O.P.A., the initials of Aircraft Owners & Pilots Association.
This logo first appeared in 1952 on the *"Navitimer"*, a word
derived from *Navi*gation, **Navi** + the word Timer. The AOPA
logo and other logos are being collected such as Blue Angles
(*U.S.Navy*), Red Arrow (*Royal Air Force*), Frecce Tricolori
(*Aeronautica Militare Italiana*), Patrouille Suisse (*Escadre de
Surveillance*), Thunderbirds (*U.S. Air Force*), Blue Impulse
(*Japan Self Defense Force*), Team 60 (*Swedish Air Force*)
Patrouille de France (*French Air Force*) and others.

BREITLING, 17 J., chronog., "Chronomat," 3 reg.
s. steel $500 $550 $650

BREITLING, 17 J., telemeter, 1 button, hinged lugs
s. steel- 44mm..........................$850 $950 $1,150

BREITLING, 17 J., **AOPA** logo Navitimer, Ca. 1952
s. steel $1,000 $1,100 $1,400

BREITLING, 17 jewels, tachymeter, Ca.1925
s. steel $1,100 $1,200 $1,500

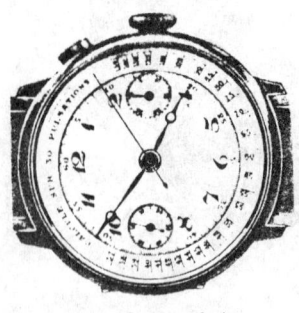

BREITLING, 17 jewels, chronog., pulsations
s. steel $600 $700 $850

BREITLING, 17 jewels, chronog., 2 reg.
s. steel $1,000 $1,100 $1,300

BREITLING, 17 jewels, tachymeter, center hinged lugs
s. steel - 35mm $800 $900 $1,200

BREITLING, 17J., chronog., RF#765, c.1960
14k $1,000 $1,200 $1,500
s. steel $400 $450 $600

BREITLING, 17 jewels, chronog., Toptime, 24 HR.
s. steel $425 $500 $650

BREITLING, 17 jewels, chronog., "Premier," 3 reg.
s. steel $500 $600 $800

BREITLING, 17 jewels, chronog., 2 reg. RF#790
18K **refinished dial** $800 $900 $1,100
18K original dial $1,200 $1,400 $1,700

BREITLING, 17 J., chronog., day-date-month, 3 reg.
18k $2,000 $2,200 $2,500
s. steel $800 $900 $1,100

BREITLING, 17J., chronog., 2 reg., "Premier", RF#790
18k $1,600 $1,800 $2,200

BREITLING, 17 jewels, chronog., 2 reg. RF 178
s. steel $375 $450 $550

BREITLING, 17J., chronog., 3 reg., RF#787, c.1942
14k C&B $1,200 $1,400 $1,800

BREITLING, 17 jewels, chronog., 2 reg.
18k $1,200 $1,300 $1,500
s. steel $275 $325 $425

BREITLING, 17 J., **split sec.** chronog., "Duograph", C.1945
18k $7,000 $8,000 $10,000
s. steel $4,000 $5,000 $7,000

BREITLING, 17J., **Super Ocean**, RF # 2005, c.1960
s. steel $1,000 $1,200 $1,500

BREITLING, 17J., chronog., 3 reg., RF#815, c.1968
gold filled................................$800 $900 $1,200

BREITLING, 17J., chronog., RF#2110, c.1970
s. steel $400 $450 $550

BREITLING, 17J., **AOPA** logo , Toptime, RF#810, c.1968
s. steel $600 $650 $800

BREITLING, 17J., chronog., RF#2009-33, c. 1975
s. steel $325 $350 $400

BREITLING, 17J., **Tour de France**, c. 1945
18K..............................$1,200 $1,400 $1,700

BREITLING, 17J., **Co-Pilot**, enamel bezel, RF # 765, c. 1960
s. steel $800 $900 $1,100

BREITLING, 17J., **Cosmonaute II**, 24 hr., Ca.1990
s.steel C&B $1,100 $1,200 $1,400

BREITLING, 17J., **Old Navitimer II**, gold bezel, Ca.1990
s.steel & G-B $1,200 $1,300 $1,500

BREITLING, 17J., **Navitimer 92**, self-wind, Ca.1992
s.steel case $1,200 $1,300 $1,500
18K case $3,500 $4,000 $4,800

BREITLING, 17J., **Chronomat**, date, self-wind, Ca.1990
s.steel $1,200 $1,300 $1,600
18K & s.steel C&B..............$2,300 $2,400 $2,600

BREITLING, 17J., **Chronomat Yachting**, date, Ca.1990
s.steel C&B $1,100 $1,200 $1,400

BREITLING, 17J., **Chrono Cockpit**, date, Ca.1990
18K & s.steel C&B..............$1,500 $1,600 $1,800

BREITLING, **UTC** (Universal Time Coordinated), Quartz
second time zone with a totally self contained quartz watch
s.steel gold bezel $300 $325 $400

BREITLING, 17J., **Corono QP**, day date moon ph., Ca.1990
18K C&B..........................$10,000 $11,000 $13,000

BREITLING, 17J., **Corono 1461**, day date moon ph., c.1990
s.steel C&B.........................$2,100 $2,300 $2,600

BREITLING, 17J., **Chrono Longitude**, date, Ca.1990
s.steel & gold C&B $1,500 $1,600 $1,800

BREITLING, 17J., **Navitimer Airborne**, date, Ca.1990
s.steel case $1,300 $1,500 $1,800

BREITLING, 17J., **Navitimer AVI**, date, Ca.1990
s.steel case $700 $800 $1,000

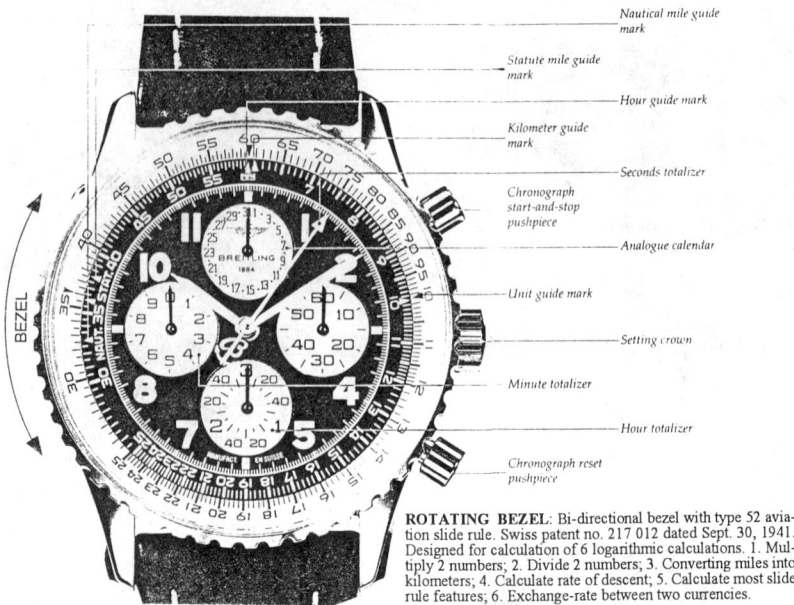

Nautical mile guide mark

Statute mile guide mark

Hour guide mark

Kilometer guide mark

Seconds totalizer

Chronograph start-and-stop pushpiece

Analogue calendar

Unit guide mark

Setting crown

Minute totalizer

Hour totalizer

Chronograph reset pushpiece

BEZEL

ROTATING BEZEL: Bi-directional bezel with type 52 aviation slide rule. Swiss patent no. 217 012 dated Sept. 30, 1941. Designed for calculation of 6 logarithmic calculations. 1. Multiply 2 numbers; 2. Divide 2 numbers; 3. Converting miles into kilometers; 4. Calculate rate of descent; 5. Calculate most slide rule features; 6. Exchange-rate between two currencies.

Complex functions

A mechanical chronograph incorporates an amazing amount and variety of horological knowhow and resourcefulness. Chronographs usually begin with a standard movement to which talented watchmakers add one or more often complex auxiliary mechanisms. Driven by the basic movement's own power, the chronograph mechanism will measure short times without affecting in the least the permanent indication of the time.

selfwinding mechanical

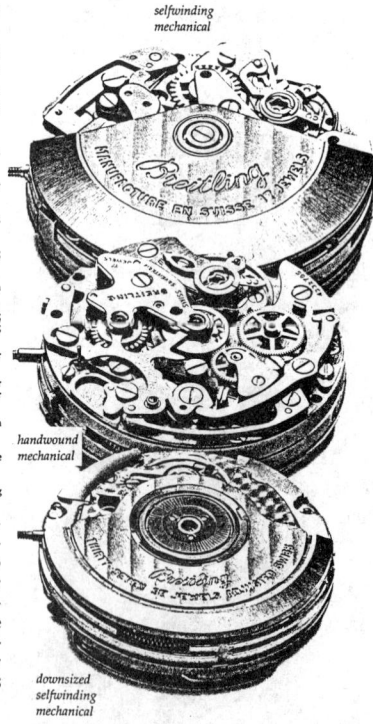

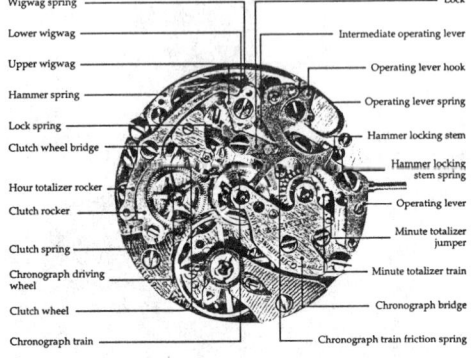

Wigwag spring

Lower wigwag

Upper wigwag

Hammer spring

Lock spring

Clutch wheel bridge

Hour totalizer rocker

Clutch rocker

Clutch spring

Chronograph driving wheel

Clutch wheel

Chronograph train

Lock

Intermediate operating lever

Operating lever hook

Operating lever spring

Hammer locking stem

Hammer locking stem spring

Operating lever

Minute totalizer jumper

Minute totalizer train

Chronograph bridge

Chronograph train friction spring

handwound mechanical

NAVITIMER movements comprise up to 250 parts, some no larger than a human hair. Unaffected by marked temperature differences, its balance spring can withstand accelerations of up to 10 G's. Three movement generations reflect, each in their own way, BREITLING's ongoing mastery of mechanical chronograph design. First, the handwound version, which alone is able to run in weightless space, for the COSMONAUTE. Then the self-winding version developed in 1969 for the NAVITIMER. Now comes the compact model, made possible by the BREITLING caliber's modular construction.

downsized selfwinding mechanical

BREITLING, 17J., chronog., RF#1450, 3 reg., c.1970
s. steel $400 $450 $525

BUCHERER,17 jewels, **note day date in lugs**
18k $900 $1,100 $1,400

BREITLING, 17J., day date month,
18k $400 $450 $525

BUCHERER,17 jewels, chronog., 2 reg.
18k $475 $500 $600

BREITLING, 21J., "UNITIME", date, 24 hour, c.1958
gold filled...............................$800 $1,000 $1,300
18k $1,650 $1,850 $2,250

BUCHERER, 17J., chronog., 2 reg., C.1959
18k $500 $600 $800
s. steel $250 $300 $375

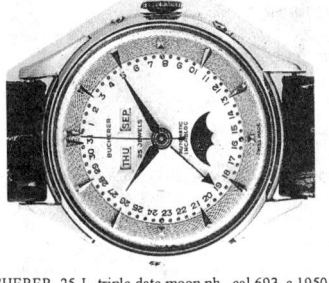

BREITLING, 21J., auto-wind, rf#2528, c.1959
s. steel $100 $125 $200

BUCHERER, 25 J., triple date moon ph., cal.693, c.1950
18k $1,200 $1,400 $1,700

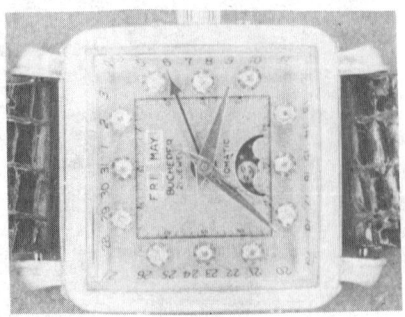

BUCHERER, 21J., 3 dates, moon ph., diamond dial
18k $2,000 $2,200 $2,500

BUCHERER, 15 jewels, **8 day** movement
18k $1,000 $1,100 $1,400
gold filled...............................$500 $600 $750

BUECHE-GIROD, 17 J., day-date-month, moon ph.
s. steel $325 $375 $500

BUECHE-GIROD, 17J., by Piguet, cal.99, c.1975
18k $400 $500 $650

🕐 Some grades are not included. Their values can be determined by comparing with **similar** age, size, metal content, style, grades, or models such as **time only**, chronograph, repeater etc. listed.

Wrist Watches listed in this section are priced at the collectable fair market **retail** level as **complete** watches having an original gold-filled case and stainless steel back, also with original dial, leather watch band, and the entire original movement in good working order with no repairs needed.

BUECHE-GIROD, 17J., dual time movements,
18k $500 $600 $800

BUECHE-GIROD, 17 jewels, tank style case
18k $500 $550 $650

BUECHE-GIROD, 17 jewels
18k C&B................................$600 $650 $800

P. BUHRE, 17 jewels, aux. sec.
gold filled $40 $50 $75

P. BUHRE, 17J., alarm, C.1956
s. steel $90 $125 $175

BULOVA, Accutron, "RF # 210" **gold bezel** & s.steel case
s.steel & **14k**............................$250 $275 $350

BULOVA, Accutron, "Spaceview Alpha" Ca. 1960
Accutron the first transistorized watch was sold Oct. 26, 1960.
14k $500 $600 $750

BULOVA, Accutron, "RF # 213"
s.steel $100 $125 $175

BULOVA, Accutron, "Spaceview B"
s.steel $150 $200 $250

BULOVA, Accutron, "RF # 214"
s.steel $100 $125 $175

BULOVA, Accutron, "Spaceview H"
gold filled...............................$175 $225 $275

BULOVA, Accutron, "RF # 216"
s.steel $100 $125 $175

BULOVA, Accutron, "RF # 202", RR approved
gold filled...............................$175 $200 $275

BULOVA, Accutron, "RF # 218" center lugs
s.steel $150 $185 $250

BULOVA, Accutron, "RF # 223"
s.steel $150 $175 $225
14k $300 $350 $425

BULOVA, Accutron, "RF # 412" gold filled bezel & s.steel
gold filled & s.steel case $100 $125 $175

BULOVA, Accutron, "RF # 400"
gold filled................................$100 $125 $175

BULOVA, Accutron, "RF # 413" gold filled bezel & s.steel
gold filled & s.steel case $100 $125 $175

BULOVA, Accutron, "RF # 401"
s.steel $100 $125 $175

BULOVA, Accutron, "RF # 417"
gold filled $150 $200 $250

BULOVA, Accutron, "RF # 403"
gold filled................................$100 $125 $175

BULOVA, Accutron, "RF # 420"
gold filled $100 $125 $175

BULOVA, Accutron, "RF # 411"
gold filled................................$100 $125 $175

BULOVA, Accutron, "RF # 500" center lugs
14k $300 $350 $450

BULOVA, Accutron, "RF # 505" Ca. 1960
14k yellow or white $425 $475 $575

BULOVA, Accutron, "RF # 513"
14k $250 $300 $425

BULOVA, Accutron, "RF # 514" Florentine engraved case
14k $300 $350 $475

BULOVA, Accutron, "RF # 560"
14k $225 $275 $400

BULOVA, Accutron, "RF # 602"
18k $500 $550 $650

🕐 NOTE: Some Bulova cases are stamped with a year date
code letter & number . L=1950s, M=1960s, N=1970s
example: L3=1953, M4=1964, N5=1975, etc.

Note: A small **predictable** position error can be taken into
consideration in the daily regulation of your Accutron. In the 12
- down **vertical** position the rate is about 5 seconds per day faster
conversely in the 6-down **vertical** position a rate of 5 seconds
per day slower. You can take advantage of this, if slow place it
in the 12-down vertical position at night and it will gain back
lost time, if fast use the 6-down vertical position to slow it down.

BULOVA, Accutron, "Mickey" day & date, **RARE**
14k C&B(original dial) ★ ★ ★$600 $700 $850

BULOVA, Accutron, date, "M 8" on back - Ca. 1968
14k $250 $300 $425

BULOVA, Accutron, "Spaceview"
s. steel $125 $150 $275

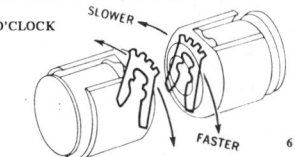

BULOVA, Accutron, **"converted dial"**, cal. 214, c.1963
gold filled $75 $100 $150
Note Below: Bulova Accutron regulator, to regulate use a
tooth pick and move regulator up or down.

12 O'CLOCK   SLOWER

FASTER   6 O'CLOCK

🕐 NOTE: Some Bulova cases are stamped with a year date code letter & number .L=1950s, M=1960s, N=1970s example: L3=1953, M4=1964, N5=1975, etc.

BULOVA, Accutron, cal. 214, c. 1963
s. steel $100 $125 $200

BULOVA, Accutron, "Spaceview," c. 1965
gold filled $125 $150 $250

BULOVA, Accutron, "Spaceview," c. 1960
14k $400 $450 $600
gold filled...............................$100 $135 $200
s. steel $100 $135 $200

BULOVA, Accutron, "Spaceview," c. 1961
gold filled $125 $150 $250

BULOVA, Accutron, "Spaceview"
s. steel $150 $200 $250

BULOVA, Accutron, "Spaceview," c. 1967
gold filled $150 $175 $300
s. steel $175 $200 $275
14k $350 $400 $500

BULOVA, Accutron, **converted dial,** Alpha, waterproof
14k $200 $225 $275

BULOVA, Accutron, "Spaceview"
18k $600 $700 $800
14k $400 $500 $600
s. steel $150 $200 $250

Accutron, reached 1/2 million in sales by 1966, 3/4 by 1968, by 1970 1 million watches, and by 1976, 2 million watches.

BULOVA, Accutron, "Spaceview," center lugs
gold filled.................................$200 $225 $300

BULOVA, Accutron, "Spaceview," center lugs
s. steel $175 $200 $275

BULOVA, Accutron, center lugs
gold filled.................................$175 $200 $275

BULOVA, Accutron, "Spaceview," center lugs
14k C & B.............................$500 $600 $750

BULOVA, Accutron, **converted** dial, date, cal.218
14k 2 tone $200 $225 $250

BULOVA, Accutron, 2 tone, Ca. 1967
gold filled $175 $200 $275

BULOVA, Accutron, Skeletonized, date, cal.218, Ca.1967
14k $350 $400 $500

BULOVA, Accutron, oval, "Spaceview"
s. steel $100 $125 $175

🕐 Some grades are not included. Their values can be
determined by comparing with **similar** age, size, metal
content, style, grades, or models such as **time only**,
chronograph, repeater etc. listed.

BULOVA, Accutron, two tone, date
14k 2 tone $225 $250 $325

BULOVA, Accutron, "Spaceview,"
s. steel $100 $125 $175

BULOVA, Accutron, "Spaceview,"
s. steel $100 $125 $175

BULOVA, Accutron, "Spaceview," gold bezel
14k $350 $400 $500
gold bezel & s. steel case $200 $225 $300

BULOVA, Accutron, M# 214, railroad approved, C. 1960s
gold filled................................$175 $200 $275
s. steel $150 $175 $250

🕐 NOTE: Some Bulova cases are stamped with a year date
code letter & number. L=1950s, M=1960s, N=1970s
example: L3=1953, M4=1964, N5=1975, etc.

BULOVA, Accutron, M# 218, RR approved, red 24 hr. dial
gold filled $175 $200 $275

BULOVA, Accutron, **quartz**, RR approved, day date
gold plate $75 $85 $125

BULOVA, Accutron, RR approved
s. steel $150 $175 $250

BULOVA, Accutron," **Mark IV" / RR approved,** date
Crown at 2 sets the hour hand, Crown at 4 sets Time & Date
two hour hands for two time zones
s. steel ....★$200 $250 $350

BULOVA, Accutron, cal. 214," Pulsation", c. 1966
gold filled..............................$125 $150 $195
14k .... ★$500 $550 $650

BULOVA, Accutron, masonic dial (all original dial)
NOTE: This dial can be printed for about $35.00.
14k $235 $265 $325

BULOVA, Accutron, cal. 214," Pulsation", c. 1966
14k $400 $450 $550

BULOVA, Accutron, asymmetric
14k $450 $475 $575

BULOVA, Accutron, "Alpha" model, cal. 214, diamond dial
14k $450 $500 $650
18K..................................... ★$500 $550 $750

BULOVA, Accutron, asymmetric, 2- tone dial, Ca.1963
14k $500 $550 $625

BULOVA, Accutron, sweep sec. hand
gold filled..................................$75 $95 $135

BULOVA, Accutron, "ASTRONAUT A", 24 hour dial
18kC&B.............................$1,200 $1,400 $1,800
14k $700 $900 $1,200
gold filled $250 $300 $400
s. steel $175 $225 $325

BULOVA, Accutron, "ASTRONAUT B", rotating bezel
s. steel $200 $250 $325

BULOVA, Accutron, "ASTRONAUT C", 18k case & band,
retail price in June, 1964 was $1,000.00.
18k C & B $1,200 $1,400 $1,800

BULOVA, Accutron, "Astronaut Mark II", time zone, window
at six o'clock, date at 12, note: red dial, on back N2 = 1972
14k $400 $450 $550
s. steel $150 $175 $250

BULOVA, Accutron, "Astronaut Mark II", time zone, original sales price was $275.00 in S. Steel.
14k $400 $450 $550
gold filled..............................$200 $275 $350
s. steel $200 $250 $300

BULOVA, Accutron, "Astronaut Mark II", auxiliary time
zone window at 6-o'clock & date at 12-o'clock.
14k $450 $500 $600

BULOVA, Accutron, "Astronaut Mark II", time zone with a
extra red hour hand, date at 3 o'clock, on back M9 = 1969
gold filled $200 $250 $325

BULOVA, Accutron
gold filled $100 $125 $150

BULOVA, Accutron, Ca. 1966
gold filled $75 $100 $135

BULOVA, Accutron, fancy lugs
gold filled...............................$100 $125 $175

BULOVA, Accutron, date, gold filled bezel
s. steel $65 $75 $95

BULOVA, Accutron
gold filled...............................$100 $135 $200

BULOVA, Accutron, date, Ca.1967
s. steel $85 $100 $135

BULOVA, Accutron, **4 diamond** dial, Ca. 1967
gold filled...............................$150 $175 $250

BULOVA, Accutron, day date
14k $175 $200 $275

BULOVA, Accutron, date
gold filled $100 $125 $175

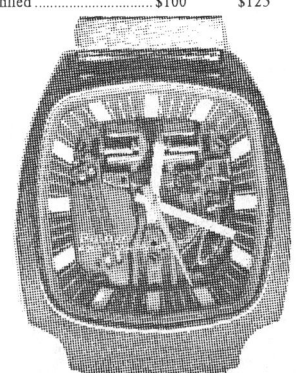

BULOVA, Accutron, **Spaceview Anniversary,** model 214
14k(large case) ....★$400 $425 $475

BULOVA, (Accu- quartz), quartz & tuning fork, day date
gold filled.................................$75 $85 $125

BULOVA, Accutron, cushion spaceview, Ca. 1970
s. steel $150 $175 $250

BULOVA, Accutron, model 2183,
s. steel $60 $70 $85

BULOVA, Accutron, **wood bezel,** day date
gold filled $75 $100 $150

BULOVA, Accutron, date, Ca.1972
base metal $60 $70 $85

BULOVA, Accutron, red dial, date
gold filled $75 $100 $125

BULOVA, Accutron, gold filled bezel, day date
gold filled.................................$75 $85 $100

BULOVA, Accutron, numbered bezel, day date
14k $300 $350 $475

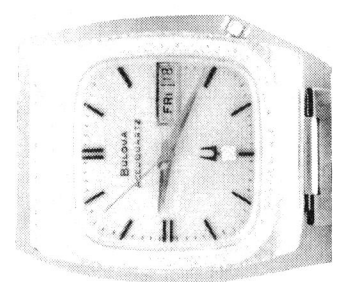

BULOVA, Accuquartz, diamond bezel, day date
14k $350 $400 $450

BULOVA, Accuquartz, note band with **accutron symbol**
18k C&B.................................$600 $700 $850

BULOVA, Accutron, day date
gold filled....................................$75 $100 $150

BULOVA, Accutron, day date, c. 1970
s. steel $50 $60 $75

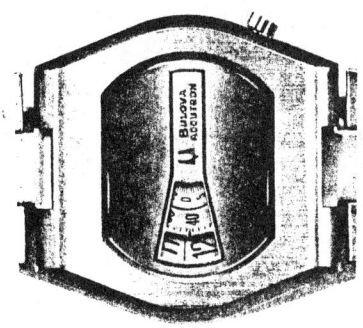

BULOVA, Accutron, day date, Ca.1972
gold filled....................................$75 $100 $150

BULOVA, Accutron, model 2186, direct read
gold filled $75 $100 $165

BULOVA, Accutron, date
gold plate $65 $75 $95

BULOVA, Accutron, **Accutron 14k Gold Band**, Ca.1972
14k C & B.............................$500 $550 $700

BULOVA, Accutron, diamond on bezel
14k(w) C&B $400 $450 $600

BULOVA, Accutron, date
gold filled.................................$75 $100 $150

BULOVA, Accutron, divers 660 ft.depth, 24 hr.dial,
rotating outside chapter, day date, Ca. 1970
s. steel $175 $200 $275

BULOVA, Accutron, **DEEP SEA**, 666 feet, date
enamel rotating bezel
s. steel $250 $300 $400

BULOVA, Accutron, day date, note <u>Accutron style sec. hand</u>
s. steel $150 $175 $225

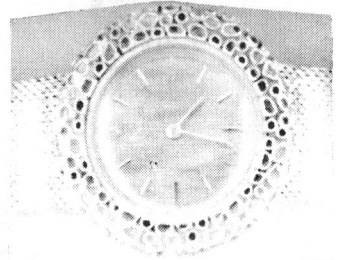

BULOVA, Accutron, fancy bezel
14k C&B...............................$350 $400 $525

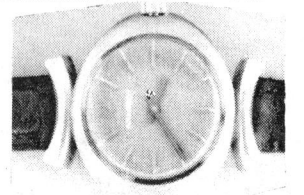

BULOVA, Accutron, lady accutron
14k $100 $110 $125

BULOVA, Accutron, note links in accutron band
gold plate $90 $125 $175

BULOVA, Accutron, date, Ca. 1968
gold filled $75 $100 $150

BULOVA, Accutron, wide oval bezel
gold filled...............................$40 $50 $75

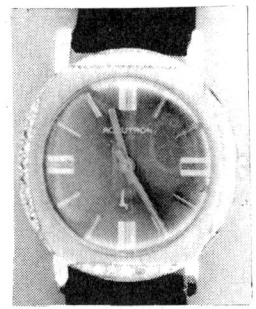

BULOVA, Accutron, 32 small diamond bezel
14k(w)....................................$250 $275 $325

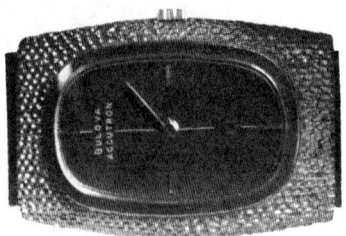

BULOVA, Accutron, cal. #221, textured bezel
sterling & 14k.........................$75 $100 $150

BULOVA, Accutron, pendant style watch
14k $125 $150 $200

🕐 NOTE: Some Bulova cases are stamped with a year date code letter & number .L=1950s, M=1960s, N=1970s example: L3=1953, M4=1964, N5=1975, etc.

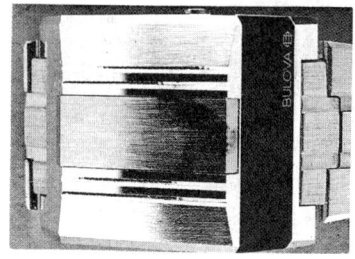

BULOVA, digital,
s. steel $100 $125 $200

BULOVA, enamel bezel
s. steel $75 $100 $150

BULOVA, 15J., one button chronog.,1/5 sec.,C.1946
14k $500 $550 $650
gold filled $300 $325 $400

BULOVA, 17J., one button chronog., cal.10BK, c.1947
gold filled $300 $325 $400

BULOVA, 17J., chronog., "660 feet" dive watch, c.1972
s. steel $100 $125 $175

BULOVA, 16 jewels, military style
s. steel $250 $300 $375

BULOVA, 17J., **Alarm**, cal.11aerc, c.1967
s. steel $100 $125 $175

BULOVA, self winding, c. 1960
14k $150 $175 $200
gold filled.................................$30 $40 $65

BULOVA, 17J., fancy lugs
gold filled $75 $90 $125

BULOVA, 23 jewels, waterproof
14k $100 $125 $200

BULOVA, 23 jewels, date, 6 adj., c. 1951
gold filled $75 $85 $100

BULOVA, 17J., cal.11 af, ca.1959
gold filled $40 $50 $75
14K $100 $125 $200

BULOVA, fancy long lugs, c. 1942
gold filled..................................$50 $60 $95

BULOVA, 17J., fancy lugs, c.1958
14k $150 $175 $225

BULOVA, 21J., fancy lugs, c.1950
gold filled..................................$75 $100 $135

BULOVA, 17J., center sec., c.1942
gold filled..................................$30 $40 $75

BULOVA, 15J., military style, c.1940
s. steel $45 $55 $85

BULOVA, cal. 700, canteen style, c. 1946
s. steel .... ★★★$375 $450 $600

BULOVA, 15J., military style, cal.10 bnch, c.1940
s. steel $45 $55 $75

BULOVA, 17J., U.S.A. military, c.1945
s. steel $45 $55 $75

BULOVA, 17J., 20 diamond dial
14k(w)....................................$175 $200 $275

BULOVA, 23J., 12 diamond dial, c. 1959
14k(w)....................................$175 $200 $275

BULOVA, 30J., diam. dial, cal#10B2AC, C.1960s
14k(w)....................................$175 $200 $275

BULOVA, **early auto wind** movement see Champ below

BULOVA, **early auto wind,** by Champ, c. 1930
gold filled.................... ★ ★ ★$400 $450 $600

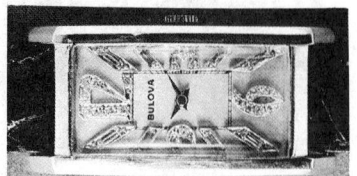

BULOVA, diamond dial, c. 1939
platinum $800 $900 $1,200
14k (w)....................................$600 $650 $800

BULOVA, 21 jewels, hidden lugs, diamond dial, c. 1935
14k $600 $650 $800

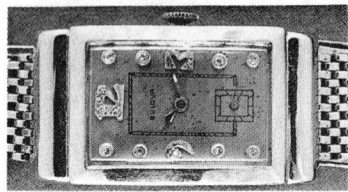

BULOVA, hidden lugs, diamond dial, c. 1945
14k $500 $550 $700

BULOVA, 21 jewels, diamond dial, long lugs, c. 1941
14k (w) $250 $300 $400

BULOVA, 17J., 3 diamond dial, cal.8ae, c.1949
14k $150 $175 $250

BULOVA, 17 jewels, curved, cal. 7AP, c. 1939
14k $250 $275 $375

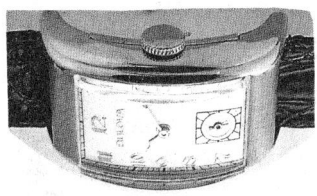

BULOVA, 17J., drivers watch, c.1935
gold filled................................$300 $350 $450

BULOVA, 17J., engraved, Ca. 1928
gold filled...................................$50 $60 $80

BULOVA, 17J., 5th ave., cal.6am, engraved bezel, c.1935
gold filled................................$50 $60 $80

BULOVA, 21J., stepped bezel, curved,
gold filled................................$75 $85 $125

BULOVA, 21J., plain bezel, curved,
gold filled...................................$75 $85 $100

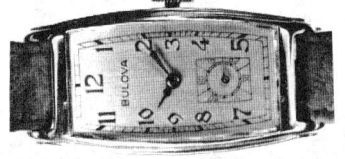

BULOVA, 17J., cal. 7ap, c.1937
gold filled...................................$75 $85 $100

BULOVA, 17J., curved, cal.7ap, c.1936
gold filled $75 $85 $100

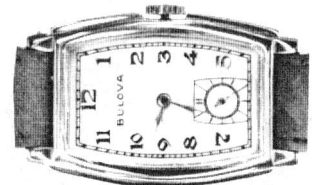

BULOVA, 17J., cal.13al,c.1935
14k $125 $150 $200

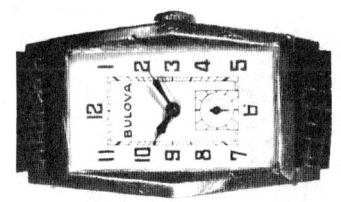

BULOVA, 17J., cal.9af, c.1929
s. steel $30 $40 $60

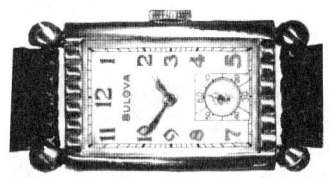

BULOVA, 17J., cal.7ap, c.1934
gold filled $75 $85 $125

BULOVA, 15J., cal.10ae, c.1938
gold filled $55 $65 $90

BULOVA, 17 jewels, curved, c. 1939
gold filled $75 $100 $150

BULOVA, 21 jewels, curved, c. 1939
gold filled..................................$75 $85 $125

BULOVA, 21J., cal# 6AE,
14k $125 $150 $225

BULOVA, 17 jewels, duo dial, c. 1935
gold filled(S.S.back)..............$175 $200 $325
s. steel $175 $200 $325

BULOVA, 17 jewels, 2 tone duo dial
s. steel $175 $200 $325

BULOVA, 17 jewels, 2 tone dial, **flexible lugs,** fancy bezel
s. steel $100 $125 $175

Wrist Watches listed in this section are priced at the collectable
fair market **retail** level as **complete** watches having an original
gold-filled case and stainless steel back, also with original dial,
leather watch band, and the entire original movement in good
working order with no repairs needed.

BULOVA, 21 J., **President, wandering sec.**, c. 1932
gold filled $100 $125 $175

BULOVA, 17 jewels, cal. 10GM, fancy lugs, c. 1953
gold filled $75 $100 $150
14k $150 $200 $300

BULOVA, 15J., fancy lugs, c.1952
gold filled $100 $125 $175

BULOVA, 21J., fancy lugs, c.1952
14k $150 $175 $225
gold filled $75 $100 $175

BULOVA, 17J., fancy lugs, cal.8an, c.1951
14k $275 $325 $400
gold filled $100 $125 $175

BULOVA, 17J., cal.8ad, fancy lugs, c.1939
gold plate $50 $75 $125

BULOVA, 17J., fancy lugs, c.1950 code on case=(LO)
gold filled $30 $40 $65

BULOVA, 21J., cal. 7ak, c.1945
gold filled.................................. $50 $75 $125

BULOVA, 17J., gold jewel settings, Ca.1923
gold filled $55 $65 $80

BULOVA, 21J., c.1950s
gold filled.................................. $40 $65 $100

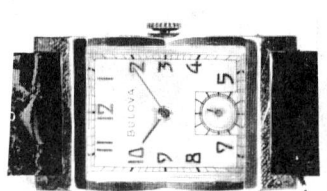

BULOVA, 21J., **carved case**, c.1948
14k $150 $175 $225

BULOVA, 21J., scalloped case, c.1950s
gold filled $75 $85 $125

BULOVA, 21J., cal.7ak, c.1945
gold filled $50 $65 $90

BULOVA, 7J., c.1945
gold filled.................................. $45 $55 $95

BULOVA, 17J., cal.8ae, fancy hidden lugs, c.1941
gold filled $50 $75 $125

🕐 Pricing in this Guide are fair market price for **COMPLETE** watches which are reflected from the "**NAWCC**" National and regional shows.

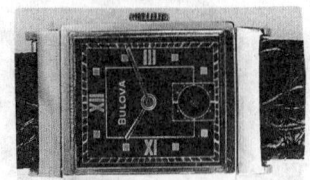

BULOVA, 21J., hooded lugs, c.1945
14k $150 $175 $225

BULOVA, 21 jewels, hooded lugs, cal. 8AC, c. 1952
14k $200 $250 $300

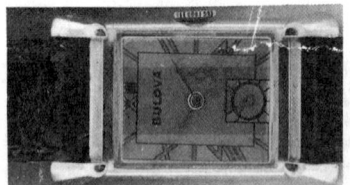

BULOVA, 17 jewels, fancy long lugs, c. 1942
14k $150 $175 $225

BULOVA, 15 jewels, **2 tone engraved bezel, flexible lugs,**
Ca. 1925
gold filled..................................$85 $100 $150

BULOVA, 17J., cal. 8AC, **flip top, photo watch,** c. 1940
gold filled..............................$250 $300 $375
14k $350 $400 $500

🕐 Some grades are not included. Their values can be determined by comparing with **similar** age, size, metal content,
style, models and grades listed.

BULOVA, 15 jewels, wandering hr. min. sec., c. 1928
s. steel $200 $250 $300

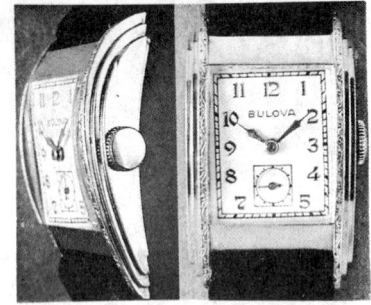

BULOVA, 17J., right angle, cal. 8AZ, c. 1938
gold filled $100 $125 $200
14k $250 $300 $400

BULOVA, 17 jewels, aux. sec.
14k $125 $150 $200

BULOVA, 17 jewels, fancy bezel
gold filled $100 $125 $175

BULOVA, 17 jewels, bell shaped lugs
14k $150 $175 $225

BULOVA, 17 jewels, fancy lugs
14k $150 $175 $225

BULOVA, 21J., hidden lugs, c.1950s
14k $150 $175 $250

BULOVA, 17J., center sec., cal.10bac, c.1935
gold filled.................................. $55 $65 $80

BULOVA, 21J., hidden lugs, c.1945
gold filled $55 $75 $125

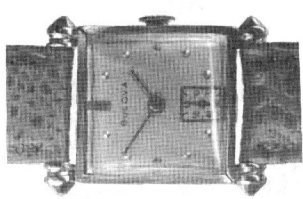

BULOVA, 17J., cal.8ac, fancy lugs, c.1940
gold plate $55 $65 $85

BULOVA, 17J., BMW- logo, c.1957
gold filled $65 $85 $125

BULOVA, 17J., flared top of case & sides,
gold filled.................................. $60 $75 $100

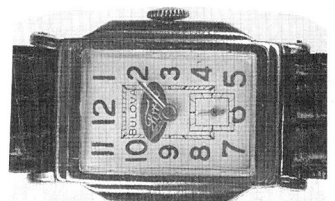

BULOVA, 17J., FORD logo, c.1947
base metal $50 $60 $90

BULOVA, 21J., hidden lugs, c.1961
gold filled.................................. $65 $85 $125

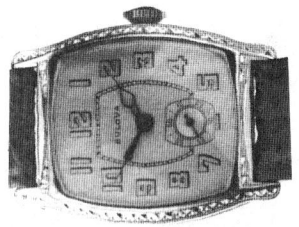

BULOVA, 17J., engraved lugs & bezel, cal.10an,c.1928
s. steel $40 $50 $75

BULOVA, 17J., engraved bezel only
base metal $30 $40 $60

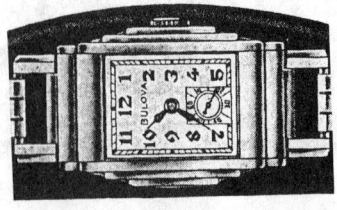

BULOVA, 15 jewels, **Senator,**
gold filled $55 $65 $85

BULOVA, 15J., cal.11ac, c.1958
gold filled..................................$65 $75 $125

BULOVA, 17 jewels, **Oakley,**
gold filled $55 $65 $85

BULOVA, 15J., cal.10ae, c.1935
gold filled..................................$50 $60 $80

BULOVA, 17 jewels, **LONE EAGLE,** stepped style case
gold filled $100 $125 $175

BULOVA, 7J., cal.10bc, c.1949
gold filled..................................$45 $55 $75

BULOVA, 15 jewels, **LONE EAGLE,** tonneau style case
gold filled $100 $125 $175

BULOVA, **Masonic** dial, Ca. 1944
gold filled..............................$100 $125 $175

BULOVA, 17J., **LONE EAGLE,** radium & cut corner dial
gold filled $100 $125 $175

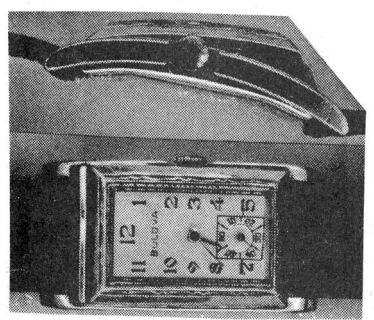

BULOVA, 17J., right angle case
gold filled..............................$100 $125 $175

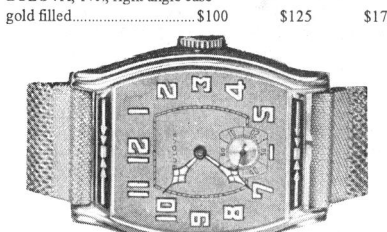

BULOVA, 17 jewels, "The Ambassador"
gold filled..................................$40 $50 $80

BULOVA, 17 jewels, "The Curtis," tank style
gold filled....................................$65 $75 $125

BULOVA, 15 jewels, "The Athelete"
gold filled....................................$75 $85 $115

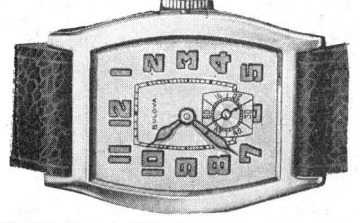

BULOVA, 17 jewels, "The Governor,"
14K...$125 $150 $200

BUREN, 17 jewels, day-date-month, moon phase
s. steel $200 $250 $350

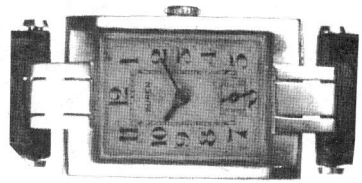

BUREN, 17 jewels, long lugs
14k $125 $150 $200

BUREN, 17 jewels, center lugs, c.1940
9k $125 $150 $250

BUTEX, 17J., triple date, moon ph.
gold filled $150 $175 $225

CARLTON, 15 jewels, **"Rite angle"** case, c. 1939
gold filled $100 $125 $200
14k $250 $300 $400

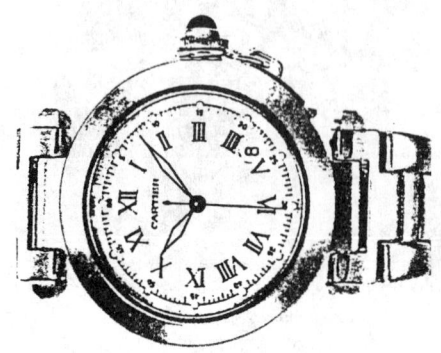

CARTIER, "Pasha", automatic, 300ft, **recent**
18k C & B..........................$8,000 $8,500 $9,500
18k leather $3,500 $4,000 $4,500

CARTIER, "Golf", automatic, 100ft, **4 counters, recent**
18k C & B.......................$14,500 $15,000 $16,500
18k leather $9,500 $10,000 $12,000

CARTIER, "Pasha", automatic, 300ft, rotating bezel, **recent**
18k C & B..........................$8,000 $8,500 $9,500
18k leather. $3,500 $4,000 $4,500

CARTIER, "Diabolo", automatic, 100ft, **tourbillon, recent**
18k leather $35,000 $38,000 $42,000

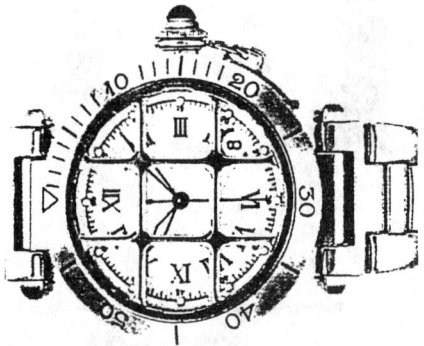

CARTIER, "Pasha", automatic, 300ft, **grill, recent**
18k C & B..........................$11,000 $11,500 $13,500
18k leather $5,500 $6,000 $7,000

🕐 Pricing in this Guide are fair market price for **COMPLETE** watches which are reflected from the "**NAWCC**" National and regional shows.

CARTIER, "Diabolo", manual w., **Min. Repeater, recent**
18k leather. $40,000 $45,000 $55,000

CARTIER, "Pasha", automatic, rotating bezel, 100 ft., **recent**
18k C & B.........................$13,000 $13,500 $15,000
18k leather $10,000 $10,500 $11,500

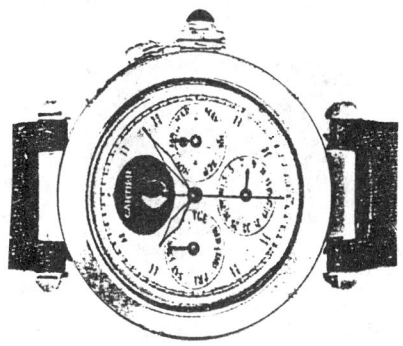

CARTIER, "Pasha", automatic, moon phases, 100 ft., **recent**
18k C & B.........................$14,000 $15,000 $17,000
18k leather $10,000 $11,000 $13,000

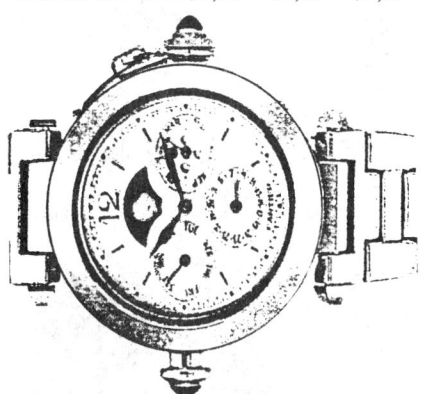

CARTIER, "Pasha", **Min. Repeater**, moon phases, **recent**
18k C & B.........................$60,000 $68,000 $75,000
18k leather $55,000 $62,000 $70,000

🕐 Pricing in this Guide are fair market price for **COMPLETE** watches which are reflected from the "**NAWCC**" National and regional shows.

CARTIER, "Tank Francaise", automatic, date, 100 ft., **recent**
18k C & B.........................$7,000 $7,300 $8,000
18k leather $2,000 $2,200 $2,500

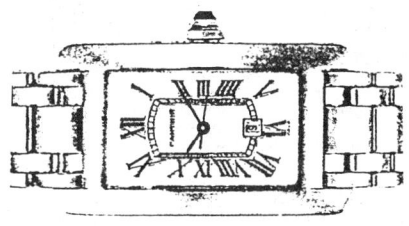

CARTIER, "Tank Americaine", automatic, date, **recent**
18k C & B.........................$9,000 $9,500 $10,000
18k leather $2,500 $3,000 $4,000

CARTIER, "Cloche", manual wind, **recent**
18k leather $7,000 $7,500 $8,500

CARTIER, "Pasha", automatic, rotating bezel, 100 ft., **recent**
18k C & B.........................$5,000 $5,500 $6,500

CARTIER, 18 J., 8 day Mvt., tank style, by E. W. Co.
18k $30,000 $33,000 $40,000

CARTIER, 18 J., sapphire crown & bezel, c. 1970
18k $2,500 $2,800 $3,500

CARTIER, 18 jewels, curved, tank style
18k $7,000 $7,500 $9,000

CARTIER, 18 jewels, curved, signed E. W. Co., c.1930s
18k $6,000 $6,500 $8,000

CARTIER, 18 J., tank style, platinum case & band
platinum C&B..................$12,000 $13,000 $16,000

NOTE: With original Cartier 18K Deployment clasp
ADD $500 to $800.

CARTIER, 18 jewels, tank style case, c. 1970s
18k $1,400 $1,500 $1,800

CARTIER, 20 jewels, tank style case, c. 1950
18k $1,800 $1,900 $2,200

CARTIER, Must de, **quartz,** tank style case, c.1980s
Vermeil =(gold over sterling)
G.P. vermeil...........................$300 $325 $400
SAME STYLE CASE AS ABOVE
CARTIER, Must de, **Mechanical,** tank style case, c.1980s
Vermeil =(gold over sterling)
G.P. vermeil...........................$300 $325 $400

CARTIER, 18 jewels, tank style, European W. Co.
platinum..............................$6,000 $6,500 $8,000

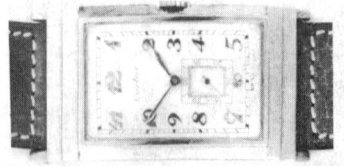

CARTIER, 18 jewels, by Movado
14k $1,000 $1,100 $1,400

CARTIER, 18 jewels, duo plan, European W. Co.
18k C&B $2,500 $2,800 $3,500

CARTIER, 18J., by Le Coultre, long lugs
18k $1,200 $1,300 $1,600

CARTIER, 18 jewels, curved, hidden lugs
18k $3,500 $3,800 $4,500

CARTIER, 18 jewels, by Universal, c. 1960
18k $800 $900 $1,200

CARTIER, 18 jewels, center lugs, c. 1930
18k $2,800 $3,000 $3,600

CARTIER, 18 J., Prince, by Le Coultre, C.1930
18k $25,000 $28,000 $35,000

CARTIER, 18 J., reversible to view 2nd **time zone**
18k $25,000 $28,000 $35,000

CARTIER, 18 jewels, by European W. Co. c. 1927
18k $3,000 $3,300 $4,000

CARTIER, 18 J., early E.W.Co., C. 1928
18k $3,500 $3,800 $4,500

CARTIER, 18 J., lady's watch by European W. Co.
18kC&B..............................$2,000 $2,400 $3,000

CARTIER, 18 J., sovonnette H.C.style, C. 1928
18k $7,000 $7,500 $9,000

CARTIER, 18 J., E.W.Co., Ca. 1925
18k $3,500 $3,800 $4,500

CARTIER,18 J., guichet tank, jump hr. & min. by E.W.Co.
18k $30,000 $34,000 $40,000

CARTIER, 18 J., jump hr. & min., E. W. Co. c. 1930
platinum $35,000 $38,000 $45,000

CARTIER, 18 J.,"Santos", cal.21
mens18k..............................$1,800 $1,900 $2,200
ladies 18k $1,600 $1,700 $2,000

CARTIER, 18 J., "Santos," 18k & s. steel case, band, Lady's
platinum & 18k C&B $12,000 $13,000 $16,000
18k & s. steel C&B.................$800 $900 $1,200

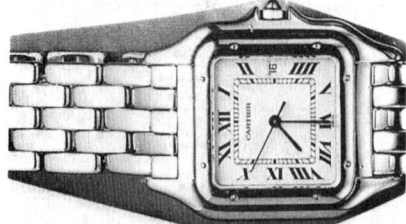

CARTIER, Panthere, large, date, water resistant
18k C & B $6,000 $6,500 $7,500

CARTIER, 18 jewels, "Santos," date
18k & s. steel C&B $1,000 $1,100 $1,400

CARTIER, 18 jewels, "Santos," octagonal, date
18k & s. steel C&B $800 $900 $1,100

CARTIER, 18 jewels, "Santos," lady's, date
18k & s. steel C&B $600 $700 $900

CARTIER, 25 jewels, chronog., European W. Co.
18k $60,000 $65,000 $80,000

CARTIER, 29 jewels, min. repeater, c. 1925
18k $100,000 $125,000 $175,000

CARTIER, 18 jewels, c. 1925
18k $3,500 $3,800 $4,500

CARTIER, 18 jewels, asymmetric, E. W. Co., c. 1928
18k $8,000 $8,500 $10,000

CARTIER, 18 J., oval maxi, C. 1968
18k $8,000 $9,000 $12,000

CARTIER, 18 jewels, by Le Coultre
18k $2,000 $2,300 $3,000

CARTIER, 18 J., bamboo style bezel, C.1970s
18k $4,000 $4,300 $5,000

NOTE: With original Cartier 18K Deployment clasp
ADD $500 to $800.

CARTIER, 18 J., large cut corner bezel, C.1970s
18k $3,000 $3,300 $4,000

CARTIER, 18 J., "Helm", single lug, C. 1950s
18k $15,000 $18,000 $25,000
platinum...........................$50,000 $55,000 $70,000

CARTIER, 18 J.,by E.W.CO., single lug, C. 1949
18k $10,000 $11,000 $14,000

CARTIER, 29 J., min. repeater, by Le Coultre, c. 1930
platinum...........................$80,000 $85,000 $100,000

CARTIER, 18 J., **triple date, moon ph.**, tear-drop lugs,
marked European Watch & clock Co., Ca.1945
s. steel $6,000 $6,500 $7,500
18K.. $8,000 $8,500 $10,000

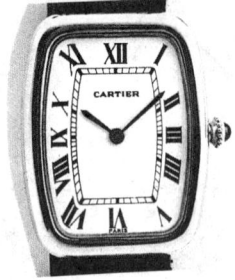

CARTIER, 18 J., **Ca. 1985**
18K.. $1,000 $1,200 $1,500

CARTIER, 18J, day of week & date chapter, by Le Coultre
14k $1,000 $1,200 $1,500

CARTIER, Quartz, 296 diamonds on bezel & 18k Band
18k $10,000 $11,000 $13,000

CARTIER, 18 J., lady's, back wind, E.W.CO., c.1940s
18k $2,000 $2,200 $3,000

CARTIER, 18J., tonneau, Ca. 1920
platinum $4,000 $4,500 $6,000

CARTIER, 18 J., lady's, E.W.Co., C.1949
14k(w) C&B $600 $650 $800

CERTINA, 17J., "NEWART", auto-wind, date, c.1965
14k $100 $110 $150

CENTRAL, 7J., cal.39, c.1937
gold filled $35 $40 $70

CHEVROLET, 6J., in form of car radiator, C. 1927
silver $400 $500 $700

CHOPARD, 18 J., 2 dial , 2 time zones, diam.bezel
18k C&B $1,500 $1,800 $2,500

CHOPARD, 18 J., skeletonized, diamond dial &hands
18k $2,000 $2,200 $3,000

CHOPARD, 28J., triple date moon ph., cal.900, c.1980
18k $900 $1,000 $1,200

CHOPARD, 20 J., RF#2113, c.1978
18k $300 $350 $400

CHOPARD, 17J., RF#2134, c.1978
18k $275 $325 $375

CLEBAR, 17 jewels, chronog., 2 reg., cal.2248, c.1952
gold filled $250 $275 $325
base metal $200 $225 $275

CLEBAR, 17 jewels, chronog., 3 reg. c.1950s
gold filled $275 $300 $350
s. steel $250 $275 $325

CLEBAR, 17J., chronog.,triple date, moon ph.
gold filled $550 $650 $800
s. steel $500 $600 $750

CLEBAR, 17 jewels, center lugs, chronog., c. 1938
s. steel $250 $300 $375

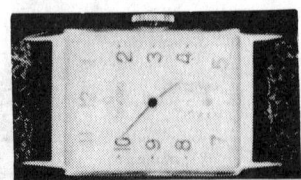

CONCORD, 17J., aux. sec., ca. 1947
14k $100 $110 $150

CONCORD, 17 jewels, center sec.
14k $100 $110 $150

CONCORD, 17 jewels, chronog. 2 reg., c.1940s
s. steel $200 $225 $300

CONDAL,15J. **hunter style**, flip top, C.1928
silver $400 $500 $650

CONTINENTAL, 17J., 3 diamond dial
14k $110 $125 $185

CORNAVIN, 17J., day date, c. 1960
gold filled $55 $65 $80

CORNAVIN, 17J., date, auto, RF#1243, C.1963
gold filled $30 $40 $55
s. steel $30 $40 $55

CORONET, 17J., chronog.
s. steel $175 $200 $250

CORTEBERT, 15 jewels, c. 1940s
gold filled $35 $45 $65

CORTEBERT, 15 jewels, c. 1941
gold filled $40 $50 $85

CORTEBERT, 17 J., "Sport," triple date, moon phase
18k $400 $500 $700
gold filled................................$150 $200 $300

CORTEBERT, 17 jewels, center sec.
s. steel $35 $45 $65

CORTEBERT, quartz, U.K. military, (CWC)
s. steel $75 $95 $135

CORTEBERT, (CWC), chronog., by Valjoux, c.1971
s. steel $200 $250 $325

CORUM, 17 J., twenty dollar gold piece 22K
22k (quartz, leather strap) ... $1,800 $2,000 $2,600
22k (M. wind, leather strap) $2,000 $2,200 $2,800
18k & 22k(manual wind) ... $2,500 $3,000 $3,800

CORUM, 24k gold ingot, 15 Grams, manual wind
24k $1,100 $1,300 $1,600

CORUM, 17 J., in form of Rolls-Royce car Grill, (large)
18k $2,800 $3,000 $3,500

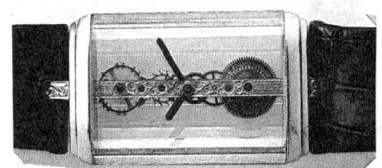

CORUM, 17 jewels, "Golden Bridge", in line train, recent
18k $2,000 $2,400 $3,000

CORUM, 17 jewels, rope style bezel
18k C&B............................$1,000 $1,200 $1,500

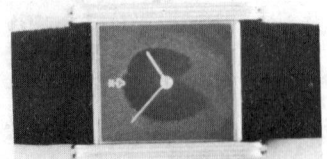

CORUM, 17 jewels, peacock feather dial
18k $700 $800 $1,000

CORUM, 21 jewels, "pave" diamond dial, c.1990
18k C&B $2,200 $2,500 $3,000

CORUM, 21 jewels, gold dial
18k $250 $300 $375

CRAWFORD, 17J., triple date, c. 1942
s. steel $95 $125 $175

CRAWFORD, 17J., chronog. engraved bezel
base metal $125 $150 $195

CRAWFORD, 17J., hooded lugs, c. 1940
14k $100 $110 $150

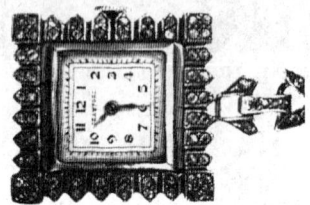

CRAWFORD, 17J., pendant watch
base metal $35 $40 $55

CROTON, 17 jewels, day date
gold filled $35 $40 $55

CROTON, 17 jewels, diamond bezel & dial
14k (w) $200 $250 $325

CROTON, 17 jewels, chronog., c. 1948
s. steel $175 $200 $275

CROTON, 17 jewels, chronog., c. 1946
s. steel $175 $200 $275

CROTON, 17 jewels, cal.630, c.1943
gold filled.................................. $35 $45 $65

CROTON, 17 jewels, Ca.1937
14k $100 $110 $150

CROTON, 17 jewels, fancy lugs
14k $200 $225 $275

CROTON, 7 jewels, **drivers** style, c.1938
gold filled.................................. $150 $175 $250

CROTON, 17 jewels, swinging lugs, cal.f3x, c.1940
14k $100 $125 $175

CROWN, 7J., luminous dial
base metal................................. $35 $45 $65

CROWN, 7J., luminous dial
gold filled $30 $40 $55

CRYSLER, 17J., aux. sec., ca. 1950s
gold filled $30 $40 $55

CYMA,7J.,enamel dial, wire lugs,(signal corp.USA),c.1928
silver $250 $300 $375

CYMA, 17 jewels, aux. sec.

18k	$175	$200	$250
14k	$100	$110	$150
gold filled	$30	$40	$55

CYMA, 15J., enamel dial, (Tacy W. Co.), c. 1925

silver	$50	$60	$75

CYMA, 15J., military style, cal.234, Ca.1945

s. steel	$100	$125	$165

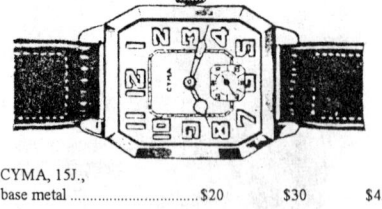

CYMA, 15J.,

base metal	$20	$30	$45

🕐 Some grades are not included. Their values can be determined by comparing with **similar** age, size, metal content, style, models and grades listed.

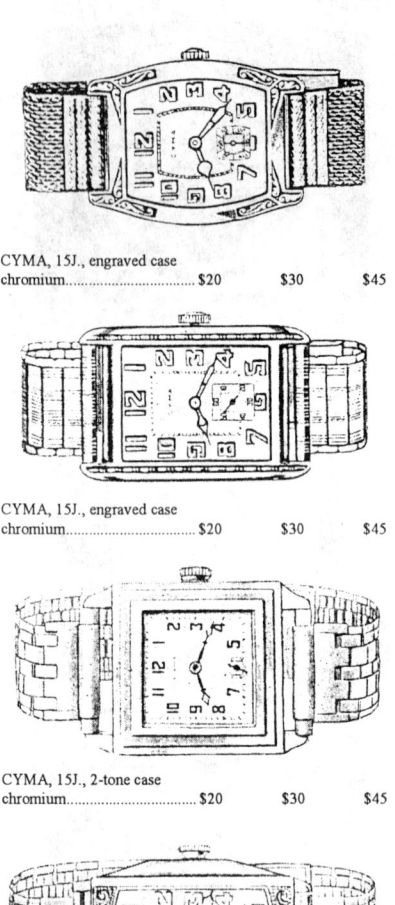

CYMA, 15J., engraved case

chromium	$20	$30	$45

CYMA, 15J., engraved case

chromium	$20	$30	$45

CYMA, 15J., 2-tone case

chromium	$20	$30	$45

CYMA, 15J., engraved case

chromium	$20	$30	$45

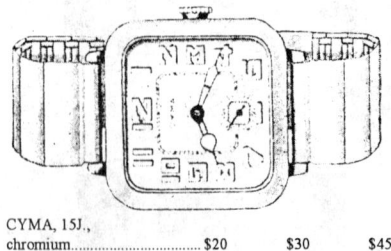

CYMA, 15J.,

chromium	$20	$30	$45

🕐 Pricing in this Guide are fair market price for **COMPLETE** watches which are reflected from the "**NAWCC**" National and regional shows.

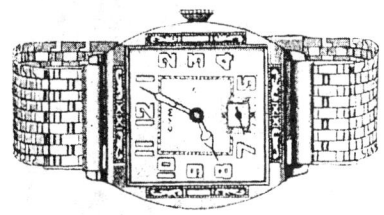

CYMA, 15J., engraved case
chromium..................................$20 $30 $45

DAU, 15J., wire lugs, c.1915
14k $60 $70 $90

DAYNITE, 7J., **8 day movement by Hebdomas**, Ca. 1920
s. steel $250 $300 $400

DELBANA, 17J., fancy hooded lugs, c.1951
14k $100 $110 $150

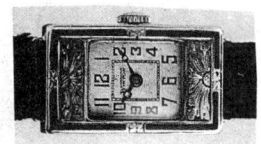

DIDISHEIM, 15J., "Winton", enamel art deco bezel, c.1927
14k(w).....................................$250 $275 $350

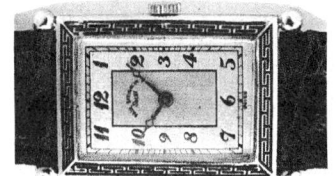

P. DITISHEIM, 16 J., "Solvil," fancy bezel, c. 1935
18k $300 $350 $425

P. DITISHEIM, 17 J., "Solvil," diamond dial, c. 1947
18K $275 $325 $400

P. DITISHEIM, 17 J., "Solvil," diamond dial, c. 1948
platinum..................................$600 $650 $800

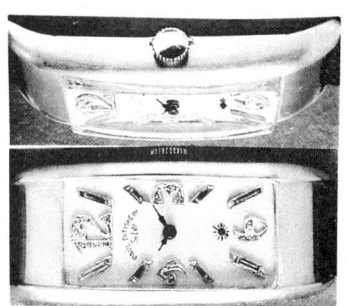

P. DITISHEIM, 17 J., "Solvil," curved, diamond dial
platinum..............................$1,000 $1,100 $1,400

P. DITISHEIM, 17 jewels, diamond dial, curved
platinum..............................$1,000 $1,100 $1,400

P. DITISHEIM, 17 J., baguette diamonds, fancy bezel
platinum $1,400 $1,500 $1,800

P. DITISHEIM, 17 jewels, hinged lugs, enameled bezel
14k $700 $750 $900

DOME, 25 jewels, triple dates, moon ph., auto wind
18k $400 $450 $550

DORIC, 17J., fancy lugs, two tone case, c.1935
gold filled..................................$60 $70 $85

DOXA, 17 jewels, aux sec.
gold filled...................................$30 $40 $55

DOXA, 17 jewels, center sec., fancy lugs
14k $125 $150 $200

DOXA, 17 jewels, chronog., fluted lugs
14k $350 $400 $475

DOXA, 17J., chronog., date, 3 reg., by Valjoux
gold filled $300 $350 $425
14k $500 $550 $650

DOXA, 17 jewels, chronog., triple dates, moon phase
14k $1,000 $1,200 $1,500

DOXA, 17 jewels, chronog., 2 reg., c. 1942
gold filled..............................$250 $300 $400

DOXA, 17 jewels, chronog., cal. 1220, c. 1940
gold filled..............................$175 $200 $275
s. steel $175 $200 $275

DOXA, 17 jewels, center sec
s. steel $35 $45 $65

DOXA, 17 jewels, center sec., c. 1949
gold filled.................................$40 $50 $70

DOXA, 17J., "Grafic" date,
14k $100 $125 $175

DOXA, 17J., cal. 1361, c.1948
14k $100 $125 $175

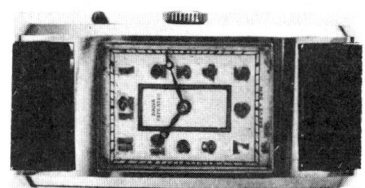

DRIVA, 15 jewels, repeater, repeats on gong, **repeater**
wound by bolt above hand, c. 1930
s. steel $3,500 $3,800 $4,500

DRIVA, 15 jewels, 5 min. **repeater**
14k $3,000 $3,300 $4,000

DRIVA, 17 jewels, double teardrop lugs, c.1945
14k $125 $150 $200

DUGENA, 17J., cal.985, c.1960
14k $100 $110 $150

DUNHILL, 17J., date, alarm by Le Coultre, c. 1965
s. steel $300 $350 $425

DUNHILL, 15J., by Bulwark W.Co., engraved bezel,c.1930
gold filled..................................$30 $40 $55

DUODIAL, 15 jewels, c. 1934
9k $900 $1,000 $1,200

EBEL, 21 jewels, chronog., self winding, perpetual cal.
18k $8,000 $9,000 $11,000

EBEL, 18 jewels, Ca.1959
18k $175 $200 $275

EBEL, 18 jewels, applied gold numbers, c. 1950
18k $250 $300 $375

EBEL, 17 jewels, slide open to wind
leather $200 $250 $325

EBEL, 17 jewels, chronog., 2 reg., enamel dial
s. steel $200 $250 $325

Wrist Watches listed in this section are priced at the collectable fair market **retail** level as **complete** watches having an original gold-filled case and stainless steel back, also with original dial, leather watch band, and the entire original movement in good working order with no repairs needed.

🕐 Some grades are not included. Their values can be determined by comparing with **similar** age, size, metal content, style, grades, or models such as **time only**, chronograph, repeater etc. listed.

EBEL, 17 jewels, chronog., c. 1955
14k $350 $400 $500
gold filled..............................$200 $250 $325

EBEL, 17 jewels, chronog., "pulsation", c. 1943
s. steel $250 $275 $350

EBEL, 17 jewels, chronog., 3 reg., c. 1941
14k $500 $550 $650
s. steel $300 $350 $425

EBEL, 17J., "sport", c.1949
gold filled..............................$100 $125 $175

EBEL, 17J., cal.119, auto-wind, c.1950
s. steel $100 $125 $175

EBEL, 17J., cal.93, center sec., c.1950
18k $200 $225 $300

EBEL, 17J., lady's watch, c.1948
14k C&B................................$200 $225 $300

EBERHARD, 18 jewels, split sec. chronog., 3 reg.
18k $5,500 $6,000 $7,500

🕐 Pricing in this Guide are fair market price for **COMPLETE** watches which are reflected from the "**NAWCC**" National and regional shows.

🕐 Some grades are not included. Their values can be determined by comparing with **similar** age, size, metal content, style, grades, or models such as **time only**, chronograph, repeater etc. listed.

EBERHARD, 17 J., tele-tachymeter, enamel dial, c. 1930
18k $1,200 $1,300 $1,600

EBERHARD, 17J., water proof, auto wind, triple date, moon phases
18k rose $1,800 $2,000 $2,400

EBERHARD, 17 jewels, chronog., 2 reg.
18k $1,000 $1,100 $1,400

EKEGREN, 18 jewels, **jumping hr.**, c. 1920
platinum...............................$6,000 $7,000 $9,000
18k $4,000 $5,000 $7,000

EBERHARD, 17 J., chronog., center lugs, 1 button, enamel dial
s. steel ....$550 $650   .$800

ELECTRA W. Co., 17J, chronog., 1 button, hinged back, enamel dial
silver $500 $600 $800

EBERHARD, 17 J., wire lugs, enamel dial, c.1928
early waterproof case
silver $400 $450 $550

ELECTRA W. Co., 17J, chronog., 1 button, hinged back, wire lugs, enamel dial
silver $600 $700 $900

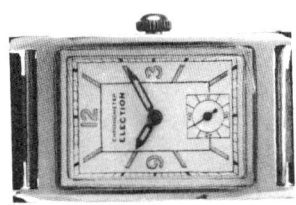

ELECTION, 17J., cal. 4019, c.1940
s. steel $60 $65 $80

LORD ELGIN, 21J., extended lugs, Ca.1955
14k $125 $150 $200

LORD ELGIN, 21J., extended lugs,
gold filled............................... $100 $125 $175

LORD ELGIN, 21J., hooded bezel, Ca. 1953
14K... $125 $150 $200

ELGIN, 19J., fancy bezel, c.1950s
gold filled............................... $150 $175 $225

🕐 Some grades are not included. Their values can be
determined by comparing with **similar** age, size, metal
content, style, grades, or models such as **time only**,
chronograph, repeater etc. listed.

ELGIN, 17J., **hidden lugs, 7 diamonds & 8 baguettes**
14K $300 $350 $550

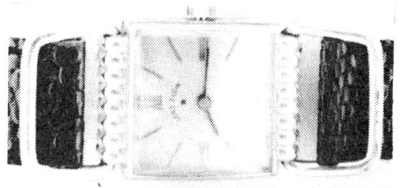

LORD ELGIN, 21J., hinged lugs
gold filled $100 $125 $200

ELGIN, 15-17J., hooded lugs, gold jewel settings, Ca. 1925
gold filled $100 $125 $175
14k(w).................................... $300 $350 $450

LORD ELGIN, 21J., Ca. 1948
14K $100 $125 $175

LORD ELGIN, 21J., **3 diamonds**, cal.626, c.1950
14k(w).................................... $150 $175 $225

ELGIN, 21J., cal.626, Ca.1950's
14k $150 $175 $225

ELGIN, 17J., stepped hooded lugs, c.1925
gold filled $75 $85 $125

ELGIN, 17J., stepped case, Ca. 1935
gold filled..................................$55 $65 $85

ELGIN, 17J., side lugs, Ca. 1958
gold filled...............................$100 $125 $175

ELGIN, 15J., cal. 554, Ca. 1950's
gold filled..................................$45 $55 $75

ELGIN, 15J., stepped case,
gold filled $35 $45 $75

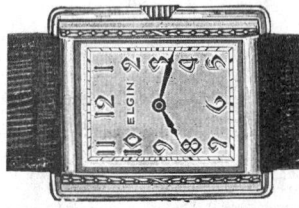

ELGIN, 15J., spur lugs, embossed dial, Ca.1929
gold filled..................................$45 $55 $75

ELGIN, 21J., Lord Elgin, Ca. 1945
14k $100 $125 $200

ELGIN, 15J., Crown Guard, Ca.1929
gold filled..................................$35 $45 $75

ELGIN, 17J., **Dollar markers,** Ca. 1955
gold filled $35 $45 $75

ELGIN, 19J., cal. 626, Ca. 1946
14k $100 $125 $200

ELGIN, 7J., tear drop lugs,
gold filled $35 $45 $75

LORD ELGIN, 21J., **11 diamonds,** Ca. 1946
14K $200 $225 $300

LORD ELGIN, 21J.,
gold filled $35 $45 $75

ELGIN, 15J., Legionnaire, Ca. 1929
gold filled $30 $40 $65

ELGIN, engraved case, Ca. 1924
14k $100 $125 $175

LORD ELGIN, 21J., cal.625, c.1950
14k $100 $125 $200

LORD ELGIN, 21J., cal. 713, GJS, c.1958
14k $125 $150 $200

ELGIN, 17J., DeLux, Ca. 1955
gold filled $50 $60 $80

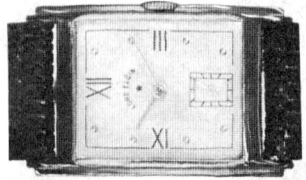

LORD ELGIN, 21J., cal.559, c.1942
gold filled $50 $60 $90

Wrist Watches listed in this section are priced at the collectable fair market **retail** level as **complete** watches having an original gold-filled case and stainless steel back, also with original dial, leather watch band, and the entire original movement in good working order with no repairs needed.

LORD ELGIN, 21J., GJS, c. 1936
14k $100 $125 $200

LORD ELGIN, 21J., GJS, cal.626, c.1940
14k $100 $125 $200

ELGIN, 17J., **Adonis**, engraved, Ca. 1929
gold filled...................................$75 $85 $125

ELGIN, 17J., "Dura Power" mainspring LOGO,
gold plate $30 $40 $60

ELGIN, 7J., **hinged case**, engraved case, c.1920s
gold filled...................................$75 $95 $150

ELGIN,15J., fancy bezel, G#554
gold filled $50 $60 $90

ELGIN, 17 jewels, raised numbers
14k $100 $125 $175

LORD ELGIN, 21 jewels, curved, raised numbers
14k $125 $150 $200

ELGIN, 17 jewels, embossed dial
14k $100 $125 $175

LORD ELGIN, 21 jewels, curved
gold filled $55 $65 $85

ELGIN, 17 jewels, curved, "Streamlined"
gold filled $75 $100 $150

🕐 Some grades are not included. Their values can be determined by comparing with **similar** age, size, metal content, style, grades, or models such as **time only**, chronograph, repeater etc. listed.

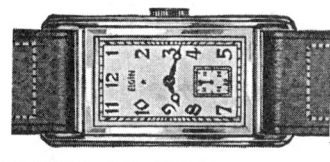

ELGIN, 17 jewels, raised numbers
gold filled.................................$35 $45 $75

ELGIN, 15 jewels, curved, fancy bezel
gold filled.................................$75 $100 $150

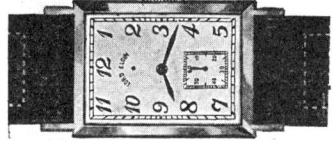

LORD ELGIN, 21 jewels, curved
platinum...............................$300 $350 $500

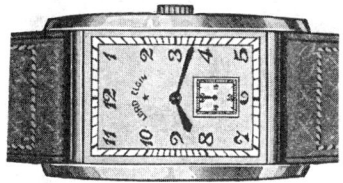

LORD ELGIN, 21 jewels, curved
14k $175 $200 $250

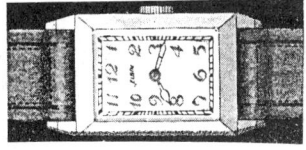

ELGIN, 15 jewels, Ca. 1929
Sterling...................................$100 $125 $175

ELGIN, 17 jewels, curved
gold filled.................................$30 $40 $60

Wrist Watches listed in this section are priced at the collectable
fair market **retail** level as **complete** watches having an original
gold-filled case and stainless steel back, also with original dial,
leather watch band, and the entire original movement in good
working order with no repairs needed.

ELGIN, 15 jewels, drivers style
gold filled $150 $175 $250

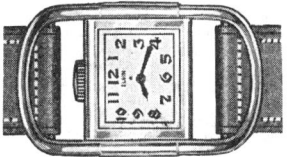

ELGIN, 17 jewels, "Ristflo"
gold filled $125 $150 $225

ELGIN, 17 jewels
gold filled $75 $85 $100

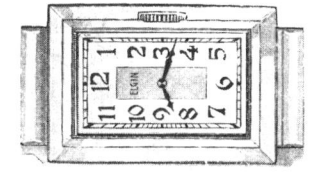

ELGIN, 17 jewels, hidden lugs
gold filled $30 $40 $60

ELGIN, 17 jewels, embossed dial, thin model
gold filled $60 $70 $90

🕐 Pricing in this Guide are fair market price for **COMPLETE**
watches which are reflected from the "**NAWCC**" National and
regional shows.

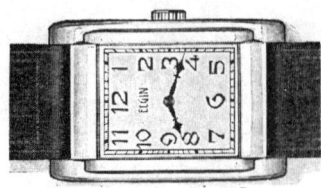

ELGIN, 17 jewels, curved, thin model
gold filled.................................$50 $60 $90

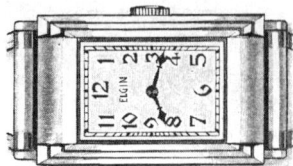

ELGIN, 17 jewels, stepped case
gold filled.................................$50 $60 $90

ELGIN, 17J., center sec., cal.11553, c.1928
gold filled.................................$75 $100 $150

ELGIN, 15 jewels, "William Osler" recess crown
gold filled.................................$75 $100 $150

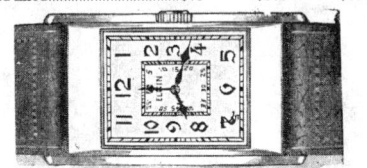

ELGIN, 7 jewels, center sec., recess crown
gold filled.................................$75 $100 $150

ELGIN, 17J., engraved case, c.1928
gold filled.................................$40 $50 $65

ELGIN, 15J., 2 tone case, recessed crown
gold filled.................................$75 $100 $150

ELGIN, 7-15J., engraved case, c. 1928
14K $100 $125 $175
gold filled $35 $45 $65

ELGIN, 15J., engraved **Mermaid** design case, c.1928
gold filled $200 $275 $350

ELGIN, 15J., engraved case, c. 1928
gold filled $55 $65 $100

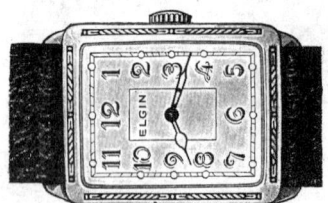

ELGIN, 15J., curved engraved case, c. 1928
gold filled $50 $60 $95

ELGIN, 17J., cal. 555, Ca. 1950
gold filled...................................$55 $65 $80

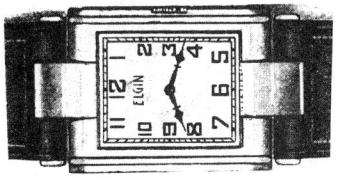

ELGIN, 15 jewels, center lugs
gold filled...............................$100 $125 $175

ELGIN, 7 jewels, fancy bezel
s. steel $45 $55 $95

ELGIN, 7 jewels, fancy bezel
gold filled...................................$50 $60 $125

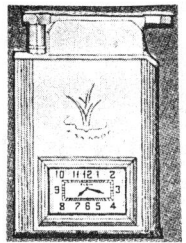

ELGIN, 15J.,combination lighter and Elgin Watch
Sterling....................................$200 $225 $300

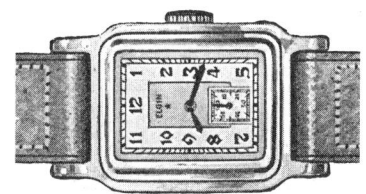

ELGIN, 17 jewels, "Crusade"
gold filled $75 $100 $150

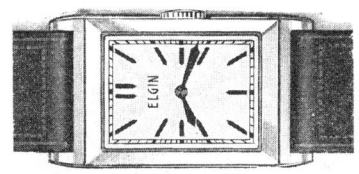

ELGIN, 7 jewels
gold filled $30 $40 $65

ELGIN, 7 jewels, stepped bezel
s. steel $50 $60 $95

ELGIN, 15J., wire lugs, stem at "12", c.1920s
silver $100 $125 $175

ELGIN, 7J., **"Recased"**, left hand wind c.1920s
base metal $30 $40 $60

ELGIN, 15J., engraved case, c.1925
gold filled..................................$55 $65 $95

LORD ELGIN, 21J., stepped case, c.1930
gold filled..................................$65 $75 $125

LORD ELGIN, 21J., stepped case, c.1930
gold filled..................................$65 $75 $125

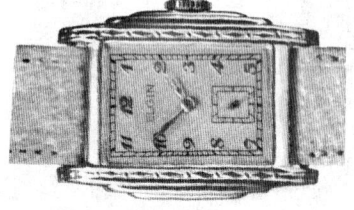

ELGIN, 7J., stepped case, c.1925
gold filled..................................$60 $75 $125

ELGIN, 17J., **BMW** logo, Ca.1955
gold filled..................................$65 $75 $125

LORD ELGIN, 21J., GJS, c.1937
14k...$125 $150 $200

ELGIN, 17J., stepped case, c.1930
gold filled $45 $55 $95

ELGIN, 17J., curved, stepped case, c.1927
gold filled $30 $40 $65

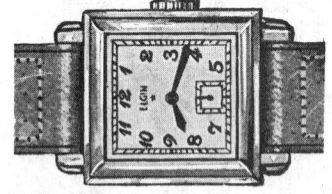

ELGIN, 17 jewels, raised numbers
gold filled $30 $40 $65

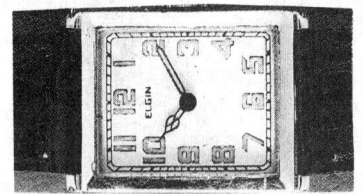

ELGIN, 17 jewels, c. 1927
14k $100 $125 $175

⊕ Some grades are not included. Their values can be determined by comparing with **similar** age, size, metal content,
style, models and grades listed.

LORD ELGIN, 21 jewels, diamond dial
14k (w)......................................$150 $200 $275

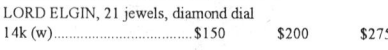

ELGIN, 19 jewels, c. 1947
14k $100 $125 $195
gold filled.................................$55 $65 $90

LORD ELGIN, 21 jewels, diamond dial
14k (w)......................................$150 $175 $250

LORD ELGIN, 21 jewels, aux. sec., fancy lugs
14k $150 $175 $225

LORD ELGIN, 21J., cal.670, c.1948
14k $150 $175 $225

Wrist Watches listed in this section are priced at the collectable fair market **retail** level as **complete** watches having an original gold-filled case and stainless steel back, also with original dial, leather watch band, and the entire original movement in good working order with no repairs needed.

LORD ELGIN, 21 jewels, flared case
14k $150 $175 $225

ELGIN, 19 jewels, flared case, fancy lugs
14k $200 $250 $300

ELGIN, 7J., cushion case, c.1930
gold filled $75 $85 $100

ELGIN, 7-15J., cushion case, c.1930
chromium..................................$30 $40 $65

ELGIN, 7-15J., solid lugs, Ca. 1925
s. steel $70 $80 $95

ELGIN, 15J., pierced shield, wire lugs, c.1918
silver $300 $350 $450

ELGIN, 15J., U.S.GOV'T grade II, c.1960s
s. steel $75 $85 $100

ELGIN, 15J., pierced shield, c.1918
silver $300 $350 $450

ELGIN, 15J., military style, 24 hr. dial, c.1942
s. steel $85 $95 $125

ELGIN, 15J., canteen style case, wire lugs, c.1919
nickel..$400 $450 $525

ELGIN, 15J., military style, cal.539, c.1940
s. steel $75 $85 $100

ELGIN, 15 jewels, ''Official Boy Scout'' model
s. steel $125 $150 $200

ELGIN, 16J., canteen style case, U.S.N.234C, c.1930s
s. steel $475 $500 $600

🕐 Some grades are not included. Their values can be
determined by comparing with **similar** age, size, metal
content, style, grades, or models such as **time only**,
chronograph, repeater etc. listed.

ELGIN, 7 jewels, "Official Boy Scout" model
s. steel $60 $75 $100

ELGIN, 15 jewels, enamel dial, wire lugs, c. 1915
silver $95 $125 $175

ELGIN, 15 jewels, enamel dial, wire lugs, c. 1915
silver $100 $125 $175

ELGIN, 15 jewels, center lugs
gold filled................................$100 $125 $175

ELGIN, 15 jewels, center lugs, c. 1922
silver $100 $125 $175

ELGIN, 15J., case by **Rolland Fischer,** c. 1928
silver $250 $300 $375

ELGIN, 17J., center sec., c.1950
base metal $30 $40 $65

ELGIN, 21 jewels, "Black Knight"
14k $150 $175 $225

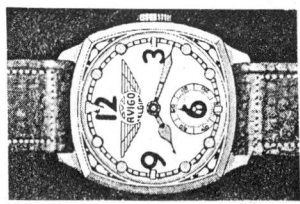

ELGIN, 7 jewels, "Avigo ", Ca. 1929
base metal $55 $65 $85

Wrist Watches listed in this section are priced at the collectable
fair market **retail** level as **complete** watches having an original
gold-filled case and stainless steel back, also with original dial,
leather watch band, and the entire original movement in good
working order with no repairs needed.

ELGIN, 21J., center sec., wire lugs, cal. 680, c.1952
gold filled.................................$30　　$40　　$65

ELGIN, 30J., auto-wind, grade 760
gold filled ....$50　　$65　　$95

ELGIN, 17 jewels, **Alarm**, Ca. 1960
gold filled...............................$100　　$125　　$175

ELGIN, 19J.,cal.681 , c.1959
gold filled ....$30　　$40　　$65

ELGIN, 21J., water-proof, c.1952
s. steel ....$30　　$40　　$65

LORD ELGIN, 21J., **enamel bezel**, cal.688, c.1948
gold filled ....$75　　$100　　$150

ELGIN, 23 J., "B. W. Raymond," R.R. approved
14k ....$300　　$350　　$425
gold filled ....$150　　$175　　$225
s. steel ....$125　　$150　　$200

🕐 Some grades are not included. Their values can be
determined by comparing with **similar** age, size, metal
content, style, grades, or models such as **time only**,
chronograph, repeater etc. listed.

LORD ELGIN, 21J., **shockmaster,** aux. sec., ca. 1955
14K...$100　　$125　　$175

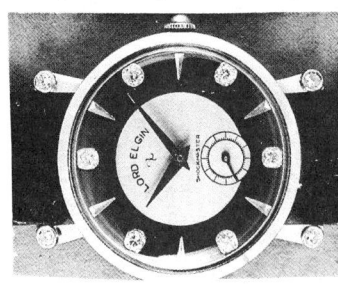

LORD ELGIN, 21 jewels, diamond dial & lugs, c. 1958
14k (w)....................................$225 $250 $300

LORD ELGIN, 21 jewels, mystery dial, c. 1957
14k (w)....................................$150 $200 $275

LORD ELGIN, 21J., direct reading, cal#719, C.1957
gold filled................................$250 $300 $375

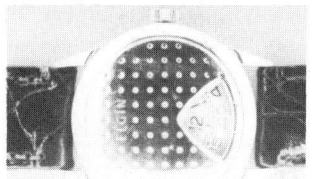

ELGIN, 17 J., in form of golf ball, rotating hr. & min.
gold filled................................$300 $350 $450

LORD ELGIN, 21 jewels, applied numbers, c. 1946
14k $125 $150 $225

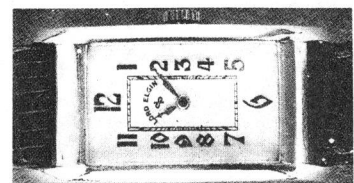

LORD ELGIN, 21 jewels, curved, applied numbers
14k $150 $175 $250

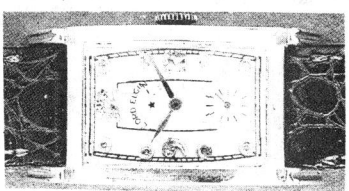

LORD ELGIN, 21 jewels, diamond dial, faceted crystal
14k $150 $175 $250

ELGIN, 17 jewels, hinged back
14k (w) $125 $150 $225

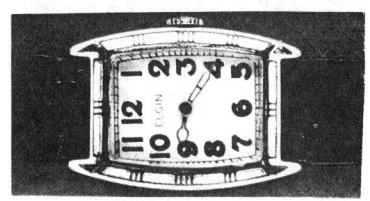

ELGIN, 17 jewels, enamel bezel, Ca. 1930
14k (w) $350 $400 $500

ELGIN, 15 jewels, Art Deco bezel, c. 1935
gold filled $85 $100 $175

🕐 Some grades are not included. Their values can be determined by comparing with **similar** age, size, metal content, style, grades, or models such as **time only**, chronograph, repeater etc. listed.

ELGIN, 15 jewels, 2 tone, c. 1930
gold filled..................................$75 $85 $125

ELGIN, 7 jewels, engraved bezel
s. steel $30 $40 $65

ELGIN, 15 jewels, enamel bezel, c. 1920
14k (w)....................................$450 $500 $600

ELGIN, 17 jewels, aux. sec., curved
gold filled $50 $60 $75

ELGIN, 17 jewels, raised numbers
gold filled..................................$75 $100 $150

ELGIN, 17 jewels, curved
gold filled $50 $60 $75

ELGIN, 17 jewels, curved
gold filled $50 $60 $75

ELGIN, 21 jewels, enamel bezel, 2 tone, c. 1931
14k $400 $450 $550
gold filled...............................$150 $175 $250

ELGIN, 21 jewels, blue enamel bezel, c. 1920
14k(yellow gold)...................$800 $900 $1,100

ELGIN, 7 jewels, fancy bezel
s. steel $30 $40 $65

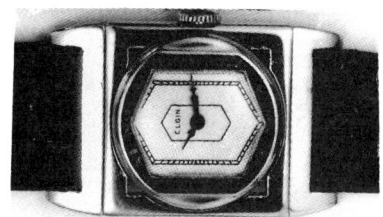

ELGIN, 21 jewels, enamel bezel
18k $1,000 $1,200 $1,500

LORD ELGIN, 21J, model 670, large lugs, anniversary of
50,000,000th watch (small run of watches),
gold plated movement, Ca. 1951
18k $1,000 $1,200 $1,500

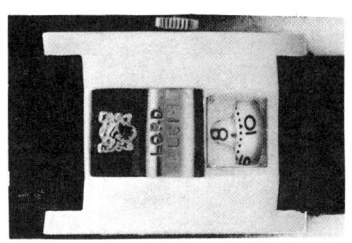

LORD ELGIN, 21 jewels, wandering hr. & min., curved
gold filled...............................$325 $400 $500

ELGIN, 17 jewels, double dial
gold filled...............................$400 $450 $550

LORD ELGIN, 21 jewels, hooded lugs, c. 1952
14k $200 $225 $325

LORD ELGIN, 21 jewels, curved, c. 1957
14k $200 $250 $325

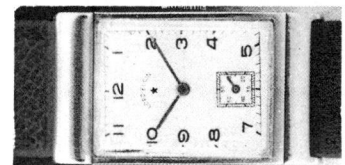

LORD ELGIN, 21 jewels, hooded lugs, c. 1950s
14k $150 $175 $250

ELGIN, 15 jewels, waterproof
s. steel $30 $40 $65

ELGIN, 15 jewels, center sec.
gold filled $30 $40 $65

ELGIN, 7 jewels, aux. sec.
gold filled $30 $40 $65

LORD ELGIN, 21 jewels, stepped case
18k $275 $300 $350

LORD ELGIN, 21 jewels, stepped case, curved
14k $150 $175 $225

ELGIN, 17 jewels, stepped case
14k $125 $150 $200

LORD ELGIN, 21 jewels, curved
gold filled................................$70 $80 $125

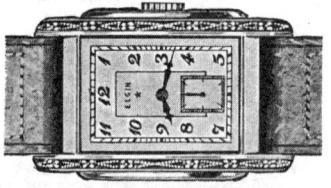

ELGIN, 17 jewels, curved, fancy bezel
gold filled................................$70 $80 $125

ELGIN, 17 jewels, curved, stepped case
gold filled................................$80 $90 $135

ELGIN, 17 jewels, curved, stepped case
gold filled................................$55 $65 $95

ELGIN, 17 jewels, curved
gold filled $50 $60 $90

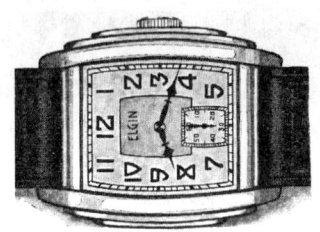

ELGIN, 19 jewels, stepped case
gold filled $75 $85 $125

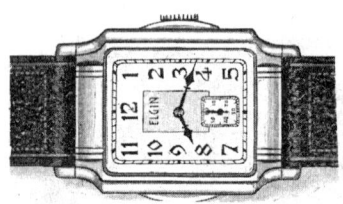

ELGIN, 15 jewels
gold filled $30 $40 $65

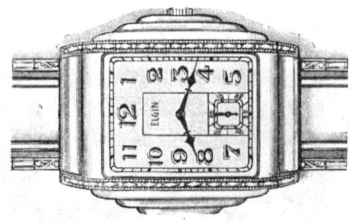

ELGIN, 7 jewels, fancy bezel
s. steel $30 $40 $65

ELGIN, 7 jewels, fancy bezel
gold filled $30 $40 $65

LORD ELGIN, 21 jewels, curved, c. 1938
14k $150 $175 $225

ELGIN, 15 jewels, fancy bezel
gold filled..................................$55 $65 $95

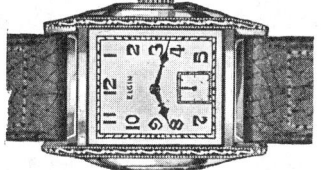

ELGIN, 21 jewels, curved
gold filled...................................$35 $45 $75

LORD ELGIN, 21 jewels, raised numbers
14k $125 $150 $200

LORD ELGIN, 21 jewels, curved
14k $125 $150 $200

LORD ELGIN, 21 jewels, curved
14k $150 $175 $225

LORD ELGIN, 21 jewels, aux. sec.
gold filled $55 $65 $95

LORD ELGIN, 21 jewels, curved
14k $150 $175 $225

ELGIN, 17 jewels, curved
gold filled $50 $60 $95

ELGIN, 17 Jewels, raised numbers
14k $150 $175 $225

LORD ELGIN, 15jewels, **electric**, 6 adj., Ca. 1962, (sold for
$89.50, July of 1962), grade 725, in **good running order**
gold filled $200 $250 $325

**Elgin pioneering effort in electric watches
started in 1955.**

LORD ELGIN, 15 jewels, **electric**, c. 1962
(back–set)
s. steel $200 $250 $325

LORD ELGIN, 15 jewels, **electric**, c.1962
(grade 725, 6 adj.)
gold filled................................$200 $250 $325

ELGIN, 17 Jewels, Lady Elgin, flared case, cal. 650, c.1950
14k $100 $125 $175

ELGIN, 15 Jewels, art deco, c.1925
gold filled................................$40 $50 $75

ELGIN, 15 Jewels, art deco, c.1928
14k $90 $125 $150

ELGIN, 17 Jewels, art deco, c.1928
18k(w)...................................$125 $150 $200

ELGIN, 15 jewels, art deco, Ca. 1929
14K(W) $100 $125 $175

ELGIN, 15 jewels, art deco, Ca. 1928
gold filled................................$40 $50 $75

ELGIN, 15 jewels, art deco, Ca. 1928
gold filled................................$25 $30 $45

ELGIN, 15 jewels, art deco, Ca. 1928
gold filled................................$25 $30 $45

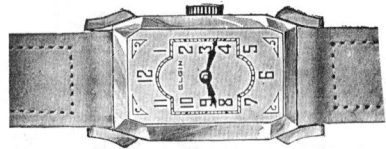

ELGIN, 15 jewels, sports model, Ca. 1928
14k...$75 $85 $125

ELGIN, 17J., 20 diamonds, art deco, Ca. 1928
18k...$225 $275 $350

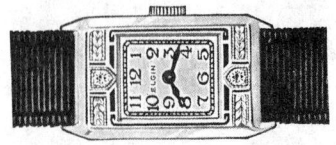

ELGIN, 15 jewels, 2 diamonds, art deco, Ca. 1928
gold filled................................$75 $85 $125

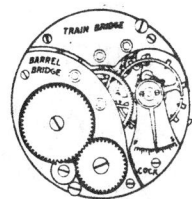   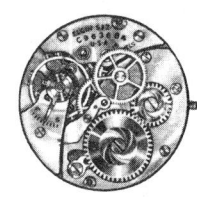

Model 3, 3-0 size, three-quarter plate, open face, pendant set, first serial number 18,179,001, Grade 414, March, 1915.

Model 1, 5-0 size, three-quarter plate, hunting, pendant set, first serial number 14,699,001, Grade 380, Feb., 1910.

Model 2, 5-0 size, three-quarter plate, open face, pendant set, first serial number 17,890,001, Grade 399, Feb., 1914.

Model 2, 8-0 size, Grade 532, 539, sweep second.

 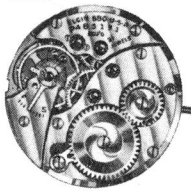  

Model 7, 8-0 size, Grades 554, 555,

Model 20, 8-0 size, Grades 681, 682.

Model 1, 10-0 size, three-quarter plate, open face

Model 2, 15-0 size, Grades 623, 624, 626.

   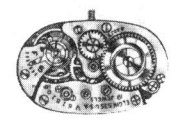

15-0 Size, movement, Grades 670, 672, 673.

15-0 size, movement. Grade 674.

15-0 size, movement, Grades 557, 558, 559.

Model 2, 21-0 size, Grade 541, 533, 535.

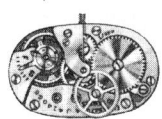   

Model 3, 21-0 size, Grade 547, sweep second.

Model 4, 21-0 size, Grades 617, 617L, 619, 619L.

Model 9, 21-0 size, Grades 650, 651.

Model 9, 21-0 size, Grades 655, 656.

 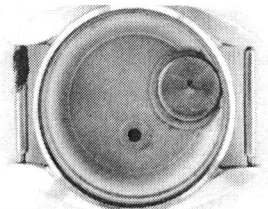

GRADE 725, 15 jewels,"electric" model movement

"ELECTRIC", case showing back—set

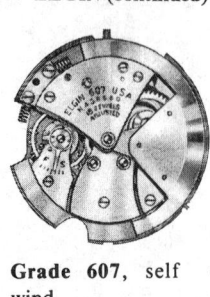  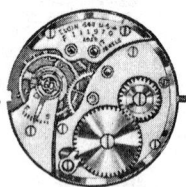 

Grade 607, self wind.

Grade 630, sweep second.

Grade 641, 642

Grade 643, self wind.

Grades 644, 645, self wind.

Grade 647, sweep second.

Grade 661

Grade 666, sweep second.

  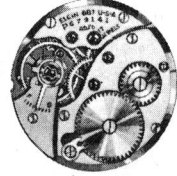 

Grade 668, sweep second.

Grade 685

Grade 687

Grade 700

 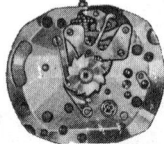 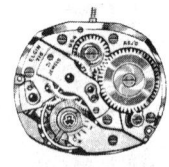

GRADE 710 & 719
719 = DIRECT READ
TRAIN SIDE

719 = DIAL SIDE
OF MOVEMENT

Grade 716

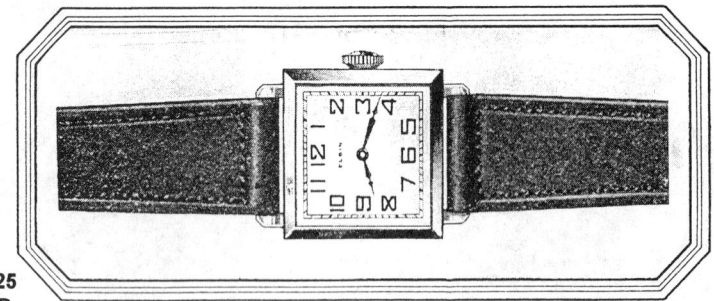

1925
AD

Elgin strap watches for men, in gold and gold-filled cases of yellow, white or green; also silver and nickel. Prices ranging from $20 to $75.

ELOGA, triple calendar,
base metal $50 $65 $95

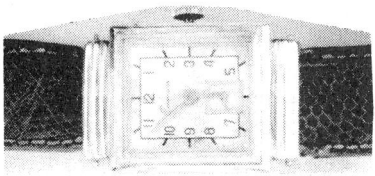

EMERSON, 17J., hooded lugs,
gold filled..................................$50 $60 $80

ENICAR, 17 jewels, center sec.
18k $150 $175 $225

ENICAR, 17J., chronograph, 2 reg. Ca. 1955
s. steel $175 $225 $300

ENICAR, 17 jewels, center sec.
s. steel.......................................$30 $40 $60

ENICAR, 17 jewels, triple date, moon phase
gold filled..............................$200 $250 $325

ENICAR, 15 jewels, egg shaped with compass, c. 1918
silver...$375 $425 $500

ENICAR, 17J., autow., date, 24 hour dial, C.1970
s. steel.......................................$75 $85 $125

ESKA, 17J.,chronog., triple date, moon phase
14k.......................................$1,400 $1,500 $1,800

ESKA, 17 jewels, chronog., 2 reg., C. 1950s
s. steel $150 $175 $225

ESKA, 17 jewels, chronog., 2 reg., c. 1940
s. steel $1,200 $1,300 $1,600

ESKA, 17 jewels, multi-colored enamel dial
18k $2,000 $2,300 $2,700

ETERNA, quartz, date, by ETA, cal#954, C.1975
s. steel $30 $40 $60

🕐 Pricing in this Guide are fair market price for COM-
PLETE watches which are reflected from the "**NAWCC**" National and regional shows.

ETERNA, 19 jewels, day-date-month
18k $300 $325 $400

ETERNA, 17 jewels, chronog., triple date, 3 reg.
s.steel $275 $300 $350
18k $600 $700 $850

ETERNA, 21 jewels, date, cal. 14390, c.1960
18k $150 $200 $275

ETERNA, 19 jewels, c.1944
14k $100 $120 $160

ETERNA, 16 jewels, aux. sec., c.1945
gold filled..................................$55 $65 $85

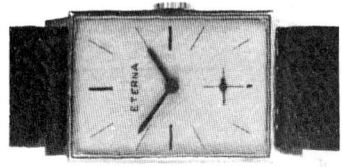

ETERNA, 19 jewels, c.1938
gold filled..................................$50 $60 $80

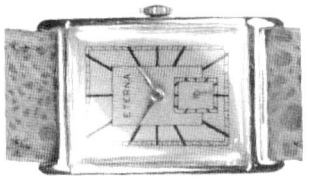

ETERNA, 17 jewels, gold jewel settings, c.1935
14k $100 $125 $175

EVANS, 17 jewels, rhinestones on bezel, c. 1948
gold plate $35 $45 $65

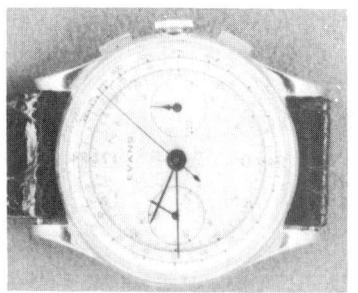

EVANS, 17 jewels, chronog., 2 reg., c. 1940
18k $350 $400 $500

EXACTUS, 17 J., chronog.,triple-date, moon ph.
s. steel.......................................$500 $550 $700

EXCELSIOR, 17 jewels, chronog., 2 reg.
14k...$375 $425 $500
gold filled..............................$150 $175 $225

EXCELSIOR, 17 jewels, chronog.
gold filled...............................$200 $225 $275
s. steel.....................................$175 $200 $250

EXCELSIOR PARK, 17 jewels, chronog.
s. steel......................................$200 $225 $275

FAIRFAX, 6J, engraved case, c.1929
base metal $30 $35 $55

FAIRFAX, 6J, engraved case, c.1929
base metal $30 $35 $55

FAIRFAX, 6J, butler finish case, c.1929
base metal $30 $35 $55

FAITH, 17J, **flip top case** HC style, by Hyde Park, c.1950
gold filled..............................$200 $250 $325

FAVRE LEUBA,17J., triple date, cal.Valj.89, c.1948
s. steel $125 $150 $200

⊕ Some grades are not included. Their values can be determined by comparing with **similar** age, size, metal content,
style, grades, or models such as **time only**, chronograph,
repeater etc. listed.

FAVRE LEUBA,17J., "Bivouac", altimeter with aneroid cap-
sule transmitting variations of atmospheric pressure to the baro-
metric mechanism, revolving bezel, Ca. 1968.
s. steel....................................$250 $300 $375

FAVRE LEUBA,17J., "Bathy 50", depth reading to about 165
feet, waterproof to 470 feet, Ca. 1968
s. steel....................................$250 $300 $375

FERRARI, quartz, chronog., c.1988
base metal...............................$200 $250 $325

FELCA, 17 jewels, auto wind
gold filled................................$30 $35 $55
14k...$100 $125 $175
18k...$175 $200 $250

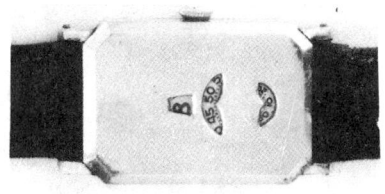

FONTAINEMELON, S. A., 17 J., gold train, digital
14k $1,500 $1,700 $2,000

FRAMONT, 17J, timer, date, cal. 290, c.1970
s. steel $75 $100 $150

FREY, 25J., rotating outside chapter, c.1970
s. steel $45 $55 $75

FREY, 17J., GJS, c.1970
s. steel $30 $35 $55

Wrist Watches listed in this section are priced at the collectable
fair market **retail** level as **complete** watches having an original
gold-filled case and stainless steel back, also with original dial,
leather watch band, and the entire original movement in good
working order with no repairs needed.

FREY, 15J., engraved case, c.1933
base metal.................................$30 $35 $55

FREY, 15J., engraved stepped case, c.1933
base metal.................................$30 $35 $55

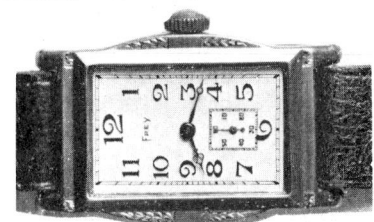

FREY, 15J., engraved case, c.1933
base metal.................................$30 $35 $55

FRIEDLI, 17 jewels, auto wind, center sec.
gold filled.................................$30 $35 $55
18k...$175 $200 $275

FRODSHAM, 17J., Ca. 1935
18k(w) $250 $300 $375

GALLET, 15 jewels, wire lugs, Ca. 1925
silver $75 $100 $150

GALLET, 15 jewels, waterproof, auto wind
s. steel $30 $35 $55

GALLET, 17 jewels, chronog., single button, c. 1950
s. steel $300 $350 $425

GALLET, 17J., chronog., by Racine, US air force, c. 1978
s. steel $150 $200 $275

GALLET, 17 jewels, chronog., 3 reg., c. 1945
s. steel.....................................$250 $300 $375

GALLET, 17 jewels, chronog., 3 reg., c. 1942
gold filled...............................$300 $350 $425

GALLET, 17J., chronog., 2 reg.,single button, C.1925,
silver"small size" $800 $900 $1,200

GALLET, 17J., chronog., 3 reg.,triple date, moon ph.
18k...$2,000 $2,300 $3,000

Pricing in this Guide are fair market price for **COM-PLETE** watches which are reflected from the "<u>NAWCC</u>" National and regional shows.

GALLET, 17J., chronog., 3 reg.,triple date,
14k $700 $800 $1,000
s. steel $350 $400 $475

GALLET, 17 jewels, chronog., 3 reg., c. 1955
s. steel $275 $325 $400

GALLET, 17 jewels, day-date-month, c. 1941
gold filled................................$350 $450 $600

GALLET, 17 jewels, chronog., 2 reg.
14k $325 $400 $525
s. steel $175 $200 $275

GALLET, 17 jewels, chronog., mid size, c. 1940
s. steel $250 $300 $375

GALLET, 17J., chronog., flying officer, cal.149, c. 1958
s. steel $350 $400 $500

GALLET, 17 jewels, chronog., waterproof
s. steel $300 $350 $425

GALLET, 17 jewels, chronog., 2 reg.
s. steel $200 $225 $300

Some grades are not included. Their values can be determined by comparing with **similar** age, size, metal content, style, grades, or models such as **time only**, chronograph, repeater etc. listed.

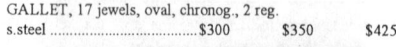

GALLET, 17 jewels, oval, chronog., 2 reg.
s.steel $300 $350 $425

GALLET, 17 jewels, chronog., 2 reg.
gold filled..............................$200 $225 $275

GALLET, 17 jewels, chronog., 2 reg.
s. steel $175 $200 $250

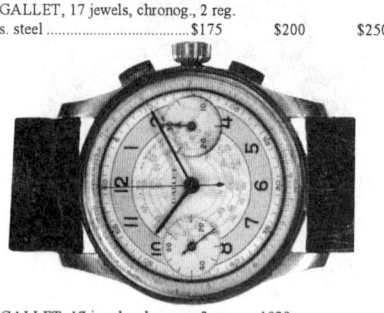

GALLET, 17 jewels, chronog., 2 reg., c. 1939
s. steel $200 $300 $375

Pricing in this Guide are fair market price for **COM-PLETE** watches which are reflected from the "**NAWCC**" National and regional shows.

GALLET, 17 jewels, time dial at 12 , chronog.
s. steel..................................$300 $350 $425

P. GARNIER, 17 jewels, minu-stop, c. 1965
s. steel..................................$50 $60 $80

P. GARNIER, 17 jewels, world time, c. 1968
s. steel.................................. $100 $125 $175

GARLAND, 17J., center sec., water-proof.
s. steel......................................$35 $45 $65

Wrist Watches listed in this section are priced at the collectable fair market **retail** level as **complete** watches having an original gold-filled case and stainless steel back, also with original dial, leather watch band, and the entire original movement in good working order with no repairs needed.

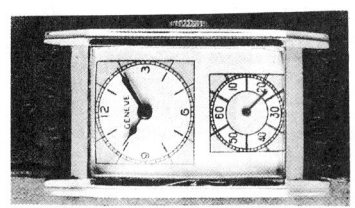

GENEVE, 15 jewels, dual dial, c. 1939
s. steel $400 $500 $650

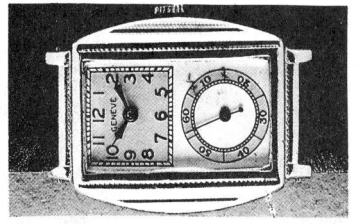

GENEVE, 15 jewels, dual dial, c. 1937
s. steel $400 $500 $650

GENEVE, 17 jewels, curly lugs, c.1950
14k $150 $175 $225

GERMINAL, 17 J., "Voltaire"
14k $100 $125 $175

GERMINAL, 15 J., early auto wind, lug action, c. 1933
s. steel $500 $600 $800

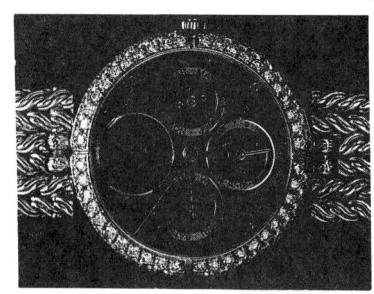

GERALD GENTA, 29J., skeletonized, auto wind,
perpetual calendar
18k C&B $12,000 $13,000 $16,000

GIRARD-PERREGAUX, 17J., auto wind, C.1951
s. steel $65 $80 $100

GIRARD-PERREGAUX, 17J., alarm, c.1960
gold filled...............................$100 $125 $175

GIRARD-PERREGAUX, 39J., center sec. c.1955
14k...$150 $175 $225

🕐 Some grades are not included. Their values can be
determined by comparing with **similar** age, size, metal
content, style, grades, or models such as **time only**,
chronograph, repeater etc. listed.

GIRARD-PERREGAUX, 17J., center sec., c.1948
18k $250 $275 $325

GIRARD-PERREGAUX, 17J., center sec., c.1960
s. steel $65 $75 $95

GIRARD-PERREGAUX, 17J., cal.47ae, c.1953
14k $150 $175 $225

GIRARD-PERREGAUX, 17J., Sea Hawk., c.1960
gold filled..................................$55 $65 $85

GIRARD-PERREGAUX, 17J., aux. sec., c.1958
gold filled..................................$55 $65 $85

GIRARD-PERREGAUX, 17J., aux. sec., c.1950
s. steel..$80 $90 $125

GIRARD-PERREGAUX, 17J., date, c.1960
gold filled..................................$55 $65 $85

GIRARD-PERREGAUX, 39J., auto-matic, date, c.1960
18k...$225 $250 $325

⊕ Some grades are not included. Their values can be
determined by comparing with similar age, size, metal
content, style, grades, or models such as time only,
chronograph, repeater etc. listed.

GIRARD-PERREGAUX, 39J., chronometre "HF", c.1970
s. steel $75 $85 $100

GIRARD-PERREGAUX, 17 jewels, triple date, center sec.
s.steel.....................................$150 $175 $225

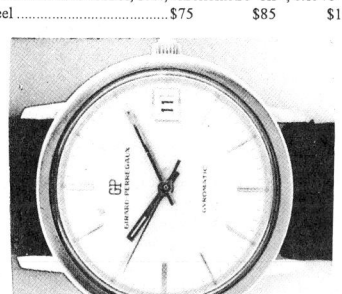

GIRARD-PERREGAUX,17J.,"Gyromatic",date
gold filled..................................$65 $75 $90

GIRARD-PERREGAUX, 17J., chronog., 2 reg.
s. steel.....................................$275 $350 $400

GIRARD-PERREGAUX, 39J.,"Gyromatic",date, Ca. 1960
18k $200 $225 $275

GIRARD-PERREGAUX, 17J., by Valjoux cal.72, c.1955
s. steel.....................................$300 $325 $400

GIRARD-PERREGAUX, 17J., triple date, autow.
s. steel $150 $175 $225

GIRARD-PERREGAUX, 17J., chronog cal.285, c.1940
gold filled..............................$200 $250 $325

GIRARD-PERREGAUX, 17J., pulsations, c.1948
14k $400 $450 $525

GIRARD-PERREGAUX, 17 J., chronog., 3 reg., c. 1952
s. steel $300 $325 $400

GIRARD-PERREGAUX, 17J, chronog., triple date, moon phase
18k $2,000 $2,200 $2,500

GIRARD-PERREGAUX, 39 J., Ca. 1955
14k $200 $225 $300
18k $275 $300 $375

GIRARD-PERREGAUX, 17J., aux. sec., Ca.1960
14k $150 $175 $225

GIRARD-PERREGAUX, 17J., "gyromatic",
14k $150 $175 $225

GIRARD-PERREGAUX, 17J., RF#2459, c.1970
14k $100 $125 $175

GIRARD-PERREGAUX, 17J., cal.a6 3606, GJS, c.1955
14k $150 $175 $225

GIRARD-PERREGAUX, 17J., recess crown, GJS, c.1954
14k $175 $200 $250

GIRARD-PERREGAUX, 17J., cal.86, GJS, c.1948
14k $100 $125 $175

GIRARD-PERREGAUX, 17J., recess crown, GJS, c.1947
gold filled................................$55 $65 $85

GIRARD-PERREGAUX, 17J., cal.86ae, GJS, c.1940
s. steel $50 $60 $80

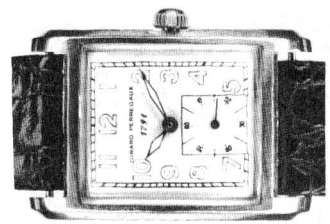

GIRARD-PERREGAUX, 17J., "1791", GJS, c.1942
s. steel.......................................$75 $100 $150

GIRARD-PERREGAUX, 17J., two tone case,GJS, c.1942
14k $250 $275 $350

GIRARD-PERREGAUX, 17J., cal.91ae220, GJS, c.1948
gold filled................................$65 $75 $95

GIRARD-PERREGAUX, 17J., GJS, c.1953
14k $125 $150 $200

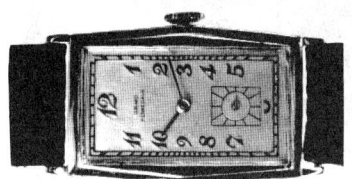

GIRARD-PERREGAUX, 17J., GJS, c.1936
gold filled................................$80 $90 $110

GIRARD-PERREGAUX, 17J., cal. 86ae, GJS, c.1942
s. steel $55 $65 $85

GIRARD-PERREGAUX, 17J., cal.86ae, GJS, c.1942
14k..$125 $150 $200

Wrist Watches listed in this section are priced at the collectable
fair market **retail** level as **complete** watches having an original
gold-filled case and stainless steel back, also with original dial,
leather watch band, and the entire original movement in good
working order with no repairs needed.

GIRARD-PERREGAUX, 39 jewels, aux. sec.
14k $150 $175 $225

GIRARD-PERREGAUX, 17 jewels, aux. sec.
gold filled....................................$65 $75 $95

GIRARD-PERREGAUX, 17 jewels, tank style, c. 1948
14k $200 $225 $300

GIRARD-PERREGAUX, 17 J., C. 1948
14k $200 $225 $300

GLASHUTTE, 17J., 2 reg., fluted bezel, c.1942
s. steel.....................................$800 $900 $1,100

GLASHUTTE, 17J., signed Uhrenfabrik Glashutte, c.1935
18k..$500 $600 $750

GLASHUTTE, 15J., signed "GUB", Ca.1950's
gold filled...............................$300 $325 $400

GLYCINE, 17J., **Airman**, auto-wind, 24hr., date, c.1970
s. steel.....................................$75 $100 $150

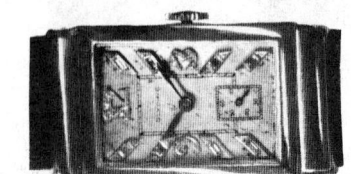

GLYCINE, 17J., 15 diamond dial, cal.4645, c.1945
14k...$350 $400 $475

GIRARD-PERREGAUX, 17 J., date, stepped case,
18k $600 $700 $850
14k $450 $550 $700

GLYCINE, 17J., 3 diamond dial, c.1950
14k(w)....................................$100 $125 $175

GLYCINE, 17 jewels, airman, 24 hr. dial, date, C.1960s
s. steel $125 $150 $200

GLYCINE, 17 jewels, **curved,** c. 1938
18k $200 $250 $325

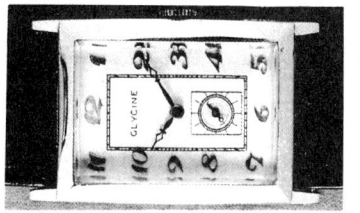

GLYCINE, 17 jewels, aux. sec., c. 1934
14k (w)....................................$150 $175 $225

GLYCINE, 18 jewels, faceted crystal & bezel
gold filled................................$40 $50 $80

GOERING W. Co., jump hr., wandering sec.,C.1935
14k.......................................$1,000 $1,300 $1,700

GOERING W. Co., jump hr., wandering sec.,C.1935
chrome...................................$250 $300 $400

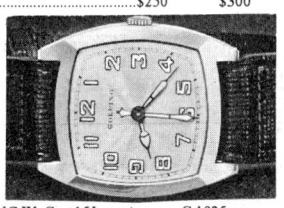

GOERING W. Co., 15J., center sec., C.1935
base metal...............................$30 $40 $65

GOERING W. Co., 15J., engraved case, C.1935
gold filled................................$30 $40 $65

GOERING W. Co., 15J., engraved case, C.1935
gold filled................................$30 $40 $65

GOERING W. Co., 15J., engraved case, C.1935
gold filled................................$30 $40 $65

GOERING W. Co., 15J., rectangular, C.1935
gold filled..................................$30 $40 $65

GOERING W. Co., 15J., ladies engraved case, C.1935
gold filled..................................$35 $45 $70

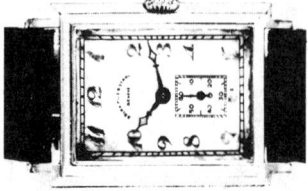

GOLAY, 18 jewels, aux. sec., c. 1928
18k & platinum...................$1,500 $1,700 $2,200

GOLAY, 32 jewels, min. repeater, adj. to 5 positions
18k $20,000 $23,000 $30,000

GRANA, 16J., **Masonic dial**, original dial, GJS, ca. 1948
14k $175 $200 $250

GRUEN, 17J., curved, precision, cal. 330, Ca. 1937
platinum............................$1,000 $1,100 $1,400

GRUEN, 15J., enamel dial, wire lugs, c. 1915
silver $150 $175 $250

GRUEN, 17J.,driver's watch, winds at 12, cal.400, c.1938
gold filled $250 $300 $375

GRUEN,17J., curved, drivers, cal.401, RF#352, c.1932
gold filled $500 $550 $625

GRUEN, 17J., extremely curved, drivers, c. 1932 , and
side view of watch
gold filled $600 $650 $725

GRUEN, 17 J., extremely curved, driver's watch
gold filled...............................$600 $650 $725

GRUEN, 17J., driver's watch , flexible long lugs , RF # 641
gold filled...............................$700 $800 $925

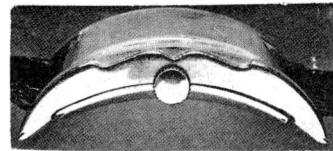

GRUEN, 17 jewels, curvex, c. 1949
gold filled...............................$250 $275 $350

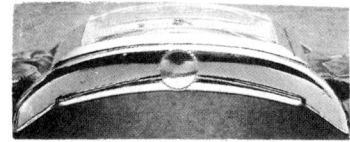

GRUEN, 17 jewels, curvex, 35mm long
gold filled...............................$250 $275 $350

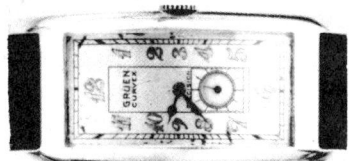

GRUEN, 17 jewels, curvex, 55mm long, C.1937
14k $900 $1,000 $1,200

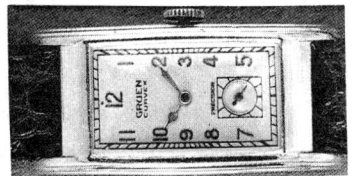

GRUEN, 17J.,curvex, precision, C. 1936
14k $400 $450 $525

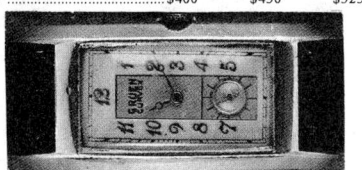

GRUEN, 17 jewels, curvex, c. 1937
gold filled...............................$200 $250 $325

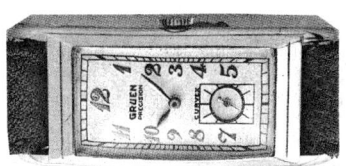

GRUEN, 17 jewels, curvex, RF# 228, c. 1935
gold filled $200 $250 $325

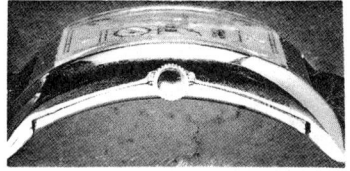

GRUEN, 17 jewels, curvex, 50mm long, c. 1937
gold filled $450 $500 $600

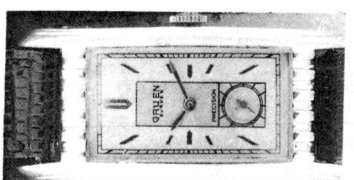

GRUEN, 17 jewels, curvex, c. 1937
s. steel $125 $150 $225

GRUEN, 17 jewels, curvex, aux. sec.
gold filled $250 $275 $350

GRUEN, 17J., note bezel,curvex, ca.1936
gold filled $200 $250 $325

GRUEN, 17 jewels, curvex, RF# 334, Ca. 1939
gold filled $200 $250 $325

🕐 First **CURVEX** was introduced on October 26, 1935, it was series # 311, the 2nd. series was 330 in 1939, and in 1940 series # 440 was issued.

GRUEN, 17 jewels, Precision, 2 Tone, Ca. 1933
18K 2 tone $300 $350 $425

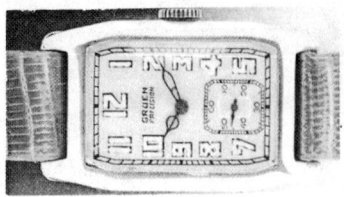

GRUEN, 17 jewels, curvex
gold filled................................$150 $175 $225

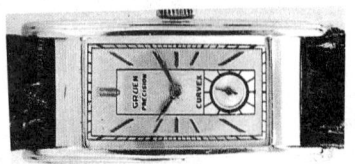

GRUEN, 17J., curvex, RF#202, cal.311, c. 1936
gold filled.............................. $175 $200 $250

GRUEN, 15J., curvex, RF#226, c. 1936
gold filled.............................. $175 $200 $250

GRUEN, 15J., curvex, stepped case, RF#278, c. 1936
s. steel $150 $175 $225

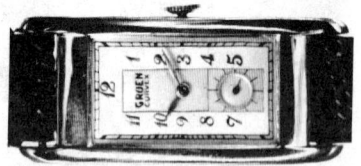

GRUEN, 15J., curvex, RF#255, cal.500, c. 1936
gold filled.............................. $175 $200 $250

GRUEN, 17J., curvex, RF#266, cal.165, c. 1935
gold filled $100 $125 $175

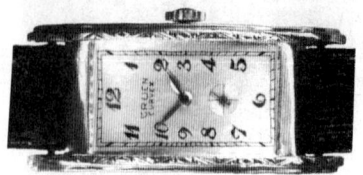

GRUEN, 17J., curvex, RF#280, cal.330, c. 1936
gold filled $175 $200 $250

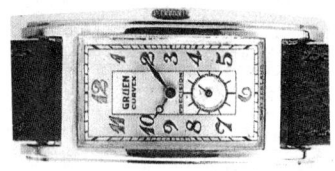

GRUEN, 17J., curvex, stepped case, RF#280, c. 1937
14k $250 $275 $350
gold filled $175 $200 $250

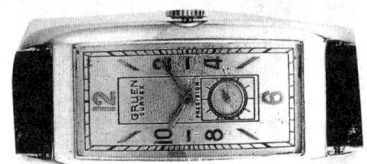

GRUEN, 17J., curvex, precision, RF#292, cal.330, c. 1937
gold filled $175 $200 $250

GRUEN, 15J., curvex, RF#324, cal.500, c. 1936
gold filled $200 $225 $275

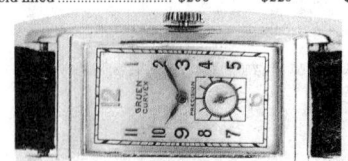

GRUEN, 17J., curvex, RF#308, cal.330, c. 1936
14k $250 $275 $350
gold filled $175 $200 $250

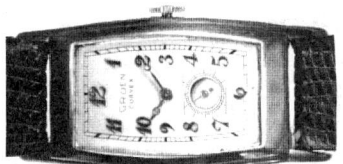

GRUEN, 17J., curvex, RF#339, cal.330, c. 1939
gold filled............................. $150 $175 $225

GRUEN, 17J., curvex, aux. sec.
gold filled.............................$100 $125 $175

GRUEN, 17J., curvex, cal#440, hooded lugs, ca.1943
14k $150 $175 $225

GRUEN, 17 jewels, curvex, fancy lugs
14k $250 $275 $325

GRUEN, 17 jewels, curvex, long lugs
14k $200 $225 $275

GRUEN, 15 jewels, **tu-tone case**, double dial, Ca. 1937
14k W & Y $3,000 $3,300 $4,000

GRUEN, 17 jewels, **jumping hr.**, double dial
14k $4,000 $4,300 $5,000

GRUEN, 17 jewels, double dial
gold filled $1,200 $1,300 $1,600

GRUEN, 17 jewels, double dial, curved, c.1930s
gold filled $350 $375 $450

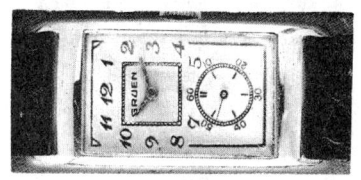

GRUEN, 17 jewels, double dial, curved, c. 1938
gold filled $900 $1,000 $1,300

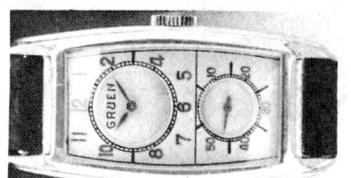

GRUEN, 17 jewels, double dial
gold filled $900 $1,000 $1,300

GRUEN, 17 jewels, double dial, c. 1932
gold filled $900 $1,000 $1,300

GRUEN, 15 jewels, in form of car radiator, curved
nickel..$800 $900 $1,300

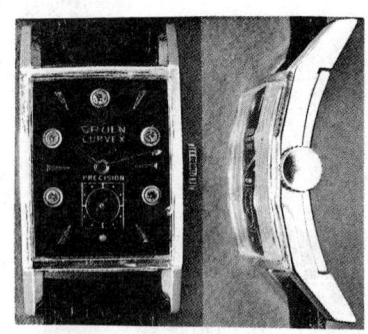

GRUEN, 17J., curvex, diamond dial, faceted crystal
14k $275 $300 $375

GRUEN, 17J., diamond dial & bezel, RF # 568, Ca. 1946
14k $450 $500 $600

GRUEN, 17 jewels, veri-thin model, fancy lugs
14k $250 $275 $350

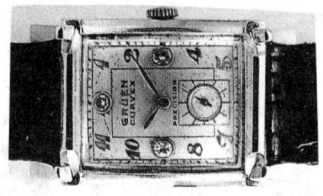

GRUEN, 17J., curvex, 3 diam., RF#568, cal.440, c. 1945
14k(w)....................................$250 $275 $350

GRUEN, 17 jewels, auto wind, cal. 840, c. 1952
18k $350 $400 $550

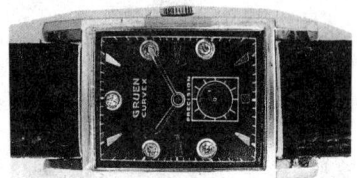

GRUEN, 17J., curvex, 5 diam., RF#615, cal.370c. 1945
14k(w)....................................$225 $250 $325

GRUEN, 17 jewels, curvex, fancy lugs
gold filled $100 $125 $175

GRUEN, 17J., stepped case, 3 diam., RF#798, c. 1950
14k(w)....................................$250 $275 $350

GRUEN, 17 jewels, curvex, diamond dial, fancy lugs
14k (w)'....................................$275 $300 $375

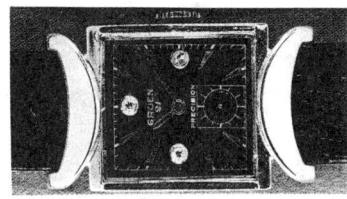

GRUEN, 21 jewels, diamond dial, fancy center lugs
14k $250 $275 $350

GRUEN, 21 jewels, fancy lugs, c. 1945
14k $300 $325 $400

GRUEN, 17 jewels, curvex, fancy lugs, c. 1943
gold filled.................................. $75 $100 $150
14k $150 $175 $250

GRUEN, 17 jewels, curvex, diamond dial, c. 1945
14k $250 $275 $350

GRUEN, 17J., **flared**, diamond dial,
14k(w)..................................... $400 $450 $550

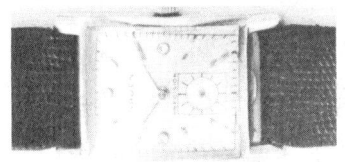

GRUEN, 17 jewels, curvex, diamond dial, c.1945
14k $250 $275 $350

GRUEN, 17 jewels, curvex, diamond dial, c. 1951
14k(w)C&B $550 $600 $750

GRUEN, 17J., so called **50th Anniversary, with a engraved**
quadron precision extra **mvt. G# 119,** Adj., also used **G# 123.**
14k(w).................................. ★$500 $550 $700

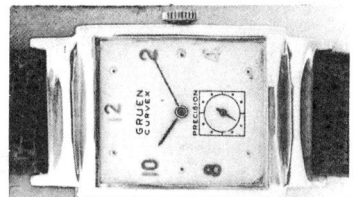

GRUEN, 17 jewels, curvex, c.1951
14k $175 $200 $275

GRUEN, 17 jewels, curvex, "Belmont"
14k $375 $400 $475

GRUEN, 21J., veri-thin, precision, swinging lugs
gold filled..............................$150 $175 $225

GRUEN, 15J., RF#467, cal.431, c. 1948
gold filled $60 $70 $95

GRUEN, 15J., RF#93, cal.179, c. 1925
gold filled.............................. $70 $85 $125

GRUEN, 17J., precision, RF#498, cal.440, c. 1945
gold filled $60 $70 $95

GRUEN, 17J., stepped lugs, RF#449, cal.440, c. 1945
gold filled.............................. $100 $110 $150

GRUEN, 17J., curvex, RF#498, cal.440, c. 1945
gold filled $100 $125 $175

GRUEN, 17J., large lugs, RF#449, cal.440, c. 1945
gold filled.............................. $125 $150 $200

GRUEN, 17J., curvex, RF#530, cal.335, c. 1948
gold filled $60 $70 $95

GRUEN, 17J., RF#449, cal.440, c. 1943
gold filled.............................$100 $125 $175

GRUEN, 17J., veri-thin, RF#530, cal.430, c. 1945
14k $125 $150 $200

GRUEN, 17J., curvex, RF#544, cal.440, c. 1942
gold filled.............................. $100 $110 $150

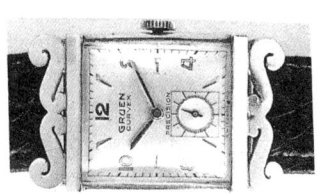

GRUEN, 17J., fancy lugs, curvex, RF#610, c. 1945
14k $300 $350 $425

GRUEN, 17J., veri-thin **3 diam.**, RF#558, cal.335, c. 1945
14k(w).................................... $150 $175 $225

GRUEN, 17J., curvex, RF#610, cal.1370, c. 1945
14k $300 $350 $425

GRUEN, 17J., curvex, RF#576, cal.440, c. 1942
gold filled..............................$100 $125 $175
14k $175 $200 $250

GRUEN, 17J., 3 diam., curvex, RF#615, cal.370, c. 1945
14k $150 $175 $225

GRUEN, 17J., curvex precision, RF#600, Ca. 1940
gold filled.............................. $100 $125 $175

GRUEN, 17J., curvex, RF#642, "Marshall", c. 1945
gold filled $75 $100 $150

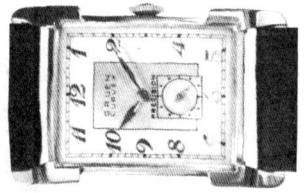

GRUEN, 17J., curvex, RF#607, "Citadel", c. 1943
gold filled.............................. $100 $125 $175

GRUEN, 17J., curvex, RF#650, cal.370, c. 1948
gold filled $100 $125 $175

🕐 Pricing in this Guide are fair market price for **COM-PLETE** watches which are reflected from the "**NAWCC**" National and regional shows.

GRUEN, 17J., twisted bezel, RF#657, cal.335, c. 1953
gold filled.............................. $150 $175 $225

GRUEN, 17J., curvex, faceted crystal, cal.440, c. 1947
14k $250 $275 $350

GRUEN, 21J., precision, RF#674, cal.430, c. 1947
gold filled................................. $60 $70 $95

GRUEN, 21J., precision, RF#801, cal335., c. 1953
14k $200 $225 $300

GRUEN, 21J., precision, RF#738, cal.335, c. 1948
14k $150 $175 $225

GRUEN, 17J., veri-thin, large lugs, c. 1950
14k $200 $225 $300

GRUEN, 17J., curvex, RF#750, cal.370, c. 1940
gold filled.............................. $100 $135 $175

GRUEN, 17J., RF # 578, Curvex Precision, Ca. 1943
gold filled $75 $100 $150

GRUEN, 17J., curvex, RF#773, cal.370, c. 1945
gold filled...............................$75 $100 $150

GRUEN, 17J., RF # 755, stepped bezel, Auto wind, Ca. 1950
gold filled $125 $150 $200

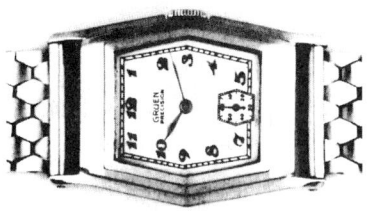

GRUEN, 19 jewels, precision, c. 1920
14k $300 $350 $425

GRUEN, 17 jewels, curvex
14k $175 $200 $275

GRUEN, 17J., RF # 575, Curvex Precision, Ca.1945
gold filled...............................$100 $125 $175

GRUEN, 17 jewels, curvex, c. 1943
14k $200 $250 $325

GRUEN, 17 jewels, cal. 440, RF#449, Ca. 1945
gold filled...............................$100 $125 $175

🕐 Some grades are not included. Their values can be
determined by comparing with **similar** age, size, metal
content, style, grades, or models such as **time only**,
chronograph, repeater etc. listed.

GRUEN, 17 jewels, Curvex, RF#610, 3 diam.dial, Ca.1945
14k(w) 6 diam.case $350 $400 $500

GRUEN, 21J., "Precision", RF#709, cal.335, Ca.1945
gold filled $65 $85 $125

GRUEN, 15 jewels, RF#8w, cal.157, Ca. 1929
gold filled $75 $100 $175

GRUEN, 15 jewels, 3 Adj., Ca.1930
gold filled $60 $70 $100

GRUEN, 17J., veri-thin, cal.405, c. 1946
gold filled $70 $90 $125

GRUEN, 17J., curvex, RF#450, cal.440, c. 1938
gold filled............................ $125 $150 $225

GRUEN, 17J., curvex, RF#448, cal.440, c. 1941
gold filled............................ $100 $125 $175
14K $200 $225 $275

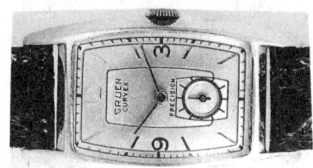

GRUEN, 17J., curvex, RF#450, cal.440, c. 1938
14k $200 $250 $325

GRUEN, 17J., curvex, RF#879, cal.370, c. 1942
14k $200 $250 $325

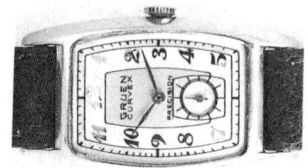

GRUEN, 17J., curvex, RF#450, cal.440, c. 1942
14k .... $ 200 $250 $325

GRUEN, 17J., curvex, RF#448, cal.440, c. 1944
14k $200 $250 $325

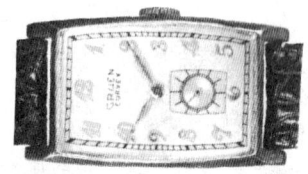

GRUEN, 17J., curvex, RF#364, cal.400, c. 1935
gold filled............................ $ 100 $125 $175

GRUEN, 17J., curvex, RF#293, cal.330, c. 1940
gold filled $125 $150 $225

GRUEN, 17J., precision, RF#271, cal., c. 1936
gold filled............................ $125 $150 $200

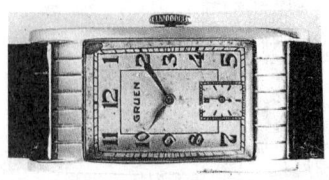

GRUEN, 17J., fluted bezel, RF#240, cal.335, c. 1935
14k $225 $275 $350

Wrist Watches listed in this section are priced at the collectable
fair market **retail** level as **complete** watches having an original
gold-filled case and stainless steel back, also with original dial,
leather watch band, and the entire original movement in good
working order with no repairs needed.

GRUEN, 17J., curvex, RF#602, cal.370, c. 1943
14k $175 $200 $275

GRUEN, 17J., curvex, RF#449, cal.440, c. 1945
14k $175 $200 $275

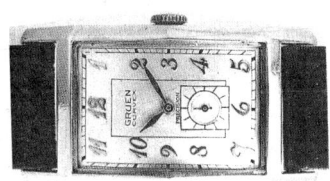

GRUEN, 17J., Curvex Precision, RF # 601, Ca. 1949
gold filled.............................. $100 $125 $175

GRUEN, 17 jewels, curvex, RF # 271, c. 1936
gold filled..............................$150 $175 $225

GRUEN, 17 jewels, precision, fancy lugs
14k $300 $350 $500

⊕ Some grades are not included. Their values can be
determined by comparing with similar age, size, metal
content, style, grades, or models such as time only,
chronograph, repeater etc. listed.

GRUEN, 17 jewels, curvex, c. 1947
14k $150 $200 $275

GRUEN, 17J., Curvex Precision, RF # 600, Ca.1945
gold filled $125 $150 $200

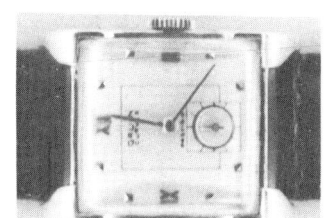

GRUEN, 17 jewels, curvex, fancy lugs
14k $150 $175 $250

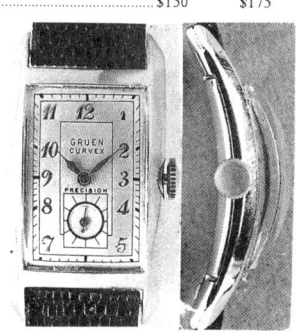

GRUEN, 17 jewels, curvex, c. 1939
14k $300 $350 $425
gold filled $150 $200 $275

GRUEN, 17 jewels, curvex, fancy lugs, c. 1961
14k $350 $400 $500

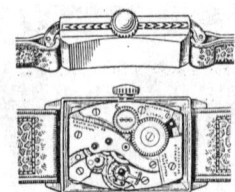

Gruen Quadron rectangular movement

GRUEN, 15J., enamel on nickel case, mvt# 158, Ca. 1927
nickel $200 $225 $275

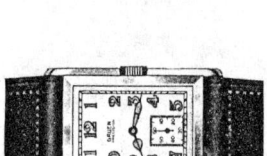

GRUEN, 17J., crown-guard, quadron mvt# 59, Ca. 1927
18K... $225 $275 $350

GRUEN, 15-17J., enamel Art Deco, Ca. 1927
gold filled $250 $275 $300

GRUEN, 15-17J., inlaid enamel case, quadron mvt, Ca. 1927
gold filled............................. $100 $125 $175

GRUEN, 15-17J., center sec., radium dial, Ca. 1927
14K $150 $175 $225

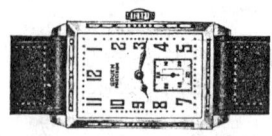

GRUEN, 15-17J., engraved case, quadron mvt# 47, Ca. 1927
gold filled................................. $65 $80 $100

GRUEN, 15-17J., engraved case, radium dial,, Ca. 1927
nickel $75 $95 $125

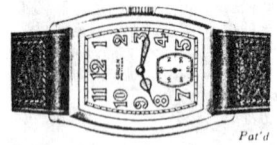

GRUEN, 17J., crown-guard, quadron mvt, Ca. 1927
14K... $200 $225 $275

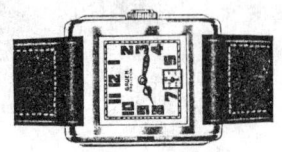

GRUEN, 15-17J., tank w/crown-guard, Ca. 1927
14K $200 $250 $325

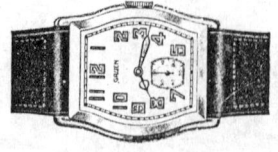

GRUEN, 17J., crown-guard, quadron mvt, Ca. 1927
gold filled............................. $100 $125 $175

GRUEN, 15-17J., tank engraved case, mvt # 13, Ca. 1927
14K... $200 $250 $325

GRUEN, 17J., pulsemeter,
s. steel $500 $600 $750

GRUEN, 17J., triple date, cal.415, c. 1953
s. steel...................................... $250 $300 $400
gold filled.............................. $250 $300 $400

GRUEN, 17 jewels, physicians chronog., screw back
18k $1,700 $2,000 $2,500

GRUEN, 17 jewels, rope style bezel with diamonds
14k...$250 $300 $400

GRUEN, 17J., jump 24 hour, c. 1970
s. steel $100 $125 $175

GRUEN, 17J., "Day-Night", cal.n510, waterproof, Ca. 1960
The "Day-night" markers have a self-powered illumination system.
base metal........................... ★ $200 $250 $375

GRUEN, 17J., alarm, date, c. 1964
s. steel $125 $150 $200

GRUEN, 17 jewels, 17 diamonds, RF# 744, Ca. 1955
14kW.....................................$250 $275 $350

🕐 Pricing in this Guide are fair market price for COM-
PLETE watches which are reflected from the "NAWCC" National and regional shows.

GRUEN, 17 jewels, veri-thin model, fancy lugs
14k $150 $200 $275

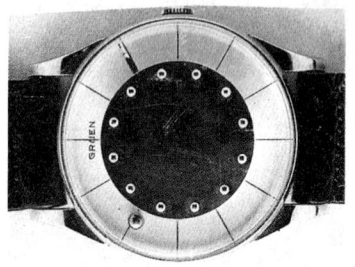

GRUEN, 17J., mystery dial, cal#215, ca.1965
gold filled................................$200 $225 $300

GRUEN, 17J., veri-thin model, fancy lugs, 24 hr. dial
14k $225 $300 $400

GRUEN, 17J., **Airflight**, jumping hours, c. 1960
s.steel $225 $250 $300

GRUEN, 17J., engraved case, cal.117, c. 1929
14k(w) $150 $175 $250

GRUEN, 15J., cushion, luminous dial, c. 1930s
gold filled..................................$85 $95 $125

GRUEN, 15-17J., barrel shaped, Ca. 1939
gold filled................................$75 $100 $150

GRUEN, 17J., veri-thin, fancy bezel, Ca. 1948
gold filled................................$75 $100 $150

GRUEN, 15-17J., RF# 544, Ca. 1949
gold filled..................................$75 $100 $150

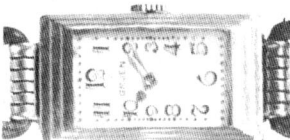

GRUEN, 17J., fluted center lugs, cal.343, c. 1936
gold filled.............................. $100 $125 $175

GRUEN, 17J., nurse style double dial, ca.1937
s. steel $150 $175 $225

E. GUBELIN, 17 jewels, chronog. 3 reg., Valj.72, c. 1950
18k (waterproof).................$1,000 $1,100 $1,300

E. GUBELIN, 19 jewels, chronog., day-date-month
18k $1,300 $1,500 $1,800

E. GUBELIN, 19J., chronog. by Valjoux, waterpf, 3 reg.
18k $1,000 $1,100 $1,300

E. GUBELIN, 29 jewels, min. repeater
18k C&B $30,000 $33,000 $40,000

E. GUBELIN, 25J., ipso-matic, triple date, moon ph.
14k & steel back $1,250 $1,350 $1,550
18k..$2,000 $2,200 $2,900

E. GUBELIN, 15J., triple date, c.1945
s. steel....................................$250 $300 $400

E. GUBELIN, 19 jewels, 18k case, 14k band
18k & 14k C&B.....................$500 $600 $750

E. GUBELIN, 17J., ca. 1970s
18k $150 $175 $250

E. GUBELIN,17J., cal#F690, center sec., ca. 1950s
18k $250 $275 $350
s. steel $100 $125 $175

E. GUBELIN, 17J., ca. 1952
s. steel $125 $150 $200

E. GUBELIN, 25J., ipso-matic, c.1955
14k $250 $275 $325

E. GUBELIN, 17J., alarm, ipso-vox, c.1960
18k $900 $1,000 $1,200

E. GUBELIN, 17J., ipso-vox, date, alarm, c.1960
s. steel $400 $450 $525

E. GUBELIN, 17J., carved lugs, center sec., c.1944
18k $300 $350 $425

E. GUBELIN, 17J., 8 baguettes, 3 diamonds, c.1948
platinum $500 $550 $625

E. GUBELIN, 15J., **back wind duoplan**, c.1935
s. steel $250 $300 $400

E. GUBELIN, 15J., ca. 1935
18k(W)..................................$700 $750 $900

E. GUBELIN, 25 jewels, milled bezel, center sec., Ca. 1955
18k...............................$350 $400 $550

E. GUBELIN, 19 J., hunter style pop-up lid, c. 1930
18k (w)................................$3,000 $3,300 $4,000

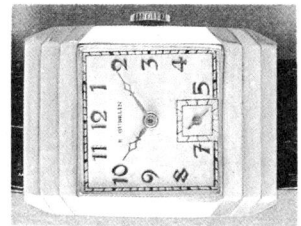

E. GUBELIN, 19 jewels, fancy hooded lugs
18k..$700 $800 $1,000

E. GUBELIN, 17jewels, jumping hr., c. 1924
14k $5,500 $6,000 $7,000

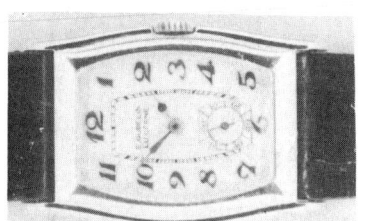

E. GUBELIN, 19 jewels, curvex, 2 tone
18k....................................$1,000 $1,100 $1,300

E. GUBELIN, 25J., triple date, moon phase, c. 1950
18k $2,500 $2,700 $3,300

E. GUBELIN, 19J., center sec., flared case, c. 1950
18k..................................$350 $400 $550

E. GUBELIN, triple date & moon ph., by Audemars-Piguet,
Ca. 1930
18k $15,000 $16,000 $18,000

E. GUBELIN, 17-21J., milled bezel, center sec., Ca. 1958
18k..$300 $350 $425

E. GUBELIN, 17 jewels, by Vacheron & Constantin
18k $1,800 $2,200 $2,800

HAFIS, 15J., luminous dial
gold plate...................................$30 $35 $50

E. GUBELIN, 18 jewels, curved, stepped case, c. 1940
18k $600 $700 $1,000

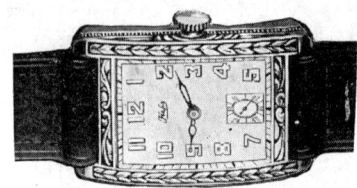

HAFIS, 15J., engraved case
gold plate...................................$50 $75 $125
14k..$150 $175 $225

GUINAND, 17J., chronog., day-date-month, 3 reg.
18k $700 $800 $1,000
s. steel $250 $300 $375

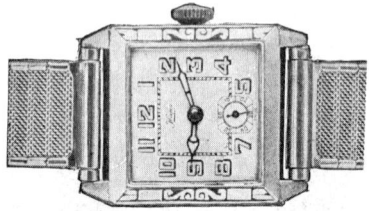

HAFIS, 15J., engraved case
gold plate...................................$40 $50 $80

GUINAND, 17 J., chronog., triple date, moon phase
18k $1,000 $1,100 $1,400
s. steel $500 $600 $750

HAFIS, 15J., engraved case
gold plate...................................$40 $50 $80

HAFIS, 15J., center sec., cushion style
gold plate $30 $35 $50

HAFIS, 15J., engraved case
gold plate...................................$40 $50 $80

HAFIS, 15J., engraved case
gold plate $40 $50 $80

HAFIS, 17 jewels, carved lugs
14k $100 $125 $175

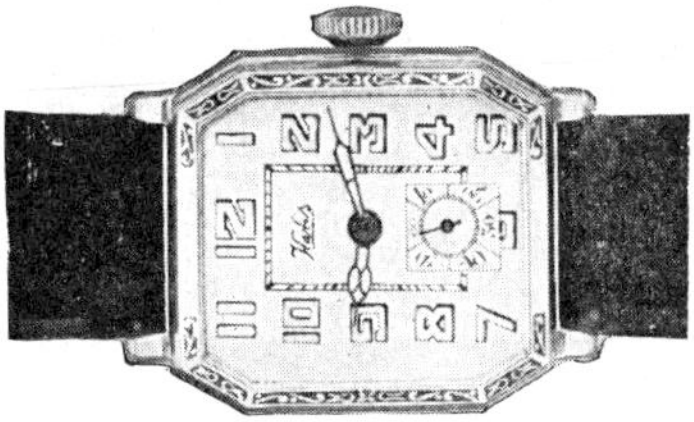

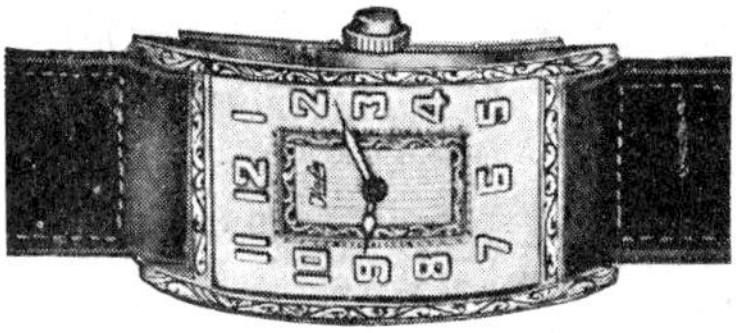

HAFIS, 15J., engraved case
gold plate $40 $50 $80

HAFIS, 15J., engraved case, curved
gold plate $40 $50 $80
14k $100 $125 $185

HAFIS, 15J., engraved case
gold plate $40 $50 $80

HAFIS, 17J., 'Queen Druga", 52 diamonds
Platinum $250 $275 $350

HAFIS, 15J., luminous dial
gold plate $30 $40 $60

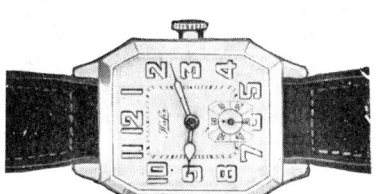

HAFIS, 15J., "Queen Marie", 26 diamonds
18k $200 $225 $300

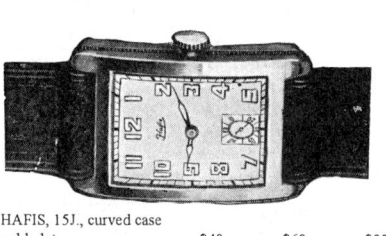

HAFIS, 15J., "Queen Charlotte", 22 diamonds
18k $150 $175 $225

HAFIS, 15J., curved case
gold plate $40 $60 $90
14k $100 $125 $175

HALLMARK, 17 jewels, day-date-month, auto wind
gold filled $100 $125 $175

Prices for electric watch to be in good running order

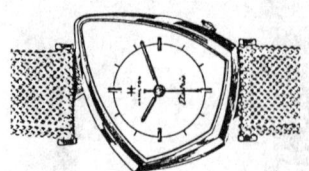

HAMILTON, electric, "Altair"
gold filled.................................$600 $700 $850

HAMILTON, electric, "Aquatel"
gold filled.................................$50 $60 $80

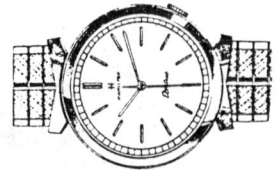

HAMILTON, electric, "Aquatel B"
gold filled.................................$50 $60 $80

HAMILTON, electric, "Atlantis"
gold filled.................................$65 $75 $100

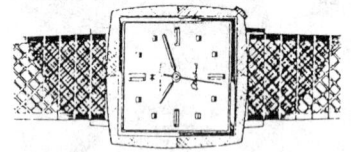

HAMILTON, electric, "Centaur"
gold filled.................................$50 $60 $80

HAMILTON, electric, "Clearview", **display back**
gold filled.................................$125 $150 $200

HAMILTON, electric, "Converta I", 18k bezel & s.s. case
18k &S.S. $75 $100 $150

HAMILTON, electric, "Converta II", 14k bezel & s.s. case
14k &S.S. $60 $70 $90

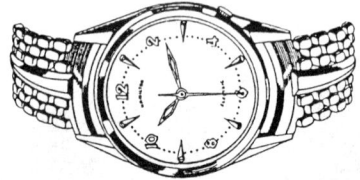

HAMILTON, electric, "Converta III", 10k bezel & s.s. case
10k &S.S. $50 $60 $80

HAMILTON, electric, "Converta IV", S.S. bezel & case
s. steel $50 $60 $80

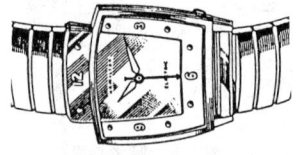

HAMILTON, electric, "Everest"
gold filled $100 $125 $175

HAMILTON, electric, "Everest II"
gold filled $75 $85 $125

Prices for electric watch to be in good running order.

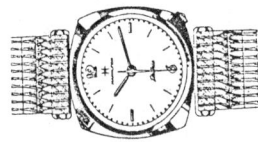

HAMILTON, electric, "Gemini" Ca.1963
gold filled $50 $60 $80

HAMILTON, electric, "Gemini II" Ca.1965
gold filled $50 $60 $80

HAMILTON, electric, "Lord Lancaster E," 12 diamonds
14k $300 $350 $425

HAMILTON, electric, "Lord Lancaster J," 8 diamonds
gold filled $225 $250 $300

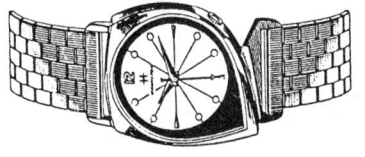

HAMILTON, electric, "Meteor," c. 1959
gold filled $225 $250 $300

HAMILTON, electric, "Nautilus" 200, single lugs
14k $125 $150 $200

HAMILTON, electric, "Nautilus" 201
14k $100 $125 $175

HAMILTON, electric, "Nautilus" 202
14k $125 $150 $200

HAMILTON, electric, "Nautilus" 400
gold filled $50 $60 $80

HAMILTON, electric, "Nautilus" 401
gold filled $50 $60 $80

HAMILTON, electric, "Nautilus" 402
gold filled $50 $60 $80

HAMILTON, electric, "Nautilus" 403, pocket watch
gold filled $75 $100 $150

Prices for electric watch to be in good running order.

HAMILTON, electric, "Nautilus" 404
gold filled...................................$50 $60 $80

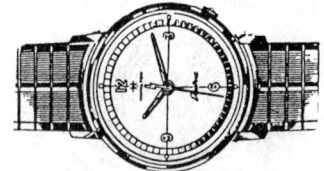

HAMILTON, electric, "Nautilus" 503
s. steel $50 $60 $80

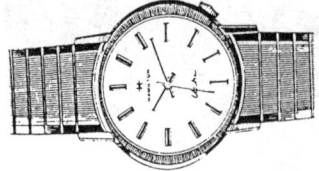

HAMILTON, electric, "Nautilus" 405
gold filled...................................$50 $60 $80

HAMILTON, electric, "Nautilus" 506
s. steel $50 $60 $80

HAMILTON, electric, "Nautilus" 450, gold filled bezel
gold filled...................................$50 $60 $80

HAMILTON, electric, "Nautilus" 507
s. steel $50 $60 $80

HAMILTON, electric, "Nautilus" 500
s. steel $50 $60 $80

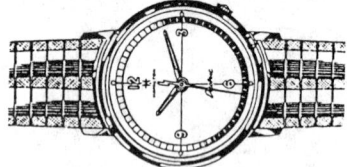

HAMILTON, electric, "Nautilus" 508
s. steel $50 $60 $80

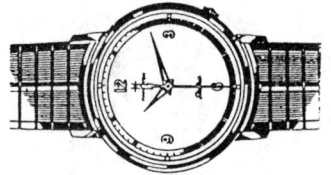

HAMILTON, electric, "Nautilus" 501
s. steel $50 $60 $80

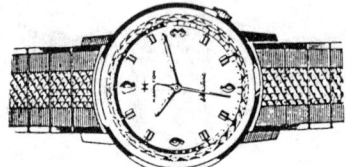

HAMILTON, electric, "Nautilus" 509
s. steel $50 $60 $80

HAMILTON, electric, "Nautilus" 502
s. steel $50 $60 $80

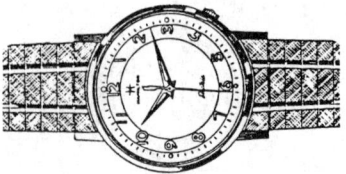

HAMILTON, electric, "Nautilus" 600
gold plate $50 $60 $80

Prices for electric watch to be in good running order.

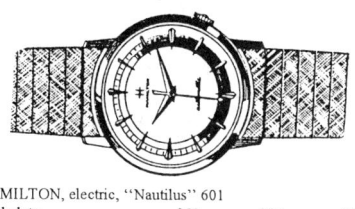

HAMILTON, electric, "Nautilus" 601
gold plate $50 $60 $80

HAMILTON, electric, "Nautilus" 602
gold plate $50 $60 $80

HAMILTON, electric, "Nautilus" 604
gold plate $50 $60 $80

HAMILTON, electric, "Nautilus" 605
gold plate $50 $60 $80

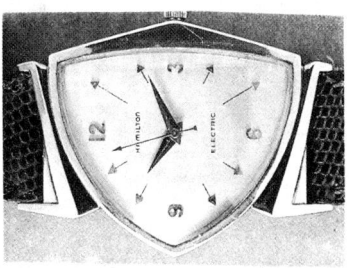

HAMILTON, electric, "Pacer," 2 tone
14k $700 $800 $1,000
gold filled.................................. $275 $300 $375
Wrist Watches listed in this section are priced at the collectable fair market **retail** level as **complete** watches having an
original gold-filled case and stainless steel back, also with
original dial, leather watch band, and the entire original movement in good working order with no repairs needed.

HAMILTON, electric, "Pegasus", engraved bezel
gold filled $100 $125 $175

HAMILTON, electric, "Polaris"
14k $250 $300 $400

HAMILTON, electric,"Polaris", diamond dial
14k $300 $350 $450

HAMILTON, electric,"Polaris II"
14k $200 $250 $350

HAMILTON, electric, "Regulus"
s. steel $100 $125 $175

Prices for electric watch to be in good running order.

HAMILTON, electric, "Regulus" II
s. steel $50 $60 $80

HAMILTON, electric, "Sea-Lectric I", GF bezel
s. steel $75 $100 $150

HAMILTON, electric, "R. R. Special"
model#52 = all 10k GF $150 $175 $275
model#51 = GF bezel only.....$125 $150 $225
model#50'= all s. steel $100 $125 $175

HAMILTON, electric, "Sea-Lectric II"
s. steel $60 $70 $90

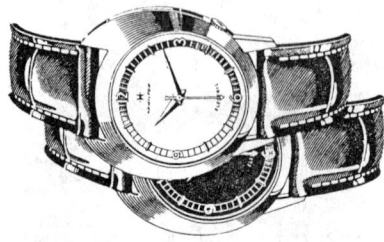

HAMILTON, electric, "Saturn"
gold filled................................$125 $150 $200

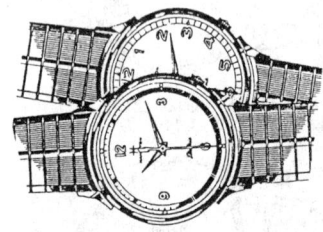

HAMILTON, electric, "Skip Jack"
s. steel $50 $60 $80

HAMILTON, electric, "Savitar"
14k $250 $300 $375

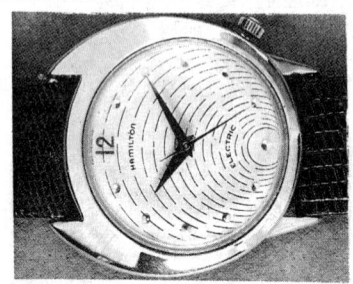

HAMILTON, electric, "Spectra"
18k **Rose gold** $600 $700 $850
14k $250 $300 $375

HAMILTON, electric, "Savitar 11", ca.1966
gold filled................................$125 $150 $200

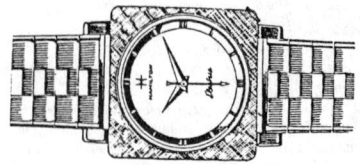

HAMILTON, electric, "Spectra" II
gold filled $50 $60 $80

HAMILTON, electric, "Summit"
14k $125 $150 $200

HAMILTON, electric, "Summit" II
gold filled.................................$50 $60 $80

HAMILTON, electric, "Taurus"
gold filled.................................$50 $60 $80

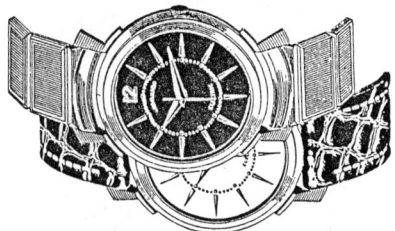

HAMILTON, electric, "Titan"
gold filled.................................$75 $100 $150

HAMILTON, electric, "Titan II"
gold filled.................................$100 $125 $150

⏱ Some grades are not included. Their values can be
determined by comparing with **similar** age, size, metal
content, style, grades, or models such as **time only**,
chronograph, repeater etc. listed.

HAMILTON, electric, "Titan III"
gold filled $100 $125 $150

HAMILTON, electric, "Titan IV-B"
14kC&B................................. $300 $350 $450

HAMILTON, electric, "Uranus"
gold filled $50 $60 $85

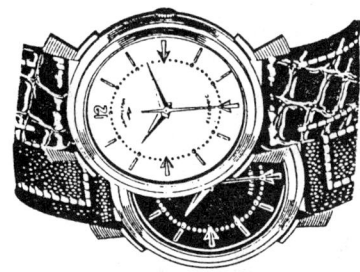

HAMILTON, electric, "Van Horn", Ca.**1957**
14k $200 $250 $350
14k +diam. dial......................$250 $300 $400

HAMILTON, electric, Vantage , ca.1959
gold filled $125 $150 $200

HAMILTON, electric, "Vega"
gold filled.................................$225 $250 $325

HAMILTON, electric, "Vela"
gold filled.................................$50 $60 $85

HAMILTON electric, "Ventura"
18k $1,200 $1,300 $1,500
14k $800 $900 $1,200

HAMILTON electric, "Ventura", **6 diamond dial**
14K..$1,000 $1,100 $1,300

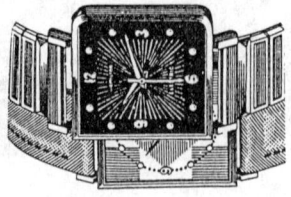

HAMILTON, electric,"Victor", ca.1958
gold filled.................................$100 $125 $175

Prices for electric watch to be in good running order.

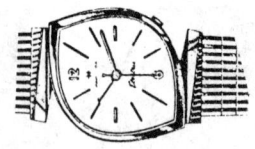

Hamilton, electric, "Victor II"
gold filled $100 $125 $175

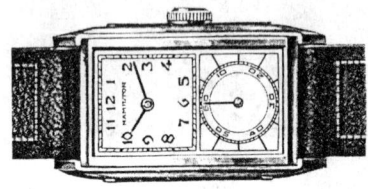

HAMILTON, 17 jewels, "Seckron," dual dial, c. 1935
gold filled $600 $650 $800

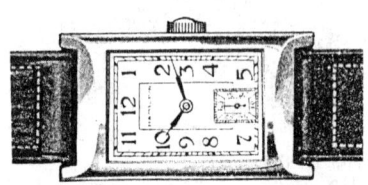

HAMILTON, 17 jewels, "Calvin," Ca. 1936
gold filled $90 $100 $125

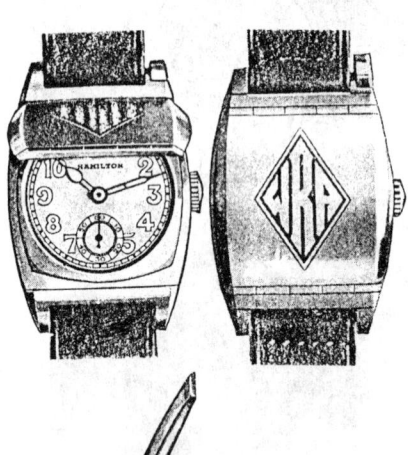

HAMILTON, "Flint Ridge," flip top is lug activated,
Grade 987=17J., Grade 979=19J.
14k $1,500 $1,800 $2,200

5 Time Zones, introduced Jan., 6 th, 1956, the G hand = Greenwich.
Pacific - Mountain - Central - Eastern

HAMILTON, 17J., "Cross Country on case", Ca. 1956
14k $500 $550 $625
gold filled................................$125 $150 $200

HAMILTON, 17J., chronog., by Valjoux cal.7733, c.1971
s. steel $150 $200 $275

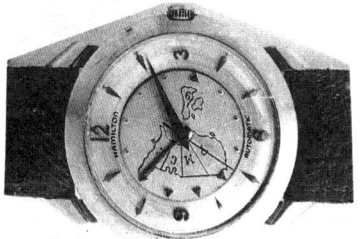

HAMILTON, 17J., "Transcontinental," auto-wind, Ca. 1963
14k $300 $350 $425
gold filled................................$125 $150 $200

HAMILTON, 17J., chronog., **DATE**, by Valjoux cal.7732,
s. steel $200 $250 $325

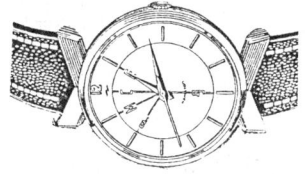

HAMILTON, "Golden Tempus", 18J., time zones, Ca. 1961
14k $300 $325 $400
14k +diamonds $350 $375 $450

HAMILTON, 17J., chronog., screw -back,
s. steel $100 $125 $175

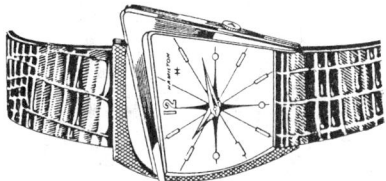

HAMILTON, 22J., above Flight I =14k MARKERS & # 12
14k case $1,600 $1,700 $1,900

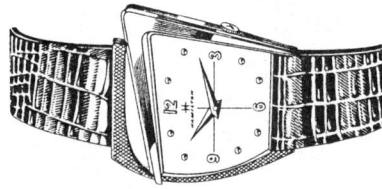

HAMILTON, 22J., above Flight II =14k dots & #s 12,3,6,9
gold filled case......................$800 $900 $1,200

HAMILTON, 22J., auto-wind, Ca. 1970
gold filled $50 $65 $95
s. steel $40 $50 $80

HAMILTON, 17J., "Heywood", grade 987, Ca. 1936
gold filled....................................$75 $100 $150

HAMILTON, 17J., hinged lugs, "Tuxedo", cal., c.1940
gold filled.................................$100 $125 $175

HAMILTON, 17J., hinged lugs, cal., c.1940
gold filled.................................$100 $125 $175

HAMILTON, 17J., drivers, cal.907, c.1938
gold filled.................................$100 $125 $175

HAMILTON,17J., drivers, **winds at 12**, ca. 1938
gold filled.................................$350 $400 $500

HAMILTON, 19 jewels, "Otis," reversible, c. 1946
gold filled..........................$1,000 $1,100 $1,300

HAMILTON, 19 J., "Coronado," black enamel bezel
14k $900 $1,000 $1,200

HAMILTON, 19 jewels, "Piping Rock," enamel bezel
14k yellow or white................$800 $850 $1,000

HAMILTON, 19 jewels, "Spur," enamel bezel
14k $1,800 $2,200 $2,500
14k(w)...................................$1,600 $1,800 $2,300

HAMILTON, 17J., 40 diamond bezel, Ca. 1955
18k (w) $300 $350 $450

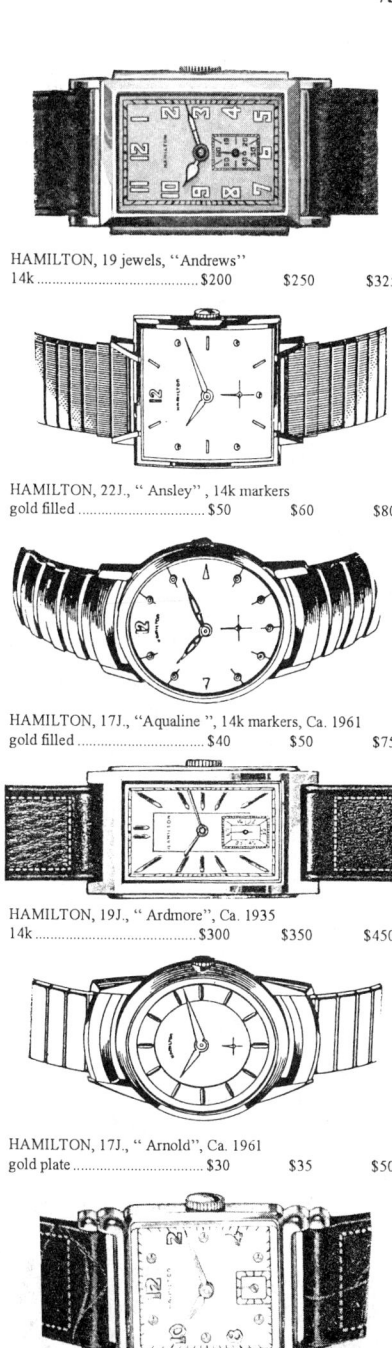

HAMILTON, 15J., "Oval", engraved or plain, Ca. 1925
14k .... ★★$600 $800 $1,100

HAMILTON, 17 jewels, cal. 987, GJS, ca. 1932
gold filled.................................$60 $70 $100

HAMILTON, 17 jewels, "Alan"
gold filled.................................$75 $100 $150

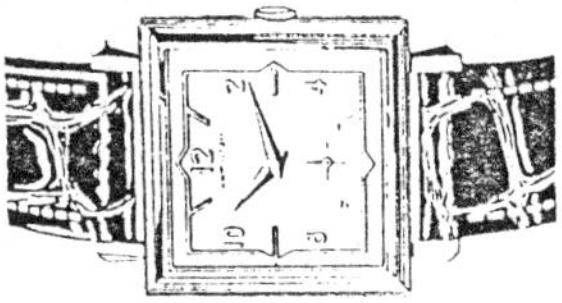

HAMILTON, 22 jewels, " Aldrich", Ca, 1961
14k $125 $150 $200

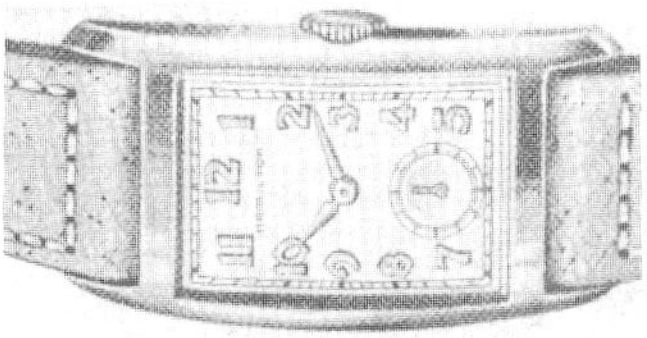

HAMILTON, 19 jewels, "Allison" , Ca. 1940
14k $250 $300 $375

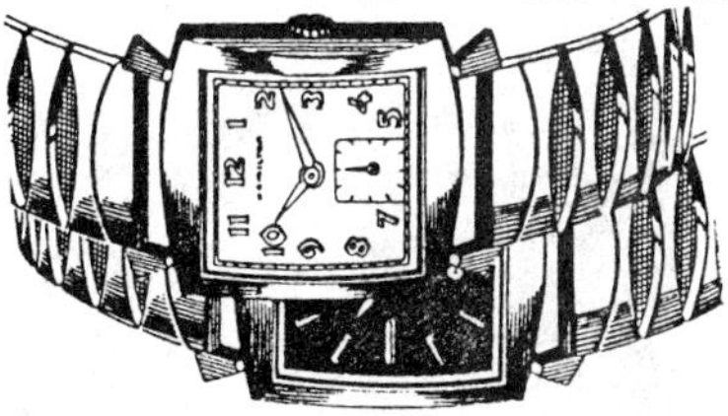

HAMILTON,17J., " Amherst", 14k markers
gold filled.................................$60 $70 $90

HAMILTON, 19 jewels, "Andrews"
14k $200 $250 $325

HAMILTON, 22J., " Ansley" , 14k markers
gold filled $50 $60 $80

HAMILTON, 17J., "Aqualine ", 14k markers, Ca. 1961
gold filled $40 $50 $75

HAMILTON, 19J., " Ardmore", Ca. 1935
14k $300 $350 $450

HAMILTON, 17J., " Arnold", Ca. 1961
gold plate $30 $35 $50

HAMILTON, 19J., " Ashley", grade 982, Ca. 1948
gold plate $60 $65 $75
14K $150 $175 $225

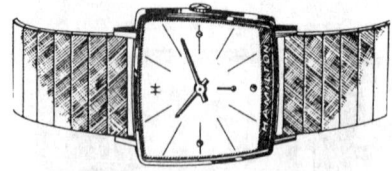

HAMILTON, 22J., "Attache", 14k markers, c.1961
gold filled..................................$70 $80 $95

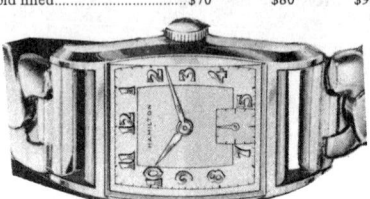

HAMILTON, 17J.," Austin ", c. 1951
gold filled..................................$80 $90 $110

HAMILTON, 17J, ''Bagley,'' applied numbers, c. 1941
gold filled..................................$90 $125 $175

HAMILTON, 19J.," Bailey ", c.1951
gold filled..................................$60 $70 $90

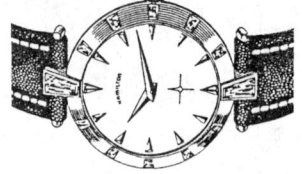

HAMILTON, 22J., " Barbizon", diam. bezel, Ca.1957
18k(w)..................................$250 $275 $350

HAMILTON, 22J., " Baron" , 5 diam. dial, BIG lugs, c.1961
14k $150 $175 $225

HAMILTON, 22J., " Baron II" , 5 diamond dial, c. 1961
14k $150 $175 $225

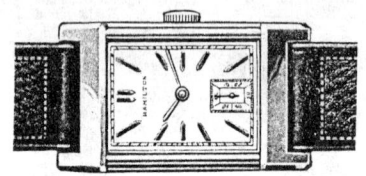

HAMILTON, 17J.," Bartley", Ca.1936
gold filled $100 $125 $175

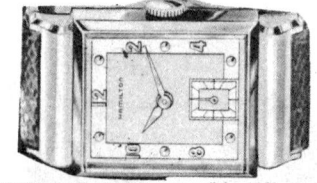

HAMILTON, 19J.,"Barton", tu tone dial, c.1951
14k $125 $150 $200

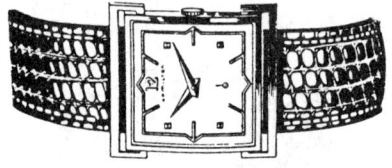

HAMILTON, 22J., "Baton", 14k markers
14k $150 $175 $225

HAMILTON,17J.,"Beldon", 2 tone dial, sealed case, c.1951
gold filled $70 $80 $100

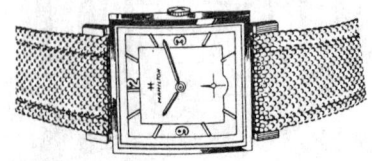

HAMILTON, 22J., " Bentley" , 14k markers, c. 1961
gold filled $50 $60 $80

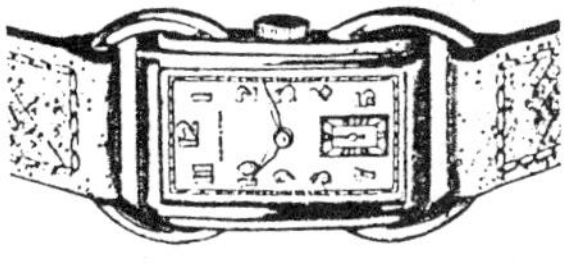

HAMILTON, 19J., " Bentley", 14k markers, Ca. 1938
14k $500 $600 $875

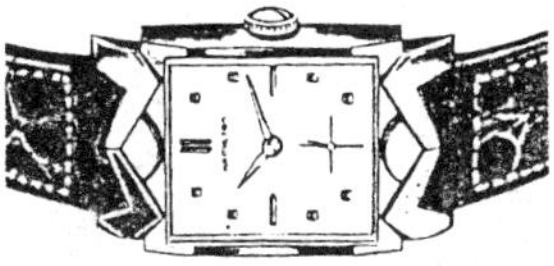

HAMILTON, 17J., "Benton" , 14k markers, c. 1954
10k $100 $125 $175

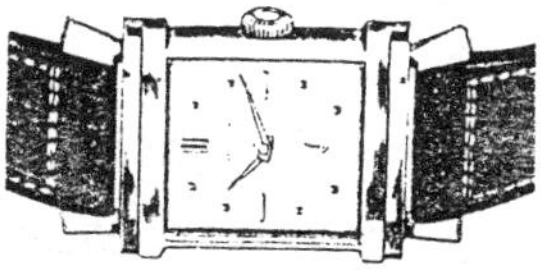

HAMILTON, 17J., "Berkshire" , 14k markers, Ca. 1952
gold filled.................................$50 $60 $80

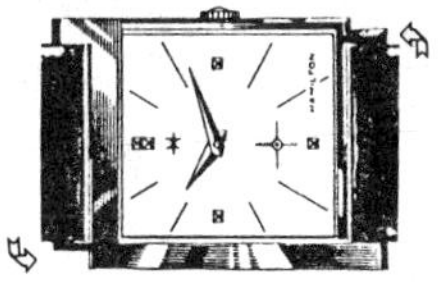

HAMILTON, 22J.,"Blade", asymmetrical note lugs, Ca.1965
gold filled........................... ★$400 $450 $550

HAMILTON, 17-21J.," Blake ", c.1951
gold filled.................................$60 $70 $90

HAMILTON, 17J., " Boatswain" , center sec., c. 1961
gold plate $35 $45 $60

HAMILTON, 17J., " Boatswain II" , c. 1961
gold plate $35 $45 $60

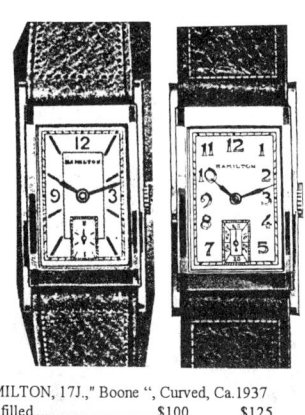

HAMILTON, 17J.," Boone ", Curved, Ca.1937
gold filled $100 $125 $175

HAMILTON, 19 jewels, "Boulton" , Ca. 1941
gold filled $75 $100 $150

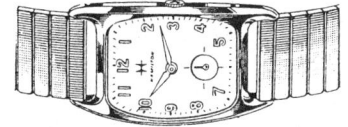

HAMILTON, 22J., " Boulton II" , 14k markers, c. 1961
gold filled $60 $70 $90

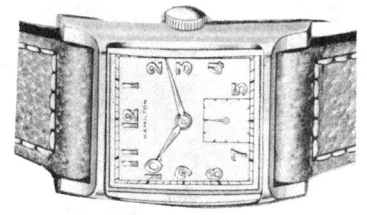

HAMILTON, 17J.,"Boyd", c.1951
gold filled $75 $100 $150

HAMILTON, 22J., "Bradford B", 14k markers, c. 1961
14k $100 $125 $175

Pricing in this Guide are fair market price for COM-
PLETE watches which are reflected from the "NAWCC" National and regional shows.

HAMILTON, 22J., "Bradford B" , **11 diam. dial,** c. 1961
14k $150 $175 $225

HAMILTON, 17J., "Brandon", swing lugs, c. 1951
gold filled............................... $100 $125 $175

HAMILTON, 17 jewels, "Brandon", Ca. 1951
gold filled................................. $80 $95 $125

HAMILTON, 19J., "Brent ", **faceted** crystal, c.1951
gold filled................................. $60 $70 $90

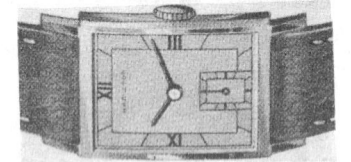

HAMILTON, 19 jewels, "Brock" , c. 1941
14k $125 $150 $200

HAMILTON, 19 jewels, "Brock" , c. 1951
14k $125 $150 $200

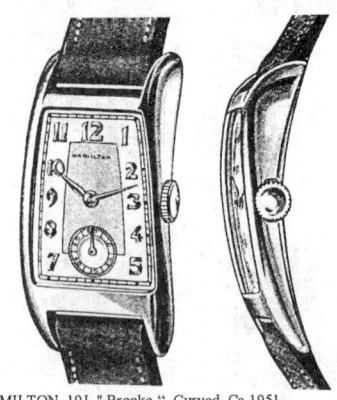

HAMILTON, 19J.," Brooke ", Curved, Ca.1951
gold filled $250 $275 $350

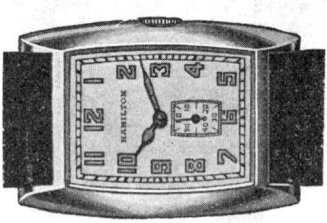

HAMILTON, 19 jewels, "Byrd"
18k $600 $650 $800
14k $400 $450 $600

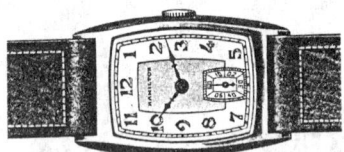

HAMILTON, 17J.,"Cabot", cal.960, Ca. 1938
gold filled $70 $80 $100

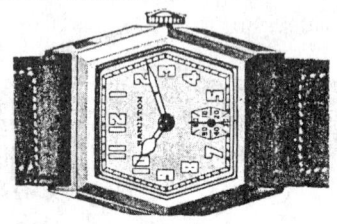

HAMILTON, 17J.,"Cambridge"
14k $500 $550 $650

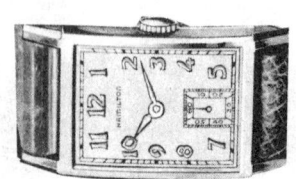

HAMILTON, 19J.," Cambridge ", c.1951
platinum................................... $400 $450 $550

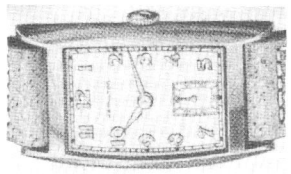

HAMILTON, 19 jewels, "Cameron" , c. 1941
14k $150 $175 $250

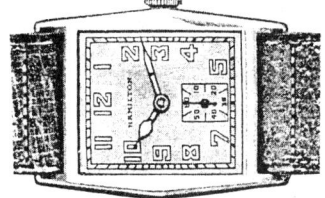

HAMILTON, 17J.,"Captain Rice"
14k $275 $300 $400

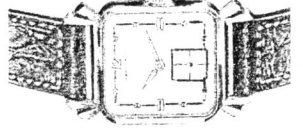

HAMILTON, 17J.," Carl ", Ca.1953
gold filled.................................$50 $60 $80

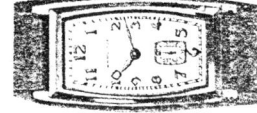

HAMILTON, 17J.," Carlisle ", 44mm, cal. 937, Ca.1937
gold filled.................................$200 $225 $275

HAMILTON, 17J.," Carson ", Ca.1935
gold filled.................................$75 $90 $125

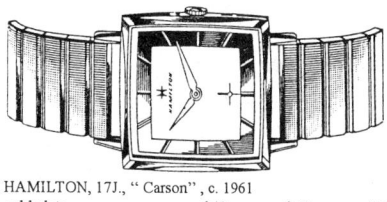

HAMILTON, 17J., " Carson " , c. 1961
gold plate $40 $45 $60

Wrist Watches listed in this section are priced at the collectable fair market **retail** level as **complete** watches having an
original gold-filled case and stainless steel back, also with
original dial, leather watch band, and the entire original movement in good working order with no repairs needed.

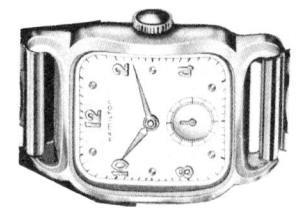

HAMILTON, 17J.," Carlton ", c.1951
gold filled $65 $75 $100

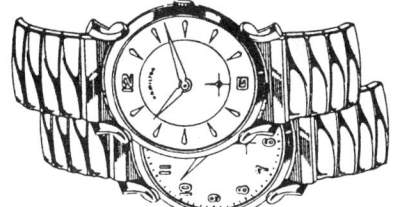

HAMILTON, 17J., " Carlyle ", c. 1961
gold plate $40 $45 $60

HAMILTON, 17J., " Carteret"   14k markers
14k $100 $125 $175

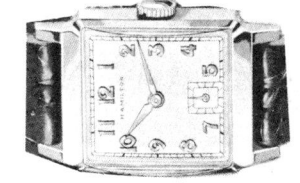

HAMILTON, 19J.," Cedric ", c.1951
gold filled $60 $70 $85

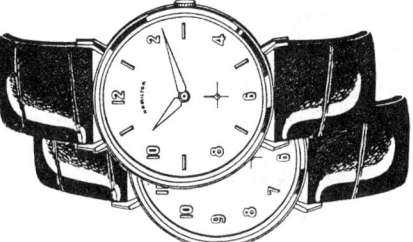

HAMILTON, 22J., "Chadwick " , 14k markers, c. 1961
14k $100 $125 $175

Pricing in this Guide are fair market price for **COM-
PLETE** watches which are reflected from the "**NAWCC**" National and regional shows.

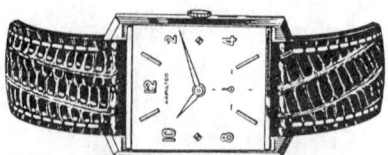

HAMILTON, 22J., "Chapman ", 14k markers, c. 1961
gold filled.................$50 $60 $80

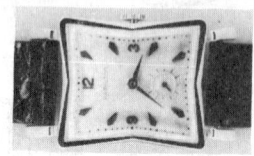

HAMILTON, 17J., " Chattam",Ca. 1953
gold filled....................$60 $70 $100
14k $100 $125 $175

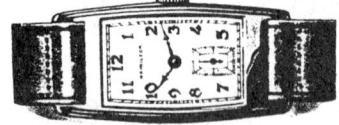

HAMILTON, 17J., " Clark", Ca. 1937
gold filled....................$100 $125 $175

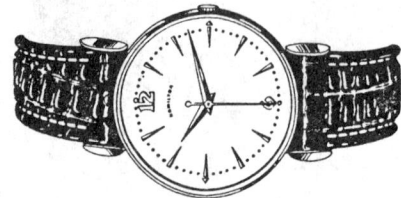

HAMILTON, 18J., "Clearview " , 14k markers, c. 1961
14k $100 $125 $175

HAMILTON, 17J.," Clinton ", c.1951
s. steel $40 $50 $70

HAMILTON, 17J.," Clyde ", c.1951
gold filled....................$75 $100 $150

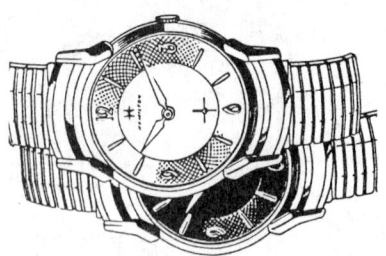

HAMILTON, 17J., "Coburn " , c. 1961
gold plate $40 $45 $60

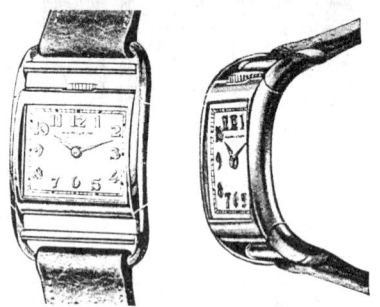

HAMILTON, 17J., "Contour " , drivers, c. 1937
gold filled $350 $400 $500

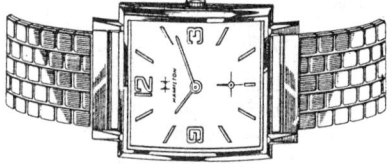

HAMILTON, 17J., "Conway ", c. 1961
gold plate $40 $45 $60

HAMILTON, 17J., " Cordell", Ca. 1961
14k C&B..............................$300 $350 $450

HAMILTON, 22J., "Corvet " , 14k markers, c. 1961
gold filled $50 $60 $80

HAMILTON, 17J., "Courtney ", 14k markers, c. 1961
gold filled...................................$60 $70 $90

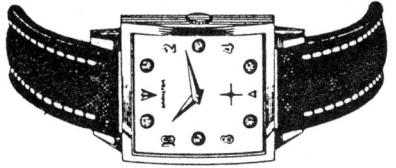

HAMILTON, 22J., "Courtney ", 6 diamond dial, c. 1961
14k $150 $175 $225

HAMILTON, 17J.," Craig ", c.1951
gold filled...............................$70 $80 $100

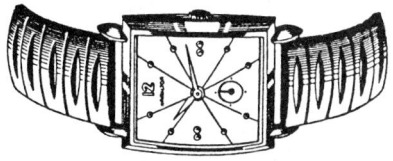

HAMILTON, 22J., " Cullen", 14k markers, c. 1961
gold filled...............................$60 $70 $90

HAMILTON, 22J., " Curtiss", Ca. 1956
14k $125 $150 $200

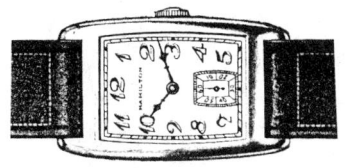

HAMILTON, 19J., " Custer", Ca. 1937
14k $200 $225 $300

HAMILTON, 17J., "Darrell", cal#747, c. 1951
gold filled $80 $90 $125

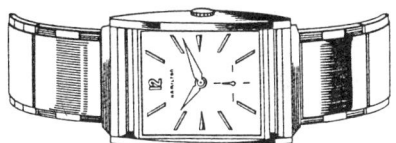

HAMILTON, 17J., "Dawson ", c. 1961
gold filled $40 $50 $70

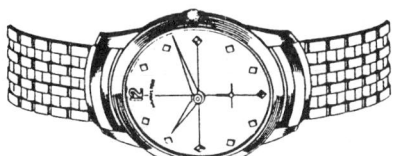

HAMILTON, 17J., "Dean ", c. 1961
gold filled $30 $40 $60

HAMILTON, 17J., "Deauville ", c. 1961
gold plate $40 $50 $70

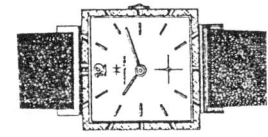

HAMILTON, 17J.," Dennis ", Ca.1961
14k $100 $125 $175

HAMILTON, 17J.," Dennis ", Ca.1951
gold filled $70 $80 $100

HAMILTON, 17J.," Dewitt ", c.1951
gold filled..............................$60 $70 $90

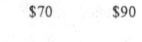

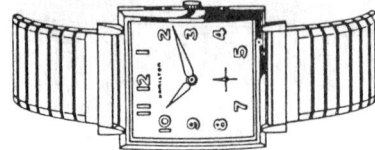

HAMILTON, 17J., " Dexter", c. 1961
gold plate $50 $60 $80

HAMILTON, 17J.," Dexter ", c.1951
gold filled..............................$70 $80 $100

HAMILTON, 17J.," Dickens ", Ca.1937
Note: Also see **Gilman** = 14k (**look-a-like**)
gold filled..............................$125 $150 $200

HAMILTON, 17J.," Dixon ", Ca.1937
gold filled..............................$100 $125 $175

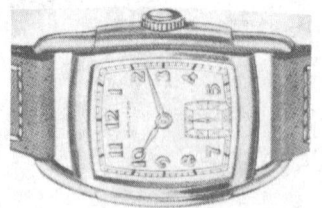

HAMILTON, 17 jewels, "Dodson" , c. 1937
gold filled..............................$100 $125 $175

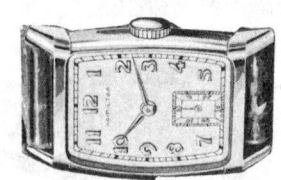

HAMILTON, 19J.," Donald ", c.1951
14k $175 $200 $250

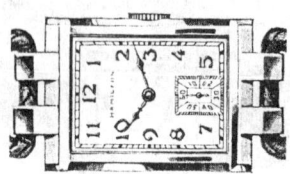

HAMILTON, 19J.," Donavan ", center lugs
14k $300 $325 $400

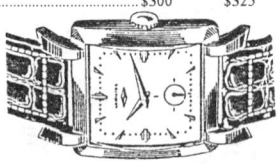

HAMILTON, 22J.," Donavan II", Ca.1961
14k $150 $175 $250

HAMILTON, 17J.," Dorsey ", Ca.1937
14k $125 $150 $200

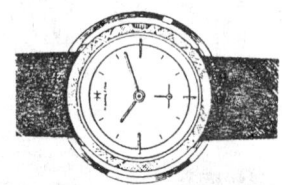

HAMILTON, 17J.," Doublet ", Ca.1961
14k $100 $120 $150

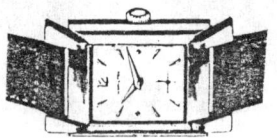

HAMILTON, 17J.," Drake ", Ca.1951
gold filled $80 $90 $110

HAMILTON, 17J.," Drake ", Ca.1935
gold filled $100 $125 $175

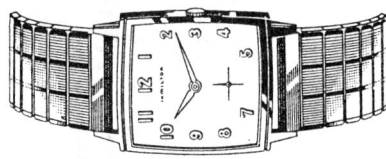

HAMILTON, 17J., "Drummond ", 14k markers, c. 1961
gold filled...................................$60 $70 $90

HAMILTON, 17J.," Dunham ", c.1951
gold filled...............................$80 $90 $120

HAMILTON, 19 jewels, "Dunkirk" , c. 1941
14k $250 $275 $350

HAMILTON, 17 jewels, "Dyson" , c. 1951
gold filled...................................$60 $70 $90

HAMILTON, 17J.," Eaton ", c.1951
gold filled...................................$80 $90 $120

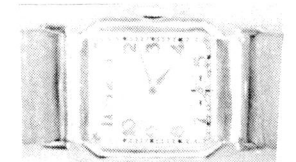

HAMILTON, 17J.," Eliott ", Cal.980
gold filled...................................$70 $80 $100

HAMILTON, 17J.," Emery ", c.1951
gold filled $70 $80 $100

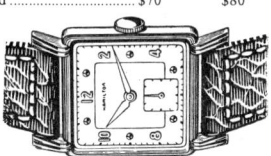

HAMILTON, 17 jewels, "Eric" , c. 1951
gold filled $70 $80 $100

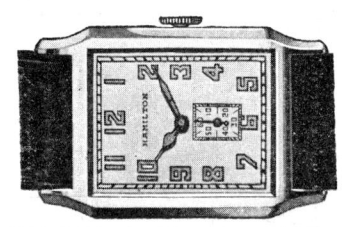

HAMILTON, 17 jewels, "Ericsson"
14k $300 $400 $600

HAMILTON, 17 jewels, "Emerson" , c. 1941
gold filled $100 $125 $175

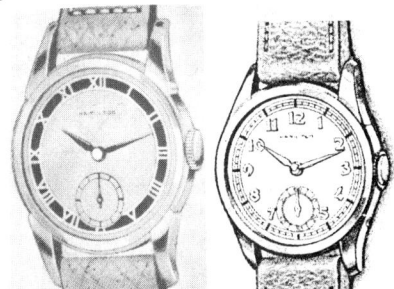

HAMILTON, 17 jewels, "Endicott" , c. 1941
gold filled $60 $75 $100

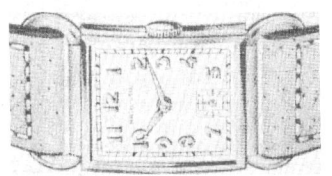

HAMILTON, 17 jewels, "Essex" , c. 1941
gold filled $125 $150 $200

HAMILTON, 17J., " Farrell", 14k # s, c.1961
gold plate $30 $35 $50

HAMILTON, 17J., " First Mate", c.1961
gold plate $30 $35 $50

HAMILTON, 18J.,"Fleetwood ", c.1951
14k $100 $125 $175

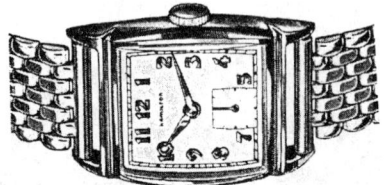

HAMILTON, 17 jewels, "Forbes", c. 1951
gold filled..............................$50 $60 $80

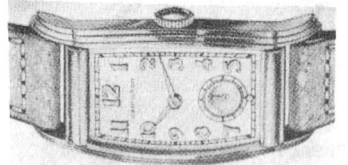

HAMILTON, 19 jewels, "Foster" , c. 1941
14k $350 $375 $450

Pricing in this Guide are fair market price for COM-
PLETE watches which are reflected from the "NAWCC" National and regional shows.

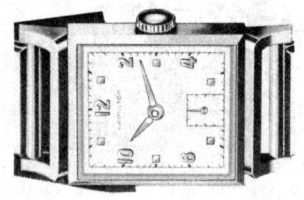

HAMILTON, 17J.," Franklin ", c.1951
gold filled $70 $80 $110

HAMILTON, 17J., " Gardner", c.1961
gold plate $40 $50 $70

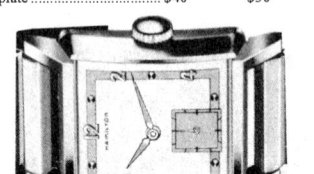

HAMILTON, 17J.," Gary ", c.1951
gold filled $75 $80 $100

HAMILTON, 17J.," Gary ", fluted lugs, Ca.1951
gold filled $50 $60 $80

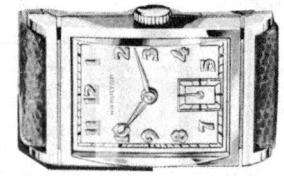

HAMILTON, 19J.," Gilbert ", c.1951
14k $150 $175 $250

Some grades are not included. Their values can be
determined by comparing with similar age, size, metal
content, style, grades, or models such as time only,
chronograph, repeater etc. listed.

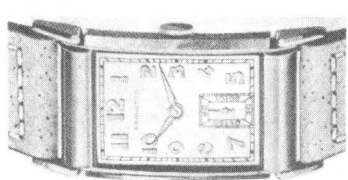

HAMILTON, 19 jewels, "Gilman" , c. 1941
Note: Also see **Dickens** = *Gold Filled* (**look-a-like**)
14k $350 $400 $500

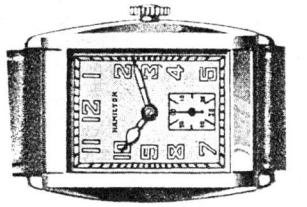

HAMILTON, 17J.,"Gladstone", cal.981, c.1951
gold filled................................$100 $135 $195

HAMILTON, 17J.," Glendale ", engraved case,
14K...$600 $700 $850

HAMILTON, 17J., " Glendon", c.1961
gold plate $40 $45 $60

HAMILTON, 17J.," Glenn ", c.1951
14k $100 $125 $175

Ⓛ Pricing in this Guide are fair market price for **COM-
PLETE** watches which are reflected from the **"NAWCC"** National and regional shows.

HAMILTON, 19 jewels, "Glenn Curtis"
14k $150 $175 $250

HAMILTON, 18J., " Golden Tempus II", 14k #s, c.1961
gold filled $40 $45 $60

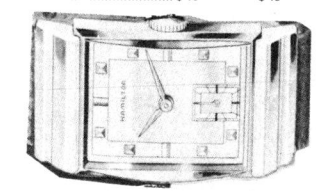

HAMILTON, 19J.," Gordon ", c.1951
18k $300 $350 $450

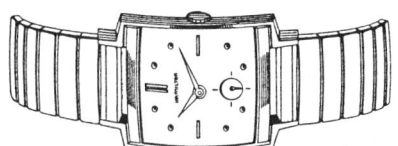

HAMILTON, 22J., " Gramercy", 14k #s, c.1961
gold filled $50 $60 $80

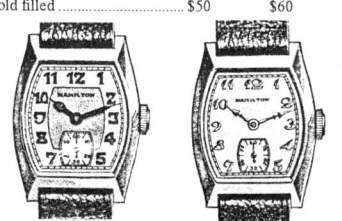

HAMILTON, 17 jewels, "Grant", Ca. 1933
gold filled $100 $125 $175

HAMILTON, 17 jewels, "Greenwich"
gold filled $100 $125 $175

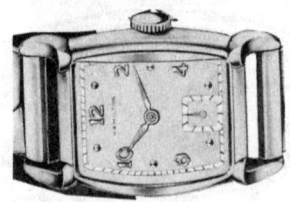

HAMILTON, 17J.," Grover ", c.1951
gold filled..................................$60 $70 $90

HAMILTON, 17J., " **Howard**", on dial & movement
gold filled $300 $325 $400

HAMILTON, 17J.," Harris ", Ca.1937
gold filled..................................$50 $60 $80

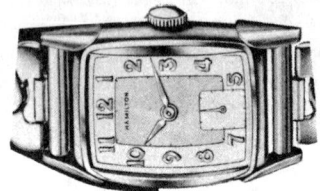

HAMILTON, 17J.," Jeffrey ", c.1951
gold filled $80 $100 $140

HAMILTON, 17J.," Hastings ", cal.987
gold filled..................................$100 $125 $175

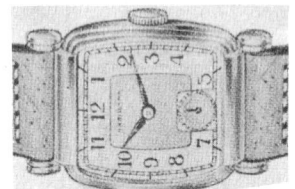

HAMILTON, 19 jewels, "Judson"
gold filled $80 $90 $125

HAMILTON, 19J.," Hayden ", c.1951
gold filled..................................$100 $125 $175

HAMILTON, 17J., " Keane", c.1961
gold plate $40 $45 $60

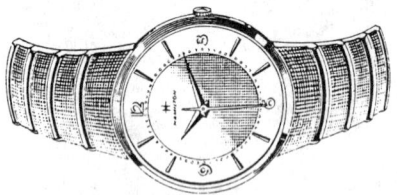

HAMILTON, 18J., " Holden", c.1961
gold filled..................................$40 $50 $70

HAMILTON, 19J.," Keith ", c.1951
14k $150 $175 $250

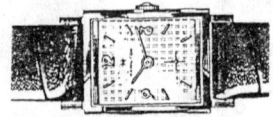

HAMILTON, 17J.," Huntley ", Ca.1961
gold filled..................................$60 $70 $90

HAMILTON, 22J.," Kevin ", hidden lugs, Ca.1951
14k $200 $250 $325

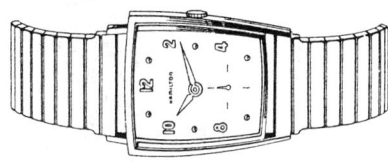

HAMILTON, 17J., '' Khyber'', 14k #s, c.1961
gold filled....................................$70 $80 $100

HAMILTON, 17J.,"Lambert '', c.1951
gold filled $80 $90 $120

HAMILTON, 17J.," Kinematic II ", Ca.1961
gold plate $40 $45 $60

HAMILTON, 17J,(Lange is =14k), Langdon is =G. filled
14k $125 $150 $200
gold filled $50 $60 $80

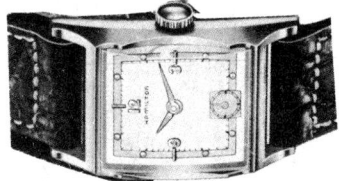

HAMILTON, 19J.," Kirby ", c.1951
gold filled..................................$80 $90 $120

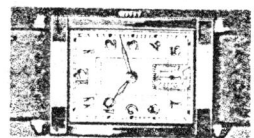

HAMILTON, 17J.," Langford ", Ca.1937
14k $150 $175 $250

HAMILTON, 17J.," Kirk ", c.1951
14k $100 $125 $175

HAMILTON, 17 jewels, "Langley"
18k $350 $400 $500

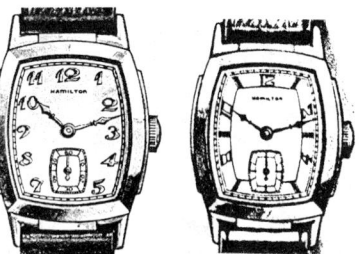

HAMILTON, 17J.," Lawrence ", Ca.1937
gold filled $80 $90 $120

HAMILTON, 17J., '' Lakeland'', c.1961
s. steel $40 $45 $60

Wrist Watches listed in this section are priced at the collectable fair market **retail** level as **complete** watches having an
original gold-filled case and stainless steel back, also with
original dial, leather watch band, and the entire original movement in good working order with no repairs needed.

HAMILTON, 17 jewels, "Lee"
gold filled..................................$200 $225 $300

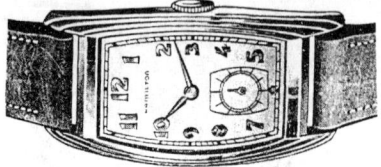

HAMILTON, 17 & 19 jewels, "Linwood" Ca. 1937
gold filled..................................$150 $200 $275

HAMILTON, 19 jewels, "Livingston"
14k $200 $250 $325

HAMILTON, 17J., " Lord Lancaster", Ca.1965
14k W..$100 $125 $175

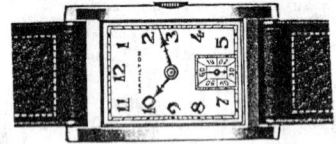

HAMILTON, 19J., " Lowell", Ca.1935
14k $175 $200 $275

HAMILTON, 17J., " Lowell", Ca.1961
gold plate $30 $35 $50

HAMILTON, 17 jewels, "Martin"
gold filled $60 $70 $90

HAMILTON, 17J., "Masterpiece", Ca.1955
14k $150 $175 $225

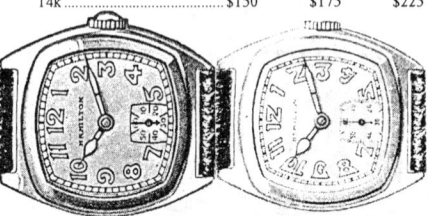

HAMILTON, 19J.,"Meadowbrook", Ca. 1933
14k $400 $450 $550
18k $550 $600 $750
Platinum..................................$800 $900 $1,100

HAMILTON, 17J., " Merritt", Ca.1937
gold filled $80 $90 $125

HAMILTON, 19 jewels, "Midas," hidden lugs , c. 1941
14k **rose**...................................$175 $200 $275

HAMILTON, 19J.," Milton ", c.1951
gold filled $80 $90 $125

HAMILTON, 17J., '' Montclair'', 14k #s, c.1961
gold filled...................................$40 $50 $70

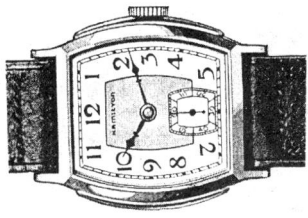

HAMILTON, 17J.,'' Morley '', c.1937
gold filled...............................$80 $90 $120

HAMILTON, 17J., '' Mount Vernon'', Ca.1932
gold filled...............................$200 $250 $325

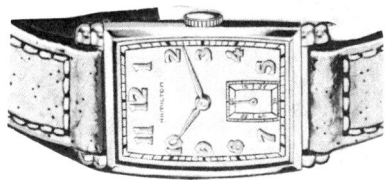

HAMILTON, 17J.,'' Myron '', c.1951
gold filled...................................$80 $90 $120

HAMILTON, 22J., '' Newlin'', 14k #s, c.1961
gold filled...................................$40 $50 $70

HAMILTON, 17J.,'' Neil '', c.1951
gold filled $50 $60 $80

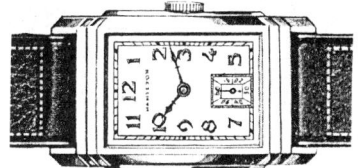

HAMILTON, 17J., '' Nelson'', Ca.1937
gold filled $100 $125 $175

HAMILTON, 17J., '' Newton'', cal.747, Ca.1951
gold filled $80 $90 $120

HAMILTON, 17J, Norde is 14k, Nordon,18J, is gold filled
14k $100 $125 $175
gold filled $60 $75 $100

HAMILTON, 19 jewels, ''Norman'' , c. 1951
14k $150 $175 $225
gold filled $80 $90 $125

HAMILTON, 17J., " Norman", 14k #s, c.1961
gold filled..................\$30   \$40   \$60

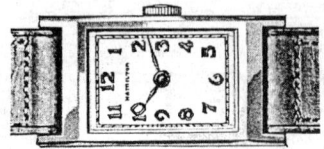

HAMILTON, 17 jewels, "Norfolk"
14k \$150   \$175   \$250

HAMILTON, 22J., " Norton", 14k #s, c.1961
gold filled..................\$60   \$70   \$90

HAMILTON, 19 jewels, "Oakmont"
14k \$300   \$350   \$450

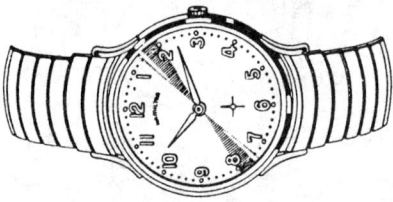

HAMILTON, 17J., "Orson", c.1961
gold filled..................\$30   \$40   \$60

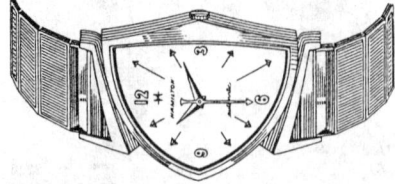

HAMILTON,17J., " Pacermatic", **auto-wind,**14k #s, c.1961
gold filled..................\$400   \$450   \$600

HAMILTON, 19 jewels, "Paige", c. 1941
gold filled \$80   \$100   \$125

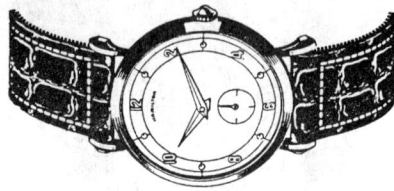

HAMILTON, 22J., " Parker B", 14k #s, c.1961
gold filled \$40   \$50   \$70

HAMILTON, 17 jewels, "Perry"
gold filled \$125   \$150   \$200

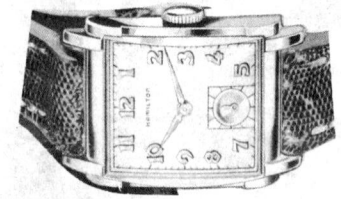

HAMILTON, 19J.," Perry ", c.1951
gold filled \$80   \$90   \$125

HAMILTON, 22J., "Peyton ", c.1961
gold filled \$30   \$40   \$60

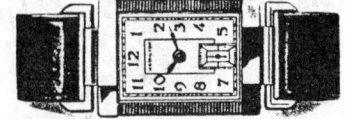

HAMILTON, 19 jewels, "Pierre" Ca. 1937
14k \$300   \$350   \$450

HAMILTON, 17J.," Pinehurst "
14k $1,000 $1,100 $1,400

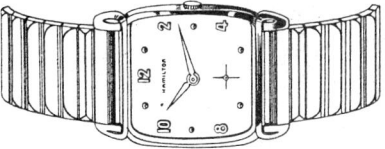

HAMILTON, 17J., " Prentice", c.1961
gold plate $40 $45 $60

HAMILTON, 17J., "Prescott ", Ca. 1937
gold filled....................................$50 $60 $80

HAMILTON, 17 jewels, "Putnam"
14k $400 $450 $550

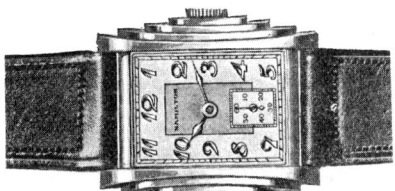

HAMILTON, 17 jewels, "Putnam"
gold filled.................................$150 $175 $225

HAMILTON, 22J.," Radburn", 14k #s, c.1961
14k $125 $150 $195

HAMILTON, 17J.," Raleigh ", Plain
14k $250 $300 $375

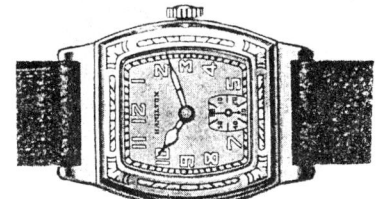

HAMILTON, 17J.,"Raleigh", Engraved
gold filled $100 $125 $175

HAMILTON, 17J., " Ramsey", c.1961
gold plate $30 $40 $60

HAMILTON, 17 jewels, "Randolph" , c. 1937
gold filled $50 $60 $80

HAMILTON, 18J., " Randolph", 14k #s, c.1961
14k $100 $125 $175

HAMILTON, 17 jewels, "Reagan" , c. 1941
gold filled $80 $90 $125

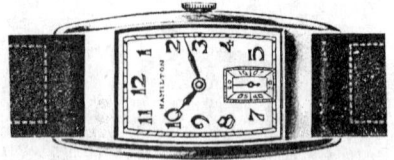

HAMILTON, 19J., " Richmond", 18K #s, Ca.1935
18k $300 $350 $450

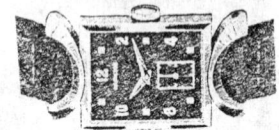

HAMILTON, 17J., " Robert", Ca.1953
14k $200 $250 $325

HAMILTON, 18J., " Rodney", 14k #s, Ca.1961
gold filled.................................$40 $50 $70

HAMILTON, 17J., "Roland", Ca.1937
gold filled.................................$80 $90 $125

HAMILTON, 22J., " Romanesque M", c.1961
14k $100 $125 $175

HAMILTON, 17J., "Romanesque N ", c.1961
gold filled.................................$30 $40 $60

HAMILTON, 22J., " Romanesque R", c.1961
gold filled $30 $40 $60

HAMILTON, 22J., "Romanesque S ", c.1961
gold filled $75 $80 $120

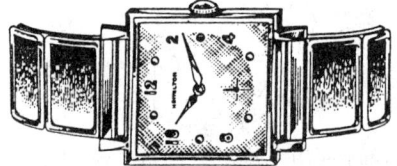

HAMILTON, 17J., " Romanesque T", c.1961
gold plate $75 $80 $100

HAMILTON, 19 jewels, "Ross" , c. 1941
gold filled $75 $95 $120

HAMILTON, 17 jewels, "Russell", hinged lugs , c. 1941
gold filled $70 $80 $100

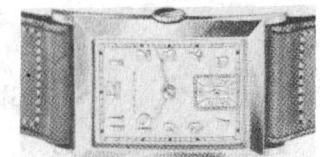

HAMILTON, 19 jewels, "Rutledge" , c. 1941
platinum.................................$700 $800 $1,000

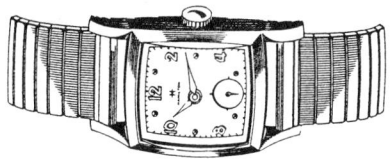

HAMILTON, 17J., " Sawyer", 14k #s, c.1961
gold filled..................................$70 $80 $100

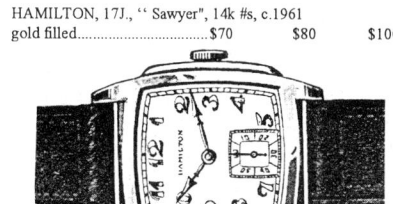

HAMILTON, 17J.," Scott ", GJS, Ca..1935
gold filled..................................$70 $80 $100

HAMILTON, 19J.," Scott ", GJS, 982, Ca.1951
14k $250 $275 $350

HAMILTON, 17J., " Sea Breeze", c.1961
gold plate $30 $35 $50

HAMILTON, 17J., " Seabrook", c.1961
gold plate $40 $45 $60

🕐 Some grades are not included. Their values can be
determined by comparing with similar age, size, metal
content, style, grades, or models such as time only,
chronograph, repeater etc. listed.

HAMILTON, 17J., " Sea-cap ", c.1961
gold plate $30 $35 $50

HAMILTON, 22J., " Sea Cliff ", 14k #s, c.1961
gold filled $40 $50 $70

HAMILTON, 17J., " Sea - crest", c.1961
s. steel $20 $30 $50

HAMILTON, 17J., " Sea- glo ", c.1961
s. steel $30 $40 $60

HAMILTON, 17J., " Sea - guard", c.1962
s. steel $20 $30 $50

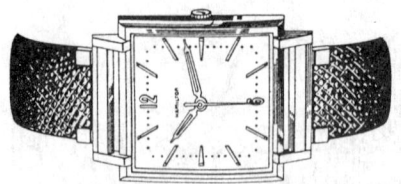

HAMILTON, 17J., '' Sea - mate'', c.1961
gold plate $50 $60 $80

HAMILTON, 17J., '' Sea - skip'', c.1962
s. steel $30 $35 $50

HAMILTON, 22J., '' Sea Ranger'' , 14K #s, c.1961
gold filled................................. $50 $60 $80

HAMILTON, 17J., '' Seaview'', 14k #s, c.1961
14k $100 $125 $175

HAMILTON, 17J., '' Sea Rover B'', c.1961
s. steel $30 $35 $50

HAMILTON, 18J.,"Sectometer B ", c.1951
gold filled $40 $50 $70

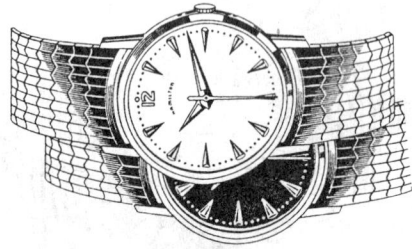

HAMILTON, 17J., '' Sea- scape '', c.1961
gold plate $30 $35 $50

HAMILTON, 18J.," Sectometer C ", c.1951
14k $125 $150 $200

HAMILTON, 17J., '' Sea- scout B '', c.1961
s. steel $30 $35 $50

HAMILTON, 17J., '' Sedgman'', Ca. 1952
gold filled $75 $100 $150

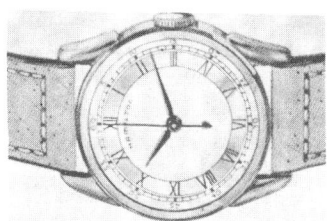

HAMILTON, 17 jewels, "Sentinel," hack setting , Ca. 1941
gold filled..................................$40 $50 $80

HAMILTON, 18J., " Seville", c.1961
gold filled..................................$30 $40 $60

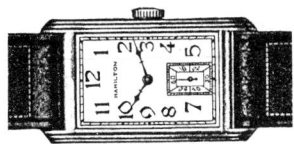

HAMILTON, 19J., " Sherwood", Ca.1935
14k $200 $225 $300

HAMILTON, 22J., " Sherwood M", 14k #s, wood dial,
American walnut wood dial, c.1961
14k $400 $450 $550

HAMILTON, 17J., " Sherwood N", 14k #s, wood dial,
Mexican Mahogany wood dial, c.1961
14k $300 $350 $425

HAMILTON, 22J.," Sherwood R", dial is made of wood,
(dial is American walnut) c.1961
14k $350 $400 $550

HAMILTON, 19J.," Sherwood", c.1951
gold filled $75 $100 $150

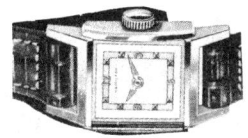

HAMILTON, 17J.," Sheryll ", small size, c.1951, also
matched styling to the Sherwood, ladies watch
gold filled $75 $100 $150

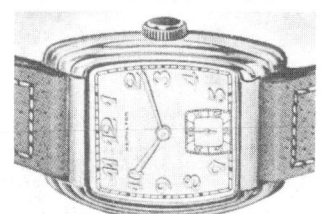

HAMILTON, 17 jewels, "Sidney" , c. 1941
gold filled $80 $90 $120

HAMILTON, 22J., " Sir Echo" ,14K #s, 6 diamond, c.1961
14k $125 $150 $200

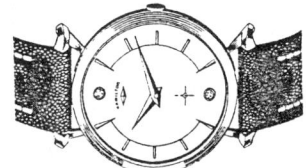

HAMILTON, 22J., " Sir Echo", 2 diamonds, 14K #s, c.1961
14k $125 $150 $200

HAMILTON, 22J., " Sir Echo" , 14K #s, c.1961
14k $125 $150 $200

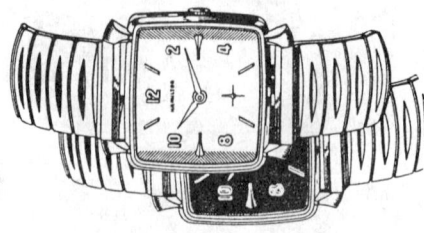

HAMILTON, 17J., "Sloane " , c.1961
gold plate $30 $35 $50

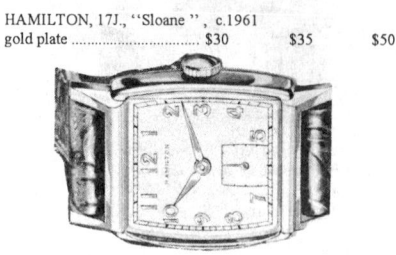

HAMILTON, 17J.," Spencer ", c.1951
10k $100 $120 $150

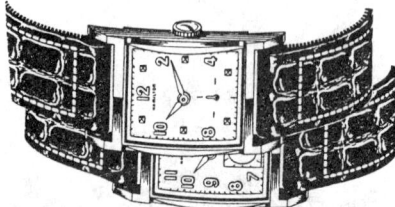

HAMILTON, 22J., " Stafford" , 14K #s, c.1961
14k $125 $150 $200

HAMILTON, 18 jewels, "Steeldon" , c. 1951
s. steel $30 $35 $50

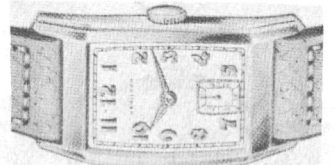

HAMILTON, 17 jewels, "Stanford" , c. 1941
gold filled..................................$80 $90 $120

Pricing in this Guide are fair market price for COM-
PLETE watches which are reflected from the "NAWCC" National and regional shows.

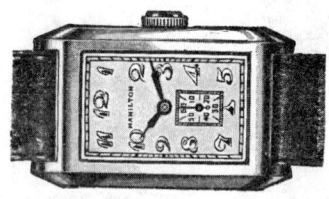

HAMILTON, 19 jewels, "Stanley"
gold filled $100 $125 $175

HAMILTON, 18J., " Stormking IV" , 14K #s, c.1961
gold filled $40 $50 $70

HAMILTON, 18J., " Stormking VI" , c.1961
gold filled $30 $40 $60

HAMILTON, 18J., " Stormking VII" , c.1961
gold filled $30 $40 $60

HAMILTON, 18J., " Stormking VIII" , 14K #s, c.1961
10k $90 $100 $120

Wrist Watches listed in this section are priced at the collectable fair market **retail** level as **complete** watches having an
original gold-filled case and stainless steel back, also with
original dial, leather watch band, and the entire original movement in good working order with no repairs needed.

HAMILTON, 17J., '' Stormking IX'', 14K #s, c.1961
14k $100 $125 $175

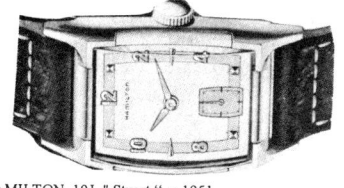

HAMILTON, 19J.,'' Stuart ``, c.1951
gold filled................................$80 $90 $120

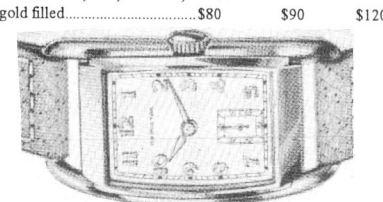

HAMILTON, 17-19 jewels, ''Sutton'', Ca. 1941
gold filled................................$150 $175 $200

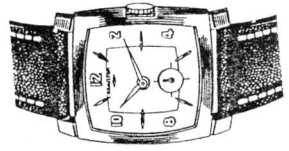

HAMILTON, 22 jewels, ''Sutton II'' , Ca. 1961
14k $125 $150 $200

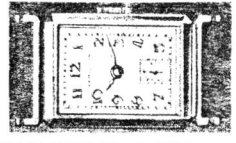

HAMILTON, 17J., '' Talbot'' , Ca.1937
gold filled................................$90 $120 $150

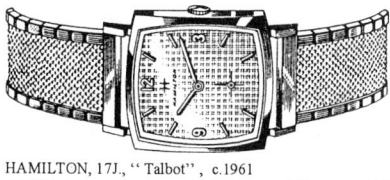

HAMILTON, 17J., '' Talbot'' , c.1961
gold filled................................ $60 $70 $90

🕐 Pricing in this Guide are fair market price for **COM-PLETE** watches which are reflected from the "**NAWCC**" National and regional shows.

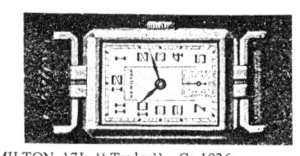

HAMILTON, 17J., '' Taylor'' , Ca.1936
gold filled $125 $150 $200

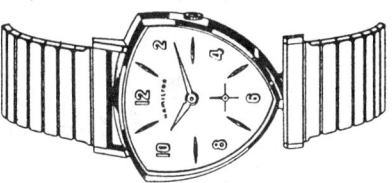

HAMILTON, 22J., '' Thor'' , 14K #s, c.1961
gold filled $175 $200 $300

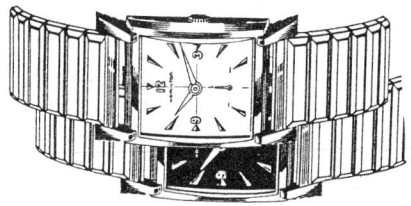

HAMILTON, 22J., '' Trent'' , 14K #s, c.1961
gold filled $90 $100 $125

HAMILTON, 18J.,'' Todd ``, c.1951
gold filled $50 $60 $80

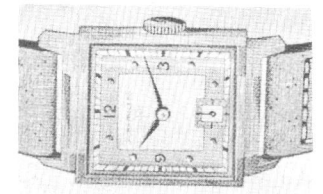

HAMILTON, 19 jewels, ''Touraine'' , c. 1941
14k **rose** $150 $175 $275

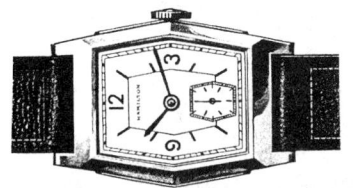

HAMILTON, 17J., '' Turner'' , Ca.1937
gold filled $100 $125 $165

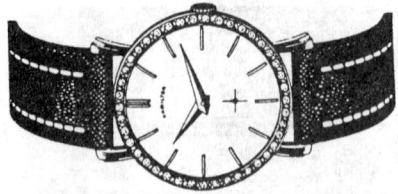

HAMILTON,22J., "Tuxedo B ", 44 diamonds,14K #s,
14k(w).................................... $250 $300 $375

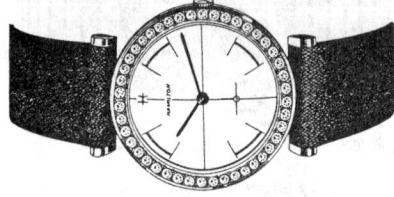

HAMILTON, 22J., " Tuxedo II", 44 diamonds,14K #s,
14k(w).................................... $250 $300 $375

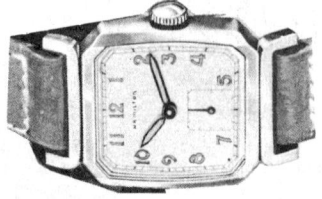

HAMILTON, 17J.," Raymon ", c.1951
s. steel $70 $90 $125

HAMILTON, 17J.," Vardon ", sealed. c.1951
s. steel $30 $40 $60

HAMILTON, 22J., " Valiant" , 14K #s, c.1961
gold filled.............................. $225 $250 $300

Wrist Watches listed in this section are priced at the collectable
fair market **retail** level as **complete** watches having an original
gold-filled case and stainless steel back, also with original dial,
leather watch band, and the entire original movement in good
working order with no repairs needed.

HAMILTON, 17J., " Viking", c.1961
gold plate $40 $45 $60

HAMILTON, 17J., " Viking II" , c.1961
gold plate $30 $35 $50

HAMILTON, 17 jewels, "Vincent" , c. 1941
gold filled $80 $90 $120

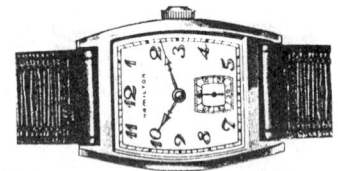

HAMILTON, 17 jewels, "Watson", Ca. 1930
gold filled $70 $80 $110

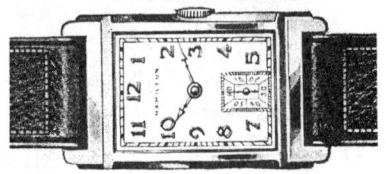

HAMILTON, 19 jewels, "Wayne", Ca. 1935
14k $125 $150 $200

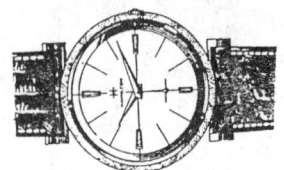

HAMILTON, 17 jewels, "Whitford", Ca. 1960
14k $100 $125 $175

HAMILTON, 17 jewels, "Webster", Ca. 1935
gold filled...............................$100 $125 $175

HAMILTON, 19J.," Wesley ", c.1951
14k $150 $175 $225

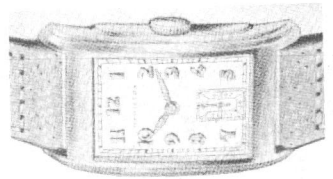

HAMILTON, 17 jewels, "Whitman" , c. 1941
gold filled...............................$100 $125 $175

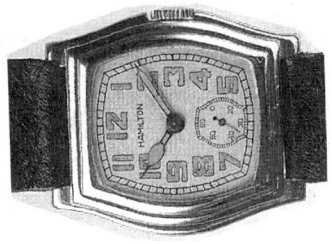

HAMILTON, 17 jewels, "Whitney"
gold filled.................... ★ ★ $200 $250 $325

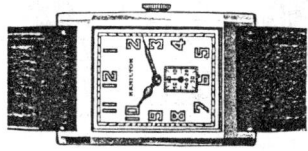

HAMILTON, 19 jewels, "Wilkinson", Ca. 1934
14k $125 $150 $200

🕐 Pricing in this Guide are fair market price for **COM-PLETE** watches which are reflected from the "**NAWCC**" National and regional shows.

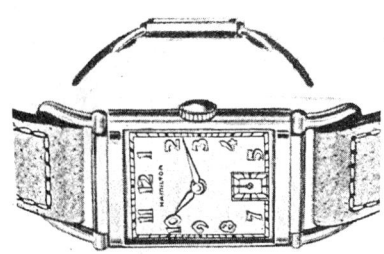

HAMILTON, 19 jewels, "Wilshire" , c. 1941
gold filled $125 $150 $200

HAMILTON, 17 jewels, "Wilson", flared, Ca. 1956
gold filled $70 $80 $100

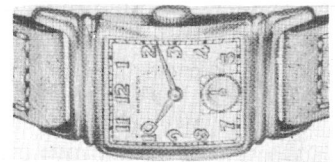

HAMILTON, 19 jewels, "Winthrop" , c. 1941
gold filled $80 $90 $110

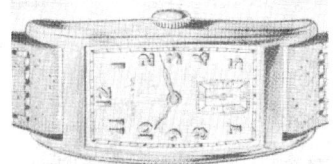

HAMILTON, 17 jewels, "Yorktown" , c. 1941
gold filled $100 $125 $175

HAMILTON,18J., (ORIGINAL) Masonic dial, Ca.1960
gold filled $80 $90 $100

🕐 Pricing in this Guide are fair market price for **COM-PLETE** watches which are reflected from the "**NAWCC**" National and regional shows.

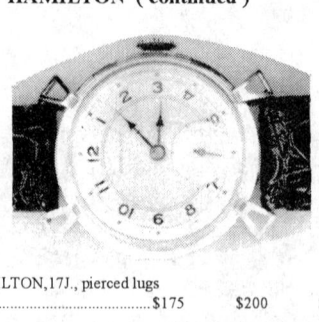

HAMILTON,17J., pierced lugs
14k $175 $200 $250

HAMILTON, 17 jewels, "Accumatic X"
s. steel $30 $35 $50

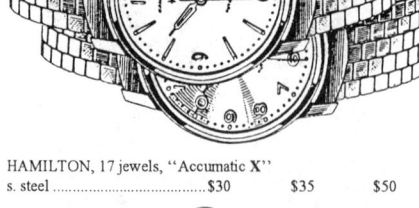

HAMILTON, 17 jewels, "Accumatic XI"
s. steel $30 $35 $50

HAMILTON, 17 jewels, "Accumatic A-575", date
s. steel $30 $35 $50

HAMILTON, 17 jewels, "Accumatic A-600"
gold plate $30 $35 $50

HAMILTON, 17 jewels, "Accumatic A-650"
gold plate $40 $45 $60

HAMILTON, 17 jewels, "Accumatic A-651"
gold plate $40 $45 $60

HAMILTON, 17 jewels, "Automatic K-203"
14k $100 $125 $175

HAMILTON, 17 jewels, "Automatic K-303"
10k $80 $90 $120

HAMILTON, 17 jewels, "Automatic K-304"
10k $80 $90 $120

Note: Hamilton acquired the Buren
Watch Factory of Switzerland in 1966
and adapted a ultra thin self-winding
movement for the **Thin-o-matic.**

HAMILTON, 17 jewels, "Automatic **K-414**"
gold filled................................ $60 $70 $90

HAMILTON, 17 jewels, "Automatic **K-417**"
gold filled $60 $70 $90

HAMILTON, 17 jewels, "Accumatic **VII**"
gold plate $60 $70 $90

HAMILTON, 17 jewels, "Automatic **K-418**"
gold filled $60 $70 $90

HAMILTON, 17 jewels, "Automatic **K-415**"
gold filled................................ $60 $70 $90

HAMILTON, 17 jewels, "Automatic **K-419**"
gold filled $60 $70 $90

HAMILTON, 17 jewels, "Automatic **K-416**"
gold filled................................ $60 $70 $90

HAMILTON, 17 jewels, "Automatic **K-420**"
gold filled $60 $70 $90

HAMILTON, 17 jewels, "**Kinematic II**"
gold plate $40 $50 $70

HAMILTON, 17 jewels, "Automatic **K-458**"
gold filled $60 $70 $90

🕐 Some grades are not included. Their values can be determined by comparing with **similar** age, size, metal content, style, grades, or models such as **time only**, chronograph, repeater etc. listed.

🕐 Pricing in this Guide are fair market price for **COMPLETE** watches which are reflected from the **"NAWCC"** National and regional shows.

HAMILTON, 17 jewels, ''Automatic **K-459**''
gold filled.................................$60 $70 $90

HAMILTON, 17 jewels, ''Automatic **K-650**''
gold plate $30 $40 $60

HAMILTON, 17 jewels, ''Automatic **K-460**''
gold filled.................................$60 $70 $90

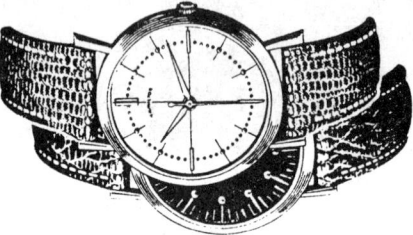

HAMILTON, 18 jewels, ''Thincraft **II**''
gold filled $30 $40 $60

HAMILTON, 17J, ''Automatic **K-475**'', *Swiss movement*
gold filled................... ★ ★ ★ $800 $900 $1,200

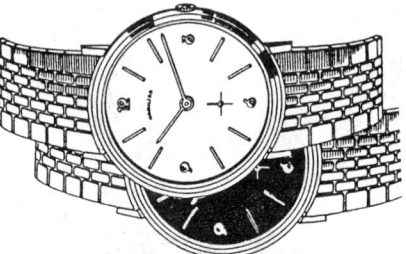

HAMILTON, 17 jewels, ''Thinline **2000**''
14k $100 $125 $175

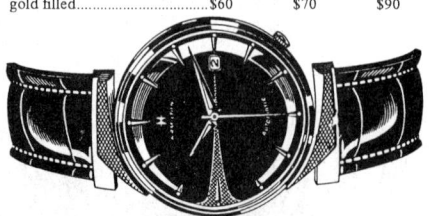

HAMILTON, 17 jewels, ''Automatic **K-503**'' Ca.1962
s. steel $20 $30 $50

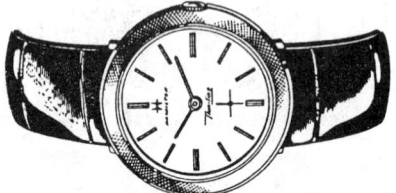

HAMILTON, 17 jewels, ''Thinline **2001**''
14k $100 $125 $175

HAMILTON, 17 jewels, ''Automatic **K-507**''
s. steel $30 $40 $60

HAMILTON, 17 jewels, ''Thinline **3000**''
10k $80 $90 $110

HAMILTON, 17 jewels, "Thinline **4000**"
gold filled..................................$30 $40 $60

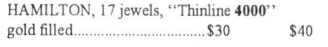

HAMILTON, 17 jewels, "Thinline **4001**"
gold filled..................................$40 $50 $70

HAMILTON, 17 jewels, "Thin-o-matic", **date**
gold plate $30 $40 $60

HAMILTON, 17 jewels, "Thin-o-matic", **Masterpiece**
14k $100 $125 $175

HAMILTON, 17 jewels, "Thin-o-matic **T-200**"
14k $100 $125 $175

HAMILTON, 17 jewels, "Thin-o-matic **T-201**", 6- diamonds
14k $150 $175 $225

HAMILTON, 17 jewels, "Thin-o-matic **T-201**"
14k $100 $125 $175

HAMILTON, 17 jewels, "Thin-o-matic **T-202**"
14k $100 $125 $175

HAMILTON, 17 jewels, "Thin-o-matic **T-300**"
10k $80 $90 $125

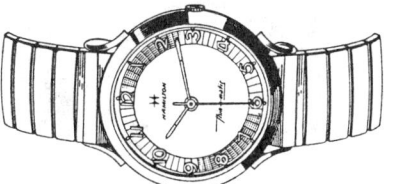

HAMILTON, 17 jewels, "Thin-o-matic **T-400**"
gold filled $40 $50 $70

Pricing in this Guide are fair market price for **COM-PLETE** watches which are reflected from the "**NAWCC**" National and regional shows.

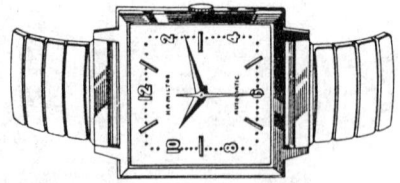

HAMILTON, 17 jewels, "Thin-o-matic **T-401**"
gold filled..................................$70 $80 $100

HAMILTON, 17 jewels, "Thin-o-matic **T-450**"
gold filled $30 $40 $60

HAMILTON, 17 jewels, "Thin-o-matic **T-402**"
gold filled..................................$30 $40 $60

HAMILTON, 17 jewels, "Thin-o-matic **T-451**"
gold filled $30 $40 $60

HAMILTON, 17 jewels, "Thin-o-matic **T-403**"
gold filled (with date)......... ★$225 $250 $325
gold filled............................ ★$200 $225 $275

HAMILTON, 17 jewels, "Thin-o-matic **T-475**"
gold filled $30 $40 $60

HAMILTON, 17 jewels, "Thin-o-matic **T-476**", date
gold filled $40 $50 $70

HAMILTON, 17 jewels, "Thin-o-matic **T-404**"
gold filled..................................$40 $50 $70

HAMILTON, 17 jewels, "Thin-o-matic **T-500**"
s. steel $30 $40 $60

HAMILTON, 17 jewels, "Thin-o-matic **T-405**"
gold filled..................................$30 $40 $60

Wrist Watches listed in this section are priced at the collectable fair market **retail** level as **complete** watches having an original gold-filled case and stainless steel back, also with original dial, leather watch band, and the entire original movement in good working order with no repairs needed.

🕐 Some grades are not included. Their values can be determined by comparing with **similar** age, size, metal content, style, grades, or models such as **time only**, chronograph, repeater etc. listed.

HAMILTON, 17 jewels, "Thin-o-matic T-501"
s. steel $30 $40 $60

HAMILTON, 17 jewels, "Thin-o-matic T-502"
s. steel $30 $40 $60

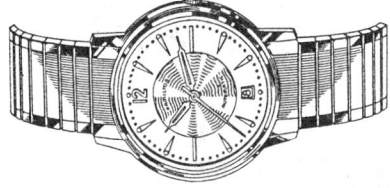

HAMILTON, 17 jewels, "Thin-o-matic T-575" date
s. steel $30 $40 $60

HAMILTON, 17 jewels, "Thin-o-matic T-650"
gold plate $30 $40 $60

HAMILTON, 17 jewels, "Thinline 5000"
s. steel $40 $50 $70

HAMILTON, 17 jewels, "Cushion B"
gold filled $60 $70 $85

HAMILTON, 17 jewels, " Cushion " plain or engraved
14k $200 $225 $275
gold filled $70 $80 $100

HAMILTON, 17 jewels, tonneau engraved
14k $225 $275 $350
gold filled $80 $90 $125

HAMILTON, 17J.,"Tonneau" plain
14k $200 $225 $300
gold filled $80 $90 $120

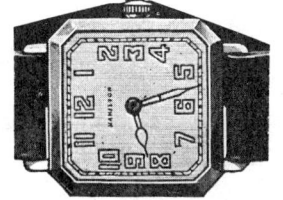

HAMILTON, 17J., " Square " cal.986 cut corner
gold filled $60 $70 $90
14k $100 $125 $175

HAMILTON, 17J., Square cut corner, **engraved** lugs
gold filled...................................$80 $90 $120

HAMILTON, 17 jewels, 2 tone dial, engraved fancy
14k $200 $250 $325
gold filled...................................$80 $90 $120

HAMILTON, 17 jewels, 2 tone dial, aux. sec.
14k $125 $150 $200

HAMILTON, 17J., cal.986, c.1928
gold filled...................................$70 $80 $100

HAMILTON, 19J., gold jewel settings, cal.982, c.1943
platinum $500 $550 $650

HAMILTON, 17J., cal.987, **enamel** on case, c.1930
gold filled $100 $125 $175

HAMILTON, 17J., "Reardon", Ca.1953
14K $100 $125 $175

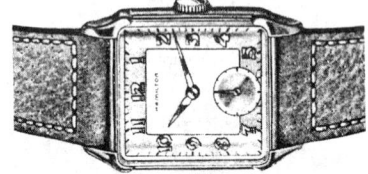

HAMILTON, 17J., "Dwight", 18K applied numbers, Ca.1948
gold filled $70 $80 $100

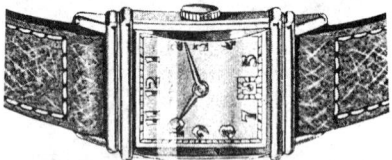

HAMILTON, 19J., "Lester", 18K applied numbers, Ca.1948
gold filled $90 $100 $125

HAMILTON, 19J., "Barry", 18K applied numbers, Ca.1948
gold filled $80 $90 $120

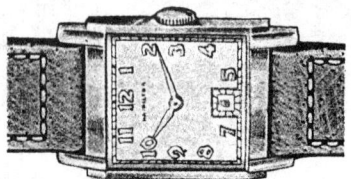

HAMILTON, 17J., "Haddon", Ca. 1953
gold filled $70 $80 $100

HAMILTON,17J., cal.980 , c.1938
gold filled................................$100 $125 $175

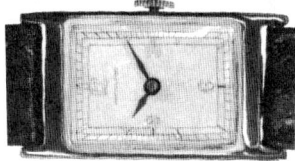

HAMILTON,17J., cal.989E , c.1936
gold filled................................$70 $80 $100

HAMILTON,17J., "Kingdon", Ca. 1943
14K..$100 $125 $175

HAMILTON, 17 jewels, engraved bezel, hinged back
14k(w)....................................$250 $275 $350

HAMILTON, 22J., "Viscount", cal.770, Ca.1959
14k $250 $275 $350

HAMILTON, 17J., "Lyndon", Ca. 1953
gold filled................................$100 $125 $175

HAMILTON, 17J., Ca.1950
gold filled $60 $70 $90

HAMILTON, 17 jewels, hidden lugs
14k $125 $150 $200

HAMILTON, 17 jewels, long lugs
14k $100 $125 $175

HAMILTON, 17 jewels, engraved bezel, c. 1920
14k $150 $175 $225

HAMILTON, 17J, *Hamilton Illinois* on dial, sold by Hamilton & Illinois marked on case with Illinois mvt. (**crossover**).
gold filled $100 $125 $175

HAMILTON, 17 jewels, "Masterpiece", Ca. 1968
14K...$125 $150 $185

HAMILTON, 19 jewels
platinum C&B.....................$1,000 $1,100 $1,300

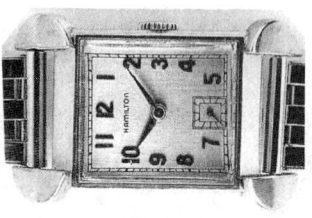

HAMILTON, 19 jewels, 18K applied numbers, Ca.1950
NOTE: Large LUGS
14K...$150 $175 $225

HAMILTON, 17J., "Beldon", Ca.1953
gold filled..............................$100 $125 $150

HAMILTON, 19J.,"bomb timer", c.1944
base metal $225 $250 $350

HAMILTON, 15 J., military frogman style, waterproof
(USN BU SHIPS on dial), canteen style
s. steel.....................................$450 $525 $625

HAMILTON, 21 J., military issue, hack setting, c.1960s
base metal.................................$80 $95 $140

HAMILTON, 17J, cut corner engraved, 987 grade, Ca. 1928
gold filled................................$80 $90 $120
14k $200 $250 $300

HAMILTON,17J, barrel engraved, 987 grade, Ca.1928
gold filled................................$80 $90 $120
14k...$200 $250 $300

HAMILTON, 17-19 jewels, diamond dial, hooded lugs
14k $800 $900 $1,100

HAMILTON, 17-19 jewels, diamond dial
14k(w).....................................$800 $900 $1,100

HAMILTON, 17-19 jewels, diamond dial , curved
platinum...............................$1,000 $1,100 $1,300
14k $800 $900 $1,100

HAMILTON, 17-19 jewels, diamond dial, c. 1940
14k $800 $900 $1,100

HAMILTON, 17-19 jewels, diamond dial
14k $400 $450 $550

HAMILTON, 17-19 jewels, diamond dial, hooded lugs
14k $500 $550 $600

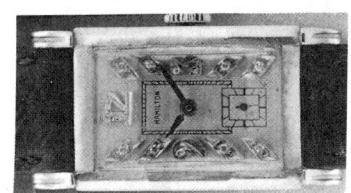

HAMILTON, 17-19 jewels,diamond dial
14k..$500 $550 $600

HAMILTON, 17-19 jewels, diam. dial, c.1948, top hat
platinum $1,200 $1,300 $1,500
14k (w)..................................$900 $1,000 $1,200

HAMILTON, 17-19 jewels, diamond dial
14k (w)....................................$400 $450 $550

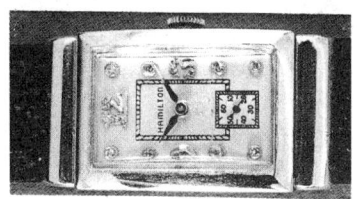

HAMILTON, 17-19 jewels, diamond dial, hooded lugs
14k..$450 $500 $600

HAMILTON, 17-19 jewels, diamond dial
platinum $1,100 $1,200 $1,400
14k (w)....................................$900 $1,000 $1,200

Wrist Watches listed in this section are priced at the collectable
fair market **retail** level as **complete** watches having an original
gold-filled case and stainless steel back, also with original dial,
leather watch band, and the entire original movement in good
working order with no repairs needed.

HAMILTON, 17-19J., mystery dial with diamonds & **bezel**
18k $550 $650 $800
14k $450 $550 $650

HAMILTON, 17-19 jewels, diamond dial
14k $200 $250 $325

HAMILTON, 17-19 jewels, diamond dial
14k (w)....................................$175 $225 $300

HAMILTON, 19 jewels, diamond dial, fancy *knotted* lugs
14k (w)....................................$200 $225 $300

HAMILTON,17J., " Belmont ", cal.955 , c.1933
gold filled..................................$30 $35 $50

HAMILTON,17J., " Ladies Tonneau "cal.987 , c.1933
gold filled..................................$40 $45 $60

HAMILTON,17J., "Bianca", diamond & sapphire, c.1933
18k(w)....................................$150 $175 $250

HAMILTON,17J., " Bryn Mawr ", c.1933
14k...$60 $70 $100

HAMILTON,17J., " Briarcliffe ", c.1933
gold filled..................................$30 $35 $50

HAMILTON,17J., " Caroline ", cal.955, c.1933
gold filled..................................$20 $25 $35

HAMILTON,17J., " Cedarcrest ", cal.955, c.1933
14k...$50 $60 $80

HAMILTON,17J., " Chevy Chase A ", cal. , c.1933
14k(w) $60 $70 $90

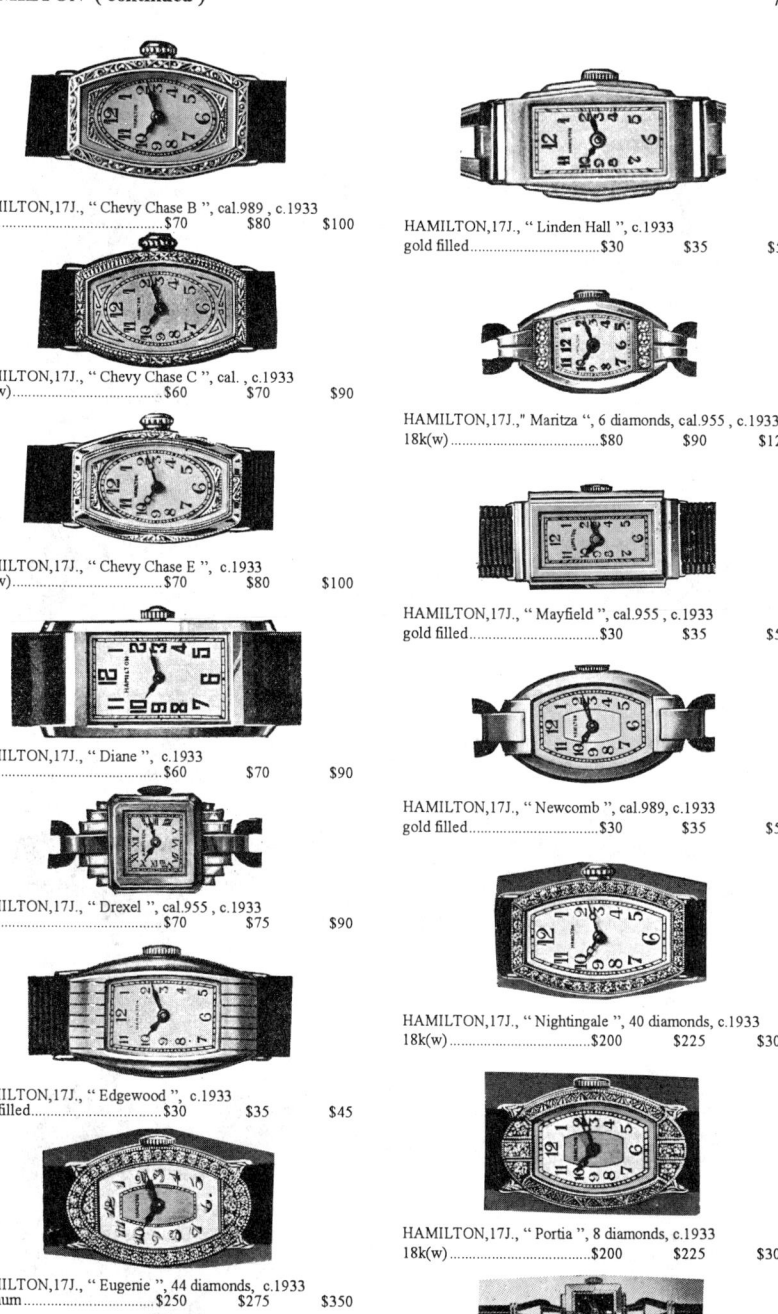

HAMILTON,17J., " Chevy Chase B ", cal.989 , c.1933
14k $70 $80 $100

HAMILTON,17J., " Chevy Chase C ", cal. , c.1933
14k(w).............................$60 $70 $90

HAMILTON,17J., " Chevy Chase E ", c.1933
14k(w)...............................$70 $80 $100

HAMILTON,17J., " Diane ", c.1933
14k $60 $70 $90

HAMILTON,17J., " Drexel ", cal.955 , c.1933
14k $70 $75 $90

HAMILTON,17J., " Edgewood ", c.1933
gold filled................................$30 $35 $45

HAMILTON,17J., " Eugenie ", 44 diamonds, c.1933
platinum.................................$250 $275 $350

HAMILTON,17J., " Glenwood ", cal.955, c.1933
gold filled................................$30 $35 $50

HAMILTON,17J., " Linden Hall ", c.1933
gold filled................................$30 $35 $50

HAMILTON,17J.," Maritza ", 6 diamonds, cal.955 , c.1933
18k(w)................................$80 $90 $120

HAMILTON,17J., " Mayfield ", cal.955 , c.1933
gold filled................................$30 $35 $50

HAMILTON,17J., " Newcomb ", cal.989, c.1933
gold filled................................$30 $35 $50

HAMILTON,17J., " Nightingale ", 40 diamonds, c.1933
18k(w)................................$200 $225 $300

HAMILTON,17J., " Portia ", 8 diamonds, c.1933
18k(w)................................$200 $225 $300

HAMILTON,17J., " Trudy ", c.1948
14k.............................$50 $60 $80

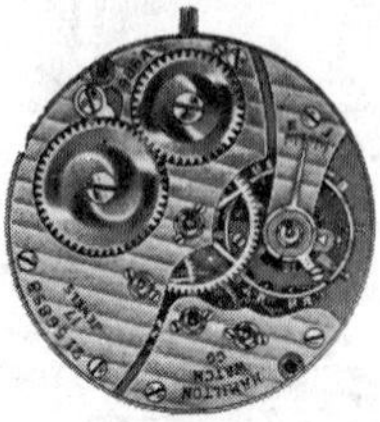

Grade 986A, 6/0 size
Open face, ¾ plate movt., 17 jewels, double roller

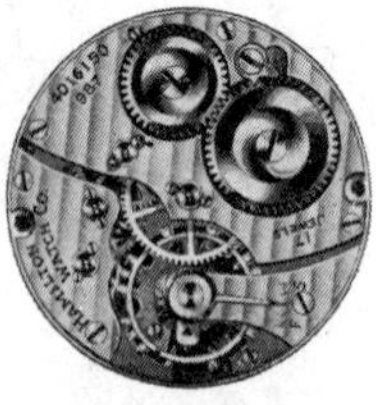

Grade 987, 6/0 size
Hunting, ¾ plate movt., 17 jewels, double roller

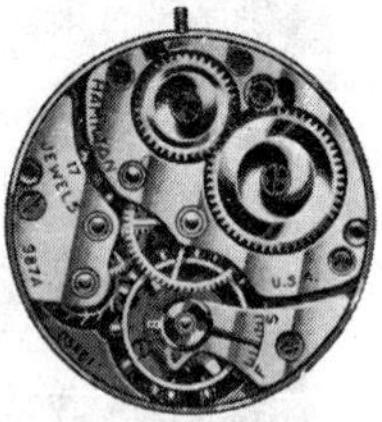

Grade 987A, 6/0 size
Open face, ¾ plate movt., 17 jewels, double roller

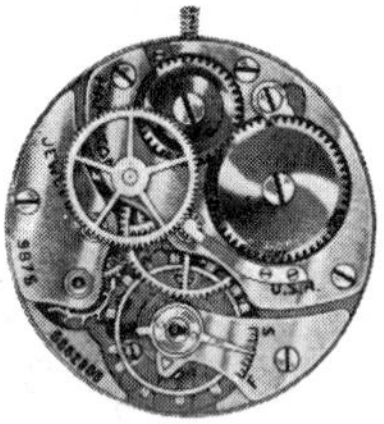

Grade 987S, 6/0 size
Hunting, ¾ plate movt., 17 jewels, double roller

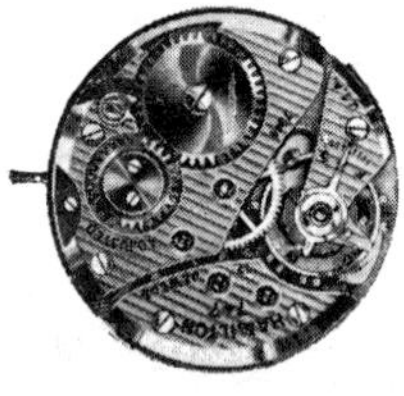

Grade 747, 8/0 size
Open face, ¾ plate movt., 17 jewels, double roller

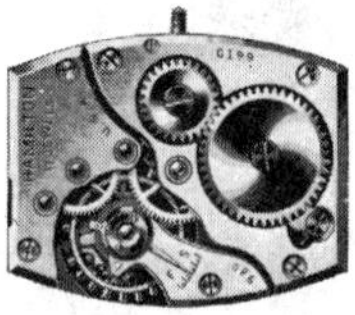

Grade 980, 14/0 size
Open face, ¾ plate movt., 17 jewels, double roller

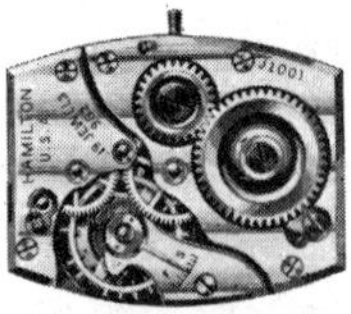

Grade 982, 14/0 size
Open face, ¾ plate movt., 19 jewels, double roller

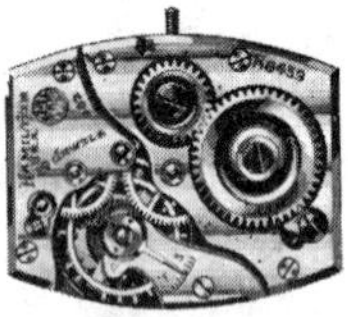

Grade 982M, 14/0 size
Open face, ¾ plate movt., 19 jewels, double roller

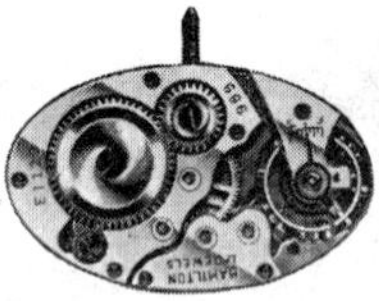

Grade 989, 18/0 size
Open face, ¾ plate movt., 17 jewels, double roller

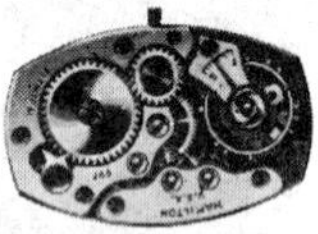

Grade 997, 20/0 size
Open face, ¾ plate movt., 17 jewels, double roller

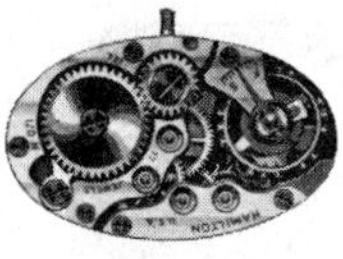

Grade 721, 21/0 size
Open face, ¾ plate movt., 17 jewels, double roller

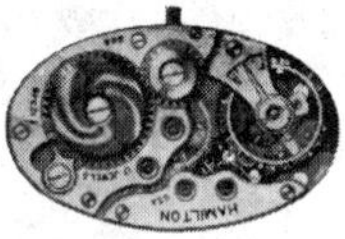

Grade 995, 21/0 size
Open face, ¾ plate movt., 17 jewels, double roller

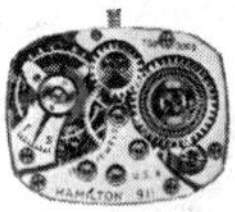

Grade 911, 22/0 size
Open face, ¾ plate movt., 17 jewels, double roller

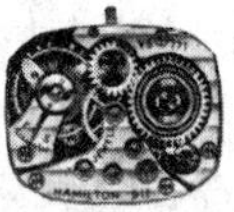

Grade 911M, 22/0 size
Open face, ¾ plate movt., 17 jewels, double roller

Grade 780, 21/0 size
17 jewels

Grade 770, 12/0 size
22 jewels

Grade 761, 21/0 size
22 jewels

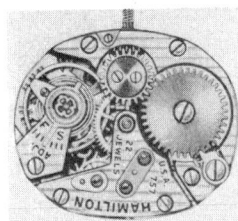

Grade 757, 21/0 size
22 jewels

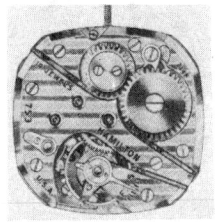

Grade 753, 12/0 size, 19 jewels
Grade 752, 12/0 size, 17 jewels

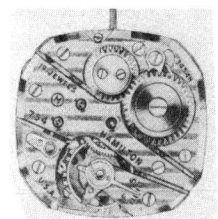

Grade 754, 12/0 size, 19 jewels
Grade 770, 12/0 size, 17 jewels

Grade 750 & 751, 21/0 size
17 jewels

Grade 748, 8/0 size
18 jewels

Grade 747, 8/0 size
17 jewels

LIGNE GAUGE

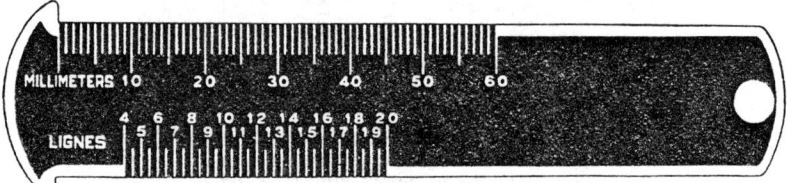

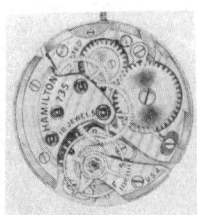

Grade 735, 8/0 size
18 jewels

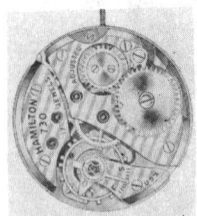

Grade 730, 8/0 size
17 jewels

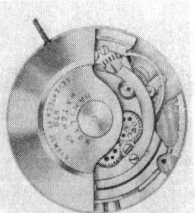

Grade 679, 17 jewels
Grade 692, 694 - calendar

Grade 666 & 663, 17 jewels
Grade 668 - calendar

Grade 658, 661, 667, 17 jewels
Grade 665, 23J, **Grade 664**, 25J
Grade 662, 690 - calendar, 17J

Grade 623 & 624, 17 jewels

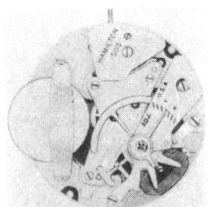

Grade 505, electric, 11 jewels

THE SPUR

1930 AD

A Hamilton the true Sportsman will
love. In either 14K yellow or white
gold with numerals of gold in a black
enamel circlet on the outside of the
case—19 jewel movement, $125

HAMPDEN, 15J., engraved case, c.1925
gold filled..............................$40 $50 $85

HAMPDEN,11J., "LEVER SET" , 3/0 size, c.1928
silver......................................$125 $150 $200

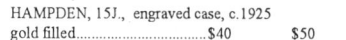

HAMPDEN, 17 jewels., c. 1936
14k $125 $150 $200

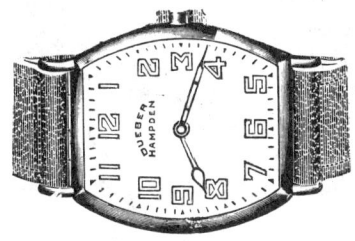

HAMPDEN, 15 jewels, c. 1928
14k..$80 $90 $150
gold filled..................................$30 $40 $60

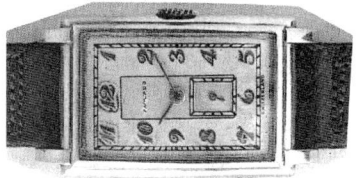

HAMPDEN, 17J., by Lonville W. Co., c. 1936
gold filled..................................$75 $80 $95

HAMPDEN, 11J., Molly Stark, c. 1928
base metal................................$30 $35 $50

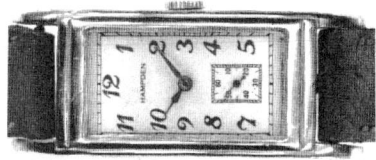

HAMPDEN, 17 jewels, double dial, c. 1930
gold filled..................................$90 $100 $150

HAMPDEN, 7J., tonneau shaped, c. 1928
gold filled..................................$30 $35 $50

HAMPDEN, 15 jewels, c. 1928
14k $100 $110 $135
gold filled..................................$30 $40 $60

🕐 Some grades are not included. Their values can be
determined by comparing with **similar** age, size, metal
content, style, grades, or models such as **time only**,
chronograph, repeater etc. listed.

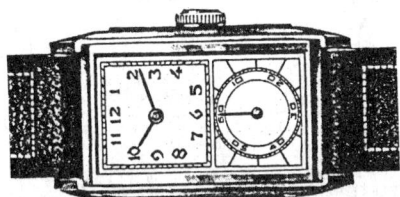

HARMAN,7J.,doctor style duo-dial,
gold filled..............................$200 $225 $275

HARMAN, 17J.,one button chronog., mid size, c.1940s
s. steel $250 $275 $350

HARVARD, 17 jewels, chronog., tach-telemeter
s. steel $200 $250 $300

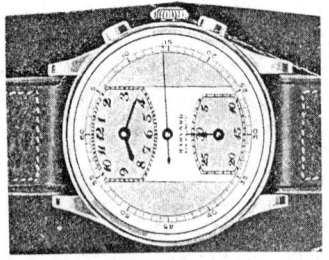

HARVARD, 17 jewels, 1/5 sec. chronog.
s. steel $250 $275 $350

HARVEL, 17 jewels, date-o-graph
s. steel $90 $100 $150

Wrist Watches listed in this section are priced at the collectable fair market **retail** level as **complete** watches having an original gold-filled case and stainless steel back, also with original dial, leather watch band, and the entire original movement in good working order with no repairs needed.

🕐 Pricing in this Guide are fair market price for **COMPLETE** watches which are reflected from the "**NAWCC**" National and regional shows.

HARVEL, 17J.,center sec.
gold filled................................$20 $30 $45

HARWOOD, 15 jewels, early self winding, c. 1928

18k (w)...................................$600	$650	$725
14k...................................$450	$500	$575
gold filled...............................$200	$250	$325
s. steel...................................$150	$200	$275

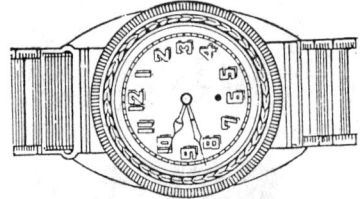

HARWOOD, 15 J., rim set by turning bezel clockwise
9k..$300 $350 $425

HARWOOD, 15 jewels, back set, c. 1925
18k...$300 $350 $425

HASTE, 17J., triple calendar moon ph.
gold filled................................$300 $350 $425

HAYDEN, 7J., by Solomax W.Co., hinged case
gold filled..................................$60 $75 $100

HELBROS, 17 jewels, aux. sec.
gold filled..................................$40 $50 $65

HEBDOMAS, 7-15 J., visible escapement, 8 day movement
s. steel $400 $500 $650

HELBROS, 17 jewels,
14k..$125 $150 $195

HEBDOMAS, 7-15 J., **8 day** movement, Ca. 1915
s. steel $200 $250 $325

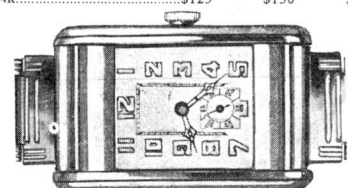

HELBROS, 7J., " Falcon ", c. 1929
base metal..................................$25 $30 $40

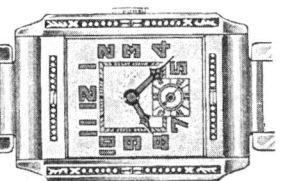

HELBROS, 7J., " Fairfax ", c. 1929
base metal..................................$25 $30 $40

HELBROS, 17 jewels, aux.sec., alarm
gold filled..................................$80 $90 $125

HELBROS, 7J., " Federal ", c. 1929
base metal..................................$25 $30 $40

HELBROS, 7 jewels, fancy bezel, curvex
gold filled..................................$70 $80 $100

HELBROS, 7J., " Filmore ", c. 1929
base metal..................................$25 $30 $40

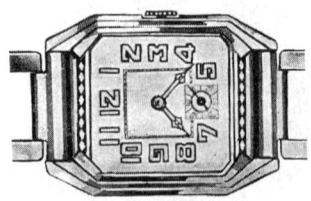

HELBROS, 7J., " Fletcher ", c. 1929
base metal $25 $30 $40

HELBROS, 7J., " Franklin ", c. 1929
base metal................................. $25 $30 $40

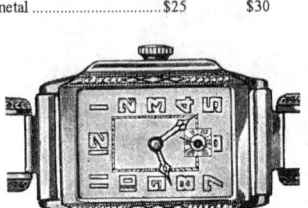

HELBROS, 7J., " Flint ", c. 1929
gold plate $25 $30 $40

HELBROS, 7J., " Frigate ", c. 1929
base metal................................. $25 $30 $40

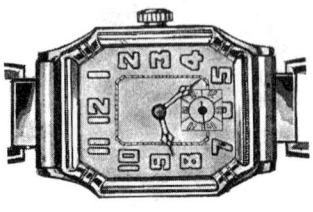

HELBROS, 7J., " Forbes ", c. 1929
base metal $25 $30 $40

HELBROS, 7J., " Fulton ", c. 1929
base metal................................. $25 $30 $40

HELBROS, 7J., " Forrest ", c. 1929
base metal $25 $30 $40

HELBROS,17J., 24 hour dial
base metal................................. $40 $50 $70

HELBROS, 7J., " Fortress ", c. 1929
gold plate $25 $35 $50

⏱ Pricing in this Guide are fair market price for **COM-PLETE** watches which are reflected from the "**NAWCC**" National and regional shows.

HENDA, 15J., direct read, c. 1930
nickel $175 $200 $250

HERMES, 17J., big wire lugs, enamel dial
14k $100 $125 $200

HELVETIA, 15 jewels, Ca. 1935
9k $90 $100 $125

HELVETIA, 21 jewels, auto wind
gold filled................................... $30 $40 $60

HEUER, 15 jewels, chronog., 2 reg., one button,
14k $1,300 $1,500 $1,800

🕐 Some grades are not included. Their values can be determined by comparing with **similar** age, size, metal content, style, grades, or models such as **time only**, chronograph, repeater etc. listed.

🕐 Pricing in this Guide are fair market price for **COM-PLETE** watches which are reflected from the "**NAWCC**" National and regional shows.

HEUER, 17J., chronog., 3 reg., 3 dates, moon phase
18k.......................................$1,500 $1,600 $1,800
s. steel...................................$500 $550 $625

HEUER, 17 J., chronog., 3 reg., "Carrera, c.1960
s. steel...................................$300 $350 $425

HEUER, 17 jewels, chronog., 3 dates, 3 reg. c.1948
14k.......................................$500 $550 $625
s. steel...................................$250 $300 $375

HEUER, 17 jewels, "Carrera," chronog., 2 reg., c.1960s
14k.......................................$400 $450 $575
s. steel...................................$275 $300 $375

HEUER,17J., "Seafarer", by Valjoux # 72, c. 1972
14k $600 $650 $800
s. steel $300 $350 $450

HEUER,17J., "Camaro", by Valjoux #7730, c. 1965
14k $250 $300 $400
s. steel $150 $175 $225

HEUER,17J., "Autavia", cal.72, micro rotor, c. 1972
s. steel $250 $300 $375

Wrist Watches listed in this section are priced at the collectable
fair market **retail** level as **complete** watches having an original
gold-filled case and stainless steel back, also with original dial,
leather watch band, and the entire original movement in good
working order with no repairs needed.

Some grades are not included. Their values can be
determined by comparing with **similar** age, size, metal
content, style, grades, or models such as **time only**,
chronograph, repeater etc. listed.

HEUER,17J., "Monaco", date, c. 1974
base metal...............................$200 $225 $300

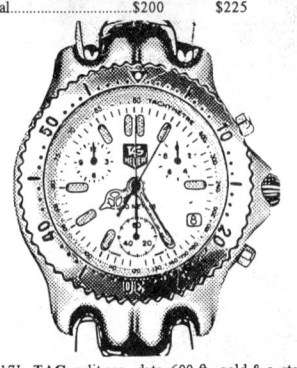

HEUER,17J., **TAG**, split sec., date, 600 ft., gold & s. steel,
sold new for $1,895.00 in Ca.1991
gold tone $300 $350 $425
s. steel & gold tone $300 $350 $425

HEUER, 17 jewels, day-date-month, moon phase
s. steel...................................$325 $400 $500

HEUER, 17 jewels, day-date-month
14k..$400 $450 $525
s. steel....................................$125 $150 $200

HILTON W. Co.,17J., chronog. by Venius W.Co.
18k $300 $325 $400

HIRCO, 17J., center sec. auto-w.
gold filled..................................$30 $40 $70

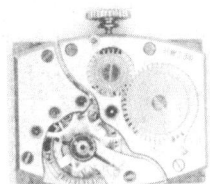

HOWARD, 17J. engraved on movement, (Howard
Watch USA, Lancaster, PA, HW138, 17J. H980)

🕐 (see HAMILTON W. CO.)

E. HUGUENIN, 17 jewels, "Black Star," c. 1940
14k $300 $350 $425

Wrist Watches listed in this section are priced at the collectable
fair market **retail** level as **complete** watches having an original
gold-filled case and stainless steel back, also with original dial,
leather watch band, and the entire original movement in good
working order with no repairs needed.

🕐 Some grades are not included. Their values can be
determined by comparing with **similar** age, size, metal
content, style, grades, or models such as **time only**,
chronograph, repeater etc. listed.

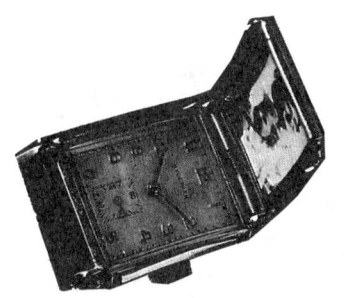

HYDEPARK, 17 jewels, flip up top
14k $400 $450 $550

ILLINOIS, 17J., GJS, model 207 on Mvt., model 250 on case
14K $300 $350 $425

ILLINOIS, 17J., **direct read**, Ca. 1925
Chrome,case & band $225 $250 $325
Aluminum, case ★ ★ ★ ★ ★ $2,000 $2,200 $2,500

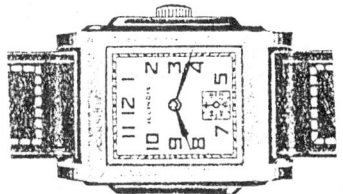

ILLINOIS, 15J., "Arlington also Hawthorne", Ca. 1929
gold filled $175 $200 $250

ILLINOIS, 17J., "Ardsley also Hudson", Ca. 1929
gold filled $150 $175 $225

ILLINOIS, 17 jewels, "Aviator"
gold filled.................................$200 $225 $300

ILLINOIS, 21J.= Beau Monde14k &17J= Beau Gest WGF
14k $400 $450 $525
gold filled **W** $200 $250 $325

ILLINOIS, 21J., " BARONET ", GJS, cal.601, c.1925
gold filled.................................$200 $225 $300

ILLINOIS, 15J., "Beau Royal "
gold filled $225 $250 $325

ILLINOIS, 19J., " Beau Brummel"
18k $700 $800 $950

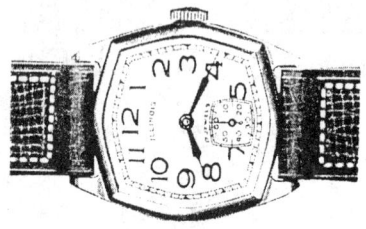

ILLINOIS, 17J., " Blackstone"
gold filled $100 $125 $185

ILLINOIS, 19 jewels, "Beau Brummel"
gold filled.................................$275 $325 $400

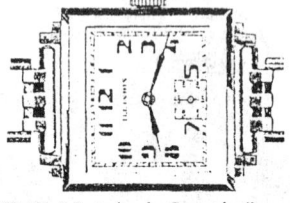

ILLINOIS, 15J., " Bostonian also Commodore"
gold filled $150 $175 $225

ILLINOIS, 17J., " Beau Brummel ", c.1929
gold filled.................................$250 $275 $375

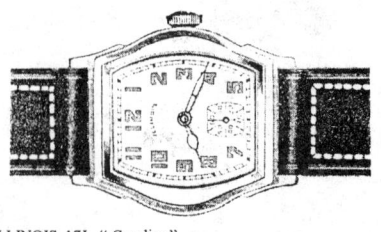

ILLINOIS, 17J., " Cavalier "
gold filled $175 $200 $250

ILLINOIS, 17 jewels, "Champion"
gold filled................................$150 $175 $250

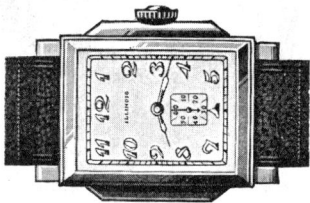

ILLINOIS, 15 jewels, "Chatham"
gold filled................................$125 $150 $225

ILLINOIS, 17J., " The Chief's", chased bezel
gold filled (w)........................$175 $200 $275

ILLINOIS, 17 jewels, "Chieftain"
gold filled................................$350 $425 $550

ILLINOIS, 17J., " Commodore also Bostonian"
gold filled................................$150 $175 $225

ILLINOIS, 19 jewels, "Consul"
14k $400 $475 $600

ILLINOIS, 21 jewels, "Consul"
14k $400 $475 $600

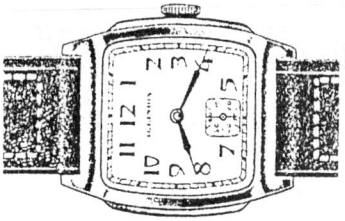

ILLINOIS, 17J., " Derby also Pimlico"
gold filled $125 $150 $200

ILLINOIS, 15 jewels, "Ensign", plain bezel
gold filled $225 $275 $375

ILLINOIS, 15 jewels, "Ensign" engraved bezel
gold filled $250 $300 $400

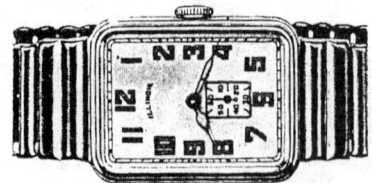

ILLINOIS, 17J., " Fontenac "
gold filled..............................$175 $200 $250

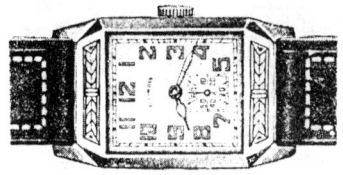

ILLINOIS, 17J., " Finalist also Chesterfield"
gold filled..............................$225 $250 $300

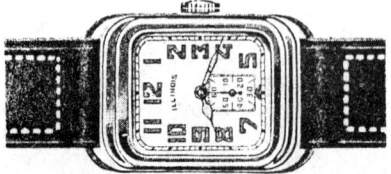

ILLINOIS, 17J., " Futura "
gold filled..............................$200 $225 $275

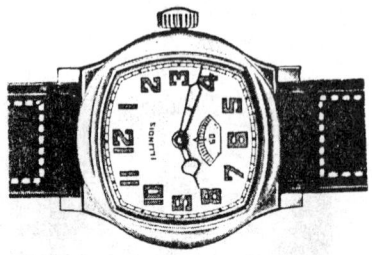

ILLINOIS, 17J., " Guardsman ", plain, rotor second dial
gold filled..............................$350 $400 $475

ILLINOIS, 17J., ''Guardsman '', engraved, cal.307, c.1929
gold filled..............................$350 $400 $475

ILLINOIS, 17 jewels, ''Jolly Roger''
gold filled..............................$300 $400 $550

ILLINOIS, 17J., " Kenilworth " also "Gallahad"
gold filled..............................$175 $200 $275

ILLINOIS, 19 jewels, ''Major'', also with plain bezel
gold filled..............................$250 $300 $400

ILLINOIS, 17 jewels, ''Major'', also with plain bezel
gold filled $250 $300 $400

ILLINOIS, 17 jewels, ''Major'', also with plain bezel
gold filled $250 $300 $400

ILLINOIS, 17-21J., " Manhattan ", aux. sec. at 9
14k $375 $425 $525

ILLINOIS, 17-21 jewels, "New Yorker", aux. sec. at 9
also "Yorktown" in smooth bezel
gold filled.............................. $200 $250 $325

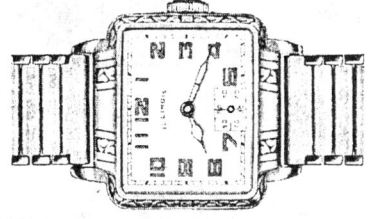

ILLINOIS, 17-21J., " Manhattan ", aux. sec. at 6
14k $375 $425 $525

ILLINOIS, 17-21 jewels, "New Yorker", aux. sec. at 6
gold filled.............................. $200 $250 $325

ILLINOIS, 19 jewels, "Marquis", engraved, curved case
gold filled.............................. $250 $300 $375

ILLINOIS, 17J., " Marquis ", plain, curved case
gold filled $200 $225 $300

ILLINOIS, 17J., " Mate ", engraved
gold filled $175 $200 $275

ILLINOIS, 17J., "Mate" , plain
gold filled $150 $175 $250

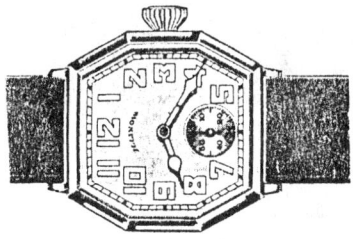

ILLINOIS, 17J., engraved case in "Maxine", plain, ladies
gold filled $75 $100 $150

ILLINOIS, 17 jewels, "Maxine", wire lugs, ladies
14k $150 $175 $225

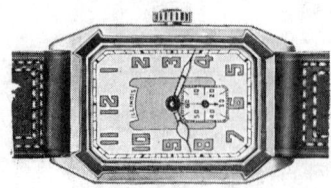

ILLINOIS, 17J., " Medalist also Wembley", c.1929
gold filled..............................$150 $175 $250

ILLINOIS, 17 jewels, "Piccadilly" in white or yellow G.F.
came with Luminous or Modern as a option
gold filled plain......................$750 $900 $1,150
gold filled engraved...............$875 $1,000 $1,250

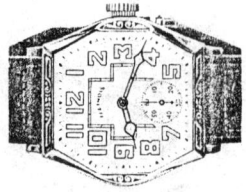

ILLINOIS, 17 jewels, "Pilot"
gold filled..............................$200 $225 $300

ILLINOIS, 17 jewels, "Prince"
gold filled..............................$175 $200 $250

ILLINOIS, 17J., "Ritz", white bezel & yellow center case
also called "Valedictorian"
gold filled..............................$375 $425 $525

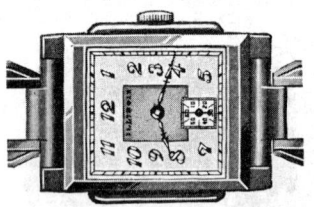

ILLINOIS, 15 jewels, "Rockingham also Potomac"
gold filled $200 $250 $325

ILLINOIS, 17J., " Rockliffe ", cal.805, c.1925
14k $350 $400 $500

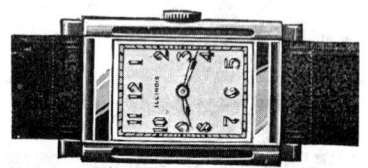

ILLINOIS, 15 jewels, "Sangamo"
gold filled $100 $150 $200

ILLINOIS, 17J., " Skyway ", engraved case, G#307
gold filled $400 $450 $600

ILLINOIS, 17J., " Special ", c.1929
silver $250 $300 $450

ILLINOIS, 17 jewels, "Speedway"
gold filled...............................$225 $275 $350

ILLINOIS, 15 jewels, "Standish"
gold filled...............................$150 $175 $250

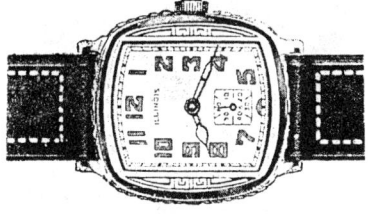

ILLINOIS, 17J., " Sterling ", direct read, c.1929
sterling silver $225 $275 $350

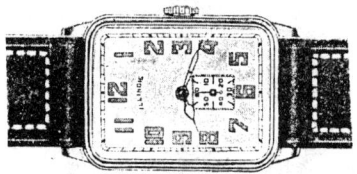

ILLINOIS, 17J., " Townsman also Metropolitan", carved
case
gold filled...............................$175 $200 $275

ILLINOIS, 17 jewels, "Tuxedo"
14k $300 $350 $450

ILLINOIS, 17J., " Viking "
gold filled $200 $225 $300

ILLINOIS, 17 jewels, "Off Duty", stars on bezel, Ca. 1927
gold filled $200 $225 $300

ILLINOIS, 15J., "Urbana",
gold filled $100 $125 $200

ILLINOIS, 17J., " Trophy also Westchester"
gold filled...............................$125 $150 $225

ILLINOIS, 17J., GENERIC, barrel & engraved side of case
base metal $100 $125 $175

ILLINOIS, 15J., GENERIC, Square cut corner
gold filled...............................$150 $175 $250

ILLINOIS, 19 jewels, GENERIC, aux. sec at 9
14k(W)....................................$400 $450 $550

ILLINOIS, 17 jewels, GENERIC, hand engraved, wire lugs
14k (W)....................................$150 $175 $250

ILLINOIS, 17J., GENERIC, tonneau style, hand engraved,
14k (W)....................................$150 $175 $250

ILLINOIS, 15J., GENERIC, seconds at "9" c.1929
gold filled...............................$200 $225 $300

ILLINOIS, 17J., GENERIC, engraved case, c.1929
gold filled $175 $200 $275

ILLINOIS, 17J., GENERIC, art deco, cal.207, c.1925
gold filled $125 $175 $250

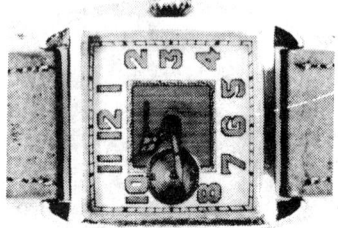

ILLINOIS, 17J., GENERIC, double hinged, GJS, c.1929
gold filled $150 $175 $250

ILLINOIS, 15J., GENERIC,, c.1926
gold filled $150 $175 $250

ILLINOIS, 17J., GENERIC, engraved bezel, Ca.1929
gold filled $150 $175 $225

ILLINOIS, 17J., GENERIC, Cushion, Shock-Proof Model,
nickel...$80 $90 $125

ILLINOIS, 17J., GENERIC, engraved case
silver $125 $150 $200

ILLINOIS, 15J., GENERIC, engraved bezel, GJS, c.1926
14k (w)....................................$250 $275 $350

ILLINOIS, 15J., **GENERIC, winds at 12:00 o'clock**
silver $200 $225 $300

ILLINOIS, 15-17J., lady's watch, black enamel on bezel
14k $100 $125 $175
gold filled................................$30 $40 $60

BELOW A JULY 1926 AD
By The ILLINOIS WATCH CO.

6-0 SIZE OR ELEVEN LIGNE

Only delivered fitted in cases supplied by Jobbers

Illustrations simply indicate some of the different styles of cases, made by
various watch case manufacturers, for these movements.

No. 907, 19 Jewels   No. 903, 15 Jewels
$35.00 *Movements Only* $26.50

19 and 15 ruby and sapphire jewels; compensating balance with timing
screws; double roller escapement; Breguet hairspring; steel escape wheel;
polished winding wheels; recoil click; silvered or gilt metal dials; full or
three-quarter open.

BELOW A JOBBERS AD Ca. 1926
ADVERTISING ILLINOIS WATCHES FOR SALE

No. 1045   The Ace $37.30
3/0 Illinois 17 Jewel
White Engraved Stellar Quality Star Case
Silver Dial Luminous Figures and Hands
Established retail price with each

No. 1047   The Whippet $36.20
3/0 Illinois 17 Jewel
Stellar White Plain Barrel Case
Silver Dial Luminous Figures and Hands
Established retail price with each

ILLINOIS, 17J., " Eliza ", c.1929
gold filled.................................$65 $75 $90

ILLINOIS, 17J., " Long Beach ", c.1929
gold filled.................................$55 $65 $80

ILLINOIS, 17J., " Lynette ", c.1929
gold filled.................................$50 $60 $75

ILLINOIS, 17J., " Mariette ", c.1929
gold filled.................................$50 $60 $75

ILLINOIS, 17J., " Marionette ", c.1929
gold filled.................................$50 $60 $75

ILLINOIS, 17J., " Marlette ", c.1929
gold filled.................................$50 $60 $75

ILLINOIS, 16J., " Mary Todd ", c.1929
18k(w)...................................$150 $200 $250

ILLINOIS, 16J., " Mary Todd ", black enamel bezel, c.1929
18k(w)...................................$150 $200 $250

ILLINOIS, 16J., " Mary Todd ", c.1929
18k $150 $200 $250

ILLINOIS, 17J., " Mateel ", c.1929
14k(w).......................................$90 $100 $140

ILLINOIS, 17J., " Miami ", c.1929
gold filled $55 $65 $85

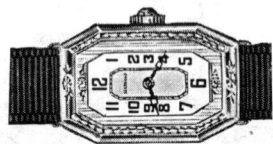

ILLINOIS, 17J., " Narragansett ", c.1929
14k $85 $95 $110

ILLINOIS, 17J., " Newport ", engraved case, c.1929
gold filled $55 $65 $80

ILLINOIS, 16J., " Queen Wilhelmina ", 22 diamonds and
8 synthetic sapphires
18k(w)....................................$200 $275 $350

ILLINOIS, rectangular, Grade 207, 17 jewels

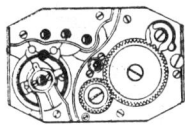

ILLINOIS, rectangular, 1st, 2nd & 3rd model

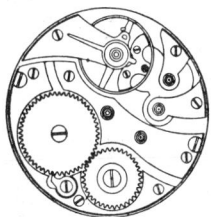

ILLINOIS, Model #4, 3/0 size, bridge, hunting, movement.

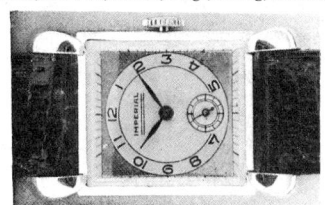

IMPERIAL, 17J., fancy lugs
14k(W) $250 $275 $350

IMPERIAL, 17J., center sec.
s. steel $30 $40 $55

🕐 Some grades are not included. Their values can be
determined by comparing with **similar** age, size, metal
content, style, grades, or models such as **time only**,
chronograph, repeater etc. listed.

INGERSOLL, 2 J.," Rist-Arch", stepped case
base metal $20 $25 $40

INGERSOLL, "Swagger",
base metal $20 $25 $40

INGERSOLL, 7 jewels
base metal $20 $25 $35

INGERSOLL, 7 jewels, radiolite dial wire lugs
W/ original band $30 $40 $60
base metal $20 $30 $40

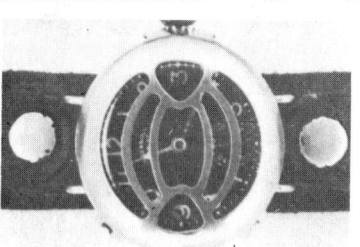

INGERSOLL, 7 J., military style, **protective grill cover
wire lugs, all original band and cover**
base metal $100 $125 $150

INTERNATIONAL W. CO., 17J., Ca. 1926
18k $500 $600 $750

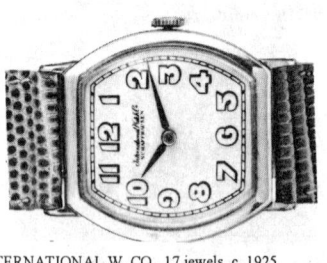

INTERNATIONAL W. CO., 17 jewels, c. 1925
18k $500 $550 $700

INTERNATIONAL W. CO., 16J., enamel dial, c. 1920
silver $400 $425 $500

INTERNATIONAL W. CO., 17 jewels
14k $350 $400 $525

INTERNATIONAL W. CO., 16J., cal.53, c. 1920
18k $400 $500 $650

INTERNATIONAL W. CO., 21 J., center sec., c. 1940
18k $500 $550 $750

INTERNATIONAL W. CO., 17 jewels, c. 1920
18k $450 $550 $700

INTERNATIONAL W. CO., 17J., "Art Deco", Ca. 1925
TU-TONE case w/ enamel on bezel
18k $1,200 $1,400 $1,700

INTERNATIONAL W. CO., 17 jewels, **curved**
14k $400 $450 $525

INTERNATIONAL W. CO., 17 jewels
14k C&B..............................$600 $650 $725

INTERNATIONAL W. CO., 17 jewels, c. 1940
18k $400 $450 $550

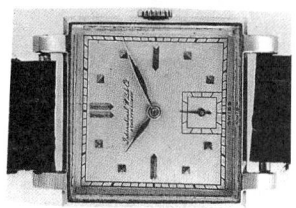

INTERNATIONAL W. CO., 17J., c. 1945
14k $200 $250 $325

INTERNATIONAL W. CO., 17J., Tiffany on dial, c. 1942
14k $350 $400 $500

INTERNATIONAL W. CO., 17 jewels, hidden lugs
14k $500 $550 $625

INTERNATIONAL W. CO., 17J., aux. sec.
14k $225 $250 $325

Wrist Watches listed in this section are priced at the collectable fair market **retail** level as **complete** watches having an original gold-filled case and stainless steel back, also with original dial, leather watch band, and the entire original movement in good working order with no repairs needed.

INTERNATIONAL W. CO., 17J., RF # 1160, Ca. 1964
18k $350 $400 $500

INTERNATIONAL W. CO., 17J., tank style, c. 1937
18k $500 $550 $650

INTERNATIONAL W. CO., 17J., c. 1926
s. steel $200 $250 $325

INTERNATIONAL W. CO., 17 J., on dial "Yard"
18k $600 $650 $750

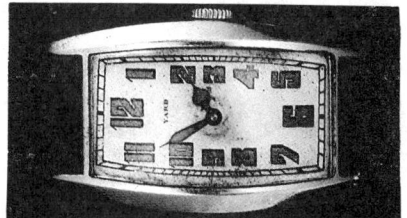

INTERNATIONAL W. CO., 17 J., curved, on dial "Yard"
platinum $1,200 $1,300 $1,600

INTERNATIONAL W. CO., 17 jewels, **hinged back**
14k $300 $350 $500

INTERNATIONAL W. CO., 17 jewels, curved
14k $500 $550 $650

INTERNATIONAL W. CO., 17J, date, auto-wind, waterproof
18k $750 $850 $1,000

INTERNATIONAL W. CO., 21 jewels, auto wind, date
18k $700 $800 $950

INTERNATIONAL W. CO., 17 jewels, center sec.
18k $500 $550 $675

INTERNATIONAL W. CO., 17 jewels, center sec.
18k $550 $600 $725

INTERNATIONAL W. CO., 17J., cen. sec., date,
platinum.............................$1,400 $1,500 $1,800

INTERNATIONAL W. CO.,17J., RF# 802a, cal.8541, c.1920
s. steel ......,...............................$300 $350 $425

INTERNATIONAL W. CO., 21J., "Ingeneur", date, c.1976
18k non-magnetic......★★ $1,600 $1,800 $2,300
s. steel non-magnetic..........★$700 $800 $950

🕐 Some grades are not included. Their values can be
determined by comparing with **similar** age, size, metal
content, style, grades, or models such as **time only**,
chronograph, repeater etc. listed.

INTERNATIONAL W. CO., 21J., date, c. 1960
18k $700 $800 $950

INTERNATIONAL W. CO., 17J., center sec.cal.89, c.1957
18k $550 $600 $725

INTERNATIONAL W. CO., 21J., cal.853, c. 1961
18k $500 $550 $675

INTERNATIONAL W. CO., 17J., wide lugs, c. 1960
18k $550 $600 $725

INTERNATIONAL W. CO.,17J.,fancy lugs,cal.C89, c.1952
18k $600 $700 $850

INTERNATIONAL W. CO., 21J., cal.C852, c. 1952
18k $500 $550 $675

INTERNATIONAL W. CO., 21J., cal.853, c. 1958
18k $550 $600 $725

🕑 Pricing in this Guide are fair market price for **COMPLETE**
watches which are reflected from the "**NAWCC**" National and
regional shows.

INTERNATIONAL W. CO., 17J., cal.89, c. 1962
s. steel $250 $275 $350

INTERNATIONAL W. CO., 17J., ca.1960s
18k C & B $800 $900 $1,100

INTERNATIONAL W. CO., 17J., auto wind, Ca. 1960
18k...$700 $750 $900

INTERNATIONAL W. CO., 17J., center sec.
18k $600 $650 $750

INTERNATIONAL W. CO., 17 jewels, center sec.
18k...$500 $550 $675

INTERNATIONAL W. CO., 17J., fancy lugs, cen. sec.
18k $650 $700 $800

INTERNATIONAL W. CO., 17 jewels, center sec., cal.402
18k...$500 $550 $675

INTERNATIONAL W. Co., 18 jewels, center sec.
18k $550 $600 $725

INTERNATIONAL W. CO., 17 jewels, center sec., cal. 89
18k...$500 $550 $675

⊕ Pricing in this Guide are fair market price for **COMPLETE** watches which are reflected from the "**NAWCC**" National and regional shows.

Wrist Watches listed in this section are priced at the collectable fair market <u>**retail**</u> level as **complete** watches having an original gold-filled case and stainless steel back, also with original dial, leather watch band, and the entire original movement in good working order with no repairs needed.

INTERNATIONAL W. CO., 17 jewels, center sec., cal.89
18k $500 $550 $675

INTERNATIONAL W. CO., 17J, for Royal Navy, ca.1950
s. steel.....................................$400 $450 $600

INTERNATIONAL W. CO., 36J., "Da Vinci," chronog.
auto wind, triple date, moon ph., center lugs
18k C & B............................$8,000 $8,500 $10,000
18k $6,000 $6,500 $8,000

INTERNATIONAL W. CO., 17J., winds at 12 o'clock
s. steel.....................................$600 $700 $850

INTERNATIONAL W. CO., 17 jewels, Autowind, Ca. 1958
s. steel.....................................$300 $350 $450

INTERNATIONAL W. CO., 17J., anti-magnet, Ca. 1942
s. steel.....................................$200 $250 $325

INTERNATIONAL W. CO., "Porsche Design", date, auto-
wind, compass, sapphire mirror, RF#3510-LMW, Ca.1988
Titanium...................................$800 $900 $1,200
base metal $400 $450 $550

INTERNATIONAL W. CO., 17 jewels, c. 1948
18k $500 $550 $650

INTERNATIONAL W. CO., 17J.,date, 30 ATM=1,000 ft.
s. steel $325 $350 $400

INTERNATIONAL W. CO., 17J., aux sec., cal.83, c.1938
14k $500 $550 $650

INTERNATIONAL W. CO., 17J., fancy lugs, Ca.1952s
18k...$550 $600 $750

INTERNATIONAL W. CO., 17J., aux. sec., cal., c.1948
s. steel $275 $300 $375

INTERNATIONAL W. CO., 15J., cal. 83, ca.1945
14k...$350 $375 $450

INTERNATIONAL W. CO., 17J., cal.461, c.1962
18k ....:.............................$500 $550 $650

INTERNATIONAL W. CO., 17J., mid-size, Ca.1945
s: steel...................................$200 $250 $325

INTERNATIONAL W. CO., 17J., 36 small diamonds
platinum $400 $450 $550

INTERNATIONAL WATCH CO.
MOVEMENT IDENTIFICATION

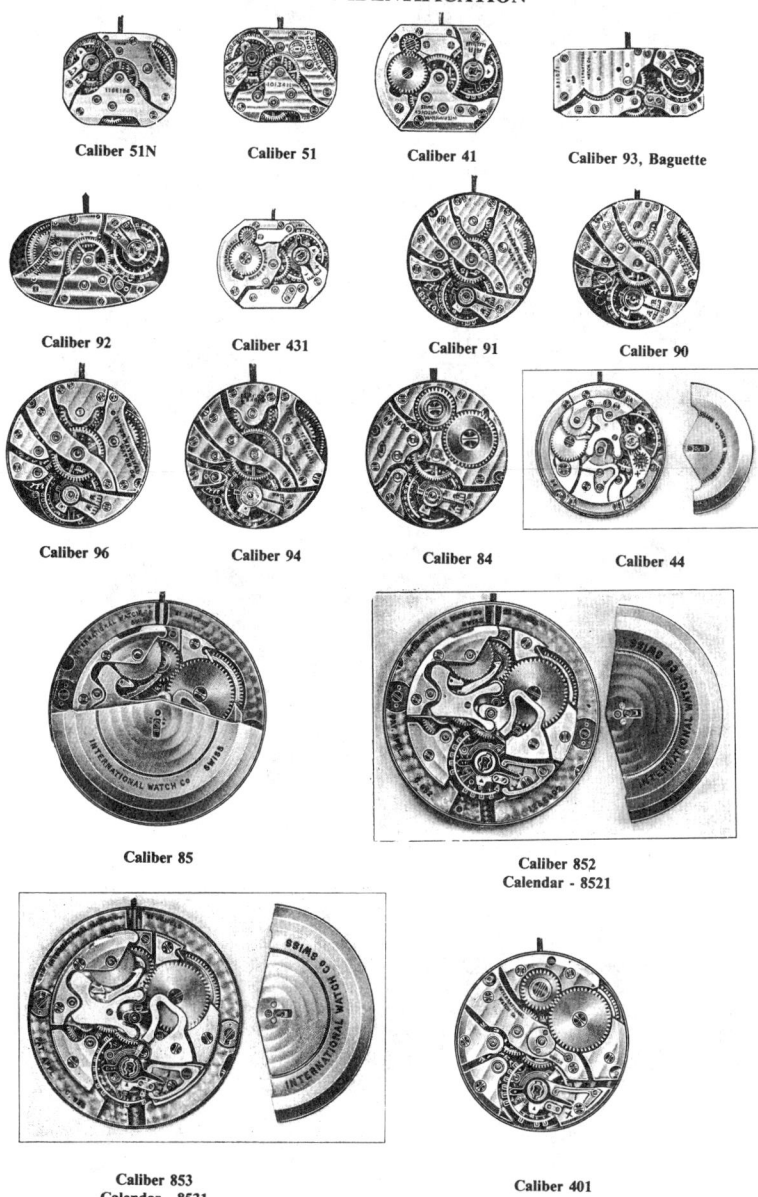

Caliber 51N   Caliber 51   Caliber 41   Caliber 93, Baguette

Caliber 92   Caliber 431   Caliber 91   Caliber 90

Caliber 96   Caliber 94   Caliber 84   Caliber 44

Caliber 85

Caliber 852
Calendar - 8521

Caliber 853
Calendar - 8531

Caliber 401

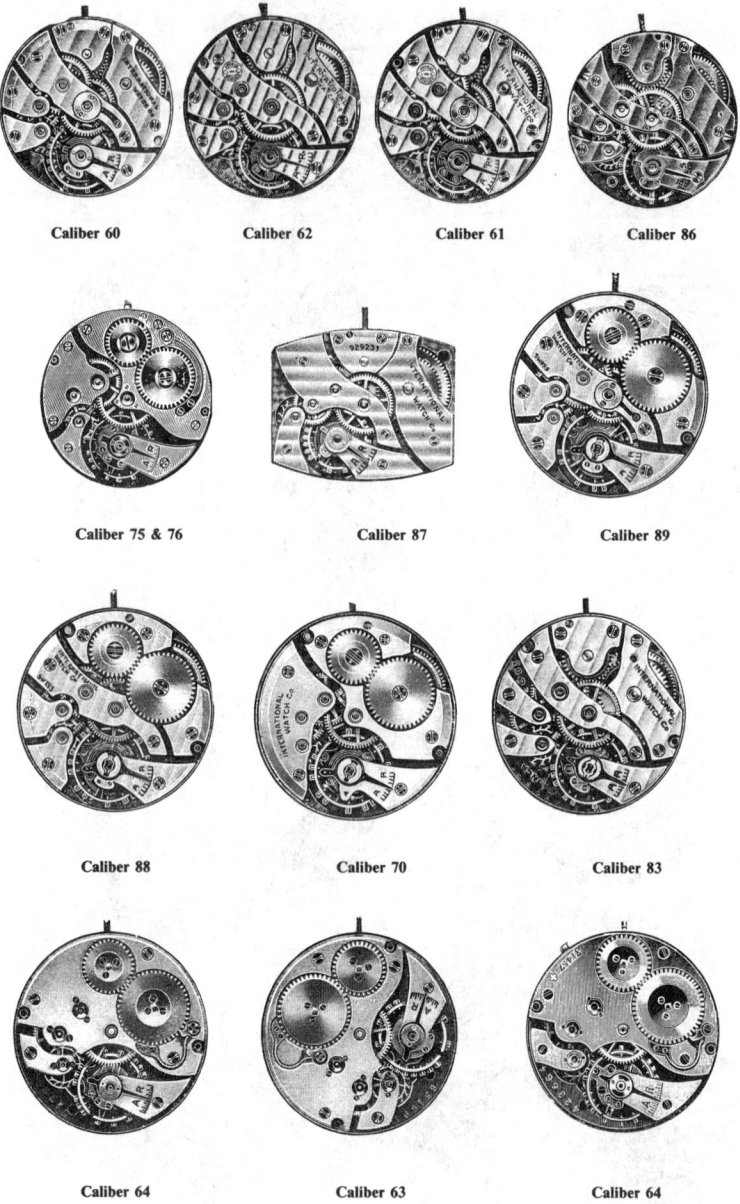

Caliber 60   Caliber 62   Caliber 61   Caliber 86

Caliber 75 & 76   Caliber 87   Caliber 89

Caliber 88   Caliber 70   Caliber 83

Caliber 64   Caliber 63   Caliber 64

INVICTA, 15 jewels, chronograph, min. reg. at 6 o'clock,
decimal aperture for sec. at 12 o'clock
18k $6,000 $7,000 $8,500

INVICTA, 17 jewels, date, center sec.
18k $200 $250 $325
s. steel $40 $50 $75

INVICTA, 17 jewels, day-date, waterproof
18k $150 $175 $225
s. steel $60 $70 $90

INVICTA, 17 jewels, day-date-month
18k $200 $250 $325
s. steel $100 $150 $225

🕐 Some grades are not included. Their values can be
determined by comparing with **similar** age, size, metal
content, style, grades, or models such as **time only**,
chronograph, repeater etc. listed.

INVICTA, 17 jewels, day-date-month, moon phase
18k $400 $500 $650
s. steel $200 $300 $450

INVICTA, 17 jewels, waterproof
18k $125 $150 $225
s. steel $40 $50 $70

INVICTA, 17 jewels, auto wind, waterproof
18k $125 $150 $225
s. steel $50 $60 $70

JAEGER W. CO., 17J., RF#5184, chronog., Ca.1942
s.steel $300 $350 $425
18k $600 $650 $725

🕐 Pricing in this Guide are fair market price for **COMPLETE**
watches which are reflected from the "**NAWCC**" National and
regional shows.

JAEGER W. CO., 15J., **duoplan, backwind,** c.1935
s steel $300 $325 $400

JOHNSON-MATTHEY, 15 J., 5-10-15 gram ingot 24k gold
24k 5 gram $200 $250 $325
24k 10 gram $600 $650 $750
24k 15 gram $850 $900 $1,000

JARDUR W. CO., 17J., RF#29840, c.1950
s. steel $300 $350 $425

JUNGHANS, 16J., chronometer, c.1965
14k..$100 $110 $150

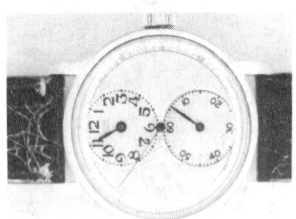

JEAN LOUIS, 17 jewels, double dial, c. 1930
14k $200 $250 $300

JUNGHANS, electronic "Ato Chron" , C.1978
14k..$90 $100 $140

J. E. Watch Co., 17J., tank style, c.1950
gold plate $40 $50 $70

JEWEL, 15 jewels, dual dial, c. 1938
gold filled...............................$250 $300 $400

JUNGHANS , 17J., cal.J88, c.1980
s. steel.....................................$150 $225 $275

Wrist Watches listed in this section are priced at the collectable
fair market **retail** level as **complete** watches having an original
gold-filled case and stainless steel back, also with original dial,
leather watch band, and the entire original movement in good
working order with no repairs needed.

J. JURGENSEN, 31J, 5 min. repeater, enamel bezel, c.1906
18k $25,000 $28,000 $35,000

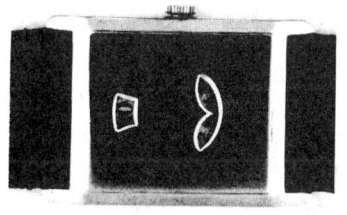

J. JURGENSEN, 15J, jumping hr., revolving min., c.1930s
18k $4,000 $4,500 $6,000

J. JURGENSEN,17J., large lugs, recess crown, c.1950
14k $200 $250 $350

J. JURGENSEN,17J., long lugs, c.1948
18k $175 $200 $275

J. JURGENSEN,17J., recess crown, fancy lugs, c.1952
14k $200 $225 $300

J. JURGENSEN,17J., 2 tone, center lugs, c.1940
14k...$300 $350 $425

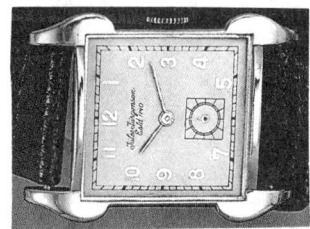

J. JURGENSEN, 17 jewels, fancy lugs, ca.1949
14k...$300 $350 $425

J. JURGENSEN, 17 jewels, fancy lugs
14k...$300 $350 $425

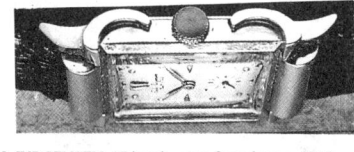

J. JURGENSEN, 17 jewels, extra fancy lugs, c. 1946
18k...$500 $550 $650

J. JURGENSEN, 17 jewels, c. 1950
18k...$150 $200 $325

🕐 Pricing in this Guide are fair market price for **COMPLETE**
watches which are reflected from the "**NAWCC**" National and
regional shows.

J. JURGENSEN, 17 jewels
18k $150 $175 $235

J. JURGENSEN,17J., center sec., c.1946
14k $100 $125 $200

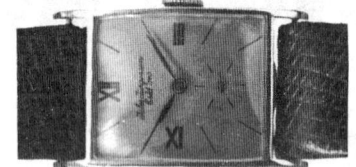

J. JURGENSEN,17J., aux. sec., c.1948
14k $100 $125 $200

J. JURGENSEN,17J., aux. sec., c.1940
14k $100 $125 $200

J. JURGENSEN,17J., textured bezel, c.1960
14k $100 $125 $175

J. JURGENSEN,17J., hidden lugs, c.1948
14k $150 $175 $225

J. JURGENSEN,17J., hidden lugs, c.1940
14k.............................$150 $175 $225

J. JURGENSEN,17J., hidden lugs, c.1952
14k.............................$300 $350 $450

J. JURGENSEN,17J., hidden lugs, c.1950
14k.............................$300 $350 $450

J. JURGENSEN,17J., hidden lugs, c.1948
14k.............................$150 $175 $225

J. JURGENSEN, 17 J., flared case, Ca. 1954
14k.............................$175 $200 $250

🕐 Some grades are not included. Their values can be determined by comparing with **similar** age, size, metal content, style, grades, or models such as **time only**, chronograph, repeater etc. listed.

J. JURGENSEN,17J., by Valjoux, cal. 69, c.1944
14K...$700 $800 $1,000
s. steel $400 $500 $700

J. JURGENSEN, 17 J., auto-w., cen. sec., ca. 1954
14k $150 $175 $250

J. JURGENSEN,17J., cal.8273, extended lugs, c.1958
14k $175 $200 $275

J. JURGENSEN,17J., extended bezel, c.1950
14k...$300 $325 $400

J. JURGENSEN,17J., cal.1139, c.1950
18k...$225 $250 $300

J. JURGENSEN,17J., center sec., date, c.1960
14k..$150 $175 $225

J. JURGENSEN,17J., center sec., mid size, c.1940
14k..$150 $175 $225

J. JURGENSEN,17J., aux. sec., c.1968
14k $100 $125 $175

Wrist Watches listed in this section are priced at the collectable
fair market **retail** level as **complete** watches having an original
gold-filled case and stainless steel back, also with original dial,
leather watch band, and the entire original movement in good
working order with no repairs needed.

🕐 Some grades are not included. Their values can be
determined by comparing with **similar** age, size, metal
content, style, grades, or models such as **time only**,
chronograph, repeater etc. listed.

J. JURGENSEN,17J., 3 diamond dial, date, c.1960
14k(w).....................................$150 $175 $225

JUVENIA, 21 jewels, **gold movement**
18k.......................................$250 $300 $400

J. JURGENSEN,17J., 40 diamond bezel, c.1960
14k(w).....................................$350 $375 $450

JUVENIA, 17J.,
s. steel.....................................$30 $35 $50

J. JURGENSEN, 17 J., 12 diamond dial, ca. 1960s
14k(W).....................................$150 $175 $225

JUVENIA, 17J.,
s. steel.....................................$30 $40 $60

JUVENIA,17J.,3 dates, moon ph., screw on back c. 1950s
18k $500 $600 $750

JUVENIA, 17J.,
s. steel.....................................$30 $40 $60

🕐 Some grades are not included. Their values can be determined by comparing with similar age, size, metal content, style, grades, or models such as time only, chronograph, repeater etc. listed.

Wrist Watches listed in this section are priced at the collectable fair market **retail** level as **complete** watches having an original gold-filled case and stainless steel back, also with original dial, leather watch band, and the entire original movement in good working order with no repairs needed.

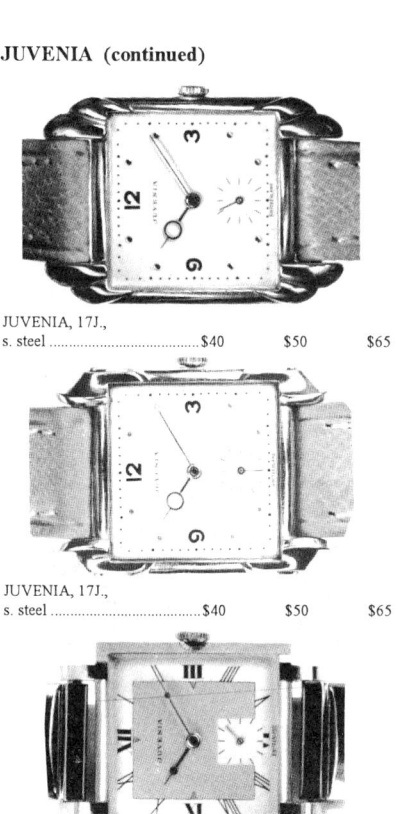

JUVENIA, 17J.,
s. steel $40 $50 $65

JUVENIA, 17J.,
s. steel $40 $50 $65

JUVENIA, 17J.,
s. steel $35 $40 $55

KELBERT, 17J., triple date, moon ph., ca.1945
s. steel $325 $350 $400

KELBERT, 17 jewels, fancy lugs, c. 1949
gold filled................................$50 $60 $80

KELEK,17J., tachymeter, auto-wind, c.1970
s. steel $100 $125 $200

Kelton, 7 jewels, curved, stepped case
gold filled $35 $45 $65

KELTON, 7 jewels, "Drake"
gold filled $30 $35 $50

KENT W. CO.,17J., Continental W.Co.(french),chronog.
s. steel $100 $125 $175

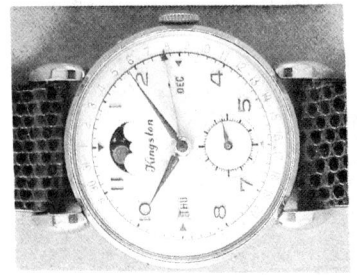

KINGSTON, 17 jewels, day-date-month, moon phase
gold filled $225 $250 $325

KINGSTON,17J., cal.G10, hidden lugs, c.1943
gold filled..................................$55 $65 $85

KORD, day date month, moon ph.
s. steel $250 $300 $400

KURTH, 17 jewels, "Certina"
gold filled..................................$30 $35 $55

LACO, 17J., center sec., c.1955
gold plate $20 $30 $45

🕐 Some grades are not included. Their values can be
determined by comparing with **similar** age, size, metal
content, style, grades, or models such as **time only**,
chronograph, repeater etc. listed.

🕐 Pricing in this Guide are fair market price for **COM-
PLETE** watches which are reflected from the "**NAWCC**" National and regional shows.

LANCEL (Paris),17J., one button chronog. by Nicolet, c.1960
gold filled $225 $250 $300

A.LANGE & SOHNE,17J., 55mm., c.1940
s. steel $1,200 $1,300 $1,600

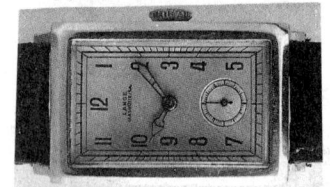

A.LANGE & SOHNE, 17J, (Glashutte), c.1936
14k $800 $850 $950

LANGE "UHR" (Glashutte),15J., c.1936
14k $800 $850 $950

LANGE "UHR" (Glashutte),17J., c.1937
s. steel $400 $450 $550

LANGE, 17J, (Glashutte), date, auto wind, waterproof
18k $600 $650 $750

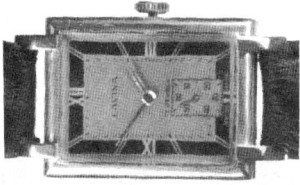

LAVINA, 17J., ca.1937
9K $100 $125 $175

LE COULTRE, 15 jewels, wire lugs, c. 1919
silver $175 $200 $250

LE COULTRE, 18J., skeletonized,
18k $1,400 $1,600 $2,000

LE COULTRE, 19 jewels, alarm
18k $650 $700 $850
14k $400 $450 $550
gold filled $200 $250 $325
s. steel $175 $225 $300

LE COULTRE, 19 jewels, alarm, c. 1950
18k $600 $650 $750
14k $350 $400 $500
gold filled $200 $250 $325
s. steel $175 $225 $300

LE COULTRE, 17J., , alarm, cal.815, c.1960
gold filled $200 $250 $325

LE COULTRE, 17J., ruby dial, alarm, c.1960
gold filled $250 $300 $375

LE COULTRE, 17J.,cal.814, memovox, alarm, c.1960
14k $400 $450 $550
gold filled $200 $250 $325

LE COULTRE, 17J., cal.p815, alarm, c.1960
gold filled...............................$200 $250 $325

LE COULTRE, 17J.,memovox , alarm, auto wind,c.1973
14k & s.s.................................$300 $350 $425

LE COULTRE, 17J., RF#3025, wrist-alarm, c.1948
gold filled...............................$200 $250 $325

LE COULTRE, 17J., RF#2676, cal.911, memovox, c.1960
gold filled ....,......................$250 $275 $325

LE COULTRE, 17J., wrist alarm, Ca.1949
gold filled...............................$225 $275 $350

LE COULTRE, 17J., date, memovox, c.1975
s. steel $100 $125 $175

LE COULTRE, 17J., "Polaris", underwater alarm tested to
600 feet, date, Ca. 1968
s. steel $700 $800 $1,000

LE COULTRE, 17J., auto wind, date, memovox, c.1976
gold filled $125 $150 $200

LE COULTRE, 19J., date, Memovox, ca. 1959

18k	$750	$800	$900
gold filled	$250	$275	$325
s. steel	$200	$225	$275

LE COULTRE, 19J., alarm, date, autowind

14k	$600	$650	$800

LE COULTRE, 19 jewels, alarm, date, autowind, ca. 1950

18k	$800	$900	$1,000
gold filled	$300	$350	$425
s. steel	$250	$300	$375

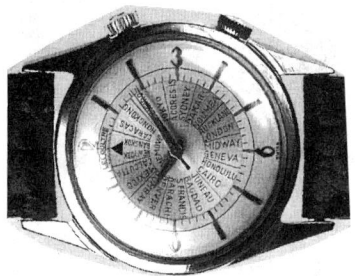

LE COULTRE, 17-19J., **World Time,** Memovox, ca. 1956

s. steel	$600	$650	$750

LE COULTRE, 17J., powermatic wind-ind., auto-w., c.1950

gold filled	$225	$250	$300

LE COULTRE, 17J., cal. 481, wind-ind., auto-w., c.1954
the cal. 481,up & down wind-ind. has **Differential Gearing**

gold filled	$200	$225	$275

LE COULTRE, 17J., auto wind, wind indicator

14k	$550	$600	$700

LE COULTRE, 17 jewels, screw back

18k	$200	$250	$325

🕐 Pricing in this Guide are fair market price for **COMPLETE** watches which are reflected from the "**NAWCC**" National and regional shows.

LE COULTRE, 17J., "Master Mariner, c.1960
14k $250 $300 $400

LE COULTRE, 17J., "Master Mariner", date, Ca. 1960
gold filled $125 $150 $200

LE COULTRE, 17J., cal.p478, center sec.c.1947
s. steel $100 $125 $175

LE COULTRE, 17J., auto-wind, cal.p812, c.1955
gold filled $100 $125 $150

LE COULTRE, 17J., "Master Mariner", c.1952
14k $250 $300 $450

LE COULTRE, 17J., RF#.480-C-380, c.1955
14k $150 $175 $225

LE COULTRE, 17J., "Master Mariner", auto-wind, c.1960
s. steel $125 $150 $225

LE COULTRE, 17J., RF#555-149, c.1955
14k $150 $175 $225

Wrist Watches listed in this section are priced at the collectable
fair market **retail** level as **complete** watches having an original
gold-filled case and stainless steel back, also with original dial,
leather watch band, and the entire original movement in good
working order with no repairs needed.

LE COULTRE, 17J., cal812, auto-wind, c.1952
s. steel $100 $125 $175

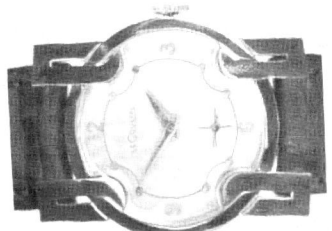

LE COULTRE, 17J.,"Coronet", cal.480cw, c.1951
gold filled.............................. $250 $300 $375

LE COULTRE, 17J., cal.480, wide bezel, c.1958
gold filled.............................. $100 $125 $175

LE COULTRE, 17J., cal.480, c.1955
14k $150 $175 $225

LE COULTRE, 17J., RF#7534, c.1960
14k $200 $250 $325

LE COULTRE, 17J., 11 diamond dial, RF#197, c.1955
14k(w)... $150 $175 $225

LE COULTRE, 17 jewels, center lugs, c. 1960
18k $250 $300 $375

LE COULTRE, 17 jewels, fancy lugs, c. 1950
14k $200 $250 $325

⏲ Pricing in this Guide are fair market price for **COMPLETE** watches which are reflected from the **"NAWCC"** National and regional shows.

⏲ Some grades are not included. Their values can be determined by comparing with similar age, size, metal content, style, grades, or models such as time only, chronograph, repeater etc. listed.

LE COULTRE, 17J., fancy lugs
14k $175 $200 $250

LE COULTRE, 17J., fancy lugs, ca. 1950s
18k $300 $325 $450

LE COULTRE, 17 jewels, fancy lugs, c. 1952
14k $300 $325 $450

LE COULTRE, 17 jewels, fancy bezel & lugs
14k $500 $550 $650

LE COULTRE, 17 jewels, fancy bezel & lugs, Ca.1953
14k $325 $350 $475

LE COULTRE, 17J., fancy bezel, Ca.1952
gold filled $75 $100 $150

LE COULTRE, 17J., auto wind, textured bezel, c. 1950
18k $200 $250 $325

LE COULTRE, 17 jewels, center sec., c. 1949
18k $200 $250   325
s. steel $75 $100 $150

LE COULTRE, 17J., cen. sec., 24 hr dial, c. 1940
s. steel $125 $150 $200

This book endeavours to be a GUIDE or helpful manual and
offers a wealth of material to be used as a tool not as a absolute document. Price Guides are like watches the worst may
be better than none at all, but at best cannot be expected to be
100% accurate.

LE COULTRE, 17J., "Quartermaster", 24 hr dial, RF#114
s.steel $400 $450 $525

LE COULTRE, 17J., cal.813, RF#388-870, Ca.1959
gold filled................................$100 $125 $175

LE COULTRE, 17J., center sec., Ca.1959
s.steel $100 $125 $175

LE COULTRE, 17J., center sec., ca. 1930s
silver $250 $300 $375

LE COULTRE, 17J., alarm, date, ca.1964
s. steel $100 $125 $175

LE COULTRE, 17J., quartz, cal.352, c.1970
gold filled $50 $60 $75

LE COULTRE, 17J., date alarm, c.1975
gold filled $100 $125 $175

LE COULTRE, 17 jewels, alarm, date, auto wind
s.steel $100 $125 $175

LE COULTRE, 17J., chronog., 2 reg.
14k $700 $800 $1,000
s. steel $350 $400 $475

LE COULTRE, 17 jewels, chronog., 3 reg.
18k $1,800 $2,000 $2,500

LE COULTRE, 17J., chronog., cal.281, c.1940
s. steel $300 $350 $425

LE COULTRE, 17 jewels, mystery dial, c. 1955
14k yellow ....,......................$400 $450 $600

LE COULTRE, 17J., chronog., FR#2644, blue dial,
s. steel $600 $650 $800

LE COULTRE, 17J., 15 diamond mystery dial, RF # 182
14k(W) $650 $750 $900

LE COULTRE, 17J., chronog. 3 reg., ca. 1958
14k $1,200 $1,400 $1,800
s. steel $600 $650 $800

LE COULTRE, 17J., 2 diamond mystery dial, RF # 182
14k(W)....................................$450 $550 $700

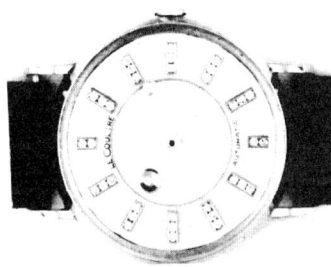

LE COULTRE, 17J., 36 diamond mystery dial, waterp.
"Vacheron Galaxy"
14k(w)......................................$800 $900 $1,100

LE COULTRE, 17J, diamond dial, textured bezel, c. 1960s
14k (w)....................................$150 $200 $325

LE COULTRE, 17J., date, cal.810, c.1952
14k $300 $350 $475

LE COULTRE, 17J., date, center sec., c.1950
14k $350 $400 $525

🕒 Some grades are not included. Their values can be
determined by comparing with similar age, size, metal
content, style, grades, or models such as time only,
chronograph, repeater etc. listed.

LE COULTRE, 15 jewels, triple-date, c. 1945
s. steel $400 $450 $600
14k $1,000 $1,100 $1,300
18k $1,300 $1,400 $1,600

LE COULTRE, 17J, triple date, moon ph., c. 1940s
18k $2,000 $2,200 $2,500
gold filled $500 $600 $700

LE COULTRE, 17J., triple date, moon ph., fancy lugs
14k $1,500 $1,700 $2,000

LE COULTRE, 17J., auto-w., Memovox, world time, c.1960
14k $1,500 $1,700 $2,000

LE COULTRE, 17J., weems style, cal.450, c.1942
s. steel $600 $650 $800

LE COULTRE, 17J., "Futurematic", auto- w., W. Ind.

18k $550	$600	$750
gold filled $250	$300	$375
s. steel ....★ $400	$500	$600

LE COULTRE, 17J., rotating chapters, date,   c.1960
s. steel $650 $700 $800

LE COULTRE, 23 J., auto-w., date cen. sec.
14k $150 $200 $275

LE COULTRE, 17J., "Futurematic", cal.817, c.1952
14k $500 $550 $650

LE COULTRE, 17J., auto-w., date
14k $150 $200 $275

LE COULTRE, 17 jewels, "Futurematic" power-reserve

18k $700	$750	$850
14k $550	$600	$700

LE COULTRE, 17J., day date, mid size, ca. 1940s
gold filled $100 $150 $200

Wrist Watches listed in this section are priced at the collectable
fair market **retail** level as **complete** watches having an original
gold-filled case and stainless steel back, also with original dial,
leather watch band, and the entire original movement in good
working order with no repairs needed.

LE COULTRE, 17J., fancy lugs, aux. sec., ca. 1948
14k $150 $200 $225

LE COULTRE, 17J., auto-w., ca. 1950s
14k $150 $200 $275

LE COULTRE, 17J., fancy lugs
14k $150 $200 $275

LE COULTRE, 17J., aux. sec. ca.1950s
14k $125 $150 $200

LE COULTRE, 17 jewels, fancy wide bezel, ca.1955
14k (W)..................................$100 $125 $175

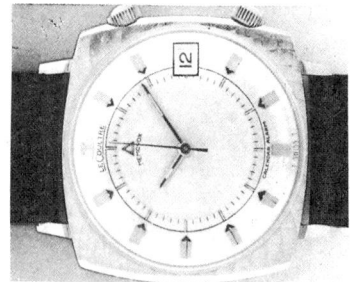

LE COULTRE, 17J., alarm, date,
14k $300 $325 $400

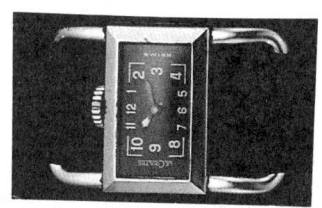

LE COULTRE, 15J., drivers style wind at 12, c.1960s
s. steel $250 $300 $375

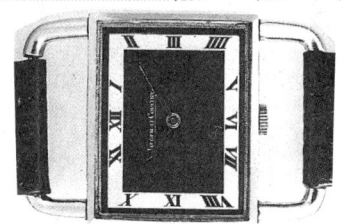

LE COULTRE,17J.,drivers style crown at 6, RF#9041
s. steel $250 $300 $375

LE COULTRE, 17J., RF#9041, cal.818, crown at 6, c.1960s
18k $500 $600 $800

LE COULTRE, 17J, "Reverso," center sec., c. 1930
18k $6,000 $7,000 $8,500
s. steel $2,000 $2,300 $3,000

LE COULTRE, 17 jewels, large fancy lugs
14k $500 $550 $650

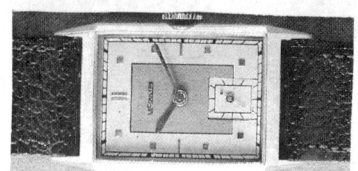

LE COULTRE, 17J., curvex,
14k $200 $250 $350

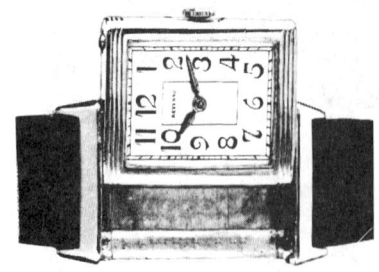

LE COULTRE, 17J., "Reverso," c. 1940s
18k $5,500 $6,500 $8,000
s. steel $1,800 $2,200 $2,800

LE COULTRE, 17J., curvex, ca. 1940s
14k $225 $275 $375

LE COULTRE, 17J., stepped lugs, ca. 1944
gold filled $75 $100 $150

LE COULTRE, 17 jewels, fancy hooded lugs, c. 1952
14k $225 $250 $325

LE COULTRE, 17J., aux. sec., ca. 1940s
gold filled $75 $100 $150

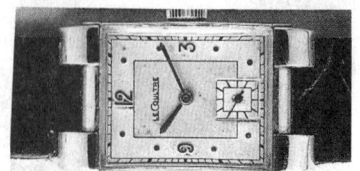

LE COULTRE, 17J., square lugs, ca. 1948
14k $400 $450 $600

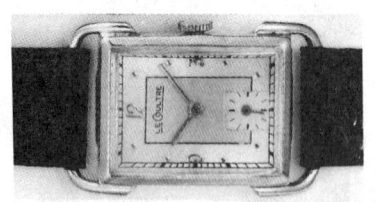

LE COULTRE, 17 jewels, fancy lugs
14k $250 $275 $350

LE COULTRE, 17J., extended lugs, c.1938
gold filled.....................................$75 $100 $150

LE COULTRE, 17J., aux. sec., c.1940
14k $100 $125 $200

LE COULTRE, 17J., tu tone dial, c.1940
gold filled.....................................$75 $100 $150

LE COULTRE, 17J., large lugs, c.1938
gold filled................................$100 $125 $175

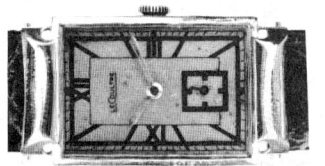

LE COULTRE, 17J.,hidden lugs, c.1942
14k $150 $200 $300
gold filled................................$100 $125 $175

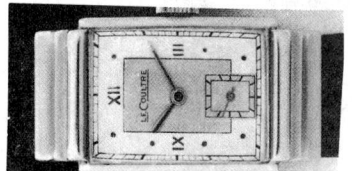

LE COULTRE, 17J., hooded lugs, ca. 1940s
14k $225 $250 $325

LE COULTRE, 17J., fluted bezel, Ca. 1949
gold filled $75 $100 $150

LE COULTRE, 17J., fancy bezel, ca. 1940s
14k $500 $550 $700

LE COULTRE, 17J, RF # 2406, 15 diamonds, Ca. 1957
14k $375 $400 $450

LE COULTRE, 17J., Asymmetric, cal.438.4cw, Ca.1957
gold filled $150 $175 $225

LE COULTRE, 17J., Asymmetric, diamond dial, RF#2406, Ca.1960
14k $300 $325 $375

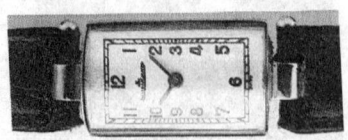

LE COULTRE, 15J., **Duoplan, back-wind,** c. 1930
18k $1,200 $1,300 $1,500

LE COULTRE, 17 jewels, **uniplan,** c. 1938
14k (w)....................................$400 $450 $550

LE COULTRE, 15J., **Duoplan, back-wind,** c. 1930
14k $1,500 $1,700 $2,000

LE COULTRE, 17 jewels, fancy lugs, c. 1948
14k $350 $400 $550

LE COULTRE, 17J., fancy lugs, cal.438-4cw, c.1951
18k $550 $600 $750

LE COULTRE, 17 jewels, fancy lugs
14k $500 $550 $750

LE COULTRE, 17 jewels, diamond dial, fancy lugs
14k $550 $600 $800

LE COULTRE, 17J., diamond dial, ca. 1940s
14k $250 $300 $450

LE COULTRE, 17J., 12 diamond dial, cal.4870cw, c.1958
14k(w)................................. $150 $175 $225

LE COULTRE, 17J., 15 diamond mystery dial ca.1940s
14k..$450 $500 $650

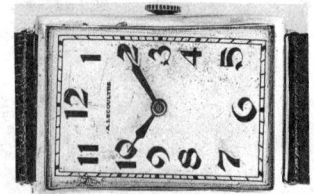

LE COULTRE, 15J., hinged case, c.1920
14k $400 $450 $525

Pricing in this Guide are fair market price for **COM-PLETE** watches which are reflected from the "**NAWCC**" National and regional shows.

LE COULTRE, 17J., stepped case & lugs, cal., c.1950
gold filled.................................$75 $100 $150

LE COULTRE, 17J., aux. sec., c.1940
14k $100 $125 $175

LE COULTRE, 17J., cal.493, c.1955
10k $100 $125 $175

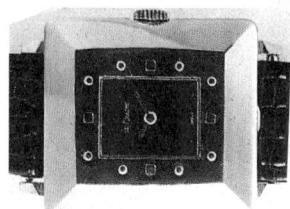

LE COULTRE, 17J., cal.438-4cw, wide bezel, c.1950
14k $250 $300 $400

LE COULTRE, 17J., textured bezel, c.1952
14k $250 $300 $400

Ⓛ Pricing in this Guide are fair market price for **COM-PLETE** watches which are reflected from the "**NAWCC**" National and regional shows.

LE COULTRE, 17J., textured bezel, c.1950
14k $250 $300 $400

LE COULTRE, 17J., RF#7540,engraved bezel, cal., c.1960
14k $250 $300 $400

LE COULTRE, 17J., cal.p812, c.1948
gold filled $75 $100 $150

LE COULTRE, 17 jewels, tank style, c.1958
18k $450 $500 $650

LE COULTRE, 17J., textured bezel, cen. sec.
18k $350 $400 $500

LE COULTRE, 17J., aux. sec., ca. 1930s
14k $200 $225 $300

LE COULTRE, 17J, triple date, moon ph., fancy bezel

18k .... ★★★	$3,500	$4,500	$6,000
14k $2,500		$3,500	$5,000
gold filled.............................$2,000		$2,200	$2,500

LE COULTRE, 17 jewels, c. 1945
18k $200 $225 $300

LE COULTRE, 17 jewels, fancy lugs, c. 1948
14k $250 $300 $375

LE COULTRE, 17 jewels, Ca. 1940
14k(rose) $150 $175 $225

LE COULTRE, 17 jewels, center lugs, c. 1945
14k $175 $200 $250

LE COULTRE, 17 jewels, c. 1950s
14k $200 $225 $275

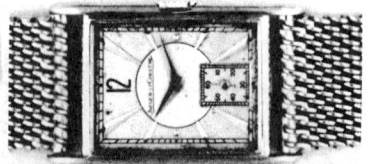

LE COULTRE, 17 jewels, 18k case & band
18k C&B................................$700 $750 $850

LE COULTRE, 17 jewels, **alarm,** date cal. 810, c. 1952
14k $600 $700 $850

LE COULTRE, 17 jewels, two tone dial
14k $150 $175 $225
18k $250 $275 $325

🕐 Some grades are not included. Their values can be determined by comparing with **similar** age, size, metal content, style, grades, or models such as **time only,** chronograph, repeater etc. listed.

LE COULTRE, 15 jewels, by Blancpain, c.1925
gold filled..................................$75　　$85　　$125

LE COULTRE, 15J., lady's
14k(W)...................................$100　　$125　　$175

LE COULTRE, quartz, date, waterproof, c. 1960s
18k ....$175　　$200　　$250

LE COULTRE, 15J., lady's art deco, by Blancpain, c.1925
silver ....$200　　$250　　$350

LE COULTRE, 15J., lady's REVERSO, c.1940
s. steel ....$700　　$800　　$1,000

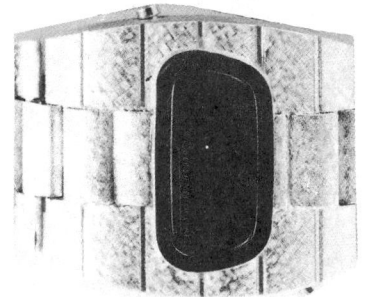

LE COULTRE, electric, digital calendar (good running order)
silver & gold...........................$150　　$175　　$225

LE COULTRE, 15J., **Duoplan, back-wind,** c. 1930
silver ....$550　　$600　　$725

LE COULTRE, 17J., lady's MYSTERY dial, c.1959
gold filled ....$100　　$125　　$175

LE COULTRE, 17 jewels, Asymmetric, c. 1953
gold filled................................$350　　$425　　$550

LE COULTRE, 17 jewels, small, Asymmetric, c. 1953
gold filled................................$300　　$375　　$475

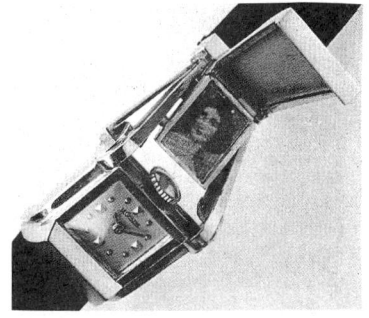

LE COULTRE, 17J., photo-watch, winds at 12, Ca. 1950
14k ....$450　　$500　　$600

LEMANIA, 17 jewels, auto wind
s. steel $50 $60 $75

LEMANIA, 17 jewels, chronog., military, ca.1970s
s. steel $350 $375 $450

LEMANIA,17J., chronog., 3 reg., c.1946
14k $350 $400 $475

LEONIDAS,17J., chronog., triple date, c.1945
gold filled $300 $350 $425

LEMANIA, 17 jewels, chronog., 2 reg., c. 1950
18k $300 $325 $400

LEONIDAS, 17 jewels, triple date, 3 reg.
18k $550 $600 $750
s. steel $350 $400 $475

LEMANIA, 17 jewels, chronog., waterproof
s. steel $200 $225 $275

LEONIDAS, 17 jewels, auto wind, triple date, moon phase
s. steel $300 $350 $425

LEONIDAS, 17 jewels, chronog., 2 reg.
s. steel $100 $125 $175

LE PHARE, 17 jewels, chronog., triple date, 3 reg.
14k $500 $550 $700

LE PHARE, 17 jewels, chronog., 2 reg.
18k $375 $425 $500
14k $275 $325 $400
s. steel $100 $150 $200

LE PHARE, 17J., triple date, moon ph., waterproof
18k $600 $700 $850
gold filled..............................$200 $250 $450

LEVRETTE,17J., chronog., (fly back), center lugs, c.1935
18k(1 button) $1,000 $1,100 $1,300

LIBELA,7J., direct read, c.1952
base metal $100 $125 $175

LIP,15J., chronog., tu-tone, center lugs, (French), c.1940
gold filled & s.steel. $450 $500 $650

LIP, electric, bulbous crown, (French)
s. steel $200 $225 $300

Wrist Watches listed in this section are priced at the collectable fair market **retail** level as **complete** watches having an original gold-filled case and stainless steel back, also with original dial, leather watch band, and the entire original movement in good working order with no repairs needed.

LONGINES, 15J., center lugs, enamel dial, ca.1923
silver $275 $325 $400

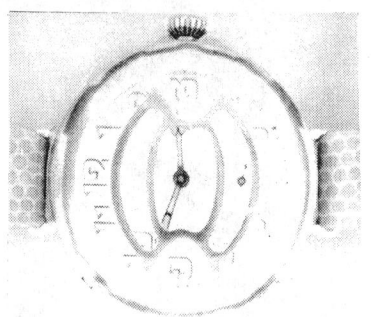

LONGINES,15J., enamel dial, pierced grill , c.1923
silver $325 $375 $475

LONGINES,15J., metal dial, GJS, c.1925
14k $150 $175 $225

LONGINES, 18J.,wire lugs, ca.1928
14k $300 $350 $425

🕐 Some grades are not included. Their values can be
determined by comparing with **similar** age, size, metal
content, style, grades, or models such as **time only**,
chronograph, repeater etc. listed.

LONGINES, 15J., wire lugs, enamel dial, c.1927
silver $250 $275 $375

LONGINES, 15J., wire lugs, ca. 1930s
silver $250 $275 $375

LONGINES,17J., tu-tone, GJS, c.1936
14k & s.s................................$200 $250 $350

LONGINES,17J., double dial, cal.932, c.1937
s. steel $700 $800 $1,000

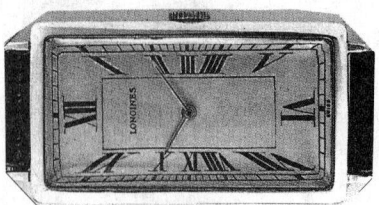

LONGINES,17J., large & curved, GJS,
gold filled $200 $250 $350

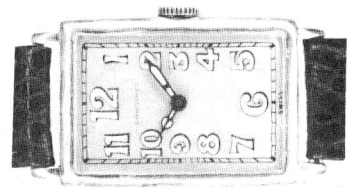

LONGINES, 15J., GJS, c.1922
silver $250 $300 $375

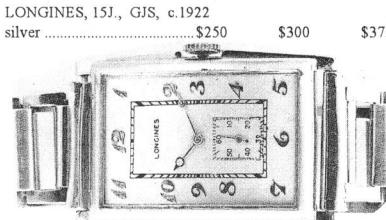

LONGINES, 17J., GJS, cal.940, c.1931
18k $500 $550 $650

LONGINES, 17J., GJS, cal.1086, c.1928
14k $250 $300 $375

LONGINES, 17J., cal.101, c.1947
14k $100 $125 $175

LONGINES, 17J., large Lindberg model 47mm., movable
bezel & center dial (weem's second setting), Ca. 1930s
18k ....★★★ $10,000 $12,000 $15,000
silver $2,500 $2,700 $3,200
nickel.....................................$2,000 $2,200 $2,600

LONGINES, 17J., small Lindberg model, original retail price
$97.50, Ca. 1930s
18k ....★★ $6,000 $7,000 $8,500
14k $4,000 $5,000 $6,500
gold filled $1,200 $1,400 $1,700
s. steel $1,200 $1,400 $1,700

LONGINES, 17J., Weems U.S. Patent 2008734 on dial
s. steel $450 $500 $650
14k $700 $800 $1,000

LONGINES, 17J., "Weems", revolving bezel, Ca. 1940s
s. steel $475 $550 $650

LONGINES, 17J., "Weems", revolving bezel, Ca. 1940s
s. steel $475 $550 $650

LONGINES,17J., fly back hand, center recording, c.1945
s. steel(1 button) $400 $450 $600

LONGINES, 17 jewels, chronog., 1 button, 2 reg., c. 1923
silver $1,400 $1,500 $1,800

LONGINES,17J., 1 button chronog., 2 reg., c.1946
14k $1,500 $1,700 $2,000

LONGINES, 17J., chronog., one button
14k $1,400 $1,700 $2,000

LONGINES,17J., 1 button, fly back hand, center recording,
RF# 5034, Ca. 1940
s. steel $400 $450 $600

LONGINES, 17J. chronog., ref. 1333, enamel dial, Ca. 1925
silver(1 button) $1,200 $1,400 $1,700

LONGINES, 17J., one button chronog., 2 reg., Ca. 1928
18k $2,000 $2,200 $2,600

LONGINES, 17J., chronog. 2 reg., tach.
14k $1,400 $1,600 $1,900

LONGINES, 17J., 1 button, chronog., ca. 1945
gold filled $300 $350 $425

LONGINES,17J., chronog., c.1942
s. steel $600 $650 $750

LONGINES, 17 jewels, chronog. 1 button
14k $1,200 $1,400 $1,700

LONGINES,17J., RF#6474, c.1955
s. steel $700 $800 $950

LONGINES,17J., chronog., cal.539, c.1969
s steel $200 $225 $275

LONGINES, 17 jewels, chronog., 2 reg., Ca. 1940s
18k $1,500 $1,700 $2,000

LONGINES, 17 jewels, chronog., 2 reg.
14k $1,300 $1,500 $1,800
s. steel $700 $800 $950

LONGINES,17J., Valjoux 726, cal.332, c.1972
s. steel $225 $250 $300

LONGINES, 16J., military issue, waterpr., ca. 1940s
s. steel $300 $350 $425

LONGINES,17J., GJS, c.1965
18k $150 $175 $250

LONGINES,17J., GJS, cal.23z, c.1958
gold filled.................................$50 $75 $125

LONGINES, 17J., GJS, cal.194, c.1963
gold filled.................................$40 $60 $90

LONGINES,17J., GJS, cal.352, c.1960
14k $100 $125 $175

LONGINES,17J., GJS, cal., c.1960
14k $125 $150 $200

LONGINES,17J., aux. seconds, Ca. 1960
gold filled $40 $60 $90

LONGINES,17J., Aux. seconds, gold jewel settings, Ca. 1957
14k $125 $150 $200

🕐 Some grades are not included. Their values can be determined by comparing with **similar** age, size, metal content, style, grades, or models such as **time only**, chronograph, repeater etc. listed.

LONGINES,17J., RF#2033p, GJS, cal., c.1958
14k $125 $150 $200

LONGINES,17J., RF#2021, GJS, cal.23z, c.1955
14k $200 $250 $325

LONGINES,17J., GJS, cal.23z, c.1955
14k $125 $150 $200

LONGINES,17J., large fluted lugs, GJS, c.1940
14k $300 $350 $475

LONGINES,17J., large lugs, GJS, c.1952
18k $300 $350 $425

LONGINES,17J., GJS, cal.18LN, c.1952
14k $250 $300 $375

LONGINES,17J., one lug at 11 & one at 5, GJS, 1955
14k $275 $300 $375

LONGINES,17J., GJS, cal.22a, auto-wind, c.1958
14k $275 $325 $400

Wrist Watches listed in this section are priced at the collectable
fair market **retail** level as **complete** watches having an original
gold-filled case and stainless steel back, also with original dial,
leather watch band, and the entire original movement in good
working order with no repairs needed.

Pricing in this Guide are fair market price for **COM-
PLETE** watches which are reflected from the "**NAWCC**" National and regional shows.

LONGINES,17J., GJS, cal.10L, c.1952
14k $100 $125 $175

LONGINES, 17 jewels, fancy lugs, c. 1954
14k $325 $375 $475

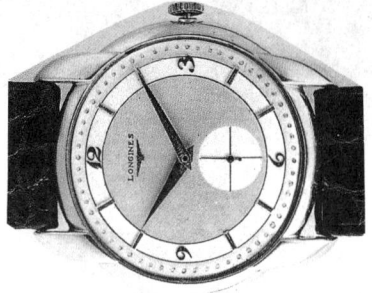

LONGINES,17J., GJS, cal.23z, c.1954
18k $250 $275 $350

LONGINES, 17 jewels, fancy lugs, c. 1949
14k $325 $375 $450

LONGINES, 15 jewels, c. 1940s
18k $200 $225 $275
14k $150 $175 $225
s. steel $75 $100 $150

LONGINES, 19J.,"Conquest", auto-wind,
14k $250 $300 $375

LONGINES,17J., GJS, cal.22ls, c.1950
14k $200 $225 $300

🕐 Some grades are not included. Their values can be determined by comparing with **similar** age, size, metal content, style, grades, or models such as **time only**, chronograph, repeater etc. listed.

LONGINES, 17J., fancy lugs, diamond dial,
14k $350 $400 $500

LONGINES,17J., "Flagship", GJS, cal.340, c.1960
18k $200 $225 $300

LONGINES,17J., RF#3759, GJS, cal.22as, c.1949
14k $225 $275 $350

LONGINES,17J., center sec., GJS, c.1948
14k $150 $175 $250

LONGINES,17J., GJS, center sec., c.1958
gold filled $100 $125 $175

LONGINES,17J., GJS, cal.19as, c.1955
gold filled.................................$75 $85 $125

LONGINES,17J., center sec., GJS, cal., c.1940
14k $150 $175 $225

LONGINES,17J., GJS, cal.340, c.1960
14k $100 $125 $175

LONGINES,17J., GJS, center sec., c.1943
14k $100 $125 $175

Wrist Watches listed in this section are priced at the collectable fair market **retail** level as **complete** watches having an original gold-filled case and stainless steel back, also with original dial, leather watch band, and the entire original movement in good working order with no repairs needed.

Pricing in this Guide are fair market price for **COMPLETE** watches which are reflected from the **"NAWCC"** National and regional shows.

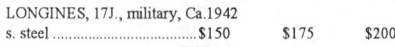

LONGINES, 17J., military, Ca.1942
s. steel $150 $175 $200

LONGINES,17J., GJS, "Flagship", date, c.1964
gold filled................................$75 $85 $100

LONGINES,17J., 36,000 (beat), auto-wind, "Ultra-Chron"
14k $200 $225 $300

LONGINES,17J., RF#9003, date, GJS, "Conquest", c.1958
18k $450 $500 $600

LONGINES,17J., a-wind, "Grand Prize", date, Ca.1960
gold filled $60 $70 $100

LONGINES,17J., oval textured bezel, cal.506, c.1965
14k $125 $150 $200

LONGINES,17J., high frequency, date, c.1972
s. steel $50 $60 $85

LONGINES, 17 jewels, ''Flagship''
14k $125 $150 $200

LONGINES, 17 jewels, gold jewel settings, Ca. 1950
s. steel $75 $85 $120

LONGINES, 17 jewels, center seconds
14k $175 $200 $275

LONGINES, 17J., aux. seconds, large lugs
14k $150 $175 $250

LONGINES, 17J., auto wind
14k $125 $150 $200

LONGINES, 19J., "Conquest", auto-w., date, ca.1962
s. steel $75 $100 $150

LONGINES, 17J., "Grand Prize", auto-w., date
14k $250 $300 $375

LONGINES, 17J., "Conquest", auto-w., date, w.-indicator
s. steel $300 $325 $400

LONGINES, 17J., date, ca. 1940s
14k $275 $300 $375

LONGINES,17J., mystery dial, cal.232 c.1960
gold filled $125 $150 $200

LONGINES,17J., mystery dial,
gold filled.............................. $125 $150 $200

LONGINES, 17 jewels, mystery hand, ca.1962
gold filled............................... $125 $150 $200

LONGINES, 17 jewels, mystery hand,
14k $300 $375 $475

LONGINES, 17 jewels, mystery hand, 12 diamond dial
14k $500 $600 $750

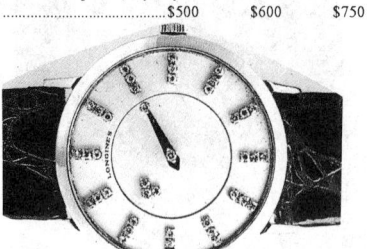

LONGINES,17J., mystery 39 diamond dial, RF#1017
14k(w).................................... $650 $700 $850

LONGINES, 17 jewels, diamond dial, center lugs
14k $500 $550 $700

LONGINES, 17 jewels, "Ultra Chrono," diamond dial
14k $200 $250 $325

LONGINES, 17 jewels, "Ultra Chrono," date, c.1949
14k $150 $175 $225

LONGINES, 17J., auto-w., aux. sec.
14k $125 $150 $200

🕐 Some grades are not included. Their values can be
determined by comparing with **similar** age, size, metal
content, style, grades, or models such as **time only**,
chronograph, repeater etc. listed.

LONGINES, 17J., auto-w., aux. sec.
14k $175 $200 $250

LONGINES, 17J., aux sec.
14k $150 $175 $225

LONGINES, 17J., diamond dial
14k(W) $150 $175 $225

LONGINES, 17J.,diamond bezel
gold filled................................$200 $225 $300

LONGINES, 17J.,3 diamond dial
gold filled $90 $110 $165

LONGINES, 17J., diamond dial,
14k(W)....................................$150 $175 $225

LONGINES, 17 jewels, cocktail style, 36 diamond dial
14k(W)....................................$275 $300 $375

LONGINES, 17 jewels, 12 diamond dial
14k (w) $175 $200 $250

LONGINES,17J., GJS, 34 diamond dial, date, c.1962
14k $300 $325 $400

LONGINES,17J., 44 diamonds bezel, GJS, cal.22L, c.1952
18k(w)....................................$350 $400 $475

LONGINES, 17J., 14 diamond dial, Ca. 1960
14k $150 $175 $225

LONGINES,17J., 14 diamonds,GJS, cal.370, c.1960
14k $150 $175 $225

LONGINES,17J., "Admiral", GJS, auto-wind, Ca. 1960
14k $300 $325 $425

LONGINES,17J., 4 diamonds, cal.194, c.1958
gold filled...............................$100 $125 $175

LONGINES, 17J., GJS, tank style
14k C&B................................$500 $550 $650

LONGINES, 17J., GJS, faceted crystal, Ca.1951
gold filled $75 $100 $150

LONGINES,17J., 37 diamonds on bezel 24 on dial, c.1958
14k(w)....................................$300 $325 $400

LONGINES, 17J., GJS, cal.9L, Ca.1939
gold filled $75 $100 $150

LONGINES, 17J., 4 diamonds, GJS, cal.23z, c.1948
14k $150 $175 $225

LONGINES, 17J., 3 diamonds, hidden lugs, GJS, c.1943
gold filled $75 $85 $110

LONGINES, 17J., 5 diamonds, GJS, cal.8ln, c.1940
14k(w)...................................$100 $125 $175

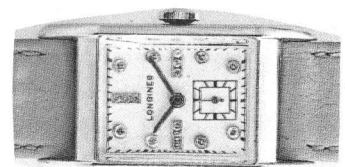

LONGINES, 17J., 17 diamonds, GJS, c.1951
14k $250 $300 $400

LONGINES, 17J., 8 diamonds, GJS, cal.22L, c.1958
14k $125 $150 $200

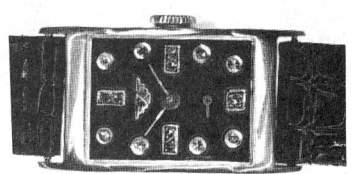

LONGINES, 17J., 15 diamonds, GJS, cal.9L, c.1945
platinum..................................$675 $775 $925
14k $300 $350 $450

LONGINES,17J.,4 diamonds, textured bezel,cal.194, c.1955
gold filled..................................$75 $85 $110

LONGINES, 17J., 18 diamonds, RF#176, GJS, c.1950
14k(w)...................................$300 $350 $450

LONGINES, 17J., 6 diamonds, GJS
14k $125 $150 $200

🕐 Pricing in this Guide are fair market price for **COMPLETE**
watches which are reflected from the "**NAWCC**" National and
regional shows.

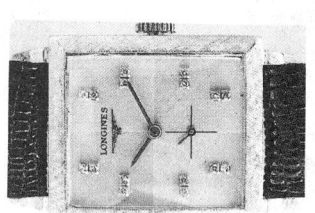

LONGINES, 17J., 16 diamonds, cal.9LT, c.1958
14k(w)...................................$200 $250 $325

LONGINES, 17J., 4 diamonds, GJS, cal.L8474, c.1960
gold filled..................................$75 $100 $150

LONGINES, 17J., 6 diamonds, RF#2763, GJS, c.1955
14k $175 $225 $300

LONGINES, 17J., 8 diamonds, GJS, cal.9LT, c.1958
14k(w).....................................$175 $225 $300

LONGINES, 17J., 5 diamonds, GJS, c.1945
14k C&B $450 $500 $550

LONGINES, 17J., 5 diamonds, GJS, cal.9L, c.1952
14k $250 $300 $375

LONGINES, 17 jewels, 17 diamond dial, c. 1951
14k(w).....................................$300 $350 $450

LONGINES, 17 jewels, diamond dial, hidden lugs, c. 1938
s. steel $125 $150 $200

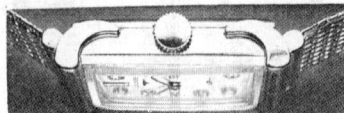

LONGINES, 17 jewels, fancy hidden lugs, diamond dial
14k (w) $300 $350 $450

LONGINES, 17 jewels, diamond dial, c. 1944
14k $300 $350 $450

LONGINES, 17 jewels, 17 diamond dial, c. 1951
14k $200 $250 $350

LONGINES, 17 jewels, diamond dial, c. 1935
platinum.............................$1,100 $1,200 $1,400
14k $750 $800 $900

LONGINES, 17 jewels, 18 diamond dial
14k (w) $150 $200 $275

LONGINES, 17 jewels, flared, 6 diamond dial
14k $500 $550 $700

LONGINES, 17 jewels, 4 diamond dial
14k $175 $225 $300

LONGINES, 17 jewels, 12 diamond dial
s.steel $150 $175 $225

LONGINES, 17 jewels, stepped case, Ca. 1951
14k $200 $225 $300

LONGINES, 17 jewels, c. 1923
gold filled................................$75 $90 $115

LONGINES, 17 jewels, flared, c. 1959
14k $450 $500 $600

LONGINES, 17 jewels, flared
14k C&B...............................$750 $850 $1,000

LONGINES, 17 jewels, fancy lugs, c. 1943
14k $350 $400 $500

LONGINES, 17 jewels, torpedo shaped numbers
14k $150 $175 $225

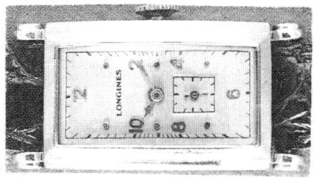

LONGINES, 17 jewels, curved, fancy lugs, c. 1939
14k $350 $400 $500

LONGINES, 17 jewels, center lugs, c. 1955
14k $175 $200 $250

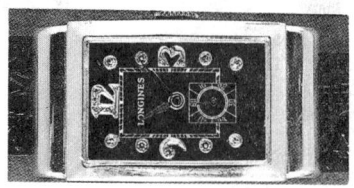

LONGINES, 17 jewels, hooded lugs, diamond dial
14k(w)...................................$700 $800 $950

LONGINES, 17 jewels, hooded lugs
14k $200 $225 $275

LONGINES, 17 jewels, diamond dial, fancy lugs
14k $675 $750 $850

LONGINES, 17 jewels, diamond dial, c. 1944
14k :...$175 $200 $275

LONGINES, 17 jewels, fancy lugs
14k $175 $200 $275

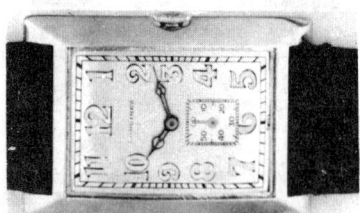

LONGINES, 17 jewels, c. 1930
18k $700 $750 $900
14k $500 $550 $700
gold filled...............................$200 $225 $300

LONGINES, 17 jewels, 20 diamond dial, Ca. 1932
platinum.................................$800 $900 $1,100

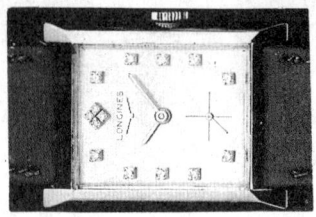

LONGINES, 17 jewels, diamond dial
14k(W)...................................$250 $300 $375

LONGINES, 17J.,curved,
14k $150 $175 $250

LONGINES, 17J., stepped case,
14k $300 $350 $425

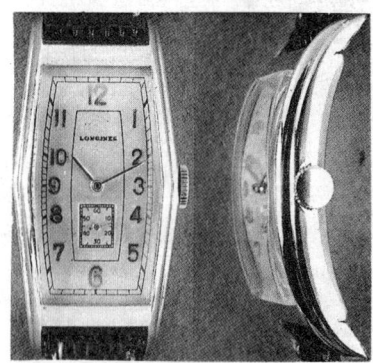

LONGINES, 17J., curvex, 52mm, ca. 1930
gold filled $300 $350 $450

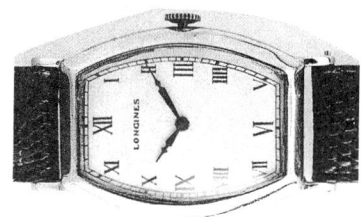

LONGINES, 15J., tonneau, GJS, c.1925
silver $350 $400 $500

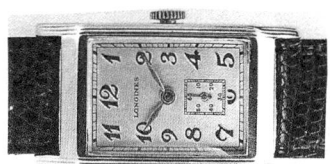

LONGINES, 17J., stepped case, GJS, cal.9L, c.1939
14k $275 $300 $375

LONGINES, 17J., extended lugs, GJS, cal.9L, c.1942
14k $200 $250 $325

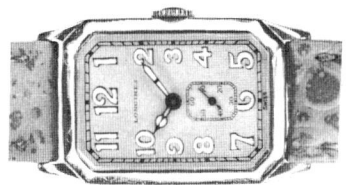

LONGINES, 17J., cut corner, cal.94w, c.1929
gold filled................................$100 $125 $175

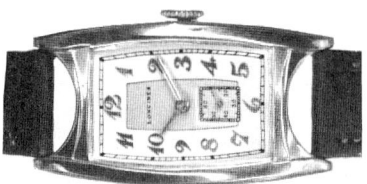

LONGINES, 17J., tonneau, cal.9L, c.1948
gold filled................................$150 $175 $225

LONGINES, 17J., carved bezel, GJS, cal.9LT, c.1950
gold filled $75 $90 $115

LONGINES, 17J., butler finish, GJS, cal., c.1951
gold filled $75 $90 $115

LONGINES, 17J., beveled bezel, GJS, cal., c.1935
gold filled $100 $125 $175

LONGINES, 17J., aux. sec., GJS, cal.9L, c.1948
gold filled $75 $90 $115

LONGINES, 17J., carved case, GJS, cal.9LT, c.1950s
14k $225 $275 $325

Wrist Watches listed in this section are priced at the collectable
fair market **retail** level as **complete** watches having an original
gold-filled case and stainless steel back, also with original dial,
leather watch band, and the entire original movement in good
working order with no repairs needed.

⊕ Some grades are not included. Their values can be
determined by comparing with **similar** age, size, metal
content, style, grades, or models such as **time only**,
chronograph, repeater etc. listed.

LONGINES, 17J., butler finish, GJS, cal.9LT, c.1957
14k $150 $175 $250

LONGINES, 15J., butler finish, c.1926
gold filled.................................$75 $90 $115

LONGINES, 17J., stepped case, GJS, cal.9LT, c.1958
14k $200 $250 $325

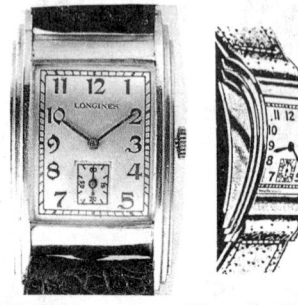

LONGINES, 17J., stepped case, GJS, curved, c.1938
gold filled................................$125 $150 $200
s. steel $100 $125 $175
14k $350 $375 $450

LONGINES, 17J., fancy lugs, GJS, cal.9LT, c.1957
14k $175 $200 $275

LONGINES, 17J., fluted lugs, GJS, cal.9L, c.1949
gold filled $100 $125 $175

LONGINES, 17J., carved case, GJS, cal.9LT, c.1959
gold filled $100 $125 $175

LONGINES, 17J., spur lugs, GJS, cal., c.1948
gold filled $100 $125 $175

LONGINES, 17J., extended lugs, GJS, cal.9LT, c.1955
14k $200 $225 $300

LONGINES, 17J., fancy bezel, GJS, Ca. 1950
14k $175 $200 $275

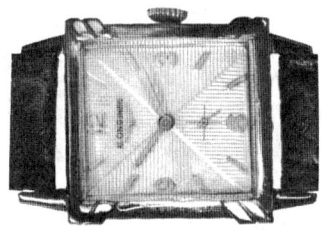

LONGINES, 17J., fluted sides, GJS, cal.9LT, c.1950
gold filled................................$100 $125 $175

LONGINES, 17J., carved case, GJS, cal.9LT, c.1955
14k $300 $325 $400

LONGINES, 17J., U shaped lugs, GJS
14k $350 $400 $500

LONGINES, 17J., gold jewel settings, Ca. 1951
gold filled................................$100 $125 $175
14k (w)....................................$175 $200 $250

LONGINES, 17J., RF#8475, GJS, cal.10L, c.1948
14k $175 $200 $275

LONGINES,17J., GJS, c.1958
14k $175 $200 $275

LONGINES, 17J., RF#3327, GJS, cal.,10L c.1948
14k $200 $250 $325

LONGINES, 17J., extended lugs, GJS, cal.9LT, c.1951
14k $225 $275 $350

LONGINES, 17J., aux. sec., GJS, Ca.1951
14k $125 $150 $225

LONGINES, 17J., butler finish, GJS, cal.9L, c.1955
14k $100 $125 $175

🕒 Some grades are not included. Their values can be
determined by comparing with **similar** age, size, metal
content, style, grades, or models such as **time only**,
chronograph, repeater etc. listed.

LONGINES, 17J., aux. sec., GJS, cal.9LT, c.1950
14k $150 $175 $250

LONGINES, 17J., fancy lugs, GJS, cal.10L, c.1951
gold filled $75 $90 $115

LONGINES, 17J., butler finish, GJS, cal.8LN, c.1942
14k $100 $125 $175

LONGINES, 17J., GJS, cal. 23Z, Ca. 1950
gold filled $100 $115 $150

LONGINES, 17J., beveled lugs, GJS, cal.8LN, c.1947
14k $100 $125 $175

LONGINES, 17J., bezeled case, GJS, cal.9LT, c.1955
gold filled $75 $90 $115

LONGINES, 17J., wide bezel, GJS, cal.23z, c.1950
gold filled................................$75 $90 $115

LONGINES, 17J., curly lugs, GJS, cal.23z, c.1950
gold filled $100 $115 $150

LONGINES, 17J., tank style, GJS, cal.23z, c.1957
14k $150 $175 $250

🕐 Pricing in this Guide are fair market price for **COMPLETE** watches which are reflected from the "**NAWCC**" National and regional shows.

LONGINES, 17J., checked dial, GJS, cal.22L, c.1957
14k $100 $125 $175

LONGINES, 17J., RF#1050, mystery dial, cal.23z, c.1960
14k $300 $325 $400

LONGINES, 17J., stepped lugs, GJS, cal.10L, c.1948
gold filled...............................$100 $115 $150

LONGINES, 17J., textured bezel, GJS, cal.22L, c.1950
14k $300 $325 $400

LONGINES, 17J., stepped case, GJS, cal.23z, c.1955
14k $125 $150 $200
gold filled...............................$75 $90 $115

LONGINES, 17J., carved case, GJS,
gold filled...............................$100 $125 $175

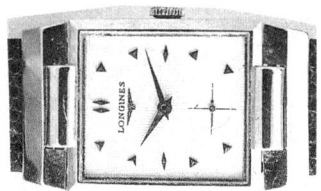

LONGINES, 17J., hooded lugs, GJS, cal.8LN, c.1942
gold filled $70 $90 $115

LONGINES, 17J., RF#2288, hidden lugs, GJS, c.1955
14k $300 $350 $425

LONGINES, 17J., hidden lugs
14k $600 $650 $800

LONGINES, 17J., **contract** case or recent case,
14k $100 $125 $175

LONGINES, 17 jewels, 42mm
14k (w) $150 $175 $250

Wrist Watches listed in this section are priced at the collectable
fair market **retail** level as **complete** watches having an original
gold-filled case and stainless steel back, also with original dial,
leather watch band, and the entire original movement in good
working order with no repairs needed.

LONGINES, 17 jewels, fancy lugs
14k $250 $275 $350

LONGINES, 17 jewels, c. 1939
14k $300 $325 $400

LONGINES, 17 jewels, curvex, slanted lugs
14k (w)....................................$150 $175 $225

LONGINES, 17 jewels, fancy lugs, c. 1942
14k $250 $275 $350

LONGINES, 17 jewels, fancy lugs, c. 1947
14k $275 $300 $375

LONGINES, 17 jewels, curved, flared
14k $150 $175 $250

LONGINES, 15 jewels, chased bezel
14k $700 $750 $900

LONGINES, 15 jewels, engraved bezel, c. 1928
14k (w) $450 $500 $650

LONGINES, 17J., faceted crystal,
14k $100 $125 $175

LONGINES, 17J., fancy lugs & diamond bezel
14k(W)....................................$500 $550 $700

LONGINES, 17J., curved case, Ca. 1930s
14k $250 $300 $375

🕐 Pricing in this Guide are fair market price for **COMPLETE**
watches which are reflected from the "**NAWCC**" National and
regional shows.

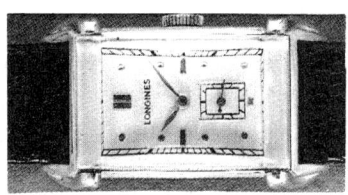

LONGINES, 17J., fancy lugs
14k $300 $350 $425

LONGINES, 17J., cal#10L, center sec.,
14k $200 $250 $325

LONGINES, 17J., fancy lugs,
14k $275 $300 $375

LONGINES, 17J., center sec., fancy lugs, ca.1946
14k $200 $250 $325

LONGINES, 17J., cal#232, ca. 1948
14k $125 $150 $225

LONGINES, 17J., fancy lugs, cal#10L
14k $150 $175 $225

LONGINES, 17J., aux. sec.
14k $200 $250 $325

LONGINES, 17J., aux. sec.
14k $125 $150 $200

LONGINES, 17J., ca. 1952
14k $175 $200 $275

🕐 Some grades are not included. Their values can be determined by comparing with **similar** age, size, metal content, style, grades, or models such as **time only**, chronograph, repeater etc. listed.

LONGINES, 17J., offset lugs
14k $250 $300 $375

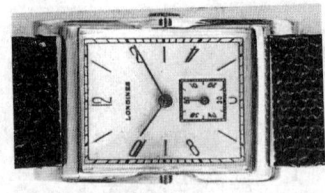

LONGINES, 17J., fancy lugs, ca. 1951
14k $175 $200 $275

LONGINES, 17J., fancy bezel
14k $125 $150 $200

LONGINES, 17J., flared case, GJS, c.1955
gold filled................................$175 $200 $275

LONGINES, 17J., flared case, GJS, cal.9LT, c.1950
gold filled................................$150 $200 $275

LONGINES, 17J., flared case, textured dial
14k $400 $450 $550

LONGINES, 17J., hidden lugs, Ca. 1940
14k(rose)................................$400 $425 $500

LONGINES, 17 jewels, enameled bezel, c. 1928
14k $400 $425 $500

LONGINES, 17 jewels, formed case
14k $175 $200 $275

LONGINES, 17J.,antimagnetic
s. steel $150 $175 $250

Wrist Watches listed in this section are priced at the collectable fair market **retail** level as **complete** watches having an original gold-filled case and stainless steel back, also with original dial, leather watch band, and the entire original movement in good working order with no repairs needed.

🕐 Some grades are not included. Their values can be determined by comparing with **similar** age, size, metal content, style, grades, or models such as **time only**, chronograph, repeater etc. listed.

LONGINES MOVEMENT IDENTIFICATION

Cal. No. 4.21, Ca.1930

Cal. No. 5.16, Ca.1922

Cal. No. 6.22, Ca.1932

Cal. No. 7.45, Ca.1916

Cal. No. 7.48, Ca.1925

Cal. No. 8.23, Ca.1931

Cal. No. 8.47, Ca.1916

Cal. No. 9.32, Ca.1932

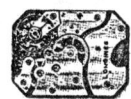

Cal. No. 9.47, Ca.1922

Cal. No. 12.19, Ca.1934

Cal. No. 13.15, Ca.1936

Cal. No. 25.17, Ca.1935

PRODUCTION TOTALS

LONGINES DATE OF MOVEMENT MANUFACTURE

DATE– SERIAL #	DATE– SERIAL #	DATE– SERIAL #
1867 --- 1	1911 - 2,500,000	1937 - 5,500,000
1870 --- 20,000	1912 - 2,750,000	1938 - 5,750,000
1875 --- 100,000	1913 - 3,000,000	1940 - 6,000,000
1882 --- 250,000	1915 - 3,250,000	1945 - 7,000,000
1888 --- 500,000	1917 - 3,500,000	1950 - 8,000,000
1893 --- 750,000	1919 - 3,750,000	1953 - 9,000,000
1899 - 1,000,000	1922 - 4,000,000	1956-10,000,000
1901 - 1,250,000	1925 - 4,250,000	1959-11,000,000
1904 - 1,500,000	1926 - 4,500,000	1962-12,000,000
1905 - 1,750,000	1928 - 4,750,000	1966-13,000,000
1907 - 2,000,000	1929 - 5,000,000	1967-14,000,000
1909 - 2,250,000	1934 - 5,250,000	1969-15,000,000

The above list is provided for determining the APPROXIMATE age of your watch. Match serial number with date. Watches were not necessarily sold in the exact order of manufactured date.

LONGINES date of movement manufacture

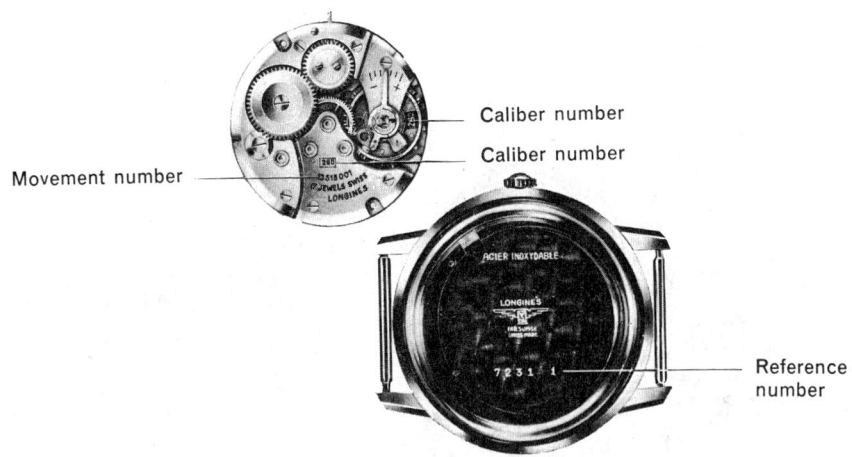

Movement number

Caliber number

Caliber number

Reference number

Cal. No. 10.68, Ca.1932   Cal. No. 10.68, Lindburg   Cal. No. 12.68, Ca.1938   Cal. No. 12.68 Z, Ca.1939

Cal. No. 14.16, Ca.1951   Cal. No. 14.16 S, Ca.1954   Cal. No. 14.17, Ca.1952   Cal. No. 15.18, Ca.1941

Cal. No. 19 A, Ca.1952   Cal. No. 19.4, Ca.1953   Cal. No. 19.4 S, Ca.1953   Cal. No. 22 A, Ca.1945

Cal. No. 22 L, Ca.1946   Cal. No. 23 Z, Ca.1948   Cal. No. 23 ZD, Ca.1954   Cal. No. 25.17, Ca.1935

Cal. No. RR 280, Ca.1963   Cal. No. 290, Ca.1958   Cal. No. 310   Cal. No. 312

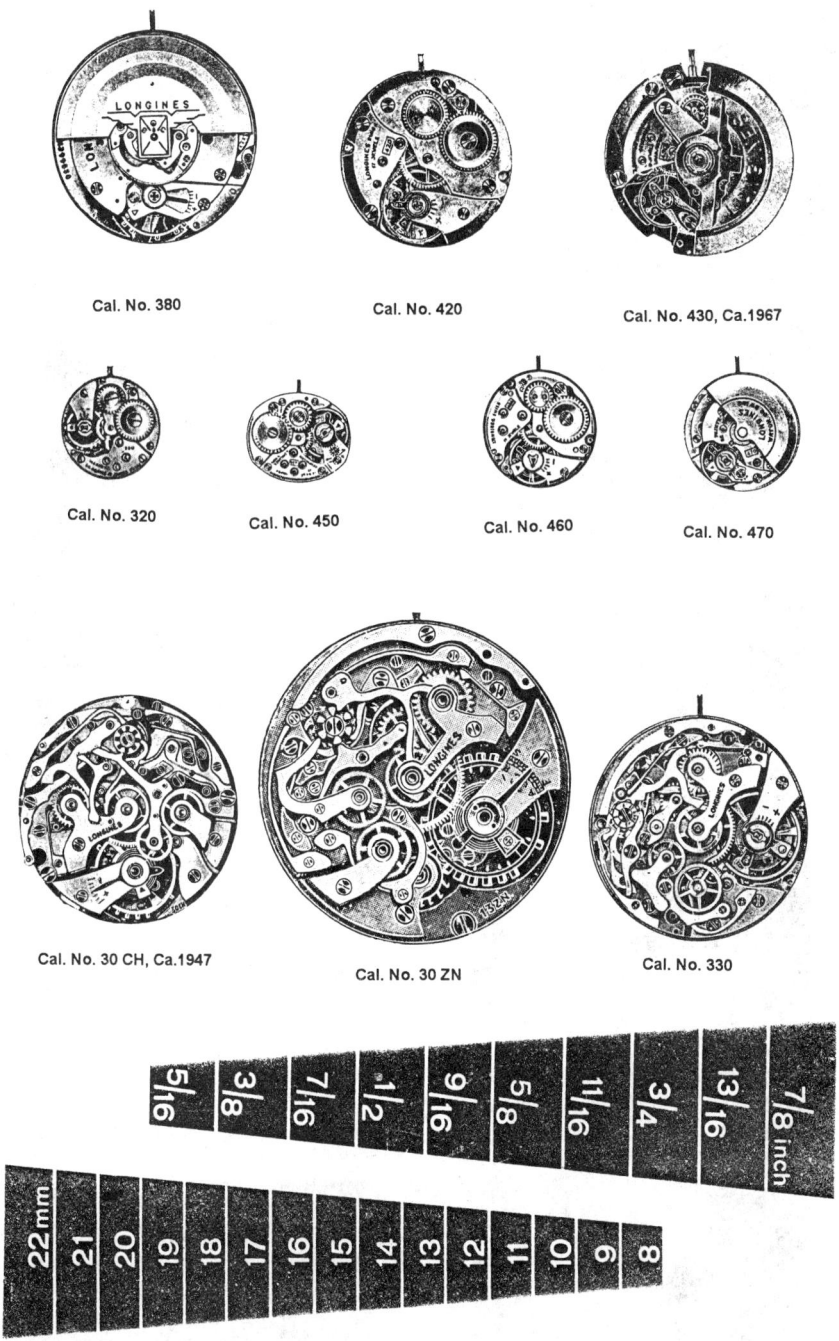

Cal. No. 380

Cal. No. 420

Cal. No. 430, Ca.1967

Cal. No. 320

Cal. No. 450

Cal. No. 460

Cal. No. 470

Cal. No. 30 CH, Ca.1947

Cal. No. 30 ZN

Cal. No. 330

To determine your wrist watch band size use the **ABOVE GAUGE** and measure between the lugs.

LONGINES, 17J., "COMET", cal.702, c.1972
s. steel $100 $135 $175

LONGINES, 17J., lady's style, center lugs, c.1948
14k C&B $200 $250 $300

LONGINES, 15J., lady's style,
14k C&B $200 $250 $300

LORTON, 17 jewels, chronog., c. 1950
s. steel $150 $175 $225

LOUIS, 17J., center sec.,
14k $100 $110 $135

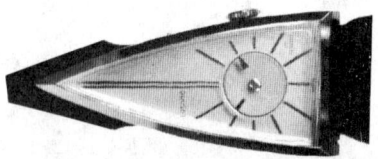

LOUVIC, 17J., mystery dial, long triangular case, c.1950
base metal $60 $75 $100

LOUVIC, 17J., hunter style case, ca. 1965
s. steel $100 $125 $175

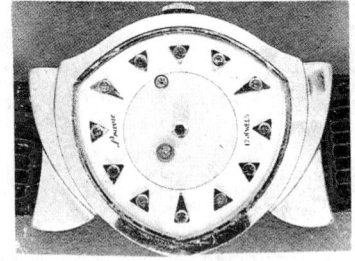

LOUVIC, 17J., mystery diamond dial, ca.1960
s. steel $200 $225 $275

LUCERNE, 17 jewels, 14k case & band , 3 diamonds
14k C&B $250 $275 $325

LUCIEN PICCARD, 17J., movement by Ditisheim
14k $125 $150 $200

LUCIEN PICCARD, 17 jewels, gem set bezel
gold filled..............................$125 $150 $200

LUSINA, 17 jewels, aux. sec., fancy lugs
gold filled...............................$40 $50 $70

LUCIEN PICCARD, 17 jewels, "Seahawk," auto wind
18k C&B.................................$400 $450 $525

LYCEUM, 17J., beveled case, aux. sec.
14k.......................................$100 $120 $150

LUCIEN PICCARD, 17 jewels, wind indicator, c. 1958
s. steel $75 $100 $150

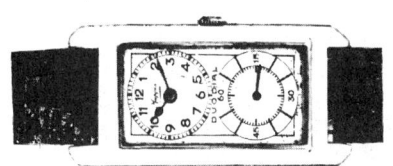

MAPPIN, 15 jewels, duo dial, c. 1930
9k $500 $600 $750

MARLYS, 15J., G.J.S., c.1935
14k $125 $150 $200

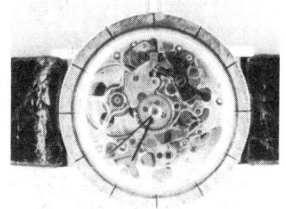

LUCIEN PICCARD, 17 jewels, skeletonized
18k $600 $700 $900

🕐 Some grades are not included. Their values can be
determined by comparing with **similar** age, size, metal
content, style, grades, or models such as **time only**,
chronograph, repeater etc. listed.

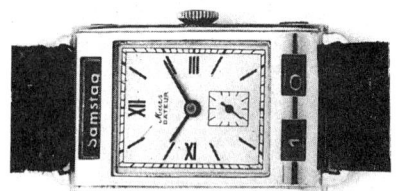

MARS, 17J, "Dateur," date on lugs, hinged back, c. 1934
gold filled $250 $300 $400

MARVIN, 17J., center sec., cal.520s, c.1943
14k $100 $110 $135

MARVIN, 17J., non magnetic,
gold filled..................................$50 $60 $80

MASTER, 17J., engraved case, c.1943
gold plate $20 $30 $45

MASTER, 17J., tonneau case, c.1943
gold plate $30 $40 $55

MASTER, 17J., stepped case, c.1943
gold plate $35 $45 $65

🕐 Pricing in this Guide are fair market price for **COMPLETE** watches which are reflected from the "**NAWCC**" National and regional shows.

C.H. MEYLAN, 17 jewels, c. 1940s
18k $275 $325 $450

C.H. MEYLAN, 18 jewels, jumping hr., c. 1920
18k $4,500 $5,000 $6,500

C.H. MEYLAN, 16 jewels, wire lugs
14k $250 $300 $375

C.H. MEYLAN, 27J, 1 button chronog., 2 reg., enamel dial
18k $2,500 $2,800 $3,500

C.H. MEYLAN, 18J., ladies , Octagon case, c.1917
platinum...................................$300 $325 $400

J.E. MEYLAN, 17J., chronograph, 2 reg., ca. 1937
14k $1,000 $1,100 $1,400
s. steel $300 $325 $400

J.E. MEYLAN,17J., stop watch,
s. steel $175 $200 $250

MIDO, 15 jewels, in form of car radiator, c. 1940s
silver $1,700 $2,000 $2,500

MIDO, 17 jewels, chronog., "Multi-centerchrono", c. 1952
s. steel $200 $250 $325

Wrist Watches listed in this section are priced at the collectable
fair market **retail** level as **complete** watches having an original
gold-filled case and stainless steel back, also with original dial,
leather watch band, and the entire original movement in good
working order with no repairs needed.

MIDO, 17 jewels, chronog., "Multi-centerchrono"
s. steel $220 $250 $325
with telemeter dial $250 $300 $375

MIDO, 17J., choronog., cal.1300, c.1954
gold filled $250 $300 $375
14k $300 $350 $425
18k $500 $550 $650

MIDO, 17J., autowind, date, Ca. 1960s
s. steel $40 $50 $65

MIDO, 17J., carved case, cal.2m, c.1947
14k $150 $175 $250

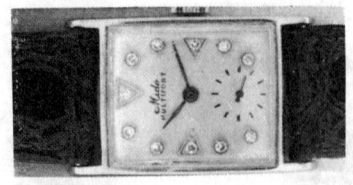

MIDO, 17 jewels, diamond dial
platinum $400 $500 $650
14k $175 $225 $300

MIDO, 17 jewels "Multifort," diamond dial
s. steel $100 $125 $175

MIDO, 17 jewels, fancy lugs, c. 1945
14k $200 $225 $300

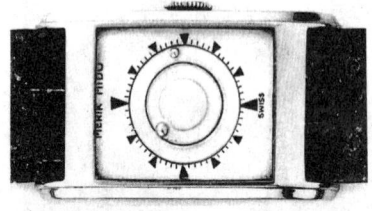

MIDO, 15 jewels, mystery dial, c. 1935
s. steel $400 $450 $525

MIDO, 17J., multifort grand luxe, date, ca. 1950s
18k C&B $400 $500 $650

MIDO, 17J., RF#7204, cal.d917b, c.1958
s. steel $60 $75 $110

MIDO, 17J., RF#228, mid size case, c.1943
s. steel $50 $60 $75

MIDO, 17J., **"Radiotime"**, to correct time push button on
crown advances minutes & seconds hand, Ca. 1939
gold filled $150 $200 $300

MIDO, 17J., mid size case, cal.917r, c.1949
s. steel $50 $60 $75

⊕ Some grades are not included. Their values can be
determined by comparing with **similar** age, size, metal
content, style, grades, or models such as **time only**,
chronograph, repeater etc. listed.

MIDO, 17J., super auto-wind, muiltfort extra,
14k $100 $110 $150
s. steel $50 $60 $75

MIDO, 17J., "power wind", c.1955
s. steel $50 $60 $75

MIDO, 17J., rotating bezel, c.1960
s. steel $150 $200 $275

MIDO, 17J., multifort grand luxe, extra-flat
s. steel $50 $60 $75

MILDIA, 17 jewels
s. steel $30 $40 $60

MIMO, 15 jewels, date
gold filled $100 $125 $175

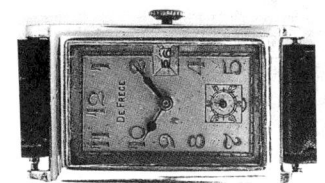

MIMO, 17J., "De Frece", date, c.1935
14k(w) $200 $250 $325

MIMO, 17 jewels, jumping hr., wandering min. & sec.
gold filled $350 $400 $500

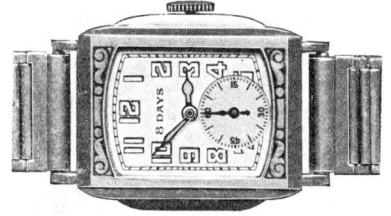

MIMO, 17 jewels, **8 day**, 6 gear train, c. 1950s
gold filled $500 $600 $750

🕐 Pricing in this Guide are fair market price for **COMPLETE**
watches which are reflected from the "**NAWCC**" National and
regional shows.

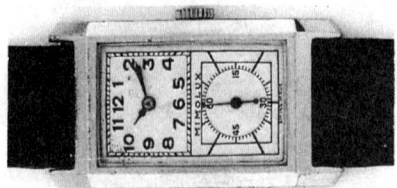

MIMO, 17 jewels, duo dial
s. steel $350 $400 $500

MIMO, 15 jewels, engraved bezel
gold filled..................................$35 $45 $75

MIMO, 15 jewels, "Mimomatic," c. 1932
s. steel $70 $80 $115

MINERVA, 29J., min. repeater, repeats on 2 gongs
18k $15,000 $18,000 $25,000

MINERVA, 17 jewels, chronog., 2 reg.
18k $900 $1,000 $1,400
s. steel $275 $350 $450

MINERVA, 17 jewels, chronog., 2 reg.
18k $300 $350 $450

MINERVA, 17 jewels, waterproof, chronog., c. 1950s
14k $400 $450 $575
s. steel $250 $275 $350

MINERVA, 17J., chronog., Valjoux cal.723, c.1955
14k $750 $850 $1,000
s. steel $500 $550 $650

MINERVA, 19 jewels, chronog., 3 reg.
s. steel $200 $250 $325

Watches listed in this BOOK as Misc. Swiss are just a few examples of miscellaneous jobbers, distributors & jewelry firms. Example Abc Watch Co., to Zuma Watch Co., etc. with the name xxxx out.

MINERVA, 17 jewels, one button chronog., c. 1942
s. steel $300 $350 $450

MISC. SWISS, 15J., shield cover, enamel dial, ca. 1927
silver $600 $650 $750

MINERVA, 17J., chronog., day-date-month, 3 reg.
18k $1,000 $1,100 $1,400

MISC. SWISS,15J., **rim wind**, wire lugs, cal., c.1920
s. steel .... ★$250 $300 $375

MINERVA, 17 jewels, center sec., auto wind
gold filled................................. $40 $50 $70

MISC. SWISS,15J., mother of pearl dial, c.1925
s. steel $200 $250 $325

MISC. SWISS, 15J., hunter style, wire lugs, ca. 1926
silver $450 $500 $600
Watches listed in this BOOK as Misc. Swiss are just a few examples of miscellaneous jobbers, distributors & jewelry firms. Example Abc Watch Co., to Zuma Watch Co., etc. with the name xxxx out.

MISC. SWISS,15J., wire lugs, exaggerated no.s, c.1925
silver $150 $175 $225

⊕ Some grades are not included. Their values can be determined by comparing with **similar** age, size, metal content, style, grades, or models such as **time only**, chronograph, repeater etc. listed.

MISC. SWISS, 15J., wire lugs, Ca. 1918
silver $100 $125 $175

MISC. SWISS, 15J., wire lugs, Ca. 1917
silver $75 $100 $135

MISC. SWISS, 15J., wire lugs, Ca. 1918
silver $125 $150 $200

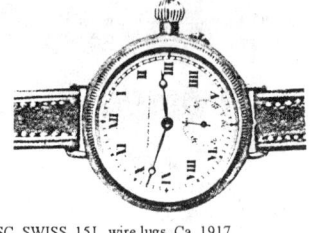

MISC. SWISS, 15J., wire lugs, Ca. 1917
silver $100 $125 $175

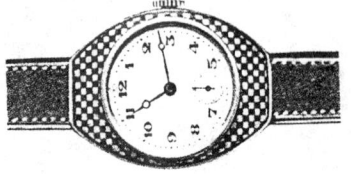

MISC. SWISS, 15J., wire lugs, Ca. 1917
base metal $75 $100 $150

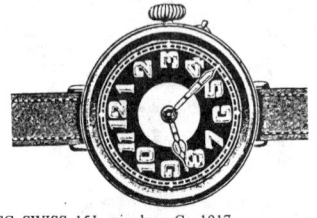

MISC. SWISS, 15J., wire lugs, Ca. 1917
silver $100 $125 $175

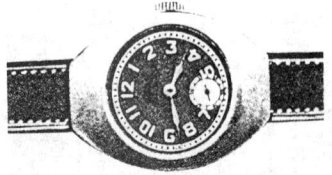

MISC. SWISS, 15J., wire lugs, Ca. 1917
silver $100 $150 $225

MISC. SWISS, 15J., wire lugs, Ca. 1917
silver $250 $300 $375

MISC. SWISS, 15J., wire lugs, Ca. 1917
base metal $75 $100 $150

Watches listed in this BOOK as Misc. Swiss are just a few
examples of miscellaneous jobbers, distributors & jewelry
firms. Example Abc Watch Co., to Zuma Watch Co., etc. with
the name xxxx out.

MISC. SWISS, 15J., wire lugs, Ca. 1919
base metal $100 $125 $175

MISC. SWISS, 15J., wire lugs, Ca. 1917
silver $75 $100 $150

MISC. SWISS, 15J., wire lugs, Ca. 1917
14K..$100 $125 $175

MISC. SWISS, 15J., wire lugs, Ca. 1917
14K..$150 $175 $250

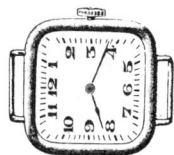

MISC. SWISS, 15J., wire lugs, Ca. 1917
14K..$100 $150 $200

MISC. SWISS, 15J., wire lugs, Ca. 1917
14K..$100 $150 $200

MISC. SWISS, 15J., wire lugs, Ca. 1917
14K..$100 $200 $300

Watches listed in this BOOK as Misc. Swiss are just a few
examples of miscellaneous jobbers, distributors & jewelry
firms. Example Abc Watch Co., to Zuma Watch Co., etc. with
the name xxxx out.

MISC. SWISS, 15J., wire lugs, Ca. 1917
14k..$100 $125 $175

MISC. SWISS, 15J., wire lugs, Ca. 1917
14K $125 $150 $200

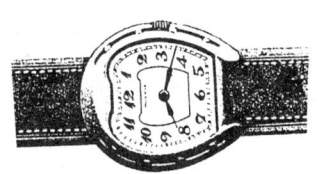

MISC. SWISS, 15J., horseshoe style, Ca. 1935
base metal $150 $200 $275

MISC. SWISS, 17J., nail set, 31 X 43mm, exaggerated no.s,
ca.1915
18k $1,200 $1,300 $1,600

MISC. SWISS, 15J., exaggerated no.s, ca.1916
silver $600 $650 $750

MISC. SWISS, 15J., exaggerated no.s,   Ca.1916
18K......................................$1,200 $1,300 $1,600

MISC. SWISS, 15J., exaggerated no.s,   Ca.1916
18K..$800 $900 $1,200

MISC. SWISS, 15J., exaggerated no.s,   Ca.1920
14K...$300 $350 $500

MISC. SWISS, 15J., exaggerated no.s,   Ca.1916
18K..$800 $900 $1,200

MISC. SWISS, 15J., exaggerated no.s,   wire lugs, Ca.1916
14K..$200 $250 $400

Watches listed in this BOOK as Misc. Swiss are just a few examples of miscellaneous jobbers, distributors & jewelry
firms. Example Abc Watch Co., to Zuma Watch Co., etc.
with the name xxxx out.

MISC. SWISS, 15J., exaggerated no.s,   Ca.1916
18K $400 $450 $600

MISC. SWISS, 15J., exaggerated no.s,   Ca.1916
18K $1,400 $1,500 $1,800

MISC. SWISS, 15J., exaggerated no.s, wire lugs, Ca.1916
silver $100 $150 $225

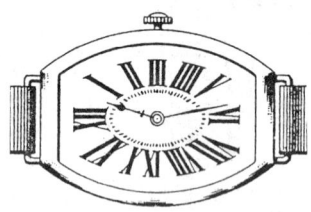

MISC. SWISS, 15J., exaggerated no.s, wire lugs, Ca.1916
silver $125 $150 $200

MISC. SWISS, 15J., exaggerated no.s,   Ca.1916
silver $100 $125 $165

MISC. SWISS, 15J., wire lugs, Ca.1917
silver $70 $80 $120

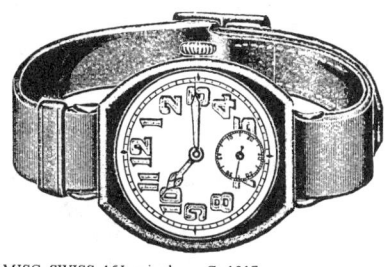

MISC. SWISS, 15J., wire lugs, Ca.1917
silver $100 $125 $175

MISC. SWISS, 15J., wire lugs, Ca.1917
silver $100 $125 $175

MISC. SWISS, 15J., wire lugs, Ca.1917
14k $100 $125 $175

MISC. SWISS, 15J., Ca.1925
14K..$250 $300 $400

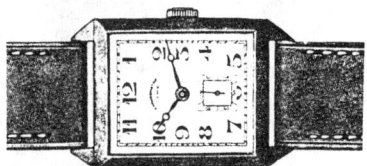

MISC. SWISS, 15J., Ca.1925
14K..$125 $150 $200

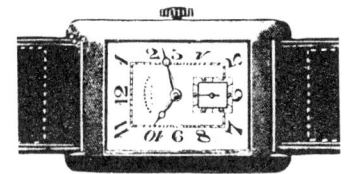

MISC. SWISS, 15J., Ca.1925
14K $125 $150 $200

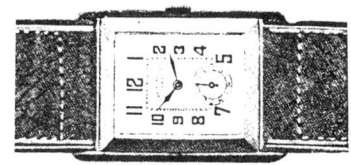

MISC. SWISS, 15J., Ca.1925
14K $100 $125 $175

MISC. SWISS, 15J., Ca.1925
14K $125 $150 $200

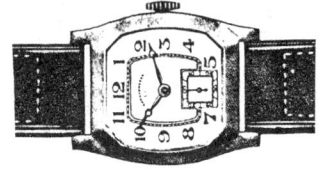

MISC. SWISS, 15J., Ca.1925
14K $125 $150 $200

MISC. SWISS, 15J., Ca.1925
14K $125 $150 $200

Wrist Watches listed in this section are priced at the collectable
fair market **retail** level as **complete** watches having an original
gold-filled case and stainless steel back, also with original dial,
leather watch band, and the entire original movement in good
working order with no repairs needed.

Watches listed in this BOOK as Misc. Swiss are just a few examples of miscellaneous jobbers, distributors & jewelry firms. Example Abc Watch Co., to Zuma Watch Co., etc. with the name xxxx out.

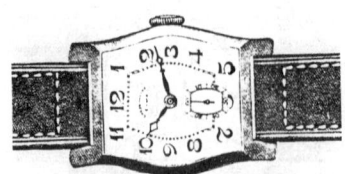

MISC. SWISS, 15J., Ca.1925
14K..$125 $150 $200

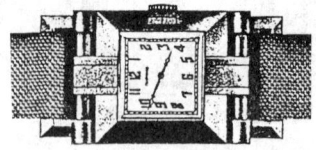

MISC. SWISS, 15J., Ca.1930
18K $350 $400 $475

MISC. SWISS, 15J., Ca.1925
14K..$100 $125 $175

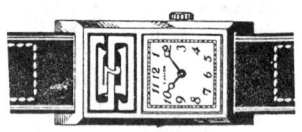

MISC. SWISS, 15J., Ca.1930
14K $300 $350 $425

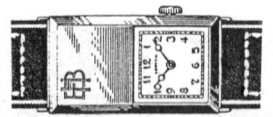

MISC. SWISS, 15J., Ca.1930
14K..$300 $350 $425

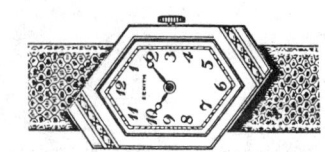

MISC. SWISS, 15J., Ca.1930
18K $350 $400 $425

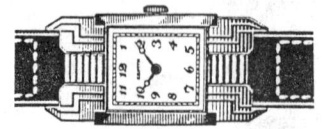

MISC. SWISS, 15J., Ca.1930
18K..$350 $400 $475

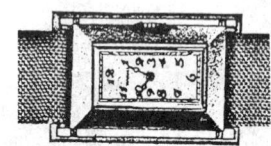

MISC. SWISS, 15J., Ca.1930
18K $250 $300 $375

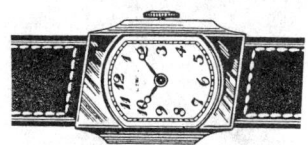

MISC. SWISS, 15J., Ca.1930
18K..$325 $375 $450

MISC. SWISS, 15J., flex lugs, Ca.1930
18K $400 $450 $525

MISC. SWISS, 15J., Ca.1930
18K..$350 $400 $475

🕓 Some grades are not included. Their values can be determined by comparing with similar age, size, metal content, style, grades, or models such as time only, chronograph, repeater etc. listed.

MISC. SWISS, 15J., wire lugs, ca. 1925
silver $100 $125 $175

MISC. SWISS, 15J., wire lugs, nail set, ca.1925
silver $100 $125 $175

MISC. SWISS, 15J., aux. sec., ca. 1930s
gold filled...................................$75 $100 $135

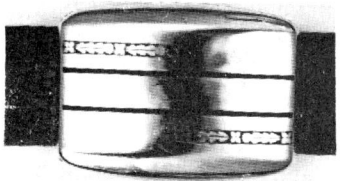

MISC. SWISS, 17 jewels, picture watch "Flip up"
gold filled................................$300 $350 $450

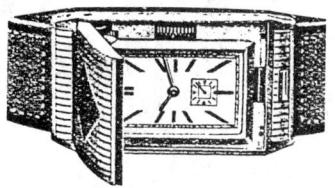

MISC. SWISS, 17J, Flip Top **winds by opening lid**, Ca.1932
base metal $800 $900 $1,100

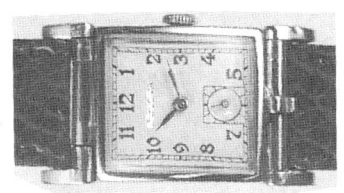

MISC. SWISS, 17J., watch top flips up to view photo, c.1950
gold filled $200 $250 $325

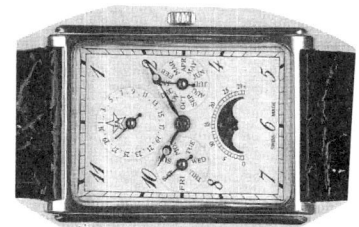

MISC. SWISS, 17J., day date month moon phase, Ca. 1955
gold filled $500 $600 $750
14K $1,000 $1,100 $1,400

MISC. SWISS, 17J., jump hr., wandering min., c. 1930
9k $500 $600 $750
14k $800 $900 $1,100

MISC. SWISS, 17J., wandering min., hr. by red mark
s. steel $250 $300 $400

MISC. SWISS, 17 jewels, fancy bezel
14k $275 $300 $350

MISC. SWISS, 17 jewels, masonic symbols, c. 1950s
s. steel & gold filled $900 $1,000 $1,200

MISC. SWISS, 17 jewels, masonic symbols, c. 1975
base metal $300 $350 $425

MISC. SWISS, 15 jewels, early auto wind, c. 1930s
s. steel $400 $500 $650

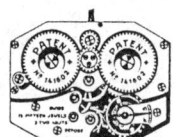

(note tandem wind)
MISC. SWISS, 15J, 2 barrels, 8 day movement , (8 JOURS)

MISC. SWISS, 15 jewels, 8 day watch, Ca. 1935
base metal $200 $250 $400
silver $350 $550 $700

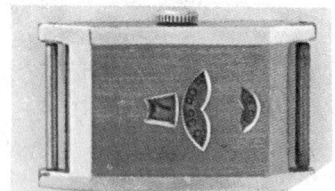

MISC. SWISS, 17 jewels, digital hr., min.& sec.
gold filled $350 $400 $500
s. steel $300 $350 $450

MISC. SWISS, 15 jewels, double dial, c.1935
9K $575 $675 $825

MISC. SWISS, 15 jewels, center lugs, c.1936
9K $150 $175 $225

MISC. SWISS, 17J, drivers style winds at 12, Ca. 1930
gold filled $200 $250 $325

MISC. SWISS, 7J, "Corvette or Mercedes Benz", c.1970
base metal $60 $75 $100

Watches listed in this BOOK as Misc. Swiss are just a few examples of miscellaneous jobbers, distributors & jewelry firms. Example Abc Watch Co., to Zuma Watch Co., etc. with the name xxxx out.

MISC. SWISS, 29J, repeater, 2 jacquemart, **all original**
18k $6,000 $7,000 $8,500

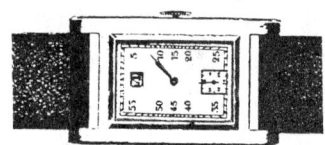

MISC. SWISS, 17J., jump hour at 12:00, Ca. 1930
14K $2,500 $3,000 $4,000

MISC. SWISS, 17J., silver coin, Ca. 1960
silver $300 $350 $500

MISC. SWISS,15J., one button chronog. wind and sets at 12, center hinged lugs, enamel dial, c.1920s
silver $1,200 $1,400 $1,700

MISC. SWISS, 17J., world time, date, Ca. 1965
s. steel $200 $250 $325

MISC. SWISS,15J., 1 button chronog., enamel dial, wire lugs, Ca.1923
silver $1,000 $1,200 $1,500

MISC. SWISS, 17J., golfers scorer, Ca. 1950
base metal $50 $60 $80

MISC. SWISS, 15-17J, enamel dial, one button chronog.
s. steel $900 $1,100 $1,400

MISC. SWISS, 17J.,early 1 button chronog., ca.1929
18k $1,000 $1,200 $1,400

MISC. SWISS, 17J., 2 reg., chronograph
s. steel $175 $200 $250

MISC. SWISS, 15J., one button chronog., ca. 1925
silver $600 $700 $900

MISC. SWISS, 17J, chronog., 2 reg.
gold filled $200 $225 $275

MISC. SWISS,15-17J, enamel dial, 1 button chronog., 2 reg.
s. steel $500 $600 $800

MISC. SWISS,17J., "chronographe" on dial, c.1940
base metal $125 $150 $200

MISC. SWISS, 17J., one button, chronog., ca. 1950
gold filled..............................$400 $450 $550

MISC. SWISS,17J., by Venus
s. steel $125 $150 $200
14k $225 $250 $300
18K $275 $300 $350

Watches listed in this BOOK as Misc. Swiss are just a few examples of miscellaneous jobbers, distributors & jewelry
firms. Example Abc Watch Co., to Zuma Watch Co., etc.
with the name xxxx out.

MISC. SWISS, 17J., triple date, chronog., 2 reg., c.1955
s. steel $350 $400 $500

MISC. SWISS, 17J., chronog., triple date, moon ph., c. 1945
14k $1,300 $1,400 $1,600
s. steel $600 $700 $900

MISC. SWISS, 17 jewels, **split sec.** chronog., 2 reg.
18k $3,200 $3,800 $5,000
s. steel $2,000 $2,200 $2,600

MISC. SWISS, 18 jewels, Jaeger,chronog., c. 1930s
18k $600 $700 $900

MISC. SWISS, 17J., triple date, moon ph., ca. 1967
gold filled $500 $550 $700

MISC. SWISS, 17 jewels, early auto wind, c. 1930s
14k $400 $450 $600

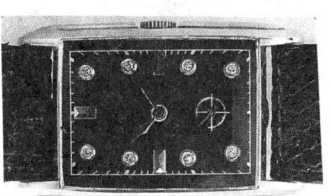

MISC. SWISS, 17J., diamond dial, Ca. 1945
14K $250 $300 $375

MISC. SWISS, 17J., diamond dial, top hat, Ca. 1945
platinum..............................$1,200 $1,300 $1,600

MISC. SWISS, 17J., mystery diamond dial, Ca. 1960
gold filled $200 $250 $325

MISC. SWISS, 17J., Rhinestone dial & bezel, Ca. 1950
gold filled.................................$80 $90 $110

MISC. SWISS, 17J., Rhinestone dial & bezel, Ca. 1950
gold filled.................................$80 $90 $110

MISC. SWISS, i7J., hidden lugs, Ca. 1934
gold filled.................................$55 $65 $80

MISC. SWISS, 17J., fancy lugs, Ca. 1945
14K..$200 $250 $325

MISC. SWISS, 17J., fancy lugs, Ca. 1940
gold filled.................................$35 $45 $65

Watches listed in this BOOK as Misc. Swiss are just a few examples of miscellaneous jobbers, distributors & jewelry
firms. Example Abc Watch Co., to Zuma Watch Co., etc.
with the name xxxx out.

MISC. SWISS, 17J., fancy bezel, Ca. 1938
14K..$150 $175 $225

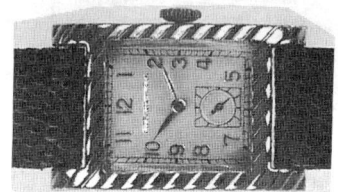

MISC. SWISS, 17J., fancy bezel, Ca. 1947
gold filled $80 $90 $125
14K $200 $225 $300

MISC. SWISS, 17J., fancy bezel, Ca. 1930
18K (W)..................................$250 $300 $375

MISC. SWISS, 7J., stepped case, Ca. 1935
gold filled $40 $50 $75

MISC. SWISS, 17J., wandering hour, Ca. 1938
base metal $100 $110 $150

Watches listed in this BOOK as Misc. Swiss are just a few examples of miscellaneous jobbers, distributors & jewelry firms. Example Abc Watch Co., to Zuma Watch Co., etc. with the name xxxx out.

MISC. SWISS, 15J., Ca. 1938
14K..$150 $175 $225

MISC. SWISS, 17J., Fancy lugs, Ca. 1950
gold filled $100 $125 $175

MISC. SWISS, 15J., Ca. 1925
silver $70 $80 $100

MISC. SWISS, 17J., Fancy lugs, Ca. 1950
14K $200 $225 $300

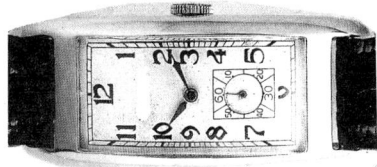

MISC. SWISS, 21J., curved, Ca. 1938
gold filled:................................$150 $175 $225

MISC. SWISS, 17J., Fancy lugs, Chronometer, Ca. 1950
14K..$150 $200 $275

MISC. SWISS, 21J., Fancy lugs, Ca. 1955
18K $300 $350 $475

MISC. SWISS, 17J., Fancy lugs & bezel, Ca. 1950
gold filled................................$100 $125 $175

MISC. SWISS, 17J., Fancy lugs, Ca. 1948
gold filled $100 $125 $175

⏱ Pricing in this Guide are fair market price for **COMPLETE** watches which are reflected from the "**NAWCC**" National and regional shows.

⏱ Some grades are not included. Their values can be determined by comparing with **similar** age, size, metal content, style, grades, or models such as **time only**, chronograph, repeater etc. listed.

MISC. SWISS, 17J., enamel & gold bezel, pin set, c.1925
18k $175 $200 $250

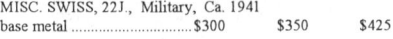

MISC. SWISS, 22J., Military, Ca. 1941
base metal $300 $350 $425

MISC. SWISS, 15J., wire lugs, Ca. 1930
14K rose $75 $90 $120

MISC. SWISS, 15J., Ruby on case, Ca. 1950
14K $75 $90 $120

MISC. SWISS, 15J., Ca. 1930
14K case & band $200 $225 $275

MISC. SWISS, 15J., Military, Ca. 1942
s. steel $75 $90 $125

MISC. SWISS, 15J., Ring watch, Ca. 1955
14K $75 $90 $120

MISC. SWISS, 16J., Military, Ca. 1940
base metal $60 $70 $90

Watches listed in this BOOK as Misc. Swiss are just a few examples of miscellaneous jobbers, distributors & jewelry
firms. Example Abc Watch Co., to Zuma Watch Co., etc.
with the name xxxx out.

MISC. SWISS, 21J., horseshoe shaped, Ca. 1939
gold filled $100 $125 $175

MONARCH, 7 jewels, stepped case
gold filled..............................$50 $60 $75

MONARCH, 7 jewels,
gold filled..............................$30 $35 $55

MONARCH, 7 jewels, engraved bezel, curved
gold filled..............................$35 $40 $65

MONARCH, 7 jewels , curved
14k $175 $200 $250
gold filled..............................$75 $100 $150

MONTBRILLANT, 15J., one button chronog. Ca 1915-20
MONTBRILLANT = early **BREITLING**
18k $1,500 $1,800 $2,500

MONTE, 16J., "Ancre", ca.1938
14k $100 $125 $175

MORIVA,17J., auto-w. with wind indicator,
s. steel $60 $70 $100

HY. MOSER & CIE., 14J., "Signal Corps USA", ctr. lugs
silver $350 $425 $550

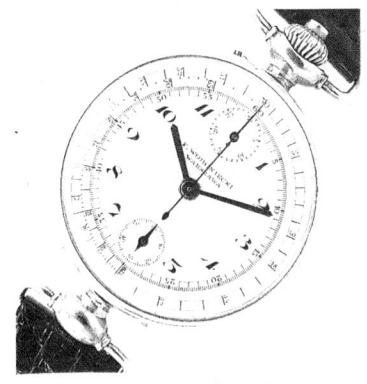

HY. MOSER & CIE., 14-18J., one button chronograph, wind
and set at 12, center lugs, 2 reg. Ca. 1920s
silver $2,000 $2,200 $2,500

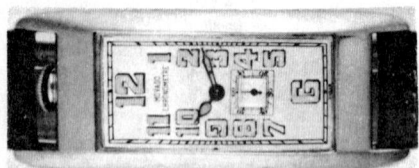

MOVADO, 15J., polyplan, winds at 12 o'clock, 46mm, curved, c. 1910
18k $4,000 $4,500 $6,000

MOVADO, 15J., polyplan, winds at 12 o'clock,
14k $3,000 $3,500 $5,000

MOVADO, 15J., polyplan, winds at 12 o'clock,
silver $2,000 $2,300 $3,000

Movado, Purse Watches See P.W. section Movado

ABOVE:
MOVADO, side view of movement with three inclined plans.

MOVADO, 15J., "Chronometre", c.1930
14k $175 $300 $350

MOVADO, 17J., day date month, "Sportsman"
14k $300 $400 $500

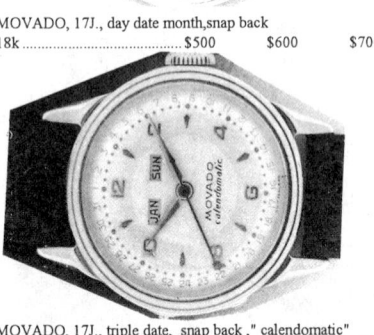

MOVADO, 17J., day date month,snap back
18k $500 $600 $700

MOVADO, 17J., triple date, snap back ," calendomatic"
18k $700 $800 $900

MOVADO, 28J., date, "Kingmatic", c.1950
s. steel $80 $100 $120
14k(w)......................................$250 $300 $350

MOVADO, 17J., month date, ca. 1950s
14k $250 $300 $425

MOVADO, 17J., 1 button chronog., c.1948
s. steel $550 $600 $700

MOVADO, 17 jewels, day-date-month, c. 1945
18k $600 $700 $900
gold filled $300 $350 $425
s. steel $275 $325 $400

MOVADO, 17J., chronog., 2 reg., c.1940
14k $1,200 $1,400 $1,600

MOVADO, 17J, triple date, moon phases, Ca. 1950
s. steel $900 $1,000 $1,200

MOVADO, 17J., 3 reg. chronog.
s. steel $900 $1,000 $1,200

MOVADO, 17J., 3 reg. chronog.,
18k $2,500 $2,800 $3,500
14k $2,000 $2,300 $3,000
s. steel $900 $1,000 $1,200

MOVADO, 17J., "tempograf, chronog., 2 reg., c.1935
s. steel $1,000 $1,100 $1,400

The Movado trademark M over flat V was Registered in 1985.

MOVADO, 17J., 3 reg. chronog., date
s. steel $300 $375 $425

MOVADO, 17J., center sec., c.1942
14k $175 $200 $275

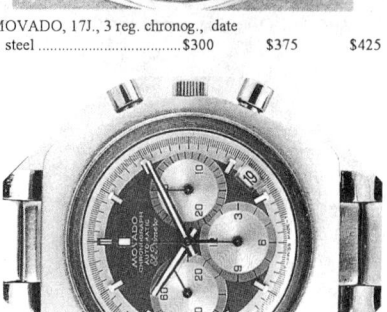

MOVADO, 17J., El Primero date at 5, c.1972
s. steel $300 $350 $425

MOVADO, 17J., center sec., c.1948
14k $200 $250 $325

MOVADO,17J., RF#2652, rotating chapter,cal.352, c.1958
s. steel $250 $300 $375

MOVADO, 17J., "Cronoplan", Ca. 1940s
s. steel $400 $450 $525

MOVADO, 15J., aux. sec., cal.75, c.1946
s. steel $75 $100 $150

MOVADO, 17J., center sec., cal.261, c.1948
18k $200 $250 $325

🕐 Some grades are not included. Their values can be determined by comparing with **similar** age, size, metal content, style, grades, or models such as **time only**, chronograph, repeater etc. listed.

MOVADO, 17J., aux. sec., cal.135, c.1955
s. steel $60 $70 $90

MOVADO, 17J., auto-wind, cal.8577, c.1957
14k $125 $150 $200

MOVADO, 17J., Tiffany & Co. on dial, center sec.,
14k $150 $175 $225

MOVADO, 15J., 2 colors of gold, tonneau, Ca. 1940
18k $500 $600 $750

🕐 Pricing in this Guide are fair market price for **COMPLETE** watches which are reflected from the "**NAWCC**" National and regional shows.

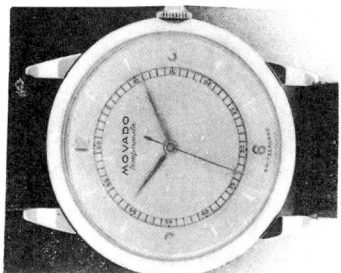

MOVADO, 17J., center sec.
14k $175 $200 $275

MOVADO, 17., center sec.
s. steel $75 $100 $150

MOVADO, 20J., auto-wind,
14k $150 $175 $225

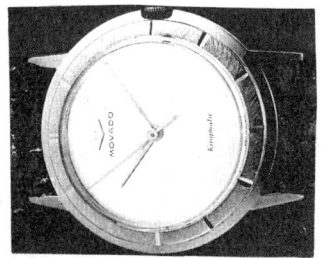

MOVADO, 28J., center sec.," Kingmatic",
14k $150 $175 $225

Wrist Watches listed in this section are priced at the collectable fair market **retail** level as **complete** watches having an original gold-filled case and stainless steel back, also with original dial, leather watch band, and the entire original movement in good working order with no repairs needed.

🕐 Some grades are not included. Their values can be determined by comparing with **similar** age, size, metal content, style, models and grades listed.

MOVADO, 17J., aux. sec.
18k $175 $200 $275

MOVADO, 15 jewels, aux. sec.
14k C&B.............................$400 $450 $550

MOVADO, 17J., auto-w., ca. 1949
14k $175 $200 $275

MOVADO, 17 jewels, aux. sec., center lugs
14k $150 $175 $225

MOVADO, 17J., nonmagnetic, RF # 11730, Ca. 1940
s. steel $100 $125 $175

MOVADO, 17J., cal.7025, GJS, c.1964
18k $200 $250 $325

MOVADO, 15 jewels, center lugs, c. 1930
18k $350 $400 $500

MOVADO, 17J., hidden lugs, tu-tone dial, c.1960
18k $300 $350 $425

MOVADO, 17J., textured 18k dial
18k $175 $200 $275

MOVADO, 17 jewels, "Museum", date at 12 o'clock
14k C&B.............................$400 $450 $600

MOVADO, 15 jewels, fancy lugs
18k $300 $325 $400

MOVADO, 17J., wide bezel, c.1958
gold filled.................................$75 $100 $150

MOVADO, 17J., diamond bezel,
18k $175 $200 $275

MOVADO, 17J., RF#621, c.1932
gold filled.................................$100 $125 $175

MOVADO, 17J., stepped case, "Curviplan", GJS, c.1942
14k $300 $350 $450

🕐 Pricing in this Guide are fair market price for **COMPLETE** watches which are reflected from the "**NAWCC**" National and regional shows.

MOVADO, 17J., aux. sec., c.1940
14k $200 $250 $325

MOVADO, 17J., extended lugs, c.1945
14k $150 $175 $250

MOVADO, 17J., aux. sec., c.1945
14k $150 $175 $250

MOVADO, 17J., extended lugs, GJS, c.1940
14k $150 $175 $250

MOVADO, 17J., tu-tone case, RF#13906, Ca.1948
14k $175 $200 $275

MOVADO, 17J.,"Andy Warhol Times/5", Ca.1988
Quartz (250 made).... ★★★$1,200 $1,400 $1,800

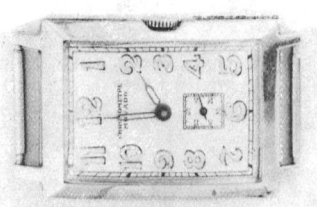

MOVADO, 15 jewels, curved, chronometre
14k $400 $450 $525

MOVADO, 17J., cal#510, ca.1941
14k $300 $350 $425

MOVADO, 17J., curviplan,
gold filled..............................$200 $250 $325

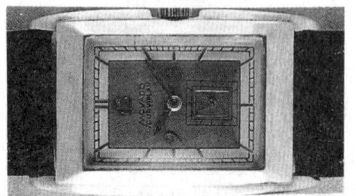

MOVADO, 17J., curviplan, ca.1941
14k $400 $450 $525

MOVADO, 17J., RF # 43872, ca.1945
14k $300 $350 $425

Wrist Watches listed in this section are priced at the collectable
fair market **retail** level as **complete** watches having an original
gold-filled case and stainless steel back, also with original dial,
leather watch band, and the entire original movement in good
working order with no repairs needed.

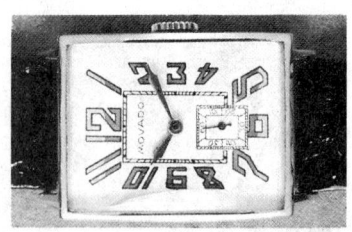

MOVADO, 15 jewels, exaggerated numbers, c. 1929
18k...$400 $450 $525

MOVADO, 17 jewels
14k $100 $125 $175

MOVADO, 17 jewels, automatic, tank style
18k $300 $350 $425

MOVADO, 17 jewels, fancy lugs, c. 1947
14k $100 $125 $175

MOVADO, 17J., Ca. 1940s
14k...$125 $150 $200

🕐 Pricing in this Guide are fair market price for **COMPLETE**
watches which are reflected from the "**NAWCC**" National and
regional shows.

MOVADO, 17 jewels
18k $300 $350 $425

MOVADO, 17 jewels, , Ca.1948
14k $300 $350 $425
18k $400 $450 $525

MOVADO, 17 jewels, hidden lugs, Ca.1940
14k $300 $350 $425

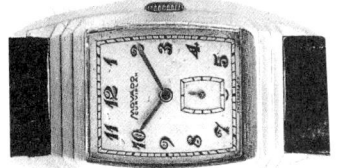

MOVADO,17 jewels, curviplan, , GJS, Ca.1937
14k $300 $350 $425

MOVADO, 17 jewels, ladies, alarm, Ca.1950
18k $175 $200 $275

SIDE VIEW

Mt. VERNON, 15 & 21 jewels, curvex style
gold plate..................................$30 $40 $55

Mt. VERNON, 15 jewels, curvex style
gold plate..................................$30 $40 $55

Mt. VERNON, 15 jewels, stepped case
s. steel.......................................$30 $40 $55

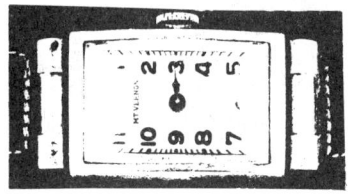

Mt. VERNON, 17 jewels
gold filled.................................$30 $40 $55

Mt. VERNON, 15 jewels
gold filled.................................$30 $40 $55

Wrist Watches listed in this section are priced at the collectable
fair market **retail** level as **complete** watches having an original
gold-filled case and stainless steel back, also with original dial,
leather watch band, and the entire original movement in good
working order with no repairs needed.

MOVADO MOVEMENT IDENTIFICATION

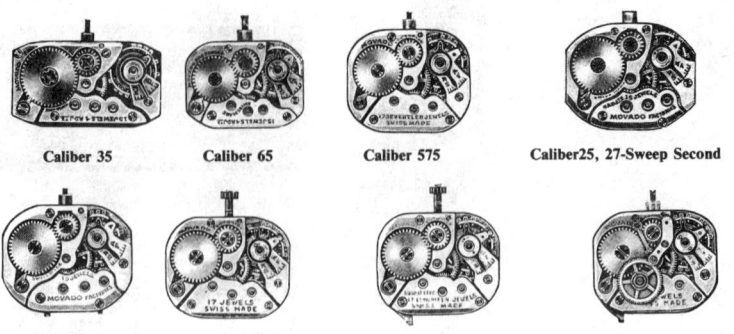

Caliber 35   Caliber 65   Caliber 575   Caliber25, 27-Sweep Second

   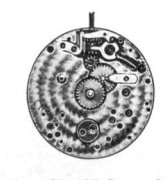

Caliber 28   Caliber 575, Ermeto-Baby   Caliber 578, Ermeto Calendine   579, Calendoplan Baby

 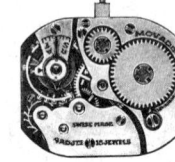 

Caliber 5   Caliber 15   Caliber 50SP   Caliber 105, 107-Center Second

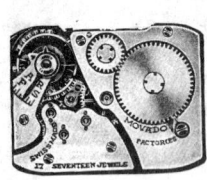  

Caliber 190   Caliber 375, 377-Center Second   Caliber 440, 443-Center Second

Caliber 510   Caliber 260M, 261   Caliber 150MN, 157-Sweep Second

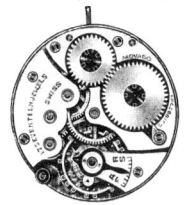

Caliber 155, Calendermeto   Caliber 470, 477-Center Second   Caliber 473, 473SC-Calendar/Moon phase

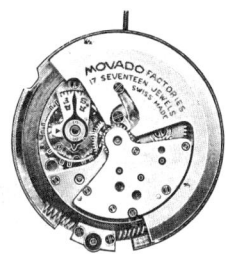

Caliber 475, 475SC-Center Second   Caliber 225, 255M

Caliber 115   Caliber 118   Caliber 220, 220M

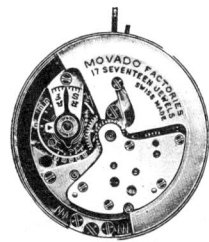
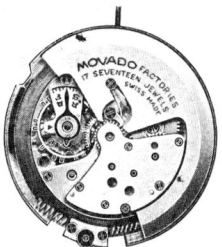

Caliber 221, 226   Caliber 223, 228   Caliber 224, 224A

Chronograph
Cal. 90M, 95M

12''' – 26,60 mm

U. NARDIN, 17 jewels, chronog., c. 1950s
18k...$1,500 $1,600 $1,900

U. NARDIN, 29 J., "Astrolabium," self wind, waterproof, local time, equinoctial time, months, signs of zodiac, elevation & azimuth of sun & moon, aspect in which sun & moon stand to each other. **recent**
18k $8,000 $9,000 $11,000

U. NARDIN, 17 jewels, split sec. chronog., c. 1910
silver.......................................$7,000 $8,000 $10,000

U. NARDIN, 17J., one button pulsations. ca.1920
18k $2,000 $2,200 $2,600

U. NARDIN, 17 jewels, chronog., 3 reg. c. 1940s
18k...$1,800 $2,000 $2,400

U. NARDIN, 17J., chronog., "Pulsations," c. 1920
18k $2,000 $2,200 $2,600

🕐 Pricing in this Guide are fair market price for **COMPLETE** watches which are reflected from the "<u>NAWCC</u>" National and regional shows.

🕐 Some grades are not included. Their values can be determined by comparing with **similar** age, size, metal content, style, grades, or models such as **time only**, chronograph, repeater etc. listed.

U. NARDIN, 25 jewels, date
14k...$200 $250 $325

U. NARDIN, 17 jewels, auto wind, c. 1952
14k $200 $250 $325

U. NARDIN,21J.,auto-wind
18k...$250 $275 $350

U. NARDIN, 17J., center sec., chronometer, c.1950
gold filled...................................$75 $100 $150

U. NARDIN, 17J., aux sec.
s. steel.....................................$100 $125 $175

U. NARDIN, 17J., center sec., auto-wind, c.1950
14k $200 $250 $325

U. NARDIN, 17J., aux. sec.
18k...$200 $225 $275

U. NARDIN, 17J., center sec., auto-wind, c.1950
18k $250 $275 $350

U. NARDIN, 17J., fancy lugs
18k...$250 $300 $425

🕐 Pricing in this Guide are fair market price for **COMPLETE**
watches which are reflected from the "**NAWCC**" National and
regional shows.

U. NARDIN, 17J., aux. sec., carved lugs, c.1950
14k $225 $275 $400

U. NARDIN, 17J., aux. sec., chronometer, c.1950
14k $125 $150 $200

U. NARDIN, 17J., aux. sec., chronometer, c.1947
18k $200 $225 $300

U. NARDIN, 17J., aux. sec., chronometer, C.1951
14k $150 $175 $225

Wrist Watches listed in this section are priced at the collectable
fair market **retail** level as **complete** watches having an original
gold-filled case and stainless steel back, also with original dial,
leather watch band, and the entire original movement in good
working order with no repairs needed.

🕐 Some grades are not included. Their values can be
determined by comparing with **similar** age, size, metal
content, style, grades, or models such as **time only**,
chronograph, repeater etc. listed.

U. NARDIN, 17J., aux. sec., chronometer, c.1964
gold plate...............................$100 $120 $165

U. NARDIN, 17J., aux. sec., chronometer, c.1948
gold filled...............................$100 $125 $175

U. NARDIN, 17J., fancy lugs
14k..$200 $250 $325

U. NARDIN, 25J., chronometer, date, c.1975
s. steel....................................$125 $150 $225

U. NARDIN, 17J., fluted case
14k $150 $175 $225

U. NARDIN, 17J., aux. sec., chronometer, c.1949
14k $125 $150 $200

U. NARDIN, 17J., aux. sec., chronometer, c.1950
18k $175 $200 $275

U. NARDIN, 17J., extended side lugs, chronometer, c.1951
14k $150 $175 $250

U. NARDIN, 17 jewels, faceted crystal & bezel
s. steel $100 $125 $175

🕐 Some grades are not included. Their values can be
determined by comparing with similar age, size, metal
content, style, grades, or models such as time only,
chronograph, repeater etc. listed.

U. NARDIN, 17 jewels, c. 1920
18k...$275 $325 $400

U. NARDIN, 17 jewels, WW I military style
s. steel....................................$450 $500 $600

U. NARDIN, 17J., lady's chronometer, c.1947
14k C&B $375 $400 $500

NATIONAL, 17 jewels,
gold filled................................$20 $30 $50

NATIONAL, 15 jewels, day-date-month
gold filled................................$50 $75 $125

NATIONAL W. Co., 16 J., 1 button Chronog., red & black color enamel dial, Ca. 1925
silver $600 $650 $750

NEW ENGLAND W. Co., 7J., Addison, Alden, Cavour, Hale, and other models, Ca.1915, colored dial add ($25)
14k $60 $70 $90
gold filled................................... $20 $30 $45

NEW HAVEN, 7 jewels, engraved bezel
base metal $20 $25 $35

NEW HAVEN, 7 jewels, stepped case
base metal $20 $25 $35

⊕ Pricing in this Guide are fair market price for **COMPLETE** watches which are reflected from the "**NAWCC**" National and regional shows.

NEW HAVEN, 7 jewels
base metal................................. $15 $20 $30

NEW HAVEN,2 jewels, "Elf" ladies, etched case
base metal................................. $10 $15 $25

NEW HAVEN, 7 jewels, "Duchess" ladies, etched case
gold plate................................... $5 $10 $15

NEWMARK, 17J., military chronog., c.1979
s. steel..................................... $200 $250 $325

NEW YORK STANDARD, 7 jewels, wire lugs
gold filled................................. $25 $35 $50
base metal................................. $15 $20 $30

NICE WATCH Co., 17J., one button chronog., c.1930
base metal $250 $300 $375

NICOLET W. CO., 17J., one button chronog., Ca. 1960
gold filled...............................$325 $375 $450

CHARLES NICOLET, 17J., chronog., ca. 1945
18k $300 $350 $450

MARC NICOLET, 17J., aux. seconds
14k $100 $125 $165

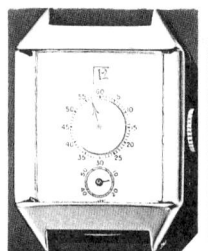 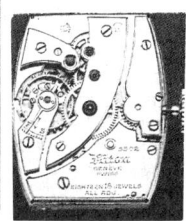

NITON, 18J., jump hr., (showing dial and movement)
(made ebauche for P.P.&CO.)
18k(W) $3,500 $4,000 $5,000

NIVADA, 21J., center sec., c.1960
base metal.................................$30 $40 $55

NIVADA, 21J., center sec., date, auto-w, c.1965
s. steel.....................................$35 $45 $65

NIVADA, 25 jewels, waterproof, c. 1940
14k..$500 $550 $650
gold filled..............................$175 $200 $250

🕐 Pricing in this Guide are fair market price for **COMPLETE**
watches which are reflected from the "**NAWCC**" National and
regional shows.

NORMANDIE, 17 jewels, compass, c. 1945
s. steel $75 $100 $150

NORMANDIE, 17J., gold train, hidden lugs, cal.4873
14k $100 $125 $175

OCTO, 17J., fluted lugs,
14k $150 $175 $200

OFAIR, 17J., chronog., cal. Valjoux 72c, c.1948
gold filled...............................$300 $350 $450
14k $600 $700 $850
18k $750 $850 $1,000

Wrist Watches listed in this section are priced at the collectable
fair market **retail** level as **complete** watches having an original
gold-filled case and stainless steel back, also with original dial,
leather watch band, and the entire original movement in good
working order with no repairs needed.

⊕ Some grades are not included. Their values can be
determined by comparing with similar age, size, metal
content, style, grades, or models such as time only,
chronograph, repeater etc. listed.

OGIVAL, 17 jewels, auto wind
gold filled....................................$30 $40 $60

OLLENDORFF, 17 jewels, fancy lugs
14k................................$150 $175 $225

OLLENDORFF, 17 jewels, movement plates made of **gold**
14k...$300 $350 $500

OLLENDORFF, 7J., direct read, stepped case, c.1930
base metal................................$100 $125 $165

OLLENDORFF, 15J., engraved bevel,
chrome plated............................$25 $30 $40

OLMA, 17J., early auto-wind, by Wyler, c.1928
s. steel $150 $175 $225

OLMA, 17J., large crab legs style lugs
gold plate $45 $55 $75

OLYMPIA, 15 jewels, double dial, c. 1938
s. steel $350 $400 $500

OMEGA, 15J., center lugs, enamel dial, Ca. 1930
18k $400 $500 $650

OMEGA, 15J., wire lugs, Ca. 1925
silver $150 $200 $275

OMEGA, 15J., wire lugs, ca. 1930s
18k $400 $500 $650

OMEGA, 15J., wire lugs,
14k $350 $400 $500

OMEGA, 17 jewels, center sec.
14k $150 $175 $225

OMEGA, 17 jewels, chronog., c. 1935
18k $2,500 $2,800 $3,500

🕐 Pricing in this Guide are fair market price for **COMPLETE** watches which are reflected from the "**NAWCC**" National and regional shows.

🕐 Some grades are not included. Their values can be determined by comparing with **similar** age, size, metal content, style, grades, or models such as **time only**, chronograph, repeater etc. listed.

OMEGA, 17J., 2 reg. chronog., ca. 1940s
s. steel	$400	$450	$550
14k	$700	$750	$900
18k	$1,000	$1,100	$1,400

OMEGA, 17J., "Speedmaster", chronog., c. 1970
s. steel	$350	$450	$525

OMEGA, 17J., 2 reg., chronog., c. 1958
18k	$800	$900	$1,100

OMEGA, 17J., "Speedmaster Pro.", chronog., c. 1969
"the first watch worn on the **moon**" on back of watch
18k C&B	$3,500	$4,000	$4,800
s. steel	$600	$650	$750

OMEGA, 17 jewels, chronog., "Seamaster," c. 1963
14k	$1,500	$1,600	$1,900
s. steel	$600	$700	$850

OMEGA, 17J., "Speedmaster Pro. Mark II", c.1975
s. steel	$250	$300	$375

⏱ Some grades are not included. Their values can be determined by comparing with **similar** age, size, metal content, style, grades, or models such as **time only**, chronograph, repeater etc. listed.

⏱ Pricing in this Guide are fair market price for **COMPLETE** watches which are reflected from the "**NAWCC**" National and regional shows.

OMEGA, 17J., "Seamaster", chronog., cal.321, c. 1962
s. steel	$600	$700	$850
14k	$1,500	$1,600	$1,900
18k	$1,700	$1,800	$2,100

OMEGA, 22J., "Seamaster", date, 2 reg., auto-wind, c.1975
s. steel $250 $275 $350

OMEGA, 17J., "Seamaster", chronostop, cal.865, c.1965
s. steel....................................$150 $175 $225

OMEGA, 17J., Speedmaster Pro. MarkIII,cal.1040,c.1978
s. steel $375 $475 $550

OMEGA, 17J., "Seamaster", chronostop., rotating bezel
s. steel....................................$175 $200 $250

OMEGA, 17J., Speedmaster, auto-wind, chronog., c.1975
s. steel $375 $475 $550

Wrist Watches listed in this section are priced at the collectable
fair market **retail** level as **complete** watches having an original
gold-filled case and stainless steel back, also with original dial,
leather watch band, and the entire original movement in good
working order with no repairs needed.

🕐 Some grades are not included. Their values can be
determined by comparing with **similar** age, size, metal
content, style, grades, or models such as **time only**,
chronograph, repeater etc. listed.

OMEGA, 17J., "Seamaster", chronog., cal.321, c.1970
s. steel....................................$200 $250 $325

🕐 Pricing in this Guide are fair market price for **COMPLETE**
watches which are reflected from the "**NAWCC**" National and
regional shows.

OMEGA, 17 jewels, chronog., "Seamaster," 3 reg.
14k $900 $1,000 $1,200

OMEGA, 17 jewels, chronog., "Flightmaster," 3 reg.
18kC&B $2,500 $2,800 $3,500
s. steel $300 $350 $425

OMEGA, 17 jewels, day-date-month, moon phase
18k $1,200 $1,300 $1,600
14k $1,000 $1,100 $1,400

OMEGA, 17J., day-date-month, moon phase, c. 1940
14k $1,000 $1,100 $1,400

OMEGA, 17J., day-date-month, moon phase, c. 1950s
14k...$2,000 $2,400 $2,800
18k...$2,500 $2,800 $3,500

OMEGA, 17J.,date, "Constellation", chronometer
18k...$600 $700 $900
14k...$400 $500 $650

OMEGA, 24J., "Constellation", auto-wind, c.1960
14k...$450 $550 $700
s. steel....................................$225 $250 $300

OMEGA, 24J., "Constellation", auto-wind, c.1968
gold filled..............................$225 $250 $300

OMEGA, 24J., "Constellation", auto-wind, c.1969
s. steel $175 $200 $250

OMEGA, 17 jewels, "Constellation," auto wind, date
gold filled................................$250 $275 $325

OMEGA, 7J., "Constellation", quartz, cal.1342, c.1970
18k & s. s. $350 $400 $525

OMEGA, 24 jewels, "Constellation," auto wind
18k C&B $900 $1,000 $1,200

OMEGA, 17J., Chronometre, auto-w.,
14k $175 $200 $275

OMEGA, 24 jewels, "Constellation," c. 1959
18k..$550 $625 $725

OMEGA, electronic, "F300," c. 1950s
18k C&B $600 $650 $800

OMEGA, 17 jewels, "Seamaster," date, waterproof
18k..$400 $450 $525

OMEGA, 24J., "Seamaster", auto-wind, c.1962
14k $275 $325 $400
s. steel $100 $125 $175

Omega, 17 jewels, "Seamaster," auto wind
14k.......................................$275 $325 $400

OMEGA, 24J., "Seamaster", auto-wind, cal.562, c.1962
gold filled..............................$100 $125 $175

OMEGA, 17J.,"Seamaster",chronometer
18k.......................................$400 $450 $525

OMEGA, 23J.,"Seamaster", auto-wind, cal.1022, c.1978
s. steel $100 $125 $175

OMEGA, 17J., "Seamaster", c.1953
gold filled..............................$100 $125 $175

OMEGA, 17 jewels, automatic, date
14k $200 $225 $300

OMEGA, 17J., "Seamaster Deluxe", auto-wind
18k.......................................$400 $450 $525

OMEGA, 20J., "Seamaster", auto-wind, cal.501, c.1957
s. steel $100 $125 $175

OMEGA, 24J., "Constellation", auto-wind, cal.551, c.1962
14k..$400 $450 $550

OMEGA, 17J., "Seamaster", auto-wind, cal.1570, c.1955
gold filled................................$100 $125 $175

OMEGA, 16-18J., gold train, center seconds
s. steel....................................$100 $125 $175

OMEGA, 17J., "Constellation", chronometer, auto-wind
18k $600 $700 $900

OMEGA, 16J., center sec., c.1940
s. steel....................................$100 $125 $175

OMEGA, 24J., "Constellation", auto-wind, cal.505, c.1958
18k $600 $700 $900

OMEGA, 16J., U.S. Army, cal., c.1948
s. steel....................................$150 $175 $250

OMEGA, 16J., center sec., c.1948
s. steel $100 $125 $175

OMEGA, 17J., auto-wind, center sec., c.1946
s. steel...................................$100 $125 $175

OMEGA, 15J., Military (**England**), c.1946
s. steel $200 $225 $300

OMEGA, 17J., Seamaster, diamond dial, cal.563, c.1955
s. steel....................................$150 $175 $225

OMEGA, 17J., "Railmaster", center sec.
s. steel $225 $250 $325

OMEGA, 17J., 12 diamond dial, center sec.
14k(W) $200 $225 $300

OMEGA, 15-17J., 24 hour marked, Ca. 1930
s. steel $225 $275 $350

OMEGA, 17J., fancy lugs, ca.1948
14k...$250 $300 $375

🕐 Some grades are not included. Their values can be determined by comparing with **similar** age, size, metal content, style, grades, or models such as **time only**, chronograph, repeater etc. listed.

OMEGA, 17J., aux.sec., cal.266, c.1956
s. steel $100 $125 $175

OMEGA, 17J., aux. sec., cal.360, c.1950
14k...$150 $175 $225

OMEGA, 17J., aux. sec., cal.266, c.1945
14k $200 $225 $275

OMEGA, 17J., auto-wind, c.1949
18k...$275 $325 $400

OMEGA, 17J., auto-wind, c.1952
18k $275 $325 $400

OMEGA, 17J., auto-wind, cal.342, c.1955
gold filled..................................$90 $110 $150

OMEGA, 17J., auto-wind, c.1949
18k $275 $325 $400

OMEGA, 17J., seamaster, auto-wind
s. steel.......................................$100 $125 $175

⊕ Pricing in this Guide are fair market price for **COMPLETE** watches which are reflected from the "**NAWCC**" National and regional shows.

OMEGA, 17J., aux. sec., cal.302, c.1948
gold filled..................................$75 $90 $120

OMEGA, 15J., extended lugs, c.1939
14k $350 $375 $425
gold filled................................$100 $125 $175

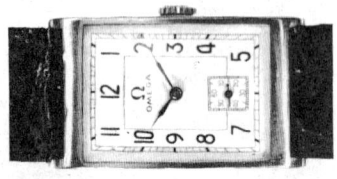

OMEGA, 15J., aux. sec., c.1937
s. steel $100 $125 $175

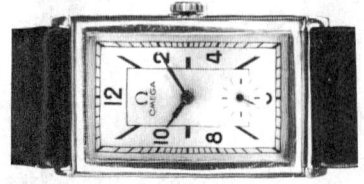

OMEGA, 15J., small lugs, c.1935
gold filled................................$100 $125 $175

OMEGA, 17J., beveled case, c.1936
s. steel $100 $125 $175

Wrist Watches listed in this section are priced at the collectable
fair market **retail** level as **complete** watches having an original
gold-filled case and stainless steel back, also with original dial,
leather watch band, and the entire original movement in good
working order with no repairs needed.

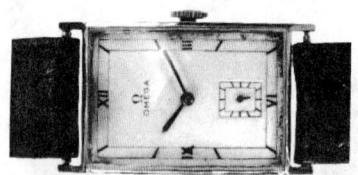

OMEGA, 15J., small lugs, c.1937
s. steel.....................................$100 $125 $175

OMEGA, 17J., fancy lugs, ca. 1950s
14k..$150 $175 $250

OMEGA, 17J., faceted crystal,
14k(W) $125 $150 $225

OMEGA, 17J., fancy lugs, ca. 1948
14k..$150 $175 $250

OMEGA, 17J., 9 diamond dial, ca. 1955
14k(W) $125 $150 $200

OMEGA, 17 jewels, aux. sec.
14k C&B $600 $650 $750

OMEGA, 17J., flared & extended lugs, cal.301, c.1948
14k $150 $175 $250

OMEGA, 17J., flared & sculptured lugs, cal.302, c.1953
14k $175 $200 $275

OMEGA, 17J., flared & hidden lugs, c.1947
14k $150 $175 $250

OMEGA, 17 jewels, hidden lugs, asymmetric
14k $600 $650 $800

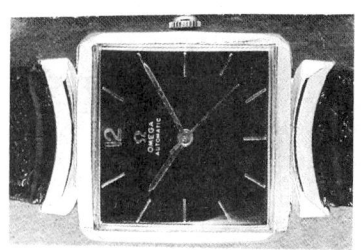

OMEGA, 17 jewels, curved center lugs
14k $200 $250 $325

OMEGA, 17 jewels, sculptured lugs
14k $600 $650 $800

OMEGA, 17 jewels, c. 1948
14k $200 $250 $325

OMEGA, 17 jewels, c. 1938
14k $175 $200 $275

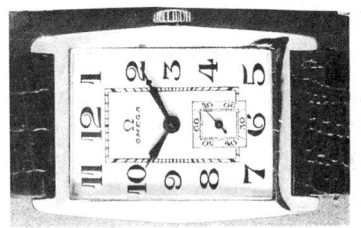

OMEGA, 15 jewels, large, c. 1935
14k $225 $250 $350

OMEGA, 17J., wide bezel, center sec.,cal.470, c.1955
14k $125 $150 $225

OMEGA, 17J., RF#347sc, cal.471, c.1956
18k $200 $250 $325

OMEGA, 17J., wide bezel & lugs, cal.369, c.1947
platinum $1,000 $1,100 $1,300

OMEGA, 17J., "De Ville",
18k $200 $250 $325

OMEGA, 17J., cal.620, c.1960
14k $100 $125 $200

OMEGA, 17 jewels, aux. sec.
18k..$200 $250 $325

OMEGA, 17 jewels, c. 1937
s. steel.....................................$175 $200 $275

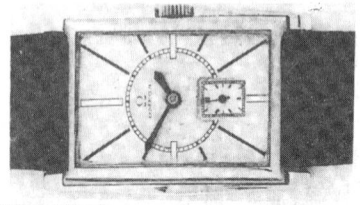

OMEGA, 17 jewels
14k..$200 $250 $350

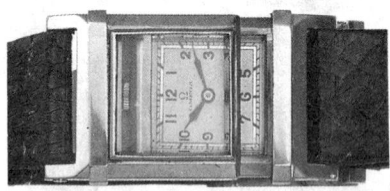

OMEGA, 15J., sliding case, winds at 12, Ca.1930s
"Marine" model
18k...$1,500 $1,800 $2,500

OMEGA, 15 jewels, hidden winding stem, c. 1930
"Marine" model, wire lugs
14k......................................$1,200 $1,300 $1,500
s. steel...................................$900 $1,000 $1,200

⏱ Some grades are not included. Their values can be
determined by comparing with **similar** age, size, metal
content, style, grades, or models such as **time only**,
chronograph, repeater etc. listed.

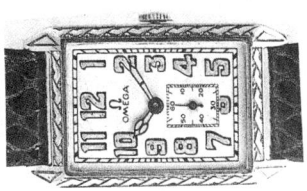

OMEGA, 15J., engraved case, c.1925
14k $275 $300 $400

OMEGA, 15J., ladies, wire lugs, c.1925
silver.......................................$50 $60 $95

OMEGA, 19J., alarm,"Memomatic", c.1975
s. steel $150 $175 $225

OMEGA, 17J., ladies center sec., c.1938
silver.......................................$150 $175 $250

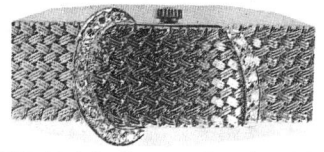

OMEGA, 17J., ladies flip open, 16 diamonds, c.1955
14k C&B $700 $800 $1,000

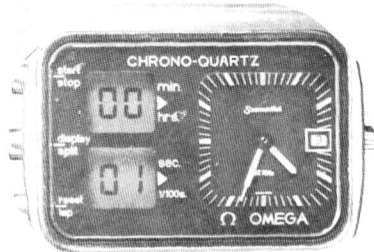

OMEGA, "Chrono-quartz, cal.1611, c.1975
s. steel $150 $175 $225

OMEGA, 15J., ladies, non-magnetic, c.1945
s. steel....................................$50 $60 $85

OMEGA, 17J., ladies, sapphire stones on lugs, c.1950
14k C&B $400 $500 $650

OMEGA, quartz, marine chronometer
s. steel $175 $200 $250

⊕ Pricing in this Guide are fair market price for **COMPLETE**
watches which are reflected from the "**NAWCC**" National and
regional shows.

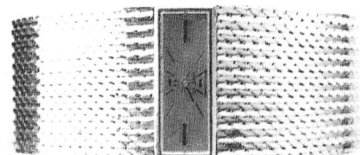

OMEGA, 17J., ladies, RF#8065, c.1965
18k C&B $500 $550 $700

OMEGA BASIC CALIBRE IDENTIFICATION

Cal. No. 100, Ca.1943   Cal. No. 210, Ca.1946   Cal. No. 220, Ca.1941   Cal. No. 230, center seconds

Cal. No. 240, Ca.1939   Cal. No. 250, center seconds   Cal. No. 260, Ca.1943   Cal. No. 280, center seconds

 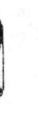  

Cal. No. 300, Ca.1944   Cal. No. 310, center seconds   Cal. No. 330, Ca.1943   Cal. No. 360, Ca.1944

Cal. No. 440

 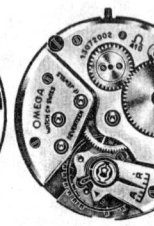 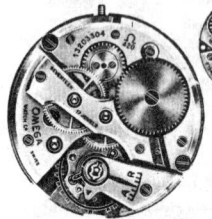

Cal. No. 372, jumping seconds   Cal. No. 410, Ca.1951   Cal. No. 420, center seconds   Cal. No. 455, Ca.1955

PRODUCTION TOTALS

DATE– SERIAL #	DATE– SERIAL #	DATE– SERIAL #
1895 --1,000,000	1944-10,000,000	1962-19,000,000
1902 - 2,000,000	1947-11,000,000	1963-20,000,000
1908 - 3,000,000	1950-12,000,000	1964-21,000,000
1912 - 4,000,000	1952-13,500,000	1965-22,000,000
1916 - 5,000,000	1954-14,000,000	1966-23,000,000
1923 - 6,000,000	1956-15,000,000	1967-25,000,000
1929 - 7,000,000	1958-16,000,000	1968-26,000,000
1935 - 8,000,000	1960-17,000,000	1969-28,000,000
1939- 9,000,000	1961-18,000,000	1970-29,000,000

Note: By 1980 ETA Calibers were being used by Omega.
The above list is provided for determining the APPROXIMATE age of your watch. Match serial number with date. Watches were not necessarily sold in the exact order of manufactured date.

Cal. No. 470, Ca.1955

Cal. No. 480, Ca.1955

Cal. No. 490, Ca.1956

Cal. No. 500, Ca.1956

Cal. No. 510, Ca.1956

Cal. No. 520, center seconds

Cal. No. 540, Ca.1957

Cal. No. 550, Ca.1959

Cai. No. 570, Ca.1959

Cal. No. 590, Ca.1960

Cal. No. 600, Ca.1960

Cal. No. 620, Ca.1961

Cal. No. 580, Ca. 1959

Cal. No. 660, Ca.1963

Cal. No. 670, Ca.1963

Cal. No. 690, Ca.1962

Cal. No. 700, Ca.1964

Cal. No. 711, Ca.1966

Cal. No. 730, Ca.1967

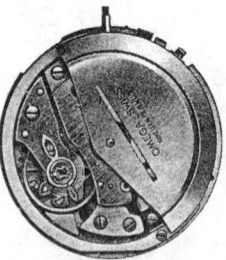

Cal. No. 980, Ca.1969

Cal. No. 1040, Ca. 1971

Cal. No. 320, chronograh

Cal. No. 321, chronograh

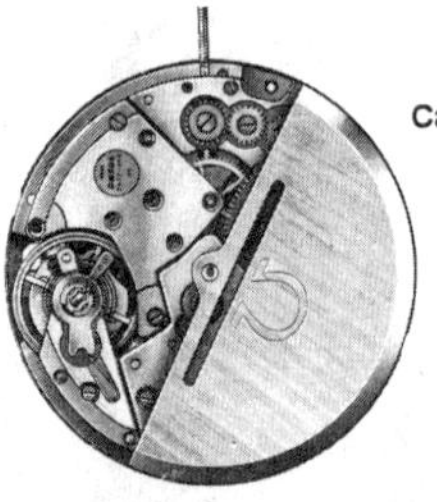

Cal. No. 1010, Ca.1973

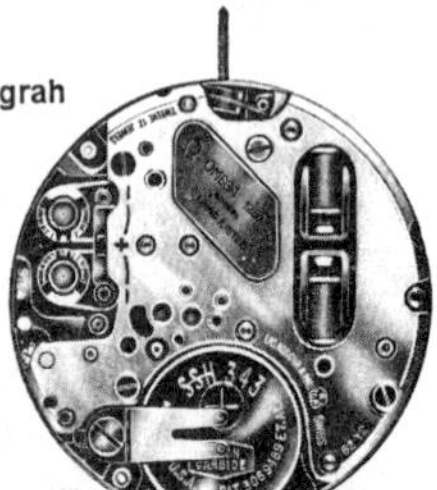

Cal. No. 1250-1260,
Ca.1970

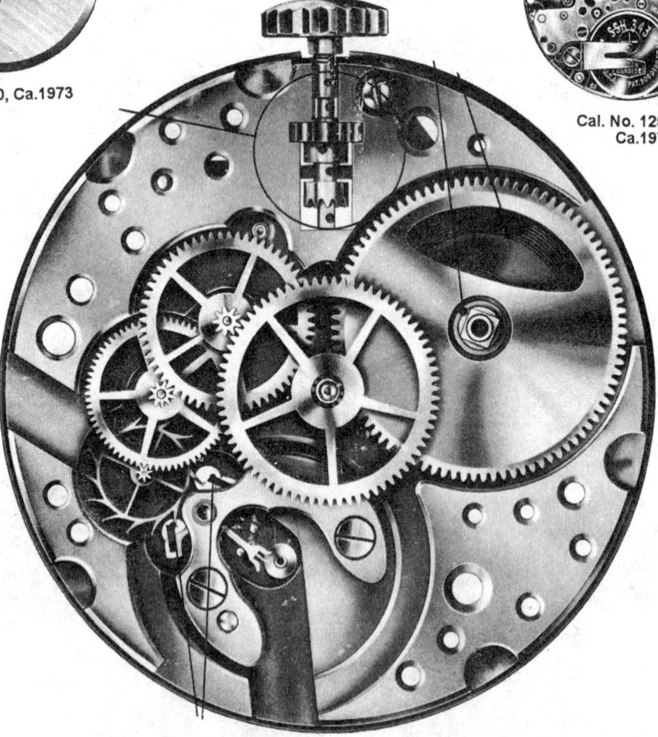

OPEL, 21 jewels, waterproof
gold filled..................................$30 $35 $50

ORATOR, 17 jewels, auto wind
s. steel $20 $30 $45

ORFINA, 17 jewels, triple date, moon phase, **bombe' lugs**
gold filled...............................$250 $300 $450

ORFINA, 17 jewels, triple date, moon phase, **carved lugs**
gold filled...............................$250 $300 $450

ORFINA, 17 jewels, day-date-month
gold filled $90 $120 $150

ORFINA, 17 jewels, date
s. steel $75 $100 $150

ORVIN, 17 jewels, day-date, c. 1945
s. steel $40 $45 $55

PABRO, 17J., ladies 76 diamond watch, c.1930
platinum..................................$300 $400 $550

PARKER, 17J., 2 reg. chronog.,ca.1948
s. steel $150 $175 $225

PATEK, PHILIPPE & CIE.
Swiss

Patek, Philippe & Cie. has produced some of the world's most desirable factory-made watches. Antoine Norbert de Patek began contracting and selling watches in the 1830's, later became partners with Francois Czapek and generally produced lovely decorative watches for a high class of clientele. In 1845 Adrien Philippe, inventor of the modern stem-winding system, joined the firm of Patek & Cie., and in 1851, the firm established its present name. Between Philippe's talent as a watchmaker and Patek's talent as a businessman with a taste for the impeccable, the firm rapidly established an international reputation which lasts to this day. A *classic* wrist watch the **"Calatrava"** model 96 was 1st used in 1932. The case and dial was designed at a time of transition from pocket watches to wrist watches. The coin was used as a perfect geometric shape to design a wrist watch case that has harmony and balance. Many varations from the classic model 96 have been used, but to most collectors the **classic** model 96 is known as the **Calatrava** model. The original 96 Calatrava model used a flat bezel, 31mm one piece case (lugs are not soldered on), manual wind, white dial, barrette-shaped hour markers, dauphine hands and aux. seconds chapter with a inside and outside circle and long 5 sec. markers. A black dial was added in 1937. The recent classic style Calatrava case is RF # 3796. To date there are many P.P. & Co. wrist watches named Calatrava.

PRODUCTION TOTALS

DATE—SERIAL #	DATE—SERIAL #	DATE—SERIAL #	DATE—SERIAL #
1840---- 100	1915----175,000	1945---- 850,000	1960----1,100,000
1845---- 1,200	1920----190,000	1950---- 860,000 *	1965----1,130,000
1850---- 3,000	1925----200,000	1955---- 870,000	1970----1,250,000
1855---- 8,000	1950----700,000	1960---- 880,000	1975----1,350,000
1860---- 15,000	1955----725,000	1965---- 890,000	1980----1,450,000
1865---- 22,000	1960----750,000	1970---- 895,000	1985----1,600,000
1870---- 35,000	1965----775,000	1940---- 900,000	1990----1,850,000
1875---- 45,000	1970----795,000	1945---- 915,000	
1880---- 55,000		1950---- 930,000	
1885---- 70,000	**DATE—SERIAL #**	1955---- 940,000	
1890---- 85,000	1920---- 800,000	1960---- 960,000	
1895----100,000	1925---- 805,000	1965---- 975,000	
1900----110,000	1930---- 820,000	1970---- 995,000	
1905----125,000	1935---- 824,000		
1910----150,000	1940---- 835,000		

The above list is provided for determining the APPROXIMATE age of your watch. Match serial number with date. Watches were not necessarily sold in the exact order of manufactured date.

Patek, Philippe & Cie. REFERENCE # INDEX

REF # PAGE	REF # PAGE	REF # PAGE	REF # PAGE	REF # PAGE	REF # PAGE
96 — 949	1432 — 940	1578 — 956	2469 — 945	2536 — 951	3519 — 941
96 — 949	1433 — 953	1579 — 946	2471 — 934	2537 — 952	3541 — 958
96 — 952	1436 — 946	1580 — 936	2472 — 933	2540 — 942	3555 — 940
96 — 953	1438 — 933	1585 — 963	2476 — 935	2541 — 957	3558 — 958
96 — 954	1442 — 935	1588 — 931	2477 — 932	2545 — 955	3569 — 959
130 — 946	1444 — 931	1589 — 958	2479 — 942	2548 — 963	3574 — 959
130 — 947	1450 — 937	1590 — 954	2480 — 937	2549 — 955	3588 — 962
137 — 930	1461 — 950	1592 — 943	2481 — 945	2550 — 955	3601 — 948
139 — 929	1463 — 946	1593 — 937	2481 — 956	2553 — 941	3604 — 949
244 — 943	1480 — 936	1595 — 958	2482 — 956	2554 — 938	3606 — 959
380 — 960	1481 — 943	2066 — 936	2484 — 951	2568-1- 958	3633 — 941
404 — 931	1482 — 934	2334 — 932	2486 — 942	2573 — 959	3700 — 961
406 — 934	1486 — 932	2403 — 936	2488 — 943	2574 — 942	3727 — 939
409 — 931	1486 — 940	2404 — 932	2491 — 940	2577 — 952	3738 — 963
420 — 935	1487 — 933	2404 — 936	2493 — 939	2588 — 960	3745 — 963
422 — 935	1491 — 957	2406 — 955	2494 — 954	2589 — 959	3800 — 961
425 — 937	1493 — 935	2414 — 934	2496 — 940	2592 — 959	" "-103-961
425 — 938	1506 — 947	2423 — 939	2496 — 941	2597 — 945	" "-105-961
426 — 929	1509 — 951	2424 — 939	2497 — 949	2597 — 946	" "-108-961
430 — 933	1516 — 953	2429 — 952	2499 — 947	3025 — 956	3834 — 929
433 — 931	1517 — 954	2434 — 935	2499 — 948	3404 — 941	3878 — 962
448 — 950	1518 — 947	2437 — 940	2500 — 953	3405 — 940	3884 — 962
490 — 932	1526 — 950	2438 — 949	2503 — 935	3406 — 940	3885 — 961
491 — 932	1530 — 935	2440 — 943	2506-1- 951	3410 — 958	3885 — 962
497 — 960	1531 — 935	2441 — 938	2508 — 957	3411 — 957	3886 — 962
497 — 964	1532 — 933	2442 — 938	2509 — 954	3412 — 930	3900-1- 960
504 — 929	1535 — 935	2443 — 936	2513 — 941	3413 — 930	3900-3- 960
513 — 932	1543 — 953	2445 — 953	2514-1- 943	3420 — 953	3900-5- 960
513-1- 933	1557 — 940	2447 — 939	2515 — 953	3424 — 930	" "-101-960
515 — 945	1559 — 932	2451 — 958	2516 — 942	3429 — 952	" "-103-960
530 — 946	1559 — 931	2452 — 951	2517 — 930	3445 — 949	" "-105-961
534 — 951	1560 — 931	2456 — 937	2518 — 933	3448 — 949	3960 — 950
556 — 942	1564 — 931	2456 — 938	2520 — 934	3450 — 949	3970-E- 947
565 — 956	1564 — 932	2456 — 939	2523 — 945	3465 — 943	3974 — 929
570 — 954	1566 — 941	2457 — 957	2524 — 929	3467 — 941	
591 — 946	1567 — 940	2459 — 951	2525-1- 951	3473 — 958	
655 — 934	1568 — 935	2460 — 957	2526 — 952	3495 — 957	
1402 — 933	1570 — 934	2461 — 931	2526 — 955	3497 — 930	
1408 — 942	1571 — 950	2466 — 956	2530-1- 942	3509 — 959	
1415 — 945	1574 — 942	2468 — 937	2531 — 931	3514 — 948	
1431 — 939	1575 — 941	2468 — 938	2533 — 956	3514-1- 948	

" **PATEK PHILIPPE**" watches should be signed on the case, dial & movement to bring the prices listed in this book.
(**triple signed P.P.CO.**)

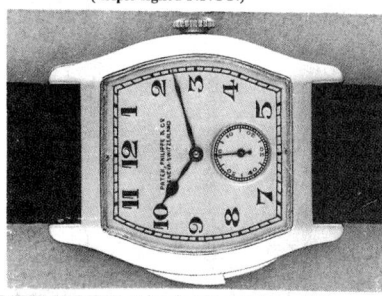

PATEK PHILIPPE, 29 jewels, min. repeater, c. 1920
platinum $250,000 $300,000 $400,000

PATEK PHILIPPE, 29 jewels, min. repeater, six watches finished by E. Gublin, 18k case & band, triple signed
18k C&B $175,000 $200,000 $250,000

PATEK PHILIPPE, 29J., min. repeater, 30 x 34mm
18k $200,000 $250,000 $350,000

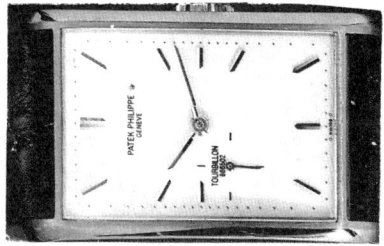

PATEK PHILIPPE, 50 sec. tourbillon, 57 hr. power reserve 5 gear train, 28 x 38mm, RF#3834
18k $185,000 $200,000 $250,000

PATEK PHILIPPE, 39J., auto-wind, min. repeater, perpetual day date month calendars, moon ph., 24 hr. ind., leap year ind., RF#3974, Ca.1989
18K...................................$200,000 $225,000 $275,000

PATEK PHILIPPE,18J., horizontal case, RF#504, 2 tone
18k $7,000 $8,000 $10,000

PATEK PHILIPPE,18 J., horizontal case, RF#139 &426
18k $5,000 $6,000 $8,000

" **PATEK PHILIPPE**" watches should be signed on the case, dial & movement to bring the prices listed in this book.
(**triple signed P.P.CO.**)

PATEK PHILIPPE, 29 jewels, min. repeater, RF#2524
18k $125,000 $150,000 $200,000

PATEK PHILIPPE, 18J., designed by Gilbert Albert, RF#3412, c. 1958
18k $18,000 $20,000 $24,000

PATEK PHILIPPE, 18J., asymmetric case designed by Gilbert Albert, RF#3413, c. 1958
18k $18,000 $20,000 $24,000

PATEK PHILIPPE,18J., fluted hooded lugs, RF#2517
18k $4,000 $5,000 $7,000

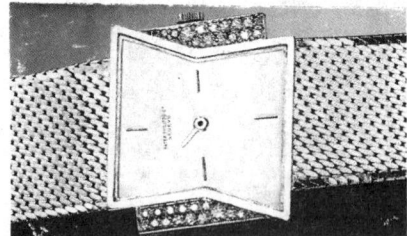

PATEK PHILIPPE, 18 J., RF#3497, diamond set case
platinum C&B...................$12,000 $14,000 $18,000

⊕ Pricing in this Guide are fair market price for **COMPLETE** watches which are reflected from the "**NAWCC**" National and regional shows.

PATEK PHILIPPE, 18J., RF#3424, asymmetric, c. 1960
18k $12,000 $13,000 $16,000

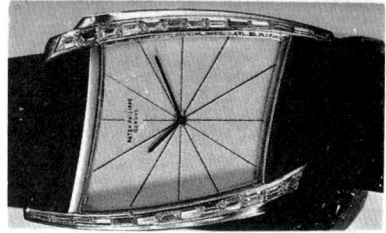

PATEK PHILIPPE, 18J., RF # 3424, asymmetric, diamond set on bezel, Ca. 1960
platinum............................$16,000 $17,000 $20,000

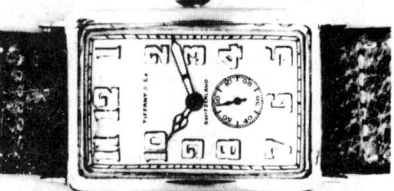

PATEK PHILIPPE, 18 J., Cal.# 9, **hinged back,** c. 1920s
18k $6,000 $6,500 $7,500

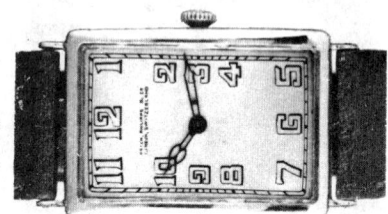

PATEK PHILIPPE, 18 J., Cal.# 10, hinged back, c. 1920s
18k $6,500 $7,000 $8,000

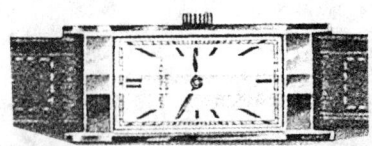

PATEK PHILIPPE, 18 jewels, RF # 137, curved, Ca. 1931
18k - 44mm $4,000 $4,200 $5,000

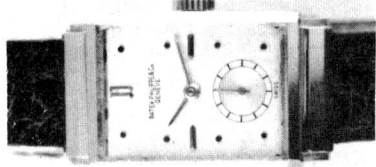

PATEK PHILIPPE, 18J., RF # 1444, Cal.# 9, c. 1940s
18k $3,000 $3,500 $4,500

PATEK PHILIPPE, 18 jewels, RF # 2461, Cal.. 9, c. 1950s
18k $3,500 $4,000 $5,000

PATEK PHILIPPE,18J., cal.990, c.1936
18K $3,500 $4,000 $5,000

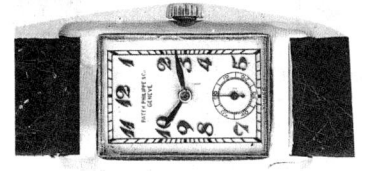

PATEK PHILIPPE,18J., RF# 409, Ca.1934
18K $3,200 $3,600 $4,200

PATEK PHILIPPE, 18 J., RF # 433, stepped case, c. 1940s
18k $4,200 $4,800 $5,500

PATEK PHILIPPE, 18 jewels, RF # 2531, c. 1950s
18k $2,500 $3,000 $4,000

PATEK PHILIPPE, 18 jewels, RF # 1564, Cal.# 9
18k $3,000 $3,500 $4,500

PATEK PHILIPPE, 18 jewels, RF# 1560
18k $2,800 $3,000 $4,000

PATEK PHILIPPE, 18 jewels, RF # 1560, c. 1940s
18k $3,600 $4,000 $5,000

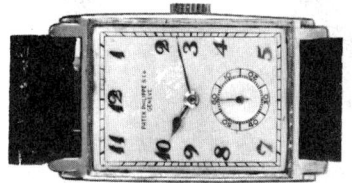

PATEK PHILIPPE, 18 jewels, RF # 1559, c. 1943
18k $3,000 $3,500 $4,500

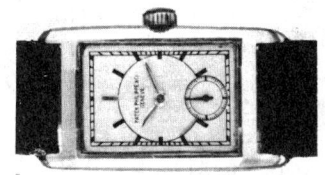

PATEK PHILIPPE, 18 jewels, RF # 404, c. 1930s
18k $2,500 $2,800 $3,500

PATEK PHILIPPE, 18J., RF # 1588, beveled crystal, c. 1945
18k $4,500 $5,000 $6,000

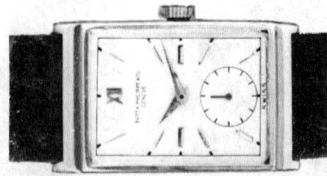

PATEK PHILIPPE, 18 jewels
18k $3,500 $4,000 $5,000

PATEK PHILIPPE, 18 jewels, RF # 2477, Cal.# 9, c. 1953
18k $4,000 $4,500 $5,500

PATEK PHILIPPE, 18 J., RF # 490 & 491, curved, cal. # 9
18k $7,000 $8,000 $10,000

PATEK PHILIPPE, 18J., decorated enamel case, c. 1920s
18k $8,000 $9,000 $11,000

PATEK PHILIPPE,18J., RF # 2334
18K.................................$3,500 $3,800 $4,500

PATEK PHILIPPE,18J., RF # 513, extended lugs, **two tone case,** cal. 885, c.1943
18K.................................$5,000 $6,000 $8,000

PATEK PHILIPPE,18J., diamond on dial & case
18K C&B.................................$3,500 $4,000 $5,000

PATEK PHILIPPE, 18 J., RF # 1486, hidden lugs, c. 1930s
18k $4,000 $4,500 $5,500

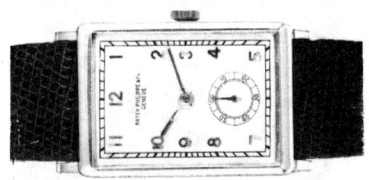

PATEK PHILIPPE, 18 jewels, RF # 1564, c. 1940s
18k $3,500 $4,000 $5,000

PATEK PHILIPPE, 18 J., RF # 1559, hinged back, c. 1920s
18k $4,500 $5,000 $6,000

PATEK PHILIPPE, 18 J., RF # 2404, applied gold numbers
18k $6,000 $6,500 $7,500

" PATEK PHILIPPE" watches should be signed on the case, dial & movement to bring the prices listed in this book.
(triple signed P.P.CO.)

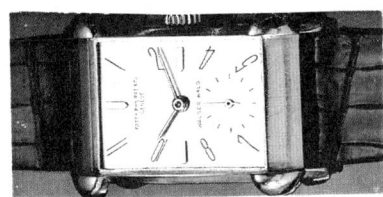

PATEK PHILIPPE, 18J., RF # 1487, Cal.#9, fancy lugs
18k $6,000 $7,000 $9,000

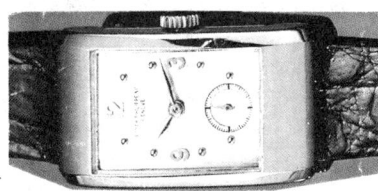

PATEK PHILIPPE, 18J., RF # 1402, hooded satin lugs
18k asymmetric $8,000 $9,000 $12,000

PATEK PHILIPPE, 18J., RF # 430, "Staybrite," curved case
s. steel $6,000 $7,000 $9,000

PATEK PHILIPPE, 18 J., RF # 1438, Cal.# 9, hooded lugs
18k $2,200 $2,400 $3,000

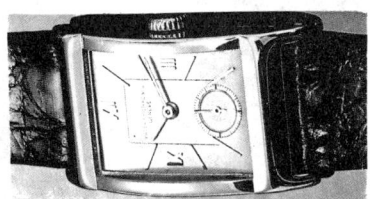

PATEK PHILIPPE, 18 jewels, RF # 513-1, curved
18k $3,500 $4,000 $5,000

⏲ Pricing in this Guide are fair market price for **COMPLETE**
watches which are reflected from the "**NAWCC**" National and
regional shows.

PATEK PHILIPPE,18J., engraved bezel,hinged back,c.1920
18k $5,500 $6,000 $7,500

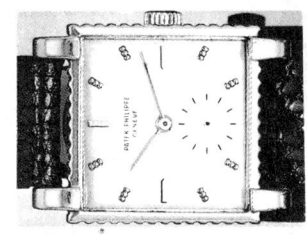

PATEK PHILIPPE, 18J., RF # 2472, ribbed case & fancy lugs
18k $3,000 $3,500 $4,500

PATEK PHILIPPE, 18 J., RF # 2518, large lugs, c. 1960s
18k $4,000 $4,500 $6,000

PATEK PHILIPPE, 18 J., RF # 1532, Ca.1940s
18k $4,000 $5,000 $6,500

PATEK PHILIPPE, 18 jewels, c. 1930s
18k $2,500 $2,800 $3,500

PATEK PHILIPPE, 18J., Cal.# 9, center lugs, c. 1940s
18k $3,500 $3,800 $4,500

PATEK PHILIPPE, 18 jewels, RF # 655, c. 1940s
18k $3,500 $4,000 $5,000

PATEK PHILIPPE, 18J., triple lugs, RF#2471, ca.1951
18k $16,000 $18,000 $22,000

PATEK PHILIPPE, 18 jewels, triple lugs, RF#1482
18k $8,000 $9,000 $12,000

PATEK PHILIPPE, 18 jewels, curved, c. 1940s
18k $3,000 $3,500 $4,500

PATEK PHILIPPE, 18 jewels, RF # 1570, Cal.# 9, c. 1940s
18k $3,500 $4,000 $5,000

PATEK PHILIPPE, 18 jewels, RF # 406, curved, c. 1940s
18k $3,500 $4,000 $5,000

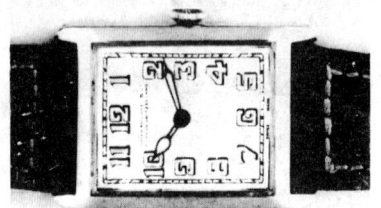

PATEK PHILIPPE, 18 jewels, hinged back, c. 1920s
18k $4,000 $4,500 $5,500

PATEK PHILIPPE, 18J., hinged back, stepped case
18k $4,000 $4,500 $5,500

PATEK PHILIPPE, 18J., RF#2520, cal. # 9, extended lugs
18k C&B..............................$7,000 $9,000 $12,000

PATEK PHILIPPE, 18J., RF # 2414, fancy lugs, ca.1949
18k $6,000 $7,000 $9,000

PATEK PHILIPPE 18J., RF# 2503, fancy lugs, ca. 1950s
18k $8,000 $9,000 $12,000

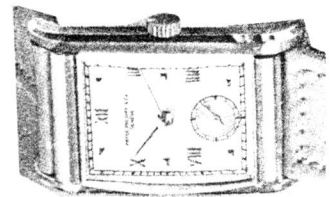

PATEK PHILIPPE 18J., RF# 1493, ca. 1940s
18k $4,000 $4,500 $5,500

PATEK PHILIPPE 18J., RF# 1530, fancy lugs, ca. 1940s
18k $3,500 $4,000 $5,000

PATEK PHILIPPE 18J., RF# 1442, ca. 1940s
18k $3,500 $4,000 $5,000

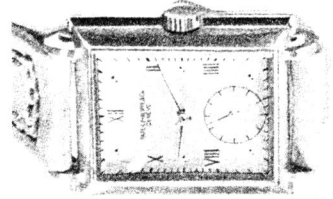

PATEK PHILIPPE 18J., RF# 1568, fancy lugs, ca. 1940s
18k $4,000 $4,500 $5,500

PATEK PHILIPPE 18J., RF# 2434, ca. 1950s
18k $3,500 $4,000 $5,000

PATEK PHILIPPE 18J., RF# 1535, fancy lugs, ca. 1940
18k $2,500 $3,000 $4,000

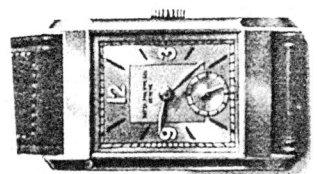

PATEK PHILIPPE 18J., RF# 420, ca. 1930s
18k $3,000 $3,500 $4,500

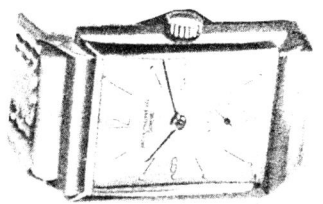

PATEK PHILIPPE 18J., RF# 1531, fancy lugs, ca. 1940s
18k $3,000 $3,500 $4,500

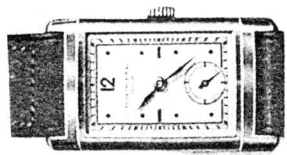

PATEK PHILIPPE 18J., RF# 422, ca. 1950s
18k $3,000 $3,500 $4,500

PATEK PHILIPPE 18J., RF# 2476, curved, ca. 1950s
18k $3,000 $3,500 $4,500

🕐 Pricing in this Guide are fair market price for **COMPLETE**
watches which are reflected from the "**NAWCC**" National and
regional shows.

PATEK PHILIPPE, 18 J., RF # 1580, Cal.# 9, concave lugs
18k $6,000 $6,800 $7,500

PATEK PHILIPPE, 18 J., Cal.#9, tank model, c.1940
18k $3,000 $3,500 $4,500

PATEK PHILIPPE, 18 jewels, RF # 2066, moveable lugs
18K..$7,000 $8,000 $10,000

PATEK PHILIPPE, 18 jewels, RF # 2403, lapidated lugs
18k $4,500 $5,000 $6,000

PATEK PHILIPPE, 18 jewels, fancy lugs, RF#1480
18k $5,000 $6,000 $8,000

PATEK PHILIPPE, 18 jewels, RF # 2404, fancy lugs
18k $5,000 $5,500 $7,000

PATEK PHILIPPE, 18J., stylized hooded lugs
18k $6,000 $7,000 $9,000

PATEK PHILIPPE, 18 jewels, RF # 2443, Cal.# 9, c. 1940s
18k $4,000 $5,000 $6,500

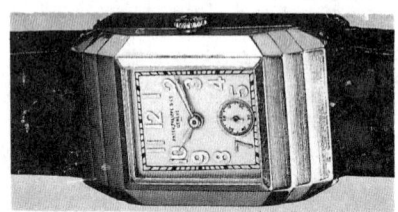

PATEK PHILIPPE, 18J., 2 tone, hooded & stepped lugs
18k $9,000 $10,000 $12,000

PATEK PHILIPPE, 18 jewels, "Reverso"
18k $20,000 $25,000 $35,000
s. steel ....★★$25,000 $30,000 $40,000

PATEK PHILIPPE, 18J., RF # 1450, top hat style, c. 1940s
18k $5,000 $5,500 $6,500
platinum $7,000 $8,000 $10,000

PATEK PHILIPPE, 18 jewels, RF # 1450, top hat style
18k C&B $6,000 $6,500 $8,000

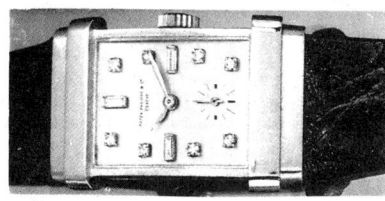

PATEK PHILIPPE, 18 J., RF # 2480, top hat, diamond dial
platinum $8,000 $9,000 $11,000

PATEK PHILIPPE, 18 jewels, M# 9, curved, tank style
18k $6,500 $7,000 $8,000

PATEK PHILIPPE, 18J., inclined & curved case, Ca.1940s
18k $16,000 $19,000 $25,000

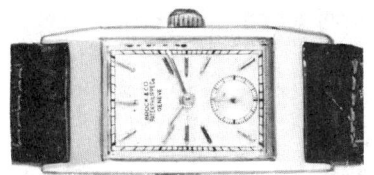

PATEK PHILIPPE, 18 jewels, RF # 425, Adj. to 8 positions
18k $4,000 $4,500 $6,000

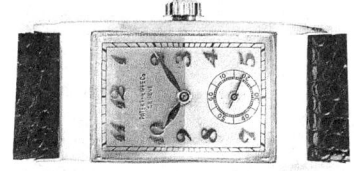

PATEK PHILIPPE, 18 jewels, RF # 425, curved, c. 1940s
18k $4,500 $5,000 $6,500

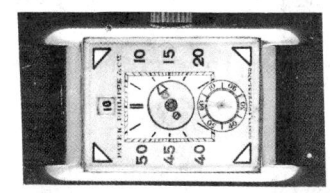

PATEK PHILIPPE, 18 J., converted to jump hr., **(recased)**
18k $3,000 $3,500 $4,000

PATEK PHILIPPE, 18 J., RF # 2468, flared case, c. 1940s
18k $6,500 $7,000 $9,000

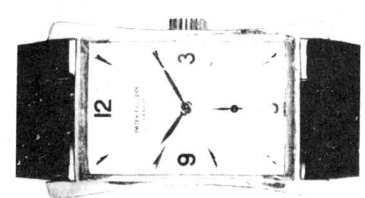

PATEK PHILIPPE, 18 jewels, RF # 1593, Cal.# 9, c. 1950s
platinum $10,000 $12,000 $15,000

PATEK PHILIPPE, 18J., RF # 2456, flared case, Ca. 1950s
18k $7,000 $8,000 $10,000

PATEK PHILIPPE, 18 J., RF # 2442, massive flared case
18k $16,000 $17,000 $20,000
platinum............................$25,000 $28,000 $35,000

PATEK PHILIPPE, 18J., RF#2441, Eiffel tower, c. 1945
18k $20,000 $22,000 $28,000

PATEK PHILIPPE,18J., RF#2441, Eiffel tower, c. 1945
18k $20,000 $22,000 $28,000

PATEK PHILIPPE, 18 jewels, RF # 2456, flared case
18k $5,000 $5,500 $7,000

PATEK PHILIPPE, 18J., RF # 2468, flared case, c. 1950s
18k(dial not original)..........$4,500 $5,000 $6,000

PATEK PHILIPPE, 18 jewels, RF # 2554, c. 1950s
18k $6,000 $6,500 $7,500

PATEK PHILIPPE, 18J., 16 diamond on bezel, ca.1960
18k C&B............................$6,000 $7,000 $9,000

PATEK PHILIPPE, 18 J., RF # 425, diamond dial, c. 1945
18k $5,500 $6,000 $7,000

PATEK PHILIPPE, 18 jewels, RF # 425, diamond dial
platinum..............................$6,000 $7,000 $8,500

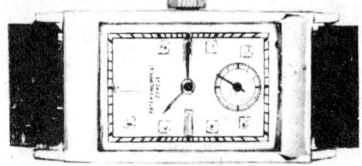

PATEK PHILIPPE, 18J., RF # 425, diamond dial, c. 1935
platinum..............................$6,000 $7,000 $9,000

PATEK PHILIPPE, 18 J., RF # 425, diamond dial & bezel
platinum..............................$7,000 $8,000 $10,000

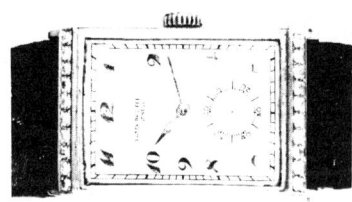

PATEK PHILIPPE, 18J., hinged back, diamond bezel
18k $5,000 $6,000 $8,000

PATEK PHILIPPE,18J., RF#2493, c.1953
18K $2,500 $3,000 $4,000

PATEK PHILIPPE, 18 jewels, Ca. 1940s
18k $3,500 $4,000 $5,000

PATEK PHILIPPE,18J., RF#1431, cal., c.1940
18K $2,000 $2,300 $3,000

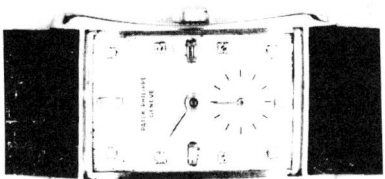

PATEK PHILIPPE, 18J., RF # 2456, diamond dial, flared
18k $7,500 $8,500 $11,000

PATEK PHILIPPE,18J., RF#2447, c.1950
18K $1,800 $2,100 $2,800

PATEK PHILIPPE, 18J, Hooded Lugs
s. steel $3,500 $4,000 $5,000

PATEK PHILIPPE,18J., carved lugs, RF#2423, c.1949
18K $3,600 $4,200 $5,000

PATEK PHILIPPE, 18J., RF 3727, **Lapis & 54 Diamonds,**
Ca.1974
18k $9,000 $10,000 $12,000

PATEK PHILIPPE,18J., RF#2424, c.1951
18K $3,600 $4,200 $5,000

PATEK PHILIPPE,18J., RF # 2437, stepped lugs, c.1940
18K.....................................$3,000 $3,500 $4,200

PATEK PHILIPPE, 18 J., RF # 1486, Ca. 1950s
18k C&B.............................$3,300 $3,800 $4,500

PATEK PHILIPPE, 18J., RF # 2496, textured bezel, c. 1940s
18k $2,500 $2,800 $3,500

PATEK PHILIPPE, 18J., RF # 2491, fancy off set lugs
18k $2,500 $2,800 $3,500

PATEK PHILIPPE, 18 jewels, RF # 1567, Ca. 1940s
18k $3,000 $3,300 $4,000

PATEK PHILIPPE, 18 jewels, RF # 3405, cal. # 9, c. 1963
18k $2,000 $2,400 $3,000

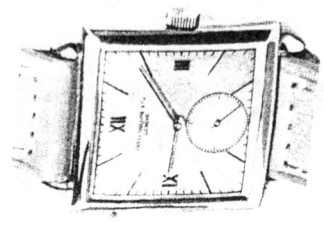

PATEK PHILIPPE, 18 jewels, RF # 1432, Ca. 1940s
18k $2,200 $2,600 $3,000

PATEK PHILIPPE, 18 jewels, RF # 3406, c. 1960s
18k $2,000 $2,200 $2,800

PATEK PHILIPPE, 18 jewels, RF # 1557, oval lugs
18k $3,500 $4,000 $5,000

PATEK PHILIPPE, 18 jewels, RF # 3555
18k $2,000 $2,200 $2,800

🕐 Pricing in this Guide are fair market price for **COMPLETE**
watches which are reflected from the "**NAWCC**" National and
regional shows.

PATEK PHILIPPE, 18 J., RF # 2553, Cal.# 9-90, Ca. 1955
18k $3,000 $3,500 $4,500

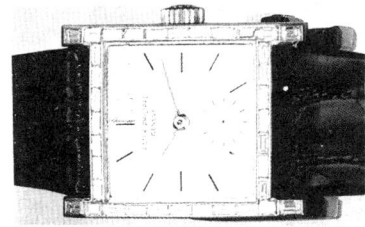

PATEK PHILIPPE, 18 J., RF # 2496, diamond bezel
platinum $8,000 $9,000 $12,000

PATEK PHILIPPE, 18 J., RF # 3519, Ca. 1967
18k(w)....................................$2,000 $2,200 $2,800

PATEK PHILIPPE, 18J., Cal.# 9, hidden dial, gold & plat.
18k & platinum..................$20,000 $22,000 $28,000

PATEK PHILIPPE, 18 jewels, RF # 3633, Cal.# 9, c. 1980s
18k C&B $3,000 $3,500 $4,500

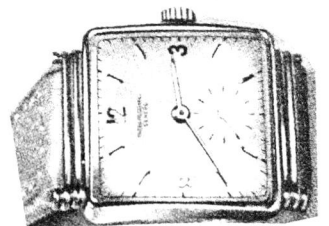

PATEK PHILIPPE, 18 jewels, RF # 1575, Ca. 1940s
18k $2,000 $2,300 $3,000

PATEK PHILIPPE, 18 jewels, RF # 1566, Ca. 1940s
18k $3,000 $3,500 $4,500

PATEK PHILIPPE, 18 jewels, RF # 3404
18k C&B.............................$2,500 $2,800 $3,500

PATEK PHILIPPE, 18 J., RF # 3467, textured dial & bezel
18k $2,200 $2,800 $3,500

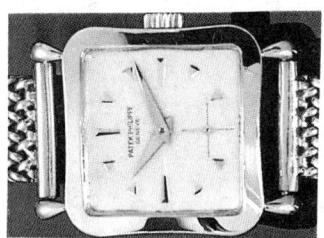

PATEK PHILIPPE, 18 jewels, RF # 2513, c. 1950s
18k $3,000 $3,500 $4,500

⊕ Some grades are not included. Their values can be
determined by comparing with **similar** age, size, metal
content, style, grades, or models such as **time only**,
chronograph, repeater etc. listed.

PATEK PHILIPPE, 18 J., RF # 2574, center sec., c. 1960s
18k C&B $3,500 $4,000 $5,000

PATEK PHILIPPE, 18 J., tank, RF#2530-1, Ca. 1959
18k C&B $3,500 $4,000 $5,000

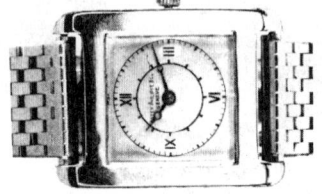

PATEK PHILIPPE, 18J., tank, Cal.# 9, c. early 1910s
18k C&B $4,000 $4,500 $5,500

PATEK PHILIPPE, 18 jewels, RF # 1408, Ca. 1940s
18k $2,000 $2,200 $2,700

PATEK PHILIPPE, 18 jewels, RF # 2486, Ca. 1950s
18k $2,500 $2,700 $3,200

PATEK PHILIPPE, 18 jewels, RF # 2516, Ca. 1950s
18k $2,600 $2,800 $3,200

PATEK PHILIPPE, 18 jewels, RF # 2540, Ca. 1960s
18k $2,500 $2,800 $3,500

PATEK PHILIPPE, 18 J., RF # 2479, guilloche bezel
18k $3,500 $4,000 $5,500

PATEK PHILIPPE, 18 J., RF # 1574, hidden lugs, c. 1945
18k $2,800 $3,000 $3,500

PATEK PHILIPPE, 18J., RF # 556, fluted cylindrical lugs
18k $6,000 $7,000 $9,000

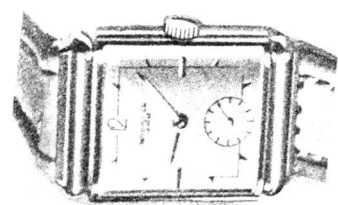

PATEK PHILIPPE, 18 jewels, RF # 1592, hidden lugs
18k $2,000 $2,200 $2,800

PATEK PHILIPPE, 18 J., RF # 2514-1, Ca. 1940s
18k $3,500 $4,000 $5,000

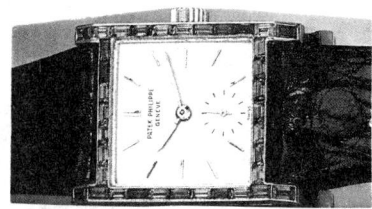

PATEK PHILIPPE, 18 J., RF # 3465, blue sapphire bezel
platinum...............................$7,000 $8,000 $11,000

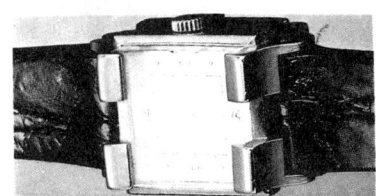

PATEK PHILIPPE, 18 jewels, RF # 1481, overhanging lugs
18k $4,000 $4,500 $6,000

PATEK PHILIPPE, 18 J., RF # 2440, fluted dropped lugs
18k $4,000 $4,500 $6,000

Wrist Watches listed in this section are priced at the collectable
fair market **retail** level as **complete** watches having an original
gold-filled case and stainless steel back, also with original dial,
leather watch band, and the entire original movement in good
working order with no repairs needed.

PATEK PHILIPPE, 18 jewels, RF # 2474, Ca. 1940s
18k $3,000 $3,500 $4,500

PATEK PHILIPPE, 18 jewels, RF # 244, large bezel
18k $2,200 $2,400 $3,000

PATEK PHILIPPE, 18 jewels, RF # 2488, Ca. 1940s
18k $2,200 $2,400 $3,000

PATEK PHILIPPE, 15J.,for Baily,Banks & Biddle, ca.1920
18k $4,000 $4,500 $6,000

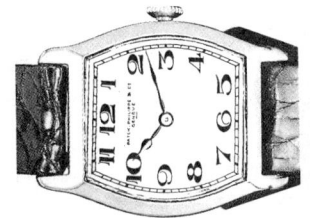

PATEK PHILIPPE, 16J., ca.1923
18k $3,000 $3,300 $4,000

PATEK PHILIPPE, 18 jewels, c. 1910
18k $3,000 $3,500 $4,500

PATEK PHILIPPE, 18 jewels, c. 1920s
18k $3,500 $4,000 $5,000

PATEK PHILIPPE, 18 jewels, c. 1920s
18k $4,000 $4,500 $6,000

PATEK PHILIPPE, 18J, **recased** & PW dial, c. 1920s
18k $1,000 $1,200 $1,500

PATEK PHILIPPE, 18 jewels, Cal.# 9, c. 1910
platinum...............................$7,000 $8,000 $10,000

PATEK PHILIPPE, 18 jewels, c. 1930s
18k $3,300 $3,600 $4,400

PATEK PHILIPPE, 18 jewels, c. 1930s
18k $3,500 $4,000 $5,000

PATEK PHILIPPE, 18 jewels, **contract case, not signed**
18k (w) $1,400 $1,600 $2,000

PATEK PHILIPPE, 18 jewels, Cal.# 9, c. 1925
18k $3,500 $4,000 $5,000

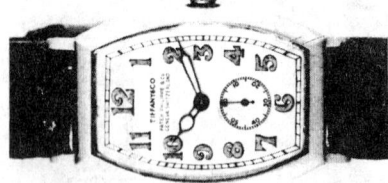

PATEK PHILIPPE, 18 jewels, M# 9, c. 1920s
18k $4,500 $5,200 $6,000

🕐 Pricing in this Guide are fair market price for **COMPLETE**
watches which are reflected from the "**NAWCC**" National and
regional shows.

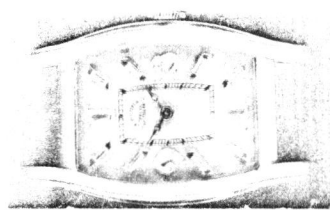

PATEK PHILIPPE, 18J, diamond dial, curved, 42mm,
Contract Case, c. 1919
platinum..............................$2,000 $2,200 $2,500

PATEK PHILIPPE, 18 jewels
18k $2,500 $2,800 $3,500

PATEK PHILIPPE, 18 J., RF # 2469, made for E. Gublin
18k $4,000 $4,500 $5,500

PATEK PHILIPPE, 18 jewels, ''Chronometro Gondolo''
18k $5,000 $6,000 $8,000

PATEK PHILIPPE,18jewels, RF#515, world time zone,
24 hr. rotating outside chapter, **tu-tone** case and band
18K C&B $200,000 $250,000 $350,000

PATEK PHILIPPE, 18 jewels, RF#2523, ''World Time,''
cloisonne polychrome enamel map on dial, **41 cities**
18k $120,000 $140,000 $200,000

PATEK PHILIPPE,18J.,''World Time,'' **41 cities**, RF#1415
18k $35,000 $40,000 $50,000

PATEK PHILIPPE, 18 jewels, RF # 2481,
landscape cloisonne polychrome enamel dial
18k $70,000 $80,000 $100,000

PATEK PHILIPPE, 18 J., RF # 2597, **2 hr. hands**,
2 time zones
18k $20,000 $25,000 $35,000

PATEK PHILIPPE, 18J., RF # 2597, **time zone**, hour hand
can be stepped forward or backward 1 hour at a time
18k $25,000 $30,000 $40,000

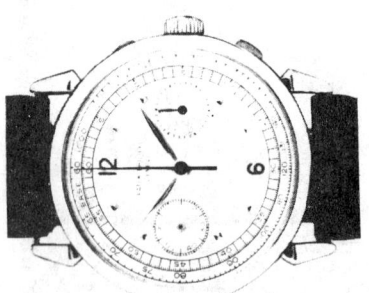

PATEK PHILIPPE,18J.,chronog., RF#1579, fancy lugs
18k $16,000 $18,000 $22,000

PATEK PHILIPPE, 18J, RF # 1436, chronog., 1940s
18k (Breguet dial) $22,000 $25,000 $35,000

PATEK PHILIPPE,18J., chronog., RF# 591, 2 reg., c.1943
18k (**black dial**) $25,000 $28,000 $35,000

PATEK PHILIPPE, 18J., RF#530, chronog.
18k $20,000 $22,000 $30,000

PATEK PHILIPPE,18J., RF# 130, chronog., **black dial**
18k & s. steel $28,000 $32,000 $38,000

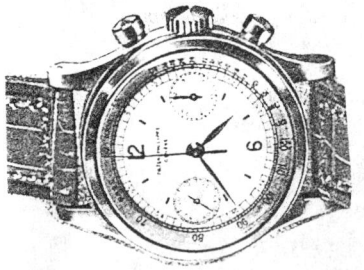

PATEK PHILIPPE, 18J., RF # 1463, 2 reg., Ca. 1940s
18k $25,000 $30,000 $40,000

🕐 Some grades are not included. Their values can be
determined by comparing with **similar** age, size, metal
content, style, grades, or models such as **time only**,
chronograph, repeater etc. listed.

PATEK PHILIPPE, 32J., **split sec**. chronog.
18k $250,000 $275,000 $350,000

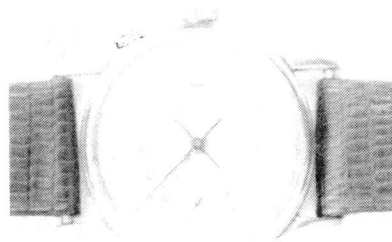

PATEK PHILIPPE, 18J., rf#3970E, chronog,triple date
moon ph., 24 hr. indicator, leap year indicator
18k $32,000 $35,000 $42,000

PATEK PHILIPPE, 26J., **split sec**. chronog. one button, for
Cartier, Sq. button for Rattrapante hand, crown for start stop
functions, RF#130, 8 adj., **Breguet dial**, ca.1938
18k $110,000 $130,000 $175,000

PATEK PHILIPPE,18J., RF#130,split sec. chronog.,c.1958
18k $100,000 $115,000 $150,000

PATEK PHILIPPE, 23 jewels, chronog., day-date month,
moon phase, made for E. Gueblin
18k C&B..........................$70,000 $80,000 $100,000

PATEK PHILIPPE,18J., RF# 1506, chronog., waterproof
18k $27,000 $30,000 $38,000

PATEK PHILIPPE, 23J., chronog., triple date, moon ph.
perpetual calendar,RF# 1518, Calatrava case, Ca.1941-54
18k .... ★ ★ $60,000 $70,000 $95,000

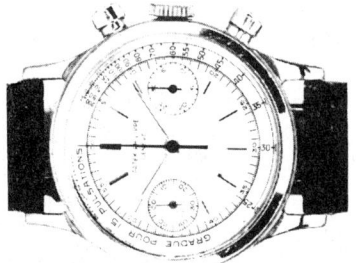

PATEK PHILIPPE, 18J., chronog., pulsometer, c. 1965
18k $32,000 $35,000 $42,000

🕐 Pricing in this Guide are fair market price for **COMPLETE**
watches which are reflected from the "**NAWCC**" National and
regional shows.

PATEK PHILIPPE, 23 J., chronog., triple date, moon ph.
perpetual calendar,ref.2499 (1 series) square button
18K $70,000 $80,000 $100,000

" PATEK PHILIPPE" watches should be signed on the case, dial & movement to bring the prices listed in this book.
(**triple signed P.P.CO.**)

PATEK PHILIPPE, 23 J., chronog., triple date, moon ph. perpetual calendar, ref.2499 (2 series)
18K..................................$65,000 $75,000 $95,000

PATEK PHILIPPE, 23J., chronog., triple date, moon ph. perpetual calendar, ref.2499 (3 series)glass crystal
18k $60,000 $65,000 $80,000

PATEK PHILIPPE, 23J., chronog., triple date, moon ph. perpetual calendar,ref.2499 (3 series)only 2 in platinum
platinum..........................$250,000 $300,000 $400,000

Wrist Watches listed in this section are priced at the collectable fair market **retail** level as **complete** watches having an original gold-filled case and stainless steel back, also with original dial, leather watch band, and the entire original movement in good working order with no repairs needed.

PATEK PHILIPPE, 23J., chronog., triple date, moon ph. perpetual calendar, ref.2499 (4 series)sapphire crystal
18k $50,000 $55,000 $65,000

PATEK PHILIPPE, 37jewels, RF # 3514, date, auto wind
platinum.............................$10,000 $12,000 $16,000

PATEK PHILIPPE, 18 J., RF # 3601, auto wind, date, Ca. 1970s
18k C&B.............................$3,000 $3,500 $4,500

PATEK PHILIPPE,37J., Auto-wind, RF#3514/1, date, c.1967
18K C&B.............................$3,000 $3,500 $4,500

PATEK PHILIPPE,37J., date, RF#3445, auto-wind, c.1961
18K.....................................$3,500 $4,500 $6,000

PATEK PHILIPPE,18J., date, RF#3604, textured dial, c.1977
18K(w)................................$2,200 $2,400 $3,000

PATEK PHILIPPE,18J., RF # 96, (**day, date, month,**
at 9-12-3), **3 known to exist**, manual wind, Ca.1934
18K................ ★ ★ ★ ★ ★$300,000 $350,000 $500,000

PATEK PHILIPPE, 18J., RF#96, Calatrava, triple date note
moon phases at 12, Ca.1936
In 1996 a similar watch sold for $1.7 million US dollars
18K..................................$300,000 $350,000 $450,000
platinum $400,000 $450,000 $550,000

PATEK PHILIPPE, 18J., RF#3450, day-date-month, moon
phase, waterproof, **perpetual date at 3**
18k $25,000 $27,000 $32,000

PATEK PHILIPPE, 37J,RF#3448, triple date moon ph, c.1968
platinum............................$35,000 $40,000 $50,000
18K $23,000 $25,000 $30,000

PATEK PHILIPPE, 37J., Perpetual, triple date, moon ph.
RF # 2497
18k $45,000 $50,000 $60,000

PATEK PHILIPPE,18J., triple date, moon ph., RF#2438,
c.1962
18k $45,000 $50,000 $60,000

PATEK PHILIPPE, 18J, perpetual, RF# 1526
18k..................................$40,000 $45,000 $55,000

PATEK PHILIPPE,18J., "Officer", RF#3960, c.1992
18k 2,000 made, 18k(w) 150 made, platinum 50 made
18K..................................$13,000 $15,000 $18,000
18k(w)..............................$15,000 $17,000 $20,000
platinum............................$25,000 $28,000 $32,000

PATEK PHILIPPE, 15J., enamel dial, c. 1910
18k $6,000 $7,000 $9,000

PATEK PHILIPPE, 18 jewels, RF#1461
18k $2,500 $2,800 $3,500

PATEK PHILIPPE, 18 jewels, RF # 1571, Ca. 1940s
18k $2,600 $3,000 $3,800

PATEK PHILIPPE, 18 jewels, RF # 1461, aux. sec.
18k $2,300 $2,700 $3,300

PATEK PHILIPPE, 18J., *Amagnetic* on dial, ca. 1960
18k $3,500 $4,000 $5,000

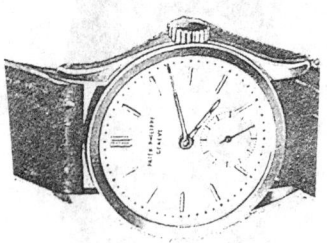

PATEK PHILIPPE, 18J.,RF # 448,"Calatrava", aux. sec.,
Ca. 1950s
18k $3,000 $3,300 $4,000

🕐 Pricing in this Guide are fair market price for **COMPLETE**
watches which are reflected from the "**NAWCC**" National and
regional shows.

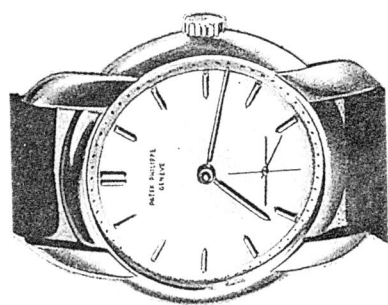

PATEK PHILIPPE, 18 jewels, RF # 2536, Ca. 1950s
18k $4,000 $4,500 $5,500

PATEK PHILIPPE, 18 jewels, RF # 2452, Ca. 1950s
18k $3,500 $4,000 $5,000

PATEK PHILIPPE, 18 jewels, RF # 2459, Ca. 1950s
18k $3,000 $3,400 $4,000

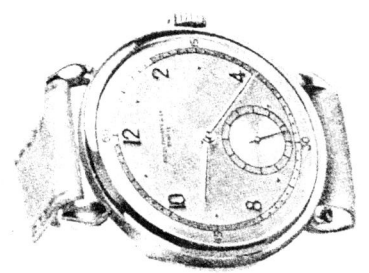

PATEK PHILIPPE, 18 jewels, RF # 1509, Ca. 1940s
18k $3,000 $3,200 $3,700

PATEK PHILIPPE, 18 jewels, RF # 2525 / 1, Ca. 1950s
18k $2,800 $3,200 $4,200

PATEK PHILIPPE, 18 jewels, RF # 2484, Ca. 1950s
18k $2,300 $2,700 $3,500

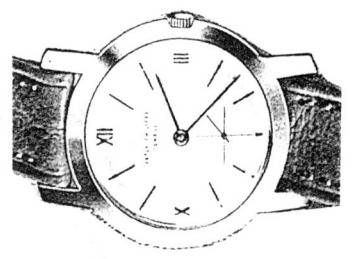

PATEK PHILIPPE, 18 jewels, RF # 2506 / 1, Ca. 1950s
18k $2,000 $2,200 $2,600

PATEK PHILIPPE, 18 jewels, RF # 534, Ca. 1940s
18k $3,000 $3,500 $4,500

🕐 Pricing in this Guide are fair market price for **COMPLETE**
watches which are reflected from the **"NAWCC"** National and
regional shows.

PATEK PHILIPPE, 18 jewels, RF # 2577, Ca. 1955
18k $2,500 $2,800 $3,500

PATEK PHILIPPE, 18 jewels, man's half size, c. 1920
18k $2,800 $3,200 $4,000
s. steel $2,600 $2,800 $3,300

PATEK PHILIPPE, 18 jewels, RF# 2429, Ca. 1950s
18k $3,200 $3,600 $4,400

PATEK PHILIPPE, 18 jewels, RF # 2537, aux. sec., c. 1950s
18k $2,600 $3,000 $3,800

🕐 Pricing in this Guide are fair market price for **COMPLETE** watches which are reflected from the "**NAWCC**" National and regional shows.

PATEK PHILIPPE, 30J., RF#3429, self-winding
18k $4,000 $4,500 $6,000

PATEK PHILIPPE, 18J., aux. sec., RF#2526, ca. 1957
RARE glass enamel dial
18k auto-w $7,000 $8,000 $12,000

PATEK PHILIPPE,18J., **CLASSIC Calatrava**, RF# 96
18k $3,000 $3,500 $4,200
s. steel $2,700 $3,000 $3,500
platinum $7,000 $8,000 $10,000
platinum + diam. dial $7,500 $8,500 $11,000

The above CLASSIC **Calatrava** case and dial model 96 was 1st used in 1932. It was designed at a time of transition from pocket watches to wrist watches. The coin was used as a perfect geometric shape to design a wrist watch case that has harmony and balance. Many variations from the classic model 96 have been used, but to most collectors the **CLASSIC** model 96 is known as the **Calatrava** model. The original 96 Calatrava model used a flat bezel, 31mm one piece case (lugs are not soldered on), manual wind, white dial, barrette-shaped hour markers, dauphine hands and aux. seconds chapter with a inside and outside circle and long 5 sec. markers. A black dial was added in 1937.
The recent classic style Calatrava case is RF # 3796.
To date there are many Calatrava styles and models.

PATEK PHILIPPE, 18J., RF# 2500, Ca. 1950s
18k $2,200 $2,400 $2,800

PATEK PHILIPPE,18J., RF # 3420, aux. sec., Ca.1943
18K $2,700 $2,900 $3,300

PATEK PHILIPPE, 18 J., RF # 2515, Ca.1950s
18k $2,200 $2,400 $2,000

PATEK PHILIPPE,18J., RF# 1433, Ca.1940s
18K $2,000 $2,200 $2,600

PATEK PHILIPPE,30J., auto wind, RF#1516, c.1950
18K....................................$6,000 $7,000 $9,000

PATEK PHILIPPE,18J., aux. sec., RF#96, cal.12-20, c.1937
18K $2,800 $3,200 $3,800

PATEK PHILIPPE,18J., aux. sec., RF#2445,
18K....................................$2,600 $2,800 $3,300

Wrist Watches listed in this section are priced at the collectable
fair market **retail** level as **complete** watches having an original
gold-filled case and stainless steel back, also with original dial,
leather watch band, and the entire original movement in good
working order with no repairs needed.

PATEK PHILIPPE,18J., RF#1543, c.1947
18K $2,600 $2,800 $3,400

Some grades are not included. Their values can be
determined by comparing with **similar** age, size, metal
content, style, grades, or models such as **time only**,
chronograph, repeater etc. listed.

PATEK PHILIPPE,18J., RF# 1590, c.1951
18K $2,800 $3,000 $3,500

PATEK PHILIPPE, 18 jewels, RF # 2509, Ca. 1950s
18k $2,800 $3,200 $4,000

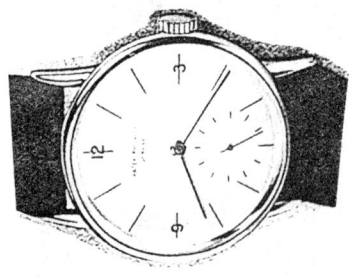

PATEK PHILIPPE, 18J., RF # 2494, extra long lugs, c. 1950
18k $2,400 $2,600 $3,000

PATEK PHILIPPE, 18J., "Calatrava", waterproof, c. 1950s
18k $3,600 $4,000 $5,000

PATEK PHILIPPE, 18 jewels, RF # 570, aux. sec., Ca. 1950s
18k $2,700 $2,900 $3,500

PATEK PHILIPPE, 30J.,"Calatrava", auto wind, gold rotor
18k $7,000 $8,000 $11,000

PATEK PHILIPPE, 18 jewels, RF # 1517, aux. sec.
18k $2,300 $2,800 $3,000

PATEK PHILIPPE,18J.,"Calatrava," RF # 96, enamel dial,
Ca.1940s
18k .... ★ $6,000 $7,000 $10,000

PATEK PHILIPPE, 18J.,waterproof, "Calatrava," rf#2545
18k $3,500 $4,000 $5,000

PATEK PHILIPPE, 18J., fancy lugs, ca. 1948
18k $6,000 $7,000 $9,000

PATEK PHILIPPE, 18 jewels, RF # 2406, Ca. 1950s
18k $2,500 $2,800 $3,500

PATEK PHILIPPE, 18 jewels, curled lugs
18k $3,500 $4,000 $5,000

PATEK PHILIPPE, 30J., RF # 2526, enamel dial, aux. sec.
18k C&B $7,000 $8,000 $12,000

PATEK PHILIPPE, 18 jewels, RF # 2549, Ca. 1950s
18k .... ★★$9,000 $12,000 $18,000

PATEK PHILIPPE, 18J., fancy lugs, c. 1940s
18k $3,500 $4,000 $5,000

PATEK PHILIPPE, 18 jewels, RF # 2550, Ca. 1950s
18k $5,000 $6,000 $8,000

PATEK PHILIPPE, 18J., RF# 2533, Ca. 1950s
18k $3,500 $4,000 $5,000

PATEK PHILIPPE, 21J., RF # 3025, "Calatrava," **Ca.1950s**
center sec., note **Breguet dial**
18k $4,000 $4,500 $5,500

PATEK PHILIPPE, 18J., center sec., rf#2466, ca.1949
18k $3,500 $3,800 $4,500

PATEK PHILIPPE, 18J., RF# 1578, center sec., c. 1950s
18k $2,500 $2,800 $3,300

PATEK PHILIPPE, 18 jewels, RF # 2482, Ca. 1950s
18k $2,600 $3,000 $3,800

PATEK PHILIPPE, 18 jewels, RF # 565, Ca. 1940s
18k $3,000 $3,300 $4,000

PATEK PHILIPPE, 18 jewels, conical lugs, center sec.
18k $3,500 $4,000 $5,000

PATEK PHILIPPE, 18 jewels, RF # 2481, center sec.
18k $3,000 $3,500 $4,500

PATEK PHILIPPE, 18 jewels, RF# 1491, Ca. 1940
18k $4,000 $4,500 $5,500

PATEK PHILIPPE,18J., center sec., RF#3411, c.1960
18K $2,200 $2,400 $2,800

PATEK PHILIPPE, 18 J., RF # 2508, center sec., c. 1950s
18k $3,000 $3,500 $4,500

PATEK PHILIPPE, 18J., RF # 2457, center sec., c. 1950s
18k $2,800 $3,000 $3,800

PATEK PHILIPPE, 18 jewels, center sec., waterproof
18k $3,000 $3,500 $4,500

PATEK PHILIPPE,18J., RF#3495, cal.27sc, c.1969
18K $1,800 $2,000 $2,400

PATEK PHILIPPE, 18 jewels, RF # 2460, center sec.
18k $2,800 $3,200 $4,000

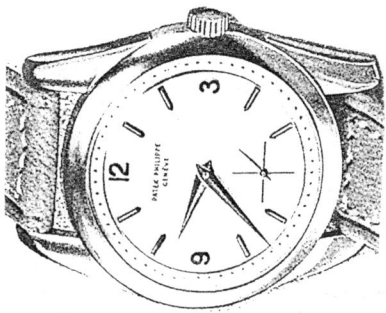

PATEK PHILIPPE, 18 jewels, RF# 2541, Ca. 1940s
18k C&B............................$4,000 $4,500 $5,500

PATEK PHILIPPE,18J., RF# 3541, auto wind, Ca. 1966
18K..................................$3,500 $3,800 $4,500

PATEK PHILIPPE,18J., RF# 3410, Ca. 1971
18K C&B...........................$3,500 $3,800 $4,500

PATEK PHILIPPE,18J., RF# 3558, auto wind, Ca. 1968
18K..................................$3,500 $3,800 $4,500

PATEK PHILIPPE,18J., RF# 3473, Ca. 1962
18K $3,000 $3,300 $3,800

PATEK PHILIPPE,18J., RF# 2451, "Calatrava", Ca. 1952
18K..................................$3,200 $3,600 $4,400

PATEK PHILIPPE,18J., RF# 2568-1, Ca. 1957
18K $2,300 $2,500 $3,000

PATEK PHILIPPE,18J., RF# 1595, Ca. 1949
18K(rose) $3,000 $3,500 $4,500

PATEK PHILIPPE,18J., RF# 1589, Ca. 1955
18K(rose)............................$2,700 $3,000 $3,500

PATEK PHILIPPE, 18 J., RF # 3569, auto wind, **back set**
18k $2,800 $3,200 $4,000

PATEK PHILIPPE, 18 jewels RF # 3606
18k C&B.............................$2,000 $2,400 $3,000

PATEK PHILIPPE, 18 jewels, RF # 3509
18k $2,000 $2,200 $2,600

PATEK PHILIPPE,18J., RF# 2573, c.1954
18K $1,800 $2,200 $2,800

PATEK PHILIPPE, 18 J., small "Calatrava," c. 1940s
18k $3,200 $3,600 $4,200

PATEK PHILIPPE,18J., RF#2592, c.1956
18K $1,700 $1,900 $2,400

PATEK PHILIPPE, 18 jewels, RF # 2589, Ca. 1970s
18k $2,600 $2,800 $3,200

PATEK PHILIPPE,18J., RF#3574, c.1960
s. steel $1,200 $1,400 $1,800

PATEK PHILIPPE, 18J., "Calatrava,", RF# 2588, c.1940s
18k $3,000 $3,400 $4,200

PATEK PHILIPPE, 18 J., RF # 497, unusual shape, c. 1940s
18k $6,000 $7,000 $9,000

PATEK PHILIPPE, 36J., RF # 380, "Nautilus", gold & steel
18K $10,000 $11,000 $13,000
18k&s. steel $5,000 $5,500 $6,500
s. steel $3,200 $3,800 $4,400

PATEK PHILIPPE, mid size, QUARTZ, rf#3900/1, date
s. steel $2,400 $2,600 $3,200

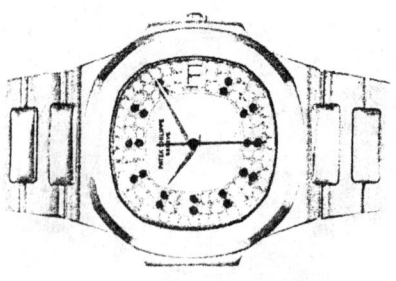

PATEK PHILIPPE, quartz, rf#3900/101, date
pave diamonds=.50ct., ruby hour markers
18k $6,000 $7,500 $10,000

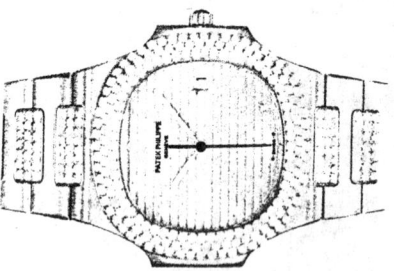

PATEK PHILIPPE, quartz, rf#3900/5, date, dia-
monds=2.27ct.
18k C&B $9,000 $10,000 $13,000

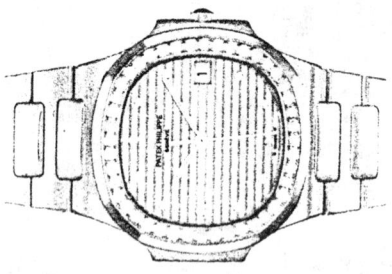

PATEK PHILIPPE, quartz, rf#3900/3, date, Carran dial
diamonds=.68ct.
platinum $12,000 $14,000 $17,000

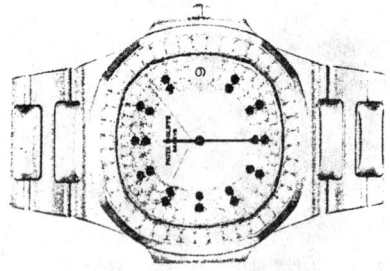

PATEK PHILIPPE, quartz, rf#3900/103, date
diamonds=.68ct, pave diamonds=.50, ruby markers
18k $7,000 $8,500 $11,000

PATEK PHILIPPE, quartz, rf#3900/105, date,
diamonds=2.27ct., pave diamonds=.50, ruby markers
18k C&B............................$10,000 $11,000 $14,000

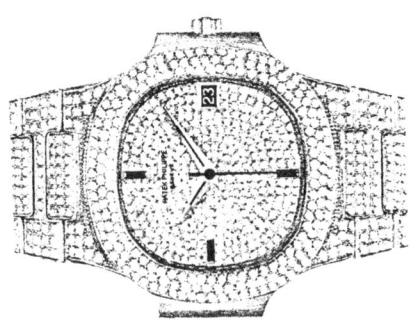

PATEK PHILIPPE, auto wind, rf#3800/108, date,
diamonds=7.46ct.,pave diam.=1.50ct.,sapphire markers
18k C&B..........................$30,000 $33,000 $40,000

PATEK PHILIPPE, auto wind, rf#3800/103, date
diamonds=.91ct., pave diamonds=63ct., ruby markers
18kC&B............................$17,000 $19,000 $23,000

PATEK PHILIPPE, 36J., RF # 3700, "Nautilus," large size
s. steel $5,000 $5,500 $6,500

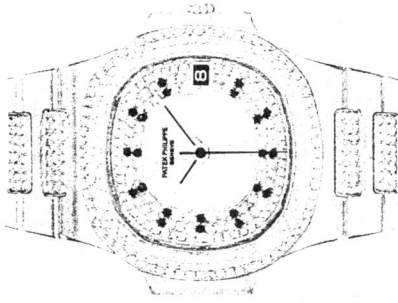

PATEK PHILIPPE, auto wind, rf#3800/105, date
diamonds=2.40ct., pave diam.=.63ct., ruby markers
18kC&B............................$20,000 $22,000 $26,000

PATEK PHILIPPE, 36 J. "Nautilus," diamond bezel
18k $12,000 $13,000 $15,000

" PATEK PHILIPPE" watches should be signed on the case,
dial & movement to bring the prices listed in this book.
(triple signed P.P.CO.)

⌚ Some grades are not included. Their values can be
determined by comparing with **similar** age, size, metal
content, style, grades, or models such as **time only**,
chronograph, repeater etc. listed.

PATEK PHILIPPE, skeleton, rf# 3885
18k $5,000 $6,000 $8,000

PATEK PHILIPPE, skeleton, rf# 3878, auto wind
18k $8,000 $9,000 $11,000

PATEK PHILIPPE, skeleton, rf# 3886
18k $7,000 $8,000 $10,000

PATEK PHILIPPE, skeleton, diamonds=.62ct., rf# 3885
18k $8,000 $9,000 $11,000

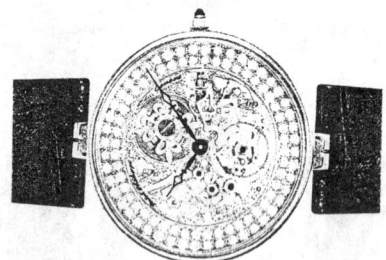

PATEK PHILIPPE, skeleton, diamonds=.85ct., rf# 3884
manual wind
18k $8,000 $9,000 $11,000

PATEK PHILIPPE, 36 J., RF # 3588, diamond dial & bezel
18k $4,000 $4,500 $5,500

PATEK PHILIPPE, 18J., diamond dial, Contract case, c. 1952
platinum...............................$6,000 $6,500 $8,000

PATEK PHILIPPE, 18J., diamond dial "Calatrava"
platinum...............................$8,000 $9,000 $11,000

PATEK PHILIPPE, 18J., "Calatrava," mid size, dia. dial
platinum...............................$8,000 $8,500 $10,000

Wrist Watches listed in this section are priced at the collectable
fair market **retail** level as **complete** watches having an original
gold-filled case and stainless steel back, also with original dial,
leather watch band, and the entire original movement in good
working order with no repairs needed.

PATEK PHILIPPE, 18 jewels, c. 1980s
18k C&B $2,800 $3,200 $3,700

PATEK PHILIPPE, quartz, c. 1980s
18k C&B $2,200 $2,400 $3,000

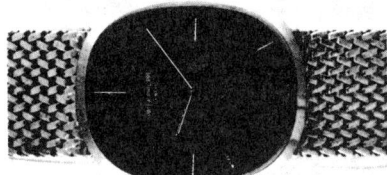

PATEK PHILIPPE, 23 jewels, RF # 3738, c. 1960s
18k C&B $3,500 $4,000 $4,800

PATEK PHILIPPE, 18 jewels, RF # 3745, c. 1980s
18k C&B $2,600 $2,800 $3,300

Wrist Watches listed in this section are priced at the collectable
fair market **retail** level as **complete** watches having an original
gold-filled case and stainless steel back, also with original dial,
leather watch band, and the entire original movement in good
working order with no repairs needed.

🕐 Pricing in this Guide are fair market price for **COMPLETE**
watches which are reflected from the "**NAWCC**" National and
regional shows.

PATEK PHILIPPE, 18 jewels, RF # 2548, massive lugs
18k.......................................$4,500 $5,000 $6,500

PATEK PHILIPPE, 18 J., RF # 1585, concave & hooded
lugs
18k.......................................$4,500 $5,000 $6,000

PATEK PHILIPPE, 18 jewels, hooded lugs, c.1930s
18K.......................................$5,000 $5,500 $6,500

PATEK PHILIPPE, 18 jewels, mid-sized, 2 tone
note: **winds at 12**
18k (y & w)........................$6,000 $7,000 $9,000

🕐 Some grades are not included. Their values can be
determined by comparing with **similar** age, size, metal
content, style, grades, or models such as **time only**,
chronograph, repeater etc. listed.

PATEK PHILIPPE, 18 J., extended lugs, 2 tone, rf#497
18k (y & w) $8,000 $9,000 $12,000

PATEK PHILIPPE, 18 jewels, lady's watch, c. 1940s
18k C&B $3,000 $3,500 $4,500

PATEK PHILIPPE, 18 jewels, lady's watch
18k $1,200 $1,400 $1,800

PATEK PHILIPPE, 18J., lady's watch, min. repeater
18k.....................................$60,000 $70,000 $90,000

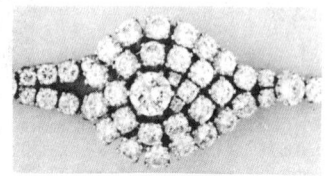

PATEK PHILIPPE,18 J., lady's, hinged lid set in diamonds
18k $6,000 $7,000 $9,000

PATEK PHILIPPE, 18 jewels, lady's watch, c. 1950s
18k.....................................$1,200 $1,600 $2,200

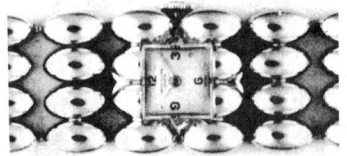

PATEK PHILIPPE, 18 jewels, lady's watch
18k C&B $2,500 $3,000 $4,000

PATEK PHILIPPE, 18 jewels, lady's watch, c. 1940s
18k.....................................$1,000 $1,200 $1,500

PATEK PHILIPPE, 18 J., lady's watch, diamond bezel
platinum $3,000 $3,500 $4,500

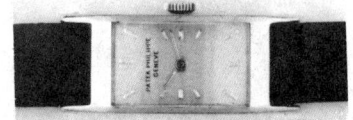

PATEK PHILIPPE, 18 jewels, lady's watch, c. 1940s
18k.....................................$1,200 $1,400 $1,700

PATEK PHILIPPE, 18 jewels, lady's watch, c. 1950s
18k $3,000 $3,500 $4,500

PATEK PHILIPPE, 18 jewels, lady's watch, c. 1950s
18k.....................................$900 $1,100 $1,400

PATEK, PHILIPPE
MOVEMENT IDENTIFICATION

Caliber 6¾, no. 60
S.no. 865000-869999
(1940-1955)

Caliber 7, no. 70
S.no. 943300-949999
(1940-1960)
S.no. 940000-949999

Caliber 8, no. 80
S.no. 840000-849999
(1935-1960)

Caliber 8, no. 85
S.no. 850000-859999
(1935-1968)

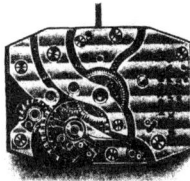

Caliber 9, no. 90
S.no. 833150-839999
S.no. 970000-979999
(1940-1950)

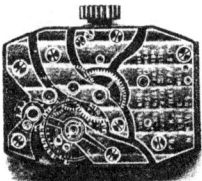

Caliber 9, no. 90a
830000-833149
(1940-1950)

Caliber 10, no. 105
S.no. 900000-909999
(1940-1945)

Caliber 10, no. 110
S.no. 910000-919999
(1940-1950)

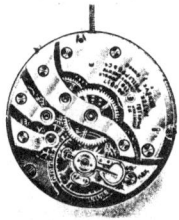

Caliber 10, no. 200
S.no. 740000-759999
(1952-1965)
S.no. 950000-959999
(1945-1955)

Caliber 23, no. 300
S.no. 780000-799999
(1955-1965)

Caliber 12, no. 600AT
S.no. 760000-779999
(1952-1960)

Caliber 12, no. 400
S.no. 720000-739999
(1950-1965)

Caliber 12, no. 120
826900-829999 (1935-1940)

Caliber 12, no. 120A
92000-929999 (1940-1950)
960000-969999 (1946-1952)
938000-939999 (1952-1954)

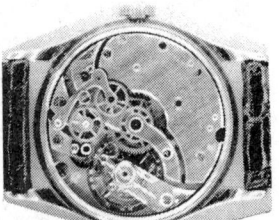

Caliber 12 , center seconds

Caliber 13, no. 130A

Caliber 13, no. 130B

Caliber 13, no. 130C

Chronograph, no. 862000-863995 (1940-1950); no. 867000-869999 (1950-1970)

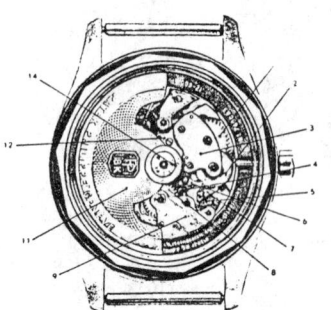

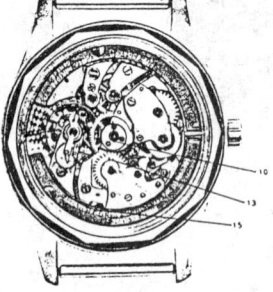

Caliber 12-600 AT, S.no. 760,000-779,999 (1960-1970)

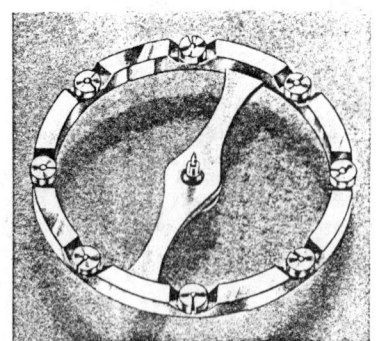

GYROMAX BALANCE WHEEL

PATRIA, 7 jewels, enamel dial, **compass**, Ca. 1920
s. steel .... ★$200 $250 $350

PATRIA, 7 jewels, enamel dial,
silver $55 $60 $85

PERFINE, 17 jewels, chronog., 2 reg.
gold filled................................$150 $175 $225
s. steel $100 $125 $175

PERPETUAL W. CO., 15 jewels, rim wind & set,
original retail price in 1933 was $31.50
14k $800 $900 $1,100
gold filled..............................$350 $375 $450
s. steel $250 $275 $350
base metal $200 $225 $300

PERPETUAL W. CO., 15 jewels, c. 1930s
14k...$600 $650 $800
gold filled...............................$350 $400 $550

PERPETUAL W. CO., 15J., fluted bezel, and sold for
$37.50 in 1933
base metal...............................$150 $175 $250

PERPETUAL W. CO., 15 jewels, fluted bezel
gold filled...............................$300 $325 $400

PERPETUAL W. CO., 15 J., diamond bezel, c. 1930s
platinum $550 $600 $700

PHILLIPE W. CO., 17J., RF#2501, chronog., c.1950
s. steel....................................$200 $250 $325

PIAGET,18J., cal.9p2 , c.1980
18k(w)......................................$500 $550 $700

PIAGET,18J., center sec., RF#1176, cal.fl560, c.1952
18k $400 $450 $600

PIAGET,18J., center sec., c.1950
18k $450 $500 $650

PIAGET, 18 jewels, 1904 $20 dollar gold piece, flip top
22k $900 $1,100 $1,400

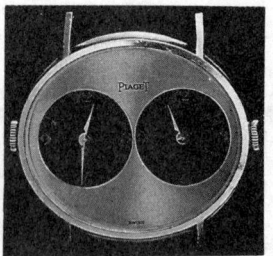

PIAGET, 18 jewels, 2 movements, 2 dials,
18k..$700 $750 $900

PIAGET, 18 jewels, black dial
18k..$500 $550 $700

PIAGET, 18 jewels, center sec., auto wind
18k..$600 $700 $850

PIAGET, 18 jewels, ref. #8177, auto wind
18k..$600 $700 $850

🕛 Some grades are not included. Their values can be determined by comparing with **similar** age, size, metal content, style, grades, or models such as **time only**, chronograph, repeater etc. listed.

PIAGET, 18 jewels
18k $500 $550 $700

PIAGET, 30 jewels, auto wind, gold rotor
18k $400 $500 $650

PIAGET, 18 jewels, 18k case, 14k band
18k & 14k C&B.....................$600 $700 $900

PIAGET, 18J., for Van Cleef, center lugs, thin model
18k $600 $700 $850

PIAGET,18J., RF#9821 , c.1975
18k C&B $800 $900 $1,100

PIAGET, 18 jewels, oval style
18k C&B $600 $700 $850

PIAGET, 18 jewels, oval style
18k...$400 $450 $525

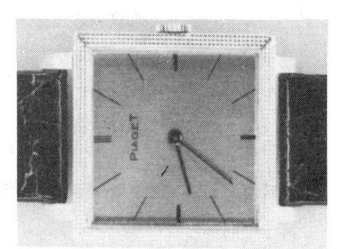

PIAGET, 18 jewels, textured bezel
18k...$700 $750 $900

PIAGET, 18J, 2 time zones & 2 movements
18k...$800 $900 $1,100

PIAGET, 30 jewels, textured bezel
18k...$500 $550 $700

PIAGET, 18J., rf#9298, c. 1970
18k $700 $800 $950

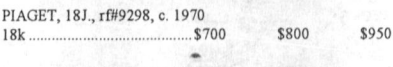

PIAGET, 18 jewels, tank style
18k $500 $550 $650

PIAGET, 18 jewels, "Executive", rf#7131C516
18k plain dial $3,000 $3,300 $4,000
18k pave dial........................$3,500 $3,800 $4,500

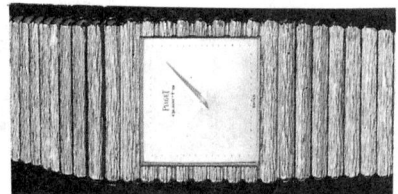

PIAGET, "Polo", rf#7131C701, quartz
18kC&B..............................$3,500 $3,800 $4,500

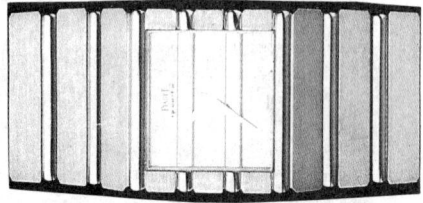

PIAGET, "Polo", rf#15562C701, quartz
18k $3,500 $3,800 $4,500
NOTE: PIAGET identification # the first 3 to 5 = case design, a letter as A, B, C, =bracelet design. All models beginning with 7, 8,15 may be worn while swimming.

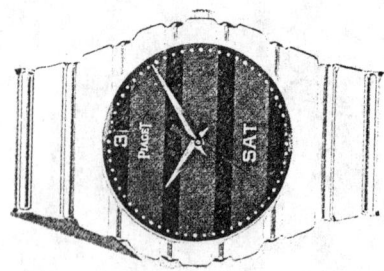

PIAGET, "Polo", rf#15562C701, quartz
18kC&B $3,500 $3,800 $4,500

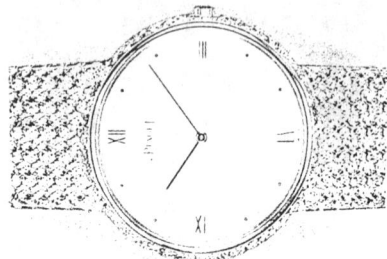

PIAGET, rf#8065D4
18kC&B $1,500 $1,700 $2,100

PIAGET, 17 jewels, Ca. 1957
18k..$500 $550 $700

PIERCE,7J., Doctors style, Ca. 1930
base metal...............................$175 $200 $250

Wrist Watches listed in this section are priced at the collectable
fair market **retail** level as **complete** watches having an original
gold-filled case and stainless steel back, also with original dial,
leather watch band, and the entire original movement in good
working order with no repairs needed.

PIERCE, 17J., early auto wind, **"Parashock,"** Ca. 1930s
waterproof, back secured by four screws.
s. steel $400 $450 $550

PIERCE, 17J., triple date, moon ph.
gold filled $250 $300 $425

PIERCE, 21 jewels, "Duofon", **2 time zones**, Ca. 1955
s. steel $95 $110 $150

POBEDA, 15J., tonneau, Ca. 1930s
14k pink $200 $225 $275

PIERCE, 17 jewels, chronog. one button
s. steel $225 $250 $300

PONTIFA, 17 jewels, chronog. day-date-month, 3 reg.
14k $400 $450 $550
s. steel $250 $300 $375

PIERCE, 17 jewels, chronog., c. 1940s
s. steel $135 $175 $225
14k $350 $375 $450
18k $425 $450 $525

PORTA, 17J., antimagnetic, c.1955
gold plate $20 $30 $50

PRAESENT, 17J., triple date, moon ph., mid size, c.1948
gold filled..................................$200 $250 $350

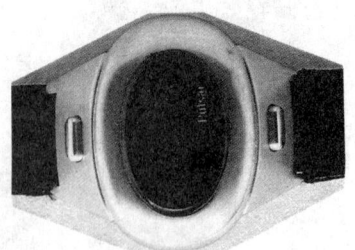

PULSAR, L.E.D. (light emitting diode), **working**, ca.1975
14k $300 $325 $400
gold filled $100 $125 $200

PREXA, 17 jewels, auto wind
gold filled....................................$30 $35 $50

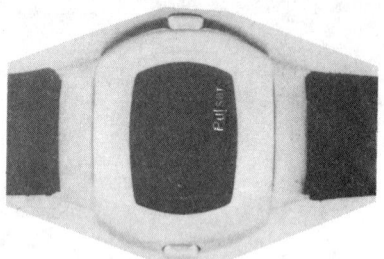

PULSAR, L.E.D. (light emitting diode), **working,**
18k $400 $425 $500
14k $300 $325 $400
gold filled $100 $125 $175
s. steel $75 $100 $150

PROVITA, 17J., cal.1525, c.1973
18k $150 $175 $250

RADO, 7J., double dial, c.1938
gold filled $200 $225 $300

PRONTO, 17 jewels, triple date, auto wind, waterproof
s. steel $75 $100 $150

RADO, 17J., date, ca.1960
gold plate $20 $30 $50

Some grades are not included. Their values can be determined by comparing with **similar** age, size, metal content, style, grades, or models such as **time only,** chronograph, repeater etc. listed.

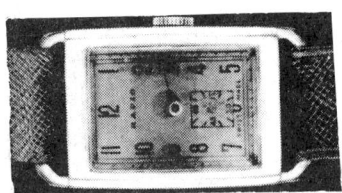

RAPID, 17J., on mvt. PATHE W. CO.
gold filled...................................$30 $35 $50

RECORD, 17J., split sec. chronog., date, moon phase
18k $5,500 $6,000 $7,000

RECORD, 17 jewels, split sec. chronog.
18k $6,000 $6,500 $8,000
s. steel $2,200 $2,500 $3,000

RECORD, 17 J., triple date, moon ph., auto wind ,
2 reg. chronograph,
18k $1,500 $1,700 $2,000

RECORD, 17 jewels, triple date, moon phase, c. 1940s
18k $1,000 $1,200 $1,500

RECORD, 17 jewels, day-date-month, moon phase
s. steel $300 $350 $450

RECORD, 17 J., triple date, moon phase, auto wind
18k $1,000 $1,200 $1,500

REGINA, enamel dial, center lugs, c.1929
silver $100 $125 $175

🕐 Some grades are not included. Their values can be
determined by comparing with **similar** age, size, metal
content, style, grades, or models such as **time only**,
chronograph, repeater etc. listed.

REMBRANT, 17J., chronog., c.1942
18k $400 $450 $550
s. steel $125 $150 $200

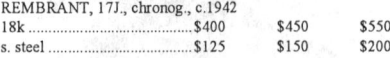

REVUE, 17J., beveled case, cal.54, c.1940
nickel $20 $30 $50

RIMA, 17J., aux. sec.,
14k $100 $110 $150

ROAMER, 17 jewels, hidden lugs
gold filled $30 $40 $60

ROCAIL, 15J., auto-wind, c.1930s
s. steel $100 $125 $165

ROCKFORD,15J., "Winona", made in USA, S#761074
gold filled $200 $250 $350
s. steel $150 $200 $300

ROAMER, 17 jewels, date, auto wind
gold filled $30 $40 $60

ROCKFORD, 17J., "Iroquois", gold train
gold filled $200 $250 $350

🕐 Pricing in this Guide are fair market price for **COMPLETE** watches which are reflected from the "**NAWCC**" National and regional shows.

ROLEX WATCH CO.

Swiss

Rolex was founded by Hans Wilsdorf in 1905, with his brother-in-law using the name of Wilsdorf & Davis and used movement supplier **Aegler** in Bienne Switzerland and bought cases in London. In *1908* the trade-mark **"Rolex"** was officially registered and by 1919, Wilsdorf started the *"Manufacture des Montres Rolex"* and the movements were manufactured in Bienne but finished and cased in Geneva. In 1926 they made the first real waterproof wrist watch and called it the *"Oyster"*. Rolex introduced a self-winding movement which they called *"Perpetual"* in 1931. In 1945, they introduced the *"Date-Just"* which showed the day of the month. In 1950 the *"Turn-o-graph"* was used, the forerunner of the Submariner & in 1953 the *"Submariner"* was introduced and in 1954 the *"GMT Master"* model. In 1956, a *"Day-Date"* model was released which indicates the day of the month (in numbers) and the day of the week (in letters).

IMPORTANT:

The following is a *guide* to help determine the age of your Rolex watches. However on some Oyster style watches Rolex added **inside** the case a Roman number (I,II,III,IV) to denote first, second third, or fourth quarter + "53", "54", "55", "56" to denote the year of production. Example outside Oyster case # 955454 inside case IV-53 which = last quarter of 1953. Example outside Oyster case # 282621 inside case III-55 which = third quarter of 1955.

ROLEX ESTIMATED PRODUCTION DATES

DATE–SERIAL #	DATE–SERIAL #	DATE–SERIAL #	DATE–SERIAL #	DATE–SERIAL #	DATE–SERIAL #	DATE–SERIAL #
1925 — 25,000	1937 — 98,000	1949 — 608,000	1961—1,485,000	1973— 3,741,000	1985— 8,810,000	1992 1/4-C000,001
1926 — 27,500	1938—118,000	1950 — 673,500	1962—1,557,000	1974— 4,000,000	1986— 9,300,000	1993 3/4-S000,001
1927 — 30,500	1939—136,000	1951 — 735,500	1963—1,635,000	1975— 4,260,000	1987— 9,760,000	1995 — W000,001
1928 — 33,000	1940—165,000	1952 — 804,000	1964—1,713,000	1976— 4,530,000	1987 1/2-R999,999	1996 — T000,001
1929 — 35,500	1941—194,000	1953 — 869,000	1965—1,791,000	1977— 5,000,000	1987 3/4-R000,001	1997 3/4-U000,001
1930 — 38,000	1942—224,000	1954 — 935,000	1966—1,870,000	1978— 5,480,000	1988 — R999,999	
1931 — 40,000	1943—253,000	1955—1,010,000	1967—2,164,000	1979— 5,960,000	1989 — L000,001	
1932 — 43,000	1944—284,000	1956—1,095,000	1968—2,426,000	1980— 6,430,000	1990 — L999,999	
1933 — 49,000	1945—348,000	1957—1,167,000	1969—2,689,000	1981— 6,910,000	1990 1/2-E000,001	
1934 — 55,000	1946—413,000	1958—1,245,000	1970—2,952,000	1982— 7,380,000	1991 1/4-E999,999	
1935 — 62,000	1947—478,000	1959—1,323,000	1971—3,215,000	1983— 7,860,000	1991 1/2-X000,001	
1936 — 82,000	1948—543,000	1960—1,401,000	1972—3,478,000	1984— 8,340,000	1991 3/4-N000,001	

The above list is provided for determining the APPROXIMATE age of your watch. Match serial number with date. Watches were not necessarily sold in the exact order of manufactured date.The above list was furnished with the help of Jeffrey P. Hess. Jeff and James M. Dowling authored a book *"The Best of Times"* a unauthorized history of the Rolex Watch Co.

ROLEX W. CO. REFERENCE # INDEX

REF # PAGE	REF # PAGE	REF # PAGE	REF # PAGE	REF # PAGE	REF # PAGE
619 —1,009	1803 —1,003	3492 —1,014	5050 —1,000	6263 — 984	7528 —1,012
678 — 979	1803 —1,004	3562 — 977	5502 — 990	6265 — 984	7610 —1,012
971 — 986	1804 —1,003	3595 — 996	5500 — 991	6266 — 994	7809 —1,012
1002 — 990	1807 —1,004	3655 — 996	5504 — 991	6284 — 991	7909 —1,012
1005 — 991	1823 —1,004	3665 — 980	5504 —1,006	6305 — 988	8094 —1,010
1007 —1,000	1862 — 986	3696 — 999	5512 —1,008	6309 —1,005	8126 —1,010
1011 — 993	1878 —1,009	3737 —1,010	5513 —1,007	6421 — 997	8171 — 985
1016 —1,006	1901 —1,004	3745 — 995	6011 —1,000	6422 — 989	8180 — 982
1018 —1,002	2010 — 991	3767 — 997	6021 — 997	6424 — 990	8206 — 982
1019 — 976	2136 — 979	3893 —1,011	6024 — 990	6426 —1,005	8405 — 992
1020 — 977	2245 — 986	3937 — 987	6024 — 991	6427 — 996	8443 — 978
1025 — 990	2280 — 997	3997 — 984	6029 — 989	6466 — 998	8952 — 992
1030 — 993	2303 — 982	4029 —1,009	6034 — 983	6536 —1,008	9083 — 995
1071 — 979	2319 — 998	4062 — 983	6036 — 983	6538 —1,006	9420 —1,013
1343 — 987	2495 — 994	4113 — 982	6050 —1,002	6541 — 977	9491 —1,011
1453 —1,002	2508 — 982	4220 — 998	6056 — 998	6542 —1,007	9659 — 977
1490 — 985	2537 —1,009	4222 — 978	6062 — 985	6552 — 995	9659 — 978
1490 — 986	2541 — 986	4325 — 989	6066 — 998	6556 — 977	9829 — 977
1491 — 985	2764 — 999	4365 — 994	6071 — 979	6558 — 977	
1500 — 987	2765 —1,013	4376 — 985	6075 — 989	6564 — 992	
1501 — 988	2940 — 976	4377 — 994	6082 — 990	6565 — 990	
1503 —1,004	2940 —1,001	4392 — 994	6084 — 992	6567 — 992	
1508 —1,004	2940 —1,003	4402 — 985	6085 — 990	6568 — 992	
1527 — 986	3055 — 982	4463 —1,013	6092 — 993	6581 — 992	
1527 — 987	3065 — 998	4467 —1,988	6094 — 987	6582 — 989	
1550 — 994	3116 — 981	4467 —1,003	6098 — 991	6585 —1,000	
1563 -3-1,012	3121 — 996	4478 — 993	6102 — 993	6590 — 993	
1600 — 995	3130 —1,001	4486 —1,014	6105 — 988	6604 — 987	
1601 — 988	3131 — 999	4554 —1,014	6511-1-1,006	6611 — 995	
1615 — 987	3133 —1,000	4547 — 980	6202 — 989	6627 — 995	
1625 —1,006	3139 — 980	4593 —1,014	6223 — 989	6634 — 989	
1665 —1,007	3233 — 982	4647 — 980	6234 — 983	6694 — 987	
1665 —1,008	3359 — 981	4767 — 983	6238 — 983	6694 — 994	
1666 —1,008	3361 — 986	4768 — 984	6238 — 984	6700-3-1,014	
1671 —1,007	3386 — 981	4891 — 995	6239 — 984	6800 — 995	
1701 —1,014	3458 —1,001	5015 —1,000	6239 — 985	6964 — 988	
1768 — 986	3478 — 997	5020 — 994	6241 — 984	7016 —1,012	

DIALS FOR MINT PRICES MUST BE ALL <u>ORIGINAL</u>.

BIENNE

ROLEX,15 jewels, enamel dial, ca.1920
silver $800 $900 $1,200

ROLEX, 15 jewels, enamel dial, flip top, c. 1918
silver $900 $1,100 $1,500

Above: Extracted from a December, 1952 AD

ROLEX, 17J., RF# 2940, back is flat & tin can shaped
non-magnetic .... ★★★ $2,000 $2,200 $2,800

ROLEX,15 jewels, enamel dial, demi- hunter style, ca.1920
silver $1,000 $1,200 $1,600

ROLEX, 26J., **Milgauss** 1st registered in 1954, RF#1019,
Ca. 1970s
s.steel $4,500 $5,000 $6,000

ROLEX, 17J, **Milgauss** in red, oyster, perpetual, RF# 6541
Lighting bolt sec. hand, Milgauss 1st registered in 1954
s. steel $4,500 $5,000 $6,000

ROLEX, 17J., "Precision"
s. steel $400 $450 $600

ROLEX, 17 jewels,"1/4 Century Club", **BOMBE**, c. 1960s
18k $1,400 $1,600 $2,000
14k $1,200 $1,400 $1,800

ROLEX,17J., center sec., RF#9829, cal.1210
s. steel $300 $350 $425

ROLEX, 17 jewels, ''Precision,'' center sec., Roman bezel
18k $1,000 $1,200 $1,600

ROLEX, 17J., rf#3562 , c.1955
14k $600 $750 $1,000

ROLEX, 26J., **jumping** center sec., RF # 6556, cal.# 1040,
Tru-beat on dial, also RF # 6558 & RF # 1020, Ca. 1960
Note: Jumping center sec. must be working to bring prices listed.
s. steel $2,200 $2,500 $3,000
14K......................................$5,000 $5,500 $7,000
18K......................................$6,000 $6,500 $8,000

ROLEX,17J., center sec., RF#9659, c.1960
14k $600 $750 $1,000

ROLEX,17J., "Chronometer", RF# 4222, Ca.1945
18k $900 $1,000 $1,400

ROLEX, 19J., RF # 8443 , c.1965
14k $700 $800 $1,100

ROLEX, 17J., "Precision", fancy lugs,
9k $500 $600 $800

ROLEX, 17 jewels, ''Precision''
18k $900 $1,000 $1,200

Wrist Watches listed in this section are priced at the collectable
fair market **retail** level as **complete** watches having an original
gold-filled case and stainless steel back, also with original dial,
leather watch band, and the entire original movement in good
working order with no repairs needed.

⊕ Some grades are not included. Their values can be
determined by comparing with **similar** age, size, metal
content, style, grades, or models such as **time only**,
chronograph, repeater etc. listed.

ROLEX, 15 jewels, enamel dial, wire lugs
9k $800 $950 $1,250

ROLEX, 15j, early waterproof,"Tropical", (case within a case)
18k $2,200 $2,500 $3,200
silver $1,400 $1,600 $2,000

ROLEX, 17 jewels, RF # 9659 , Ca 1960s
14k C&B..........................$1,200 $1,300 $1,600

ROLEX, 17 jewels, ''Precision''
gold filled $300 $400 $650

ROLEX,15J., wire lugs, c.1925
silver $400 $500 $700

ROLEX, 15J., oyster, royal, 2 tone dial, c. 1930s
9k $1,200 $1,400 $1,700

ROLEX,15J.,"Aqua", RF # 2136, c.1928
s. steel $500 $600 $900

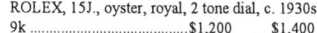

ROLEX, 15J., RF # 1071, oyster, ca. 1930
silver $800 $900 $1,100

ROLEX,15J., RF # 6071, c.1926
s. steel $500 $600 $900

ROLEX, 15 jewels, oyster, center sec.

18k	$3,400	$3,800	$4,500
14k	$2,200	$2,500	$3,200
9k	$1,400	$1,600	$2,000
silver	$1,000	$1,200	$1,500
s. steel	$600	$700	$1,000

ROLEX,15J., by OYSTER W. CO., c. 1927
s. steel $300 $400 $700

ROLEX, 17 jewels, RF # 678, oyster, c. 1934

18k	$3,200	$3,400	$4,000
14k	$2,200	$2,500	$3,000
9k	$1,400	$1,600	$2,000
silver	$800	$1,000	$1,500
s. steel	$600	$700	$1,000

ROLEX, 15 jewels, oyster, center sec, Ca. 1930

9K	$1,500	$1,700	$2,500
14K	$1,800	$2,200	$3,000

DIALS FOR MINT PRICES MUST BE ALL <u>ORIGINAL</u>.

ROLEX, 17 jewels, oyster, center sec.
18k	$2,500	$2,700	$3,200
14k	$2,000	$2,200	$2,600
9k	$1,400	$1,500	$1,800
s. steel	$600	$700	$1,000

ROLEX, 17 jewels, graduated bezel, c. 1928
silver $900 $1,000 $1,300

ROLEX, 18J., note dial top half & bottom, RF # 3139
s. steel $600 $725 $1,200

ROLEX,17J., RF # 4647, c.1948
s. steel $600 $700 $1,000

ROLEX, 18J., Viceroy, center sec. ca. 1937
s. steel $600 $700 $1,000

ROLEX,17J., RF # 4647, 2 tone dial, c.1943
s. steel $550 $650 $950

ROLEX,17J., RF # 3665, enamel dial, Ca.1930
s. steel $600 $800 $1,200

ROLEX, 17 jewels, oyster, RF # 4547
s. steel $650 $700 $1,000

🕐 Pricing in this Guide are fair market price for **COMPLETE** watches which are reflected from the **"<u>NAWCC</u>"** National and regional shows.

DIALS FOR MINT PRICES MUST BE ALL <u>ORIGINAL</u>.

ROLEX, 17 jewels, oyster, c. 1930s
18k $2,800 $3,000 $3,600
14k $2,200 $2,400 $2,800

ROLEX,17J., "Observatory", RF # 3386, c.1940
gold filled..............................$700 $800 $1,000

ROLEX,17J., Viceroy, RF # 3116, c.1942
14k $2,000 $2,200 $2,600

ROLEX, 17 jewels, oyster, cushion, 2 tone, c. 1943
14k & s. steel $1,400 $1,600 $2,000

🕐 Pricing in this Guide are fair market price for **COMPLETE** watches which are reflected from the "**NAWCC**" National and regional shows.

DIALS FOR MINT PRICES MUST BE ALL ~~ORIGINAL~~.

ROLEX,17J., "Viceroy", RF # 3359, c.1943
14k & s. steel......................$1,300 $1,500 $2,000

ROLEX, 17 jewels, oyster, extra prima "Viceroy"
18k $2,500 $2,800 $3,500

ROLEX, 26 jewels, "Viceroy", center sec.
9k $1,500 $1,700 $2,200

ROLEX,17J., "Skyrocket", Ca.1944
gold filled $500 $600 $800

DIALS FOR MINT PRICES MUST BE ALL ~~ORIGINAL~~.

🕐 Some grades are not included. Their values can be determined by comparing with **similar** age, size, metal content, style, grades, or models such as **time only**, chronograph, repeater etc. listed.

ROLEX,17J., 28mm, small one button chronog., RF # 2303
9k .... ★ ★ ★$20,000 $22,000 $25,000

ROLEX,17J., Chronograph, triple date & **moon-phases**,
about **12 made**, RF# 8180 & RF# 2508, Valjoux cal. 72C,
This chronograph is being FAKED so beware.
18k .... ★ ★ ★ ★ $65,000 $70,000 $85,000

ROLEX,17J., split second chronog., RF # 4113, **15 examples**, large 43mm, Valjoux caliber 55 VBR, Ca.1943
s. steel .... ★ ★ ★ ★ $30,000 $35,000 $50,000

ROLEX, 17 J., chronog., 70-made, flat, tachometer, "Gabus",
RF # 8206,c.1940s
18k .... ★ ★ ★$15,000 $18,000 $25,000

ROLEX, 17J., one button chronog. 2 reg., curved back
18k .... ★ ★ ★$25,000 $27,000 $32,000

ROLEX, 17 J., chronog., center lugs, RF#3233, c. 1940s
18k $8,000 $9,000 $11,000
14k $5,000 $5,500 $7,000
9k $3,000 $3,500 $4,500
s. steel $2,500 $2,800 $3,500

🕐 **Note: Rolex chronographs must have original dial, deduct 30% for refinished dial.**

ROLEX,17J., RF # 3055 , Antimagnetique, 200 made, c.1956
18k $12,000 $14,000 $18,000

ROLEX, 17 jewels, chronog., mid-sized, c. 1950s
18k $8,000 $8,500 $10,000
14k $7,000 $7,500 $9,000

ROLEX,17J., Valjoux cal.23, RF # 4062, c.1940
18k $6,000 $6,500 $8,000

ROLEX, 17 jewels, chronog., 3 reg. oyster, RF # 6238
s. steel $5,000 $5,200 $6,000

ROLEX, 17J., chronog., 3 reg., RF # 6234, Valjoux 72bc
s. steel $5,000 $5,500 $7,000
14k $9,000 $10,000 $14,000

ROLEX,17J., triple date, RF # 4767, c.1948
Beware of **FAKES**
s. steel .... ★ ★$12,000 $14,000 $18,000

ROLEX, 17J., chronog., triple-date, diamond style chapter,
RF # 6036, about 175 made in Y. gold , 144 made pink gold
18k $24,000 $26,000 $30,000
14k $20,000 $22,000 $24,000
s. steel $13,000 $15,000 $18,000

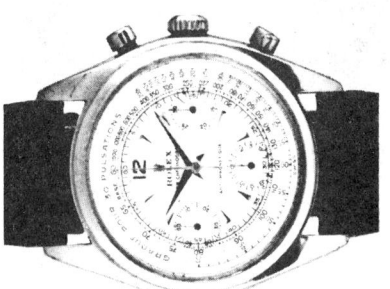

ROLEX, 17J., **pulsation**, 3 reg., RF # 6234, Ca. 1960
s. steel $6,000 $7,000 $10,000

ROLEX,17J., Antimagnetic chronog., 3 reg., RF # 6034,
about 45 made, Ca.1950s
18k .... ★ ★ ★$12,000 $13,000 $16,000

Wrist Watches listed in this section are priced at the collectable
fair market **retail** level as **complete** watches having an original
gold-filled case and stainless steel back, also with original dial,
leather watch band, and the entire original movement in good
working order with no repairs needed.

ROLEX, 17J., RF # 6238, 3 reg., c. 1950s, rect. markers
18k $8,000 $9,000 $11,000

ROLEX,17J., exotic dial, RF#6239, Valjoux 727, c.1965
"PAUL NEWMAN", (_beware of reproduction dials_)
s. steel $9,000 $10,000 $12,000

ROLEX, 17J., RF # 4768, 3 reg., date, tear drop lugs, 1950s
18k $9,000 $10,000 $12,000
14k $7,000 $8,000 $10,000
s. steel $4,000 $4,500 $6,000

ROLEX,17J., "Daytona", RF#6263, c.1978
s. steel $5,500 $6,000 $7,000

ROLEX, 17J., triple-date, 3 reg., square markers
s. steel .... ★★★$12,000 $14,000 $18,000

ROLEX,17J., screw down pusher 1st used 1976, RF#6265,
s. steel $5,500 $6,000 $7,000

ROLEX, 17J., Daytona, red outside chapter exotic dial
RF# 6241, **"PAUL NEWMAN"**
s. steel $8,000 $9,000 $12,000

ROLEX, 17 jewels, RF # 3997, chronog., Ca. 1940
s . steel $2,000 $2,400 $3,000

ROLEX, 17 J., tachometer, 3 reg., RF # 6239, c.1960s
18k $10,000 $11,000 $14,000
14k $9,000 $10,000 $12,000
s. steel $4,800 $5,200 $6,000

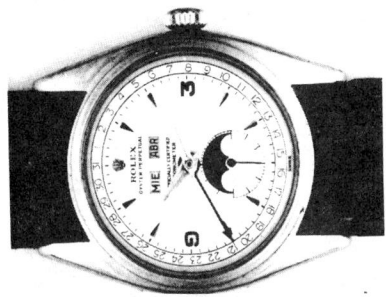

ROLEX,17J., triple-date, moon ph., RF # 8171, **1,000 made**
18k .... ★★★$12,000 $14,000 $18,000
14k .... ★★★$9,000 $10,000 $12,000
s. steel .... ★★★$6,000 $7,000 $9,000

★ **FAKE** ★
ROLEX on dial & movement, day-date-month, moon ph.

ROLEX,17J., STARS on dial, triple date, RF # 6062, Ca.1945
18k Pink Gold..... ★★★★$25,000 $30,000 $40,000
18k .... ★★★★$22,000 $28,000 $36,000

ROLEX,17J., day-date-month, moon ph., RF # 6062,c.1945
18k .... ★★★$20,000 $25,000 $33,000

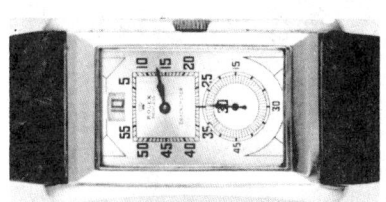

ROLEX, 15J., jumping hr., duo dial, RF # 4402 &
RF # 1491, Ca. 1930s
platinum............................$14,000 $16,000 $19,000
18k $12,000 $14,000 $16,000
14k $10,000 $11,000 $13,000
9k $7,000 $8,000 $10,000
silver $6,000 $7,000 $9,000
gold filled $4,000 $5,000 $7,000
s. steel $5,000 $6,000 $8,000

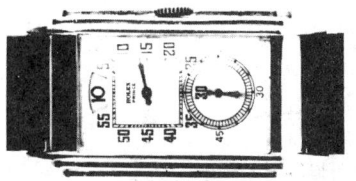

ROLEX,17J.,jump hr., duo dial, stepped case, RF# 4376
18k 2 tone $15,000 $18,000 $22,000
18k $12,000 $13,000 $16,000
14k $9,000 $10,000 $13,000
9k.....................................$7,000 $8,000 $11,000
s. steel $6,000 $7,000 $9,000

ROLEX, 17 jewels, ''Prince,'' duo dial, RF#1490
18k C&B.............................$5,000 $6,000 $8,000

🕐 Pricing in this Guide are fair market price for **COMPLETE**
watches which are reflected from the "<u>**NAWCC**</u>" National and
regional shows.

DIALS FOR MINT PRICES MUST BE ALL <u>ORIGINAL</u>.

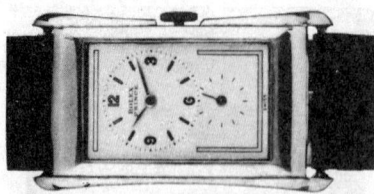

ROLEX, 17 jewels, RF # 1490, flared, duo dial, c. 1930s
9k $3,700 $4,250 $5,500

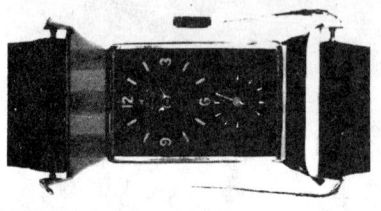

ROLEX, 17J., RF # 2245 & RF # 1768, 2 tone case,
   beware of **FAKES**
18k $12,000 $14,000 $19,000

ROLEX, 17 jewels, "Prince," duo dial, stepped case
18k $6,200 $7,200 $9,000
14k $4,700 $5,200 $7,000
9k $3,700 $4,200 $5,500
silver $3,700 $4,200 $5,500
s. steel $3,200 $3,700 $5,000
gold filled............................$2,500 $2,800 $3,500

ROLEX, 17J., RF # 971, 2 tone stripes, Adj. to 6 pos.
   beware of **FAKES**
18k $12,000 $14,000 $20,000
14k $10,000 $11,000 $15,000
9k $7,000 $8,000 $10,000

ROLEX, 15 jewels, RF # 971, flared, duo dial, Adj. to 6 pos.
9k $3,800 $4,200 $5,000

ROLEX, 15 jewels, RF # 971, "Prince," duo dial, c. 1930s
s. steel $3,500 $4,000 $5,000

ROLEX, 15 J., RF # 1862, chronometer, duo dial, c. 1930s
s. steel $3,000 $3,500 $4,500

ROLEX, 15 J., RF # 1527, "Railway," stepped case, 1930s
18k 2 tone $8,000 $9,000 $12,000
18k $7,000 $8,000 $10,000
14k 2 tone $6,000 $7,000 $9,000
14k $5,000 $6,000 $8,000
9k 2 tone $5,000 $6,000 $8,000
9k $4,000 $4,500 $5,500
s. steel $4,000 $4,500 $5,500

ROLEX, 15 J., RF # 3361, "Prince," center sec., c. 1930s
18k $8,000 $10,000 $14,000

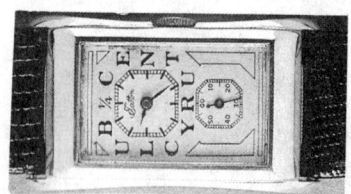

ROLEX, 15 jewels, 1/4 century club, RF # 2541
14k $4,500 $5,500 $7,500

🕐 Pricing in this Guide are fair market price for **COMPLETE** watches which are reflected from the "**NAWCC**" National and regional shows.

DIALS FOR MINT PRICES MUST BE ALL <u>ORIGINAL</u>.

ROLEX, 15 jewels, RF # 3937, 1/4 century club,
14k $5,000 $6,000 $8,000

ROLEX, 15 jewels, "Prince," RF # 1343, c. 1935
platinum $12,000 $14,000 $20,000
18k $6,000 $7,000 $9,000
14k $5,000 $5,500 $6,500
gold filled..........................$2,000 $2,500 $3,500

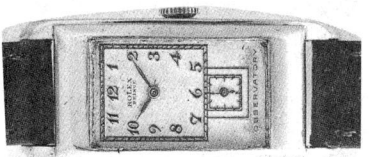

ROLEX, 17J., RF # 1615, "Observatory", c.1938
gold filled..........................$1,200 $1,400 $2,000

ROLEX, 15 jewels, stepped case, RF # 1527
18k $8,000 $9,000 $12,000

ROLEX, 17J., date, mid size,
s. steel $400 $450 $600

🕐 Pricing in this Guide are fair market price for **COMPLETE**
watches which are reflected from the "**NAWCC**" National and
regional shows.

DIALS FOR MINT PRICES MUST BE ALL <u>ORIGINAL</u>.

ROLEX, 25J., RF # 6604 , date, c.1958
s. steel $500 $550 $700

ROLEX, 25J., RF # 1500 , date, c.1963
s. steel $575 $650 $850

ROLEX, 26J., RF # 6694 , date, c.1971
s. steel $350 $425 $600

ROLEX, 17J., RF # 6094 , date, Ca.1951
s. steel $350 $425 $600

ROLEX, 26J., RF # 1501 , c.1970
s. steel $550 $650 $850

ROLEX, 17 jewels, oyster, perpetual, date, ca.1950s
14k $1,700 $1,900 $2,400

ROLEX,25J., date, **marked gold bezel**, 2 tone case, RF#6305
s. steel/gold bezel $600 $800 $1,100

ROLEX, 25J., **"Ovettone"**, RF # 6105, auto wind, oyster,
note thin milled bezel, Ca.1953
14k Pink......................★★$2,800 $3,100 $4,000
14k ....★★$2,500 $2,800 $3,700

ROLEX, 17J., date, RF # 6964, ca.1953
s. steel $400 $500 $700

ROLEX, 25J., oyster, perpetual, date, **"Ovettone"**,
note thin milled bezel, RF # 4467, Ca. 1950s
18k Pink......................★★$3,300 $3,800 $4,600
18k ....★★$3,000 $3,500 $4,200

ROLEX, 26J., 2 tone, date just, RF # 1601, Ca.1968
s. steel / gold $700 $800 $1,000

ROLEX, 17 jewels, ''Speed King''
14k $800 $950 $1,200
s. steel $350 $500 $700

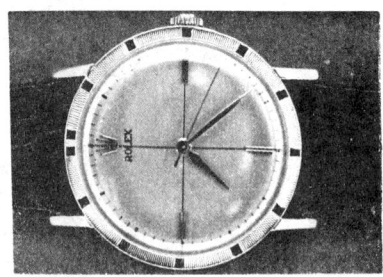

ROLEX, 17 jewels, ref. #4325
14k $600 $700 $850

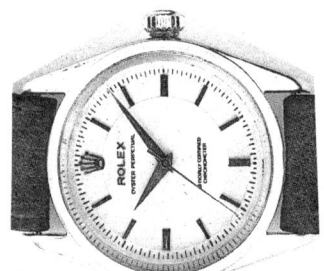

ROLEX, 19-25J., RF # 6634, center sec.,gold & s. steel 2
tone case, Ca. 1952
Gold & steel............................$600 $700 $900

ROLEX, 18J., RF # 6075, 2 tone, Ca. 1951
s. steel & 14k.......................$1,000 $1,100 $1,400

ROLEX, 17J., RF # 6029, marked bezel, rose gold, c.1940s
18k $2,000 $2,200 $2,600

ROLEX, 17J., RF # 6223, oyster, manual wind, Ca. 1954
18k $1,000 $1,200 $1,500
14k $900 $1,000 $1,400
9k $550 $700 $1,000
gold filled..............................$400 $450 $700
s. steel $350 $400 $650

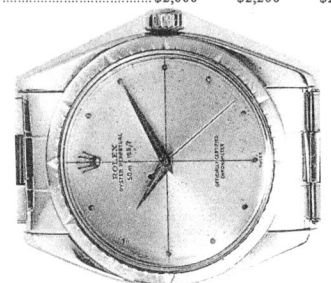

ROLEX, 17J., RF # 6582, marked bezel 2 tone, ca. 1955
gold & s. steel........................$550 $700 $900

ROLEX, 25J., RF # 6202, marked bezel, "Turnograph"
ca.1962
s.steel $1,000 $1,200 $1,800
14k & s.steel.......................$1,400 $1,600 $2,200

ROLEX, 17J., center sec., precision, RF # 6422
s. steel $400 $450 $600

ROLEX, 26J., RF # 1002, c.1965
14k $1,300 $1,400 $1,800

ROLEX, 25J., RF # 5502 , Ca. 1955
s. steel $500 $600 $800

ROLEX, 17J., RF # 6085, marked bezel, Ca. 1951
14k $1,300 $1,400 $1,800

ROLEX, 16J., RF # 6082 , c.1950
s. steel $350 $400 $550

ROLEX, 25J., RF # 6565 , c.1958
s. steel $600 $700 $1,000

ROLEX, 25J., RF # 1025, c.1960
14k $1,200 $1,500 $1,900

ROLEX, 25J., RF # 6024, c.1953
s. steel $400 $450 $600

ROLEX, 17J., RF # 6424, c.1965
s. steel $400 $500 $700

ROLEX, 17J., RF # 2010 , Ca. 1960
s. steel $400 $500 $650

ROLEX, 26J., perpetual oyster, **recent**
s. steel $800 $900 $1,200

ROLEX, 17J., RF # 6284 , c.1955
18k $1,800 $2,000 $2,500

ROLEX, 25J.,RF # 6098 , star dial, c.1956
18k rose $2,000 $2,500 $3,200

ROLEX, 17J., RF # 6024 , c.1952
s. steel $450 $500 $650

ROLEX, 25J., "Air King", RF#5500, c.1962
s. steel $500 $600 $800

ROLEX, 26J., RF # 1005 , c.1964
14k & S.S...............................$600 $700 $1,000

ROLEX, 25J., "Air King",RF # 5504, c.1959
s. steel $400 $500 $700

ROLEX, 17J., RF#6084, c.1951
14k $1,400 $1,500 $1,800

ROLEX, 25J., RF#6568, c.1956
s. steel $450 $500 $700

ROLEX, 25J., RF#6084, textured dial, c.1953
14k $1,600 $1,800 $2,400

ROLEX, 18J., RF#8405, c.1950
18k $900 $1,000 $1,300

ROLEX, 25J., RF#6564, c.1955
s. steel $450 $500 $700

ROLEX, 25J., RF # 6567, center sec., Ca. 1960
14k $800 $900 $1,200

ROLEX, 25J., marked bezel, RF#6581, c.1954
14k $1,600 $1,800 $2,200

🕐 Pricing in this Guide are fair market price for **COMPLETE** watches which are reflected from the "**NAWCC**" National and regional shows.

DIALS FOR MINT PRICES MUST BE ALL <u>ORIGINAL</u>.

ROLEX, 18J.,RF # 8952, center sec., Ca. 1950s
14k $700 $800 $1,100

ROLEX,17J., RF # 4478, 9 diamonds, Ca.1948
18k $1,300 $1,500 $2,000

ROLEX, 25 jewels, "Bomb'e", RF # 6102, c.1953
14k $1,600 $1,800 $2,200

ROLEX, 25J., "Bomb'e"12 diamond dial, RF # 1030, c.1958
s. steel $900 $1,000 $1,500

ROLEX, 26 jewels, "Bomb'e", RF # 6102, c. 1950
18k $2,200 $2,400 $3,000

ROLEX, 17J., Linz 1877, oyster, "Bomb'e", c. 1950s
18k $2,200 $2,400 $3,000

ROLEX, 19 J., RF # 6092, "Bomb'e", center sec., c. 1950s
18k $2,200 $2,400 $3,000
18k Pink...........................$2,600 $2,800 $3,500
14k $1,600 $1,800 $2,200
14k Pink...........................$1,800 $2,000 $2,500
9k $1,000 $1,200 $1,400
s. steel $600 $700 $1,000

ROLEX, 26 jewels, "Bomb'e", RF # 6590, c. 1950
14k $1,600 $1,800 $2,200

ROLEX, 26J., RF # 1011, "Bomb'e", center sec., Ca. 1960
14k $1,500 $1,600 $1,800

ROLEX,17J., RF # 4365, Oyster, Ca.1951
s.steel (redone dial) $500 $600 $800

ROLEX,15J., RF # 2495, "Extra-Prima", Ca.1937
9k enamel dial $600 $800 $1,100
9k $400 $500 $700

ROLEX,17J., RF # 5020, 2 tone, Ca.1943
14k & s. steel (redone dial) ... $700 $800 $900

ROLEX,17J., RF # 6694, Oyster, Date, "Honey Comb"
textured dial, Ca.1952
s. steel $500 $600 $800

ROLEX,15J., RF # 4377, "Oyster", Ca.1944
s. steel $900 $1,000 $1,400

ROLEX,17J., RF # 6266, Oyster, Date Ca.1937
s. steel $500 $600 $800

ROLEX,17J., RF # 4392, Ca.1948
s. steel $1,000 $1,200 $1,700

ROLEX,25J., RF # 1550, Oyster Perpetual, Ca.1960
s. steel $500 $600 $800

DIALS FOR MINT PRICES MUST BE ALL <u>ORIGINAL</u>.

ROLEX,17J., RF # 3745, Precision, Ca.1949
18k $1,000 $1,200 $1,600

ROLEX,26J., RF # 6627, Oyster, date, Ca.1971
18k $1,500 $1,700 $2,200

ROLEX 18J., RF # 4891, Chronometer, Ca.1957
18k $1,200 $1,400 $1,800

ROLEX,28J., RF # 6800, Oyster, date-just, Ca.1982
s. steel $1,000 $1,200 $1,500

ROLEX,25J., RF # 6611, day date, Ca.1956
18k $3,000 $3,200 $3,700

ROLEX,26J., RF # 1600, Oyster, date-just, Ca.1987
s. steel $1,000 $1,200 $1,500

ROLEX,17J., RF # 9083, Precision, Ca.1955
s. steel $300 $400 $600

ROLEX,25J., RF # 6552, Oyster, Chronometer, Ca.1958
s. steel $500 $600 $850

ROLEX, 17 jewels, center sec., gold bezel
18k & s. steel $600 $700 $900

ROLEX, 26J., bubble back, hooded lugs, rf#3595
18k $8,000 $9,000 $11,000
14k $6,000 $6,500 $7,500
9k : $3,500 $4,000 $5,000
s. steel & gold $2,000 $2,200 $2,800
s. steel .... ★★★$12,000 $14,000 $16,000

ROLEX, 17 jewels, black dial, center sec., c. 1945
18k $2,000 $2,200 $2,600
14k $1,200 $1,500 $1,800
9k $1,000 $1,100 $1,400
s. steel $450 $525 $700

ROLEX, 17J., Pall Mall, manual wind, Ca. 1949
s. steel .... ★★$1,200 $1,500 $1,700
14k $600 $700 $900

ROLEX, 18J., RF # 6427, center sec. Ca. 1962
s. steel $450 $500 $650

ROLEX, 17J., "Royal Observatory" , RF#3121, c.1937
s. steel $500 $550 $700

ROLEX, 15J., RF # 3655, aux. sec. Ca. 1945
s. steel $450 $500 $650

ROLEX, 17J., Oyster Co., "Record", manual wind, c.1940
s. steel $300 $350 $600

🕐 Pricing in this Guide are fair market price for COMPLETE
watches which are reflected from the "NAWCC" National and
regional shows.

ROLEX, 17J., "Neptune", mid-size, manual wind, c.1939
gold filled...............................$300 $400 $600

ROLEX, 17J., RF # 2280, manual wind, c.1951
s. steel $500 $550 $625

ROLEX, 17J., RF # 6421, Speedking, Ca.1960
s. steel $400 $500 $700

ROLEX, 17J., Speedking, Oyster, RF # 6021, c.1953
index on bezel
s. steel $450 $500 $700

ROLEX, 17J., RF # 4302, 2 tone, Ca. 1944
gold filled & s. steel $600 $700 $900

ROLEX, 18J., RF # 3767, mid size, Ca.1940
s. steel $400 $475 $550

ROLEX, 26 jewels, bubble back, hooded lugs, 2 tone
18k & s. steel $6,000 $7,000 $9,000

ROLEX, 17J., mid size,RF # 3478, c.1940
gold filled $300 $350 $400
s. steel $300 $350 $400

ROLEX, 26 jewels, bubble back, hooded scalloped lugs
18k & s. steel $6,000 $7,000 $9,000

Some grades are not included. Their values can be
determined by comparing with **similar** age, size, metal
content, style, grades, or models such as **time only**,
chronograph, repeater etc. listed.

ROLEX, 17J., "Speed King", RF#4220, c.1945
s. steel $400 $500 $700

ROLEX, 17J., "Speed King", RF#6056, c.1952
s. steel $400 $500 $600

ROLEX, 17J., mid size,RF#6066, c.1951
s. steel $400 $500 $700

ROLEX, 17J., mid size, RF#6466, c.1957
s. steel $400 $500 $700

ROLEX, 18J., "Royal", mid size, aux. sec.
s. steel $450 $550 $750

ROLEX, 18J., "Speed King", mid size, center sec.
s. steel $400 $500 $700

ROLEX, 18J., RF # 3065, B.B., hooded 2 tone yellow gold
14k Gold & steel $2,000 $2,500 $3,500

ROLEX, 18J., RF # 2319, B.B., hooded 2 tone rose gold
14k Gold & steel $2,500 $3,000 $4,000

Wrist Watches listed in this section are priced at the collectable fair market **retail** level as **complete** watches having an original gold-filled case and stainless steel back, also with original dial, leather watch band, and the entire original movement in good working order with no repairs needed.

🕐 Pricing in this Guide are fair market price for **COMPLETE** watches which are reflected from the "**NAWCC**" National and regional shows.

DIALS FOR MINT PRICES MUST BE ALL ORIGINAL.

🕐 Some grades are not included. Their values can be determined by comparing with **similar** age, size, metal content, style, grades, or models such as **time only**, chronograph, repeater etc. listed.

ROLEX, 18J., B.B., center sec.
s. steel $1,200 $1,400 $1,800

ROLEX, 18J., B.B., not 2 tone, RF # 3131
14k $2,800 $3,200 $3,800

ROLEX, 18J., RF # 3696, B.B., oyster perpetual, Ca. 1948
9K...$2,200 $2,400 $2,800

ROLEX, 25J., RF # 2764, B.B., marked bezel, 2 tone, c.1945
14k & s.steel. $1,400 $1,600 $2,000

⊕ Some grades are not included. Their values can be
determined by comparing with similar age, size, metal
content, style, grades, or models such as time only,
chronograph, repeater etc. listed.

ROLEX, 18J., RF # 2764, B.B., marked bezel,
18k $3,500 $4,000 $5,000

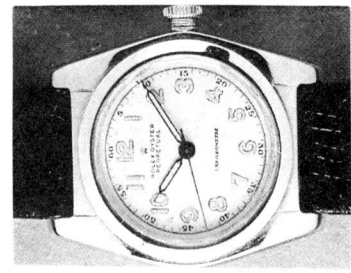

ROLEX, 18J., B.B., chronometer, RF # 3131, cal#600
14k $2,800 $3,200 $3,800
s. steel $1,200 $1,400 $1,800

ROLEX, 18J., B.B., cal. # 600, aux. sec., ca. 1945
s. steel $1,200 $1,400 $1,800

ROLEX, 18J., B.B., self winding on dial
14k $2,800 $3,200 $3,800

ROLEX, 17J., BB,RF # 6011, c.1948
14k $3,000 $3,200 $3,800

ROLEX, 25J., RF # 6585, index on bezel, c.1958
14k $900 $1,000 $1,400

ROLEX, 17J., BB,RF # 3133, tu-tone, c.1940
14k & s.steel. $1,600 $1,800 $2,200

ROLEX, 26J., RF # 1007, Chronometer Oyster, index on bezel, c.1965
14k $900 $1,000 $1,400

ROLEX, 18J., BB, RF # 5050, Oyster, c.1945
9k $2,000 $2,200 $2,800

ROLEX, 17J., RF # 5015, BB, marked bezel, c.1949
s. steel $1,200 $1,400 $1,800

ROLEX, 17J., center sec, cal.1530, c.1955
gold filled..............................$400 $500 $700

🕐 Pricing in this Guide are fair market price for **COMPLETE** watches which are reflected from the "**NAWCC**" National and regional shows.
DIALS FOR MINT PRICES MUST BE ALL ORIGINAL.

ROLEX, 18J., B.B., center sec. ca. 1940s
14k $3,000 $3,200 $3,800

ROLEX, 18J., RF # 3130, B.B.,ca. 1945
14k $3,000 $3,200 $3,800

ROLEX, 26J., bubble back, graduated bezel , aux. sec.
14k $3,000 $3,200 $3,800

ROLEX, 19 jewels, bubble back, 2 tone
18k & s. steel $1,800 $2,000 $2,500

ROLEX, 26 jewels, bubble back, Arabic & Roman no.'s
14k $3,000 $3,500 $4,000

Wrist Watches listed in this section are priced at the collectable fair market **retail** level as **complete** watches having an
original gold-filled case and stainless steel back, also with
original dial, leather watch band, and the entire original movement in good working order with no repairs needed.

ROLEX, 26 J., bubble back, aux. sec., RF # 3458, Ca. 1940s

18k	$3,500	$4,000	$5,000
14k	$3,000	$3,200	$3,800
9k	$2,000	$2,200	$2,800
gold filled	$1,100	$1,200	$1,500
s. steel	$1,200	$1,400	$1,800

ROLEX, 26 J., bubble back, RF # 2940, c. 1940s

18k	$3,500	$4,000	$5,000
14k	$3,000	$3,200	$3,800
9k	$2,000	$2,200	$2,800
gold filled	$1,100	$1,200	$1,500
s. steel	$1,200	$1,400	$1,800

ROLEX, 26 J., bubble back, mercedes hands, c. 1930s

18k	$3,500	$4,000	$5,000
14k	$3,000	$3,200	$3,800
9k	$2,000	$2,200	$2,800
gold filled	$1,100	$1,200	$1,500
s. steel	$1,200	$1,400	$1,800

⊕ Some grades are not included. Their values can be
determined by comparing with **similar** age, size, metal
content, style, grades, or models such as **time only**,
chronograph, repeater etc. listed.

ROLEX, 26J., bubble back, marked bezel, c. 1940s

18k	$3,500	$4,000	$5,000
14k	$3,000	$3,200	$3,800
9k	$2,000	$2,200	$2,800
gold filled	$1,100	$1,200	$1,500
s. steel	$1,200	$1,400	$1,800

ROLEX, 26 jewels, bubble back, c. 1940s

| s. steel | $1,200 | $1,400 | $1,800 |

ROLEX, 26 jewels, bubble back, c. 1940s

| 14k | $2,800 | $3,200 | $3,800 |

ROLEX, 19 jewels, bubble back, center sec., rf#1453

18k	$3,500	$4,000	$5,000
14k	$2,800	$3,200	$3,800
s. steel	$1,200	$1,400	$1,800

ROLEX, 25J., RF # 6050, BB, Ca. 1949

| s. steel | $1,200 | $1,400 | $1,800 |

ROLEX, 26 jewels, bubble back

| 18k | $3,500 | $4,000 | $5,000 |
| s. steel | $1,200 | $1,400 | $1,800 |

ROLEX, 26 jewels, RF# 1018, Oyster, Chronometer, c. 1967

| s. steel | $600 | $700 | $900 |

ROLEX, 26 jewels, bubble back, c. 1945

| 14k | $2,800 | $3,200 | $3,800 |

ROLEX, 26 jewels, bubble back, c. 1940s
18k $3,700 $4,000 $5,000
14k $2,800 $3,200 $3,800
s. steel $1,200 $1,400 $1,800

ROLEX, 18 jewels, bubble back, RF # 2940, c. 1940s
s. steel $1,200 $1,400 $1,800

ROLEX, 18 jewels, bubble back, c. 1942
18k $3,700 $4,000 $5,000
14k $2,800 $3,200 $3,800
s. steel $1,200 $1,400 $1,800

ROLEX, 18 jewels, bubble back, original gold & s. steel band
14k & s. steel C&B..............$2,600 $2,800 $3,500

ROLEX, 18 J., RF # 4467, date, left hand winds at 9 o'clock
s. steel .... ★$1,800 $2,000 $2,500

ROLEX, 30 jewels, "Presidential," 44 diamonds on dial &
bezel, day-date, oyster, perpetual, RF # 1803
18k C&B (non-Quick) $6,500 $7,000 $8,000

ROLEX, 26 jewels, day-date, 10 diamond dial, **old model**
RF # 1803
18k C&B........................... $4,000 $4,500 $5,800
18k (w) $4,500 $5,000 $6,200

ROLEX, 26 jewels, "Presidential," diamond dial, day-date,
perpetual, oyster, RF # 1804, quick set
18k C&B............................. $6,500 $6,800 $7,500

ROLEX, 30 jewels, "Presidential," (Tridor), oyster, daydate, diamond dial, perpetual, oyster,

18k (y & w) single quick.....	$6,500	$7,000	$7,800
18k (y & w) double quick ...	$7,000	$7,500	$8,800

ROLEX, 26 Jewels, "Presidential," day-date, Single Quick set model RF # 1803, double quick-set RF# 1823

18kC&B double quick-set...	$7,000	$7,500	$8,500
18k C&B single quick-set...	$6,000	$6,300	$7,000
18k Single Quick................	$4,000	$4,300	$5,000

ROLEX, 30J., "Presidential," bark finish, RF # 1803, c.1971
18k C&B(non quick)...........$5,500 $5,800 $6,500

ROLEX, 26J., "Presidential," day-date, perpetual, note textured dial, **Pink gold**, RF#1803 old model
18k C & B $5,000 $5,500 $6,500

ROLEX, 30 jewels, "Presidential," day-date, perpetual, oyster, diamond bezel, bark finish, RF # 1807
18k C&B(quick set).............$7,000 $7,500 $8,500

ROLEX, quartz, RF # 1901
diamond dial & diamond bezel add $1,000-$1,200
18k $5,000 $5,500 $6,500

○ Pricing in this Guide are fair market price for **COMPLETE** watches which are reflected from the **"NAWCC"** National and regional shows.

DIALS FOR MINT PRICES MUST BE ALL ORIGINAL.

ROLEX, 26 Jewels, RF# 1503, index bezel, date, Ca. 1973
14k $2,200 $2,400 $2,800

ROLEX, 26 J., jubilee band, 10 diamond dial, date just
18k C&B quick set $4,500 $5,000 $6,000
14k C&B non quick.............$2,200 $2,500 $3,500
18K & s. steel C&B quick...$2,000 $2,200 $3,000

ROLEX, 26 jewels, date, oyster, mid-size
s. steel C&B............................$450 $600 $750

ROLEX, 26 jewels, date, perpetual, oyster
18k $2,000 $2,200 $2,600
14k $1,600 $1,800 $2,300
s. steel $550 $600 $750

ROLEX, 21J., RF # 6309, "Thunderbird", Ca.1955
14k gold bezel, s.steel case........ $1,000 $1,100 $1,400

ROLEX, 26J., quick set, date, Oyster bracelet, c.1965
14k C&B.............................$2,400 $2,700 $3,200

ROLEX, 17J., RF#6426, manual wind, c.1961
s. steel $350 $450 $650

ROLEX, 21 jewels, date just, center sec., c. 1965
18k non quick set................$2,800 $3,000 $3,500

ROLEX, 26 J., sapphire crystal, perpetual, oyster, date just
18k $4,000 $4,500 $6,000
18k & s. steel $1,600 $1,800 $2,200
s. steel $800 $1,000 $1,400

ROLEX, 26J., perpetual, oyster, date, graduated bezel

14k	$2,600	$2,800	$3,200
s. steel	$700	$850	$1,200

ROLEX, 21 jewels, perpetual, oyster

18k	$1,800	$1,900	$2,300
18k & s. steel	$800	$900	$1,300
14k	$1,400	$1,500	$2,000
14k & s. steel	$700	$800	$1,200
s. steel	$600	$700	$1,000

ROLEX, 26 jewels, oyster, date-just, ref. #1625

18k & s. steel quick set	$2,200	$2,400	$3,200
14k & s. steel C&B non Q.	$1,200	$1,500	$1,900

ROLEX, 25J., **gold bezel**, ''Explorer,'' RF # 5504, Ca. 1959

s. steel & gold bezel	$2,000	$2,500	$3,500

ROLEX, 25 J., early Submariner, RF# 6538, Ca.1958
Note:This style watch worn by **007** Sean Connery (rf# 6538)

s. steel	$900	$1,000	$1,200

ROLEX, 26 jewels, ''Explorer,'' RF # 1016, perpetual, oyster

s. steel	$2,200	$2,500	$3,300

ROLEX, 21 jewels, perpetual, oyster date just, 2 tone

Gold & steel	$1,200	$1,300	$1,600

ROLEX, 17J., **''Luminor Panerai,''** Italian military diving, RF# 6151-1, Ca. **1940s**, Note: look for reproduction 1992

s. steel	$2,200	$2,300	$2,600

ROLEX, 26 jewels, "GMT-Master," perpetual, oyster, date
ruby & diamond dial, sapphire crystal
18k $5,500 $6,500 $8,000

ROLEX, 26 J., "Submariner," non quick set, RF # 5513
s. steel $1,000 $1,200 $1,600

ROLEX, 26 J., RF # 1671,"GMT-Master II," date
sapphire crystal, quick set
18k $5,000 $5,500 $7,000
s. steel $1,500 $1,800 $2,300

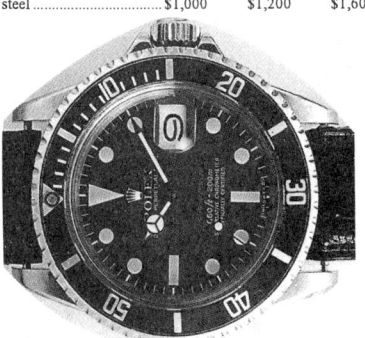

ROLEX, 26 J., "Submariner," perpetual, oyster, date
sapphire crystal, quick set
18k C&B.............................$8,000 $8,500 $11,500
18k & s. steel C&B $3,000 $3,200 $3,800
s. steel $1,600 $1,800 $2,400

ROLEX, 26 J., "GMT-Master", RF # 6542, c.1957
s. steel $1,400 $1,600 $2,500

Single quick set Presidential & Jubilee use 6 screws.
Double quick set Presidential & Jubilee use 7 screws.
Presidential or Jubilee gold link $250.00
Jubilee or Oyster s. steel link $40.00
Oyster gold link $200.00
ROLEX first used **HACK** system in Ca. 1972
ROLEX first used the Quick Set feature Ca. 1977
Sapphire crystals were added in U.S.A. Ca.1989= gents $100.
steel screw-on crown=$20., gold screw-on crown=$35.

ROLEX, 26J., "SEA-DWELLER," RF # 1665, 2,000 ft, date
all with Fliplock Band
s. steel plastic crystal...........$1,200 $1,300 $1,600
s. steel sapphire crystal $1,400 $1,600 $2,000
s.steel (Seadweller in red letters)$1,800 $2,200 $2,600

ROLEX factory only, mens diamond dials & bezels
Bezel 18k or platinum, W/44 full cut $3,000 $5,000
Dial W/8 brilliants & 2 baguetts for Oyster Perpetual &
DAY DATE.................................. $1,000 $1,600
Dial W/ 10 baguettes for Oyster Perpetual &
DAY DATE.................................. $2,000 $3,500
Dial W/ 10 brilliants for Oyster Perpetual &
DATEJUST or DATE.................... $700 $1,500

ROLEX, 21J., "SEA-DWELLER," up to 4,000 ft.,
RF # 1666, date, sapphire crystal, quick set
s. steel $1,800 $2,000 $2,400

ROLEX, 26 jewels, "Explorer II," RF # 1665, date
s. steel $2,200 $2,500 $3,300

ROLEX, 26 jewels, "Submariner," RF # 5512, 200M
s. steel non quick set............$1,000 $1,200 $1,600

Wrist Watches listed in this section are priced at the collectable
fair market **retail** level as **complete** watches having an original
gold-filled case and stainless steel back, also with original dial,
leather watch band, and the entire original movement in good
working order with no repairs needed.

ROLEX, 26J., "Submariner", RF # 6536,100M,c.1958
s. steel (no crown guard) ... ★ ★$1,200 $1,600 $2,000

ROLEX, 15J., ca. 1935
s. steel $800 $900 $1,200

ROLEX,18J., hooded lugs
14k $1,200 $1,400 $1,800

ROLEX, 18J., stepped case, 2 tone, ca. 1940s
G & steel............................$1,500 $1,700 $2,200

🕐 Pricing in this Guide are fair market price for **COMPLETE**
watches which are reflected from the "NAWCC" National and
regional shows.

DIALS FOR MINT PRICES MUST BE ALL ORIGINAL.

ROLEX, 15J., ca. 1937
s. steel $500 $600 $800

ROLEX, 15J., engraved case, c.1930
s. steel $800 $900 $1,200

ROLEX, 15J., GJS, c.1935
9K...$1,000 $1,200 $1,500

ROLEX, 18J., RF # 4029, c.1945
18k $1,000 $1,200 $1,500

ROLEX, 17J., RF # 619, ROSE gold,c.1948
18k Pink.............................$1,600 $1,800 $2,200

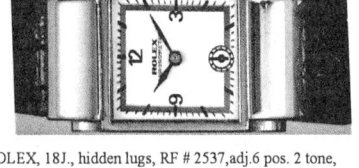

ROLEX, 18J., hidden lugs, RF # 2537,adj.6 pos. 2 tone,
Ca.1940s
gold & steel $2,500 $3,000 $4,000

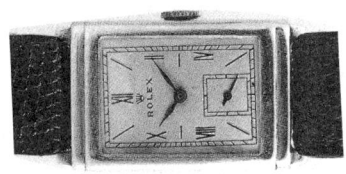

ROLEX,15J., stepped case, c.1938
18k $1,800 $2,200 $2,800

ROLEX, 17J., 2 tone, center lug "Standard", c.1940
14k & s.s...............................$700 $1,000 $1,400

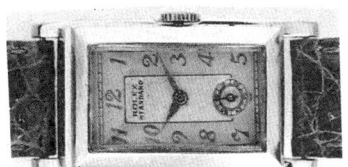

ROLEX, 17J., "Standard", c.1940 (no brass for mint)
gold filled $500 $600 $900

ROLEX, 15J., RF # 1878, beveled case, c.1927
s. steel $700 $800 $1,200

⊕ Some grades are not included. Their values can be
determined by comparing with **similar** age, size, metal
content, style, grades, or models such as **time only**,
chronograph, repeater etc. listed.

ROLEX, 17J., hidden lugs,
14k $1,500 $1,800 $2,200

ROLEX, 18J., round movement, ca. 1947
18k $1,000 $1,200 $1,500

ROLEX, 17J., "31 Victories",
18k $1,400 $1,600 $2,000

ROLEX, 17 jewels, RF # 8126, "Precision", manual wind
18k $1,000 $1,200 $1,800

ROLEX, 18J., fluted bezel, RF # 3737
18k $1,400 $1,600 $2,000

ROLEX, 17 jewels, curvex
18k C&B.............................$3,500 $4,500 $6,000

ROLEX, 18J., RF # 8094, 3 diamond dial , ca. 1940s
18kC&B.............................$1,500 $1,800 $2,200

ROLEX, 17 jewels, curved, c. 1940s
gold filled $400 $500 $700

ROLEX, 18J., ca. 1940s
s. steel $500 $600 $900

ROLEX, 17 jewels, "Ultra Prima," gold train
18k $1,500 $1,800 $2,400

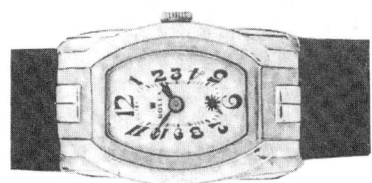

ROLEX, 17 jewels, hooded lugs, 2 tone
Pink & White gold...............$2,600 $2,800 $3,500

ROLEX, 17 jewels, "Precision," c. 1940s
18k $1,600 $1,800 $2,200
14k $1,000 $1,200 $1,700

ROLEX, 17 jewels, "Standard," c. 1939
gold filled.............................$1,000 $1,200 $1,500
14k ....:$2,500 $2,800 $3,800

ROLEX, 17 J. , "Precision," tank style, faceted bezel
18k $1,200 $1,500 $2,000

ROLEX, 15 jewels, hooded lugs, "Precision", Ca. 1945
14k $800 $900 $1,200

ROLEX, 17 jewels, extra flat, c. 1950s
18k $1,200 $1,500 $2,000

ROLEX, 17 J., RF # 9491, "Precision", Ca. 1958
18k $1,400 $1,600 $2,000

ROLEX, 21 jewels, perpetual, oyster, c. 1945
18k $2,500 $2,800 $3,500

Wrist Watches listed in this section are priced at the collectable
fair market **retail** level as **complete** watches having an original
gold-filled case and stainless steel back, also with original dial,
leather watch band, and the entire original movement in good
working order with no repairs needed.

ROLEX, 17J., RF # 3893, hidden lugs, Ca. 1943
14k $1,500 $1,700 $2,200

ROLEX, 17J., "Victory", Tudor, mid size, Ca. 1940
s. steel $400 $500 $700

ROLEX,17J., "Tudor", auto-wind, RF # 7909, c.1955
s. steel $125 $150 $200

ROLEX, Quartz, RF # 1563-3, 2 tone, "Tudor", Ca. 1993
18k & s. steel $300 $350 $425

ROLEX, 25J., "Tudor", RF # 7016, submariner, by ETA
s. steel $275 $325 $425

ROLEX, 17J., RF # 7528, "Tudor", ETA cal. 2438, Ca. 1968
s. steel $300 $350 $450

ROLEX, 25J., "Tudor", submariner, date, by ETA,
RF # 7610, Ca.1985
s. steel $300 $350 $475

ROLEX, "Tudor," (Prince)
s. steel $250 $300 $375

ROLEX, 25J., "Tudor", RF # 7809, auto-wind, c.1978
s. steel $100 $125 $175

ROLEX, 17J., "Tudor", auto-wind, c.1955
18k $400 $450 $550

ROLEX, "Tudor," chronog., date, RF # 9420,
s. steel model sold for $1,200 retail Ca. 1992
s. steel $800 $900 $1,250

ROLEX, 17J., "Tudor", SOLAR, RF # 4463, c.1955
s. steel $225 $250 $300

ROLEX, 25J., Prince Oyster Ranger II, Ca.1973
s. steel $250 $350 $550

ROLEX, 17J., "Tudor", RF # 2765, TURTLE, Zell Bros
Gold filled...............................$125 $150 $200

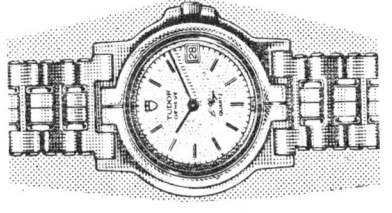

ROLEX, quartz, "Tudor," date, Ca. 1992
s. steel & gold plate...............$150 $200 $275

ROLEX, "Tudor," chronog., date, 165 ft., **auto-wind**
s. steel $900 $1,000 $1,250
Tiger Wood's model.........$1,200 $1,400 $1,800

ROLEX, 17J., **Drivers**,Ca. 1935
gold filled $700 $800 $1,100

ROLEX, 18J., lady's, Ca. 1948
18k $250 $325 $450
14k $200 $250 $400

ROLEX, 17J., ladies, "Oyster",
14k $1,000 $1,200 $1,500

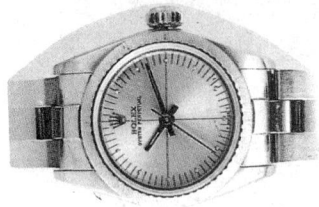

ROLEX, 29J., ladies, "Oyster", RF#67003
s. steel &14k,C&B...............$1,000 $1,100 $1,300

ROLEX, 17J., ladies, "Oyster", RF#4486, c.1957
14k & s.s.case $400 $450 $600

ROLEX, 17J., BB, ladies, "Oyster", c.1948
s. steel $600 $700 $900
s. steel & gold.........................$800 $1,100 $1,500
18k $1,800 $2,000 $2,300

ROLEX, 17J., RF # 1701, ladies, fancy lugs, Ca. 1950
14k $300 $400 $600

ROLEX, 17J., ladies, "Oyster", RF # 3492
s. steel....................................$300 $350 $500

ROLEX, 17J., ladies, RF # 4593, c.1954
s. steel....................................$200 $250 $350

ROLEX, 15J., 54 diamonds, 9k band 18k(w) case, c.1930
9k & 18k $1,600 $1,800 $2,500

ROLEX, 17J.,RF # 4554, "Precision", ladies, Ca. 1955
gold filled...............................$125 $150 $200

ROLEX, 15J., lady's, curved, ca.1925
9k..$250 $300 $400

ROLEX, 15J., lady's, center lugs, ca.1925
9k enamel dial.........................$400 $500 $650

ROLEX, 18J., lady's, ca. 1930s
18k $400 $500 $650

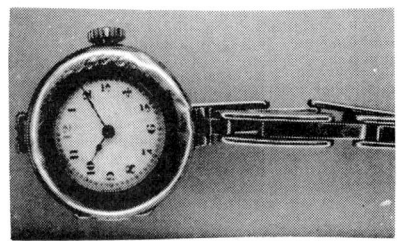

ROLEX, 15J., lady's, Ca.1925
18k band.................................$400 $450 $600

ROLEX, 18J., wire lugs, diamond bezel, ca. 1940s
18k(W)....................................$500 $550 $700

ROLEX, 18J., lady's,
14k $300 $350 $450

ROLEX, 18J., lady's,
14k(W) C&B $350 $450 $650

ROLEX, 18J., lady's, bubble back
18k pink $1,600 $1,800 $2,800
18k $1,400 $1,600 $2,600
s. steel & gold.........................$800 $1,100 $1,500

Wrist Watches listed in this section are priced at the collectable
fair market **retail** level as **complete** watches having an original
gold-filled case and stainless steel back, also with original dial,
leather watch band, and the entire original movement in good
working order with no repairs needed.

ROLEX, Oyster Perpetual Datejust, diamond dial &bezel
Sapphire Crystal, Quick Set
18k C&B $6,500 $7,000 $8,000

ROLEX, Oyster Perpetual Datejust, Plastic Crystal
18k C&B $4,000 $4,500 $5,500

ROLEX, Oyster Perpetual Datejust, Sapphire Crystal,
Quick Set
18k & s. steel $1,700 $2,100 $2,600

ROLEX, Oyster Perpetual Sapphire Crystal, no Date
18k & s. steel $1,200 $1,400 $1,800

6694

1705215

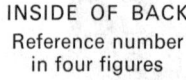

Reference number,
four figures engraved
between the lugs

INSIDE OF BACK
Reference number
in four figures

NON-OYSTER CASE

Serial number,
six or seven figures
engraved between the lugs

On recent OYSTER models the number is engraved
on the outside of the case between the lugs. Reference number of earlier models will be found engraved on the inside of the back of the case.

Reference number for NON-OYSTER models will
be found engraved on the inside of the back of the
case.

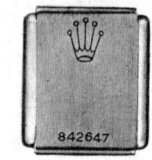

OUTSIDE OF BACK
Serial number
in six or seven figures

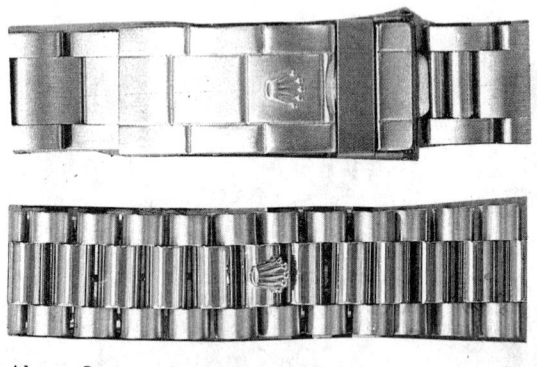

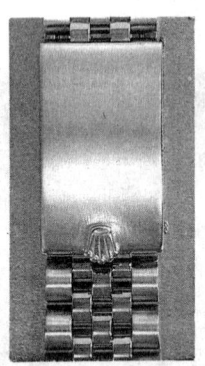

Above: Oyster style bracelet. **Below:** Presidential style band with hidden clasp.
Right: Jubilee style bracelet.

Current *double quick set* Presidential and Jubilee bracelets use **7 screws** for adjustment links.
The older models *Single quick set* Presidential and Jubilee bracelets use **6 screws** for adjustment links.

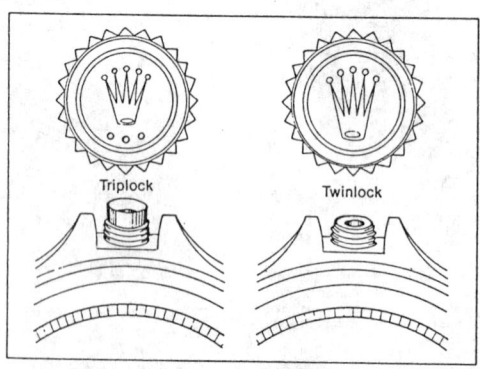

Triplock   Twinlock

ROLEX
MOVEMENT IDENTIFICATION

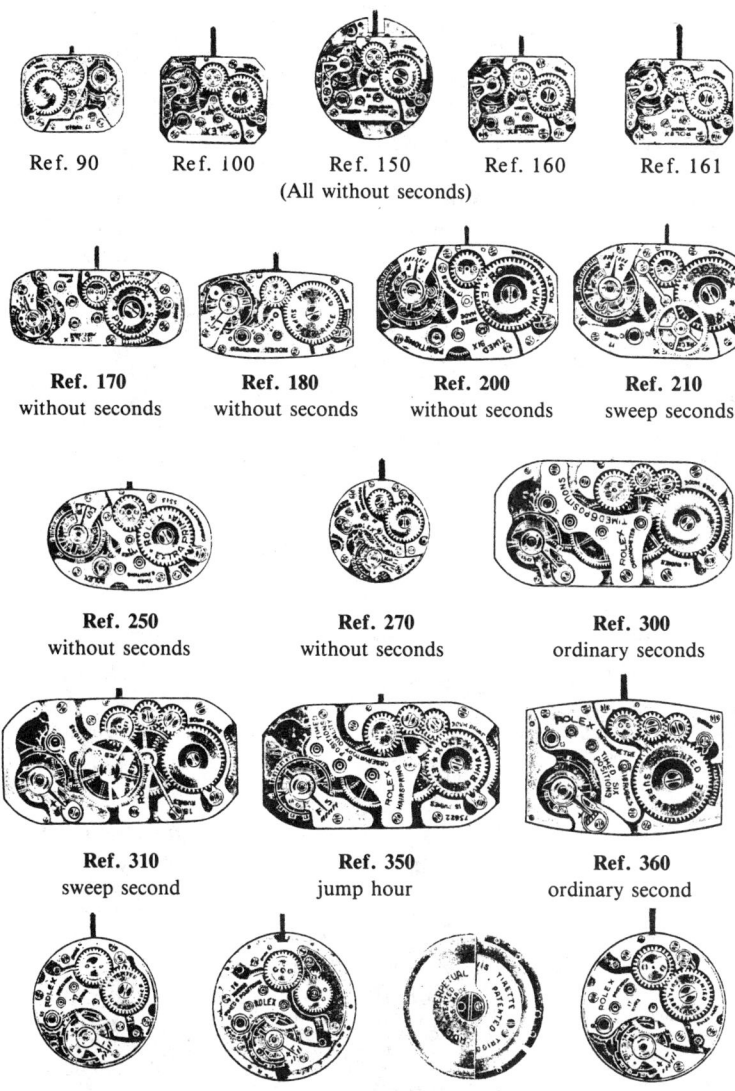

Ref. 90   Ref. 100   Ref. 150   Ref. 160   Ref. 161
(All without seconds)

Ref. 170   **Ref. 180**   **Ref. 200**   **Ref. 210**
without seconds   without seconds   without seconds   sweep seconds

Ref. 250   **Ref. 270**   **Ref. 300**
without seconds   without seconds   ordinary seconds

Ref. 310   **Ref. 350**   **Ref. 360**
sweep second   jump hour   ordinary second

Ref. 400   **Ref. 420**   **Ref. 420**   **Ref. 500**
ordinary seconds   ordinary seconds   rotor   ordinary seconds
Ca. 1941   **Ca. 1941**   **Ca. 1941**   **Ca. 1936**

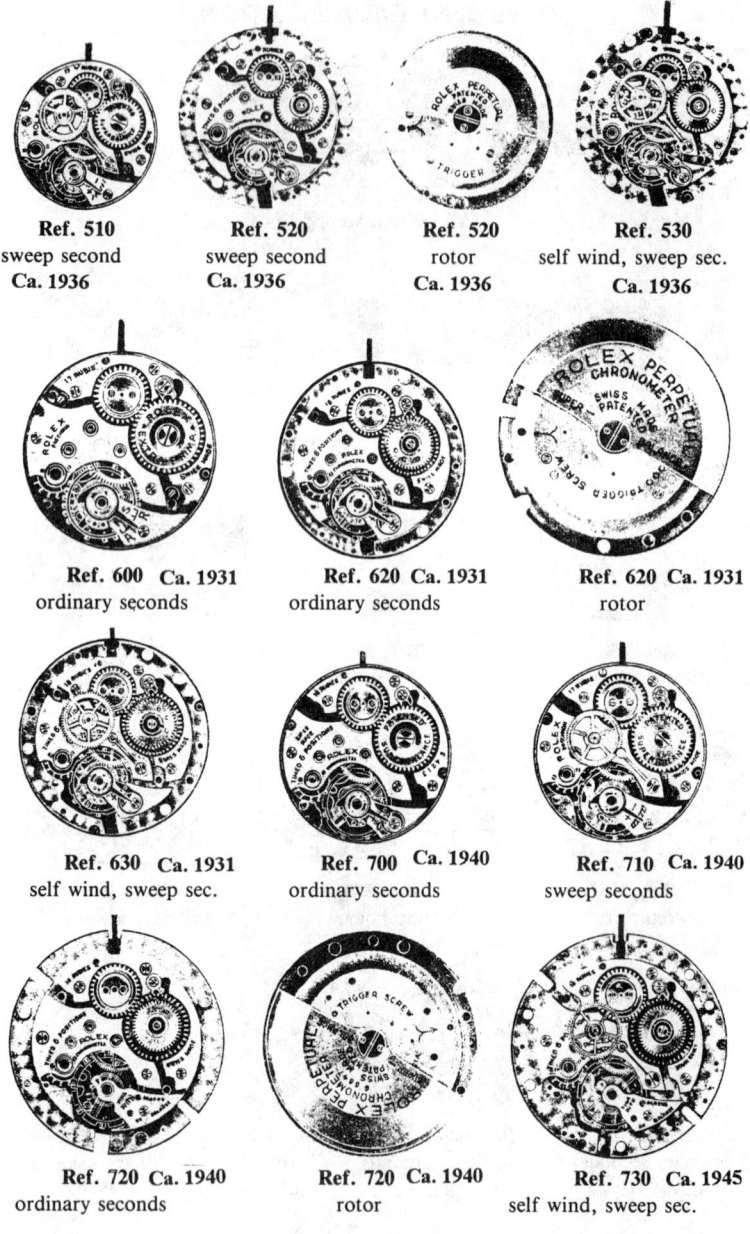

Ref. 510
sweep second
Ca. 1936

Ref. 520
sweep second
Ca. 1936

Ref. 520
rotor
Ca. 1936

Ref. 530
self wind, sweep sec.
Ca. 1936

Ref. 600 **Ca. 1931**
ordinary seconds

Ref. 620 Ca. 1931
ordinary seconds

Ref. 620 Ca. 1931
rotor

Ref. 630 Ca. 1931
self wind, sweep sec.

Ref. 700 **Ca. 1940**
ordinary seconds

Ref. 710 **Ca. 1940**
sweep seconds

Ref. 720 Ca. 1940
ordinary seconds

Ref. 720 Ca. 1940
rotor

Ref. 730 Ca. 1945
self wind, sweep sec.

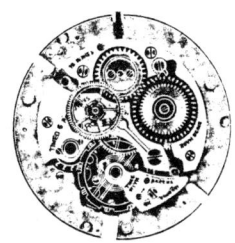

Ref. 740 **Ca. 1945**
self wind, calendar, sweep sec.

Ref. 850
ordinary seconds

Ref. 72
chronograph, 3 registers

Ref. 23
chronograph, 2 registers

POSITIONS OF THE WINDING CROWN FOR CALENDAR MODELS

Pos. 1
Crown fully screwed down.
In this position the Rolex Oyster is warranted pressure-proof to a depth of 330 feet/100 m.
The watch is ready to be worn.

Pos. 2
Crown unscrewed.
When the crown is free of the screw threads, the watch is in position for handwinding, if necessary.
In quartz models, this is a neutral position.

Pos. 3
Crown pulled out to the first notch.
When turning the crown from three to six o'clock, the date will change rapidly.
This position is used to correct the date when months have less than 31 days.
The timing of the watch will not be altered.

Pos. 4
Crown pulled out to the last notch.
Position for setting the correct time, the date and the day.
The watch stops and enables adjustments to be made, for Day-Date models, when the hands are turned counter-clockwise, the day of the week changes while the date remains unchanged.
Change the day before correcting the date.

ROLLS, 15J., early auto wind, by Leon Hatot, movement inside case moves back & forth to wind, c. 1920s
s. steel $600 $700 $900

ROLLS, 15 jewels, early auto wind, c. 1920s
s. steel $700 $800 $1,000

ROLLS, 15 jewels, "ATO," flip top
s. steel $700 $800 $1,000

ROLLS, 15 jewels, ladies, "ATO," flip top, by Blancpain
18k $800 $900 $1,100

ROTARY, 15J., aux. sec., ca.1934
9k $100 $110 $150

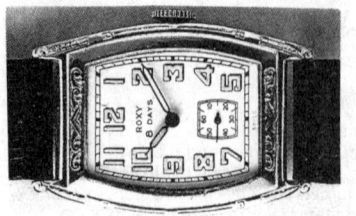

ROXY, **8 day**, engraved case, ca. 1930s
s. steel .... ★$200 $250 $400

RULON, ca. 1940s
gold filled $30 $40 $60

RULON, 17J., 3 diamonds on dial
gold plate $70 $80 $100

SCHILD, 17J., "Aqua lung", tach.chronog., ca.1972
s. steel $250 $275 $350

SCHULTZ, 17J., diamond dial, c.1930
platinum C & B $1,800 $2,000 $2,500

J. SCHULTZ, 17J., enamel hunter style, ca. 1949
18k $1,500 $1,700 $2,000

SEELAND, 17J., aux. sec., Ca. 1955
14k $90 $100 $135

SEELAND, 7J., ca. 1950s
gold filled.................................$30 $40 $75

SEELAND, 17J., "Quadramatic" auto-wind, c.1947
s. steel $25 $30 $65

SEELAND, 17J., manual wind, c.1947
chrome $25 $30 $45

SEIKO, quartz, rope style bezel
14k $100 $110 $125

SEMCA, 17J., day-date-month, moon phase, c. 1950s
18k $800 $900 $1,200

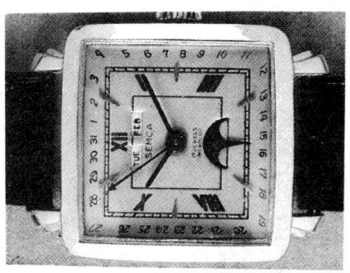

SEMCA, 17J., day-date-month, moon phase, c. 1950s
14k $500 $600 $1,000

SETH THOMAS, day date, moon phases, ca. 1949
s. steel $200 $225 $300

Some grades are not included. Their values can be
determined by comparing with **similar** age, size, metal
content, style, grades, or models such as **time only**,
chronograph, repeater etc. listed.

SEIKO, 6J., wire lugs, on dial "LAUREL", ca.1925
s. steel $20 $30 $45

SHEFFIELD,17J., chronog., by Venus, cal.189
s. steel $125 $150 $200

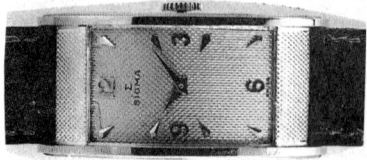

SIMGA,17J., textured dial,c.1940
18k $200 $225 $300

SMITH, 17J., military , Ca.1969
s. steel $100 $125 $165

SPERINA, 7 jewels, day & date on lugs
s. steel $40 $50 $95

🕐 Pricing in this Guide are fair market price for **COMPLETE**
watches which are reflected from the "**NAWCC**" National and
regional shows.

SOUTH BEND,17J., multi-color dial, made U.S.A.
base metal $250 $300 $400

STANDARD,17J., 24 hr. dial, world time, c.1965
s. steel $100 $150 $225

STOWA, 20-22J., Military watch, Ca. 1942
s. steel $350 $400 $500

TAVANNES, 15J., enamel dial, flip top, c.1915
silver $300 $350 $425

TAVANNES, 17J., chronog., c.1940
s. steel $125 $150 $200

TAVANNES, 17J., extended lugs, c.1955
gold filled..................................$30 $40 $60

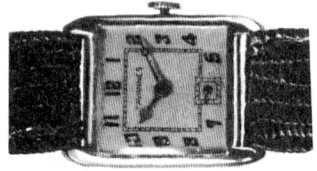

TAVANNES, 17J., aux. sec., c.1935
14k $100 $110 $150

TAVANNES, 17J., GJS, cal.365k, c.1938
14k $110 $125 $160

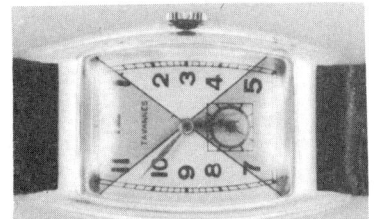

TAVANNES, 17 jewels, hour glass dial, **curved**
14k $125 $150 $200

TAVANNES, 15 jewels, "334," c. 1939
14k (w) $100 $110 $150

TAVANNES, 17 jewels, aux. sec. ca. 1940s
s. steel $30 $40 $60

TAVANNES, 17 jewels, aux. sec.
14k $100 $110 $150

TECHNOS, 17J., "Sky Diver", auto-wind, 500m., c.1970
s. steel $55 $65 $125

Wrist Watches listed in this section are priced at the collectable fair market **retail** level as **complete** watches having an original gold-filled case and stainless steel back, also with original dial, leather watch band, and the entire original movement in good working order with no repairs needed.

🕐 Some grades are not included. Their values can be determined by comparing with similar age, size, metal content, style, grades, or models such as **time only**, chronograph, repeater etc. listed.

TELDA, 17J., chronog.,3 reg, date, moon ph., c.1980s
s. steel $300 $350 $425

TELDA, 17J., center sec., c.1948
gold filled................................$30 $40 $60

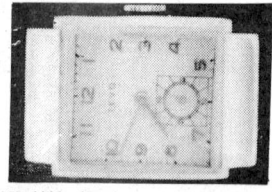

TEVO, 17J., hidden lugs
14k $100 $110 $125

NOTE: Examples of Tiffany made up watches are listed but were not sold by Tiffany & Co.. These off-brand watches will be listed but not priced as true Tiffany & Co. watches. EXAMPLES: *Kingston, Emerson, Banner*, ETC. were not sold by Tiffany.

TIFFANY & CO.,17J., exaggerated numbers, Ca.1920
silver $400 $450 $600

TIFFANY & CO., 18J., by P.P.& CO., exaggerated numbers, Ca. 1920s
18K $4,000 $4,500 $6,000

TIFFANY & CO., 17J., curved, mvt. by P.P. & Co., c. 1910
18k $5,000 $5,500 $6,500

TIFFANY & CO.,17J., by Banner"?" , c.1926
18k $250 $300 $375

TIFFANY & CO.,17J., by Wheeler "?", c.1930
14k $100 $125 $175

TIFFANY & CO., 26 jewels, min. repeater, slide repeat, automaton, 40mm
18k $5,000 $5,500 $7,000

TIFFANY & CO., 15J., wire lugs, ca. 1928
silver $200 $250 $300

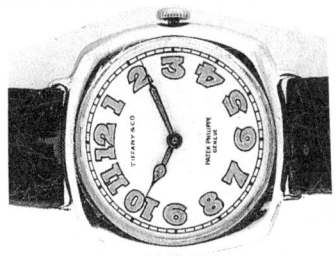

TIFFANY & CO.,17J., by P.P. & Co., wire lugs, c.1915
18k $3,500 $3,800 $4,500

TIFFANY & CO.,17J., by I.W.C., wire lugs, c.1918
14k $600 $650 $800

TIFFANY & CO., 15J., enamel dial, ca. 1930s
silver $450 $500 $600

TIFFANY & CO., 17J., Concord W. C0.
14k $600 $700 $900

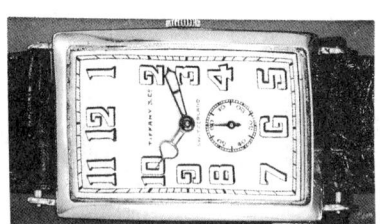

TIFFANY & CO., 18J., by P.P.& CO., Ca. 1930s
platinum...............................$6,000 $6,500 $7,500

TIFFANY & CO., 15 jewels, Swiss, Ca. 1926
18k $500 $550 $700

TIFFANY & CO.,17J., by Longines, c.1928
14k $250 $275 $350

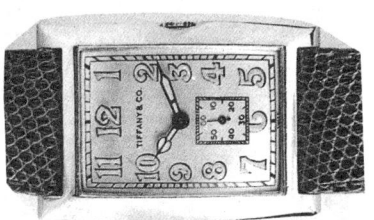

TIFFANY & CO.,17J., aux. sec., Swiss, c.1926
18k(w).......................................$500 $600 $750

TIFFANY & CO.,17J., by Fidea "?", c.1930
14k $175 $200 $250

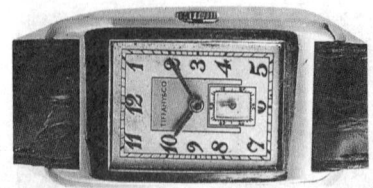

TIFFANY & CO.,17J., GJS, by Movado, c.1940
14k $400 $450 $525

TIFFANY & CO.,17J., by Kingston "?", hidden lugs, c.1943
14k $100 $125 $175

TIFFANY & CO.,17J., by Charlin W. Co. "?", GJS, c.1940
14k $100 $125 $175

TIFFANY & CO.,17J., by Hampden "?", c.1949
14k $100 $125 $175

TIFFANY & CO.,17J., by I.W.C., c.1942
14k $500 $550 $625

TIFFANY & CO.,17J., by I.W.C., hidden lugs, c.1942
14k $600 $650 $725

TIFFANY & CO., 17J., top hat, by I. W. CO.
14k $1,000 $1,100 $1,400

TIFFANY & CO., 30J., auto-wind, date, Ca.1955
18K $500 $550 $700

TIFFANY & CO.,15J., one button chronog., by Goering, Cal. 69 mvt., c.1925
silver $1,000 $1,100 $1,400

TIFFANY & CO.,17J., Valjoux cal.72c., c.1948
s. steel $550 $650 $750
14k $1,200 $1,300 $1,500
'8k $1,400 $1,500 $1,700

Some grades are not included. Their values can be determined by comparing with **similar** age, size, metal content, style, grades, or models such as **time only**, chronograph, repeater etc. listed.

TIFFANY & CO.,17J., by Movado, c.1947
14k $800 $900 $1,100

TIFFANY & CO., 17J., chronog., day-date-month
14k $1,000 $1,100 $1,300

TIFFANY & CO.,17J., by Bovet"?", c.1940
18k $600 $700 $850

TIFFANY & CO., 21J., mvt. by P.P. & Co., c. 1950
18k $2,000 $2,200 $2,600

TIFFANY & CO., 17J., curved , ca.1920s
platinum..............................$1,000 $1,200 $1,500

TIFFANY & CO.,17J., by Tourneau , Valjoux 72c, c.1950
s. steel $400 $450 $525

TIFFANY & CO.,15J., engraved bezel, c.1919
18k $1,000 $1,100 $1,300

Wrist Watches listed in this section are priced at the collectable
fair market **retail** level as **complete** watches having an original
gold-filled case and stainless steel back, also with original dial,
leather watch band, and the entire original movement in good
working order with no repairs needed.

TIFFANY & CO., 31J., chronog., triple date, moon ph. screw-
back, note window for date at 4 & 5
18k $2,000 $2,400 $3,000

TIFFANY & CO., 15J., ca. 1920s
14k $500 $550 $700

TIFFANY & CO.,17J., by Zodiac , c.1942
14k $125 $150 $200

TIFFANY & CO.,17J., by Hampden "?", c.1945
gold filled $75 $85 $125
14k $125 $150 $200

TIFFANY & CO.,17J., by Glycine "?", c.1945
gold filled $75 $85 $125
14k $125 $150 $200

TIFFANY & CO.,17J., by Ollendorf "?", c.1945
14k $125 $150 $200

TIFFANY & CO.,17J., extended bezel, c.1942
14k $250 $300 $400

TIFFANY & CO.,17J., by Crawford "?", c.1947
14k $125 $150 $200

TIFFANY & CO.,17J., by Wyler "?", c.1950
gold filled $60 $80 $125

TIFFANY & CO., 17J., fancy lugs & bezel,ca.1950s
14k $300 $350 $500

TIFFANY & CO.,17J., by Tissot, c.1948
14k $150 $175 $250

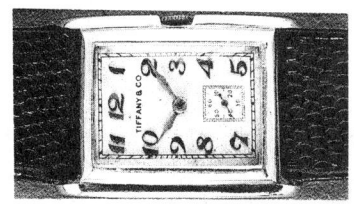

TIFFANY & CO., 17J., applied numbers, ca. 1950s
14k $200 $250 $350

TIFFANY & CO., 17J., flared & stepped, ca.1950s
14k $300 $350 $500

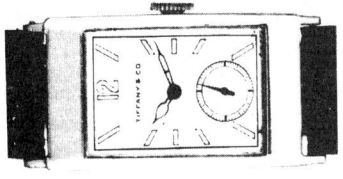

TIFFANY & CO., 17 jewels, Swiss, c. 1935
18k $500 $550 $700

TIFFANY & CO., 17 jewels, fancy bezel, c. 1942
14k $400 $450 $550

TIFFANY & CO., 17 jewels, sculptured lugs, c. 1948
14k $700 $800 $1,000

TIFFANY & CO.,17J., 3 diamond dial, by Lathin "?",
14k(w)......................................$175 $200 $250

TIFFANY & CO.,15J., rhinestones "?", c.1948
base metal $40 $50 $75

TIFFANY & CO., 17J., "Movado", triple date, center sec.
s. steel $350 $450 $550

TIFFANY & CO.,17J., by Movado, triple date, c.1948
gold filled $350 $400 $550
14k & s.s..................................$550 $600 $750

TIFFANY & CO.,17J., by Tissot, triple date moon ph.,
14k $900 $1,000 $1,200

TIFFANY & CO., 17J., triple date, moon ph.
s. steel $400 $450 $600

TIFFANY & CO.,17J., by Ardath "?", auto-wind, c.1950
14k $100 $125 $175

TIFFANY & CO.,17J., by Nicolet, c.1955
gold filled....................................$65 $75 $125

TIFFANY & CO.,17J., by Helvetia , c.1948
gold filled $100 $110 $135
14k $150 $175 $225

TIFFANY & CO.,17J., "?", c.1940
gold filled $65 $75 $125

TIFFANY & CO.,17J., by Mepa "?", GJS, c.1949
gold filled $50 $60 $80
14k $100 $125 $175

TIFFANY & CO.,17J., by Zenith, c.1939
14k $150 $175 $225

TIFFANY & CO.,17J., c.1948
18k $500 $550 $700

TIFFANY & CO.,17J., carved lugs, c.1950
18k $300 $325 $400

TIFFANY & CO.,17J., ladies, by Longines, c.1920
18k $100 $125 $175

TIFFANY & CO.,17J., ladies, by I.W.C., c.1948
18k $100 $125 $175

TIFFANY & CO.,17J., ladies, I.W.C., c.1955
18k $125 $150 $200

TIFFANY & CO., 15J., 2 tone , ladies, ca. 1939
18k C&B................................$250 $275 $325

TIFFANY & CO., 15J., early ladies, wire lugs ca.1925
14k $200 $225 $275

TIFFANY & CO., 17J., ladies, aux. sec., Ca.1940
gold filled $40 $45 $60

TIMECRAFT, 17 jewels, chronog., Ca. 1950
s. steel $125 $150 $185

TIMEX,**chronog.**, slide to start, stop & return to zero
base metal $65 $75 $125

TISSOT, 17 jewels, 1898 USA 20 dollar gold piece
24k $1,000 $1,200 $2,000

TISSOT,17J., military, chronog., Valjoux cal.225, c.1955
s. steel $325 $350 $425

TISSOT, 21 jewels, world time, 24 hr. dial, 24 cities
s. steel $700 $750 $900
18k $2,000 $2,200 $3,000

TISSOT,17J., Valjoux cal.726, c.1965
18k $800 $900 $1,100
14k $700 $750 $900

TISSOT, 21J, world time, 24 hr. dial, 24 cities, mid-size
18k $2,500 $2,800 $3,500

TISSOT,17J., auto-wind,"Navigator", date, c.1972
s. steel $150 $175 $225

TISSOT, 17J., "Stadium", tachymeter, c.1960
gold plate $150 $175 $225

TISSOT, 17 jewels, chronog., 3 reg., c. 1956
s. steel $325 $350 $450

TISSOT, 17 jewels, chronog., 3 reg.
gold filled................................$325 $375 $500
s. steel $275 $300 $400

TISSOT, 17 jewels, chronog., 3 reg.
18k $700 $750 $900
s. steel ....:.$250 $275 $350

TISSOT, 17 jewels, chronog., 3 reg., c. 1940s
14k $1,200 $1,300 $1,600

TISSOT, 17 jewels, chronog., triple date, moon phase
s. steel $900 $1,000 $1,200
14k $2,300 $2,500 $2,900
18k $2,750 $3,000 $3,300

TISSOT, 17J., day-date-month, moon phase, ctr. sec.
18k $900 $1,000 $1,200

TISSOT, 17J., "UHF", date, auto-wind, c.1960
14k $100 $125 $200

TISSOT, Worlds first transparent plastic watch, "Idea 2001",
with model "Synthic, Astrolon & Sytal", cal.2250, Ca. 1971
plastic(working) ....★$75 $100 $175

TISSOT, 17J., hidden lugs, c.1938
14k $125 $150 $200

TISSOT, 17J., 4 diamonds on dial, GJS, hooded lugs
gold filled $100 $125 $175

TISSOT,17J., aux. sec., c.1951
18k $200 $225 $300

TISSOT, 15 jewels, wire lugs, aux. sec., Ca. 1915
silver $250 $275 $350

TISSOT,17J., hidden lugs, c.1950
14k $175 $200 $250

TISSOT,17J., aux. sec., c.1942
s. steel $30 $40 $60
18k $125 $150 $200

TITUS, 17 jewels, chronog., 2 reg.
18k $300 $325 $400
14k $200 $225 $300
s. steel $100 $125 $200

TISSOT, 17 jewels, large lugs,
14k $125 $150 $200

TORNEX-RAYVILLE,17J., military, "SEAL", auto-wind,
water-proof, 150M or 490 ft., Ca. 1966
s. steel .... ★ ★$500 $550 $650

TISSOT, 17J., open shutters to reveal dial
base metal $150 $175 $225

TOUCHON,17J., tonneau case, c.1928
18k(w)...................................$175 $225 $300

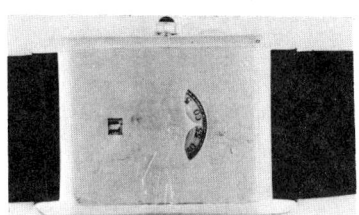

TOUCHON, 17J., jump hr., wandering min., c. 1930s
18k $3,000 $3,500 $4,200

TOURNEAU,17J, triple date, 3 reg., moon ph., c. 1952
s. steel $700 $750 $900

TOURNEAU,17J.,chronog. by Valjoux cal.886, c.1965
18k $800 $900 $1,100

TOURNEAU,17J., day date , c.1945
s. steel $175 $200 $275

⊕ Pricing in this Guide are fair market price for **COMPLETE** watches which are reflected from the "**NAWCC**" National and regional shows.

TOURNEAU,17J., beveled lugs, c.1945
14k $125 $150 $200

TOURIST, 17J., by MEPA, timer, c.1958
s. steel $30 $40 $65

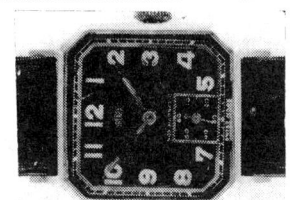

TREBEX, 15 jewels,cut corner dial, c. 1940
gold filled $40 $45 $60

TREBEX, 15 jewels, c. 1940
gold filled $30 $35 $50

TREBEX, 15 jewels, c. 1940s
gold filled $30 $35 $50

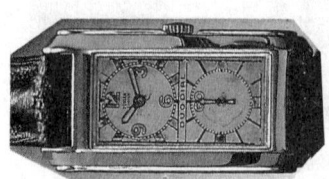

TURLER, 15-17J., duo-dial, Ca.1930s
18k $1,000 $1,200 $1,500

UNITAS, 17 jewels, triple date, moon phase, c. 1948
s. steel $250 $300 $450

TURLER, 17 jewels, chronog., triple date, 3 reg.
18k $900 $1,000 $1,300

URANIA, 15 jewels, military style grill, c. 1915
silver $150 $200 $300

UHRENFABRIK GLASHUTTE, 17J., chronog., c. 1940s
s. steel $500 $600 $800

UNIVER, 17J., triple date , moon ph., chronog.
14k $1,400 $1,700 $2,200

ULTIMOR, 17J., chronog., cal.51, c.1945
18k $325 $400 $550

UNIVERSAL,17J.,"medico compax", c.1949
18k $900 $1,000 $1,200

Wrist Watches listed in this section are priced at the collectable
fair market **retail** level as **complete** watches having an original
gold-filled case and stainless steel back, also with original dial,
leather watch band, and the entire original movement in good
working order with no repairs needed.

UNIVERSAL,17J., "uni compax", c.1942
s. steel $350 $400 $500

UNIVERSAL,17J., tri-compax, day date moon ph.,c.1955
s. steel $1,500 $1,800 $2,200
14k $4,000 $4,300 $5,000

UNIVERSAL, 17J., chronog., triple date, moon phase
18k $1,800 $2,000 $2,500
14k $1,600 $1,800 $2,300

UNIVERSAL, 17J., chronog., aero compax, diff. meridian,
square pushers
14k $1,800 $2,000 $2,400

UNIVERSAL, 17J. chronog., tri-compax, day date
s. steel $1,100 $1,200 $1,400

UNIVERSAL, 17 jewels, chronog., M. #281, c. 1950s
18k $2,200 $2,400 $2,800

UNIVERSAL, 17J., chronog., tri-compax, moon phase
s. steel $1,200 $1,300 $1,500

UNIVERSAL, 17J., chronog., aero compax, diff. meridian,
round pushers
18k $2,000 $2,200 $2,600

UNIVERSAL, 17J., chronog., compax, massive case
18k $1,100 $1,200 $1,400

UNIVERSAL, 17 jewels, c. 1952
14k $275 $300 $375

UNIVERSAL, 17J., chronog., dato-compax, c. 1950s
14k $1,500 $1,700 $2,000
s. steel $500 $550 $700

UNIVERSAL, 17 jewels, day-date-month
14k ....j..................................$600 $650 $800

UNIVERSAL,17J., compax, RF#885107, Valj.cal.72,c.1965
s. steel $500 $550 $625

UNIVERSAL,17J., "Polerouter Sub", date, auto-w., c.1960
14k $350 $400 $500
s. steel $150 $200 $300

UNIVERSAL, 17J. chronog., 10 ligne size,uni-compax
s. steel ....$ 700 $750 $900

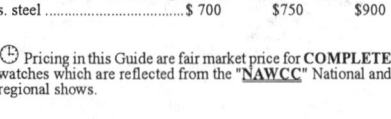

🕐 Pricing in this Guide are fair market price for **COMPLETE** watches which are reflected from the "**NAWCC**" National and regional shows.

UNIVERSAL,28J.,"Polerouter Sub",rotating bezel, c.1980s
s. steel $200 $225 $300

UNIVERSAL, 17 jewels, "Polerouter", auto wind, day date
18k $400 $500 $650

UNIVERSAL, 23J., auto-wind, date, c.1965
14k $100 $125 $175

UNIVERSAL, 28J., center sec., date, auto-wind, c.1958
18k $200 $250 $325

UNIVERSAL,17J., cal. 138c, date, c.1952
18k $150 $175 $250

UNIVERSAL,17J., cal.52, date, c.1965
18k $150 $175 $250

UNIVERSAL, 17 jewels, day-date-month, moon phase
18k $1,200 $1,300 $1,500

UNIVERSAL,17J., Unisonic chronometer, date, c.1968
s. steel $100 $125 $175

UNIVERSAL,17J., m#264, large lugs, c.1957
gold filled $75 $100 $150

🕐 Pricing in this Guide are fair market price for **COMPLETE** watches which are reflected from the "**NAWCC**" National and regional shows.

UNIVERSAL,17J., cal.267g, date, center sec. c.1948
18k $300 $350 $425

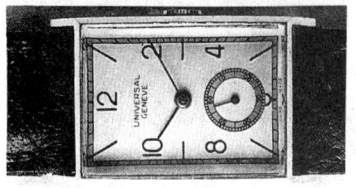

UNIVERSAL, 16J., cal#230,ca. 1940s
s. steel $100 $150 $225

UNIVERSAL, 17J., fancy lugs, Ca. 1948
14k $250 $275 $350

UNIVERSAL, 17J., fancy lugs
14k $250 $275 $350

UNIVERSAL, 17 jewels, "Cabriolet," reverso, c. 1930s
s. steel $3,500 $3,800 $4,400

UNIVERSAL,17J., center sec., cal.263, c.1950
18k $200 $225 $300

UNIVERSAL,17J., center sec., cal.138, c.1950
s. steel $75 $100 $150

UNIVERSAL,17J., center sec., cal.236, c.1955
18k $150 $175 $350

UNIVERSAL,17J., aux. sec., Ca.1955
s. steel $100 $125 $175

Wrist Watches listed in this section are priced at the collectable
fair market **retail** level as **complete** watches having an original
gold-filled case and stainless steel back, also with original dial,
leather watch band, and the entire original movement in good
working order with no repairs needed.

UNIVERSAL, 17 jewels, auto wind, c. 1955
14k $300 $325 $400
gold filled................................$100 $110 $140

UNIVERSAL, quartz, day-date, center sec., c. 1960s
18k $200 $225 $300

UNIVERSAL, quartz, , c.1981
18k $175 $200 $250

UNIVERSAL, 17 jewels, auto wind
gold filled................................$80 $90 $110

🕐 Some grades are not included. Their values can be determined by comparing with **similar** age, size, metal content,
style, models and grades listed.

Wrist Watches listed in this section are priced at the collectable
fair market **retail** level as **complete** watches having an original
gold-filled case and stainless steel back, also with original dial,
leather watch band, and the entire original movement in good
working order with no repairs needed.

VACHERON, 36J., skeletonized, triple date, moon phase,
leap year, gold rotor
18k $17,000 $18,000 $20,000

VACHERON, 36J., diamond bezel, triple date, moon ph.,
leap year, gold rotor
18k C&B..........................$14,000 $15,000 $18,000

VACHERON, 17J., triple date, moon phase, c. 1947
18k $12,000 $13,000 $16,000

VACHERON, 17J., triple date, moon phase, c. 1945
18k $5,000 $5,500 $6,500

VACHERON, 17J., triple date, moon phase, c. 1950s
18k manual wind $4,500 $5,000 $6,000

VACHERON, 29 jewels, waterproof, auto-w, c. 1960s
18k $1,500 $1,800 $2,300

VACHERON,17J., triple date, fancy lugs, moon ph.,
c. 1940s
18k manual wind ....:$5,000 $5,500 $6,500

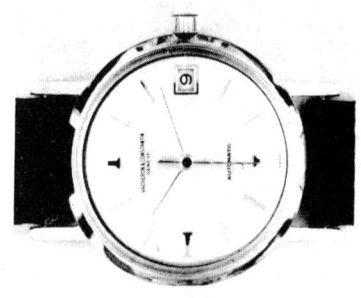

VACHERON, 29 jewels, auto wind, c. 1960s
18k $1,200 $1,400 $1,800

VACHERON, 17J., triple date, fancy lugs, c. 1940s
18k $2,000 $2,400 $3,000

VACHERON, 17 jewels, RF # 6094, Ca. 1955
18k $1,000 $1,200 $1,500

VACHERON, 17 jewels, day-date-month, c. 1940s
18k $2,000 $2,400 $3,000

VACHERON, 29 jewels, center sec., auto wind, date
18k $1,500 $1,800 $2,300

VACHERON, 29 jewels, gold rotor, date
18k $1,500 $1,800 $2,300

VACHERON, 18J., chronog. 2 reg., ca.1942
s. steel ....,..................... $5,000 $5,500 $7,000

VACHERON, 33J., auto-wind 21k rotor, cal.1124 , c.1980s
18k & s.s. $1,000 $1,100 $1,400

VACHERON, 17 jewels, chronog., 2 reg. Ca. 1934
18k & 14k band.......⌐.........$16,000 $18,000 $22,000

VACHERON,17J., enamel dial,1 button chronog.,c. 1910s
18k $25,000 $28,000 $35,000

VACHERON, 19 jewels, chronog., 2 reg., c. 1950s
18k C&B.............................. $6,000 $6,500 $8,000

VACHERON, 15J., early chronog.,2 reg.,one button,
ca. 1921, large in size
18k $16,000 $18,000 $22,000

VACHERON, 17 jewels, chronog., 2 reg., c. 1945
18k $4,500 $5,000 $6,000

VACHERON, 29J., min. repeater, slide repeat, c. 1950
18k $50,000 $60,000 $75,000

VACHERON, 29J., min. slide repeater, diamond dial
platinum.............................$75,000 $80,000 $90,000

VACHERON, 29J., min. slide repeater, ca. 1950s
18k $55,000 $60,000 $80,000

VACHERON, 18J., diamond set case, skeletonized
18k(W)................................$4,500 $5,000 $6,000

VACHERON, 18J., skeletonized,diamond bezel
18k $3,000 $3,500 $4,500

VACHERON, 17 jewels, skeletonized
18k ......,.:............................$2,500 $3,000 $4,000

VACHERON, 17 jewels, skeletonized, c. 1960s
18k $2,500 $3,000 $4,000

VACHERON, 17 jewels, mystery dial with diamonds
18k C&B.............................$1,000 $1,200 $1,500

VACHERON, 17 jewels, textured bezel
18k $800 $900 $1,100

VACHERON, 18 jewels, center sec., c. 1940s
18k $1,200 $1,400 $1,700

VACHERON, 18J., fancy graduated bezel, c. 1950s
18k $4,000 $4,500 $5,500

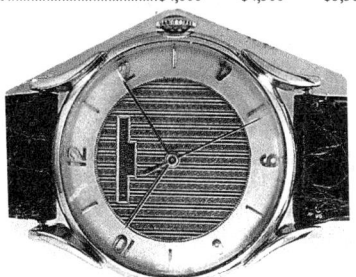

VACHERON, 18 jewels, auto wind, center sec., Ca. 1945
18k $1,500 $1,600 $1,900

VACHERON, 18 jewels, center sec., Ca. 1945
18k $900 $950 $1,100

VACHERON, 18 jewels, center sec., Ca.1945
s.steel $600 $650 $800

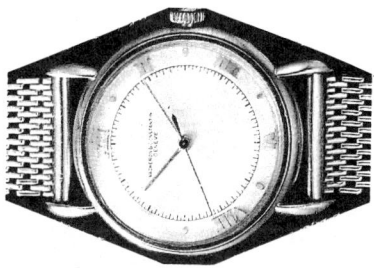

VACHERON, 18 jewels, center sec.
18k C&B.............................$1,400 $1,600 $2,000

VACHERON, 18 J., center sec., waterproof, c. 1950s
18k $1,700 $1,900 $2,200

VACHERON, 21J., auto wind, gold rotor, center sec.
18k $1,800 $2,000 $2,400

Pricing in this Guide are fair market price for **COMPLETE**
watches which are reflected from the "**NAWCC**" National and
regional shows.

VACHERON, 18J., center sec., ca.1940s
18k $1,200 $1,400 $1,700

VACHERON,17J., center sec., c.1940
s. steel $600 $650 $800

VACHERON, 18J., rf#6903, center sec., ca.1958
18k $800 $900 $1,100

VACHERON,17J., center sec., large lugs, c.1949
18k $2,400 $2,600 $2,900

VACHERON, 18J., center sec., ca.1953
18k $1,100 $1,200 $1,400

VACHERON,17J., center sec., c.1940
s. steel $600 $650 $800

VACHERON, 18J., textured dial center sec.
18k $1,200 $1,400 $1,700

VACHERON,17J., center sec., c.1940
18k $900 $1,000 $1,200

VACHERON, 18J., center sec.
s. steel $600 $650 $800

VACHERON, 18J., fancy large lugs, center sec., ca.1953
18k $1,600 $1,800 $2,200

VACHERON, 18J., center sec.
18k $900 $1,000 $1,200

VACHERON, 18J., rf#4730, fancy lugs, ca. 1950s
18k $1,700 $1,800 $2,300

VACHERON, 18J.,textured dial, center sec.,ca.1947
18k $1,300 $1,400 $1,600

VACHERON, 18J.,textured dial, fancy lugs
18k $1,800 $1,900 $2,400

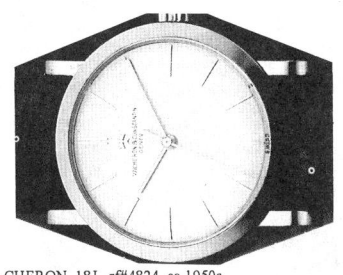

VACHERON, 18J., rf#4824, ca.1950s
18k(W)..................................$1,000 $1,100 $1,300

VACHERON, 18J., center sec., ca.1944
14k $800 $900 $1,100

VACHERON, 18J., royal chronometer, ca.1950s
18k $1,500 $1,700 $2,000

VACHERON, 17J., center sec.auto-w., ca.1945
18k $1,500 $1,700 $2,000

VACHERON, 29J., center sec., auto wind, c. 1950s
18k $1,500 $1,700 $2,000

VACHERON, 29 jewels, center sec., auto wind, c. 1949
18k $1,500 $1,700 $2,000

VACHERON, 29 jewels, textured dial, c. 1948
18k $1,500 $1,700 $2,000

VACHERON, 29 jewels, 2 tone dial, center sec.
18k $1,500 $1,700 $2,000

VACHERON, 29 jewels, center sec., center lugs,c. 1950s
18k $1,200 $1,300 $1,500

VACHERON, 29 jewels, center sec.
18k $1,000 $1,100 $1,300

VACHERON,17J., diamond dial, aux. sec., fancy lugs
platinum...............................$2,500 $2,600 $3,000

VACHERON,17J., aux. sec., c.1945
18k $1,200 $1,300 $1,500

VACHERON, 18J.,aux. sec., fancy lugs,ca. 1944
18k $1,400 $1,500 $1,800

VACHERON,17J., aux. sec., RF#4073, c.1942
s. steel $700 $800 $1,000

VACHERON, 18J., aux. sec.
18k $1,300 $1,400 $1,700

VACHERON,17J., aux. sec., tear drop lugs, c.1945
18k $1,600 $1,800 $2,200

VACHERON, 18J.,fancy lugs
18k $1,300 $1,400 $1,700

VACHERON,17J., aux. sec, fluted lugs, c.1950s
18k $2,000 $2,200 $2,600

🕐 Some grades are not included. Their values can be determined by comparing with **similar** age, size, metal content, style, models and grades listed.

VACHERON, 18J., cal#p453/3b,aux.sec.
18k $1,300 $1,400 $1,700

VACHERON, 18J., aux. sec.,
s. steel $500 $550 $700

VACHERON, 18J., aux. sec., thin model
18k(W) $900 $1,000 $1,100

VACHERON, 18J., aux. sec., long lugs, ca.1942
18k $1,000 $1,100 $1,300

VACHERON, 18J., aux. sec., ca.1951
18k $1,000 $1,100 $1,300

🕐 Pricing in this Guide are fair market price for **COMPLETE**
watches which are reflected from the "**NAWCC**" National and
regional shows.

VACHERON, 18J., **winds at 12,** ca. 1928
18k $3,000 $3,300 $4,000

VACHERON, 15J., champagne dial, long lugs, ca.1935
18k $1,000 $1,100 $1,300

VACHERON, 17 jewels, aux. sec., fancy lugs
18k $1,400 $1,500 $1,800

VACHERON, 17 jewels, aux. sec., Ca. 1950
18k $1,100 $1,200 $1,400

VACHERON, 17 jewels, aux. sec., stepped lugs
18k $1,800 $2,100 $2,500

VACHERON, 17 jewels, 2 tone dial, aux. sec.
18k $1,400 $1,500 $1,800

VACHERON, 17 jewels, aux. sec., c. 1940s
18k $1,400 $1,500 $1,800

VACHERON, 17 jewels, aux. sec.
18k $1,200 $1,300 $1,600

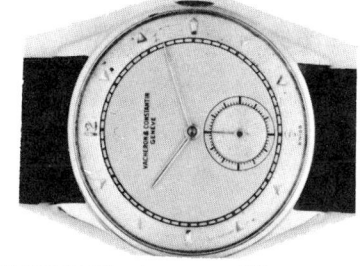

VACHERON, 17 jewels, aux. sec., c. 1940s
18k $1,200 $1,300 $1,600

VACHERON, 17 jewels, aux. sec.
s. steel $500 $550 $700

VACHERON, 17 jewels, aux. sec., large lugs, c. 1950s
18k $1,600 $1,800 $2,200

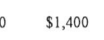

VACHERON, 17 jewels, aux. sec.
14k C&B.............................$1,000 $1,100 $1,400

VACHERON, 17 jewels, aux. sec.
18k $1,400 $1,500 $1,800

VACHERON, 17 jewels, aux. sec., c. 1940s
18k $1,100 $1,200 $1,500

VACHERON, 17 jewels, aux. sec.
18k $1,200 $1,400 $1,700

VACHERON, 17 jewels
18k C&B.............................$1,800 $2,000 $2,500

VACHERON, 17J., RF# 6498, Ca. 1965
18k $1,200 $1,300 $1,600

VACHERON, 17 jewels
18k $1,000 $1,100 $1,300

VACHERON, 18J., no sec. hand,
18k $800 $900 $1,100

VACHERON,17J., RF#6099, cal.1003, c.1960
18k $800 $900 $1,100

VACHERON, 17J., 20 dollar gold piece, RF # 4928
18k $2,200 $2,500 $3,000

VACHERON, 16J., hidden lugs, Ca. 1945
14k $1,200 $1,400 $1,700

Wrist Watches listed in this section are priced at the collectable
fair market **retail** level as **complete** watches having an original
gold-filled case and stainless steel back, also with original dial,
leather watch band, and the entire original movement in good
working order with no repairs needed.

🕐 Some grades are not included. Their values can be determined by comparing with **similar** age, size, metal content,
style, models and grades listed.

VACHERON, 16J., wire lugs, silver dial, ca.1917
14k $3,000 $3,300 $4,000

VACHERON, 18J., tonneau shaped, ca. 1930s
18k $2,500 $2,800 $3,500

VACHERON, 15J., lady's with wire lugs,ca.1920
18k(W) $400 $500 $650

VACHERON, 15 jewels
18k C&B $2,000 $2,200 $2,600

VACHERON, 17 jewels , 2 tone case yellow & white
18k $1,800 $2,000 $2,400

🕐 Pricing in this Guide are fair market price for **COMPLETE** watches which are reflected from the "**NAWCC**" National and regional shows.

VACHERON, 36 jewels, auto wind
18k C&B.............................$1,500 $1,800 $2,200

VACHERON, 21 J., date, auto-w. ca. 1980s
s. steel $1,000 $1,100 $1,400

VACHERON, 15J., shutters with center slide to view dial, 2 tone case, ca. 1933
18k $10,000 $11,000 $14,000

VACHERON, 17J, with shutters, crowns at 3 & 9
18k $12,000 $13,000 $16,000

🕐 Some grades are not included. Their values can be determined by comparing with **similar** age, size, metal content, style, models and grades listed.

VACHERON, 18J., heavy case,ca.1930s
18k(W) $2,500 $2,800 $3,500

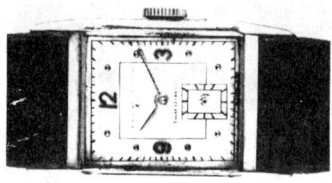

VACHERON, 18J., silver dial, ca.1941
18k $1,700 $1,800 $2,000

VACHERON, 18J., applied numbers, ca.1940
18k $1,700 $1,800 $2,000

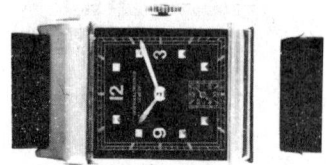

VACHERON, 18J., black dial, aux. sec.,ca.1937
18k $1,800 $1,900 $2,100

VACHERON, 18J., silver dial, ca.1942
18k $2,000 $2,200 $2,500

Wrist Watches listed in this section are priced at the collectable
fair market **retail** level as **complete** watches having an original
gold-filled case and stainless steel back, also with original dial,
leather watch band, and the entire original movement in good
working order with no repairs needed.

VACHERON, 18J., hidden lugs, ca.1940s
18k $1,700 $1,800 $2,100

VACHERON, 18J., off set lugs,
18k $2,000 $2,200 $2,500

VACHERON, 18J., off set lugs,
18k $2,000 $2,200 $2,500

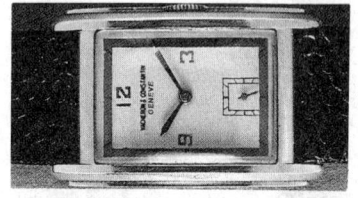

VACHERON, 18J., aux .sec.,
s. steel $1,200 $1,300 $1,600

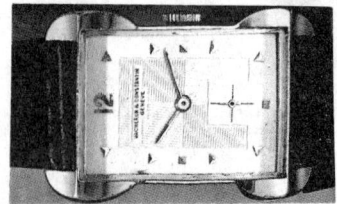

VACHERON, 18J., textured dial, large lugs, ca.1951
18k $4,000 $4,300 $5,000

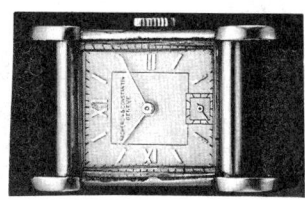

VACHERON, 18J., fancy lugs,ca.1938
18k $2,800 $2,900 $3,200

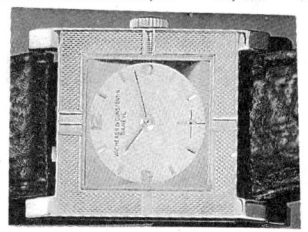

VACHERON, 18J., textured bezel,ca.1950s
18k $1,700 $1,800 $2,100

VACHERON, 18 jewels, aux. sec., c. 1950s
18k $1,500 $1,600 $1,900

VACHERON, 18 jewels, aux. sec., c. 1940s
18k $1,500 $1,600 $1,900

VACHERON, 17J., applied gold numbers, c. 1940s
18k $1,400 $1,500 $1,800

VACHERON, 17 jewels, aux. sec., c. 1945
18k $1,000 $1,100 $1,400

VACHERON, 17 jewels, applied gold numbers
18k $900 $1,000 $1,200

VACHERON, 17 jewels, fancy lugs
18k $1,800 $1,900 $2,200

VACHERON, 17 jewels, c. 1950s
18k $1,500 $1,600 $1,900

VACHERON, 17 jewels, fancy lugs
14k $1,200 $1,400 $1,700

VACHERON, 17 jewels, aux. sec., Ca. 1945
18k $1,600 $1,700 $1,900

VACHERON, 17 jewels, stepped bezel, fancy lugs, Ca. 1940
18k $2,700 $2,900 $3,200

VACHERON,17J., hidden barrel shaped lugs, c.1943
14k $1,200 $1,400 $1,700

VACHERON,17J., aux. sec., c.1947
18k $1,500 $1,600 $1,900

VACHERON,17J., aux. sec., c.1942
18k $1,300 $1,400 $1,700

VACHERON,17J., RF#6249, aux. sec., c.1963
18k $1,500 $1,600 $1,800

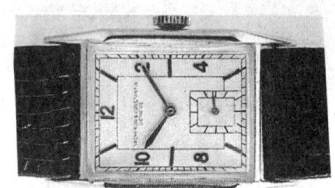

VACHERON,17J., aux. sec., c.1934
18k $1,500 $1,600 $1,800

VACHERON, 17 jewels, aux. sec., Ca. 1946
18k $1,500 $1,600 $1,800

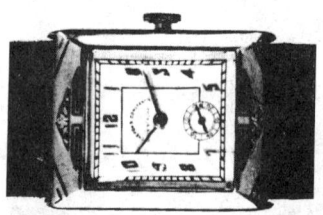

VACHERON, 17 jewels, Art Deco bezel, c. 1925
18k $5,000 $5,300 $6,000

VACHERON, 17 jewels, long lugs, applied numbers
18k $1,800 $2,000 $2,500

🕐 Pricing in this Guide are fair market price for **COMPLETE** watches which are reflected from the **"NAWCC"** National and regional shows.

VACHERON, 17 jewels, aux. sec.,
18k $2,200 $2,400 $2,800

VACHERON, 15J., hinged back, ca. 1930
18k $2,500 $2,600 $3,000

VACHERON, 18 jewels, aux. sec.
18k C&B..............................$2,000 $2,100 $2,300

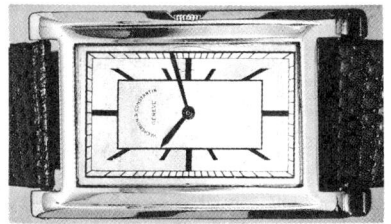

VACHERON, 18J., large 2 tone mans watch, ca.1928
18k $4,000 $4,500 $5,500

VACHERON, 15 jewels, heavy bezel, c.1925
18K C&B $2,600 $2,800 $3,200

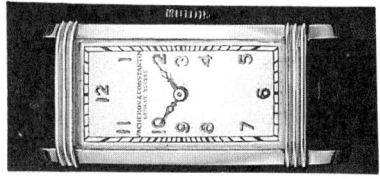

VACHERON, 18J.,long curved case, ca.1929
platinum..............................$4,500 $5,000 $6,000

VACHERON, 17 jewels, fancy long lugs, Ca. 1940s
18k $1,600 $1,700 $2,000

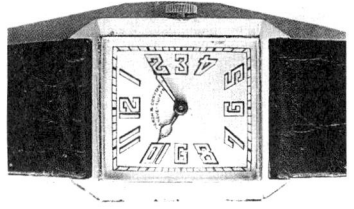

VACHERON, 18J., ca. 1926
18k $1,600 $1,800 $2,200

VACHERON,15J., curvex,wire lugs,33mm long,ca.1923
18k $2,500 $2,700 $3,200

VACHERON, 18J., ca. 1950s
18k $900 $1,000 $1,200

VACHERON, 15J., early movement, ca.1925
18k $1,300 $1,400 $1,800

VACHERON, 15J.,2 tone case, ca. 1926
18k $1,400 $1,600 $2,000

VACHERON, 18J., tank style, ca.1960s
18k $1,200 $1,300 $1,500

VACHERON, 17 jewels, hinged back
18k $1,400 $1,500 $1,800

VACHERON, 15J., wire lugs, enamel dial, Ca.1920s
18k $2,000 $2,200 $2,500

VACHERON, 17 jewels, aux. sec.
14k $900 $1,000 $1,200

VACHERON, 17 jewels, flat & thin model, c. 1960s
18k $1,000 $1,200 $1,500

VACHERON, 17 jewels
18k C&B.............................$1,500 $1,700 $2,000

VACHERON, 18 jewels, stepped case & beveled lugs
18k $1,600 $1,700 $2,000

VACHERON, 15 jewels, c. 1920s
18k $1,200 $1,300 $1,600

VACHERON, 17 jewels, 2 tone, 24mm, c. 1920s
18k $2,000 $2,200 $2,500

VACHERON, 17 jewels, 68 diamond bezel
18k $2,200 $2,500 $2,800

VACHERON,17J., RF#7252, c.1962
18k $1,000 $1,200 $1,500

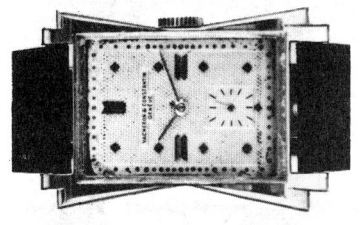

VACHERON, 17 jewels, flared, curvex, c. 1940s
18k $4,000 $4,500 $5,500

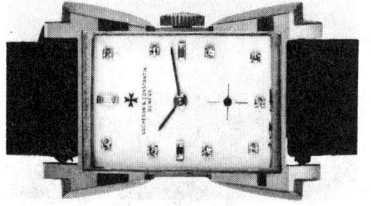

VACHERON, 17J., flared,12 diam. dial, aux. sec., c. 1948
platinum $4,500 $5,000 $6,000

VACHERON, 17 jewels, flared, c. 1948
18k $3,500 $3,800 $4,500

VACHERON, 17 jewels, flared, c. 1940s
18k $3,500 $3,800 $4,500

VACHERON, 17 jewels, "Chronoscope," jumping hr.,
revolving ruby min. indicator, c. 1930s
18k $20,000 $22,000 $26,000

VACHERON, 20 jewels, Adj. to 5 Pos., c. 1970s
18k $2,000 $2,200 $2,500

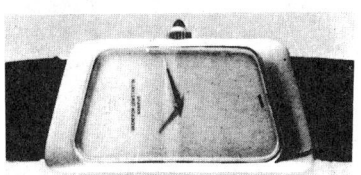

VACHERON, 22 jewels, lady's watch, c. 1970s
18k $1,000 $1,100 $1,300

🕐 Pricing in this Guide are fair market price for **COMPLETE**
watches which are reflected from the "**NAWCC**" National and
regional shows.

VACHERON, 17 jewels, aux. sec., ruby dial
18k $1,600 $1,800 $2,100

VACHERON,16J., black star & forrest, wire lugs, c.1919
18k ladies............................... $400 $450 $600

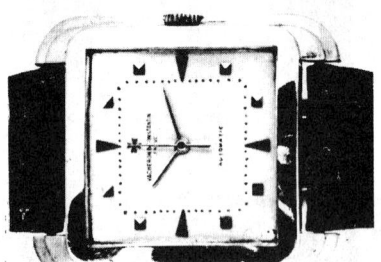

VACHERON, 21 jewels, center sec., c. 1950s
18k $3,000 $3,300 $4,000

VACHERON, 17 jewels, heavy bezel
18k ladies.............................$1,200 $1,400 $1,700

VACHERON, 17 jewels, aux. sec., fancy lugs, c. 1947
18k $2,200 $2,500 $3,000

VACHERON,17J., ladies, c.1948
18k ladies............................... $800 $900 $1,100

VACHERON, 15 J., lady's, wire lugs, ca.1919
18k $400 $450 $600

VACHERON, 17 jewels , swinging lugs
14k $1,200 $1,400 $1,800

Wrist Watches listed in this section are priced at the collectable
fair market **retail** level as **complete** watches having an original
gold-filled case and stainless steel back, also with original dial,
leather watch band, and the entire original movement in good
working order with no repairs needed.

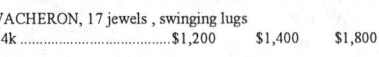

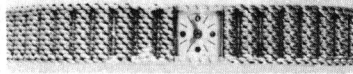

VACHERON, 17 jewels, lady's watch, c. 1960s
18k C&B.............................$1,200 $1,400 $1,600

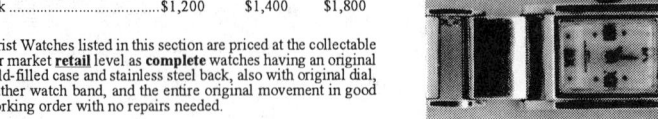

VACHERON, 17J., cased & timed in U.S.A. by Vacheron &
Constantine , heavy 14k gold bracelet, ladies, Ca.1950s
14k heavy C&B $1,000 $1,100 $1,400

VAN CLEEF & ARPELS,17J., center lugs, c.1970
18k $250 $300 $400

VULCAIN,17jewels
s. steel $30 $35 $50

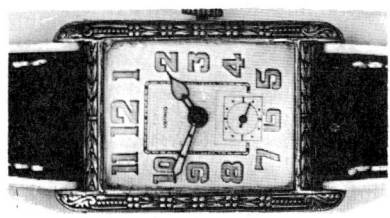

VERNO, 15 jewels, chased bezel
gold filled (w)...........................$30 $40 $75

VULCAIN,17J., ''Cricket'', alarm, c.1960
base metal $60 $70 $100

VULCAIN, 17 jewels, ''Cricket,'' alarm
s. steel $60 $75 $100

VULCAIN,17J., ''Cricket'', alarm, c.1948
s. steel $70 $80 $125

VULCAIN, 17 jewels, ''Cricket'', alarm
14k $125 $150 $200

VULCAIN,17J., center sec., alarm, c.1940
s. steel $70 $80 $125

VULCAIN, 17 jewels, "Cricket," alarm
gold filled..................................$70 $80 $125

WAKMANN,17J., "Gigandet" Valjoux cal.72, c.1955
18k $1,200 $1,300 $1,600

VULCAIN, 17 jewels, "Minstop"
s. steel $70 $80 $125

WAKMANN, 17J., chronog., 3 reg., triple date
14k $400 $500 $650

WAKMANN,17J., 24 hr. dial, c.1955
s. steel $75 $100 $150

WAKMANN,17J., chronog., 3 reg., triple date, sq.buttons
s. steel $175 $225 $300

WAKMANN, 17 jewels, chronog., 3 reg., c. 1958
s. steel $200 $250 $325

WAKMANN,17J., chronog., Valjoux cal.188, c.1960
s. steel $150 $175 $225

WAKMANN,17J., chronog., Valjoux cal.236, c.1968
s. steel $175 $200 $250

WAKMANN,17J., chronog., c.1955
18k $500 $550 $650
s. steel $175 $200 $250

WAKMANN,17J., chronog., c.1970s
s. steel $100 $150 $225

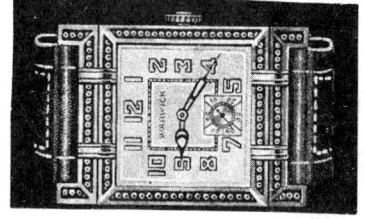

WARWICK, 6J., hinged back, 1930s
gold plate $30 $40 $60

WARWICK, 15J., 1930s
gold plate $30 $40 $60

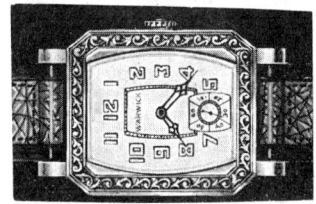

WARWICK, 15J., 1930s
gold plate $30 $40 $60

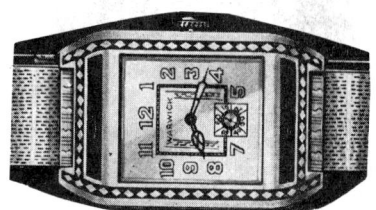

WARWICK, 6-15J., 1930s
gold plate $30 $40 $60

WARWICK, 6-15J., 1930s
gold plate $30 $40 $60

WARWICK, 6-15J., 1930s
gold plate $30 $40 $60

WARWICK, 6-15J., 1930s
gold plate $30 $40 $60

WARWICK, 15J., 1930s
gold plate $30 $40 $60

WARWICK, 15J., 1930s
base metal $20 $30 $45

WATEX, 7J., fluted case, c.1940
gold filled...............................$100 $125 $175

WEISCO, 7J., aux. sec., wire lugs, c. 1928
base metal $30 $40 $60

WELDON,17J., aux. sec., large lugs c.1950s
gold filled $75 $100 $150

WELSBRO ,17J., single button chronog., c.1940
s. steel $150 $200 $275

WELTALL W. Co., floral enamel on case, cylinder escp.
wire lugs, Ca. 1910
14k $100 $125 $175

WEST END, 17 jewels, "Keepsake," c. 1925
silver $150 $175 $250

WEST END, 17 jewels, center lugs
18k $200 $225 $300

WHITE STAR, 17J., triple date, moon phase, c. 1948
s. steel $400 $500 $650

WITTNAUER, 17 jewels, chronog., c. 1948
s. steel $250 $300 $375

WINTON, 17J., hooded lugs
14k $100 $125 $175

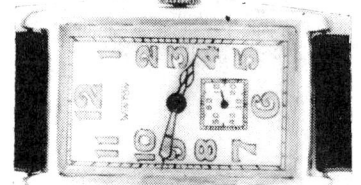

WINTON, 16J., curvex, hinged back, c.1930s
silver $150 $200 $300

WITTNAUER,17J., "Professional", RF#6002, c.1955
18k $600 $650 $725
s. steel $275 $325 $400

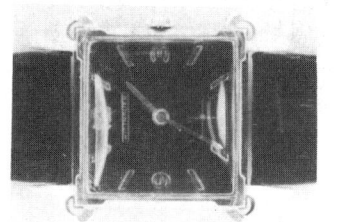

WITTNAUER, 17 jewels, fancy lugs
14k $125 $150 $200

WITTNAUER,17J., chronog., waterproof, c.1958
18k $400 $450 $550
s. steel $200 $250 $325

WITTNAUER, 17 jewels, chronog., day-date-month
s. steel $375 $450 $550

WITTNAUER,17J., chronog., by Venius, **Time Zone Bezel**,
Ca. 1955
s. steel $350 $400 $500

WITTNAUER,17J., chronog., by Valjoux, #72, cal.13w1
s. steel $175 $200 $250

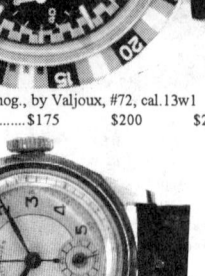

WITTNAUER,7J., mid size , stop watch, c.1940
s. steel $125 $150 $200

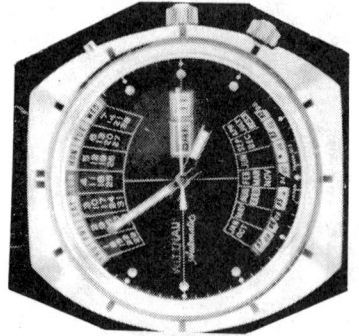

WITTNAUER, 17 J., day date, set year by button
s. steel $75 $85 $100

WITTNAUER,17J., perpetual calendar
base metal $75 $85 $100

WITTNAUER,7J., "Electronic", day date, c.1968
s. steel $20 $30 $45

WITTNAUER,17J., direct read, c.1970
s. steel $30 $40 $55

WITTNAUER,17J., Zircon on dial, direct read, c.1970
base metal $25 $30 $45

WITTNAUER, 17 jewels, auto wind, sector, date
gold filled $350 $375 $450
s. steel $300 $325 $400

WITTNAUER, 17 jewels, fancy lugs, Ca. 1955
14k $100 $125 $185

WITTNAUER, 17 jewels, curved case, c.1950
14k $200 $225 $300

WITTNAUER,17J., aux. sec., c.1958
gold filled....................................$75 $85 $125

WITTNAUER, 17 jewels, cal.9wn, fancy lugs, c.1954
gold filled $100 $125 $175

WITTNAUER,17J., aux. sec., c.1950
14k $175 $200 $275

WITTNAUER, 17 jewels, fancy lugs, GJS
14k $175 $200 $275

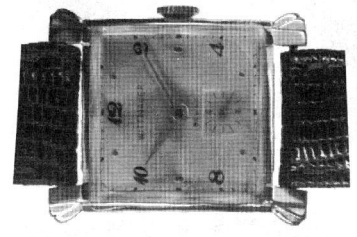

WITTNAUER,17J., aux. sec., GJS, c.1948
14k $175 $200 $275

WITTNAUER,17J., aux. sec., GJS, large lugs, c.1950
14k $200 $225 $275

WITTNAUER,17J., aux. sec., fancy lugs, c.1955
gold filled....................................$70 $80 $100

WITTNAUER,17J., aux. sec., fancy case, c.1950
gold filled $80 $90 $135

WITTNAUER,17J., aux. sec., flared case
14k $250 $275 $325

WITTNAUER,17J., aux. sec.
gold filled..................................$75 $85 $110

WITTNAUER, 17 jewels, fancy lugs, c. 1950s
14k $200 $250 $325

WITTNAUER,17J., aux. sec., GJS, c. 1955
14k $125 $150 $200

WITTNAUER,17J., aux. sec., tu-tone dial, c. 1950
gold filled..................................$70 $80 $125

WITTNAUER,17J., aux. sec., c. 1950
gold filled $50 $60 $80

WITTNAUER,15J., aux. sec., tonneau case, c.1945
gold plate $50 $60 $80

WITTNAUER,17J., aux. sec.
gold filled $50 $60 $80

WITTNAUER,17J., aux. sec.
14k $100 $125 $175

WITTNAUER,17J., flared case, Ca.1949
14k $150 $175 $250

⊕ Some grades are not included. Their values can be determined by comparing with **similar** age, size, metal content,
style, models and grades listed.

⊕ Pricing in this Guide are fair market price for **COMPLETE**
watches which are reflected from the "**NAWCC**" National and
regional shows.

WITTNAUER,17J., RF#2067, c.1950
gold filled..................................$55 $65 $85

WITTNAUER,17J., auto-wind, c.1960
base metal $40 $50 $70

WITTNAUER,17J., cal.7630, aux. sec., c.1955
14k $100 $125 $175

WITTNAUER,17J., "Alarm", c.1960
gold filled..................................$60 $70 $125

Wrist Watches listed in this section are priced at the collectable
fair market **retail** level as **complete** watches having an original
gold-filled case and stainless steel back, also with original dial,
leather watch band, and the entire original movement in good
working order with no repairs needed.

WIG WAG, 15 jewels, early auto wind, c. 1932
s. steel $500 $550 $700

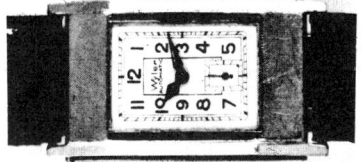

WYLER, 17 jewels, early auto wind, watch winds by using
the muscular movement of the wrist, back set
gold filled $400 $450 $600

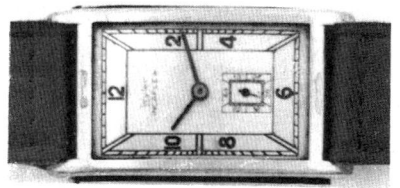

WYLER, 17 jewels, early auto wind, back set
gold filled $400 $450 $600

WYLER, 17 jewels, center sec.
s. steel $50 $60 $75

WYLER, 17 jewels, aux. sec., Ca. 1955
s. steel $40 $50 $65

🕐 Some grades are not included. Their values can be determined by comparing with **similar** age, size, metal content,
style, models and grades listed.

WYLER, 17 jewels
s. steel $75 $100 $150

WYLER, 17 jewels, diamond dial, c. 1946
s. steel $60 $70 $90

WYLER,17J., center sec., c.1945
s. steel $50 $60 $80

WYLER,17J., center sec., waterproof, ca.1941
s. steel $50 $60 $95

WYLER,17J., aux. sec., c.1938
s. steel $50 $60 $75

Wrist Watches listed in this section are priced at the collectable fair market **retail** level as **complete** watches having an original gold-filled case and stainless steel back, also with original dial, leather watch band, and the entire original movement in good working order with no repairs needed.

WYLER,17J., auto-wind, c.1932
chrome $50 $60 $75

WYLER,17J., day date month, c.1946
gold filled $100 $125 $175

WYLER, 17 jewels, chronog., c. 1940s
14k $400 $450 $525
s. steel $200 $225 $300

YALE, 15 jewels, calendar, c. 1939
14k $250 $300 $400
gold filled $100 $150 $200

🕐 Some grades are not included. Their values can be determined by comparing with **similar** age, size, metal content, style, models and grades listed.

🕐 Pricing in this Guide are fair market price for **COMPLETE** watches which are reflected from the "**NAWCC**" National and regional shows.

ZELIA, 17 jewels, chronog.
18k $275 $300 $375

ZENITH,15J., enamel dial, wire lugs, c. 1918
silver $250 $300 $375

ZENITH,15J., signal corps on enamel dial, center lug, 1918
silver $275 $325 $400

ZENITH,17J., Chronog., Ca. 1930
18k $1,200 $1,300 $1,600

ZENITH, 19 jewels, 33mm, c. 1950s
gold filled $50 $60 $75

ZENITH, 17 jewels, chronog., Ca. 1950
18k $275 $300 $375

ZENITH, 36 jewels, chronog., auto wind, c. 1969
s. steel $200 $225 $300

ZENITH,17J., Chronograph 3 reg., Ca.1965
14k $400 $450 $525
s. steel $175 $225 $300

ZENITH, 36J., "El Primero", RF#502,auto wind, c. 1970
18k $600 $650 $750

ZENITH, 36 jewels, "El Primero," chronog., triple date
moon phase, c. 1970s
18k $1,200 $1,300 $1,500

ZENITH,36J., chronog., auto-wind, triple date, moon ph.
base metal $300 $350 $425

ZENITH, 17 jewels, fancy bezel
18k $200 $225 $300

ZENITH, 17J., auto-wind, date at 5, Ca. 1959
18k $200 $250 $325

ZENTRA, 24 jewels, ladies,auto wind, c. 1958
14k $75 $90 $125

ZODIAC, 17J., chronog., 2 reg., fancy lugs, c.1948
gold filled $200 $225 $300
14k $425 $450 $525
18k $500 $550 $675

ZODIAC, 17J., chronog., auto-wind, date, c.1971
s. steel $100 $125 $175

ZODIAC, 17J., center sec., auto-wind, c.1959
s. steel $40 $50 $70

ZODIAC, 17J., day-date-month, moon phase, c. 1957
s. steel $300 $350 $425
14k $600 $700 $850

ZODIAC, 17 jewels, 24 hour dial
s. steel $70 $80 $100

ZODIAC, 17J., center sec., power reserve, cal. 1094, c. 1959
s. steel $75 $100 $150

ZODIAC, 17 jewels, ref. #8088
14k $100 $110 $130

ZODIAC, 21J., date, "Olympos", date, auto-wind,c.1965
s. steel $40 $50 $70

ZODIAC, 17J., auto wind with reserve power indicator, cal. 1225 with **differential gearing**
14k $200 $225 $275
gold filled................................$75 $100 $150

ZODIAC, 17J., center sec., Ca.1948
s. steel $50 $75 $125

Wrist Watches listed in this section are priced at the collectable fair market **retail** level as **complete** watches having an original gold-filled case and stainless steel back, also with original dial, leather watch band, and the entire original movement in good working order with no repairs needed.

ADJUSTED-Derived from Latin *ad justus*, meaning just right. Adjusted to compensate for temperature, positions, and isochronism.

ALARM WATCH-A watch that will give an audible sound at a pre-set time.

ALL or NOTHING PIECE-A repeating watch mechanism which ensures that ALL the hour & minutes are struck or sounded or nothing is heard.

ANALOGUE-A term used to denote a watch dial with hands rather than digital display.

ANNEALING-Heating and cooling a metal slowly to relieve internal stress.

ANTI-MAGNETIC-Not affected by magnetic field.

ANTIQUARIAN-Of antiques or dealing in, also the study of old and out-of-date items.

Arbor

ARBOR-The mechanical axle of a moving part; on the balance it is called the staff, on the lever it is called the arbor.

ASSAY-Analyzing a metal for its gold or silver content.

AUTOMATON-Automatic working figures moving in conjunction with the movement mechanism. Striking *Jacquemarts* or jacks which are figures (may be humans provided with hammers) striking bells to supply the sound for the hour & quarter hours. The hammers take the place of the bells clapper. *Automata* plural of **automaton.**

AUXILIARY COMPENSATION-For middle temperature errors found on marine chronometers.

AUXILIARY DIAL - Any extra dial for information.

AWI - American Watchmakers-Clockmakers Institute, 701 Enterprise Drive, Harrison, OH 45030. Tel # **(513) 367-9800**

BAGUETTE-A French term for oblong shape. A watch having it's length at least 3 times it's width. A long narrow diamond.

Balance Cock

BALANCE COCK-The bridge that holds the upper jewels and the balance and secured at one end only.

Balance Spring

BALANCE SPRING-Also called the hairspring; the spring governing the balance.

Balance Staff

BALANCE STAFF -The shaft of the balance wheel.

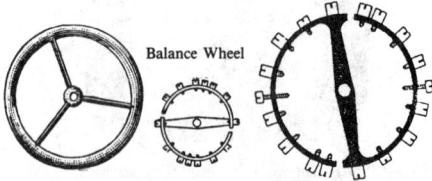

Balance Wheel

BALANCE WHEEL-A device shaped like a wheel that does for a watch what a pendulum does for a clock.

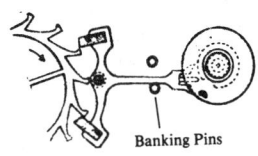

Banking Pins

BANKING PINS-The two pins which limit the angular motion of the pallet.

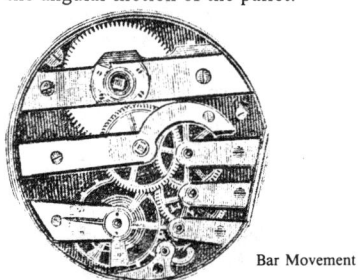

Bar Movement

BAR MOVEMENT-A type of movement employing about six bridges to hold the train. In use by 1840.

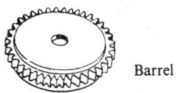

Barrel

BARREL-Drum-shaped container that houses the mainspring.

BEAT-Refers to the tick or sound of a watch; about 1/5 of a second. The sound is produced by the escape wheel striking the pallets.

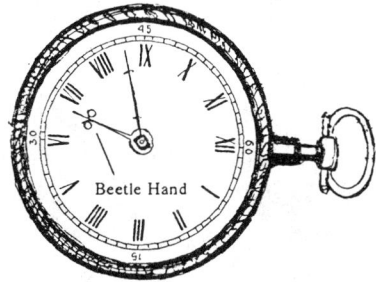

Beetle Hand

BEETLE HAND-Hour hand resembling a stag beetle; usually associated with the poker-type minute hand in 17th and 18th century watches.

BELL METAL-Four parts copper and one part tin used for metal laps to get a high polish on steel.

O S. Htg. Bezel,

BEZEL-The rim that covers the dial (face) and retains the crystal.

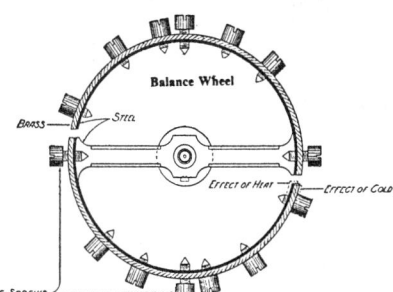

Balance Wheel

BI-METALLIC BALANCE-A balance composed of brass and steel designed to compensate for temperature changes in the hairspring.

BLIND MAN'S WATCH- A Braille watch; also known as a tact watch.

BLUING or BUING-By heating polished steel to 540 degrees, the color will change to blue.

BOMBE'- Convex on one side.

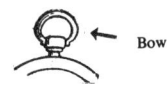

Bow

BOW-The ring that is looped at the pendant to which a chain or fob is attached

BOX CHRONOMETER-A marine or other type chronometer in gimbals so the movement remains level at sea.

BOX JOINTED CASE-A heavy hinged decorative case with a simulated joint at the top under the pendant. (BOX CASE)

BREGUET KEY-A ratcheting watch key permitting winding in only one direction.

Overcoil Hairspring

BREGUET SPRING-A type of hairspring that improves time keeping also called over-coil hairspring.

BRIDGE-A metal bar which bear the pivot of wheels and is supported at both ends .(see cock.)

BUBBLE BACK-A Rolex wrist watch which were water proof (Oyster) and auto wind (Perpetual) Ca. 1930 to 1950's.

BULL'S EYE CRYSTAL-Used on old type watches; the center of the crystal was polished which achieved a bull's eye effect.

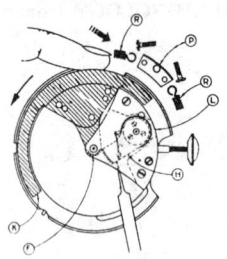

Top Side

BUFFER SPRING - Buffer spring "R" is a stop spring for oscillating weight.

CABOCHON - An unfaceted cut stone of domed form or style. (on some crowns)

CALENDAR WATCH-A watch that shows the date, month and day.

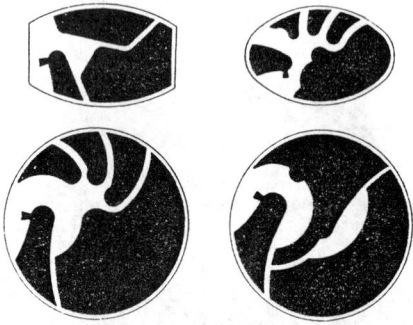

CALIBRE or CALIBER-**Size** of a watch movement also to describe the model, style or shape of a watch movement.

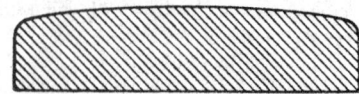

CAP JEWEL-Also called the end stone, the flat jewel on which the staff rests.

CASE SCREW-A screw with part of the head cut away.

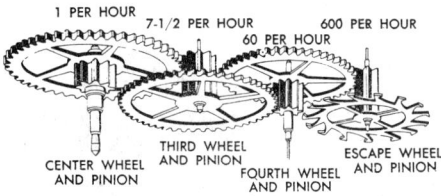

CENTER WHEEL-The second wheel; the arbor for the minute hand; this wheel makes one revolution per hour.

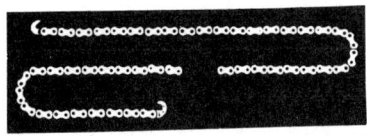

CHAIN (Fusee)-Looks like a miniature bicycle chain connecting the barrel and fusee.

CHRONOGRAPH-A movement that can be started and stopped to measure short time intervals and return to zero. A stopwatch does not keep the time of day.

CHRONOMETER ESCAPEMENT - A detent escapement used in marine chronometers.

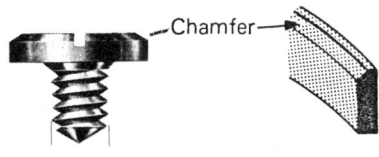

CHAMFER-Sloping or beveled. Removing a sharp edge or edges of holes.

CHAMPLEVE-An area hollowed out and filled with enamel and then baked on.

CLICK-A pawl that ratchets and permits the winding wheel to move in one direction; a clicking sound can be heard as the watch is wound.

CLOCK WATCH-A watch that strikes the hour but not on demand.

CLOISONNE-Enamel set between strips of metal and baked onto the dial.

CHAPTER-The hour, minute & seconds numbers on a dial. The chapter ring is the zone or circle that confines the numbers.

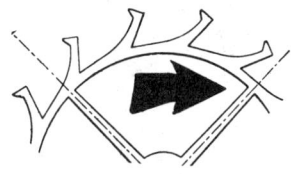

CLUB TOOTH-Some escape wheels have a special design which increases the impulse plane; located at the tip of the tooth of the escape wheel.

COARSE TRAIN-16,000 beats per hour.

COCK -The metal bar which carries the bearing for the balance's upper pivot and is supported at one end.

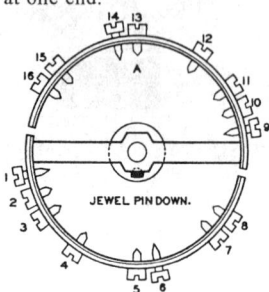

COMPENSATION BALANCE-A balance wheel designed to correct for temperature.

COMPLICATED WATCH-A watch with complicated works;other than just telling time, it may have a perpetual calendar, moon phases, up and down dial, repeater, musical chimes or alarm.

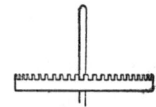

CONTRATE WHEEL-A wheel with its teeth at a right angle to plane of the wheel.

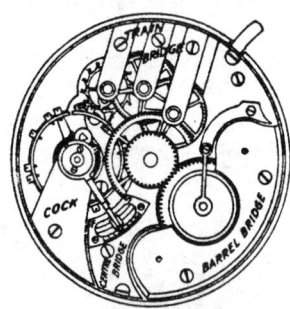

CONVERTIBLE- Movement made by Elgin & other companies; a means of converting from a hunting case to a open-face watch or vice-versa.

CRAZE(crazing)-A minute crack in the glaze of enamel watch dials.

Railroad Style

Round Style   Antique Style
CROWN-A winding button.

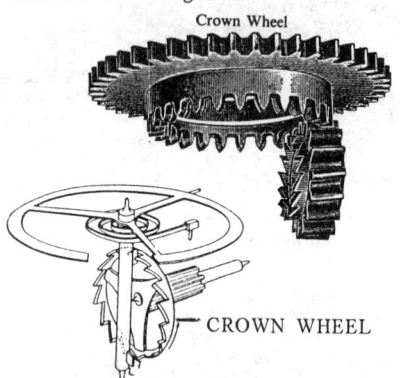

CROWN WHEEL-The escape wheel of a verge escapement; looks like a crown. Also the lower illustration shows a crown wheel used in a stem winding pocket watch.

CURB PINS-The two pins that change the rate of a watch; the two pins,in effect,change the length of the hairspring.

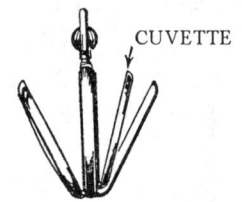

CUVETTE-The inter dust cover of a pocket watch.

CYLINDER ESCAPEMENT-A type of escapement used on some watches.

DAMASKEENING-The art of producing a design, pattern, or wavy appearance on a metal. American idiom or accepted expression of the watch term for damascene.

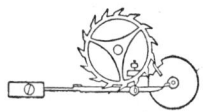

DEMI-HUNTER-A hunting case with the center designed to allow the position of the hands to be seen without opening the case.

DETENT ESCAPEMENT-A detached escapement . The balance is impulsed in one direction; used on watches to provide greater accuracy. Detent a locking device.

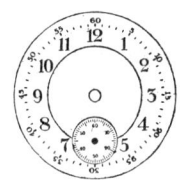

DIAL-The face of a watch. Some are made of enamel.

DISCHARGE PALLET JEWEL-The left jewel.

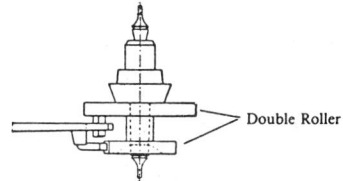

DOUBLE ROLLER-A watch with one impulse roller table and a safety roller, thus two rollers.

DRAW-The angular position of the pallet jewels in the pallet frame which causes those jewels to be drawn deeper into the escape wheel under pressure of the escape wheel's tooth on the locking surface.

DROP-The space between a tooth of the escape wheel and the pallet from which it has just escaped.

DUMB –REPEATER-A repeating watch with hammers that strikes a block instead of a bells or gongs.

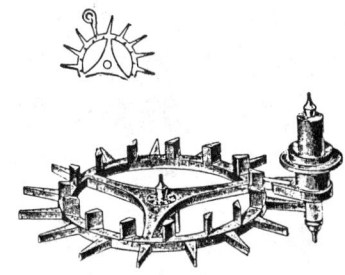

DUPLEX ESCAPEMENT-An escape wheel with two sets of teeth, one for locking and one for impulse.

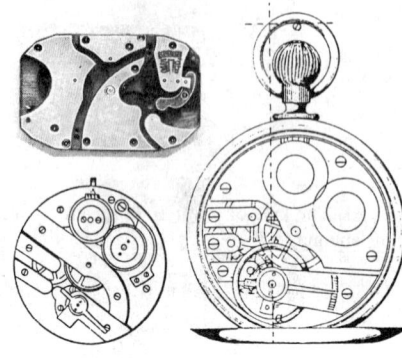

EBAUCHE(ay-boesh)-A movement not completely finished or in the rough; not detailed; a raw movement; a movement made up of two plates ,train, barrel & did not include a dial, case, or escapement.

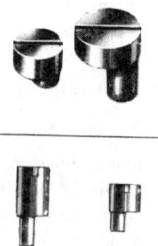

ECCENTRIC-Not exactly circular, *Non-concentric*. A cam with a lobe or egg shape.

ENGINE TURNING-Engraving a watch case with a repetitive design by a machine.

ELECTRONIC WATCH-Newer type watch using quartz and electronics to produce a high degree of accuracy.

ELINVAR-A hairspring composed of a special alloy of nickel, steel, chromium, manganese and tungsten that does not vary at different temperatures. Elinvar was derived from the words elasticity invariable.

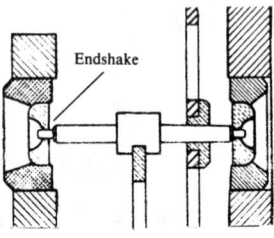

END SHAKE-The up and down play of an arbor between the plates and bridge or between the jewels.

END STONE-The jewel or cap at the end of the staff.

EPHEMEROUS TIME-The time calculated for the Earth to orbit around the sun.

ESCAPE WHEEL-The last wheel in a going train; works with the fork or lever and escapes one pulse at a time.

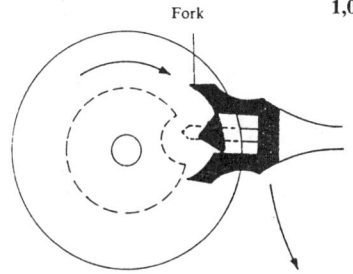

Fork

FORK-The part of the pallet lever that engages with the roller jewel.

FREE SPRUNG-A balance spring free from the influence of a regulator.

FULL PLATE -A plate (or disc) that covers the works and supports the wheels pivots. There is a top plate, a bottom plate, half, and 3/4 plate. The top plate has the balance resting on it.

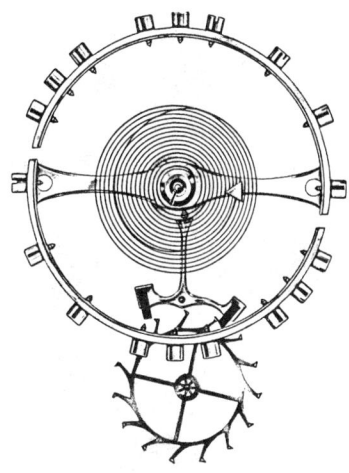

ESCAPEMENT-The device in a watch by which the motion of the train is checked and the energy of the mainspring communicated to the balance. The escapement includes the escape wheel, lever, and balance complete with hairspring.

FARMER'S WATCH(OIGNON)-A large pocket watch with a verge escapement and a farm scene on the dial.

FECIT-A Latin word meaning"made by ".

FIVE-MINUTE REPEATER-A watch that denotes the time every five minutes, and on the hour and half hour, by operating a push piece.

FLINQUE-Enameling over hand engraving.

FLY BACK-The hand returns back to zero on a timer.

FOB-A decorative short strap or chain.

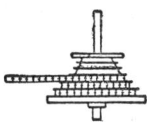

FUSEE-A spiral grooved, truncated cone used in some watches to equalize the power of the mainspring.

GRANDE SONNERIE-(**Grand strike**) a watch or clock that strikes the hour, 1/4 hours and minutes if minute repeater, a Petite Sonnerie strikes hour only.

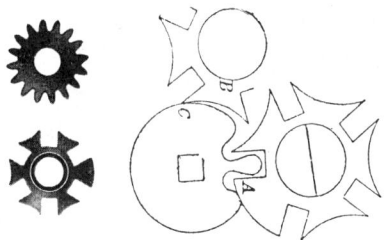

GENEVA STOP WORK-A system used to stop the works preventing the barrel from being over wound.

GILT (or GILD)-To coat or plating with gold leaf or a gold color.

GOING BARREL-The barrel houses the mainspring; as the spring uncoils, the barrel turns, and the teeth on the outside of the barrel turn the train of gears as opposed to toothless fusee barrel.

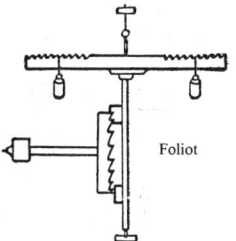

Foliot

FOLIOT-A straight-armed balance with weights on each end used for regulation; found on the earliest clocks and watches.

GOLD-FILLED-Sandwich-type metal; a layer of gold, a layer of base metal in the middle, another layer of gold-then the layers of metals are soldered to each other to form a sandwich.

GOLD JEWEL SETTINGS-In high-grade watches the jewels were mounted in gold settings.

GREAT WHEEL-The main wheel of a fusee type watch.

GUILLOCHE - A decorative pattern of cross or interlaced lines. (engraving style)

HACK-WATCH-A watch with a balance that can be stopped to allow synchronization with another timepiece.

HAIRSPRING-The spring which vibrates the balance. Above flat style hairsprings. Also called balance spring

HAIRSPRING STUD-A hairspring stud is used to connect the hairspring to the balance cock.

HALLMARK-The silver or gold or platinum markings of many countries.

HEART CAM-PIECE-A heart-shaped cam which causes the hand on a chronograph to fly back to zero.

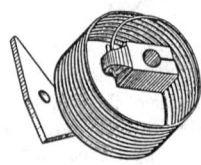

HELICAL HAIRSPRING-A cylindrical spring used in chronometers.

HOROLOGY (haw-rahl-uh-jee)-The study of time keeping.

HUNTER CASE-A pocket watch case with a covered face that must be opened to see the watch dial.

IMPULSE-The force transmitted by the escape wheel to the pallet by gliding over the angular or impulse face of the pallet jewel.

IMPULSE PIN(Ruby pin)(roller jewel)-A pin or jewel on the balance roller table which keeps the balance going.

INCABLOC-A patented shock absorbing device which permits the end stone of the balance to give when the watch is subjected to an impact or jolt. 1st. used in 1933.

INDEX-Another term for the racquet-shaped regulator which lengthens or shortens the effective length of the hairspring.

INDEPENDENT SECONDS-A seconds hand driven independently by a separate train but controlled by the time train.

ISOCHRONISM-"Isos" means equal; chronos means time-occurring at equal intervals of time. The balance and hairspring adjusted will allow the watch to run at the same rate regardless whether the watch is fully wound or almost run down.

JEWEL-A bearing made of a ruby or other type jewel; the four types of jewels include; cap jewel, hole jewel, roller jewel or ruby pin, pallet jewel or stone.

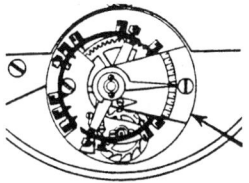

KARRUSEL-An invention of Bonniksen in 1894 which allows the entire escapement to revolve within the watch once in 521/2 minutes (in most karrusels), this unit is supported at one end only as opposed to the tourbillon which is supported at both ends and which most often revolves about once a minute.

KEY SET-Older watch that had to be set with a key.
LEAVES-The teeth of the pinion gears.

L'Epine' CALIBRE-Introduced by J.A. L'Epine about 1770. Swiss for **open face.**

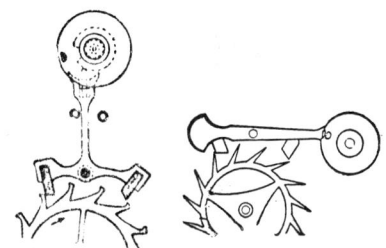

LEVER ESCAPEMENT-Invented by Thomas Mudge in 1760.

LEVER SETTING-The lever used to set some watches.

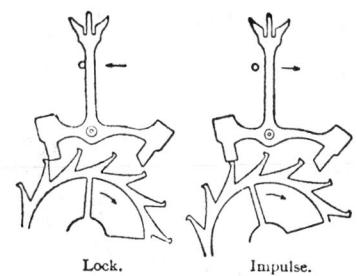

Lock.   Impulse.

LOCKING-Arresting the advance of the escape wheel during the balance's free excursion.

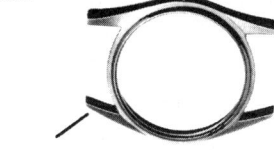

LUGS-The metal extensions of a wrist watch case which the bracelet or band are attached usually with a spring bar.

MAIN SPRING-A flat spring coiled or wound to supply power to the watch. The non-magnetic mainspring, introduced 1947.

MAIN WHEEL-The first driving wheel, part of the barrel.

MALTESE CROSS-The part of the stop works preventing the barrel from being over wound.

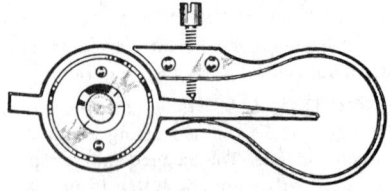

MICROMETRIC REGULATOR-A regulator used on railroad grade watches to adjust for gain or loss in a very precise way.

MICRO-SECOND-A millionth of a second.

MINUTE REPEATER -A watch that strikes or sounds the hours , and minutes on demand.

MOVEMENT-The works of a mechanical watch without the case or dial. (quartz watches have modules)

MARINE CHRONOMETER- An accurate timepiece; may have a detent escapement and set in a box with gimbals which keep it in a right position.

MEAN TIME- Also equal hours; average mean solar time; the time shown by watches.

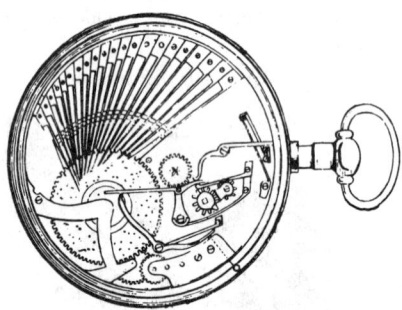

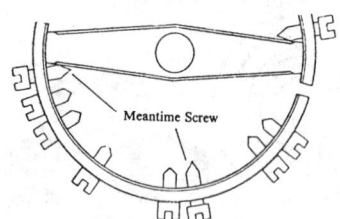

Meantime Screw

MUSICAL WATCH-A watch that plays a tune on demand or on the hour.

MULTI-GOLD-Different colors of gold- red, green, white, blue, pink, yellow and purple.

NANOSECOND-One billionth of a second.

MEANTIME SCREWS-Balance screws used for timing,usually longer than other balance screws; when turned away from or toward the balance pin, they cause the balance vibrations to become faster or slower.

N. A. W. C. C. - National Association of Watch and Clock Collectors 514 Poplar St. Columbia, Pa.   17512.

TEL. 1- 717- 684- 8261

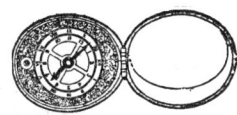

NURENBURG EGG-Nickname for a German watch that was oval-shaped.

OVERCOIL-The raised up portion of the balance hairspring, not flat. Also called Breguet hairspring.

PATINA-Oxidation of any surface & change due to age. A natural staining or discoloration due to aging.

PAIR-CASE WATCH-An extra case around a watch-two cases,hence, a pair of cases. The outer case kept out the dust. The inner case could not be dustproof because it provided the access to the winding and setting keyholes in the watch case.

PALLADIUM-One of six platinum metal used watches in place of platinum because it is harder, lighter and cheaper.

OIGNON-Large older (1700s) style watch in the the shape of a onion or *in the shape of a bulb.*

OIL SINK-A small well around a pivot which retains oil.

PALLET-The part of the lever that works with the escape wheel-jeweled pallet jewels, entry and exit pallets.

Parachute

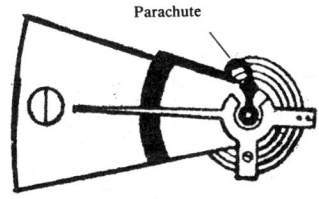

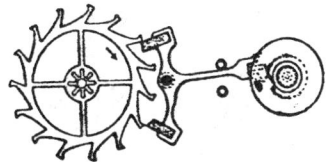

OVERBANKED-A lever escapement error; the roller jewel passes to the wrong side of the lever notch, causing one side of the pallet to rest against the banking pin and the roller jewel to rest against the other side, thus locking the escapement and stopping the motion of the balance.

PARACHUTE-An early shock proofing system designed to fit as a spring on the end stone of balance.

PAVE'- A number of jewels or stone set close together. Paved in diamonds.

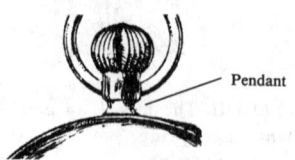

PENDANT-The neck of the watch; attached to it is the bow (swing ring) and the crown.

PILLARS-The rods that hold the plates apart. In older watches they were fancy.

PINCHBECK-A metal similar in appearance to gold. Named after the inventor. Alloy of 4 parts copper &3 parts zinc.

PINION-The larger gear is called a wheel. The small solid gear is a pinion. The pinion is made of steel in some watches.

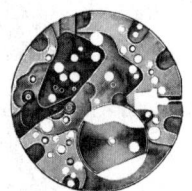

PLATE-A watch has a front and a back plate or top and bottom plate. The works are in between.

POISE-A term meaning in balance to equalize the weight around the balance.

PONTILLAGE(bull's eye crystal)-The grinding of the center of a crystal to form a concave or so called bull's eye crystal.

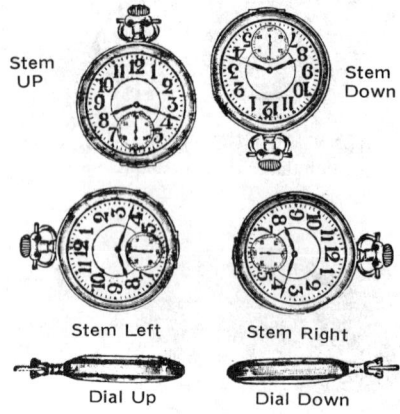

Stem UP   Stem Down

Stem Left   Stem Right

Dial Up   Dial Down

POSITION-As adjusted to five positions; a watch may differ in its time keeping accuracy as it lays in different positions . Due to the lack of poise, changes in the center of gravity, a watch can be adjusted to six positions: dial up, dial down, stem up, stem down, stem left, and stem right.

QUICK TRAIN-A watch with five beats or more per second or 18,000 per hour.

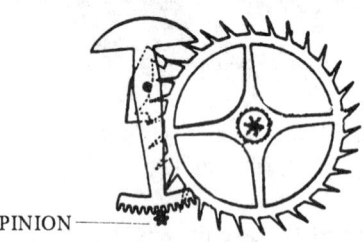

PINION

RACK & PINION LEVER ESCAPEMENT-Developed by Abbe de Huteville in 1722 and by Peter Litherhead in 1791; does not use a roller table, but a pinion.

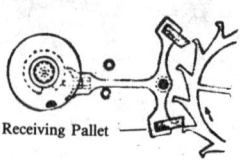

Receiving Pallet

RECEIVING PALLET-Also called left or entrance jewel, the first of two pallet jewels with which a tooth of the escape wheel comes into engagement.

ROLLED GOLD- Thin layer of gold soldered to a base metal.

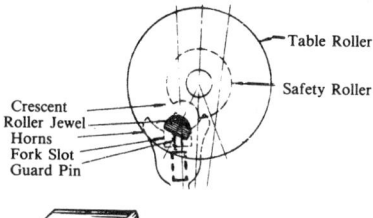

ROLLER JEWEL-The jewel mounted or seated in the roller table, which receives the impulse from the pallet fork.

ROLLER TABLE-The part of the balance in which the roller jewel is seated.

ROTOR-Oscillating weight for self-wind watches.

SAFETY PINION -A pinion in the center wheel designed to unscrew if the mainspring breaks; this protects the train from being stripped by the great force of the mainspring.

SAFETY ROLLER-The smaller of the two rollers in a double roller escapement.

SAPPHIRE CRYSTAL - Scratch resistant glass with a hardness of 9. Mineral glass has a hardness of 5.

SHAGREEN-The skin of a horse, shark, ray fish & other animal usually dyed *GREEN* or a *BLUE GREEN*. Then used as a ornamental covers for older watch cases.

SIDEREAL TIME-The time of rotation of the Earth as measured from the stars.

SIDE-WINDER-A mismatched case and movement.; a term used for a hunting movement that has been placed in an open face case and winds at 3 o'clock position. Open face winds at 12 o'clock.

REPEATER WATCH-A complicated watch that repeats the time on demand with a sounding device.

REPOUSSE'-A watch with hammered, raised decoration on the case.

RIGHT ANGLE ESCAPEMENT-Also called English escapement.

SILVEROID-A type of case composed of alloys to simulate the appearance of silver.

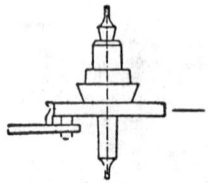

SINGLE ROLLER-The safety roller and the roller jewel are one single table.

SIZE-System used to determine the size of the movement to the case.

SKELETON WATCH-A watch made so the viewer can see the works. Plates are pierced and very decorative.

SKULL WATCH-A antique pendant watch that that is hinged at jaw to reveal a watch.

SLOW TRAIN-A watch with four beats per second or 14,000 per hour.

SNAIL-A cam shaped much like a snail. The snail determines the # of blows to be struck by a repeater.(A count wheel)

SNAILING-Ornamentation of the surface of metals by means of a circle design; also called damaskeening.

SOLAR YEAR-365 days, 5 hours, 48 minutes, 49.7 seconds.

SOUSCRIPTION- The cheapest Breguet watch which he made with high quality made in batches or group lots in advance to lower the cost.(ebauches)

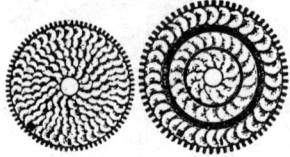

SPOTTING-Decoration used on a watch movement and barrel of movements.

SPRING BAR-The metal keeper that attaches the band to the lugs of a wrist watch & is spring loaded.

SPRING RING-A circular tube housing a coiled type spring.

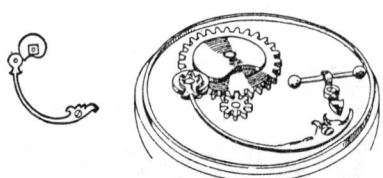

STACKFREED-Curved spring and cam to equalize the uneven force of the mainspring on 16th century German movements.
STAFF-Name for the axle of the balance.

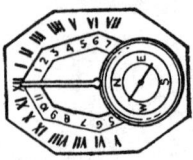

SUN DIAL-A device using a gnomon or style that cast a shadow over a graduated dial as the sun progresses, indicating solar time.

SWIVEL-A hinged spring catch with a loop of metal that may be opened to insert a watch bow.

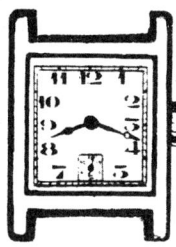

TANK WATCH-A wrist watch case design which the shape looks like the track & body of the military tank.

TOP PLATE-The metal plate that usually contains the name and serial #.

TORSION-A twisting force.

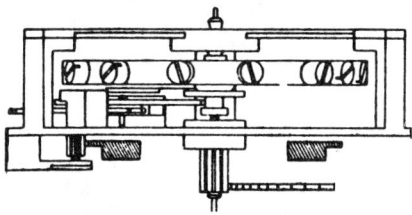

TOURBILLON-A watch that uses a escapement mounted on a platform and pivoted at both ends and revolves 360 degrees at regular intervals most often once a minute. This design helps to eliminate position errors.

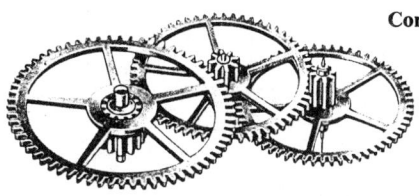

TRAIN-A series of gears that form the works of a watch. The train is used for other functions such as chiming. The time train carries the power to the escapement.

TRANSITION WATCH - Watches sold with both key and stem-winding on same movement.

TRIPLE CASE WATCH-18th and 19th century verge escapement, fusee watches made for the Turkish market. A fourth case sometimes added in Turkey.

UP AND DOWN DIAL OR INDICATOR-A dial that shows how much of the mainspring is spent and how far up or down the mainspring is.

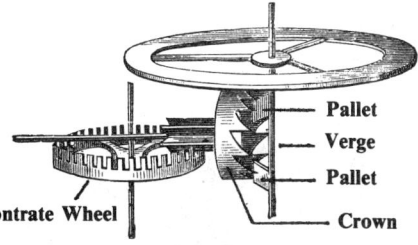

Pallet
Verge
Pallet
Contrate Wheel
Crown

VERGE ESCAPEMENT-Early type of escapement with wheel that is shaped like a crown.

VERMEIL-Gold plated over silver.

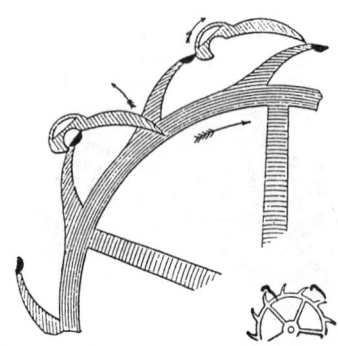

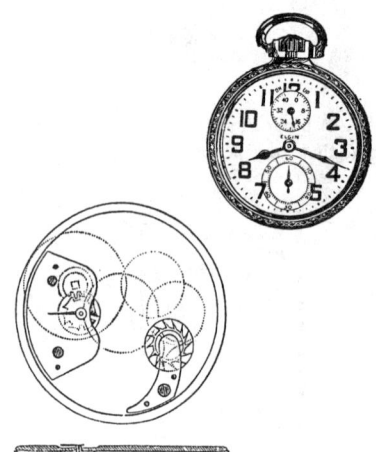

VIRGULE ESCAPEMENT-Early escapement introduced in the mid 1700s .

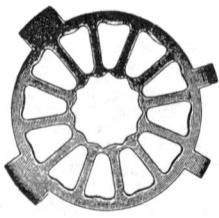

WIND INDICATOR-A watch that indicates how much of the mainspring is spent. The **illustration** shows a modified Geneva stop works. (see up and down dial)

WATCH GLASS PROTECTOR- A snap on metal grill that covers the crystal .

WATCH PAPER-A disc of paper with the name of the watchmaker or repairman printed on it; used as a form of advertising and found in some pair-cased watches.

WOLF TEETH-A winding wheel's teeth so named because of their shape.

Accutron — AC-kew-tron
Agassiz — A-guh-see
Antiquarian — an-tih-KWAIR-ee-un
Art Nouveau — art noo-VOE
Astrolabe — AS-trow-labe
Atelier — a-teh-lee-ay
Audemars, Piguet — aw-dee-MAR, PEE-gay
Automaton — aw-TAW-muh-tahn
Baguette — bah-get
Bannatyne — BAN-uh-tyne
Basse-Taille— boss-tie
Basscine — bah-seen
Basel — BAH-zuhl
Baume & Mercier — bome-MAY & mair-cyay
Beaucourt— boe-koor
Benrus — BEN-rus
Bergeon — BEAR-juhn
Berne — bairn
Berthoud — bair-TWO
Besancon— buh-sahn-son
Bezel — BEZ-EL
Biel — beel
Bienne — by-en
Blancpain — blahnk-PAn
Blois — blu-wah
Bombe' — boom-bay
Bovet — boe-vay
Bras en L'Air— brah on lair
Breguet et Fils — bruh-GAY ay fee
Breitling — BRITE-ling
Brevet — bree-VET (or) bree-VTAY
Bucherer — boo-shay-er
Cadrature — kad-ruh-chur
Calibre — KAL-ih-breh
Capt — kapt
Carillon — KARE-il-lahn
Cartier — kar-t-yay
Cartouche — kar-toosh
Champleve — shamp-leh-VAY
Chatelaine — SHATT-e-lane
Chaton — sha-tawn
Chopard — show-par
Chronograph — Kronn-oh-graff
Chronometer — kroe-NOM-meh-tur
Cie — see
Cloisonne' — kloy-zoe-NAY
Cortebert — coh-teh-ber
Courvoisier — koor-voo-see-ya
Corum — Kore-um
Craze — krayze (or) crazing — krayze-ing
Cuvette — koo-vet
Cyma Travannes — SY-ma TA-VA
Damaskeen — dam-us-KEEN
* damaskeen = A special terminology or American idiom
Detent — dee-TENT
Ditisheim — DI-tish-heim
Doxa — docks-uh
Droz — droze
Dauphine — doug-feen
Ebauche — AY-boesh
Ebel — AY-ble (sounds like **Abel**)
Elinvar — EL-in-var
Ermeto — air-MET-oh
Escapement — es-cape-ment
Escutcheon — es-KUHCH-un
et Fils — AY feece
ETA — EE-ta
Fahys — fah-z
Fasoldt — fa-sole-dt
Favre Leuba — fahv-ruh lew-buh
Fecit — FEE-sit =(made by)
Fleur de lis — flur duh lee
Foliot — FOE-lee-ut
Fontainemelon — fone-ten-meh-loh
Francillon — fran-see-yoh
Freid — freed
Frodsham — FRAHD-shum
Fusee — few-ZEE or few-zayh
Gadroon—ga-drewn
Gallet — gah-lay
Girrard Perregaux — jir-ard per-ay-go
Glashutte — GLASS-hew-tay
Glycine — gly-seen
Gouache — goo-wash
Grande sonnnerie — grawnd shon-uh-ree
Grenchen — GREN-chun
Gublin — goo-blin
Guilloche — gill-LOWSH
Guinand — gwee-nahnd
Hampden — HAM-dun
Hebdomas — heb-DOM-us
Helical — HEL-ih-kul
Helvetia — hel-VEE-shuh
Henlein — HEN-line

Heuer — HEW-er (the watch Co.)
Heuer — oo-air also eu-air (French for time or hour)
Horology — haw-rahl-uh-gee
Huyghens — hi-guhnz
Illinois—ill-ih-NOY
Ingraham — ing-gram
Invar — in-VAR
Isochronism — eye-SOCK-roe-nism
Jacot— zha-koe
Jaeger — YAY-gur
Japy — zja-pee
Jaquet Droz — zha-KAY droze
Jours — goo-or (French for days)
Jura — joo-rah (moutains on French & Swiss border)
Jurgensen — JUR-gun-sun
Karrusel — kare-us-sell
Kessels — KESS-ulz
La Chaux de Fonds — lah show duh Fawn
A. Lange & Sohne — A. lahng un zoo-nah
Landeron — lan-der-on
Lapis LAZULI — lay-pis laz-you-lye
Lavaliere — la-vahl-yare
Le Coultre — luh-kool-tray
Le Locle — luh LOKEl
Lemania — leh-mahn-yuh
Leonidas — lee-OH-ih-dus
Le Phare — luh-fahr
Lepine — lay-peen
Le Roy — luh roy
Le Sentier — la sant-ya
Leschot—leh-show
Ligne — line
Longines — LAWNG-jeen
Loupe—loop
Lucien Piccard (Arnex) — lew-see-en pee-kar (ar-nex)
Lyon — lee-OHn
Mathey — ma-tay
Mido — me-DOE
Mollineaux — MOLE-ih-noe
Montre — MON- tru (Swiss name for WATCH)
Moser, Henri & Cie—awn-ree mow-say eh see
Movado — moe-VAH-doe
Mozart — MOE-tsart
Nardin — nar din
Nivarox — niv-ah-rocks
Neuchatel — noo-sha-TELL
Nicole — nee-kol
Niello— nye-el-oh
Oignon — ohn-yoh
Omega — oh-me-guh
Osaka —oh-sah-kah
Otay — oh-tay
Oudin — oo-dan as in (soon)
Paillard — pay-lar
Pallet — PAL-let
Parachute — PAR-ah-shoot
Patek, Philippe — Pa-tek fee-leep
Patina—pah-teen-ah
Pave' — pah-vay
Piaget — pee-uh-jaay
Piguet — pee-gay
Pique — pee-kay
Quare — kwair
Rado — rah-doe
Remontoire — rem-on-twor
Repousse' — reh-poo-say
Rococo — roe-ko-ko
Roskopf — ROSS-cawf
Sangamo — san-guh-moe
Schaffausen — shaf-HOW-zun
Schild — sheild
Shugart — sugar with a T, or Shug-gart
Sonnerie — shon-uh-ree
Sotheby — SUTH-ee-bee
Souscription — sue-skrip-tshown
Stackfreed — stack-fried
St. Imier — sahnt imm-yay
Tavannes — ta-van
Tempus Fugit — TEM-pus FYOO-jit = (time flies)
Tissot — tee-SOh
Tobias — toe-bye-us
Tonneau — tun-noe
Touchon — too-shahn
Tourbillon — toour-bee-yohn
Vacheron & Constantin — VASH-er-on , CON-stan-teen
Valjoux — val-goo
Vallee de Joux — valley duh Zhoo
Verge — vurj
Veritas — VAIR-ih-tas
Vermeil — vair-may
Vertu — ver-too
Virgule — VIR-gool
Wittnauer — Wit-nower
Woerd — verd

European Terminology — U. S. A. Terminology

European Terminology	U. S. A. Terminology
ACIER	Steel or Gunmetal
AIGUILLES	Hour Hand
ALARUM	Alarm
ANCHOR or ANCRE	Lever Escapement
ATELIER	Small Workshop
BAGUETTE	Long & Narrow
BALANCIER	Balance
BOITE-DOUBLE	Pair-case
BOMBE'	Convex or Bulges
BRAS EN L'AIR	Arms in the Air
BREVET	Patented
CADRATURE	Attachment (as repeater or chronograph)
CALIBRE	Model
CHASED	Embossing
CHATON	Jewel Setting
CHRONOMETRE	Chronometer
CIE	Company
COMPENSE	Compensating
CUVETTE or DOME	Inside Hinged Dust Cover
CUIVRE	Copper or Brass
DEPOSE	Registered Trademark
DOG SCREW	Case Screw
EBAUCHE	Raw Blank Movement
EMPIERRE	Jewelled
ECHAPPEMENT A' ANCRE	Lever escapement
FAUSSE COTES	Damaskeening
FILS	Sons
FLUTED	Grooved
GENEVE STRIPES	Damaskeening
GUILLOCHE	Engine Turned
HOOK	Pin Lever Escapement
INVENIT ET FECIT	Made By
JACQUE-MART	Figures That Strike Bells
JOURS	Days As In 8 Days
LE PINE	Open Face
LIGNE	Size
MONTRE	Watch
MONTRE A' TACT	Watch by Touch
MARQUE DEPOSE (M.D.)	Registered Trademark
OIGNON or TURNIP	Large Bulbous French Watch
PARACHUTE	Shock Resisting
PAVE	Cover
PIQUE	Pin Work Decoration
PERPETUELLE	Self-Winding
POLYCHROME	Color
POUSETTE	Push Piece
REPOUSSE	Embossing
RATTRAPANTE	Split Seconds
REFERENCE #	Case # & Style
REMONTOIRE	Constant Force or Keyless Winding
RESSORT DE CROCHEMENT	All-or-Nothing
RESSORT SPIRAL	Hairspring
ROSKOPH	Dollar Watch
RUBIS	Ruby Jewel
SAVONETTE	Hunting Case
SHAGREEN	Shark or Ray Fish Skins
SPIRAL BREGUET	Overcoil Hairspring
TANGENT SCREW	Endless Screw
TONNEAU	Barrel Shaped
TOUT-OU-RIEN	All-or-Nothing
UHR	Timepiece (German)

Vallee de Joux (Swiss - French cradle of watch making)

8 DAYS = 8 DIAS, 8 CIOANI, 8 JOURS, 8 TAGE

WATCH terminology or communication in this book has evolved over the years, in search of better & more precise language with a effort to purify, adjust itself & make it easier to understand.

Timeless & Terrific
WHOLESALE LOTS

LOT # 1- Running Wrist Watch lot: Ten piece lot, including six gent's (mostly round) styles and four ladies. Brands comparable to Bulova, Benrus, Elgin and miscellaneous Swiss. YGF and Steel, Circa 1930-1965.
All mechanical. Super mix. Great for resale! **$195.00**

LOT # 2- Gent'sWholesale Gold Wrist Watches: Three piece lot, all name brands. Circa 1930-1955. All 14K and in good running order. Near mint or better round style cases. Leather straps, Sharp dials. Values of approx. $225 to $275 if sold individually! - **$465.00**

LOT # 3- Five Men's Open Faces, engraved and plain cases, 7-15 jewels, excellent to near mint, 12 S. to 18S. running and ready to sell! **$225.00**

LOT # 4- Gold investment Package: This lot includes two men's 14K open face pocket watches plus two ladies 14K gold hunters case watches.
A great investment in gold at only! **$850.00**

LOT # 5- Five Rectangular Men's Gold Filled Wrist Watches. Popular deco styles, mint cases, superb dials, professionally restored, and fitted with new leather straps! - **$350.00**

LOT # 6- Ladies Gold Wrist Watch Lot: Four super pieces, 14K cases with strong antique and collector's styling. Some with diamonds. All clean and running. Brands like Hamilton, Bulova, Elgin. Circa 1930-1955. A pretty lot! **$295.00**

LOT # 7- Unused Super-hero character Wrist Watches! New-old stock warehouse find, Circa 1970s D.C. Comics. Limited quantities. Two piece lot. Wonder Woman with blue / white / red dial. Robin Boy Wonder with yellow / black / red dial. 31mm, steel back cases, manual movement, mint!........................... **$260.00**

LOT # 8- Unused 25 Jewel Compass Wrist Watch With Date: This new-old stock watch has a central compass located on its' 41mm white enamel dial. Made by Breil (Swiss) C. 1970, and is an auto-wind movement. Watch has a steel, water-resistant case with movable bezel **$150.00**

LOT # 9- Leather Watch Bands! A great inventory lot for the collector or dealer with mixed sizes, colors and leather designs.
New old stock: 200 pieces total **$295.00**

LOT #10- Watch Keys! Set of watch keys from 0 to12 assortment.
25 Pieces **$74.50**

LOT # 11- Ten Men's Watch chains all Gold Filled, Medium to heavy link in a variety of sizes and styles. 8" to 15" with swivel and swing ring or "T" bar **$135.00**

LOT # 12- Supreme Lot of Chains! Ten men's watch chains all gold filled with medium to heavy links all with beautiful charms attached. 1 miniature knife, 2 Sardonyx cameos, and 7 other great charms. 8" to 15" with swivel and swing ring or "T" bar ... **$210.00**

LOT # 13- Dealer or Investor Starter Group: Lot contains 15 pocket watches total as described; three ladies' gold filled hunter cases, 7-15 jewels, 0s - 6s; three men's hunting cases, 7-15 jewels; 12s - 18s; three mens' open face key winds; three men's open face, 7 - 15 jewels; three American railroad watches, 16s-18s, 2 -21 jewel, and 1 - 19 jewel movements. Cases are excellent to mint and dials are fine to superb. Running and ready to sell.
Bonus - 5 watch chains free with order of this lot!........................... **$1,750.00**

LOT # 14- Wholesale Pocket Watch Lot! Super assortment of antique pocket watches, circa 1890-1930, open face cases, 6 through 18 size. This mixed lot (50% U.S. /50% Swiss) needs repair & is a terrific value. In restored condition these watches will have a resale value of $75.00 to $100.00 per piece.10 piece lot **$195.00**

LOT # 15- Five Open Face American Railroad Pocket Watches: Including Waltham, Elgin, and others. Lot contains 4 - 21 jewel and 1 - 19 jewel timepieces. All dials are very fine to superb. Cases are excellent to mint.
Running and ready to sell $1,050.00

LOT # 16- Grab Bag Lot! Cigar box filled with 100's of parts, partial movements, dials and cases. All watch related and well worth the money!
Note this lot is sold as it is, and is not returnable.. **$37.50**

LOT # 17- Dealer's Wrist Watch Lot! A dozen easy to sell vintage watches in all. Three men's round runners and two ladies in steel or YGF cases, near mint and nice brand names, three ladies 14K gold antique pieces with pretty cases in mint condition, and finally two great vintage gent's rectangle watches in gold filled cases nicely restored. Twelve pieces, all running and ready to go................... **$675.00**

LOT # 18- Complete Wrist Watch Movements: All ladies' sizes and types, runners and non-runners. **50 for $175.00 - 100 for $295.00 - 500 for $695.00**

*POSTAGE AND HANDLING
PLEASE ADD $6.00 TO ALL ORDERS
*Canadian customers add additional $12.00 P&H *Foreign customers add additional $30.00 for P&H (Florida residents add 7% sales tax)
ASHLAND pays P&H for any order over $1,000.00

BUYING

Over 35 Yrs. Buying & Selling Vintage-Hi-Grade Watches — Specializing in Patek Philippe, Rolex, Vacheron & Constantin, Audemars Piquet, LeCoultre, Gruen & IWC — As Always Still Paying Highest Prices — Same Day Payment — All Phone Calls Will Be Returned Shortly — Bank References Furnished — Member of "National Watch & Clock Association "For 30 Yrs. — Co-Author Of The #1 Selling *Complete Price Guide To Watches* 18th Edition. We Insure Fair, Honest, Confidential Transactions.

RICHARD E. GILBERT

Rolex Moon Phase
Paying up to
$65,000

Patek Philippe
Moon Phase
Paying up to
$100,000

CATALOGS
and
FREE MONTHLY
WATCH LISTS
AVAILABLE!

One of the
finest inventories
in the world.

SEND YOUR NAME AND ADDRESS TO RECEIVE THESE SPECIAL PUBLICATIONS!

GIVE ASHLAND A CALL WHEN YOU WANT TO SELL

ASHLAND INVESTMENTS
Sarasota Art & Antique Center . Suite 200
640 South Washington Blvd.
Sarasota, Florida 34236-7108

RICHARD E. GILBERT
NAWCC#34777

For purchases or
sales only call

1-(941) 957-3760   1-(800) 424-5353 or Fax 1-(941) 365-4931

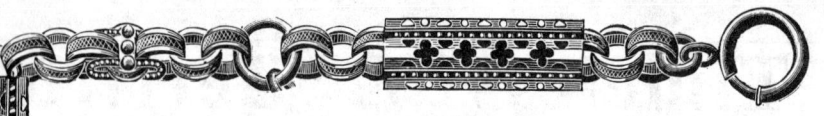

ADVERTISE IN THE GUIDE

ATTENTION DEALERS: This book will receive world-wide <u>BOOKSTORE</u> distribution, reaching thousands of people buying & selling watches. It will also be sold directly to THE WATCH COLLECTOR'S MARKET as well. We will be offering limited advertising space in our next edition. Consider advertising in the Guide, as it is an annual publication, your ad will pull all year long or longer. Unlike monthly or quarterly publications, your ad will stay active for years at a *cost savings* to YOU.

PRINTED SIZES
FULL PAGE — 7 1/2 " LONG X 4 3/4" WIDE
HALF PAGE — 3 1/2" LONG X 4 3/4" WIDE
FOURTH PAGE — 1 7/8" LONG X 4 3/4" WIDE

<u>AD RATES</u> ARE SET IN THE LATE SUMMER PRIOR TO EACH EDITION'S RELEASE. CONTACT US FOR AD RATES BETWEEN **(AUGUST & SEPTEMBER)**.

NOTE: Submit your ad on white paper in a version of the actual printed size. We must ask that all ads be neatly & professionally finished, *camera ready.* **FULL PAYMENT** must be sent with all ads. Your ad will be run as received.

← 4 3/4 →	
1/2	3 1/2
1/4 th	1 7/8
1/4 th	1 7/8

7 1/2

TARGET YOUR MARKET

AD DEAD LINE NEXT EDITION IS - OCTOBER 15

This "GUIDE" is the PROFESSIONAL STANDARD and used by collector's and dealer's throughout the world. <u>Do not miss this opportunity to advertise in the guide.</u>

SEND YOUR AD TO:
COOKSEY SHUGART PUBLICATIONS
P. O. BOX 3147
CLEVELAND, TN. 37320-3147
Office: (423) 479-4813 — Fax: (423) 479-4813

LANCE THOMAS

The Original Vintage ## LOS ANGELES

Established 1968

Wrist and Pocket Watch Dealer

P. O. BOX 3758
SANTA MONICA, CA 90408-3758

POCKET: (310) 453-0107
WRIST: (310) 449-1008
FAX: (310) 453-8008

Home Page: www.watchcompany.com   E-Mail: www.watchcompany@earthlink.net

THE WATCH CO.
BUY SELL

11 12 1
10 *Lance* 2
9   3
8 *Thomas* 4
7 6 5

TOP $$$ PAID!

* ROLEX - CARTIER
* PATEK - BREITLING

* AMERICAN POCKET
* E-MAIL or S.A.S.E. FOR PW LIST

CALL US FOR YOUR ROLEX SERVICE NEEDS

ALWAYS BUYING — GET MY OFFER BEFORE SELLING

Hamilton Watches

Specializing in HAMILTON *Electric* Watches

Expert Repair Service for All HAMILTON Electric Watches

HAMILTON Wrist Watches Bought and Sold

René Rondeau
P.O. Box 391
Corte Madera, CA 94976-0391
Tel: 415-924-6534 - Fax: 415-924-8423
Web Site: http://rondeau.net
E-mail: rene@rondeau.net

ADVERTISE IN THE GUIDE
OVER <u>375,000</u> IN PRINT WORLD WIDE

 TARGET YOUR MARKET

ATTENTION DEALERS: This book will receive world-wide **BOOKSTORE** distribution, reaching thousands of people buying & selling watches. It will also be sold directly to **THE WATCH COLLECTOR'S MARKET** as well. We will be offering limited advertising space in our next edition. Consider advertising in the Guide, as it is an annual publication, your ad will pull all year long or longer. Unlike monthly or quarterly publications, your ad will stay active for <u>years</u> at a cost savings to YOU.

SEE AD THIS SECTION FOR MORE
INFORMATION

EXTEND THE LIFE OF YOUR GUIDE
(COMPLETE PRICE GUIDE TO WATCHES)
WITH A CRYSTAL CLEAR BOOK COVER
ADD'S LUSTER & LIFE TO YOUR BOOK.

LIBRARY & SCHOOL TESTED

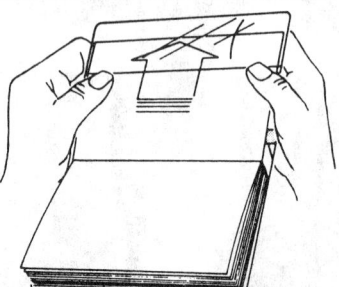

ECONOMICALLY PRICED AT $2.95
POSTAGE AND HANDLING CHARGES = $2.05
TOTAL PRICE = $5.00
★ <u>SPECIFY</u> FOR **EITHER** SOFT BACK OR HARD BACK BOOK

send **CHECK OR MONEY ORDER** <u>only</u>, sorry no **C.O.D.**, no **CREDIT CARDS.**

TO: **COOKSEY SHUGART PUBLICATIONS**
P. O. BOX 3147
CLEVELAND, TN. 37320-3147

Money
to Loan
We Buy and Loan Money
on Diamonds, Jewelry, Rolex and
other Fine Watches.
Antiques ♦ Collectibles ♦ Furs

The Area's Largest Estate & Diamond Brokers

NEW LOCATION *Annette's*

Fine Jewelry	North Stockton
DIAMONDS	Jewelry & Loan Co.
Buy Factory Direct	

7201 Pacific Ave . ♦ Stockton CA 95209

209-474-7532
1-800-54 ROLEX or 1-800-547-6539

JOIN THE NAWCC

The National Association of Watch & Clock Collectors, Inc.
invites you to become an active member of the
world's largest horological association.

BENEFITS OF MEMBERSHIP

Subscription to the BULLETIN
Subscription to the MART
Participation in National Conventions
Participation in Regional Conventions
Participation in local Chapter activities
Advance notice of National Seminars
FREE Research services of the NAWCC Library & Museum
FREE Admission to the Watch & Clock Museum
Use of the NAWCC Lending Library

Establish friendships with others who share a fascination
for watches and clocks. Time is wasting! **JOIN TODAY !!**
Annual NAWCC membership dues are only **$40.00 (US)**
or **$50.00 (Non-US)**. Payment must be in US funds
drawn on a US bank or International money order.

MEMBERSHIP APPLICATION

To enjoy the benefits of membership, please complete this form and
send it, with your check or money order to:
NAWCC, 514 Poplar St, Columbia PA 17512-2130
(717) 684-8261

Name _____

Street _____

City _____ **State** ____ **Zip**_____

Phone (____)_____ **Amt Enclosed $40** [ ] **$50** [ ]

Were you previously an NAWCC member?   Yes [ ] No [ ]

What was your previous Member Number? _____

If recommended by an NAWCC member, please give name and number:

COOKSEY SHUGART NAWCC # 23843

Chicago's
Vintage Watch Source
Assisting Collectors Since 1979
♦ BUYING and SELLING ♦
♦ All Famous Maker Timepieces
♦ Estate Jewelry
♦ OUR SPECIALTY: Buying Estates, Collections, or a Single Item. Confidential, knowledgeable quotes.

Old World Jewelers
OAK BROOK, ILLINOIS
(708) 456-7730 • 1-800-322-3871
http://www.antiqnet.com/oldworld

*An international
nonprofit corporation
dedicated to the
advancement of the
art and science of horology*

FOR THOSE INTERESTED IN HOROLOGY AS A PROFESSION OR AVOCATION

Publishers of *Horological Times*

For a brochure & sample copy of *Horological Times*

Phone	(513) 367-9800
Fax	(513) 367-1414
E-Mail	info@awi-net.org

American Watchmakers-Clockmakers Institute
701 Enterprise Drive
Harrison, OH 45030

http://www.awi-net.org

ANTIQUE WATCH CO. OF ATLANTA

–REPAIR–

Antique Watch Company of Atlanta is an established company specializing in the *RESTORATION* of *"CAN'T BE FIXED"* and complicated Pocket and Wrist Watches including Railroads, Fusees and Repeaters. *ALL WORK GUARANTEED. ESTIMATES FREE OF CHARGE.*

Antique Watch Co. of Atlanta

RUSTY TUGGLE
TEL. 770-457-9686
FAX: 770-457-0163

4335-B N. Shallowford Rd.
Atlanta, GA 30341

www.antiquewatchco.com

– CUSTOM LATHE WORK – APPRAISALS – SALES –
While in Atlanta come visit us in our railroad cabooses.

*Member: National Association of Watch & Clock Collectors,
American Watchmakers Institute*

ESCONDIDO COIN SHOP

Dealers in Vintage Timepieces

Buy • Sell • Trade • Repair

RAY LOVELL NAWCC No. 77064
H. RAY ELLIS NAWCC No. 70809

Send name and address
for free list of pocket and
wrist watches for sale.
Please mention this ad.

E mail ray@escondidocoin.com   http://www.escondidocoin.com

241 E. Grand Ave. • Escondido, California 92025 • 760/489-6058 • FAX 760/745-4816

Buying Exclusively

Patek
Philippe

Paul E. Gabriel

Los Angeles, Calif.

Tel: (310) 397-0902
Fax: (310) 390-4204

★★★★★★★★★★★★★★

Buying & Selling

High Grade & Rare

Clocks

Music Boxes

Paul E. Gabriel

Offering Complete

Repair &
Restoration

LosAngeles,Calif.

(310) 397-0902

★★★★★★★★★★★★★★

THE BEST OF TIMES

vintage watch repair and restoration

Specializing in vintage watch repair -
including Rolex, Accutrons, chronographs,
and other complications.

Write or call anytime for a free brochure with
pricing and customer testimonials.

Tom Gref, Certified Master Watchmaker (AWI), BSME
P.O. Box 794 • Wakefield, RI 02880 • phone/fax 401.789.8463

RESTORING VALUE AND PRIDE OF OWNERSHIP TO YOUR FINE WATCHES

Tom Chapman

USA
Vintage Watches

Newly Updated
Auction Software!
Now Powered by:
AUCTIONKING
YOUR INTERNET SOURCE FOR $$$

Phone: 217-423-7155
FAX: 217-423-7121
NAWCC Member #0136368

PO Box 866
Decatur, Il
62525

Actively Seeking Estates, Timepiece Collections and Consignments

The First & Largest Online Vintage Watch Store on the Internet!
http://www.timeauction.com   http://www.pocketwatches.net

POCKET WATCH COLLECTIONS WANTED

American and European Pocket Watches

If you have a single piece or an entire collection—I want to hear from you. I also keep want lists—call and let me know your needs.

Complicated Watches, Repeaters, Enamels

Also interested in collections of movements, cases, dials, parts

Special interest in early complicated unusual watches by American Waltham Watch Co. All 19 & 21 jewel 72 models. Also Waltham Watch Co. automated machinery, tools, historic documents, catalogues, advertising, etc. — for research or purchase.

GEORGE L. COLLORD III

watches, clocks, mechanical antiques

295 Forest Avenue, Suite 262 · Portland, ME 04101-2000

207-773-6803   FAX (207) 773-6750

HAMILTON   HAMILTON   HAMILTON

Wanted By Serious Collector:
HAMILTON vintage wristwatches,
especially platinum, 18K, 14K, pink or green gold, enamel and
gold, gold or asymmetrical electrics, Deco style, military,
new old stock, anything unusual, esp. Glendale, Oval,
Pierre, Donovan, Pinehurst, Cambridge, Byrd, Oakmont,
Altair, Flight, Langley, Pacermatic, Spur, Otis, Seckron,
Bentley, Rutedge, etc.

Also **HAMILTON** *memorabilia, advertising material,
watch boxes, catalogs, display cases, signs, bands,
buckles, key chains, dials, new old stock etc.*

Bob Toborowsky
NAWCC #00903737
823 Oxford Crest
Villanova, PA 19085

Telephone
Days: (215) 829-5206
Eves: (610) 519-9858
Fax: (215) 829-5176

HAMILTON   HAMILTON   HAMILTON

RAILROAD WATCH TOOLS

Specializing in New & Used Equipment for the Watch, Clock or Jewelry Trades

Watch Making Equipment:

Timing and cleaning machines, hand tools, benches, pocket watch parts, movements, cases, dials and parts systems.

Clock Making Equipment:

Lathes and accessories, bushing tools, ultrasonic tanks, staking sets, rolltop benches.

Jewelry Making Equipment:

Authorized Foredom dealer, Smith Torch dealer (the mini-torch), casting equipment, buffers, steam cleaners.

GARY ROWLAND OF RAILROAD WATCH TOOLS
830 SHEPARKON   MIDLOTHIAN, TX 76065   (972) 723-8665

The WATCHMAKER

A specialist with 30 years experience in the repair and resealing of high quality water resistant watches, both mechanical and quartz. All repairs are made with genuine parts, tested with state of the art Witschi Swiss equipment, and guaranteed. Free estimates. *Jack Kurdzionak*

379 Main Street
Stoneham, MA   02180
(781) 438-6977 voice   (781) 438-6954 fax
watchmaker1@juno.com

Looking to bring in
Mint and Extra Fine Prices for your
Wrist and Pocket Watches?

In order to do so, you need all original factory parts. S. LaRose has the remaining stock from the Hamilton, Illinois, Elgin, and Waltham factories, not to mention old and new swiss parts from Omega, Wittnauer, Longines, Bulova, and many other Swiss factories! We've also got displays to show off pocket watches as well as wrist watches.

Orders only: 1-888-SLAROSE
(752-7673)

S. LaRose, Inc.
Worldwide Distributors to Horologists

3223 Yanceyville St. • P.O.Box 21208
Greensboro, N.C. 27420 USA
Technical info: (336) 621-1936
Orders only 1-888-SLAROSE(752-7673)
Fax: 1-800-537-4513
E-Mail: SLAROSE@worldnet.att.net
http://www.slarose.com

Point.
Click.
Buy A Watch.

www.antiquewristwatches.com

P.O. Box 5120, Elgin, IL 60121-5120
Phone : 800-908-6349   Fax : 847-468-9651

OLD NAVITIMER

JOHN D. HUNTLEY, INC.
313B. South College Ave.
College Station, Texas 77840
409 - 846 - 8905

INSTRUMENTS FOR PROFESSIONALS

Professional Horology
The Art of Mechanism.

A s with other art forms, international and regional conventions and auctions help determine prices and appreciation for fine watches and clocks almost on a weekly basis.

Professional Horology is a recognized specialist in the evaluation, purchase & sale of fine pocket and wrist watches, clocks, and other ingenious mechanisms from the 15th century to the present.

Clients both here and abroad will attest to the confidential, courteous and patient handling of appraisals as well as purchase and sale negotiations entered into on their behalf.

Victor Kullberg minute repeater, #4000: Presented by King George V of England to Shah Reza I Pahlevi, in 1925, to commemorate the founding of the sovereign nation of Iran: 6 Carats in fine diamonds, ruby eyes, enamel sun, platinum sword.

LeRoy à Paris #3138 (CA1800): Extremely rare example of a first class execution of the Pinwheel Escapement for use in a pocket watch.

If your travels take you to the Boston area, schedule a visit to my premises for an examination of my current inventory. If you are looking for a particular timepiece or wish to discuss the liquidation or sale of a collection, or individual item, please do not hesitate to contact me (interesting trades or upgrades will always be considered). I will gladly travel to facilitate a mutually rewarding transaction.

Joseph Conway, Horologer
Fine Watches & Clocks, Ingenious Mechanisms & Instrumentation

P.O. Box 60008, Newtonville, MA 02460-1638
1-(800) 542- 7771 / FAX (617) 244-5290
Shop (617) 244-0066 / Cell (617) 365-6279

TAGHeuer
SWISS MADE SINCE 1860

The S/el Series.
Water-resistant to
200 meters.

© 1997 TAG Heuer USA

JOHN D. HUNTLEY, INC.
313B. South College Ave.
College Station, Texas 77840
409 - 846 - 8905

An authorized TAG Heuer dealer.

DON'S WATCH SHOP

Quality Sales & Service

BUY • SELL • TRADE • REPAIR
All Types Pocket Watches, Wrist Watches
We Are Interested In Buying Your Watches, Parts & Bands
CERTIFIED ACCUTRON TECHNICIAN
ACCUTRON Repairs & Spaceview Conversions

BUY

SELL

TRADE

DON & SANDY ROBBINS
1838 MONROE STREET
P. O. BOX 416
SWEETWATER, TN. 37874
TEL. (423) 337-7067
FAX (423) 337-0172
Member: A W I & N A W C C
VISA & MASTERCARD

ALL HOURS

Diane & Dave Resnick

*Specializing in
Quality Sales & Service*
Clocks ● Watches ● Phonographs

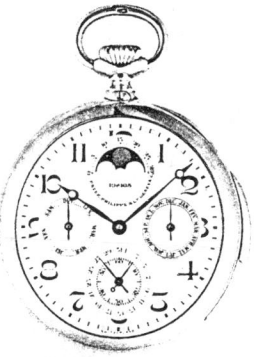

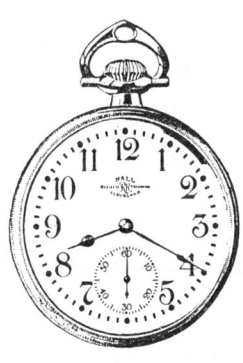

**POCKET WATCHES
BALL
HOWARD
ELGIN
WALTHAM
HAMILTON
ILLINOIS
ALL FOREIGN MAKERS**

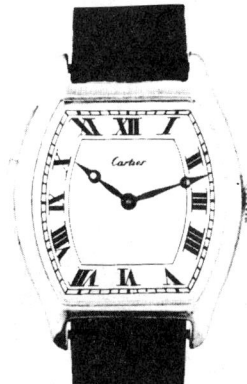

**WRIST WATCHES
PATEK PHILIPPE
VACHERON CONSTANTINE
CARTIER
GRUEN
HAMILTON
& ALL OTHERS BRANDS**

1414 South Broadway
Denver, Colorado 80210

(303) 777-3264

YOUR CANADIAN CONNECTION

WANTED TO BUY

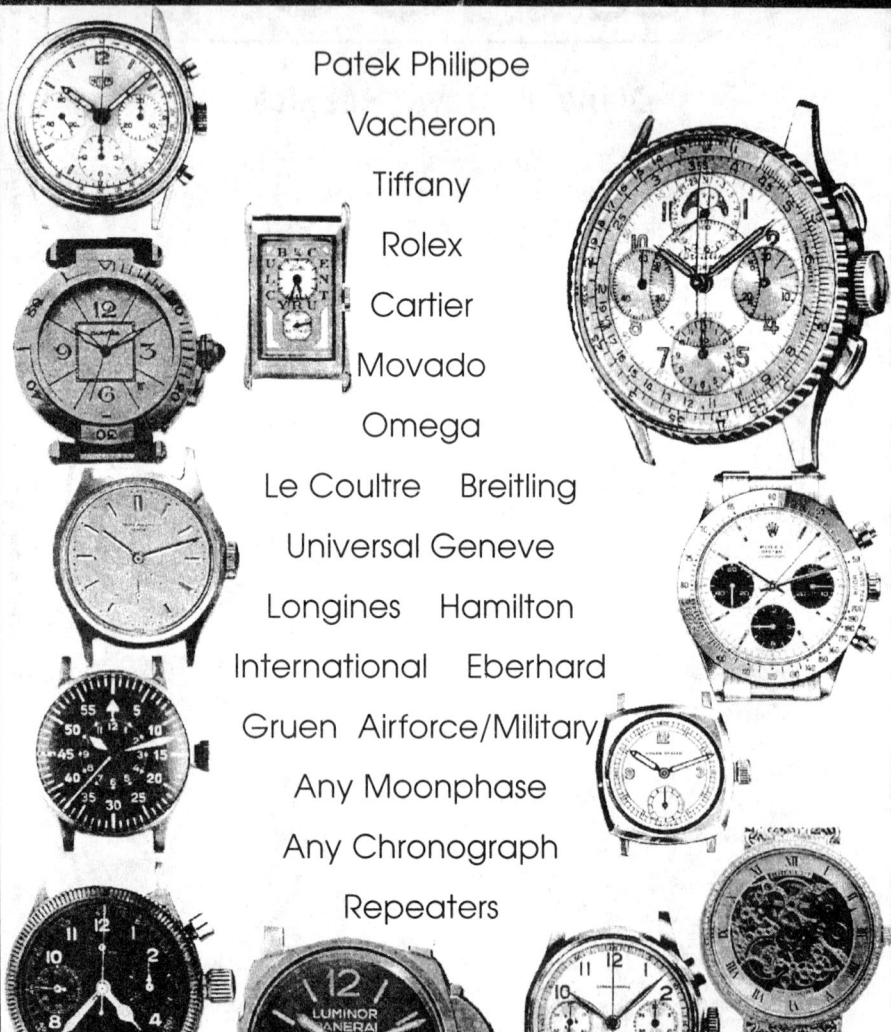

Patek Philippe

Vacheron

Tiffany

Rolex

Cartier

Movado

Omega

Le Coultre   Breitling

Universal Geneve

Longines   Hamilton

International   Eberhard

Gruen Airforce/Military

Any Moonphase

Any Chronograph

Repeaters

© Touch of Gold

TOLL FREE 1-888-671-3038
TORONTO 416-260-2182

VISIT OUR WEB SITE - www.touchofgold.on.ca
E-MAIL - jfk@touchofgold.on.ca

Attention: Watchmakers, Jewelers, Flea Marketers, Auctioneers, and Repair Shops! Mixed Wholesale Lots Now Available!

WFN Enterprises, Inc. has been liquidating jewelry and gift stores since 1974 and constantly has available both unpicked up repairs and customer reject quartz watches. These are excellent for parts or secondary market sales. Lots include popular brands such as Pulsar, Seiko, Casio, Timex, Lorus, etc. but with no specific brand guarantee in any given lot. These quartz watches are sold in mixed brand lots and are priced as follows:

Grade A: Like new, minimum wear, watch may or may not be working but 90% of time only needs battery. $5.00 each. *Minimum lot size: 20 pieces.*
Above: Add $6.00 U.P.S. (USA)

Grade B: Light to medium used, 75% of time needs only battery. Attractive to consumer eye. $3.00 each. *Minimum lot size: 35 pieces.* Add $6.00 UPS (USA)

Grade C: Heavily worn but servicable. 50% of the time needs only a battery to work but might have heavily scratched crystal or heavy wear on bezel. $2.00 each. *Minimum lot size: 50 pieces.* Add $7.00 U.P.S. (USA)

Grade D: Good for parts only. May be analog or digital. May be damaged and some pieces missing. $1.00 each. *Minimum lot size: 100 pieces.*
Above: Add $8.00 U.P.S. (USA)

Mechanical lots sometimes available. Your inquiry welcome.
TERMS: Check, Money Order, in advance, credit to JBT or D&B rated accounts.
All prices add U.P.S.; COD available in U.S.A. Only.
We also BUY - Call for details

New Closeouts Available

Seiko, Pulsar, Hamilton, Movado, Baume Mercier and other popular brands!
Prices range from $.25 to $.50 on retail dollar for most items.
All new with factory warranty. Selection always changing. Call for details.

Contact Mr. Neff:
Phone: (770) 396-1787 Fax: (770) 395-6959
E-mail: wfn@mindspring.com
WFN ENTERPRISES, INC.
Dept. C99
5579B Chamblee Dunwoody Rd. Suite 215
Dunwoody, GA 30338

NEW for 1999 !!
LUMINOX®
Navy Seals
Dive Watches
Now Available

Open
24 Hours
A Day.

www.antiquewristwatches.com

P.O. Box 5120, Elgin, IL 60121-5120

Phone : 800-908-6349   Fax : 847-468-9651

POCKET WATCHES – WRIST WATCHES

Bought ★ Sold ★ Traded

34 Years of Business
in San Francisco
Bay Area

★ **Please call or send in
  your want list**
★ American Railroads a Speciality
★ We trade U. S. and Swiss High-Grade
  Wrist Watches including Rolex, Patek,
  Vacheron, Gruen, Hamilton, etc.

COLLECTORS AND DEALERS WELCOME AT OUR SHOWROOM

Our Company also buys and sells Gold & Silver
Rare Coins – Diamonds – Estate Jewelry

MISH INT'L MONETARY INC.

1154 University Drive
P. O. Box 937
Menlo Park, California USA
Zip Code: To Street 94025
        To Box 94026

IRA P. MISH

Tel: (650) 853-TICK
Fax: (650) 322-6091
NAWCC No. 70123
I.W. J. G. No. 472

WANTED

GOLD FILLED SCRAP
SILVER, GOLD, PLATINUM
BATTERIES

NO ASSAY or REFINING COSTS

NO MINIMUM AMOUNT

DAILY QUOTES – FAST PAYMENT

ARE YOU PLANNING TO RETIRE?

WE BUY... Watch & Jewelry Repair Shops
- All Equipment, Tools, Material Systems, Crystals, Movements, Cases, Books

WE BUY... Jewelry Stores
- All of Your Inventory

GF SPECIALTIES, LTD.

P.O. Box 17216 • Milwaukee, WI 53217

1-800-351-6926 • IRV BARD

— 30 Years of Experience —

Don & Linda Levison
Antiquarian Horology

P. O. Box 22262, San Francisco, Ca., 94122
TEL. (415) 753 - 0455   FAX (415) 753 - 5206
WWW.antiquehorology.com   •   E MAIL: dlevison@juno.com
We Welcome Inquiries to Buy, Sell, Trade Rare and Antique Wrist / Pocket
Watches, Clocks, Music Boxes, Bird Boxes / Cages, Automata, Barometers
CONSIGNMENTS ACCEPTED SASE For List (No WW), Please Specify Interests

WatchWare

WatchWare
Great for Insurance and
Safeguarding your collection
Used by COLLECTORS
around the **WORLD!**

4130 Terrace Drive, Anchorage, AK 99502
http://www.alaska.net/~watch
e-mail: watch@alaska.net
Ph: 907-243-8894

WatchWare 3.0 for Win 95,98	$79.95
ClockWare 2.0 for Win 95,98	$49.95
SwatchWare 1.0 for Win 95,98	$49.95
Shipping/Handling	$6.00

Software for **Watch** or **Clock** Collectors. Features include **multiple input screens** to track all your watches or clocks, miscellaneous items, repair parts needed, suppliers, literature/books, tools, and more! **Multiple drop down menu lists** to choose manufacturer, size, jewels, movement type, winding mechanism, case metal, case condition, case features, etc. Now you can add **Pictures** of your watches! These programs are intuitive and easy to use. Multiple printouts let you keep hardcopies and even create 'For Sale' lists and HTML. Keep track of cost and values. Too many features to list.

COME SEE THE LARGEST SELECTION OF VINTAGE WRISTWATCHES ON THE NET

www.finertimes.com

Exclusive Internet Distributor of Fully Restored
Vintage Wristwatches From Watch Wyse

City Bank Antiques
Buy, Sell, Repair Pocket Watches and Clocks

Specialize in Webb C. Ball and high grade railroad & gold watches. We want to buy watch collections and accumulations of watch makers parts, tools, etc. Will Travel! Don, Karen & Donnie Barrett 115 S. Water St., Kent, OH. 44240
wk phone (330) 677-1479hm (330)673-4246

WATCHES WANTED

HIGH PRICES PAID FOR ALL QUALITY WATCHES
WE BUY WRIST & POCKET, MODERN & VINTAGE

BUY ALL
ROLEX
PATEK PHILIPPE
CARTIER
VACHERON CONSTANTIN
AUDEMARS PIGUET
LANGE
BULGARI
PIAGET - POLO
CORUM $20 COIN
BREGUET

WE BUY
CHRONOGRAPH
DOCTORS WATCHES
ENAMEL DIALS
ROLEX DIALS, BEZELS
BOXES & LINKS
REPEATERS
ENAMEL CASES
JUMP HOURS

ALSO BUYING: BETTER ESTATE JEWELRY,
SIGNED PIECES BY CARTIER, VAN CLEEF,
BULGARI, BUCCELLATTI, JENSEN,
AND OTHER FINE MAKERS.

*WE SELL NEW & PRE-OWNED ROLEX, PATEK, AUDEMARS, BREITLING, AND
ALL BETTER WATCHES PLUS CUSTOM DIAMOND DIALS & BEZELS.*

TARRYTOWN JEWELERS
273 NORTH CENTRAL AVE.
HARTSDALE, N.Y. 10530
TEL. (914) 949-0481 FAX (914) 949-0546

IMMEDIATE
$$ CASH $$ PAID!!

. . . $100 To $1,000,000 Available . . .
IMMEDIATE CASH FOR. . .
. . . Unsalable & Unwanted Items . . .
. . . Contents of Entire Jewelry Stores . . .

BUYING . . .
WATCHES
*High Grade
*Low Grade
*New & Used
*Watch Related Items, Such As
  Watch Bands & Watch Material
*Ladies/Mens - Pocket & Wrist

BUYING . . .
FLATWARE
*Sterling Silver
*Silverplate
*Stainless Steel
*Dirilyte
*Pewter
*Large quantities always needed

BUYING . . .
JEWELRY

*Karat Gold Jewelry
*Platinum Jewelry
*Scrap Jewelry
*Gold-Filled Jewelry
*Sterling Silver Jewelry
*Costume Jewelry
*Diamonds & Colored Stone Items
*Coin & Related Items

BUYING . . .
MISC.
*China & Crystal Tableware
*Gift Items
*Collector Plates
*Christmas Tree Ornaments
*Old Fountain Pens
*Sterling Holloware & Tea Sets

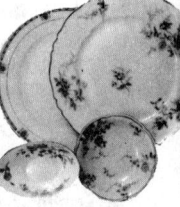

. . . OR . . .

Trade your old items for popular American
Silver & Gold Eagle Coins, as well as
Pandas and other popular coins, usable
in current style jewelry.

JEWELRY FOR SALE!!
Purchase At...
UNDER WHOLESALE PRICES
(Usually 1/2 to 2/3 of normal wholesale cost)
Selection changes constantly

Items Such As. . .
* Closeout Watches & Watch Bands
* Gold Filled & Sterling Carded & Boxed Jewelry
* Diamonds & Colored Stones
* Karat Gold Jewelry
All items from stores we have previously liquidated.

Call or write Mr. Neff
Phone (770) 396-1787 Fax. (770) 395-6959

ENTERPRISES, INC
DEPT. C 99
5579B Chamblee - Dunwoody Road, Suite 215
Dunwoody, GA 30338
Hours by appointment only.   E-mail: wfn@mindspring.com

* Member of Jewelers Board of Trade
* Member SJTA, ICTA, ANA, JVC, Coin Net
* Bank & Trade References Available
* Will Travel for Major Deals

Serving The Jewelry Industry Since 1974

Retiring? WFN can also arrange quitting business, retirement, liquidation and promotional sales. Call for
complete details! Like to travel? Finders Fees Paid! Know of a business or an estate for sale? WFN pays top
finders fees (usually 2 - 10%). Fees can be paid in cash, wholesale merchandise or vacation certificates. Your
choice!

 # MODESTO HOROLOGY

Manny and Liz Trauring

2616 Bardolino Lane • Modesto, CA 95356

e-mail: watches@modesto-horology.com • web site: http://www.modesto-horology.com

inquiries (209) 579-2824 • fax (209) 579-0901 • for orders only 1-800-833-8425

OUR CATALOGS OFFER LARGE SELECTIONS OF OUTSTANDING VALUES IN INTERESTING AMERICAN AND EUROPEAN POCKET WATCHES AND MOVEMENTS. WE ALSO HAVE GREAT CHOICES OF GOLD AND GOLD FILLED POCKET WATCH CHAINS AND GOLD POCKET WATCHES. ORDER OUR CATALOGS ($6.00 INCLUDES POSTAGE) FOR COMPLETE LISTINGS. OUR STOCK IS FREQUENTLY UPDATED. (ALL ITEMS SUBJECT TO PRIOR SALE.)

WE CARRY ONLY WHAT IS ADVERTISED IN OUR CATALOGS

"YELLOW PAGES MATERIAL CATALOG" IS AVAILABLE FOR $1.00 WHICH LISTS MATERIALS AND SUPPLIES, CRYSTALS, STAFFS, CROWNS, BOWS, HANDS, MAINSPRINGS, BALANCE JEWELS, ETC. *ALSO AVAILABLE, GLASS POCKET WATCH CRYSTALS (HUNTING AND OPEN FACE),* INDIVIDUALLY BY LIGNE SIZE AND ASSORTMENTS *AND POCKET WATCH CASE LIFT AND LOCK SPRINGS.*

We are Proud to be one of the World's Leading Horological Dealers, offering a Large Selection of Pocket Watches, Movements, Watch Chains, Crystals, Material and Supplies with Prompt, Reliable and Efficient Service for over 40 Years.
Thank You for Your Continuing Horological Interest.
We Appreciate Your Business!

Original 8" x 12" Waltham Watch Company Stock Certificates in Various Colors. They date back to 1950 or Earlier. Excellent for Collecting, Framing, Gifts or Decorating your Watch Show Cases. Only $3.00 Each..............5 for $10.00 15 for $25.00 ....(plus $2.00 postage)

Oversize Black Suedette Cloth
WATCH POUCHES
$8.50 Dozen
Actual Size 4" x 4 3/4"

We also Purchase Horological Collections at Fair Prices (no wristwatches, only Pocket Watches, Chronometers and related items).
Experience Counts!

Order our latest Catalog for only $6.00 or an Annual Subscription (last year we published 12 GREAT Issues). *You will receive the Finest Selection of Reasonably Priced American and European Pocket Watches, Movements, etc.*

"THE MODESTO HOROLOGIST"
"THE WONDERFUL WORLD OF WATCHES"

Order an Annual Subscription to our Unique Catalogs...

MasterCard, Visa and American Express gladly accepted		U.S.A (via First Class Mail)..............................$45.00
		Canada/Mexico (via Air-Mail)......$55.00 (U.S. Funds Only)
		All Other Foreign (via Air-Mail)...$65.00 (U.S. Funds Only)

We are currently interested in purchasing the following Wrist and Pocket Watches!

AUDEMARS PIGUET: All Royal Oak models, dates, calendars, perpetuals, any vintage makes, call today.

BREITLING: Any Navitimers (Ref. 806, 809), Chronomats, Premiers, all square chronos, unusual lugs, split seconds, SS, GF, 14kt, 18kt models needed.

CARTIER: All mens and ladies 18kt Tanks, all Pasha's, any type of Panthere's; Santos models. Vintage make all models needed. Clocks from the 20's, 30's, 40's etc., pocket watches.

CORUM: Need $20, $10, $5, Coin watches, 18kt or platinum 15 gr., 10gr., 5gr., Ingot watches. All Rolls Royce Radiator Grill watches.

EBERHARD: Chronographs any model SS, Gold.

GRUEN: Curvex Majesty - any drivers, also Doctor's watches, 47mm - 51mm.

GUBELIN: Call for quotes.

IWC - SCHAFFHAUSEN: All 18kt Rounds, manual and automatics with dates. All Ingenieur's with dates.

JAEGER LECOULTRE: All Reverso models from the 30's to 50's, any chronographs. Any Alarms in 14kt and 18kt, calendars, need full mystery dials.

LONGINES: All stainless, 14kt and 18kt chronographs, square or round pushers, rectangular diamond dials.

MOVADO: Any chronographs, moon-dials, gold or stainless purse watches.

OMEGA: Speedmaster chronographs (man on moon) other chronographs from the 30's, and 40's, S/S, 14kt, 18kt.

PATEK PHILIPPE: All types vintage to current. Any Nautilus models mens and ladies. Call today.

PIAGET: All types needed, Polo's, Dancer, Auto's Quartz. Ladies Diamond Watches any model.

ROLEX: Bubble Back to Prince Models, any vintage make. All sport models, mens and ladies S/S - 2 tone, gold. Daytona's—New—Exotic 50's, 60's makes. All types of 14kt and 18kt Date, Datejust and Day Date models. Milgauss, King Midas, Explorer I & II, Submariner, GMT, Sea Dweller. Call today we buy all models of Rolex.

TIFFANY: Any Rolex with Tiffany Dial. Call for quote.

ULYSSE NARDIN: All chronographs, S/S and 18kt.

UNIVERSAL GENEVE: Chronographs, any Tri-Compax or Compax.

VACHERON & CONSTANTIN: Vintage models, chronographs, mystery.

ALSO: Very interested in watch lighters, small desk clocks etc. Dunhill, Cartier, Gubelin, Jaeger LeCoultre, call today.

VINTAGE WRISTWATCH & JEWELRY

P.O. Box 542235, Houston, TX 77254-2235

GREGG ESSES

Phone: **713-523-5508** or FAX: 713 - 523 - 5551

Member: National Association of Watch & Clock Collectors (NAWCC)
and International Watch & Jewerly Guild (IWJG)

COLLIERS'

Sales Service Purchase

$$Cash$$ paid for all watches. Service and restorations on chronographs, chronometers, all complications, wrist and pocket. Obsolete parts are no problem. Ph. 918 7420701 or 800 9335562, Addr. 4310 S. Peoria, Tulsa Okla. 74105

BUYING

TOM ENGLE & COOKSEY SHUGART
BUYING WATCHES
Specializing in "Patek Philippe" & "A. Lange"
FOR OUR PRIVATE & PERSONAL COLLECTION
TOP PRICES PAID TO YOU FOR **OUR** PERSONAL WATCH COLLECTION

WILL PAY TOP **"$"** FOR YOUR QUALITY WATCHES
OR LARGE COLLECTIONS OF
BOTH WRIST WATCHES & POCKET WATCHES
WILL PAY POSTAGE BOTH WAYS
SAME DAY PAYMENT
CALL

TOM ENGLE
SUMMER # **(502) 969-9778**
WINTER # **(813) 360-6645**

COOKSEY SHUGART
SUMMER # **(423) 479-4813**
WINTER # **(813) 367-9278**

TOM ENGLE
4809 FAMOUS WAY
LOUISVILLE, KY. 40219

COOKSEY SHUGART
P.O. BOX 3147
CLEVELAND, TN. 37320

Watches
Wanted

Top prices paid for all pocket watches and wrist watches from single watches to large collections as well as watchmakers' estates of tools, parts, crystals, cases, dials, etc. Immediate confidential payment by overnight mail or wire transfer.

Always in stock: A fine selection of premium condition wrist watches and pocket watches. If you are searching for something special, please call. I may have it.

Ray Porter, Fine Watches

395 Rand Pond Road ▪ **Goshen, NH 03752**

603/863-4708   **Fax: 603/863-4490**

THERE'S A TERRIFIC DEMAND FOR VINTAGE WATCHES
IT'S TIME TO LET GO!
WE'RE READY TO BUY YOURS FOR THE HIGHEST PRICE

ROLEX	Jaeger	*Cartier*	MOVADO	OMEGA	LONGINES	Vachero
IWC	Breguet	BREITLING	PATEK PHILIPPE	*Tiffany*	Audemars	and mar more...

◆ FOSSNER ◆
TIMEPIECES INC

J&P
TIMEPIECES INC

TELL US YOUR SPECIFIC NEEDS & WE CAN QUOTE PRICES & AVAILABILITY. PLEASE DO NOT ASK FOR STOCK LIST, IT CHANGES DAIL
● NEW WATCHES AVAILABLE, AT PRICES YOU CAN PROFIT FROM! ●

1059 2nd AVE. NEW YORK CITY N.Y.10022
BRANCH OFFICES GENEVA ● VIENNA ● MONTE CARLO ● LONDON

CALL 800-828 8004 FAX 212-935 0339
OVERSEAS ENQUIRIES PLEASE CALL 212-980 1099 or 212-249 2600

WE BUY WE SELL WE SERVICE
NOW AVAILABLE, MERCEDES HANDS FOR BUBBLE BACKS

Maundy International
Pocket Watches

Post Office Box 13028-PR
Shawnee Mission, Kansas 66282, U.S.A.
Wire Connection: CALL TOLL FREE
1•800•235•2866

Specializing in the Purchase & Sale of Fine Pocket Watches Since 1976.

Especially Interested in Rare & Unusual Timepieces.

Maundy International offers one of the most complete services for buying watches in the world. We offer catalogs by mail on a regular basis. Everything from Audemars to Patek Philippe. From Illinois to Waltham. From Moonphase to Repeater. Experience the infinite possibilities.

When you are ready to sell, give us a call. Estates, collections and accumulations a specialty. We are serious buyers of Pocket Watches. CALL US TODAY TOLL FREE for more information at 1•800•235•2866.

We look forward to your business in the near future.

Send a self-addressed stamped envelope for a free copy of our latest catalog.

All the Best from,

Maundy International

Celebrating Our 18th Consecutive Year of Advertising in this Publication.

©1999 MAUNDY INTERNATIONAL

LOOK FOR US...

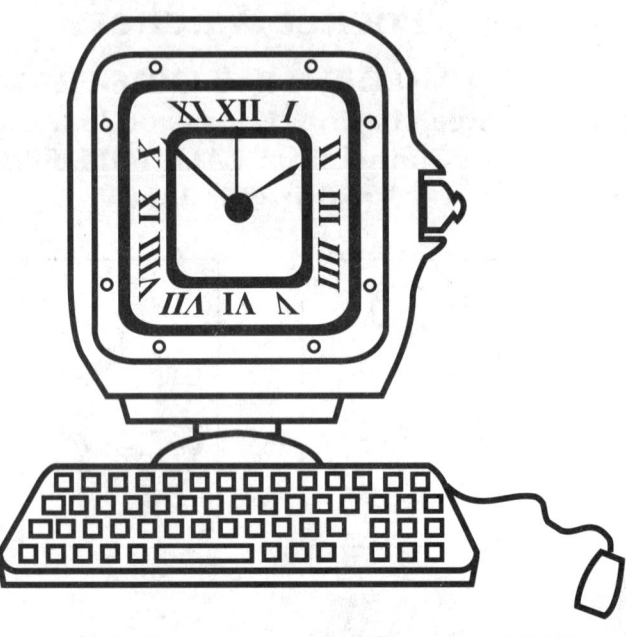

WE'LL WATCH FOR YOU

BERNARD
ENTERPRISES

Dallas • Austin

1-800-200-2724

bernardwatch.com

Hundreds of watches, pictures and prices

WATCHES

We buy & sell most fine brands

New - Used - Vintage

Rolex Specialist sales/service
Diamond dials/ bezels

Need info on a watch? call us!

415-283-1930

Let's make some $ together

Select

TIMEPIECES & JEWELRY

210 Post St. 712 • San Francisco, CA • 94108
Not an official Rolex Jeweler

See Us on the INTERNET!

It's Time To
Surf Our Turf!

Visit us on the World Wide Web
Hundreds of fine watches
Full color photos – Updated weekly

http://www.tic-tock.com/wingates

Fine Vintage & Contemporary
Wrist & Pocket
WATCHES

ROLEX · CARTIER · PIAGET
PATEK PHILIPPE · CORUM
VACHERON & CONSTANTIN
AUDEMARS PIQUET · EBEL
BREITLING & OTHERS

Call Toll Free
1-800-842-8625

QUALITY WATCHES

Write for a FREE Catalog (Specify Wrist or Pocket)
P.O. Box 59760 · Dallas, TX 75229-1760
Fax: 972-392-2304 · E Mail: wingates@tic-tock.com

THIS SIZE
COLOR AD
MADE

$200,000.00

PROFIT
RECENTLY
FOR ONE OF OUR ADVERTISER'S
FROM A 1984 AD

WE THOUGH
YOU MIGHT BE INTERESTED IN KNOWING WHAT
ONE AD....
ONE WATCH
MAY DO FOR YOU!!!
WE THINK YOU CAN DO
JUST AS WELL

IT PAYS TO ADVERTISE
CALL OR WRITE US
FOR NEXT YEARS RATES

COOKSEY SHUGART PUBLICATIONS
P. O. BOX 3147
CLEVELAND, TENN. 37320 - 3147
(423) 479 - 4813

AD DEAD LINE OCTOBER 15th EACH YEAR.

NATIONAL WATCH EXCHANGE
1-800-8-WATCHES

Visit Our Web Site: nationalwatch.com
Send e-mail to: info@nationalwatch.com

OVER 300 ROLEX'S IN STOCK

Also Cartier, Breitling, Ebel, Patek, Vacheron, Audemar and a large assortment of diamond bezels and dials.

BUY · SELL · TRADE

Shipping Nationwide for Over 10 Years. Each watch is inspected and refurbished by our watchmakers and warrantied for one full year.

Call for FREE! Pre-Owned Rolex Price List.

NATIONAL WATCH EXCHANGE

Proudly Not Affiliated with Rolex USA
N.W.E is not an official Rolex dealer and Rolex's warranty no longer attaches.

107 S. 8th Street, Philadelphia, PA 19106

Whether it's a Hamilton 992B or rare Patek Philippe Moonphase Minute Repeater pocketwatch, **Hess Fine Art** is there for you. **Jeffrey P. Hess**, Owner of **Hess Fine Art** is a noted Horological researcher and can answer any horological question. If you have a watch to sell, or an entire collection, please give us a call. Our courteous staff is standing by. Call anytime.

We urge you to get several offers before you sell.

• • Please make ours one of them • •

HESS
FINE ART

1131 4th STREET NORTH
ST. PETERSBURG, FL 33701
Hours: M-F 9:00-5:00
(813) 896-0622 • (800) 922-4377 • FAX: (813) 822-8899

PAUL A. DUGGAN CO.

fine watches bought and sold

15 Fletcher Street, Chelmsford, MA 01824, USA
Telephone: (978) 256-5966 • Facsimile: (978) 256-2497
Email: Paul @ Pduggan.com

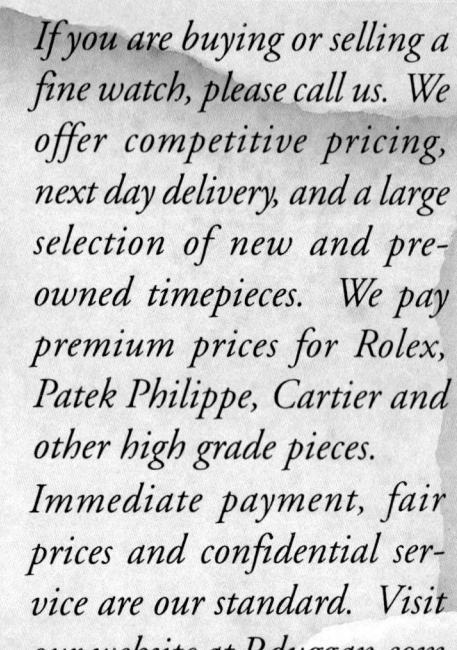

If you are buying or selling a fine watch, please call us. We offer competitive pricing, next day delivery, and a large selection of new and pre-owned timepieces. We pay premium prices for Rolex, Patek Philippe, Cartier and other high grade pieces. Immediate payment, fair prices and confidential service are our standard. Visit our website at P.duggan.com

Rolex is a trademark of Rolex USA. Paul Duggan Co. is not an authorized Rolex dealer.

ORIGINAL NEW OLD-STOCK BREITLINGS

FROM THE 60'S AND 70'S

#7102.3 TRANSOCEAN, CIRCA 1972, **$1,090**
#7104.3 LONG PLAYING TACHOMETER DATE, CIRCA 1972, **$850**
#2016 SPRINT, CIRCA 1972, **$490**
#820.3 LONG PLAYING, CIRCA 1968, **$800**
#815.4 LONG PLAYING, CIRCA 1974, **$1,450**
#809.4 COSMONAUT NAVITIMER, CIRCA 1967, **$1,990**

**FIND ADDITIONAL MODELS
ON WORLD WIDE WEB**
http://www.antiqnet.com/oldworld

#2016

#7104.3

#7102.3

#809.4

#815.4

#820.3

Old World Jewelers

Oak Brook, Illinois
708-456-7730 · 1-800-322-3871

BUYING

ANTIQUE WATCH INVESTMENTS
TOM ENGLE & JOYCE ENGLE
4809 FAMOUS WAY LOUISVILLE, KY. 40219
Summer (502) 969-9778 - Winter (727) 360-6645
FAX NO. (502) 969-9795
TOLL FREE 1-800-T. E. ENGLE – 1-800-833-6453

UNUSUAL RARE REPEATERS - MOONPHASES, ETC.

CHRONOGRAPHS - SPLIT SECONDS - RAILROADS, ETC

BUYING
Patek Philippe - A. Lange - ROLEX
COLLECTIONS WRIST AND POCKET WATCHES
POSTAGE PAID BOTH WAYS - SAME DAY PAYMENT
FOR MY PRIVATE & PERSONAL COLLECTION

TOM ENGLE
SAME ADDRESS - SAME PHONE NUMBER 30 YEARS
STILL BUYING
FAIR HONEST PRICES

Summer (502) 969-9778 - Winter (727) 360-6645
FAX NO. (502) 969-9795 - TOLL FREE 1-800-833-6453